T0330375

HARVARD STUDIES IN BUSINESS HISTORY • 45

Published with the support of the Harvard Business School
Edited by Thomas K. McCraw
Isidor Straus Professor of Business History
Graduate School of Business Administration
George F. Baker Foundation
Harvard University

JEFFREY R. FEAR

Organizing Control

August Thyssen
and the Construction of German
Corporate Management

HARVARD UNIVERSITY PRESS
Cambridge, Massachusetts, and London, England
2005

Library of Congress Cataloging-in-Publication Data

Fear, Jeffrey R.
Organizing control : August Thyssen and the construction of
German corporate management / Jeffrey R. Fear.
p. cm. — (Harvard studies in business history ; 45)
Includes index.
ISBN 0-674-01492-8 (alk. paper)
1. Industrial management—Germany—History.
2. Industrialists—Germany—History.
3. Thyssen, August, 1842–1926.
4. Dinkelbach, Heinrich, b. 1891.
5. Thyssen & Co. (Mèlheim an der Ruhr, Germany)—History.
6. Vereinigte Stahlwerke Akiengesellschaft—History.
I. Title.   II. Series.

HD70.G3F43 2005
658—dc22   2004054313

To Cathy

Contents

List of Figures and Tables   ix

Acknowledgments   xiii

Introduction   1

I. Thyssen & Co., 1871–1914   39

1 August Thyssen, Victorian Entrepreneur   43

2 If I Rest, I Rust   74

3 Creating Management   104

4 Accounting for Control   150

5 Sustaining Innovation   190

II. The Thyssen-Konzern, 1890–1926   231

6 Cartels and Competition   235

7 Rushing Forward and Backward   261

8 Managing a Konzern   296

9 Organizing Financial Control   337

10 Revolutionizing Industrial Relations   380

11 Centralization or Decentralization?   431

12 The Demise of the Thyssen-Konzern   478

III. The Vereinigte Stahlwerke, 1926–1936   519

13   The "Rationalization Company"   523

14   Contested Terrain   569

15   Business Practice and Politics   618

16   Heinrich Dinkelbach, Organization Man   677

Conclusion   711

Appendix A: Tables   751
Appendix B: Accounting as Symbolic Practice   770
Notes   789
Index   935

Figures and Tables

Figures

1.1	August Thyssen at Schloss Landsberg Gate, 1912	48
1.2	Thyssen's children with nanny, ca. 1900	63
2.1	Turbine distribution pipe of the Ontario Light and Power Co., Niagara Falls	95
3.1	Thyssen & Co.'s first headquarters	106
3.2	Thyssen & Co.'s second headquarters	109
3.3	Thyssen & Co. organization, 1903	113
3.4	Thyssen & Co. advertising brochure, 1906	115
4.1	Thyssen & Co. management at headquarters, ca. 1900	160
5.1	Gas dynamo hall of the GDK steelworks	203
5.2	Thyssen & Co. Machine Company, 1913–1914	214
7.1	Four Thyssen headquarters	273
7.2	Thyssen-Konzern, 1914—extended konzern	294
8.1	Core Thyssen-Konzern firms, 1914	298
8.2	Thyssen & Co. Berlin structural steel warehouse and grounds, 1889 and 1913	306
9.1	Phoenix-Konzern, 1925	366
10.1	Institutional levels and main organizations/actors, 1918–1920	383
11.1	Thyssen & Co., 1918	442
11.2	Thyssen-Konzern, 1919	444
11.3	Thyssen & Co., machine engineering division, 1922	462
11.4	Headquarters of Thyssen & Co. rolling mills, 1922	463

12.1	Extended Thyssen-Konzern, ca. 1924	480
12.2	Consolidated Thyssen-Konzern, end of 1925	487
13.1	Corporate headquarters of the Vereinigte Stahlwerke, Düsseldorf	542
14.1	Vereinigte Stahlwerke, 1930	572
14.2	VSt Central Administration, Düsseldorf, 1930	577
14.3	The "modern office": VSt's Hollerith department, 1933	590
15.1	Vereinigte Stahlwerke AG, 1934	646
16.1	Heinrich Dinkelbach	679
16.2	Thyssen headquarters, Düsseldorf, 1950s	701

Tables

4.1	Monthly financial reports, plate and sheet department, November 1888	164
4.2	Cost accounting for boiler plates (2-meter mill)	178
4.3	Cost accounting for patent lapwelded boiler tubes	180
9.1	Profitability ratios of various Ruhr steel firms, 1909–1913	357
9.2	Cash flow (ROI) of various Ruhr steel firms, 1909–1913	358
9.3	Cash-flow ratio generated by total fixed assets of various Ruhr steel firms, 1909–1913	359
11.1	Key financial accounts of the GDK, 1915–1918	436
11.2	IG financial redistribution among Thyssen firms, 1915–1918	437
11.3	IG financial redistribution among Thyssen firms, 1919–1922	449
13.1	Capacity and production of the four VSt merger groups, 1925	528
13.2	VSt quotas in steel cartels, 1926 and 1929	552
13.3	Comparison of Vereinigte Stahlwerke with the four largest American steel companies	554
13.4	Approximate annual capacity of the VSt and four American companies, 1926	556
13.5	Comparison of 1925 production and revenues, VSt, U.S. Steel, Bethlehem Steel	557
13.6	Rationalization of production units of the VSt, 1926–1933	558
14.1	Basic expense categories of the VSt	601
A.1	Selected financial statistics of the GDK, 1892–1913	752

A.2   Thyssen & Co. credits and debits to the Thyssen-Konzern,
      1909–1914   754
A.3   CAO-prepared Thyssen-Konzern financial statement,
      1912   756
A.4   Thyssen & Co. banking relations, 1908–1914   758
A.5   Thyssen-Konzern balance analysis, 1909–1913   760
A.6   Selected financial statistics of the GDK, 1910–1918, and
      ATH/Friedrich Thyssen, 1919–1925   764
A.7   Liquidity analysis of the GDK/ATH, 1897–1925   766
A.8   Financial analysis of the ATH, 1924–1925 (Price
      Waterhouse figures)   768

Acknowledgments

I wish to thank the many people and institutions who made this book possible. First and foremost, the archivist of the Mannesmann Archiv, Dr. Horst A. Wessel, and of the Thyssen Archive, the late Dr. Carl-Friedrich Baumann, and its present archivist, Dr. Manfred Rasch, provided a great deal of impeccable help. Accomplished scholars themselves, they tolerated my early guesses and hypotheses, and proved more than willing to impart what they knew about August Thyssen and the German steel industry. They and their staffs acted as models of support. Dr. Wessel's generosity and enthusiasm in particular has consistently gone well beyond the call of duty. The charming Dr. Stephan Wegener made my time in Düsseldorf exceptionally pleasant. That year in the archives was an austere one and they made it a joy to go to work.

Thanks to both the Mannesmann-Archiv, Mülheim/Ruhr, and the ThyssenKrupp Corporate Archives in Duisberg for permission for the photos and the logos used on the three part openers of the book.

I would also like to thank Werner Plumpe, Christian Kleinschmidt, Lutz Budrass, and Thomas Welskopp for the wonderful discussions at numerous "beer evenings," where I learned much about German industry. This work clearly builds on their own research.

At Stanford, where the first draft of this book was written, I benefited considerably from the sage counsel of James Sheehan, my primary dissertation advisor. His ideas about German history permeate this book, although he is in no way responsible for its interpretation.

Stephen Haber sparked my interest in Mexican economic history, which may appear tangential on the surface, but his sharp comparative and analytical instincts inform this book, although he is certainly not to blame for its length or the various postmodernist leanings in some of its discussions.

More research was accomplished at the Baker Library of the Harvard Business School, which has an extensive collection of early German management literature. My year on site as a Harvard-Newcomen fellow proved invaluable. The chapter on cartels, for instance, is based entirely on this new material. The Business History Seminar run by Thomas McCraw proved an intellectually invigorating forum for presenting some initial conclusions. I cannot say enough about Tom, who has inspired me with his ability to fuse biography, intellectual history, and business history. The biographical chapters owe much to him. I also learned a great deal from Debora Spar, Richard Tedlow, and Richard Vietor, especially regarding many of the ideas about cooperation and competition expressed here.

At the University of Pennsylvania, I had the pleasure of working with a number of wonderful colleagues, but would like to highlight a special few. I am grateful to Jamshed Ghandhi and Ginger Mace of the Huntsman Program, who made my first teaching forays into global economic history so enjoyable. The Penn Economic History Seminar, a seminar series that brings together a range of disciplines and schools, helped me to hone a number of key arguments. Bruce Kogut, Mauro Guillen, Dan Raff, Adrian Tschoegl, and Walter Licht proved rich in ideas, which has influenced this work. Lynn Lees inspired me with her ability to transform herself constantly as she too ventured into world history; she has become a role model for her rare ability to bridge disciplinary boundaries. I owe her an overwhelming amount of thanks for showing such a sparkling, enthusiastic interest in my work and teaching. Although he came late to Penn, more than any other person, Jonathan Steinberg got what I was trying to do. His words of encouragement came at a particularly opportune time as I was beginning to doubt seriously certain aspects of this project. Not everyone automatically sees how important internal transfer prices are to the overall argument. I thank him for noting that alone. Finally, close friends such as Warren Breckman, Matthew Sommer (now at Stanford), Peter Siskind, Rohit (Dan) Wadwhani, Elisa von Joeden-Forgey, and Jerry Drew made my time there more than pleasant. I also owe a debt of gratitude to the University of Pennsylvania for a sabbatical year when the bulk of the revisions and new chapters were written.

Gerald Feldman has proven to be an inspiration both intellectually and personally. I hope readers will not draw the conclusion that his mentorship led to this big book, although the joke is that any study about German heavy industry has to result in a heavy book. Gerry also holds the dubious distinction of having read lengthier drafts and I thank him for his time. A great thanks to the numerous anonymous reviewers who also read an early version. Caroline Fohlin, Geoffrey Jones, and Christopher Kobrak also helped and I look forward to working more closely with them in the future.

Last and certainly not least, I owe everything to my wife, Cathy Belcher, who has recently done double duty giving birth to and raising our daughter Aitana while also giving birth to her own dissertation.

ORGANIZING CONTROL

Introduction

One of the special features of a modern industrial capitalist society, central to its strengths and problems, is the modern business corporation. Corporations command a high degree of market power, straddle national and cultural boundaries, and organize both time and space. Railroads and telegraphs gave rise to our clock-time scheduling. Corporate skyscrapers sculpt our city skylines. The local supermarket supplies exotic fresh fruit even in the winter. Industrial artifacts such as automobiles are not just products; consumer advertising is not mere packaging. Such commodities and marketing techniques help *make* meanings in our greater culture. Automobiles and the freeway embody such values as freedom and mobility. Advertising catchphrases reshape our everyday language.

If big business has helped manufacture our culture, then managers have helped make the modern corporation. Understanding the twentieth century means comprehending the growth and activities of this important group of people working inside this uniquely modern institution. Ronald Coase had long viewed the business firm as a "governance structure" for reducing transaction costs. He asked: if the market works by itself and mediated supply and demand through the price mechanism, then why do firms exist? Even in small firms, why is the coordinating power of entrepreneurs needed to direct production if the price mechanism does so?[1] For Alfred D. Chandler, Jr., large-scale business corporations replaced the "invisible hand" of the market with the "visible hand" of managerial hierarchy.[2] William Lazonick went one step further, declaring that business organizations have called into question the belief in the inherent efficiency of markets.[3]

In this study, I examine how this visible hand of management has operated in Germany. One of the classic dilemmas of German history is the problem of continuity in a national history marked by violent, destructive political change. Yet a number of corporations with global reputations, such as the Deutsche Bank, Daimler-Benz, Siemens, and the subject of this book, Thyssen (now ThyssenKrupp), attest to those firms' ability to bridge the political chasms of modern German history. They have also managed to export all around the globe in the teeth of strong international competition for more than a century in spite of Germany's turbulent political history. These firms and people also reflect a significant strain of German national identity that finds its strength in its national economic competitiveness, technical expertise, long-term solidity, and industrial tradition. Germany was never just a land of poets and thinkers, but entrepreneurs, managers, scientists, craftsmen, and skilled workers.[4] Yet its managerial styles and strategies remain an "enigma."[5]

In this study, I want to show how managers actively made and remade the modern German business enterprise. Those managers, to paraphrase Olivier Zunz, helped "make Germany corporate."[6] Analyzing *management* in an industrial capitalist organization, even a company with a strong entrepreneur like August Thyssen, is one of the most important perspectives for understanding how corporations make, regulate, and legitimize their decisions. Business histories that focus on the great entrepreneurial figure have hidden how managers have made, and remade, the modern corporation. However brilliant August Thyssen may have been as an entrepreneur, if his firms had not developed a competent managerial staff, they would have failed. With some outstanding exceptions, we have little sense how these famous large firms, let alone innumerable Mittelstand firms, confronted as organizations, their economic and political worlds.[7] We do have a considerable literature on individual entrepreneurs and firms, but it tends to offer little information inside the business firm showing how these firms worked.

This book concentrates on the development of managerial organization and practice inside the Thyssen-Konzern and the Vereinigte Stahlwerke (United Steel Works) between 1871 and 1934. August

Thyssen can best be described as the Andrew Carnegie of Germany. He founded his first, family-owned steel firm, Thyssen & Co., in Mülheim (Ruhr) in 1871, the same year that Otto von Bismarck united Germany by "blood and iron." Thyssen's fortunes rose along with the wealth of the German nation. By World War I, Thyssen's total assets vied with Krupp and Siemens and a number of Silesian magnates as the largest industrial operation in Germany. In 1926, Thyssen along with three other major concerns, merged to form the Vereinigte Stahlwerke AG (VSt), the second largest corporation in Germany and the second largest steel corporation in the world behind U.S. Steel. By 1933, when Hitler came to power, the VSt proved to be too unwieldy, so its executives, especially a young Thyssen manager named Heinrich Dinkelbach, redesigned the VSt along the organizational lines pioneered by the Thyssen-Konzern. This reorganization paralleled similar changes in U.S. Steel, Du Pont, and General Motors in the 1920s and 1930s. These two figures, August Thyssen, a classic Victorian entrepreneur, and Heinrich Dinkelbach, a prototypical systems manager, frame this history of German management in the steel industry. Dinkelbach's generation helped create the West German economic miracle. The contrast between the two figures symbolizes many of the dramatic changes in business between the 1870s and the 1960s.

Following a line of continuity in German business history running from Thyssen & Co. to the VSt, from a proprietary enterprise to a managerial corporation, from the rudimentary beginnings of industrial management to its rationalization and professionalization, from August Thyssen to Heinrich Dinkelbach, the business firm was transformed from an entrepreneurial expression of personal property to a managerially organized expression of institutionalized property relations. These abstract managerial practices have found concrete expression in the architectural monuments of twentieth-century business corporations. In fact, the narrative can be read symbolically through the erection of ever more elaborate corporate headquarters (see the series of photographs in this book). This line of inquiry follows the conceptual and organizational logic internal to Thyssen & Co. (Part I), the Thyssen-Konzern (Part II), and the Vereinigte Stahlwerke (Part III). Following this underlying logic uncovers continuity in specifically German management practices. It also exposes a debate about the best manner in which to organize large-scale business, which ex-

pressed an ongoing, universal tension between centralization and decentralization.

In a strict sense, this study is not really a business history, but a history of corporate management, focusing particularly on commercial
administration, rather than on factory management.[8] The persistent
tendency to emphasize production, which can be found in diverse figures such as Marx, Taylor, or Ford, is a historically contingent (and
gendered) way of conceiving the business corporation and capitalism.[9]
Instead, this book focuses primarily on the evolution of a particular
management model that differs from our standard image of German
entrepreneurs and industrial bureaucracy. I am primarily interested in
how managers coordinated their activities *inside* the business firm—
the processual world of management and organizational change. This
study is probably best likened to the forensic reconstruction of a human face from skeletal remains. It is not primarily concerned with how
Thyssen asserted himself on particular product markets against other
competitors, which assumes the (legitimate) perspective that his organization was a unitary actor acting strategically on markets. The story
is written from perspective of senior management and the central
headquarters, not the owner or the shop floor. The organizational capabilities of large-scale business enterprises—that is, their ability to
know how to make and do things—are crucial drivers of innovation as
well as of sustained growth. In this respect, this study follows Richard
Nelson's and Sidney Winter's insight, whereby routines underlie an organization's competence or capabilities as a sort of genetic code or organizational memory within organizations. Routines both constrain
and enable people to manage the complexity of a large-scale business.
Routines enable an organization to know, grow, and do things over
time. Moreover, once an organization has learned to do certain things,
it is often difficult for the organization to change. As such, this study
contributes to the recent notion of organizational learning.[10]

By focusing on the internal corporate decision-making process, one
gains a critical perspective on how management coped with crisis and
change, shedding important light on continuity, rather than discontinuity, in German history. Too often business histories relate what the
company's management decided, its strategy, or its policies, without
relating how they made these decisions, how they formed strategy, and
how they created new policies. Business histories often present a view

from the boardroom, but only after debates quiet and decisions are announced. Moreover, the long-term perspective offered here also allows one to make explicit comparisons to other international business developments rather than implicit claims for a peculiar German development.

By taking this perspective, I call into question four major, conceptually interrelated themes or arguments, whose historiographical background is elucidated below. First, we should call into question the notion of the peculiarly German, state-bureaucratic, authoritarian model of entrepreneurship and organization. This conception of German industrialism stems from the political role of German industry in the "special path" of German history, which led to the Third Reich. No one epitomized the image of the *Herr im Hause* (master of the house or lord in the manor) more than August Thyssen, who along with Alfred Krupp and Hugo Stinnes represents the paradigm of the classic German entrepreneur. But this image describes his person and politics, not his business firm.[11]

Yet Thyssen's management practices fit neither the Krupp absolutist model nor the Siemens state-bureaucratic model, which are the two most influential models of German management. The decentralized, decidedly unbureaucratic methods inside the Thyssen-Konzern are a useful antidote to widely held notions of bureaucratic mentalities permeating German business. Initiatives for organizational and strategic change did not necessarily come from the entrepreneur or senior management, but frequently from young managers deep inside the business organization. Thyssen's management forged final strategies, often after intensely competitive negotiations among executives, as much in a middle-up process of managing tradeoffs and learning rather than a top-down process from the entrepreneur.

I advance the following base argument: Managing a large-scale business corporation was fundamentally different than running a state bureaucracy. There were few precedents for dealing with high-fixed-cost industries that had to sell and service their complex products in an increasingly international and export-oriented economy. These organizations and new techniques resulted from problems of constructing large-scale capitalistic enterprises that forced management to deal with fundamental issues of *monitoring, coordination,* and *control* inside the firm. German firms were just as advanced as many companies in the U.S., the alleged "seedbed of managerial capitalism."[12] They operated with extensive managerial systems and used complex financial reporting that had no precedent in the civil service, although military models clearly had an influence. Military influence on corporate organization, however, was hardly specific to Germany.

In addition, the Thyssen-Konzern, in parallel with Mitsui and Siemens, developed an early version of a multidivisional structure (M-form) by pioneering the management of *Konzerne,* multisubsidiary corporate complexes. *Zaibatsu* and *Konzerne,* Mitsui or Thyssen, for example, are most comparable in their formal organizational structure to family-led enterprise groups.[13] Both faced similar problems caused by the relationship of the family, the desire to retain family control yet the need for expansion and capital, and similar managerial problems involving autonomy and control, decentralization and centralization. Thyssen's Konzern organization was truly innovative and modern, not a product of preindustrial or civil-service mentalities. The multidivisional form has regularly been called one of the most significant achievements in the twentieth century for managing large-scale business.[14] It is a testament to how little we know about structure, let alone internal organizational process and learning, that the most vaunted organizational form of the twentieth century appeared in Japan and Germany before its ostensible home in the U.S. More surprising is that this occurred while Thyssen-Konzern remained a family enterprise, and it stemmed from German steel companies, the conservative-reactionary *bétes noires* of German history. The VSt, moreover, developed state-of-the-art management practices that paralleled U.S. developments and influenced German business well into the 1950s.

Second, this book calls into question the ubiquitous notion of the Americanization of German business. Judging from the vast amount of literature written about the obvious influence of America on Germany, especially after 1945, one would think that the German business world would be a very familiar place to Americans. In a recent article, Ulrich Wengenroth characterized the entire century of German business development as a series of successive waves of Americanization.[15] Yet at the end of this 120-odd-year process, Germans still have a distinct form of capitalism. Michel Albert called it the "Rhine model" of capitalism.[16] After all this Americanization, how can this be? In the end, it may be a far better question to ask how these American influences became

Germanized. This Americanization thesis casts German methods as somehow unmodern or as a catching up to the U.S. This portrayal is both a result of German historiography about its "special path" as well as Alfred Chandler's immense influence on business history (explained below).

A straightforward Americanization thesis obscures indigenous trajectories and continuities within German business. All that appears as "American" did not have American origins. Many institutional, professional, and organizational developments were true parallels, rather than imitations. Clearly, American ideas filtered into German business, but one could just as well call this borrowing the Germanization of American techniques, rather than Americanization. German management did (and does) differ from American management, but these techniques were by no means necessarily developed backward; indeed many German practices were more sophisticated than American ones. Additionally, to be modern implies a normative, best-practice model stemming from America. If one follows the trajectory of German industry offered here, German management appears to be more modern than a "preindustrial tradition" would imply, and German management appears to be more American than the standard portrayal of German industry allows. In fact, August Thyssen had the reputation for being the most American of German industrialists, so he serves as an ideal point of study; a constant comparison with Andrew Carnegie highlights these differences. Just how American was Thyssen really? Like Carnegie, Thyssen confronted a choice in 1926 of whether or not to merge his family industrial dynasty into the VSt, an anonymous "trust" modeled explicitly along the lines of U.S. Steel.

Third, Chandler's enterprise classifications have contributed to misleading conclusions about German business. Just as German "special-path" historiography established a path of modernization using Anglo-Saxon countries to highlight German deviancy, Chandler's classifications and organizational forms based on American examples skews results by making U.S. developments the ultimate yardstick by which to judge other national business enterprises. Yet German business developed different forms of organizational design that do not fit into his typologies, which have influenced German business historians to presume that family-run enterprises such as Thyssen did not have a managerial revolution. Yet the Thyssen-Konzern was a modern managerial enterprise, which happened to have an entrepreneur at its head. Much of Chandler's discussion of organizational design is built around two ideal-types of managerial structures cut from the American experience: the unitary, multiunit, multifunctional enterprise (U-form); and the multidivisional structure (M-form). These, too, do not effectively describe Thyssen's organizational structure or its management practices. They do, however, fit the VSt experience more closely. In this study, I will focus explicitly on Thyssen and VSt's organizational forms, managerial practices, the use of information (particularly accounting reports), and debates among managers to arrive at a more adequate formulation.

The book develops an alternative typology based on the development of the managerial hierarchy itself, described here as built around three conceptions of control—i.e., ways of running a business. Thyssen & Co. (Part I) manifested a mercantile conception of control from the 1870s to the turn of the century. Entrepreneurs had to develop new techniques for the growth and control their operations. After the turn of the century, a shift to a manufacturing or productivist conception of control ensued (Part II), which continued into the 1930s. This phase saw focus shift to the development of manufacturing productivy or technical efficiencies, i.e., the classic realm of scientific management, engineers, and rationalization. The traditional bias of much business history, to the neglect of commercial administration, stems from this perspective. The third technocratic systems conception of control appeared in the 1930s (end of Part III), which was dominated by a new attention to financial and organizational ways to create greater administrative efficiencies—and was arguably more prevalent after the war. This managerial-finance conception of control was oriented to issues of organizational design, financial liquidity, and efficient use of investment capital.

The advantage of these conceptions of control is that they historicize particular notions of how managers think they can generate profits (strategy), for whom does the firm work, and how they conceive of a firm, i.e., what they think a business enterprise is.[17] The notion of a conception of control stresses the types of information and the rationales by which executives ground their decisions. Finally, it describes the main concerns of the managerial hierarchy itself. Whether this typology fits other kinds of enterprise is a matter for further research.

The fourth line of argument critiques Weberian notions of the business firm, i.e., bureaucratization and rationalization, and his methodology of "ideal-types," which has underpinned and propelled literature on German history as well as Chandler's business classifications. The argument calls into question Weber's notion of capital accounting as the epitome of formal rationality; instead the formally rational procedures of accounting are filled with conceptual content (substantive rationality in his terms) that construct organizational reality and guide action. Internal transfer prices, for instance, became a political point of contention, not a signifier of formal, instrumental rationality. The accounting system creates critical information and guides an active communicative process among managers. Accounting is the beginning of discourse, rather than the end of rationality. This information system offers an "account"—a story—about the enterprise, to which management must react. Accounting practices provide the best representation, in its discursive sense, about the changing nature of business corporations.

Drawing on organizational theory and new accounting theory, I analyze the different formal and (where possible) informal organizational dynamics that led to new formulations of policy and strategy. This approach allows different, conflicting, yet legitimate, points of view with different reasonings and criteria to emerge at different time periods. Business firms face constant tradeoffs that cannot be rationalized out of existence, and the notion of bureaucratization is too vague to describe the development of modern organizational life.

For this reason, this study underscores where possible the disputes among managers, because they illustrate particular problems of running a complex organization. Focusing on the entrepreneur or chief executive officer, as a shorthand for the company, effaces the process of coming to a decision. The economy is filled with living, breathing human beings making decisions characterized by a mixture of calculative rationality, cultural norms, and power. The challenge is to find a way to mix these three elements of rational choice, normative values, and power-seeking behavior into the analysis.[18] Hence I have freely drawn upon social history, business history, biography, economics, sociology, and the insightful field of organizational theory to build this story.

This book is written as a series of nearly self-contained chapters that create a thematic narrative of organizational change and choice. Part I focuses on Thyssen & Co., but deals explicitly with German business historiography about the levels of bureaucratization and their alleged preindustrial patterns. It establishes a methodology for understanding the "conception of control" governing the business enterprise. Part II focuses on the growth of the Thyssen-Konzern, but more generally addresses the interaction between cartels and concerns and the development of a highly sophisticated managerial organization epitomized by the Central Auditing Office of the Thyssen-Konzern. Part III focuses on the managerial organization of the Vereinigte Stahlwerke, but addresses most directly the thematic issue of Americanization. Each of the three parts has a brief outline of the individual chapters and main arguments.

I make three general claims in this study. First: Before they could influence the German state and national economy to the extent they did, German heavy industrialists had to run their businesses successfully. Constructing a large-scale industrial firm was by no means an easy task, and is a story in itself. This book focuses on this story. Second: Their professional achievements have had as much (or more) long-term influence on societies than their more notorious forays into high state politics. For instance, Hamborn's existence as a major city was inextricably bound to Thyssen's decision to establish a firm at the train station on the green fields outside the village. The growth—or decline—of entire metropolitan areas is unthinkable without such industrial firms. Third: The growth of large-scale industry and a management profession is not only a national, but also an international phenomenon. One cannot understand the trajectory of business corporations only in terms of national politics. The consequences of big business are international in scope.

This perspective thus tends to trade off potentially important stories about the short-term relationship between economics and politics in favor of a long-term, comparative story on the growth of business. It can better explain why Thyssen AG exists today as a capitalist enterprise than can explain Thyssen's political involvement in industrial associations or Albert Vögler's political stance toward Hitler. Moreover, many leading directors and middle managers, like Heinrich Dinkelbach, continued to work through Weimar, the Third Reich, and the early Federal Republic. In such a manner I hope to contribute to a general theory of the business enterprise in a national and international context.

Because of this approach, I stopped this study at the 1933 reorganization of the VSt, although the last chapter on Heinrich Dinkelbach provides some insight into the postwar period. As I argue, the 1933–1934 reorganization of the Vereinigte Stahlwerke had less to do with the unfortunate new political order than coping with its financial and organizational problems. While there were amazing parallels with U.S. companies, this critical juncture in time completely altered the political *meaning* of this corporate restructuring. While the interests of the VSt were not entirely congruent with those of the newly installed Nazi government, this restructuring did depend on an active, rhetorical accommodation with the regime. This important shift in meaning and involvement during the Third Reich requires that business–government relations rightly overshadow the long-term lines of continuity developed in this book. But taking a business–government approach to the period of the Third Reich would break the parameters of this work, and one study on the VSt already exists.[19] There are too many important issues that would have to be discussed first: political contacts with the Nazis, exploitation of captured territories and properties, Aryanization, and the employment of forced labor. Such a study would demand a different approach than the one offered here. This study tends to assume that business corporations are relatively autonomous governance structures, which rest on a space accorded to the private sector. Just as in the revolution of 1918–1919, this space broke down during the Third Reich. For this reason, the chapter on war and revolution reads like a sociopolitical history of Germany told from the point of view of a company. The serious issues raised by business complicity during the Nazi period, combined with the vast amount of archival material to research, means that the 1933–1945 VSt still awaits its historian.

On the "Special Path" of German Business Historiography

Since this book addresses the work of both German historians and international business historians, it is worth reviewing how the two distinct literatures collide in German business history. This broader debate about Germany's *Sonderweg* ("special path") has shaped considerably the way German historians have conceptualized business and industrial developments over the last thirty years. Above all, this two-decade old controversy sought to explain the particularly violent course of German history.[20] Code words such as "lateness," "backwardness," "preindustrial," "state–bureaucratic traditions" have dominated discussion for decades and try to capture the phenomenon that made German economy, business, and society so different that Germany took a "special path" away from Anglo-American models of economic and political development until 1945. After 1945, German society has allegedly been Americanized, that is, normalized and integrated into the peaceful pattern of historical development found in the West. In German historiography, the Americanization of West Germany plays a crucial role in explaining the gradual conforming of German business to generally accepted Western business practices. Not surprisingly, one of the leading proponents of the *Sonderweg* thesis, Volker Berghahn, also has written one of the best books on the Americanization of West Germany.[21]

In this section, I want to briefly outline the research tradition against which I am arguing, and call into question the methodology implicit in the concepts of the "special path." The notions of "special path" and Americanization both rest upon a normative model or yardstick by which deviations are measured, a methodology based on the theories of Max Weber.

The original *Sonderweg* interpretation argues that German history took a "special path" because of the "lateness" of German industrialization or its "relative backwardness"—both are phrases taken from Alexander Gerschenkron's influential tract, *Economic Backwardness in Historical Perspective*.[22] Gerschenkron cast a wide, theoretical net that is still of fruitful heuristic value, even if it has become a bit dated along strict interpretive lines. Gerschenkron's ideas went well beyond a discussion of Germany's economic development, but found special resonance there.

According to Gerschenkron, late-developing countries overcame economic backwardness by resorting to special "substitutes," which replaced the institutions, capital, and people found in more advanced economies. The more backward the country, the more reliance it placed on the newest technology, on a greater size and scale of enterprises to match and compete with leading countries, and on producer-goods industries. The emphasis on producer goods derived from the fact that domestic purchasing power would naturally be weaker because the country was poorer. Latecomers would also have to rely on some sort of directed institutional substitutes to replace the shortage of capital, (perhaps) market demand, and managerial know-how. If this was done, however, the more backward the country, the more rapid the growth spurt—in part because the distance to be made up was greater. From this description, it is easy to see how follower countries would have to make up the degrees of "deviation" from the industrialized countries by relying on substitute institutions such as large investment banks, the state itself, or even further down the backwardness path, on foreign investment, multinationals, and know-how. Under the Gerschenkron model, the industrialization of latecomers becomes an "orderly system of graduated deviations from that [first] industrialization."[23]

For Germany, this backwardness model, this deviation from the British path of industrialization, meant that it was producer- rather than consumer-oriented. Great universal banks were formed to amass the little capital available to entrepreneurs. These banks played a role similar to the one played by an independent, decentralized (and democratic) commercial class in Britain. The universal banks also helped to direct investment in an industry that had to play catch-up. Germans established cartels and protective tariffs to counteract the superior productivity of English industries. State–bureaucratic models of organization made up for weak markets. Aggressive exporting overcame weak domestic demand. Finally, the state played a much more active role in subsidizing and directing the economy.

Gerschenkron's economic analysis had political implications for Germany that were more fully developed by other historians. His model of late industrialization implied that early industrializers would be democratic (Britain), relatively late industrializers would espouse a more or less mild form of authoritarianism (Germany), and late industrializers, who needed a strong central state to generate growth, would be autocratic (Russia). Gerschenkron's classic *Bread and Democracy in Germany*, in which he advocated the expropriation of the Junker ruling class, can be seen as a direct predecessor to the *Sonderweg* interpretation of German history.[24] To paraphrase: democracies eat wheat, while autocracies eat rye. Future historians focused on the close relationship of big business to a politically reactionary and militaristic state. In this view, the industrialization process occurred swiftly in Germany, but a significant number of preindustrial traditions remained in German society and business, preventing the middle class from having political power. Instead of modernizing German society, the German *bourgeoisie*, epitomized by German entrepreneurs and industrialists, failed to fulfill its historical mission. Instead of forcing greater democratic reforms, it became feudalized because of the continuing influence of aristocratic elements in German politics. Squeezed between the continuing hold on the political levers of power by the aristocracy and the ever-rising threat of a socialist-influenced working class, the *bourgeoisie* and entrepreneurs sided with those in power. The structural disjunction between a preindustrial politics and culture coupled with a modern industrial capitalist economy dominated by premodern, illiberal elements left Germany a fundamentally flawed society.

This general view that Germany failed to rid itself of its preindustrial traditions found additional support from a long line of historiography which tapped into the authoritarian, patriarchal nature of German industrial authority. Decision-making within German firms has traditionally been described as deriving from authoritarian military or state-bureaucratic models. Krupp's *Herr im Hause* stance has been held to be typical for German industry. The discipline of workers and staff consisted of strict military lines of command within the firm.[25] At the same time, strong welfare policies such as housing cushioned this authoritarianism but bound workers tighter to the patriarchal company in a type of capitalist serfdom. These policies also helped to counteract working class radicalism. Finally, industrialists' collection of official orders and medals, construction of huge villas, and other symbols of status and authority indicated a process of feudalization.[26]

Heinz Hartmann attempted to capture the link between accepted national cultural value systems and the specifics of industrial authority inside German business firms. He found that "German management holds predominantly ultimate, value-oriented authority" based on a fused triad of "ultimate values": the calling *(Beruf)*, private property, and elite ideology. Entrepreneurial authority based itself on property, loyalty, and discipline, which were held as self-evident values for their own sake. In contrast, American management oriented itself more toward "functional authority," toward competence, efficiency, and performance.[27] This ultimate authority found its linguistic roots in the "guiding model" of the entrepreneur *(Unternehmer)*. Hartmann spent a great deal of time outlining the differences between entrepreneurs and the then disparaged term *management,* between leadership *(Führung)* and administration *(Leitung),* between "creative destroyers" and routine organization. Hartmann quotes one entrepreneur: "We have no use for the manager farms which are America's pride, where managers are 'made' like chickens in the incubator. Please don't overlook the difference between *Führung* und *Leitung. Führung* needs personal qualities which cannot be replaced by mechanical instruction, even though that may help considerably in other instances." *Führung* was much less rational, and rested on loyalty and unquestioned rule. Needless to say, the emphasis on ultimate values and creative destroyers smacked suspiciously of a *Führer* ideology, making entrepreneurs charismatic leaders in their own firms.[28]

The interpretations of Jürgen Kocka, the leading historian on German business organization, act as a weathervane indicating changes in the winds of German business history. His works, moreover, represent the most sophisticated interpretations of organizational developments inside the business firm and the most influential in the context of German historiography.[29]

Kocka's case study of Siemens between 1847 and 1914 has set the standard for studies on internal industrial organization to this day.[30] Kocka traced the changes in organizational structure, the formalization of business procedures, and especially the growth of white-collar jobs and their professionalization from "private civil servants" to "salaried employees" (*Privatbeamte* to *Angestellte*). The growth of a white-collar class created an entirely new middle social class *(Mittelstand),* which redefined social relations.[31] Kocka argues that in Germany the work ethic, the managerial style, the general mentality and behavior of these white-collar employees continued to be characterized by state–bureaucratic traditions. Significantly, German white-collar employees in business firms were termed *Beamte,* or civil servants. Implied is that Siemens, and German firms in general, tended to be more bureaucratic—both in terms of the size of their managerial staffs and mentality—than comparable U.S. and British firms.[32] Without question Kocka's book on Siemens succeeds brilliantly in combining business history, general sociology, a history of professionalization, and a critique of Max Weber.[33]

Kocka's work on German business, however, modulates strangely between backwardness and modernity. On one hand, Kocka generally adheres to the argument that interprets Germany's special path as caused by continuing preindustrial traditions. On the other hand, Kocka has done more than any other German historian to show that German industrial techniques were as advanced as those of the United States. For instance, Kocka demonstrated that Siemens moved before 1914 to a weak form of the multidivisional structure—predating American developments.[34]

Kocka's overall interpretation remains indebted to Gerschenkron and is surprisingly tied to the concept of backwardness. After his work on Siemens, Kocka moved on to a more comprehensive assessment of German entrepreneurship and economic organization.[35] Kocka argued that the relative backwardness of Germany as compared to Britain led to a greater reliance on organizational than on market mechanisms. A weak market forced a greater reliance on product diversification, a greater internalization of market functions, and a higher degree of integration. Germans' cultural predilections to organize privately alongside the long tradition of public bureaucracy reinforced this structural deficit, which then insinuated preindustrial authoritarian patterns into industrial decision-making.[36]

By the early 1980s, however, Kocka had largely ceased to use the backwardness argument as an explanation for distinctively German bank–industry relations, cartels, and degree of state intervention. Banks, for instance, "acted like large flywheels; they did not initiate most changes but, rather, reflected and strengthened existing trends." Cartels ceased to be a result of bank pressure, but a result of industrialists' initiatives; banks "facilitated" mergers and cartel formation, with neither side dominating the other. The backwardness argument no longer carried the inevitable implication of a fusion of industrial and banking capital, but the relative backwardness of the market still explained the size, extent of diversification, and degree of vertical integration of German firms.[37]

The drift away from backwardness as an explanation for German business was a result of Kocka's own work. Kocka has been at the forefront of those arguing that German managerial hierarchies (apparently in spite of their preindustrial, illiberal baggage) were as (or more) sophisticated than their American counterparts.[38] The separation between ownership and control had progressed to a high level, which meant salaried entrepreneurs, not owners, ran large enterprises. These managers were well educated and academically trained. Highly differentiated middle-management staffs could be found in a wide variety of industries. Furthermore, especially close relationships between science and engineering, and universities and industry had developed—more so than in Britain or the United States. On the commercial side of business (marketing and finance), however, the connections were less close and less well developed. Still, a commercial and organizational literature did develop that discussed in detail various accounting techniques and factory controls. In fact, a sophisticated and systematic factory-management system sprang up well before Taylor's ideas crossed over to Germany.[39]

It is precisely these modern elements of German managerial capitalism outlined by Kocka that forced Alfred D. Chandler, Jr., to reevaluate some of his basic theses after publication of his classic *Visible Hand*. In 1979 and 1980, Chandler could confidently proclaim that the United States was the "seed-bed" of managerial capitalism.[40] He argued that other countries failed to develop an impersonal, managerial capitalism and remained tied to a family or personal capitalism—by implication, less advanced. Yet at the same time, Kocka and Hannes Siegrist argued that the hundred largest German firms were in roughly the same industries as the United States, but Germany had a greater proportion of firms in the producer-goods industry. Additionally, German firms had diversified, integrated, and expanded to much the same degree as their American counterparts. The similarities between German and American firms were "striking."[41]

The Kocka-Siegrist article marked a turning point in German business history. It was the first to compare explicitly and statistically Chandler's model of American business historical development to the German model. Three general differences were found between the largest German and American firms. First, German firms tended to be smaller. Second, they remained more tied to the family and entrepreneur. Third, they were more heavily concentrated in producer goods. Not surprisingly, given the implicit Gerschenkronian, *Sonderweg* line of argumentation, Kocka and Siegrist attributed the German drive toward large-scale business organizations, in particular their level of diversification, to the "relative economic backwardness" of German markets in comparison to Britain and the U.S.

By contrast, the confrontation with German managerial capitalism forced Chandler to revise some of his earlier assertions. *Scale and
Scope* summarizes the state of the literature on the rise of managerial
capitalism in America, Great Britain, and Germany.[42] While Kocka's
work presents the growth of managerial bureaucracies largely in a national context, with an eye toward explaining the sociopolitical implications of German relative backwardness, Chandler seeks to explain
the growth of large-scale business in an international context. It is instructive to read the conclusions reached by an historian working un-
burdened by the weight of the *Sonderweg* debate.

Chandler advances the thesis that the German development of big
business was more like the United States than Great Britain in terms
of the number, extent, and sophistication of managerial hierarchies.
When German firms made the "three-pronged investment in manufacturing, marketing, and management essential to exploit fully the economies of scale and scope, they became first movers in many of the new
capital-intensive industries, not only in their homeland but in all of
Europe." Chandler attributes Germany's rapid industrial comeback,
despite a lost world war, a revolution, and hyperinflation, to the resil-
iency of its managerial or "organizational capabilities." In terms of the
"basic dynamic of industrial capitalism," that is, this three-pronged investment, the Germans and Americans were comparable.[43]

While the Americans developed a "competitive managerial capitalism," the Germans created a more "cooperative managerial capitalism." By this distinction, Chandler summarized clear differences
between the German and American experience. Most importantly,
the Germans permitted cross-firm cooperation, such as cartels, close
bank–industry ties, peak industrial associations, etc., that mediated industries' and individual firms' relations with one another. Many of
these arrangements were illegal in the United States or not enforceable in Britain. The argument Chandler advances is a reformulation of
what the Germans have long called *Organisierter Kapitalismus*—a term
first coined by Rudolf Hilferding.[44] The German version of "organized
capitalism" goes beyond the increasingly organized nature of corporation and market control expressed by the American terms "corporate capitalism," "oligopoly capitalism," Chandler's "visible hand," or
"cooperative managerial capitalism." It encompasses the interdepen-
dence of highly influential trade and manufacturing associations, car-

tels, and growing state intervention. The American terms emphasize how the economy regulates itself. But the German use of "organized capitalism" emphasizes the fusion of state and economy into a new system of domination or hegemony—with insidious results for the history of Germany.

By the end of Chandler's analysis, however, one wonders how the theory of German backwardness, which is contingent on the positive model of English industrialization, ever came about. Chandler argues: "By World War I the British had become 'late industrializers' (to use Alexander Gerschenkron's widely applied term) in the new industries that were the dynamos driving the growth of industrial capitalism after the 1880s."[45]

Thus viewing essentially the same set of materials, Kocka and Chandler came to nearly opposite conclusions about Germany's lateness and special path. In his largely positive assessment of Chandler's *Scale and Scope*, Kocka retreated still further from his older position in order to save the explanatory effectiveness of backwardness; he pointed out the disjunction "between the relative backwardness of an economy at large and the relative modernity of some of its largest firms." The "Gerschenkronian idea is not incompatible with Chandler's analysis."[46] Kocka argued that German firms internalized market mechanisms more quickly as a compensation for "deficient markets." Then German firms could fall back on a long-standing tradition of German public bureaucracy. Ironically, since Kocka's seminal work on Siemens, backwardness as an explanatory concept has continued to drift away from the main phenomena that it purported to explain.

The tension between preindustrial influences and modern innovations reappears in a 1993 article significantly entitled "The Impact of the Preindustrial Heritage," by Kocka and Bernd Dornseifer, who argue that "preindustrial factors" in the 1830s and 1840s significantly modified the "German pattern of corporate development."[47] By "preindustrial heritage," they meant a curiously toothless "institutional structures and resources which had originated before industrialization proper." These factors include the handicraft and guild tradition, the educational system, and the "massive neoabsolutist state-bureaucracy and the corresponding experience of state-intervention and modernization 'from above'."

The craft and guild tradition, coupled with relatively low German wages, assured German firms comparative advantage in high value, low-volume niche goods. Many entrepreneurs stressed product quality and service with a "strong aversion against 'cheap production' and price competition, sometimes with an anti-capitalist or even anti-western undertone." Neoabsolutist state policy "propelled" university and technical traditions, which in their "core were of preindustrial origin" to create an abundant supply of engineers and scientists for industry. The emphasis on low-batch, customized production also depended on the craft and apprenticeship tradition: "The technological capabilities of German enterprises on the shop floor were thus shaped by a peculiar symbiosis of educational and craft traditions. Both traditions were of preindustrial origin."

Finally, the "accepted indicators of industrial modernity" *(sic)*, that is, the degree of capital intensity, the extent of mechanization and standardization of production, the level of information controls, and the intensity of the division of labor, show that Germany's industries— particularly the machine-engineering industry—were "relatively backward" compared to the United States. German organizational structures were heterogeneous and complex with a symbiosis of modern and traditional elements, particularly in decentralized nonstandard areas of business firms. After having retreated from the commanding heights of the German economy, Kocka sought to find "backwardness" in small and medium-sized *(Mittelstand)* business.

While their description is generally correct, the analysis of Kocka and Dornseifer turns on the terms *modern* or *advanced* or *backward* or *preindustrial.* We have little criteria for judging the terms rigorously, or if they are used rigorously they are arbitrary. An absurd argument can make this objection more obvious. In the beginning of the 1990s, the American government proposed to improve American vocational and apprenticeship training along German lines. Second, Michael Porter recommended a more German-style governance structure to ensure long-term investment horizons in American companies to make them less hostage to short-term fluctuations in the stock market.[48] Third, management literature of the 1990s seeking to revitalize the concept of the creative entrepreneur expressly reached back to the strategic thinking of Helmuth von Moltke, the Prussian chief of the general staff, as one model.[49] Are these three recommendations an attempt to insinuate German preindustrial traditions into American business?

A second problem is the long-running German effort to use Britain or America as the yardstick for modernity itself. The sociological (Weberian) method of setting up standards or criteria, an ideal-type, to measure difference, quickly turns into a normative presumption. At bottom, the attempt to use Max Weber's method of ideal-types shades over into idealist-types. For instance, the "accepted indicators of industrial modernity" used by Kocka and Dornseifer tend to idealize American factory-based, Fordist, mass-production methods. Even if the German machine-tool industry was relatively backward by these standards, it still has managed to be one of Germany's most successful export industries over the last one hundred years. Arguably, the long-term success of the German economy as a whole owes a good deal to this backward *Mittelstand* of small and medium-sized businesses, backward only if judged according to these "(allegedly) accepted indicators." The *Mittelstand* occupies a special role in Germany's long-term competitiveness.[50] There simply is no compelling economic reason why the German machine-tool industry should look like the American one, or that one should generalize about the American system from its mass-production firms.[51]

Finally, being the second or third industrializer in the world is hardly a sign of "lateness." Can only England be on time and the rest of the world late? A close relationship to the state or a state-directed industrialization is not inherently neoabsolutist nor should it be condemned outright. If a close symbiotic relationship between state and industry exists in most industrializing countries today because it plays a crucial role in creating opportunities for industry, then German development may be closer to the norm, rather than the exception or deviation.[52] As Gerschenkron noted, Britain in fact is the exception only because it was first. The United States was exceptional because it had a large (protected) domestic market that enabled large-scale mass production.[53] Maybe the German experience could be a model or yardstick for the rest of the world?

Still, Kocka and Dornseifer subtly shift the basis on which their article's main arguments rest. The article modulates less between backwardness and modernity than the tension between Germany's comparative advantage in world markets and its existing traditions.[54] It is unclear whether the use of such a loaded phrase, "preindustrial heritage," is still useful. Is it really helpful in illuminating questions of comparative advantage, historical traditions, and differences in the way firms operate within national economies? Which country does not have a "preindustrial heritage?" The intellectual shift implicit in the article begins to move the study of German business away from its highly normative, inappropriate, and misleading comparative methodology.

The thrust of the *Sonderweg* debate has also tended to interpret German business in light of political events. One could say that in the historiography of German political economy, we are long on politics and short on business practice, although this appears to be changing. (I am not arguing that this is not a valid research area, but that it blends out other approaches.)

The historiography of German business and, in particular, business–government relations has been dominated by "structures" and "fractions": heavy vs. light, export-oriented vs. domestic-oriented, dynamic vs. stagnant, producer vs. consumer goods, liberal versus conservative industries, etc. These categories are too loose to describe individual firms' interests or actions accurately.[55] Heavy industrial firms such as the VSt ranged from traditional coal mining to highly innovative machine engineering, were heavily oriented to export markets around the world, and borrowed state-of-the-art American managerial practices. Leading VSt figures were instrumental in establishing the International Steel Cartel, arguably a precursor of the European Economic Community, yet they also occupied key positions inside the Third Reich.[56] Furthermore, historians have portrayed the political ideology of a handful of industrialists as proxies for whole industries, firms, structures, or mentalities.[57] Fritz Thyssen, who "paid Hitler," illustrates most clearly the limitations of this approach.[58] Neither his support nor his subsequent imprisonment explain much about the Thyssen-Konzern or the VSt. Even as chairman of the VSt supervisory board, his initial support of Hitler did not reflect the mind-set of his colleagues. As I will demonstrate, the alleged interests of firms did not follow directly from structural positions or from individual leaders, but were formulated in a complex and contested negotiation process within the firm itself. If we want better studies of business–government relations, we need better business histories that go inside the firm.[59]

The literature on the Americanization of German business, especially after 1945, stands in direct and inverse relation to the pre-1945

Sonderweg debate. If the period before 1945 is interpreted as an aberrant, deviant history relative to Britain and the United States, then the period after 1945 is interpreted as a period of normalization, integration, modernization, democratization, Americanization, or Westernization. The conflation of those categories is a product of postwar modernization theory itself. Most business-history literature has focused on the decartelization process and the impact of the Marshall Plan commissions. While the prohibition of cartels is of critical importance to understanding post-1945 dynamics, this focus is too narrow to encompass an entire Americanization process for Germany—or even German business history. This begins to show a critical problem of the Americanization literature: how only a few criteria are somehow sufficient to Americanize German business. (Part III addresses this literature more explicitly.)

Volker Berghahn, for instance, focuses most intently on the heated battles surrounding the introduction of anticartel legislation, the development of American-style oligopoly capitalism after the breakup of large firms such as IG Farben or the VSt, and the introduction of codetermination. Berghahn equates Americanization largely with the advent of anticartel legislation, oligopoly competition, and much less authoritarian managerial attitudes of the younger generation after the 1960s. Indeed, the prohibition of cartels is the most robust example he could choose to make his case. Granted this transition is true, but his analysis is loaded with a curious tension between the very American decartelization and the very unAmerican codetermination act. Berghahn tends to use codetermination as a litmus test to see if the older authoritarian mentalities of German industrialists faded, but what if he were to impose the same test on present-day American executives? Finally, along with John Gillingham, Berghahn identified Heinrich Dinkelbach as the "one potential Americanizer."[60] Interestingly, the same Dinkelbach who broke up the German steel industry advocated codetermination on the employer side. This same Dinkelbach, however, could introduce modern American methods in the VSt in the 1920s in spite of the existence of cartels and backward, autocratic attitudes.

Berghahn ends his 1986 book and his 1997 article with a call for further national comparative studies about the impact of Americanization. He believes that the United States should still serve "as the *tertium comparationis* in the background that most comparative historians now-adays agree is the indispensable reference point for any viable comparison, because without this yardstick it will never be possible to know whether we are dealing with phenomena that are, in fact, comparable."[61] Without denying the vast assymmetry of power at the end of WWII, I will demonstrate that this is simply the wrong method, as it makes America the end of history, the yardstick of modernity itself.

Chandlerian Typologies of the Modern Business Corporation

Underlying Kocka's, Berghahn's, and Chandler's approaches is the ideal-type methodology of Max Wcbcr.[62] This section analyzes the (changing) Chandlerian classification of the business enterprise. Chandler's theoretical approach has influenced business history on four continents.[63]

To see what is at stake, one must clarify some of Chandler's terms. In the *Visible Hand,* Chandler divides firms into three types: family enterprises, entrepreneurial or personal enterprises, and managerial enterprises. A family enterprise refers to a firm owned and controlled by a family or a single figure. An entrepreneurial or personal enterprise refers to a firm in which the owner holds significant control, but employs a managerial staff; the owner still personally manages the firm in varying degrees. A managerial enterprise refers to a firm, usually a joint-stock corporation, in which salaried managers make strategic investment decisions; control has been separated from ownership. This classification scheme also explicitly underlies most German business historiography.[64]

In Chandler's *Visible Hand,* these ideal-types shade over into explanations with strong claims attached to them. In the *Visible Hand,* family or entrepreneurial enterprises failed to develop "systematic, impersonal techniques" of management and had strategic goals different from managerial enterprises. Owners continued to be too involved in day-to-day management. Long-range planning based on statistical material, the collection of information, and "formal capital appropriation procedures" were absent. Family and entrepreneurial enterprises "assured income rather than appreciation of assets," paid out dividends rather than reinvesting, and opted to retain personal control over the enterprise—thus inhibiting the competitive advantages of a manage-rial hierarchy. Virtuously, the managerial enterprise did just the oppo-site, managing its way to competitiveness over the long term.[65]

The *Visible Hand* formulation actually describes very little. It asks whether the top person in the firm is a family member, an owner-man-ager working with other salaried managers, or a salaried manager. This definition of the enterprise, which is really a definition of entrepre-neurship, privileges the *site* of strategic control, not how decisions about strategy and investment are made, or how they are implemented by the organization, or who initiates them. In ideal-type fashion, a whole slew of qualities follows from this shorthand description of the figure at the top. But these imputed set of qualities and claims do *not* necessarily follow.[66] Chandler confirms as much in *Scale and Scope,* as his *Visible Hand* classification scheme broke down—less for Britain than for Germany.

In *Scale and Scope,* Chandler critically revised the old classification scheme to incorporate the German case, which contradicted many of the tenets of the old typology. Successful firms such as Krupp, Siemens, the Haniel-owned Gutehoffnungshütte (GHH), and Thyssen, who were not mere exceptions to the rule in Germany, re-tained the strong presence of family members at the head and remained successful over the long term. A recent study of Krupp de-scribed it as an "entrepreneurial enterprise" until 1968.[67] Another 1969 study estimated that 60 of Germany's 150 largest firms were still owned by family members.[68] The huge Franz Haniel & Cie. firm re-mains entirely owned by family members today. As a result, John Wilson argues that before 1914 German business should be labeled "cooperative entrepreneurial capitalism."[69] In the *Visible Hand,* the presence of family and strong entrepreneurs (let alone cartels) im-plied a lack of competitiveness and failure; in *Scale and Scope,* Chandler altered his theoretical categories so that such entrepreneurial firms could remain competitive. Even family capitalism (in *Visible Hand*) is not necessarily personal capitalism in *Scale and Scope.* In fact, Chan-dler's earlier *Visible Hand* classification reverses the traditional Ger-man business historical interpretation. An older generation of Ger-man business historians tended to argue that continuing owner involvement led to long-term growth and reinvestment, while joint-stock companies and managerial enterprises were more interested in short-term financial success and dividends—behavior confirmed by the VSt.[70]

In effect, Chandler detached the negatives of personal management from the categories of entrepreneurial and family firms. He did this by redefining personal management to refer to a firm run *without* a broad administrative hierarchy or impersonal techniques. The second category encompasses entrepreneurial or family firms whose owners run their firms with managerial hierarchies or systematic, formal techniques. Such family-owned firms could be successful if they developed organizational capabilities. The third classification, the managerial enterprise, still refers to firms with hierarchies but without direct owner control. Not surprisingly, Chandler labels the section on British capitalism "Personal Capitalism." British firms' "continuing commitment" to personal capitalism led to its failure to retain its competitive status vis-a-vis the United States and Germany.[71] In *Scale and Scope,* the critical factor is the size and competency of managerial staffs. The question is not who the chief executive of the firm is, but whether the family, entrepreneur, or chief executive officer is to create, maintain, and improve the firm's "organizational capabilities." Following this shift in perspective, the development of Thyssen and VSt organizational capabilities is the centerpiece of this study.[72]

But August Thyssen's career glaringly exposes the weaknesses of Chandler's classification schemes in both their old and new guises. August Thyssen's longevity holds the person at the top as a constant, forcing a shift of attention to the structure of the enterprise, its scale and scope, its managerial competencies, and its decision-making process. As owner-manager in 1872, Thyssen employed roughly 150 workers. By 1884 the firm employed around 1,000 workers, including numerous salaried managers, who ran the firm on a day-to-day basis, and introduced organizational reforms that undergirded operations until 1926. Relying on these managers and this system, by 1913 Thyssen built up one of the largest industrial complexes in Germany. Just before his death in 1926, the Thyssen-Konzern employed roughly 50,000 employees and was widely considered to be the most efficient steelmaking complex in Germany. Classifying Thyssen's operations as a family enterprise *(Visible Hand)* cannot distinguish the changes from a 150-employee firm in 1872 to a 1,000-employee firm in 1882 to a 50,000-employee firm in 1926. Labeling Thyssen's firms as entrepreneurial *(Scale and Scope)* is somewhat better, but leads to the problem of distinguishing in an effective manner the tremendous changes in industrial organization between 1884 and 1926. We need to describe more forcefully shifts in managerial organization itself.

Otherwise the merger of Chandler's typology and *Sonderweg* historiography leads to misleading conclusions. As an example (and I am critiquing the categories of analysis from these two theoretical streams of thought, not her work), Suzanne Hilger argued that Germany did not have a "managerial revolution," especially in heavy industry, because entrepreneurs continued to have direct influence on the affairs of their firms. Following Chandler, family or personal enterprises precluded managerial enterprises. Then, activating the logic of the *Sonderweg,* Germans vehemently maintained their "traditional," reactionary, and "authoritarian, ideological commitment of German entrepreneurs—the 'Herr-im-Haus' or 'Lord in the Manor-attitude'—toward his company affairs" (quoting Richard Tilly). They despised any sort of third-party intervention on the part of the state or workers in their business affairs.[73]

First, there is *nothing* peculiarly German about this attitude. If one means by the "lord-of-the-manor" description the exclusion of an institutionalized voice for labor inside the enterprise, such as factory councils, collective bargaining, or greater state regulation, then business greatly resisted such encroachments all across the world—especially in the United States. Unlike Andrew Carnegie, an alleged friend of the working class who was hoisted on his rhetorical petard at the Homestead strike, no one would have ever caught August Thyssen in such hypocrisy; Carnegie's rhetoric was also the exception to the rule even in American industry. French or British or American entrepreneurs hardly countenanced sitting around a table with union representatives or allowing state inspectors into their firms. Such refusal to stomach any intervention in free enterprise has an arguably stronger tradition in the United States than in Germany. This attitude should not be viewed as the residue of a peculiarly German preindustrial tradition. One might even view this opposition as deriving from *liberal* principles, as a conflict between the private-property rights and public regulation.

Secondly, as will be shown, the heavy industrialist August Thyssen developed a sophisticated managerial hierarchy. Chandler's classification system privileges the type of person who has ultimate strategic control over the firm, not the "organizational capabilities" of the firm itself. Above all, this concept emphasizes the ability of the firm itself (regardless of who stands on the hierarchical apex) to generate, use, and commercialize knowledge in order to sustain innovation, and implicitly emphasizes learning over time. The evolution of these firm-specific capacities should be classified more adeptly, not imputed through ownership.

Thirdly, the link between family and business is not necessarily dysfunctional in a global perspective—if the family or entrepreneur develops a firm's organizational capabilities and does not use the firm as a golden goose. By this chain of logic, no other country in the world had a managerial revolution *á la* the U.S. All countries would fall short of this standard. From a global perspective, then, German big business tended to follow a *Normalweg* instead of a *Sonderweg*.

For years, Kocka has pointed out the need for more research concerning the organizational structure and procedures of large-scale business in Germany.[74] In his still unsurpassed article on German management, Kocka distinguished various models, but derived his conclusions mostly from published literature. Youssef Cassis reiterates that we know very little about the internal organization of most European business before 1945. We know very little about the depth or size of middle management, let alone how managers actually made their decisions and strategic choices. Research on the internal life of business corporations is "still in its infancy."[75] Two recent histories make organization a variable, but tend to be descriptive rather than analytical.[76]

Kocka critiqued Chandler's *Scale and Scope* by writing that the "real working of the managerial structures remain something of a "black box."[77] Chandler's famous formulation, "structure follows strategy," tends to make organization a structure, not a process or a culture. Yet in order to refine his historical, evolutionary theory of the modern business enterprise, Chandler has increasingly emphasized the importance of organizational capabilities and continuous learning to explain the competitive strengths and weaknesses of firms.[78] Although Chandler makes organizational learning central to his discussion—that is, problem-solving through trial and error, feedback, and evaluation—his definition of the corporation remains largely defined in the structural terms of his "three-pronged investment" in manufacturing, marketing, and management. Paradoxically, as Chandler has spread his theoretical scope to more countries, his writing has become more structure-oriented, yet to an inversely proportional degree his *theory* stresses *process:* organizational evolution, capabilities, and learning. Moreover, his emphasis on internal organizational form misses the "inter-subjective dimension of structure," that is, "managers' shared ideas and beliefs and the way these shape decision-making."[79] Although Chandler "places the problem of coordination squarely at the center of business history . . . [and] focused attention on large firms' dependence on managerial coordination, he actually had surprisingly little to say about how this coordination was achieved throughout the organization."[80] *Strategy and Structure* actually emphasizes internal organizational process and learning more than do *Visible Hand* or *Scale and Scope*. We need to reconstruct decision-making processes, organizational routines, and management styles inside individual business firms to bring organizational learning processes to light.[81]

Behind Kocka's, Berghahn's, and Chandler's comparative approaches discussed above, and our understanding of organizations, looms Max Weber.[82] In his general body of thought, Weber created a strict separation of ends and means, which affects his theory of bureaucracy. Values, often formed by a charismatic personality, are institutionalized in rules and regulations; a division of labor set by strict competencies and offices ensure regularity and enforcement.[83] Implicitly, organizations are conceived as internally consistent, somewhat mechanical, and organic wholes. In Weber's theory of organization, bureaucracy is an instrument, a tool, or a technology of power *(Herrschaft)*.[84] Crucially, bureaucracy is not defined as a field of social processes or rich, intersubjective human behavior, but as a set of functions or offices (roles). Bureaucratization meant the growth of formally rational rules and procedures, a set of offices, files, paperwork, a hierarchy, a career path, and so on, but defined as structural characteristics. Bureaucracies also have a power–political dimension in that they institutionalize a given value-orientation, usually through a charismatic, visionary figure. In a strict theoretical sense, bureaucracies do not learn, but execute. They alter their functioning as values generated from the top trickle down. Moreover, the tension between bureaucracy as a system of efficiency (as a means of getting things done effectively) and as a system of domination (a means of authority over people) is a basic characteristic of Weber's thought.

In business history, this translated into the notion that the entrepreneur sets the goals and strategy for the firm, while the firm's managers execute those desires and values: structure follows strategy; *Leitung* follows *Führung;* administration follows leadership. Hartmann's and Chandler's analysis of ultimate authority and values positively rings with Weberian analysis. The strongest statement of this notion came from Josef Schumpeter, who saw the entrepreneur as a "creative destroyer" and the growing bureaucratization of companies as the death-knell of the great entrepreneur. In one respect, Schumpeter's reliance on the mythic, creative hero-entrepreneur as an agent of change disguised the fact that he was at a loss to explain change.[85]

Based on the Thyssen story, strategic decision-making did center on the entrepreneur and senior management, but no strict separation between the entrepreneur and management, leadership and administration, values and means should be made. Moreover, the relationship between the entrepreneur and management shifted as the firm grew larger, as the separation of ownership and control grew, and as the nature of management and the business firm developed over time. A qualitative shift in decision-making occurred between 1871 and 1930 from a rather simple entrepreneur-set strategy to a fluid political process involving powerful internal and external constituencies, which does not describe just the transition of Thyssen & Co. to the VSt, but the transition to large-scale business enterprises everywhere.

At the level of theory, this transition to a political process calls into question the idea of bureaucracies as internally consistent wholes, particularly in the Weberian framework. Business firms become contested terrains. Positing an entrepreneurial/managerial intention or a vague rationalization process serves only to conceal the internal decision-making process forming corporate strategy and policy.

Kocka, too, relies heavily on the Weberian notion of bureaucratization. This reliance helped to bolster his thesis that the German state–bureaucratic tradition shaped its company management, but ironically the great theoretical achievement of his work on Siemens was to show that capitalist organizations do not mesh easily with Weber's model of bureaucracy. He found Weber's model insufficient for capitalist administration because of business' fundamental market orientation. A degree of flexibility, improvisation, and reaction had to be built into the organization to allow some degree of lateral communication between departments and offices, circumventing a strictly vertical, rule-bound decision-making process built around regularity. Moreover, clear standards of success largely defined by profitability legitimized organizational behavior and change. Seniority and tenure rights were not strictly adhered to. Instead of (rational) regulations, (market and meritocratic) performance became a new means and measure of legitimate domination.[86]

But Kocka does little to develop an alternative framework for describing industrial bureaucracy, that is, management. Kocka is able to point out differences in industrial organization, but cannot break the yardstick of the Weberian theory of bureaucracy. In historical literature, we are left with Weberian terms of bureaucratization and rationalization, which are too vague to distinguish various factors and conceptions structuring organizations and too broad to capture the decision-making process inside the business firm. Kocka himself argued that it was crucial to differentiate business management from Weber's theory of bureaucracy.

If, as Kocka argues, (measurable) standards of performance are one of the critical distinguishing characteristics between management and bureaucracy, then we need to know how performance is assessed and evaluated. But in Kocka's work, we rarely get a sense of how performance was defined except that the company was profitable. We rarely see how those managers worked inside Siemens, what they did, or how they were evaluated. The analysis is largely structural; managers have functions or roles, rather than agency.[87]

A Strategy for Analysis

This study is designed to cast light on issues inside the black box of the modern corporation. Although the focus on Thyssen and the VSt has all of the problems of a case study, I have attempted an approach sufficiently robust to rethink the history of German management more generally. If Thyssen had run his company as a state–bureaucratic, *Herr im Hause* entrepreneur, he would have failed miserably. Personal, paternalistic capitalism can work well in a small firm where the owner can oversee all of the operations of the enterprise. Once a company moves to larger-scale operations, numerous problems arise that have to be surmounted, redefining the role of the entrepreneur and the nature of the firm.[88]

If we think of a firm as a human hand, then a firm has four fingers (manufacturing, finance, marketing, and personnel) and a thumb (management). A successful business firm must manage constant tradeoffs among these functions and learn to make adjustments among them over time. Manufacturing scale itself engenders qualitative change in managerial practices, and places pressure on the quality of the product. Management must sustain product innovation over time. Expansion places pressure on finance, and managers must find new sources of internal and external finance with their own claims on the firm. The marketing department must find buyers willing to buy the product at a profitable price. A product is expensive junk unless it is sold. The sales staff and customers might want the lowest possible price even at the cost of lower product quality, which engineers in manufacturing might not want. Complex products such as sewing machines or steam turbines need servicing. As the firm grows, it must develop a personnel policy that can attract and retain good people, yet management might not want to pay the higher wages or salaries that employees desire. The firm must also develop employee technical skills or knowledge over time.

Then, firms must face ongoing problems of coordination among these four functional areas. Franz Dahl, one of Thyssen's most trusted technical directors, related one incident that illustrates the inherent tradeoffs among these activities. At the beginning of the 1890s, Dahl and Thyssen used to stand in the middle of the steelworks and discuss new investments, which Thyssen approved or rejected on the spot. Afterwards, an "immense" (Dahl) commercial apparatus had been built up, which mediated the information received by Thyssen. Thyssen listened increasingly to the recommendations of his purchasing office, which naturally wanted to minimize procurement costs. Dahl urged Thyssen to buy a heavy, expensive crane from one company for the steel mill, but the purchasing office rejected Dahl's recommendation in favor of a lighter, less expensive crane from another company. Thyssen sided with his purchasing manager. Shortly after they installed the crane, it collapsed, killing the crane operator. This "drastic and deeply regrettable" incident, which cost a worker his life, ended up costing more than Dahl's first choice of the more expensive crane. From then on, the purchasing offices had to adhere to the guidelines laid down by the production departments, reasserting the priority given to technical engineers on the factory floor.[89] The Dahl example shows how organizations learn and institutionalize new routines to overcome past mistakes.

Similarly, Henry Ford's wonderful marketing strategy meant that his customers could have any color Model T—as long as it was black. This marketing strategy, arguably more a manufacturing strategy, proved to be immensely successful for a time, but it also eventually allowed General Motors to overtake Ford after the mid-1920s. Ford sold his famous $5.00/day wage as a way for workers to purchase his cars, but he offered the $5.00/day to overcome workers' distaste for working on the assembly line, a type of disgust premium. He had to originate a new personnel policy to enable his manufacturing strategy. In short, what may be good for marketing may be bad for manufacturing. What may be good for manufacturing may be disadvantageous for workers. What may be good product design for engineers, might be bad for the sales force or customers. What may be good for shareholders, might be bad for stakeholders. Even within one functional area such as manufacturing, the tradeoffs between standardized mass production and diversified flexible production are well known.

Senior management must fuse these four areas (production, finance, marketing, and personnel) together into a more or less coherent corporate strategy. Strategy is a set of overall objectives and methods designed to assert the firm on the market by reducing transaction costs and developing organizational capabilities that add value. Corporate policy is the underlying set of rules, procedures, and conventions governing the firm at the organizational level, which should be designed to realize the firm's overall strategy. In Chandler's famous formulation, structure follows strategy, meaning that a firm's internal organization and institutionalized practices must eventually conform to strategic goals. That, too, is not always easy. Management must continually redefine corporate strategies and policies through a complex decision-making process inside the firm.

Yet different people within the organization might offer different rationales for coordinating how strategy and organizational policies should fit together, let alone how the four fingers of the business firm should work with one another. Since the entrepreneur cannot make all of these decisions, they help formulate strategies and policies with their personal judgments of the situation based on organizational routines and the information available to them. Often their own professional training shapes their decision-making. Lawyers think differently than engineers.[90] The use of the term *policy*, moreover, opens the firm to negotiation—politicking—among advocates of these rationales.[91] Both corporate strategy and policy are often an end result of negotiation among myriad coalitions, interests groups, stakeholders, rationales, and world views.

Then, the firm must ensure that the rest of the organization executes or adheres to the goals or policies selected. Formulating a strategy or creating policies are one thing, but senior management must also manage the inevitable tradeoffs or setbacks. Implementation is just as important as having the correct strategy. All of this leads to complex internal issues of organization, coordination, and monitoring— a problem of control and surveillance, which inform top management about what is going on in the firm. Thyssen and VSt managers' solutions to the problems of coordination and control depended on changing ideas about efficiency, profits and profitability, performance, and on the evolving nature of the firm itself. These conceptions became embodied—institutionalized—in the standard operating procedures (routines) and the corporate culture of the firm. Corporate culture simply refers here to the general set of implicit or explicit values, often a vague "the way we do things here," which in turn shapes corporate strategy and policy.

Understanding this decision-making and organizational learning process inside the firm provides the main focus of this book. For my purposes, process is more important than final outcome. Debates about the direction of the company are more important than the final strategy eventually decided upon.[92] How did management inside Thyssen and the VSt evolve over time? Why did changes in management occur? What triggered changes in managerial practice? One of the key problems in business history is the sample of firms studied tends to be success stories, yet this book seeks out the mistakes, failures, or setbacks that were corrected and institutionalized in new procedures like the crane disaster, which in turn affected how decisions were made at later points. The creation of offices or routinized tasks and its communication system coded information in specific ways. By doing so, one can gain a critical perspective on how management coped with crisis and change.

Understanding the methods of organizing managers is a crucial variable for understanding a firm's capabilities. Organization consists of the formal lines of hierarchy, which obviously structures decision-making by choosing who has more power and influence, but it also consists of routines and techniques of management. Then there is also the less formalized, intersubjective aspect of organization, but formal lines of authority help structure this intersubjective process. Organizational design also matters because it coordinates the interactions between the various members in the corporation by a mixture of control and function, authority and volition, hierarchy and autonomy, centralization and decentralization. It is an instrument for implementing company goals, especially as defined by senior management, but it is also an inadvertent result of historical circumstance, market relations, technological necessity, economic efficiency, ideology, and power. The hierarchy of offices constrain and channel information flows within the firm in particular ways.

Aside from outlining critical internal debates and sketching organizational change, I pay special attention to the accounting and information system of Thyssen and the VSt. First, accounting in capitalist firms differs significantly from the budget of a bureaucracy, single office, or a household because it fundamentally defines the performance of the business. Weber himself viewed accounting's calculability and "formal rationality" as one of the distinguishing features of capitalist enterprise because it measured profits earned on the market.[93] But Weber viewed accounting more as a system of formally rational rules rather than as a *communicative process* that shapes managerial perceptions and actions. Accounting is not just an information-processing service, but rather organizes knowledge about the firm and acts as a crucial signaling device. Like all codes, it transforms action and helps to create organizational reality.[94]

Second, the accounting system provides a sort of bottom line for the firm by implicitly conceiving the enterprise as a coherent, unified whole that makes sense of the firm's activities and performance. Like archaeological artifacts, one can interpret such business practices not only as instrumental techniques, but also as signifiers of the social, organizational, and conceptual world they express.[95] Reading accounting information provides the historian with an insightful method for entering into the life of an organization. By analyzing a firm's accounting and information systems, one can track the evolving *conception of control* operating inside management, which refers to the relationship between strategy, organization, information, and accountability. Andrew Carnegie, for instance, felt profits would follow if he drove direct manufacturing costs down, which meant that he stressed a strategy of economies of scale (strategy), factory and labor management (organization), prime costs (information about a particular definition of manufacturing costs), and holding people accountable for these costs.

If the remnants of this management control system are analyzed as conceptual and procedural remnants of a previous organizational order, they can provide insight into key measures of performance, linking the information system to the firm's strategy and core organizational values.[96] Accounting provides a feedback loop for managers precisely because it informs them about the success or failure of a firm's strategy. Moreover, a business may aim the antennae of its accounting and information system to signal some changes in performance more sensitively than other issues.[97] Firms design accounts in very different ways, with different categories, different principles, and different conceptions underlying the calculable figures and ratios. Moreover, at different times and for different people, some figures are more convincing and persuasive than others. Once the categorization of these accounts and the role they play inside an organization is deconstructed, the Weberian distinction between formal rationality and "substantive rationality" blurs considerably. This conception of control helps disclose how management defines profits and how they attempt to realize profits. Ultimately, by tracing the historical uses of accounting information inside the business firm more effectively, one can shift the Chandlerian classification scheme onto the managerial hierarchy itself.

Third, the information and accounting system is also a crucial aspect of corporate governance—of maintaining control. A firm's conception of control is not just an attempt to improve efficiency or maintain authority, but a basic problem of ensuring accountability and trust. The firm develops a surveillance system designed to monitor, inform, coordinate, and manage its diverse people and operations. Yet this surveillance creates a tension between decentralized autonomy and centralized standards, between flexibility and rigidity, between informal exchange and formalized procedure, between independent decision-making and accountability to the firm. All firms must confront this fundamental problem of trust or control to grow. Heinrich Dinkelbach summed this up concisely as "Delegate as much as possible, but supervise." The German word he used, *überwachen*, translates literally to "watch over." I prefer the term *control* because it retains the Weberian tension between authority and market rationality. The business firm operates "between power and [the] market" with a curious mixture of authority and efficiency, surveillance and trust.[98]

From this perspective, accounting systems are coded surveillance systems that define, construct, and delimit the performance of the firm and its managers in specific ways. The control system of the organization shapes the conceptual lens of top management, "deciding" for management, and helping to form the future strategy of the firm. Moreover, following the double meaning of the word, control also implies a degree of power and authority, of disciplining, of potential sanctions and rewards. In this system of controls that tracks and records the activity of a firm over time, with its implicit values and concerns and with its explicit routines and procedures, alterations best signify the evolving, historical nature of the business enterprise and managerial knowledge that makes firms' operations intelligible.[99] (For those readers interested in a richer discussion of the methodology associated with "new accounting theory," or for readers unfamiliar with reading accounts, Appendix B discusses some of the main ideas associated with this approach.)

At an empirical and theoretical level, this book also demonstrates how financial and accounting criteria, accounting conventions, and financial ratios inform organizational decision-making. They help guide the formulation of business strategy. They confer organizational legitimacy on those managers who make such signals: Those who gather, frame, and report this information gain special power within the business. From this perspective, there is little wonder that discussions about the proper organization of the firm were closely associated with the central auditing offices of German firms. This link between organizational knowledge and power was particularly true for Albert Killing (inside Thyssen & Co., Part I), Carl Rabes (inside the Thyssen-Konzern, Part II), and, Heinrich Dinkelbach (inside the VSt, Part III).

This book implicitly leans on postmodernist organizational-learning literature of the 1990s, which has tended to call into question the definition of control as performance management. From this perspective, management tries to design an organizational form that optimally aligns individual incentives. This modernist conception of management tends to view the organization as a closed set of more or less efficient functions, as if they were the gears of a clock, while the postmodernist views it as an open, holistic system of built-in reception, knowledge-creating, learning processes.[100] German steel's method of organizing control remains well within this modernist conception, yet the postmodernist approach still provides considerable insights into life in such early organizations.

In the end, this study addresses the theory of the firm and the structure of modern society. Business corporations are not uniquely German phenomena, so I draw freely on U.S. business history and recent organizational theory to provide access to the corporate world. The contrast with U.S. developments provides a useful analytic foil, but the assumptions of American historiography about its model quality cannot be sustained. The challenge, therefore, is to wed business history with economic theory, empirical evidence with theoretical analysis, narrative with explanation. The thematic chapters serve to highlight conceptual points less possible in a conventional narrative, and to illustrate the diverse array of influences affecting management. The modern business corporation is not a closed, internally consistent organization, but a contested field of people and operations attempting to manage their internal and external environment.

PART I

Thyssen & Co., 1871–1914

August Thyssen is one of Germany's best-known entrepreneurs, largely because of his activity at the Gewerkschaft Deutscher Kaiser (GDK), one of the historical roots and legal predecessors of today's Thyssen-Krupp AG. His Mülheim experience has largely been overlooked. The first two decades at Thyssen & Co. created the organizational and financial foundation for the wave of expansion that made Thyssen one of Germany's most famous captains of industry, by 1900 vying with the nineteenth-century leader, Krupp, for leadership in the twentieth. At Thyssen & Co., August Thyssen forged his entrepreneurial style and fashioned a corporate culture that would permeate his other firms for the next five decades. In Mülheim, Thyssen first learned how to manufacture using economies of scale and scope, to delegate wide-ranging responsibility to dynamic managers, to account for and control them, and to sustain technological innovation by incorporating research and development. He needed all of these qualities to compete in the brave new world of steel. Paradoxically, although he ostensibly sought to create a family dynasty, Thyssen kept his sons distant from company affairs until after World War I. A brief biography of August Thyssen shows how certain traits in his personality chilled his relationship to his children and markedly influenced his business strategy and corporate culture.

This story of Thyssen & Co. actually encompasses three distinct business operations. The original core of the firm consisted of four product departments, which were eventually referred to as the Thyssen &

Co. Steel and Rolling Mills. This part of the firm manufactured strip steel, heavy-gauge plates and lighter sheets, and small-diameter pipes and large-diameter tubes. Thyssen & Co. also built one of Germany's premier machine engineering departments, which they spun off in 1911 as an independent firm, the Thyssen & Co. Maschinenfabrik AG. Thyssen & Co. finally established a gas and waterworks department that supplied the surrounding region, which they also made an independent firm, the Wasserwerke Thyssen & Co. GmbH. The Gas and Waterworks firm essentially made Thyssen & Co. part of the region's infrastructure. While the rolling mills division depended essentially on mastering economies of scale and scope, the Machine Company and the waterworks firm owed their success to sheer entrepreneurial opportunism and science-based technical capabilities. Germany's "national innovation system" (Richard Nelson) provided the necessary foundation for the Machine Company's success. A positive, virtuous feedback loop between company experience and academia, practice and theory came into existence, allowing Thyssen & Co. to sustain innovation. Finally, the commercialization of high-horsepower gas engine, and dynamos by the Machine Company exemplified the shift to new methods of manufacturing control after the turn of the century, and epitomizes a distinctly "German path" of rationalization. While American scientific management focused on economies of task and labor (Taylorism), German rationalization focused on "economies of energy" (Christian Kleinschmidt).

Just as Thyssen & Co. provided the financial and experiential foundation for Thyssen's more famous wave of expansion, the following chapters build a conceptual framework for understanding the history of organizing control. Thyssen & Co. had to build manufacturing capacities that rested on the technical expertise of engineers. Then it had to find ways of coming to terms with fast growth. Thyssen established a modern managerial hierarchy built around product departments that forced these department chiefs to organizationally combine their engineering expertise with commercial success. Thyssen & Co.'s modular management system does not fit Alfred Chandler's ideal-type organizational structures but represents a distinct and fairly common form of German management. Thyssen & Co. also does not fit our stereotypical view of German managers as following state-bureaucratic or civil-service traditions. Thyssen expected the chiefs of these commercial-technical product departments to act as inside entrepreneurs and to demonstrate "self-sufficient," "managerial leadership" *(Dispositions-Fähigkeit)*. Finally, this specific corporate culture of Thyssen & Co. derived as much from August Thyssen's expectations, as from the various trials and failures his firm had to overcome in an organizational learning process.

Thyssen relied on a modern managerial system, built around a highly sophisticated accounting and information system—a system of surveillance. Thyssen & Co. managers introduced new procedures, routines, and controls as a type of nerve-and-sinew network, binding the firm together. Ultimately, the accounting system provides an account—a story—about the firm. Like all narratives, there are *genres* of internal business communications that shape knowledge about the firm's activity and performance. This system also allowed it to branch out into machine engineering and gas and water supply without these ventures spinning out of control.

These symbolic, communicative practices inside the business enterprise provide the best guide for conceiving the managerial system of the firm as a whole. Thyssen & Co. moved from a merchant-industrial conception of control to a manufacturing-engineering conception of control around the turn of the century. Before the turn of the century, accounting reports tended to emphasize sales and commercial surpluses, but after the turn of the century Thyssen & Co. turned greater attention to rationalized manufacturing efficiencies. In Thyssen & Co. and other German businesses, the turn of the century marked a shift to more American-style practices in economies of scale. In both cases, the ultimate goal was to earn profits in the market, but the strategies signified by changes in the accounting, information, and control systems shifted dramatically. Finally, I demonstrate how Thyssen & Co.'s managerial practices were as advanced, if not more so, than American techniques. While German companies tended to excel in managerial accounting, American firms tended to excel in workshop or cost accounting. This emphasis grew out of the relatively high costs of labor in the United States, but also from their respective differences in the strategy, structure, and institutional contexts of their business organizations. None of these methods derived from alleged preindustrial or state-bureaucratic traditions.

CHAPTER 1

August Thyssen,
Victorian Entrepreneur

August Thyssen's personal life is nearly inseparable from his professional work. He poured his great personal pride, as molten metal is casted into forms, into his machines, his factories, his business ventures—his work.[1] From 1871 to 1926, the Thyssen-Konzern remained independent, entirely owned by his family. Dolores Augustine argued that August Thyssen wanted to create a family industrial dynasty.[2] Yet, paradoxically, because of his miserable relations with his children, he kept them at arms length from his business throughout his life. Yet family issues still intruded upon some of the most momentous decisions of his long career, including the decision to end his steadfast independence.

The fundamental tension between two of Thyssen's most cherished principles, the desire for independent family control versus the desire to create Germany's premier steelworks, came to a head in 1925 with the negotiations to found the Vereinigte Stahlwerke (VSt). Like Andrew Carnegie before him, Thyssen had to decide whether to join this new venture and thus terminate his control over his empire of firms. In fact, August Thyssen (1842–1926) can best be described as Germany's version of Andrew Carnegie (1835–1919). Their lives overlapped for all but seven years. Contemporaries viewed the absorption of the Thyssen-Konzern into the VSt as either a sad end to a family business in a new age of anonymous corporate capitalism, or as a triumph of Thyssen's goal to build an American-style "trust" along the lines of U.S. Steel. Paul Arnst, who wrote the first comprehensive overview of Thyssen's career in 1925, appeared to be prescient in predicting the merger when Thyssen joined the VSt just one year later. International newspapers reinforced this interpretation by claiming that Thyssen was the great "Americanizer" and "trustmaker" among German industrialists. The *New York Times* dubbed Thyssen the "Rockefeller of the Ruhr."[3] The decision to join the VSt provides one of the knottiest interpretive points for any Thyssen biography, which one can only resolve if one considers his sad, strained, and often solitary family life.

This brief sketch of his family life and his character, both personal and political, provides a window onto the fundamental values and tensions underlying his strategic vision and the corporate culture inside his firms. The reader should also contrast August Thyssen with Heinrich Dinkelbach, an organization man *par excellence,* to personify some of the many changes in business life between the 1870s and the 1950s.

Thyssen remained a classic Victorian-age entrepreneur. His formative years lay well before the founding of the German Reich, well before the wealthiest members of the middle class evolved into a *parvenu* elite that incorporated elements of aristocratic, upper-class culture. Thyssen remained attached to this pre-Bismarckian *Bürger* world of thrift, frugality, industriousness, middle-class values, patriarchalism, and conservatism. But the brave new world of corporate capitalism, which he helped to create, undermined this older pattern of *bourgeois* behavior, which helps explain his children's rebellion against him.

Thyssen's milieu and career up to 1871 was fairly typical for Ruhr industrialists.[4] In contrast to many later myths about his being a self-made man rising from rags to riches, August Thyssen came from an established, upper middle class, Catholic family in the Rhineland.[5] He was born in Eschweiler outside of Aachen on May 17, 1842, to Johann Friedrich and Katharina Thyssen. His father, Friedrich, was a local merchant-banker. Some measure of Friedrich's success can be gleaned from the substantial inheritance (230,000 marks) he left to his children after his death in 1877. Signifying the unity of homelife and worklife, Friedrich Thyssen's bank was located downstairs in his home, typical for the time.

August Thyssen had an unusually good education for the time, attending a leading technical university in Karlsruhe in 1859.[6] There he found himself inclined toward commerce rather than technical matters, foreshadowing a lifelong tendency in his business style. In 1861, at the age of 19, Thyssen moved to Antwerp, Belgium, to study at the renowned *Institut Supérieur du Commerce de l'Etat,* one of the first academic institutes for commercial administration. After finishing a one-year stint in the military, he then joined his father's banking business in Aachen for a two-year apprenticeship.

Thyssen grew up in one of the most vibrant clusters of small merchants and industrialists in Germany. Just as knowledge about steel-making methods drifted from England through Belgium to Germany, the cultural fluidity of the Rhineland and Belgium and his contacts there influenced Thyssen's career in the same way that outside knowledge decisively affected early German industrialization. Through his father's business activities, he developed numerous contacts with leading merchant families in the Aachen area, such as the Poensgens, Bicheroux, and Piedboeufs, who would later move to the Ruhr alongside Thyssen. The Ruhr was not yet Germany's great industrial smithy, but an area largely of agricultural fields, river-based commerce, small villages, and rabbits. Thyssen's later defense of economic liberalism and world trade owed much to his own interpretation of his early life, which was open to foreign influence.[7]

Thyssen's first major business opportunity arose through the 1867 marriage of his sister, Balbina, to Désiré Bicheroux, a Belgian manufacturer. The young August followed his sister and the Bicheroux family to Duisburg, where they founded a rolling mill in 1865. In 1867 the Bicheroux family helped finance Thyssen's first venture, a small partnership called Thyssen, Foussoul & Co. Thyssen was its commercial director; Noel Fossoul, another Belgian, managed the manufacturing side. Their firm was located next to the Bicheroux rolling mills near the Duisburg train station, and Thyssen took up residence in the home of Désiré and Balbina, also directly adjacent to the rolling mills. Family and business remained tightly entwined. The firm had numerous puddling furnaces producing hoop iron (medium-width strip steel used as hoops for barrels, crates, or wheels), merchant bars, and angle iron. Here Thyssen gained his working knowledge of the steel industry. Fifty years later Thyssen paid tribute to these years: "I was lucky to enter into a new business immediately, which was directed by very energetic, farsighted people. The Bicheroux were extraordinarily significant for my future development."[8] The company expanded quickly, so that his investment of 8,000 taler (24,000 marks) grew fourfold to 32 taler (96,000 marks) by 1871.

According to his own account, Thyssen struck out on his own in 1871, the same year Germany became unified through blood and iron "because I did not find enough freedom for my business activities there." There is some question how proactive Thyssen was in deciding to leave, especially as Fossoul and the elder Bicheroux were no longer there (possibly as a result of the war), which left the Bicheroux mills in the hands of his three sons. However, there is no question that a basic urge for independence propelled Thyssen's business strategy for the next fifty-five years.[9]

With his father as silent partner, Thyssen established his new firm, Thyssen & Compagnie, Commanditgesellschaft, Styrum bei Mülheim a/d Ruhr on April 25, 1871, in the middle of the speculatory euphoria following unification. The history of the Thyssen-Konzern properly begins here.[10] His first step into independence was by no means a heroic pioneer performance with a vision of large industrial combines, nor was it an attempt to break free from tried and true methods of commerce and industry. Instead it was a sense for opportunity combined with a strong streak for independence.

Thyssen's early biography illustrates a typical path for Ruhr entrepreneurs of his day.[11] At roughly the same age as other area entrepreneurs, thirty, Thyssen married Hedwig Pelzer, the eighteen-year-old daughter of two leading Protestant merchant families in Mülheim (Ruhr). Typical for the time, the "mixed" marriage (Catholic-Protestant) was as much a business arrangement as a romantic liaison: Hedwig's marriage dowry found prompt use in Thyssen's new firm. Son Fritz was born in 1873; August, Jr., in 1874; Heinrich in 1875; and finally, Hedwig in 1878.

In three ways Thyssen's career path proved exceptional. First, he had a high degree of prior technical and commercial education. Second, he came to the steel industry rather late, as most of his primary rivals had already migrated to the Ruhr and established their factories before 1870. Capital-intensive heavy industry quickly grew out of the reach of single owner-founders.[12] Finally, Thyssen was Catholic. Catholics were severely underrepresented in the German business elite (more on this below).[13]

Overall, however, Thyssen's early career typified the mid-to-late nineteenth-century connections among family, the entrepreneur, the local community, and the business. Nineteenth-century company letterheads usually showed the family home directly adjacent to the factory, signifying the close relationship between family and business. In 1873, August and Hedwig Thyssen moved into a medium-sized house on Froschenteich Street (today Friedrich-Ebert-Strasse) in Styrum, directly next to the railroad lines and the hoop-iron mill. Thyssen lived there for the next thirty years, increasingly squeezed in amongst the railway loading docks, the gasworks, his own rapidly expanding firm that belched ever larger quantities of dense black smoke, and the Friedrich-Wilhelms-Hütte, one of the largest steel and machine engineering factories in the Ruhr. The house was subject to the constant rumblings of freight cars and enveloped in black smoke. Thyssen's butler called the area flat-out "ugly."[14] Whatever one might say about his Victorian equation of industry and progress, he at least breathed his own smoke.

The next generation of entrepreneurs, epitomized by Fritz Thyssen and Hugo Stinnes in Mülheim, constructed magnificent villas in exclusive residential suburbs.[15] These villas were separate from the factory works, symbolizing the transition from family capitalism to corporate capitalism, with its separation of homelife and worklife, ownership and control. Thyssen's eventual move to a renovated castle at the turn of the century was as much a reaction to the growing pollution and traffic enveloping the house on Froschenteich, as it was a symbol of Thyssen's rise to the heights of economic power in a newly confident, if not increasingly bellicose, Germany.

Thyssen Personal

Thyssen was a creature of Bismarckian Germany, increasingly as outmoded as the stiff, rollover collars and black frock coats he preferred to wear his entire life, somewhat quaint and old-fashioned in appearance even in his own time.[16] The future president of the Reichsbank, Hjalmar Schacht, once remarked that August Thyssen looked like a wizened Lenin (Figure 1.1).

In person, Thyssen had a distant friendliness about him that was accessible and unfailingly polite, but not sociable or gregarious. On one hand, he could be friendly, genteel, and respectful.[17] On the other

Figure 1.1 August Thyssen at seventy at Schloss Landsberg Gate, 1912. Note the expression of pride that Thyssen has for his castle and his accomplishments. (Reproduced with the permission of the Mannesmann-Archiv, Mülheim/Ruhr)

hand, he considered himself a "mistrustful" person.[18] His letters betray a matter-of-factness, largely unadorned with sentiment. They generally give the impression of a very busy person, written in a rushed, nearly illegible scribble that worsened with age.[19] He had incoming letters read to him so as to imprint its contents on his excellent memory, and he remained mentally sharp throughout most of his long life.[20] His negotiating style was characterized by a penetrating focus, and he did not allow himself to be easily deflected from his goal.[21] He became renowned as a decidedly uncomfortable business partner, who could abruptly change his mind without much personal tact. Though he kept up the appearance of diplomacy, he always had one fixed eye on his own business interests, which led to accusations that he disregarded the larger implications of a given project. Although Hugo Stinnes found his partnership with Thyssen on various major projects to be essential, he also found Thyssen to be more financially cautious than himself.[22] His fellow industrialists had warned Hugo Stinnes not to work with Thyssen because of his difficult nature, which Stinnes did anyway because he wanted to learn from a master of business. However, Stinnes felt he had to break away from Thyssen when Thyssen could no longer treat him as a junior partner, which led to jealousy and resentfulness.[23] If people crossed him, Thyssen could summon up a cold ruthlessness, bordering on pettiness. If trusted executives disappointed him, this often resulted in a pained, even wounded sensibility. He would usually attribute this failure to the alleged character flaws of that person.[24]

The ethos of hard work neatly summed up Thyssen's worldview. Thyssen stressed that while he might belong to the capitalist class, there was also no worker who labored harder than he did.[25] Thyssen regularly astounded his executives at early morning breakfast meetings with a stack of letters already in hand, although he was one of the last to go to bed; he was "tireless" on business trips.[26] Thyssen demanded no less from his colleagues and subordinates. Most of his executives felt that Thyssen had just as much respect for a skilled craftsman as a top executive.[27] Thyssen represented an older school of Bismarckian entrepreneur who was still close to the workers and the shopfloor, something that the next generation had lost touch with. Fritz Thyssen enviously related how his father would tour the company in his free time and confidently talk with workers.[28]

To outsiders, Thyssen gained a reputation for being a hard-driving, cold-hearted capitalist with little regard for social niceties. According to Thyssen, creating the opportunity for work *was* his social contribution.[29] This work ethic garnered Thyssen respect, but he was "indeed not particularly popular with his workers and the local population but neither was he particularly unpopular or hated."[30] Without a trace of irony, he could advocate hard work and increased savings on the part of every individual as a way out of the macroeconomic problems of the post-Versailles world. Thyssen bound together very different issues of social welfare, savings, and public policy by the ideology of hard work, which he felt was the key to his long-term success. (He still established a number of social welfare policies and contributed to churches, consistent with many other German firms, not on the scale of Krupp, but more than most American firms). Not surprisingly, the caricatures of George Grosz show two figures in particular as representatives of the capitalist class: Hugo Stinnes and August Thyssen.[31]

Thyssen had a legendary, if somewhat undeserving, reputation for stinginess that could be supported by just enough of his behavior to lend it some credence.[32] Legend has it that he regularly took third- and fourth-class seats in trains. He never used a valet to carry his bags. He walked to work except when it rained. When he invited guests to his castle, he would mention that the walk was only ten minutes by foot from the train station in Kettwig; only in bad weather would he pick his guests up.[33] He never did own an automobile, that became practically a required status symbol of the wealthy. Thyssen was extremely cost-conscious, especially at work. He hounded his sales managers about their travel expenses.[34] One top sales executive of the Thyssen & Co. once received a letter from Thyssen complaining that expenses (a mere 8.10 marks) charged to the firm for a conference sponsored by the foremost iron and steel journal in Germany should be a private expense, not a company one.[35] Once when he was purchasing a large mine for several million marks, he pointed out to the seller that the envelopes used for their contracts were so heavy that they had to pay double postage.

The legends spun about the ostensible miserly quality of August Thyssen should be taken with a grain of salt. The popular media portrayed Thyssen in the stock, heroic image of German entrepreneurs, who picked up rusty nails on the factory grounds as scrap for recycling. Thyssen did not really adhere to this image. The thriftiness was less stinginess than ingrained frugality for his personal self, but not for official "representation". Thyssen allowed himself a degree of good living appropriate to his position and for cultivating good public business relations. For instance, he tended not to stay in the top hotels where the high society of Berlin met, but in hotels where businessmen stayed. It was said that he was too cheap to pay the bridge toll if he drove, but he used walking as an opportunity for exercise, relaxation, and as a period for thinking.[36] Especially when people came to dinner, Thyssen knew "how to keep up appearances in princely fashion."[37] He enjoyed lavish, semi-official meals with the elite of the German business and political community at his castle. Thyssen thrived on the posh and genteel atmosphere of dinner parties. He was very form-conscious. Dinners at his castle were black-tie, frock-coat affairs. Such dinner parties got on the nerves of Clara Stinnes, who loved to hear Hugo Stinnes and Thyssen discuss business, but not the "superficial talk" and barbs about women's makeup and clothing.[38] Thyssen was merely unostentatious relative to his considerable means as one of the richest persons in Germany.

Extraordinarily secretive, Thyssen did little to suppress false rumors about him, preferring a kind of disinformation campaign. One interviewer and industry expert once tried to piece together the strategy and extent of Thyssen's assets, but after Thyssen corrected his ideas, he demanded that the researcher not update his original conclusions for publication. The scholar refused to publish false information, but felt compelled to respect Thyssen's wishes for discretion: "With that he was pleased, even happy, and I can boast that I once brought the old man to real laughter, what many could not say about him."[39] After Paul Arnst published one of the first scholarly overviews of his career, Thyssen refused to comment on any mistakes "because I like to spread censures of the public, even when they are not justified."[40] Not for nothing, the German Metalworkers Association termed him the "Sphinx" among German industrialists.[41]

Thyssen's innate personal modesty did not extend to his burning pride in his work, his companies, his products, and his role as one of Germany's leading businessmen. Thyssen felt immensely honored at one official ceremony when Field Marshal Paul von Hindenburg went out of his way to shake his hand.[42] Clara Stinnes felt this pride bordered on vanity. Thyssen wanted recognition and prominence, but not fame. He never became boastful. One time, Thyssen warned his executives against expressing *Schadenfreude* about his rivals. He urged them to display calm dignity:

> In case the commission today decides in our favor, I ask of you to act quite friendly nevertheless quite modestly in the railway ministry so that we will injure no one and remain simple and calm even in our joy.

I think that the calmer and more dignified our attitude the more
friends we will win and the larger our reputation will become with all
those people who love the truth.[43]

Fritz Thyssen attributed his father's success to his ability to remain
modest in good times and bad.[44]

Thyssen's largest extravagance was his purchase of Castle Landsberg
in Kettwig just outside Mülheim, which showed how he began to adhere to new standards of upper-*bourgeois* representation after the turn
of the century. Despite a rather imposing south view from the bottom
of the hill, the castle appears much smaller from the entrance to the
courtyard, more the size of a large house. It snuggled into the side of
the hill rather than ranging over it. Unlike Carnegie, Thyssen made
sure that his new home was within a few easy minutes by carriage to his
company office, an important consideration.[45] Even the largest rooms
in the house were not awe-inspiring and lavish like Krupp's luxurious
Villa Hügel. Many contemporary commentators thought that Thyssen
attempted to "keep up with Krupps," but Thyssen compared himself to
Krupp only in terms of business, not in personal lifestyle. He was
proud to have matched Krupp, especially in market competition, but
not for monopolies, or high prices lobbied from the Reich bureaucracy, or for personal favors from the Kaiser, whom Thyssen had little
respect for anyway.[46]

Thyssen's castle artfully combined traditional and art-nouveau elements with calm, clean lines.[47] At her first visit to Thyssen's new home,
Clara Stinnes found it "tasteful" without "extravagances and sumptu-
ousness;" she especially liked Thyssen's workroom, which impressed
her as "calm and refined." Thyssen led her through the house with
"unmistakable pride; today he already speaks of his 'castle,' yet a few
months ago only about 'Landsberg'."[48] One gains the overall impression that the castle was certainly designed to represent the master
of the house, but that it was still someone's home, not a museum.
Thyssen's taste was basically conservative, especially in his paintings,
which tended toward standard representational, landscape, or allegor-
ical nineteenth-century art. (Many of them were copies, but as Thyssen
reminded one visitor, copies also cost money). On the other hand,
Thyssen intensely admired Auguste Rodin, from whom he bought
seven originals, ordering them sight unseen and paying an exorbi-

tantly high price for them.[49] Thyssen felt especially strongly about Rodin's *Christ and Madelaine* sculpture, which he felt to be the "height of beauty."[50] This particular sculpture, which shows Christ and Mary Magdalene locked in a deeply erotic embrace of tormented suffering, found a special place in his heart, perhaps because of his own pain caused by his divorce. He requested that this sculpture be placed at his gravesite.

All in all, Thyssen's castle distinguished itself with its smooth and seemingly effortless mixture of traditional and modern motifs, much like the traits in his personality. He was princely but not ostentatious, modest but not retiring, prideful but not boastful, simple but often magnanimous, civil but not warm, wealthy but not *nouveau riche,* old-fashioned in dress but modern in furnishing and technology. While his Victorian sensibility moderated his behavior and consumption, when his passions broke through they could lead to dramatic excesses, as evidenced by the purchase of a spectacularly gaudy and beautiful, *art nouveau* bathtub for the guestroom, which seemed incongruous and not entirely integrated into the rest of the house.

Thyssen's Politics

Thyssen's political views were conservative and patriotic. In general, he tended toward the conservative Prussian nationalism of Bismarck, not the Teutonic pride of the bombastic Wilhelm II. He admired Bismarck as a "great statesman," and the unification of Germany remained one of the seminal political milestones of his life. By contrast, Thyssen had less respect for Kaiser Wilhelm II. Thyssen thought the Kaiser focused too much on appearances rather than realities. He also objected to Wilhelm's inability to listen to criticism. At a 1912 dinner-table conversation in the midst of the second Moroccan crisis, Thyssen stated presciently: "He is a disaster for our people. He needs only to start a disastrous war, and it will come, then they will sweep him from his throne."[51]

While he could differentiate versions of monarchist rule, he had little understanding of the social or democratic aspirations of the vast majority of people. In 1890, for instance, Thyssen suggested "more decisive" action on the part of government against the "socialist cravings of the workers" which, in Thyssen's eyes, seemed to be rooted more in the "bars, dances and other such amusements" than in the working conditions of his own factory. Socialism was just the attempt to consume more, to get more money by working less, and ultimately the result of "moral negligence." He did not hesitate to equate social democracy with the destruction of industry, progress, and "human civilization" itself.[52] Morality, work, respectability, politics, and civilization fused into a single worldview.

For Thyssen the social democratic revolution of 1918–1919 was a complete disaster, but his rhetoric betrays his political assumptions. In his words, the higher salaries and wages of the postwar period could only have been tolerable if they were "combined with a great desire to work, a great desire to save as well as with discipline and order."[53] Socialism and the nationalization of industry were impractical. It replaced the entrepreneur with a "thousand-headed working class" that could not possibly direct a company; besides, workers would rather not work to earn more money. Discipline was a favor to workers. Socialism would lower productivity, eventually leading to a "creeping infirmity" of German industry.

Under his conception, the entrepreneur became a patriarchal disciplinarian, who acted for the good of others. This attitude wreaked havoc on his family life, let alone on his business during the revolution, which became one of the epicenters of strike action. Thyssen placed the majority of the blame for Germany's worsening economic situation squarely on the "unfulfillable Diktat called the Treaty of Versailles," along with the eight-hour day that sapped the productivity of German industry, productivity that was all the more necessary to reassert Germany's economic and export potential. Thyssen advocated a "struggle" *(Kampf)* to eliminate the eight-hour day because: "It is now a matter of being or not being. The majority of the people—if necessary against their own fierce resistance—must be protected from total ruin."[54] His whole tone betrays Thyssen's authoritarian streak that allowed him to act in the "true" interests of others, be they the German people, the workers, or his own children.

A conservative Catholicism reinforced his political views. Thyssen, Sr., as well as his son Fritz, were long-standing members of the Catholic Center Party, a political haven for most Catholics in Imperial Germany. Although he rarely spoke publicly about his politics, Thyssen maintained close behind-the-scene contacts with important Catholic

Center party politicians such as Matthias Erzberger and Konrad Adenauer. In 1925, he wrote Adenauer, then the mayor of Cologne, that he should become Chancellor of the Reich because Adenauer understood "our needs." Adenauer considered Thyssen one of his friends and admired him greatly.[55]

His Catholicism made him exceptional among German industrialists, yet Thyssen's religious convictions played a strangely inverse role in his business affairs. If anything, Thyssen became more objective and meritocratic, to head off any potential criticism. He took great care to appear neutral, supporting both religions inside his companies, and he made significant financial contributions to building both Catholic and Protestant churches just outside the factory gates in Styrum. In the interests of "parity" among office workers, he allowed everybody to have half a day off on Catholic holidays; anyone could attend church on those days.[56] Thyssen did think that churches (of both sorts) around the factory would dampen worker radicalism. Before he would hire a prospective executive, he would ask about the man's religious views because good relations with both religions were a prerequisite of employment. When he hired Franz Dahl, he explicitly stressed that only performance mattered; religion and other matters were secondary.[57] Such agnosticism extended to the Jewish religion as well.

This sort of aggressive neutrality was important at the time. In the 1870s, during the "cultural struggle" against Catholicism, Thyssen had to pull Fritz from school.[58] At the turn-of-the-century, one such attack accused Thyssen of running a Catholic firm to the detriment of Protestants.[59] In response, Thyssen conducted a complete survey of his management and workers to counter these charges. At Thyssen and Co., Thyssen did employ a higher proportion of Catholic managers than was usual, near parity, but only about twenty percent at the GDK, although Catholics predominated in the area. The GDK was closer to the norm for German big business. The representation at Thyssen & Co. could probably be traced to hiring from Thyssen's personal network in churches, schools, and community clubs or, more simply, to a lack of prejudice against Catholics.

Thyssen's political ideology helps to explain his views but not his political actions, which were always refracted through the economic interests of his companies. What was good for Thyssen's business *was* his politics. When a planned canal threatened to erode the value of a

Thyssen waterworks, Thyssen came out against it—even threatening to close the plant and discharge its workers to spite everyone. Clara Stinnes perceptively saw that "Thyssen unfortunately only knows his interests, that is, the interests of his works; despite the significance of these questions for him in this matter the city has no interests as soon as a collision with his own business interests presents itself."[60] Thyssen had a single-minded focus on his economic interests that acted as an abrasive and sometimes unattractive personality trait.

Ideologically, Thyssen tended to advocate a policy based on private enterprise and economic liberalism (understood in its classic sense). In the prewar period, he consistently advocated the further "internationalization of the national economy, trade, and commerce" on the basis of international agreements (i.e. price agreements for coal to eliminate "dumping"). He stressed the importance of the exchange of goods, ideas, and experiences. Americans learned from Germans and *vice versa;* English-German relations should be improved. At the height of the Anglo-German trade rivalry, he argued that the tension surrounding the building of the German navy was a symptom, not a cause, of growing economic competition. (Karl Marx might not have put it any better.) Yet Thyssen felt there was "enough room" for both countries on the basis of new division of labor and product specialization. England had no reason to worry about intensified German competition in a few areas; its high standard of living required that other countries produce for its needs. For Thyssen, the most important political questions of the age were also economic. Naively, he wanted a select group of experts who could "correctly and practically deal with and solve economic questions" to regulate trade and commerce between nations. Thyssen expressly cited his early business world of fluid borders and international contacts, where experiences crossed from England to Belgium to Germany. Thyssen had a continental, if not Western, vision of a relatively open international economy among "civilized nations" based on comparative advantage and trade. Not surprisingly, such an open-borders vision conformed to his economic interests; he had extensive foreign investments all over the world.[61]

World War I put a swift end to Thyssen's "internationalization of national economies and values." Nationalism and economic advantage gained the upper hand. Thyssen joined those "annexationists" who demanded wide-ranging border changes.[62] His claims followed his business interests: Belgian coalfields, the iron ore of Longwy-Briey, and the manganese and iron ore from Russia. Each would ensure a competitive position for his steel on the world market at the end of the war. Thyssen placed great importance on the lands in eastern Europe annexed after the treaty of Brest-Litovsk.[63] Unlike the pan-Germanists, who envisioned a political, cultural, and even racial continental Germany, Thyssen's reasoning concentrated on securing his business interests after military gains.[64] Competition for advantage among business rivals amplified their annexation claims. Thyssen meant to create a "great Middle European customs union," admitting that it might take some coercion to create. This customs union would include Holland, France, Denmark, Switzerland, Austria, and the Balkans. It would be directed essentially against Britain and its empire, but he also had one eye on a continental market along the lines of the United States.[65]

In order to realize these goals, Thyssen enlisted Matthias Erzberger, a prominent Catholic politician, who for two years during World War I held a post on the board of directors of the GDK—the only outsider ever to hold a position on a Thyssen board of directors.[66] Thyssen wanted Erzberger's clout in Berlin to clarify the messy political and legal matters involved with the conquered territories in the interest of the Thyssen-Konzern, particularly in Longwy-Briey. Thyssen also felt that the Prussian (Protestant) bureaucracy consistently awarded contracts to his rivals because they were discriminating against his Catholic firm, or because he did not have an inside relationship to the Kaiser, as did Krupp. Erzberger resigned from Thyssen's board at the end of 1917, reversing his political stance in response to unrestricted submarine warfare and the weakening state of the German army. He began calling for peace without annexations, a diplomatic end to the war, and greater power to the *Reichstag,* positions that the Social Democrats had long advocated and that Thyssen rejected.[67] In the end, Erzberger could cull few advantages for Thyssen, but both managed to accumulate negative publicity claiming that Erzberger was in Thyssen's back pocket.

By the end of the war, Thyssen was more interested in securing a "good peace" that "might make the awful sacrifice and the tremendous efforts worth it."[68] By late 1918, a "good peace" still meant the annexation and the economic exploitation of eastern Europe—for Thyssen, the manganese ore of Georgia. Along with other German industrialists, Thyssen planned to divvy up the French de Wendel firm among themselves.[69]

As Thyssen predicted, the 1918 revolution did sweep Wilhelm II from the throne, and the war victors imposed their claims at Versailles. Thyssen permanently broke with Erzberger after he signed the Versailles Treaty as head of the Armistice Commission. Thyssen lost his most modern steel plant with the loss of Alsace-Lorraine. Both August and Fritz Thyssen walked away from the Center Party—and by implication out of the compromise policies of the new, shakily democratic Weimar Republic. Thyssen never really recovered from these financial losses, which contributed to his decision to join the VSt. For a man whose business interests formed his politics, his ventures into politics revenged themselves on his business.

Thyssen's Relationship to His Family

Joseph Thyssen (1844–1915), August's younger brother, became his lifelong business partner two years after the death of their father in 1877. Like his brother, Joseph had apprenticed in his father's banking business in Eschweiler. After liquidating his father's business, Joseph brought with him a considerable amount of money from his inheritance that immediately flowed into Thyssen & Co.'s coffers. In 1879, August and Joseph transformed Thyssen & Co. into a private partnership, which it remained until 1918. In addition, their sister Balbina left much of her inheritance and her husband's to her two brothers to use in the expansion of their firm. Balbina's husband, Désiré Bicheroux, had passed away in 1875, whereafter Balbina moved to Düsseldorf and cared for their mother.[70] By the end of the 1870s, August Thyssen had reassembled a good portion of his family's capital and these funds were decisive for the firm's survival in the recessionary 1870s.

The two brothers divided all securities and assets 75% to 25%, reflecting August's clear dominance in their business relationship. The Thyssens agreed to take little out of the business for private use, reinvesting most of their profits back into the business. Only around the turn of the century did both begin to spend more on themselves by building or buying larger homes. The reticent Joseph deferred to his older brother's judgment in business matters and August used Joseph as a sounding board for his ideas. Relations between August and Joseph remained amicable throughout their lives, seemingly without strain. Moreover, as August's relationships with his sons grew increasingly distant, he relied on his brother for companionship and advice.

Within a year of moving to Mülheim, Joseph married Klara Bagel, from a leading Protestant entrepreneurial family, who also brought a significant dowry to Thyssen & Co. The Bagels had built their fortune publishing children's textbooks and increasingly popular stories about the American Wild West. The Bagel publishing house printed most of the advertising brochures and financial reports for the Thyssen firms. Like August, Joseph and Klara lived modestly for twenty-five years in a simple brick row house near the factory on the Bahnstrasse. Unlike August's wife, Hedwig, Klara handled with solid yet simple aplomb the considerable demands of entertaining business and social contacts. She eventually replaced Hedwig in these matters after August's messy divorce.

Joseph was an enigmatic figure, acting as a true silent partner in the business. While August constantly traveled on business, Joseph remained in the central office in Mülheim. Although Joseph worked long hours, he was so retiring that traces of his influence on Thyssen & Co. over forty years are difficult to find. According to his wife, Joseph never felt comfortable in industry and would have preferred to remain in the more rarefied air of banking.[71] The future managing director of Thyssen & Co., Carl Wallmann, thought that Joseph Thyssen was "completely unimportant."[72] Thyssen's closest confidante in financial matters, Hermann Eumann, did not have a high opinion of Joseph. Eumann had close contact with both Thyssens; he worked in the central office between 1882–1926 as chief financial officer and as a kind of personal financial secretary for them. Eumann thought that Joseph did not have good business sense, made too many mistakes, and did not have a good knowledge of the industry. He thought that Joseph "rather feared" his brother. Eumann also felt that Joseph could also be "extremely mean and petty." When August was away, Joseph would come to life and feel like the boss.[73] While August Thyssen gained an undeserving reputation for miserliness, the true pennypincher and disciplinarian of the family was Joseph.[74]

On the other hand, Jakob Hasslacher, of the rival Rheinische Stahlwerke, found Joseph Thyssen very nice, warm, and modest. He felt that August conveniently used Joseph as a "scapegoat" to break off negotiations or as a delaying ploy.[75] Joseph remained especially active in the management of the pipe department and wrote most of the recommendations for outgoing salaried managers. But perhaps the most telling sign of Joseph's quiet importance is the fact that August was willing to work across a double desk from his brother for over forty years; August proved utterly unwilling to tolerate poor business performance from any of his managers or his sons.

So it would be wrong to accept Eumann's assessment of Joseph at face value, but his critique points out a personality streak of pettiness common to both Thyssen brothers, as a type of perverted outgrowth of their Victorian *bourgeois* virtues of modesty, frugality, patriarchalism, seriousness, and industrious ways.

Unlike the close relationship to his brother, Thyssen's marriage to Hedwig proved deeply unhappy for both partners. According to Fritz, Hedwig married August on the wishes of her parents.[76] By all accounts, Hedwig was a sociable, light-hearted, and rather happy-go-lucky personality who contrasted dramatically with her husband's single-minded, obsessive absorption in his work.[77] Their bedroom contained a desk where Thyssen often worked late into the night or before he went to work in the morning. While this focus and zeal probably saved his company at critical points, those same qualities cost him his marriage. Thyssen demanded a good deal of help from his young wife, which even Klara Thyssen seemed to think excessive.[78] He constantly entertained local businessmen at his home, a nineteenth-century version of networking, yet Hedwig yearned for a different type of socializing. Thyssen, however, was famous for turning social gatherings into business meetings. After one dinner, Thyssen suggested a walk in the woods around his castle, which was completely inappropriate for the women, who were dressed in bustles, long dresses, and thin-soled shoes. The men disappeared into the woods for hours to talk business.[79]

Hedwig herself entertained higher ambitions, perhaps ennoblement, a trait she passed on to her children, much to Thyssen's chagrin. Thyssen had little desire to join "high society." To the great disappointment of his family, Thyssen adamantly turned down the Kaiser's offer of nobility, which would have only distracted him from his business. He and his brother would remain "simple people." As with many

Victorians, he reinforced his moral backbone with a strict fashion distinction from a decadent aristocracy. While they wore colors, he wore black.[80]

Hedwig, who never felt at home with Thyssen's other relatives, felt increasingly isolated. His frequent business trips only heightened that sense of emotional coolness that kept his immediate family at arm's length. To alleviate her loneliness, Hedwig took to visiting the elegant spa resort of Wiesbaden, one of the centers for European high society. There she met others who had more on their minds than business. At the beginning of the 1880s, Hedwig had a miscarriage, but Thyssen denied that he could have been the father. The miscarriage set in motion divorce proceedings. (It is not exactly clear who pursued it.) The divorce agreement transferred ownership *(Eigentum)* of Thyssen & Co. to the four children equally and paid Hedwig a substantial alimony, but gave August lifelong use *(Nutzniesser)* over these possessions *(Besitz)* until he agreed to relinquish control or in the event of his death. In strict legal terms, the 1885 divorce settlement ushered in a separation of ownership and control. He became a type of trustee over his children's fortune. Thus, his children became owners without any legal voice in decision-making.

The divorce contract led to years of misunderstandings, crossed expectations, and permanently soured Thyssen's relationships with his children. For twenty years, the terms remained unclear to the children who felt themselves owners of the firm with legitimate claims on its assets. The divorce agreement applied only to Thyssen & Co., yet Thyssen owned a great many more firms by the turn of the century. Thyssen, Sr.'s accumulation of immense assets combined with the rising desires of his children to join high society led to periodic family crises and legal battles. August Thyssen, Jr., pressed his claims especially forcefully. An additional ruling in 1907 further clarified that the divorce did not actually transfer property rights to the children. Instead, the divorce contracts amounted to a statement of intent: transfer of possession remained contingent on Thyssen's approval or his death.[81]

This 1885 divorce was probably the defining moment of Thyssen's personal and family life. As a devout Catholic and upstanding member of the community, Thyssen found this divorce embarrassing. It tore the family apart and had major consequences for the business. For the rest of his life, Thyssen felt wounded by the family troubles stemming from it. The psychological dimensions of the divorce permanently aggravated his relationship to his children. In 1919, Thyssen wrote to his son Heinrich: "The 1885 divorce contract between your mother and me has provoked so much disaster that I have the most overwhelming desire to compensate for the damages that have come from it, as much as I possibly can, although I wanted to carry out these agreements only in the interests of my children."[82] Over the decades, however, Thyssen managed to come to some sort of civil terms with his ex-wife. After World War I, Hedwig would visit Thyssen's castle for a few weeks each year. She remarried three times into nobility, outliving each one of her aristocratic husbands. She eventually moved to Brussels, where she entered into the elite of Belgian society, and died there in 1940, just before the Vichy authorities delivered Fritz Thyssen to the Gestapo. Fritz had delayed his escape from the Third Reich to visit her bedside, a final sign of his emotional dedication to his mother.

Thyssen's children remained emotionally attached to their warmhearted, accessible, and fun-loving mother, rather than to their busy, distant, and cold father. One leading industrialist, Jakob Hasslacher, noted that Thyssen had a "coldness" about him that made him an extremely effective businessman, but a stern, intolerant, unsympathetic father.[83] While believing profoundly that he was acting in his children's interests, his effective control over their lives and his emotional distance created scars that no amount of generous living expenses could heal. In the end Thyssen never really trusted his children to run the company—and they knew it.

After the divorce, Thyssen employed a nanny to help raise the children at home, which also permitted him to continue his frequent business travels. From reports, the children constantly fought with the nanny and squabbled amongst themselves.[84] As adults (Figure 1.2), the differences among the Thyssen children continued. Fritz and Heinrich had fundamentally different ideas about how to run the family business. August, Jr., ultimately refused to work with Fritz.

Among the children, Fritz most willingly accepted his father's leadership. He worked most closely with his father in the Gewerkschaft Deutsche Kaiser (GDK), but the relations between the two were tense, punctuated by frequent fights. When Fritz was learning the ropes, his father initially treated him as low as the lowest clerk. Thyssen, Sr., did

Figure 1.2 Thyssen's children with their nanny, ca. 1900. From left: August Jr., Fritz, Heinrich, Hedwig, and nanny Minna Schlömann (seated). (Reproduced with the permission of the ThyssenKrupp Corporate Archives, Duisburg)

not have a high opinion of Fritz and he was renowned for his assessment of business character. He once wrote to his close friend, Carl Klönne of the Deutsche Bank: "Fritz's character is unpredictable; he is too easily swayed by outside influences"—a judgment which tragically proved to be all too correct.[85] Forty years later, two leading executives in the VSt echoed Thyssen's character evaluation. Heinrich Dinkelbach thought "Fritz Thyssen became intoxicated with big ideas ... Very clever, volatile, accessible to insinuations, became enthusiastic for everything great, saw the light sides, but only thereafter the dark sides."[86] Albert Vögler thought that "Fritz Thyssen [was] a clever man with a good understanding of technical things, but above all an excellent financial man, but volatile. He had not learned to work systematically. His desk [was always] full of documents, moreover [he was] mistrustful and accessible to insinuations." The famous Ruhr industrialist, Hugo Stinnes, once joked that he would hand the Saar-Mosel mining company over to Fritz and see what Fritz would make out of it.[87] Fritz was a naïve idealist who tended to jump at grand ideas, which unfortunately included those of Adolf Hitler. Fritz Thyssen became one of the few major industrialists who actively supported Hitler and contributed money to the Nazi party, but he just as impetuously became disenchanted with the Nazis and openly rejected their war aims, which nearly cost him his life.[88]

While differences in personality underlay many of their quarrels, in the end, the father's inability to accept the life decisions of his children led to unbecoming and cruel attempts to control their choices. (Joseph Thyssen had a similar experience with one of his sons.)[89] Thyssen, Sr., tried to block Fritz's marriage to Amelie Zur Helle by claiming a hereditary disease in her family. When he could not change Fritz's mind about the marriage, which was based largely on love, he then tried to place humiliating conditions on the bride's parents, hoping to change their minds. He failed. In 1900, Fritz and Amelie married with at least the blessing of Fritz's mother. Their marriage proved to be the most lasting one among August's children.

If Thyssen's relationship with Fritz was tense but tolerable, his relationship to his second and favorite son, August Thyssen, Jr., bordered on the pathological. Many thought that August, Jr., was endowed with the highest raw intelligence of all the children, which he unfortunately put to use in an original, vindictive way. "Little August" inherited the same high voice, short stature, and cunning ruthlessness for which the elder Thyssen was known. But he inherited none of his father's interest in business. Together, August Sr. and Jr. made a volatile cocktail of frustrated hopes and crossed ambitions.

In training at Thyssen & Co.'s Berlin office, August, Jr., soon became seduced by the capital city. He joined the feudal Bodyguard Squad of the Hussar Guard Regiment of the Kaiser in Potsdam and advanced quickly in its ranks because of his father's wealth. He became the first *bourgeois* officer of the regiment, well on his way toward entering the Kaiser's court. He also joined the exclusive, aristocratic Union Club. Although Thyssen, Sr., provided substantial allowances to all his children, these sums were not sufficient for August, Jr.'s (and Hedwig's) high-flying plans. August, Jr., also engaged in a number of romantic liaisons and near marriages in an ultimately futile attempt to join the nobility. Such affairs made him a favorite of Berlin high society and gossip columns, whose press mortified the secretive father. August, Jr., also purchased noble lands just west of Berlin, the Rittergut Rüders-dorf, squandering company and family money.

Thyssen wrote to Carl Klönne about the deep disappointment that August, Jr., caused him:

> My sons should be striving wholeheartedly with me and my brother to develop our ventures into really great and independent enterprises. Our future does not lie in Potsdam; our greatness and significance lies in our coal and soon in our iron-ore mines. Only these factors will se-cure us for a long time the justified influence and the great reputation that a world-class firm must achieve in order to create and sustain, freely and independently and with all its power, a great, flourishing ex-port industry for the Fatherland.[90]

The quote illustrates wonderfully the confluence of Thyssen's per-sonal, professional, and political values that permeated the corporate culture of the Thyssen-Konzern. Thyssen never understood what drove August, Jr., to devote such energy to becoming an aristocrat of the Kai-ser's court. Thyssen felt that his son had used all means "fair and foul," costing millions of marks and the respect of the family: "I see all of my hopes destroyed because my children want and will turn my achieve-ments toward the most unworthy and unbelievable uses."[91] All wanted greater access to the family fortune. His siblings joined August, Jr., in his goals, but not his means.

The means by which August, Jr., pursued his ends brought utter scandal. Around 1901–1902, as Thyssen was launching a major expan-sion drive to construct the largest steel-making operations in Germany and his finances were stretched to their limit, August, Jr., approached his father's major banks and brokers, hinting that his father's credit rating was not as solid as it should be. August, Jr., along with Fritz and Heinrich, wanted to be named to the board of directors of the GDK, and all the children wanted to receive a higher monthly allowance. Thyssen wrote Klönne that he had "never felt so unhappy in my en-tire life."[92]

Unfortunately, family relations went even further downhill. In 1902, in the midst of a major recession and financial crisis, all the children allied themselves with August, Jr., against their father to change the conditions of the divorce agreement. Hedwig sided with her children. Joseph Thyssen and Carl Klönne of the Deutsche Bank tried to mediate, but to little avail. Even Thyssen's friend, Klönne, felt that he was being too intransigent.

At this point, the story becomes murkier. The press got wind of his children's court cases against their father. Allegedly the elder Thyssen tried to declare August, Jr., mentally incompetent and forcibly commit him to an insane asylum. The papers reported that at a reception, he attempted to place his son in a straitjacket, but August, Jr., escaped and doctors found nothing wrong with him. Berlin's top tabloid, strongly on the side of August, Jr., who did nothing to deny the truth of this story, gleefully ran a six-part article on the affair, humiliating his father in public. August, Jr., sued his father for defamation of character. Adding a libel suit brought by August, Jr., against Fritz Thyssen, who allegedly spread rumors that August, Jr., was homosexual, created a first-class celebrity scandal. The article framed it—not entirely wrongly—as a conflict between two worldviews, between two generations, and an old and a new Germany—a real life *Buddenbrooks*, Thomas Mann's great novel of family degeneration, which had appeared just two years before. Revealing the silly sensibility of the tabloid, the article alleged that August, Jr., would have chosen a more generous social policy than the miserly elder Thyssen and met the "just demands" of workers. There is still disagreement among researchers as to whether this incident actually occurred, but the fact that August, Jr., attempted to put such public pressure on his father indicates the deep animosity between the two, and the extent to which both were willing to go to assert himself over the other.[93]

August, Sr., refused to concede any control over the finances of "his" firm. His children argued that they should be allowed to use the firm's assets as they saw fit, corresponding to their moral and legal position as owners. In 1906, they met in Hamburg to wrest more money out of their father. They took out loans from a Dutch bank secured by the 1885 divorce agreement. They mutually agreed to back one another financially with long-term loans. This plan, however, quickly collapsed when Fritz and Heinrich refused to support the enormous financial expenditures required for August, Jr., and Hedwig's aristocratic life. Fritz and Heinrich may have wanted more control over their own lives, and may have wanted to become nobles, but they were by no means profligate people. In any case, August, Sr., was horrified. Even August, Jr.'s brothers were shocked by his methods.

August, Jr., and Hedwig, who tended to ally with each other, turned to a fellow Mülheim industrialist, Hugo Stinnes, in March 1906 to act as an intermediary. At the time, Stinnes was as much a (junior) partner as direct rival, having invested jointly with Thyssen in a number of important ventures.[94] August, Jr., explained to Stinnes how he would use the Rüdersdorf lands to make his way into the aristocracy. He even offered Stinnes part of his inheritance if Stinnes would help pressure Thyssen into changing the divorce agreement. August, Sr., also turned to Stinnes for advice, who found his position highly "embarrassing."[95] All he heard from August, Jr., was "disgusting filth" about his siblings and relatives.[96] In the midst of all these schemes, Thyssen suffered medical problems from a near fatal nose operation before the courts issued the 1907 ruling. In the same year Stinnes, however, did manage to arrange a settlement with Hedwig, whereby she relinquished her ownership rights in exchange for a financial settlement, which eliminated her debt, provided her an allowance of 60,000 marks per year, and guaranteed one million marks to each of her children after they turned twenty-five.[97]

While these rulings helped to clarify property relations between father and children, it by no means ended August, Jr.'s attempts to secure his inheritance through a larger allowance and a greater field of activity by working on one of his father's boards of directors. After he purchased the noble lands of Rittergut Rüdersdorf, August, Jr., briefly attempted to run it as a business. Thyssen, Sr., gladly supported this pursuit, for it would give August, Jr., his own independent field of activity, perhaps turning him into an honest businessman. But August, Jr., quickly became dissatisfied and demanded that he be placed in charge of his father's newest venture in Alsace-Lorraine, the Stahlwerke Thyssen AG, the linchpin of Thyssen's world export strategy. August, Jr., wrote his father in May 1910:

> I am hereby posing the question to you whether you are willing to provide me with the necessary means and allow me to take over the management of the ore fields. I am once more giving you the opportunity to provide me with an employment that is suited to me and if possible in an area of activity separate from that of Herr [*sic*] Fritz Thyssen so

that we may at last work peacefully next to one another. I am also prepared, in order to put an end to the perpetual family quarreling, to
have myself naturalized here.

August, Jr.'s tone of voice is insistent and demanding. Thyssen retorted that August, Jr., should "renounce any claim to a position that
you cannot and may not occupy."[98]

However, August, Jr.'s costly lifestyle had reached its limits. In September 1910, he declared bankruptcy, bringing down the Nieder-
deutsche Bank, which had loaned over one million marks to him. He
racked up at least eleven million marks in liabilities versus two million in Rittergut Rüderdorf company assets, using its assets less to run
a business than as a magnet for attracting credit. Moreover, at least
four million marks in claims were from August, Jr.'s three siblings.
Court proceedings began that stretched over years because of August,
Jr.'s many creditors, who naturally made claims on August, Sr.'s fortune on the basis of the 1885 divorce agreement.[99] August, Jr., failed to
show up at his own bankruptcy proceedings. Unlike Fritz or Heinrich,
who were capable businessmen, or Hedwig, who was excluded from
the management of the firms because of her gender, August, Jr., saw
no reason to run a business except as a treasure chest for status advancement.

This new August, Jr., affair started another round of gossip. In 1911,
August, Jr., accused his managing director of negligence. The newspapers reported that at a breakfast table at a well-known Berlin hotel, the
managing director slapped August, Jr. The scene led to an arranged
duel by pistols. Tipped off by his creditors, the police arrested August,
Jr., before he could make it to the arranged site. Thyssen, Sr., whisked
him back to Mülheim. There he said that he would take care of all of
his son's debts if he gave up all claims on his inheritance. August, Jr.,
refused.[100]

Thyssen hired a lawyer, Carl Härle, to help deal with the myriad
legal claims and once again turned to Hugo Stinnes. Once Härle
entered the dispute, August, Jr., knew that he had crossed a decisive
line in the father-son relationship. Knowing that Härle had previously
fought a duel, August, Jr., insulted Härle, trying to provoke him. Härle
refused to answer letters from August, Jr.[101] However, August, Jr.'s
bankruptcy briefly called into question Thyssen's financial condition.

The huge steelworks in Alsace-Lorraine did seem to be financed out of thin air. The business press openly doubted Thyssen's ability to pay his creditors.[102] August, Jr., engaged more lawyers to sue his father and demanded a place on one of his French-German joint ventures, which Thyssen, Sr., naturally refused because of the high level of diplomatic tact needed to run them. Stinnes felt that August, Jr., would hardly be satisfied with a settlement on par with that of Hedwig.[103]

August, Jr., sued once again in 1913 on the grounds that his portion of Thyssen & Co. property should be used to clear up his bankruptcy, which Thyssen, Sr., refused to do unless August, Jr., gave up his inheritance. This round of court battles led to another alleged attempt by Thyssen to declare his son mentally incompetent. By 1914, August, Jr., managed to reenlist the help of his sister, who felt the 1907 settlement was not adequate.[104] The disputes, complicated by myriad creditors' claims on August, Jr., dragged on throughout the war. When Joseph died in 1915, his sons, Hans and Julius, joined the owner group of Thyssen & Co., but they too were explicitly excluded from executive direction of the firm.[105] By the end of the war, August, Jr.'s bankruptcy proceedings still threatened Thyssen & Co. so Härle refounded Thyssen & Co. as a joint-stock company, which voided any creditors' claims to the private assets of the original partnership, to which the 1885 divorce agreement applied. Explicit legal clauses in the firm's new statutes voided any financial or leadership claims August, Jr., might make on the new firm.[106] In conjunction, Härle and Thyssen finally arranged a financial settlement for August, Jr., and Hedwig; they also transferred ownership of Thyssen & Co. to Fritz and Heinrich. After this effective disinheritance, the unhappy August, Jr., traveled far and wide, engaging in numerous romantic encounters that did not bring him marriage, ennoblement, or children. He died mysteriously in 1943 in Munich. When the coroner began to autopsy the body, he found instead the body of a young soldier; August, Jr.'s body was never found.

The third son, Heinrich, inherited his father's broad streak of independence. Heinrich probably took the smartest way out of the "perpetual family quarrels" by leaving the country. He studied natural sciences and art history in Munich, Berlin, and London and took a doctorate in chemistry in 1899 from the University of Heidelberg. In 1905, he moved to Budapest, and a year later married a Viennese baroness, Margareta Bornemisza, who "even made quite a good impression" on Thyssen.[107] His father-in-law then adopted Heinrich by order of the Emperor of Austria-Hungary, entitling him to carry the full noble name of Baron Heinrich Thyssen-Bornemisza de Kászon. His Hungarian citizenship later saved his assets from Allied confiscation at the end of World War II. Thyssen-Bornemisza remained distant from most of the disputes over management of the Thyssen companies, appearing on Thyssen executive boards before World War I only as a formality. After the revolution broke out in Hungary in 1919, however, Thyssen-Bornemisza moved to the Netherlands, where he took over primary responsibility for Thyssen's foreign financial transactions, basing his operations in Rotterdam. In this manner, Heinrich Thyssen-Bornemisza maintained independence from his father as well as from his older brother, Fritz, who was more actively involved in his father's industrial operations in the Ruhr.

Where did such familial dysfunctionality come from? The ambiguity surrounding the divorce agreement combined with August, Sr.'s cold authoritarianism proved to be a potent brew. All of them lived a good portion of their adult lives in the monumental shadow of their father. None of Thyssen's sons could have full claim to entrepreneurial leadership or financial independence as long as he lived. Thyssen's longevity and the curious divorce contract extended this period of adolescence for his sons even longer than normal. Then Thyssen, Sr.'s sheer force of personality and will, which worked so well in business life—although not without garnering him the reputation for ruthlessness and ambition that Clara Stinnes found so off-putting—helped push his children into a revolt against him. From the point of view of August or Joseph Thyssen, his children appeared well on their way to becoming something no longer respectably *bourgeois* and certainly no longer capable of running the family business. Since his children did not share the same priorities, and remained loyal to their mother, a woman who had fallen out of Thyssen's favor—probably not without causing feelings of hurt, disgrace, and embarrassment—they threatened to call into question the financial stability of the family business, Thyssen's obsessive lifework. Because of his messy divorce and troubled family life, his life and work, the personal and the professional, fused into a whole.

In conclusion, for Thyssen's early business career, technical and commercial knowledge, family, friends, relatives, home and work remained tightly interwoven. Family provided a crucial support base in his early years, but the fraying of family capitalism clearly showed by the turn of the century. Judging from the conflicts with his children, it would seem that his business might go the way of the burgher family in *Buddenbrooks*. If Thyssen had died, as he nearly did in 1907, or retired in his mid-sixties, his name would not have garnered the same reputation that it did by World War I. The classic problem of succession in a family business was less solved than delayed by Thyssen's longevity. The divorce agreement, moreover, made him a lifelong trustee for the property of his children—in this narrow sense—a kind of manager rather than an entrepreneur. And the divorce only reinforced an obsessive focus on business as his lifework.

Although distinguished by its melodramatic excesses, the Thyssen family was not alone in its conflicts.[108] Thomas Mann's great novel, *Buddenbrooks,* appearing in 1901, crystallized the fear of degeneration and decadence of the old burgher family world. The Thyssen scandal broke in 1904. Thyssen's relationship with his children only seemed to confirm *Buddenbrooks*. Contemporary articles rhetorically framed their scandal as a battle between two different worldviews: one bourgeois, the other aristocratic; one modest, the other luxurious, one liberal and rational, the other illiberal and drawn to irrational impulses, even mysticism; one of upright moralism, the other of decadent intoxication; one of unquestioned progress, the other of decline; one of tradition, the other of modernity. These dichotomies are too broad to capture the economic, psychological, and power dynamics within the Thyssen family (and other families), but *Buddenbrooks* appeared true enough in its sensibility to provide contemporaries a more or less persuasive portrait of a society wracked by class and familial revolt as well as foreboding decline. *Buddenbrooks* confirmed a sense of *fin-de-siécle* contradictions marked by a fascinated, insatiable appetite for the "new" that simultaneously engendered a diffuse set of anxieties about the future.

The old patriarchal authoritarianism and classic Victorian values of Joseph and August, Sr., *were* giving way to new modes of family life. His attempt to control his children's lives "in their own interest" was self-serving and patriarchal, but not cynical. The individualistic desires of children asserted themselves against the decision-making power of the father. Some questioned the seemingly inevitable participation in the family business as new career paths opened up. Lengthening periods of education extended adolescence. Daughters began to question paternal authority in the family and society. Some desired careers; universities grudgingly opened their doors to women at this time. Arranged marriages began to be superseded by marriages based on romantic love—which led to major rows within the Thyssen family. Companionate marriages like that of Fritz and Amelie increasingly challenged the traditional arranged marriage of the business elite. (Still, Heinrich's and Hedwig's marriages and August, Jr.'s near-marriages contained a heavy dose of self-conscious social climbing. The marriages were just not in the direction that their fathers desired.)[109] With the rise of the corporate form, inheritance and the dowry became less important than good relations with the large investment banks, undermining the economic justification for a conscious and careful fusion of two families. Despite these changes, in the end, most sons of the industrial elite still entered their father's world in some capacity, just as Fritz and Heinrich did. Fritz was more representative of the German business elite, whose sons did follow, uneasily, in their father's footsteps; August, Jr., was least typical of sons of businessmen.[110]

Finally, dramatic changes in lifestyle characterized the turn of the century, especially for the wealthiest *bourgeoisie*. The *fin-de-siècle bourgeoisie* found itself in a faster, more intoxicating and exhilarating, more anxious, somewhat confusing, emerging modern world. Conflicting messages and new opportunities brought on by spectacular new wealth affected the Thyssens as it did many others. Luxury and progress was a natural result of masculine hard work, but also appeared to lead to decadent, effeminate softness. As in *Buddenbrooks,* wealth was double-edged: a signifier of success and of potential decline; consumption in the sense of acquire and use was a sign of comfort and ease, but also in a second sense of wasting and as a metaphor for disease (tuberculosis). A feeling of degeneracy arose within a *bourgeoisie* that had apparently reached the height of civilization, yet felt irritatingly discontented, undermined from within.[111] Solid *bourgeois* values appeared to melt into the air.

Perhaps because of family tensions, Thyssen relied on his managers, whom he trusted more with the operations of the family business than his sons. His sons clearly sensed this and resented him for it. Paradoxically, for someone ostensibly building a family dynasty, his obsessiveness, his distrust of his children, and his strong work and performance ethos allowed him to trust (successful) managers whom he granted wide-ranging autonomy and decision-making powers. What is striking and surprising about Thyssen's relationship with his managers is how collegial they were. His closest intimates were executives such as Albert Killing, Franz Wilke, Franz Dahl, Conrad Verlohr, Julius Kalle, and Carl Rabes. While he refused to let outsiders influence his business decisions, his up-close managers influenced him considerably. He could take reasoned criticism, and all of his managers praised his ability to listen to them.[112] His reliance on good managers was the key to his business success. Thus, in spite of Thyssen's obvious patriarchal authoritarianism, the classic *Herr im Hause* mentality is not a good description of how his enterprise operated. This mentality describes his person, not his company. The 1904 move to his castle confirmed that a growing distance between personal or family ownership and managerial control had already taken place, even in a "family" enterprise.

CHAPTER 2

If I Rest, I Rust

Rast' ich so rost' ich.
August Thyssen

When Thyssen founded his small hoop-iron mill on the green fields outside of Mülheim, he had little idea that this company would become the root of a massive steel complex eventually rivaling Krupp. In 1872, Krupp already employed more than 10,000 people, including its coal-mining operations. Thyssen employed just over 140. As far as anyone can tell, he had no plans to build a massive industrial empire, just a solid, reputable, leading business for finished rolled-steel goods in the region.

Yet by choosing to make a career in the steel business, Thyssen became subject to certain dynamics of scale and scope in one of the most expansive, capital-intensive industries of the late nineteenth century. Other industries rivaled steel's growth, such as chemicals or electrical equipment, but none could match steel's significance as a symbol of industrial society.[1] Steel-making formed the foundation of modern economic and military power—one reason why Ruhr steel became associated with German militarism. Steel revolutionized bridge and building construction. A modern skyscraper was unimaginable without massive steel girders creating its internal skeleton. Electrification was not possible without miles of wire and cable. Water and gas pipes penetrating every home, and the huge sewage and drainage systems of modern cities were inconceivable without steel. Steel could even serve as a symbol of civilization and cultural achievement, offering a new aesthetic. Gustav Eiffel, for instance, designed his famous Tower (1889) as a tribute to French power, culture, and technological prowess.

74

Thyssen & Co. made its fortune by supplying the massive expansion of urban infrastructure around the world with small gas and water pipes, large-diameter conduits and pipelines, and the ubiquitous plates and sheets. As a whole, the Thyssen-Konzern supplied nearly every steel product necessary for modern infrastructural growth.

Although one of Thyssen's favorite sayings—"If I rest, I rust"—neatly encapsulates his near indefatigable personal drive, the economics of steel necessitated such restless behavior. He had incessantly to race to develop unprecedented economies of scale and scope. If Thyssen had not kept expanding and innovating at the pace of the industry, his steel products would have rested unsold on the factory grounds, left to rust away in the cold, damp air of the Ruhr. He also had to come to terms with the dramatically new technologies of making steel, which nearly destroyed Thyssen & Co. in the 1880s. These early years set the tone for future Thyssen strategy and corporate behavior, whose leitmotifs would reoccur over the course of the next half-century.

Thyssen & Co., 1871–1882

The founding of Thyssen & Co. in 1871 came in the midst of a unification euphoria called "founding fever," which propelled the German economy to giddy new heights.[2] Some of Germany's most famous companies were established in this period, including such luminary firms as the Deutsche Bank, Dresdner Bank, and two of Thyssen's rivals, the Rheinische Stahlwerke and Hoesch.

Family played a crucial role in the early period. The start-up capital for the new firm came entirely from family funds.[3] August Thyssen became the general partner of the new company, with full liability. His father had limited liability as a silent partner; he contributed 35,000 taler (105,000 marks). August Thyssen's equal contribution of 35,000 taler (105,000 marks) raised the total equity of the company to 70,000 taler (210,000 marks), a not inconsiderable sum at the time. According to fire-insurance records, Thyssen & Co.'s total assets at its opening amounted to 250,860 marks. The other 40,000 marks probably came from other family members or possibly friends.[4]

What attracted Thyssen to Styrum on the edge of Mülheim? With his move to Styrum, Thyssen began a long history of locating his firms on green-field sites next to critical train junctions.[5] The first lines directly

linked Styrum to the main regional railways, not Mülheim, which was
still attempting to improve its harbor on the Ruhr. Styrum's other advantages pale in comparison with proximity to the railroad, but constituted important secondary considerations. Mülheim had long been
a center of an active coal-mining industry. Companies at the center
of the coal trade in the western part of the Ruhr were owned by the
families of Mathias Stinnes and Franz Haniel, two future rivals. Mülheim was also an important center of the machine-tool industry. The
Friedrich Wilhelms-Hütte (FWH) lay directly adjacent to Thyssen &
Co. Thyssen could also count on relatively favorable wages because
the labor market was not stretched thin, as in the larger cities of
Dortmund or Duisburg. Finally, Styrum lay just outside the legal
boundaries of Mülheim, and was not subject to its municipal taxes.
Styrum was only a community on the tax census. In 1877, five years after Thyssen moved there, it inaugurated its first mayor. Not until 1904
did Mülheim incorporate Styrum, providing it for the first time with
street names.[6]

Unfortunately, the timing of Thyssen's start-up could not have been
worse. The heady "founding bubble" after unification soon turned
into a type of economic hangover called the "founding crisis" after
the May 1873 stock-market crash. Metaphorically speaking, Thyssen &
Co.'s first locomotive, which he had purchased second-hand to replace
horses, exploded.[7] By the end of 1873, about one-third of all Prussian
banks had failed. The total-value curve of new start-ups begun before
1913 bottomed out in 1878. The wholesale price index plummeted by
one-third. Coal, pig iron, merchant bars, and rail prices fell by 50–
60%. In 1874 and 1875, the average gross profits in the iron and steel
industry dropped by 50% each year. About one-half of all Ruhr blast
furnaces shut down; those still in operation ran at roughly 50–60% capacity. The downswing caught even powerful firms like Krupp and the
Gutehoffnungshütte (GHH); both suffered a major liquidity crisis.
Prices did not begin rising until after 1879.[8]

How did Thyssen survive the macroeconomic disaster of the 1870s?
Clearly understanding the principle of economies of scale, he kept expanding and diversifying as much as possible. As early as 1876, Thyssen
wrote the Chamber of Commerce declaring that Thyssen & Co. did
not yet have to cut its working hours despite the "miserable" state of affairs; Thyssen found it "disheartening" to watch government officials

piling together statistical material instead of applying themselves to alleviating the onerous economic situation.[9] Although information about the exact financial and productive condition of Thyssen & Co. is sparse, Thyssen managed to put a leading finished steel products company on its feet during the economic misery of the 1870s. It took a tremendous amount of capital, credit, ingenuity, and effort on his part. Lutz Hatzfeld called this period Thyssen's "true time of heroics."[10] Thyssen's continuing expansion did not depend as much on increasing productivity or technical improvements (these would come later), but on a close attention to input costs, marketing (especially exporting), technological innovation, vertically integrating into pipes, joining the pipe convention (a cartel), and resorting to heavy debt financing. Finally, he received a bit of morbid luck when his father died, and his brother joined Thyssen & Co.

Thyssen focused on hoop iron (strip steel). According to its letterhead, Thyssen & Co. specialized in strip steel with widths ranging from 13 mm to 260 mm.[11] Medium-width strips were often used as the hoops for barrels or crates or wheels—hence its somewhat archaic name "hoop iron." The thinnest strips of steel were used for a host of binding materials such as cotton bales or packaging. The widest strips of steel, called tubing strips or skelp, were used for fashioning welded pipes and tubes.

A mill train flattened puddled iron "loops" into thin strips of steel or hoops using an array of heavy rollers. Thyssen added four rolling-mill trains by January 1875. Housed in a low-slung, sooty, brick-and-mortar factory building with few windows, poor gas lighting, and even poorer ventilation, these mill trains ran parallel to one another. The third and fourth rolling-mill trains produced broad steel strips with straight edges for sale to gas and boiler pipe producers.[12] At the height of the recession, in 1876, Thyssen intended to add a fifth rolling-mill train along with the accompanying furnaces and equipment, but it did not go into operation until August 1883.[13]

Like most German mills, Thyssen & Co. relied on a number of puddling furnaces, which converted pig iron into a more malleable and durable form of steel. Puddling was one of the most difficult types of labor in the world. Not for nothing did Germans call the final product "sweat iron" *(Schweisseisen),* a pun referring both to the welding process needed to make larger pieces of metal and the enormous effort paid for in sweat on the part of the worker.[14] Puddling took a great deal of time, almost an entire twenty-four hour day, to produce one ton of steel. Creating large quantities of steel depended entirely on the strength of the puddler, which limited the size of the charges. The puddling process also created a severe bottleneck in the manufacture of steel products. Nonetheless, it remained the best manner for producing good-quality steel and it could use the phosphorous-rich iron ore mined in Germany.[15]

The seven-year delay before the fifth mill train went into operation was due not only to the strained financial situation of the mid-1870s, but to Thyssen's strategic redirection of investment toward pipes and tubes. Illustrating an early link between cartelization and vertical integration, in October 1877 six pipe works (among them Poensgen, Piedboeuf, and Tellering) founded the first gas-pipe price convention in Düsseldorf to prop up the price for gas pipes for one year. As with most price agreements that stabilize or raise prices above market levels, they attracted outsiders. Immediately in the winter of 1877–1878, Thyssen decided to move into gas and boiler pipe production; the Düsseldorfer pipe industry already purchased much of Thyssen's hoop iron sold domestically. By adding the next, downstream stage of production, Thyssen helped to assure a steady demand for his own tubing strips and diversified his production palette. He moved from a pure intermediate-product manufacturer to a finished-goods manufacturer. When, in July 1879, the pipe producers established another convention for boiler pipes, Thyssen promptly joined it to help maintain steady, higher prices for his products. The pipe producers kept renewing price agreements each year until May 1883, when the convention collapsed because Thyssen broke the agreement that had allowed him to enter the pipe industry in the first place.[16] Thus began Thyssen's reputation as an uncomfortable member, if not hostile enemy, of cartels. This behavior became a hallmark of Thyssen's strategy over the following decades.

In 1878, Thyssen hired Emil Bousse to erect a new pipe-and-tube mill as quickly as possible. Thyssen gave him full responsibility for the new plant. By October 1878, Thyssen & Co. had speedily hired a full contingent of new workers and charged its first gas-pipe furnace *before* authorities granted Thyssen the license to build the plant—another leitmotif of Thyssen business behavior.[17]

In 1879, the first Thyssen Patent Pipes came out of the furnaces. Until the Mannesmann brothers invented and commercialized the seamless pipe process in the 1890s, Thyssen's lapwelded pipes proved to have a crucial competitive advantage. These innovative pipes had a diagonal or overlapped welded edge. The factory beveled the edges of the metal strip so that when the metal was bent into a cylinder, the edges overlapped instead of being merely pressed up flat against one another. The seam's weld sealed much more effectively. Boiler pipes could be made stronger using this method because the weld could withstand greater levels of pressure—a particularly important innovation as boiler-pipe explosions were not uncommon.[18] By 1882, a third mill for lapwelded tubes went into operation.

This rapid expansion, which doubled the number of employees and pipes produced by 1882, did not not have the expected results. Although Bousse outfitted the pipe mill with the most advanced manufacturing technologies of the time, he "demoralized" many of the pipe mill's best workers and productivity fell. Thyssen fired Bousse for lack of people skills and commercial success. Thyssen always demanded that technology serve commerce, not the other way around.

After 1879, the state of the iron and steel industry improved as general economic growth accelerated. Thyssen & Co. took advantage of the brief upswing to integrate vertically and diversify into a number of new product lines, erecting a plate and sheet mill, a Siemens-Martin steel mill, and a galvanizing plant. In November 1881, the puddling works of the new plate and sheet mill went into operation.[19] The mill could produce metal plates and sheets with a width of 90 mm to 310 mm; its lifelong specialty became boiler plates. In 1883, Thyssen & Co. added a forge and an iron construction workshop for fashioning boilers themselves, which too became a Thyssen & Co. specialty.

The Siemens-Martin (open-hearth) steel mill represented an attempt by Thyssen & Co. to break the bottleneck in steel production caused by the labor-intensive puddling process. By its very nature, workers could not cast or form puddled iron into a homogenous block large enough to make the plates or sheets needed for larger diameter pipes.[20]

By 1881 the galvanizing plant went into operation. It included two vats for tin-plating pipes and for tin-plating sheet metal; both were open tanks that generated considerable chemical fumes. By galvanizing pipes and sheets, it helped retard rust. A year later, the galvanizing plant added an open tank for pipes but was used only as a reserve tank to handle peak production periods. It did not enter continuous operation until 1904.

Thus, by 1882, at the end of a decade of work, the five workshops or mills manufacturing strip steel, steel, plates and sheets, and pipes and tubes, and the galvanizing plant, formed the basis of the Thyssen & Co. steel and rolling mills. Thyssen's initial expansion tended to follow the technological logic of the manufacturing processes, called *related diversification*.[21] The steel mill and galvanizing plant largely supported the plate and pipe mills, while the strip steel and plate mill also supplied intermediate materials to the pipe mill; they both sold their individual products on the open market as well. This modest combination of vertical integration and diversification positioned Thyssen & Co. in at least three different product markets and stabilized demand for the other plants. Such a strategy would be repeated again and again in the course of Thyssen's development.

How could Thyssen expand so quickly during the difficult 1870s? In both mills, labor productivity (measured in workers/ton sold and wage levels/1,000 tons sold) did not improve in both the hoop-iron and pipe mills until after 1883. Under Bousse, they worsened; productivity in the pipe mill did not improve until after 1883.[22] Yet between 1873 and 1879, during the brunt of the recession, the hoop-iron mill expanded from 125 workers to 470 workers and increased its sales from 3,802 tons to 13,125 tons. (Revenue or earnings figures are not available.) Just after the economy began to pick up, the pipe mill expanded from 165 workers in 1879 to 505 workers in 1883 and increased its tonnage sold nearly fourfold, from 2,700 to 8,118. In short, it took roughly as much in wages, workers, and effort to produce strip steel or pipes in 1883 as in 1873. Internal productivity gains did not drive expansion.

In 1875, Thyssen wrote to the Mülheimer Chamber of Commerce that the key to staying afloat in these years was to pay attention to the difference between production costs and sale price. Thyssen also admitted to having accepted losses in the short term.[23] According to the available figures, overall wage levels advanced in the same proportion as the number of workers, so Thyssen did not inordinately depress wage levels. There is some evidence to suggest that the cost of inputs (coal and pig iron) dropped faster than the cost of finished products in the 1870s, giving some advantage to finished-goods rolling mills such as Thyssen & Co. In the desperately competitive atmosphere among pig-iron producers, for instance, Thyssen could always cut better deals. He gained a reputation for hard bargaining in these years. If one compares market prices for pig iron with the amounts purchased from the Ilseder Hütte, one finds that Thyssen & Co. purchased pig iron at significant discounts of up to 50%.[24]

Surprisingly, Thyssen also managed to augment his securities portfolio in these years. Most of his investments appear to have been part of a portfolio strategy of spreading his financial risk and maintaining contact with important collieries in the northern area of the Ruhr. By October 1882, the Thyssens purchased a not inconsiderable 286,000 marks in stocks and possessed 1,450 mining company shares around the Ruhr.[25] Some investments, however, were designed to secure a steady supply of raw materials (coal) and intermediate materials (pig iron). By far, Thyssen's most important outside investment was the Schalker Gruben- und Hüttenverein, one of the most important "mixed works" in the Ruhr. Thyssen used this investment, above all, to secure a reliable source of pig iron. At the time, very few heavy industrial firms combined coal-mining operations and blast furnaces with rolling mills for intermediate steel products. Later, this sort of vertical integration would become standard practice. Thyssen accumulated invaluable experience and contacts at the Schalker Verein, foreshadowing his entry into integrated steel-making after 1890s.[26]

A sure sign of Thyssen's influence in Schalker Verein emerges as yet another leitmotif in his career. In 1877, Thyssen became a member of the Schalker Verein's board of directors. Between 1880 and 1888, the Schalker Verein earned more than 6.8 million marks, but paid *no* dividends to shareholders; Thyssen reinvested all the profits and expanded. Under Thyssen and Friedrich Grillo (one of the most important bankers in the Ruhr), the Schalker Verein became one of the leading pig iron producers in the Ruhr.[27] Ultimately, Thyssen's active involvement in the Schalker Verein represented an important capital reserve for Thyssen & Co., not a new field of manufacturing activity. Thyssen would buy and sell Schalker Verein stock as needed, and acquiesced to extraordinarily high dividends, to enable his own expansion.[28]

Thyssen's investment here hints at the second possible strategy of full *vertical integration*—a strategic choice *not* taken until a decade later after input prices began to rise. Despite Thyssen's heavy financial commitment, the Schalker Verein never became a core Thyssen operation. A number of considerations were probably paramount. Prices remained stagnant until the late 1880s. Thyssen's independent personality made him uncomfortable dealing with other shareholders, the same reason he left the Bicheroux; differences with Grillo provided an excuse to sell his Schalker shares in 1886. Having other shareholders meant the reservoir of available capital expanded, but with that capital came claims and potentially diverging interests. Few investors would be willing to forgo dividends over the long term, a policy he ruthlessly followed with his Gewerkschaft Deutscher Kaiser (GDK). Thyssen also could not build the Schalker Verein without a secure, nearby source of coal. Finally, he decided to devote all available capital to expand the GDK.[29]

While the Schalker Verein helped to lower input costs, another ingredient crucial to Thyssen & Co.'s initial survival was marketing. Thyssen discovered new markets through incessant travel and cut-rate pricing, selling even at a loss to break into new markets. His own best traveling salesman, Thyssen went as far afield as Russia to find new customers. In 1878, Thyssen wrote the Chamber of Commerce that he exported most of his production.[30] In 1887, he wrote that so far Thyssen & Co. had exported one-third to one-half of its strip-steel production, but by 1887 profits from exports had dried up and no longer covered production costs. But Thyssen continued to orient his firms to the world export market, literally cutting Thyssen & Co. pipes to English standards (in inches). For Thyssen, exports were not a "safety valve," but a primary target market, another hallmark of his business strategy. Thyssen would remain one of Germany's leading exporters.

As at other points in his career, family played an important role in Thyssen's initial expansion. In 1875, with rather macabre timing, Désiré Bicheroux, the husband of Thyssen's sister, Balbina, died; Balbina loaned Thyssen & Co. a significant, though unspecified, portion of her inheritance. Thyssen's father died in 1877, leaving an inheritance to Thyssen. Joseph then joined Thyssen & Co. in 1879 after he liquidated their father's banking business in Eschweiler. These personal losses injected additional funds into Thyssen & Co.'s strapped coffers.[31]

Still, by the early 1880s, Thyssen had butted up against the limits of family financing. Thereafter, *the* fundamental tension of Thyssen's career made itself manifest: the desire to retain total financial control, yet continue to expand to become a leading firm in an increasingly capital-intensive industry. In Thyssen's own words, the reasons for his initial success were that:

> The new firm turned a profit through extreme thrift in production as well as in purchasing and sales. The firm could retain its earnings in order to strengthen its working capital and operations *(Betriebsmittel)*. By this means it was possible to achieve [additional] savings and funds needed to enlarge the existing production facilities and to build new ones. In order to do so, I naturally had to take out loans numerous times which were indeed quite modest in the beginning, but which were later made available to me in greater amounts. Most of the time, I succeeded with the planned expansion and new production facilities in attaining profits. We also urgently needed these profits not only to proceed with the necessary complementary additions, but also to cover the losses that appeared on occasion. Everything that was undertaken did not always succeed. Wrong decisions and failures also occurred in the process. These were all the more severe when some credit had been borrowed for new equipment on which nothing could be earned because the debts incurred had to be paid back.[32]

Thyssen's emphasis on the utmost savings, continuous reinvestment of profits, thrift, and industriousness recalls classic Victorian entrepreneurial virtues, but his heavy use of credit and rapid expansion to *create* additional cost savings to finance even more expansion did not.

Thyssen found rather adventurous ways of tapping new lines of credit. He rightfully became notorious for his rather unusual financing techniques. A letter from December 1883 provides some insight into Thyssen's financial strategy, as well acting as a touchstone for assessing the success of Thyssen & Co. by the early 1880s. In an unusual move, he took out an advertisement in a trade publication announcing that an unnamed Rhenisch steel company sought a loan of one million marks. After receiving inquiries, August Thyssen wrote back to one prospective creditor, describing the state of the firm:

> ... [O]ur production facilities, which we would be willing to mortgage, consist of a strip steel works with five rolling mill trains operating at full

capacity, a plate mill, a pipe mill, a steel mill, and a galvanizing plant. Each of these plants are at the highest state of perfection and are running at full capacity with satisfactory financial results despite the adversity of the present times.

These facilities represent at least four to five times the value of the above loan! For the most part, the requested sum will be used to pay off the remaining small amount of debts, but mostly for the expansion of existing equipment.

Any firm in the local area or any larger iron and steel company in Rhineland and Westphalen will be able to tell you about our reputation and our position achieved in the iron industry![33]

One can sense the considerable pride Thyssen had in his firm and reputation. The sum of four to five million marks probably referred to the fixed assets of the firm, since he offered to mortgage them. Thyssen had increased his original investment by roughly twelve times in twelve difficult years of business. Thyssen also made absolutely clear on what terms he would accept a loan: "[W]e would like to know if the relevant bank wants to invest its own money in us with the mortgage or wants to trade it on the market: in the latter case, further negotiations would be pointless!" Thyssen distrusted any financial machinations that might mean a loss of control. At this time, Thyssen even entered into negotiations for a joint venture to develop manufacturing capabilities for steam boilers, but after 1883, when his financial position and productivity figures improved, Thyssen abruptly withdrew from the negotiations. He justified the withdrawal on the grounds that Joseph did not agree with the project, a ploy he often used.[34]

By 1882, the firm had weathered the downcycle of the mid-1870s, altered its legal form to a private partnership, consolidated a good portion of the family's financial assets, achieved vague but "satisfactory" financial results, and embarked on a strategy of rapid expansion and diversification. Thyssen & Co.'s total employment had risen from 95 people in 1872 to over 1200 in 1882. During the upswing of 1880–1882, its workforce doubled. In 1882, as if to mark the transition from small-scale enterprise, Thyssen & Co.'s wage and salary payments also broke the one million marks level. These two figures signified the point at which Thyssen could no longer run the company largely alone, but had to create a sophisticated industrial bureaucracy to manage Thyssen & Co.'s increasingly complex operations.

This early history of Thyssen & Co. highlights a number of leitmotifs of Thyssen strategy that contributed to his tremendous success.
Thyssen's future behavior became manifest before he ever set up operations at the GDK: the tendency to secrecy and self-sufficiency; an indefatigable sales effort; an export orientation; the sheer speed with
which he launched new operations; the instrumentalization of cartels
to his own ends; a constant reinvestment of any profits; his dependence on the technical advice of managers combined with a fundamental *commercial* orientation; and finally, his preference for family or
self-financing. Only if self-financing fell short did he resort to outside
financing, and then largely through highly leveraged and risky debt.
Equity would only lead to a loss of his "freedom."

A considerable portion of Thyssen's success in the 1870s derived
from his ability as a Victorian-style *merchant,* with its corresponding values of thrift, industriousness, solidity, constant reinvestment of profits,
and the cultivation of extensive sales contacts to build a personal reputation (or brand). Throughout his life—and with noteworthy implications for the organization and corporate culture of his firms—Thyssen
ran his companies with an eye to long-term *commercial* success. But
his use of debt and attention to scale and maximum capacity utilization indicate he understood the economic dynamics of the brave new
world of steel.

Strategies of Scale, 1882–1895

Thyssen clearly understood the logic of economies of scale as early as
the 1870s. In January 1884, he wrote to all of his department chiefs
that hard times lay ahead. Without an apparent end, prices for strip
steel and plates were dropping below production costs. He explained
how Thyssen & Co. had to compete:

> In such a situation, it is absolutely necessary, yes to avoid another re-
> duction in wages in which we want to take refuge only in the most ex-
> treme emergency, to run our factory operations to their utmost limit.
> The only way [to achieve this end] is if the greatest thrift acts as the rul-
> ing guide . . . that only the most necessary workers remain active, that
> all superfluous people or those who can be made superfluous be dis-
> charged, that the energies of the individual be intensified as much
> as possible, and that new expenses of any type be reduced to the min-

imum. In other words: Do everything to press production costs to their minimum, be it through direct savings in operations, [or] be it through the improvement of our equipment without increasing production costs, so that production can be raised![35]

A clearer statement about the need for economies of scale can scarcely be imagined.

Expansion did not derive *from* financial success but *created* the basis for success. Thyssen achieved his "satisfactory" results by producing at capacity, that is, running operations "at their utmost limit," even in the face of an unfavorable economy. Indeed, before 1895 the German economy remained stalled in what has classically been called the "Great Depression," but was rather a period of slow but grudging growth. Thyssen became a fanatic about scale and tonnage figures.[36] Thyssen executives thought this obsessive focus on scale brought Thyssen his cost advantages. Thyssen's choice to enter the steel manufacturing industry placed him in an ever-spiraling race to achieve economies of scale.[37]

Capital-intensive industries in manufacturing distinguish themselves by the immense size of the investments needed to start operations, which—potentially—could lead to lower average costs per unit of output *if* the volume of production is raised. (High-volume economies also depended considerably on the extent of the market, which the railroads and steam shipping had enlarged considerably.) Like Thyssen, Andrew Carnegie understood that "cheapness is in proportion to the scale of production. To make ten tons of steel a day would cost many times as much per ton as to make one-hundred tons. . . . Thus the larger the scale of operation the cheaper the product."[38]

As scale rose so did the minimum investment to enter the industry and remain competitive. If capital-intensive operations prove profitable, these profits naturally attract competitors who build larger plants to achieve even lower production costs. Over time, the industry's minimum efficient scale of plant grew ever larger. One had to keep up or get out. As plants grew larger, the industry itself became characterized by high fixed costs. The original capital invested in the firm represented a significantly larger cost sunk into the venture before it ever began manufacturing. As the term suggests, fixed costs are constant costs that the firm incurs whether or not it sells a single unit of product. By definition, fixed costs do not fluctuate with the volume of production. Fixed costs include expenses such as interest on debt, depreciation of buildings and equipment, overhead expenses for a managerial staff, insurance, pension plans, taxes, even long-term investments in training new personnel (if we use a more expansive definition of human capital). Interest on debt was always a huge consideration for Thyssen.

Critical, then, to industries characterized by high fixed costs is the ability to operate at capacity over the long term—"to run our factory operations to their utmost limit." Alfred Chandler has termed this acceleration of production and distribution *throughput,* or economies of speed, which are actually scale economies resulting from speeding up the flow of work and the flow of product through the manufacturing process and onto the market. The greater the speed of transformation of raw materials into finished products, the more fully capacity becomes used, thereby lowering a company's average fixed unit costs. A firm's management could intensify capacity use by speeding up the manufacturing process or extending working hours by adding shifts. (Needless to say, workers did find both strategies objectionable.)

A third major consideration, however, is finding enough market demand to keep running "factory operations at their utmost limit." And the market price may not cover even the lowest possible production costs. Hence, potential economies of scale and the subsequent rise of fixed costs helped encourage fundamentally new marketing strategies (advertising), often created out of sheer desperation. As initial investments mounted into the millions (or billions), the stakes, and the anxiety, rose geometrically with every new investment, which is why such businesses were among the first to resort to cartels to fix prices.

Because of high fixed costs and greater financial risks, capital-intensive businesses altered their competitive behavior on the market, perverting the classical model of market competition. As the Thyssen experience demonstrated, instead of reducing production in difficult times to match demand, high fixed-cost businesses kept producing, expanding, putting more product on the market although that practice often drove prices down even further. Economies of scale implied pricing and selling products at their last (marginal) unit cost, rather than average cost. Because fixed costs remained constant, if one limited production, the average unit cost of the product would rise dramatically. Thus it paid to run full, as close to capacity as possible, even in bad times. Such practices may have paid very little, but one lost less money if one could recoup some revenue rather than none. This practice conferred advantages to those with deep financial pockets. Or one could fix prices through cartels to avoid "ruinous" competition. Or one could engage in so-called "predatory pricing" that might drive out weaker competitors. Not surprisingly, under these competitive dynamics, "monopoly" became one of the most important words of the late nineteenth century.[39]

This capitalist race called for a confluence of personality and profession that Thyssen embodied in his favorite phrase, "If I rest, I rust." Yet Thyssen & Co. nearly did founder in the 1880s, caused by "wrong decisions and mistakes" surrounding the start-up of the Siemens-Martin steel mill. This steel mill was one of the severest setbacks of Thyssen's career, as both the new steel mill and new plate mill were built on extensive lines of credit. Until Thyssen's move to the GDK after 1890, Thyssen & Co. relied mostly on outside supplies of coal, iron ore, pig iron, and crude steel. The Mülheim mill filled only the supply needs of the plate and sheet mill. Thyssen & Co. was what the Germans then called a "pure" rolling mill because it did not combine other stages of the steel-making process.

In the early 1880s, Thyssen did not only have to achieve economies of scale, but also master new technologies of steel-making. In order to break the bottleneck caused by puddling, Thyssen chose the Siemens-Martin or open-hearth process. Open-hearth steel was most appropriate for Thyssen & Co.'s palette of goods. Unlike the Bessemer process, it could make higher quality steel, particularly appropriate for plates and ship plates. It was less capital-intensive than the Bessemer or Thomas processes. It could also recycle relatively plentiful Bessemer scrap, turning this waste into higher value-added steel. With careful selection of phosphorous-free materials (iron ore, pig iron, or scrap), it allowed a greater flexibility in input materials and even could compete with lower-end crucible steel casting products. It did not compete directly with mass-production steel. Over time, the open-hearth process became increasingly important as the demand for quality became paramount.

Unfortunately for Thyssen, the acid-based Siemens-Martin process used in the early 1880s also quickly destroyed the furnaces and produced inferior products. Because of the high heat reached in the regenerative firing system, the furnaces needed constant repair. The open hearth contained the heat, and the acidic limestone furnace lining chemically reacted with materials found in the slag, quickly destroying the furnace. Products suffered from numerous cracks, holes, and other imperfections. Not until engineers pounded dolomite into magnesite hearths that could better withstand the heat and convert the acid process to a basic process did the open-hearth process become successful. [40]

For Thyssen & Co., and other German steelworks, this conversion to the basic process first occurred in 1888, four difficult years after he was forced to shut it down. From the time the steel mill opened in 1881, it caused Thyssen nothing but grief. He went through numerous chief engineers. In 1884, he shut down the whole mill and added more puddling furnaces. Thyssen remembered the setback as one of the worst in his life.[41] Thyssen & Co. still managed to increase overall sales in each of the main product areas by relying entirely on outside intermediate materials. Once Thyssen & Co. engineers mastered the open-hearth process, which came on line in 1888, its overall production increased rapidly. Unfortunately, Thyssen & Co. encountered another general slowdown in the economy, which stalled after 1889.

August Thyssen portrayed the general stagnation at the end of the 1880s and beginning of the 1890s as a time of "general economic misery," even the "decline" of the German iron and steel industry.[42] Then, in a characteristic rhetorical move common to Thyssen and other industrialists, he claimed that exports had dried up because of the excessive burdens placed on industry by government as well as the growing demands of workers. Over the next few years, Thyssen reiterated the same complaints. By 1895, he claimed that Thyssen & Co. could barely meet the minimum interest payments on its debt. Continuing expansion and improvements to the factory's equipment still had not led to better financial results. Before 1895, the reduction in production costs only seemed to chase a greater drop in market prices. Indeed, the price of heavy plates, for instance, dropped by almost half, from 220 marks/ton to 126.25 marks/ton, between 1890–1894. Thyssen continued to invest in the newly renovated steel and plate mill, but a continuing strategy of economies of scale and debt financing was born out of the sheer necessity of reducing manufacturing costs faster than market prices.

What Thyssen neglected to mention was that he also began a huge wave of investment activity at the GDK to secure his raw material and intermediate input materials, which would explain why he could barely keep up with his interest on debt and capital improvements. The firm continued to "run full" by accepting various export con- tracts below cost in 1891; exports amounted to approximately 50% of sales. Franz Wilke, Thyssen's top factory director, could ask the mayor of Styrum to allow the factory to work through the holidays in both 1889 and 1890. This sort of hard-driving was characteristic of Thyssen. Wilke also argued that keeping the factory open would be in the inter- ests of the public order because it would keep workers out of the bars after recent strikes and layoffs elsewhere. The combined effect of idle- ness and alcohol would only make the workers susceptible to the argu- ments of "unscrupulous agitators."[43] The discrepancy between the real economic reasons for poor profitability (a slowdown in the economy and high fixed costs) and the rhetoric of business politics is another leitmotif of Thyssen (and other steel industrialists), which grew to par- ticularly egregious proportions during the days of Weimar Republic.

Until the late 1880s, the strip-steel department remained the driving force behind Thyssen & Co.'s growth in terms of tonnage and value. After 1887, the steel plant and plate mill (Department II) became the most important department in terms of tonnage and general revenues until the turn of the century. Thyssen & Co. also became one of the leading pipe producers in Germany.[44] By the mid-1890s, the produc- tion emphasis of Thyssen & Co. shifted to the plate and pipe depart- ments, with the strip steel, Siemens-Martin mill, and galvanizing plant largely acting as support.

Although production grew impressively, profits did not necessarily follow. The steel and plate mill revenues (for which we have a near complete run) make it clear that the fast growth period after 1895 dif- fered significantly from the period before. After 1895, the German economy entered a period of intense, sustained growth, interrupted by only two brief but harsh downturns in 1902–1903 and 1909–1910.[45] By 1898, Thyssen could complain to the Chamber of Commerce only about the lack of workers caused by high turnover—a byproduct of a good economy. His reports to the Chamber of Commerce became considerably more cryptic as he became unwilling to trumpet his suc- cesses.[46]

Plate-mill revenues mirrored general trends, conveyed the depth of the recessions, and stand as a rough proxy for Thyssen & Co.'s growth. In 1883, its sales totalled roughly 2 million marks (on 10,800 tons of production); in 1895 about 6.7 million marks (54,700 tons); in 1900 almost 20 million marks (94,600 tons); but dropped in 1902 by one-quarter to 15 million marks (105,400 tons) because of price deflation. Prices quickly recovered, dropping again in 1909 and recovering once again, to provide just under 31.7 million marks in revenue (203,400 tons). Yet, on the available evidence, profit margins per ton of plate-mill product dropped from roughly 20–25 marks/ton between 1887 and 1889 to just 4.1 marks/ton in 1905, although sales grew sevenfold between 1887 and 1905. In 1889, the plate department had higher total profits with less than one-third of 1905 sales.[47] In 1901–1902, Thyssen had to cut bonuses by one-third in the plate mill and the pressing works due to "difficult times."[48] In spite of massive improvements in manufacturing processes around the turn of the century, the pipe department worked in the red. All in all, higher and higher volume chased smaller and smaller profit margins. Heavy plates, for instance, quickly became commodity products and sensitive to economies of scale. Increasing volume was a survival strategy.

Rapidly declining profit margins, particularly in commodified steel goods, reflected the dynamics of the industry:

> The entrepreneur or the director of a company can only care for the good of its operations if the workers and the company earn the means that are required for the development of the works and for its appropriate costs for all participants. If the equipment and facilities of my domestic or international rivals are substantially better than mine and if my [financial] means are not adequate to improve them, then a creeping infirmity *(Siechtum)* sets in, which will not be possible for us to halt.[49]

Strategies of Scope, 1895–1914

In order to keep up with the scale necessary in mining coal and manufacturing commodity steel goods, Thyssen found it necessary after 1887 to build a whole new scale of operations in Hamborn-Bruckhausen, located about ten miles northwest of Mülheim and directly north of Duisburg. Mülheim did not have the space for greater expansion, nor such geographical advantages as rich coal seams and inland river harbors located on the Rhine. In Bruckhausen, Thyssen located the Gewerkschaft Deutscher Kaiser (GDK), Thyssen & Co.'s "sister firm," to integrate vertically into coal mining and high-volume steel-making.

While the GDK competed in the market for mass-production goods, Thyssen & Co. increasingly positioned itself in world markets as a highly diversified finished-goods manufacturer with an array of specialty products. After 1895, Thyssen & Co.'s strategy shifted to emphasize economies of scope rather than economies of scale, although the two strategies were not mutually exclusive. Thyssen & Co. offered a full range of products with particular types of niche products nestled among them. The Thyssen & Co. plate department supplied all types and sizes of specialty heavy plates, sheets, and boilers for sale to other machine companies and shipbuilding docks. In addition to commodity pipes and tubes, it offered as full a range as possible of specialty pipes and tubes, as well as the largest-diameter pipes for waterlines and turbines then in existence.[50] Specialty product lines could be found especially in the welding and pressing works of the plate mill, the pipe and tube mill, and the machine-engineering department. By 1914, these specialty products made a name for Thyssen & Co. around the world. This strategy helped combat rapidly fluctuating prices through product diversification. Economies of scope offered distinct cost advantages, since the same unit used the same raw materials, input goods, and production processes to manufacture a large number of related products. This diversification strategy helped to keep the plant running at capacity and positioned the firm in a varied set of individual product markets, which spread risk.

Thyssen & Co. published advertising brochures in English, French, Russian, and Italian, and in a 1906 version stressed that each of the departments of the rolling mills offered a full range of products in "all dimensions," "for all purposes," "up to the largest sizes," "for every description," "to any shape and of any length," "galvanized or plain."[51] The brochures always emphasized that Thyssen & Co. would customize any product to the customers' needs. Thyssen & Co. exported heavily, so its output conformed to many different national and regional standards; even pipe threads differed among countries.

The following statistics provide some measure of Thyssen & Co.'s export orientation and the relative size of its departments. The plate department (without the steel mill) contributed 44% of all sales, 42% of which derived from exports. The pipe department's revenues nearly equalled that of the plate department, contributing 38% of total sales, one-third of which were exported. The starting point of Thyssen & Co., the strip-steel mill, contributed just 9% of total sales, and it exported 38% of its production. Finally, the galvanizing plant added an additional 7% of sales, exporting 33% of its production.[52]

Thyssen & Co.'s product-diversification strategy can best be viewed by examining the development of the plate-mill department. The press works and welding works within the plate department represented Thyssen & Co.'s commitment to specialty products. As early as 1884, Thyssen's factory director, Franz Wilke, erected a small pressing works in the plate department. Wilke carried out his own primary research and developed a patented press for using corrugated plates in steam boilers and other such vessels. In 1887, Thyssen & Co. advertised that its main product line was wide plates for welded pipes, but it also offered top-class (*Lowmoor*-quality) plates for high-stress, high-heat work; plates for ships; thin and medium-sized sheets; and manhole covers.

The next head of the plate mill, Franz Metzmacher, expanded the pressing workshop with a plate forge. The press works eventually manufactured all sorts of boiler ends, pressed parts for railway rolling stock and carriage construction, coke-furnace doors, bottoms for furnaces, firebox plates, and so on; it also placed a greater weight on bending plates and sheets used in furnaces and large-diameter tube-making.[53] The plate forge welded steel vessels of all types, including locomotive boiler parts, fireboxes, supports, gas boilers, and vessels for chemical works. In 1901, Thyssen & Co. completely renovated and enlarged the press works.

Between 1893 and 1895, Metzmacher erected a corrugated-sheet mill and pipe-rolling mill using water gas welding for manufacturing large-diameter water, gas, and steam conduits for pipelines, as well as high-pressure boilers of all types. Water gas welding, which produced combustible gas from heated charcoal and water, significantly improved the quality of the welds necessary for high-pressure work and large-diameter pipes for gas, water, steam, or drainage that became a Thyssen & Co. specialty. The welding tube workshop did not start production until 1895, but quickly doubled its production after 1900. Diversity and scale of products increased as Siemens-Martin steel completely replaced puddled steel. The shaping machines of the welding shop grew from being able to bend plates up to four meters in 1888, to five meters in 1893, to 8 meters in 1904, to 8.5 meters in 1912. They added an electrically driven crane in 1899 and a hydraulically driven plate shears in 1906; both innovations, along with modified floor plans, sped up product flows within the mill. In 1906, Metz-macher added a metals-testing laboratory and an experimental office for quality control, signifying the strong commitment to value-added specialty production.

The welded-tube and boiler workshop of the plate department grew to be one of the most important production areas within the firm, delivering large water mains to major cities all over the world. The 1896–1898 deliveries to Hamburg, for instance, made Thyssen & Co. one of the major suppliers of materials for urban infrastructure, just as Germany underwent a swift and massive urbanization process. In 1906, the Thyssen & Co. welding workshop alone supplied 43% of the total sales of corrugated tubes in Germany.[54] Thyssen & Co. also delivered pipelines for major infrastructural projects in major cities and hydro-electric power stations over the entire world: the U.S., Canada, Holland, Denmark, France, Italy, Romania, Switzerland, Chile, Mexico, Argentina, Japan, India, and South Africa.[55] It offered specialty designs as well: for instance, the distribution conduit for turbines delivered to Niagara Falls (Figure 2.1).

Until the expansion of Thyssen trading firms just before the war, Thyssen & Co. worked through agents such as Robert Brown in New York and Drummon, McCall & Co. in Montreal.[56]

The Thyssen & Co. welding workshop in the plate mill offered all types of pressing, flanging, and welding products made from plates, especially for marine and stationary boilers. After taking out a license for the Fox & Morison process to make corrugated furnaces with flanged tubes, Thyssen & Co. became one of the premier suppliers of corrugated furnaces to navies and merchant marines in Europe. Thyssen & Co. supplied its products according to the specifications of the German, French, Italian, Dutch, and Belgian navies. The Thyssen staff also worked through the varied tests required by other European countries' standards offices.

Figure 2.1 Turbine distribution pipe of the Ontario Light and Power Co., Niagara Falls. (Reproduced with the permission of the Mannesmann-Archiv, Mülheim/Ruhr)

The most important field for the long-term growth of the company, however, was the rapid expansion of plates for conduit tubes and corrugated tubes and furnaces, growing to nearly one-quarter of total plate production by the beginning of World War I. Production of large conduit tubes rose dramatically from 1400 tons in 1898 to more than 24,000 tons in 1913. Massive, large-diameter conduits for pipelines became a specialty of the Mülheim works, exporting to such places as Carp River and Tallulah Falls in the United States. They remained its signature product until the present time, when one can still see long lines of large-diameter pipes sitting on railroad tracks outside the factory. Thyssen & Co.'s press and welding works supplied for such pipelines all sorts of auxiliary parts as well, which included welded fittings, sockets, boiler ends, flanges, and manhole covers.[57]

After 1900, in particular, the diversification of products broadened revenues of the plate mill from more than just the sale of commodity heavy plates and universal flat bars (an intermediate product for tubing strips). Until 1900, price movements for plate-mill products, heavy plates, and boiler plates paralleled one another in a fairly regular cyclical pattern of fluctuation. After 1902, however, the average price per ton of plate-department products shot upwards as a result of the diversification into higher-value-added goods. The Thyssen & Co. plate department exported a significant portion of each of its products, ranging from a low of 13% in 1904 to a high of 37% in 1901 and 1913. While it still offered commodity products, it specialized in boiler plates and heavy plates of up to 35 tons and 100 square meters. Boiler plates had constituted about three-quarters of all of Thyssen & Co. manufactured plates, but after 1904, the proportion of boiler plates manufactured dropped in favor of tubing plates and sheets for conduits, ship plates (especially after 1909), and for construction activity. Plates and sheets for construction activity hovered relatively steadily at just over 20% of total production. With the expansion of the German merchant marine and navy, the demand for ships' plates grew dramatically. (Thyssen & Co. did not supply armored plates for warships until the war broke out). Ship-plate sales grew dramatically after 1909.

Thyssen & Co. engineers perfected the quality of the steel produced by the Siemens-Martin mill, which turned it into a solid asset. An entirely new Siemens-Martin steel mill went into operation in 1907, with a new Harmet pressing process capable of shaping steel blocks directly out of the furnace while the steel was still in a semi-liquid state. This open-hearth steel could be cast and pressed into forms of greater density, homogeneity, and with fewer surface imperfections, producing plates of greater strength and durability. By 1912, ten Siemens-Martin ovens with a total daily capacity of 800 tons were operating in Mülheim. The basic Siemens-Martin process positioned Thyssen & Co. to compete on world markets, especially against the British, with high-quality products for the shipping industry, a market niche where Germans previously had had difficulty competing. Altogether, the Thyssen & Co. product line was more diversified than those of many large American companies, which tended to concentrate on fewer lines of standardized products to achieve economies of scale.

In spite of increasing product diversity, technical improvements in the manufacturing process drove productivity way up in the firm. For instance, the strip-steel department's technical director, Nowack, tied the mill more closely to the production of tubing strips for pipe manufacture; in 1909 he phased out puddling altogether. In 1911, Thyssen & Co.'s first electrically driven rolling mill train went into operation.

The results of these technical innovations showed quickly. If before 1885 it took roughly thirty-five workers to produce 1,000 tons, and before 1900 about twenty, by 1912 Thyssen & Co. needed just five.[58] In 1912, the number of workers and wages needed by Thyssen & Co. to produce 1,000 tons of strip steel reached its lowest point in the prewar period. Not until 1929 and 1933 was this productivity figure equalled. This was one reason why German industrialists viewed the Imperial period as a golden age. Even the stable years of the Weimar Republic did not match the productivity gains and levels of the prewar period.

While the plate mill developed an entirely new range of products, the pipe and tube mill benefited more fundamentally from process innovations. After 1900, three engineers, Willy Trapp, Alfred Drieschner, and Aloys Fassl, created huge productivity gains by introducing U.S.-style production practices. Always aware of new business developments, Thyssen (and others) became increasingly conscious of the massive production potential being created in the United States, and he shipped a number of his senior technical directors off to America on industry tours. This included sending Trapp to America to find new ways of using Siemens-Martin steel instead of puddling steel for pipes.

Within a few years after his American trip, Trapp introduced three American-designed gas-tube furnaces in rapid succession. By 1910, all three were in full production and used Siemens-Martin steel exclusively. Siemens-Martin steel pipes and pipe fittings offered greater malleability and tensile strength than did iron tubes. After 1900, the pipe department's English advertising brochure could emphasize the advantage of manufacturing "the necessary Raw-Material in our Steel Works by the approved Siemens-Martin Process, and also of rolling the Strips in our own Rolling Mills. We therefore need not to depend upon other works for the necessary material to make the tubes and can therefore guarantee the quality of the material as well as prompt delivery."[59] The use of liquid steel for pipes, moreover, enabled new economies of speed to be introduced. As a result of the third new American-designed furnace alone, three older gas-tube furnaces could be shut down. By 1910, none of the older gas-tube furnaces were still in operation. Puddling had ended.

After 1900, Trapp's introduction of American-designed gas-pipe ovens dramatically lowered the labor intensity of pipe production. Since the 1870s, productivity in the pipe mill had hardly improved at all. In fact, productivity had slowly worsened over time, probably due to the constant customizing of pipes and tubes for various uses. In 1899–1902, it took more than seventy workers to manufacture 1,000 tons, yet by 1906 less than half that number, and by 1913 just twenty workers. Just as in the strip-steel mill, the pipe mill's productivity tripled between 1900 and 1912 and its sales quadrupled. In 1899, it sold more than 20,000 tons of goods, by 1906 more than 43,000, and by 1912 more than 85,000 tons. These turn-of-the-century innovations turned Thyssen & Co. into the largest producer of welded gas pipes in all of Germany.[60]

At the same time, Thyssen & Co. continued to diversify the types of pipe products offered. The pipe mill extended the range of its production to include specialized forms of pipes and tubes and added six patented tube furnaces for gas pipes and boiler tubes. Trapp and Drieschner also added numerous workshops and foundries to the pipe department to produce specialty products to exact specifications. These included all types of variations on pipes and pipe products: socket tubes, heating coils, flanged tubes, drilling pipes, enamel-lined tubes for coal sluices, and steel masts and poles for lighting fixtures. These products demonstrate how Thyssen's fortunes depended heavily on the growth of urban and industrial infrastructure.

In order to achieve the new process innovations, Thyssen & Co. completely rebuilt the layout of the pipe mill. One former pipe-mill employee remembered how the newly erected production halls towered "monstrously" over the "oldest workshops with their gloomy lowness and their sooty timbers." Although the old gas-pipe works had used hydraulics and electricity to some extent, continuous processing became the norm. Thyssen & Co. engineers equipped the new fitting workshops with numerous flexibly moving electric cranes instead of the "ungainly" hydraulic crane that moved on one track, so that "eternal mechanical movement is above all a particular characteristic of the new workshops." Instead of the dark, dusty, brick-lined workshops, one of the effects of the modernization was to fill the halls with light and air, made possible by new steel-girder and sheet-metal construction. The effect was so dramatic, and the new facilities projected such an aura of state-of-the-art modernity, that Thyssen & Co. sales managers featured them in their advertising brochures.

Those new halls of internal steel skeletons and skins of sheet metal marked a significant discontinuity in the manufacturing history of Thyssen & Co. New attention was brought to bear on manufacturing process technologies that quantitatively and qualitatively dwarfed anything that had come before.

So as not to lose time or money, the older mill continued to produce, as Thyssen & Co. erected the new building to use new processes. Once the new building engulfed the old, workmen razed the old brick mill and restarted production with new equipment as quickly as possible. Achieving economies of scale and speed meant creating a continuous flows of people and products inside the factory walls. Inside the new buildings, product flows from the unloading of raw materials to the storage of finished products to the loading of the finished plates and pipes fell under the oversight of management. Thyssen & Co. had suffered under space constraints since the 1890s, and its management surveyed space continually, creating maps to rationalize more broadly the use of space. Previously, department managers laid out single workshops wherever space was available, but after the turn of the century Thyssen engineers redesigned combinations of halls and departments to ensure a smooth overall flow of product, so that loading, furnaces, blocks of intermediate materials, rolling mill trains, cooling beds, storage areas, and shipping areas all streamed into one another. Electrically driven cranes moved product along planned lines. A well-designed layout minimized the loss of heat and the number of people on the shopfloor, reduced heavy lifting, and sped up material flows to create economies of speed. The creation of plant layout maps signified to what degree space was rationalized, altered, and managed according to efficiency and productivity criteria. Management rationalized space itself. Electricity, cranes, and improved layouts created "eternal mechanical movement" inside the factory halls, resulting in unprecedented productivity gains, which were not surpassed until the 1930s.

While new volume economies in pipe manufacture relied a good deal on American mass production lines, new technological advances in pipe manufacturing owed more to German know-how. Until 1900, Mannesmann controlled the patent rights to the seminal invention of the seamless tube-making process, which gave it a monopoly and permitted it to earn exceptional profits in this sector of the pipe market. According to Fritz Bethlehem, seamless pipes were one of the most significant inventions of the nineteenth century. Thomas Edison remarked at the Chicago World Exhibition of 1893: "The seamless Mannesmann pipe—a masterpiece of men as men should be."[61] In Germany, Mannesmann acted as the great competitive thorn in Thyssen's side in the pipe and tube market until 1970. Since the 1890s, Thyssen had his engineers in the machine department devote a considerable amount of energy to figuring out the process, but to little avail.

An opportunity arrived in 1900, when Mannesmann's patent elapsed. Thyssen immediately hired away Aloys Fassl, a Mannesmann engineer, to build a seamless tube facility at Thyssen & Co.'s "sister work" in Dinslaken. The Thyssen & Co. machine engineering department formally employed Fassl. Fassl combined the Mannesmann seamless tube process, which actually formed a semi-finished, hollow, cylindrical block of metal that still need to be further shaped into pipes, with American-style continuous processing. Fassl's process innovation creatively combined the best of both worlds. The first Fassl pipe mill train, located at the GDK Dinslaken, could manufacture seamless tubes of 8–10 meters in length, which eventually stretched to 20–25 meters. These long seamless tubes could be formed into coils, drilling pipes, and boiler tubes capable of withstanding great pressures.

Drieschner introduced Fassl's seamless tube production to the Mülheim production palette in 1911, mostly for coils for heating, superheating, and refrigeration. As the advertising brochure highlighted, these coils could be made into one continuous length without joints, which minimized the danger of explosion. For his efforts, Fassl received the highest severance award ever paid out by Thyssen, 500,000 marks. He left Dinslaken and Mülheim for the United States, where he introduced his mill trains to the American steel industry.[62] The Fassl process clearly shows that the Germans did not simply imitate American methods, but creatively blended them with their own methods. German pipe-making technology transfers contributed to the creation of the American mass-production model.

This manufacturing history of Thyssen & Co. has highlighted a number of leitmotifs of Thyssen strategy. The steel business of the late nineteenth century rewarded hard-driving, near-obsessive behavior, and Thyssen clearly understood the new logic of running a capital-intensive business, which necessitated running his "factory operations to their utmost limit." He oriented himself to export markets with an eye to marketing, often acting as his own best salesman. His personal reputation was wrapped around his products' reputation.

Always attentive to new business opportunities and technical developments, Thyssen invested heavily in state-of-the-art equipment, which mixed volume with diversification, scale with scope. However, as important as August Thyssen was for his own economic fate, he relied entirely on engineers and shopfloor masters for their technical expertise. Thyssen did not design any of these technologies or run the manufacturing operations. His top technical managers, Bousse, Blasberg, the Wilkes (Franz, August, Robert), Nowack, Metzmacher, Matzek, Trapp, Drieschner, Wallmann, to mention a few, did. Thyssen remained a merchant. In this respect, Thyssen was the complete opposite of Werner von Siemens, who viewed himself as a scientist and inventor, proud of his technical reputation, and his firm as a technical research and development institute.[63] Siemens denigrated "money-making" merchants and businessmen such as his rival, Emil Rathenau, who did not invent or design, and merely transplanted "American designs and methods of production into German soil."[64]

Thyssen's success was more analogous to Rathenau's. Thyssen & Co.'s performance rested on the commercialization of largely existing products. With a few exceptions of singular technological improvement (patented lapwelded pipes, the Fassl seamless tube, continuous-process manufacturing of large diameter welded pipes), Thyssen & Co.'s overall success did not rest on new inventions *per se* (such as Mannesmann's seamless pipe process, Siemens' telegraphs or electric dynamos, or Krupp's casting process for cannons), but on constant, incremental innovations. Thyssen & Co. patents also rested on continuous improvements of existing technical capabilities and product lines. Thyssen & Co. often bought licensing rights to important process innovations such as the Fox & Morrison system for corrugated furnaces, Morgan cooling beds, Harmet pressing processes for steel, or Trapp's patent of the production process for pipes and fittings. Not until its machine engineering department developed the large, coking-gas-powered engine did Thyssen & Co. create a breakthrough invention.

Because it remained a private partnership in the interests of secrecy, was somewhat hidden behind the more famous and larger GDK, and because many archival materials have been lost, the extent of Thyssen's success in Mülheim has been obscured. It does not appear on the lists of Germany's largest firms. (Thyssen would have found some joy in this fact.) Yet Thyssen & Co. did grow into one of Germany's largest firms, with a significant presence on world export markets.

We have only a few points of reference to anchor an evaluation. In 1899, Thyssen & Co. had revenues totalling 34.6 million marks. This made Thyssen & Co. roughly the same size as Hoesch, slightly smaller than the Bochumer Verein, larger than the Rheinische Stahlwerke, and twice the size of Mannesmann. The integrated steelworks, Phoenix, however, was twice as large as Thyssen & Co., Krupp almost four times its size.[65] The comparison with the other major steel firms is somewhat misleading, though, because they were very different types of firms. Thyssen & Co. was a "pure" rolling mill. The partner firm of Thyssen & Co., the GDK, was comparable to Krupp or Phoenix.

By 1913, Thyssen & Co. brought in 60.8 million marks of sales, nearly doubling its turnover in just over a decade. It remained about the size of Hoesch or the Bochumer Verein, but smaller than the Rheinische Stahlwerke.[66] In 1913, its total assets amounted to 130.6 million marks (without the machine engineering department). According to Feldenkirchen's listing of the fifty largest German enterprises, Thyssen & Co. would have ranked twelfth, slightly ahead of the Haniel's GHH, Bayer, and BASF. In Chandler's listing, which does not include coal companies, it would rank sixth among all industrial firms.

Thyssen & Co.'s total assets, however, are somewhat misleading because Thyssen & Co. acted as a type of financial holding company for the rest of its "sister firms." And Thyssen's private equity accounts further inflate this figure. If these accounts are subtracted, Thyssen & Co.'s total assets are reduced to 94.5 million marks, ranking it 27th according to Feldenkirchen, and 20th according to Chandler. Companies such as Mannesmann, Hoechst, or MAN would be slightly larger, but Thyssen & Co. was still larger than such other notable firms as Blohm & Voss in the shipping industry, the Rheinische Stahlwerke, the Bochumer Verein, or Hoesch in the steel industry. Thyssen & Co. would have fallen just out of Leslie Hannah's global top 100 firms of 1912. If we look at Thyssen & Co.'s employment figures in 1907 (with its attendant machine company), about 6,958 people, it ranked

60th. It was slightly smaller than the chemical company, Bayer, but larger than Hoechst. It remained considerably smaller than other heavy-industry firms of the Ruhr such as Thyssen's own GDK, which employed just under 19,000; Phoenix, 32,000; Siemens, 34,000; and Krupp, 64,350.[67]

That Thyssen & Co. grew to be one of Germany's largest industrial operations has important analytical implications. Since Thyssen & Co. was as large as comparable German, British, or American firms, its organizational structure and specific corporate culture cannot be functionally derived from its scale or scope, its technology, or its product markets. Clearly, its managerial organization had to come to terms with these factors. *Provided* Thyssen & Co. management met the challenging technological and economic requirements for competing in this industry, which was by no means a given, the particular internal organization of Thyssen & Co. resulted primarily from the interaction of managers with the entrepreneur's expectations and strategies.

CHAPTER 3

Creating Management

The present state of things leaves little doubt that all of our attempts and requests to reach this goal have to be judged as failed—
failed only because of your insufficient management capability!

August Thyssen to Emil Bousse, May 27, 1882

One of the greatest challenges facing any business is not the inevitable crisis, but coming to terms with growth. By the end of the 1870s, a classic business dilemma faced Thyssen: how to turn a small, private partnership into a large-scale industrial enterprise without losing control over the strategic direction of the business, the cost and quality of its products, and the coordination of an ever-growing number of people. As Thyssen did not have the technical expertise to build his own machines or the inclination to operate them himself, and as he often traveled throughout Europe selling his wares or could not be in Mülheim to oversee operations, he had to hire others to help run his new venture. These new managers *(Beamte)* were the critical figures behind Thyssen & Co.'s long-term success. While one could make the argument that the initial success of Thyssen & Co. in the 1870s rested in good part on August Thyssen's personal initiative and entrepreneurship, after the 1880s this was no longer the case.

By 1884, Thyssen had introduced a modern managerial hierarchy with novel procedures, as a foundation for long-term growth. Unlike at Siemens or Krupp, it did not take a crisis of owner-manager control to initiate these organizational innovations.[1] In the early 1880s, Thyssen & Co. established a centralized formal internal communication system to bind Thyssen's "diverse", in Thyssen's own words, operations together, which empowered middle-level managers by according them a high degree of decision-making autonomy. They also had an active role in formulating top-level strategy; initiatives often arose from high-level middle managers, not just from Thyssen. Department heads not only had to produce in a cost-effective manner (manufacturing), but manage sales activities (marketing) and lead their subordinates (personnel)—at least three fingers of the business-management hand. Unlike most American corporations before World War I, which operated with a unitary, functional model of organization, Thyssen & Co. built itself on semi-autonomous, commercial–technical centers—what I term modular management—not production workshops. Thyssen & Co.'s organizational structure thus does not fit Chandler's ideal-types and offers a view of a distinctive German model.

Thyssen & Co.'s managerial structure reinforced Thyssen's high expectations that his managers should exercise a good deal of internal entrepreneurship. He insisted on self-sufficiency, energy, and activism, characteristics and values that permeated the Thyssen-Konzern corporate culture for the next half-century. This combination of autonomy and system was an integral component of Thyssen & Co. management. Above all, how he dealt with the failures of his various managers exposes the fundamental boundaries of Thyssen's tolerance, shows a process of organizational learning, and discloses the values underlying Thyssen & Co.'s organizational life. Most business histories stress achievements, but here I want to stress cases of failure inside a clear success story; successful organizations overcome and learn from failure. Internal correspondence offers us a rare chance to reconstruct the inter-subjective dimension of corporate culture at the moment when Thyssen & Co. tried to form an effective management team.

Building an Organizational Structure

When Thyssen opened his Mülheim firm in 1871, he converted a bakery into his headquarters (Figure 3.1). The fire-insurance policy listed the building as a horse stall, which left the impression that Thyssen, like his American counterparts, was a self-made man who had risen from a lowly background.[2]

The bakery provides an early view into Thyssen's organization. Thyssen subdivided the one-room house into three rooms: a commercial office, a technical operations office, and a stockroom, a predecessor of the inventory and purchasing office. He thereby introduced the classic German administrative separation between commercial offices

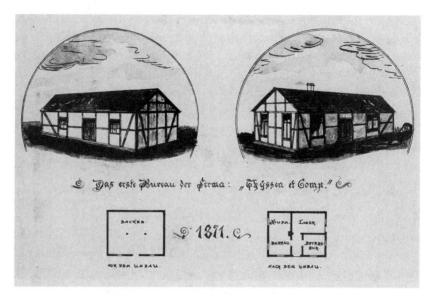

Figure 3.1 Thyssen & Co.'s first headquarters. (Reproduced with the permission of the Mannesmann-Archiv, Mülheim/Ruhr)

and technical offices.[3] Two years later, Thyssen moved into a slightly larger residential building on the same grounds, to accommodate a growing staff of salaried employees.

In 1873, two of the most important managers in the history of Thyssen & Co. joined the firm: Albert Killing and Franz Wilke. Albert Killing, twenty-seven years old (five years younger than Thyssen), headed the *Centralbureau* in charge of general administration, sales, central-office personnel, salaries, and record-keeping.[4] One long-time employee remembered: "Herr Procurist Killing, who retired in 1904, sat in the plain conference room behind the thick salary book and paid the office employees, who were always warmly asked to take a seat, a greater or lesser number of shiny gold pieces and other coins on the large desk. The sum was entered in the book, 'thank yous' said, and the next employee entered through the high double doors into the shrine."[5]

Killing acted as a general administrator and chief of staff to Thyssen. From the beginning, Thyssen delegated a good deal of his firm's administrative affairs to him. Killing ran the day-to-day business from within the *Centralbureau*. He wrote a good portion of all the external and internal correspondence and directives for the firm. It is not clear whether Killing actively formulated the letters, which he then presented to Thyssen for signature, or whether Killing passively took dictation from Thyssen or Franz Wilke, the chief factory director. We cannot fully ascertain the division of responsibility among Thyssen, Killing, and Wilke because they worked so closely together in a collegial fashion. General directives or reprimands generally have the same tone whether Thyssen was away or not. If Thyssen wanted to highlight points, he would make addendums in his own scribble.

Franz Wilke ran Thyssen & Co.'s factory operations. A former steel puddler, Wilke had a commercial apprenticeship degree, worked in various industrial firms in Wickede, and rose to become a factory inspector by the 1850s. Lutz Hatzfeld called Wilke a type of "exchangeable manager" who could have run any type of firm.[6] Wilke held final authority over all operational management, as well as all new construction projects. As Thyssen & Co. added pipe, steel, plate, and galvanizing plants, Wilke's responsibilities became more that of a general director, as individual department engineers wielded direct authority over their mills. Given his experience, Wilke continued to take personal charge of the firm's puddling operations. That Thyssen & Co. became one of Germany's leading manufacturers owes much to Wilke and his sons, who succeeded him.

Thyssen held Wilke in immeasurably high regard. He was older (by fifteen years), had more experience, and was the highest paid person in the firm. Because of his technical expertise, Wilke became the crucial advisor to Thyssen as to factory operations and any capital improvements. When Thyssen purchased a manor near the Ruhr River *(Schloss Styrum)*, he permitted the Wilke family to live in it with the full use of a horse and carriage, although Thyssen's home was a much less pleasant place to live. The Wilke family continued to live in it long after Franz Wilke died in 1891.[7] His son, August Wilke, took over for his father and stayed until 1908.

Wilke handled all personnel decisions below the level of department chiefs. Thyssen hired senior engineers directly, but they were then subordinated to Wilke. Wilke hired or fired all operations managers below the level of department heads. A tough commander, he readily fired workers for showing up late, being lazy, talking back, insubordination, or drunkenness.[8] Wilke chaired the factory insurance office, a nascent social policy forum, and handled all the disciplinary affairs of the factory's workers. Until the 1882 reorganization of Thyssen & Co. into product departments, Wilke also dealt with all the administrative work inside the production workshops. His son, August Wilke, assisted him in the hoop-iron mill. His two other sons also began their careers inside Thyssen & Co. Together, Wilke and Killing coordinated supplies, parts, and raw materials for the "storage room," or stockroom. Finally, Wilke acted as Thyssen & Co.'s main liaison with the mayor of Styrum. He acted as Thyssen's troubleshooter, dealing with such company–community problems as building concessions, the selling of allegedly tainted and stale beer (to quell schnapps consumption), pollution affecting a local baker, and even the bad cooking of a local housewife who boarded some of Thyssen & Co.'s managers.[9]

Wilke and Killing formed a dual-headed senior management, with formal equality between the technical and commercial sides of the business, common to many German but not American firms.[10] Wilke and Killing were considered equals by Thyssen, and implicitly by the organizational structure, although Wilke earned more, with an annual salary of 6,000 marks, 2,400 marks more than Killing, the next highest.[11] Killing sat in the "plain conference room" in Thyssen & Co.'s first administrative building. Wilke's office was in the brickworks of the hoop-iron mill adjacent to the *Centralbureau*. The layout of Thyssen & Co. reproduced the standard staff-line distinction for large-scale industrial firms, and the link between buildings, organizational structure, and office space remained quite close throughout the history of Thyssen & Co.

Both Killing and Wilke became active co-formulators of company strategy and policy, as Thyssen's myriad business activities took him away from Mülheim. In 1879, both Killing and Wilke received the power of attorney to sign *individually* as agents of Thyssen & Co, the only individuals to receive this power; the sole limitation concerned the buying or selling of land. Later, other executives received collective power of attorney, which permitted them to make legally binding contracts in the name of the firm, but only with another executive's countersignature.[12] Naturally, Thyssen remained ultimate arbiter over any major financial investment, but delegation of individual power of attorney is striking. The explicit trust in Wilke and Killing was much higher than at Krupp, which was a much larger firm and whose

Figure 3.2 Thyssen & Co.'s second headquarters, as the building looked around 1900 after two stories were added. (Reproduced with the permission of the Mannesmann-Archiv, Mülheim/Ruhr)

chief executives suffered under incessant owner interventions.[13] Unlike Krupp, Thyssen always respected the established line of command through Wilke and Killing, and never undercut their authority. Subordinates dealt with Wilke and Killing first. Thyssen was strict about this principle.

As if to embody the legal administrative changes in mortar and stone, in 1879 they also built Thyssen & Co.'s first new administrative building near Gate I, directly adjacent to the hoop-iron mill (Figure 3.2).[14] This building had a large, single, hall-like room for sales, central cashier, bookkeeping, and auditing. The lack of distinct workspaces— they had desks, but no offices or cubicles—for the different functions indicates that the differentiation of skills implicit in each functional activity had not yet progressed very far. Beginning as clerks, apprentices gained experience in all commercial functions of the *Centralbureau*.[15] Initially, the central office was housed in a one-story brick building. Thyssen & Co. enlarged it after 1900 to include an additional two stories because of the growth of the central staff.

Initially, administrative work inside Thyssen & Co.'s *Centralbureau* resembled a classic merchant house, which had changed little over the centuries, rather than a modern business. The physical attributes of the single room and its administrative activity tended to reinforce the slightness of differentiation in functions. Most bookkeeping entries were recorded in large, quite heavy, hard-bound journals like the order books (rather than in modern filing systems).[16] Each worker-roll book, located in the individual mill offices, alone weighed about fifteen pounds. The letter-press journals were also thickly bound books of tissue paper rather than separate (carbon) copies on single leaf forms. Clerks placed the individual, outgoing letters between the pages of the press book while the letters' ink was still wet. Protecting the previous pages with paper or cloth, the book was then closed and a mechanical screw (developed by James Watt, the inventor of the steam engine) pressed the pages of the book together so as to leave a clean imprint (in theory) of the letter. This letter-press journal held key accounts, directives, and circulars largely in chronological order, with little functional or subject differentiation. As in many other industrial firms in the world, Thyssen & Co. used this process up until the turn of the century. Office workers could not file letters separately until better facsimiles could be reproduced.[17]

The upshot was that most of the books in the central office would lay open at particular workstations on a podium or on a desk or shelf within the hall. People would move around to the journals, which anchored the circulatory communication patterns of the office. Letter-press books lay near the desks of senior managers, so permission was needed to view relevant letters, which reinforced authority and possibly hindered the free flow of pertinent information across the firm. The relative lack of differentiation as well as the spatial layout of administrative work had important consequences for managerial sociability. Lines would form behind the journals as the employees waited for their turn, creating pauses and a space for discussion—a space analogous to that created by copy machines today.

The hierarchy in the operations side of the business started with mill heads or department chiefs (termed *Betriebs-Chef, Betriebsführer*), followed by varying levels of engineers who directed individual product lines along with *Meister. Meister* were key shopfloor supervisors, not just work foremen *(Vorarbeiter)*. The 1870s had largely completed the devaluation in the status (not importance) of the *Meister* within large

German firms from top-middle management to middle-lower management.[18] *Meister* received a salary, not a wage, indicating that the boundary of management lay just below them. But because of their technical and craft skills, they retained a good deal of leverage, control, and authority over the shopfloor and its workers until after 1900.[19]

Authority within the factory and its workshops followed a military-style line of command emanating from Wilke. The 1871 Thyssen & Co. *Reglement* (list of regulations) indicates that a military-style hierarchy pervaded the whole firm. This reliance on military-style organization was not peculiar to Germany. In many countries, including the United States, large-scale organizations arose out of experience with the army. The *Reglement* applied to both the *Meister* and workers, and not *Beamte*.[20] The *Reglement*'s very first article emphasized that all *Meister* and workers had to subordinate themselves unconditionally to the "rules of work." They had to follow commands from superiors and carry them out in a conscientious way. Both *Meister* and workers should "always behave with an official demeanor of duty and service." The regulations concerning time and work behavior were by far the most detailed—and typical for this historical period. Above all, the *Reglement* sought to regiment behavior. As a whole, it was a strange mix of sharply phrased rules such as no drinking on the job, and petty rules such as no smoking in front of a superior, or where not to eat on the factory grounds. The *Reglement* was an expression of the entrepreneur's central claim to authority and obedience; the regulations represent a kind of ideal state as envisioned by the entrepreneur.

After a decade as a family enterprise, Thyssen & Co. should be described as entrepreneurial when Wilke and Killing gained individual powers of attorney. As other symbolic markers, by 1882 Thyssen & Co. crossed the 1,000-employee mark, paid out more than one million marks in wages and salaries, completed its basic product lines, became an increasingly diversified firm, and was housed in a specially-built but rudimentary headquarters.

Between 1882 and 1885, Thyssen's managerial hierarchy took a quantum leap in sophistication that set the tone for the rest of Thyssen's career. Thyssen, Wilke, and Killing began thinking systematically about the state of Thyssen & Co.'s organization, and undertook a series of major reforms. The goal of this managerial system was to decentralize operational authority and decision-making to departments, while maintaining tight supervision of finances and production from above through standardized, regular statistical reporting and expense accounting, one of the salient principles of modern management.

In 1882, they reorganized Thyssen & Co. into a series of product departments (Figure 3.3). The hoop-iron mill became known as Department I; the steel mill and plate mill, Department II; the pipe and tube mill, Department III; and the tin-plate or galvanizing plant, Department IV. When Thyssen & Co. took over a neighboring machine company in 1884, it became Department V. The manufacturing workshops *(Werke)*, with their individual product lines, also became departments *(Abteilung)*, equipped with administrative functions including sales, accounting, shipping, technical, and personnel responsibilities—all the fingers of the business hand except finance and auditing functions. They were not considered just production sites. The 1882 reforms endowed each of the departments with a distinct commercial or sales office, initially consisting of only one manager.[21] In the same year, they also added at least one additional manager for the technical side. Thyssen & Co. reproduced the typically German dual-headed senior management structure (administrative and technical) at the level of the department, freeing Killing and Wilke from day-to-day operations to concentrate on general supervisory tasks. Indeed, in 1883, the steel mill and plate mill were merged into a single department with a single technical director because Wilke was "overloaded" with work.[22]

By 1891, the main extensions to Thyssen & Co.'s basic structure lay in the proliferation of workshops within the main departments, such as the pressing works. Additionally, Thyssen & Co. added new departments, like the short-lived nail factory, but also the longer-lived brick works, gas works, and the important machine engineering department. In 1884 Thyssen also established a branch sales office in Berlin led by one of Thyssen's most trusted executives, Ernst Nölle. Thyssen also purchased Bad Tönnistein, a bottler of spring water in 1885, to provide his employees with something less alcoholic. It remained largely independent, held as a strategic portfolio investment.[23] Wilke had ultimate responsibility for most social-policy functions, such as factory health insurance, company store, mechanical testing laboratory, wage office, and a boarding house.

The succession of Franz's son, August Wilke, to factory director in

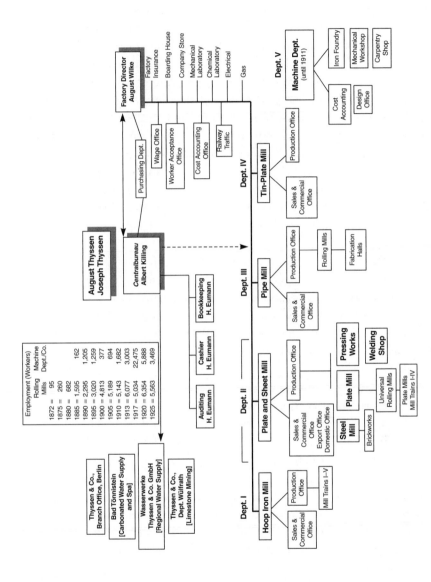

Figure 3.3 Thyssen & Co. organization, 1903

1891 exemplified the continuity in senior management. August Wilke followed closely in his father's footsteps, but the extent of his activities differed slightly from that of his father. August Wilke had less specific responsibilities than his father, including less direct personal intervention in manufacturing operations. He presided over the proliferation of auxiliary offices, which included an independent construction department and a distinct railway department. August Wilke also became the point man in the scrap trade for all the Thyssen firms, including the GDK.[24] With a good deal of freedom, he handled job searches for prospective technical managers and other personnel. With Thyssen's ultimate approval, he hired executives up to the position of workshop technical supervisor *(Betriebsleiter)*. In 1891, for instance, August Wilke hired one supervisor for a fabrication workshop in the pipe mill that alone employed about 600 workers.[25] Moreover, August Wilke signed his letters with a stamp "Thyssen & Co. in Vollmacht," indicating his full authority.

Inside Thyssen & Co., the number of executives endowed with the important power of attorney remained small, which kept centralized control of binding obligations with the external world, while handling of internal affairs was decentralized. In August 1890, Hermann Eumann and August Wilke received collective power of attorney.[26] Until 1906, just six people held power of attorney in a firm that employed roughly 6,000.

By 1900, the central office grew, though remaining relatively lean and with strong supervisory powers, but the product departments expanded considerably. Thyssen expected the product departments to act as small enterprises—semi-autonomous modules. An increasing differentiation of functions *within* the four main commercial-production departments occurred in the 1890s. By integrating commercial, technical, and shipping offices into each department, department heads *(Betriebs-Chefs)* became responsible for a wide range of activities: for manufacturing, technical innovations, sales, personnel, and increasingly some financial questions. The organizational structure of the firm required that department chiefs find some manner of combining their technical expertise (almost all were engineers) with commercial success. Finding this combination of capabilities proved to be the faultline in the careers of many Thyssen & Co. department chiefs.

As clearly stated in its advertising brochures, Thyssen & Co. asked its

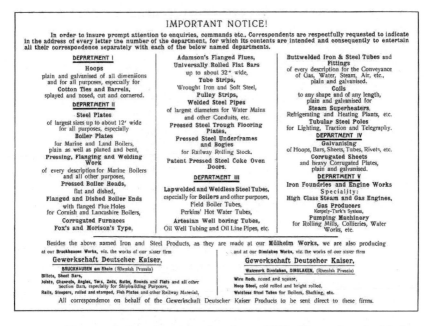

IMPORTANT NOTICE!

In order to insure prompt attention to enquiries, commands etc., Correspondents are respectfully requested to indicate in the address of every letter the number of the department, for which its contents are intended and consequently to entertain all their correspondence separately with each of the below named departments.

DEPARTMENT I

Hoops
plain and galvanised of all dimensions and for all purposes, especially for Cotton Ties and Barrels, splayed and nosed, cut and cornered.

DEPARTMENT II

Steel Plates
of largest sizes up to about 12′ wide for all purposes, especially

Boiler Plates
for Marine and Land Boilers, plain as well as planed and bent,

Pressing, Flanging and Welding Work
of every description for Marine Boilers and all other purposes,

Pressed Boiler Heads,
flat and dished,

Flanged and Dished Boiler Ends
with flanged Flue Holes for Cornish and Lancashire Boilers,

Corrugated Furnaces
Fox's and Morison's Type,

Adamson's Flanged Flues,
Universally Rolled Flat Bars
up to about 32″ wide,

Tube Strips,
Wrought Iron and Soft Steel,

Pulley Strips,

Welded Steel Pipes
of largest diameters for Water Mains and other Conduits, etc.

Pressed Steel Trough Flooring Plates,

Pressed Steel Underframes and Bogies
for Railway Rolling Stock.

Patent Pressed Steel Coke Oven Doors.

DEPARTMENT III

Lapwelded and Weldless Steel Tubes,
especially for Boilers and other purposes,
Field Boiler Tubes,
Perkins' Hot Water Tubes,

Artesian Well boring Tubes,
Oil Well Tubing and Oil Line Pipes, etc.

Buttwelded Iron & Steel Tubes and Fittings
of every description for the Conveyance of Gas, Water, Steam, Air, etc., plain and galvanised.

Coils
to any shape and of any length, plain and galvanised for

Steam Superheaters,
Refrigerating and Heating Plants, etc.

Tubular Steel Poles
for Lighting, Traction and Telegraphy.

DEPARTMENT IV

Galvanising
of Hoops, Bars, Sheets, Tubes, Rivets, etc.

Corrugated Sheets
and heavy Corrugated Plates, plain and galvanised.

DEPARTMENT V

Iron Foundries and Engine Works
Speciality:
High Class Steam and Gas Engines,
Kerpely-Turk's System,

Gas Producers

Pumping Machinery
for Rolling Mills, Collieries, Water Works, etc.

Besides the above named Iron and Steel Products, as they are made at our **Mülheim** Works, we are also producing at our **Bruckhausen** Works, viz. the works of our sister firm

Gewerkschaft Deutscher Kaiser,

BRUCKHAUSEN am Rhein (Rhenish Prussia)

Billets, Sheet Bars,
Joists, Channels, Angles, Tees, Zeds, Bulbs, Rounds and Flats and all other Section Bars, especially for Shipbuilding Purposes,
Rails, Sleepers, rolled and stamped, Fish Plates and other Railway Material,

and at our **Dinslaken** Works, viz. the works of our sister firm

Gewerkschaft Deutscher Kaiser,

Watzwerk Dinslaken, DINSLAKEN, (Rhenish Prussia)

Wire Rods. round and square,
Hoop Steel, cold rolled and bright rolled,
Weldless Steel Tubes for Boilers, Shafting, etc.

All correspondence on behalf of the Gewerkschaft Deutscher Kaiser Products to be sent direct to these firms.

Figure 3.4 Thyssen & Co. advertising brochure, 1906. (Reproduced with the permission of the Mannesmann-Archiv, Mülheim/Ruhr)

customers to send their orders directly to the departmental commercial offices, not the central office (Figure 3.4). The 1908 German version was quite adamant, and less polite, about the proper address:

> *In order to process the correspondence promptly and correctly,* it is absolutely essential that the letters, enquiries and orders are held strictly separate from one another for bookkeeping and for the various product lines listed above, and that the respective department address be expressly indicated on every letter, even if they are sent in a common envelope.[27]

The tone suggests that many customers were accustomed to sending their orders to a central sales office. Evidently, the advantages of decentralizing the firm were partially offset by the difficulties of sorting out various orders from one another, since many orders crossed departmental boundaries, let alone other Thyssen firms. After the mid-1890s, these brochures also advertised the products of "firms closely affiliated with our firm," referring to the GDK steel firm and the Thyssen rolling mills in Dinslaken.[28]

We do have some record of these departmental offices' operations during this period. Ernst Brökelschen, who later became director of the purchasing office, entered the firm in 1890. Brökelschen described the plate mill technical office as "primitive:"

> The one-storied, long building with a flat roof lay in the corner between the puddling works and the plate mill, stuck between the puddling ovens, rolling mill, loading hall, and storage place for ingots. Every once in a while the walls would be freshly plastered to make them white again for a time. The whistling from the locomotives traveling by, the rattling of the rolling mill trains, and the booming of the steam hammers was not an enjoyable accompanying music to the very intense work, which had to be performed there.[29]

Significantly, until the 1920s the departmental offices remained physically closer to the manufacturing operations across the factory grounds than to the central office.

Orders came directly into the commercial offices, where the clerks recorded them in large "commission books." They then sent them to the department technical office, where Brökelschen recopied the orders into his books. Later, the commercial and technical office managers cross-checked the copies against the originals to make sure they squared. Brökelschen had other duties as well, including the writing of accident reports in triplicate. This was his favorite task because it took him away from the "monotonous" office work; the task allowed him to visit homes outside the factory or wander around the shop floor. Clearly, as one moved down the hierarchy, the more bureaucratic and mundane the work became.

In the real world of business, the division of labor between the central office and the departmental offices was not always clear. Sometimes third-party firms ordered materials from a number of departments, yet the orders needed to be coordinated centrally. A tradeoff, for instance, existed between the relative effectiveness of each department handling its orders separately, while the central office wished to minimize shipping costs by doing bulk or joint shipments, especially of foreign orders. At one point the *Centralbureau* attempted to centralize the processing of foreign orders, but after numerous "irregularities," Killing transferred responsibility back down to the departments. (Departments retained responsibility for domestic orders.)[30] The plate and pipe departments established separate commercial offices for foreign and domestic orders. The degree of decentralization required in these matters can be seen in the fact that correspondence overwhelmed the shipping and postal office of the *Centralbureau,* which had only one employee in the mid-1880s—*fewer than the departments.*[31]

Individual department directors also had ultimate responsibility for all necessary personnel matters, setting of wages, and hiring or firing within the department: "At the same time we order, as a general rule, that a *Meister* or an *Obermeister* is not permitted to hire or fire any worker. Instead, the department chief must decide what is necessary in each individual case and is held responsible for his rules by the firm."[32] This order reinforced executive and engineer control over the *Meister.* Within a given range, department heads and key shopfloor supervisors became responsible for setting wages. These figures, whose orders and whims ruled shopfloor labor relations, were the most important people for understanding labor relations inside Thyssen & Co.

Finally, the product departments were also given responsibility for a number of accounting functions. Thyssen required that the department submit uniform, standardized financial reports that included manufacturing costs and sales revenues each month. This provided a rough but fairly sophisticated approximation of its operating profits for the month. Department cash accounts reimbursed salesmen for travel and sales expenses directly, although this caused some difficulties. The departments also put a value on their own inventories. Disputes arose *within* departments on the proper division of labor between the commercial and technical offices on this issue. Until 1903, department technical offices had been solely responsible for inventory control, but Thyssen had Wilke order that the commercial offices participate in the proper valuation of inventories. The top technical and commercial officers of each department were jointly responsible for the accuracy of the inventory lists. They then passed these lists on to the *Centralbureau.*[33]

After the turn of the century, there was some evolution in this basic structure, an evolution that tended to modernize the central office and make it more powerful. Almost as an organizational countercurrent to its emphasis on economies of scope, Thyssen & Co. increasingly centralized information flows and functionalized authority more along American lines inside the *Centralbureau.* But these reforms did not call into question its basic modular structure. The most significant change involved the proliferation of a number of functional staff offices responsible for the whole firm, especially regarding workers.[34] They included a central wage office, a worker acceptance office to track turnover, a cost accounting office for product lines, a railway office (which had been subsumed under the strip-steel department), and a chemical laboratory.

In 1891, Thyssen & Co. strengthened the functions of the wage office. The previous incarnation of the wage office merely monitored payments, but in the interests of a "sharper control" of wages to reduce irregularities, Thyssen gave it the authority to distribute wages from time to time to ensure the proper handling of these payments by the departments. In this respect, the wage office partially checked the independence of the departments, but departments continued to disburse wages.[35]

In 1905, Thyssen & Co. set up a "workers acceptance office" (Arbeiterannahmebüro) to track more precisely worker turnover throughout the firm. In part, this was a reactionary move, as worker turnover reached record highs after the 1902–1903 recession ended. It created blacklists for the regional Employer Union, a confidential agreement among some Ruhr heavy industries to slow labor turnover and discipline unwanted laborers. The office had little authority over the departments, which were the primary site of record-keeping. Ironically, the blacklists turned out to be ineffective, as workers could change firms faster than the acceptance office could draw up the lists.[36]

Other major organizational changes after 1900 were made at the level of senior management in the Centralbureau. A whole new generation of leading managers came to the fore, as the unbroken line of Wilkes on the production side and Killing on the commercial side left the firm. In May 1907, August Wilke recommended that Ernst Becker take the new intermediate position as the vice-director of the factory, with power of attorney for the four departments, which eventually became known as the Thyssen & Co. Steel and Rolling Mills.[37] Becker's main purpose was to "carefully supervise" and coordinate the needs of all four departments. Joseph Thyssen reminded everyone that Becker's orders should be "observed and followed as if they came from Herr Direktor Wilke." One year later, when Wilke left the firm because of eye trouble, Becker took his position as Fabrikdirektor. A thirty-seven-year old engineer from the plate department, Carl Wallmann, replaced Becker as second-in-command of the steel and rolling mills.[38] Wallmann and Becker would be the decisive figures in the Thyssen & Co. rolling mills for the next twenty years.

Through reforms initiated by Becker, Thyssen & Co. became more centralized. Along with his position as factory director and formal head of the purchasing office, Becker became the director of the strip-steel department, the galvanizing department, and the pipe department. The strip-steel department and the galvanizing department lost their commercial offices to the *Centralbureau*. Both departments became essentially intermediate suppliers to the pipe and plate departments. Becker also became technical director of the pipe department, but it retained both commercial and technical personnel. The pipe and tube department and plate and sheet department retained their modular organization to maintain the proper coordination of manufacturing and marketing because of their direct contact with customers and the specialized requirements of the products. Technical specifications were wrapped up in the sales requirements, and *vice versa.*

The two departments remained organized along self-sufficient, modular lines, with a high degree of organizational differentiation within them. The pipe department had special offices to coordinate its relations with the Thyssen & Co. waterworks, and a separate machine-maintenance office to keep close contact with the design offices of the Thyssen & Co. Machine Company. It also had its own shipping offices, cost accounting office, and a special office to handle accidents.[39] The sheet and plate department under Carl Wallmann had a relatively autonomous position *vis-à-vis* Becker, and was even more complex than the pipe department. Each of the main production plants—plate mill, universal rolling mills, steel mill, welding plant, and pressing works— had its own production supervisor and administrative office supervisor. The welding plant had its own technical statistical offices, a purchasing office, a cost- and wage-accounting office, and its own shipping office, among other technical offices. The cost-accounting office handled the complicated pricing of products, particularly for contracts involving large-diameter welded conduits and pipelines, and their accoutrements. The steel mill had its own chemical laboratory for testing special qualities of metal. The pressing works had a shipping office, forge, and fitting area. Most importantly, the plate department had research and experimental testing offices for quality control of metals and chemicals. Finally, Wallmann had an important machine-maintenance section responsible for the central boiler facilities and general equipment maintenance for the whole firm. This section became very important when the Thyssen & Co. machine engineering department and waterworks began recycling energy and gas from Thyssen coke and steel plants to generate heat and energy.

At Wallmann's side in the commercial offices of the plate department were Heinrich Martini and Alfred Gilles, who managed the department's burgeoning sales. Both were highly important figures. Wallmann had line authority as *Direktor,* but Martini and Gilles also had collective power of attorney and were actually senior in age to Wallmann. They worked together collegially in the classic dual-headed fashion inside the department. The plate department established a formal division of commercial operations into domestic (Gilles) and foreign sales offices (Martini). It also had formal invoice offices to handle trade with Thyssen-Konzern firms and third-party firms. Finally, the commercial department had its own registration office and visiting rooms, as if it were an independent firm unto itself.

The correspondence of the department commercial office shows how independently and un-bureaucratically Wallmann, Gilles, and Martini could act. For a contract with the city of Steglitz, Martini had to handle a wide array of problems: shipping details, changing technical specifications of the city project, financial arrangements through the Rheinische Bank, problems of war production, changing cost calculations and prices, and legal issues.[40] None of his arrangements with Steglitz needed to go through Becker, Phillip Neuhaus (Killing's successor), or the Thyssens for approval.

Departmental commercial offices also gained some accounting and financial functions after 1900. Each of them began keeping track of its own inventories, and even had accounts for estimating the value of departmental capital equipment.[41] In Thyssen & Co.'s annual financial statements, the departments remained distinct from one another in all accounts except land valuations. They reported profits independently of one another. Alongside the central cost-accounting office, the plate and pipe departments had their own cost-accounting offices. One series of cost accounts still extant shows that the pipe department tracked twenty different types of indirect costs for each product line before 1914.[42] Thyssen & Co.'s essentially modular management structure remained the organizational form for the business until its merger into the VSt in 1926.

This skeletal description of Thyssen & Co.'s organizational structure contradicts the principles on which Chandler's standard American ideal-type was built.[43] In standard American models, sales, personnel, and financial "functions" (so-called staff functions) remain organizationally distant from production operations. Function, instead of product-orientation, guides the organizational structure. In the United States, production engineers focus exclusively on shopfloor management. Middle managers of a typical American-style central office become general managers, who organizationally and statistically combine sales and production functions, but not in their daily activities, as at Thyssen & Co. This means that power within the firm tends to move upwards into the central office, where executives manage difficult issues of coordination and combination. Middle managers oversee more functionally oriented sales operatives and technicians.

In Thyssen & Co., the organizational structure pushed authority downward into the department and away from the central office and its middle managers—away from "general management." Departmental engineers managed the important task of combining and coordinating sales, production, and personnel questions. Financial questions, particularly regarding new investment, remained largely out of their hands. The central office monitored, controlled, and assessed departmental financial performance. As Bernd Dornseifer has stressed, the formal and collegial cooperation between the technical and commercial sides of the business, especially at the level of top management, did not correspond to the "monochromatic pattern of the bureaucratic model" either.[44] Thyssen & Co. reproduced this dual-headed structure at the level of the department as well as at the senior level.

Dornseifer has also argued that, in general, German firms tended to be much less homogenous than American firms. Susanne Hilger's illustrations of various Ruhr steel companies before 1880 (GHH, Krupp, Hörder Verein, Bochumer Verein) also show a great variety of organizational forms, although most of her examples except the Bochumer Verein might well be subsumed under Chandler's ideal-type.[45] Dornseifer's argument, however, rests on examples taken from the machine engineering, electrotechnical (Siemens), and chemical industries, which offered technically complex goods and services. Quite possibly, the technical sophistication of these products required closer cooperation between marketing and manufacturing. However, Thyssen also differentiated his firm into product departments, so this sort of organization did not require technological complexity to justify it. Similar German and U.S. steel companies did not systematically push responsibility downwards in the same way that Thyssen & Co. did. In short, there is no necessary structural-functional reason why Thyssen & Co. should have organized in such a fashion. Ultimately, it was a product of entrepreneurial and organizational choice, which had implications for managerial behavior inside the firm.

Forging an Organizational Culture

The formal delegation of responsibilities to department chiefs provides some indication of Thyssen's expectations. Yet, while formal hierarchy writes the organizational script, much like a plot line structures a narrative, it is not the story.[46] What sort of personal qualities did Thyssen expect from his managers? How much autonomy did they really have? The corporate culture at Thyssen & Co. resulted from the personal interaction between the owners and its managers, especially during the 1880s. It did not spring from Thyssen's will as a fully articulated entrepreneurial intention or strategy. The precise level of freedom, or play, inside Thyssen & Co. resulted as much from trial and error, new problems, setbacks, debates, frictions—in short, an organizational learning process. Language, tone, and particular phrases used are especially critical to revealing the constellation of values articulating Thyssen & Co.'s corporate culture.[47] Thyssen tried to instill an entrepreneurial ethos into his top executives.

Thyssen's first major row was with Emil Bousse, who launched the pipe department. Bousse's failure illustrates how the appearance of new organizational routines can indicate failure and how Thyssen defined performance as commercial, not technical success. In December 1881, he awarded Bousse a generous year-end bonus and made it known that he wanted the pipe mill to operate in two shifts by the end of February 1882. He asked Bousse to place his

entire ambition now, and to draw the consequences from it, to perform
. . . work and to fulfill the wishes of the customers with the greatest circumspection *(Umsicht)* for this is the only way that we will succeed to
create an estimable name *(Renomme)* and to maintain completely and
steadily the planned expansion of operations. Most of all, every link in
the largest chain [must] fulfill its duty with enthusiasm *(Freudigkeit)* and
sacrifice![48]

Throughout his career, Thyssen linked customer satisfaction with
his own personal reputation. Thyssen also had a clear sense of the firm
as a hierarchy, as a chain of command. Although a sense of duty, sacrifice, and service played a role, Thyssen built in a series of performance-oriented incentives into his payment system to spur his subordinates. In addition to offering bonuses, Thyssen appealed to Bousse's
own interests and career trajectory. (As a general practice, Thyssen extended this bonus system to all line managers down to the level of
Meister). Thyssen wanted ambitious, enthusiastic managers under his
command.

The new incentives failed. In spring 1882, Bousse again delivered
pipes late to customers. In mid-May, Thyssen & Co. introduced a new
business procedure, a new method of control: all new orders had to
have the delivery date clearly written next to the appropriate order in
the department commission books with the delivery date in chronological order. If the delivery date could not be met, the department
chief had to submit a written justification to the *Centralbureau* well before the deadline. Bousse complained that he did not have enough
staff to deal with orders, but Thyssen had little patience for his complaints, reminding Bousse that the hoop-iron and plate mills were capable of delivering its products "in abundance" and with similar staff.
(The plate mill had just started up in the previous year.)

We expect, and we can demand, that everyone involved in this matter
will do his part with energy and enthusiasm to fulfill these regulations
with the utmost degree of punctuality in order to achieve the final goal
of regaining and maintaining our reputation with our customers (especially in terms of prompt delivery) which has been lost. We owe it to
our reputation as well as to our own interests to find a thorough rem-

edy in this respect and we would regret it deeply if we would be forced to take measures in this matter.[49]

Although the emphasis on punctuality could be interpreted as a bureaucratic principle, Thyssen put this virtue mainly in the context of customer relations and the creation of a reputable brand. When Thyssen threatened a "thorough remedy" *(eine gründliche Remedur)*, this usually meant that a manager would lose his job. Once again, Thyssen called for greater vigor and attention on the part of Bousse.

Just two weeks later at the end of May 1882, Thyssen discovered that Bousse had allowed a customer to pay in advance for hundreds of pipes although the pipe mill had manufactured and delivered a mere tenth of the order. This boosted Bousse's department sales for the month (and his bonus), but was not backed up by pipe production, let alone a satisfied customer. Disgusted, Thyssen fired Bousse. According to his hiring contract, Bousse had a nine-month grace period, drawing salary and still legally under contract to the firm. Such long grace periods following dismissal were an exceptional incentive practiced by Thyssen to attract the best engineers. Thyssen's reasons for firing Bousse went well beyond a single incident:

> It is known to you that we have endeavored for years to create order in the relationships with the workers and to improve the operating results of the pipe mill. The experiences which we have had during this time have proven more than enough, and the present state of things leaves little doubt that all of our attempts and requests to reach this goal have to be judged as failed—failed only because of your insufficient management capability *(Dispositions-Fähigkeit)!* It can be attributed to this shortcoming that the operating results, i.e., meaning the production per worker and per shift, have dropped instead of rising as should be the case in a well-ordered operation despite the fact that we, on our part, have done everything to bring our pipe mill to the highest level of production capacity with the best facilities and equipment. It can also be attributed to this shortcoming that many of the better workers have departed, leaving us reliant on those less capable! It has come to light that your authority is no longer recognized by people because they are not treated according to their performance, which is the only correct way, but according to [your] favor.

Thanks to these circumstances, a great demoralization has set in amongst the workers of the pipe mill and grows clearer from day to day, nourished by lax practice, demonstrated by the fact that people who have committed great offenses have not been discharged and are still employed and other such cases!

But we no longer want to dwell on listing all of these sad and distressing events. They explain sufficiently in themselves why it has not been possible for you to retain or attract competent people to our works. They also have convinced us to make an end to these sad conditions. With this letter we are left with no other choice than to release you from the direction of the factory.

You can be assured that it has been very difficult for us to take this measure. The conviction, which we have held for a long time, that all of our endeavors to lead you in the proper direction, which we have brought to bear for years, have been in vain and that a fundamental improvement is not otherwise possible, has [enabled] us to take this step. We owe it to ourselves and our customers, who still write us with feelings of bitterness and disappointment, to find a thorough remedy.[50]

Thyssen ultimately judged Bousse using clear, statistical performance standards, in this case production per worker and per shift. Most of these early records have been lost, but we do know that yearly productivity figures worsened under Bousse's watch. Thyssen felt Bousse had no excuses since the mill's equipment was state-of-the-art. In a confidential letter to another pipe-company director, Thyssen felt that Bousse had proved to be "headstrong." He had tried to "raise his stature by trying to turn the workers to his side, at least as *we* judge the affair; we could not possibly approve of this in our diversified production relationships over time." Bousse apparently did not adhere to the uniform disciplinary and performance standards that Thyssen felt were needed. Thyssen fired Bousse in spite of the fact that Bousse had developed innovative technical processes and had started the pipe mill. Ultimately he was fired for his lack of leadership ability, which Thyssen expected from his engineers, and which was his central expectation for executives over the next forty years. Thyssen forbid Bousse ever to set foot on the factory grounds again.

The Bousse affair did not end there, however. In the summer of 1882, Bousse apparently offered the design of a new machine to another firm while still under his grace-period of his contract. With this violation, Thyssen voided Bousse's contract. Bousse lost his remaining salary. Thyssen kept the design for a new, Bousse-designed machine. Bousse received a terse recommendation emphasizing only his "good technical knowledge."[51]

After this debacle, Robert Blasberg and Robert Wilke, the second son of the factory director, took over the direction of the pipe mill, which they placed on a relatively smooth operating and profitable basis. They managed the pipe mill until after the turn of the century. Willy Trapp followed them. Trapp, as mentioned earlier, dramatically enhanced the productivity of the pipe mill by introducing American-inspired manufacturing operations.

Yet Trapp, who achieved the greatest productivity gains in the history of Thyssen & Co., ran into the same profitability problems as Bousse and had to leave. Thyssen reprimanded Trapp for the "thoroughly unsatisfactory financial success of your department." His recommendation for Trapp mentioned only that he was technically competent, which angered Trapp, but Thyssen reminded him that he did Trapp a favor for not mentioning his commercial failure, and would not revise it. Technical proficiency without profitability or leadership skills did not impress Thyssen. He judged engineers by their commercial as well as technical success.[52]

Thyssen also fired August Schmitz, the unfortunate engineer at the head of the Siemens-Martin steel mill of the early 1880s, for lack of managerial competency. The mill suffered from fundamental technological problems associated with the acidic Siemens-Martin process. Schmitz suffered a constant rain of reprimands from both Wilke and Thyssen, who complained that he did not set a good example for other employees because he was not at his workplace and did not check the furnace often enough. Like Bousse, Schmitz had difficulty completing orders on time. When he complained directly to Thyssen, Thyssen reminded him to follow the proper channels and first write to Wilke. Customers continued to complain about the poor quality of the hoop iron and plates. Thyssen wanted more "care and circumspection" *(Sorgfalt und Umsicht)* in the steel mill. Moreover, Schmitz could not keep up with the written work required of the department although he, too, had enough office personnel. Moreover, Schmitz could not account for over 12,000 marks worth of materials. After this, Thyssen felt that there were no further excuses for the "gross negligence of the mill's management." He wrote Schmitz that it was not only in the interests of the business but "in your own interests to try to fulfill your functions in the future with the [necessary] circumspection and conscientiousness" [double underlining in original] or else expect a "decisive remedy" of the situation.[53]

Schmitz was unlucky in arriving when the steel-making process itself was insufficient, but the case of Wilhelm Deussen, Schmitz's immediate successor, demonstrates that Thyssen could distinguish between problems due to technology and problems due to leadership. Thyssen did *not* blame Deussen for the continuing poor quality of the steel (he had had little prior experience with the Siemens-Martin process) or even the failure to turn a profit, which Thyssen did not expect that early. He did become angered at the lax manner in which Deussen treated his personnel.[54] Most damningly, he left management of the steel mill in the hands of the *Meister,* and set wage rates too high and paid too many workers for too little work:

> As sorry as we are about it, we cannot avoid reproaching you that you have not proceeded with the necessary vigor and circumspection *(Umsicht)* in this regard and have not at least reduced the production costs in this manner! The people themselves show little thanks to you for your lenient treatment granted them—the countless anonymous letters sent to us, and that have of course always ended up in the wastepaper basket, prove that for us. Now we have gathered from them as well as other signs, which we have come across, that an evil spirit has descended upon the people of the steel mill! This awareness has been the direct cause for us to discontinue the operations of the steel mill. We believe that a thorough clearing away of the present personnel will do you, and us, the greatest favor.

Thyssen decided to rebuild the mill "on fresh grass." The whole tone of the letter shows how Thyssen gained his reputation as a hard-driving disciplinarian, which would come back to haunt him at times. Still, Thyssen did not fire Deussen. Instead he asked him to concentrate all his "vigor" on the new press machine, the universal rolling mill, and the puddling furnaces. Deussen could stay if he had the character to find "a comprehensive remedy" to improve the "department's results" *(Betriebs-Resulte)*. His year-end bonus depended on it.

When unilateral modifications were made to his contract, Deussen promptly gave notice. After June 1884, their relationship, which had been disappointing but civil, turned ugly. Despite numerous visits by Wilke, Deussen had refused to behave with an "appropriate" degree of restraint, even though the Thyssens remained civil, while the plate mill lost money and the number of complaints from Deussen's subordinates increased. Thyssen agreed to terminate Deussen's contract immediately and the whole affair took on a "bitter aftertaste." Deussen's successors, Hermann Löhrer and Paul Schmidt, also met similar fates, largely because they could not lead and set an example for their colleagues and subordinates.[55]

Thyssen's reprimands of Bousse, Trapp, Schmitz, Deussen, Löhrer, and Schmidt consistently emphasized a number of salient principles. First, Thyssen emphasized customer satisfaction tied to his personal and professional pride and reputation, a Victorian value on the borderline between a family-named business and modern brand-name marketing. Second, Thyssen judged his top managers according to clear, statistical performance standards: production per worker, per shift, and per wages and salaries; sales revenues; and especially departmental profits—in short, what he called the "results." These statistical measures acted as the ultimate arbiter. Third, Thyssen took great pains and pride in providing state-of-the-art technical equipment. Given this advantage, the lack of commercial and productive success, in Thyssen's eyes, became a failure of character, which says a lot more about August Thyssen than his managers. Fourth, Thyssen required that his top managers act as role models for their colleagues and subordinates. They all failed in this regard. The Deussen case also began a pattern that can also be seen with Willy Trapp in the pipe mill, Ernst Nölle in Berlin, and Hans Richter in the machine department. Thyssen placed great expectations and responsibility on a new executive, remained firmly polite as conflicts arose, but then became bitterly disappointed when he felt crossed. Carl Wallmann, the director of Thyssen & Co. in the 1920s, felt that Thyssen could react very "sensitively" to setbacks.[56] Thyssen often tried to cut his losses, sometimes with rather generous severance settlements, so that the person would leave as quickly as possible and Thyssen could move on.

Sometimes conflict among his executives led to a clearer formulation of fundamental principles and organizational lines of respon-

sibility. Among his managers (including *Meister*), Thyssen tried to instill a level of collegiality and flexibility as part of Thyssen & Co.'s
corporate culture. (Workers were an entirely different matter.) For instance, Adolf Reussner successfully ran the galvanizing department
from its inception in October 1881. By 1883, the demands of his job
grew so large that Bruno Heil was hired as his assistant.[57] Heil was
prone to vehement outbursts, which Thyssen termed "fierceness of
character." When Deussen asked *Meister* Daub to contact *Meister* Bene
of the galvanizing plant directly about a roofing problem, Heil felt that
Daub had improperly passed over him. Heil confronted Deussen in a
harshly phrased memo and then wrote directly to Thyssen. Thyssen
stepped in to criticize Heil for a "highly *inappropriate* and *inadmissable*"
behavior *vis-à-vis* a superior, let alone one of the top executives of
the firm [underscores in original]. Thyssen felt it was irrelevant to accomplishing the task at hand that Daub and Bene could not talk directly with one another, rather than through their supervisor as a strict
line of command might dictate. In any case, Heil should have gone
through Wilke first. After requesting that Heil apologize, he wrote:
"But also we can only urgently ask you to observe the most tactful behavior in general, not only in dealing with higher ranking managers,
but also with equally ranked managers, through which alone true collegiality is awakened and the interests of the business are best guaranteed!"[58]

Reussner and Heil, however, did not work together well. This forced
Thyssen to make unusually explicit the areas of managerial responsibility within the galvanizing plant. Reussner was made exclusively responsible for sales, customer relations, administrative matters (design,
material purchases, estimates), as well as the technical direction of any
assembly work. Heil, "just as exclusively," took over line authority for
manufacturing operations. Thyssen asked the department to support
Reussner and Heil "so that the benefits emerging from this division of
labor were carried out in the interests of the whole."[59] The technically
expert Reussner had started up the state-of-the-art galvanizing plant,
but Thyssen placed him in sales; less trusted, Heil remained on the
line.[60]

Heil remained on shaky ground. According to Thyssen, Heil kept
designing new machines without showing that the "foundation" of the

tin-plate mill was "healthy and promising." Heil continued to object to Reussner's supervision and standard Thyssen & Co. cost reporting. Thyssen retorted:

> The task of the Department IV [commercial] office is to report to us immediately on income and expenses of the department and to keep us informed moreover by means of monthly statistical reports. If you do not succeed as expected inside a short time to convince us that the production of the boiler smith shop is profitable, we would have no other choice but to shut it down. We declare to you in the clearest manner that we will not hesitate in this case to resort to this [measure], because the unfavorable business conditions at present are the least of all suitable to keep a shop running which does nothing but require subsidies and therefore does not justify its existence![61]

Finally, Heil promised to deliver a galvanized boiler to the *AG für Stahlindustrie* in Bochum by the end of the month, yet various people stated that its fabrication would take at least three more weeks. Thyssen recommended to Heil that he put aside all of his other projects, his scientific journals, and "devote all of his effort, energy and circumspection exclusively to shopfloor operations and achieving better operating results" or else Thyssen would find a "thorough remedy." Heil's name does not appear in the records again.

The contradiction between formal line authority and pragmatic business operations became a running problem with the machine engineering department, which employed a high proportion of academically educated engineers who tended to look down on the *Meister* of the steel and rolling mills, who were largely trained on the job. In 1891, Thyssen released a top-ranking director of the machine engineering department, W. Surmann, for his "high-handed and superior" behavior with *Meister* Reining. Reining was responsible for the equipment maintenance in the rolling mills and one of Thyssen's most "proven and respected" executives. He had complained in the "most bitter tones" to Wilke, while Surmann complained to Thyssen that Reining had abused his authority as director. Thyssen wrote back:

> If you believe your rights to have been offended, the proper way of lodging your complaints with Herr Director Wilke or the firm stands open to you in an oral and written manner. But we find it impossible to

consent that such behavior among the personnel could come to be practiced, just as we, in contrast, are strictly attentive to ensuring that high-handedness or arrogance from one department opposite another will not become a habit. We cannot help but remark in this affair that the machine department has up to now not taken notice of this obvious directive. We have to request of you to observe a more appropriate and peaceful behavior with the personnel of this firm in light of its consequences.[62]

Thyssen eventually revised his employment contracts to make polite and professional behavior explicit. For instance, the 1887 contract with Diedrich Overdieck, who revamped the Siemens-Martin mill, read "that relations with superiors and colleagues always be concluded in the most pleasant manner."[63] When the engineer E. Schwarz took over the technical supervision of the iron foundry of the machine department in 1893, his contract reflected recent problems in the machine engineering department:

We greatly and confidently hope that you meet our high standards with your knowledge and abilities, your industriousness and thriftiness in the factory, your vigor and correct treatment of the foremen and workers, in particular we hope that you will do everything possible to carry always out willingly the directives of your superior, or the firm and its owners, to reinforce your position and to make our relationship a pleasant and lasting one.[64]

These examples confirm the decades-later memories of two of Thyssen's most senior executives, that Thyssen respected the many competent *Meister* as much as he did senior directors.[65]

One personal quality stood out in almost every contract for new department chiefs: self-sufficiency *(Selbständigkeit)*. Thyssen required that directors run their departments productively and profitably *without* his direct intervention. The formal structure of the departments, which combined manufacturing and commercial operations, reinforced this subjective value. The clearest example can be found in the contract of E. Münsterberg, who Thyssen hired in 1891 to construct the welding workshop of the plate mill:

I declare myself capable of directing this area in a self-sufficient manner, to equip the facilities, insofar as they are not already extant at

[Thyssen & Co.], exactly as those of Schulze-Knaudt in Essen, and indeed, to bring its operations to the same level which the above firm has achieved![66]

The remarkable aspect of this contract was that Thyssen wanted Münsterberg to take a small workshop of the plate department to a level competitive with another leading firm. And he wanted Münsterberg to do it himself. Thyssen intervened only—and then decisively—when he saw unsatisfactory "results." Similarly, when in 1887 he hired Diedrich Overdieck to restart the Siemens-Martin steel mill, he wanted to make it "equal" to the best that other firms had to offer. Thyssen demanded entrepreneurial performance. His incentive system offered long grace periods after dismissal (six to nine months for directors; three months for *Meister*) as well as a bonus based on departmental operating profits in an attempt to align managers' interests with his own.

In the 1880s, fixed salaries remained stable in contracts, with raises possible only through performance bonuses, much to the chagrin of many people. But departmental performance depended on many factors, such as technology, competition, business cycles, or accounting standards (like depreciation), which individual managers had little control over. This performance-based principle often worked counterproductively with line managers, especially in the 1880s. Initially, Thyssen followed this practice with his executives and *Meisters*. But he lost numerous (good) managers because of it, including Julius Wallmann, who later advised him on the startup of GDK and whose son became Thyssen & Co.'s future executive director: "As usual, we regard, and continue to regard, an expansion of production as the only permissible and natural means of improving your income."[67] Later Thyssen would admit that he had had "bad experiences" with fixed salaries.[68] By the 1890s, Thyssen changed his contracts by stipulating regular yearly raises along with performance incentives, eliminating this problem. In this respect, he had to adjust to the expectations of his managers.

Thyssen frequently used the phrase *Dispositions-Fähigkeit,* meaning "the ability to make arrangements." *Disposition* (the verb is *disponieren*) means being capable of being in charge, to have at one's disposal, to make plans or preparations, to place things in an appropriate order, to prepare oneself for eventualities. In an organization, the *Disponent* is roughly interchangeable with the position of *Vorsteher,* chief or supervisor, of an office with some degree of planning or decision-making power. As used by Thyssen, circumspection *(Umsicht),* the most often used word in his reproaches, had a similar meaning—to observe one's surroundings, to observe vigilantly and thoughtfully changing circumstances or events of the business environment. Circumspection also implied a level of care, thoughtfulness, and attention to detail without necessarily being cautious. With both words, *Disposition* and *Umsicht,* the emphasis was not on the ability to maintain loyalty, and discipline, or follow rules, but to engage actively and insightfully with one's area of competency and the surrounding world. Thyssen generally fired department heads because they lacked such leadership and managerial skills.

Department chiefs had to "self-sufficiently" bring their operations up to the level of market competitors. They had to manage almost all business activities except strategic investments—and even then they had an important voice in formulating strategy. The dualistic structure reinforced corresponding value expectations that required coordinating manufacturing and commercial ends in a collegial, cooperative, and profitable manner. Technical requirements had to meet customer needs, not the other way around. Thyssen demanded of departmental executives prompt and quick reactions to customers, flexibility, planning, decision-making autonomy, and leadership, so that the departments reacted appropriately to the outside market, not to internal, top-down rules and procedures. If anything, Thyssen transferred *merchant* and *entrepreneurial* expectations onto his managers. He consistently wanted to transform engineers into good businessmen.

Ernst Nölle and the Berlin Office

Designed to break Thyssen & Co. products into a lucrative urban market, the Berlin branch office experienced periodic crises, which provide an excellent view into the *process* of forming top-level strategy at Thyssen & Co. Thyssen managers did not merely execute Thyssen's strategic vision, but actively formulated it. Moreover, the tribulations of the Berlin office offer one of the best inside views of the tension between overall company strategy and departmental decentralization, and between Thyssen's expectations and individual managers' autonomy. It foreshadowed a more comprehensive move into marketing after 1906, but initially acted as a field of experimentation, disappointment, and failure.[69] According to Philip Neuhaus, Killing's successor, the resistance and "ill-will" of the more established commercial houses towards Thyssen & Co. slowed the Berlin startup. Only after a "period of development filled with change and purified by various crises . . . [could] Thyssen & Co. stand today [1918] on equal footing with the representatives of the old Berlin iron traders."[70] While stiff competition curtailed its performance, the Berlin office constantly tripped over internal problems, demonstrating what can occur when corporate controls are weak.

In February 1884, Thyssen established Thyssen & Co., Berlin as a branch office and made Ernst Nölle its supervisor.[71] At the time, Nölle was one of Thyssen's most trusted executives, who created Thyssen & Co.'s reporting system. After February 1891, the relations between Thyssen and Nölle began to sour badly. Nölle had built up the business in Berlin much more quickly than expected because of "his devoted activity, vigor, and circumspection," but at the same time Nölle was closing large deals with customers without first getting permission from the *Centralbureau*. He also sold Thyssen & Co. goods without respect to their production costs, and finally, was not keeping the departments "*au courant*" (*sic*). As Killing and Thyssen reminded Nölle, the branch office was designed "(1) . . . to achieve the largest possible turnover, primarily in our own products and (2) to keep [the departments] constantly well informed as to the prices and fluctuations in the market."[72]

Nölle achieved a high sales volume without regard to other consequences. The end result was that, as Albert Killing wrote to Nölle, the "home office and branch office are today, in a business sense, just as distant from one another as would be the case if they had nothing in common. That this [state of affairs] cannot be the right one and cannot correspond to our intentions is obvious and needs no further remarks!" Killing cut Nölle's freedom of action, which he had had for nearly seven years, by initiating rigorous new controls for contracts of 100 tons, which needed "our expressed permission." When Nölle objected, Killing countered Nölle, stressing "that the business there is not an end in itself, but is viewed as a means to an end."[73]

Nölle became deeply dissatisfied with Thyssen's new strictures and marketing strategy. He wanted to bring the Berlin office into some sort of larger sales combination with a Herr Steffens, a businessman from St. Petersburg. Thyssen admitted that the present state of the branch office was "all too much a product of necessity," but it still was the linchpin of his long-awaited and expensive plan to bring Thyssen & Co.'s sister firm, the GDK, into operation. The GDK would not join the steel cartel so as not to limit its output and Nölle's plans jeopardized it. Thyssen felt he needed every bit of sales volume that he could muster as a negotiating lever in any sort of cartel negotiations "because we *want to* and *must* remain independent in all respects."

Thyssen rejected any change in the "organic" relationship between Mülheim and Berlin.[74] Nölle argued again for a revision of the terms on which the branch office stood, but Thyssen reiterated, in the strongest terms,

> It is simply *impossible* to let our branch office fall into other hands because it alone guarantees us the absolutely necessary security to develop or expand the amount of production continually and under all circumstances, be it with or without profit and be it even with losses. For my firm and me, this is an issue that is *completely out of the question.*[75]

Thyssen even offered to provide capital for Nölle and Steffens' new business if they would move outside his "sphere of interest" to Leipzig, Hamburg, Hannover, or Frankfurt. Nölle gave notice. Thyssen genuinely regretted losing him: "in spite of it all, I am grateful for your friendly attitude and warm feelings with which you accompanied your intention to leave, which are, just like our long and untarnished relations with one another, naturally reciprocated in the most sincere and heartfelt way!" In 1892, to Thyssen's chagrin, Nölle formed a new firm called Steffens & Nölle, which eventually became one of the more important iron-and-steel wholesalers in Berlin—and the branch office's direct rival. The business rivalry became personal, and six years later, Thyssen ordered everyone not to entertain any further correspondence with Nölle.[76]

Before Nölle's departure, Thyssen moved to secure his two other senior executives, Bellmann and Oparka. He urgently instructed them to meet him in Mülheim on Christmas morning (!) to discuss contracts and salaries. When he learned that that Nölle had "incomprehensibly" granted Bellmann and Oparka advances on their raises without notifying Thyssen & Co., he felt compelled to honor the advances to retain them. Then, he discovered Nölle advanced them a share of the profit *before* they prepared the annual financial statement, which Nölle partially covered by manipulating the value of a mortgage. Finally, Nölle's successor, August Buff, discovered that Nölle had inflated sales figures by counting unpaid accounts. The following year's sales figures would actually have closed with a net loss if those "sales" were not included. Killing reminded Buff to go forward *"with the greatest possible care and circumspection" (Vor- und Umsicht)* and concentrate on sales only to financially solid businesses, rather than recklessly raising revenues.[77]

As a result of this loss of control, from this point on the Berlin branch office took directives from the Mülheim *Centralbureau*. Thereafter, Thyssen personally kept an unusually close watch on the development of the branch office and deducted any expenses deemed excessive directly from executives' personal salaries. He once reprimanded Bellmann for his traveling expenses, which were higher than his own.[78]

In spite of these safeguards, another scandal rocked the branch office. Thyssen discovered that Buff had risked more than 17,000 marks in order to save 1,100 marks, and did so without notifying Mülheim. Then, in 1896 Buff retired Oparka without the *Centralbureau*'s knowledge. Oparka promptly accused Buff of falsifying Berlin's financial statements and of engaging in risky real-estate and money-market speculation—with little success. Thyssen had to send two of his most trusted executives, Hermann Eumann, his chief financial officer, and Otto Garrey, head of the commercial office in the pipe department, to verify Oparka's claims. They substantiated all the accusations.[79]

The revelations created a new dilemma. There was little question that Buff would have to be held accountable, but the manner in which Oparka brought the irregularities to light did little to comfort Thyssen. Oparka had his own "hidden motives," and the manner in which he confronted Buff was patently "unfair." Most damningly, Oparka had done little to prevent or blow the whistle on Buff's poor business practices until after Buff dropped him.

Thyssen asked Eumann and Garrey to reflect on whether the Berlin office should be shut down, especially as it had operated for years at a loss and with great "unpleasantries." More irregularities came to light.

Thyssen briefly considered legal action, but waited on their judgment of the situation. Eumann and Garrey ordered a definitive end to all credit acceptances or extensions. They rehired Oparka and dismissed Buff. Thyssen then named Garrey the new director *(Disponent)* and gave him power of attorney. At the end of 1896, Thyssen again contemplated closing the branch office, but Eumann and Garrey recommended keeping it open.[80]

The Mülheim *Centralbureau* closely monitored Garrey, who remained the director of the Berlin office until 1907. In 1897, they beefed up the number of managers—including Phillip Neuhaus, who would succeed Killing—who controlled accounts and correspondence. August Thyssen, Jr., was moved to Berlin, in theory to make him a respectable businessman. The Berlin office underwent another round of serious cost-cutting.[81]

Killing micromanaged the office to such an extent that the minutia inadvertently discloses some standard informal practices that are normally difficult to reconstruct. First, such a level of oversight was very unusual. Killing went so far to advise August, Jr., to assign one manager to handle the accounts A–M, another N–Z, to ensure that each would correspond with the same firms all the time. In case Garrey was absent, these two managers would set final prices themselves and "in case of differences of opinion, Herr Weisskopf, as the older of the two (but not as a superior!) will decide and of course be held responsible. . . . We think that with such an arrangement all petty jealousies will be held at bay and a harmonious collaboration guaranteed; we trust that you and Herr Garrey will agree to our opinion."[82]

Killing distributed functions in a highly bureaucratic manner to minimize open frictions inside the Berlin office, but still attempted to discourage a rigid hierarchy. Seniority or rank did not imply superiority or subordination. When Thyssen recalled Neuhaus to Mülheim in 1904 to replace Killing, he wrote Neuhaus: "we do not wish to omit that our Herr Eumann, as the most senior member by far in our service, actually holds the director's position in the [central] office and you should see him as a *primus inter pares*."[83] Decisions were to be made on the basis of competence, i.e., responsibility, expertise, experience (seniority), and results, not authority based on rules, regulations, and functions. Bureaucratic controls grew out of scandals, irregularities, and petty "jealousies," not a general civil-service orientation. Just as

with the case of Reussner and Heil in the galvanizing plant, bureaucracy grew, so to speak, from the bottom up.

Although sales at Thyssen & Co. Berlin more than doubled between 1897 and 1906, sales or profit levels never lived up to Thyssen's
or Garrey's wishes.[84] The 1902 recession hit Berlin's sales hard. Structural steel sales, for instance, had risen to over 23,400 tons in 1901
(10,000 more tons than 1900), but dropped back to 12,000 tons in
1902. Thyssen again faced the choice of whether to close the branch
office or expand it even further. He postponed all raises. When Garrey
protested that one of his salesmen deserved a raise or else would leave,
Thyssen retorted that this proved that rival firms were earning more
than the Berlin office because they obviously could afford higher salaries.[85]

Garrey became increasingly frustrated by the tight scrutiny of the
Centralbureau. Mülheim did not allow the Berlin office much leeway in
constructing its financial statements in the "interests of the whole of
our firms over and above interests of each individual [firm] or special
interest."[86] Thyssen would not allow Garrey to set competitive prices
(based on rivals' prices in the Berlin market); instead Thyssen's manufacturing firms set prices for the Berlin office as they saw fit. Thyssen
refused to offer an obviously dissatisfied Garrey a raise; he felt additional earnings should only come through bonuses based on operating profits. But Garrey felt that profit levels lay outside his hands,
especially as he had no control over transfer prices from the manufacturing firms. Almost two decades later, Thyssen still had trouble with
his system of bonuses based purely on "results." After the 1906 financial statements came in, Thyssen summarily fired Garrey, accusing him
of failure in spite of a "glorious business conjuncture in which the entire world profited." Echoing his reprimand of Nölle, Thyssen stated:

> Moreover, we want to call attention to our explication in today's letter
> to the whole firm. In particular, we cannot avoid emphasizing that we
> entirely condemn the series of deals that you are pursuing. Such con-
> tracts that you have negotiated for our firms here and in Bruckhausen,
> Dinslaken, etc., were made without any regard for them. We must char-
> acterize this contracting policy as damaging to the prosperous develop-
> ment of the business there.[87]

As with Nölle, the later managers of the branch office failed properly to coordinate manufacturing and marketing, so that even high

sales did little to promote the well-being of the Thyssen manufacturing plants.

The Berlin experience illustrates a number of important points regarding Thyssen management. First, a full-blown strategy did not arise from the mind of August Thyssen alone. His strategy was formed after frequent setbacks, numerous adjustments, and with considerable advice from his executives. Killing, Eumann, Garrey, and Neuhaus were as, if not more, responsible than Thyssen for formulating Berlin's organizational policies. They also all had an active say in entrepreneurial or strategic decisions. Second, the eventual successful expansion of Thyssen marketing efforts rested on twenty years of hard, somewhat unsuccessful, perseverance. The Berlin experience "planted and matured" Thyssen's marketing policy. Only after learning how to operate in the Berlin market and managing the tradeoffs between manufacturing and marketing, did Thyssen executives learned to sell their products more profitably. Third, the extreme degree of control over Berlin contradicted the normal level of delegation inside the firm. Finally, Thyssen & Co. Berlin provides a perfect example of the results of delegation *without* enough supervision or control. Thyssen trusted Nölle enough to send him to Berlin, but the high level of autonomy granted, combined with Nölle's ambition, meant that the Berlin office was essentially independent of Mülhiem. At issue were the limits of Thyssen's organization. No controls and the organization ceased to exist. Thyssen management worked out those boundaries over time in a complex learning process. As the Thyssen-Konzern grew larger, this supervision became even more of a problem, giving rise to stronger, central statistical control measures that both limited *and* enabled higher degrees of autonomous action.

Formulating Investment Strategy

As shown by the Berlin experience, Thyssen managers had a profound influence on company strategy. The standard definition of entrepreneurship looks merely at the site of strategic control; that is, who has ultimate authority about new investment and strategy; not at *how* decision-making takes place *at* this site. This approach elides the organizational decision-making process itself. At Thyssen & Co., initiatives for new strategic directions often came from middle management. The examples of Martin Roeckner and Rudolf Traut, two important mid-tier engineer-managers, highlight this decision-making process, which involved significant tradeoffs among various options. They succeeded in persuading Thyssen to rethink his strategy and illustrate how well Thyssen listened to his managers. This documentation permits one of the rare behind-the-scenes looks at a major investment decision of Thyssen & Co., and demonstrates the pattern of behavior and persistent continuity of corporate values fostered by Thyssen's organizational culture.

After 1917, Thyssen management placed three separate but interrelated expansion plans on the table, one each for the pipe mill, the plate mill, and a new water-gas pipe-welding shop (for boilers, high-pressure drums, and wide-diameter pipes). At some points, each complemented one another, but at other points they conflicted with one another. All three expansion plans vied with one another for levels of financing and factory space. Since the city of Mülheim resisted any Thyssen & Co. expansion plans, which might raze private homes, and the war ministry did not permit the Thyssen & Co. Machine Company to give up any of its production halls because of important war contracts, Thyssen & Co. had no chance of finding new land. This situation created a type of zero-sum game, heightening the competition among Thyssen managers.

Discussions about how to make the firm competitive on the world market began before the cessation of World War I hostilities. War production had brought the equipment in the plate mill to the brink of ruin due to the lack of standard maintenance and repair. Carl Wallmann, the factory director and head of the plate department, wrote: "We had hoped to be able to wait until the end of the war, but the old mill train simply does not work any more, and subsequently, we are forced already to get on with the installation of the new mill train." The smelting furnaces of the steel mill were completely worn out because of the scarcity of fireproof materials; all drives, gears, and belts had been worn out because of the lack of lubrication; spare parts were gone; and building supports were weakened by rust. Thyssen had already placed 10.4 million marks in reserve for maintenance and renovation.

But in order to install a replacement rolling mill train, with its new dimensions, they had to build a new foundation, remove the old pillars, replace the wooden roof of the old hall because it was old and a fire hazard, and construct a new, modern hall with the requisite cranes, conveyors, cooling beds, and plate shears. Large cooling beds allowed the plates and sheets to lie flat and cool evenly to improve their tensile quality, particularly important for minimizing defects in high-pressure boilers, drums, and conduits. These cooling beds in particular required a great amount of space. Moreover, Thyssen & Co. had to retrack the railway lines running among the water-gas pipe-welding department, the plate mill, and the Machine Company, but they could only lay the tracks by cutting into the welding workshop's floorspace. All these improvements were necessary only to renovate the old mill train, let alone enable the expansion plans of the plate mill and welding workshop. At the same time, they needed to modernize the water-gas pipe-welding workshop to improve its operations. Thyssen & Co. had thought of upgrading the water-gas pipe-welding shop as early as 1911, but the war interrupted those plans. Management would prepare six different designs for its expansion between 1911–1921 before the new welding-gas pipe-welding shop finally began construction.[88]

On top of this conflict between the plate mill and the water-gas pipe-welding shop, Thyssen wanted to mass-produce drilling pipes and high-pressure pipelines, which meant expanding the pipe mill. Thyssen thought that demand for such pipes for the international oil industry and chemical industry would be high in the postwar period. He also felt it was of utmost importance to remain competitive with Phoenix and Mannesmann, his main rivals in manufacturing pipes, who were drawing up similar plans. Closely associated with the pipe mill diversification was Martin Roeckner's new design for high-pressure safety drums of great wall thickness, to be produced by the renovated water-gas pipe-welding plant.

The strategic, financial, technical, and spatial interrelatedness of these improvements caused a running series of competitive negotiations among Thyssen & Co. directors, mediated by Thyssen. Any change in the floorspace or financing of one department initiated a series of counterclaims by the other departments. At one meeting in September 1918, they discussed all options. Thyssen approved the modernization of the replacement mill train for the plate mill, but the discussion about the water-gas pipe-welding shop versus drilling-pipe production went nowhere. Wallmann, who felt market demand for drilling pipes and pipelines would be too weak in the foreseeable future, came out against Thyssen's plan to enter the mass production of them. Thyssen defended his position. So Wallmann and others modified Thyssen's riskier approach by beginning moderate quantities of drilling-pipe production in the old welding department until they found space elsewhere.[89]

The key figure for building the new water-gas pipe-welding shop was Martin Roeckner, who would become one of the most important engineers in Thyssen & Co., remaining until the 1940s. Roeckner had entered the firm just before the war and quickly made a name for himself with his designs. Although he did not have seniority or formal authority, Roeckner set the tone for the debates. Roeckner prepared all of the reports regarding the new welding shop. He combined various technical discussions with precise cost estimates for each of the potential options.[90] Roeckner's reports placed a particular emphasis on the costs of depreciation, interest payments, debt burden of each potential new plant design, the change in market prices, and the necessary volume and margins in order to turn a profit—especially important if he was to persuade Thyssen. As with so much of Thyssen corporate culture, the Thyssen engineers had to take responsibility for more than just their functional task. Financial and commercial issues were primary; one can perceive that layer of commercial orientation so typical of Thyssen practices.[91]

Because of political upheavals, macroeconomic difficulties, and space limitations, they still did not reach any agreement on the water-gas pipe-welding shop's expansion for another three years. In August 1921, another senior-level discussion took place. Again the cautious Wallmann felt that, given existing economic conditions, the full productive capacity of any new version of the welding shop would not be commercially viable. Weak demand would not provide enough volume to justify the high fixed cost of the new facilities, which would then not lower conversion costs. Roeckner's own plan projects a 4,000-ton/month production level in order to be profitable, which Wallmann thought excessive, given existing market conditions. Wallmann advocated instead the establishment of a syndicate. The other directors present disagreed with Wallmann, their formal superior. Most argued that a completely new and enlarged version of the welding shop would be the "technically correct solution." (An engineering bias is clearly evident here.)

Thyssen objected to Roeckner's plan on financial grounds. It was simply too expensive. Thyssen would only approve the plan if the welding shop could be built with the same productive capacity, but for half the projected cost. Thyssen postponed final approval until they drew up another profitability analysis and contemplated whether to build the new plant elsewhere at another Thyssen-owned firm, the *Press- und Walzwerke* in Reisholz.[92] By the end of the year, however, Roeckner's arguments and financial calculations managed to override Wallmann's objections and convince Thyssen. The modernization of the welding shop, which enabled the production of Roeckner's high-pressure safety drums, took another two years because of the upheavals of hyperinflation and the French invasion of the Ruhr.[93] These high-pressure drums eventually became a Thyssen & Co. specialty.

They again tried to convince the city of Mülheim to allow them to purchase land, but failed.[94] Eventually, they forced the organizationally weaker galvanizing department to give up its space in the interest of the water-gas pipe-welding shop. After 1923, Thyssen & Co. built a second galvanizing plant in Aschaffenburg outside of Frankfurt/Main in order to solve the space issue and establish a better presence in the south German market.

The case of Rudolf Traut, another young engineer in the pipe mill, exemplifies the latitude and entrepreneurial initiative desired by Thyssen. In 1911, Traut joined the Thyssen Machine Company as a leading engineer. Traut had special expertise in the design of rolling mills for pipe manufacturing. During the war, he transferred to the pipe department. Traut would become one of the most important figures in Thyssen & Co. history.

The disruptions of the postwar period had also delayed the modernization of the pipe mill, in spite of Thyssen's continued advocacy for entering the drilling pipe business. Traut argued for more expansive plans than did Thyssen. While Thyssen focused on drilling pipes, Traut wanted to transform the Mülheim pipe mill into a major center for seamless pipes of all possible sizes. Up to this point, Mülheim had concentrated on welded pipes, except for small-diameter boiler pipes. He also wanted to introduce expensive electric turbines instead of steam engines.

In the course of the negotiations, Traut took nearly complete control of the strategic direction of the pipe department. In an October 1920 conference, Traut presented a carefully prepared set of plans to persuade Thyssen to invest in seamless pipe production. Like Roeckner, Traut estimated costs and potential financial burdens of various plans. Prior to this meeting, Traut experimented with different technical processes for creating the intermediate seamless blocks to ensure that they would work. He took the initiative to negotiate with the director of GDK Dinslaken on the proper division of labor between Dinslaken and Mülheim so as not to generate rivalries between the two firms. Finally, Traut had discovered that DEMAG, an important machine engineering company, already had a large pilgrim's-step rolling mill available, which it had built for another firm, and was willing to sell it more cheaply than usual. Traut's presentation was convincing: Thyssen agreed with all of Traut's recommendations, especially the strategy of having the Mülheim factory produce all diameters of seamless pipes, and approved more than 36 million marks of investment funds on the spot.[95]

Traut also had to overcome internal organizational frictions, which caused further delay. By purchasing a rolling mill from DEMAG, the Thyssen & Co. Machine Company's archrival, Traut upset its director, Edmund Roser. Roser agreed that Traut could purchase the large pilgrim's-step machine and rolling mill train from DEMAG, but only if the pipe mill bought a smaller diameter rolling mill train from the Machine Company. Wallmann stepped in, arguing that the director of GDK Dinslaken be consulted first about this move. But Traut argued that the pipe mill needed the small diameter rolling mill train quickly because the old boiler-pipe plant would shut down at the end of the year. DEMAG could supply one within eight to ten months, while the Thyssen & Co. Machine Company was already operating at full capacity and they would have to draw up whole new designs. Eventually, Roser agreed that if DEMAG could deliver it sooner than they could, then DEMAG could supply it, but only if DEMAG ordered parts from Thyssen & Co. in return. Thyssen arbitrated at this point and agreed that time was of the utmost importance and entrusted Traut with full authority to negotiate the price of the machine, whose purchase he had authorized.[96] All in all, the decision to diversify into manufacturing a full range of seamless pipes in Mülheim and its realization owed most to Rudolf Traut, not Thyssen, who merely gave his final approval for investment financing.[97] Cumulatively, the decisions taken in the plate mill, water-gas pipe-welding department and pipe mill during a difficult period after the war kept Thyssen & Co. one of the premier pipe and tube producers in Germany. For his efforts, Traut received power of attorney in 1921 and became chief of the pipe mill.

The way these weighty, expensive strategic decisions were made show that Thyssen did not decree, but argued with his managers, fielded reasoned objections, and took them seriously.[98] He anchored a very competitive process of negotiation among his top managers. Such intra-organizational competition was a regular occurrence among Thyssen managers. In many of these protocols, Thyssen sat in the background of the discussion, but interjected points or came down on one side or another at the end. Managers led the debates independently. The best way to convince Thyssen on a project was to combine arguments for technical improvements with the project's present cost and estimated future profitability. Commercial and financial considerations overlaid and tempered the best technical solution; Thyssen & Co.'s organizational structure and corporate culture institutionalized this orientation. Key factors in the profitability assessments were depreciation and interest payments, especially since debt financed most of Thyssen's expansion. Strategic initiatives could originate from middle-level managers, even relatively young ones. Both Roeckner and Traut are prime examples of how young managers could move quickly upward through the Thyssen hierarchy as a result of their initiative and planning. Roeckner and Traut were not reduced to solving technical problems or to losing their "economic and entrepreneurial-organizational interest."[99] Thyssen expected his engineers to act as good businessmen.

In summary, after the reforms of the early 1880s, a distinctive Thyssen & Co. management system developed out of an integrated, multi-departmental structure organized around product line (instead of function), and monitored primarily through tight statistical controls developed by the *Centralbureau*. The departments had control over almost all operations except financial decisions regarding new investment; the department chiefs retained a strong say in the strategic direction of their individual departments. The organization of the departments themselves reproduced the classic German dualism between commercial and technical offices, but at the next level below senior management. The departments acted as semi-autonomous modules; the department heads as entrepreneur-engineers. Thyssen & Co.

Betriebs-Chefs had to run these departments as "self-sufficiently" as possible. The key to Thyssen & Co.'s success was to find a director who could combine both the commercial and technical sides of the business in a profitable manner; otherwise, it "did not justify its existence."

Above all, Thyssen demanded *Dispositions-Fähigkeit.* We might translate this as "managerial leadership." Certain managerial qualities became leitmotifs of Thyssen corporate culture for decades to come. Such language can consistently be found from the 1880s through the 1920s, demonstrating a persistent corporate culture that reflected a constellation of such values:

- ambition, energy, and vigor
- care, conscientiousness, and circumspection, especially in the interests of customers
- maintenance of authority over workers by example
- judging employees by their performance, not by personal favors or social status
- collegiality, civility, and politeness toward others, including subordinates
- the ability to fuse the technical and commercial aspects of the business so that departments rise to the level of rival competitors
- the ability to think ahead and to deal with complex problems
- "self-sufficient" leadership, independence of judgment, and planning skills.

Obviously, at lower levels work was more clerical, routine, and "monotonous," but promotion depended entirely on the qualities listed above. Thyssen regularly promoted numerous talented young managers, who bypassed the ladder of bureaucratic seniority. This anti-bureaucratic nature of the Thyssen hierarchy helped keep it at the forefront of the German steel industry. Thyssen became renowned for his ability to find vibrant young executives, and his management culture helped form them.

Thyssen & Co. operated with a merchant-entrepreneurial corporate culture that contrasted greatly with both Krupp and Siemens. Because of Krupp's status, historians have generalized from his particular entrepreneurial style as a model of other German enterprises. Krupp's administration was cut to Alfred Krupp's strict patriarchal leadership style. At Krupp, the entrepreneur continually undercut the authority of his senior executives and engineers, *the* fundamental managerial tension prevailing inside Krupp. Krupp never held himself to the same rules of his engineers or managers, and demanded a high degree of subordination and subservience. The highly patriarchal, "precapitalist craft tradition" set the ideological tone in the corporate culture of Krupp's works. Krupp tried to engender in his employees a sense of dependence and loyalty to the firm, especially through extensive social welfare programs.[100] Under the impact of sickness and the fear that he would lose control over his firm, Krupp composed his 1872 *General Regulations*. The level of authority accorded to lawyers and commercial functions, the detailed nature of the statutes, the emphasis on exact roles and competencies, the regular conferences, and the amount of written documentation all point to a centralized, rule-bound, bureaucratic, machine-like model of organization, accessible through its files. Krupp once stated that "one should be able to study and survey the factory's past and its probable future in the office of the central administration, without having to question a single mortal."[101]

At Siemens & Halske, Werner Siemens similarly acted as a "preconstitutional monarch," refusing to be bound by his own rules, yet he created a great many new rules for his management. Kocka found at Siemens & Halske "even a fetishization of internal written business communication" exemplified by the overly formal, bureaucratic discussion about whether to add another middle-level supervisor to a workshop office.[102] At Thyssen & Co. such a pedantic tone simply did not exist. In the case regarding the Berlin office, where one might hear such a tone, the necessity to overcome running managerial tensions forced them reluctantly to devise overly formalized distinctions. Still, the tone of Thyssen & Co. correspondence was businesslike, civil, and functional. Kocka also argued that in the 1880s Siemens & Halske missed the "necessary transition" to a "constitutional monarch," whereas Thyssen & Co. did make that transition.[103] The corporate culture of Siemens & Halske also contrasted dramatically with Thyssen's in that technical innovation, often for its own sake, was valued more than commercial considerations. Compare the values demanded by Thyssen (listed above) with the values found in a standard 1914 questionnaire at Siemens:

Capabilities (theoretical, practical, business attitude, memory, personability);

Character traits (loyalty, honesty, energy, steadfastness, thoroughness);

Industriousness;

Relationship to alcohol;

Punctuality;

Previous job experience?

How is his performance?

Does his performance correspond to his renumeration?

Personal relationships with superiors, colleagues, subordinates,
    customers?

Health;

Can the person be recommended for further employment?

Do you consider the person capable of being promoted to more
    important positions?[104]

At Siemens, values tended to cluster around reliability, dependability, and the ability to perform assigned roles and tasks. At Thyssen & Co., they clustered around initiative, energy, and the ability to achieve competitive goals.

Thus, if Alfred Krupp or Werner Siemens acted as absolutist rulers, August Thyssen was the strong executive in a constitutional government. Thyssen *freed* himself from day-to-day activities to concentrate on strategic decision-making and the attainment of new business contacts. He did *not* want to meddle in departmental affairs. Thyssen acted respectfully and collegially with his senior executives, using their advice. Thyssen encouraged entrepreneurial and commercial values, not civil service or bureaucratic ones. Without question, Thyssen built an industrial bureaucracy as well. Thyssen & Co. added new layers of hierarchy, formal offices, written procedures and routines, and a greater number of statistical controls to measure performance. But Thyssen built in a high degree of autonomy inside this hierarchy and required behavior consistent with this delegation.

As illustrated by problems at the Berlin office, Thyssen paid extremely close attention to organizational questions when he thought that the lack of control would cost him money. Thyssen & Co.'s relatively high degree of delegation and organizational decentralization was predicated on its systematic standards of supervision, embodied in the *Centralbureau* and its required statistical reports. When Thyssen reprimanded his department directors, he rarely questioned their technical competence, but rather their ability to lead and maintain authority within their departments, their ability to satisfy the customers, and to produce in a commercially successful manner. The accounting and information system established between 1882 and 1884 formed the basis for Thyssen's judgments about the departments and their "operating results." In fact, Thyssen's success has a good deal to do with his skills as an *Organisator.*

CHAPTER 4

Accounting for Control

Finance and accounting are the "heart of the enterprise."
Karl Härle, Commercial Director of the Thyssen Machine Company

If Thyssen required wide-ranging autonomy and "self-sufficiency" of his departmental managers, how did Thyssen & Co. align these managers' interests with his strategy? If they acted entirely independently, they would not necessarily have acted in Thyssen's interest or remain within the control of Thyssen & Co. Modern economic thinking terms this dilemma an *agency* problem. Why should and how do agents (managers) act in the interests of the principal (the owner)? In certain respects, the history of the creation and use of information inside business firms is "also a history of trust and distrust," a means of establishing coordination and control over these agents. Counterintuitively, trust and control are flip sides of the same coin.[1]

Most German business historiography tends to emphasize the importance that leading German entrepreneurs and salaried managers placed on authority, loyalty, and discipline in their subordinates. Bernd Dornseifer hints at an inverse correlation between the level of loyalty and discipline demanded by those "lords" and the lack of a formal information and control system. His critique of Kocka's bureaucratization thesis stresses the relative underdevelopment of formal, bureaucratic control measures inside German enterprises relative to American ones. Hence German entrepreneurs relied more than American ones on "ultimate authority" and loyalty of subordinates to overcome the agency problem.[2]

The inverse case can be found at Thyssen & Co. Precisely because of the existence of a systematic information and control system, Thyssen could demand self-sufficient leadership capabilities. Delegation and systematic control went hand in hand. Above all, Thyssen judged his managers by their "results" as defined by his accounting, information, and control system. Thyssen attended quite closely to the challenges of establishing what we call a modern industrial organization.

The crucial time period in the organizational history of Thyssen & Co. was between 1881 and 1885, when Thyssen, Wilke, Killing, and Nölle introduced a new framework. At the same time Thyssen & Co. delegated functions to the modular commercial-technical departments, it centralized an important set of procedures that routinized communication inside the business firm. Management circulars (downward communication) and the monthly departmental operating results (upward reporting) epitomized this new communication system. This self-conscious implementation of a "system" in the early 1880s created new procedures and tied them to regular, uniform information channels. This controlled accountability acted as a system of surveillance, that is, monitoring, supervision, and control. In these respects, Thyssen & Co. was as advanced (if not more) than many innovative U.S. firms.

Most modern business decision-making rests on statistical information, but until the physical apparatus we now take for granted was created, such as typewriters, telephones, carbon copies, and filing systems, all of which create, manage, and store organizational memory, such information was not easily accessible or disseminated. Organizational knowledge depended on certain types of information, but information technologies first had to be assembled before they could replace more informal, personal ways of managing a business.[3]

The new demands of business activity combined with these new technical practices produced new *genres* of business communication. JoAnne Yates shows how tables, graphs, and forms enhanced the efficiency of managerial reporting. She nicely calls them a *genre,* but uses the term in a functional way, as a generic formatting of information that became more effective and efficient over time. Such genres include circulars, directives, manuals, corporate magazines, reports, tables, forms, graphics, memos, and face-to-face conferences—each with its own manner of communicating—which affect behavior in much the same way that literary genres alter reading habits. Specific written documents embodied these new procedures and arranged the data in formatted reports, the essence of informing or reporting. These forms created information flows that linked people and tasks across increasingly differentiated offices, which occupied distinct organizational and physical space within the firm. Eventually they became housed in the specific architecture of the central office. Altogether this collection of people, procedures, written forms, and (architectural) space constructed an organizational system of controlled accountability.

I want to push this concept of genre one step further than Yates does by emphasizing how this formatting packages information, revealing certain aspects of the business or disguising others, creating organizational knowledge, and conceptually constructing the firm as a unified, coherent whole. Hayden White demonstrated how literary genres map information in particular ways so as to create meaning and turn information into relevant and significant knowledge. White has shown how the narrative genre of history itself mobilizes a particular developmental story, a particular set of expectations, prefiguring how information becomes evidence and how knowledge becomes constructed. Genres or "emplotment," that is, the "encodation of the facts contained in the chronicle as components of specific kinds of plot structures," actually constitute knowledge and make sense of reality.[4] The form of a communication helps create significance and a story. For a richer discussion about genre and accounting information, see Appendix B.

Analogously, these internal business reports, written communiqués, and year-end financial statements subtly construct the story, the reality, of organization life. Like any other texts, these statistical accounts create a particular developmental story about the business organization that can be deconstructed.[5] But in this case, when Thyssen read the "results," people could lose their jobs.

Centralizing and Standardizing Communication

Crucial reforms of the early 1880s created the basic organizational system that Thyssen & Co. would use well into the 1920s. This proliferation of written procedures and forms certainly represent a type of bureaucratization, but they did not grow out of an alleged German state-bureaucratic tradition. The most advanced U.S. firms introduced the same type of systematic methods largely in parallel with Thyssen & Co. These forms and procedures represented new types of genres and rou-

tines that addressed the growing complexity and issues of agency—
control and trust—inside the business firm.

Thyssen & Co. introduced management circulars *(Circulairs)* in May
1882 to regularly inform department executives about new organizational procedures. These circulars differed from general bulletins, orders, or factory regulations posted onto company blackboards or gates
in that they were specifically oriented toward middle to upper-level departmental managers, not the company as a whole. They provided
a degree of procedural consistency and uniformity across all the departments, reducing the risks of misunderstanding involved with numerous, *ad hoc* individual orders or oral communications. In the beginning, the circulars contained a host of unrelated issues, but once
established, they addressed specific problems arising out of irregularities. The first *Circulair* explained the need to "simplify," speed, and
standardize. Until 1904, Killing wrote most of the *Circulairs,* which
were successively numbered. August Thyssen usually signed them by
using the firm's official name, not with his own name. Department
clerks copied the original by hand and placed it in a department
folder; managers initialed and passed them on to the next department. The collected circulars helped create a kind of organizational
memory about proper routines.

The Thyssen management circular appears to have been unique in
industrial operations at the time in Germany and the United States.[6]
Siemens generally used regular conference meetings among the various department directors, but after the 1880s, it also used management circulars. They tended to be signed but not copied and retained
by the individual department until the advent of carbon paper, which
eased duplication.[7] Some U.S. manufacturing firms also introduced
such management circulars at roughly the same point. At Lammot
du Pont's organizationally innovative Repauno Chemical Company,
founded in 1880, a similar set of reforms as Thyssen & Co. introduced
the same type of management tools: circulars and formal written sales
reports to ensure uniform upward and downward flows of information. Not before the 1890s, however, did systematic management replace the rather staid, personal managerial style at DuPont.[8] Based on
admittedly sketchy evidence, my conclusion is that Thyssen & Co. advanced largely in parallel with U.S. developments and perhaps at the
frontier of German techniques.

Early circulars centered on issues of authority, coordination, and timing. For instance, the second circular clarified questions of authority regarding personnel matters. Local officials had complained about the hiring of adolescent workers without working papers, so Thyssen & Co. initiated a new rule requiring all new hires have them. Moreover, *Meister* would no longer have control over the hiring and firing of workers.[9] Here circulars reinforced executive control over the *Meister.* Similarly, the U.S. brass company, Scovill, used circulars to "curb the power of foremen and other lower-level managers."[10]

The earliest circulars concern themselves with proper "office-order," routines to ensure the speed and timeliness of all correspondence, accounts, and information among the departments, and between the departments and the central office. In one case, the plate mill had come to a complete standstill due to the lack of reserve materials. Many workers simply left, dissatisfied with the paucity of available work. Fritz Wilke initiated a new procedure that required department chiefs to update "punctually and conscientiously" a list of all necessary reserve equipment and spare parts ahead of time "so that the matter can be taken care of by this office calmly and without rush, which, in terms of the quality of the materials or their price, cannot be underestimated." Similarly, the fourth circular regularized the procedure for creating bills of lading because the railroads were charging Thyssen & Co. extra when the bills did not reach the railway loading zone on time or were poorly numbered. Such difficulties resulted from each department's having its own shipping office.[11] The seventh circular stated that no letter could rest in a department for more than one day. The ninth circular regulated telegram correspondence among the customers, departments and central office.[12]

The circulars more precisely circumscribed the boundaries of the firm. All visitors, except very "important customers," had to receive prior permission of *die Firma* before entering the factory grounds.[13] Another case involved deductions from workers' paychecks. Until 1882 Thyssen & Co. had deducted non-business-related claims such as rents or the delivery of goods directly from workers' pay. Rumors had cropped up that the firm was making arbitrary and unfair deductions. To minimize any perception of misappropriation, Thyssen & Co. decided it would henceforth deduct only advances or regular contributions to the sickness insurance fund from workers' paychecks. The circular specified that workers' pay was a departmental responsibility, and that the order required strict compliance.[14] Essentially, the circulars announced that Thyssen & Co. would become more responsive to its internal organizational procedures than to the outside world. Thyssen & Co. defined its borders more rigidly, physically in terms of the factory gates and fence, and administratively in terms of its organizational practices. Internal procedures and modes of communication became the new sinews of its governance structure.

Other early circulars addressed the problem of regular upward communication from the departments to the central office. In 1882 Thyssen & Co. introduced monthly departmental reports and standardized accounting procedures. The monthly reports represented the key organizational innovation in upward communication. A group of distinct functional offices coalesced in the *Centralbureau* to collect this information: a cashier's office, a bookkeeping/accounting office, and (after 1885) an independent internal auditing office. Three important managers in the history of Thyssen & Co. also entered the firm at this time: Ernst Nölle, Hermann Eumann, and Moritz Pickhardt.

The creator of this sophisticated reporting and information system was Ernst Nölle, the second highest paid commercial executive, who later moved to Berlin.[15] After intensive discussions with Wilke, Killing, and department heads, Nölle designed a standardized reporting "scheme" for each department. Thyssen and Nölle relied on proper accounting practice by the department commercial offices. The *Centralbureau* did not create department monthly balances, but audited and consolidated them.[16]

In spite of the very different production programs, Nölle standardized the monthly accounting reports so that they provided a coherent statement of a department's business performance, providing a rough approximation of *sales* and *profits*.[17] These reports created a good deal of inter-organizational tension because they controlled and checked (in the double meaning of the word) the autonomy of the departments. Effectively, the reports reproduced the departmental management system of Thyssen & Co.

The departments handed these monthly "results" to Wilke by the fifteenth of the following month. The regularity of the reports created an organizational calendar, much like a forty-hour workweek creates a weekend. Yet a ten-year running struggle ensued between the departments and the *Centralbureau* over these monthly reports because department heads, especially those in the machine department, had great difficulty presenting them on time. In August 1884, Thyssen sent out yet another circular reminding the departments to submit their balances "absolutely finished" *(fix und fertig)* by the fifteenth. He expected the subsequent auditing of the final results to be completed by no later than the twenty-fifth of the same month: "We expect in the future that this extremely late deadline be strictly adhered to! [double underlining in original]" A delay by one department affected the whole firm because it caused a backlog in the work of the *Centralbureau*.[18] After numerous complaints from the auditing office, Thyssen wrote another circular in June 1885 reiterating the "serious" complaints about the "lackadaisical manner in which the departments finished their monthly account reports."[19] Thyssen felt that this timeliness was the highest priority. Not handing in these reports on time became one of the greatest vices in Thyssen's eyes.

This organizational calendar created a point of conflict between the central office and the departments. Thyssen expected the department heads, mostly engineers, to bring the department up to the latest technical and quality standards, fulfill orders promptly, satisfy the customers—and now prepare statistical reports. But which practice should take priority? What if the processing of sales orders needed extra time? How could department chiefs justify this paperwork when they had products to manufacture and customers to deliver to? This conflict of priorities could rarely be easily solved—except by working longer hours.

Thyssen & Co. did try to reshape the working day. In May 1884, it attempted to introduce a new "office order" based on "English time," a nine-hour day without the standard two-hour lunch. This met with practical difficulties (other firms did not work this way) as well as the adamant resistance of managers. Thyssen gave up. (Ironically, after 1917, white-collar employees tried to reintroduce "English" time because it would allow them to go home earlier to work on garden plots or shop for food. This time, management rebuffed them.)[20]

After Nölle left for Berlin, Hermann Eumann replaced him in Mülheim. In early 1882, at the age of twenty-five, he had joined the firm, beginning in the bookkeeping and cashier offices. He quickly gained responsibility for the entire financial and managerial reporting system of the firm and tracked Thyssen's burgeoning securities transactions. As part of these organizational innovations, in October 1882 Eumann established a consistent securities portfolio book for Thyssen & Co., for which until 1918 he took the personal responsibility of posting each individual transaction. Eventually Eumann specialized in high finance and banking relations. He became one of Thyssen's most important confidantes, working with him for nearly forty years until Thyssen's death in 1926. After the death of Joseph Thyssen in 1915, Eumann moved to the desk across from Thyssen's. Essentially, Eumann acted as chief financial officer of the Thyssen-Konzern. Sitting at the center of such financial controls and information conferred great organizational power.

In 1885, Eumann established a distinct internal auditing office, which had an explicit *"kontrollierende Funktion"* of bookkeeping procedures.[21] Each department had its own cash box from which it paid wages, some salaries, and miscellaneous expenses. After Eumann rechecked the amount in each box, the cash left was sent to Killing at the end of the month.[22] In this respect, Eumann "controlled" the autonomy of the department chiefs. This close central monitoring of the cash boxes allowed the departments to maintain their own cash accounts.

Along with procedural reforms of the central office, Thyssen & Co. established a distinct inventory and purchasing office, with Moritz Pickhardt at its head, who remained with the firm until 1910. The reforms of the early 1880s strengthened his control over all inventory questions, spare parts, and prices for inputs. Pickhardt, however, never received *Prokura* (power of attorney), so all contracts needed the signature of Killing, the Wilkes, or the Thyssens. Wilke ultimately had final approval of all prices and bids. In consultation with department heads, Pickhardt helped set monthly price levels for goods and inventories with the important exception of strip steel, plates and sheet metal, steel blooms and slabs.[23]

Why were these products exempted from Pickhardt's control? The question is of utmost importance because the answer exposes one of the most important faultlines of the organizational structure and explanation for managerial behavior at Thyssen & Co. All of the above were intermediate products manufactured for sale using internal transfer prices to other departments. Internal transfer prices are the value of products passed from one part of the firm to the next in a value chain. For instance, the strip steel department "sold" its products to the pipe department as intermediate material for making pipes. Transfer prices are artificial because the products are not sold on the open market, but priced bureaucratically. *Die Firma,* that is, the Thyssens, set the internal transfer price for intermediate products. Only gas and boiler pipe prices did not have internal transfer prices, because Thyssen & Co. sold the vast majority as end products on the open market.

By taking personal control over the setting of prices for these crucial intermediate products, Thyssen helped eliminate potentially divisive negotiations between each of the departmental heads. Less important prices for other intermediate goods could be left in the hands of Pickhardt and the department heads. Naturally, the department head supplying the input material (strip steel) had an interest in the highest possible internal price, while the department head purchasing the input (for pipes) had an interest in the lowest possible price. Departmental profits depended crucially on such considerations and such prices could be easily manipulated. Any complaints or questions about these critical prices had to go through Thyssen, Killing, Wilke, Nölle, and Eumann; in other words, through senior management.

It is impossible to reconstruct whether Thyssen & Co. used production costs or approximate market prices as transfer prices. Setting internal transfer prices at production cost would mean that the next downstream stage in the value chain accrued most of the profits. Profits would come out of the high end of the production chain. Setting transfer prices at market prices, however, would build in constant pressure to drive production costs lower than market prices to increase profit margins. Since the monthly reports calculated "results" as a measure of profits, chances are Thyssen set internal transfer prices close to market levels except for the steel mill, whose prices were definitely set near cost. If Thyssen's subsequent behavior is a guide, the firm used market transfer prices or some middle ground after much negotiation about prices among the departments and the central office. We also know that when Thyssen & Co. spun off the machine department, its director, Carl Härle, commented:

> What it [the machine department] delivered to the other departments,
> it used the prices agreed upon [with these departments] just as it pur-

chased the materials produced for it by the other departments. In this sense, certain autonomy existed internally, which could not be shown externally in the form of statistics and bookkeeping, because the commercial organization, the accounting [of the machine department], was unified. This had the consequence that internally and externally as well only the entire firm could balance.[24]

Each department bought and sold "self-sufficiently." Accounting and organizational procedures bound them together as a unified, coherent firm. These procedures also reinforced the autonomous leadership behavior that Thyssen expected from his department chiefs.

These reforms of the early 1880s created the organizational sinews of Thyssen & Co. The sudden 1881–1882 spurt in the number of higher management positions reflected the amount of written work now needed to process the new bureaucratic procedures. Central office and senior management figures numbered just ten in Jan. 1881, but grew to roughly forty by the end of 1882.[25] By the turn of the century, the Thyssen & Co. central office and departmental management grew to roughly one hundred people (Figure 4.1). By 1910, managers of all grades in the Rolling Mills numbered 349 people, rising to 479 people by 1913.

The systematization of Thyssen & Co. management controls appeared to have moved along relatively smoothly, but not all the new procedures easily found space inside the *Centralbureau* or the departments. Certain control functions, such as the reimbursement of expense accounts and the handling of freight charges, bounced back and forth between the *Centralbureau* and the departments.

The same held true for the use of two new important communication technologies at Thyssen & Co., the telephone and the typewriter. Over decades, beginning in the 1880s, both technologies generated entirely new jobs, and were used by male clerks on a potential career path to management; not until roughly the war did women begin using them, without a chance of moving into management, thereby creating the jobs of operators and secretaries. Paradoxically, the telephone first served to centralize communication through the *Centralbureau* rather than diffuse it. Killing felt it disturbed the routine in the *Centralbureau*. After any call, the central office had to send a clerk out to the department offices, spread throughout the factory grounds (a disadvantage of decentralization), to find the appropriate person

Figure 4.1 Thyssen & Co. management at headquarters, ca. 1900. Joseph Thyssen and Albert Killing sit in the middle first row. (Reproduced with the permission of the Mannesmann-Archiv, Mülheim/Ruhr)

while the caller remained on hold. Customers complained that Thyssen managers spoke too softly and not distinctly enough. In view of these inconveniences, Killing requested that most business be conducted in writing rather than through the telephone. But by 1891, Killing had hired someone to handle telephone conversations; he could refer to the new job only as "someone [male] servicing the telephone."[26] Not until after 1900 did Thyssen & Co. build a private telephone network for the company. And only during the war did Thyssen & Co. hire women as telephone operators.[27]

The typewriter, too, made a brief appearance in the 1880s; in 1890, Killing figuratively pulled the ribbon out of it. Killing continued to rely on handwritten letters and the letter-press book until the end of his tenure in 1904. The typewriter reappeared in the *Centralbureau* after March 1901, and within a few years became the standard means of creating correspondence. As far as the records permit conclusions, Fritz Schaaphaus, the commercial director of the pipe department, appears to have been the first to use the typewriter consistently. August Wilke, the factory director, used a typewriter after January 1903 but inconsistently. After 1910 Thyssen & Co. began hiring female typists.[28]

There was nothing particularly German about resisting the adoption of these technologies. Various aspects of the company could lag or speed ahead with no necessary tight coupling of all the new genres, procedures, or technologies. Initially, moreover, the technologies first led to difficulties; efficiency gains did not immediately become apparent. Thyssen & Co. followed a pattern of halting organizational innovation similar to that found in the United States. Just as at Thyssen & Co., telephone communication at DuPont, for example, first went by messenger. In general, however, American firms integrated typewriters more swiftly.[29] Compared to American firms, Thyssen & Co. (and Siemens) adopted the typewriter about two decades later, but the telephone at about the same time.[30]

The introduction of formal communication systems in manufacturing firms accelerated on both sides of the Atlantic after the 1880s.[31] As the administrative spread of the firm grew beyond the reach of personal leadership and management, the means of communication and the standard operating procedures became more formal. Scale alone was not the only factor contributing to reorganization. Ten times the size of Thyssen & Co, Krupp introduced similar organizational reforms in the 1870s; Siemens was roughly twice as large when its reforms took place in the early 1880s.[32] Thyssen and his managers proactively initiated these organizational innovations. Serious attention to organizational questions would prove typical of the Thyssen-Konzern.

Accounting for Control

The central documents in the Thyssen & Co. accounting system were monthly departmental reports, cost-accounting worksheets, and year-end financial statements.[33] In order to assess company and departmental performance accurately, Thyssen & Co. needed sophisticated, comparable standards that were consistent across diverse products and over time. In the early 1880s, managerial accountancy was in its infancy, with few standard outside conventions. Managerial accounting reports the results of (internal) operations to managers for decision-making purposes. Even today, managerial accounting methods remain relatively heterogeneous depending on the type of firm, type of products, and strategic objectives of the company.[34] In our case, the diversity in managerial accounting proves advantageous because it provides a glimpse into the imaginations of the five main players at Thyssen &

Co. (the Thyssen brothers, Killing, Wilke, and Nölle) and their conception of control.

Nölle's accounting innovations set rigid accounting conventions—codes—for Thyssen & Co. If the first rule of Thyssen accounting was handing in the monthly reports punctually, the second rule distinguished new investments from operating expenses. All wages and associated expenses for acquisitions or modifications would be assigned directly to the operating budget of the department and not to the new investment account. Department heads needed the explicit consent of *die Firma* to post any expenses to the new investment account. And in the early 1880s, Thyssen considered the expansion of the departments as largely closed. He found the practice of classifying operating expenses as new investment to be a deliberate "obfuscation of the department's results."[35] In March 1885, Thyssen repeated once again the rigid guidelines for department accounts:

> We remark respectfully that our bookkeeping office will proceed strictly despite any contradictory notes contained in the accounts. All such margin comments are thus completely useless, if they cannot rest upon a previous understanding with *die Firma;* the same holds true when the purpose of the expenditures is not clearly apparent from their description.[36]

This primary rule of Thyssen & Co. accounting generated a classic conflict of interest between the central office and the production departments, between administrative and operating interests, between the firm and the operating departments, between owners and management, between principal and agent. Every expense classified as new investment rather than operating expense added to (or padded, depending on the point of view) monthly operating profits. If, as Thyssen wished, the departments booked almost all expenses into operating cost accounts, the end effect reduced their profitability. The department chiefs had a personal stake in moving expenses to the new investment accounts, thus increasing their department profits and, conveniently, their take-home pay.

While the theory of distinguishing new investment from operating expenses, and general overhead from department expenses, was (is) impeccable, sufficient grey zone still existed for honest disagreement. Far from being a neutral assessment of expenses, accounting guidelines shape the politics of a firm. They draw potential fault lines of conflict and represent power within an organization. Accounts are more or less standardized conventions more or less useful to somebody.[37] Obviously, these classifications were most useful to August Thyssen, and he consistently sided with commercial administration, not production.[38] By radically limiting charges to the new investment account, he followed a conservative accounting policy that depressed immediate profits in favor of long-term financial substance. Thyssen did not have to answer to shareholders. In these matters, his tenacity reinforced the financial foundation of his enterprise, an accounting counterpart to his personal sense of bourgeois solidity. Moreover, the practice of clearly distinguishing investment accounts from operating expenses demonstrates that Thyssen employed rather sophisticated capital-accounting techniques for the time, even compared to U.S. firms.[39]

The construction of these monthly reports (an example of which is shown in Table 4.1) demonstrates how Thyssen & Co. devolved accountability to the departments, reproduced the modular structure of the firm, and reinforced Thyssen's fundamental commercial orientation.[40] At first glance, the monthly reports appear to be mere lists of transactions, but the flurry of postings at the end of the month nullify this first impression. It is also not immediately obvious that the original report acts as a double-entry balance sheet (with a 10-pfennig discrepancy here). They do not show total debits and total credits. Excepting minor credits, the monthly sales can largely double as the total credit sum or balance.

Nölle formatted the original report so that two figures jumped out: the monthly sales and the cumulative profit balance to date, not monthly profits. One can derive the monthly operating surplus by laboriously adding up (no calculators!) all the expenses for the month and subtracting the debit total from total credits, or by subtracting the cumulative total of the previous month from the present month's cumulative total. The report stresses sales and surpluses—the primary criteria for assessing "results"—consistent with the commercial orientation of Thyssen & Co. organizational culture.

The debit side of the monthly report was consistently classified into six constituent parts: (1) rent reimbursements for housing for key *Meister* every few months; (2) corrections for miscellaneous trans-

Table 4.1 Example of monthly financial reports, plate and sheet department, November 1888 (completed March 20, 1889)

Nov.

		Debet (Marks)
2	Rent to H. Jürgens from 1/5–31/10	212.50
2	Rent to H. Adams from 1/5–31/10	133.35
2	Rent to Fr. Backhaus from 1/5–31/10	130.00
2	Rent to B. Lock from 1/5–31/10	75.00
2	Rent to H. Rosstroff from 1/5–31/10	97.50
2	Cash	800.00
3	Cash	500.00
3	Cash [Wages]	21,300.00
3	Gasseth Smith & Co. returned plates	227.39
3	Eduard Stier, traveling expenses	8.00
5	Cash	500.00
7	E. Tielmanns & Co, commission	7.47
8	J. G. Schmidt, freight difference	16.10
8	Gasseth, Smith & Co., returned plates	233.52
9	Fischer & Rechsteiner, expense receipt	499.12
10	Gewerkschaft Orange, returned bottoms	40.28
14	Heinr. Lang, weight difference	8.62
15	De Leema & Philippsen, expense receipt	1.60
15	Railway "Die Altona," weight difference	4.48
17	Cash [Wages]	24,900.00
19	Contract Notarization, Linksrhein. Bahn	4.05
20	Thyssen & Co., Berlin, weight difference	18.19
20	Henck & Hambrock, retr. plates, discrepancy	48.31
20	Carl Sträfer, discrepancy	4.39
21	Nederl. Staatschappy, miscell. freights	46.38
21	Aug. Reinstragen, retr. plates	118.50
22	Gewerkschaft Orange, retr. plates	249.27
22	Gusstahlwerk Witten, discrepancy	2.72
23	E. Benninghaus, price discrepancy	4.60
25	Cash	1,100.00
27	L. Radoux, weight excess	24.00
29	Vereing. Ges. Kohlscheid, weight difference	1.63
30	Salaries of the *Meister*	1,187.00
30	Salaries of the *Beamten*	898.33
30	Deliveries from the nail dept., costs	1.00
30	Deliveries from the gas central, costs	871.03

Table 4.1 (continued)

Nov.

		Debet (Marks)
30	Deliveries from the strip steel dept., costs	5.43
30	Deliveries from the strip steel dept., costs	1,228.80
30	Deliveries from the machine dept., costs	6,815.88
30	Deliveries from the pipe and tube dept., costs	969.05
30	Deliveries from the steel mill, costs	108,795.31
30	Percentage of general overhead account	6,960.00
30	Depreciation	10,000.00
30	Deliveries from the galvanizing dept., sales and costs	2,684.98
30	Deliveries from the Purchasing, pig iron	84,787.68
30	Deliveries from the Purchasing, ingots	38,801.74
30	Deliveries from the Purchasing, coal	20,275.90
30	Deliveries from the Purchasing, general expenses	13,455.86
30	Deliveries from the Purchasing, sales expenses	4,810.44
30	Freight costs, Bergisch-Märkische RR	4,131.90
	[Subtotal of debits—not in original]	357,997.30
		Credit
2	1 sold chest	0.20
7	1 sold keg	2.40
31	**Sales for November [highlighted by J. F.]**	**395,163.16**
	[*Total credits—not in original*]	**395,165.76**
	On 1 December 1888, the value of the balance in favor of the plate mill [highlighted by J. F.]	**698,652.30**
	[*Balance, 1 November—not in original*]	*661,483.94*
	[*December surplus—not in original*]	*37,168.36*
	[*Balance sum = Dec. surplus + subtotal debits—not in original*]	*395,165.66*

actions and commissions; (3) wages and salaries at regular intervals throughout the month; (4) deliveries from other departments, including purchasing; (5) general overhead and depreciation, and (6) freight costs.

Thyssen & Co. classified rents for *Meister* as operating expenses for the department, not as an extraordinary expense for the firm. Somewhat inconsistently, rents covered six months, rather than one. The categorization implies that Thyssen & Co. considered the social policy of the firm as an integral part of departmental production operations. The second section concentrated on correcting discrepancies in weight and prices, and included returns. This section also included sales commissions paid every six months to a number of independent agents. The department debited year-end royalties or bonuses, production premiums, and contributions to professional associations. In the third section, Thyssen & Co. distributed its wages through the department accounts in cash, indicating that departments had final responsibility over their workers. Finally, the department distributed salaries for master craftsmen *(Meister)* and managers *(Beamte)* (considered distinct from one another). Thyssen & Co. considered departmental managers' salaries as an operating expense for the department, not as general overhead. The sixth section handled running accounts with railroad companies.

The fourth section concentrated on deliveries from other Thyssen & Co. departments. By far, these debits outweighed other expenses. Most of the deliveries to the plate and sheet mill came from the steel mill and the purchasing department. Thyssen & Co. broke these accounts down into the major basic input materials of the department—pig iron, ingots/blocks, and coal—and general and sales expenses. In effect, Thyssen & Co. treated shipments among the departments in same manner as those from outside suppliers—as if the departments were independent entities. The major difference was that the transactions among the departments did not go through the market but as internal transfer prices. All the departments had account books that were crosschecked against the other departments for errors (debits and credits appear when discrepancies arose). Each department had its own shipping and weighing station headed by a weighing master, who controlled for deliveries. The *Centralbureau* did not have to mediate departmental transactions directly, giving it a supervisory and arbitration role, rather than a direct bookkeeping role. The auditing office verified the accuracy of the departments' account books. Department audits occurred monthly—probably based on sampling as the number of transactions skyrocketed.

Conceptually, the most interesting section is the inclusion of general overhead and depreciation accounts. Both accounts represent an attempt to apportion overall firm expenses across the departments on a proportional and monthly basis. Significantly, after adding these two accounts into the monthly reports, Thyssen & Co. called the resulting surplus (or loss) the "net profits" *(Reingewinn)* of the department for the month and year. If the two accounts had not been taken into consideration—as with most U.S. accounting methods at the time—the surplus of the plate and sheet mill in one month would have been 17,000 marks higher.

The general overhead account incorporates all shared indirect expenses, such as administration, interest on debt, sales, indirect labor, maintenance, utilities, taxes, insurance, and so on, associated with the overall operations of the company. Allocating joint costs accurately across different products or departments was (and is) difficult. As a solution, Thyssen & Co. subtracted every month a "percentage of the firm's interest and general overhead costs in installments and moreover in proportion to the number of workers of the various departments!"[41] *Die Firma* reserved the sole right to readjust the exact level of general overhead or extraordinary depreciation apportioned. Department chiefs waived their right of disclosure: "It was recognized that the firm, Thyssen & Co., has the sole decisive and ultimate right to ascertain net profits according to its accounting so that a recourse to the legal means or disclosure of the accounts is rendered completely impossible." Legal and accounting standards provided one way in which owners exerted their "ultimate authority." Every contract contained the phrase "according to our judgment" *(nach unserem Ermessen)* regarding accounting policies. (The root of judgment in German, "messen" means to measure.) *Die Firma* maintained full informational and decision-making control over key internal transfer prices, general overhead, interest, depreciation rates, and final bonus levels.

Thyssen & Co. deemed the number of workers employed the best approximation for allocating interest and general overhead expenses to the department. This measure assumes that labor was the main cost driver. For the nineteenth century, this was not necessarily a wrong assumption.[42] Thyssen & Co. did not use other potential proxies to allocate general overhead costs. For instance, sales revenues, the total amount of wage and salary payments, a percentage of total capital stock (land, buildings, equipment, machinery), a percentage of total interest payments incurred by this capital stock (as a measure of total firm debt generated by the costs of capital), or even floor space—all might have served as alternative proxies. This allocation formula underscores the fact that Thyssen & Co. could only estimate the exact amount of joint overhead expenses used by individual product departments. Thyssen & Co. could ascertain overall expenses, but with the information technology available at the time, assessing and allocating these costs more accurately was cost prohibitive.

For our purposes here, the use of this proxy shows how a degree of fungibility was built into Thyssen's accounts (as with all accounts) and how it shaped the ultimate measure of performance inside Thyssen & Co. Other proxies would lead to different results. Later such allocation formulas (as in cartels or the VSt) became the source of considerable controversy. Thyssen & Co. avoided potential infighting by holding central financial statistics close to their vests. A simple accounting figure such as general overhead disguises the potentially messy faultline between owners and managers—as well as among managers. This seemingly straightforward accounting convention, which creates a hard figure of numerical rationality, disguised wide discretion. Accounting is thus embedded in the organizational values, strategic objectives, and system of authority and accountability inside the business firm.[43]

The second conceptually interesting account, depreciation, was also considered a departmental expense on the debit side. Depreciation, too, is an estimate, but in a dual sense. First, like general overhead, the depreciation figure allocates an approximate portion of the overall depreciation of buildings, equipment, or machinery of the firm to the department. Similar problems of joint allocation are involved as with general overhead. The use of large round numbers also indicates that they were approximate. Second, depreciation is fundamentally an act of imagination, an accounting device to allocate the costs of using an asset (building, equipment, or machinery), which will physically deteriorate, become obsolete, or become inadequate for some reason or another over time. In effect, management tries to "take into account" a deteriorating asset and time itself. The simple figure implicitly relies on an estimate of a piece of equipment's service life and the rate it deteriorates. By dividing this expense evenly over time (straight-line method), depreciation accounting mimics the loss in service value of the asset in question. (It says nothing about the actual use of an asset, as a particular piece of machinery may be in operation years after it is written off; depreciation affects book value, not an asset's true market value.)[44] We do not know how Thyssen & Co. set final depreciation figures, except that *die Firma* had ultimate control over setting them. This practice started as early as 1884 inside Thyssen & Co.[45] Around 1908, the departments gained primary responsibility for taking stock of their own equipment and inventories. Unlike the general overhead account, depreciation bore some relationship to the assessed value of a department's fixed assets.[46]

Of what significance was general overhead, depreciation, and interest expenses? Depreciation in the department monthly reports represented yet another attempt by Thyssen, Killing, and Nölle to apportion capital expenses to departments as a standard operating procedure, rather than relying on a year-end adjustment at the enterprise level. By including interest in general overhead as well, they also tried to create some rudimentary sense of the cost of capital used by the departments. Nölle tried to provide a mirror-like rendition of the true costs of operating individual departments. His reasoning appears to be guided by two principles. First, it shifted accountability for the firm's performance downward in the hierarchy. It reinforced the organizational conception of the department as a semi-autonomous module— as "self-sufficient" as possible, responsible for manufacturing, marketing, and personnel questions, accountable for its full costs, including some capital expenses. Second, Thyssen and Nölle did not want to overstate income levels that would make the department (and firm) appear more profitable than it actually was. Since depreciation and interest are capital expenses, they depressed net profit levels, providing the firm with more substance, more solidity, and hidden reserves of strength.

The fact that Thyssen & Co. viewed monthly surpluses as "net profits" and that department directors received "royalties" *(Tantieme)*, not "bonuses" or "premiums" *(Gratifikationen, Prämien)* that master craftsmen received, indicates that Thyssen and Nölle thought that the figure represented a good assessment of the final profits made by the department. The overall results calculated in these monthly reports could be neatly dovetailed into the firm's financial statements at the end of the year. With minor adjustments, the cumulative figures provided by the monthly reports essentially reproduced the year-end gross revenues and net surplus of each department in the profit-and-loss sheet of the year-end financial statements, and official anniversary issues of yearly sales. They provided a bridge between a management information system and the financial accounts of the firm.

In effect, Thyssen & Co. viewed the departments as profit centers, not as production workshops. However, these departmental net profits would be construed more as gross operating margins or as a departmental surplus (sales minus expenses plus departmental operating expenses) than as net profits. Modern accounting methods would use the term "net profits" only if changes in inventories (and their costs), new investment, interest on debt, and an exact assessment of all general costs were taken into account. Only later did Thyssen & Co. integrate new plant investment and change in inventories into monthly department profits.[47] Most importantly, the departments would have to account more fully for the cost of capital to become true profit centers in modern terms. Thus, despite the terminology used by Thyssen & Co., the departments cannot quite be construed as profit centers, only as cost centers—even though Thyssen and Nölle conceived them as profit centers. Thyssen & Co. just tried to be more comprehensive than usual in its inclusion of expenses. Of the basic functions and expenses of any enterprise (manufacturing, marketing, personnel, and financing), the departments controlled three out of four. Still, judging from published literature, the early integration of depreciation and interest expenses into department operating costs represented a novel and innovative attempt to shift costs downwards.[48]

Thyssen & Co. managerial and financial accounting was more advanced than corresponding American practices. In the nineteenth century, many English and American firms (such as the American Tobacco Company, McCormick Harvester, or Standard Oil) did not depreciate even on a yearly basis for the enterprise as a whole. They preferred the older renewal or replacement accounting method stemming from the railroad experience that "delayed the recognition of capital consumption until expenditures were made for renewals."[49] Carnegie Steel did not recognize depreciation in any systematic way, and excluded overhead costs, preferring to focus on a ruthless drive to cut prime manufacturing costs.[50] The accounting system designed by Thyssen & Co. proved to be as sophisticated in the 1880s, for instance, as that of the Dow Chemical Company in the 1900s. Despite the recommendations of its auditors, Dow did not include regular depreciation charges in its monthly company-level financial reports until after 1909.[51] Thyssen & Co. (and other German firms such as Krupp) paid much more attention to overhead costs and depreciation than most American companies, including the pioneering Standard Oil. DuPont introduced the clean separation of new investment expenses and operating expenses only after 1900, which Thyssen & Co. forcefully introduced in the 1880s. In historical terms, only DuPont's pioneering use of return on investment (ROI) ratios after 1900, which integrated depreciation and assessed the efficient use of capital, proved to be more advanced than Thyssen & Co. But DuPont was the American pioneer and thus not representative of American firms. In addition, DuPont's mill superintendents concentrated exclusively on the physical manufacturing efficiency of their departments, particularly labor productivity and raw material consumption, not the mill's financial profitability—unlike Thyssen & Co.'s engineers who always had to have one eye on department commercial profits. At DuPont, the Executive Committee or central office handled such matters, typical for a unitary, functional structure.[52]

Ultimately, which country's companies were more modern is a less important question than how differently German and American firms tended to organize control. The Fall River Iron Works in Massachusetts provides an illuminating contrast. Founded by Richard Borden in 1821, this firm also produced hoop iron. By the 1880s the Iron Works remained but it had spun off a number of allied subsidiaries: the Annawan Mill (cotton textiles) and its machine shop; the Metacomet Mill (cotton textiles); a railway and steamboat line; and a Gas Manufactory. The companies represented independent capital assets for the Bordens and other stockholders, with no overarching central office.[53]

After being spun off as independent companies in 1880, each of the subsidiaries kept its own standard set of general account books, using a particularly American style of double-entry journal bookkeeping that Thyssen & Co. (Heinrich Dinkelbach) introduced to the Machine Company during World War I.[54] As at Thyssen & Co., each subsidiary kept ledgers, the key book of financial consolidation in which trial balances, accounts receivable and payable, and eventually the annual balance and profit-loss statement formed.[55]

All of the Fall River subsidiaries—independent companies, not internal departments—prepared quarterly trial balances from the led-ger accounts, but these did not include inventory accounts, overhead, or any capital accounts (depreciation). Unlike Thyssen & Co., the Fall River rolling mills made no attempt to factor in returns, freight costs, inventories, overhead, or capital accounts such as depreciation and interest. Only after the central office generated gross profit calculations did they include overhead (repairs, taxes, insurance, team labor, outdoor labor, interest, stock shrinkage) in their annual profit-loss statement. These quarterly trial balances acted as the closest equivalent to Thyssen & Co.'s monthly departmental reports, but these trial balances did not function as a means of assessing profitability, but monitoring whether accounts properly balanced. Other firms such as the Lowell Machine Shop, the Stanley Manufacturing Company, and the Portland Company had similar account structures. None took into account depreciation.[56]

Fall River's accounting system mirrored the typical American enterprise before World War I: Chandlerian ideal-type, unitary and functionally organized. The structure of the firm placed a greater emphasis on tracking functional activities, especially manufacturing. The Fall River firms kept detailed production records and created their own monthly, even weekly, statements about their transactions. Functionally separate accounts were kept in both textile mills (cloth books, dept. books, weekly statements, cloth stock, cloth produced, waste books, cotton mixing accounts, sales accounts, and labor accounts). These accounts were an excellent means of tracking department labor and production costs, but not in relation to revenue, sales, or profits. They provided monitoring, but were less useful for decision-making, especially about finances. Fall River (and other American firms) were focused on activity and workshop accounting.

Significantly, none of the activity accounting (manufacturing, sales, personnel, and financial information) was combined below the level of central office or owner-manager. The central office sewed these figures together into relationships or ratios. For instance, the Fall River Iron Works central office created numerical ratios for the different functional activities, i.e., sales expense per keg of nails. They calculated the profit margins for the rolling mills as "net average per keg of sales of nails," and came up with a figure representing the "profit per keg" of nails. They also calculated profits per ton of iron or rails as the average revenue minus the average cost of a ton of the respective product, so that "profits" really referred to profit margins.[57] This accounting and information structure tended to grant the power of decision-making to central management, who could formulate such relationships. Since information conveys power, *general management* had a lock on its ability to process this information, coordinate functional activities, and form strategy.

As in other U.S. companies, the Fall River Iron Works (which included a puddling flat, hoop iron, and wire mill), as well as the Annawan and Metacomet textile mills, paid minute attention to workshop production costs, and were biased toward assessing the effectiveness of manufacturing—a particular conception of enterprise control. In trial balances, they calculated quarterly profits simply by taking "Account receipts for Quarter" minus expenditures to equal "Actual Gain by Manufacturing." Unlike Thyssen & Co.'s commercially oriented "net profits," they termed these profit margins as "gain by manufacturing."[58] Shops and "shop accounting," which in American parlance could refer to workshops, mills, even whole factories, treated the firm as a shop, or the factory as a "production function." The relatively high labor costs in the United States certainly drove this obvious desire to minimize labor costs, but the functional activity-based approach to administration fostered an atmosphere of tight, obsessive, Tayloristic cost controls.

Such measurements caused particular systemic biases within the organization. For instance, Carnegie emphasized the reduction of prime costs for his rails. It meant that lower average unit costs became the main criteria of performance, appropriate to a strategy of scale, but this measurement could come at the expense of product quality in the name of driving prices lower. To counteract this potential consequence, Carnegie, like Thyssen, regularly reminded his plant managers about customers' expectations and quality requirements so they would not cut corners. Thyssen & Co.'s accounting *system,* not just entrepreneurial exhortation, built in a degree of sales and profit accountability, thereby checking a potential tendency to cut corners. Unlike Carnegie, who always wanted to know the costs, Thyssen always wanted to know the profits.[59]

As American firms were generally single-activity firms with one or two productive activities (say Carnegie and rails), a focus on driving down production costs translated relatively directly into company-wide

profits. American firms could focus more intently on cost accounting and workshop control measures, because fewer financial transactions occurred within the scope of the enterprise as a result of standardized production.[60] Emphasizing critical accounting figures such as
cost per unit, operating ratios, or cost per labor hour "assumed a life
of its own by driving the search for labor-saving efficiencies, say from
improved machinery." Before 1900, American accounting literature
concentrated on designing systems to track prime costs (direct labor
and materials).

However, the limits of this approach became manifest as American
firms moved from single-activity to multi-activity, so that single measures of manufacturing efficiency did not translate directly into company-wide profit. Relative to German firms, U.S. firms lacked the accounting techniques to manage the coordination of various product
lines and of "internal resource flows from raw material to final customer," let alone assess the costs of administration (overhead), depreciation, and capital (debt). After 1900, American management literature shifted to issues of overhead and the relationship between cost
accounting and financial accounting. Eventually, U.S. managerial accounting developed new techniques (such as budgeting and return-
on-investment ratios) to dovetail activity accounting into company-
wide financial systems. Kocka points out that a full-scale discussion in
published literature about corporate accounting and management began in the U.S. about a decade later than in Germany.[61]

German firms involved in steel, finishing, machine engineering,
and chemicals developed more quickly than did American firms into
multi-activity firms through product diversity and vertical integration.
By 1887, GHH and Krupp were active in more than ten different
diversified fields. In 1887, two-thirds of large German steelmakers and
manufacturers were already diversified. In 1907, over one-half of German large enterprises were either fully or strongly diversified, while in
1909 under one-fifth of U.S. large enterprises had the same degree of
diversification.[62] This meant that Germans confronted the problems of
accounting and coordinating the flow of information and materials in
diversified or vertically integrated firms *before* Americans.

In the 1920s, a number of German accounting analysts argued that
Americans tended to have an advantage in developing methods of
factory cost accounting (particularly standard rates, efficiency cost

accounting, and budgetary analysis). U.S. firms tended to excel in workshop and activity accounting. According to them, Germans had an advantage in the area of general costs, depreciation, and internal transfer prices, that is, in areas of managerial administration.[63] Thyssen & Co.'s managerial reporting confirms their argument. Such methods might signify that Germany had more of a managerial revolution than the alleged home of the managerial revolution, the United States.

It simply became easier in the United States to imagine workshops, departments, even whole firms as "production functions." Workshops did not have accounts, but were accounted *for* by a supervisory office, separating supervision or general management from work activity. American-style Taylorism with its obsession for workshop minutiae and efficiency grew out of the combination of these characteristics. If one follows this relationship between accounting measures and the conception of control, then the American conception of the firm was much more manufacturing-oriented, while Germans were much more managerial—a counterintuitive twist on stereotypical notions about German business.

Not surprisingly, as German industrialists visited America around the turn of the century, German companies adopted more of the cost accounting or activity measures pioneered by the Americans. Indeed, we might then speak of the Americanization of German cost-accounting methods. The turn-of-the-century recession brought a new emphasis on workshop techniques, manufacturing costing, and labor control.[64] But as American firms grew into multi-activity firms, they had to develop more sophisticated managerial accounting that focused on problems of overhead, internal transfer prices, depreciation, relatively well-developed areas of German managerial accounting. In this respect, we might speak of an American convergence to the German model.

The so-called Americanization of German cost accounting found expression in Thyssen & Co.'s most important cost-accounting innovation. In 1904, Thyssen & Co. established a central production-cost office *(Kalkulations-Büro)*. Up to this point, the departments independently maintained their own cost accounting. This central cost-accounting office tightened controls by standardizing costing procedures across the four rolling-mill departments. Above all, the central office measured conversion costs (i.e., the costs of transforming raw materials into a finished product defined as direct labor plus factory overhead) for each individual product line in each department in a standard, consistent, and comparative fashion.[65] Unlike the monthly reports, these accounts did not estimate profitability, but assessed manufacturing efficiency, production costs, and relative input costs.

(Richard Woldt, a contemporary organizational theorist, stressed that in order to introduce the correct method of calculation, the accountant had to shed light on the best possible organizational form for the firm by describing its present processes and operations. To include costs properly and show where costs emerged in manufacturing operations, the accountant had to imagine and reimagine the firm.[66])

These standardized cost-accounting worksheets express a shift of managerial attention to manufacturing costs after the turn of the century and had major organizational implications. In order to construct the detailed worksheets, the departments and the cost-accounting office had to track more precisely a host of detailed expenses in a standard fashion. Not only did this allow a more complete monitoring of the cost performance of product lines and workshops, but it also took a certain amount of information (and power) away from the shop floor and department chiefs. The standardization of cost accounting left less leeway for the workshop supervisors to juggle costs. The consistent representation of all manufacturing costs also immediately pointed senior-level managerial attention to any deviations in individual product expenses. Finally, the formatting of the cost sheets set clear, rigid cost categories that lower-level managers had to "account for" consistently, thereby creating new organizational routines, shifting information patterns, and altering power relations inside the firm.

The central cost-accounting office created a yearbook for the period 1904–1918 with printed column headings for each of the individual product lines (workshops or rolling-mill trains). It calculated all of the expense items in absolute monetary terms along with a derivative second figure, the cost per unit of net product (per metric ton). These cost worksheets show the variety of direct and indirect costs that Thyssen & Co. could track.

I have chosen two examples from roughly 50 different product lines, boiler plates (Table 4.2) and patent-lapwelded boiler tubes (Table 4.3), which were two important Thyssen & Co. products, to show how the worksheets could tell different stories. These cost worksheets make possible a comparison of conversion costs across the whole enterprise for all types of expenses.

In the original, managers of the cost-accounting office highlighted in red in each column the two most important derived figures: the cost per unit of net product of various costs and conversion costs. For instance, in 1904 it cost the boiler plate plant about 7.70 marks worth of coal to produce 1000 kilograms of boiler plates, but about 5.16 marks by 1913, a cost reduction of one third. The cost of input materials (blooms or slabs), however, fluctuated greatly, reflecting broader economic cycles. Bloom or slab prices rose from 80 m/ton in 1904 to 98 m/ton in 1907 before falling back roughly to its original levels by the war. By 1916, one could clearly see the inflationary effects of the war. Before the war, the cost of labor stayed roughly the same, between 10 and 11 marks per ton of product except in 1904 (12.23 marks) and 1912 (8.80 marks). Thus, the price of inputs most explained fluctuations in product costs of boiler plates.

The boiler-tube plant tells a different story. The fluctuations in input prices (i.e., strip steel in the last column) also reflect the macroeconomic cycle, but coal costs per ton of boiler tubes dropped dramatically after 1907, nearly two thirds. If one takes 1904 as the base point, coal costs dropped by nearly one half. In addition, labor costs per ton produced dropped dramatically from about 50.41 marks in 1904 to just 24.67 marks in 1914, another drop of 50 percent. These dramatic cost reductions owed much to the American-style manufacturing designs and Siemens-Martin steel introduced by Trapp. Reflecting the improvements in gas supply, the cost of gas also dropped dramatically, but as in both the boiler-plate and boiler-tube plants, the cost of steam heating rose.

In contrast to the boiler-plate plant, the story told by the boiler-tube plant testifies to the impact of new manufacturing efficiencies. Unlike the boiler-plate plant, where fluctuations in bloom prices provided the best indicator of changes in final product costs, product costs in the boiler-tube mill dropped from roughly 250 m/ton to 207 m/ton (a 17% cost reduction) in spite of wide fluctuations in the price of strip steel. The standard categories and formats of the worksheet allowed one to tell different stories about all the product lines in the factory.

The cost-accounting office designed the worksheets to calculate av-

Table 4.2 Cost accounting for boiler plates (2-meter mill)—cost per unit of net product per ton (1000 kg)

Year	Input (kg.)	Net production (kg.)	Net (%)	Block price	Coal	Input	Wages	Storage material	Replacement parts	Electricity	Gas	Water/steam
1904	12,206,059	8,371,975	68.6	79.65	7.70	116.14	12.23	0.92	2.60	0.39	0.40	0.10
1905	16,125,039	10,733,495	66.6	79.56	6.90	119.55	10.56	0.84	2.90	0.39	0.38	0.16
1906	17,899,298	12,041,857	67.3	87.87	6.76	130.62	10.80	0.97	3.88	0.74	0.38	0.19
1907	20,959,593	13,767,221	65.7	98.01	8.27	149.20	10.95	0.97	2.54	0.82	0.31	0.25
1908	17,821,665	12,021,375	67.4	83.90	7.65	124.38	10.16	0.76	1.43	1.09	0.21	0.22
1909	15,794,096	10,574,751	67.0	75.89	6.61	113.30	10.43	0.76	1.33	1.06	0.14	0.22
1910	25,384,941	16,432,218	64.8	80.74	6.26	124.69	10.33	0.63	1.45	1.02	0.12	0.20
1911	24,620,940	16,147,687	65.6	83.75	6.38	127.67	10.10	0.72	1.62	0.71	0.11	0.21
1912	27,467,671	18,240,698	66.4	86.42	3.53	130.12	8.80	0.67	1.17	0.34	0.05	2.63
1913	15,172,566	10,002,360	65.9	87.08	5.16	132.12	10.65	0.74	1.67	0.36	0.06	3.63
1914	13,078,730	8,680,833	66.4	79.71	5.10	120.10	10.61	0.90	1.69	0.39	0.08	3.71
1915	8,245,700	5,522,424	67.0	90.22	4.78	134.71	10.42	1.35	1.34	0.41	0.12	5.81
1916	10,821,076	7,191,560	66.5	119.85	4.64	180.34	10.45	1.80	1.50	0.44	0.10	6.78
1917	10,619,203	7,216,360	68.0	185.54	5.81	273.04	14.09	2.49	3.44	0.61	0.13	13.17
1918	3,909,119	2,683,385	68.6	202.22	8.62	294.59	19.96	4.66	5.01	1.10	0.27	17.88

Year	Alteration funds	Operating overhead	General overhead	Amortization of rolling mills	Depreciation	Credit (Gutschrift)	Production costs (Selbstkosten in original)	Prime cost (calc.)	Product costs (calc.)	Conversion costs (original)	Remarks
1904	1.00	2.10	2.09	1.00	1.74	27.16	121.25	136.07	138.17	32.27	
1905		2.44	1.89	1.00	1.99	28.01	120.99	137.01	139.45	29.45	
1906		2.50	2.31	0.55	2.38	27.69	134.39	148.18	150.68	31.46	
1907		3.91	2.32	0.60	4.04	32.04	151.14	168.42	172.33	34.98	
1908		3.70	1.76	0.60	3.63	26.47	129.12	142.19	145.89	31.21	
1909		2.72	1.28	0.40	3.27	26.48	115.04	130.34	133.06	28.22	
1910		2.53	1.97	0.60	2.73	30.74	121.79	141.28	143.81	27.84	
1911		2.61	1.72	0.60	2.66	29.35	125.76	144.15	146.76	27.44	
1912		4.75	1.90	0.50	1.82	28.12	128.16	142.45	147.20	26.16	
1913		5.25	1.97	0.40	2.15	28.92	135.24	147.93	153.18	32.04	
1914		5.39	2.23	0.50	1.33	25.08	126.95	135.81	141.20	31.93	
1915		7.41	2.46	0.50	1.57	26.78	144.1	149.91	157.32	36.17	
1916		8.74	2.45	0.60	1.22	33.27	185.79	195.43	204.17	38.72	
1917		13.01	2.58	0.60	1.30	36.23	294.04	292.94	305.95	57.23	
1918		19.82	3.14	1.00	1.62	35.98	341.69	323.17	342.99	83.08	

Table 4.3 Cost accounting for patent lapwelded boiler tubes—cost per unit of net product per ton (1000 kg)

Year	Input (kg.)	Net production (kg.)	Net (%)	Coal	Input	Wages	Storage material	Replacement parts	Electricity	Gas	Water
1904	12,611,228	9,594,358	76.1	24.86	155.46	50.41	2.15	12.90	1.07	1.84	0.47
1905	16,881,787	12,861,906	76.2	24.79	152.94	41.94	2.15	9.21	1.07	1.78	0.47
1906	20,104,907	15,740,923	78.3	21.59	166.99	36.22	1.93	7.05	1.01	1.63	0.41
1907	15,500,625	12,022,257	77.6	30.57	183.11	40.81	2.01	6.06	0.99	1.73	0.64
1908	6,894,317	5,164,418	74.9	17.23	159.10	43.15	1.70	6.97	2.35	0.77	2.87
1909	7,091,605	5,489,804	77.4	13.08	145.99	37.33	1.30	5.98	2.58	0.53	0.52
1910	7,683,855	6,064,008	78.9	12.66	148.37	32.98	1.31	4.02	1.21	0.45	0.50
1911	7,893,113	6,262,222	79.3	11.31	145.10	28.41	0.94	3.76	1.05	0.41	0.45
1912	6,330,336	5,065,947	80.0	11.86	155.80	28.00	0.83	4.23	2.61	0.36	0.53
1913	6,544,882	5,275,231	80.6	11.47	152.11	24.67	0.71	4.86	2.11	0.46	0.45
1914	5,306,911	4,262,224	80.3	11.74	129.61	24.99	0.68	3.07	2.19	0.47	0.47
1915	1,582,460	1,352,830	85.5	14.80	155.35	33.02	1.59	3.53	5.06	0.85	0.85
1916	3,351,200	2,612,254	77.9	18.20	234.67	38.60	2.14	7.25	5.90	0.72	0.47
1917	2,059,399	1,597,078	77.5	24.94	352.60	57.60	3.66	16.12	5.22	1.71	0.28

Year	Steam	Alteration funds	Operating overhead	General overhead	Depreciation	Credit (Gutschrift)	Production costs (*Selbstkosten* in original)	Prime costs (calc.)	Product costs (calc.)	Conversion costs (original)	Price of strip steel
1904		0.50	5.39	6.99	4.33	15.99	250.38	230.73	236.12	110.91	118.27
1905			5.76	7.15	4.98	13.35	238.89	219.67	225.43	99.30	116.54
1906			7.35	7.09	4.35	11.69	243.93	224.80	232.15	88.63	131.41
1907			6.61	7.36	4.50	15.77	268.92	254.49	261.10	101.28	142.47
1908	9.86		13.39	9.74	4.36	18.37	253.12	219.48	232.87	112.39	119.18
1909	7.09		10.89	7.00	4.62	13.32	223.59	196.40	207.29	90.92	113.01
1910	6.13		8.99	7.71	5.04	12.56	216.81	194.01	203.00	81.00	117.1
1911	5.28		6.88	6.53	3.24	11.81	207.55	184.82	191.70	68.26	115.1
1912	5.74		7.46	6.52	3.34	12.37	214.91	195.66	203.12	71.48	124.65
1913	4.86		6.89	6.30	3.22	11.00	207.11	188.25	195.14	66.00	122.6
1914	6.42		7.72	6.45	1.96	10.38	185.40	166.34	174.06	66.16	104.13
1915	6.26		10.69	6.90	0.42	10.89	228.43	203.17	213.86	83.97	132.78
1916	4.89		11.07	6.42	0.00	17.90	312.43	291.47	302.54	95.66	182.92
1917	12.17		22.71	8.27	0.00	23.63	481.65	435.14	457.85	152.68	273.44

erage *product costs (Selbstkosten),* but especially *conversion costs (Umwand-lungskosten).* The latter was highlighted in red, and stood alone in the last column of each page for each product line. The eye gravitated naturally to this line of figures. Conversion costs attempt to measure the costs, or changes in relative efficiency, of the manufacturing process itself. Here conversion costs equal the cost of coal, plus the sum of columns for wages through and including depreciation. This calculation method is consistent across all product lines. Unlike product costs, they do not include the cost of input materials. In effect, the accounts isolate the process of transforming inputs, deleting the effect of varying input prices on final product costs. For instance, the manufacturing efficiency of the boiler plate, two-meter mill train improved by 15% between 1904 and 1911, before falling back to its original levels by the outbreak of the war. By contrast, the introduction of American-style continuous process improvements in the boiler-tube mill dropped conversion costs from 111 m/ton to 66 m/ton, roughly a 40% improvement in manufacturing efficiency.

Some ambiguity surrounds production cost figures because it is not clear if the phrase *"Selbstkosten"* refers to prime costs or average product costs. (It remains unclear how Thyssen calculated their production-cost figures in the original.) Production costs tend to mean a factory-oriented cost calculation, which generally subtracts general company expenses; they are considered to be a rough break-even point. Prime costs equal those expenses directly traced to the finished product, i.e., direct materials and direct labor. Carnegie, for instance, emphasized reducing prime costs. I calculated prime costs of Thyssen & Co. by adding together the cost of coal, inputs, and wages. While prime costs for the boiler-plate plant showed a fluctuating, if not a rising, tendency based on the price of inputs, by 1914 the boiler-tube plant showed a 30% drop in its prime costs. Calculating prime costs in this manner (which should approximate the production costs given in the original), one arrives at a figure consistently higher than the production costs of boiler plates, but consistently below the production costs of boiler tubes. Another potential calculation of production costs is product costs, i.e., the costs of the product as if the product went straight into inventory unsold; this figure includes direct materials, direct labor, and factory overhead. This calculation also emphasizes a factory-based outlook, where all costs derive from the shopfloor. But, however calculated, all sets of figures tell the same story. Production costs in the boiler-plate mill depended mostly on input prices, but for lapwelded boiler tubes on improvements in manufacturing efficiency. These costs would also imply two different sorts of managerial attention—one more interested in controlling price fluctuations (purchasing), the other more on continuing to improve (manufacturing) efficiency.

Despite the clear shift of attention to manufacturing efficiency by central management, the cost-accounting worksheet still attests to the fundamental commercial outlook pervading Thyssen & Co. Although conversion costs as the main figure tacitly highlights the importance of manufacturing efficiency, the worksheet took into account all direct and indirect costs per product, including depreciation, factory and general overhead, and even interest payments for equipment. Thyssen & Co. distinguished factory and general overhead. It is not known how these were apportioned across products, but most likely they bore some relation to the number of workers or wages, as per standard practice. Like the monthly department reports, Thyssen & Co. cost-accounting practices took into consideration the total proportional costs of transforming product, not just the physical or technical efficiency of the process. The yearbooks represent an accounting attempt to link the technical, manufacturing process with the overall commercial, even financial, expenses arising from the technical operations of individual product lines and to embed those costs into product costs.

The accounting historians, H. Thomas Johnson and Robert S. Kaplan have shown that the 19th century accounting theorist, Alexander Hamilton Church, also wanted to go beyond the physical conversion-cost-accounting methods advocated by Frederick Taylor. Church wanted to link more accurately the profitability of the firm as a whole to the efficiency of making and cost of individual products. The worksheets seem to put Thyssen & Co. (and Krupp) in this alternative tradition.[67]

There are problems with Thyssen & Co.'s methodology. The more expenses one includes in the product costs, the messier and less comparable the measurement of manufacturing efficiency becomes. Such accounting methods also do not seem to represent the steel industry as a whole. We do know that when Thyssen merged into the VSt, only Thyssen included both commercial and technical costs in its average product prices.

Including both types of costs highlights another significant aspect of Thyssen corporate culture. Thyssen remained highly sensitive to the costs of capital (depreciation, interest, debt) because he had to finance all expansion himself. The inclusion of depreciation and overhead meant that Thyssen measured his costs higher than he might have otherwise done, setting the breakeven point for profit higher. Such cost calculations forced his department managers to become even more efficient on the technical side to drive costs lower, especially if market prices dropped to the level of average product cost. This method of cost accounting ultimately depressed Thyssen & Co.'s potential profit margins and profitability. But Thyssen seemed to place greater weight on having a solid enterprise than on higher profitability (defined as a relative return on assets or investment or revenues). As he never had to answer to outside shareholders, short-run profitability appeared to be less important to him than keeping track of investment costs and long-run viability.

All in all, the advent of a central accounting office signified a fundamental shift in the strategic and organizational principles governing Thyssen & Co. at the turn of the century.[68] At Thyssen & Co., a new type of language appeared in top executive's contracts. The up-and-coming Ernst Becker, who replaced August Wilke in 1907 as director of the rolling mills, received a new contract that stressed, for the first time:

> On your side, you commit yourself to offer everything just as before in order to construct the [strip steel] department in a rational and profitable manner, to allow the greatest thrift to prevail, to discern and represent the interests of the business in general, in all ways, and in the most conscientious manner, to always be willing to comply *(enstprechen)* with the directives of the firm or the leading director of the factory [August Wilke], and to precede in the exercise of your occupation as a good example for your subordinates.[69]

Thyssen clearly emphasizes the importance of following directives of superiors, but uses the term comply, which can certainly mean to follow superiors' instructions, but falls short of associated meanings: to correspond, fulfill, carry out, or to live up to expectations. Becker's contract still emphasized the importance of managing the strip steel department with the greatest attention to thrift or savings, but introduces the dual goals of "rationally and profitably" managing the rolling mills. Becker had to combine manufacturing rationalization and commercial profitability. In informational terms, the monthly reports highlighted sales and surpluses and the cost accounting worksheets highlighted manufacturing efficiencies. In verbal terms, the phrasing "rationally and profitably" reproduces the dual orientation required of Thyssen executives.

Combined with the new stress on manufacturing efficiencies and measuring techniques, the use of the term "rational" marks a turning point toward a more complex notion of performance and profit based on efficient techniques or measures. Saving *(Sparsamkeit)* is a classic merchant virtue, which emphasizes the reduction of expenditures; if one spends less money, profits will increase; if one spends more money, profits will decrease. Rational efficiency, however, is a relative value (profits/per unit cost or output/input), a relationship, rather than the absolute value implied by saving or thrift, leaving aside its moral and behavioral overtones. One could actually spend more and profits might increase because of the greater efficiency or productivity of a new (manufacturing) process. The turn of the century ushered in a new language that stressed rationalized manufacturing or productivist efficiency, the age of the engineer, as the dominant mode of running large-scale industrial operations. The turn of the century really began the German rationalization movement that the war interrupted, and that became famous in the 1920s.[70] Indeed, German firms began incorporating more American-style production methods and American-style cost-accounting techniques into their already relatively sophisticated managerial enterprises.

The ability of Thyssen & Co. to delegate wide-ranging, "self-sufficient" powers to departments, decentralizing decision-making in the firm, owed much to Thyssen & Co.'s ability to standardize information flows into the central office, centralizing the supervision of the firm. The dialectically related process of greater delegation combined with greater formal control drove organizational change within Thyssen & Co., and later, the Thyssen-Konzern and the VSt. The design of a control or surveillance system is as important as acquiring manufacturing equipment, using new technologies, arranging shopfloor activities, or erecting factory buildings in creating a coherent firm. Increasingly complex informational demands also created a need for more middle managers and larger headquarters.

Thyssen & Co. organized control differently than did U.S. firms. If

Thyssen & Co. had been organized along the Chandlerian unitary-functional model, then the central office would have handled the salaries of all engineering and commercial employees. A central wage office would have controlled and disbursed workers' wages. Sales and shipping offices would have belonged to the central administration instead being associated with a particular product department. Finally, department chiefs would have been expressly responsible for manufacturing only (with a fierce attention to labor control and costs), not manufacturing and marketing as well. Its accounting and information system would have correspondingly tracked expenses functionally; the central office would have had general management roles rather than supervisory and monitoring roles. Thyssen & Co. did establish a central office for collecting and evaluating product or conversion costs, but without the centralization implied by a Tayloristic planning department.[71]

The introduction of management circulars and Nölle's accounting reports in the early 1880s represented a self-reflexive attempt by Thyssen & Co. management to organize the firm using formal management procedures. They formed the accounting and information framework—the conceptual girders and scaffolding—of the firm's operations forward into the twentieth century. With the growing internalization of a number of conventions and codes, firms (not just Thyssen & Co.) increasingly made decisions based on those operating procedures. The arbitrariness inherent in personal ownership became more limited—even in a family enterprise.

If any symbolic point can be used to mark this transition to an abstract managerial enterprise, then August Thyssen's request at the end of 1884 to discontinue the patriarchal custom of congratulating the owners for another successful year might act as a good marker. August Thyssen unceremoniously brought an end to this preindustrial practice because of the time needed to reply properly to all of the greetings. Thyssen stated that he would just "assume that benevolent feelings from all sides were present."[72] The cessation of this custom, along with the addition of circulars and monthly departmental reports effectively marked the end of the personal enterprise. By the 1880s, Thyssen & Co. was a modern managerial enterprise

Ironically, given Siemens' reputation for bureaucracy, Thyssen & Co. had a more coherent system of controls than Siemens & Halske. In somewhat of a contradiction to his portrayal of Siemens as fetishizing bureaucracy, Kocka points out that Siemens evinced a "type of conceptionless bureaucracy."[73] Even in the 1880s, Siemens simply "lacked" a "functioning reporting system" with regular controls and clear standards. Siemens developed nearly autonomous departments complete with "separatist commanders." Unlike Thyssen & Co. circulars, written memos lacked a binding generality and focused on immediate, single events. Indeed, by the turn of the century, Wilhelm von Siemens lamented the lack of central coordination among the directors of the departments. In 1898, Siemens noted: "our company consists in a certain sense of a series of factories and enterprises, which for the most part could also exist in entirely independent forms."[74] Kocka's own evidence calls into question the extent of Siemens' bureaucratization. In this respect, Thyssen & Co. had more authoritative central control than Siemens & Halske because it bound its "self-sufficient" departments or subsidiaries together with a goal of overall profitability. Thyssen could control this degree of delegation through centralized and coherent accounting, monitoring, and reporting, i.e., by using modern managerial methods, not just an authoritative personality.

The sophistication of Thyssen & Co.'s administrative techniques was on par with or more advanced than American developments. Along with other German firms, Thyssen & Co. appears to have been more advanced in terms of managerial accounting techniques (issues of overhead, internal transfer prices, or depreciation), while Americans excelled in workshop or cost accounting methods. After the turn of the century, Thyssen & Co. and other German firms turned greater attention to manufacturing efficiencies and cost accounting.[75] In this respect—only—can we speak of an Americanization process. Thyssen & Co. incorporated such American innovations into an already sophisticated managerial system.

Finally, the accounting and reporting system reconceptualized the enterprise. New measures brought different processes, costs, and stories to the attention of central management. New cost-accounting methods made transparent the sources of manufacturing costs, just as electric lights lit up the dark recesses of the old brick halls. Thus these measures provide an indication of the conception of control operating within the firm—the way the firm governed itself.

At Thyssen & Co., Thyssen's virtues as a Victorian-age merchant-businessman underlay the values and operations of the firm. A fundamental commercial orientation guided the internal policies of the firm throughout his life. Thyssen defined performance, the "results," as commercial success, customer satisfaction, company reputation, and departmental profitability, not engineering expertise, high production levels, or even manufacturing efficiency. The monthly departmental reports institutionalized this outlook by defining performance as sales and surpluses. By 1900, however, Thyssen & Co. turned a greater attention to manufacturing efficiencies, signified by a stronger emphasis on input efficiency and cost conversion figures. Without neglecting the first measure of managerial performance, but by adding another criteria or measure, Thyssen & Co. placed greater emphasis on workshops' ability to produce a good at a competitive cost with a lower proportional share of inputs. Productivist efficiency became the dominant manner of managing large-scale industrial operations. This emphasis lasted until well into the 1930s, if not longer. The power to supply ideas and initiative moved to engineers, even about organizational questions.

This statement does not imply that engineers or manufacturing efficiency were not important inside Thyssen & Co. before this time. Any company must simultaneously combine sales, production, finance, and personnel management into some coherent whole, but the dominant types of management controls imply the dominant strategy of the firm. At heart was the redefinition of performance and control based on rationalized efficiency, not sales, savings, or thrift. Emergence of new accounting practices to create new types of knowledge also signified a shift in the type of business culture inside Thyssen & Co.[76] Still, Thyssen & Co. classified as many commercial and financial expenses as possible (and apparently more than was usual) as part of production costs and conversion costs.

This turn-of-the-century shift in conceptual framework implicitly viewed a business as an organizational efficiency machine that makes things, not as entrepreneurial property that sells things. (In both cases, the ultimate goal is still to earn profits.) In the 1870s and 1880s, merchant/entrepreneurial performance was implicitly defined as the ability to cut costs, be thrifty and frugal, and by implication, raise profits; profitability was defined absolutely as savings. These savings and profits added value to the business as the property of the entrepreneur. Creating manufacturing efficiencies—rationalizing—became the dominant strategy of adding value to the enterprise. The company redefined performance and control as manufacturing efficiency, not sales, savings, or thrift. As long as Thyssen was alive, however, this first sense continually vied with the second.

Essentially, Thyssen & Co. moved from a merchant-business model of enterprise to an engineering-manufacturing model of enterprise. The study of Thyssen & Co.'s organizational practices confirms Kocka's general conclusions about German changes in corporate management. While U.S. firms concentrated on workshop issues, German firms tended to concentrate on the collection of offices, interoffice procedures and rules, accounting fundamentals, and a more comprehensive view of *Organisation.* In the 1880s, organizational questions about how to bind a series of production units together to form a coherent business preoccupied Thyssen & Co. management. But by the turn of the century, German companies focused more intently on manufacturing innovations. Thyssen & Co. management concentrated more heavily on cost-accounting methods within its workshops.[77]

It extended this organizational system to activities such as machine engineering and water and gas supply, which were largely unrelated to manufacturing in the rolling mills. This expansion tested Thyssen & Co.'s organizational culture to its limits. The supple combination of extensive delegation and a sophisticated surveillance system provided the organizational nerve system holding together these diverse activities, augmenting Thyssen & Co.'s corporate coherence. This corporate culture with its informational sinews contributed to the sustained technological innovation and financial profitability of Thyssen & Co. over the long term. This was the "heart of the enterprise" as Carl Härle, the commercial director of the Thyssen Machine Company, once said.[78]

CHAPTER 5

Sustaining Innovation

> Until quite recently it was a common opinion often voiced to us
> that we would never succeed in turning the Thyssen & Co.
> Machine Company into a flourishing enterprise.
> Karl Härle, March 22, 1913

The success of the Thyssen & Co. steel and rolling mills, the first four departments, rested on the development of economies of scale and scope. But the history of the Thyssen & Co. machine-engineering and gas-and-waterworks departments owed more to science-based capabilities and sheer entrepreneurial opportunism. The machine-engineering department occupied a special place in the history of the Thyssen-Konzern. In 1911, Thyssen & Co. spawned the Thyssen & Co. Machine Company AG *(Maschinenfabrik Thyssen & Co. AG)* with the express purpose to "conquer the domestic and world market."[1] Under Hans Richter, the machine department commercialized the high-horsepower gas engine, arguably the most important new invention for the German steel industry of the early twentieth century. It transformed the energy economies of German steelworks, literally electrifying entire firms. German steel firms led the world in the development of regeneration economies, that is, the recycling of waste-gas energy from coking and blast furnace operations to drive powerful engines and turbines. These gas engines subsequently generated the electricity for lighting and driving mill trains, blew compressed air into blast furnaces and steel converters to improve the quality of the steel, and even supplied electricity to regional electrical companies. Thyssen & Co. helped pioneer the German variant of rationalization built on "economies of energy," a distinctive form of technological as well as corporate development.[2]

The Thyssen & Co. Machine Company epitomized German companies' integration of R&D facilities into their business organizations, along with the more famous examples of the chemicals and electro-technical industries.[3] This integration, and close ties to academic research institutions, helped differentiate German business culture from the American, British, French, and Japanese in degree, if not in kind.

The combination of theoretical science, applied research, and commercialization is neatly combined in the German term, *Verwissenschaftlichung*, the "scientific professionalization" of production. At its foundation lay a coherent university and vocational schooling system, which set high standards built on the mastery of theoretical knowledge. This technical education system trained a significant number of students. In the first decade of the twentieth century, for instance, Germany trained about 30,000 engineers compared to 21,000 in the United States, roughly twice as many relative to total population. There were ten times more engineering students in Germany than in England or Wales.[4] In addition, professional societies such as the Association of German Engineers, the Association of German Iron and Steelmakers, and the Association of German Machine Engineering Firms anchored and facilitated the exchange of information about new developments between firms in their respective industries. Each of these societies had its own magazines. For the steel industry, journals such as *Stahl und Eisen* and *Gemeinfassliche Darstellung des Eisenhüttenwesens* [Common Overview on the Nature of Steelmaking] outlined state-of-the-art equipment and practices. German steel firms drew upon a deep well of trained people and knowledge in these social institutions and professional associations.

Despite the institutional reservoir of people and know-how, business firms (the organizational sites of manufacturing and commerce) still needed to transform technical knowledge into profitable activity. One historian of technology, Joachim Radkau, emphasized that everyday practical experience with a new technology or process constituted an important part of technological progress. Despite theoretical training, much of the successes of industrial firms still rested upon skilled, experienced line managers who made the ideas work through trial-and-error methods; there was still no substitute for practical experience in learning the science. Many processes such as the chemical transformation in blast furnaces or the seamless tube process remained theoretical mysteries at this time.[5] The business firm had to overcome everyday practical challenges, integrate these learning experiences, and then manage to achieve profits using this knowledge and experience—with no guarantee of success. Thyssen & Co.'s machine-engineering department was both embedded in Germany's "national innovation system" and helped to reinforce it.[6]

The department generated positive feedback loops between German technical education and practical business experience that helped it sustain innovation over the long term. The machine department's capabilities then spilled over to propel the fast growth of auxiliary departments like the gas and water works. While the rolling mills supplied critical products for urban infrastructure, the gas and water works became an integral part of the region's infrastructure. Both departments linked Thyssen & Co. to the infrastructure of the Ruhr, blurring the boundary between firm and region, testing the limits of what it meant to be one corporation.

Finally, Thyssen & Co. managed to sustain innovation through its manner of organizing control, not only its technological competencies. The histories of the Thyssen & Co. Machine Company and Gas and Waterworks reveal the inner coherence of Thyssen's combination of overall strategic vision, entrepreneurial opportunism, common corporate culture, and policy of profitable commercialization.[7]

Thyssen & Co. Machine Department

The machine department, Department V, initially grew out of the attempt to maintain secrecy, to service and maintain rolling mill equipment, and to reduce transaction costs (the costs of market exchanges). Its purpose mutated in the 1890s into an innovation center for rolling-mill technology largely used inhouse at the Thyssen & Co. and GDK rolling mills. After 1900, its purpose mutated one again into the design, creation, and serial production of powerful gas engines and turbines for sale on the open market.[8]

The machine department began modestly as a small auxiliary repair shop responsible for maintaining equipment for the rolling mills. Thyssen & Co. relied on a small local company, Jordan & Meyer, located directly adjacent to the plate and pipe mills. It specialized in rock-drilling machines and air compressors with a panoply of other small equipment and tools.

An incident concerning one of Thyssen's suppliers of rolling-mill equipment, the *Duisburger Maschinenfabrik AG* (later DEMAG), forced Thyssen to rethink his relationship with Jordan & Meyer, which already had difficulties servicing Thyssen & Co. The *Duisburger Maschinenfabrik AG* had "repeatedly" conveyed vital information about his new universal rolling mill train to Thyssen's archrival, Albert Poensgen of the *Düsseldorfer Eisen- und Röhrenindustrie*. Thyssen felt betrayed. His comments about Poensgen are instructive. They express Thyssen's business values and future objectives of the new machine department: "It is certainly very convenient . . . for that company, and completely in accord with its familiar reputation, only to use its considerable means to discover successes elsewhere, but not to construct its own production facilities on the basis of its own experiments and experiences."[9] Fearing that independent machine-engineering contractors would disclose his expansion plans and technical problems to rivals, Thyssen began building his own rolling mill equipment.

Thyssen bought out Jordan & Meyer (all 150 shares), and in May 1883 founded the *Actien-Gesellschaft Mülheimer Maschinenfabrik*.[10] August Thyssen became chair of the supervisory board; Rudolf Meyer, Joseph Thyssen, and August Baertl, a Thyssen & Co. engineer, were placed on the executive board. Meyer's partner, Jordan, refused to participate in the new venture.

According to standard operating procedure, Thyssen immediately required monthly financial reports. They showed, however, that the new machine company operated in the red, in spite of upgraded facilities. Its machines were shoddy; it still could not make timely repairs. Most damning was that no sales orders were coming in for the alleged "specialties" of the firm, which Thyssen argued "in reality did not deserve the term." Thyssen found the state of affairs "no longer compatible with our business principles" and unceremoniously fired Rudolf Meyer.[11] In April 1884, Thyssen liquidated the company, absorbing it into Department V, and completely renovated the Thyssen & Co. machine department.

The beginnings of Department V were not auspicious. The iron foundry, despite its managers' and workers' best efforts, continued to deliver unusable stoppers to the pipe mill. Thyssen attributed this failure to a "lack of vigor and all too great laxness" on the part of Baertl.[12] Baertl proved incapable of preparing his monthly financial reports on time, a deadly managerial vice.[13] In January 1887, Thyssen ordered Baertl to turn over the direction of the machine department to Edgar Widekind, then chief of the design office. Apparently Thyssen remained impressed enough with Baertl's technical expertise, but not his leadership abilities. Thyssen offered him a new three-year contract and ordered him to concentrate all of his energies on competing with the new Mannesmann seamless pipe process, which threatened the existence of all welded pipe manufacturers.[14] Thyssen essentially demoted Baertl, but assigned him to a central position in research and development, now one of the main objectives of the machine department.

The machine department held a special organizational position inside Thyssen & Co., though it was subordinate to Wilke. Machinery-building created different types of management problems. Few economies of scale were possible because of constant design changes and small-batch production. Its production schedule differed from that of the rolling mills, which ran up fairly regular sales per month, subject to seasonal fluctuations. The machine department would have little sales volume for months, then would sell enough equipment in one month to make up for the operating losses in the other months. Cost accounting was infinitely more difficult because of the number of specialized parts. Overhead and labor had to be accounted for in a different manner. R & D constituted a larger portion of its overhead.

Not surprisingly, the machine department established Thyssen & Co.'s first distinct, formal cost accounting office (1885). By 1890, the machine department included a number of specialized technical offices, including a design office, a cost-accounting office, a carpentry workshop for models, a mechanical workshop, and an iron foundry for casting parts. It also had a relatively high percentage of salaried employees and engineers relative to its total employment. Before 1914, roughly 10% of its total employees were white-collar employees, compared with just 2–3% in the strip steel or pipe departments. The machine department carried more indirect employees ("unproductive" in the parlance of the time).

The startup of Thyssen's GDK in Bruckhausen, one of the largest steelmaking complexes yet seen in Germany, marked a turning point. Between 1890 and 1894 Thyssen made the machine department almost entirely responsible for building the GDK rolling mills, although it had barely begun to develop its own manufacturing capabilities.[15] Essentially, Thyssen placed the machine department in a sink-or-swim situation, equivalent to an entrepreneurial startup. At first, Thyssen still had to rely on outside suppliers for the GDK's first steam engines. But by the mid-1890s, the machine department developed enough expertise to manufacture its own engines and equipment, largely by borrowing ideas and designs. For instance, in 1891 Thyssen wrote a local official for help finding information regarding an American machine used to shape plates into pipes.[16] By the late 1890s, its managers managed to transform the machine department into a dependable contractor of rolling-mill-train equipment and steam engines. Throughout the 1890s, the GDK startup accounted for almost two-thirds of the machine department's total sales. Total sales of the machine department quickly rose from under 400,000 marks in 1887 to 1.3 million marks in 1892, to 1.6 million marks in 1899. It employed 300 people by 1899. Until 1900, almost all sales went to Thyssen & Co. and the GDK.

In spite of solid growth, the statistics conceal the considerable difficulty of putting a full-fledged machine-engineering operation on its feet. The immense difficulties and psychological strain of supplying equipment to the GDK took its toll directly on its chief executives. Between 1890 and 1893 alone, the machine department went through three department heads because of defective machinery and the "arrogance" of the directors toward *Meister.* Not until Thyssen hired C. Ebeling from Saxony in 1893 did the machine department stabilize.[17]

Ebeling turned the machine department into a thoroughly reliable inhouse contractor. Before 1900, the machine engineering department specialized in all types of rolling-mill-train equipment for blocks, billets, plates, sheets, bars, rods, and wires. It also supplied a complete set of the auxiliary equipment needed for rolling mills, including shaping machines, saws, shears, and mechanical cooling beds. Thyssen & Co. later licensed the cooling beds from the Morgan Construction Company in Massachussetts and began building them for other firms. Fitted with hundreds of small wheels, long cooling beds became immensely important for the quality of large plates and for facilitating continuous-process operations. The company also began building pumping equipment for waterworks. The machine department also created a number of patented processes for manufacturing boil-

ers and pipes. Ebeling's achievement was not easy, because Thyssen reserved the right to turn to outside suppliers if the quality or cost of the
machine department's equipment was not competitive.

Thyssen's manufacturing expansion provided the experimental
proving ground for the technical and organizational learning process of the machine department's personnel. Without this built-in demand, it would have been much more difficult to enter the machine
engineering field. The learning curve in machine engineering was
much steeper than in coal mining, steel works, or rolling mills because
people had to imagine, design, and create new techniques, equipment, and processes, incorporating theoretical know-how into the machines.

After the turn of the century, the machine department made a national reputation with the manufacture of its powerful gas-powered engines. For almost a century, inventors had eyed the potential in recycling the gas emitted from coking and blast-furnace operations. Until
then, the coking and steel industry simply let the gas burn off through
smokestacks, giving the Ruhr (and other steel-producing regions) a
distinctive night glow of hundreds of gas fires. The appearance of
Nikolaus August Otto's and Eugen Langen's internal combustion engine (1876), Gottlieb Daimler's gasoline engine (1885), and Rudolf
Diesel's self-named motor (early 1890s) finally offered a promising
substitute for the steam engine. Steam engines tended to explode and
consumed vast quantities of coal. Coal and coke remained significant
input costs in a steel works.

But before German engineers could reuse blast-furnace gas, they
had to overcome two problems: capturing the hot gas from coking and
blast furnaces without it bursting into flames in contact with oxygen,
and purifying the gas of unwanted dust and chemicals. By the 1890s,
engineers had developed rudimentary technologies to solve these
problems. In 1898, the *Hörder Verein* (consistently one of the technical
pioneers in the steel industry) installed the first 600-horsepower gas-
powered engine; the *Gutehoffnungshütte* (GHH) followed suit with an
engine built by its own renowned machine company. Thyssen's GDK
continued to power its newly installed electrical central with three
steam engines of 400, 600, and 1500 horsepower (all supplied by the
Thyssen & Co. machine department). But Thyssen & Co.'s electrical
use skyrocketed beyond the capacity of these machines. In addition,

Thyssen wanted to fully electrify his rolling mill operations. Typically, Thyssen did not want to rely on outside suppliers.

In 1899, sensing that gas-powered engines and dynamos were the wave of the future, Thyssen hired R. Hoffman, formerly of the *Elsässischen Maschinenbau-Gesellschaft* in Mühlhausen. Thyssen wanted Hoffmann to develop commercial production of gas engines "on the basis of [the machine department's] own experiments and experiences"—to quote his earlier reasons for establishing the department. Hoffmann's technical expertise appears to have been so valuable to Thyssen that he allowed him to keep extra patents in his own name. Moreover, Hoffmann was to act as "technical advisor" for all other departments at Mülheim, as well as for the other "associated" Thyssen firms.[18] Essentially, Thyssen wanted Hoffmann to convert completely the energy supply for all of his major firms. Finally, Hoffmann assumed the position of *Direktor*, expressly under the authority of the Thyssens and outside the line authority of August Wilke—the first to do so. Organizationally, the machine department became independent of the rolling mills.

Despite this clear vote of confidence, the transition to commercial production of gas engines nearly failed. The period between 1900 and 1905 was yet another transition period for the machine department, whose sales reached 3 million marks before falling back again in 1905; employment reached 779 people. Under Hoffmann, Thyssen & Co. made a concerted effort to expand its outside sales. From a miniscule 2% before 1900, outside sales immediately expanded to 12% in 1900 and up to 25% by 1903 before they collapsed to 6% in 1905, the last year of Hoffmann's directorship. Sales stalled at 2.5–2.9 million marks in this period, yet the number of employees nearly doubled from 413 to 779.

This expansion of outside sales had come at the expense of product quality. The machine department could not construct an acceptable plate shears; Thyssen & Co. was forced to purchase one from competitors. Equipment delivered to GDK collieries proved defective. Finally, in 1904, when the GDK erected a second power central, Thyssen had to award the contracts to rival M. A. N.

In addition, Hoffmann could not manage the machine department's personnel. Indicating that Thyssen did not micromanage this transition, Thyssen had found out "by chance" that Hoffmann granted a number of subordinates long vacations over and above their contracts. Thyssen found this unacceptable, in light of the particular difficulties in the machine department at the time. Thyssen felt that "the bad consequences of your [Hoffmann's] policies have appeared in every corner of our machine factory and have plunged us into endless difficulties." Thyssen felt that "a complete change in the management *(Disposition)* of the machine engineering department" was urgently required.[19] Thyssen also attributed the 1905 sales collapse to Hoffman's leadership.

Despite the generous financial support for the design and construction of gas engines, Hoffmann proved incapable of delivering a single gas engine during his directorship. This was the last straw. The engines remained in the development stage, and the energy needs of the GDK, the AGHütt, and Thyssen & Co. continued to outpace the steam engines supplied by the machine department. Even if he had been able to deliver his machines, Hoffmann's designs and prototypes remained under 1,600 horsepower, the technical limit at the time. In cost-effective terms, they offered few advantages over steam engines in the short term. Hoffmann did not fulfill his potential in the technical arena and proved incapable of managing the machine department in a commercial manner. Thyssen let him go.

On one of his many trips to M. A. N., Thyssen noticed a young machine engineer named Hans Richter. Richter had developed a novel design that would ostensibly double the gas engine's horsepower. In 1905 Thyssen offered the 37-year old Richter the reins of the machine department. The choice of Richter was a classic example of Thyssen's practice of handpicking young managers and transferring full responsibility to them. The trust he placed in Richter was a bold move—and Thyssen expected entrepreneurial behavior from Richter.

Richter proved to be a genius of machine design whose talents knew little bounds. Richter came to Thyssen & Co. without design blueprints, and immediately began constructing high-horsepower gas machines for full-scale serial production for the GDK and AGHütt electrical power facilities. His rapid promotions left many other engineers and managers envious of his success. Born outside of Berlin and the son of a priest, Richter graduated from the Technical University of Charlottenburg, where he proved himself a star pupil. After a brief stint in academia, he switched to the industrial world at M. A. N. There he was placed in charge of steam-engine construction, and was promoted swiftly to assistant director of the Nürnberg facility. Richter designed M. A. N.'s showcase engine, demonstrated at the 1900 world exhibition in Paris. His generators for the Hamburg and Berlin electrical power stations became models for other companies and cities.[20] It was at this stage of his career that he came to the attention of Thyssen.

Initially, Thyssen considered working with M. A. N. and Hugo Stinnes in a joint venture to transform the machine department into a fully independent, limited-liability subsidiary. Stinnes thought he and Thyssen would be able to control the new venture through shareholding and exploiting the differences among the Augsburg and Nürnberg factions within M. A. N. Thyssen felt M. A. N. was a "very solid" enterprise. Richter, however, did not want to remain in a potentially subordinate position to his former M. A. N. directors, of whom he was somewhat "mistrustful," and Stinnes wanted to be sure that M. A. N. would not hinder their joint control over the new operations. Stinnes saw the new venture as the first step toward moving into the lucrative shipbuilding industry. This step by Thyssen & Co. foreshadowed the takeover movement by steel firms of machine companies of the 1920s.

In any case, Thyssen felt they were probably better off not working with M. A. N.; negotiations fell through by September 1905. Conrad Verlohr had serious objections. He wanted to build an iron foundry for casting parts at Thyssen's AGHütt, which he directed. Cartels also played a role because if the iron foundry was not located at the AGHütt but at another firm, the iron production might not be considered as self-consumption, and this could affect Thyssen's cartel quotas. Thyssen still contemplated working with Stinnes and was very "sympathetic" about the idea of fusing Stinnes' *Friedrich Wilhelms-Hütte* with his up-and-coming machine department. He also thought that joining with a locomotive construction company would diversify his product lines and help smooth Thyssen & Co.'s business cycle. In the meantime, however, he wanted Richter to concentrate on getting operations up to speed as quickly as possible. Thyssen eventually decided to take Stinnes' offer of going it alone if it would be easier for Thyssen.[21]

During his brief three-year stint at Thyssen & Co., Richter transformed it into one of the pacesetting firms for the entire world. Thyssen provided the financing, but everything else depended on

Richter. Richter's success, in turn, rested considerably on his academic training and the decades-long construction experience of the machine department. Karl Schneider, a machine designer and Richter's eventual right-hand man, thought the Thyssen machine department was "hardly known by the broad public or even by the industrial public" until Richter came along.

Influenced by Thyssen's insistence on dependability and serial production, Richter placed particular emphasis on good accessibility of the machine for quick repair and maintenance, and above all, the highest possible reliability for demanding, continuous use. This meant simplifying and standardizing parts as much as possible. Richter constructed his first machine "almost exclusively" from the point of view of operational durability.[22] Finally, the emphasis on standardization of the gas engines helped reduce the fixed cost of the new facilities for Thyssen & Co. through some scale economies. This is another good example how Thyssen always tied technical innovation to clear commercial goals. Unlike a Werner Siemens, his goal was not technical innovation for its own sake, or experimentation to push the bounds of scientific research, or prestige value, but immediate operational, commercial, and profitable "results." Thyssen needed these profits because throughout this period his finances were stretched by multiple lines of expansion.[23]

Before Thyssen & Co. could introduce the first gas engine, Thyssen and Richter put the machine-engineering department on a crash expansion course. The machine department exploded into activity. Whole new workshops were built. After 1906, the iron foundry expanded even more until it could supply huge specialty cast-iron pieces for use in the largest steel mills and blast furnaces. The foundry now could mold cast-iron pieces up to 80 tons. Sales from the machine department's iron foundry alone tripled from 9,800 tons in 1904 to 32,700 in 1908, doubling again to 66,700 tons by 1910. Even Krupp, the most renowned casting goods producer in Germany, would order specialty casting products from Thyssen & Co.[24] In order to support this expansion, Thyssen & Co. installed new heavy cranes, which required that construction halls have special reinforcements. Twenty years later, industry analysts still considered the layout, cranes, and the design of the Thyssen & Co. machine-engineering facilities as state of the art.

The iron foundry provided crucial support for gas-engine production. The sheer power and stresses created by the powerful new engines required low tolerances. Machine department engineers and technicians had to carefully test and select the quality of the steel parts and iron castings before use. In turn, low tolerances and high quality meant that modern measuring and testing techniques had to be introduced. For that reason, in 1906 Richter established an experimental station and laboratory. In the space of just two years, 1905–1907, the total number of machine department employees jumped from 779 to 1750. The number of salaried employees rose to a new high of 134. A new electrical generation plant was also built, but suffered an explosive setback, killing one person, injuring others, and destroying a number of buildings.[25]

In 1907, the main technological achievement of the machine department finally arrived, Richter's first high-powered gas engine, which proved capable of 2,000 horsepower, the most powerful yet manufactured in Germany. (By the postwar period, the machine department could build gas engines up to 6,000 horsepower.) Richter's design of critical aspects and parts became standards for all German gas engines.

The gas engine had many applications, affecting a good portion of the technical operations of German steel firms. It could generate more horsepower than steam engines, yet use less total energy. After the technical problems of removing impurities from coking oven and blast-furnace gases were overcome, the gas engines could be used as air compressors. By pumping oxygen into the very middle of huge iron and steel converters, it accelerated the heat and chemical transformations of the metal, created a controlled heating process, and enhanced the quality of iron and steel. This, too, required improvement of measuring techniques in the gauges to monitor and control air and gas pressure and temperature in blast furnaces and converters. Technicians could manipulate the chemical composition of the gas and iron with a greater degree of control, leading to varying qualities of iron and steel. Gas engines, moreover, were used to preheat air to higher temperatures before being blown into the converters, further reducing the use of coal and improving the quality of the iron. Best of all, the newly generated gas from the blast furnaces could again be recycled through the cleaning process to power the engines, thus creating an energy loop which drove total energy costs for iron and steel down dramatically.

When used in the coking process, gas-powered engines had even more dramatic effects. The gas released from coking ovens burned three to four times more powerfully and more cleanly than blast-furnace gases. Once cleaned, this gas could be used more generally in an integrated, "linked" company economy *(Verbundwirtschaft)* for almost all types of heating and the generation of electricity. In 1911, Thyssen's GDK, and the neighboring *Friedrich-Wilhelms-Hütte* (FWH) owned by Hugo Stinnes, became the first steel firms to use the lower quality blast-furnace gas to heat coking ovens, whose higher quality gas could be used elsewhere. In addition, by using gas engines in the coking process, coal could be converted to coke in half the time. The coking-gas-powered engines were also used for compressors, heating furnaces, warming cool air prior to introducing it into converters (or just vented through buildings for heating), keeping intermediate materials warm before finishing, and most importantly, for generating electricity through massive turbines. By 1913, gas power supplied 70% of Thyssen & Co. energy needs.

A high-powered gas dynamo accelerated the electrification of Thyssen's entire steelworks. Under Richter's tenure, the machine-engineering department built the first electrically driven rolling-mill train in Mülheim.[26] The gas engine propelled the shift away from coal to gas and electricity. Edmund Roser, the technical director of the Thyssen & Co. Machine Company, estimated that a full shift from coal to gas and electricity at Thyssen & Co. would save a whopping 650 of 950 tons of coal used per day, a savings of almost 70%.[27] Although electrification of the GDK began with steam engines, it was completed with gas engines.

As Figure 5.1 illustrates, the machine department's engineers designed, built, installed, and aligned the gas engines in a standard series. The formidable array of machines leaves the impression of a military line formation. On the engine room floor, the standardization reduced the need for a wide range of spare parts in inventory as well as the number of personnel needed to service the engines. The machines appear as if they could operate the factory untended, like an underground industrial scene from the Fritz Lang film, *Metropolis*.

Arrays of gas engines located in central power stations, so-called

Figure 5.1 Gas dynamo hall of the GDK steelworks. Note the two types of logos vying to brand these gas dynamos. (Reproduced with the permission of the Mannesmann-Archiv, Mülheim/Ruhr)

Zentrale, had wide-ranging effects on factory operations in Germany. Beforehand, each of the individual stages of steelmaking and rolling mill operations needed its own engine and power source. Now, fewer men were needed to operate the engines, and they monitored dials, switches, and gauges instead of operating the engines manually on the shop floor. The proliferation of new electrical power stations also led to great improvements in measuring techniques and monitoring methods. Although the GDK electrical power station and steelworks were 900 meters apart, a single person could coordinate the power generation, speed, and air pressure needed by the steelworks.

The centralization of power machinery eased the supervision of plant power needs, as the engines were no longer spread throughout the plant. Electricity, for instance, enabled a more flexible crane system, since the cranes were no longer tied to a specific location and power source. Rolling mill trains were fully electrified. Electric power tools and lighting became more prevalent. As a technological counterpart to central accounting control, the centralization of power sources enabled greater supervision of energy allocation, and more even diffusion of electricity to the far confines of the factory grounds, thus enhancing the flexibility of machinery placement throughout the firm and freeing newly available floor space for other uses.

The success of the gas engines and turbines allowed Thyssen to expand well beyond his original plans. By 1911, the gas and electrical central of the GDK in Bruckhausen included twelve gas dynamos for the generation of electricity, nine air compressors for the blast furnaces, and two for the steel works—altogether a total of just over 30,000 horsepower, generating over 110 million kilowatt/hours. At Thyssen's iron works in Meiderich, the AGHütt, a new gas and electricity power station had ten gas dynamos and five air compressors for the blast furnaces, generating about 75 million kilowatt/hours. The tremendous surplus of electrical energy also permitted the introduction of new electric-arc furnaces for very high quality steel and recycling of scrap. Thyssen's GDK introduced its first electric-arc furnaces in 1911, first 6 tons, then 25 tons in 1913.[28] When Thyssen began building his massive new steelworks in Alsace-Lorraine in 1911, it led the continent in the use of gas energy and the electrification of the works. Thyssen's gas and electrical power stations had set the standard for the steel industry.

The machine-engineering department's gas engine proved to be the key link in an integrated energy economy for the Thyssen-Konzern, and the "hub" of the new style of technical rationalization which dominated German steel strategies after 1900. The high-horsepower gas engine not only extended Thyssen's general strategy of diversification and self-sufficiency, but also proved to be the key invention or "catalyst" for the "German path" of rationalization.[29] While the Americans concentrated on economies of scale and speed, the Germans pioneered in the creation of energy economies, which stressed the efficient use of energy and reuse of so-called waste material. While Taylorist scientific management focused obsessively on reducing wage costs, German scientific management focused on reducing fuel costs. This sort of scientific management cannot be conflated with an alleged Americanization of German practices. It was not necessary to read Taylor's *Scientific Management* (1911) to find the winds of scientific management blowing through German industry. Unlike Taylorism, such rationalization did not focus on the minutia of the shopfloor, but on systematic integration of factory (or factories') operations. The proliferation of gauges, levers, and dials signified the increasing degrees of metering, monitoring, and measuring production. Although rationalization and efficiency became catchwords across the industrial world, considerable variation existed among countries (or industries). The phrases often carried different components, associated meanings, varying corporate strategies, and sometimes, political implications. For most German industrialists, energy economies justified extensive vertical integration from coal to machine engineering on technical and cost-saving grounds. This logic came into conflict with those contemporaries who wished to limit the expansion of German steel firms, and later with the Allies after World War II who sought to deconcentrate them.

The high-horsepower gas engine acted as the linchpin of a completely integrated energy circuit based on regeneration economies. German heavy industry led the world in regeneration economies and coking technology. Reversing the usual pilgrimage to the United States at the time, American engineers came to Germany to learn about coking technology and the commercial use of byproducts made possible by the application of science. In 1908, measured in horsepower, Germany produced 46.5% of all the world's energy generated by gas engines; the United States followed with 32.5%, while Britain and France generated just 2.4% and 5.4%, respectively. Heavy industry alone consumed more than 80% of Germany's gas-engine horsepower. In the same year, Germany managed to reuse almost a quarter of all the blast furnace and coking oven gas. Belgium followed with 20.8%, the United States with 12.9%, France with 12.3%, and Britain with only 1.5%.

The use of gas and gas engines also created a series of energy loops with wide-ranging implications outside the business firm. The quality of the coking-oven gas was high enough that it could be piped to cities for gas lighting, or to a regional utility company to generate electricity. Thyssen and Stinnes supplied their own excess coking oven gas to the regional electricity company, the *Rheinisch-Westfälische Elektrizitätswerke* (RWE), which they owned, for municipal lighting, starting with Mülheim. The machine department's gas dynamos generated so much electricity that Thyssen's GDK and AGHütt also sold surplus electricity to the RWE. By 1913, German heavy industry produced five times more electrical energy than did public utilities. In addition, this connection conveniently created a new demand for Siemens-Martin seamless steel pipelines to transport the gas. The energy economies created by the high-horsepower gas engine helped drive the growth of Thyssen & Co.'s pipe department, as well as its auxiliary water and gas department.

Richter's gas engine proved to be the dramatic breakthrough ("killer app") for Thyssen & Co., and it opened a lucrative new market. Under Richter, the Thyssen & Co. machine department became a full-fledged capital goods producer (that is, a producer of investment goods used by other industrial companies). It offered a full range of gas engines and dynamos of varying sizes, steam engines, conveyance systems, air compressors, pumping machines for water works, irrigation systems and mines, coal generators, and all types of rolling-mill trains and their accessories.[30] In 1905, when Richter took over, total department revenues were 2.5 million marks. By 1908, the last year of Richter's tenure, these revenues had quadrupled to 10.3 million marks. More importantly, outside sales to third parties were now 25–50% of total department sales.

Richter's talent and the industry links created by sales of the department's machinery made him indispensable in a range of other ventures. Thyssen named him as one of the directors for the *Bohr- und Schachtbau-Gesellschaft,* a Thyssen company for the construction of mining collieries and deep shaft operations. The machine department built all sorts of conveyance machines, compressors, cooling towers, and condensation plants. Richter helped guide the sinking of a new deep shaft at the *Gewerkschaft Lohberg,* which used a new freezing process to harden the ground around the shaft. He was instrumental in designing the equipment for the mine, which the machine department and welding works of the plate department made. Thyssen made Richter responsible for the welding works as well—a move he would later regret. Thyssen appointed Richter to the supervisory board of his *Oberbilker Stahlwerk,* which concentrated on specialty steels. Finally, Richter played a critical role in negotiating with Hugo Stinnes and the RWE, because Richter best understood the technical requirements. Richter's responsibilities grew as Thyssen underwent a nose operation in 1907, suffered from a series of bouts with a near fatal illness in 1908, and endured his childrens' demands.

Yet just at the moment when Thyssen became seriously ill, the machine department went through one of its periodic management crises. In technical and production terms, the department's operations proved to be an unqualified success, but this very success caused serious problems of organization and marketing. Both Richter and Thyssen felt that a sales organization was urgently required. Thyssen admitted that he had given Richter too many responsibilities, especially since the quality of product in the welding works suffered, and crucial large customers such as the Bremer Vulkan and the City of Berlin complained. Thyssen blamed himself for their strained relationship and wanted to give responsibility for the welding works back to rolling mill directors so that Richter could focus on the machine department and the mine construction company. But he still demanded that Richter deliver the required monthly reports and year-end financial statements, and he suspected that the machine department operated at a loss. Richter apparently lost patience with Thyssen's sickness, overwork, the loss of responsibility in the other departments, running conflicts with Ernst Becker of the rolling mills, and the lack of an effective commercial organization. Richter was, after all, a machine designer, not an administrator or salesman.[31] His myriad responsibilities with a bare-boned commercial staff left him overwhelmed and frustrated. In 1908, he left.

Richter moved on to the position of director at Krupp's *Germaniawerft* machine engineering and shipbuilding operations. At Krupp, the ultra-talented Richter quickly achieved a number of early successes. However, just two years later he contracted typhus and died at the age of 42, an abrupt end to a stellar personality.

The machine company's spectacular growth and "complicated organization" necessitated a new basis for its operation.[32] For Thyssen, growth again posed the greatest challenge. Since at least 1906, Thyssen had intended to spin off the machine department as an independent company. In 1907, Thyssen began negotiations to form a joint venture, a long-term "community of interest" (*Interessengemeinschaft*, IG), with an established machine-engineering firm, *Ehrhardt & Sehmer GmbH* in Schleifmuehle-Saarbrücken. An IG often began as the first step to a full merger. This new IG would have been called the *Ehrhardt-Sehmer'schen Maschinenfabriken, GmbH,* whose goal was "above all to strive to strengthen the competitiveness of both firms on the world market."[33]

Why did Thyssen, this notoriously do-it-yourself entrepreneur, opt for a joint venture? First, the German machine-engineering industry was (and still is) one of Germany's leading industrial sectors. The machine department would have to compete on the international market against some of the best companies in Germany. Moreover, the machine department's specialties, such as rolling mills, gas engines, high-powered air compressors, and mining equipment machines, would have to be sold to Thyssen's main rivals. The IG or joint venture's name at least disguised the fact that Thyssen would have had a substantial stake in the firm. Pooling their efforts would also help ease some of the financial risks. The initial financial objective for the new firm, for instance, was quite modest; they just wanted to be able to cover the interest payments on the start-up expenditures.

Most importantly, however, Erhardt & Sehmer had an established sales organization with an extensive set of domestic and foreign sales agents. Going alone, the Thyssen machine department would have had to create from scratch a new sales organization with the necessary technical expertise to market and service complicated machinery. Moreover, the two firms complemented one another, as Thyssen's facilities were geared toward producing heavy machines while Erhardt & Sehmer concentrated on lighter machinery. Both companies would set up the IG as a legal/administrative holding to run both factories (Saarbrücken and Mülheim) according to "unified standards" which would "simplify" and standardize both operations, particularly for those products like rolling mill construction, which they both manufactured. Technical developments and experience in their specialties would be shared. Using the most favorable transport situation in Saarbrücken or Mülheim would reduce shipping costs. By eliminating duplicate expenses, particularly in design and development, and by purchasing common required materials in greater bulk, production costs could be reduced.[34] Provided that the initial merger difficulties could be sorted out, the new firm could also use the existing capital more effectively.[35] Essentially, the proposed joint venture was a division of labor between Thyssen & Co.'s capital and Erhardt & Sehmer's marketing expertise.

But two years of intensive negotiations came to naught. The IG contract clearly favored August Thyssen. Thyssen & Co. would have provided the bulk of the capital (75%). The IG had to retain all earnings until start-up costs were covered. The firm had to prove commercially viable before it would distribute dividends, and Thyssen would set the accounting policy of the new firm.[36] And it had to purchase supplies from Thyssen firms *if* the inputs were "at equivalent or cheaper prices than comparable competitors." This would guarantee "self-consumption rights" with the cartels that would allow Thyssen to sell intermediate products beyond the cartel quotas, allowing him to run more fully.[37] (It was precisely these types of arcane cartel considerations that distinguished German entrepreneurship from American.)

Ehrhardt & Sehmer backed out at the last minute, even after the IG had hired a new technical director, a new commercial director, and set the legal founding date.[38] At bottom, Erhardt & Sehmer would have lost control of the company. The supervisory board and all accounting stipulations were controlled by Thyssen—another way in which accounting standards convey power. Sehmer objected to the fact that his firm would become the junior partner, with a declining influence over the joint venture.

Thyssen & Co. Maschinenfabrik AG

The surprising end to these negotiations forced Thyssen to set up his own company. Between 1906 and 1911, the machine department operated in an organizational limbo, more than a department, not quite an independent firm. The obstacles facing this transition were high. Karl Härle, the commercial director of the new firm, commented: "Personally, we were certainly convinced that we would succeed in moving the machine company forward . . . [But] actually, until quite recently it was a common opinion often voiced to us that we would never succeed in turning the Thyssen & Co. Machine Company into a flourishing enterprise." [39] The potential new company had to invest heavily in new equipment, an administration and sales staff, establish a network of foreign agents, and create an entirely new central office and administrative building distinct from that of the rolling mills.

A complete leadership void also affected the machine department. The first executive Thyssen hired to organize the commercial and administrative side of the machine department failed badly.[40] Thyssen had no technical or commercial director, and only a temporary operations supervisor. A number of middle managers left, disgusted. In

March 1911, Gottlieb Fassnacht became the official new production supervisor, after proving himself; he had joined the firm in 1909.

Most critically, Thyssen needed to find someone competent enough to build on Richter's technological leadership. He found Edmund Roser, whose specialty was the design of gas engines.[41] Thyssen could again dip into Germany's deep well of technical education. The son of a housepainter and craftsman, the modest and reserved Roser began his career in a craft apprenticeship as a mechanic in Freudenstadt in the Black Forest. Showing more than the usual talent, he began to study mechanical engineering after he graduated from the *Realschule,* the vocational track of the dual German educational system. In 1895, he took his exam as a government official in construction and building. But instead of moving directly into nonacademic life, he came to the attention of Dr. Julius Carl von Bach, who had recently established a state-of-the-art engineering and materials testing laboratory at the Technical University of Stuttgart. This laboratory had gained a worldwide reputation for machine design and construction. Roser became his assistant and collaborated on Bach's book, *Maschinen-Elemente,* a textbook on machine technology. Roser eventually took over the direction of the regional government's materials testing laboratory, which became a model institute for many others. In 1901 Roser graduated with a Ph.D., the first doctorate granted by the faculty specifically for gas-machine engineering. Thereafter, Roser moved into more applied work as technical director of the *Maschinenfabrik G. Kuhn* in Stuttgart-Berg.

Roser joined Thyssen & Co. in January 1909 as chief technical director, with power of attorney *(Prokura)*. He contributed in a major way to new, larger gas-turbine designs, which eventually became known as "Thyssen Gas Rams" because of their great horsepower. He became known especially for the development of the Holzwarth-Gas Turbine, which in 1921 was the most powerful gas-powered turbine in the world. Along with Franz Bartscherer of the GDK, Roser was given responsibility for handling all the energy needs of the Thyssen-Konzern. Because of his expertise, Roser became one of Thyssen's closest advisors, often walking home after work with Thyssen over the Ruhr River bridge. He remained one of the most important figures at the Thyssen & Co. Machine Company until it merged into the VSt in 1926.[42]

The new commercial director of the Machine Company, Karl Härle, cut an imposing and flamboyant figure. Härle joined the Thyssen machine department in the fall of 1909, along with Fassnacht and Roser. Härle made himself indispensable to Thyssen in both personal and professional ways. After his transfer to Mülheim, Härle began a nearly half-century relationship with the Thyssen family. In personal terms, he became Thyssen's point man in the dispute with August, Jr., and later became executor of August and Fritz's estate. As a legal expert, Härle guided the transformation of the machine department into a joint-stock company. But above all, Härle enabled the machine department to come to terms with its immense organizational, commercial, and accounting needs.

Born in Königseggwald in Württemberg, Härle came from a Catholic family of seven children. His father owned a small pub and brewery, which Härle found embarrassing. He received a gymnasium education in Ulm before going abroad to London for an apprenticeship in banking. When he returned he spoke fluent English and was hired by a local firm as a foreign correspondent. In 1901 he enrolled at the University of Tübingen, one of the leading law centers in Germany. The first in his family to receive a university education, he graduated three years later after writing a dissertation on contracts between ship owners and ship officers. (We would now assign this work to issues of incentives and agency.) In 1908 passed the Royal Justice Testing Commission's exam (the equivalent of a bar exam), entitling him to become a state lawyer and civil servant in Württemberg. Instead, he chose to work in the private economy. A relative suggested that he apply for a position as the chief legal officer (*Justitiar*) for the *Krefelder Stahlwerke*, a quality steel goods producer in the Ruhr and a joint venture involving August Thyssen, Peter Klöckner, and Franz Burger (of the *Schalker Verein*).

Once in Krefeld, Härle realized that the director was ruining the firm. He accused the director of cheating the company and its shareholders, which led to a brief arrest for slander and defamation of character. When the director then sued him, Härle challenged him to a duel: three shots at ten steps. Only at the last minute was the duel called off, but not before it created a public spectacle. Thyssen, however, was impressed with Härle's ferocious honesty and brought him to the machine department to create some order there.

It was just one measure of Härle's blunt, bulldog approach to any issue that he managed to get himself arrested three times on political grounds. In 1919, the socialist revolutionary councils arrested him; his attitude was in no small measure the reason why the Thyssen Machine Company was the target of one of the largest strike actions in Germany before the war ended. During the Ruhr Struggle of 1923, the French arrested him. Then again, in 1939, the Gestapo placed him under house arrest. Not everyone could boast of such credentials. His legal interpretations turned any loophole to his advantage and once he found one, he did not let go. Just before his death, a local newspaper once described Härle in the following understated terms: "With a talent for recognizing the essential, once he held something to be right, Dr. Härle pursued it with all of his power. He expressed his opinions clearly and distinctly. This stance combined with his prominent position brought many conflicts with it." [43]

With this trio of Swabians—Fassnacht "the director," Roser "the doctor," and Härle "the lawyer"—the Thyssen & Co. Machine Company gained the informal reputation as a Swabian firm in the Ruhr. (In Germany, Swabians have long had a reputation as mechanically adept people.) Although their common regional heritage and dialect should have facilitated their friendship, they instead fought amongst themselves. It is perhaps a tribute to Thyssen's management of men that the Machine Company ever got off the ground. Ongoing heated disputes characterized their relationships, with two against the other, but not always the same two. Härle and Fassnacht could not stand one another. [44] But these three figures, Roser, Fassnacht, and Härle, transformed the Thyssen Machine Company into one of the leading machine engineering firms in Germany.

On March 3, 1911 the machine department was officially entered in the commercial register as the *Maschinenfabrik Thyssen & Co. AG*. [45] (To avoid confusion, I will henceforth refer to the Thyssen Machine Company and the Thyssen & Co. Rolling Mills.) As usual, August Thyssen owned three-quarters of the stock; Joseph Thyssen the other quarter. It remained essentially a private partnership in the guise of a joint-stock company. They chose the joint-stock form in case they needed to resort to capital markets to raise new capital. Company statutes kept key investment decisions firmly in the hands of the supervisory board (August, Joseph, and Fritz). [46] In practice, most of the strategy and recommendations for new investment originated with the managing directors (Roser, Härle, and Fassnacht). For instance, Härle and Roser felt that the machine department building and crane facilities were designed only for heavy engineering work on the high-horsepower gas machines, and not a "rational way" to produce lighter goods, "as the sharp competition in these goods require." They recommended that a new facility with cranes be erected for the lighter goods and submitted their reasons and plans to August Thyssen for approval, who was at a spa for his health.[47]

Unlike the Thyssen & Co. Rolling Mills, which were organized into commercial-technical departments, they organized the Machine Company along centralized, functional lines—more along American lines (Figure 5.2). At the senior level, the Machine Company had a German-style dual-headed managerial structure with a commercial director and a technical director, who in principle acted on equal terms with one another. The Machine Company had three main areas: production workshops, design and development, and commercial administration. As production director, Fassnacht had formal equality with both Härle and Rose, but in practice tended to take orders from them. Roser had ultimate authority over design and development. Fassnacht focused on production, which had five operating plants: workshops for machine construction (gas and steam engines), rolling-mill equipment, parts production, an iron foundry, and an assembly hall. The workshops were organized by product line. Each workshop had its own workshop supervisor. The design offices included sections for gas engines, steam engines, rolling-mill equipment, pumps, turbines, pipelines, and refrigeration units, along with various support offices, including a patent office.

Härle was fully in control of the commercial side of the business and introduced state-of-the-art managerial methods. The organizational performance of the Machine Company must have been enhanced by the entirely new organization using the newest methods to monitor its complicated operations. Härle established special offices for cost-accounting for machines and for casted goods. The most innovative aspect of the Machine Company organization lay in the introduction of a Hollerith (IBM) office for tracking materials and inventories, as well as for aiding cost calculation. The Hollerith machine was the first punch-card computing machine to be used in business firms. It marks the beginning of the mechanization and standardization of office work.[48] Härle placed a twenty-three-year-old employee, Heinrich

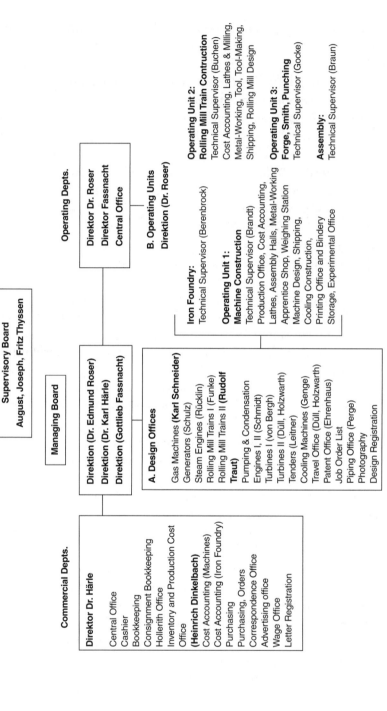

Figure 5.2 Thyssen & Co. Machine Company, 1913–1914

Dinkelbach, in charge of it. Dinkelbach's swift rise in the Thyssen-Konzern rested on the sponsorship of Härle and an attention to innovative organizational methods.[49]

By the end of 1912, the new organization of the Machine Company was fully in place. So many contracts poured in that the Machine Company worked day and night. Total sales rose almost geometrically, from 5 million marks in 1906, to 9.1 million marks in 1909, 14.3 million marks in 1911, and 23.8 million marks by 1913. Third party sales hovered around 50% of total company sales in the last few years before the war. In the same period, the number of employees rose from 1,600 in 1909 to 2,100 in 1911 to just over 3,000 in 1913. And this growth came in spite of the fact that the profitable cast-iron foundry, which produced 66,000 tons in 1910, was shut down. The foundry was transferred to a new, larger facility at the AGHütt in Meiderich, closer to Thyssen's main source of specialty iron. Despite the loss of the foundry, the Machine Company's capital stock rose from 3.5 million marks in 1911 to over 8 million marks in June 1914. In just a few years, the Machine Company proved to be the most profitable firm relative to size in the Thyssen-Konzern. Typically, Thyssen retained all profits for further expansion.

In 1912, the premier journal on the German iron and steel industry, *Stahl und Eisen,* devoted a special article to the Thyssen Machine Company. The author tended to emphasize the difficulties involved in machine-tool construction and concentrated on the importance of cranes and hall design as organizational means for rational operations. The article considered the layout of the machine department as state of the art. The *Stahl und Eisen* article was so glowing that Thyssen & Co.'s marketing department simply added more photographs and turned the article into an advertising brochure.

Within a few years after independence, the Thyssen & Co. Machine Company could measure itself in the high-powered gas engine sector only against one of the largest and most renowned machine-engineering firms in Germany, M. A. N. In typical German fashion, a syndicate for large gas engines was established in which M. A. N. received a quota of 22.8% and the Machine Company 20%. No other company even came close. In revenues from the sale of high-powered gas engines, the Thyssen Machine Company received 17.7 million marks, and M. A. N. 16.6 million marks.[50]

In 1911 Thyssen & Co. finished constructing a new central administration building for the machine company (see Figure 7.1). The new
building exuded a monumental solidity, a solidity that the organization of the Machine Company did not yet have internally, as if the Machine Company needed a building as imposing as the massive machines it manufactured. Unlike the GDK central administrative
building, a Gothic style typical of the highly detailed Wilhelmine architecture of the time period, the Machine Company's administrative
building pared away the ornamentation in favor of massive, clear horizontal and vertical lines. From the front, the building leaves the impression of a series of superimposed blocks, but the side view leaves an
even more bare functional approach. The massive seriality of the design provides a nice parallel to the imposing line of Thyssen & Co. gas
dynamos. The complex organizational relations between the Rolling
Mills and the Machine Company were neatly illustrated by the fact that
the plate department's administrative staff also occupied the first floor
of the new administrative building. Excepting the plate department,
the offices of the Rolling Mills remained spread across the factory
grounds, embodying the different organizational structures in architectural and spatial terms.[51]

Within the space of a few years, the Thyssen & Co. Machine Company could count itself among Germany's top machine-engineering
firms. But Thyssen's entrepreneurial opportunism by no means guaranteed success. Nor could technical genius alone build a business.
While its success certainly rested on the technical competency of its
engineers, it also rested on the department's ability to overcome and
learn from numerous setbacks. These failures lay less in the realm of
technology, than in organization and commercial operations. While
the rapid expansion of the firm in the last years before the war appears
nearly miraculous, in reality, the Machine Company built upon almost
thirty years of good but decidedly more modest experience. Finally, its
individual success rested on the broad, collective system of German
technical education. Most of the Machine Company's technical managers did not move up from within the Thyssen organization itself, but
were rotated in from the outside. If Hoffmann failed, Thyssen could
find Richter; if Richter left, he could find Roser. Without this national
system of technical education as a foundation, Thyssen and his Machine Company would have stalled like an engine without gas.

Wasserwerk Thyssen & Co. GmbH

Proving that the success of the Machine Company was no fluke, Thyssen & Co. spawned a number of other ventures. These followed a similar pattern of opportunism and organizational learning. The most important of these new subsidiary activities was the gas and water works, *Wasserwerk Thyssen & Co., GmbH,* which became part of the infrastructure for the region. Other such auxiliary departments included *Bad Tönnistein,* a mineral water company, and *Thyssen & Co. Abteilung Wülfrath,* which mined limestone. Here I want to concentrate only on the development of the gas and water works, as it quite unexpectedly grew out of energy economies.[52]

Established in 1893, the Thyssen & Co. waterworks department initially grew out of a market failure. Thyssen again turned a disadvantage into an entrepreneurial opportunity. As Thyssen & Co. expanded, it utilized ever more water for cleaning and cooling purposes. At first, Thyssen drew water from a local well on the grounds, but the company quickly exhausted this source. He then turned to the Mülheim municipal water supply because Styrum did not have a waterworks of its own (one of the problems of greenfield sites). But by 1892, the Mülheim waterworks could no longer supply Thyssen & Co. and it lacked the necessary funds to enlarge its municipal waterworks by itself. Thyssen & Co. responded by setting up its own waterworks department. The Thyssen & Co. machine department equipped the waterworks with pumps and steam engines to draw water from the Ruhr River. Thereafter, water pumps became a specialty of the machine department. Within two years, the waterworks proved so successful that Styrum asked to have its water supplied by Thyssen & Co.

The next stage in the waterworks' development also grew out of the deficiencies of the Ruhr's infrastructure. In 1895, the Thyssen-owned mine, *Graf Moltke,* flooded because of an inadequate pumping station. Moreover, the water in the surrounding area had a high saline content, ruining it for industrial operations. After trying in vain to get a neighboring municipal waterworks to supply fresh water, Thyssen decided to supply the mine through his own waterworks department. In order to do so, Thyssen & Co. had to lay a long pipeline from Mülheim to Gladbeck, directly to its north, a distance of approximately 10 miles (16 km). But the intervening communities, Dümpten, Borbeck,

Bottrop, and Gladbeck, would only allow Thyssen & Co. to lay the pipeline through their districts if they could draw water from pipeline. By 1896, Thyssen & Co. finished the pipeline, delivering 2 million cubic meters of water to these communities and the Gladbeck mine. In the end, Thyssen & Co. not only gained a number of new customers to defray some of the costs of laying the pipeline, but also created a market demand for its own pipes and pumping equipment! Immediately thereafter, Thyssen & Co. began building another pipeline to the GDK in Hamborn, connecting the communities of Hamborn, Alsum, and Marxloh to its water network. By 1900, the Thyssen & Co. waterworks department delivered 10.3 million cubic meters of water, of which about 70% went to other *Thyssen'schen Conzern* firms. The rest went to other large-scale businesses or communities, but over time smaller customers accounted for an increasing amount of volume. By 1900, the waterworks department delivered water to more than 1,300 different customers, and had built a network of more than 85 kilometers of pipeline.[53]

In 1903, the surprising success of the waterworks led Thyssen to spin off the department into a separate firm, the *Wasserwerk Thyssen & Co., GmbH,* under the commercial direction of Moritz Pickhardt (also supervisor of the purchasing department in Thyssen & Co.), and with Walter Pouch as technical director. In 1903, Pickhardt and Pouch arranged to build a separate waterworks station at the GDK because the facilities in Styrum proved to be too distant and too small to supply adequately the huge demand created by the GDK.[54] By 1905, the Waterworks delivered 20.7 million cubic meters of water, 63% of which supplied other Thyssen firms. The number of customers expanded to 4,368, large and small, and the Thyssen water network expanded to 245 kilometers.

In 1905, the Waterworks development moved into another stage. It began to deliver refined gas from the GDK coking operations in Hamborn. Thyssen then consolidated the Mülheim and Hamborn gas operations. At this point, the refining and recycling of excess gas from coking and blast-furnace operations, the supply of gas and water to surrounding communities, the demand for pipes, and the growth of the machine department combined to form an integrated and complementary system.

With the move into gas refining and supply, Thyssen again dipped into the pool of university expertise. He hired a young chemist of twenty-eight, Franz Lenze. Lenze became the decisive figure in the Waterworks. Just as infrastructure tends to be invisible, Lenze tended to remain quietly in the background, but his decisions underlaid the strategy of the Waterworks for the next thirty years. Typically, Lenze was trained in the sciences but was expected by Thyssen to act as a businessman; in fact, Lenze became *commercial director* of the firm.

Lenze had grown up, so to speak, in the infrastructure business. His father was a director of the municipal works in Düren. Like Thyssen, Lenze studied at the Technical University of Karlsruhe, graduating in 1903 with a degree in chemistry. He briefly worked in the gasworks in Thüringen, then in Mülheim, where he came to the attention of Thyssen. By almost all accounts, Lenze was a "burning patriot inside and out," complete with an upturned handlebar moustache, like the Emperor. He combined his belief in Christianity with a love of the Fatherland and duty into a soldierly "upright" spirit. Like Härle, he was during World War I decorated with the Iron Cross, First Class.

Soon after he was hired, Lenze built the first gas manufactory in Hamborn, directly adjacent to the coking facilities. He developed a special patented process to clean and purify coking gas. His facilities remained in operation until 1971 when natural gas replaced it.[55] After hiring Lenze, Thyssen began closing a series of deals with local communities to deliver his excess coking gas to their citizens: Walsum in 1905, Hamborn and Dinslaken in 1906, Oberhausen in 1907, and Mülheim in 1908. By 1909, the GDK fed its excess supply of coking gas through 65 kilometers of pipelines to almost 1,900 customers. The Waterworks supply network also continued to grow to 7,400 customers and 325 kilometers, delivering more than 35 million cubic meters of water.

The expansion of the gas network, however, brought Thyssen into direct conflict with the expansion of the *Rheinisch-Westfälische Elektrizitätswerke* (RWE), whose leading investors included himself (the "old man") and Hugo Stinnes (the young "merchant of Mülheim"). Stinnes was one of the more outspoken public figures in German industrial and political history. While Thyssen preferred to stay in the background, Stinnes stepped willingly onto the public stage and carried out a lot of the public relations work that Thyssen was unwilling to do. Stinnes could negotiate almost anything, and was the driving force behind the RWE's rapid expansion. At the same time, Stinnes was in the midst of building Deutsch-Luxembourg into one of the leading coal and steel combines in the Ruhr. Increasingly, their initially cooperative relationship became highly competitive once Stinnes became Thyssen's direct rival. Their colliding interests and competitive–cooperative solutions for electricity, water, and gas supply best typify the sort of capitalism that existed in Germany.[56]

In 1902, Stinnes and Thyssen formed a partnership to take over the majority of RWE shares from the *Elektrizitätswerke AG vorm W. Lahmeyer & Co.* With the support of two banks, this company had founded the RWE in 1898 to build for the city of Essen a modern electrical power station. Conveniently, this station, which went into operation in 1900, was located on land owned by Stinnes and adjacent to a Stinnes-owned coal mine. The RWE had great cost advantages over the municipal electricity works, not the least because Stinnes could draw a cheap supply of coal and gas from his own operations.

Stinnes sought to have the RWE extend its electrical cables and streetcars, as well as gas and water pipelines, into every community of the Ruhr. Not only did Stinnes see the clear advantages of economies of scale and the potentially lucrative interconnections among these businesses, but this extension matched his own empire-building ambitions. Stinnes admitted to Thyssen that this would also give him political influence with other firms and cities.[57] More than once, Thyssen advised him not to overextend himself, personally or financially.[58] Stinnes framed his expansion as cost savings for everyone and in the general interest, yet it also clearly meant a monopoly, a term that Stinnes sometimes used in correspondence.[59] Sensitive to public opinion and the potential demands of cities for costly safety and maintenance, Thyssen advised against connecting electrical generation with transportation.[60] In general, Thyssen was more cautious than Stinnes. Thyssen sought to find an outlet for the excess gas and electricity generated by his own manufacturing plants and machine department's dynamos; at the same time, he focused on the electrification of his own plants rather than on entire cities. Moreover, he was suffering a liquidity crisis, which constrained his expansion.[61]

At the time, the general public, neighboring firms, cities, and the electrical industry feared a dangerous monopoly controlled by Thyssen and Stinnes. Their partnership had already led to some of the largest mergers of the period.[62] Stinnes openly strove for a monopoly, yet "monopoly" was one of the worst words in the political lexicon at the time. Both Thyssen and Stinnes were attacked as trying to build an American-style trust, and accused of unalloyed greed and craving for power. It also appeared that a key public good, transportation, would fall into private hands. All this scared off various cities from the network. Cologne, Düsseldorf, Mönchen-Gladbach, Neuss, and Rheydt signed an agreement not to sign any contract with the RWE. Bochum, Dortmund, and Hagen resisted RWE's embrace until it signed an agreement that it would not extend its influence into certain areas. In order to assuage these fears, Stinnes and Thyssen were willing to allow communities and the government to buy a majority shareholding in the new company, which not only helped overcome political resistance to the venture, but also attracted cities to the RWE network and helped raise capital.

Over time, however, Stinnes' general strategy collided more often with Thyssen's plans. It interfered with Thyssen's plans to supply gas to Borbeck and Walsum and his intention to deliver electricity to cities located directly around his core companies: Hamborn, Bruckhausen, Meiderich, and Dinslaken. Stinnes' high-flying expansion also financially overextended the "nervous" Thyssen, who was already investing heavily elsewhere.[63] During negotiations with Stinnes, the GDK expressed dismay that the RWE balked at a suggested paragraph that would have guaranteed Thyssen the right to deliver gas, electricity, and water to firms in which Thyssen owned a majority interest (over 50%). This paragraph would have considerably extended the definition of Thyssen's sphere of interest outside his core (100%-owned) group of firms. Both Thyssen and Stinnes wanted to develop economies of scale as much as possible. But here they began to clash rather than cooperate. On top of this, Emil Rathenau of the AEG entered the Ruhr, wanting to build his own regional electric company.

In 1905, Thyssen and Stinnes entered into exceedingly complicated negotiations involving gas, water, and electricity supply. Most of the detailed negotiations with Stinnes went first through Hans Richter of the Thyssen & Co. machine department. Thyssen expected Richter to handle the first-draft negotiations. Walter Pouch of the Thyssen & Co. Waterworks also corresponded through Richter. Correspondence with the mayors of Borbeck and Walsum tended to pass through

the Thyssen & Co. central office, through the hands of Hermann
Eumann, Thyssen's chief financial advisor, and Philip Neuhaus, the
commercial director and successor to Albert Killing. The GDK also
sent a stream of correspondence to Richter, arguing its position on the
various drafts of the contracts. Only after the Waterworks, machine department, the GDK, and the RWE drew up a final contract, would
Thyssen scribble in the margins and return it to Richter, who renegotiated with Stinnes. This complicated, tedious negotiation process went
through a series of "final drafts" until Thyssen and Stinnes agreed
upon amicable spheres of interest. Thyssen managers were important
formulators of Thyssen strategy here as well.

The upshot of these negotiations was that the Thyssen & Co. Waterworks gave to the RWE its rights to supply electricity for streetcars in
Borbeck, northeast of Styrum. In return, it gained the exclusive right
to supply water to all the communities between Borbeck and beyond.[64]
Pouch still objected to this arrangement because he felt that the
Waterworks should have had a guarantee to lay a gas line to Walsum,
lying northwest of Hamborn. Clearly, there continued to be conflict
over the supply of water, gas, and electricity to the region.[65] It did not
help that they had sharp differences about the director of their jointly
owned Saar-Mosel venture.[66]

While they cooperated in electricity, Thyssen and Stinnes clashed on
gas and water supply. For the most part, gas pipelines laid before 1910
supplied the communities found in and around Thyssen firms. In December 1909, however, the city of Barmen, located far to the southeast
of Mülheim where the Ruhr meets the Bergisches Land in the direction of Remscheid, decided to shut down its gas manufactory in favor of Thyssen's coking gas. Thyssen made this surprise announcement—not so tactfully—at a dinner at Stinnes' home. Stinnes and his
wife, Clara, were shocked. This arrangement obstructed Stinnes' plans
to push beyond Barmen into the Bergisches Land to the cities of
Solingen and Remscheid with RWE gas pipelines, and Stinnes thought
he had already gained Barmen's acceptance.

On top of this, a few days later Thyssen announced that he would
leave the supervisory board of the RWE because he "must remain independent and unhindered in this development also in this direction." Their disputes spread into the board of the Saar-Mosel mining
company, into the coal and steel cartel negotiation, and into Mülheim

politics regarding canal-building off the Ruhr river, which would harm the growth of Thyssen's Waterworks. Their personal differences grew so strained that it ruined the baptism of her daughter for Clara Stinnes, which was carried out in tense silence.

In the gas dispute, the Prussian state had to step in to arbitrate. Stinnes and Thyssen agreed to another complicated sphere of interest. Thyssen could supply gas to Barmen and all the communities in between, but the RWE would have the exclusive supply of gas beyond Barmen into the Bergisches Land.[67] Within a few years, a number of other communities between Mülheim and Barmen hooked onto the Thyssen gas and water pipelines. While this agreement regulated the southern and eastern areas of the Ruhr, Stinnes and Thyssen continued to carry their conflict over the supply of gas on to the north and west of Mülheim.

As part of the negotiation of spheres of influence, Thyssen retreated from any more claims to supply the communities surrounding his firms with electricity, which he left to the RWE. In return, after 1910 the RWE agreed to draw a portion of its electrical power from Thyssen's coking, blast furnaces, and steelworks of the GDK and the AGHütt—generated by Thyssen & Co.'s gas turbines. The RWE also guaranteed a regular supply of electrical power to Thyssen firms in case of shortfalls. The importance of the gas engines to the whole division of labor between the RWE and the Wasserwerk, between Stinnes and Thyssen, explains why the negotiations centered on the Machine Company. In spite of this division of labor, the friendship between Thyssen and Stinnes remained chilly. It never really warmed again.

By 1912, the Thyssen & Co. Waterworks completed gas and water pipelines stretching on a diagonal from one end of the Ruhr to another.[68] Thyssen firms supplied gas for all communes between Walsum to Mülheim to Barmen, while it supplied water all the way to Dinslaken and Hiesfeld in the northwest and up to Gladbeck and Dorsten in the north. The two Thyssen Waterworks built well-water pumping stations and pipelines from Mülheim to Borbeck, Bottrop, Gladbeck to Dorsten and from Mülheim over Meiderich, Ruhrort, Beeck to Walsum and Dinslaken. During and after the war, the Thyssen network extended in a northerly direction, continuing nearly to the Dutch border. The water pipelines extended roughly 400 kilometers, transporting 50 million cubic meters of water. Over 9,000 large and small customers connected themselves to Thyssen-supplied water. By 1912, Thyssen gas pipelines covered 143 kilometers, shipping 29 million cubic meters of gas and supplying gas for over 2,000 customers.

Lenze and Pouch had built the Thyssen & Co. and GDK gas and water works into the largest long-distance supplier of gas and water in Europe, the first of its kind. Although it created a considerable demand for Thyssen & Co. pipes, it also posed a considerable challenge to the pipe department to seal pipe joints correctly. In mid-1912, Thyssen took the opportunity to sell off his Mülheim-based waterworks to a joint venture of the RWE and the city of Mülheim. Mülheim had suffered a cholera epidemic in the previous year and wanted more control over its water supply. In addition, the canal-building in the Ruhr would constrain its development, so Thyssen sold out. Thyssen retained the GDK waterworks in Beeckerwerth, which had been incorporated as a department of the Thyssen & Co. Waterworks. It became an independent division, called the *Gas- und Wasserwerke Gewerkschaft Deutscher Kaiser.* The war interrupted its spinoff into a fully independent company.

The key to Thyssen's success in fields quite unrelated to his original rolling-mill operations was his reliance on trained engineers and talented managers who actively helped to formulate business strategy and to realize his high-flying plans. Andrew Carnegie once credited a trained, "thorough" German mind for his early success in the steel industry: A German partner, Andrew Kloman, helped establish the reputation of Carnegie's Keystone Works by developing cold saws, upsetting machines, and the first universal mill used in the United States. Carnegie trusted this "young genius" so much that when Kloman said he could make something unprecedented, Carnegie entered "unhesitatingly" into the contract or venture. When Carnegie's famous Lucy furnace had troubles due to the varying qualities of ore, limestone, or coke, he hired a chemist, an educated German, Dr. Fricke, to solve the problem. Fricke introduced chemical testing for input materials and persuaded Carnegie of the efficacy of "scientific management" in a traditionally hands-on, empirical activity.[69] In this respect, Thyssen's trust in "young geniuses" made him similar to Carnegie. Both examples attest to an ongoing German–American dialogue on technical practice.

Thyssen could rely on the strong German technical education system as a reservoir of innovation. Much like the water drawn from the

Ruhr by the Waterworks, Thyssen continually drew talented newcomers from German technical universities into his firm. This reservoir of theoretical knowledge met empirical experience through applied practice and learning inside the business firm. Thyssen still had to choose the right people, incorporate their personalities and abilities into his organization, and make them work in accord with his very high expectations and within his corporate culture. The Thyssen & Co. Machine Company was not always successful for various technological, organizational, commercial, and personal reasons. It achieved profitability only after considerable investment and perseverance.

The reservoir metaphor, however, fails to draw the circle of innovation and learning from the business firm back into the educational system, from practice back into theory. Engineers' applied experience inside the business enterprise fed back into the technical university system. This institutional learning loop can best be represented by Lenze's career in the Thyssen & Co. Waterworks. After World War I, Lenze continued to extend the wasserwerk until it could supply over 100,000 people with drinking water. Lenze also developed new ways of cleaning the coking gas through high towers and new cooling processes. In Thyssen's coking facilities, he also fully mechanized the entire operation. His work was so pioneering that the Technical University of Karlsruhe, the same university where Thyssen briefly studied, established a new specialty of gas engineering based on Lenze's recommendations and experience. Lenze also actively participated on the board of directors of the Kaiser-Wilhelm-Institute for coal research. (Richter surely would have been just as important in his specialty if not for his untimely death.) Lenze's career trajectory, from university-trained engineer to practical experience in the business world, and then back to provide new technical theory in the university system, represents just one case among thousands.[70] Ultimately, this "academic–industrial-knowledge network" (to quote Johann Peter Murmann) created positive feedback that kept Thyssen and the German "national innovation system" on the cutting edge of technological leadership. Production capacities may have been lost or disrupted or destroyed and dismantled during the two world wars, but institutional, technological, organizational and personal capabilities continued.

Forgetting for the moment the expansive vertical integration of the Thyssen-Konzern that most directly compares to Carnegie's steelmaking operations, Thyssen entered into a range of activities rarely envisioned by Carnegie. By World War I, Thyssen & Co. had developed into a widely diversified set of firms: rolling mills for pipes and plates; machine engineering with its high-horsepower gas engines and turbines, and water and gas supply. The Thyssen & Co. Machine Company and Waterworks extended outside the steel industry *per se*, blurring the boundaries between the concepts of related and unrelated diversification (conglomeration), between the firm and the region's infrastructure.

At stake in this argument is how Thyssen & Co. created corporate coherence. The diversification of Thyssen & Co. clearly rested in part on the technological interconnections growing out of its industrial operations. The Thyssen machine department helped fulfil the equipment needs of all Thyssen firms. The Waterworks grew out of the heavy demand for water to clear out mines and cool equipment. The excess waste gas emanating from Thyssen's coking, iron-, and steel-making operations was then recycled to power the gas engine or sold off to local communities. In this respect, the coherency of this diversification lies in its related technological interconnections. The coherency of the business firm appears to rest on a core set of technological imperatives.[71]

Indeed, the gas engine turned a former waste material from the coking and steelmaking operations into a positive source of energy, recycling the gas, which lowered the use of coal, and in turn reduced the cost of producing coke and steel. The increasing electrification of the mills created widespread changes on the manufacturing floor (cranes, shopfloor organization), and central energy surveillance system, which put pressure on the development of more precise dials, gauges, and measuring techniques. The capture and cleaning of the gas to drive the engines in turn created a surplus that could be supplied to other customers in the region. The communities in the region required that Thyssen & Co. supply them with water and gas, driving Thyssen into becoming a regional water, gas, and later electricity supplier. The growth of water and gas pipelines in turn created an in-house demand for pipes and fittings that rebounded to the good of the scale economies for the plate and pipe mills. These positive production interconnections put pressure on upstream and downstream stages of production, like a series of interlocking gears, or of pressures and responses, actions and reactions.[72]

Yet the creation of these interconnections neither followed naturally from the potential technologies nor was a necessary outgrowth of Thyssen's industrial operations. The danger of this argument is that one can imagine almost any new technology as connected to another set of technologies in some manner or another. Why did Thyssen not enter the oil industry with its huge demand for pipes, or the lubricating oil business, because his firms certainly used a good deal of it? Deriving coherency from technological imperatives can explain the drive to greater diversification on the basis of complementary assets or transaction costs, but not the direction, pattern, or timing of diversification. Can the transition into machine engineering or water and gas supply really be described as a kind of clustering of technical competences?[73]

Both the Machine Company and the Waterworks began as auxiliary departments, internalizing the costs of subcontracting. Transaction-cost theory explains the initial decision to enter the market. But there was no necessary reason to commercialize these operations as full-fledged, competitive industrial firms except Thyssen's sense of opportunism, and entrepreneurial principle that they support themselves on their own, otherwise they "did not justify their existence." Before the war, only a few heavy industrial firms, such as the GHH, the Friedrich-Wilhelms-Hütte, and Krupp, integrated machine engineering into their operations. American steel firms rarely ventured into mechanical engineering, although one can imagine how technological interrelatedness might have existed there as well. Thyssen & Co.'s move into gas and water supply, moreover, made it the first long-distance gas supplier in Germany and made it unique among German firms. Other German steel firms found it unnecessary or did not take advantage of the opportunity to pump their own water and gas, let alone supply it to outside communities—Stinnes excepted. Moreover, the move out of larger scale electricity generation was due to the complicated competitive–cooperative rivalry of Hugo Stinnes and August Thyssen, along with the mediation of community governments and the Prussian state, both of which feared an RWE monopoly controlled by Thyssen and Stinnes. Otherwise Thyssen & Co. might have also entered the field of electricity supply. In short, politics, institutions, personal qualities and conflicts, agency, chance, and timing mediated the decision to diversify in the way that Thyssen did.

In short, the coherency of Thyssen & Co.'s technological competencies rested on the successful *commercial* and *organizational* realization of these projects. Above all, August Thyssen's strategic vision, Thyssen & Co.'s relatively uniform organizational controls, policies, and procedures, and Thyssen & Co.'s corporate culture created this technological coherency—after the fact.[74] That Thyssen had to keep drawing from the well of educated engineers (if not Ebeling, then Hoffmann; if not Hoffmann, then Richter; if not Richter, then Roser) showed that Thyssen & Co. could not supply all of the competencies necessary to compete in these diverse fields. In spite of this reservoir of talented, educated people, Thyssen & Co. still had to fold them into its own specific organizational patterns.

How was Thyssen & Co. as an organization able to sustain innovation and compete effectively over time in these diversified fields? Unlike the competition in the water and gas market, which was largely an open field for first movers, the machine engineering field was one of the strongest in Germany. One factor was certainly the series of positive feedback loops created by Thyssen's manufacturing operations themselves. The growth of the Thyssen-Konzern provided a relatively safe set of orders for the machine department before 1900 to develop its manufacturing competencies. When Thyssen & Co. moved into the water business, the Waterworks also acted as a source of demand for both pumping equipment and pipelines provided by the machine department and rolling mills. When the machine department moved into gas-engine production, it could build upon twenty years of previous experience of building steam engines and machinery.

Technical expertise was not the main problem for the Machine Company. Its commercial and marketing organization was, which is why Thyssen at first turned to joint ventures. Pressures from one stage of production to another did not automatically generate technological, commercial, or organizational solutions. Those intermeshing gears of technological determinism could just as well lock up. Such an action–reaction description might work on an industrywide basis (if one firm does not pick up on the next stage of technological development, another does), but it cannot explain why a particular firm managed to diversify and develop these processes.

Less appreciated as a source of sustained (technological) innovation is the powerful coherence created by the firm's control system and corporate culture—the system of the business firm itself—not just its structure, or scale and scope.[75] Clearly Thyssen & Co. imposed a consistent set of commercial values and controls on these new scientists and engineers as they moved into Thyssen's corporate world. The significant turnover of machine-department executives reveals the considerable tension between Thyssen & Co. routines (monthly financial reports, successful results, commercialized applications) and the expectations of the new machine department directors. So many of Thyssen & Co. department chiefs, such as Richter or Lenze, began as engineers/scientists, yet were made to perform as "ordinary businessmen." Thyssen made Lenze a commercial director of the Thyssen & Co. and GDK Waterworks. Thyssen & Co.'s ability as an organizational culture to extend these fundamental corporate values, policies, and internal routines to new fields of endeavor created a baseline of organizational competency and internal coherence that allowed it to diversify beyond the bounds of the steel industry and sustain innovation without crumbling apart, without losing control.

PART II

The Thyssen-Konzern, 1890–1926

THYSSEN

The rapid growth of the *Gewerkschaft Deutscher Kaiser* (GDK) made Thyssen famous, yet it remained only the largest firm in a complex of firms known as the Thyssen-Konzern. Although Thyssen became most famous for pioneering the vertical integration of "mixed firms" (as contemporaries called them), which incorporated coal, steel, and finished products, I argue that Thyssen should instead be known more for his pioneering efforts as a modern *Organisator*. The Thyssen-Konzern developed a multidivisional (more precisely, a multisubsidiary) form with its characteristic "decentralized centralized" organizational structure. Thyssen personally attended to the creation of the crucial Central Auditing Office (CAO), a central corporate supervisory office for financial and organizational affairs. The CAO acted as an inhouse management consultancy. How Thyssen and his directors formed their strategy under the competitive dynamics of the German steel industry and why they chose the organizational form of the *Konzern* are the central issues covered in this section.

I first analyze why Germans felt cartels were an appropriate part of economic life, and show how they altered the competitive dynamics of the German steel industry. As a response to cartels in particular, German heavy industrial firms integrated vertically. The rise of the Thyssen-Konzern is a clean, almost ideal example of such vertical integration. Other German *Konzerne* developed in a messier fashion because they grew largely as a result of mergers and acquisitions.

The paramount organizational problem facing German heavy industrialists was how to manage a firm within a heavily cartelized world, with a high degree of vertical integration, highly diversified product lines, and small-batch production in a highly capital-intensive industry. Running a coal company was different than operating a pipe mill or managing a machine-engineering firm. This institutional environment, combined with vertical integration, created very different organizational dilemmas than those faced by most American firms, with their focus on scale economies in a few product lines. German steel industrialists had essentially three organizational choices: (1) combine multiproduct operations into a unified corporation structured along functional lines, (2) create one large corporation subdivided into relatively autonomous commercial-technical departments (as did Thyssen & Co.), or (3) form *Konzerne*, multisubsidiary structures of affiliated but legally independent firms. Before 1914, Thyssen's highly coherent *Konzern* management was unique in German heavy industry, but that industry moved to this organizational solution as they acquired other finishing and machine-engineering firms after the war.

Owning an array of interrelated firms, however, did not make a coherent *Konzern*. True to the principle of "delegate but supervise," Thyssen and his directors developed a relatively sophisticated set of central corporate offices to monitor and evaluate the performance of individual firms. Only by grasping the Thyssen-Konzern as a whole can one make sense of the interlocking arrangements of Thyssen's financial organization, which reproduce the basic financial principles and advantages attributed to the multidivisional enterprise. The Thyssen-Konzern offers a striking parallel to other leading companies' organizations around the globe (Mitsui, Mitsubishi, DuPont, and General Motors). Indeed, the vaunted "M-form," *or multidivisional*, which Oliver Williamson and Alfred Chandler termed the most significant organizational innovation of the twentieth century, first appeared in Germany and Japan. Analyzing Thyssen's financial machinations also provides a unique vantage point from which to study German bank–industry relations.

The Great War and subsequent hyperinflation knocked the financial coherency of the Thyssen-Konzern off of its hinges. Thyssen and his managers spent much of the postwar period trying to restore the balance of control found in the Thyssen-Konzern before the war and come to terms with revolutionary activity and the effect of new forms of industrial relations, such as works councils and collective bargaining. Pressure by labor altered key aspects of Thyssen's organizational culture, forcing greater central coordination of social policy. Along with financial travails, and tax and legal issues, the new political situation led to a fundamental debate among Thyssen managers whether to centralize the *Konzern* into a unified corporation or retain its decentralized management structure. The stabilization crisis of 1924 threw the Thyssen-Konzern into a major liquidity crisis, forcing Thyssen and his sons to make hard choices. They turned to Wall Street for financial respite. They debated centralizing the Thyssen-Konzern into a single legal entity to attract American money and reduce their tax burden. Those revisions tested the limits of German corporate law and the legal definition of the corporation. Such debates about financial relations with America, organizational change, law, and the nature of the corporation foreshadowed future issues inside the *Vereinigte Stahlwerke* (VSt). The stabilization crisis also sparked a crisis of succession. Thyssen and his sons had to decide whether to join this new trust modeled on U.S. Steel. Ultimately, the decision to join the VSt came down to family relations, especially the sibling rivalry between Fritz Thyssen and Heinrich Thyssen-Bornemisza. Just one month after the VSt officially came into existence, August Thyssen died, taking the entrepreneurial, financial, and economic unity of the Thyssen-Konzern with him to his grave.

CHAPTER 6

Cartels and Competition

It may not be pretty but it is practical.
August Thyssen

For nearly two decades (1871–1886), August Thyssen focused on his partnership in Mülheim. Alone, Thyssen & Co. was a successful, profitable industrial firm among the elite of German industry. Yet suddenly, after 1887, he ventured into constructing a larger integrated combine (coal mines and steelworks) in Hamborn-Bruckhausen near Duisburg: the *Gewerkschaft Deutscher Kaiser* (GDK), for which he became famous as the Carnegie of Germany. Why did Thyssen begin investing directly in his own coal-mining and steelmaking operations when beforehand, especially through the *Schalker Verein,* he had maintained a degree of influence over his input supplies through his financial portfolio?

In order to answer this question correctly, we need to sketch one of the most distinctive aspects of German capitalism before 1945: the capacity of German industrialists, most particularly those in the coal and steel industries, to organize sophisticated cartels and syndicates. Cartels changed the competitive environment of German capitalism, and are crucial for understanding the strategies of individual steel firms. Cartel contracts had a profound impact on business, and could affect even the minutest aspects of internal operations. The presence of cartels lay at the heart of the rubrics "cooperative managerial capitalism" and "organized capitalism."

Yet such formulations fundamentally overplay the amount of cooperation, and underplay the level of competition, inside cartels. Business historians have tended not to analyze cartels' effects on competitive behavior and their impact on organizational change within business firms. German firms certainly could and did collude, but what difference did this make? Contrary to most commonsense notions about them, cartels did not eliminate, but rechanneled and restructured, competition among firms, much like state regulation.[1] German industrialists claimed, however, that they regulated themselves *(Selbstverwaltung)*. One result was the growth of vertically oriented *Konzerne*.

American Anti-cartel and German Antitrust Legislation

Why did Germans feel that cartels were an appropriate, even necessary, part of economic life? In general, German affirmation of cartels was as "populist" as the American prohibition of them. Moreover, Germany followed no *Sonderweg* or "special path" regarding cartels.[2] From a global perspective, the United States did.

German industrialists did have a well-deserved ability to organize cartels and syndicates. The expressed goals of the cartels were usually threefold: to ensure producers and financiers with an adequate return on their investments by avoiding excessive competition; to coordinate supply and demand in the face of business cycles by regulating competition through production or sales quotas; and to represent the marketing interests of the industrial sector as a whole.

Friedrich Kleinwächter, a respected economist, set the tone. He concluded that cartels were "children of necessity" designed to save entrepreneurs from "ruinous competition."[3] One of Germany's leading intellectuals, Lujo Brentano, felt cartels were "parachutes" that softened landings after a high-flying business cycle. Cartels moderated the egoistic price-undercutting practices of individual firms and regulated wasteful competition and overproduction.[4] Even Karl Bücher, the speaker most critical of cartels at the famous meeting of the Association for Social Policy *(Verein für Socialpolitik)*, still justified cartels as a necessary stage in the cultural evolution of economies.[5]

Along these lines, much of the literature on cartels conflated the common interests of producers with the good of society as a whole, quite unlike Anglo-Saxon assumptions, which tended to equate individualistic self-interest and the lowest possible prices for consumers as good for society as a whole. German economic theory tended to distinguish between private/individualistic economies and a public/national economy, which found expression in Friedrich List's critique of Adam Smith.[6] Not surprisingly, German economists called themselves *Nationalökonomen*. Generally, the tradeoff between purely price-based, individualist economic efficiency and its social costs was decisive in their argument. Cartels ameliorated the severe social costs of industrial change *without* eliminating such change altogether. The higher prices charged by cartels were viewed as the necessary cost of stability and gradual adjustment, as opposed to anarchic competition and disorderly change. At bottom, it was a pro-producer, conservative point of view. German national economists were skeptical of Adam Smith's arguments that the unlimited pursuit of private gain always served the public interest, and that a host of uncoordinated individualistic decisions automatically added up to a superior economic order.

Cartels were viewed in Germany as a particular form of self-regulation, as intermediate organizations that helped to coordinate individual actions with the greater goals of the community, industry, and the nation. Clearly, a nostalgic vision of corporate estates and guilds lay behind these notions, but the legal basis for permitting cartels was based on *liberal* principles of law. Industrialists' defense of cartels also contained a significant, but underappreciated, associational and anti-statist moment that asserted private interests and self-regulation.

The debate about cartels involved a conflict between two liberal (not corporatist) values. For the German Imperial Court, the crucial legal issue that needed to be adjudicated was whether freedom of association (or freedom of contract) had precedence over freedom of competition (or no restraint of trade). One lawyer stated the issue clearly: "The cartels want to restrain competition through freedom of contract, while their opponents want to attain free competition by limiting freedom of contract." Another lawyer skeptically pointed out that the cartels were an organization "in which free competition freely dissolved itself."[7] We should not be too quick to draw a sharp contrast between Anglo-Saxon and German (or Continental) traditions in this matter; both British and American courts wrestled with this very same conflict.[8] (American courts simply obliterated this tension by arguing that cartel agreements would regulate interstate commerce, and hence encroach on the Constitutional powers of Congress.)[9] This conflict took place *within* liberalism itself, as the growing power of big business threatened the "industrial liberty" of a world of small consumers, producers, shopkeepers, traders, and merchants.

At roughly the same time as it surfaced in American and British courts, the contradiction between liberty of contract and freedom of competition reached the German Imperial Court in 1897 in a case about the Saxon wood-pulp producer association.[10] The Imperial Court had to decide whether the cartel's attempt to set minimum prices for its products contradicted the intentions of the state's legislature to promote freedom of trade, and whether cartel contracts could be enforced.

The 1897 Imperial Court decision clearly stated that cartels helped manage crises engendered by ruinous competition and permitted them as long as they did not monopolize or abuse their market power. Raising prices was not a sufficient criterion for prohibiting cartels, because state-sponsored tariffs did the same, yet were deemed in the national interest. "Properly used," cartels could provide a "particularly appropriate service to the entire national economy" by preventing "wasteful overproduction" and "catastrophes." A cartel contract "does not violate the principle of freedom of trade, insofar as the interest of the whole should be safeguarded against the self-interest of the individual, if members of a common trade join together in good faith to maintain the viability of a branch of trade by protecting the devaluation of their products and other resulting disadvantages from the price-cutting by individuals." Only if cartel agreements intended to create a "monopoly" or cause "usurious exploitation of the consumer" should they be banned.[11] Unlike the situation in America, where cartels were illegal and criminal, or in Britain, where cartel agreements were condoned but leniently enforced, German cartel agreements became both legal and enforceable.

Ultimately, the Imperial Court justified enforcing cartel contracts on the grounds that they represented a legitimate form of "cooperative self-help." Cartels were regarded as measures to prevent economic turmoil, agreed upon by voluntary association for purposes of private self-regulation. The legal justification for cartels rested firmly on the liberal principles of freedom of contract and association. Members of cartels freely agreed to the stipulated rules, so the courts, as with any other contract, could enforce fines and sanctions levied by the cartel.

Many German entrepreneurs, *die Wirtschaft*, viewed cartels' self-regulation as a means of making state regulation and intervention superfluous. The term means not only a self-regulating market, but also an active collection of individuals and firms working in the economy. Cartels acted as a means of "self-government," that is, a type of private business management of the economy and industry.[12] German entrepreneurs vehemently opposed any sort of cartel supervisory office. In this respect, Americans and British were much more interventionist than the Germans, reflecting a greater faith in the "visible hand of the lawmaker" to counter growing economic power.[13]

The Imperial Court's decision to permit cartels overwhelmingly reflected public opinion. The German public perceived cartels as legitimate instruments of economic order. German advocacy of cartels was an expression of fundamental social values, just as the Sherman Act articulated American populist reaction against price-fixing. The desire for cartels also had important legal ramifications for the Social Democrats, who realized that freedom of association was critical for legitimizing workers' unions. Their belief was borne out by the use of the Sherman Antitrust Act against the American union movement—just one way in which the American experience was used as a negative argumentative foil.[14] Negative American examples, such as Standard Oil's predatory practices, pervaded German discussions.

The Imperial Court also based its decision on mainstream economic thought regarding cartels, especially as expressed by the economists Friedrich Kleinwächter and Lujo Brentano. But in terms of economic justification for cartels, the two most important theorists were Robert Liefmann and Gustav Schmoller, the latter being Germany's leading economist. Their arguments rested on the problems of managing business cycles in a capitalist economy by firms saddled with the problems of high fixed costs, long investment horizons, the necessity to ensure volume or throughput, and attendant social issues such as employment and costs of social change.[15]

But the distinction between huge American firms and German cartels is critical for understanding why cartels were viewed positively. Germans found "trusts" (a derogatory term) to be more dangerous than cartels. Cartels were contractual associations of legally independent firms. American-style trusts and mergers, by contrast, merged the legal and economic independence of individual firms into one big corporation under a single management. Liefmann, in fact, argued that cartels were more "democratic" than "monarchical" American trusts. In comparison to the "unbelievably ruthless" American practice of "throwing workers into the streets," cartels would help German firms maintain a steadier overall employment level by moderating price fluctuations. Liefmann thought this made planning more calculable, thus enhancing technological progress by reducing risk.[16] The sheer size of trusts concentrated unprecedented financial power in the hands of few people, "in particular because anyone can get anything with money in America."[17] To Liefmann, systematic elimination, predatory pricing, or absorption of one's competitors hardly seemed to be "free competition." The big U.S. trusts such as Standard Oil and U.S. Steel epitomized the German horror of wide-open American capitalism. If there were no other competitors left because of so-called free competition, then free competition apparently ended in monopoly, the antithesis of competition.[18] Cartels were allegedly immune to such practices, but some members of the German Parliament pointed to the marketing strategies of Standard Oil and the Rheinisch-Westphalian Coal Syndicate: "The similarity is so great that one can practically see the coal dust on these petroleum contracts."[19]

Schmoller and Liefmann granted that many large trusts were more efficient manufacturers, but stressed that the social costs of trusts outweighed their advantages. Liefmann, for instance, found a few virtues in American-style trusts. They could adjust to market demand more quickly by shutting down less efficient plants and allowing the best facilities to run at capacity. Trusts could also introduce new technologies faster, but at the cost of employment. Their scale brought them advantages in purchasing or freight costs. They could produce higher profits for their shareholders more quickly than cartels. And since the trust operated with just one will, rather than a collective will, it could also confront rivals more coherently. According to Liefmann: "With the above, however, the advantages making a trust superior to a cartel are exhausted."

Germans thus tended to view cartels as a middle way between egoistic anarchy and monopolistic trusts, between unfettered capitalism and state socialism. Schmoller called them "the correct middle road between socialist experiments and the previous organization of the economy." For Schmoller, cartels were a form of "cooperative competition." Only "childish hot-heads" and "fanatics of individualism" would want to ban them. Schmoller argued: "On the whole they [cartels] are either as beneficial or as disastrous in the measure that their leadership are moderate and statesmen-like or short-sighted and greedy."[20]

Just as there were good trusts and bad trusts in the United States, there were good cartels and bad cartels in Germany.

In the end, Germans viewed cartels as a "dike" against further trust-making. Cartels *reduced* the level of industrial concentration and permitted smaller, family-owned firms to stay in business. Schmoller regarded the Sherman Antitrust Act as "overhasty" and "clumsy." It unintentionally promoted rather than prevented trusts (as many contemporaries and business historians today have argued.)[21] A parliamentary representative, Theodor Vogelstein, commented in 1906: "if we had trustification today in the German coal and steel industry, we would see no other people left except Mister Kirdorf and Mister Thyssen."[22]

Unlike American oligopolies such as U.S. Steel, which alone accounted for 45–77% of various product lines in the American steel market in 1901, the ten largest German integrated combines produced about 50% of German crude steel, while the ten largest German mining firms (often the same as the steel companies) had just under a 30% share in 1913. By 1925, the concentration level had increased in all primary goods sectors, but the ten largest German steel combines still had under a 70% market share. Not until the founding of the VSt in 1926 did Germans reach American-style concentration levels in the steel industry.[23] Cartels did help to keep German steel firms relatively small compared to American firms in any given product line. There was always just enough truth in cartel theorists' contentions to lend them plausibility.

Paradoxically, then, the Sherman Antitrust Act acted mostly as an anti-cartel law that encouraged trusts, while the affirmation of cartels by the German Imperial Court was a form of antitrust action. Counterintuitively, *laissez faire* was practiced in this regard more consistently by Germany, which allowed industry to collude.[24] The United States intervened with politicians and lawyers.

Cartels in Practice

The existence of cartels cannot itself explain the competitive dynamics of individual industries. The economics of the industry, the form of cartel, and the specifics of the individual cartel contract shaped its growth. In theory, cartels were an orderly means of distributing contracts, stabilizing prices, keeping smaller firms in business, and reducing concentrations of property. In practice, they were a motley collection of disorderly organizations and messy compromises, shaky frameworks hammered together after very competitive haggling about quotas. They restructured competition in different industries by varying degrees.

Acceptance of interfirm agreements gave German entrepreneurs a range of strategic options not available to Americans. German cartel theory distinguishes at least twelve to fourteen different types of cartels, ranging from relatively weak "condition cartels" that set only terms of sale, to full-scale syndicates that set prices and marketed their members' wares. Price-fixing was not necessarily the only or main goal of cartels. Improving market organization, standardizing products or sales terms, rationalizing production, exchanging information, ameliorating the social and economic costs of downsizing industries, and even reducing marketing costs, as in some export cartels.[25] Even an IG (*Interessengemeinschaft*), or "community of interest," which resembled an American holding company, was a coalition of companies who voluntarily gave up part of their entrepreneurial autonomy to the IG—a kind of holding cartel. IG's could be relatively weak profit-pooling arrangements or strong rationalizing instruments, depending on the collective agreement. IG's were one of the strongest forms of interfirm alliances along the spectrum of market-bridging instruments; they were viewed as a prelude to merger.

German heavy industry had three of the most important cartels: the Rhenisch-Westphalian Coal Syndicate, the Düsseldorf Pig Iron Syndicate, and the Steel Works Association. All three were significantly strengthened after the turn of the twentieth century—forming a German version of the American "Great Merger Movement." In 1907, the coal syndicates covered about 80% of total German coal production, the pig iron syndicates about 25% of pig iron, and the steel works association about 50% of steel. Collapsing after the war, cartels reasserted themselves in the mid-1920s. In 1925, they controlled 100% of coal production, and roughly 90% of primary steel production.[26]

The Rhenisch-Westphalian Coal Syndicate was Germany's most stable model cartel. It was founded in 1893, and controlled about 87% of Ruhr coal production. The syndicate itself was a joint-stock corporation that operated without profits in the interests of its members. By 1913 it employed about 500 in administrative and marketing jobs, managing about 1,400 prices for different qualities of coal.

Belying many theories about the inherent instability of cartels with a large number of members, the coal syndicate consisted of 98 firms in 1893, 83 in 1903, and 67 in 1912. The affiliated coke syndicate consisted of 53 members in 1890 and 46 in 1912. The coke syndicate held together in spite of the size difference between large and small producers. In 1912, 22 firms had quotas above one million tons (five about three million), while the rest ranged down to a low of 135,000 metric tons. In 1913, the five largest coal producers mined about 20% of German coal, more than the ten largest in 1893. By 1925, the five largest firms mined about 25% of all German coal, while the ten largest produced about 40%.

The pricing policy of the coal syndicate can best be described as moderate; English coal prices fluctuated both higher and lower than the German syndicate's prices. Coal prices in Germany rose steadily, but not dramatically. One reason why the syndicate could not raise prices higher was that significant areas of Germany were still competitive. In the north, English coal competed with syndicated coal. In the east, and in the important Berlin market, Upper Silesian coal and English coal vied with Ruhr coal. In southern German markets, Saar coal mines could successfully compete. Moreover, the Ruhr coal syndicate was joined by Silesian and Saar coal cartels (the latter run by the Prussian state). The Rhenisch-Westphalian Coal Syndicate had a near monopoly position only within a 250 km radius of the Ruhr. By 1925, the regional syndicate mined 78% of Germany's coal, allowing it to act as a hegemon or collective oligopoly, but it still was not a monopoly.

Coal cartel contracts illustrate the way cartels rechanneled competition. The 1893 contract stipulated that sinking new shafts would raise the production quota of any company. Suddenly a boom of new shafts occurred, many with no intention of mining coal (so-called "syndicate rubber shafts"). Capacity outstripped production quotas within the cartel. While the coal syndicate's production rose 60% between 1893 and 1902, the integrated combines outside the cartel doubled their production. They were led by Thyssen's GDK, whose production rose 450%. The syndicate had to incorporate this production or collapse.

The growing contradiction between the small and "pure" coal-mining firms (such as Kirdorf's Gelsenkirchen, the largest) and the integrated combines (such as Thyssen, Phoenix, the GHH, or Krupp) became the single greatest source of tension inside the syndicate. Until 1903, the syndicate could not entice the integrated combines like

Thyssen's to join. Only by conceding them generous self-consumption exemptions (right to consume one's own production without being limited by cartel quotas), did the cartel persuade them to join. Thyssen's GDK, the leading outsider, negotiated this concession. Eliminating the "rubber shaft" loophole, the 1903 contract stipulated that firms could raise their production quotas only by taking over existing mines rather than by sinking new ones. Naturally, this provision gave considerable incentive to incorporate mines or vertically integrate to take advantage of self-consumption rights and raise quotas. In 1904, roughly 19% of the syndicate's coal production was mined by integrated combines and 24% of its coke refined by them. By 1909, this proportion rose to 29% and 40%, respectively. The uncontrolled growth of integrated combines increased tension within the syndicate.

Under great pressure from the pure coal-mining companies, the 1909 renewal contract finally limited self-consumption rights. Krupp, Thyssen's GDK, and Phoenix, which had the highest self-consumption exemptions, managed to set these rights still high enough so that they did *not* affect internal operations or hinder growth. But the pure mining companies gained a significant concession, in that self-consumption quotas could only be raised in the same proportion as that of the pure mining companies. Still, the independent mining companies bore a disproportionate share of the costs of running the syndicate. The conflict between the two types of firms was so great that the coal syndicate would have collapsed in 1915 if the state did not persuade industrialists like Thyssen to agree "voluntarily" to its renewal, or face its forcible extension in the interest of war production. Temporary extensions and contract revisions kept the coal syndicate together through the revolutionary years. While most (90%) of Ruhr coal producers agreed to join the 1924 extension, a number of strong producers, including Thyssen, refused to join. Again the state stepped in. A revised contract went into effect in 1925, extending until 1930, by which the syndicate retained jurisdiction over the "uncompetitive" parts of the domestic market (a radius of 250 kilometers around the Ruhr), but lost control over marketing in competitive and foreign markets.[27]

Unlike the Ruhr coal syndicate, the twenty-member Düsseldorf Pig Iron Syndicate, founded in 1896, did not have the market power to act as a price-setter. Unlike the coal syndicate, it had no legal status as a company and little staff, limiting its ability to enforce agreements. It nearly went under during the boom of 1899, because its members refused to sell their pig iron through it. It had little power over members until its renewal in 1903. When the economy went into a recession in 1902–1903, the integrated combines put a large amount of their cheap iron on the market, depressing prices even further, and took a significant share of the market away from the pure iron-making firms inside the cartel.

The 1903 pig-iron contract renewal brought significant improvements. The syndicate was made responsible for domestic and foreign sales. It negotiated some temporary agreements with its rival pig-iron syndicates in the Saar, Lorraine-Luxembourg (only until 1906), and Upper Silesia, but it remained in competition with them. Many integrated combines, including Thyssen, joined at this point, but the syndicate collapsed in 1908 because outsiders aggressively undercut its prices. Prices dropped to roughly 25% of pre-syndicate days. Desperate, the integrated combines breathed new life into the syndicate in 1910 by reforming it, and it now included forty-one producers. In 1912, the syndicate made arrangements with both Saar and south German ironmakers. By 1915, it was able finally to collude successfully with Luxembourg producers.

In 1907, cartels controlled only about 25% of German pig-iron production. Not until 1925 did a national cartel control all of Germany's production. Concentration in the pig-iron industry continued to rise slowly. At the time of the cartel's founding in 1896, the five largest firms in the Ruhr produced roughly 20% of the nation's pig iron; by 1913, they produced 30%.[28] By comparison, U.S. Steel alone produced over 45% of blast-furnace products for the U.S. market in 1913.[29]

Unlike the coal and pig-iron cartels, which handled relatively homogenous products, the important Steel Works Association was a comprehensive, national cartel that encompassed an extensive array of heterogenous steel products.[30] It consisted of a number of sub-cartels to coordinate production and sales of specific product lines. After difficult negotiations, made more complex by the diverse range of goods to be regulated, thirty-one member firms—led by August Thyssen—founded the cartel in 1904. Previously, industrialists formed numerous, short-lived, shaky cartels in structural steel, rails, pipes, strip steel, and so on, but none had been able to put a serious check on production or firmly regulate prices.

The association distinguished between A-products (semiprocessed material, structural steel and joists, heavy and light railway material) and B-products (bar iron, rolled wire, sheets and plates, pipes and tubes, railway axles). While A-products were syndicated, little agreement could be reached for B-products, which returned to an unregulated status after 1912 when negotiations collapsed. In 1913, the ten largest producers of crude steel had about a 50% market share, the top three about 20%. By 1925, the ten largest producers held over a 60% share, the top three just under 30%. Rather than merging horizontally, most of the integrated combines saw better profit opportunities in further vertical integration into B-Products.

Again, the conflict between pure and integrated mills was a great source of debate within the Steel Works Association, but one could find both types of companies on either side of the fence between syndicating or not syndicating B-products. Although there were fewer firms making B-products (many firms often having oligopolistic positions in tubes, plates and sheets, or axles), B-products were even harder to cartelize than A-products, which involved 24–28 firms. Standard cartel theory suggests that the fewer firms in negotiation, the more likely an agreement, but this idea was counterbalanced by the greater heterogeneity of B-products relative to the more homogenous A-products. Another problem for the B-product sector was the existence of a strong outsider making pipes (Mannesmann). A third problem was August Thyssen, who insisted on having B-products completely syndicated or not at all. Thyssen tried to break his B-product pipe quotas in the cartel, and threatened its entire existence with his request for a huge quota in A-products for his new steel works in Alsace-Lorraine, the *Stahlwerke Thyssen*. Additionally, steel industrialists found it harder to agree on B-products after an A-product cartel was successfully formed. The large integrated combines, in particular, threw their immense financial resources (partially generated by the cartelization of A-products) into B-products through additional internal expansion or by mergers and acquisitions. The integrated combines had great cost advantage over independent mills (explained below), which increased over time. While syndicate sales in A-products rose by 32% from 1904 to 1911, B-product sales rose 106%. B-product quotas were raised considerably in the 1907 renewal contract, but the internal conflicts over B-products resulted in failure to set controls over B-products in the 1912 renewal agreement.[31] This imposing steel sounding cartel, then, had decent control over A-products, but little over B-products, which saw vicious price competition.

The Steel Works Association limped along without any controls on B-products until the World War I, when the government took over the steel cartel for war production, extending it in 1917 without any significant changes. In 1919, it collapsed. Industrialists called the period of the great inflation the "cartel-less" period. When Germany received tariff sovereignty after January 1925, German industrialists quickly restored their syndicates. Eventually, a European-wide steel cartel was established in 1925 and solidified in 1926.

What is striking about German coal and steel cartels is less their inherent instability, but their relative longevity—all the more surprising considering the number of firms involved. They survived because of revisions made in their contracts every three to five years. The regional nature of German cartels has also been underestimated. As their names indicate, they reproduced regional disparities in the German economy and *competed* with one another.[32] The Ruhr coal syndicate could act as a price leader—a collective price-setting oligopoly. Finally, we must not forget the huge number of local or regional cartels, estimated in the thousands in the 1920s, that existed among small and middling size businesses—the collusive barbers or fishmongers or shopkeepers. The German cartel system remained patchy. And it remained subject to high levels of competition, especially among integrated combines and pure firms, between the largest and smallest firms. German steel industrialists demonstrated a continuing commitment to cooperative agreements in principle, but objected to specific terms at specific times. Heated competition took place over cartel contracts *and* in markets. A good deal of competition remained built into even the strongest cartel. Cartels slowed but did not eliminate concentration. And by 1913, the coal and steel cartels were stretched to their limits. The strongest firms, like Thyssen, were more and more willing to break them.

Why were cartels relatively stable in German heavy industry? First, their contracts were legal and enforceable, which gave cartels recourse to the courts to penalize transgressors. Their widespread legitimacy and perceived efficacy made steel industrialists predisposed toward cartels. As with any industry anywhere characterized by heavy fixed costs, a tendency to regulate competition cropped up. But two other factors contributed to this relative stability: tariffs and the great universal-credit banks.

Tariffs helped prevent foreign firms from taking advantage of the relatively high German domestic prices. The economic historian Steven Webb argues for a tariff-cartel system.[33] After the war, during a period when it was prohibited from establishing protective tariffs, Germany could not establish cartels. On the other hand, German tariffs on manufactured goods were not unusual by world standards; it offered moderate protection, lower than that of the United States.[34]

It has long been argued that the great universal banks also propelled this cartel movement. Alexander Gerschenkron felt that the "cartelization movement of German industry cannot be fully explained except as the natural result of the amalgamation of German banks," since "banks refused to tolerate fratricidal struggles among their children."[35] Indeed, bank representatives sat on the supervisory boards of most major Ruhr steel companies, and banks had considerable financial stakes in them. Personal friendship or familial relations reinforced financial and institutional ties. Werner von Siemens' cousin, Georg von Siemens, for instance, occupied a seat on the board of directors of the Deutsche Bank. Even August Thyssen, a notorious financial maverick, maintained an intimate, consultative friendship with Carl Klönne of the Deutsche Bank, who advised him on economic as well as family matters.[36]

Recent archival studies about bank–industry relations have, however, undermined this thesis. Powerful banks with financial interests across many firms did not necessarily promote cartels at all times. Often banks had diverging interests in one or more firms. For instance, Mannesmann was viewed as the great outsider in the pipe industry, yet the Deutsche Bank engaged itself heavily in the company. It was once said: "Anyone who is familiar with the German industrial and financial world answers questions about Mannesman with the information: It is the Deutsche Bank."[37] Simultaneously, the Deutsche Bank could promote the Steel Works Association, yet support Mannesmann's desire to stay away from it, especially from its attempt to syndicate B-products. Most steel firms could generate enough cash flow to finance their investments internally, at an average of 80% before 1914, which reduced the leverage that banks could have over industrial enterprises. As companies grew larger than the financial resources of single banks, consortiums of banks supplied the necessary financing, but this only increased competition among banks for the favor of industrialists, who could play banks off one another.[38] Thyssen and Stinnes managed to turn this competition into an art form. Stinnes even grew disgusted with the petty groveling of some banking officials who coveted his business.

The complex calculations involved among cartels, combines, and banks can best be observed from the forced entry of Phoenix into the Steel Works Association. For many, this example almost singlehandedly demonstrated the power of *Finanzkapital* over industrial firms.[39] Ironically, Phoenix, an integrated combine and one of the largest steel companies in Germany, had always been one of the most active promoters of cartels. Yet in an unusual move, Phoenix's chief executives *(Vorstand)* refused to join the cartel, because

- the proposed quota was too small and did not take into account unfinished capacity that was not yet operating;
- the syndicated A-products covered only 40% of Phoenix's total production, and quotas for B-products remained an open question;
- Phoenix would be obligated to share in the marketing costs of exports for joists, structurals, and intermediate materials, but would have to bear the costs for wire exports itself.

The *Schaaffhausen'sche Bankverein, the Bank für Handel und Industrie* (Darmstädter), and the *Disconto-Gesellschaft,* Phoenix's main banks on its supervisory board, differed with management. They agreed that the proposed quotas and arrangements were inadequate, but thought that the collapse of the cartel would be a "disaster" for the German steel industry. They had stakes in other firms and a keen desire to participate in the cartel's transactions. In public, they backed the Phoenix objections. But within a few months, the banks changed their tune. Promoters of the steel cartel had threatened to boycott Phoenix's intermediate products and target Phoenix by undercutting its prices in its important rail market. For insiders, there was little question who stood behind this threat—August Thyssen. Playing hardball, Thyssen threatened to cut any bank out of the cartel's financial transactions that did not promote Phoenix's entry into it. Phoenix offered an explanation of his reasons:

> Thyssen is greatly interested in the establishment of the Steel Works Association because on one hand he has completed his production facilities and runs them full, and would gladly see hoisted on the shoulders of his competition the burdens of his large export business. He is going through the fire for it with his renowned energy and does not spare those who stand in his way. Unfortunately our president [Albert von Oppenheim of the *Disconto-Gesellschaft*] does not have as much courage and endurance as the other . . . You will have already gathered by which means Thyssen & Co. has influenced our president and has frightened him.[40]

Thyssen became an ardent advocate of the cartel when the recent recession left his decade-long expansion plans for the GDK in financial disarray. The cartel would help stabilize his earnings on the domestic front and enable him to export more cheaply to world markets. Since syndicates were collective marketing organizations, Thyssen's sales would spread the costs of marketing and overhead over numerous firms rather than just his own.

Thyssen had leverage over the banks because they competed vehemently with one another for the opportunity to do business with the cartel, which promised to be so lucrative that no bank could afford to stay away from it. Thyssen's personal friend Carl Klönne, of the Deutsche Bank, wrote a series of nearly identical letters to all the major steel-company directors. He let it be known that the Deutsche Bank stood in the service of the steel cartel.[41] Steel industrialists should place the Deutsche Bank at the top of the list and cut out any nonsupportive banks.

Thyssen's heavy-handed maneuvers left the Phoenix banks little choice but to override the managing board. Up to the last minute, the executive directors still held out some hope that their house banks would not let Phoenix be "raped." But at the shareholders meeting in April 1904, the banks, who held a majority of shares, overrode the executive board and minority shareholders. Phoenix joined the Steel Works Association. The directors of Phoenix had to accept the *fait accompli:*

Thyssen let it be known to me that he wanted to visit me if I wanted to speak to him, but not about the quota. I answered him that I would have nothing to speak with him then, but would be available if he wanted to speak to me. The messenger then said that it was certainly not necessary to wash our dirty laundry in front of others, whereby I answered that we did not have any dirty laundry. Yesterday though, I heard from the last directors' meeting [of the Steel Works Association] that the Thyssens and their advisors were indeed not completely sure of their victory. It is too bad that our banks did not completely and wholeheartedly support us, then the decision would not be in doubt. I have therefore little hope although a great number of shareholders will express their support for us. Unfortunately their stockholdings are too small. You would be interested to know that even the upper circles of the coal syndicate are of the opinion that his actions violate common decency.[42]

As Thyssen said about hardboiled solutions: "It may not be pretty but it is practical."[43]

The intricacies of cartel-combine-bank relations could often mystify the participants themselves. Just two years after the steel cartel debacle, August Thyssen and Hugo Stinnes maneuvered Phoenix's reluctant main banks into a merger of Phoenix with the *Hörder Verein.* Their intentions and plots completely baffled the *Schaffhausen'sche Bankverein:*

I can understand that the question Hörde-Phoenix arises again. But I cannot find any reason whatsoever what interest Thyssen or Stinnes can have in the project. Both men are not represented on the boards of both companies, do not have, as much as is known, any large amount of shares and certainly do not belong to those people who make recommendations to other people from pure altruistic goodwill . . . [44]

Schaafhausen initially resisted the merger because it had invested a great amount of money in the *Hörder Verein,* which had just been completely reorganized. Schaafhausen would lose its leading position in Hörder if it fused with Phoenix. It would then have to share its influence with the *Darmstädter* or *Disconto-Gesellschaft.* Schaafhausen pointed out the difficulties in its position to Thyssen, and asked Thyssen to use his influence with other banks to help alleviate any rivalry. Thyssen agreed, for instance, to keep the Deutsche Bank in the dark about the state of the merger negotiations. Thereafter, Schaafhausen came around to accepting the advantages of such a merger. Schaafhausen then loaned Phoenix enough money to cover the merger costs. The merger made Phoenix one of Germany's largest prewar enterprises.

Why did Thyssen and Stinnes engage in such behavior? Both Thyssen and Stinnes realized that only larger combinations would keep German industry competitive. This was not an altruistic move. Conveniently, larger mergers would serve to simplify cartel negotiations, strengthen the bargaining positions of integrated combines in the cartels against independent mills, as well as lead to greater economic efficiency in the industry as a whole.

Thyssen and Stinnes backed another merger, one of the largest of the time: the 1905 merger of *Gelsenkirchener Bergwerks AG,* the *Schalker Verein,* and the *Aacher Hütten-Aktien-Verein* into a community of interest (IG). (Recall that Thyssen had been involved with the *Schalker Verein* since the 1870s.) Gelsenkirchen was by far the largest independent and "pure" coal producer in Germany, headed by Emil Kirdorf, who also directed the coal syndicate. Gelsenkirchen anchored the interests of independent coal-mining companies in the syndicate, and Kirdorf had a near "pathological suspicion" of Thyssen. Suddenly, at a 1904 shareholders meeting, Thyssen and Stinnes appeared. They controlled nearly 50% of the stock, and advocated a merger; it was widely interpreted as the decisive step toward the building of a trust in the steel industry. This fusion brought Gelsenkirchen into a vertically integrated structure that undercut its interests in defending pure coal-mining companies, brought it into the fold of the integrated combines, and neatly eliminated Gelsenkirchen as an object of state attention.[45]

We cannot speak of bank dominance over industry or a bank-driven cartelization movement. Around 1900, Emil Kirdorf thought that banks' influence on industry was the smallest that it had ever been: "Never has the influence of the great banks on the heavy industry of Rhineland and Westphalia been so small as it is now. We can even venture to say the opposite: the great banks court the favor of industry, not the opposite."[46] Instead, a dense, complex web of interdependency, often riddled with unintended consequences, characterized bank-industry-cartel relations. Cross-shareholdings could certainly encourage cooperation, but they also could immobilize bank strategy.

Cross-shareholdings could just as well generate crosscutting interests, not common interests. Finally, enough rivalry existed among the big universal banks to give individual industrialists, as exemplified by Thyssen or Stinnes, considerable room to maneuver.

In the end, we can endorse Adam Smith's opinion that industrialists of the same trade seldom need encouragement to contrive higher prices. German steel industrialists needed little prodding from banks to form cartels. However, the presence of a relatively small number of universal-credit banks involved in this highly capital-intensive industry raised another barrier to entry. The structure of German capital markets dampened competition by making it more difficult, but not impossible, for new firms to enter the sector to take advantage of higher prices. But the banks did not engineer cartel formation.

Cartels and Steel-Firm Strategy

Cartels did not banish competition, but recast competition. They primarily, but not exclusively, channeled German steel firms into a strategy of vertical integration. Cartels also encouraged a diversification of their product lines to take advantage of economies of scope, and to circumvent cartel agreements by branching into non-syndicated goods.

Before the 1890s it was generally cheaper to buy coal on the open market than to own mines. The advent of the coal syndicate changed everything. Steel industrialists had to be careful about the crisscrossing of short-lived cartel agreements, which might make a firm susceptible to sudden rises in crucial input prices. In addition, new steelmaking processes required different qualities of coal, coke, pig iron, and steel, which caused myriad problems of supply. Finally, the coal and steel cartels allowed generous self-consumption rights to their members. These self-consumption rights were key. The combination of avoiding higher transaction costs *and* being permitted to produce for one's own use provided a huge incentive to integrate vertically. One could use capacity more effectively if one could assure upstream *and* downstream demand.

From their various starting points, all of the dominant German steel firms followed a remarkably similar pattern of vertical integration, ranging from coal mining to finished steel goods—and eventually to machine engineering and shipbuilding during and after World War

I.[47] Krupp and the Bochumer Verein began with high-quality casted goods. The GHH began with machine construction and coal shipping. Hoesch and Rheinische Stahlwerke began with crude steel. Phoenix began as an integrated coal, pig-iron, and steel producer. Mannesmann began with pipes and tubes. Thyssen started with strip steel and pipes. Each of these firms had special strengths and weaknesses, which they sought to overcome either through mergers and acquisitions, new investments, or new cartel negotiations. The goal was a self-sufficient, well-balanced, and financially profitable vertical steel operation.[48] In general, they first moved backward into coal and pig iron, especially in the 1890s, and then, after the turn of the century, forward into finishing and distribution.

The German cartel order channeled the strategy of German steel firms into vertical integration, economies of scope, product innovation, and exports. (For the most part, exports did not necessarily fall under the cartels' quota system.) By differentiating specialty products from those whose output was regulated, firms could exempt them from cartel jurisdiction as well as use capacity that might be underused because of quotas. For example, Mannesmann joined only the 1902 pipe syndicate, because it could still sell older products and develop new specialty products outside the syndicate.[49] Cartels encouraged a strange type of niche strategy. The cartels unintentionally subsidized their members' advances into new, potentially risky, capital-intensive, and higher value-added product lines.[50] Such strategies of scope then led to immensely complicated negotiations, to the annoyance of everyone involved.

Competition remained within the cartel system through a number of mechanisms. First, since sales or production quotas would be renegotiated in the near future, industrialists attempted to put themselves in the best possible position for the next round of negotiations. The coal syndicate agreement was renegotiated every five years, and the steel works association agreement every three or four. Since quotas were usually based on capacity, an incentive to grow still existed. Quotas often were set higher than present capacity in order to allow for growth, or to give time for projects underway to come on line, or to persuade annoying outsiders to join. Producers who could threaten others with their potentially unregulated productive capacity gained leverage in quota negotiations. At minimum, cartels encouraged excess capacity as a negotiating ploy. Steel executives might be content to let the cartel work for them, but this was not an effective long-term strategy. If the cartel agreement ended, they would be at a disadvantage on the open market. Moreover, they would lose negotiating power and quota share over time because they had failed to innovate or enlarge their plants. Thus, cartel quotas were less expressions of "delicate" technological balance of multiples or "defensive investment to protect [them]" than the result of fierce market competition translated by hardboiled bargaining into formal cooperative structures.[51]

Second, instead of battling one another directly and primarily through economies of scale in one or two categories of goods, German steel industrialists competed across a broad array of syndicated and non-syndicated goods. The byzantine and tedious cartel negotiations among vertically integrated firms ranged from the amount of coal mined to the quality of castings and forged parts. Bargaining strength in one product line could be enhanced by expansion into another product line. Threatening a rival's competitive advantage in one product line could force concessions elsewhere. For instance, Thyssen could bring to bear his immense new investments in A-products to influence negotiations on B-products. In the torturous 1915 renewal negotiations, steel syndicate advocates put pressure on Thyssen to give on B-products by threatening his coal position. Indeed, in 1910 Stinnes threatened to bring down the entire Steel Works Association as the only way to force Thyssen to join the coal syndicate.[52] The quotas themselves were calculated down to the rounded hundred-thousandth decimal place (such as 8.158%), which often meant quite a bit of money, but nonetheless signified the tightness, and sometimes the pettiness, of negotiations. "Higgling and bargaining" was the norm.

Third, cartels altered the strategic incentives of German steel companies. Financially stronger producers could buy out less efficient companies for their quotas and shut them down. This practice was one of the most notorious side effects of the German cartel system, because it contradicted one of the main goals of cartels: to help keep more firms in business. The director of the coal syndicate, Emil Kirdorf, defended the practice by arguing that at least less efficient firms would receive some sort of compensation instead of simply being bankrupted with nothing to show for it. Essentially creating a market for quotas, this practice ended with the reestablishment of cartels after

1924, which permitted members to buy and sell quotas in the interest of rationalization.

Fourth, because the prices of raw materials and of many intermediate products were guaranteed, profit margins could rise by increasing the difference between the cartel-set price and production costs through greater scale or scope economies, or higher technical efficiency, or both. One contemporary American consultant emphasized that in the cartel world "the main factor in establishing low costs is therefore the efficiency of the plant and its management."[53] Cartels thus placed a premium on knowing one's production costs; deciding and negotiating cartel quotas meant that cost accounting became a crucial variable. Finally, cartels reinforced the strong tendency toward a production engineering perspective of German firms. Since German (and French) cartels were particularly adept at organizing syndicates, instead of forming one corporate structure, as in America. Syndicates took over marketing functions, so the business firm had fewer internal tradeoffs between manufacturing and marketing.[54] (To be sure, engineering innovations inside German steel firms were not simply the result of market failure induced by cartels).

Fifth, since domestic market share was regulated, the export market was one way of dumping excess production. German industrialists had long viewed foreign markets as a "safety valve" to keep production volume high. Exports became increasingly important to steel industrialists, especially as domestic production overshot domestic demand. (By 1913, domestic consumption of pig iron, for instance, was just 45% of total domestic production.) Germany became the world's leading exporter of steel products, mostly cheap commodity Thomas steel products, which could use the phosphorus-rich iron ore in Germany. Thyssen's GDK became the most aggressive exporter in the German steel industry. While comparable firms regularly exported 20–30%, the GDK exported about 30–40%.[55] Although German products made up about one-third of all exported iron and steel in the entire world, German firms still ran at much less than capacity. As a result, all of the complicated steel cartels came under tremendous strain to maintain prices.[56] International market prices were consistently below domestic cartel-set prices, which led to many problems with German finished goods manufacturers, who could often purchase steel products cheaper outside Germany. For instance, Thyssen & Co. explicitly prohibited the resale of export products in its advertising brochures.[57]

The relatively high, cartel-stabilized price of domestic coal and steel contributed to the dampening of domestic demand.

Finally, excess production could be consumed by oneself if downstream parts of the vertical combine processed materials into finished products. This practice allowed production of intermediate materials—usually more homogeneous and cartelized—to maintain a steady volume. All of these advantages or side effects of the interaction between cartels and combines were only available if industrialists integrated vertically. Cartel self-consumption rights virtually guaranteed that much of the excess capacity would be channeled in that direction. Integrated combines had an increasing cost advantage over independent firms because they controlled their own inputs. These cost advantages allowed them to produce downstream goods more cheaply than independent or pure firms. After 1900, the integrated combines increasingly pushed into finished goods manufacturing. It is not surprising that the conflict between the pure independent producers and the integrated combines became one of the most divisive political topics after the cartel mergers at the turn of the century.[58]

The dysfunctions of this competition came home to roost in the years before the war, especially in the failure of the Steel Works Association to cartelize B-products; the stagnation of domestic demand; and the forced extension of the coal syndicate by the state just after the war began.[59] It is unlikely that the coal, pig-iron, or steel cartels would have survived without state intervention during the war. In any event, they immediately collapsed during the postwar period.

Ironically, instead of orienting themselves purely toward profitability, German steel producers haggled over quota shares, chased after productive efficiency, and attempted to reduce transaction costs arising from the cartels that they themselves erected. For industries like German coal and steel, cartels were the German version of entrepreneurship. Hugo Stinnes neatly capsulized the German philosophy: "I do not share the view of the creators of the great American trusts, that every branch of industry must be separate from the others and take care of itself with the single purpose of the greatest possible return."[60] Cartels often prevented an industry as a whole from matching production capacity to market demand in the long run precisely because of its market-mediating role. This unintended consequence contradicted the basic theory of cartels as outlined by cartel advocates.

Cartels only slowed but did not halt consolidation. A relatively small number of vertically integrated firms came to dominate the German steel industry before the war. Instead of tacit oligopoly pricing, as in America, German steel firms could explicitly cooperate to set prices. The cartel system did not work if any one of the big German integrated combines could not come to an agreement with the others. The cartels most certainly did not provide "a market for everyone [or make] even the smallest firms viable."[61] But they did allow a greater number of vertically integrated firms with smaller scale and market share to remain extant in Germany than in the United States. In general, U.S. firms tended to grow horizontally first, focusing on a few product lines, then moved into vertical integration. German firms did the reverse. Unlike American oligopolies, which showed a high degree of market concentration among a few large firms, German integrated combines had smaller shares of individual product markets but a greater degree of vertical integration and a more diversified product line. American firms were shorter, broader, and concentrated on one or two standardized products, while German firms were taller and thinner with branched, diversified product lines.[62]

Although it appeared that Ruhr heavy industry was swallowing up the rest of the economy, some perspective is in order. German steel firms were closer to the size of the fast-moving independent steel firms clustered around U.S. Steel, the true anomaly, and monster company in the world, with over one billion dollars in assets. In total fixed assets, Thyssen, Krupp, and Phoenix roughly equalled Republic and Bethlehem Steel together. However, comparable German firms employed approximately three times more workers than did American firms (although average American wages were three to four times higher than German wages).[63] These figures also show just how much more capital-intensive and efficient American steel firms were than German steel firms, which became problematic in the mid-1920s.

European firms are better yardsticks than American ones to judge German developments. On the whole, German firms were comparable in total assets and employment to British firms, while significantly larger than most French companies. Krupp was the giant of the continent. Krupp employed nearly six times the employees at Republic or Bethlehem; nearly three times as many as Vickers, Sons & Maxim, Phoenix, or Gelsenkirchen; and 2.5 times Armstrong Whitworth & Co. and Thyssen's GDK, largely because of its extensive finished and specialty steel production (armaments). By the turn of the century, German heavy industry firms in this sector (but not overall) had clearly taken the lead in terms of size over their European counterparts. (These statistics, however, disguise the robustness of the British economy in almost every other sector before 1914.)[64]

Despite admittedly less-than-efficient allocation of resources across the steel industry and the economy as a whole, Germany still managed to create some of the most innovative steel firms in the world, particularly in energy economies and important niche sectors.[65] They continued to innovate, not stagnate. The blunt Anglo-Saxon notion that cartels inevitably lead to disastrous economic performance should be parsed. Cartels fulfilled a range of responsibilities and objectives beyond raising prices. Without question, the cartel system led to a number of critical structural problems in the industry. One result was the founding of the VSt, which industrialists conceived as a solution to the weird competitive dynamics of German steel.

In summary, cartels were important, pervasive institutions of the pre-1945 world economy, and restructured the competitive dynamics of numerous industries. The cartel question involves important value questions about economic and political power, size, concentration, family ownership versus corporate control, legitimate market behavior, freedom of association and the right of contract or freedom of competition, labor employment, individualism, the value of competition versus cooperation, the virtues of *laissez faire* versus a managed economy, the boundaries between public and private, and the state and civil society. It is ironic that the dominant vision today of cartels as mere price-fixers stems from the United States, which has the least historical experience with cartels.

Organized cartels regulated and structured competition in the German coal, iron, and steel industry. They did not eliminate competition, but rechanneled it. For the steel industry, cartel capitalism made the dominant (but not exclusive) strategy in German steel one of vertical integration rather than horizontal expansion. The two strategies were complementary, but the necessity for vertical integration was greatly enhanced in the context of German cartels, but this put pressure on German steel industrialists to find an organizational solution for broad vertical integration.

Paradoxically, since Thyssen drove the cartel movement at the turn of the century, it was Thyssen himself who recognized the greater advantages large-scale mergers held over cartels. In 1902, just after Franz Dahl and Fritz Thyssen returned from the U.S., Thyssen wrote to his personal friend, Carl Klönne, of the Deutsche Bank:

> The time of syndicates is past and we must move on to the time of trusts. . . . German syndicates performed well in the beginning. Now they are obsolete, because they continually multiply the competition and raise production costs. Also the coal and coke syndicate has reached its high point and will be very weakened by the building of syndicate collieries. German industry cannot bear over the long term the burdens of its expensive railway monopoly, the coal and coke syndicate, the pig iron, semi-processed and finished product syndicates. We have to work cheaper and nevertheless make money, which will only be possible by fusing the works, creating larger companies and by a better division of labor.[66]

Thyssen even made a prescient case for greater banking concentrations, urging the Deutsche Bank to merge with the Disconto bank. Such thinking would lead to the formation of the VSt in 1926 as well as the fusion of both banks in 1929, but Klönne felt the time was not yet ripe in the public's mind for an American-style trust; syndicates could be improved.[67]

For such statements, Thyssen became known as the "American" among German steel industrialists. Elimination of cartels was a radical idea, one that did not sit well with German public opinion or with his competitors. Thyssen quickly became labeled as an "enemy of cartels" and an "American-style" entrepreneur—a robber baron as opposed to a civilized steward of the nation's industry. His seemingly inexplicable behind-the-scenes maneuvering to promote mergers and volatile, uncomfortable personality in cartel negotiations contributed to the widely held belief that his true goal was an industry-wide monopoly under his own leadership.[68]

CHAPTER 7

Rushing Forward and Backward

If the few Lorraine mines still available for us fall *into others' hands,*
then our position would become untenable because we would have
to fear at any point that a strong syndicate of iron ore mine owners
[would move] against us.

August Thyssen to Carl Klönne of the Deutsche Bank, July 16, 1902

Those convoluted competitive dynamics of the industrial branch
were decisive for understanding entrepreneurship in German steel.
Thyssen represents a near ideal-type picture of how cartels altered the
strategies of German industrialists and how closely the twin processes
of cartelization and vertical integration were entwined in German economic history.[1] Unlike other firms, which merged and acquired other
firms, often in an *ad hoc* fashion, Thyssen managed to create a balanced Konzern structure from his own efforts. The threat of cartels
only intensified Thyssen's natural tendency toward independence and
self-sufficiency. If Thyssen was Germany's version of Andrew Carnegie,
he operated in a significantly different economic and social environment, which made Thyssen behave differently than his American
counterpart.

The centerpiece of Thyssen's efforts lay in Hamborn-Bruckhausen
with the integrated steelworks of the *Gewerkschaft Deutscher Kaiser*
(GDK). By 1913, in terms of total assets, the GDK (alone) was the sixth
largest industrial firm in Germany and broke into the top fifty capitalist industrial firms in the world.[2] By 1907 it ranked nineteenth in
terms of employment.[3] The history of Thyssen's efforts at the GDK has
already been well told. (It is the official, legal predecessor of Thyssen
AG, the fifteenth largest company in Germany in 1994; now part of
Thyssen-Krupp AG, the largest steel company in Germany). Yet the
GDK represented just one part of the larger Konzern, which arose because of the dynamics of German cartel–concern capitalism. Talented

executives played a decisive role in helping Thyssen master these dynamics and build a Konzern.

Gewerkschaft Deutscher Kaiser

In the late 1880s, Thyssen confronted one of the critical turning points in his career. He could remain an important regional producer by specializing in high-quality niche products, or he could move into coal and steel production to secure his supply of the input materials needed for mass production in Mülheim. In 1887, he wrote the Mülheim Chamber of Commerce:

> At the end of the previous year, an upwards movement of all prices took place as a result of more or less stable associations of firms [formed], conventions, syndicates, etc. Namely, it is the rolling mill branch that threatens to find itself in a very adverse position over time due to the significant rise of pig iron and coal prices. The latter still continues to climb. Because of this, its export capability will be completely undermined. Without exports, the many companies in this branch absolutely cannot exist.[4]

Thyssen's complaint is ironic because he expressed an argument that many German finished goods manufacturers would make against primary steel producers such as Thyssen over the next forty years.

Thyssen & Co. was what the Germans then called a pure rolling mill, largely a finishing mill. (Its Siemens-Martin mill only covered the demand of the plate department.) Growing cartelization efforts in coal jeopardized its fuel supply. In his 1922 autobiographical article, Thyssen stated that secure control over his own coal supply became a "matter of survival."[5] While the final consolidation of the coal syndicate would take another five or six years, Thyssen sought to head off this threat. Note it is the perceived *threat* and *expectation* of a cartel, not its actual existence, which was decisive. If a solid cartel formed, it might already be too late.

The linchpin of Thyssen's strategy was the *Gewerkschaft Deutscher Kaiser* (GDK). The GDK allowed Thyssen & Co. to survive in the "organized capitalism" of Germany. The name translates to "Mining Company German Emperor," which, like Germany itself, had been founded in 1871. Like Thyssen & Co., it too remained a private company, not subject to the laws of public financial disclosure. Before Thyssen started operations, only 3,000 souls inhabited the entire sleepy district of Hamborn. It was said, not entirely wrongly, that the city began as a Thyssen train station. Like Styrum, Hamborn was not incorporated and was largely agricultural greenfields. By 1900, it had 34,144 inhabitants; of these the GDK supported 8,750 workers along with their families so that a majority of Hamborn's population was dependent on the GDK. By 1914, Hamborn had become a teeming city of around 120,000 inhabitants in the "Wild West" of the Ruhr. Perhaps more than any other large municipal area in Germany, Hamborn was almost entirely the product of a single industrialist.[6]

August Thyssen first involved himself in the GDK in May 1883 with the purchase of ten shares, part of his general strategy of keeping abreast of mining developments in the Ruhr. After March 1887, Thyssen & Co. initiated a flurry of investment activity. By February 1890, Thyssen had managed to purchase all 1,000 shares of the GDK mining stock, at a total cost of four million marks and had bought nearly all the land around the small villages of Hamborn-Bruckhausen. The official founding date of the GDK (or Thyssen AG) is September 29, 1891, the date of the general assembly meeting in Duisburg, when the Thyssen brothers officially announced that they owned all 1,000 mining shares.[7] Just like Styrum in 1871, Hamborn provided good railway line connection to the main branches. Moreover, the GDK was located directly on the Rhine and Ruhr rivers, a superb location for shipping coal to south German and export markets. The Rhine also provided easy transport of foreign iron ore.

In August 1890, the GDK and Thyssen & Co. signed a 99-year lease for the land on which the GDK stood. In effect, the GDK began as a subsidiary of Thyssen & Co.[8] This formal leasing arrangement signified that the GDK had to compete as much as possible as a separate enterprise: otherwise it "did not justify its existence."

GDK Mining (Hamborn)

When Thyssen moved into the western area of the Ruhr, the area was largely an untapped territory for deep mines because of its geological characteristics. The proximity to the Rhine held great advantages for shipping coal but great disadvantages for excavating it. The ground of shifting sandstone layers was waterlogged from constant seepage, and the pitheads were only a few meters above the level of the Rhine. Deep sinkholes and sagging ground resulted from mining. Such occurrences would threaten not only Thyssen's own commencing steel operations, but also the increasingly populated area of Hamborn-Bruckhausen.[9]

When Thyssen began to take over the GDK, its first colliery had already surpassed a production mark of 300,000 tons/year. In 1888, he convinced the wary remaining stockholders to begin another mineshaft. Colliery 2 did not, however, begin to mine a single ton of coal until *eight* years later. Colliery 2 required that Thyssen sink a shaft more than 100 meters deeper than Colliery 1, in very dangerous territory; it eventually reached 233 meters underground. Begun a year later than Colliery 2, Colliery 3 came into operation a full year before Colliery 2, still an investment horizon of *six* years. A full decade went by before Thyssen had the financial resources to begin in 1899 drilling a fourth mineshaft, which went on line *four* years later. Colliery 5 was begun in 1901, but did not begin producing until 1909 because of its immense depth (243 meters). The GDK started sinking Colliery 6 in 1903, which began production in 1907. Because of the immense resources literally sunk into the soil, Thyssen's finances remained stretched thin for more than a decade. Not surprisingly, the long time horizons before mines brought even one lump of coal to the surface made coal industrialists hypersensitive to price falls, explaining why coal companies were among the first to establish cartels.

Under the resolute direction of Otto Kalthoff, the GDK managed to overcome the geological difficulties faced, especially by Colliery 2. Like Thyssen, Kalthoff was born in Eschweiler and moved to the Ruhr. He started at the very bottom as a miner, and eventually became a pit foreman in various Bochum and Essen mines. At Rheinpreussen, directors named him as a department chief *(Betriebsführer)*. In 1884, he had a brief stint at the GDK before leaving one year later for another mine. He returned to the GDK at about the same time that Thyssen began purchasing GDK shares. In 1890, Thyssen gave Kalthoff complete authority over all GDK mining operations. Kalthoff was an imposing, big, burly, red-bearded man with a reputation for being hard but fair. Along with his appearance, his experience as a former miner must have conveyed a great deal of authority. He was known for his quick temper but also for his ability to lay it aside quickly. Having been a miner since childhood, he had a clear sense of its dangers. He had a sharp eye for mistakes and negligence which he did not tolerate.[10]

Kalthoff was above all responsible for the success of the GDK's mining operations. It was Kalthoff who advised Thyssen on how best to round out his purchase of fields and where to drive new mineshafts. By the turn of the century, Kalthoff had Collieries 1, 2, and 3 in operation, mining 1.2 million tons of coal annually and employing roughly 4,000 workers. Production rose almost geometrically after 1898 as the new mineshafts began operating. By 1913, the GDK's yearly output reached nearly 4.5 million tons and it employed nearly 15,000 workers.

GDK Schachtbau

GDK's proximity to the Rhine proved both a boon and a curse, a curse because of the unprecedented dangers of sinking deep mineshafts. Again Thyssen turned disadvantages into advantages. Similar to the examples of the Thyssen & Co. Machine Company or the Gas and Waterworks, Thyssen created his own mineshaft construction department in the GDK, eventually called the *GDK Bergbau Abteilung Schachtbau*.[11]

The *GDK Schachtbau* began out of opportunism and some desperation. Since 1898, the GDK had done some of its own trial drilling, but tended to rely on other firms. After 1903, the Prussian Mining Authority required that Thyssen completely fill in the mined-out coal veins to shore up the layers of rock and soil above them. It had been standard practice to flood the empty caverns with wet sand as fill, but the GDK lacked sand or other fill. As a substitute, they used the hardened slag from the GDK's blast furnaces heaped up in huge mountains around the steel mills. Again, Thyssen managers turned waste materials into useful ones. But it proved difficult to put the slag into the ground. They granulated the slag and sluiced it down in iron pipes, but the sharp edges of the slag quickly destroyed the pipes. This problem led to another technical innovation: lining the iron pipes were with baked-on porcelain to protect them. Eventually, Thyssen engineers developed an entire patented process system *(Spülversatzverfahren)* to recycle slag and refill hollowed out mine shafts.

The GDK mining construction department did not just develop a few new techniques, but transformed itself into an independent contractor for entire mineshaft construction. The expectation that the Prussian state would end further drilling in the Ruhr propelled a boom in exploration. In order to expand his capabilities, in 1903 Thyssen secretly purchased all of the shares of the drilling company, *Tiefbohr-AG vorm. Hugo Lubisch*. In December 1905, the GDK founded a legally independent subsidiary called the *Bohr- und Schachtbau GmbH* in Mülheim, which consolidated the GDK and Tiefbohr AG.

The new firm expanded its technological capabilities to include novel means of constructing mineshafts. After five years of fruitless endeavor, the construction of Colliery 5 at the GDK, its deepest mineshaft, had stalled because of incessant water seepage. No other mineshaft construction firm was willing to undertake the risks involved in sinking this shaft. With no alternatives, the *Bohr- und Schachtbau* undertook the project itself and succeeded in opening Colliery 5 as the first shaft to use a new freezing method *(Gefrierverfahren)*. In essence, this new method involved freezing the water around the shaft, then bolstering the mineshaft walls with cement and steel lining. Hans Richter of the Thyssen & Co. machine department played a critical role here in developing equipment for the *Bohr- und Schachtbau*. The wide-ranging work of this mine construction division brought further contracts to Thyssen & Co. for support tubings, pipes, pumping machines, steam engines, and other accessories. Again Thyssen & Co. created an internal demand for its own products with its characteristic mixture of desperation, swift opportunism, and clever but solid scientific engineering. The new process turned into an unprecedented success. The company managed to sink two other extraordinarily deep mineshafts (over 400 meters) at Thyssen's Lohberg mines using the technique. Again Thyssen engineers turned a potential disaster into a gold mine.

When Prussian law limited further exploratory drilling after 1909, Thyssen liquidated the *Bohr- und Schachtbau* company and turned it into a separate internal division of the GDK, entitled the *GDK Bergbau Abteilung Schachtbau*. Contracts with third parties in the region faded away because rivals did not necessarily want to contract with Thyssen, but the new division attracted contracts from a number of firms in the Netherlands and Belgium, and became an immensely profitable venture.

GDK Iron and Steel (Bruckhausen)

At the same time he was confronting these considerable difficulties in his mines, Thyssen began a hurried expansion of the GDK into steel, directly on top of the coal reserves. The GDK was primarily conceived as a supplier of coal and intermediate material (blocks, blooms, billets) for Thyssen & Co., as well as an independent producer of heavy formed and structural steel.

The first few years of the GDK's development—mistakenly—owed much to the organizational experience of Thyssen & Co. Much like the Mülheim works, they planned to build a Siemens-Martin open-hearth mill with rolling mills that were heavier and had more capacity. Symbolizing the continuity, first Wilhelm Overdieck, then Fritz Wilke from the Mülheim steel mill, took over the direction of the new GDK Siemens-Martin mill.[12] They charged the first 15-ton Siemens-Martin furnace on December 17, 1891, but since none of the rolling-mill trains had been built yet, they initially stacked the ingots to the side. Thyssen had built the new mill so quickly that neighbors of the factory could look in and see the red-hot glow of molten metal inside the factory. By the end of 1894, all five rolling-mill trains for intermediate materials and heavy structural steel went into operation. Unlike Thyssen & Co., the financial results of the GDK did not match its expansion in capacity. The GDK steel and rolling mills ran in the red for the first three years of operation.

The GDK's initial travails derived largely from Thyssen's attempt to replicate the Mülheim model of production on a larger scale. While Siemens-Martin steel remained competitive for high-end goods, it could not compete in heavy, low-end goods with Thomas steel.[13] Thomas steel was more appropriate for mass produced goods such as rails, joists, structurals, heavy plates, and wire and could use the high phosphoric content of iron ore largely available to Germans. Just as Thyssen began constructing the open-hearth plant, Thomas steel production began to dominate the liquid-steel production of Germany.[14] Siemens-Martin open-hearth production, moreover, depended a great deal on the price of scrap, which was relatively high compared to Thomas pig iron. The 1893 GDK annual report admitted as much and the poor financial results confirmed this assessment. Additionally, the rolling mills incurred considerable losses because of their inadequate design and layout. Thyssen's expensive new GDK was behind the competitive curve.

To break out of the organizational pattern set by Thyssen & Co., Thyssen brought in an outside consultant, Franz Dahl. Dahl thought that the equipment was "solid and appropriate," but that the mill trains were built too close together to allow good working space. Betraying the great financial strain that he was in, Thyssen touchily replied, "The plant cost eight million marks and will not be changed."[15] Julius Kalle, another future Thyssen director, happened to visit the GDK in 1894. He remembered it as "simply a disorganized hovel. Everything there was over and under one another, and not laid out well."[16] Thyssen nonetheless invited Dahl to a discussion with three other outside steel works engineers about building a Thomas mill. The three outside consultants recommended a converter size of 12 tons, which was exactly the size of the converter at the *Burbacher Hütte* where they worked. Dahl, however, recommended one of 20–25 tons. They eventually compromised on 16 tons because Thyssen did not want to (or could not) spend more. Dahl portrayed Thyssen as "a very careful man, somewhat anxious," who was constantly short of cash.[17] Dahl's assessment, however, did not take into account the considerable financial risks that Thyssen was already taking. In the early 1890s, he struggled with losses in the rolling mills and the expenses caused by the slow sinking of Colliery 2. Thyssen had initially offered Dahl a position as director of the GDK steel and rolling mills, but his criticism was not appreciated. Thyssen retracted the offer. When the 16-ton converter came online in July 1897, the converter quickly proved inadequate, as Dahl had predicted.

Six months later Thyssen came back to the thirty-five year old Dahl and asked him to head the construction of the heavy block rolling mills.[18] Dahl became responsible for the extensive redesign of the Bruckhausen works, which placed Thyssen at the forefront of German steel development. Dahl also began diversifying Bruckhausen's production program and constructing better production flows within the plant. By 1895, it began to generate an operating profit.

Franz Dahl was to Thyssen what Alexander Holley was to Carnegie. By the end of his career, Thyssen freely granted Dahl the financing to realize his ideas for production, because they almost always worked. Dahl had worked himself up from the shopfloor rather than through engineering school. He had a vocational education. After the postal service rejected him, he began his career at the *Burbacher Hütte* in 1878 as a puddler, rolling mill foreman, and as a smith for harnesses. He worked eleven years there before reaching a leading position. He left the *Burbacher Hütte* for the *Gutehoffnungshütte* (GHH) although he earned half as much there, because he wanted to learn more about liquid steel processes. He thought puddling was on its way out. In 1891, he went to the *Röchlingschen Eisen- und Stahlwerken* to direct the expansion of the rolling mills. Thyssen found him at Röchling and outbid his Essen rival, Schulz-Knaudt, for Dahl's services. Although Dahl had a hand in practically every major technical venture in Bruckhausen, he was most renowned as a specialist in rolling mills. He was a first-class plant designer who knew how to blend seamlessly the peculiar technical demands of individual processes with the layout of plant as a whole. After the retirement of Fritz Sültemeyer in 1904 due to hearing problems, Thyssen appointed Dahl general director of the GDK.

Dahl was a maker of crude steel but also a grower of delicate roses, remembered as having a hard exterior but a soft core. He retired in 1920 to become a rose gardener and vintner, which was how he described himself for the rest of his life. Like Thyssen, he was obsessed with work. He lived in a modest house. He never married. He was always one of the first at work, although he was known to be a very "spirited" wine-drinker and consistently one of the last to leave the table at the company *Casino*, the restaurant/bar for salaried executives. As a respite from work, he gardened in the backyard near the factory. His subordinates learned how they could manipulate his soft side. He retired in 1920 because he no longer felt he could work in the altered postwar circumstances that allowed workers greater voice.[19]

Dahl placed the GDK on a crash expansion program that focused the GDK on Thomas steel for commodity goods and export markets. By the turn of the century, three-quarters of the GDK's crude steel production consisted of Thomas steel, although Siemens-Martin steel remained important, especially for deliveries to Thyssen & Co. and the GDK's new pipe works in Dinslaken. According to Dahl, Thyssen seemed pleased with the progress of the new Thomas works, which he thought would enable him to produce cheap steel blocks, but Dahl reminded him that the price of the steel was entirely dependent on the price of pig iron. Dahl urged Thyssen in 1895 to move into pig-iron production. The expansion of the GDK's steel capacity had created a bottleneck for pig-iron production, making the GDK subject to price fluctuations in the pig-iron market. The 1894 annual report remarked that only those large firms producing their own intermediate materials would remain competitive and profitable.[20] In 1895, moreover, the threat of a pig-iron cartel loomed as the Düsseldorf Pig Iron Syndicate (1896) began to form. Thyssen asked Dahl whether he should build a new block mill train or a blast furnace first. Dahl recommended blast furnaces. Thyssen chose the blast furnace to minimize his exposure to market (*potentially* cartel) prices.

Before he received legal permission to begin, Dahl began building the first two of five blast furnaces in August 1895 over the protests of numerous farmers. The upset farmers must have been horrified by this imposing modern steel structure, resembling as it did a rocket launching pad, which sprouted monstrously skywards from the flat greenfields. The first blast furnace went into operation at about the same time as the Thomas works in July 1897; Dahl completed the fifth and last by 1901. True to his growing reputation as a master of factory design, Dahl took the innovative step of building a tunnel underneath the street between the blast furnaces and the steelworks to connect them. By improving production flows, the tunnel reduced heat loss. A block rolling-mill train went into operation just after the blast furnaces and steel mills were finished.

By the logic of the German steel industry, Thyssen began constructing a new coking plant near Colliery 3, immediately after it began mining coal. Its construction had begun in 1895, the same year as he began building the Thomas works and blast furnaces.[21] The coking plant made him independent of the powerful coke syndicate.

The GDK increasingly linked all of these individual plants—coal pitheads, coking furnaces, blast furnaces, steel works, and rolling-mill trains—through an extensive private railway network. Dahl made sure that the GDK became mechanized as much as possible. Cranes were built within the individual plants. Steam engines drove most of the conveyance systems, but after the turn of the century, the GDK increasingly used electricity. Locomotives then linked the whole factory to the state-operated railway junctions and Thyssen's private harbor at Alsum. The harbor itself was quickly outfitted with huge cranes towering over the water. The turnover at the harbor alone testifies the swift growth of the GDK. In 1890, the harbor processed about 53,800 tons of material, and by 1900 ten times as much.

By the turn of the century, the GDK's production capacity dwarfed Thyssen & Co.'s and created considerable cost advantages for the Mülheim works. The GDK was solidly based on economies of scale in low-value-added commodity goods based on Thomas steel, high-volume throughput, and integrated flow production, while Thyssen & Co. focused on high-end, high-value-added goods using Siemens-Martin steel—a *Qualitätswerk,* concentrating on a strategy of scope and diversification. Together, the two firms represented nearly the full spectrum of vertical integration.

GDK Rolling Mills (Dinslaken)

To secure downstream demand and restore balance to higher value-added product lines, Thyssen planned to build a high-quality strip steel mill. After the 1890s, new products, primarily in the electrotechnical branch, such as sewing machines, watches, electrical appliances, etc., but also bicycles and cans, made increasing demands on the quality and quantity of strip steel. (One can hear this in the semantic transition from the relatively crude term *hoop iron* to *strip steel.*) Unprecedented lengths, surface quality, tolerances, and coatings made the old hoop-iron mill in Mülheim increasingly obsolete.

In 1896, Thyssen & Co. hired Julius Kalle to become the director of an entirely new strip-steel mill.[22] Mülheim was out of the question as a location because of the scarcity of land. (Only after he bought out a neighboring glass factory could Thyssen & Co. expand.) Hamborn and Bruckhausen were unacceptable because Thyssen would have to build a new house for each new worker. The considerable housing shortage was one of the major disadvantages of starting up a greenfield operation. One day when Kalle and Thyssen were scouting land for possible purchase, Thyssen noticed an entire train filled with young workers traveling to Oberhausen from Dinslaken. Dinslaken was located directly on the railroad line between Oberhausen and Wesel and on the Rhine north of Duisburg. Thyssen decided to locate the new factory where the workers already lived, thus avoiding additional housing costs. In the fall of 1895, August Wilke negotiated with the mayor of Dinslaken about locating the firm there, but only if Dinslaken agreed not to raise taxes on commercial business.

Typical for the way that Thyssen could choose talented but relatively young managers and place them in positions of great responsibility, Kalle was only twenty-seven years old when Thyssen handed him the reins of the GDK Dinslaken. Kalle was born in Dortmund, the son of a master metalworker who ran a small machine shop for agricultural implements. After receiving a basic education, Kalle apprenticed at the *Maschinenfabrik Geb. Wagner & Co.* in Dortmund, the first machine-engineering company founded in the Ruhr. It built equipment for heavy industry. Thereafter Kalle studied machine engineering at a technical university in Chemnitz before Thyssen hired him in 1896. At first, Kalle was subordinated to the more proven August Wilke of Thyssen & Co., but in the second draft of his contract he was granted full independence from Wilke's direction and reported directly to Thyssen.[23] Rather than the normal German dual-headed collegial directorship, Kalle had complete control over both sales and production at the GDK Dinslaken.

Like Willy Trapp, Thyssen sent Kalle on an extensive trip to the United States to study the latest techniques in strip-steel manufacturing. When he returned, Kalle designed and built the new factory with three mill trains and a cold rolling mill to complement the Mülheim factory. The Thyssen & Co. machine department built all of the mill trains, driven by steam engines from Ehrhardt & Sehmer. On New Year's Eve 1897, the first strip-steel mill train began operations. Within two years, the other mills went on line.

Sales of GDK Dinslaken products, cold and warm-rolled strip steel, rolled wire, and seamless pipes, grew rapidly, even outstripping the supply of intermediate material from Bruckhausen. Warm-rolled strip steel production grew from 10,000 tons to nearly 60,000 tons in just over a decade. The important cold-rolled strip steel tripled its production between 1901 and 1913, to just under 30,000 tons. In addition, the GDK Dinslaken began producing expensive seamless pipes production after the Mannesmann patent rights expired. By 1911 (one of the few revenue figures available), warm and cold-rolled strip steel and seamless pipes brought the GDK Dinslaken about six million marks worth of revenues, while rolled-wire production earned about 1 million Marks. By the war, it employed nearly 1800 people and turned a residential suburb of Duisburg into a major center of production. The GDK Dinslaken proved so successful that it ran up a loss only in the first year of its operations; it turned a profit every year until 1944.[24]

Figure 7.1　Four Thyssen headquarters. (Reproduced with the permission of the Mannesmann-Archiv, Mülheim/Ruhr)

The GDK Dinslaken proved to be crucial for the overall profitability of the GDK.

Just like the GDK and Thyssen & Co., Kalle and the GDK Dinslaken received its own central administrative building, which attested to its autonomy (Figure 7.1), as well as the others'.

After 1900, the GDK represented a nearly complete integrated steel works situated on top of large coal reserves, and ranged from coal mining to strip steel and seamless pipe production. By integrating the GDK vertically, Thyssen outraced the cartelization movement in German heavy industry after the turn of the century. Had he failed, Thyssen & Co. might have been destroyed or gobbled up along with many other independent rolling mills and steelworks.

After a decade of expansion, Thyssen's GDK entered into the leading ranks of coal and crude steel producers in Germany, just as Thyssen reached the age when many began to think of retirement. In 1899, the GDK posted revenues of 46.9 million marks, making it roughly the size of the Hörder Verein, the GHH, or the Dortmunder Union, but still less than the 73.9 million marks earned by Phoenix or the 119.7 million marks of Krupp.[25]

Although ultimately successful, the startup of the GDK coal-mining and steelmaking operations was considerably more difficult than can be conveyed in this brief exposition. Thyssen confronted unprecedented difficulties opening the new mineshafts, which took years of financial investment, hard work, and sweat to complete. Thyssen and his management underwent a clear organizational learning process as they tried to break into new areas of steelmaking. Thyssen made mistakes. His ultimate success in these fields rested on the advice, initiative, and talent of important executives such as Kalthoff, Dahl, and Kalle. Strategic initiatives often came from them. Finally, the logic of economies of scale combined with vertical integration to avoid cartels propelled Thyssen just as much as his personal preference for independence. These continuing investments pushed Thyssen's finances to their limit. Dahl actually thought that cartels and the necessity for scale drove Thyssen into larger financial expenditures than he really wanted, which his caution demonstrated at times. The increasingly cartelized world of German steel required him to create a balanced, self-sufficient, vertically integrated firm, which became the holy grail of German heavy industry.

Crisis

Expansion threw August Thyssen into one of the major financial crises of his career. Thyssen & Co.'s twenty years of financial reserves and solid credit rating, based entirely on Thyssen's personal reputation rather than any clear knowledge about his assets, had financed the GDK's growth. Remarkably, Thyssen still did not sell equity, in spite of the fact that the GDK did not generate enough internal profits to cover its capital expansion until 1897, almost *eight* years after he took it over. It was symptomatic of his tight financial situation that short-term credits extended to Thyssen & Co. actually constituted a good portion of the "equity" of the GDK. Luckily, Thyssen's expansion was pace by an extremely favorable economy. In spite of the vast expansion of capacity in the coal and steel industry, the overall economy grew fast enough that shortages of labor, coal, coke, and steel products still appeared. Around 1900, prices reached their prewar highs.

A sharp recession caught Thyssen in the middle of his expansion plans, causing a severe liquidity crisis. In 1901–1902, for instance, the price of pig iron suddenly dropped by 50%, for intermediate materials 40%. In December 1901, Thyssen could write Klönne at the Deutsche Bank that the coal and coke prices set by the syndicate were too high because they dampened overall demand in the economy, although Thyssen admitted that "good" coal and coke prices were certainly in his interest. Thyssen had to ask some of his creditors if he could delay payments. According to Joseph Thyssen's wife, Klara Bagel, she even had to dip into her private funds to help pay the wages.[26] Making matters worse, the troubles with his children, especially August, Jr., came to a head. Little wonder Thyssen felt that this was the unhappiest time in his life.

The Prussian state proved an unlikely and inadvertent savior by purchasing some of Thyssen's most important mining companies. After considerable public outrage about the market practices of the coal syndicate, which kept prices stable during the recession, the Prussian state attempted to penetrate the Ruhr coal business to gain influence over the coal cartel. This tension between the state and the private coal industry eventually ballooned into the 1904 Hibernia affair, when the coal syndicate formed a consortium of industrialists and bankers to prevent the Prussian state from purchasing the Hibernia, the third largest mining operation in the Ruhr.[27]

In 1902, Thyssen's financial crisis prevented him from engaging in this ideological conflict. In March, Thyssen righted his financial ship by selling off his stock in a number of major mining companies (Gladbeck, Graf Moltke, Simson, Graf Bismarck, Bergmannsglück, and Berlin) from his securities portfolio, which now proved its worth as a financial reserve. The Prussian Mining Authority paid more than 37 million marks for them. It was not conceived as a bailout for Thyssen. After all of the costs associated with the sale were deducted and his debt reduced, Thyssen made a net profit of just under 7 million marks. When Stinnes heard of the sale, he intimated that they could apply the funds long-term to two of their joint enterprises, the RWE and Saar & Mosel, but Thyssen informed him that the funds were already spent.[28] The sale of the Gladbeck fields restored his liquidity and allowed him to clear up the considerable debt carried on the books of his companies. Fortunately, the recession proved to be brief. Thyssen later commented that foreign contracts, especially exports to the United States, had again pulled him and the entire German steel industry out of a very difficult situation.[29]

Aktiengesellschaft für Hüttenbetrieb, Meiderich

Without "resting or rusting," Thyssen immediately launched another round of expansion to fill in his vertically integrated structure. All of the profits of the Gladbeck sale went to Thyssen's next major project: the April 1902 founding of the *Aktiengesellschaft für Hüttenbetrieb in Ruhrort-Meiderich* (AGHütt), an independent iron works, located in the city of Ruhrort-Meiderich between Oberhausen and Hamborn. The location took advantage of the harbor in Alsum and the train stations in Neumühl and Oberhausen. Fritz Sültemeyer, the GKD general director and technical director of its blast furnaces, conceived of the AGHütt to supply the GDK, Thyssen & Co., and the open steel market with special qualities of pig iron. They had designed the GDK blast furnaces to supply its Thomas converters, whose quality proved entirely inappropriate for Thyssen's Siemens-Martin products of the GDK Dinslaken and Thyssen & Co, both of which were growing rapidly.

Thyssen and Sültemeyer had planned since the late 1890s to build the AGHütt, but the recession, Thyssen's financial situation, and numerous problems with government authorities delayed its construction.[30] The district president in Düsseldorf initially refused to permit Thyssen to pour waste and sewage into the Emscher river. In addition, Thyssen's plans for a new train station in Ruhrort-Meiderich conflicted with the construction of a new canal (today the Rhein-Herne-Kanal). Largely due to the lobbying efforts of Conrad Verlohr, who worked at Thyssen's former Gladbeck operations, in March 1901 the district president finally approved the construction of the AGHütt. Then Thyssen's liquidity crisis delayed its startup once again.

In an unusual move, Thyssen established the AGHütt as a public, joint-stock company with a share capital of 1.5 million marks. Thyssen chose the joint-stock form so that he could quickly issue more shares if needed.[31] The AGHütt was the *only* core Thyssen manufacturing firm in which other investors held any ownership. In 1906, the GDK owned all but 108 of a total of 4,500 shares in AGHütt. Three other investors held those 108 shares. Even these few shares of outside ownership would cause Thyssen major headaches.

Over the years, the AGHütt grew into one of the most consistently profitable parts of the Konzern. In later years, Thyssen gave the credit for its success largely to its long-time general director, Conrad Verlohr, who he retained from Gladbeck: "We have treated Meiderich too stingily *(stiefmütterlich)* in spite of the great amount of money that it always earned. The management of Meiderich always worked excellently and we always had excellent directors, which we owe to Herr Verlohr in particular, who has a great talent for training new managers."[32]

Conrad Verlohr belonged to Thyssen's intimate circle of friends. They remained in constant contact with one another between 1889 and 1923, leaving a veritable treasure trove of over 1,000 letters that has yet to be fully examined. Most of the letters, of course, involved business. In spite of their close contact, the two men continued to use the formal "you." Verlohr had received practical commercial training in an iron wholesaler. He then moved on to the pig-iron sales department of the *Niederrheinische Hütte* in Duisburg. In 1889, Verlohr met Thyssen for the first time. In the following year, Thyssen hired him as the commercial director of the *Gewerkschaft Graf Moltke* in Gladbeck. Verlohr was thirty. He remained commercial director of the company when it merged with the Nordstern mining company in 1899. Verlohr's continuous stream of advice in land matters and his handling of the government negotiations for starting up the AGHütt made him indispensable. Thyssen made him commercial director, and Sültemeyer technical director. After Sültemeyer retired from both the GDK and the AGHütt, Thyssen replaced him with Aloys Melcher. The AGHütt was an exception for Thyssen firms (and for most German steel firms) in that it had a commercially trained director as *de facto* chief executive of the company, instead of an engineer. The AGHütt also had its own headquarters building, which reinforced Verlohr's organizational independence inside the Thyssen-Konzern.

Thyssen wrote Verlohr in February 1904 about the role that the AGHütt played in his plans:

> I am glad to see from your friendly letter that you are intervening personally in the pig-iron business. This is the only correct way to become independent. We must become self-sufficient by all necessary means in pig iron so that the relatively small earnings in this sector are retained. You and Herr Melcher have still another task. Together you

must think about and care about how we can lower production costs. I think there is a lot we can do to save and improve in this respect. The Meiderich works must and will pay off its interest well if we are thrifty *(sparsam)*.[33]

One can almost hear an undertone of desperation as Thyssen stressed paying off his interest rather than becoming profitable. But clearly, Verlohr's main objective was to make Thyssen independent of the pig-iron market, a commodity product whose price fluctuated widely. In 1903 Thyssen and other steel industrialists founded the Düsseldorf Pig Iron Syndicate to prop up prices. Verlohr became an expert in cartel questions and advised Thyssen on a continuous basis.

Verlohr also became Thyssen's point man in all matters regarding lime, limestone, and dolomite, necessary for iron production. It was Verlohr who dragged the *Rittergut Rüdersdorf* out of bankruptcy after Thyssen, Jr., ran it aground, and transformed it into a successful limestone mining operation. Verlohr also helped to train Carl Rabes, the new GDK commercial director, when he took over the commercial operations of the GDK after 1904. Rabes would later become one of the most important people in the Thyssen-Konzern and the VSt.

Under Verlohr's leadership, the AGHütt grew to include five major blast furnaces. It also built an entirely new state-of-the-art gas central in Meiderich that eventually had eight large gas dynamos and numerous gas compressors, allowing all five blast furnaces to be operated simultaneously. The AGHütt grew into one of the major centers of iron production in the Ruhr. In 1912, its production peaked at 384,000 tons of pig iron, and more than 50% of this figure went to other Thyssen firms. In the same year, its revenues reached 39 million marks, with 39% of its revenues from the Thyssen-Konzern, which it supplied at somewhat below market price. Its employment rose swiftly from 379 workers and 18 "officials" in 1903 to over 1300 workers and 97 "officials" by 1913. Using highly advanced chemical and material testing, the AGHütt gained the nickname "apothecary of the Ruhr" because of its diverse assortment of high-quality specialty pig iron. The Thyssen & Co. Machine Company eventually closed its highly profitable iron foundry in favor of the new one, built at AGHütt three years before the war. The economies of scale, flow, and energy provided by the AGHütt blast furnaces allowed the new iron foundry to be constructed so that the liquid pig iron could cast into molds directly out of the furnace. This saved reheating time, energy, coal, and money. In the first full year of operation (1911), it produced 60,000 tons of foundry goods and in 1913 67,617 tons.[34] The center for cast iron shifted to Meiderich, away from Mülheim, as the Machine Company phased out its foundry production.

The AGHütt also had a number of subsidiary investments, particularly the *Rheinische Kalksteinwerke, GmbH, Wülfrath,* founded jointly by the AGHütt, GDK, and the Schalker Verein to open up new fields of limestone.[35] To ensure downstream demand for the AGHütt's specialty pig iron, Thyssen himself became the majority shareholder in two other steel works, the *Krefelder Stahlwerke AG* and the *AG Oberbilker Stahlwerke* in Düsseldorf. The *Oberbilker Stahlwerke* produced railway, locomotive, ship, and machine parts. In 1900, Thyssen, along with Franz Burger, Peter Klöckner, and Carl Spaeter founded the *Krefelder Stahlwerke AG* as an integrated quality steel works. When the digging of a nearby canal did not pan out, Thyssen began buying up the majority of Krefelder stock. After gaining control, he eliminated production overlap with his core firms, and moved it into high-quality steel products.[36] The integration of these two companies typified the next wave of vertical integration into finished goods sectors by German heavy industry after the turn of the century.

Continuing Expansion at the GDK Bruckhausen

Franz Dahl and Fritz Thyssen could, in part, trace the necessity for even greater expansion to a 1901 tour of American steel works. They came back with a great appreciation for the sheer scale, flow economies, and cost reductions achieved by American steel firms. This next round of investment rested on six key factors:

1. concentration on greater economies of scale;
2. diversification into mass-production finished goods on the basis of flow production using "one heat" processes;
3. the growing interconnection and mechanization of all major production processes by means of cranes, inclines, sluices, and internal railways, which put a premium on proximity, and plant design, i.e., layouts;

4. reuse of waste products, such as tar, benzene, ammonia, nitrogen, slag, etc.;

5. development of integrated "economies of energy," based on the high-horsepower gas engine;

6. electrification of the entire Konzern, exemplified by the full electrification of the GDK Dinslaken.

Each of the means of cost reduction supplemented one another, and could be found in varying degrees in the technical modernization of the Bruckhausen works. While one could argue that the first three trends were inspired by American models of production, the last three factors grew out of a particular "German path" of rationalization based on institutionalized R&D and "economies of energy" exemplified by the Thyssen & Co. Machine Company.

In terms of American-style rationalization, Dahl placed two new 40-ton Siemens-Martin furnaces into operation in 1907–1908 and two new 25-ton Siemens-Martin furnaces in 1910–1911.[37] Each of the furnaces came equipped with modern Harmet presses, which could shape the steel right out of the furnaces in a nearly continuous process. Backed by the tremendous energy generated by the gas dynamos, Dahl also added three electric-arc steel furnaces, including one of 25 tons. No one had had experience with that amount of electrical energy. Coking facilities were expanded and refurbished. In 1911, Dahl completely shut down the first Thomas steel works, which had proven to be too small; he brought a new one on line in 1914. The expansion of the new Thomas works proved to be a particularly complex undertaking because production in the older Thomas works could not be interrupted.

The scale of investment in Bruckhausen completely transformed the GDK in the last years before the war. The older buildings were adorned with simple ornamentation, but even the heavy stone facades of the older steel works could not stand their ground against the enveloping advance of the new Thomas steel works, with its towering skeleton of structural steel girders and sheet metal. This new type of building construction allowed management to design the internal layout of the plant so as to streamline the flow of men and materials.

Dahl also moved the GDK into specialized forms of rolling-mill products as part of the product diversity needed to penetrate world export markets. He improved the older set of rolling-mill trains with the introduction of electric motors, and built a new set of heavy rolling mills to make quality plates for turbines and transformers. An entirely new rolling-mill department after 1910 was added that used specialty rolling-mill trains to make sheets, turbine plates, and blocks for seamless pipe production. The production capacity of this last rolling-mill train alone could reach 60 tons per hour. Dahl placed all of them in continuous movement to minimize heat loss. Dahl specialized in linking production operations together in well-laid out plant designs using mechanical conveyance methods, which minimized hand loading and reduced the number of workers needed. For instance, the new rolling-mill department built just before the war was linked to the Siemens-Martin ovens by a 900-meter-long tunnel. Dahl introduced American-style slanted furnace inclines, instead of the older German vertical elevators to load coal and iron ore directly into the coking ovens and converters.[38] These inclines eliminated the heavy, dirty work of loading, as well as numerous other jobs. In short, the Bruckhausen works made increasing use of large-volume, Americanized flow economies.

These innovations in conveyance, in turn, forced a greater attention to service, maintenance, and technically rational planning in terms of factory layout. Dahl expanded the GDK mechanical workshop and carpentry shop for the first rolling-mill department to include the production of railway wagon materials and small iron goods. Along with the rapid growth of the Thyssen private railway network between Thyssen departments and firms, the railway workshop grew in the space of a few years from 200 men in 1910 and to 450 men by 1912. When the *Stahlwerke Thyssen* in Lorraine was being built, this GDK workshop turned out 30 new wagons a month, as well as all the railway junctions for the new firm.

The GDK Dinslaken rolling mill under Kalle also underwent major expansion after the Gladbeck sale. The Dinslaken plant added four continuous mill trains for seamless pipes after the patent rights on the Mannesmann patent had run out, and a fourth continuous-strip-steel mill train.[39] In 1905, Kalle and Fassl introduced the first continuous pipe production process in Germany. In the previous year, Kalle had made another pilgrimage to the United States and found that the Morgan Construction Company in Worcester, Massachusetts, had developed a continuous strip steel process whereby the mill train produced a thin strip of steel in lengths up to one kilometer. This long strip steel was used for protecting electrical cables, whose demand was booming. Lengthening the strips reduced the amount of welding together shorter strips, so the costs of the strip steel dropped dramatically. On the advice of Kalle, Thyssen bought a license to build an American-style cold-rolling strip-steel mill. By cold-rolling strip steel at room temperature, the surface quality of the metal could be improved. This strip-steel mill came into operation in 1905 and for twenty-five years was the only one of its type in Europe. The cold-rolling mill made an "extraordinary" amount of money, and was considered one of the "most important facilities of this type in Europe."[40] In addition to new scale and continuous flow processes, Kalle continued to diversify the GDK Dinslaken, expanding it into seamless pipe production, higher qualities of strip steel, wire, masts, and poles, and finally in 1914 into high-pressure seamless steel tanks for carbon dioxide, oxygen, and nitrogen.

While one could construe all these economies of scale, flow, and mechanization as the Americanization of the GDK, the broad diversification, the reuse of waste products, and "economies of energy," were distinctly German ways of rationalizing factory processes.

As did other German steel firms, the GDK metamorphed waste material into new products, new cost reductions, new sources of revenues, and new markets. The GDK granulated the blast-furnace slag used as ground filler for the hollowed-out coal veins, instead of just piling it up in huge mountains, as did Carnegie around Pittsburgh. (These mountains can still be seen today.) The slag from the Thomas converters made excellent fertilizer because of its rich nitrogen content. The GDK coking ovens generated such byproducts as tar, ammonia, benzine, etc., which were extracted, distilled, and sold on the open market. With their strong scientific training and theoretical knowledge of chemicals, German engineers and chemists took full advantage of these byproducts and led the world in coking technology and the use of byproducts. In 1909, 84% of all coking operations in Germany had associated byproduct facilities, compared to 18% in Great Britain.[41] The GDK recycled the tremendous amount of gas from the coking ovens and blast furnaces into a virtually unlimited renewable energy source. But before the gas could be reused, impurities had to be filtered out from the downtake of the blast furnaces. At first, this dust was left in huge mounds around the steel plants. But after chemical analysis, it was discovered that the dust itself had an iron content of 40%. Dahl himself patented a system just before the war that recycled the dust by forming it into briquets, which could then be reintroduced into the steel converters as another source of iron.

The first gas high-horsepower engines went into operation at the GDK in 1906 (four gas-blowing engines) and 1907 (four gas dynamos). By 1909–1910, three further gas-blowing engines and four dynamos were added. The old steam engine center was then completely shut down. The results were dramatic. While crude steel production doubled between 1901 and 1910, coal use remained essentially the same. Coal consumption dropped so dramatically by 1926, the crude steel-making stage of production did not need a single ton of coal because it used the ample surplus gas energy generated by the coking and blast furnace processes.[42] Moreover, the offices created to statistically assess the efficiency of technical processes *(Wärmewirtschaftsstellen)* provided the starting point for many factory efficiency measures and comparisons *(Betriebs-wirtschaft)*, which saw its full fruition in the rationalization measures of the 1920s. By 1914 the GDK Dinslaken ran entirely on electricity.

All of these innovations rested on and attested to the close relationship in Germany between production and research. Inside the GDK itself, Dahl set up in 1896 a sophisticated laboratory for organic and synthetic testing for both the blast furnaces and steel furnaces. According to Chandler, research and development played an extremely small role in the American steel industry.[43] Science-based commercialization in the German steel industry, however, played a central role.

Altogether the GDK had numerous advantages: a favorable transport situation on the Rhine at the head of one of the largest inland harbors in Europe; a first-class staff of (often young) plant managers; integrated state-of-the-art facilities; a high degree of mechanization and factory layout designed for flow production; and laboratory testing of metals. GDK's manufacturing success rested on its combination of capital-intensive, American-style volume production, along with German-style diversification and science-based commercialization, making it by 1914 one of the premier steel companies in the world. By the time the war began, the GDK was producing 800,000 tons of crude steel per year (three-quarters Thomas steel) and employ-

ing 9,000 workers (not including those employed in mining and coking operations).

Thyssen and the Cartels

With the completion of the GDK and the AGHütt, Thyssen had largely
outraced the cartelization movement in German heavy industry. Cartels and vertically integrated combines eventually destroyed many
pure mines, steelworks, or rolling mills—a fate which would have be-
fallen Thyssen & Co. had its owners not constructed the GDK and the
AGHütt.

In the German version of the American Great Merger Movement,
characterized by the 1903 renewal of the Coal Syndicate, the 1903
refounding of the Pig Iron Syndicate, the 1904 creation of the Steel
Works Association, and with a host of mergers and acquisitions,
Thyssen created a sensation when the cartel quotas in the steel industry became public. Until then, only insiders knew of the tremendous
capacity and cost advantages being created by the privately owned
Thyssen works in Hamborn, Bruckhausen, Dinslaken, and Mülheim.
When the GDK joined the Coal Syndicate in 1903, it ranked third
among the integrated combines, behind Deutsch-Luxembourg and
the GHH, but ahead of the Schalker Verein, Rheinische Stahlwerke,
Hoesch, the Dortmunder Union, Bochumer Verein, Phoenix, and
Krupp.[44] Compared with the great pure coal mining firms, however,
the GDK sales quota of 1.2 million tons placed it only sixteenth, well
behind the top three: Gelsenkirchen (7.7 million tons), Harpener
Bergbau (7.2 million tons) and Hibernia (5.4 million tons). The syndicate quotas, however, are misleading in this case because they do not
include coal production for self-consumption rights. Judged by total
coal production, the GDK placed fifth. Moreover, Thyssen owned the
mining rights *(Gerechtsame)* to the largest area of untapped coalfields
in Germany (even after the sale of Gladbeck)! Wielding it as a club
in coal syndicate negotiations, Thyssen threatened to mine this land
reserve.[45]

When Thyssen entered the Pig Iron Syndicate in 1903, the GDK received a quota at 3.16%; the AGHütt received 7.59%.[46] Together, they
held 10.75% of the entire quota. Moreover, the cartel agreement considered all pig-iron deliveries to Thyssen & Co. and the GDK as self-

consumption, thus not calculated into the quota. This meant that Thyssen gained all of the cost advantages deriving from economies of scale, but did not have to limit his production to the cartel quota. Thyssen then transferred the entire quota to the AGHütt so that the cartel quota would not limit the AGHütt's *future* capacity. The transfer of the syndicate quota between the two firms shows just how Thyssen understood that all of his legally independent firms acted as "one company." The transfer also shows the extent to which industrialists could manipulate cartel agreements.

The biggest surprise, however, came with the 1904 founding of the Steel Works Association. While the general public was mildly surprised to see the GDK in fifth place in coal, the announcement that Thyssen received 9.3% of the total quota of the steel cartel created a sensation; Krupp, the traditional leader in the nineteenth century, had received 6.1%. In 1902, the GDK surpassed Krupp for the first time in crude steel production, breaking the half-million-ton mark.[47] For A-products (intermediate goods, structural steel and formed material, heavy and light railway superstructural material), the GDK received the highest quota, 6.18%, ahead of the Rheinische Stahlwerke at 5.45%, Hörde at 5.42%, and Krupp at 5.07%. (The small quota shares also attest to the relatively low firm concentration in the steel industry.) In B-products (rod iron, rolled wire, plates and sheets, pipes and tubes, railway axles), the GDK and Thyssen & Co. had a decided advantage over all other firms except Phoenix. Of the syndicated B-products, the GDK and Thyssen & Co. led with 11.9%, ahead of Phoenix with 9.93%; Krupp followed with a quota of 6.3%.

The surprise created by Thyssen's leading position in these heavy industrial cartels was such that August Thyssen, who had just passed sixty, came to be known as an "upstart" *(Eindringlinge)* in the steel industry, along with his much younger partner and rival, Hugo Stinnes of Deutsch-Luxembourg.[48] At this point, "Old August" increasingly became known as the "American." After Dahl and Fritz Thyssen returned from the United States, Thyssen began to wonder in private whether the German cartel system might soon give way to even larger consolidations, like U.S. Steel. In 1902, he wondered aloud to Carl Klönne of the Deutsche Bank and drew the conclusion "the time of syndicates is past and we must move on to the time of trusts." In public, he increasingly made derogatory comments about the extensive cartel systems, especially and conveniently if he did not receive the quota he demanded. In 1906, regarding the extension of the steel cartel, Thyssen argued that only "a trust could help to rectify all present troubles," which only confirmed to contemporaries his American bent.[49] Indeed, after such comments—and behavior—Thyssen became known as an "enemy of cartels." Along with Stinnes, he actively engaged in a number of behind-the-scenes maneuvers to force a number of spectacular mergers. His speed, cold ruthlessness, cunning to the point of unscrupulous maneuvering, relatively minimalist social policy, and single-minded devotion to the bottom line did appear to follow an American model of entrepreneurship—a "robber baron" rather than a benevolent paternalist like Krupp. It became a widespread conviction that Thyssen's ultimate goal was an American-style trust under his own leadership. (Thyssen's basic line of thought did find resonance in the founding of the Vereinigte Stahlwerke twenty years later.)

But can we really call Thyssen an Americanizer or trustmaker? Thyssen was probably the most "American" among Ruhr steel industrialists, but he worked in a significantly different regulatory environment that ultimately made him very German. Dahl and Kalle did not think he had American models in mind, although they agreed that he used technical aspects that were useful to him; this stance was typical for most German industrialists. Cartels forced Thyssen to move into vertical integration to maintain his independence and self-sufficiency. Just two years after his famous comment disparaging cartels, he became the crucial figure in launching three great cartels in 1903–1904, even forcing the reluctant Phoenix and its banks into it. Because he was joining the heavy industry club (coal, pig iron, crude steel), Thyssen remained aloof from the major cartels until after the turn of the century. Arguably, his short-term liquidity crisis made him predisposed to join at this juncture. Thyssen combined this theoretically American viewpoint with a hard-hitting promotion of cartels when it suited him.

Dahl actually thought that Thyssen was "cartel-friendly" because they gave Thyssen some relief from his persistent shortage of cash.[50] Cartels allowed efficient works to reap additional profits from higher, stabilized prices, which was necessary because Thyssen operated at the margins of his financial liquidity. Here is one key to understanding Thyssen's behavior. Cartels provided a welcome respite from the tension between expanding so as to achieve leadership in the industry, yet maintain personal and family control.

Moreover, after 1900, Thyssen's managers consistently played leading roles in various cartels. Carl Wallmann of Thyssen & Co., for instance, played a leading role in the various plate and sheet cartels even before the turn of the century. Thyssen followed the strip-steel cartel with particular interest because he felt it was his specialty. For years he shadowed the strip-steel-cartel price policy without undercutting it, before finally joining it in 1907.[51] Thyssen had also long been an active member of the gas and boiler pipe cartels, though he jumped ship from time to time. Thyssen often used the pipe cartel against the true outsider of the industry, Mannesmann. By avoiding cartels and concentrating on one type of product, Mannesmann actually followed a more American-style development than did Thyssen.

But Thyssen was just as willing to wreck cartels. For instance, in 1910 Thyssen insisted on having B-products in the steel cartel completely syndicated or not at all. Syndication would help control cheaters, as well as push marketing expenses off on the industry as a whole. Anything less would be to his disadvantage because it would limit his flexibility, that is, his ability to cut prices and keep running as "full" as possible. In both cases, his position derived from his competitive strength. Thyssen had just wrecked the boiler pipe cartel because it limited his ability to compete against Mannesmann. At the same time, he tried to break his pipe quotas in the Steel Works Association and threatened the entire syndicate with huge quota requests for his Stahlwerke Thyssen (below).[52] In 1913, Klönne wrote apprehensively to Thyssen:

> As you know, I personally regret the competitive race of our large industries. I would rather see that the urge to expansion, and therefore the demand for credit from industry, be held within natural bounds. With this opinion, however, we bankers cannot get through to the industrialists. Now that the battle in the pipe sector will expand even more is extremely regretful. It is inexplicable to me that especially you do not see any way of ending this struggle.[53]

Klönne was naturally representing the Deutsche Bank's stakes in Mannesmann in this struggle, but his comments also reflected their general differences about cartels and competition. As did other industrialists, Thyssen steeled himself for the next round of competition. If cartels allowed him time to become more competitive, then he used them.

He remained personally skeptical about the long-term effectiveness of cartels and advocated large trusts *in principle*. Thyssen did think that trusts were more efficient. At least, they did not have to support the weak. Although Thyssen advocated a trust, it was also unlikely that he would have given up his own hard-fought independence. He hated to deal with messy shareholding relations that might call into question the family ownership of his firm or limit his freedom. Given his aversion to large boards, it is unlikely that he would have participated in a huge merger. Above all, greater consolidations would simplify complicated, if not obscure, cartel negotiations. He tended to advocate, and push, mergers on *other* firms.

In short, "he had one foot in the syndicates, the other outside."[54] Andrew Carnegie, for instance, made sure that both feet remained outside the despised pools. Thyssen, on the other hand, was willing to work with them. Carnegie was also much more willing to work with shareholding partners, although the so-called Iron Clad Agreement gave him full control. Carnegie, like Thyssen, had little desire to sacrifice his company to so-called "speculators."[55] Thyssen had a purely instrumental view of cartels. They were useful if they helped him earn money, and he destroyed them if they did not.

Stahlwerke Thyssen AG (Alsace-Lorraine)

True to the competitive nature of German "cooperative" capitalism, Thyssen could not allow himself to rest or rust. In 1905, the GDK was again surpassed in crude steel production by Krupp, and by Phoenix in 1906. In 1910, both Phoenix and Krupp broke the million-ton mark, twice as high as the largest firms in 1902. Minimum scale in the industry climbed ever higher. In addition, the only real gap in Thyssen's vertical integration was in the supply of iron ore. The rapid expansion of the AGHütt placed greater pressure on him to secure his iron ore supply. To close this gap, in 1910, at nearly seventy, he began the construction of the Stahlwerke Thyssen AG in Alsace-Lorraine, the apex of his expansion. Stahlwerke Thyssen further solidified Thyssen's reputation as the American, yet its motivation stemmed from very German considerations.

By purchasing iron ore fields, Thyssen hoped to gain near total independence from *potential* competitors or cartels. One Thyssen executive remembered Thyssen saying: "If we attain the iron ore fields for Hagendingen, we will be secure for one hundred years. That was how he thought."[56] Thyssen clearly revealed his reasoning in a *1902* letter to Klönne:

> After we have succeeded in making the GDK to one of the greatest companies on the continent, [there] remains still one great job left to do and that is the creation and securing of our iron ore supply. [. . .] If the iron ore question is not regulated, the GDK and the Meiderich iron works could probably expect difficulties, which could cost us our entire position in the iron business. If the few Lorraine mines still available to us [fall] *into others' hands* [underline in original], then our position would become untenable because we would have to fear at any point that a strong syndicate of iron ore mine owners [would move] against us.[57]

One can sense the immense pride that Thyssen felt. Thyssen essentially admitted that he came to the iron ore question late. Phoenix, the GHH, the Rheinische Stahlwerke, and the Hörder Verein had already purchased the best lands. This lateness would prove to be aggravating and costly.

The search for a regular supply of iron ore already took Thyssen far afield. In 1901, he had fields in Lorraine, including the later important field of Jacobus. He participated in a joint venture there with a Belgian firm. He tried to secure supplies in Sweden. He also concentrated on fields in France through two attempts at joint ventures, which never really paid off because of French nationalist resistance. In Luxembourg, he was labelled a "Teutonic intruder." There, Thyssen unsuccessfully tried to play a political game in order to turn the mining rights to his advantage. Party-political maneuvering laced with anti-Catholic sentiment and nationalism slowly ground down his plans.[58] Finally, Thyssen tried to extend his influence over iron ore areas with further investments in Morocco, southern Russia in the Caucasus along the Black Sea, Norway, and British India.[59] War, of course, ended more such ventures.

With the construction of the Stahlwerke Thyssen AG in Hagendingen on the railway line between Metz and Diedenhofen, near the

Jacobus iron ore fields, Thyssen tried to close the main gap in his vertical manufacturing structure. Thyssen and Dahl planned to move the GDK Bruckhausen into higher quality rolling mill goods, while Hagendingen would take over the role of basic intermediate material supplier for the rest of the Konzern and compete in commodity steel goods on the world market. The Stahlwerke Thyssen AG would compete directly with the round of expansion initiated by Krupp and Phoenix. Thyssen also rushed its construction as part of his cartel policy. In 1912, the Steel Works Association agreement was up for revision and Thyssen wanted to negotiate from a position of strength using the threat of unbridled extra capacity.

Within four years, Thyssen managed to raise 85 million marks (65 million marks for fixed assets alone) to build the new steel firm. In 1921, Thyssen estimated total construction costs at 101 million marks.[60] In February 1911, Thyssen established the Stahlwerke Thyssen AG as a joint-stock company. He chose the joint-stock form in case his private funds proved insufficient. The Stahlwerke Thyssen remained entirely private.

Dahl designed the whole manufacturing process along wide-ranging, technically rational lines on greenfields outside of Metz.[61] He built the steel works in Hagendingen from scratch, using the latest techniques. Its construction took less than three years, and it became the best-designed, most modern, most "American" steel factory on the continent. The speed of the construction was so "ruthless" that Thyssen received numerous complaints from Lorraine authorities about the number of accidents, the disrespect for the Sabbath, the work at night, and the lack of proper written authorization to build.[62] There, Thyssen reproduced an entrepreneurial pattern established well back in the 1870s.

The Stahlwerke Thyssen combined Thyssen's German-style vertical integration with American-style capital-intensive, volume economies. The finished factory consisted of six blast furnaces, an electrical center equipped with twelve gas dynamos and twelve gas blowers (all built by the Thyssen & Co. Machine Company), a Thomas plant with five converters, an 80-ton Siemens-Martin work, three electric-arc steel furnaces, a block rolling mill train, and five rolling-mill trains for heavy steel goods. Gas dynamos attached to the blast furnaces generated enough electricity for the entire works. A central crane line ran through each department of the factory. More than 127 kilometers of track connected the various plants; the railway stock consisted of 27 locomotives and more than 500 wagon cars. Extensive housing facilities were built for the workers as well. The Stahlwerke Thyssen also built its own streetcar line, directly connecting two train stations to the factory gates. By 1913, it employed roughly 3,500 people. In the same year, the *unfinished* production facilities of the factory managed to produce up to two-thirds of the GDK Bruckhausen's yearly rate. The degree of plant mechanization was unparalleled on the continent. A particularly impressive example of Dahl's design achievement was the fact that *eight* people could run the 550,000 ton-per-year (1,800–2,000 ton-per-day) blast-furnace operations. Individual batches were, moreover, 35–40% larger than any produced thus far on the continent. In spite of the disappointingly poor quality of the iron ore, which raised production costs considerably, and the fact that it was not yet fully in operation, in 1913 the Stahlwerke Thyssen could produce roughly 20% more cheaply than the GDK Bruckhausen.[63]

There was little question at the time that the Thyssen's Lorraine steel company in Hagendingen was the best-designed, most modern steel factory on the continent. German, American, and European newspapers admitted as much as well. The Stahlwerke Thyssen AG marked the high point of Thyssen's expansion and the crown of Franz Dahl's technical and design achievements.

Ironically, the main purpose of building the steel works on this spot—next to a regular supply of iron ore—was only partially fulfilled. The Lorraine ore proved to have a relatively low iron content. In this question, Thyssen had largely followed the advice of Alfons Horten, the first director of the Gewerkschaft Jacobus and the Stahlwerke Thyssen AG. As usual, Dahl put the problem most bluntly: "Horton said 30% iron ore was present; it was not." Thyssen eventually replaced Horten after differences of opinion. The Stahlwerke Thyssen remained somewhat hamstrung by the constant tensions between the iron ore mines and the steelworks. The poor quality of the Jacobus and Pierrevilles mines put tremendous pressure on Thyssen to find new fields with richer iron ore. Thyssen still had to rely on the purchase of high-iron-content Swedish ore. In addition, the poor iron-ore content combined with the high production capacity of the Stahlwerke Thyssen placed tremendous pressure on Thyssen's supply of coke.

Thyssen could only partially cover this supply through his own coking facilities.

Thyssen's competitors found no little satisfaction in his difficult iron ore situation. The State Mining Authority in Metz blocked one of Thyssen's attempts to purchase other lands in the Lorraine area. The Reich military blocked another attempt to gain access to other iron ore fields. The military believed that underground mining would damage its military fortresses. Kaiser Wilhelm II personally intervened against Thyssen's new project.[64]

Thyssen's poor iron ore situation negatively affected his negotiating position in the cartels. In the last round of cartel quota negotiations in the Steel Works Association before the war, Thyssen managed to get only a quota of 100,000 tons in A-products. That meant that of the Stahlwerke Thyssen's total production, less than one-quarter could be marketed through the syndicate. Other firms could cover approximately half their total production through their quotas.[65] While roughly 40% of the Stahlwerke Thyssen's production went to the GDK Dinslaken and Thyssen & Co. Mülheim as intermediate products, the rest had to be unloaded or dumped somewhere on the world market. Such discrepancies between industry production and cartel sales quotas were becoming endemic. Thus, the Stahlwerke Thyssen AG not only completed Thyssen's vertical integration, but it also pressed against the limits of the German cartel system.

It also stretched the limits of Thyssen's financial capability. Once the war broke out, it suffered considerable labor unrest, further reducing its use below capacity. Then, its proximity to the war front created myriad problems. It is not surprising that Thyssen became among the most vehement about additional annexations, which had as much to do with his extended business position as with his burning patriotism. Thyssen became most ruthless when business interests combined with his fundamental belief system.[66]

When the French took over the Stahlwerke Thyssen at the end of the war, it put Thyssen permanently on the financial defensive, a blow from which the Thyssen-Konzern never quite recovered. As a result, while the Stahlwerke Thyssen was a technical marvel for the time, it became a major "headache" of a business operation. Great factory operations do not necessarily make great businesses. Even without the intervening war, Thyssen later admitted that it had simply cost too much money.[67]

But to return to the world before June 1914, the Stahlwerke Thyssen completed the Thyssen-Konzern's vertical integration as he reached a very active seventy-two years of age (Figure 7.2). From his modest beginnings in hoop iron, he had built a complete, vertically integrated manufacturing apparatus stretching from coal to machine engineering that now rivalled the largest coal and steel companies in the world except for U.S. Steel.

Around 1900, most German steel companies remained tightly packed at between 200,000 and 400,000 tons of crude steel production, but by 1913 clear leaders broke out of the pack: Krupp, Thyssen (Stahlwerke Thyssen, AGHütt, GDK, and Thyssen & Co.), Phoenix, and the fast growing Deutsch-Luxembourg. By 1913, these all reached one million metric tons of production. A second tier of firms also formed, which would include the GDK (alone), the Rheinische Stahlwerke, the GHH, and Hoesch. While both Phoenix and Deutsch-Luxembourg grew through mergers and acquisitions, Thyssen and Krupp (Rheinhausen) rapidly expanded by building entirely new steelworks. A similar overall pattern emerges if one examines the course of competition among rolled finished goods production, which ranged from heavy rolled steel products to seamless pipes. In 1899, the major German steel companies clustered around 200,000 tons of finished rolled goods production; in 1913, Phoenix and Thyssen (as a whole) reached 1.4 million tons. After 1900, it was Thyssen again who broke away from the pack. The GDK (alone) managed to maintain a lead against all other companies except Deutsch-Luxembourg and Phoenix. Deutsch-Luxembourg managed to make a strong push to surpass the GDK in these product lines after 1909. But only Phoenix and Thyssen had clear dominant strengths in so-called B-product goods, that is, finished goods such as plates, sheets, and pipes, which put them in a class by themselves. Krupp did not have the same presence in commercial rolled products that it had in crude steel production, but retained its dominance in casting and forged goods. If Thyssen struggled to catch up to the other firms in coal, coke, pig iron, and crude steel in the 1890s, other steel firms had to struggle to catch up to Thyssen in finished goods manufacture after 1900. At sixty years of age, Thyssen suddenly made a push to lead in nearly every sector of heavy industry. Thyssen clearly took to heart his favorite maxim: "If I rest, I rust."[68]

Without this vertical integration, Thyssen & Co. could not have continued to produce effectively in the cartelized German business world,

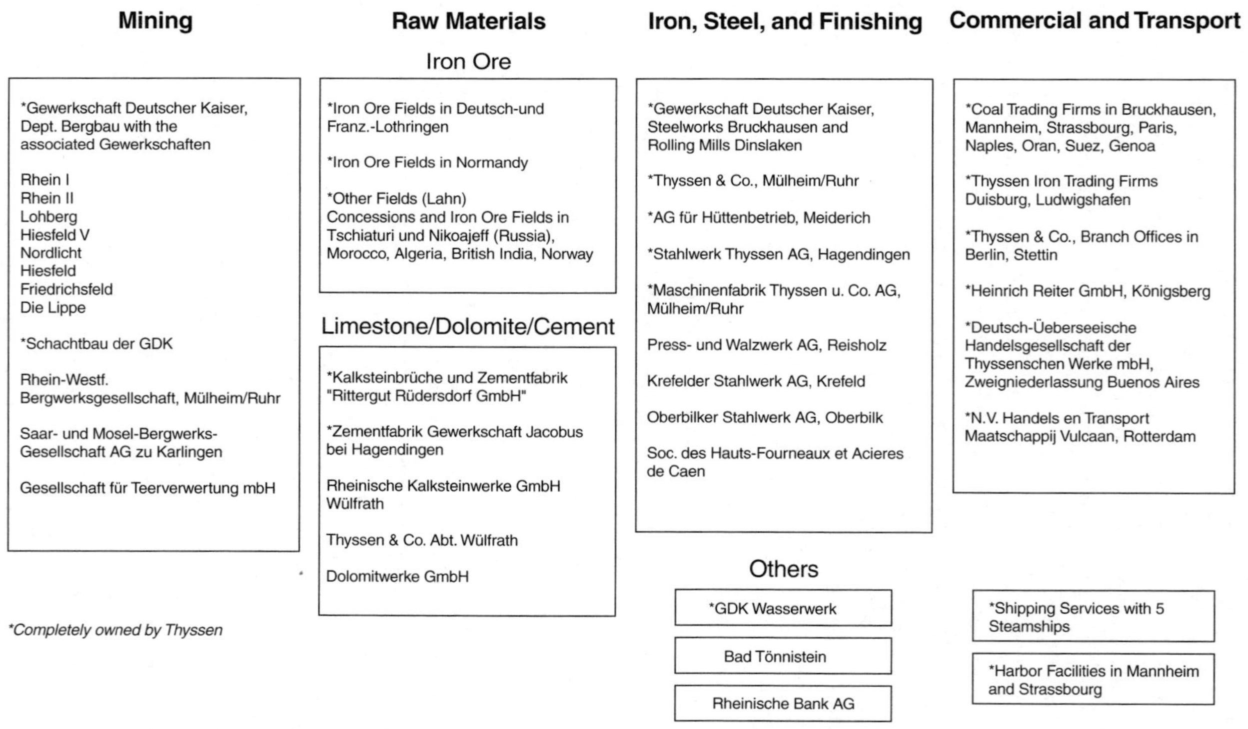

Mining

*Gewerkschaft Deutscher Kaiser, Dept. Bergbau with the associated Gewerkschaften

Rhein I
Rhein II
Lohberg
Hiesfeld V
Nordlicht
Hiesfeld
Friedrichsfeld
Die Lippe

*Schachtbau der GDK

Rhein-Westf. Bergwerksgesellschaft, Mülheim/Ruhr

Saar- und Mosel-Bergwerks-Gesellschaft AG zu Karlingen

Gesellschaft für Teerverwertung mbH

*Completely owned by Thyssen

Raw Materials

Iron Ore

*Iron Ore Fields in Deutsch-und Franz.-Lothringen

*Iron Ore Fields in Normandy

*Other Fields (Lahn)
Concessions and Iron Ore Fields in Tschiaturi und Nikoajeff (Russia), Morocco, Algeria, British India, Norway

Limestone/Dolomite/Cement

*Kalksteinbrüche und Zementfabrik "Rittergut Rüdersdorf GmbH"

*Zementfabrik Gewerkschaft Jacobus bei Hagendingen

Rheinische Kalksteinwerke GmbH Wülfrath

Thyssen & Co. Abt. Wülfrath

Dolomitwerke GmbH

Iron, Steel, and Finishing

*Gewerkschaft Deutscher Kaiser, Steelworks Bruckhausen and Rolling Mills Dinslaken

*Thyssen & Co., Mülheim/Ruhr

*AG für Hüttenbetrieb, Meiderich

*Stahlwerk Thyssen AG, Hagendingen

*Maschinenfabrik Thyssen u. Co. AG, Mülheim/Ruhr

Press- und Walzwerk AG, Reisholz

Krefelder Stahlwerk AG, Krefeld

Oberbilker Stahlwerk AG, Oberbilk

Soc. des Hauts-Fourneaux et Acieres de Caen

Others

*GDK Wasserwerk

Bad Tönnistein

Rheinische Bank AG

Commercial and Transport

*Coal Trading Firms in Bruckhausen, Mannheim, Strassbourg, Paris, Naples, Oran, Suez, Genoa

*Thyssen Iron Trading Firms Duisburg, Ludwigshafen

*Thyssen & Co., Branch Offices in Berlin, Stettin

*Heinrich Reiter GmbH, Königsberg

*Deutsch-Überseeische Handelsgesellschaft der Thyssenschen Werke mbH, Zweigniederlassung Buenos Aires

*N.V. Handels en Transport Maatschappij Vulcaan, Rotterdam

*Shipping Services with 5 Steamships

*Harbor Facilities in Mannheim and Strassbourg

Figure 7.2 Thyssen-Konzern, 1914—extended Konzern. *Source:* adapted from W. Treue, *Die Feuer Verlöschen Nie,* pp. 156–157.

which put a premium on controlling the supply of raw and intermediate input materials. The GDK and Stahlwerke Thyssen relied heavily on capital-intensive, American-style volume production. Not only was Thyssen one of the largest, most efficient coal producers, but at the other end of manufacturing, he owned one of the premier machine engineering companies in the world. It was precisely the extent, the balance, and the quality of his endeavors that set Thyssen apart from other industrialists. Since Thyssen built his core firms from scratch rather than through merger and acquisition, each of his firms complemented each other's product arrays in the coal and steel market with little overlap—a coherent manufacturing and marketing strategy bound the firm's together.

He did not do this alone, but relied on his managers to advise, formulate, and design efficient strategies for both manufacturing and marketing. As epitomized by Kalthoff's gruff leadership in Hamborn, Dahl's design activities in Bruckhausen and Hagendingen, Kalle's in Dinslaken, and Verlohr's in Meiderich, Thyssen relied heavily on his managers to advise, formulate, and design whole companies. Significantly, when Thyssen established a commercial shipping company in Rotterdam in 1910, Thyssen named its five ocean-going steamers after his key managers: the "Franz Wilke," "Albert Killing," "August Wilke," "Otto Kalthoff," and later, the "Franz Dahl."

While Thyssen was Germany's version of Andrew Carnegie, the emphasis should be on the phrase "Germany's version." The competitive dynamics of the steel industry altered German entrepreneurialism into vertical integration and diversification. Like others, Thyssen had to follow the logic of German cartel-concern capitalism or else suffer a slow loss in his competitive position. Once he moved into this fast-moving stream, he had to continue expanding to keep up with minimum efficient scale. This vertical integration eventually confronted German business with unprecedented problems of coordination and control, which eventually resulted in a typically German *Konzerne* structure. Thyssen pioneered the management of such an organizational structure, which rested not only on economic and technological interrelatedness, but also on its coherent strategic, organizational, and corporate culture. Paradoxically, Thyssen excelled less as a pioneer of vertical integration (he actually followed a half-step behind the others and often reluctantly), than in his ability to manage this extended vertical integration.

CHAPTER 8

Managing a Konzern

> You [Berlin] and "Deutscher Kaiser" along with this firm [Thyssen
> & Co.], together build a *single* enterprise . . . you should certainly
> not forget this fact, but rather know to *give precedence* to the overall
> interest over the individual interest and begin from this fundamen-
> tal premise.
>
> August Thyssen to Thyssen & Co. Berlin and the GDK,
February 12, 1898

August Thyssen became renowned as one of Germany's leading entre-
preneur-industrialists. His standard image as a pioneer of vertical integration neglects his qualities as an *Organisator.* The Thyssen-Konzern
epitomized a healthy combination of family *and* managerial capitalism.[1] There is no necessary contradiction if the entrepreneur or family
values and attends to questions of management. Thyssen's pioneering
achievement actually lay in the field of managerial innovation, not of
vertical integration.

The paramount problem facing German heavy industrialists was
how to manage a firm within a heavily cartelized world, with a high degree of vertical integration, diversified product lines, and often small-
batch production, in a highly capital-intensive industry. German steel
industrialists had essentially two organizational choices. Either they incorporated all of the operations into one legally unified firm subdivided by product line or function (Krupp, Phoenix, or the GHH) or
they formed a *Konzern.*

By definition, a Konzern was a multisubsidiary organization with a
parent company that controlled the financial and strategic direction
of legally independent subsidiary firms. The parent company could
take many different forms: it could be an official holding company,
a "community of interest" (IG), or simply the strongest firm in the
group. Inside the Thyssen-Konzern, the parent company was first
Thyssen & Co. and then the GDK. In its formal structure, a German
Konzern most resembled a Japanese *zaibatsu.* Like zaibatsu, a family

or single powerful entrepreneurial figure owned Konzerne. Unlike *zaibatsu*, Konzerne did not command the market share of the largest Japanese *zaibatsu*, tended not to incorporate banking operations, and remained largely committed to related product areas.[2]

In everyday speech the word "Konzern" is not precise. Similar to the English word "concern" (such as an ongoing concern), it generally applied to any very large company or set of companies. The word connoted a certain threatening immensity. For this reason, Siemens preferred "House of Siemens," not the Siemens-Konzern.[3] In this study, I would like to use the term *Konzern* precisely as a multisubsidiary structure to avoid confusion. The difference between a single legally unified corporation and a multisubsidiary structure had decisive financial and tax implications for German steel firms in the 1920s. The term *zaibatsu* has a similar ambiguity. Prewar *zaibatsu* also tended to organize themselves into one large corporation with numerous semi-autonomous groups or divisions. In both guises, one can still call them *zaibatsu*.

Before 1914, Thyssen's multisubsidiary management structure was unique in German heavy industry. Thyssen kept his core companies (GDK, AGHütt, Stahlwerke Thyssen AG, Thyssen & Co., Maschinenfabrik Thyssen AG) legally separate entities (Figure 8.1), while other heavy industrial firms (such as Phoenix, the GHH, or Krupp) incorporated their core holdings into a single large corporation. These unified companies did have a satellite system of affiliates, joint ventures, or auxiliary enterprises, typical of prewar integrated combines.

Why did Thyssen prefer the multisubsidiary form? Thyssen and his managers developed an organizational design which derived from the basic principles governing the corporate culture of Thyssen & Co.—"delegate as much as possible, but supervise." The Konzern organization built on the autonomy, responsibility, and "managerial leadership" Thyssen required of his top executives. Because other German coal and steel firms were roughly the same size, were also vertically integrated, used similar technologies, competed on the same product markets, and had a similar degree of product diversification (with variations, of course), one cannot explain Thyssen's organizational structure on the basis of structural-functional characteristics alone. Ultimately, the organization design of the Thyssen-Konzern depended on managerial choice and agency.

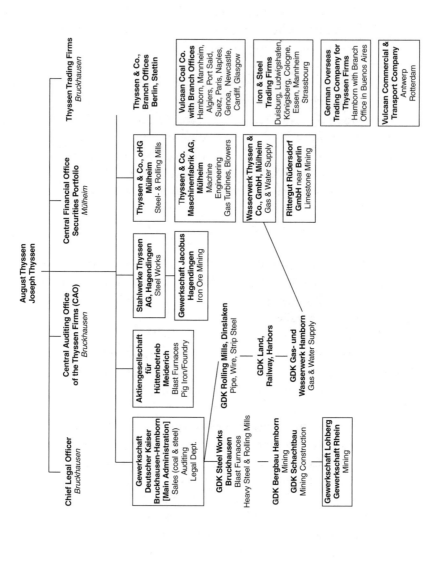

Figure 8.1 Core Thyssen-Konzern firms, 1914 (boxed = independent firms)

Thyssen's reprimand to the GDK and Thyssen & Co., Berlin illustrates these fundamental values. Nearly eight years after the GDK steelworks had gone into operation, Thyssen regretted reminding the Berlin trading office and the GDK of their place in his corporate world; they should have known that they constituted a "single enterprise." Thyssen sent identically worded letters to both parties. The tone of the letters reflected Thyssen's characteristic blend of adamant politeness and concern for profitability and performance. Demonstrating that he was no micro-manager, Thyssen only "happened" to see the correspondence. Thyssen broke through the bounds of individual entrepreneurialism and could manage a large enterprise because he worked through a well-designed organization. He let his managers do their work and intervened only when necessary. He based these interventions largely on the information and reporting system provided by his accounts, his system of organizing control.

Decentralization

The Thyssen-Konzern included almost all of the legal forms available to industrialists at the time: a personal general partnership (oH), limited liability companies (GmbHs), joint-stock companies (AGs), and numerous mining companies (Gewerkschaften). The trading firms, proliferating after 1906, were generally set up as limited-liability companies (GmbH). Thyssen & Co., Berlin, however, had no legally independent status as a branch office because of previous managerial difficulties. It acted, however, as if it were an independent trading firm. As such, the Thyssen-Konzern was a motley collection of legal forms. What advantages did Thyssen gain from this structure?

Streamlined Management

By keeping individual companies legally independent, he retained a relatively simple, clear administration in each of his companies with little overlap in managerial competencies, product lines, and labor markets. Running a labor-intensive coal mine in Hamborn was a significantly different enterprise than the high-technology machine-engineering company in Mülheim. For this reason, once the Thyssen & Co. machine department, the Thyssen & Co. Waterworks, or the

GDK Schachtbau began selling to third-party customers on the open market, Thyssen wasted little time spinning them off as independent firms. Delays in making them legally independent owed more to management or financial difficulties.

Thyssen kept the boards on his firms extremely lean, not top-heavy:

GDK Grubenvorstand (Board of Directors) 1912:
Family: August, Joseph, Fritz, Heinrich, Julius Thyssen
Managers: Franz Dahl, Arthur Jacob, Julius Kalle, Wilhelm Kern,
    Carl Rabes

Aktiengesellschaft für Hüttenbetrieb 1913:
(Supervisory Board): August, Joseph, Fritz Thyssen, Franz Dahl
(Managing Board): Conrad Verlohr, Alois Melcher

Stahlwerke Thyssen AG 1914:
(Supervisory Board): August, Fritz Thyssen, Franz Dahl
(Managing Board): Franz Theis, Wilhelm Verlohr

Thyssen & Co. oHG 1914:
(Owners): August, Joseph Thyssen
(Managing Board): Hermann Eumann, Philipp Neuhaus, Ernst
    Becker

Maschinenfabrik Thyssen & Co. AG 1914:
(Supervisory Board): August, Joseph Thyssen
(Managing Board): Karl Härle, Edmund Roser, Gottlieb Fassnacht

Thyssen firms had small corporate boards with only a few people endowed with executive authority to sign for the company *(Prokura)*. Lean boards reduced the level of bureaucracy. Large central boards would have created an organizational nightmare—a lesson later learned by the VSt. Small boards also effectively reduced the amount of people who received bonuses or dividends on the profits. While other heavy industrial enterprises (i.e., Phoenix or Krupp) had supervisory boards of twenty people, a managing board of ten, and perhaps thirty *Prokuristen,* the GDK operated with nine to ten board members and four *Prokuristen.* The Stahlwerke Thyssen in Hagendingen was even leaner. Six members on the supervisory board, two managing executives, and three managers with power of attorney *(Prokuristen)* ran one of the largest steel companies in the world.[4] This decentralization gave senior managers wide-ranging freedom as lords in their independent industrial fiefdoms.

Above all, according to Heinrich Dinkebach, Thyssen valued "leadership personalities:"

The August Thyssen-Konzern was not a unified Konzern. A[ugust]. Th[yssen]. wanted to rock back and forth *(schaukeln)*. He did not like the joint-stock company form. [He] valued *leadership personalities (Führerpersönlichkeiten)*. In a single corporation the management *(Haupt)* would have been either too large or too small. The Thyssen-Konzern was never fused together.[5]

The decentralized organization with its numerous firms multiplied the total number of board chairmen. This allowed a greater number of young, talented, and often assertive people to move up into full leadership positions than in a single, unified firm. Thyssen valued the personnel implications of a decentralized structure.

The GDK was a particularly strong example of managerial autonomy. Despite nearly a decade of working in the same company, Wilhelm Späing, the chief legal officer *(Justitiar)* of the Thyssen-Konzern, could not say very much about Franz Dahl, the technical director of the GDK, because they had so little contact with one another. Despite its formal unitary, functional structure and central administration building, the GDK was organized into three "strictly self-enclosed administration centers, which rose above the other offices like fortresses." These administrative centers included the main administration with all sales and commercial offices under Fritz Thyssen, Rabes, Filius, Hofs and Späing, the blast furnaces and steel works in Bruckhausen under *Generaldirektor* Franz Dahl, and the mining operations in Hamborn under *Generaldirektor* Jacob. Both Dahl and Jacob acted as "absolute dictators" *(Alleinherrscher)* within their respective areas. Dahl's office literally sat behind a huge wall, which no one could see over. Dahl hardly ever came to the main administration building except when it was absolutely necessary to talk with Carl Rabes about the iron ore supply or about product costs. Dahl and Jacob had a decade-long running dispute about how much coal to mine around the security column supporting the steel works. Jacob always wanted to mine more; Dahl wanted to avoid any chance of sinkings ground that might endanger his steel manufacturing operations. Such rivalries among strong-willed managers permeated the Thyssen-Konzern. Späing even attributed Dahl's early retirement in 1920 to Fritz

Thyssen's recurrent surprise visits to Dahl's "fortress."[6] Unlike August Sr., Fritz did not respect Dahl's sphere of influence by giving notice before he arrived to discuss matters.

At the Konzern level and inside individual firms, clear lines of authority were drawn, reinforcing the strong individual personalities of its directors. The best example can be found in the GDK Dinslaken under Julius Kalle. The GDK Dinslaken had a similar modular structure as Thyssen & Co., built along product departments uniting manufacturing, sales, and shipping offices. Kalle managed Dinslaken as a fully independent "profit center," or division of the GDK (like Buick or Chevrolet inside General Motors). The GDK Dinslaken had its own fully independent accounting staff, which calculated its annual balances, capital accounts, and all of its commercial and financial transactions independently from the rest of the GDK. Until 1905, the GDK final balance did not even include GDK Dinslaken (thereafter it consolidated that balance into the GDK balance at the end of the year). Inside Thyssen-Konzern accounts, GDK Dinslaken finances, loans, and credits remained entirely distinct from the rest of the GDK. GDK Dinslaken even extended credits to other firms as if it were a separate firm. Its geographical separation from the main GDK works in Bruckhausen and the strong personality of Kalle helped keep it autonomous. Thyssen spoke of the GDK Dinslaken as if it were a separate firm. In debates with the rolled-wire cartel, he claimed that the GDK Dinslaken should have a distinct quota itself, but could not convince the cartel.[7] It is unclear why Thyssen did not turn it into a legally independent firm. Possibly its revenues and profits helped bolster the revenue and cash-flow streams inside the GDK. Only in the eyes of the law was Kalle's GDK Dinslaken not an independent company. When, in 1924–1925, the Thyssen-Konzern was legally unified for tax purposes, the divisional status of GDK Dinslaken provided the basic organizational template, so that the Konzern retained the autonomy of individual executives.

When the question arose in the early 1920s of whether or not to unify the Konzern, the most controversial question was which directors would be appointed to oversee the consolidated firm. None of the Thyssen companies' board members was willing to be subordinated to any of the others. The extreme independence of Thyssen directors made a central organization almost unthinkable.

Financial Advantages

What did Dinkelbach mean when he said that Thyssen liked to "rock back and forth?" The legal decentralization of the Konzern afforded the Thyssen companies a great deal of financial flexibility. Expanding their credit possibilities, each could extend and receive credits through their current accounts with one another and with outside firms. Thyssen followed a regular practice of extending loans from one firm to another to finance his start-ups, a rather strange capability. Throughout the 1890s, the GDK's equity was actually covered by long-term credits through Thyssen & Co., which borrowed from banks. When Thyssen made the Thyssen & Co. Machine Company independent, the company took out long-term bonds worth 4 million marks, but other Thyssen firms credited it a further 4.8 million marks. These inner-Konzern credits carried interest, just as with any other firm or bank.

This legal decentralization allowed Thyssen to multiply sources of credit, which would not have been possible under a consolidated framework. Thyssen's most irregular, but legally permissable practice, was the issuing of acceptances. Acceptances are usually short-term bills of credit that act much like a line of credit or promissory note, whereby the acceptor agrees to pay the amount before the due date. In effect, Thyssen was loaning money to a trusted, first-class, reliable customer—himself. This was one of the main advantages of a multi-subsidiary structure that Dinkelbach highlighted when he argued for decentralizing the VSt in 1932/34: "*Main point:* One can extend acceptances with independent firms."[8]

One of the leading directors of the Deutsche Bank, Oscar Schlitter, pointed out the curious nature of Thyssen finances:

> Thyssen operated a lot with credit, but he apprehensively avoided committing himself to an overly close relationship with a single bank. He played them off one another and when the banks at the time criticized the abuse of acceptances, that criticism was directed above all at Thyssen. In the construction of his financial transactions, he was a master. Bonds, loans, personal credit—it was all arranged in such a way [so] that he would not feel restricted in his leadership.[9]

The multisubsidiary form also maximized Thyssen's ability to hide the true financial state of his Konzern, especially to the general public or even historians today. The interlocking nature of Thyssen-Konzern finances made generalizations difficult. A few times this lack of transparency played to Thyssen's disadvantage, as when August, Jr., threatened to expose Thyssen's financial overextension.[10]

Internally, however, the Konzern structure provided Thyssen with a high degree of financial transparency. The creation of the Central Auditing Office (CAO) further enhanced transparency. Thyssen and the CAO could more easily assess profit levels than in a centralized structure with a huge overhead and central staff, helping to identify financial weaknesses of individual Thyssen firms. Each firm and its chief executives became directly responsible for the profitable "results" of their firm. Each firm or division (like the GDK Dinslaken) carried all of these credits and loans on their financial statements and had to act as an independently financially viable entity. In a unified firm, overhead, depreciation, other common expenses, and the level of cross-subsidies would have been spread across each operational area, muddying accounting and financial clarity. While Thyssen's loans to various firms could be seen as a form of subsidy, they carried interest charges as if they came from outside capital sources and were clearly laid out in the accounts. Thyssen thus expected the new firms to generate their own internal cash flow as quickly as possible to pay off their loans and build up their equity and reserves: "otherwise they did not justify their existence."

Beating the Cartels

The legal structure of the Konzern proved extremely useful to Thyssen in his off-and-on battles with the cartels. By setting up new companies, Thyssen could expand production outside of existing cartel agreements. For instance, around 1910 Thyssen established two new mining companies Gewerkschaft Lohberg and Rhein, for tactical reasons *vis-à-vis* the coal syndicate. He could now expand coal production beyond the terms of the 1909 coal cartel agreement. (After 1909, the new syndicate contract limited self-consumption rights of the integrated combines by quotas, even though they remained high. The GDK, for instance, produced about 3 million tons of coal in 1908, yet received a quota in the new syndicate contract of 4.08 million tons.) Not only did this contract create an incentive to expand as quickly as possible, but the legal independence of the two companies technically placed them outside of the 1909 syndicate agreement! Legally, the GDK would remain below its production quota. Thyssen played the disjunction between the obvious economic unity and the legal decentralization of the Konzern to his advantage.[11] Such maneuvering did not endear Thyssen to his rivals.

Enhanced Sensitivity to Market Performance

As could be seen by the failure of the Thyssen & Co. model of Siemens-Martin production at the GDK in Bruckhausen, each of the firms had to address different sets of product markets and demands. The GDK Hamborn collieries, employing tens of thousands of (sometimes rebellious) miners, were labor-intensive operations. The Machine Company dealt with highly paid, highly educated, sometimes arrogant engineers. By keeping them distinct, each firm could react flexibly to the nuances of its product and local labor markets.

By far the best example of administrative decentralization in the interest of enhanced market sensitivity and performance stems from Thyssen's marketing operations, eventually called *Thyssenhandel*. By 1913, an ingenious marketing strategy had evolved based on the learning experience "planted and nurtured" in Thyssen & Co. Berlin. The juxtaposition of the two photographs in Figure 8.2 not only illustrates the greater internal rationalization of Thyssen & Co.'s Berlin operations after the rough first two decades, but can also symbolize the greater sophistication of Thyssen's marketing operations and organization as a whole.

Philip Neuhaus, the successor to Killing in the *Centralbureau*, termed the relationship between the home office *(Stammhaus)* and trading firms as one of manufacturing works with marketing firms, rather than marketing firms with manufacturing works:

> The Thyssen firms are therefore—deliberately and intentionally— companies that have created trading firms as a means to promote their interests and distinguish themselves sharply from other companies such as Rombach, Kneuttingen, and Deutsch-Luxemburg which should be termed merchant firms *(Händlerwerke)* because they are dominated by a commercial firm which subordinates them to their

Figure 8.2 Thyssen & Co. Berlin structural steel warehouse and grounds, 1889 (top) and 1913 (bottom). Note the effect of rationalization measures and the use of cranes. (Reproduced with the permission of the ThyssenKrupp Corporate Archives, Duisburg)

goals. The marketing firms of the Thyssen-Konzern are the organic extension of the sales departments of their firms; the firms named above though have sold themselves out to their commercial firms because they have relinquished their own marketing activities. In terms of the connection to the traders, the entire center of gravity at Thyssen firms has been at the [manufacturing] plants *(Werke)* for the entire duration of [the Konzern's] historical development, rather than in the hands of the commercial houses as at Rombach, Kneuttingen, and Deutsch-Luxemburg. The organization of the Königs- und Laurahütte, which is again different, is due to the peculiar relations in Silesia and would only be possible for the Thyssen-Konzern, if the existing system, which grounds the essence and goals of the trading firms, were to be broken.[12]

The trading firms operated as a sales buffer for the manufacturing units. Their main objective was to achieve direct contact with customers, especially those small to middling size customers who might work outside of the commercial areas of the large-scale wholesalers, in order to achieve the broadest possible customer base. The trading firms also received commissions from the manufacturing works' departments if they helped arrange large contracts with other commercial houses.

The trading firms were granted wide-ranging autonomy. Because "a Thyssen trading firm, which purchases on its own *(selbständig)* and of its own accord like an independent *(freier)* commercial firm, it must also go after business like independent firms." In short, the trading firms had full "autonomy" *(Selbständigkeit)* over their internal affairs *(Innenbetriebe)* and marketing operations. Thyssen products had *priority* in the trading firms' marketing plans, but they did not have to market Thyssen wares exclusively. The trading firms' independence was limited by the priority (not necessity) assigned to marketing Thyssen products as well as the "type, scale, and scope of the firms' production program." They had to award contracts, insofar as they corresponded to the Thyssen range of products, first to Thyssen firms. As a counterpoint to this maxim, Thyssen manufacturing firms had to give Thyssen marketing firms the most favorable deals so that they would have the most flexibility in tendering new offers.

An example of this flexibility was the fact that Thyssen allowed his trading firms to market *other* firms' products and thereby built a financial cushion through outside profits and commissions. Thyssen trading firms had free rein to supplement their customer's main order with complementary products from another firm in order to meet the needs of the customer. The sale of Thyssen products would be assured, and a commission made from the sale of both Thyssen and the other firm's products. This policy also helped to spread financial risk. Finally, the Thyssen trading firms expressly helped Thyssen manufacturing firms break into new markets. Knowing that one Thyssen firm would introduce a new product, the trading firm would close a deal with a customer and purchase the desired products from a third-party firm, but then substitute the Thyssen product at a later date. According to Neuhaus, the key to marketing success of the trading firm was based on the offering a full range of steel goods, which spread risk. He also argued that the trading firms worked somewhat anticyclically for Thyssen products on the basis of the flexibility created by the sales of products from other firms.

The flexibility accorded to the Thyssen trading firms was also one manner of dealing with the very regional nature of markets in Germany. Even the unifying presence of such an important cartel like the Steel Works Association did little to standardize marketing around Germany. The Steel Works Association set up five different regional offices *(Kontoren)* in structural steel alone; each region had different legal forms, charters, and statutes. Neuhaus' memorandum maintained that flexibility was of paramount importance because Thyssen trading firms needed freedom of maneuver *(Spielraum)* for their operations.

To enhance market responsiveness and performance, the Thyssen-Konzern used market transfer prices for deliveries between manufacturing and trading firms. The manufacturing works and trading firms *negotiated* these transfer prices according to an organizational rule of thumb. The trading firms had to give the most favorable deals to the manufacturing firms, while the manufacturing firms had to give the trading firms the most favorable conditions on their products. Thyssen trading firms bought from the manufacturing works at cartel prices for syndicated goods but at the most favorable market price for nonsyndicated goods. The trading firms had liaison officers in each of the manufacturing works to help coordinate pricing transfers. Before 1918, the negotiations were carried out informally and centered on setting the "most favorable" market price, which remained open to interpretation and made negotiations competitive. In case of disputes, the Thyssen & Co. *Centrale* or the CAO arbitrated. After a Konzern-wide conference on marketing in 1918, a formal transfer-price formula was specified to calculate transfer prices.

How did this market transfer price affect Thyssen operations? First, the transfer price forced the manufacturing units to make a profit on the most favorable market price from the point of view of the trading firms, at least for nonsyndicated goods. (Clearly, the manufacturing works held the organizational upper hand in cases when disputes about conditions, contracts, or transfer prices arose.) A similar set of negotiations occurred among Thyssen manufacturing works with August Thyssen or the CAO acting as the ultimate arbiter. The supplying firm earned a modest profit on its deliveries in intra-Konzern trade, while the purchasing firm still had to pay attention to its input and production costs in order to turn a profit on its downstream sales. Unlike the trading firms, however, the manufacturing firms did not have to pay syndicate prices for their product. The supplier firm sold neither at cost nor at cartel prices, but at some measure of "most favorable" market prices. Presumably the trading firms helped establish some baseline for price calculations within the Konzern. Second, it forced the trading firms to find new customers willing to accept syndicate prices. In short, both manufacturing and marketing firms had to demonstrate initiative, profitability, and performance based on market criteria. The market transfer prices built in a level of internal competitive pressure or "otherwise it should not exist."

This attempt to build in competitive market pressures applied as well to machinery purchased from the Thyssen & Co. Machine Company. Thyssen directors could freely tender outside offers for new equipment, forcing the Machine Company to outbid or outclass other suppliers. Unlike other Konzern firms, it sold its products to other Thyssen firms at cost. When they transformed the machine department into a legally independent firm, Thyssen executives drew up a formal contract to govern their relationship. Only *after* a number of drafts and considerable negotiation among Thyssen directors did the final draft reach Thyssen for approval.[13]

The differences in the various drafts exhibited a highly politicized decision-making process among executives. The first draft clearly favored the Machine Company (probably written by Carl Härle), but the second version favored other Konzern firms, probably written by Carl Rabes and Wilhelm Späing. The Machine Company's draft obligated all Thyssen firms to order their entire machinery requirements from it unless they could prove that it could not compete in design or construction; only then could they order from a third party. The burden of proof lay on the ordering companies. The Machine Company also wanted a 5% profit on all supplied equipment. The second draft written by GDK managers placed the burden of success squarely on the Machine Company, keeping it in its traditional role as an in-house contractor which supplied equipment at cost. Konzern firms could even deduct 0.5% from the sales price for any delays on the part of the Machine Company. It bore all risks. Both drafts agreed that the Machine Company was to provide access to all cost calculations on demand and roughly stipulated how production costs should be assessed.

Thyssen and the directors of each firm eventually decided against the Machine Company. Even a risky start-up like the Machine Company had to compete as a technologically and financially viable enterprise. Thyssen would not coddle it. It would have to make its profits on the market, not from relatively safe Konzern deliveries.

The legal autonomy and pricing mechanisms of its governance structure kept each firm responsive to market pressures. It kept every Thyssen director on his toes. Because a great part of all directors' yearly income was based on the financial success of their companies, they had a built-in incentive to remain as profitable as possible.[14] Not surprisingly, pricing issues became highly competitive, if not politicized. If the Thyssen-Konzern had been unified, these pressures and incentives would have been softened, cushioned by bureaucratic procedures, additional administrative costs, overhead, conscious and unconscious internal subsidies, and pricing practices. A large central staff and administration would have greatly complicated pricing decisions, especially overhead costs. Because Thyssen included overhead and salaried costs in his production prices, it would have added to product costs and complicated pure internal transfer prices. The larger a central administrative bureaucracy, the more it would have decoupled the definition of performance from market success. It was as if Thyssen had institutionalized his favorite saying: "If I rest, I rust."

The real organizational winner in these intersubsidiary conflicts within the Thyssen-Konzern was the CAO, which arbitrated cost disputes, standardized procedures, checked for competitiveness, evaluated (internal) transfer prices, assessed performance, provided all financial information to the supervisory board, evaluated purchasing policies, and audited the year-end results of the manufacturing and trading firms. Again we see that curious dialectic whereby decision-making inside the Konzern was decentralized as much as possible, but combined with concomitant centralization of evaluation standards and measurements. Increasingly, the directors of the CAO saw themselves as the appointed guardians of the Konzern as a whole.

Supervision

Thyssen excelled at an ever-larger scale of operations by reinventing his fundamental principle of "delegate, but supervise." The defining characteristic of the Konzern system was not just the legal independence of its constituent firms, but rather the high degree of supervision and of interlocking controls that made a Konzern a unified economic and administrative unit. Obviously family property relations provided an important source of cohesion, but by itself this was not sufficient. Latin American *grupos,* Japanese *zaibatsu,* South Korean *chaebol,* or an agglomeration of firms, do not necessarily make a coherent enterprise. Most important for understanding Thyssen's organization was the creation of a series of overarching corporate offices inside the parent companies that administratively bound the separate companies into a coordinated and systematic whole (see Figure 8.1). Thyssen remained sovereign in his corporate house because of his organization of control.

Thyssen & Co., *Centrale*

In the beginning, Thyssen & Co. acted as the corporate headquarters. With the rise of the Thyssen-Konzern, the Thyssen & Co. *Centralbureau* became a coordination center, a type of junction point *(Schaltstelle),* for financial decisions regarding the whole Konzern. Albert Killing played a critical role controlling the GDK's financial activities.

Throughout the 1890s, Thyssen & Co. treated the GDK as a subsidiary. August Thyssen and the Thyssen & Co. *Centralbureau* sent a continuous stream of advice and warnings to Berlin and the GDK:

You [Thyssen & Co., Berlin] and "Deutscher Kaiser" along with this firm [Thyssen & Co.], together build a *single* enterprise. And if you are at first called upon to represent the interests of the branch office there, you should certainly not forget this fact, but rather know to *give precedence* to the overall interest over the individual interest and to begin from this fundamental premise. I must therefore implore you *not* to continue the correspondence concerning the disputed affair with the "Deutscher Kaiser", but rather summon up everything to create a relationship between . . . and this firm, which is as refined as possible and that is just as civil *(correctes)*, pleasant, and profitable for all sides. You and "Deutscher Kaiser" should not fight one another, but rather complement and support one another. Commensurately, the correspondence with one another must always be carried on in a professional *(sachgemäss)*, dignified, yes, even distinguished form.[15]

In one 1893 case, Killing and Thyssen became upset that the GDK claimed compensation for a transaction already arranged with Krupp through Thyssen & Co., and Thyssen wrote the GDK:

My firm can claim a replacement rolling mill from Krupp at no cost and this was guaranteed without burdening your firm in any way. The combination of both transactions occurred at Krupp's request, which apparently did not want to admit [directly] that the rolling mill delivered was defective. The compensation that you claim of 1,400 marks is entirely unjustified, apart from the fact that nothing could be further from my mind and my firm's intentions [*mir u. m. Firma*] to take even a penny from you. With this in mind, I ask of you to confirm the transaction with Krupp and express the definite expectation for the consequences, that the agreements concluded by myself will be carried out completely and entirely, so that such embarrassing episodes are avoided.[16]

Thyssen still distinguished between "my firm" (Thyssen & Co.) and "your firm" (the GDK). The two firms lacked coordination. In fact, Thyssen had to write back two days later apologizing to the GDK for a 400-mark error in his own calculations. Thyssen & Co. would credit the GDK for it. Thyssen also reminded the GDK that "my firm" had suggested using the GDK as collateral *(Bürge)* for another transaction with Baden railway authorities; the GDK should make appropriate arrangements because they had accepted the offer. In another case, Thyssen regretted hearing from an Antwerp firm, with whom he had worked with for twenty years in the most "pleasant manner" and who required a steady delivery of material, that the GDK could not fulfill its orders. Thyssen called for an immediate meeting to assess why.[17] At this point, Thyssen & Co. kept the GDK on a very short organizational leash. The correspondence also begins to hint at the growing rivalry between the two firms' managements. In the end, the business relationship between Bruckhausen and Mülheim was more mutual and complementary than antagonistic. Both firms exchanged information rapidly and learned to integrate their experiences into their operations.[18]

We can also see the difficult process of translating the same guiding business policies of Thyssen & Co.'s corporate culture to greater spheres of activity. Initially, Thyssen & Co. treated the GDK exactly as it did its own departments. The GDK directors faced the hardheaded emphasis on financial "results," the same problem of clearly distinguishing new investments from operating costs, and Thyssen's characteristic exhortations to create the greatest possible savings and cost reduction. The following letter written by Killing is a prime example of Thyssen's business philosophy, his curious mixture of firm but polite admonishment:

I permit myself again to turn your attention to the enormous expenditures, which the Gewerkschaft Deutscher Kaiser has and which [handwritten insert by AT: "even still today"] do not at all match the incoming earnings in spite of the fact that the blast furnaces have gone into operation.

Under these circumstances I consider it my duty to point out that it is absolutely necessary for the managing board of the firm to keep production up at the same pace [insert by AT: "if possible"], and that means that inventories [insert by AT: "for the operations"] be held as small as possible. Moreover, the treatment of the wage question [should] be handled with the highest conceivable thrift, and, in particular, that all somehow dispensable laborers involved in new construction projects be discharged and for those considered necessary be employed only by day (not by night).—Therefore, all new construction not absolutely required must be postponed; also, only [expenses], which have been expressly approved of by me, be credited to the "new investment" account.—Wages from those people who are used alternately in "new investment" and operations *(Betrieb)*, are to be exclusively debited to the latter!—

I can only ask of you in the most serious and urgent manner to turn your very special attention to the previous points, so that these justified requests are carried out to the full and that after January 1 the income at least covers the expenditures under all circumstances.—

[P. S. handwritten by AT: "I would be very grateful to you, if I can completely count on your support to the greatest extent."][19]

Thyssen softened Killing's insistent tone in this letter. In January 1898, Thyssen wrote confidentially to both Director Raabes and Dahl that they had improperly booked over 100,000 marks to the new investment account. He reminded them that he needed to approve beforehand all such postings.[20] In February 1898, he reminded the GDK to be prompt about the monthly financial and cost-accounting reports so that he could draw the proper conclusions:

With this letter I intend to ask of you just as friendly and urgently, from now on to send to me the reports on the mines, the steel and rolling mills, and the Thomas phosphate mill under all circumstances before the final closing of the accounts for the following month (not any later!). Otherwise they, or the warnings *(Monita)* drawn from them, have little or no value to me!—In addition, I ask of you to strictly ensure that every one of your departments, including the railway department, reports monthly on the amount of wages for new investment and for operations . . . and to pay attention that wages, whose classification are somewhat doubtful, always be posted to operations! [Added at end of letter:] (Similarly I ask you to send the monthly cost accounting of the steel and rolling mills). Also I would like to be informed in monthly reports about the amount of railway fines incurred by each department and on what grounds they have arisen![21]

Thyssen applied to the GDK the same procedures and expectations pioneered at the departmental level within Thyssen & Co. in the 1880s with the same strictness and same business style in the 1890s. All of the letters illustrate Thyssen's style of "remote control."[22] Thyssen relied on monthly cost accounting and financial reports as his main method of control.

Over time, a portion of the Thyssen & Co. *Centralbureau* specialized in Konzern-wide activities. Konzern correspondence and statistical material regularly flowed specifically to an office within the *Centralbureau* in Mülheim, which after 1907 was called the "Thyssen & Co., Centrale." The office centered on Phillip Neuhaus, Friedrich Riepelmeier, and especially Hermann Eumann, the *"Finanzminister"* of the Konzern.[23]

Eumann and his assistants (Heinrich Hofs, H. von Kamp, and W. Kocks) headed all auditing operations for the Konzern before the CAO was founded. They continually audited the GDK in the 1890s and the AGHütt thereafter, playing the same role as outside chartered accountants.[24]

The *Centrale* acted as a financial control office for the entire Thyssen-Konzern. All land purchases or sales went through this office. All the balances and financial statements of Thyssen firms circulated back and forth between the CAO to the *Centrale*. Numerous letters filled with information regarding revenues, production, worker statistics, and general financial and statistical matters attest to its role in general management. The Centrale also had an especially important mediating role between the GDK and the regional Reichsbank branch office in Mülheim. The Centrale and the CAO jointly handled tax, loans, and insurance questions. The *Centrale* acted as the primary mediator of the relationships between the Thyssen & Co. Waterworks, the Hamborn waterworks and the communities of the Ruhr. It also handled commercial transactions with its branch offices in Berlin and Stettin.

Finally, the *Centrale* conducted a great portion of the current account financing with banks and among Thyssen firms, as well as transfer pricing issues for the Konzern. These accounts required a thorough knowledge of the operations of the entire Thyssen-Konzern. Friedrich Riepelmeier, who entered Thyssen's service around 1900, monitored all of the intra-Konzern financial transactions. Riepelmeier himself set up the entire internal transfer pricing work process *(Geschäftsgang)* inside Thyssen & Co. and prepared account statements for each Thyssen-Konzern firm every six months.[25] This task was complicated by the fact that each Thyssen firm charged interest (5%) on the current account credits to one another—another indicator that each firm had to remain financially viable on its own.

A number of Konzern functions also remained at Thyssen & Co. without a formally distinct office. Before he retired in 1908, August Wilke coordinated the entire scrap trade for the Konzern, a task that would also fall to his successor, Ernst Becker.[26] Becker would become known as the "scrap baron" of the Thyssen-Konzern.[27] Wilke, Becker, and the *Centralbureau* could also sign agreements with the cement syndicate, binding for the entire Konzern. In May 1906, for instance, the AGHütt signed an agreement with the *Rheinisch-Westfälische Zement-Syndikate,* whereby all the Thyssen firms agreed to buy their cement at syndicate prices.[28]

The *Justitiar,* Wilhelm Späing

The financial and legal dilemmas caused by the construction of the Thyssen-Konzern created enough work to justify in 1910 the hiring of a chief legal executive (*Justitiar*), Wilhelm Späing, one of the most important figures in its history. Späing increasingly played the point position for the Thyssen-Konzern in its complicated, and sometimes antagonistic, relations with communities, competitors, cartels, courts, tax ministries, and the government. He would play a similar role for the VSt.

Wilhelm Späing was born in 1882 in the small town of Wriezen, northeast of Berlin near the Oder River. His father was a Prussian judge. Späing attended Gymnasium in Königsberg and then moved to Cologne to study law, earning his doctorate in 1906 in Bonn. During this time, his studies took him all over Europe, to widen his knowledge of comparative law. He moved back to Berlin, passed the bar exam in 1909, and immediately took on a number of positions in the Berlin court system. There he happened to hear that the GDK was searching for a chief legal officer. Without expecting much, Späing applied, along with fifty other applicants. Späing did not expect to receive the job at all after he arrived three hours late for the interview due to train delays. Thyssen worried, however, that they would not be able to retain Späing because Hamborn would turn him off as an ugly industrial city; Hamborn could not compete with the attractions of Berlin.

Späing reassured Thyssen by replying that he could live in any city of 100,000 people, especially in a city where he could live on a river in green fields, which he had spied on a map. Thyssen quickly disabused Späing, calling the Emscher the "sewage canal" of the GDK and Ruhr; those green fields on the map were mounds of Thyssen slag and iron ore. In spite of this, in 1910 Späing decided to move to Hamborn-Bruckhausen.[29] As a bit of compensation, Späing tried to turn the GDK Casino into a major social club for important figures in the area.

Späing became Thyssen's leading authority on tax and corporate law. Although Härle and Späing represented Thyssen with equal tenacity, Späing's legal mind worked as precisely, diplomatically, and with nuance as Härle's worked single-mindedly and bluntly. Späing had a sharp mind, much like a chess master, with a good eye for the long-term consequences and political implications of the strategies under question. He could see the legal implications for the opposing side, not only for his own, like Härle. This quality made him an effective diplomat and advocate for Thyssen. He also had a keen interest in politics. After the war, Späing became a representative for the German People's Party (DVP) in the Hamborn city council. (The DVP was a moderately conservative party with close ties to industry, best known as the party of Gustav Stresemann.) During the postwar revolution, he ardently defended Thyssen and the sanctity of private property. By then, Hamborn had gained the reputation as one of the "reddest" (i.e., socialist) cities in Germany. Späing recalled how vegetables and fruit would fly at city council meetings.

In the same way that knowledge and experience circulated among engineers and technicians, Späing actively engaged in the associational life typical of the way Germans managed their distinct variety of capitalism. He sat on a number of other supervisory boards of area firms, often as chairman of the board. Toward the end of his life, he held the chair of the committees on law and taxes for the notorious *Langnamverein,* the most influential association of Ruhr heavy industrialists. He became chairman of the tax committee and a member of the legal council for the *Reichsgruppe Industrie* (the major industrial lobby in Germany). He played leading roles in local chambers of commerce. Eventually, the Düsseldorf Chamber of the Economy *(Wirtschaftskammer)* appointed him as an honorary member of the Finance Court of the State Finance and Tax Office of Düsseldorf *(Finanzgericht, Landesfinanzamt)*. One could say he became an honorary member of the opposing side.

Späing considerably expanded the scope of his activity inside the Konzern. According to Späing, his predecessor had managed to build a free-standing legal office from its initial base in the mining division—apparently against resistance from GDK directors. Späing quickly gained full authority over the legal affairs of the GDK, which ranged from mining compensation cases to cartel questions to eviction notices against renters of Thyssen-owned housing. As one of his first major Konzern-wide tasks, he redesigned the pension plan for Thyssen executives. He replaced Härle as the key figure in Thyssen social policy.[30] Thyssen put him in charge of the written protocols of the board meetings, which met more frequently to cope with increasing differences of opinion among Thyssen directors. Within four years of his hiring, he had gained full authority over all legal questions *(Einzelvollmacht)* in the Konzern.[31] In 1915, Thyssen named him an executive board member of the Stahlwerke Thyssen AG. By 1919, he became a member of the board of directors of the GDK. By his thirty-third birthday, Späing had made himself absolutely indispensable.

One of his first major cases set a precedent for German corporate law. Späing took particular pride in this case, which revolved around the rights of minority shareholders and the fundamental disjunction between the economic unity and legal divisibility of the Konzern, which pointedly exposed one of the major disadvantages of this decentralized form. This case acted as a kind of shot across the bow of the Thyssen-Konzern ship. The question of when and if a collection of legally independent companies constituted a single corporation would form an important new body of case law built up over the next thirty years. This question fundamentally affected the organizational options, level of taxes, and corporate strategies of the Thyssen-Konzern and the VSt.

The case: At the end of 1903, the GDK received permission to erect a harbor along the Rhine at Walsum. But the minister of public works and other officials would not allow the AGHütt or Thyssen & Co. to use the harbor because they had granted permission only to the GDK "in a narrow sense."[32] If the AGHütt used an alternative harbor in Ruhrort, it would have increased the cost of iron ore deliveries approximately 500,000 marks per year. The GDK protested the ruling on the grounds that the "most closely related" Thyssen firms constituted a unity:

> On this point, please permit us to argue that Thyssen & Co., the Gewerkschaft Deutscher Kaiser, and other companies, for whom we are applying of the right of use, have been systematically built up by the present owners of these companies. We do not understand why the Imperial Government is apparently making difficulties particularly with us and is trying to tear apart an economically related whole. Especially because we believe that the state as such is being provided a service by the development of the firms belonging to the Thyssen Concern *(sic)*.—The local communities as well as the state have a not inconsiderable interest on the further undisturbed development of this enterprise, at least for the reason that it is selling exports in constantly rising quantities on which the economic condition of our fatherland depends quite essentially. We therefore have confidence that our completely justified and loyal wishes will be met and a right not withheld from us that other equally large or larger economic units, which are represented under one name, have been granted without hesitation.

Aside from the obvious rhetorical plea for the mercantile health of the nation, the GDK's argument rested on the economic unity of the Thyssen-Konzern in spite of the legal independence of its individual firms. Other firms operating under one name (such as Phoenix, Krupp, or the GHH) confronted no such problem. In strict legal terms, Thyssen & Co. and the AGHütt each had to be treated as a contractually independent individual.

There was one legal escape hatch for Thyssen. The authorities agreed that the AGHütt could use the harbor, *if* Thyssen owned all its shares. Unfortunately, the AGHütt was the first and only time he had offered equity in a core Thyssen firm. In 1906, the GDK offered to buy out the last three AGHütt investors who held 108 shares (of 4,500). The troubles would have vanished, but one shareholder with just nine shares held out until the end of 1909. That shareholder was August Haniel, who was related to the great Haniel family controlling the rival GHH; he had received the shares as an inheritance from his mother. Haniel agreed to sell his shares only if the GDK agreed to share the Walsum harbor with the GHH.[33]

Thyssen refused, so Haniel sold his shares directly to the GHH. The dispute became a direct confrontation with the GHH's powerful general director, Paul Reusch. In a series of decidedly unlegalistic tit-for-tats, the Thyssen had the GDK begin mining on land close to if not underneath the GHH steelworks. In a midnight action, Reusch sent in a truckload of pigs and set up a pig stall located on GHH-owned land next to GDK housing. The squeals and smells of the pigs created such a ruckus that GDK employees could not sleep.

Meanwhile, back in the courts, the AGHütt announced that it would reduce its share capital by 100,000 marks in such a manner that for every 45 old shares, the stockholders would receive 44 new shares. This heavy-handed maneuver effectively eliminated the GHH's nine shares. The GHH sued Thyssen for loss of shareholder and property rights. For the first three years of Späing's tenure, the case dragged on through the lower courts. After numerous appeals and counter-appeals, which Thyssen often lost, in November 1913 Späing won the case before the highest German court, the Imperial Court. The case set a precedent. It provided legal grounds for removing unwanted minority members of the shareholders' general assembly under certain conditions in the interests of the majority and the administration of the firm.[34] Thyssen already despised the joint-stock company form and this case did little to change his mind.

The legal complexities of the economic unity yet legal divisibility of the Thyssen-Konzern proved to be a continuous source of friction. One time the municipality of Steglitz actually sued Thyssen & Co. for breach of contract because it had supplied pipes made by the GDK Dinslaken.[35] During and after the war, the lack of a standardized wage policy among Thyssen firms would prove highly divisive. Such dilemmas increasingly called into question Thyssen's governance structure. The added tax burden eventually proved to be decisive in ending the Konzern structure. Such legal ramifications raised by the multisubsidiary form made Späing one of the major players inside the Thyssen-Konzern and later, inside the VSt.

Thyssenhandel, Carl Rabes

For decades, Thyssen's forward integration into sales distribution languished because of heavy competitive pressures from the iron and steel wholesalers, as well as organizational difficulties. Except for Berlin, until 1906 Thyssen tended to rely on domestic wholesalers and overseas agents. Carl Rabes, who became the commercial director of the GDK after 1905, promoted improved distribution channels in both domestic and foreign markets. Like many other important Thyssen managers, Rabes too was relatively young at thirty-three when he took over. If anyone was the true successor to Albert Killing, who retired in 1904, it was Carl Rabes.

Rabes began his career under the supervision of Conrad Verlohr, the commercial director of the AGHütt. Thyssen wrote Verlohr in 1905:

> The main point is and remains that Meiderich, Bruckhausen, and Schalker [Verein] cooperate and that we support Herr Rabes if he earns our full trust, which appears to be the case. I ask of you your sworn and secret statement in this matter. I am of the opinion that you and Herr Melcher must monitor (*kontrolliert*) Rabes in a respectful (*vornehmer*) way, which can best be carried out by a common weekly conference in Bruckhausen.[36]

Rabes informal subordination to Verlohr did not last long. Rabes was an extremely ambitious, competent person. Rabes knew how to exploit his working long hours (including Sundays) and his close contact with August and Fritz Thyssen to his own advantage. On one business trip to Sweden with Späing and Thyssen to purchase iron ore, Rabes sat at the typewriter for Späing around midnight when no one else was available. Späing thought this was remarkable for a top director of a major firm, but it was typical for Rabes. Such dedication allowed Rabes to pull together a good deal of the commercial, financial, and administrative threads of the Thyssen-Konzern by 1926. Like Späing, he then worked with the same drive and in the same capacity for the VSt.[37] He tended to hide his accomplishments behind Thyssen, later Albert Vögler. Rabes once refused an interview on grounds that his achievements were more a result of "teamwork by numerous good people daily, and over the years."

Rabes was born near the French-Luxembourg-German border in Saarlouis, northwest of Saarbrücken. After graduating with distinction from the gymnasium, he gained his commercial apprenticeship at a firm in the area. From 1897 to 1905, Rabes held power of attorney for the machine-engineering firm, Ehrhardt & Sehmer. (Recall that Thyssen tried to establish a joint venture with Ehrhardt & Sehmer in 1906. Conveniently, Rabes headed the merger negotiations of his former firm with the Thyssen & Co. machine department—a good example how Thyssen's mode of operation was practical, but not always pretty.)

Rabes' French and English were so fluent that he could astound native speakers. After days of fruitless negotiation, Rabes could summarize the essential results and divergences of opinion in a short memo, which he himself dictated in the other language. This put the talks on an entirely new basis. Instead of coming back to the GDK empty-handed, he could come back with a closed deal, which saved months of correspondence. It did not hurt that Rabes gained nearly full authority to close large-scale deals for Thyssen. Rabes' authority became so great that he almost singlehandedly closed Thyssen's huge multi-million-dollar 1924 bond issue with Dillon, Read & Co., a New York investment house.

Rabes' favorite saying was: "Only growth is life!" Making this thought a reality, Rabes spearheaded Thyssen's move into direct coal and iron ore distribution. In 1906, Thyssen & Co., the GDK, and the AGHütt founded the *Transportkontor Vulkan GmbH* in Bruckhausen. It quickly added a number of steamers, which plied the Rhine between Lorraine and the Ruhr. Rabes essentially fused the coal and iron-ore trades, so that iron ore was shipped north to the Ruhr, and coal shipped south. Thyssen's distribution network shipped coal and iron ore to England, the Mediterranean, and to the Black Sea. As Thyssen did not yet control his own iron-ore reserves, Rabes personally handled Thyssen's iron-ore purchases. Rabes traveled widely across Europe in search of new sources and better prices for coal and iron ore. In 1910, Rabes and Thyssen established another transport firm, the *N. V. Handels en Transport Maatschappij Vulcaan* in Antwerp and Rotterdam and the Vulcaan Coal Company in Rotterdam. Together, these shipping firms quickly opened new markets to England and the Mediterranean. After months of travel, Rabes personally set up a system of ports and docks for storing and loading coal for export throughout the Mediterranean. Just before the war, the Vulcaan Coal Company had subsidiaries and agents in Newcastle, Cardiff, Glasgow, Naples, Genoa, Algeria, Port Said, Oran, and the Suez. The Newcastle and Cardiff agents also traded English coal and became significant players in the English export business. For France, the Vulcaan Coal Company worked its business through the *Société Anonyme Charbonnière Kronberg* in Paris. Additionally, Rabes set up a joint venture with Gelsenkirchen for loading and shipping iron ore from Russia. The war abruptly halted plans to open agencies in Finland, Russia, Romania, Belgium and Holland.[38] Just before the war, Rabes began to cultivate contacts across the Atlantic. In 1913, Thyssen founded the *Deutsch-Überseeische Handelsgesellschaft der Thyssenschen Werke mbH* in Hamborn with a branch office in Buenos Aires, which traded in all the main and secondary products of the Thyssen-Konzern. The war cost Thyssen this entire sales network.

Thyssen's on-again-off-again battle with cartels accrued to the organizational advantage of Rabes. Since Rabes knew more than anybody else about the coal trade and had daily reports about coal and coke production cross his desk, Rabes became Thyssen's top negotiator in the coal syndicate talks. This expansion into direct distribution and export played a critical role in cartel negotiations. As the two new mining collieries, Gewerkschaft Rhein I and Lohberg, began mining coal after 1912 and remained outside the syndicate, Rabes designed this coal distribution network expressly to unload this new surplus of coal outside syndicate channels.

In addition, Rabes urged the expansion of Thyssen's steel-goods distribution network. He warned Thyssen about the imminent collapse of the Steel Works Association and the inadequacy of Stahlwerke Thyssen's quotas. As a result, just before and during the war, Thyssen trading firms multiplied, to include the Heinrich Reiter GmbH in Königsberg (1906), Köln (1912), Stettin (1913), Essen (1914), Mannheim and Hamborn-Duisburg (1915), Halle and Erfurt (1916), and Leipzig and Hamburg (1918). All were established to solidify Thyssen's independence from the cartels and prepare him for the expected harsh competitive realities of the postwar period.

In early 1918, a central advisory board, called *Thyssenhandel*, fused these trading firms together into a systematic, coordinated whole. This advisory board did not centralize marketing operations, but helped to ensure a uniform execution of a general marketing strategy. It became responsible for all decisions to establish or expand the trading network and the hiring of leading directors. Finally, it arbitrated the relationships among the manufacturing firms' production departments, their sales offices, and the trading firms. Over time, Rabes came to control this board, to the disadvantage of the first chairman, Herr Sandmann.

Späing, one of Rabes' closest colleagues, explained how Rabes managed to make himself so important. Späing believed that Rabes felt himself to be the "executive organ of Herr August Thyssen and Fritz Thyssen, whose views he accepted without contradiction." According to Späing, Rabes was "not above taking the low road when necessary:"

> Because of his outstanding competence, he was a dangerous rival to business *(kaufmännischen)* colleagues in his own firm. And he did not use this superiority and his close cooperation with the Thyssens always collegially and was therefore partly guilty that so many good colleagues like Herr Filius, Kern, Wilhelm Verlohr, and Sandmann among others left Hamborn because they saw that they could not advance further. But that is what one calls the struggle of life. Herr August Thyssen saw through him completely in this regard, but felt his great adaptability no doubt [to be] more an advantage.[39]

Rabes gathered a great many organizational threads to himself. By World War I, the sheer complexity of managing the Thyssen-Konzern forced Thyssen to pay greater attention to issues of coordination *among* Thyssen firms. As a result, more and more central corporate offices were established, usually at the GDK, usually headed by Rabes. Rabes' ability to excel in the managerial competition only accelerated this process of consolidation around the GDK, away from Thyssen & Co. Not surprisingly, during the war he became head of the CAO, the supreme center of control inside the Konzern.

The Central Auditing Office (CAO), Heinrich Hofs

In 1906, Thyssen established the Central Auditing Office (*Revisionsbüro der Thyssen'schen Werken,* CAO) at the GDK Bruckhausen. The CAO would exercise control *(Ausübung der Kontrolle)* over the entire Thyssen-Konzern's financial and accounting affairs. The information collected was considered a business secret. Heinrich Hofs, who had worked under Hermann Eumann in the Thyssen & Co. *Centralbureau,* became its first supervisor. The CAO was the first Konzern-wide corporate office completely separate from the day-to-day operations of individual Thyssen firms, and one of the first of its type in the world. When Dinkelbach argued that Thyssen had the "first specialists," he was referring above all to the CAO.[40] But most importantly, the tasks and type of controls used by the CAO made it innovative, as innovative as managerial practices anywhere in Germany, or for that matter, the United States. With it, the Thyssen-Konzern had a nascent multidivisional form, one of the twentieth century's most important organizational structures.

Like Thyssenhandel, the CAO had a board of trustees *(Kuratorium)*. The owners named the members of the board, consisting of two or three trustees. The internal organization of the CAO consisted of its director, his representative, other auditors, and their assistants. This arrangement was similar to that of a supervisory board and an executive board. The CAO director personally handled all correspondence with the general directors of each respective firm. A daily journal was kept for all incoming and outgoing correspondence. Any discrepancies between the firms' books and the CAO's audits were listed in a *Differenzen-Journal* and given to the firms' directors at the end of the year. The CAO additionally handed over to the *Direktion* (directors) of the individual firm its comprehensive annual audit results. The individual firm directors then decided on the proper course of action and reported back to the CAO. The last article made it clear that the directors of each Thyssen firm had final discretion over the CAO's recommendations.

Initially, the CAO did not have powers of command, only of disclosure and recommendation, but it created a powerful consulting presence, close to Thyssen, and thus it increasingly accrued power. Hofs gained a powerful position as a central advisor. Little is known about Hofs. He joined Thyssen & Co. in 1892 and died in 1916, just one year shy of his twenty-fifth year of service. Hofs also became one of the crucial point men for Thyssen's (acrimonious) relations with the city of Hamborn, which always felt that he did not pay enough taxes. Dinkelbach felt Hofs was "excellent" and one of the crucial figures in the history of the Thyssen-Konzern.[41] After Hofs died, Heinrich Kindt replaced him, and then in November 1918, Carl Rabes.

The CAO was one of the few offices at this time that had formal written procedures governing its operations. (Thyssen management generally operated more by experience and corporate custom.) Moreover,

August Thyssen composed the ordinances *(Geschäftsordnung)* himself, so they express his fundamental principles. They also prove how closely Thyssen attended to organizational matters.

Thyssen divided the statutes into three main categories: its tasks, its internal administration, and the scope of its authority over the other Thyssen firms, the latter being a particularly sensitive issue.[42] All Thyssen firms were required to disclose to the CAO any information regarding their finances. The CAO monitored all financial transactions and contracts. In its review of contracts, the CAO ensured "that by contracting to carry out any work or have any goods delivered, *competition* [ital added] was brought into play and utilized."

Thyssen stressed that an individual firm's management answer any requests by the CAO in a professional and objective *(sachgemäss)* manner; the dialogue between the CAO and the individual subsidiaries should be carried out in an appropriately civil form. One can almost hear Thyssen's caution in assigning powers to a central office over his strong-willed "lords." The members of the CAO had to be diplomatic. In one case, Heinrich Kindt of the CAO arbitrated an intense dispute between the Thyssen & Co. Rolling Mills and Machine Company: Härle and Roser felt that the Rolling Mills company was overcharging them for the use of its railway loading docks. Diplomatically, Kindt defused the situation by reporting that the overcharges were unintentionally incurred by the complicated nature of the loading process, but that the railway department of the Rolling Mills needed to calculate the charges with more care.[43] Hofs once praised one colleague in the CAO for his skill, his wide-ranging knowledge, but also that he "understood how to handle suitably the work assigned to him with the required tact *(Takt)*. He always knew how to strike the right note with his subordinates. We found his quality of character to be impeccable in every way."[44]

The CAO provided an increasingly sophisticated overview of the Thyssen-Konzern, enhancing its cohesiveness as a single enterprise. The CAO became the key agency for assessing the profitability of various Thyssen firms, as well as for evaluating their budget and capital allocation needs. Exemplifying this close monitoring were the year-end audits of the financial statements for the Thyssen trading firms. The CAO prepared fifty-page-plus audits of the balance statements with detailed explications of the firms' accounting methods and yearly activities as if it were an independent auditing commission.[45]

The CAO acted as a mediator of intra-Konzern relations, a function that became more and more important as the centrifugal tendencies among Thyssen firms increased. It arbitrated the incessant pricing disputes among Thyssen firms. In one case, Hofs and Kindt found that the Machine Company was overcharging the rest of the "Thyssen-Conzern." The Machine Company had initiated a new set of indirect cost surcharges after June 1913 because the present surcharges did not cover all of the "unproductive" costs and general overhead. This move increased the amount of surcharges from 161% of productive wages to 229%. But Hofs checked Härle's accounting assumptions and found that the Machine Company had added numerous expenses to the general overhead account, which did not conform to "generally prevailing opinion in theory or practice." Hofs found the basic bookkeeping system in order, but that indirect costs were inexplicably set higher in the sales records than in the general ledgers. Hofs showed that these indirect costs were higher than the Machine Company's own accounts could justify. In effect, it had padded its indirect expenses and overhead by including numerous small losses. Thus, it had turned an "indirect profit" on the Thyssen-Konzern that contradicted the production-cost agreement made amongst the Thyssen firms. As a solution, Hofs recommended that the 1913 overcharges be reimbursed proportionally according to the amount of sales to each of the firms, instead of recalculating each individual transaction, and that the calculation of surcharges for the next year be revised. The whole tone of Hofs' evaluation made it absolutely clear that the CAO acted in the "interests of the Conzern" (Hofs) as a whole.[46] The position of the CAO as an independent and objective corporate office not tied to the interests of any one firm ensured it a great deal of organizational power.

The CAO audits took it deeper and deeper into the organizational recesses of the Konzern. Hofs even prepared annual reports regarding the activities of the CAO, to inform Thyssen of its progress. The CAO extended its influence to every page of the Thyssen-Konzern books. The size and scope of the CAO grew accordingly. (Unfortunately, only indirect information is available, which indicates that its staff also grew considerably.)

In practice, the CAO did not always fulfill its wide-ranging objectives. Until 1910, Hofs did not yet have the personnel to regularly audit the cash accounts of all the firms. Thereafter, the CAO attempted to check the cash accounts of each Thyssen firm on a monthly basis by introducing pre-formatted, standardized auditing books. By 1912, the CAO had achieved a complete set of cash-account audits for the whole Konzern. It also made organizational suggestions. For instance, in 1912 it helped reduce wage costs in the Thyssen & Co. Machine Company by designing better controls for workshifts. It also helped to standardize wage levels for job classifications among the firms for similar work, but this made little headway, and proved particularly aggravating during the war and revolution. The CAO added managers whose sole purpose was monitoring the inventory changes of all firms, creating a central set of statistics. By 1911, the CAO could systematically check invoices for almost all Thyssen firms. By 1911, the CAO could completely audit the new investment accounts of the GDK and AGHütt, and was seeking to do more than sample these accounts for other firms. According to the statutes of the Thyssen & Co. Machine Company, each firm had a yearly budget (Etat) to manage its new investment.

The CAO also tried to ensure comparable cost-accounting results by standardizing production costs. Hofs intended to undertake the standardization of production costs (Vereinheitlichung der Selbstkosten) for all Thyssen blast furnaces because each firm's technical offices calculated them differently. This project moved very slowly. The pipe mills were also not outfitted with consistent cost-accounting methods. Only the coking ovens of the GDK had "comparable production costs."[47] These were classic problems throughout German industry until the 1920s and 1930s. Although the CAO was able to become more systematic about its audits and standardization of production costs, Hofs' intentions outstripped actual results.

Still, the CAO became the premier authority on the effectiveness of the firm's management. Essentially, the CAO acted as an in-house consulting firm that carried out explicit "organizational studies" (Organisationsarbeiten). It made extensive analyses and recommendations for the operations of Thyssen firms. For instance, the CAO noted how sloppy the Thyssen & Co. Rolling Mills and the Machine Company had been in calculating their accounts before 1911. The CAO suggested that more wage offices be established and that a clear separation of operating inventories (Betriebsmaterial) and storage inventories (Magazinmaterial) be carried out. It sent out more-or-less permanent liaisons to the individual firms to help coordinate and standardize their accounting systems. A similar case occurred with the Stahlwerke

Thyssen. In November 1912, Härle and Roser requested an even closer monitoring of their departments because of the Machine Company's rapid expansion. They wanted the CAO to send a permanent liaison officer to Mülheim to ensure "the most regular and therefore the sharpest possible control *(Kontrolle)* of our machine factory." They felt that the CAO was not doing enough. Hofs apparently felt this was an insult, but Härle and Roser made clear that they were not suggesting *how* the auditing should be done. They felt it could only enhance the CAO's activities.[48]

Finally, the CAO constructed overall financial/auditing statements for Thyssen firms. Some of its annual financial reports were incredibly detailed assessments of the performance, accounting system, and organization of individual Konzern firms.[49] One 1913 CAO audit of Thyssen & Co. Berlin demonstrates the professional quality of the CAO. After checking the basis for each of the individual posts on the balance sheet and profit-loss statement, found largely to be in order, the CAO turned to a market analysis of the "unsatisfactory" profits made by Berlin. In 1913, its profit consisted largely of interest on capital reserves and from a reduction of inventories, but a measly 862 marks of actual operating profits. The CAO ascertained that the miserable level of profits had three causes: First, Berlin allowed merchant bar inventories to rise considerably in the last quarter of 1912 because the manufacturing units required longer delivery periods. With high inventories, the branch office could still deliver goods quickly to customers, thus fulfilling its role as a buffer for the manufacturing units. But a "surprising" price crash in the merchant bar market cost the Berlin trading office, the CAO estimated, roughly 77,000 marks. Second, in 1913 the structural steel cartel dissolved itself for eight days. In just those eight days, more than 2000 tons of structural steel, about one-quarter of the entire year's sales, were sold at competitive predatory prices *(Kampfpreisen)*, leading to losses of 70,000 marks. Thirdly, high levels of inventory cost the trading house additional interest on outstanding debt of roughly 26,000 marks. Altogether the Berlin office incurred 170,000 marks in extraordinary losses, without counting the usual operating loss in its fabrication workshop.

In this and other auditing reports, the CAO took into consideration expenditures that included wages and transport costs, operating costs *(Betriebs-Unkosten)*, overhead costs including salaries, interest on debt, interest on inventories, depreciation, and interest on capital—in contrast to most pricing and evaluation mechanisms of the time. Moreover, the CAO distributed these general overhead figures proportionally over the four main commercial "centers" of the Berlin operations: warehouse sales of structural steel and merchant bars, commissioned sales, and workshop sales *(Fabrikationsgeschaeft)*. We can see how basic Thyssen & Co. accounting principles were being extended to the whole Konzern. Such monitoring of branch sales offices was at least as advanced as that of the pioneering U.S. company, DuPont. Both Thyssen and DuPont incorporated decentralized decision-making into a pricing procedure through market transfer prices and an "incentive-compensation scheme." (They constructed these accounts slightly differently, though.)[50] Annual profit calculations became a particularly tricky affair of corporate high diplomacy, because each Thyssen director's annual royalties depended on the results. Roser and Härle of the Machine Company became notorious for quibbling about these calculations. Härle threatened to quit every year because he felt that his bonuses were never sufficient.[51] Hofs, and later Rabes, mediated disputes about proper amounts and guided Thyssen's judgment.

The CAO could make wide-ranging recommendations that fundamentally altered how the Thyssen firms interacted with one another. For instance, the CAO ended its 1913 report on Thyssen & Co. Berlin with a plea to revise inventory valuations for all of the trading firms, which skewed their financial results in both good and bad years. If inventories were high but valued low during boom years, the results would show depressed earnings. Conversely, if inventories were low but valued low during poor years, the results would show high earnings although business was bad. In short, Thyssen's inventory policy created or destroyed hidden financial reserves that the balance sheet did not reflect.[52]

In effect, the CAO became an all-purpose, in-house management consultancy. In policy and practice, CAO management self-reflectively viewed organizational design as a variable in itself. The CAO embodied the notion of "audit" as a means of seeing, of super-vising, of "watching over" *(überwachen)*. The German term *Revision*, which has Latin roots, clearly associates monitoring and examination with vision and visibility. The CAO created self-reflexive, organizational transparency.

Why was the CAO set up at this point in time, and at the GDK in Bruckhausen, not Thyssen & Co. in Mülheim? Office space was one problem in Mülheim.[53] Also the sheer financial weight of Thyssen's activity shifted to the Hamborn-Bruckhausen area. A new generation of top executives had entered the firm, especially at the GDK; Carl Rabes just started as commercial director in 1904. In short, the GDK Bruckhausen most needed auditing and control. These considerations must have played a role, but the immediate reason for establishing the CAO in Bruckhausen was *to facilitate company–community relations*— surely one of the few times in business history that key corporate offices (except perhaps for public-relations work) were created to improve community relations.

Some background is needed here. The GDK acted as the proverbial eight-hundred-pound gorilla in Hamborn-Bruckhausen life, engendering a good deal of hate, envy, and resentment. Hamborn was splitting at the seams with people attracted by industrial jobs, with 100,000 inhabitants by World War I. Financed with public funds, new streetcar lines ran from privileged GDK factory gates. The GDK's company store undercut prices of many local small businesses. With growth, new competitors challenged the old retailers and elite. An influx of foreigners, especially Poles, changed the entire character of the town. Land speculation was rampant; rents ballooned. Hamborn was no longer a quaint village, but a roaring industrial city, coated in soot and enveloped in smoke.

Yet not *until 1911* was Hamborn legally considered a city, with powers of self-government. This had major political implications. Thyssen supported the application of Hamborn to become a city partially because it would cut out many of the old landowners and property owners (*Meistbegüterte* or *Meistbeerbte*) of Hamborn from the city council (*Gemeinderat*). In Hamborn, an 1856 law allowed all (male) citizens over 24, who were not foreigners or felons, who owned a house and land, and who paid at least 150 marks in taxes, automatic and permanent representation in the district parliament. In October 1906, for instance, this old middle class had a 30:28 advantage over all others in Hamborn's parliament. By 1911, the old elite of Hamborn had managed to *increase* their representation to 59 members. If Hamborn became districted as a city, the Prussian three-class voting system would be introduced. Although this notorious voting system severely skewed parliamentary representation based on wealth (i.e., to Thyssen), it would still have been more inclusive than the existing system.[54] Making Hamborn into a full-fledged city would undermine the power base of the old class of property owners, as well as privileging the GDK in the new city parliament. In fact, the old Hamborner ruling elite raised the dark threat of a "Thyssen-Parliament" in the event of redistricting. This threat was not entirely paranoid. In the 1913 election after Hamborn officially became a city, the so-called "Schnapps election" saw the foremen and *Meister* of the GDK lead the workers to the voting booths. The directors sat at voting tables and handed out bottles of schnapps to those voting for the GDK-supported party list.[55]

The largest running problem between Hamborn and the GDK concerned taxes.[56] Thyssen's main argument against taxation was that he had never taken a single penny out of the GDK (true enough). But Hamborn desperately needed more tax revenue. Until 1906 Thyssen & Co.'s *Centralbureau* in Mülheim arranged all of the financial affairs *(Dispositionen)* for the GDK through the Mülheim Reichsbank branch office, particularly Thyssen's voluminous and lucrative discount business. The Hamborn city administration requested that Thyssen transact the GDK's financial business through the Reichsbank branch office in Hamborn, thus supporting the tax base of the booming city. Thyssen voluntarily complied, although it would "strongly impair the longstanding and proven unity of our financial management *(Dispositionen)*."

Thyssen wanted to reunify such transactions in the Mülheim central office. Thyssen had the director of the Mülheim Reichsbank office, Eduard Schmid, draft a letter from Thyssen & Co. to his superiors in Berlin suggesting that the Hamborn and Mülheim banking districts be fused into one. (Joseph Thyssen's son, Hans, later married Eduard Schmid's daughter, in spite of his father's obstinate resistance.) If Thyssen unilaterally ran GDK financial transactions again through Thyssen & Co., such a solution "would indeed restore again the desired unity of our financial management *(Dispositionen)*, but would bring us into a conflict with our promise to the community of Hamborn regarding tax support." Thyssen and Schmid ended the letter with a plea to incorporate the Hamborn Reichsbank district into Mülheim, arguing that a larger, more encompassing banking area would allow the city of Mülheim to bolster its own finances.

Thyssen's request failed. The branch office in Hamborn remained separate; he was forced to continue the division of his financial management.[57] This division caused such egregious problems that Thyssen even considered fusing Thyssen & Co. with the GDK. Schmid had actually mentioned this option in his first draft, but Thyssen cut it out as it might "weaken our argument, rather than strengthen it."[58] Ultimately then, Thyssen placed the CAO in Bruckhausen instead of Mülheim in order to monitor more closely the newfound financial autonomy of the GDK. The new CAO provided central control, enabling financial decentralization.

The CAO's powers and responsibilities grew over time, especially during the confusing financial conditions of the war. The exact scope of its authority over the individual firms' directors (those lords) proved to be the most contentious issue, but was always postponed in favor of more pressing matters. However, after discovering that a high-ranking manager inside the AGHütt was cheating the AGHütt (much to the embarrassment of Thyssen's close friend and director, Conrad Verlohr), the GDK board of directors again raised the question of the CAO's authority.

Späing drafted new statutes, explicitly reaffirming the CAO's main objectives:[59]

1. to avoid discrimination against the Thyssen-Group, whether it be due to executives or suppliers,
2. to strive to achieve savings through comparative use of production costs of similar manufacturing operations,
3. to make equally accessible to all relevant positions the experiences assembled by the control audits, and accordingly
4. to monitor *(wachen)* that all of the improvements and innovations approved of by the supervisory board of the Central Auditing Office are also actually implemented.

The first three points emphasized the greater need for standardization, not just in the name of efficiency, but also to minimize organizational frictions among Thyssen firms by setting fair and uniform standards. Thyssen management explicitly viewed the CAO as an organizational learning instance to assemble "experiences" and improve the managerial capabilities of the Thyssen-Konzern, an extremely modern formulation. Today, we might call it a central office for organizational learning or knowledge creation.

Finally, the last point increased the CAO's authority, implying that the CAO was now less a central *advisory* board than an office with direct powers of intervention. The new 1918 statutes also created a new, formal supervisory board *(Aufsichts-Rat)* for the CAO. This board consisted of six members: one from the GDK steel mills (Dahl), the GDK mines (Jacob), the GDK Dinslaken (Kalle), the AGHütt (Schuh), Thyssen & Co. AG (Becker), and a representative of the Thyssen marketing firms *(Thyssenhandel)*. Fritz Thyssen held the chair while Dahl and Jacob acted as first and second vice-presidents. The equal representation speaks volumes about the Thyssen-Konzern's internal organizational politics.

This board then named Carl Rabes managing director "to whom the control *(Kontrolle)* for the entire directorship *(Geschäftsführung)* was transferred." Heinrich Kindt and an unnamed engineer became office supervisors. (Inside the CAO, the commercial and technical sides of the business were corepresented to evaluate production costs in particular.) Rabes provided regular written reports to the chair of the supervisory board. But most importantly, "the orders given by the managing director are therefore to be observed, as if they came directly from the supervisory board (i.e., Fritz or August Thyssen) and should be acted upon on the part of the executive director [of the individual firm]."

With this line, The CAO gained executive powers and Rabes solidified his position in the center of Thyssen's financial control system. Unlike the 1906 ordnances, which kept most of the power in the hands of the firms' directors, the 1918 ordinance gave Rabes and the CAO powers to decree organizational change. The individual works' directors still had to be informed properly *(ordnungsgemäss)* as to regular audits. Moreover, the entire supervisory board had to approve, in written form, any special audits, unless one of the board members ordered an extraordinary audit for the firm which he himself directed. This clause kept one firm from interfering in the affairs of another. But the CAO now was equipped with full authority over the internal organization of the entire Konzern. The war had forced a greater centralization of authority, which individual firms' directors had successfully resisted until this time.

Thus, the establishment of the CAO at the GDK Bruckhausen in

1906 marked a turning point. Thyssen & Co.'s parent role ended for the GDK and AGHütt. Symbolically, in 1904 Thyssen & Co. transferred the ownership of most of its GDK shares; in 1906 they transferred those of the AGHütt to the GDK.[60] Since the beginning of the 1890s, *die Firma* Thyssen & Co. had legally owned the GDK, not August or Joseph Thyssen. Both became equal partners in GDK, rather than its being a property holding of Thyssen & Co.

As if to represent its newfound legal independence in architecture, Thyssen built a new *Central-Büro* in Bruckhausen to house the new administrative capacities of the GDK (see Figure 7.1). In rather typical Wilhelmine fashion, the building alluded to a whole mishmash of past styles of churches, castles, and city halls.[61] The creation of the CAO administratively cemented this newfound independence, but by placing supreme control of the Thyssen-Konzern at the GDK, the center of power inexorably moved there.

Before the creation of the CAO, the Thyssen-Konzern could best be described as a federation of firms bound together by a strategic conception of self-sufficiency and balanced vertical integration under the control of Thyssen property holdings. With the construction of these four offices (Figure 7.1) and their sophisticated control functions, the legally independent subsidiaries of the Thyssen-Konzern were bound together as a coherent, coordinated, economic, and strategic unity— as a "single enterprise." The formal structure and internal behavior of the Thyssen-Konzern is a near equivalent to one of the twentieth century's most important organizational forms, the multidivisional structure. It would be an analytical mistake to reduce the Thyssen-Konzern to that of a "family enterprise."

The CAO mediated Thyssen's judgement. It constructed his knowledge about his far-flung activities. Thyssen knew about the performance of his firms through the auditing reports of the CAO or the *Centrale*. The very independence of this office ensured a degree of objective or fair standards. By objective standards, I do not mean any ideal Archimedean point, but simply that the accounting conventions used by the CAO were not subject to the particular interests of any one firm in the Konzern. A good case could be made, however, that its directors (Hofs, Kindt, Rabes) tacitly favored the GDK.

The CAO's activities predate the more public discussion of rationalization and standardization, which became a near-mania in the 1920s under the guise of "Americanization" of the German economy. Such rationalization of management (of corporate management, not just the shopfloor) clearly had German roots and derived in good part from the complexity of modern corporate life. That the Thyssen-Konzern developed such clear-headed and innovative control owes much to Thyssen and his managers. Showing a keen interest in organizational matters, Thyssen personally composed the statutes of the CAO.

Surprisingly, community relations and taxes induced the organizational innovation of the CAO. They also forced Thyssen to consider fusing the GDK and Thyssen & Co., a question that would continually arise over the next twenty years. For Thyssen, a unified firm would have also contradicted all of his historical experience since the 1880s, let alone create organizational dissension among his independent industrial "lords." Thyssen kept his boards lean, and institutionalized market pressures through market transfer pricing and bonuses based on profits in order to avoid slow, bureaucratic decision-making. If anything, he created a highly competitive, politicized atmosphere among the independent subsidiaries.

Precisely because of this new *centralized* instance, Thyssen could retain control over a *decentralized* multisubsidiary form. Standardized, systematic controls enabled a division of his financial management and allowed him to delegate authority to powerfully autonomous directors with good leadership capabilities. In short, in order to delegate effectively, one had to create a system of monitoring and surveillance. The same type of dialectical relationship that we saw inside Thyssen & Co. in the 1880s reappeared at the level of the Konzern after the 1900s. The CAO helped give the Konzern organizational coherency. The next chapter analyzes this system of surveillance by analyzing the principles underlying its financial reporting, which betrays Thyssen's fundamental commercial/financial conception of control.

CHAPTER 9

Organizing Financial Control

If we have succeeded in building our work over the last fifteen
years to its present height, then we have to attribute this above all
to the fact that we have never distributed one penny.
August Thyssen to the GDK Board of Directors, December 30, 1905

Thyssen's ultimate authority rested on his property relations and his financial system of organizing control. Thyssen paid utmost attention to financial questions, because finance was *the* constraining factor on his industrial empire. This limitation was a personal choice. He remained suspicious about issuing equity that might lead to "speculation" or constrain his "freedom." This commitment to personal ownership, however, had distinct advantages for the Thyssen-Konzern.

Although the Thyssen-Konzern was privately owned, the CAO provided an important, pioneering managerial perspective on his enterprise. Specifically, an analysis of the CAO's methodology provides an insight into how Thyssen conceived his enterprise. This analysis reinforces the argument that the Thyssen-Konzern represented one of the first examples in the world of a nascent multidivisional form because of its sophisticated managerial and financial controls.

Volker Wellhöner and Wilfried Feldenkirchen had already analyzed the financial statements of the GDK, but Wellhöner noted that Thyssen & Co. acted "quasi as a holding company for the Konzern." Because the financial statements of Thyssen & Co. were not available, they could not analyze the complicated, interlocking financial relations of the Thyssen-Konzern, which must be understood collectively.[1] From reconstructed trial balances of Thyssen & Co. and the few CAO financial statements remaining, however, I have consolidated the finances of the core parts of the Thyssen-Konzern (Thyssen & Co. Rolling Mills, the Machine Company, the AGHütt, the GDK, and Stahl-

werke Thyssen) for the years 1909–1914. They provide the fullest picture yet available for understanding Thyssen's financial practices. The
financial statements reproduce the guiding organizational principles
underlying Thyssen operations and show the dual headquarters of the
Konzern at the GDK and Thyssen & Co., the latter acted as a kind of
"house bank" for the Konzern. Contrasting Thyssen's financial organization with international developments demonstrates that it represented one of the most innovative firms in the world.

Finally, this inside perspective on Thyssen finance sheds light on
one of the most vibrant questions in German economic and business
history: the impact of universal banks. The traditional view of German
universal banks and bank–industry relations, was built on a version of
Rudolf Hilferding's *Finanzkapital,* which stressed the "dominance" of
German universal banks over major industrial firms. Viewing it in a
more positive light, Alexander Gerschenkron interpreted the institution of universal banks as a "substitute" for the relative scarcity of capital and entrepreneurship in Germany.[2]

Recent work, however, has called into question these traditional
views. Researchers have gone back to the archives instead of relying on
formal structures and then presuming particular power relations or
consequences.[3] These revisions allow one to recontextualize Thyssen's
financing practices. In the earlier literature, Thyssen was viewed as an
outstanding exception to the rule, valiantly managing his firm independent of banks' attempt to control him. In the newer literature,
Thyssen is still seen as exceptional in his ruthlessly independent financing practices, but similar to Krupp or GHH or Hoesch or Siemens or
thousands of Mittelstand firms as a successful family enterprise.

At first glance, the Thyssen story is a poor vantage point from which
to analyze bank–industry relations, because bankers rarely had leverage, insight, or control over Thyssen. But the great universal banks remained valuable, even to notoriously independent people like August
Thyssen, because of the crucial role of credit. Providing lines of credit
is what *Kreditbanken* do, not guiding investment or forming industrial
strategy.

The CAO: Accounting for Control

What makes a multidivisional company is not its formal organizational
form, but how it accounts for itself. How did the CAO itself and

Thyssen use such information to analyze the financial condition of the firm? What evaluative criteria or ratios did they feel were most relevant and significant to their decision-making? These measures show quite clearly a new conception of the firm emerging from problems of managing a multiactivity, vertically integrated enterprise that made the Thyssen-Konzern among the most modern business firms in the world.

Before Thyssen transformed the Thyssen & Co. machine department into a joint-stock company, Heinrich Hofs prepared a detailed financial analysis in order to estimate the appropriate level of its capitalization and its necessary performance levels relative to other publicly held companies.[4] This report provides a clue to the way the CAO conceived of the new firm and its performance. The CAO judged the potential performance of the new Machine Company according to various explicit profitability criteria utilizing a comparative method. As outlined in Appendix B, these evaluative criteria betray a particular way of analyzing and thinking about business. The CAO could certainly apply the same criteria to evaluate the Thyssen-Konzern's financial performance.

The CAO analyzed the entire machine-engineering branch for the years 1907–1910 by creating a spreadsheet—a method taught to all students of business today. The new Thyssen & Co. Machine Company would have to compete internally and—maybe—on the capital markets to raise investment capital. On the left-hand side of this sheet, the CAO planning report divided the machine-engineering branch into six main sectors: general machine construction; locomotive manufacturing; shipbuilding machinery; machine tools; textile machinery; agricultural machinery; and mass-production or specialty machines. The CAO subdivided each of these sectors into firms with a nominal capitalization of 3 million marks or more, 1.5–3 million marks, and less than 1.5 million marks. Such a subdivision would analytically isolate firms with higher capitalization that managed to achieve higher profitability rates. This assumption generally proved to be correct. The CAO then compared the profitability achieved by six direct competitors, including M. A. N. and the *Duisburger Maschinenfabrik vorm. Bechem & Keetman,* which merged in 1910 to form the *Deutsche Maschinenfabrik AG* (DEMAG).

At the top, the CAO cross-divided the spreadsheet into five forms of profitability ratios. To measure returns to shareholders, the CAO used three forms of a *return on equity* (ROE) ratio (i.e., the amount of returns to shareholder investment) and two forms of a *return on investment* (ROI) figure. At the bottom of the sheet, the CAO averaged each column of figures.

The first three ratios viewed the enterprise from the point of view of owners, and measured the rate of return on their investment in the enterprise. The return on equity ratios placed the level of *dividends* (1) in relation to the nominal or par value of enterprise equity; (2) in relation to actual proprietary investment (which might include reserves, deposits, or other owner liabilities); and finally, (3) dividends per share in relation to the market value of shares—a price-earnings (P/E) ratio (actually an earnings-price E/P ratio). The CAO then multiplied all ratios by 100 to form a percentage. In addition, for the Machine Company's six direct competitors, Hofs also placed dividends in relationship to total invested capital and their sales turnover. If the machine company had to raise capital on the stock market, it would have to match the profitability rates of other machine companies to attract new capital.

Realizing that high dividends might mean that potential funds for reinvestment were taken out of the business, sometimes to the firm's detriment, the CAO created two forms of return-on-investment ratios. (Certainly Thyssen's dividend policy—if one could call it that—was to plow most earnings back into the company.) The CAO placed the year's net profits in relation to the gross assets of the enterprise to form one basic ROI ratio. But it also calculated another version of ROI by adding together net profits plus interest expenses of long-term debt, divided by invested capital *(dem werbenden Kapital)*. By adding interest expenses to net profits, the CAO created a figure that highlighted how asset investment was actually used, regardless of the associated costs of a firm's investment resources. The figure calculates how well a firm's investment, however attained, generates profits.

These equations have important implications for understanding how managers governed their businesses. Such equations have strategic biases and a history. To the CAO, returns to owners in the form of dividends did not necessarily mean that the firm itself was financially healthy. The CAO made a clear distinction between the performance of the enterprise and its returns to its owners. Moreover, the return on investment (ROI) figure indicated that the standard definition of profit, which in the nineteenth century equaled revenues minus costs (however defined), was insufficient. Often firms placed net profits in relation to sales revenues to define rate of return. But firms also needed to measure the cost of and returns to capital itself. This insight reshaped strategic decision-making and investment decisions. For instance, if Firm 1 had assets of $100, sold $5,000 of goods and earned $1,000 in net profits, and Firm 2 had assets of $5,000, sold $20,000 of goods and earned $10,000 in net profits, a definition of profitability as earnings to turnover would signal to the investor to place her money in Firm 2. Firm 2 earned a 50% rate of return on a dollar of sales, while Firm 1 earned 20%. However, profitability defined as return on investment would tell an owner or manager to invest in Firm 1 because it earned ten times the firm's total investment, versus two times for Firm 2. Finally, Firm 1 and Firm 2 might have distinctly different dividend policies. Simply put, different target ratios mean different decision paths.

Third, the CAO's financial-planning sheet emphasized profit-loss statements and profitability ratios, rather than assets alone. This was a remarkable shift in business perspective. In the nineteenth century, lawyers tended to dominate German accounting practice. For instance, Herman Veit Simon wrote the standard work on the evaluation of company financial statements.[5] Simon interpreted balance statements largely in legalistic terms, that is, that they reflected (or should reflect) the true wealth of the corporation or as statements of the value of enterprise assets at the end of the year—a static analysis of an enterprise. In this conception, the asset/liability financial statement had priority over the profit/loss statement. But the next wave of balance theoreticians viewed balance sheets as indicators of economic success over time—"dynamically."[6] The most important German accounting and organizational theorist, Eugen Schmalenbach, who influenced a good part of Europe, pointedly stated that the calculation of a firm's assets was a "fiction." The profit/loss statement was the key indicator for the success and efficiency (*Wirtschaftlichkeit*) of the firm; moreover, he conceived it as a managerial *instrument* to better steer and coordinate the enterprise.[7] In brief, Schmalenbach's ideas shifted the balance sheet from a representation of the absolute conception of wealth of a firm to a relative conception of its financial efficiency. The return on investment ratio also turned managerial attention to the efficient use of capital.

Moreover, the CAO's method of analysis implied that a *comparative* approach to analyzing profitability was appropriate. The CAO's accounting methodology again foreshadowed the theoretical accounting innovations of Schmalenbach. Schmalenbach emphasized that the performance of a particular enterprise needed to be placed within the context of comparable firms and the industry to compensate for industrial or macroeconomic conditions. Practice led theory. This is another reason why Dinkelbach later felt that Heinrich Hofs was one of the most important figures in the history of the Thyssen-Konzern.[8]

Fourth, the pathbreaking DuPont corporation first explicitly developed and implemented this approach in the United States, *independently and at the same time* as Thyssen's CAO. By 1910, DuPont "developed accounting methods and controls that were to become standard procedure for twentieth-century industrial enterprises." The ROI ratio, "for the first time ever" turned managers' attention to the "productivity and performance of capital itself."[9] The use of a return-on-investment ratio ushered in a new era of twentieth-century management accounting. Turning attention to the costs of capital, rather than cost efficiencies in manufacturing, implied a different manner of viewing a corporation and new modes of managing corporations. No longer did the market alone decide how capital was allocated. Managers mediated market signals and decided where new investment should go, especially in vertically integrated, multiactivity manufacturing firms. The return-on-investment figure became a key evaluative device for determining capital allocation. The development of ROE/ROI and internal transfer prices were both new symbols of bureaucratic rationality and new symbols of managerial control. The use of such innovative profitability ratios indicated that Thyssen and the CAO conceived the firm more as a set of financial assets that earned a return on capital investment, not just a set of manufacturing facilities that earned profits—a financial rather than a manufacturing conception of control. Thyssen had long innovated in terms of its capital accounting, but this use of ROI accounting placed Thyssen's CAO among the pioneers.

At least for Thyssen, profitability figures did not necessarily dominate investment decisions, but remained one consideration among others.[10] Thyssen's close attention to financial questions had as much to do with the limits of his internal financing capacity and potential dependencies on banks, as with ROI-based decision-making, which might orient Thyssen to those sectors offering the highest rate of return on investment capital. Unlike at DuPont, ROI figures did not appear to be applied to individual manufacturing lines or areas, only to entire firms. Thyssen firms also generally operated with top directors, who were usually engineers (Verlohr being the exception to the rule). Most of them thought primarily in production-technical and engineering terms. The emphasis on accounting and financial criteria expressed the outer limits of Thyssen's control, rather than defining the decision-making within the Konzern. Third, the cartel-concern dynamics of German steel ensured that profitability would not be the main consideration because they placed a premium on securing control of upstream and downstream activity without regard to profitability. It was more important to ensure control over backward and forward linkages than to be most profitable at any given stage of production. Stinnes could argue that the American single-minded emphasis on single-branch activities and the greatest rate of return made little sense. Combined with a growing structural crisis in coal and crude steel (lower value-added commodities), such competitive dynamics built a considerable degree of unprofitability into German steel, a situation which came home to roost by the 1920s.

Thyssen-Konzern Finance

Thyssen & Co. raised most of the additional funds for the GDK's first decade from its own capital reserves and creditable reputation. During 1888–1892 alone, Thyssen & Co. called upon roughly 10 million marks of reserves and additional credits to finance the GDK. Thyssen sold off some of his security portfolio or used others as collateral to take on more debt. Before 1895, any growth in GDK assets derived from external sources. During 1892–1897 the GDK showed no net profit; Thyssen used all operating surpluses for depreciation.[11] Moreover, the second GDK colliery, a sinkhole for investment funds, did not mine coal until 1897. In a letter to a foreign consulting firm, Hermann Eumann, Thyssen's chief financial officer, replied that the main bankers for the GDK were *Schaaffhausen'sche Bankverein,* the *Disconto-Gesellschaft,* and the *Essener Credit Anstalt* (where Carl Klönne worked before going to the Deutsche Bank). Thyssen always worked through a consortium of banks so that no one bank's influence grew too great.[12]

Until the turn of the century, Thyssen & Co. financed the GDK as a subsidiary. The GDK's nominal equity rose from 12 million marks in 1894 to 25 million in 1898, and 30 million by 1899. This equity actually consisted of short-term bank credits funneled through Thyssen & Co.[13] Because the GDK and Thyssen & Co. were private, such financing practices did not come to light until Thyssen's liquidity crisis.

The recession caught Thyssen at a delicate point in time. The interlocking financial relationship between Thyssen & Co. and the GDK proved to be dangerous. The recession led to a brief stock-market selloff that depressed the value of his securities, which Thyssen had used as collateral for his loans. Banks nervously held back further credit. By the end of 1901, Thyssen could no longer meet his payments. Then, in March 1902, Thyssen reluctantly sold his shareholdings in Gladbeck and other mining companies. Only *after* the crisis had passed did Thyssen reveal to Carl Klönne of the Deutsche Bank that Thyssen & Co. and the GDK had operated for years with 30–40 million marks of short-term debt. In 1901, Thyssen admitted to Conrad Verlohr that Thyssen & Co. alone operated with a debt of 15–20 million marks, although it was a considerably smaller firm than the GDK.[14] Debt levels easily matched (and really exceeded) the owner's equity in the GDK, amounting to nearly half its total assets. Bank monitoring played little role here. Basically, Thyssen bet on his ability to speed the GDK through its start-up phase.

It worked. According to Wilfried Feldenkirchen, the GDK showed the fastest overall growth rate (14.3%/yr.) of all top fifty German enterprises between 1890 and 1913.[15] In spite of sharp recessions, its total assets never shrank until the war (see Appendix A, Table A.1). (The 1913 decline was a result of extraordinary writeoffs.) Owner's equity rose just as consistently from 14.5 million marks in 1895 to 69.5 million marks in 1905, accelerating to 169 million marks by 1912. Even though Thyssen was financially stretched, the equity/debt ratio never fell below 1, what Germans then called the "golden rule of finance." It signifies that owners and creditors furnished equal amounts of funds for the business.

But the GDK rarely adhered to another "golden balance rule," which states that owner's equity be greater than the firm's total fixed assets. A ratio of greater than 1 signals that long-term fixed assets are covered by long-term owner's commitments, not outside debt. Thyssen rarely came close to this "golden" ratio; his owner's equity amounted to an average of 82% of total fixed assets, and was especially low between 1904 and 1909, at roughly 75%. These figures indicate that the GDK was highly leveraged. If we had exact figures on the amount of credit granted by Thyssen & Co. as equity, such a ratio would only worsen.

Since Thyssen never distributed profits from the GDK, the additions to reserves doubles as a figure for net profits; cash flow equals gross profits. Only after 1898 did the GDK generate internal profits with returns running roughly 6–11% of owners' equity, a rate of return *under* the average earned by other steel industrialists (see below).[16] Between self-generated returns and liberal depreciations, which created additional hidden reserves but depressed official net profit levels, the GDK began to carry its own financial weight for expansion. If cash flow (net profits plus depreciation plus addition to reserves) is placed in relation to total assets as a return-on-investment figure, Thyssen's cash flow averaged 8.4% after 1898, the end of its start-up phase. In addition, the more Thyssen could rely on self-financing, the less leverage banks had on his actions. In short, his initial investments eventually generated enough return to stave off any influence that outsiders might have had.

Thyssen pushed the GDK to the heights of German steel by plowing *all* profits back into the firm. He did this throughout the *entire* history of the GDK. At a 1905 GDK shareholder and directors' meeting, Thyssen stated the financial secret to his success: "If we have succeeded in building our work [the GDK] over the last fifteen years to its present height, then we have to attribute this above all to the fact that we have never distributed one penny."[17] Not once in the forty-year history of the GDK did Thyssen pay out dividends—a fact that gave Thyssen considerable leverage in his negotiations with Hamborn tax officials and communists in its city council.[18] To overstate the point, one might describe the GDK as an auxiliary firm. Its relatively low—but by no means poor—profitability allowed other firms in the Thyssen complex to operate at higher levels of profit.

Thyssen resorted to two other means of raising capital. First, as one of their myriad joint ventures before the turn of the century, Thyssen and Stinnes founded their own bank, the Rheinische Bank in Mülheim. In this respect, both acted very American by founding their own bank so that they might tap into pooled funds. Yet the

Rheinische Bank never fulfilled their expectations. It lost money. In 1903, to curry favor with Thyssen and Stinnes, the Dresdner Bank saved the Rheinische Bank with a 3-million-mark infusion. This bailout was also part of the Berlin bank strategy to penetrate the Ruhr.[19] Once stabilized, the Rheinische Bank supplied between 516,000 and 2 million marks to Thyssen & Co. for its short-term current-account credits between 1908 and 1914 (Appendix A, Table A.2).

The second aspect of Thyssen's financing practice was his direct, special and personal relationship with the Reichsbank. Eduard Schmid, later to become Joseph Thyssen's son in law, worked closely with Thyssen in Mülheim. In order to support the community of Hamborn, Thyssen began running his voluminous discount business through the Reichsbank's branch office there. (He did the same for the Reichsbank's office in Mettmann.) Thyssen also offered to discount his withdrawals and drafts *(Tratten)* from the GDK's current account transactions with all the other Thyssen firms directly through the Reichsbank in Hamborn. By doing so, Thyssen withdrew a sizable portion (6–7.5 million marks) of the GDK's draft-account transactions from private banks. At Thyssen & Co., these current-account drafts from private banks represented a hefty portion of its total bank credits (Table A.2). This special relationship with the Reichsbank meant that he too received the most advantageous rates, undercutting private banking rates. The Reichsbank Hamborn also let it be known that it felt its "most noble duty" was to support important large enterprises in critical times for the good of the fatherland.[20] This obliging attitude reinforced Thyssen's general sense that what was good for his business was also good for those communities—and the fatherland.

The GDK financial statements provide an important but circumscribed view of Thyssen's financial practices. One example of a trial CAO consolidated Konzern financial statement for the fiscal/calendar year of 1912 has survived (Appendix A, Table A.3). It acts as an anchor for reconstructing consolidated financial statements for 1909–1914. This statement included financial figures for three mining companies (Lohberg, Rhein, and Jacobus), and the core Thyssen firms, the Stahlwerke Thyssen, the GDK, AGHütt, Thyssen & Co. Rolling Mills, the Machine Company, and one trading firm, Vulcaan AG. Thyssen owned 100% of these firms. These figures do not include the assets of the extended Thyssen-Konzern.[21]

This financial statement shows the considerable results of Thyssen's forty years in business. The total assets of the Thyssen-Konzern were 562.2 million marks (ca. $2.4 billion in 2003). If only Thyssen's main manufacturing works are counted (Stahlwerke Thyssen, GDK, AGHütt, Thyssen & Co. Rolling Mills, and the Machine Company), the figure becomes 504.2 million marks (ca. $2.2 billion), which vied for leadership in German industry with Krupp (587.2 million marks or ca. $2.6 billion), and Siemens (consolidated) at 500.9 million marks (ca. $2.19 billion). Alone, the GDK ranked seventh in 1913 behind the AEG, GBAG, Siemens-Schuckert, and Deutsch-Luxembourg, and ahead of Phoenix and Siemens & Halske. From an international perspective, Christopher Schmitz estimated that Krupp and Siemens ranked as the fourteenth and fifteenth largest industrial companies in the world, which would place the Thyssen-Konzern at roughly the same spot.[22]

The 1912 financial statement provides a clear overview of the financial constitution of the Konzern. It clearly shows that the Konzern had dual financial centers. The GDK owned the great proportion of Thyssen affiliated subsidiaries *(Beteiligungen)*, amounting to 25.5 million marks out of a total of 27.5 million marks. Thyssen & Co., however, controlled almost all of the securities of the Thyssen-Konzern except for a small amount owned by the Stahlwerke Thyssen AG and Vulcaan AG. Moreover, those 2.6 million marks of Thyssen & Co. securities represented a considerably more valuable packet of stocks than this book value suggests.[23]

Thyssen & Co. and the GDK held most of the Konzern's accounts receivable. (Contemporary balance practices included intra-Konzern assets and liabilities.) Although Thyssen & Co. had a relatively small amount of fixed assets, it distributed roughly the same amount of credits as the GDK. Thyssen & Co. had accounts receivable worth 89.8 million marks, while the GDK credited 102.8 million marks, nearly 80% of its total accounts receivable. Of the total 192.7 million marks of accounts-receivable assets, Thyssen & Co. and the GDK distributed 81% (156.5 million marks) as credits to other Thyssen-Konzern firms.

If we break down the accounts-payable column, the internal financial organization becomes transparent. While the GDK and Thyssen & Co. distributed 81% of total credit in the Konzern, together they were held liable for just 52% of total Konzern accounts payable. About 77%

of total accounts payable at Thyssen & Co. came from short-term and medium-term bank credits, while the GDK accounts payable consisted of just 23% of bank credits. Roughly 60% of all credits extended to the GDK came from other Thyssen firms. Yet other Thyssen firms credited Thyssen & Co. with an insignificant amount of funds (1.1%). A majority (57%) of all short-term bank liabilities for the Konzern went through Thyssen & Co., but Thyssen & Co. immediately transformed these debts into credits to other Thyssen-Konzern firms. Credits to other Thyssen firms amounted to 57% of Thyssen & Co.'s total assets. Almost 30% of Thyssen & Co.'s total liabilities consisted of bank credit. Proportionally, Thyssen & Co. carried much higher debt levels relative to its equity, fixed assets, or revenues than other firms.

Thus, banking relations for the Thyssen-Konzern primarily went through Thyssen & Co., which acted as a financial sluice for capital funds to the rest of the Konzern. While the manufacturing center of the Konzern lay at the GDK, which controlled almost half of all fixed assets and the ownership of Thyssen subsidiaries, the financial parent of the Thyssen-Konzern was in Mülheim. Thyssen & Co.'s equity represents a good portion (43%) of the formal equity of the Thyssen-Konzern; its equity actually pertains to the Konzern as a whole.

Because of the interlocking nature of the whole Konzern, generalizations are difficult when one considers only one firm in the complex from the outside, but a high degree of transparency existed on the inside. From the accounts one can ascertain that Thyssen financed each of his firms in a slightly different way, a tribute to his legendary financial flexibility. Thyssen financed the two new mining companies (Lohberg, Rhein) and the cement firm Jacobus in Alsace-Lorraine through Konzern current-account credits. They had no equity, mortgages, acceptances, or long-term loans. Short-term Konzern credits covered their long-term fixed assets. Likewise, Thyssen firms primarily financed the Stahlwerke Thyssen through short-term loans, although it had a small amount of share capital. The newly independent Thyssen & Co. Machine Company, however, took out long-term bond worth 4 million marks; other Thyssen firms extended it short-term credits equalling 4.8 million marks. The AGHütt had a normal financial statement, possibly because of public disclosure requirements. It financed its operations largely internally or by mortgaging part of its assets; the GDK followed a similar pattern with mortgages amounting to 44.5 million marks. Unlike the GDK, Thyssen & Co. resorted to mortgaging its property more moderately, but used its property and securities as collateral to float bonds, as in the case of the 4-million-mark loan for the Machine Company, or as a basis for further credit lines.[24] In Thyssen's financial scheme, firms had to repay these credits/debts as quickly as possible by generating their own independent cash flows and by earning profits.

The formal legal independence of individual Thyssen firms gave him important financial advantages. Each Thyssen firm could grant acceptances, a kind of short-term bill of credit or promissory note, to one another. The GDK (13.2 million marks), Thyssen & Co. (11.3 million marks), and the AGHütt (7.9 million marks) held acceptances worth over 32 million marks. The 7.9 million marks held by the AGHütt represented a short-term personal credit from August Thyssen himself. His use of acceptances pushed the limits of good business practice.[25] But the legal decentralization of the Konzern multiplied credit possibilities that would not have been available if the firm had been consolidated in a unified corporation.

Thyssen made good use of his depreciation accounts to build hidden reserves. According to this balance, the GDK, the AGHütt, and the new mining companies did not depreciate that year. Yet based on their original or published balance sheets, the GDK depreciated 8.9 million marks or 4.9% of its fixed assets (land, buildings, and equipment), and the AGHütt 1.3 million marks or about 6%. In fact, the GDK and the AGHütt depreciated through the profit-loss statement, but did not carry a depreciation account on the liability side of the balance.[26]

Thyssen & Co. and the Machine Company did not use their depreciation accounts in the same way. The depreciation account for Thyssen & Co. in 1912, for instance, equaled 20.1 million marks, while its fixed assets amounted to 29.2 million marks. In Thyssen & Co. annual statements, the depreciation figure is actually a cumulative figure; the difference from one year to the next equals the depreciation for the year.[27] In effect, the depreciation account acted more as a type of capital reserve (where it was lined up in the liability column) or as a form of accumulated retained earnings. The depreciation figure in Thyssen & Co. largely helped to cover short-term loans to other Thyssen-Konzern firms. The size of the figure, moreover, implies that Thyssen

& Co. had largely written off its equipment. The Machine Company used the depreciation account in the same way, but this account covered the rapid expansion of its own fixed assets. This might also be the case for the Stahlwerke Thyssen AG and the Gew. Jacobus.

Without information from Thyssen & Co., the core financial state of the Konzern remains in the dark. From reconstructed trial financial statements between 1909 and 1914, we can show these shifting financial relations more dynamically. Thyssen & Co. had a unique role as house bank of the Konzern. (Table A.2 isolates these intra-Konzern accounts.) Except for the consistently profitable GDK Dinslaken, which Thyssen treated as a financially independent firm, relatively few Thyssen firm accounts appear on the liability side. In 1909, Thyssen & Co. credited the rest of the Konzern with just under 50 million marks, rising by 1913 to over 80 million marks. By far, the GDK accounted for most of this credit, which rose from roughly 50% to 81% of total short-term credits. Thyssen immediately transferred these funds into the new subsidiary mining companies and the Stahlwerke Thyssen. Each of the main firms in the Thyssen-Konzern had three to five different types of short-term accounts, which Thyssen used to extend credit. The exceptions to this general rule were the AGHütt, which had a loan account *(Darlehen-Konto)*, and the Machine Company, which in 1911 had a capital account *(Kapital-Konto)*. After the Machine Company became a joint-stock company, the bulk of Thyssen & Co. credit then appeared in current accounts, which was usual for Thyssen's financing practices.

These practices demonstrate how Thyssen could invisibly shift funds to other parts of his firm through current accounts. Since most of the Konzern's internal sales (excepting the Machine Company) were priced at the "most favorable" market value, Thyssen could technically finance a firm by allowing current accounts to rise or fall as needed without manipulating internal transfer-pricing procedures or providing outright subsidies. This practice can be illustrated by Thyssen & Co.'s loan credit to the AGHütt between 1909 and 1911, which the AGHütt then paid off by extending credit through its current accounts to Thyssen & Co. between 1912 and 1914. The legal independence of Thyssen firms also allowed them to extend lines of credit based on the volume of transactions among various Konzern firms or third-party firms, which was large relative to total current accounts. Importantly, on intra-Konzern current accounts, each Thyssen firm charged other Thyssen firms a standard 5% interest on these credits, so that such short-term credits were treated in financial terms as if they were from third-party firms or banks, but more flexible. Over the long term, one firm did not prop up another firm without incurring expenses. One might consider them as temporary subsidies with interest.[28] Such practices implied that each Thyssen firm had to act as much as possible as economically viable units—"otherwise it should not exist."

Thyssen & Co. continued to act as the main organizational liaison with banks. Between 1912 and 1914, it operated with over 36 million marks of banking liabilities. Thyssen & Co. had account liabilities (debts) with twenty-eight different banks (Appendix A, Table A.4). About two-thirds of Thyssen's short-term bank credits came from the great investment banks of Berlin, that is, the *Bank für Handel und Industrie,* the *Commerz- und Disconto-Gesellschaft Bank,* the Deutsche Bank, the *Disconto-Gesellschaft-Gesellschaft,* the Dresdner Bank, the *Nationalbank für Deutschland,* and the *A. Schaaffhausen'sche Bankverein.* His main banks, the Deutsche, Dresdner and Schaaffhausen, lent him money largely through draft accounts *(Tratten-Konto).* But important private, regional, and foreign banks supplied a significant and growing portion of Thyssen's credit. In spite of rising international tensions, Thyssen added a number of London and Paris banks to his credit line, particularly Kleinwort Sons & Co. and Lazard Brothers & Cie. in London, and A. J. Stern & Co. in Paris. Bank liabilities represented about 74–85% of all his current-account liabilities and 27–32% of total liabilities between 1909–1914.

The consolidated Konzern balances illustrate the growing financial strain caused by continuing expansion just before the war. Although the GDK posted enormous levels of profit just before the war (over 20 million marks), its internal financing slowly began to unhinge; the war only further aggravated its financial condition. For instance, between 1909 and 1913, Thyssen & Co. short-term credits to the GDK ballooned from 26.3 to 66.6 million marks. As a proportion of Thyssen & Co.'s fixed assets, such GDK credits grew from 18.6% to 37%; as a proportion of its gross assets, these GDK credits nearly doubled from 14.3% to 26.6%. In the same period, total GDK current liabilities moved from 34.9 million to 57.7 million marks, while its long-term debt nearly doubled from 36.7 million to 65.3 million marks. Both grew much faster than the GDK's rate of growth of its fixed assets. Much of this additional credit burden supported the expansion of the Stahlwerke Thyssen and the Rhine-based mining fields, but the GDK increasingly drew a greater proportion of Thyssen financing to itself as a huge, high-volume producer of commodity goods. One can see another sign of Thyssen's financial strain in the acceptance accounts of Thyssen & Co. (Table A.4). Thyssen & Co.'s questionable practice of extending acceptances grew from 7.9 million at the beginning of 1908 to 13.5 million marks in 1913, the last full peacetime year; the next year they more than doubled to 31 million marks after the war began. The war broke the financial balance of the Thyssen-Konzern.

How profitable were different areas of Thyssen's industrial empire? How much did his expansion depend on internal or external (bank) financing? Derived from a consolidated Konzern balance (Appendix A, Table A.5), we may offer a selective quantitative analysis.

The GDK generated the vast majority of total Thyssen-Konzern profits. Between 1909 and 1913, the operating or gross profits of the Thyssen-Konzern nearly doubled from 20.3 million to 39.6 million marks. Before the Stahlwerke Thyssen began generating significant surpluses, the GDK supplied roughly three-quarters of all Konzern gross profits. By 1913 the Stahlwerke Thyssen began generating profits, dropping the GDK's share of gross profits by nearly a quarter. Thyssen & Co. and the AGHütt supplied 12–15% and 8–12% of total gross profits respectively; the Machine Company about 4%.

Because of Thyssen's conservative business policy emphasizing liberal depreciation rates and the build-up of financial reserves, the net profits of the Konzern consistently amounted to roughly 50% of gross profit levels. Net profits rose from 10.1 million to 16.7 million marks in the same time period. All of the gross profits from the Stahlwerke Thyssen, for instance, went into depreciation or various reserve accounts so that the proportion of net profits supplied by the GDK, AGHütt, and Thyssen & Co. rose slightly. The GDK clearly generated most of the net profits for the Konzern (79–64%) while Thyssen & Co. delivered between 14–22% and the AGHütt between 3–14%. (The move of Thyssen's specialty iron foundry to the AGHütt accounts for its sudden rise of gross and net profit levels.) The Machine Company quickly found its feet before the war and immediately began to generate up to 6.5% of total Konzern net profits.

The absolute amount of profits, however, does not necessarily provide a good indicator of the *profitability* of these firms. Profits need to
be placed into relation to the amount of fixed assets, owner's shares,
total investment, or other variables to be meaningful. Total fixed assets
rose over 110 million marks in just five years, from 182.7 million to
293.3 million marks between 1909 and 1913, a remarkable 60% increase. The Stahlwerke Thyssen accounted for most of this increase,
but the GDK also registered a 28% increase, or roughly 40 million
marks, in its fixed assets. The AGHütt assets also grew strongly. The
Thyssen & Co. Rolling Mills registered no gains, while the Machine
Company's fixed assets doubled.

If net profits are placed in relation to each firm's fixed assets, we arrive at a profitability ratio that emphasizes how well these fixed assets
generated profits. For instance, there is little question that the GDK
supplied the bulk of net profits, but relative to its scale, the GDK returned 6% of its investment in fixed assets, while the Machine Company returned a 9–15% rate, Thyssen & Co. 6.6–13%, and the AGHütt
1.7–12.4%. The GDK clearly generated the most profits, but the
AGHütt and Machine Company were more profitable ventures.

If the GDK Dinslaken had balanced independently of the GDK,
which it did prior to 1908, the GDK's gross profits would still have
been lower. In 1913, for instance, the GDK Dinslaken generated 3 million marks of gross profits with just 10 million marks of fixed assets, a
high rate of return of nearly 30%. If GDK Dinslaken's net profits bore
the same relationship to gross profits as the rest of the Konzern, it
would have had a return of roughly 15%, matching that of the Machine Company. The GDK (including Dinslaken) generated 20 million marks with 180.9 million marks of fixed assets—a proportion of
1:3 vs. 1:9 when compared to Dinslaken alone. In general, the GDK
Dinslaken, with its seamless pipes and cold-rolling mills, and the Machine Company tended to be the most profitable areas of the Konzern
relative to the amount of fixed capital invested. After the AGHütt received its specialty cast-iron foundry, it too jumped to the same profitability levels as the GDK Dinslaken and the Machine Company.

The net profit figure, however, is subject to considerable manipula-
tion through financial accounting techniques, especially by Thyssen.
Thyssen once admitted to Klönne that he felt depreciation rates at the
GDK were too low; the government regulated such matters. He did not

want to become the target of tax officials, who already regularly objected to his depreciation policies, which built considerable hidden reserves and underestimated his actual profit levels. Thyssen admitted
that he quietly depreciated in a disguised fashion, especially on land.[29]
A better indicator is cash flow, which circumvents such accounting
problems with net profits by adding depreciation as well as increases in
reserves. The cash flow figure is one of the best indicators of the financial *potential* of a company because it registers the amount of internally
generated fungible capital funds. Cash-flow figures indicate the level
of internal funds in the firm's cash reservoir that management can use
in different ways: further expansion, distributed as dividends, to build
reserves, or whatever. It indicates a degree of financial maneuverability.[30]

Thyssen directors realized the importance of cash flow rather than
net profits since their annual bonuses *(Tantieme)* were contingent on
cash flow rather than on net profits. Both Härle and Roser continually
badgered Hofs, Rabes, and Thyssen in five-page reports which outlined what they felt was a proper calculation of cash flow. In 1913,
for instance, Thyssen understandably refused to consider the 70,000
marks presented to him by the Machine Company for his seventieth
birthday as part of cash flow, which would have increased their bonuses![31]

As an individual figure, cash flow says very little about the state of
the firm, but must be placed in relation to other variables. Such cash
flow-based ratios measure the firm's potential to finance various demands. One of the most significant ratios for our purposes is the
amount of cash flow in relation to the net increase in fixed assets. This
ratio is a particularly good indicator of how well a firm could internally
finance its expansion of fixed assets. The net increase in fixed assets
is simply the difference from the previous year and the present year,
plus any depreciation. If the ratio is more than one, it means that the
level of cash flow could fully cover increases in fixed assets; if the ratio
is less than one, then the firm resorted to external funds to finance expansion.

Most of the Thyssen firms could largely cover their internal expan-
sion except the Stahlwerke Thyssen (Table A.5). Except in 1911, the
GDK could generate enough cash flow just to cover its own expansion.
The expansion of the AGHütt's iron foundry, which went on line after

1912, temporarily strained its internal financing capacity, but thereafter this ratio improved dramatically. In only one year (1910), did the Machine Company and Thyssen & Co. not cover increases in fixed assets; both easily covered expansion with high ratios. Only Thyssen & Co. and the AGHütt had cash flows well above their expansion rates— Thyssen & Co.'s assets actually contracted in 1913. Since the GDK just covered the rate of its own expansion, Thyssen & Co. and the AGHütt supplied the bulk of internally financed and *distributed* funds for overall Konzern expansion. The Machine Company plowed back all of its profits and used its cash flow for its own expansion. The expansion of the Stahlwerke Thyssen, however, came almost entirely from external funds.

If the AGHütt and the Machine Company provide a rough indicator of Thyssen's general pattern of behavior, Thyssen temporarily extended himself using short-term credits, but expected to make back the shortfall inside 2–4 years. The most important figure, however, might be the consistent shortfall of internally generated financing for the overall Konzern in this period. External sources financed about 15–30% of total expansion. The business historian Wilfried Feldenkirchen found similar internal financing ratios for Hoesch, GHH, and Deutsch-Luxembourg, but Krupp, Phoenix, and the Bochumer Verein covered their expansion entirely by internal financing.[32]

The financial statements of Thyssen & Co. are useful for identifying particular sources of outside funding (Table A.4). Thyssen & Co. took out an additional 10 million marks in bank credits, which rose from 25.7 million in 1910 to 36.8 million marks by 1913. Thyssen & Co. relied particularly on the largesse of the Dresdner Bank, whose draft account rose from 5.6 million in 1910 to 8.3 million marks by 1913. Additionally, in 1912 the Deutsche Bank set up a special Lombard account of 2 million marks, whereby Thyssen & Co. pledged a given sum of securities. Surprisingly, Thyssen & Co. accounts with most other domestic banks remained relatively steady. But in 1913, Thyssen & Co. took 4 million marks of additional credit from foreign banks. In short, banks certainly aided Thyssen's great push of expansion, but cannot fully explain it—which is why outsiders felt it appeared to be financed out of thin air.

With Thyssen & Co.'s annual financial statements as a guide, Thyssen's financing practices become clearer. In addition, Thyssen &

Co.'s total long-term debt rose from 14 million in 1909 to 19.7 million marks by 1913 before ballooning to 37.7 million marks by the end of 1914. This consisted mostly of acceptances, which rose from 6.9 million to 13.5 million marks, before exploding to 31 million marks at the same dates. Reflecting the financial strain of expansion, Thyssen & Co. allowed its current account liabilities to rise from 2.1 million in 1909 to 10.3 million marks in 1912 before cutting it in half by 1913. Finally, Thyssen & Co. increasingly drew upon current-account credits (short-term loans) from the more profitable GDK Dinslaken and AGHütt. The jump in current account credits from the AGHütt from 2.8 million in 1913 to 7.8 million marks in 1914 foreshadows a trend that would accelerate during the war. As the war began, Thyssen & Co.'s financial stability began to erode.

Another standard indicator of the relative financial performance of any company is a return on equity (ROE) coefficient. But one of the problems of assessing returns to equity inside the Thyssen-Konzern is that the equity or share capital of any individual company was unevenly distributed throughout the Konzern. On one hand, the Stahlwerke Thyssen had a minimal share capital figure, skewing a return-on-equity figure. On the other hand, Thyssen & Co. would have extremely low profitability figures because its financial accounts included the personal accounts of August and Joseph Thyssen, which actually belonged to the whole Konzern. So I redistributed the total amount of nominal Konzern equity (share capital) *as if* Thyssen covered each firm's fixed assets by the same proportional amount of nominal share capital (Table A.5). Then I calculated a return on equity figure based on the ratio of net profits to this redistributed owner's share capital. From the point of view of the owners, the Konzern returned 18–22% on their personal capital. The AGHütt and the Machine Company were the most profitable parts of the Konzern by this recalculation.

Nominal share capital, however, severely underestimates the actual level of proprietary capital inside the company, which could be found in various reserve funds and owner's "deposits." Combining the GDK's nominal share capital, owners' "deposits," and various reserve funds (a *de facto* measure of owners' equity) forms a ratio comparable to other Ruhr steel firms' return on equity based on net profits (Table 9.1).

The GDK, which generated the bulk of the Thyssen-Konzern's

Table 9.1 Profitability ratios of various Ruhr steel firms, 1909–1913

Year	GDK	GHH	Krupp	Phoenix	BV	RSW	Hoesch	Deutsch-Lux
1908–09	6.7	12.3	7.6	10.1	10.6	4.8	11.9	8.0
1909–10	7.8	12.2	10.3	15.9	8.6	5.0	15.2	7.6
1910–11	7.3	12.0	13.7	16.0	10.4	6.4	16.3	8.6
1911–12	7.4	13.8	13.4	17.2	11.6	8.4	18.3	7.0
1912–13	7.0	15.1	15.7	19.1	12.1	8.6	21.4	7.7
1913–14	9.3	11.0	14.2	16.9	8.6	8.0	9.0	5.0

Source: TKA: A/1754 and Feldenkirchen, *Eisen- und Stahlindustrie,* Tab. 77b, 125b.

GHH = Gutehoffnungshütte; BV = Bochumer Verein; RSW = Rheinische Stahlwerke.

profits, consistently had some of the lowest return-on-equity ratios in Ruhr steel. The GDK's returns matched most closely those of the Stinnes-controlled Deutsch-Luxembourg. There are a number of reasons for this pattern. The GDK's returns were lower because of the high level of reserves held inside the firm and Thyssen's general inclination to depress net profits. But since Thyssen did not have to answer to shareholders and could retain all earnings, the lower rate of return made little difference. Moreover, the high level of proprietary capital in the GDK also belonged to the Stahlwerke Thyssen and new mining fields, Rhein and Lohberg (Table A.3). Finally, in certain respects, the GDK is *not* comparable to the above firms because other Ruhr steel firms incorporated their high-value-added activities into a single, unified enterprise, while Thyssen did not.

If net profits are placed in relation to the total level of investment (ROI), the GDK generated a more consistent rate of return, around 4%, slightly higher than the Konzern average (Table A.5). Again, the Thyssen & Co. Machine Company and AGHütt became (after 1912) the most profitable areas of the Konzern. Thyssen & Co. became the least profitable. Its profits bore less relationship to its total investment because of its financial holding function. Compared to other Ruhr steel firms, only the AGHütt had comparable ROI ratios of 6–8.8% in these years.

Since net profits have less meaning for a Thyssen firm than a cash-flow-based ratio, the next set of figures calculate a different version of return on investment, which is how well these investments generated a

Table 9.2 Cash flow (ROI) of various Ruhr steel firms, 1909–1913 (cash flow ÷ total investment × 100)

Year	Thyssen	GHH	Krupp	Phoenix	BV	RSW	Hoesch	Deutsch-Lux
1908–09	—	12.52	7.11	12.16	9.63	8.03	16.98	9.21
1909–10	—	11.71	8.30	15.12	8.61	8.33	17.83	8.75
1910–11	6.31	11.35	9.29	15.56	9.73	9.26	18.51	8.92
1911–12	6.45	12.84	8.47	16.82	10.02	10.64	18.02	7.99
1912–13	4.07	14.20	9.55	18.79	11.41	13.82	21.32	10.38
1913–14	8.51	10.54	9.10	16.08	12.34	12.00	10.95	8.18

Source: TKA: A/1754 and Feldenkirchen, *Eisen- und Stahlindustrie,* Tab. 74b, 100b, own calculations.

GHH = Gutehoffnungshütte; BV = Bochumer Verein; RSW = Rheinische Stahlwerke.

cash flow that the owner could use as needed (Table A.5). The GDK had rates of return most similar to the overall financial potential of the Konzern. Both the AGHütt and the Machine Company showed the highest returns, while Thyssen & Co. had the lowest. Despite having no net profits, the Stahlwerke Thyssen began to show its potential for generating high rates of return (cash flow) on its investment.

If one compares this cash flow ratio of the Thyssen-Konzern as a whole to other Ruhr steel firms (Table 9.2), Thyssen generated a remarkably low return on his investment, especially as compared to Phoenix, Hoesch, or the GHH. In part, Thyssen's low figure reflects the start-up phase for Stahlwerke Thyssen. But even if one subtracts the effect of Stahlwerke Thyssen (especially affecting the 1912 ratio, which would change to 7.5% instead of 4%), the ratios still do not appreciably change. Only the AGHütt and the Machine Company generated comparable returns (Table A.5). These consistent results appear to indicate that Thyssen's growth (in sheer size second only to Krupp) rested less on absolute profitability rates and more on the ruthless long-term reinvestment of all possible financial resources to remain competitive. This result gives credence to Dahl's comment about Thyssen that he always seemed short of cash.

Finally, in order to eliminate the biases associated with the high total assets resulting from Thyssen & Co.'s and the GDK's role as financial centers of the Konzern, I placed the amount of cash flow in relation to

Table 9.3 Cash flow divided by total fixed assets (× 100) of various Ruhr steel firms, 1909–1913

Year	Thyssen	GHH	Krupp	Phoenix	BV	RSW	Hoesch	Deutsch-Lux
1908–09	—	18.80	15.86	17.18	17.28	10.35	28.29	10.75
1909–10	—	17.97	19.96	22.45	16.07	12.78	31.29	13.06
1910–11	10.54	17.20	24.32	24.03	16.85	13.84	36.64	12.37
1911–12	11.47	19.09	24.22	26.52	15.49	15.23	39.12	11.80
1912–13	13.77	22.09	26.03	30.03	17.88	20.13	36.29	14.01
1913–14	14.80	14.82	22.45	25.24	17.47	17.80	21.19	11.12

Source: TKA: A/1754 and Feldenkirchen, Eisen- und Stahlindustrie, Tab. 83b, with own calculations added.

GHH = Gutehoffnungshütte; BV = Bochumer Verein; RSW = Rheinische Stahlwerke.

total fixed assets (Table A.5). This ratio indicates the ability of these fixed assets to generate an internal stream of capital, thus isolating their manufacturing capacity's ability to generate a rate of return. Again, roughly the same relationship among Thyssen firms result. The GDK had average to lower than average rates of return, the Machine Company and AGHütt had the highest rates. Thyssen & Co. remained in a holding pattern, with generally lower than average returns.

Compared to other rival steel firms, the Thyssen-Konzern cut a somewhat better figure, similar to Stinnes' Deutsch-Luxembourg, the other upstart firm after the turn of the century (Table 9.3). Only the AGHütt and the Machine Company could push to the 20% rates of return (Table A.5) other steel firms regularly achieved. The Machine Company, in fact, achieved a 40% rate of return, surpassing any rate achieved in the steel industry proper. This result foreshadows why most of the steel firms began incorporating machine-engineering companies at the end of World War I to supplement weaker returns in other sectors and to secure downstream demand.

In conclusion, in spite of the lower absolute profit levels created by the GDK, it acted as a kind of manufacturing workhorse, enabling the rest of the Konzern to operate. Thyssen & Co. remained in a holding pattern in terms of manufacturing, but still acted as the house bank of the Konzern. The AGHütt and the Machine Company demonstrated their high profitability, while the Stahlwerke Thyssen had just begun to show earning potential when the war broke out. In spite of reliance on banks for credit, Thyssen's financial viability rested largely on internally generated funds and the ruthless reinvestment (rather than absolute profitability) in his core companies. Except for brief bursts, such as the expansion just before the war when Thyssen extended himself using short-term credits, the firms had to become competitive, profitable, and generate as quickly as possible their own internal funds to cover expansion. Thyssen relied on the speed of his start-ups, new cost reductions from new plants, and the quality of his products to overcome (he hoped) brief periods of financial overextension. Thyssen also did not carry the complications caused by mergers and acquisitions or the immense managerial or financial overhead expenses incurred by comparable firms (see below on Phoenix). He did not have to answer to outside shareholders, who might demand higher dividends and profits. Financial solidity, not profitability, guided Thyssen. His accounts testify to his relentless focus on long-term competitiveness.

Yet these rather low profitability rates also hint at an underlying weakness in the Thyssen-Konzern. Even before the war, Thyssen had to invest more and more in expensive scale in coal and crude steel production to remain competitive, which might have called into question his financial policy of not issuing equity. Without the GDK workhorse or the new Stahlwerke Thyssen, which would take over low-end commodity-steel-goods production from the GDK, the profitability of the AGHütt and the Machine Company could not remain secure in the cartelized world of German steel. In short, ever-increasing minimum-efficient scale in commodity goods areas was required, yet the GDK operated with relatively lower rates of return, and Thyssen refused to offer equity. Hints of a structural crisis also began to appear. If one followed profitability rates instead of production in a less cartelized system, Thyssen could have expanded more into specialty and finished goods to increase his profitability rates. But instead he had to continually improve his commodity goods production first, which challenged his financing capacity to the utmost.

Then, just the Stahlwerke Thyssen began to cover its own rate of expansion, the war forever disrupted Thyssen's financial balance. One can see this initial strain by a near three-fold jump in acceptances (Tables A.2–4) and a dramatic 20 million mark reduction in August

Thyssen's personal accounts after the war began. Aside from the huge loss of the Stahlwerke Thyssen after the war, the above financial analysis also shows how the GDK quickly became the financial weakpoint in the Konzern. Although the GDK earned massive amounts of profits, it was generally not as profitable as other sectors of the Konzern and not as profitable as comparable Ruhr heavy industrial firms. By no stretch of the imagination could one argue that the GDK was a weak firm, but its profitability rested fundamentally on high-speed, high-scale, high-volume activity in markets with relatively low profit margins. It generated high levels of profits only after extremely high levels of investment, which were difficult for a family-owned firm. Once Thyssen lost the Stahlwerke Thyssen, the GDK once again had to take over again the role of basic and intermediate goods manufacturer, which further strained Thyssen's financial capacity in the postwar period. Increasingly, other Thyssen firms had to support the GDK financially.

The Thyssen-Konzern in International Historical Perspective

Thyssen's pioneering achievement lay not in his ability to vertically integrate (the contemporary view), but in managerial innovation—that is, how he managed this vertical integration. The CAO's methodology and financial management represent distinctively modern aspects of Thyssen management—on par with the most innovative American corporations. After 1906 the Thyssen-Konzern began to act as a nascent multidivisional structure with a small central staff. This central staff, split between Bruckhausen and Mülheim, the CAO and the *Centrale,* advised Thyssen on planning, monitoring, and allocation of funds across all the technical-commercial operations in the firm. The organizational structure of the Thyssen-Konzern can best be described as a multisubsidiary structure controlled through a series of central offices with an entrepreneurial head.

From different theoretical starting points, two important scholars of business, Alfred Chandler and Oliver Williamson, have called the multidivisional structure "the most significant organizational innovation of the twentieth century."[33] Such an assessment is exaggerated because it sets up an American "Harvard Business School-approved M-form as a clue to the organisational efficiency of individual business systems," implying a one-world standard for best practice.[34] But if we follow their line of argument for the time being, then Thyssen is one of its first formulators. All of the basic tenets of a multidivisional structure were in place inside the Thyssen-Konzern before American firms such as DuPont and General Motors developed the M-form in the 1920s.

According to Chandler and Williamson, the multidivisional structure's crucial advantage was its organizational distinction between long-term (financial/organizational) strategic planning and short-term, day-to-day, tactical (manufacturing) operations.[35] Thyssen found distinct advantages in this type of organization, with its characteristic emphasis on "centralized control with decentralized responsibilities," to use a phrase by an architect of GM's management system.[36] According to the literature, the crucial advantage of the multidivisional form rests on this *combination* of centralized financial controls with decentralized responsibilities. A distinct specialization of labor among product lines is a secondary advantage. An entrepreneur or a holding company with a collection of specialized product departments or subsidiaries (as with many German IGs) does not make a multidivisional structure. Divisions differed from the self-contained commercial-technical modules of Thyssen & Co. (or as at Phoenix or Krupp) in that they accounted for their own fixed and liquid capital *as if* they were fully independent firms. Unlike General Motors or DuPont, which established *internal* corporate divisions along the lines of the GDK Dinslaken, Thyssen preferred legally independent subsidiaries (more like Mitsui or Mitsubishi). According to this argument, the central offices of a multidivisional structure provided a resource (financial) allocation capability and formulated strategic planning based on the monitoring and control of operational divisional performance through its financial accounting system. Such a distinction allowed the firm to manage a diversity of product lines through a coherent administrative apparatus. Because the future allocation of investment funds to divisions or subsidiaries came from these central offices, the central offices acted as an internalized "capital market." Managers made investment decisions across divisions that rested on rational managerial routines oriented to maximizing the use of available capital. (This is a theoretical, not an empirical quality.) Accordingly, the central offices judged the diverse individual divisions or subsidiaries according to some standardized financial criteria, thus creating a financial conception of control.

Before World War I, Thyssen-Konzern management was unique in German heavy industry. Thyssen kept his *core* companies as legally separate, decentralized entities, while most other heavy industrial firms incorporated their core holdings into single, large, unified corporations organized into more or less autonomous departments. Moreover, he created at least four independent central offices to control them in a systematic manner. Phoenix, Krupp, or the GHH better typified prewar integrated combines.

One of Thyssen's main rivals, Phoenix, was a nearly complete historical and organizational opposite to Thyssen. While Thyssen grew from internal expansion, Phoenix extended itself largely through merger and acquisition. A brief sketch of the history of Phoenix also illustrates why Phoenix chose a single, unified corporation, and provides another perspective on the logic of German cartel-concern capitalism.

Founded in 1852, Phoenix began its corporate existence as a vertically integrated and geographically decentralized firm.[37] By 1860, its central administration was in Cologne, its puddling work in Eschweiler near Aachen (Thyssen's hometown), its steelworks in Laar near Ruhrort, its copper-wire factory and another steelworks in Essen, and a series of mines in various locations. In the 1860s, Phoenix suffered severe organizational difficulties: its executive board was too large, transportation and communications among the units were erratic, and it lacked any sort of a uniform administration across its operating units.

As for Thyssen, the founding of the coal syndicate spurred a second major round of expansion for Phoenix. In 1896 Phoenix and the *Meidericher Steinkohlenbergwerke AG* (which had coal mines and coking plants) merged. As an outsider to the syndicate, *Meidericher Steinkohlenbergwerke* needed to secure downstream sales to make its recent mine improvements profitable. Phoenix and Meidericher chose a unified company to minimize administration costs and to ensure the technical coordination of moving coking gas to the blast furnaces. In addition, Phoenix was simply the financially stronger company and so refused to consider a looser IG, which might have allowed Meidericher executives a greater degree of autonomy. In 1898, to secure upstream demand, Phoenix absorbed the *Westfälischen Union* in Hamm, which manufactured rolled goods, wire products, springs, rivets, and nails. The shareholders of the *Westfälischen Union* agreed to the merger to minimize the risks of working on a fluctuating open market for intermediate products. As the financially more powerful enterprise, Phoenix again chose full merger to ensure greater administrative coordination. In 1906, Phoenix and the Hörder Verein merged, causing a stock-market spectacle. This merger grew out mutual needs for a secure supply and demand and also syndicate and banking politics. Phoenix and Hörder Verein shareholders chose a single unified corporation for a host of reasons. A full merger guaranteed self-consumption rights for both firms. It also ensured that Phoenix's house banks received the profits from issuing new shares, especially as both companies' stocks soared in expectation of the merger. Finally, a full fusion avoided certain taxes, minimized financial costs, and avoided potential personnel losses associated with the alternative, a leasing arrangement. A leasing arrangement would have kept Hörder executives in a subordinate position, but in a unified corporation they would move onto Phoenix boards. Clearly, Phoenix had a welter of considerations that Thyssen could simply avoid.

As a result of its expansion of capacity in steel, Phoenix became more vulnerable to the syndicated coal market, so in 1907, it annexed the mining company Nordstern. With this move, Phoenix wielded more influence in the coal syndicate and gained control over its coal supply, thus undercutting syndicate prices for downstream use. Much like the Hörder Verein, only a full fusion would allow syndicate self-consumption rights to go into effect. Banks again profited greatly from issuing new shares to finance the large firm. Finally, a centralized administration improved coordination among previously independent firms.

In 1910, Phoenix incorporated Thyssen & Co.'s main rivals in the welded pipe business, the *Düsseldorfer Röhren- und Eisenwalzwerke AG* (DREW), run by Ernst Poensgen. Until then, the DREW, like Thyssen & Co., was a pure rolling mill. The merger allowed Phoenix to expand its plate production; DREW secured its raw-material and intermediate-product supply. Cartel politics drove vertical integration and strategic choices. In fact, competing against Thyssen helped drive the DREW into the merger because it could no longer compete as an independent. Supplied by the GDK, Thyssen & Co.'s transition to liquid steel, along with its three American-style gas-furnace pipe operations, left DREW undercapitalized, unable to compete, and unable to match Thyssen's expansion. All of the DREW's puddled strip steel for pipes went straight into inventory, but the DREW kept manufacturing them so as to keep older workers (over 25 years of age!) employed.[38] In reaction, the DREW's main allied bank urged Poensgen to merge with an integrated combine before it would grant more credit to modernize DREW's facilities. Pushed by cartels, the competitive environment, and banking pressure, the DREW fused with Phoenix. It chose full fusion to ensure self-consumption rights in the steel cartel. Additionally, the fusion followed Phoenix's long-standing policy to centralize administrative coordination as much as possible.

Phoenix's history of mergers and acquisitions shows that a single, unified corporation had definite advantages. A full fusion ensured some degree of standard administration as a means to overcome organizational difficulties associated with mergers. Other considerations included improved technical coordination among the stages of vertically integrated production processes, and a better internal exchange of experience and information. Financial factors included financial pooling, profit or stock manipulations, cross-subsidization of product lines, and tax considerations. Intangible factors included the prestige value of being large. Size also carried weight in cartel negotiations and political power. Finally, a unified firm eliminated many of the hassles of working with cartels, especially by working under one legal name; it guaranteed those all-important self-consumption rights. (All of these reasons would underlie the resistance to decentralizing the VSt into a multisubsidiary structure in 1932–1934.) Only after 1920 did Phoenix a multisubsidiary form, with the formation of IG's for its additional mining firms and the acquisition of machine-engineering companies (Figure 9.1).

If we go inside Phoenix, we can see how it organized control. Both Phoenix's supervisory and managing boards grew to considerable size, as the acquired firms sent their shareholders or executives to them. Its board acted as a type of parliament, with representatives from the provinces (former firms). In 1913, the Phoenix supervisory board carried 28 members, the managing board 10, along with 26 who had power of attorney.[39] (The GDK had 10 members on *both* boards; the Stahlwerke Thyssen just 8). The Phoenix management experience would resemble that of the VSt between 1926 and 1932.

To clarify the specific lines of responsibility of each executive in the managing board, Phoenix composed a 17-page "business directive" (*Geschäftsanweisung*), with 33 paragraphs detailing the managerial com-

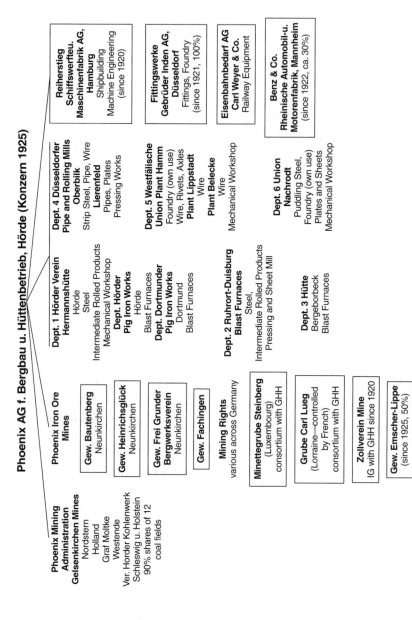

Phoenix AG f. Bergbau. Hüttenbetrieb, Hörde (Konzern 1925)

Phoenix Mining Administration Gelsenkirchen Mines
Nordstern
Holland
Graf Moltke
Westende
Ver. Horder Kohlenwerk
Schleswig u. Holstein
90% shares of 12 coal fields

Phoenix Iron Ore Mines

Gew. Bautenberg
Neunkirchen

Gew. Heinrichsglück
Neunkirchen

Gew. Frei Grunder Bergwerksverein
Neunkirchen

Gew. Fachingen

Mining Rights
various across Germany

Minettegrube Steinberg
(Luxembourg)
consortium with GHH

Grube Carl Lueg
(Lorraine—controlled by French)
consortium with GHH

Zollverein Mine
IG with GHH since 1920

Gew. Emscher-Lippe
(since 1925, 50%)

Dept. 1 Hörder Verein Hermannshütte
Hörde
Steel
Intermediate Rolled Products
Mechanical Workshop
Dept. Hörder Pig Iron Works
Hörde
Blast Furnaces
Dept. Dortmunder Pig Iron Works
Dortmund
Blast Furnaces

Dept. 2 Ruhrort-Duisburg Blast Furnaces
Steel,
Intermediate Rolled Products
Pressing and Sheet Mill

Dept. 3 Hütte
Bergeborbeck
Blast Furnaces

Dept. 4 Düsseldorfer Pipe and Rolling Mills Oberbilk
Strip Steel, Pipe, Wire
Lierenfeld
Pipes, Plates
Pressing Works

Dept. 5 Westfälische Union Plant Hamm
Foundry (own use)
Wire, Rivets, Axles
Plant Lippstadt
Wire
Plant Belecke
Wire
Mechanical Workshop

Dept. 6 Union Nachrodt
Puddling Steel,
Foundry (own use)
Plates and Sheets
Mechanical Workshop

Reiherstieg Schiffswerfteu. Maschinenfabrik AG, Hamburg
Shipbuilding
Machine Engineering
(since 1920)

Fittingswerke Gebrüder Inden AG, Düsseldorf
Fittings, Foundry
(since 1921, 100%)

Eisenbahnbedarf AG Carl Weyer & Co.
Railway Equipment

Benz & Co. Rheinische Automobil-u. Motorenfabrik, Mannheim
(since 1922, ca. 30%)

Figure 9.1 Phoenix AG f. Bergbau. Hüttenbetrieb, Hörde, Konzern, 1925 (boxed = legally independent firm). *Sources:* Walther Kunze, "Der Aufbaudes Phoenix-Konzerns" (diss., Universität Frankfurt a. Main, 1926); Arnold Tross, *Der Aufbau der Eisen-undeisenverarbeitenden Industrie-Konzerne Deutschlands* (Berlin, 1923), pp. 43–47; Harold Wixforth, *Banken und Schwerindustrieinder Weimarer Republik* (Koeln, 1995), pp. 358–407.

petencies of the executive board and department directors.[40] The degree of explicit bureaucratic formality contrasts greatly with Thyssen *precisely because of the absence* of clear organizational rules of the game. The *Zentraldirektion,* with its *Generaldirektor* (Wilhelm Beukenberg), had control over all financial questions, tax and legal considerations, cartels, relationships to the shareholders, central statistics, contracts, and general administration. But there was little distinction between the general and day-to-day administration in this large, unified firm. Directors of the individual departments *(Abteilungen)* also had general responsibilities. The general director could intervene directly into the departments in wage questions, or large-scale hirings or firings. If anything, the statutes suggest an increasing amount of power and responsibility given to the central board, probably to counteract the former independence of the acquired firms in the interests of uniform administration. Indeed, in many firms, the directors of acquired firms retained a good deal of autonomy within the corporation, hindering uniform, clean bureaucratic administration of new acquisitions.

Phoenix organized itself along the product lines of its acquired firms, essentially the commercial-technical lines seen in Thyssen & Co. Each department had joint commercial and technical directors (usually with the technical director as *de facto* head of the department). These directors ran their department "self-sufficiently," but within the overall guidelines of Phoenix. Like Thyssen & Co. departments, they were run as operating units.

The lack of a clear distinction between the central board and departments, strategy and operations, reproduced itself in the system of accounting for control. (We can see again how an accounting system helps imagine an enterprise as well as define the operating responsibilities and performance of its managers.) Phoenix departments supplied the central administration with biannual operating balances (quarterly after 1924).[41] (Recall that Thyssen & Co. departments submitted *monthly* balances.) The format of the reports remained roughly the same between 1912 and 1925; they were not typewritten until 1925. Until 1913, none of Phoenix's departments could finalize the biannual balances in the same way; thereafter the central administration worked out a preformatted form to follow. Importantly, these balances did *not* include any capital accounts for fixed assets or departmental liabilities, although they did include accounts payable and receivable.

The profit/loss statement included various sorts of overhead costs, along with depreciation for equipment. The central administration then allocated general overhead costs according to a "production cost" formula. In short, Phoenix treated these operating departments as cost centers, just as at Thyssen & Co. The commercial-technical operating units were not divisions because production costs were placed in no direct relation to capital assets or investments. Not until the year-end balances did capital-asset accounts appear. Phoenix then transferred departmental operating profits directly to central reserve accounts. In the central internal preparations for the year-end balance, Phoenix management subdivided capital accounts by production sectors, starting with mining and ending with pipes, but the lack of distinction between central administrative costs and the operating units caused considerable difficulty in estimating true earnings for each of the departments.[42]

Phoenix had the utmost difficulty creating some sort of financial and organizational standard. The expansion-through-acquisition strategy frustrated bureaucratic uniformity. For instance, when Phoenix merged with the Hörder Verein, the new accounting formats met with a good deal of resistance from Hörder executives. Many discussions turned on the proper cost calculation of Thomas slag. In any case, the "profit-loss" accounts established a type of gross profit margin for the month (like Thyssen & Co.'s).[43] Just before the war, Phoenix created standard procedures for auditing the departments' cash accounts.[44] Not until June 1925 did central administration create standard account forms for departmental creditors and debitors.[45] Phoenix did not have anything along the lines of Thyssen's CAO or Krupp's *Revisionsbüro*. In short, although Phoenix was as large and diversified as the Thyssen-Konzern, it organized control in almost the exactly opposite manner. Its organizational form did not directly follow its structure or strategy. Entrepreneurs and executives both had room for choice.

Ironically, Krupp, usually held as typical of German firms, organized itself before the war in a functional, unitary fashion, typical of U.S. corporations. Krupp roughly followed the Phoenix pattern of growth through incorporation, but had a much stronger foundation, consisting of internal growth through vertical integration and diversification.[46] Starting from its near invincible position in casted goods, using its famous crucible steel process, Krupp grew through a flourishing armaments-export business and its infamous, scandalous relations with the German Imperial Government.[47] By 1913, it had vertically integrated from mining to shipbuilding. Unlike Thyssen & Co., the decisive managerial issues inside Krupp centered on the degree of independence of the *Direktorium* (executive board) from the owner, who continued to intervene directly in day-to-day affairs. Just before the war, Krupp had 4 to 6 supervisory board members and 10 to 12 executive directors.

For Krupp, the relevant organizational unit used to control these acquisitions and growth through diversification was the internal product departments called *Ressorts* or branch offices *(Zweigniederlassung)* within the unified corporation. By July 1914, Krupp had 31 *Ressorts*. Unlike Thyssen or Phoenix, the *Ressorts* were largely functionalized production units, with specialized offices *(Dezernate)* located at Krupp's central headquarters in Essen. Unique to Krupp, it also subdivided its central commercial offices into those that handled peacetime products, and armaments. The main exceptions to Krupp's functional, unitary managerial lines were the relative independence of its Grusonwerk in Magdeburg, because of geographical distance (and perhaps its former rivalry), and the shipbuilding department, Germania. Grusonwerk and Germania came closest to Phoenix's commercial-technical departments, but not Thyssen's independent subsidiaries.

From the available literature, however, it is impossible to say how Krupp constructed its accounts, that is, how it organized control. It did, however, have an "astonishingly modern" internal auditing office, with strong powers of recommendation. Unlike Thyssen's CAO, Krupp's auditing office focused more heavily on the control of cash and other accounts, but Krupp's fast growth outpaced its powers. After 1900, Krupp expanded its powers to include the control of Krupp's "external relations," and eventually subdivided it into commercial and technical control functions. It did not, appear, however, to play the powerful Konzern-wide consulting and financial auditing role that Thyssen's CAO did.

The Haniel-Konzern provides an exemplary case of the differences between prewar and postwar Konzerne. By the war, the Haniel-owned *Gutehoffnungshütte* (GHH) under Paul Reusch stretched from mining to machine-engineering operations within one legally unified corporation. The GHH organized its machine engineering as a department, much like Thyssen & Co. Moreover, the GHH remained closely allied through property relations with the Franz Haniel & Co., the largest coal-shipping company in the Ruhr. But the two major corporate centers of Haniel family activity lacked central coordination, except in family ownership, which might have made it a more coherent Konzern. That changed after the war, as the GHH and the Haniel family swiftly moved forward into distribution and machine engineering. The GHH's merger with the *Maschinenfabrik Esslingen,* M. A. N., the *Deutsche Werft,* and the *Zahnräderfabrik Augsburg* counted among the more spectacular acquisitions of the postwar period. In addition, the GHH and the Haniels acquired numerous trading and distribution companies, including Steffens & Nölle, the firm Ernst Nölle cofounded after he left Thyssen & Co. The Haniels and Reusch organized these acquisitions into a multisubsidiary form that became more commonplace in the postwar period. Not until 1925, however, did they found the *Gutehoffnungshütte AV* as a holding company, which gave the Haniel-Konzern a formal coordinating superstructure for this collection of firms. We do not know, however, the common organizational or accounting procedures that bound this Konzern together, but they apparently remained minor. After 1910, Reusch introduced an internal auditing office for the GHH, along the lines of Krupp. But before the war, GHH had great difficulty even auditing the cash flows of its departments.[48] For the Haniel-Konzern, central auditing and control functions remained underdeveloped.

Before 1913, Siemens came closest to resembling the Thyssen-Konzern in its organizational form.[49] Siemens, in fact, represented an array of firms built around two core companies: Siemens & Halske (the original company) and the Siemens-Schuckertwerke (SSW). In 1903, the Siemens family organizationally detached the heavy-current business from Siemens & Halske and founded the SSW as an independent company. Siemens & Halske concentrated on light-current engineering (telecommunications, signaling, magnetic, and measuring devices), while Siemens-Schuckert concentrated on heavy-current power engineering. It had an array of wholly owned satellite subsidiaries and joint ventures, including such luminary firms as Osram (light bulbs), Telefunken (radio, television), and the *Deutsche Grammophon-Gesellschaft.* Siemens & Halske acted as a quasi-holding company for the SSW and a host of affiliated independent companies.

Although Siemens, too, had a huge multisubsidiary structure, the family avoided the term *Konzern* like the plague. They preferred their coinage, the "House of Siemens." Such phrasing was a deliberate attempt on the part of the founder and his sons to avoid the "vague and unpleasant" connotations of "concern" *(Konzern)*.[50] Thyssen tended to use the phrases "Thyssen Gruppe" or "Thyssen Concern." Siemens viewed a Konzern as a purely financial and administrative holding with a tendency toward abstract financial manipulations and ominous monopoly tendencies, instead of a technical-industrial enterprise bound together by family. By calling themselves a "house," they retained familiar and safe-sounding connotations. Even Siemens & Halske considered itself not as a financial holding but rather as a "technical holding," a place where ideas, inventions, knowledge, and innovations flowed into the parent company much like a financial holding pools profits.[51]

In actuality, Siemens & Halske and SSW had an increasingly interconnected joint management, although they retained their legal independence. Siemens & Halske's departments remained more loosely organized, "side-by-side," and "self-contained," while the SSW had a tighter, more intricately connected administration.[52] Siemens & Halske, like Thyssen & Co. or Phoenix, was organized along product or regional lines, which combined development, manufacturing, and marketing, while the SSW, like the GDK or Krupp, was organized along functional lines. Siemens & Halske retained its "product-centric principle." On the surface, the SSW followed a more American-style organizational development. Still, even inside the SSW, as at Thyssen & Co., each workshop had to deal with customers' orders directly and created their own internal balances. (How they constructed them is not detailed.) The central factory administration, moreover, created individual workshop balances as a control measure. Still, one director could complain in 1906 that this control was too "loose" and there was not enough uniformity. As a result, in 1913 the SSW united central finance, plant, and commerce administration into a new central administration that would create more uniform standards, disseminate technical information, and monitor plant equipment. Carl Friedrich von Siemens played a particularly strong role in reforming the SSW.[53]

The diversity and centripetal tendencies of the Siemens firms' product lines always threatened to pull it apart. Thus, although Siemens gained a somewhat stuffy, bureaucratic reputation for its management style, internally it had difficulty asserting the bureaucratic principle. As part of the rationalization measures since the 1890s, both Siemens companies had detailed, centrally issued procedures regulating behavior and responsibilities down to a burgeoning middle management. In this respect, Siemens was decidedly more bureaucratic than Thyssen, which rarely had such written codes. Ironically, this sort of bureaucratic movement worked against the organic, pragmatic, family-oriented, even "anti-commercial resentment" of Wilhelm and Werner von Siemens.[54] It was under Carl Friedrich's reign that Siemens issued brochures on organization with systematic descriptions of rules and responsibilities.

Most important was the 1907 establishment of a joint Managerial Secretariat *(Direktionssekretariat)* "to ease the burden on the management of both companies (S&H and SSW) and to ensure that issues affecting both companies are dealt with in a uniform manner."[55] This secretariat was comparable to the Thyssen CAO. Both Siemens' firms had interlocking directorates. The two boards met regularly concerning strategy. Top directors had considerable freedom from day-to-day operating responsibilities. The staff of the Managerial Secretariat officially belonged to Siemens & Halske after 1913, and included such important offices as the legal department, patent department, the economic policy department, and the press department.

In addition, the SSW contained a number of joint departments with Siemens & Halske, especially those centering on the finance department of Siemens & Halske and the central finance department of the SSW, which jointly administered their shareholdings in other companies. These two general administrative offices prepared reports, statistics, and facilitated uniform standards and control, especially in finance and accounting areas. The finance department concentrated specifically on financial planning every six months and new investment decisions.[56] Especially under Carl Friedrich von Siemens, the critical joint central offices gained more power, very similar to the power accruing to Thyssen's CAO under Hofs and Rabes. In addition, a number of joint offices helped to coordinate purchasing and sales, product design, overseas exports, legal matters, public relations, archival matters, and the assembly of general economic information.

It was that combination of centralization of strategy formulation and general administration, along with the decentralization of day-to-day decision-making, which made the two Siemens companies a "single enterprise," very much like a multidivisional. The exact type of central financial and accounting coordination, however, still needs to be outlined more precisely in order to ascertain what sort of capital controls and on what type of accounting principles these central offices evaluated the operating units. Given that Siemens generally viewed itself as a technical research institute, rather than a somewhat distasteful commercial-financial operation (such as the AEG), it is unlikely that financial criteria (as at Thyssen or DuPont) gained the upper hand as the dominant conception of control. In any case, the central offices did ensure that the extremely diverse product lines of the two Siemens companies had more uniform financial accounting statistics and that the House of Siemens had a coherent strategy and policy.

From these brief descriptions, the essential *heterogeneity* of German organizations becomes clear. As at Thyssen or Krupp or Siemens, two different types of organizational structures could exist within one economic enterprise. The degree of organizational clarity inside the Thyssen-Konzern was exceptional in German steel, largely because Thyssen retained complete financial, strategic, and organizational control over his enterprises. The Thyssen-Konzern also grew less through merger and acquisition of existing enterprises than by concentrating and extending core operations, a corporate policy that continued into the inflationary 1920s. But Thyssen and his managers' commitment and attention to organizational questions also mattered considerably. Thus, especially with the construction of the CAO or the *Centrale,* the Thyssen firms became less a federated, family-owned group of firms (such as the Haniel-owned firms before 1913 but not after 1925), than a coherent Konzern with a definite, overarching managerial structure (like Siemens). Because of the central offices, the legally independent firms could act as a "single enterprise."

Ultimately, it is of profound irrelevance which firm in which country developed the multidivisional form first in some magical race to modernity. An international perspective reveals that a number of important corporations, independently of one another, began developing such organizational designs and patterns of control within a decade of one another. The best confirmation comes from the other side of the planet, in Japan.

Mitsui and Mitsubishi offer striking parallels with the Thyssen-

Konzern. At exactly the same time (1906–1909) that Thyssen nearly fused Thyssen & Co. and the GDK into a single enterprise but then reaffirmed the multisubsidiary form, Mitsui moved to a multisubsidiary structure. Moreover, Mitsui created a Management Department of the Family Council's Secretariat (1902–1909), the equivalent of Thyssen's CAO (1906) or Siemens' Managerial Secretariat (1907).

Mitsui's history goes back three centuries, to when its founder set up dry-goods shops in Edo (Tokyo) and Kyoto to sell high-quality kimonos. Its dry-goods shops branched out into a variety of goods. Mitsui dry-goods shops also anticipated nineteenth-century innovations such as department stores, fixed prices, even chain stores by nearly two centuries.[57] During the Meiji regime, it established a trading company (Mitsui Bussan), the Mitsui Bank, the Miike Coal Mining Company, and diverse manufacturing ventures, as well as real estate and banking. It continued its dry-goods operations as well. Except for the Mitsui Bank, each of these enterprises had been independent firms with long histories and had leading roles in their respective industries. Like Phoenix, which acquired independent companies, considerable centrifugal tendencies existed within Mitsui. As in the Thyssen-Konzern, strong-willed directors, preferring decision-making autonomy, became one of the main managerial problems faced by Mitsui. Mitsui retained a multisubsidiary form to deal with these issues. The main difference between *zaibatsus* and *Konzerne* was the zaibatsu inclusion of huge general trading companies and banks as well as its unrelated diversification.

In 1896, Mitsui set up a board of directors, its first central committee or office, under the Mitsui Family Council to coordinate and control more closely the operations of the companies. The Family Council concentrated on the affairs of the "house," while the board of directors focused on formulating overall strategy for the allied firms. Each subsidiary had a top director on this board, which approved all major transactions. A series of reforms in 1900 failed to resolve conflicts among Mitsui's firms and directors. An internal memorandum written in 1901 by one of Mitsui's top directors criticized these arrangements. The individual directors in the board represented their own "one-sided viewpoints of their respective subsidiaries and tend[ed] to forget their duty not to be prejudiced in favor any particular unit but to decide policy in terms of the overall, balanced management of the Mitsui zaibatsu." This criticism echoed Thyssen's criticism of the GDK and Thyssen & Co, Berlin. Above all, the board of directors lacked an "effective adjunct body to provide detailed studies of those [subsidiaries'] proposals."

In 1902, Mitsui established the Management Department of the Secretariat of the Mitsui Family Council, which carried out organizational studies for the subsidiaries. It focused on overall policy and finance for the zaibatsu, much like Thyssen's CAO. Its managing director had wide-ranging advisory and deliberative powers, who, like the CAO's Heinrich Hofs, could *not* immediately impose his will on the independent directors, but who could advise and recommend. Mitsui's Management Department, like the advisory board of the CAO, had representatives from each of its subsidiaries. It still failed to curb the "harmful effects of each subsidiary's representative sticking to the point of view of his company and never giving way." These centrifugal tendencies continued to be a running problem inside the Mitsui organization. Inside Thyssen, the lordly behavior and rivalry among Thyssen directors also effectively slowed greater centralization and blocked fusion attempts.

At essentially the same time that Thyssen contemplated the fusion of the GDK and Thyssen & Co. (1906), a top Mitsui director and some family members thought of merging the independent companies into a single, large corporation, a *Mitsui Gōmei Kaisha*. As at Thyssen, the subsidiaries' directors bitterly opposed this move. The proposal died. Instead, in 1909, they reaffirmed the decentralized structure of the zaibatsu, but founded the Mitsui Gōmei as a central holding company, which incorporated the Management Department of the Family Council Secretariat. They then transformed the subsidiaries, which had been unlimited partnerships, into joint-stock companies. Thus between 1906 and 1909, both Thyssen and Mitsui debated the same set of issues, only to reaffirm the advantages of the Konzern or zaibatsu organizational form.[58]

Mitsubishi faced similar internal organizational issues as Mitsui.[59] Mitsubishi began in the shipping business. Mitsubishi grew enormously with the help of the Japanese government, eventually driving out American and British firms. After considerable tensions within the government and a vicious price war with a rival shipping firm, the government helped arrange a merger between the two firms, establishing the Nippon Mail Steamship Company (NYK). Tired of the political infighting, its director, Iwasaki Yatoro, diversified into a host of businesses. Mitsubishi became one of Japan's most diversified zaibatsu: coal mines, copper and metal (gold, silver) mines, ship repair facilities, shipyards, warehousing, financial exchange offices, banking, even a public water company for Tokyo (until 1908). Mitsubishi hosted the leading shipyard in Japan by 1913. Its close government–business relations mirrored that of Krupp. Somewhat like the Haniels, the Iwasaki family also invested independently of Mitsubishi in railroads, insurance, general trading companies, real estate, government securities, paper mills, fertilizer, and the famous Kirin brewery. Profits gained from the nationalization of the railroads in 1906–1907 (much like Thyssen's sale of his Gladbeck mines) financed much of this diversification.

Initially, Iwasaki constructed Mitsubishi Ltd. as a single large corporation. Unlike Mitsui, which had difficulties centralizing because of its acquired independent firms, Mitsubishi began with a great deal of centralization and worked its way toward a decentralized system. Mitsubishi had separate divisions for metal mining, coal mining, banks, coal-distribution, shipyards, and real estate. At first, headquarters set the level of capital for the units (fixed and liquid assets), the depreciation rate, and calculated each units' net profits. The head office directly managed the divisions. In this respect, Mitsubishi followed an organizational pattern similar to that of Phoenix, Krupp, or the GHH. But Mitsubishi treated the divisions more as financial units rather than commercial–technical operating units, than did the German firms. Only Mitsubishi's banking division actually had an independent accounting and formal capitalization.

Such a system of direct management, however, overloaded the central office. As a result, Mitsubishi undertook a major reorganization in 1908, which created internal financial divisions. Now, unlike Phoenix, Krupp, or the GHH, these *divisions* independently accounted for their own capital, both fixed and liquid assets, as well as depreciation and net profits *as if* they were legally independent firms. They also could institute their own rules and regulations, handle their personnel questions self-sufficiently, and institute their own cost and financial accounting standards (within the overall financial guidelines of the corporation). In this respect, they resembled Thyssen's GDK Dinslaken or

GM's automobile divisions. The 1908 Mitsubishi reorganization established these divisions as profit centers.

By 1919, however, Mitsubishi had moved to a multisubsidiary system
governed by a holding company responsible for general administration, operations, personnel, and general affairs. By 1926, the administration of the holding company became increasingly differentiated
and sophisticated. Mitsubishi set up a series of central councils for
finance, operations, and technical matters to manage common affairs of the subsidiaries. Like Thyssen, the Mitsubishi holding company created distinct central offices for accounting and legal matters.
Mitsubishi's holding company also included an additional office for
general affairs.

The organizational strategies of Japanese zaibatsu and German
Konzerne proved remarkably similar. Like Konzerne, zaibatsu confronted first the difficulties of managing diversification rather than
scale. By the 1920s, Japanese managers viewed the multisubsidiary
form as one of the best ways to manage their highly diversified businesses. Family ownership proved critical in binding these diverse operations together. Eventually, they introduced sophisticated, centralized
managerial controls to reinforce family ownership. Both countries'
firms fundamentally wrestled with the problem of finding the appropriate balance between control and autonomy, centralization and decentralization. Above all, finding means of establishing standardized
controls across multiactivity firms proved to be the most difficult task.

All of these organizational changes at Thyssen, Siemens, and Mitsui
predate DuPont and General Motors, which according to Chandler,
pioneered the multidivisional system in the early 1920s. Again, who
was first is irrelevant. Within roughly a decade of one another, leading
and major German, Japanese, and American firms moved to a similar
organizational design to cope with the pressures of vertical integration, different product markets, geographic dispersion, different labor
markets, and related or unrelated diversification. Such integration of
complexity forced them to devise new organizational systems to minimize administrative discordance and solve coordination difficulties.

From a global perspective, the Japanese *zaibatsu*, Latin American
grupos, South Korean *chaebols*, or German *Konzerne* (all family-owned,
multisubsidiary forms) were more typical or representative of big businesses in late-industrializing countries than early U.S. or British corpo-

rations. Family ownership anchored all of these types of firms and is not necessarily dysfunctional in a global perspective. It is more pervasive than not. On the basis of the massive, isolated—protected—and relatively wealthy North American market, U.S. firms could afford to expand first horizontally in one product market, maximizing capital-intensive economies of scale. Such a degree of standard product facilitated the development of standard cost accounting, which was infinitely easier than in a vertically integrated or highly diversified firm. Thereafter they integrated vertically, introduced more economies of scope, and diversified. Not surprisingly, then, American firms confronted the problems of managing diversity and complexity. In Germany or Japan, problems of managing diversity arrived first; issues of scale arrived a half-step behind.[60] From a global perspective, German business development thus tended to follow a *Normalweg* instead of a *Sonderweg*. If any country followed a "special path," then it would be the United States. Thus, one should not clumsily use the development of U.S. corporate organization as norm to judge other countries' business developments, let alone modernity. The United States is simply the wrong yardstick. I have only emphasized the M-form because it has played such a central role in corporate scholarship as a symbol of best-practice *modern* organizational forms. We should not reify or deify it.

The shift to the multidivisional or *Konzern* did imply a new way of organizing business in the twentieth century. The growing complexity of business organization forced managers to find a means of intelligently allocating capital internally, rather than by using capital markets. Such holding or parent companies became house banks, in a certain sense, usurping or internalizing the role that banks or capital markets or even shareholders might play in a capitalist system.

As practiced by Thyssen, internalizing such decisions turned managerial attention to the efficient use of financial capital itself, above and beyond manufacturing efficiency. For Thyssen, this grew out of his fundamental refusal to issue equity. He could not afford to be wasteful. The multisubsidiary system combined with the financial control of the CAO built in a high degree of financial clarity and made sure that each individual firm justify its financial existence. Unlike single, unified corporations, which cross-subsidized manufacturing lines through administrative means at no cost, Thyssen's multisubsidiary form meant that funds transferred from one firm to another bore a finance charge, which was still less than relying on banks. Each firm had to compete for additional investment capital from Thyssen & Co. Over the long term, they had to finance their own expansion. By treating them as much as possible as independent firms, Thyssen paid particularly close attention to their relative profitabilities and their efficient use of his investment capital.

In Thyssen's case, the GDK did not have to be as profitable as other German steel firms to play a critical manufacturing role inside the Konzern. Unlike other steel firms, however, Thyssen's multisubsidiary, modular system ensured that all firms earned enough to finance their own expansion, except for short-term subsidies, and that that they had to be profitable (but not at the highest possible rate). The governance structure of the Thyssen-Konzern attempted to fuse both objectives.

For *short-term* bursts of expansion, Thyssen relied heavily on the great German banks. They provided valuable services through their consulting, credit, and general information capacities—not their ability to monitor his borrowing or any form of direct investment. Banks' value to industrialists like August Thyssen lay in the volume of short-term credit they provided, their mediation of stock and securities transactions, the information they provided (not the information supplied by industrialists), and their ability to float loans. For other firms, their ability to issue shares was obviously an important service. To be clear, I am not arguing that such levers of power as German banks could at times wield over industrial firms were unimportant. From the vantage point of the Thyssen story, I am merely suggesting the answer to the effectiveness of German universal banking might lie more on the banking, finance, and capital markets side of the equation, especially banks' implicit "liquidity guarantee" with the Reichsbank and their legislated role in issuing securities, rather than on issues of bank control of industrial firms.

CHAPTER 10

Revolutionizing Industrial Relations

It is now a matter of being or not being. The majority of the people—if necessary against their own fierce resistance—must be protected from total ruin.

August Thyssen to Chancellor Joseph Wirth, October 14, 1922

World War I changed everything. The war transformed the central government into a new, more powerful force regulating the economy. At the same time, organized labor sought a stronger voice in government and firms. The subsequent abdication of the Kaiser and the November 1918 revolution ushered in Germany's first experiment in parliamentary democracy, with new forms of industrial relations. The Weimar Republic pioneered many of the innovations in corporate social policy, industrial relations, rationalization measures, and managerial practices later found in the highly successful Federal Republic of Germany. However, this new framework for industrial relations became *the* point of contention between largely conservative industrialists and the young social democracy. Unfortunately, conservatives and social democrats never reached a lasting political compromise, which had devastating consequences for the history of the world.

For Social Democrats, the November revolution apparently began a "new dawn," but opened the question of whether the new republic would be a social or socialist democracy. If socialist, the nationalization of private property appeared possible. If social, at a minimum new legislation would transform industrial relations and alter the one-sided system of authority, previously characterized by a military-command model and softened somewhat by a paternalist social-welfare policy. The Weimar Republic secured the right of unions to organize and bargain collectively, established state arbitration of wage disputes, introduced factory councils, and finally, created the eight-hour day. Labor viewed the eight-hour day as Weimar's major achievement.

Employers like Thyssen elevated the eight-hour day to a doomsday scenario, construing it as a symbol for all that was wrong with Weimar. Only a few, such as the "Red" Robert Bosch, argued that the length of the day was not the main issue, but that increased productivity within an eight-hour day was more important.[1] Most German industrialists felt an overwhelming nostalgia for the Wilhelmine golden age, which allowed employers a relatively free hand with their allegedly apolitical, internal affairs. Economic conditions during Weimar became an abominably negative contrast with the peace, prosperity, and pride of the Imperial period. Moreover, business strategies had to incorporate complicated political machinations after 1914. Along with collective bargaining agreements and state arbitration, the eight-hour day became a potent symbol, fusing politics and economics, with deeply unhealthy consequences for the Weimar Republic. Altering these key compromises meant undercutting the new democracy.

This story has been well told as national or regional political history, but less so at the company level.[2] Only recently has Werner Plumpe definitively explored the history of factory councils inside the chemical industry (Bayer) and coal (esp. Gelsenkirchen/GBAG).[3] Following Plumpe's company-based approach, I focus on labor-management relations inside Thyssen & Co. from 1914 to 1923. Thyssen & Co. is particularly interesting because, after 1918, it combined two industrial branches (manufacturing and machine engineering) inside one firm, and its two divisions manifested distinctly different labor-management dynamics. We should take into consideration the organizational culture of the firm as well as individual managers below the company figurehead to understand working-class dynamics inside and outside the firm.[4]

Historians have tended to view conflicts about factory councils as measures of the success or failure of the larger political revolution. As Plumpe contends, this perspective reduces the impact of factory councils to a crude thermometer of class struggle, and traps further analysis in contemporaries' own discourse.[5] This chapter confirms Plumpe's overarching thesis that the success or failure of factory councils was dependent on the capacity of participants, both workers and managers, to *learn* from experiences gained from it. Indeed, the more participants viewed factory councils as a positive or negative signifier of something else, the less effective the forum became. Paradoxically, just as German companies needed maximum internal cooperation to overcome the myriad traumas of the postwar world—cooperation the factory councils at Thyssen & Co. (as at Bayer) actually helped create in practice—entrepreneurs especially and workers often proved unwilling to acknowledge factory councils' potential and positive achievements. As with so much in Weimar, this story discloses another missed opportunity.

To understand this complicated story, it is useful to delineate four distinct political-institutional levels and their main actors (Figure 10.1). The first level represents national party politics. On the left, the major groups were the Social Democratic Party (SPD), the Independent Social Democrats (USPD), and the nascent Communist party (KPD). On the right, various bourgeois parties [German Democratic Party (DDP), German People's Party (DVP), and German National People's Party (DNVP)] sought to hold the line against a further drift to the left. For all practical purposes, Germany operated under a military dictatorship and command economy between 1916 and 1918. The regional arm of the High Command, the Military Command, acted ambivalently, sometimes siding with industry, sometimes with labor in order to keep the social peace and win the war. The second level encompasses relevant regional associations. On the left, Ruhr industry faced three major unions plus a radical, syndicalist movement, which was especially active inside the GDK mines in Hamborn and the Thyssen & Co. Machine Company in Mülheim. Opposing them, on the right, were the powerful Northwest Group and its closely affiliated Employer Association, the mouthpiece of Ruhr heavy industrialists. The third level consists of the main actors inside the firm: the representatives of the workers' and white-collar employees' committees for labor, as well as the four top directors of the Thyssen & Co. Rolling Mills and Machine Company. The fourth level represents the individual shop floor labor committees and various department heads inside the firm.

These institutional levels are important for understanding how unity (on both the right and the left) formed—or did not form. To make matters more complicated, while the main antagonism arose between left and right, between workers and employers, it proved extremely difficult to coordinate actions, words, and policies along the vertical—for both the political left and right. In general, the grassroots on the shop floor offered the most radical demands, while the senior

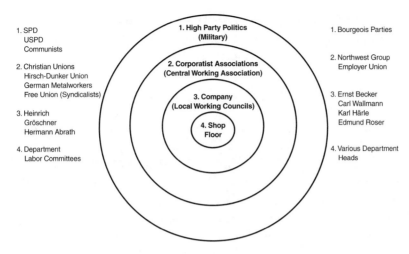

1. SPD
USPD
Communists

2. Christian Unions
Hirsch-Dunker Union
German Metalworkers
Free Union (Syndicalists)

3. Heinrich
Gröschner
Hermann Abrath

4. Department
Labor Committees

1. High Party Politics
(Military)

2. Corporatist Associations
(Central Working Association)

3. Company
(Local Working Councils)

4. Shop
Floor

1. Bourgeois Parties

2. Northwest Group
Employer Union

3. Ernst Becker
Carl Wallmann
Karl Härle
Edmund Roser

4. Various Department
Heads

Figure 10.1 Institutional levels and main organizations/actors, 1918–1920

level of the SPD proved most moderate. Workers often accused their factory committees of being too conciliatory or having sold out to management. Management, of course, saw these labor committees as radical interventions in their decision-making. On the other hand, factory councils were more responsive to the radical demands of the grassroots and conditions within particular factories than the trade unions could tolerate, especially if they wanted to reinforce the collective bargaining process. The trade unions initially viewed the company worker committees as a potential rival power base, only later as an active arm of the unions. But the needs of one factory committee could conflict with the demands of another, which regional unions sought to reconcile. Unions tended to react more quickly to regional or national issues than to issues within individual companies.[6] They also competed strongly with the councils for the loyalties of workers.

Finally, each of the main trade unions had more or less close ties to various political parties, with their own agendas. At the national level, these parties had to deal with highly controversial political issues (ending the war, demobilizing the army, suppressing violent coups, taking the blame for Versailles, paying reparations, and setting up a new democratic government), let alone issues of industrial relations. The Social Democrats, above all, tried to become a responsible, governing party, but conflicting goals and ideological differences had divided the party by 1916. By 1920 the governing SPD managed to alienate much of its working class support. Labor *and* employer unity proved highly elusive in spite of their alleged common, structural interests.

Forcing Corporatism

Thyssen and his managers took an extraordinarily long-term and far-sighted approach to their marketing, manufacturing, and investment strategies, but they took a short-term and nearsighted approach to their labor policies. They tried *not* to make any decisions, or in their words, concessions. Like most other German employers, Thyssen management considered any alterations to its labor policy as onerous, temporary, emergency wartime measures.

The mobilization of all possible energies to arm the nation, however, created a dynamic among army, industry, and labor that eventually destroyed employers' exclusive right to determine working conditions. The war and attendant labor scarcity gave labor unprecedented leverage over employers, although workers' political unity should not be overstated.[7] Growing material deprivations and the frustrating inability of labor unions to bring industrialists into open, direct negotiations provided an initial basis for a common negotiating position among the three major Ruhr unions.[8] While they differed in their ultimate political aims, all eventually agreed on the "stomach question." By August 1915, unions collectively demanded higher wages and cost-of-living increases from Thyssen & Co.[9]

Employers found it difficult to find unity in spite of their common structural interests. The Northwest Group and its associated Employer Association provided the main forums for confronting the growing strength of organized labor and attempted (unsuccessfully) to bring firms together along a common front. Before the war, the infamous German industrial associations had had little influence on the employment policies of individual firms; they focused more on questions of general market order.[10] During the war, the Northwest Group took a more active role in resolving conflicts among Ruhr firms, but still remained dependent on the good faith of individual employers.[11] As usual, Thyssen best epitomized the sheer willful independence of many employers. He refused to join the largely sympathetic Northwest Group and Employer Association. Thyssen willingly agreed to help reduce worker turnover, but only on a non-contractual, non-binding basis. He did not want incur any disadvantages for the Thyssen & Co. Machine Company in the distribution of workers *vis-à-vis* Krupp or Rheinische Metallwaren. Still he regularly sent Ernst Becker of Thyssen & Co. and Herr Surmann of the GDK as his main liaisons with the Northwest Group. Additionally, the legal construction of his Konzern allowed Thyssen to exempt some of his firms from the Employer Association agreement. The Employer Association, for instance, pleaded with the GDK Gas & Waterworks to join the agreement.[12]

As a general rule of thumb, in the same proportion that labor grew scarce, the common collective interests of industrialists grew that much stronger, but their individual interests pulled them farther apart—a classic problem of collective action. Krupp, for instance, complained that Thyssen & Co. advertised in Essen, which violated a tacit agreement among industrialists not to advertise in other "industrial cities" so as to avoid "unrest" and wage competition. Ernst Becker replied that he also disapproved of such ads, but a department chief had placed it in the newspaper without the knowledge of senior management. A corporate culture virtue before 1914, departmental autonomy turned into a vice. To help solve such disputes, Thyssen & Co. and Krupp turned to the military to enforce measures against their own undisciplined poaching of workers.

Competition among Thyssen firms for labor exemplified the lack of coordination across firms in the Ruhr. Thyssen directors hurled a continuous stream of accusations against one another for poaching workers. In 1917, the Thyssen & Co. Rolling Mills and the Machine Company signed a formal agreement promising not to steal workers from each other. In such a case, one firm could levy a 10,000 mark fine against the other.[13] Moreover, the Thyssen-Konzern's traditional decentralization and vertical integration made employment policies that much more difficult to standardize. Regional trade unions effectively pointed out the opaque confusion regarding wages, cost-of-living increases, additional welfare support, supply of food, and the employment of women and foreigners across Thyssen firms. After 1916, Thyssen & Co. tried to introduce standard employment policies to conform more closely to Konzern-wide practices, but these proved difficult to implement.[14] The Machine Company offered the highest wages in the area to attract workers, which exacerbated relations with neighboring firms, including the Rolling Mills.

Forced to keep up with rising competition and inflation, employers commonly granted cost-of-living raises to retain workers, but with the caveat that these were voluntary and temporary. Employers usually granted such cost-of-living raises as surcharges to normal wage or salary rates according to the type of work, individual, department, number of children, or worker pressure. Härle of the Machine Company gained the nickname "Surcharge 80 = Härle."[15] The multiplication of special considerations complicated administrative operations and eventually generated dissatisfaction with workers who desired higher and standard minimum wage levels.[16] Becker wrote the regional Military Command: "If such conditions are already very worrisome, then the repercussions in particular on the development of all working conditions can hardly be foreseen after the end of the war."[17]

As at Bayer, organized labor compelled the Thyssen-Konzern to alter its administrative practices, which resulted in a greater degree of consistency in its employment policies. Wilhelm Späing and Carl Rabes played particularly important roles in this, which enhanced the status of the GDK board of directors in formulating Konzern-wide personnel policies. In May 1916, for instance, Späing set up non-binding *"recommendations"* (underlining is Späing's) to standardize cost-of-living subsidies for all Thyssen white-collar employees, including female secretarial staff, with the exception of the AGHütt and the Stahlwerke Thyssen. GDK directors reiterated again that these measures were "merely temporary" and that individual firms remained responsible for determining wage levels.[18] If Thyssen's firms had difficulty arriving at any coherent personnel policy, one can only imagine the dissonance among hundreds of competing firms across the Ruhr.

Since industrialists relied on the military to quell labor unrest and enforce their own agreements, they ironically brought the state into their company affairs. The Military Command, however, acted as a wild card in labor-management relations. On one hand, the army backed the strict discipline of employers. On the other hand, the army also backed union demands for better working conditions, cost-of-living raises, the prohibition of blacklists, and higher wages, in the interests of social peace.[19] As the war dragged on, the regional Military Command stepped in to persuade employers to grant so-called voluntary cost-of-living raises.

The Military Command undermined the Northwest Group's strategy (if we can call it that) of answering union demands with shattering silence. The fear of setting irreversible precedents underlaid the refusal to reply to labor unions and recognize, however implicitly, collective bargaining rights. The army refused to countenance strikes as a legitimate means of bargaining, but it upheld the idea of companies negotiating with labor instead of rejecting their demands out of hand.[20] Most egregiously to employers, the military advocated greater collective bargaining procedures even before the passing of the Auxiliary Service Law. In February 1916, the military floated the idea of "war committees" inside Ruhr industry based on the Berlin model. The war committees might satisfy worker demands for representation.[21] Unlike the introduction of war committees in Berlin, established only after strikes, the Military Command viewed them as a preventive measure for the Ruhr. Relative to Berlin and other areas, the Ruhr had been "astonishingly moderate" until this point.[22] The Military Command also suggested raising wages and salaries.

The Military Command's announcement set off a round of confidential communiqués among Thyssen directors, resulting in a central conference at the GDK to clarify their position.[23] Personally affronted, Becker of Thyssen & Co. and Rabes of the GDK tersely replied to the Military Command that company directors would continue to regulate all personnel matters. Becker refused to alter traditional wage and salary levels, but would continue to rely on temporary surcharges to individuals.[24]

In the end, military intervention proved disappointing to employers. When strike threats arose, the military wanted industrialists to negotiate, not stonewall. Even the Military Command noted that it was "unmistakable" that employers had little desire to negotiate. In its survey, only 565 of 876 firms had any type of negotiating forum and these forums did not necessarily exist in the most important firms. In any case, they had little influence. More forcefully, the Military Command reserved the right if tensions rose to establish unilaterally arbitration committees, with a military official as chair. This sort of triangular dynamic among army, industry, and labor eventually resulted in forced corporatism.

As the demand for war production increased, so did the role of the central government. The Hindenburg Program and the Auxiliary Service Law, both passed in 1916, proved to be major turning points for the war, and for the history of German industrial relations in the twentieth century. The Hindenburg Program was designed to maximize war production with little regard for economic or social costs. Industry, for instance, managed to block caps on war profits, which generated hate for war profiteers, as many Germans starved under the impact of the Allied sea blockade and wartime controls. The Hindenburg Plan also established a new War Office to mobilize manpower resources and centralize military procurement. It had prominent industrialists on its advisory council and a technical staff.

Passed by the Reichstag on December 2, 1916, the Auxiliary Service Law mobilized most German civilian men for war-related work and allowed the state to shut down small firms to transfer labor (increasingly women) to high-priority armament factories. However, it also forced employers to recognize collective bargaining, affirmed unions' right to organize, and secured worker representation in firms and factories. It was a decisive breakthrough in labor relations.[25] The Auxiliary Service Law established worker committees and salaried employees' committees inside firms. (Henceforth, the term employees will refer only to salaried employees, and workers to wage earners). The Auxiliary Service law also established arbitration councils that mediated wage and labor disputes.[26] These new committees added a whole new level of micropolitics to firms.

The Military Command enforced these new laws. Industrialists gritted their teeth, insisting that the reforms were only emergency measures. They derided them as a type of "war socialism" or as "concessions to the street." Such furious animosity plagued business–government relations for the next fifteen years. The Auxiliary Service Law had the unintended effect of *increasing* labor turnover, exacerbating one of industrialists' major headaches. The arbitration committees, originally designed to stem labor fluctuation, generally took the position that higher wages represented an "appropriate" improvement in the income of the workers, encouraging them to move to firms that bowed to labor pressure or shortages more readily than others. Unsuccessfully, the Northwest Group tried to prevent this wage competition.[27] Now, even the alleged good aspects of the law provided little comfort.

After stalling, in May 1917 the Thyssen firms held their first elections. Labor officially became part of the constitution of the firm. With their new foothold, worker and employee committees provided a direct, face-to-face forum to pressure Thyssen management. The overall tone of these committee meetings conveyed the escalation of tensions. In the beginning, workers and employees addressed their superiors with polite, deferential phrasing common to Imperial Germany. By 1919, they dropped this pretense entirely.[28]

In order to understand the dynamics of labor–management relations in the heart of the firm, it is necessary to sketch briefly the different wartime experiences of the Thyssen & Co. Rolling Mills, the Machine Company, and the GDK. Despite historically close relations and an October 1918 fusion, labor–management relations at Thyssen & Co. followed two distinct paths because of the internal organizational structure of the firm itself, the type of worker it employed, and the personalities of the senior directors. While the Machine Company developed into one of the "reddest" centers of syndicalist activity in the Ruhr—second only to Thyssen's Hamborn mining operations—the Rolling Mills' workers proved to be less radical. By January 1919, however, the Rolling Mill workers became as radical as Machine Company workers; also thereafter, workers and employees coordinated their actions.

The Rolling Mills had a different war experience than the Machine Company. In 1913, the Rolling Mills employed just over 6,000 workers, which dropped to under 5,000 after the first wave of conscription. Its employment continued to sink throughout the war. The Machine Company also saw a quick drop of employment after the first callups, dropping from a record high of 3,000 workers in 1913 to 2,700 workers in 1914. Thereafter, its employment doubled in each successive year to reach 22,000 by 1917. The composition of its workforce also changed dramatically. Both firms employed few women or foreigners before the war. While the Rolling Mills employed about 800 female workers in 1916 (ca. 17%), the number of female wage earners in the Machine Company reached a peak of almost 8,500 (ca. 38%) by 1917.[29] Unlike the Rolling Mills, the Machine Company completely transformed its shopfloor organization to take advantage of (mostly) unskilled women workers, particularly in shell and artillery-piece production. Moreover, the average yearly figures hide tremendous turnover. In June 1917 alone, the Machine Company added 3,000 new workers and 1,600 left. This turnover rate was by no means unusual.

The Rolling Mills had higher prewar turnover rates, so they did not jump as dramatically as that of the Machine Company.[30]

The massive growth of the Machine Company's workforce skewed the entire labor and housing market in Mülheim. An invasion of new workers moved in from the countryside, attracted by the high wage rates paid by the armament industry. A dire need for housing arose. Mülheim did not have the "rental barracks" so typical of major industrial cities, but relied on family homes. Thyssen did not provide the same proportion of company housing in Mülheim as in Hamborn or Bruckhausen, which meant that workers were subject to huge rent increases. At the end of the war, the Machine Company, which employed about 20,000 workers, laid off at least 14,000, whose resentment at unemployment helped feed revolutionary, syndicalist activity in Mülheim. As late as 1926, 20% of the unemployed and emergency part-time workers in Mülheim had migrated there during the war. Most lived in Styrum and Heissen, where most Thyssen & Co. workers also lived, and contributed to heightened tensions.[31]

Hamborn also saw a similar invasion of rural workers who likewise fueled a radical syndicalist movement. Nowhere was the work probably more miserable than in the GDK mines in Hamborn and Lohberg. The GDK mines lost many workers to conscription, yet output remained relatively high. New workers flooded in from the countryside, attracted by high wages and secure provisioning, and foreigners and some prisoners-of-war replaced the loss of manpower. In spite of coal's high priority and the fact that financially powerful companies such as Krupp, the Rheinische Metallwaren, and Thyssen could monopolize black markets for food (and hoarded vast quantities of it), rations never matched their physical exertions, especially for miners. (Krupp and Thyssen's purchasing power alone distorted the entire market for meat in the Ruhr.) According to regulations, the state allotted miners a 1,900-calorie/day ration, but they needed approximately 4,000–5,000 calories/day. Naturally, productivity suffered. The already dangerous job of mining became even more dangerous as less experienced workers replaced those at the front, and hunger levels grew, which led to fatigue and a multiplication of dangerous mistakes underground. Sloppy work practices and the shortage of wood for tunnel frames also meant more accidents. Almost 3,000 miners across the Ruhr lost their lives during the war. Not surprisingly, the strongest demands for a shortened workday, first eight hours, then seven, then six by 1919, came from physically exhausted miners.[32] Malnourishment and exhaustion provoked intermittent wildcat strikes.

The GDK steel works also hired women in the same proportion as the Thyssen Rolling Mills (1,500 out of 8700 or 17%) and also employed foreigners. Although steel was a high-priority good, the GDK's employment in the steelworks rose by only 7%, as opposed to almost 700% in the Machine Company. Still, the new workers, the constant shortage of supplies, the exhaustion, and nagging hunger led to a decline in pig-iron production (18%), steel (5%), and rolled goods (7%) from 1913 to 1917.[33]

The Thyssen & Co. Rolling Mills and Machine Company also had two different types of management systems. The Rolling Mills' product departments displayed a striking lack of coordination as a result of its modular organizational design. In general, Rolling Mills workers dealt directly with individual department heads; each department had its own worker committee. Over time, workers pressured management for more common conferences, especially in regards to working hours.[34] They pointed out numerous inconsistencies to managers, even bringing them to the attention of the mayor of Mülheim. The Rolling Mills did not standardize wage levels or piece rates across its departments until after the 1918 revolution; even functionally similar jobs in different departments of the firm could have different renumeration levels.[35] In April 1918, the strip-steel-department committee could argue that the wages of craftsmen and machinists were "insufficient" and did not stand in the "correct relationship to the wages of other workers and to the same work in other departments."[36] Attempts to standardize wage rates across the Rolling Mills failed, in part due to the traditional independence of the department managers. The workers' committee of the pipe department, for instance, brought their demands directly to the head engineer, who independently raised piece rates and permitted greater flexibility in working hours. Because department chiefs in the Rolling Mills, who often worked directly on the shopfloor, handled many of the negotiations regarding work policy, negotiations remained more personal, individual, and flexible than in the Machine Company. There was little intentional guile in these methods nor a divide-and-conquer motive, because management had run the company in this manner since the 1880s.

Pressure from labor committees forced Thyssen & Co. management to standardize wage levels for similar work across individual departments and eventually across Thyssen companies. In one case, the shop-floor foremen in the pipe mill wrote to their supervisor that they wanted a brief holiday to recuperate just like that granted by the Machine Company.[37] Often workers' committees were better informed than management. For instance, Wallmann reported to Becker that his workers had told him that other firms, including the GDK rolling mills in Bruckhausen, were paying 100% surcharges for overtime work on Sunday. At first Wallmann thought this was "impossible," but after calling the GDK he found out that it was partially true.[38]

By contrast, the Machine Company organized itself along central, functional lines, closer to an American-style organization. The basic organizational unit was the manufacturing workshop, not a semi-autonomous operating unit as in the Rolling Mills. Central management had authority over sales, wage and piece-rate levels, general administration, and accounting standards. Machine Company worker committees brought unified demands forward to central, not departmental, management. Shopfloor superintendents had less autonomous negotiating power. This organizational design tended to focus negotiations at the top, with Härle and Roser, leading to a stop-start pattern of negotiations.

The distinct differences of workforce, the internal organizational structure of firms, and the type of work resulted in differing levels of labor militancy. The workforce of the rolling mills in Mülheim, Bruckhausen, and Dinslaken remained less radical relative to the syndicalism that arose in the Machine Company and the GDK Hamborn. If they joined, they did so later. And while the Rolling Mills remained relatively calm before 1918, the Machine Company had to avert strikes. Likewise, the GDK mining operations became the sites of massive labor unrest near the end of the war, becoming the pacesetter for other uprisings in the Ruhr.

By 1917–1918, strikes over the "stomach question" fused with political demands to end the war and for radical political change. Ordinary German citizens suffered horribly from wartime conditions. Malnourishment, rising food prices, black markets, tattered clothing, sheer exhaustion from overwork, and excessive overtime intensified working-class discontent. In June and July of 1917, a wave of short strikes hit

Mülheim because of poor food supply and the infrequency of cost-of-living raises. In November 1917, the Thyssen Machine Company suffered a brief work interruption (only 10% of its workforce went out) for similar reasons, but the radical workers failed to spark a major city-wide strike. Strike waves throughout the Ruhr in the harsh "turnip" winter of 1917–1918 did not affect either Mülheim firm because Thyssen & Co. labor committees felt that management negotiated in good faith. The Thyssen & Co. *worker committee* successfully quelled one strike movement in favor of sending a delegation to the District President in Düsseldorf to report on the miserable state of workers. It transformed the more radical workforce's call to end the war into less politicized demands for better food supply, wage raises, and shorter working hours. As late as July 1918, the worker committee of the Thyssen & Co. Rolling Mills advocated shortening the workweek not on the grounds of a programmatic eight-hour day, but because of the worsening food situation. Workers would have more time to scrounge for food. As at the Bayer works in Leverkusen, the worker committees despised by industrialists helped moderate worker demands.[39]

At the height of the last-gasp German offensive in France, on July 13, 1918, the workforce of the Machine Company peacefully laid down their tools four hours earlier than usual on Saturday to protest the long workweek. Historians consider this to be one of the most significant strikes leading to the November revolution. The next weekend, Machine Company workers repeated their action, which a number of other firms' workers in the western region of the Ruhr imitated. Management threats and attempts by the moderate worker committees failed to stop the strike. On the same day as the second strike, industrialists met with military officials, and August Thyssen and Carl Duisberg (of Bayer) said that one "could not confront union agitation energetically enough" and felt that the army had allowed labor too much "freedom."[40]

Why did Machine Company workers strike when so few others did? In Mülheim, Härle and Roser's hardline approach and unsympathetic tone proved decisive. Even after the strike, they remained completely unmoved by workers' complaints. They refused to believe that there was widespread discontent and instead blamed the strike on a few outside agitators. Such a deluded misreading angered workers. Härle and Roser had conceded so little that its workers committee had nothing with which to pacify workers. At one Machine Company assembly, the workforce interrupted the directors and workers' committee with catcalls of "down with the war" and criticism directed at their own workers' committee. Workers seemed to want some concessions, some sense of shared sacrifice, or at least, empathy or respect on the part of management. The GDK and the neighboring Rolling Mills did not strike, just as Krupp did not strike. As one of the union representatives at Krupp explained, Krupp workers did not follow the Thyssen Machine Company's example because its directors worked "more diplomatically."[41]

Härle steered the Machine Company's ship. His colleagues described Härle as the "iron backbone" of the Machine Company. Dressing in a frock coat and side-striped pants, he often appeared at work at 5:00 in the morning and left late in the evening. His demeanor was that of an aristocrat and soldier with a strong sense of honor. He felt it was a permanent blemish on his social standing that his father had run a pub. Härle had been a reserve officer in the Ulmer field artillery regiment, and had eagerly volunteered for service, fighting at the Argonne, Flanders, and Ypres and earning an Iron Cross. He was a soldier "heart and soul." In 1917, the Military Command recalled him to fight on the home front.

Härle ran his office like a military operation, famous for its high work tempo. His subordinates considered him a holy terror, trembling when they had to appear before him. When Härle walked through the office, everyone fell silent. He did not hesitate to fire people, which kept him constantly before the local arbitration court. Heinrich Dinkelbach called his office an "assembly line" of firings. In political terms, Härle remained entirely loyal to the emperor and he brutally stated his opinions. In 1930, he once embarrassed his fellow Swabians (the area roughly around Stuttgart to Ulm) at his regular drinking table with a bombastic speech lauding the monarchy. (And those in Härle's circle were not liberals or social democrats.) Unlike many German Catholics, Härle's political sympathies lay with the ultraconservative German National Party. Another colleague related how Härle would leave any social gathering precisely at 11:00 in the evening. Likewise, if he had guests over, they too would have to leave precisely at 11:00. He had principles.[42] Härle's unforgiving, upright, soldierly attitude threw the Machine Company into periodic turmoil, generating a pattern over the next four years of harsh confrontation followed by capitulation on the part of management.

In response to the July strike, the Military Command came down strongly on the side of Thyssen & Co. It argued that conditions on the front were worse, tried to move the strikers into legal channels through the local arbitration committee, and finally, threatened striking workers with the trenches of France. But the strike actions forced Härle and Roser to meet jointly with the Military Command and workers' committee, something they were otherwise loathe to do. Härle and Roser declared themselves willing to reexamine the question of shorter working hours after the end of hostilities. The lack of immediate concessions, moreover, took some wind out of the workers' sails. But this July strike marked the point when radical workers managed to place the Military Command, industrialists, and moderate labor unions on the defensive.

Tensions remained high throughout the end of 1918, but did not erupt into open strikes. The workers committee of the Machine Company had again staved off a broader strike movement in the interests of the war effort and union solidarity at the corporate level. The workers' committee gave voice to workers' interests, but also acted as a tempering influence on activist workers at the grassroots. Unions wanted to come across to management as responsible negotiating partners, rather than as agitators, so they too defused strike situations. No further strike actions occurred in the Ruhr before the November revolution, since they seemed counterproductive also to the major organized parties. The moderation of unions, including the socialist-oriented Free Unions, helped keep the Ruhr relatively calm until the Revolution.

In Mülheim, a joint council meeting between labor and management was held at the end of October 1918 to manage the transition to peacetime. The council epitomized the potential for cooperation. This council, consisting of representatives of the SPD and Catholic Center party, labor unions, company directors (for Thyssen & Co., Härle, Roser, and Becker), the mayor, and an editor of the local newspaper, foreshadowed Weimar's future political constellation.

But in the Ruhr mines, wildcat strikes erupted with increasing ferocity, triggered by the mining companies' stance that wage raises had to be coupled with rises in productivity, and their absolute refusal to negotiate with worker organizations. This intransigence forced the government and the Military Command to intervene, which satisfied no one.[43] To head off further strikes, mining owners (including Thyssen) finally met with miners in Essen in October to discuss a rise in wages, extra pay for overtime work, abolition of blacklists, and introduction of the eight-hour day. The meeting alone was a dramatic concession by industrialists. Results were inconclusive, but Thyssen and other mining owners recognized unions as *de facto* "social partners." Yet, even as the war wound down, workers did not programmatically link at company, associational, and political levels their demands for reduced working hours, the eight-hour day, and an end to the war.[44] Most importantly, SPD-oriented unions tried to calm their workforces. However, miners at the GDK in Hamborn would explode this moderating cap, much like an oil well might gush forth under enormous pressure.

A Revolution in Industrial Relations

For a brief period, strike action did appear to be superfluous. The old order appeared to crumble without a fight. At the beginning of October 1918, General Ludendorff, still deep in the heart of France, admitted to a shocked German public that the country needed to seek an immediate armistice. He left the onerous task of accepting surrender to the newly empowered Reichstag and a coalition government of the SPD, Center Party, and moderate bourgeois parties. Unfortunately, the new government inherited the demoralizing defeat. Starving, resentful—armed—soldiers streamed home.

One month later, sailors in Kiel began a mutiny after refusing to carry out a suicide mission for the honor of the fatherland. Within days, mutinies spread like wildfire across Germany and merged into a nationwide revolution. On November 9, 1918, a democratic republic was proclaimed in Berlin. The Kaiser abdicated and fled the country. The warring sides of World War I signed an armistice a few days later.

In Mülheim, as elsewhere, the revolution occurred quite swiftly and peacefully. Workers' and Soldiers' Councils (or soviets) took over municipal government on November 9; of the ten members of the inner circle of the worker's council, eight were Thyssen Machine Company workers; of the 39 extended council members, 22 were Thyssen workers. Until February 1919, the Workers' and Soldiers' Council acted as the new ruling government of Mülheim. In Hamborn, the revolution occurred just as peacefully, although the Hamborn Workers' and Soldiers' Councils proved to be more radical. The Hamborn Councils called immediately for an armistice, democracy at all levels of government, a eight-hour work day, a National Assembly to form a constitutional government, and the socialization of mining firms. Unlike Carl Duisberg of Bayer, who acquiesced to the new politics and even joined his local Council to influence its decisions, August Thyssen, not surprisingly, maintained his hard line against the new powers.[45]

If the wartime dynamic created by army, industry, and labor generated a great deal of political pressure for change, it now created a basis for stability. Industrialists as well as Social Democrats felt a deep uneasiness about the political status of the Councils or soviets. The threat of further chaos and the spectre of a Russian-style revolution scared moderate politicians on both the left and the right. The Councils initially acted as a stabilizing factor in German life.[46] The SPD, unions, and most of the Councils condemned wildcat strikes because they disrupted the coal supply and the employment potential of area firms. But they encountered an increasingly powerful syndicalist movement, particularly strong at the GDK Hamborn and Thyssen Machine Company, which advocated direct worker control over big businesses and government.

Led by Hugo Stinnes, Ruhr employers quickly realized that they would have to rely on organized labor unions and the moderate Social Democrats to stabilize the political situation. This insight found expression in one of the founding political compromises on which the Weimar Republic built its shaky house, the "central working association" (Zentralarbeitsgemeinschaft, ZAG) or the Stinnes-Legien agreement. On November 15, Stinnes and Carl Legien, the union trade leader, agreed to introduce collective bargaining on a permanent basis. The ZAG guaranteed employment for veterans in their former firms, reconfirmed the status of worker and salaried employee committees, reaffirmed arbitration procedures and committees with state mediation, and introduced the eight-hour day.[47] The ZAG agreement essentially conceded the workers some rights, while heading off immediate efforts on the part of the more radical socialists to call into question property ownership. This national corporatist agreement found its regional counterpart one week later with a joint interpretation of the

Stinnes-Legien agreement, signed by the Northwest Group's director, Dr. Hoff, and the head of the Metalworking Unions, Karl Spiegel.[48] The agreement took overall wage levels out of the hands of management and placed them in regional collective bargaining associations. Pressure grew intense to standardize wages around functional job descriptions across companies in the region. The Stinnes-Legien agreement represented a fundamental limitation on the prewar powers of industrialists, and they knew it.

The Mülheim Council began to influence Thyssen & Co. corporate policies. The Council agreed not to "intervene in the technical operations" of Thyssen & Co., since they found it necessary that firms continue to employ workers during demobilization. The Machine Company directors, however, wanted the Council to refrain from all "political interventions"—which was precisely the problem. To Härle and Roser, the introduction of the eight-hour day through legislation had effectively altered their company statutes and constituted a political intervention in their "technical operations." They subsequently refused to establish minimum salaries for white-collar employees and retained the exclusive right to fire workers, which the Council saw as a means (and it was) to eliminate uncomfortable members of the committees.[49]

Despite clear left-wing tendencies on the part of the Mülheim Council, the Mülheim mayor had to admit that the council and the city government worked well together.[50] The Council calmed a march on city hall and joint strike action by the Rolling Mills and Machine Company workforces on November 23, 1918. Thyssen directors had ordered unpaid "vacation shifts" caused by the lack of coal, which greatly upset workers living on the edge of subsistence. During the war, payments had continued for "vacation shifts," but Thyssen & Co. unilaterally discontinued this practice. The Council decreed that companies would still have to pay 80% compensation for any temporary shutdowns due to lack of coal or materials. At the same time, the Council helped prevent further strike actions regarding the coal supply, which became an issue because GDK miners caused myriad "vacation shifts" throughout December 1918 at Thyssen & Co. by their strike activity.

The overall situation in the Ruhr remained tense. Thyssen miners at Hamborn and Lohberg tried to win additional gains through highly visible strikes. A day before the Stinnes-Legien agreement went into effect, unions pressured mine owners into the eight-hour day, 25% over-time pay on weekdays, 50% on Sundays, and a minimum wage. The mine owners made these concessions with the *caveat* that the miners remain disciplined and at work. But no more than three days after the Stinnes-Legien agreement, on November 18, individual Thyssen collieries shut down due to wildcat strikes. The dispute centered on the interpretation of the eight-hour day for miners. If the descent and ascent of the miners were included in the eight-hour day, it effectively made it a 7.5-hour day, according to Thyssen managers; ironically their arguments clung to the negotiated agreement. Despite considerable grumbling, moderate unions managed to hold the line on an eight-hour day that did not include ascent and descent.

GDK miners broke through the moderating dam created by the alliance of moderate SPD, trade unions, and industrialists. The revolt of GDK miners against their union representatives began the "real revolution in the Ruhr."[51] Hamborn miners additionally demanded a 7.5-hour workday (seven hours if ascent/descent are included), even a six-hour shift, further raises, and fundamental alterations to work organization.

The atmosphere had also worsened dramatically in Mülheim after December 7 when a radical wing of the Council summarily arrested eighty-year old August Thyssen, Fritz Thyssen, Carl Härle, Edmund Roser, and Ernst Becker, along with Hugo Stinnes' son and three other Mülheim firm directors. The Council charged Thyssen with high treason, accusing both Thyssen and Stinnes of supporting the separatist movement in the Rhineland and advocating an invasion by French troops to stop the revolution. The Council unceremoniously schlepped the aged Thyssen off, wrapped in a blanket, on a night train to Berlin.

Within twenty-four hours, Friedrich Ebert, the president and leader of the SPD, personally intervened on Thyssen's behalf. Berlin police directors dismissed the charges and released the men. Thyssen's arrest undermined the legitimacy of the Councils and was a harbinger of impending lawlessness. Still, the end of the year, Thyssen & Co. and the city of Mülheim had suffered from little open violence.

But in Hamborn, GDK miners organized huge public rallies and shut down all of Thyssen's mines in response to the accusation of treason. The Hamborn Workers' and Soldiers' Council supported their

demands and urged GDK management to give up or else face pro-
longed strike activity. In order to halt potential violence and imminent
destruction of property, senior GDK mining director Arthur Jacob sur-
rendered to miners' demands, under protest, on the condition that
unions and the government permit a rise in coal prices. The Council
also insisted that the miners go back to work. Thereafter, trade unions
and coal producers met in Essen to forge a uniform, regional agreement on wage levels and coal prices, which would have taken effect after January 1919.

However, when Thyssen returned from Berlin, he overturned Jacob's verbal concessions to the workers, which prompted the radical
miners to resume their strike. GDK miners now marched to nearby
collieries, forcing many of them to shut down. Miners physically
hauled three GDK directors to Mülheim to talk with Thyssen, who was
not in town and, in any case, refused to meet with them on principle.
Holding fast to their agreement with the moderate unions, the GDK
refused to grant a Christmas bonus or new cost-of-living raises. Jacob
accused the radical miners of using terror and refusing to negotiate. A
stalemate, with sporadic violence, ensued. Two days after Christmas,
the Military Command, supported by right-wing *Freikorps* troops armed
with machine guns, marched against Thyssen miners, and killed three
miners. In retaliation, the Hamborn workers' army sent two trucks and
machine guns in support of the miners. A company of sailors came to
the aid of the Freikorps troops. A short skirmish ensued, resulting in
two dead on each side, an unfortunate prelude of things to come.
Lines hardened. Everyone feared further escalation.[52]

In spite of the nearly two-week strike and ugly skirmish, the Prussian
Minister of the Interior (a Social Democrat) managed to subdue the
violence. A December 28 meeting in Mülheim arranged a compromise, granting Hamborn miners a one-time payment and a bonus for
workers with children. Thyssen directors placed great weight on the interpretation that these payments represented compensation for wages
lost during strikes, not a general cost-of-living increase, and that they
would again begin the agreed-upon eight-hour day. The compromise
temporarily dampened Hamborn strike fervor, but, as Ruhr industrialists feared, the settlement encouraged strike movements elsewhere.
Within days, Essen miners wanted the same "Hamborn awards."

After January 1919 perceived fears drove real events. The trigger occurred in Berlin. Karl Liebknecht and Rosa Luxemburg reorganized the small Spartacist movement into the Communist party (KPD) and held a protest rally on January 5, 1919. It began as a symbolic protest, but turned into a national disaster. The Social Democratic minister of the interior, Gustav Noske, ordered the German Military Command to clear out the Spartacists. He permitted the use of Freikorps groups made up of demobilized officers, drifters, students, nationalists, and mercenaries—men hardened by war who felt themselves defenders of all that was most German. They were often little better than vigilantes and thugs, with little or no loyalty to the new government.[53] Troops put down the Spartacists with flamethrowers and machine guns. They killed or wounded hundreds, including Luxemburg and Liebknecht, whom they mutilated and dumped into the river Spree. Relatively powerless in life, Luxemburg and Liebknecht became powerful as martyrs. Noske's "bloodhound" tactics discredited the SPD's compromise tactics and reinforced the split in the left for the remainder of the Weimar Republic. The new democratic republic received its name, in fact, when its first parliament fled to Weimar for protection from the violence in Berlin.

Across the Ruhr, wildcat strikes, uncoordinated violence, intermittent demonstrations, and occupations of newspaper buildings spontaneously erupted everywhere in support of the Spartacists—or rather against the government for its ferocious response. An estimated 16% of all miners struck. In the western Ruhr, nearly all the Independent Social Democrats went over to the Communist party.[54]

Wildcat strikes at the GDK Hamborn shut it down. Jacob disappeared into a Duisburg apartment on the advice of its mayor. Accusing Jacob of "deserting the flag," a particularly harsh insult among conservative patriots, Thyssen summarily fired him after fifteen years of service. He was obviously punishing Jacob for failing to hold the line. Ironically, Thyssen blamed the discontent on Jacob for his incentive schemes designed to squeeze the utmost performance out of individual workers. Jacob countered, correctly: "To get as much as possible from the individual is rather exactly the fundamental principle that has made the Thyssen works so large so quickly and that has made you the pacesetter for all of German industry. This system has proved itself wonderfully for you personally and for every one of your executives and workers."

This performance-oriented system gave Thyssen a reputation as one of Germany's hardest driving mine owners, but Jacob now paid the cost. In front of other Thyssen executives, Thyssen humiliated Jacob, accusing him of destroying all that he had worked for. Thyssen pettily accused Jacob of failing to file his reports on time and keeping him informed. Jacob retorted that Thyssen simply ignored him, never visited him in his office like other executives, and did not approve more funding. Thyssen retorted that he paid out the highest wages and salaries in the district and therefore expected the highest performance. Jacob accused Thyssen of "hanging him out to dry" and not offering enough protection against leftist attacks. He felt justified moving to Duisburg under these conditions.

The ugly exchange between Thyssen and Jacob is interesting because it shows how much Thyssen's business policies and values exacerbated working relations around his firms. One former Thyssen executive related that Stinnes did not feel that Thyssen treated Jacob appropriately. These recriminations also confirm Cläre Stinnes' devastating criticism of Thyssen's treatment of his managers from a prior case before the war: "Again he throws the baby out with the bathwater, forgetting every reason for justness and thankfulness. It always makes one feel sorry and suffer when one finds yet another proof of this great flaw of Thyssen. If he does not like someone anymore, he must go, regardless of what he has so far performed." Ironically, Thyssen had sent Jacob down to evaluate a director whose company suffered considerably from labor strife, which Thyssen blamed on the man's management.[55] While protests were nationwide, individual companies could handle them more or less well. Thyssen's and other employers' defense of their so-called social policy rested on a direct correlation between renumeration and performance, which did not allow much room for extras or concessions: work as world view.

Events in the Ruhr now reached a critical stage. The direct action of Hamborn miners appeared successful in forcing owners to make concessions. On January 11, 1919, the Essen Workers' and Soldiers' Council occupied the buildings of the coal syndicate and mine owners' association. They proclaimed the immediate socialization of Ruhr mines; the proclamation found considerable support among Ruhr Councils, trade unions, and left-wing politicians. In part, Councils and trade unions tried to stay ahead of more radical claims by Ruhr miners, who wanted greater material rewards than the collective bargaining agreements permitted. But the Social Democrats and national government refused to entertain any immediate plans for socialization, which frustrated Ruhr workers. On February 6, another joint declaration of Ruhr Councils threatened to call a general strike. The government answered with the threat that any such strike would be met with regular troops and Freikorps battalions already assembling in the region. One future VSt mining director, Gustav Knepper, suffered two physical attacks by miners; mine owners formed their own police forces to protect their property.[56] Noske wanted a "strong man" as the regional Military Command in the Ruhr and appointed the monarchist General Oskar von Watter.

With help of the *Freikorps Lichtschlag* battalion [nicknamed by workers the "death blow" *(Totschlag)* battalion], von Watter arrested on February 12th the Münster Soldiers' Council, who had tried to disarm the Freikorps. After two Communists murdered the president of the association of colliery clerks in Hervest-Dorsten in the northern Ruhr, von Watter ordered Freikorps troops into that city. Roughly 100 armed workers, recruited mostly from Hamborn and Mülheim, marched against von Watter's troops. After short battles, the Freikorps prevailed, losing only two men to the miners' forty, and occupied the mining settlements. It was the first armed red-white clash. The Ruhr verged on civil war.

On February 16 the Mülheim Council along with delegates from the western Ruhr declared a general strike against the national government for not "suppressing the dictatorship of the Freikorps officers."[57] Between February 18 and 23, about one-half of all Ruhr miners acted on the call for a general strike. In Düsseldorf, Remscheid, Mülheim, Hamborn, Dinslaken, Oberhausen, and Wuppertal, factories fell silent. Armed strike guards ensured that all work stopped. Even white-collar employees participated in the strike in Mülheim, although for different reasons. A "Red Army" appeared in Gelsenkirchen and Bottrop, and occupied Bottrop after bloody fighting. Their success was brief. After Bottrop, the army began systematically to seize power from the Councils across the Ruhr

Mülheim had surprisingly seen little violence before a battalion of Freikorps troops entered the city on March 9. They easily disarmed the Council and arrested its leaders. Despite protest strikes at Thyssen &

Co. and Stinnes' Friedrich Wilhelms-Hütte, the political revolution effectively ended for Mülheim.[58] On March 14, 1919, the Freikorps battalion placed an advertisement in the newspaper thanking the city of Mülheim and Thyssen & Co. for their generous financial donations.[59]

Hamborn offered the fiercest resistance. Hamborn miners threw themselves into pitched battles against Freikorps troops that even included artillery. After several hours of fighting and numerous casualties, the miners gave up. GDK Hamborn directors immediately announced a reduction in wages and an increase in overtime, although the new moderate-to-right Hamborn executive council tried to dissuade Thyssen management from provoking the miners further. Not surprisingly, Thyssen miners went off on another two-week strike protesting the occupation of the city and the lack of political representation.[60]

At the end of March, however, another major general strike convulsed the Ruhr. By April 10, approximately three-quarters of all miners in the Ruhr went on strike. Coal deliveries dwindled to almost nothing. Sympathy strikes shut down Essen, Mülheim, Hamborn, and Bruckhausen mines.

The national government declared martial law, lifting citizen's rights, and moving Freikorps troops into all major cities. Incidents with the Freikorps multiplied. In Mülheim, the Freikorps assaulted a syndicalist meeting, killing four and arresting 150. In Düsseldorf, almost forty people (including four children) died as a result of clashes. But the general strike lost steam. Mineowners compromised, offering the seven-hour shift. By mid-April government troops had unseated all Councils across the Ruhr. Noske appointed Carl Severing of the SPD as state commissar for the Ruhr. In late April, the last major general strike of the year collapsed because of concessions, lack of wages, food, and sheer exhaustion.[61]

After the April general strike, the Ruhr returned to a relative state of calm. By October 1919, mining unions and employers finalized the first regional wage contract for Ruhr mines, which included the seven-hour shift (not including ascent/descent) along with regulations regarding vacations, night-time, and holiday pay. At the end of the year, Hamborn miners once again tried to force a shorter workday through direct action, but Severing and von Watter suppressed these movements.

The intervention of government troops successfully ended attempts to socialize the mines or heavy industry. The SPD-led national government ensured that Germany would remain within the bounds of a capitalist system, but at a tremendous cost. The manner in which the government reconstituted law and order by using some of the most lawless, vile elements in German society, the Freikorps, scarred the new republic. Noske's "bloodhound" techniques alienated a good portion of the left from the SPD and Weimar democracy. The willingness to tolerate right-wing violence helped transform the Ruhr into one of Germany's bastions of Communism. One minister living in Hamborn in the summer of 1918 remarked that the miners were Social Democrats, but by April 1919 now almost all were Communists. Hamborn became the first city with a majority of Communists.[62] Mülheim still had a moderate to conservative government. As in the national government, the Mülheim SPD had to ally itself with parties on the right that showed little desire to compromise with the SPD except under extraordinary pressure. Such political divisions contributed to the demise of Germany's first experiment in democracy.

Institutionalizing Industrial Relations

After the breakdown of the April 1919 general strike, business firms began using collective bargaining procedures, but within the bounds of a capitalist system. Many of these innovations still determine the German way of doing business.

By June 1919 local "working associations" were formed as local wage-negotiating forums in Mülheim, analogous to the national "central working association" (ZAG). Participating unions attempted to standardize wage rates across Mülheim in order to avoid a "guerrilla war" among individual firms.[63] Amidst mutual recriminations about delaying tactics, Thyssen & Co. management took an active part in these local wage agreements, but this guerrilla war continued even within Thyssen & Co. Management refused to consider any local wage agreement valid and binding for both the Rolling Mill and Machine Company, although they were now joined as one legal company. Additionally, Thyssen & Co. would not respect the validity of any local agreement with other Mülheim firms; in particular, that of the neighboring Friedrich Wilhelms-Hütte. Following Stinnes' more conciliatory approach, the Friedrich Wilhelms-Hütte had joined the Northwest Group's collective bargaining agreements on the regional level.[64]

Like the trade unions, the employers' Northwest Group advocated standard regional wage and social policy agreements so that member firms would not be "played off one another."[65] But Thyssen firms refused to join the Northwest Group's regional agreements, while temporarily tolerating local ones. As if to stress their principled independence, the Thyssen-Konzern felt that a recently created central board of Thyssen technical directors (March 1920) made the Employers Association of the Northwest Group "dispensable."[66]

After months of negotiations, in February 1920 a collective bargaining agreement for Ruhr iron and steel industry fell through. Industrialists adamantly refused to make May 1 (a labor holiday) and November 9 (the founding date of the Weimar Republic) legal holidays. Again symbolic issues of political culture like the eight-hour day, May Day, or the color of flags (the democratic black-gold-red vs. the Imperial black-white-red) drove real politics. Once employers balked at introducing the holidays, collective bargaining moved back to square one, to local working associations and individual firms.[67] The same guerrilla war arose all over again at the local level, which made regional agreements more desirable for both sides. The upshot of all these negotiations meant that the *status quo*—and the freedom of individual companies—was unintentionally reaffirmed.

Regional collective bargaining negotiations, however, did manage to institutionalize salary agreements for white-collar employees at Thyssen & Co. due to the intransigence of the Machine Company directors, Härle and Roser. Their behavior sparked a major confrontation with salaried employees in the difficult month of February 1919.[68] Their lack of tact helped to forge a unity among blue-collar workers and white-collar employees in both the Rolling Mills and the Machine Company—each of which had followed separate tracks up to this point. Härle and Roser abruptly fired an engineer of the salaried employee committee named Schlusen. The head of the employee committee of the Rolling Mills, Heinrich Gröschner, threatened a citywide strike of salaried employees if they did not reinstate Schlusen. The timing of the strike coincided with the workers' February general strike, and the Machine Company had to capitulate.[69]

Gröschner thought their victory to be a major turning point because they had now gained the initiative. Salaried employees could pressure management just as much as workers could.[70] The resulting April 4, 1919 agreement represented the first time that the two Thyssen & Co. divisions' directors and employees' committees signed a joint agreement on standard minimum salary levels. A number of regional salaried employee associations also signed the agreement. The April 1919 agreement also marked a turning point in labor relations because by the end of the year white-collar and blue-collar employees for the whole Thyssen-Konzern managed to link their demands. Any rejection of their united demands could shut the whole Konzern down, which Becker noted, changed everything.[71]

Labor forced Thyssen's management to standardize its personnel policies to a greater degree than ever before. Gröschner consistently linked the demands of the Rolling Mills salaried employees with those of the Machine Company because the Machine Company employees had the highest salaries in the area. Just as in the July 1918 sitdown strike, the aloof obstinancy displayed by the Machine Company's directors helped forge broader collective actions among workers and salaried employees.

Worker and employee committees did exert a greater influence on Thyssen & Co. personnel policies, though with some perverse effects. The Rolling Mills employee committee's first demand required the immediate reinstatement of former employees who had fought in the war. Their second demand asked Thyssen & Co. to fire all female employees. In the important April 1919 agreement, Thyssen & Co. conceded the committees' demand not to discharge any male employee as long as any female employee still worked in the same office (provided she was not dependent on the job for her livelihood). Judging from the numerous recommendations (and the fact that women asked for recommendations meant that they wanted or needed to be employed somewhere), Thyssen & Co. let some women go very "reluctantly." Becker expected that only three or four women salaried employees would remain in the Rolling Mills by May. In May 1919, the employee committee tried to have these few remaining women laid off as "double-earners."[72]

The revolution took lower to middle-level salary questions, and to a lesser extent, wages, out of the hands of individual companies and placed them into an institutionalized system of regional collective bargaining. For white-collar employees, the most important forum was the regional "working council" located in Düsseldorf, which began to set minimum salary rates for certain classes of white-collar employees. Although Thyssen still refused formally to join the Northwest Group, he had to tacitly match salary levels inside the region, a process Plumpe neatly termed "crypto-collective bargaining." This collective bargaining process mediated industrial relations of white-collar employees for as long as Weimar lasted.[73]

Wages remained subject to a more difficult bargaining process, which brought in the final player in this dance among labor, industry, and regional bargaining associations—the Prussian state. The government now took on an intermediary role analogous to that of the military during the war. Carl Severing, the Reichskommissar for the Prussian government, adjudicated disputes when negotiations between workers and management threatened to stall at critical junctures. At a formal conference on the matter, Ruhr employers agreed to abide by the "content" of the arbitration agreements, but not to step on letter beyond it since they had no "legal" obligation to do so.[74]

Due to the chaotic situation, rising inflation, and wage and salary rivalries among firms, however, these agreements frequently lasted only a few months before another round of negotiations began again. The collective bargaining process was often too slow to react to changes on the ground or too normed to take into account individual factories or workers. As labor-management disputes heated up, the state stepped in to arbitrate, but this dynamic had disastrous long-term results for the Weimar Republic. From the point of view of industrialists, wages no longer corresponded to market rates or to individual performance but to politics. The constant "arbitrary" interventions in internal firm matters by the Prussian (SPD-led) state not only helped to politicize individual collective bargaining agreements, but also helped to delegitimize the state itself. For this reason, industrialists often called the Weimar Republic a "union state." (The bad results of compulsory arbitration in Weimar explain why the Basic Law of the Federal Republic of Germany expressly forbids compulsory intervention.)

The accusations that Weimar was a "union state" were entirely misleading. The actions of Severing against Ruhr miners in the winter of 1919–1920 are the best counter-example. The coal supply remained one of the major bottlenecks throughout the economy. Miners' working and living conditions after five years of war, revolution, blockade, and rising prices, left them undernourished, eating moldy bread, wearing tattered curtains for clothing.[75] In October 1919, trade unions and mine-owners had signed the first regional, uniform wage and work condition agreement. But by the end of the year, miners demanded a six-hour shift and higher wages. Driven by hunger and political determination, they carried their demands forward. Backed firmly by Severing, mineowners blocked any attempt to introduce the six-hour day in spite of a February 1, 1920, deadline for strike action.

On January 11, 1920 Friedrich Thyssen miners (formerly GDK Hamborn miners) again took matters into their own hands and launched a campaign of direct action by storming the Hamborn town hall. Severing called in von Watter's troops, who arrested over 350 people. A few days later, Severing announced that he would use "all means at his disposal, even against the trade unions themselves" to halt strikes. At the same time, Severing sweetened the deal by increasing wages, overtime pay, extra rations and clothing, and vacations for miners, and for mine owners raising coal prices and adding an extra shift of work.[76] Naturally, industrialists grumbled. Throughout the troubled years of inflation, the government followed this general pattern of mediation. It firmly blocked "blackmail" attempts by radical workers to overturn the existing economic order, but allowed wage or work-oriented concessions to blunt worker anger and improve their living standards.

Such actions might have brought some semblance of peace to the Ruhr, if not for a virulent, resurgent right-wing movement. Backed tacitly by General Ludendorff and overtly by General Lüttwitz (who commanded rabidly nationalistic Freikorps battalions), Wolfgang Kapp of the "German Fatherland Party" launched a counterrevolutionary putsch on March 13 from Berlin. For the first time, some Freikorps units wore swastikas emblazoned on German military helmets. (The government's attempts to disband the Freikorps in line with the requirements of the Versailles Treaty sparked the coup.) After regular army troops refused to fire on their brothers-in-arms, the government again had to flee Berlin, first to Dresden, then to Stuttgart. The SPD and trade unions called an immediate nationwide general strike, which found impressive resonance in all parts of Germany except Bavaria.

At Thyssen & Co., workers and white-collar employees went on strike. The local *Freikorps Schulz* battalion supported the putsch and raised the black-white-red colors of the former empire. Thyssen & Co. shut down. The massive national response against the putsch attempt isolated Kapp and his band of followers. By March 17, the coup had fizzled out.[77]

The Kapp putsch revitalized radical left-wing movements, especially in the Ruhr. The general strike continued well on after the collapse of the attempted coup. Once again, the Ruhr plunged into violence, a true civil war. In the Ruhr, spontaneous "Red Army" units formed. Heavily armed, they disarmed local police and civilian forces; they even beat back *Freikorps* units.

The "Red Army" achieved a spectacular quick takeover of the Ruhr, with violence particularly strong around Thyssen firms. Schulz and von Watter ordered their demoralized troops to evacuate all Ruhr cities and collect themselves outside of Dinslaken before they became encircled. The line of retreat for the Mülheim-based *Freikorps Schulz* troops took them through Hamborn, a "Red Army" stronghold. Street-fighting broke out there. When they turned south to circumvent Hamborn, they met sporadic resistance in Alsum, the site of Thyssen's harbor. Schulz's battalion answered with a spray of machine gun fire into workers' houses until "deathly silence" reigned (Schulz's own words). Schulz sent a company with an artillery piece into Hamborn from the north, but armed workers killed or wounded the entire company. Another Freikorps regiment fought its way through Hamborn-Bruckhausen from house to house, street to street, with bullets and mortar fire coming from all directions. The fighting damaged Thyssen's administrative building. Carl Rabes remembered how a solid, oak door was all that stood between him and an angry crowd who attempted to set his house on fire during the street fighting. Both corps eventually escaped Hamborn with remarkably few deaths (about thirty), many fewer casualties than suffered by workers.

The troops retreated to an area just outside of Dinslaken, where another Thyssen colliery, the Gewerkschaft Lohberg, lay. By the evening of March 21, in the open fields outside Dinslaken, both sides set up artillery positions, trenches, foxholes, and machine-gun nests as if they were fighting the last war. Artillery shots rained into Dinslaken and Lohberg. In the midst of this fighting, "Red Army" workers killed one of Thyssen's managing directors, Heinrich Sebold. They found his body in the woods, shot execution style. Although the murder of a leading director was exceptional, his murder struck holy terror into management. Sebold's death proved the danger of the "red terror."

Organized trade-union representatives (Carl Legien) tried to end the Ruhr uprising by promising wider ranging changes if workers disarmed, including the socialization of the coal and potash industry. Such appeals did not prove to be effective. Another general strike hit the Ruhr at the end of the month. All Thyssen's miners voted to join the strike. With little coal reserves left, Thyssen pleaded that these strikes would shut down the rest of the firm, throwing 50,000 workers and their families out of work and bread. Without coal to make electricity, the mines would flood.[78] Desperate, all Thyssen and other industrialists could do was implore the SPD-led coalition government for help.

The national government then sent into the Ruhr regular army troops—reinforced once again by the Freikorps (some of whom had just supported the Kapp putsch). Throughout April 1920, vicious fighting took place between the "Red Army" and "White" government troops before order was restored. The ultimate loser in all this violence was Weimar democracy. In national elections (June 1920), the moderate Weimar coalition no longer carried a majority of German voters. In the Ruhr, the SPD, which had done so much to restore order, lost credibility with workers and gained little favor with industrialists and those with whom it compromised.[79] From this point on, supporters of Weimar democracy had to find coalition partners with those who wanted to end it or who merely tolerated it.

The Factory Council of Thyssen & Co.

Thyssen and his managers could only react to these national events. Likewise, Parliament's ratification of the Factory Council Law on February 4, 1920, which resulted in mass demonstrations and over forty deaths, seemed to come from above as yet another "political intervention" and did little to dispel fears that labor dominated Weimar. While industrialists had always viewed committees as an emergency wartime measure, the Factory Council Law made them permanent features in business enterprises. The new Weimar constitution, itself ratified only a few months earlier in August 1919, anchored some sort of institutional representative for workers and salaried employees in German companies. The Factory Council Law, however, set the boundaries for this new negotiating forum. This now distinctive part of German industrial relations introduced a "factory council" and "salaried employee council" into firms of over twenty people. A smaller factory council committee of five people negotiated directly with senior management. By law, management had to consult the councils regarding decisions affecting labor, especially discharges, and to disclose company financial statements to the committee. A subsequent revision in February 1922 permitted workers to send two representatives to supervisory boards of joint-stock, limited liability, or mining companies, but they had no voting rights.[80] We can only speculate as to the choice words Thyssen had for these laws.

The Factory Council Law passed in spite of great resistance from employers and those on the radical left, many of whom felt it "ridiculously distorted," the goal of direct industrial democracy (syndicalism).[81] Rhetorically, factory councils did evoke revolutionary councils or soviets, which the Social Democrats had helped disarm. However, both employers and moderate Social Democrats approached the new factory councils warily, because they felt they tended to undermine the system of collective bargaining through "working associations." Union leaders also felt that factory councils gave an institutional voice to radical workers inside the company. In fact, the actual wording of the law made factory councils responsible for the overall health of the firm and improving its productivity, which stemmed from a longer tradition of social reform and moderate Catholic unionism.

The reaction of Thyssen management to the Factory Council Law epitomized employer hostility. Unlike Bayer (IG Farben), Thyssen managers wasted no time minimizing its potential influence.[82] Assuming the worst, at the end of October 1919—years before the Council act regarding supervisory boards actually passed—Härle suggested altering the Machine Company's corporate charter: "The draft has been made necessary due to the proposed Factory Council Law. Its objective is to withdraw all rights from the responsibility of the supervisory board, and therefore from the responsibility of the factory council, which can possibly be withdrawn according to the law."[83] Härle altered the formal decision-making script of the company by literally pasting a strip of paper over any phrase that endowed ultimate decisions in the supervisory board with a new phrase that all final decisions rested exclusively with the chairman of the board, i.e., August Thyssen.[84] Paradoxically, the Factory Council Law served to centralize managerial decision-making (formally, but not in reality) back into Thyssen's individual person. In December, the AGHütt also changed its statutes in accordance with Härle's suggestions. Thyssen works' directors formulated a unified position: "As regards the factory council law it was unanimously agreed not to overstep the legal obligations in any way."[85] Their position conformed to the stance laid out by the Northwest Group, which had outlined a common response.

Typically for Weimar, the first elections and first meeting of the Thyssen & Co. factory council came at the worst possible time, on March 25–26—just at the end of the Kapp putsch, in the midst of the general strike and Ruhr civil war.[86] The first two chairs of the factory council, Hermann Abrath and Theodore Lohschelder, were members of the radical Free Unions. The chair of the salaried employee council of the Rolling Mills was Heinrich Gröschner. (We do not have the protocols of the factory council for the Machine Company.)

The first meeting of the new factory council did not begin auspiciously. Directors Ernst Becker and Carl Wallmann questioned the legality of the factory council elections. Abrath retorted that they were the official representatives of workers and salaried employees; they would have to deal with them whether they liked it or not. The Factory Council Law did not exist for the workers anymore because the March revolution had voided it and the workers in the firm did not agree with it anyway. Abrath then announced that the goal of the factory council was to socialize the firm and turn it over to the public good.[87]

The Rolling Mills director, Ernst Becker, also hardly distinguished himself. Once the employees committee wanted to know if Becker would show up at the next scheduled meeting so they could avoid being present as "statues." Becker often allowed Härle or Roser to negotiate for him—not a good idea. Becker also did not inform other directors of the committees' requests. Becker sometimes did not sign an agreement that Härle or Roser of the Machine Company negotiated, which left a question mark over whether or not the agreement applied to the Rolling Mills.[88] After June 1920, however, Becker moved to Thyssenhandel Duisburg.

After this decidedly inauspicious beginning, the factory council took a surprising turn. The new director of the Rolling Mills, Carl Wallmann, altered the tone. Tension dropped markedly once Wallmann took over as the main negotiator for Thyssen & Co., sometimes for both the Rolling Mills and the Machine Company. Wallmann is a good example of how individual managers can make a positive difference. Born just outside of Mülheim, Wallmann remained deeply committed to his community throughout his life. He joined Thyssen & Co. in 1895 after finishing his studies at the Technical University in Berlin. In 1908, Thyssen named him chief of the plate department; in 1915 he advanced as second-in-command to Becker. When Thyssen & Co. merged into the VSt in 1926, Wallmann remained director of the Mülheim plant until 1939.

Wallmann belonged to Thyssen's inner circle. It was largely due to Wallmann that Thyssen & Co. remained at the cutting edge of technical change throughout his tenure. Wallmann's proximity to Thyssen allowed him to lobby successfully for continuing investment in Mülheim. His specialty remained plates and boilers, which provided the base for a slew of specialty goods. He promoted the use of laboratory techniques to improve their quality. He became one of the most influential figures in engineering associations and headed numerous technical commissions and cartels. Although he had an experimental spirit in terms of technology, Wallmann was a cautious man in commercial matters. He preferred to work through cartels and usually urged a conservative course.

Wallmann's even keel in his professional and personal life was a consistent character trait. Wallmann was remembered as having a "serious, sensitive nature" that could turn melancholy if troubled. He was genuinely respected in business and community life. Voted chairman of the Mülheim emergency aid commission during the depression, he was one of the few people that diverse interests in Mülheim, including the Communists, could agree upon to head the commission. A devout Catholic, he appealed to the consciences of well-off citizens to do more for the poor. The commission itself operated its many soup kitchens and charitable works almost as a business operation without regard for class, religion, or political opinion.[89]

After the initial poses and confrontation, the Thyssen & Co. factory council developed into a highly pragmatic forum, which took on a firmly contested but cooperative venture. Unlike Becker, who treated employees with disdain, and Härle and Roser, who alternated between high-handed contempt and collapse, Wallmann ensured that difficult negotiations moved steadily along. Similar to Carl Duisberg of Bayer, Wallmann acknowledged that times had changed.[90] He recognized the new forum, but required it to work for the good of the firm and not insist on rights beyond its legal status. Wallmann was no pushover and represented employer interests, but negotiations did not stall in petty bickering either.

At the second meeting, Abrath offered the chair of the factory council's conference, which was legally entitled to workers, to Wallmann: "for it appears to us that the person of Herr Director Wallmann can ensure to be a fair *(unparteiisch)* chairman." (Not surprisingly, a worker representative remained chair at the Machine Company.) This gesture owed much to Abrath, who wanted the factory council to "achieve practical work."[91] Abrath stressed, however, that the workers did not give up their legal right to chair the council. When Becker appeared at the next meeting for the last time, Abrath openly announced to Becker that he had given the chair to Wallmann, the person, not the firm.[92]

The factory council inserted a communication forum inside the business firm that helped create greater transparency and consistency for *both* labor and management. For instance, Abrath complained that the Machine Company was "raping" the workers of the Rolling Mills of food. The Rolling Mills management agreed with the factory council that it was a considerable mistake to entrust the purchasing department of the Machine Company (Härle) with their food supplies. The Rolling Mills then set up its own supply commission in the purchasing office. The factory council also ensured that the Rolling Mills paid the same amount of child support as the Machine Company.[93]

In a less successful example, the factory council made suggestions on how to better organize the personnel offices. They felt shortchanged because the management of the Rolling Mills *and* the Machine Company would declare themselves not responsible for certain matters because of confusing lines of authority. They objected to a reorganization of the Rolling Mills, which would have subordinated its wage office, the calculation office, bookkeeping, and purchasing offices to the Machine Company division—to Härle. By 1922, Härle formally united these offices, but kept two office supervisors for both divisions. Thus, the factory council helped perceive organizational difficulties not only regarding labor, but also for management.[94]

The factory council could also act as a mild disciplinary instance against labor.[95] In one case, the municipal government gave the Rolling Mills permission to work on a holiday, so Wallmann wanted to clarify the situation first with the factory council—a remarkable change in itself from prewar years when directors would have decided it unilaterally. Wallmann wanted some departments to shut down but keep others open. The factory council, however, wanted the whole firm to stay open. Management compromised by keeping the entire factory open during weekday holidays, but would not pay the Sunday premium. After agreeing to this plan, it became the duty of the factory council to head off any objections by the workforce.[96] Management relied on the factory councils' influence to persuade the workforce to conform to these measures.

As required by law, the factory council participated in the creation of new company statutes, accomplished in February 1921 for the Rolling Mills division.[97] In contrast to earlier versions of the statutes, which represented an ideal order exclusively from the point of view of the entrepreneur, these new statutes contained clauses concerning freedom of association and an outline of the duties of supervisors, not just subordinates. Superiors, for instance, had to treat workers in "quiet and just" tones; criticism had to be professional, not "injurious." These reforms acted at least as symbolic limitations on the imperious attitudes of many German managers.

The degree of constructive cooperation created by the factory council was often surprising. In May 1921, the factory council met with directors to discuss a brief shutdown of the plate mill. The factory council found it unnecessary; they felt other work could be found, especially in repair and maintenance work. Wallmann asserted that the firm had been "very loyal" because of its relatively low level of "vacation shifts." The salaried employees' representative, Gröschner, objected that management had not informed them about the firm's commercial condition; they were unaware that the firm did not have enough sales orders. Gröschner wanted an overview of incoming sales orders and to know whether Thyssen & Co. would continue to operate in spite of losses. The commercial director of the plate mill, Heinrich

Gilles, replied that the Rolling Mills were already operating in the red. Strikes in England and Scandinavia had cancelled larger orders. Given Gilles' portrayal of the situation, one of the *factory council members* suggested that they temporarily layoff one-quarter of the workers from parts of the plate mill, but employ the rest in miscellaneous repair and cleaning work. The technical director of the plate mill argued that there was little outstanding repair work to accomplish. The discussion then turned on the question how many workers to lay off. They eventually agreed to give one-half of the workers leave, but to employ the other half full-time.[98] Neither side achieved what they wanted, but they did come to an agreement. Negotiations were not easy and could become testy, but neither did they collapse or reflect worker powerlessness. The councils acted as a moderating forum for both sides.

As inflation dominated the years 1920–1923, the factory council meetings often reflected the difficulties that workers and employees had in managing the mundane matters of everyday life. The factory council facilitated the process of muddling through. One could say that in rough proportion to the devaluation of the currency, the more discussions turned into debates about natural goods such as clothing, shoes, potatoes, foodstuffs, better rations in the canteens, bicycles, cheese, or cigars. Because the accelerating inflation quickly negated wage and salary agreements, often within days of signing them, factory council meetings were filled with detailed wage and salary rate discussions, disputes over work breaks, and a host of minor adjustments.

Convening long before the currency astronomically devalued, a September 1920 meeting epitomizes the eminently "practical work" of the factory council. In this brief session, the factory council arranged, with management, installment payments for new suits, a new storage room for potatoes, sales of cheese, the purchase of shoes, rewriting the company statutes, the possible purchase of reasonably priced underwear, the appropriate price for the evening meal in the boarding house, and the purchase of a couple of thousand cheap cigars. (It was apparently very important that the Rolling Mills match the Machine Company's purchase of cigars by buying three different types of cigars, all of which would not be more expensive than 0.98 marks.)[99] At another meeting in November 1922, they discussed a range of issues, from accident protection to the growing problem of theft, to the proper departure times of local trains.[100] As silly or petty as these matters sound, Thyssen & Co. had to provide workers with basic necessities because it had deeper pockets and better connections. The largest industrial firms had great advantages in procuring goods. Such provisioning ensured that production continued as well as possible, promoted some form of willingness to work for the company, and helped legitimize its existence. Moreover, with the accelerating collapse of basic public functions, the tasks of management changed dramatically—so much so that Nowack, the head engineer of the strip-steel mill, had to travel to Cologne to arrange the purchase of underwear for his workers. The ATH even printed its own scrip and ration coupons.[101] By the end of 1923, when normal currency meant nothing, the firm had become much more of a social-welfare agency than a capitalist enterprise.

If all these unending postwar difficulties were not enough, on January 11, 1923, the French and Belgians invaded the Ruhr, beginning the so-called "Ruhr Struggle" *(Ruhrkampf)*. The French intervened on the pretext that the Germans were not delivering enough coal and steel goods (so-called "productive guarantees") in lieu of monetary reparations. Workers and industrialists agreed on very little, but they united in an emotional and patriotic campaign of passive resistance. The German government subsidized the passive resistance, whose ultimate effect was the complete destruction of its own money.

The height of cooperation between Thyssen & Co. management and its factory council occurred during the Ruhr occupation. The factory council played a key role in helping management arrange provisions and organizing passive resistance. At Krupp, occupying troops killed a number of workers.[102] On the initiative of the factory council, a meeting was called with management to discuss options for confronting the French if they decided to confiscate property at Thyssen & Co. Labor and management jointly organized their initial response to avoid similar incidents.

Worsening living conditions, combined with greater agitation by the Communist party, led to a series of wildcat strikes in April, May, and August 1923. In May, 300,000 workers went on strike in the western Ruhr, which shut down all Thyssen's plants. In the middle of June, occupying troops tore up critical railway lines, effectively dividing Thyssen plants from one another. In July, French troops occupied the ATH in Bruckhausen, forcing the ATH to shut down until August. In September, French troops physically hauled away remaining coal and steel reserves, including locomotives, railway cars, and any other equipment and tools that they could carry. The French even took the water spigots from the ATH headquarters, causing water damage. They completely destroyed the ATH chemical laboratory. In October, the ATH entirely shut down, Thyssen & Co. soon thereafter.

The factory council inside Thyssen & Co. ended up creating a pragmatic forum for managing the firm during crisis—in spite of huge differences in ideological positions. Once calls for immediate socialization of heavy industry quieted, the factory council became a relatively successful organizational forum for coping with the sociopolitical nightmare of the postwar period. If not for the "practical work" of the factory council, the tribulations of the postwar world would have upset production even more. The factory council forum acted as a moderating instance, smoothing extreme positions on both sides. It also helped Thyssen management earn a modicum of legitimacy in the eyes of the workforce.

But Thyssen and other employers chose not to build upon the council's potential cleansing effects of what has nicely been called "economies of atmosphere."[103] Unlike Bayer, where radical workers provoked a lockout, steel industrialists answered this pragmatism at the company level with their own lockout, in a concerted effort on the corporatist and political level to void most of labor's claims on them since the revolution—including and especially the despised eight-hour day.

The End of the Eight-Hour Day

If the Versailles Treaty struck Thyssen and many other Germans as a *Diktat,* then the French invasion of the Ruhr forced industrialists to face squarely that they had lost the war. They, too, now followed their own policy of "fulfillment," a policy that they ridiculed when the national government followed it. Stinnes spearheaded negotiations with the French General Degoutte of MICUM *(Mission Interalliée des Mines et des Usines),* a French engineering commission in charge of securing German reparations. Although industrialists were in denial, MICUM negotiations made them just as complicit in a second sort of German surrender as any politician who signed at Versailles. (Not surprisingly, Stinnes reacted vehemently against this analogy when portions of the public called him a traitor.)

Industry representatives made painfully clear that the first MICUM agreement, signed on November 23, 1923, represented a private contract, not a treaty. The MICUM agreement regulated reparation payments in coal, coke, and steel to France and protected German industry from arbitrary confiscations. It allowed them to start production again on harsh but regular, calculable terms. These private negotiations defused tensions with the French.[104] Moreover, the Weimar government promised Ruhr industry financial compensation for losses incurred during the Ruhr occupation and for MICUM-based payments.

When workers, factory councils, and unions argued to restart operations, employers rebuffed them. Ruhr steel industrialists first wanted the political situation clarified and reparation payments, in hard goods or taxes, placed on a calculable basis before they would begin production again. They instrumentalized the Ruhr crisis as a means of ridding themselves of the detested eight-hour day and other regulations in place since the end of the war. Thyssen exemplified this attitude:

> But we have to ascribe a good portion of fault to ourselves. The greatest misfortune that the Revolution could bring to us has been the undifferentiated introduction of the eight-hour day for all workers and salaried employees. Because of it, work performance and thus production was severely reduced . . . [after losing the war, the fleet, colonies, and all overseas assets]. . . .
>
> And now the German people, who in peacetime had to work ten hours a day in order to feed themselves, believe that they only need to work eight hours and that they can live better than before the war . . .
>
> It is now a matter of being or not being. The majority of the people—if necessary against their own fierce resistance—must be protected from total ruin.[105]

Enraging workers and trade unions across the country, industrialists even tried to urge the French occupiers to abrogate the eight-hour day, thus circumventing German laws.

The attack on the eight-hour day epitomized German industrialists' inability to view the eight-hour day as other than a political intervention in their private affairs. Irmgard Steinisch made the important point that ideologically American and German industrialists did not differ much from one another in their views of the eight-hour day. American steelmen hardly embraced the eight-hour day, even in good economic conditions, but in Germany the eight-hour day was introduced at the worst possible time, in the worst possible circumstances, and in the worst possible way. The American debate eventually came to be dominated by the code word "efficiency" (not least due to Herbert Hoover's national efficiency commission). The German debate, however, remained wrapped up in questions of political order, the loss of the war, a government led by Social Democrats, a deep shift in industrial relations, and the expansion of the social welfare state. The demobilization and inflation then aided and abetted industrialists by negating any chance of distinguishing questions of economic efficiency from those of political economy. Because of postwar disruptions, no one could possibly demonstrate that the eight-hour day was or was not more productive than ten hours. Finally, while the American steel industry introduced the eight-hour day gradually, Weimar introduced a whole range of progressive measures at one political stroke. The eight-hour day played a critical symbolic role, representing all these gains for labor after the democratic revolution. It acted as the cornerstone of the ZAG agreement between industry and organized labor; the ZAG, in turn, was one of the critical sociopolitical compromises establishing the Weimar Republic.[106]

At the end of October 1923, Labor Minister Heinrich Brauns delivered an important arbitration decree. But separatist uprisings in the Rhineland, attempted Communist takeovers in Hamburg and Saxony, Adolf Hitler's failed beer-hall putsch in Bavaria, and the introduction of the new currency, the Rentenmark, drowned out realization of its importance. The decree allowed the Labor Ministry to appoint state arbitrators and issue compulsory arbitration agreements if employers and labor could not agree through collective bargaining. Brauns, a long-time supporter of the Christian trade-union wing of the Catholic Center Party, maneuvered the Labor Ministry into a decisive position to mandate working hours and work legislation after postwar demobilization decrees dissolved. While Brauns advocated stronger social legislation and collective bargaining through trade unions, he also felt that wage increases needed to be tied to increases in productivity. He realized that the national government planned to let the hours-of-work decree of November 23, 1918, lapse on November 17, 1923, leaving industrialists in all sectors free to discharge workers unilaterally and to renegotiate workers' contracts on their terms. One month after the 1918 hours-of-work decree expired, Brauns ordered a new hours-of-work decree on December 21, 1923. The decree allowed the ten-hour day to be introduced in most factories and a twelve-hour day in continuously operating plants, but only if industrialists, after giving three-day notice, initiated a collective bargaining process or appealed to the appropriate authority in the Labor Ministry to permit exceptions to the eight-hour day.[107] In effect, Brauns sacrificed the eight-hour day in practice (not in principle) in order to reinforce the role of trade unions and the Labor Ministry in collective bargaining.

Thyssen management jumped at the opportunity presented when the demobilization decrees lapsed. Thyssen & Co. Rolling Mills, for instance, never employed as many workers or had such low productivity as it had in September 1923. Along with other Thyssen firms, Thyssen & Co. reduced working hours at the beginning of October. After a Konzern-wide board of directors meeting in Bruckhausen at the end of October, Thyssen unilaterally shut down all of his firms. Roser of the Machine Company admitted to the employees committee that this was not entirely legal, but they were living in a situation where little legality prevailed. The French had just confiscated most of their inventories, gold reserves, and anything else they could carry away; there was little else Thyssen & Co. could do.[108]

On the advice of his managers, Thyssen used these plant shutdowns as an excuse for mass layoffs. At the end of November, the Rolling Mills officially employed only 158 workers, out of 7,100 workers employed in September. Similarly, the Machine Company reduced its workforce from 6,052 to 153 workers. After the District President of Düsseldorf agreed that no labor law remained after the demobilization laws expired, Thyssen & Co. began hiring back employees in early December. However, they had to sign a contract waiving any claims they had had from their previous engagement with the firm. In contrast to his post-World War II approach to industrial relations, when he advocated codetermination, a young, ambitious Heinrich Dinkelbach organized the administrative aspects of the lockout and reinstatement of workers at Thyssen & Co. Dinkelbach caused a row among its managing directors because he had signed the hiring regulations himself without the signatures of both divisions' directors; he had no power of attorney. Thyssen & Co. executives found this highly "impertinent."[109]

In effect, Thyssen & Co. (and other Ruhr firms) initiated a type of preemptive lockout—in expectation of the new hours-of-work de-cree—voiding most claims on them. Thyssen & Co. made it clear to workers and salaried employees that the layoffs, justified by French confiscations, were indeed mass firings. The lockout generated quite a bit of legal fallout, which was not resolved completely until a year later. The factory council immediately sued Thyssen & Co. for lost earnings and actually won their case. But their success was as short-lived as the value of a mark. The court sided with Thyssen & Co. on grounds of an emergency situation, but it also forced Thyssen & Co. to pay out one-time compensation to workers, distributed through unions. In ex-change, workers dropped all outstanding suits.[110]

On November 30, 1923—three weeks before Brauns' new hours-of-work decree went into effect—Thyssen & Co. issued new company stat-utes applicable to both divisions (an exception), instituting the twelve-hour shift, that is, ten hours of work with breaks amounting to two hours a day. Cynically, Roser and Härle announced the new labor stat-utes "in order to give the workforce the opportunity to go back to work as quickly as possible." They needed to hold new elections to the fac-tory council; the trade inspection could approve of it at a later date.[111] In principle, they reestablished the top-down management methods of the Imperial period. Brauns' hours-of-work decree merely reaffirmed the Thyssen management *fait accompli*. After the decree went into ef-fect, Thyssen & Co. announced via circular new shift hours, which they based explicitly on the Berlin agreement between the Labor Ministry and industry associations.[112] Production would begin again after Janu-ary 2, 1924.

In this way, Thyssen & Co. managed to restart with a relatively clean slate and, at the same time, eliminate the eight-hour day even before laws changed. The unilateral willfulness exhibited by Thyssen and his managers is astounding. Such speed, initiative, and foresight—leitmo-tifs of Thyssen corporate culture—made for great business practice, but miserable political behavior.

Employers' successful rollback of the eight-hour day signalled the end of labor's revolutionary momentum. The last quarter of 1923 marks the end of the postwar period, although negotiations contin-ued to be hammered out throughout 1924 in the courts, in the gov-ernment cabinet, in government ministries, in the Reichstag, and among international authorities attempting to regulate the sticky reparations question. In May 1924, 300,000 bitter Ruhr miners went out on strike in defense of the seven-hour (underground) shift. Thyssen mines shut down and discharged all of their workers. Labor Minister Brauns stepped in and decreed the eight-hour day for miners working underground; nine hours for those working above ground. Despite this rearguard action on the part of miners, labor remained on the defensive for the remaining life of the Weimar Republic. Wages during the initial stabilization period after the hyperinflation period tended to be set well below prewar levels, often 20–50%. This helped stave off further inflation, but workers felt they bore a disproportionate share of the costs of war and inflation, especially as foodstuffs and manufactured goods prices could freely adjust to market prices.

The loss of influence of trade unions and the power of Social Democrats in the contemporary political constellation left workers with little choice but to rely on binding arbitration through Labor Ministry boards to protect them against resurgent employer demands. Despite the loss of the eight-hour day, employers still had to activate a contentious collective bargaining process that kept them from acting entirely unilaterally. Brauns' defense of trade unions and arbitration continued to frustrate employers. Unions remained involved in the bargaining process, even if they resorted to binding arbitration. In the short term, binding arbitration helped to stabilize production operations and inflation—no small achievement. But in the long term, one of the casualties of the reliance on binding arbitration through the state rather than collective bargaining through associations was the collapse of the ZAG agreement. The ZAG agreement presumed some degree of civility, mutual dependency—even if from sheer desperation—some form of willingness to compromise. Led by Ruhr heavy industry, employers gradually dissociated themselves from the process, hollowing out the forum. The final blow came in 1924, when Socialist union representatives walked out of the negotiating forum. In the medium term, Labor Ministry's binding arbitration allowed both sides to take irresponsible positions, until the state stepped in to decree new wage levels or work rules. Now employers and labor could feel dissatisfied with the results—and with the government. Wage levels thus became more "political;" from the industrialists' point of view, more arbitrary and "forced" (*Zwangsschlichtung*) than ever before. Employers would launch an all-out assault on binding arbitration in the great Ruhr Iron Lockout of 1928.

At the broadest level, we see a pattern of Weimar politics. The moderate left was (too) willing to work with reactionary elements like the *Freikorps,* often at the cost of their own grassroots support, while conservative industrialists could not bring themselves to work even with the moderate Social Democrats, whose actions saved them at decisive points. The ultimate casualty was Weimar democracy. Yet on the micropolitical, company level and on the corporatist level of labor unions and employer associations, both sides had a range of options—a space for constructive collaboration—even in the most radical times. Epitomized by Thyssen, Ruhr industrialists showed little inclination to build upon the pragmatism shown by some factory councils or the willingness of the trade unions and Social Democrats to compromise, cooperation that foreshadowed the industrial relations success of the post-1945 "German Model."

Just as the Council movement was far more stabilizing in practice than perceived by contemporaries, the Thyssen & Co. Rolling Mill factory council proved to be more moderate and pragmatic than expected. Far from being disruptive to Thyssen & Co. company practices, the factory council tended to allow the firm to react more quickly, flexibly, and in a more coordinated fashion to the myriad crises of the postwar period—if company directors tolerated it. At the Machine Company, the poor diplomacy of its directors radicalized its workforce, who already needed little excuse to strike. Once political posturing on both sides ended, "practical work" characterized relations between the factory council and Thyssen & Co. management in mid-1920–1923. In the difficult inflation years, the Thyssen & Co. factory council acted as a critical communication channel, helping the company maintain itself. This turn of events had little to do with August Thyssen—one of the most hardline of industrialists—but with Thyssen & Co.'s director, Wallmann, and the labor leader, Abrath. In part, this cooperation was related to the defeat of extra-legal, direct action in the Ruhr, but clearly Wallmann and Abrath steered the council toward "practical work." Individual figures below the entrepreneur played crucial roles in determining labor relations inside the firm.

One also need not have liked the factory councils to make them work for the firm. By accepting, or merely tolerating, the forum and working within the boundaries of the law, Wallmann helped to make it work for management, Abrath for workers. At Thyssen & Co., managers chose not to learn from the experience; at Bayer radical workers chose not to learn; and at the GDK Hamborn both managers and workers chose not to learn. Indeed, in mining firms, the authoritarian tradition and the structure of mining organization combined with the violent experience of the revolution to create a "pathological learning process," which led to a pitiful paralysis of the factory council. This process "taught" both sides that this communication forum could never work.[113] Ironically, both Thyssen and Stinnes had found workers' committees valuable as early as 1908 in their Saar-Mosel joint venture in Lorraine.[114]

The acceptance and effectiveness of factory councils varied from industry to industry, from firm to firm, from director to director, and from time to time. Siemens used factory councils to improve internal communication. By 1931, the director of the social-political office of IG Farben in Leverkusen (Bayer) could actually find a few managers who enthusiastically endorsed the forum, although relations with the factory council deteriorated markedly after 1920. The GBAG stalled any type of factory council initiative through "petty legalisms." At the neighboring Friedrich Wilhelm-Hütte in Mülheim, directors urged its elimination because it cost too much.[115]

The dual-track negotiations of Thyssen & Co. Rolling Mills and the Machine Company isolates crucial variables of internal organization, political ideology, and participants' openness to learning. Although the Machine Company was more profitable and had more complex technical operations, it operated with a centralized, functional structure that put labor negotiations in the hands of Härle. The Rolling Mills had highly integrated but simpler production operations, and worked on a departmental, decentralized basis, diffusing collective action and personalizing negotiations. Moreover, the contrast between the personalities of Wallmann and Härle could not be starker. No amount of moderation by labor would have ever convinced Härle, Becker, or Thyssen of the efficacy of the factory council.

The experience at Bayer provides another useful contrast, since Carl Duisberg, unlike Thyssen, proved willing to work with the factory council. Plumpe attributed this cooperation to Duisberg's leadership, Bayer's organizational flexibility, the technical complexity of its work operations, and its historical attention to social policy issues. For these reasons, Bayer experienced a considerable degree of cooperation between 1916 and 1920, until "politicized workers lightly played away" the potential of the new forum.[116] Cooperation with the factory council collapsed after early 1921, while the Thyssen & Co. Rolling Mill factory council became a fairly effective forum after June 1920.

Daimler's experience paralleled that of the Machine Company. Daimler also had great difficulties because of its complete conversion to wartime, serial production. Its peacetime production, too, rested on highly complex, technically differentiated production processes. It also paid some of the highest wages in its area and accrued massive wartime windfall profits, yet suffered from intense labor disputes. In June 1918, workers struck at Daimler, remarkably similar in process and timing to the July strike at the Machine Company. At Daimler, blatant financial cheating seriously discredited management, creating a national scandal. The army even had to place it under military supervision. The scandal accelerated the loss of trust by labor and undermined the legitimacy of management. As at Thyssen & Co., the revolution radicalized workers' committees. Just after the Kapp putsch, radical leftists increased their representation in Daimler's factory council elections.

Unlike Abrath's call to do "practical work" at Thyssen & Co., Daimler's factory council formed a "political workers council" to prepare Daimler for the proletarian revolution. As in Ruhr mines, it acted as a mouthpiece and forum for the most radical workers and for organizing demonstrations in response to national and international events, for instance, against the use of military force on Ruhr workers, against inflation, "on behalf of Soviet Russia," or against the new, nationwide ten-percent income tax on wages. In September 1920, Daimler (and other Stuttgart metalworking firms, including Robert Bosch) closed down unilaterally, initiating a lockout that rid themselves of all previous legal obligations. This action was parallel to Bayer's 1920 action and Thyssen's 1923 lockout.[117] As at the Machine Company or in the GDK mines, the factory council of Daimler remained a sore point of contestation, not cooperation.

The Machine Company, Bayer, or Daimler were all more profitable, more technologically complex operations than the Rolling Mills, which suggests that perhaps the most decisive variable was the political ideology of the participants. The more participants (labor *or* management) construed the factory council in political, ideological, and symbolic terms—as a signifier of the November revolution writ large—the less effective it was at the "practical" level of the firm. Viewed from the right, the factory council symbolized a fundamental breach of the rights of management and private property. Viewed from the left, its lack of direct control over the means of production, its incomplete powers due to an "incomplete revolution," meant that the factory council was a hapless compromise. Workers with higher hopes of political revolution or greater material gains became disappointed. Thus the factory council's effectiveness (or lack thereof) derived less from its organizational role in the firm than its symbolic relation to the new economic order. This symbolism in turn helped unleash a chain of events that eventually confirmed the *a priori* reasoning on the part of intransigent industrialists or revolutionary workers.[118]

Differences in the course of labor militancy within one firm and the varying acceptance of factory councils did not just derive from the class structure or culture of the workforce, important enough, but from particular process dynamics created by labor and managers inside the business firm. Precisely because of the difficulty of upholding broader political or corporatist agreements, the business firm by default became one of the primary collective actors in this period. The firm, its formal organization, its corporate culture, and personalities of its directors acted as crucial intervening variables affecting the course of labor activism.

An examination of company management will obviously not provide some magic key to understanding working-class formation, but it does need to be placed in the mix more adroitly. It is impossible to understand the actions of labor without understanding organizational variables and the actions of management, especially since they stood in dynamic relation and face-to-face with one another. Diplomacy and tone of management mattered. The relative neglect of management and company policy on the part of labor historians is curious, since management has largely set the conditions to which labor must react, reconstitute, and reinvent itself, or is, at the very least, the primary antagonist over the contested terrain of the business firm itself.[119]

Viewed from the other side of the labor–management dynamic, labor helped to redefine management itself. Labor demands forced Thyssen management to alter key parts of its corporate culture. Coordination issues called into question one of the salient features of the organization of the Thyssen-Konzern—the wide-ranging decentralization of decision-making in the hands of the individual firm directors. Labor called into question the traditional departmental organization at Thyssen & Co. As Plumpe has smartly argued, worker committees uncovered considerable arbitrariness in managerial behavior and now had a forum to voice their complaints (at least for Bayer). Collective bargaining and factory councils compelled greater transparency and consistency, which turned managerial attention to the standardization of piece rates and wages. In turn, ironically, this awareness promoted performance-based pay, rationalization, and the systematization of shopfloor management itself.[120] Such change was not always in the best interest of workers, but the council helped to legitimize these changes if management addressed such complaints.

Pressure from labor also called into question the traditional autonomy of Thyssen firms, which suddenly exposed a major disadvantage of decentralization because workers could play individual Thyssen firms against one another. Although Thyssen tried to retain his "freedom," he still had to conform in practice to regional renumeration levels. The more frequent meetings in Bruckhausen, the creation of specialized boards, the growing standardization of internal business policies, the addition of new social policy offices, and the strengthening of the CAO's role all indicated the need to ensure overall direction and control. Such central offices also coordinated relations with regional corporatist institutions.[121]

Before the war, Thyssen management could largely set the terms for workers inside the individual business, but after the war, individual firms had to negotiate and coordinate with external agencies—with other Thyssen firms, with other firms in the region, with relevant interest groups, with associations, with lawyers, and with politicians. The contrast between establishing new work statutes in the 1870s versus the 1920s at least symbolically attests to this change. However reluctantly, managers had to combine these various claims into a more or less legitimate corporate policy acceptable to stakeholders, be they perceived as hostile or friendly. The firm's central office was embedded in a denser web of external legal, associational, and political constituencies and stakeholders. Thus managers became policy makers, not just economizing agents of the owner, by their expanded role as key intermediaries between stakeholders and stockholders, the environment and the firm, and the public and the private. Labor and labor legislation redirected the attention of German managers whose tasked shifted, reluctantly, from being three-pronged (management, marketing and manufacturing) to include personnel issues and political arrangements at the local, regional, and national level—a four-pronged approach one could say.

CHAPTER 11

Centralization or Decentralization?

Herr Thyssen's greatest concern with the fusion was that Herr General Director Silverberg's leadership would probably build a top-heavy general administration, which in his opinion would be less able to direct the self-sufficient individual firms of the Thyssen-Konzern as of now with such expertise, circumspection *(Umsicht)*, and zeal that has so far been the case.

Directors Meeting, January 25, 1921, regarding a merger
with Paul Silverberg's Rheinische Braunkohle AG

In spite of the fact that August Thyssen belongs to the ranks of "war profiteers" and "winners" of the great inflation, the war and postwar upheavals cracked the financial foundation of the Thyssen-Konzern. Thyssen once wrote that the war "first intervened" in his company "between 1918 and 1925."[1] The war and postwar upheavals left the House of Thyssen standing, but with a fallen annex and numerous cracks in the façade and foundation.

Thyssen and his managers had to cope with strikes and new forms of industrial relations. They had to convert his companies to war production and then convert them back. They had to reinvest in new manufacturing capacities to compensate for the loss of Stahlwerke Thyssen, the confiscated overseas assets, and the results of French occupation. They had to reconstruct his marketing operations under highly competitive market conditions. Finally, they had to manage an inflationary fiasco. Thyssen and his managers coped by resorting to increasingly complicated maneuverings in order to restore some semblance of organizational, and especially, financial balance. The crises engendered an ongoing internal discussion on whether to centralize strategic decision-making or continue to rely on the decentralized, multisubsidiary form.

431

The Organizational and Financial Impact of the War

World War I interrupted Thyssen's long-range plans to "conquer the world market" and the long-term rationalization drive in German steel beginning at the turn of the century. Throughout the war, the question in the back of the minds of Thyssen managers was how to reestablish their competitiveness on the world market at the end of hostilities.

Until WWI, Thyssen's Mülheim firms had supplied not one piece of armament. The Imperial Navy once approached Thyssen & Co., but Thyssen's terms were too high.[2] The *Oberbilker Stahlwerke, Krefelder Stahlwerke,* and the *Press- und Walzwerk Reisholz,* all involved in high-value-added steel products, did supply armored plates and torpedo hulls to the Imperial Navy before the war, but Thyssen's growth rested solidly on market-oriented, peacetime manufacturing. Carl Wallmann was proud that Thyssen's success rested on competitive markets rather than on monopolies and government contracts, like Krupp.[3]

By 1918, however, war production engaged the entire Konzern. By 1915, the GDK had already achieved full capacity.[4] Centers for Thyssen's war effort included the mechanical workshops of the GDK, which manufactured grenade blocks, and a munitions plant built in 1916 three months after the announcement of the Hindenburg plan. The GDK Dinslaken concentrated on barbed wire. The Oberbilker Stahlwerk delivered a range of materials and products to the navy. The *Press- und Walzwerk Reisholz* produced high-pressure containers for submarines, grenades, torpedos, and large-diameter shells for munitions. Thyssen & Co. Rolling Mills developed lines of armored plates, pipes, and boilers for the navy; its plate department became the center of the Rolling Mills war production. Converting entirely to munitions and artillery production, the Machine Company became one of the main centers of armaments production in the Ruhr. Before the war, the Machine Company had three main production workshops, but by 1916, twenty-five different workshops. By February 1918, these workshops had manufactured five million mines by February 1918, thousands of carriages for artillery pieces *(Lafetten),* various types of artillery pieces, and millions of shell casings. Thyssen executives later credited Edmund Roser for managing this difficult and expensive but successful conversion.[5] Unlike the Rolling Mills, the Machine Company's war production capabilities would largely be useless at the end of the war.

The onset of war put Thyssen's extensive international marketing operations on hold and cost him dearly. The Allies froze Thyssen's overseas assets at the beginning of the war. They confiscated his extensive foreign holdings in France, England, and Russia, which were permanently lost. Literally closing its books at the end of June 1914 to start afresh, the Machine Company placed 3 million marks of contracts into inventory, which they considered lost.

Converting to war production proved to be extremely expensive. (Not surprisingly, German industrialists refused to entertain any discussion about limitations on their war profits.) For Thyssen, coping with these enormous costs immediately demanded a new financial organization. The explosion of new workshops at the Machine Company created a dire financial situation. The Rolling Mills loaned the Machine Company 9 million marks, which the Machine Company then converted to stock of the same value, raising its equity to 15 million marks.[6] In November 1915, the Thyssen & Co. Rolling Mills and Machine Company took a first step toward their 1918 fusion when they formed an *Interessengemeinschaft* (IG), a community of interest. This IG pooled both firms' profits and divided them evenly. In effect, additional funds flowed to the Machine Company. This arrangement, however, did not even begin to cover the financial needs of the Machine Company, let alone that of the Konzern.

The idea of a profit-pooling IG quickly took hold at the GDK. A few weeks after the Mülheim firms formed their IG, Späing drafted a contract incorporating Thyssen's core manufacturing works into an IG.[7] This IG arrangement pooled and redistributed total Konzern profits in proportion to the individual firm's total salary, wage, and bonus payments. All losses were "borne collectively" in the same proportion. After redistributing Konzern profits to each individual firm, the firms then constructed their annual financial statements according to standard statutory regulations. Thyssen firms, "economically entwined together in the closest way," ratified this IG arrangement on December 20, 1915.[8]

They designed this profit-pooling arrangement to transfer additional funds to Thyssen companies with the largest employment, the GDK and the Machine Company. While the Machine Company became immensely profitable, the GDK needed constant subsidies. Organizationally, the IG ensured that the CAO (esp. Hofs and Rabes) played a greater role in the internal politics of the Konzern. Moreover, this IG agreement provides the first evidence for the growing self-assertion of Thyssen's sons. The IG formalized the joint financial relationship among Thyssen firms in the event of the now 73-year-old August Thyssen's death. The war raised difficult questions regarding the strategy and structure of the Konzern as well as the inevitable problem of succession.

The IG opened the first of many recurring discussions over the next nine years as to whether the Konzern should create a single, unified corporation. The relative simplicity of the final IG contrasted sharply with the draft that Späing had drawn up for Fritz Thyssen. The first version of the IG would have established a central board of directors *(Verwaltungsrat)* with full control over all strategic decisions for the Konzern. Explicit clauses of its responsibilities included:

- the division of labor among the firms included in the IG;
- plant expansion, large new investments, comprehensive renovations;
- manufacturing or selling new products;
- entering or exiting syndicates, and negotiating quotas or cartel questions,
- joining or exiting economic associations;
- carrying out litigation against cartels or other authorities;
- participating in exhibitions or fairs;
- changing the statutes of any one of the IG member firms;
- hiring or discharging managing board directors, or any other questions which concerned the relationship of one firm to another according to the "responsible" judgment of the directors of the firms in the IG.

In short, the draft IG fundamentally revised the corporate structure, policy, and culture of the Thyssen-Konzern. Its board would convene regularly to execute the provisions of the IG. Each firm could name at least one representative to the board. This board would consist of August Thyssen (as chair), Fritz Thyssen, Heinrich Thyssen-Bornemisza, Julius Thyssen, Matthias Erzberger (a parliamentary representative on the board of the GDK), Dahl, Jacob, Kalle, Rabes, Verlohr, Melcher, Becker, Roser, and Späing. With the majority of those present, this central board could decide for all Thyssen firms. Since this board of directors would always meet at the GDK headquarters in Hamborn-

Bruckhausen, it gave a perceptible advantage to GDK executives—one of those organizational intangibles. This draft version also gave Thyssen's sons a clear and decisive veto right over management, which they had never had. The Thyssen brothers could veto a proposal if all three family members voted against it. This draft clearly reflected the objectives of Fritz Thyssen, who made his own amendments to the draft.

But August Thyssen did not allow this proposed form of the IG to take effect. Presumably he found support from non-GDK managers who rejected this version just as they resisted future attempts at centralization. Thyssen always remained highly sensitive to the problem of advantaging one firm or its managers over others. In fact, *the* main reason for the continued decentralization within the Konzern was its long tradition of decision-making autonomy by its leading executives. (We have no direct evidence of their resistance at this point in time.) The final version of the IG watered down the powers of the central board. In the ratified version, the central board met irregularly and had little explicit decision-making power. The stipulation giving Thyssen sons veto rights disappeared, reducing the IG to a profit-pooling arrangement.

Above all, the IG helped alleviate the tremendous financial strain of the war on the GDK (Table 11.1). As set up by Heinrich Kindt, one of the GDK's main accountants, these figures are *balances*. (It was customary at the time to subtract bank credits from bank debits and Konzern credits from Konzern debits, to achieve a plus or minus balance.) Surprisingly, bank debt and long-term mortgages hardly rose during the war. But the level of total liabilities, that is, the financial claims on the GDK, nearly doubled between 1915 and 1918 from 127 million to 246 million marks. Part of the growth can be traced back to inflation, but the level of liabilities grew mainly in the GDK's current accounts and acceptances. Current accounts were short-term accounts whose payments the GDK delayed. The GDK also paid for its Swedish iron-ore deliveries almost entirely on credit, leading to a spectacular rise in acceptances from 4 million to 57 million marks. The government requested that steel industrialists defer payments until the end of the war, and industrialists figured someone else would end up paying for them.[9] Like that of Germany, the war at the GDK was fought on credit and with expectations of winning.

On the debitor side, the level of financial claims *owed to* the GDK rose nearly three times, from 87 million to 244 million marks. Most of

Table 11.1 Key financial accounts of the GDK, 1915–1918

GDK selected liabilities, 1915–1918

Year	Banks	Current accts.	Other creditors	Acceptances	Mortgages	Total creditors
1915	20,117,943	5,232,110	40,370,869	4,072,869	56,889,257	126,683,048
1916	11,718,373	8,966,523	39,687,615	4,124,460	62,609,232	126,981,743
1917	2,516,981	27,061,875	46,786,249	16,324,204	54,698,718	147,388,027
1918	19,428,089	50,373,058	67,038,425	56,998,000	52,110,968	245,950,740

GDK selected assets, 1915–1918

Year	Konzern	Current accts.	Other debitors	Total debitors
1915	43,482,960	5,232,110	38,312,078	87,027,148
1916	60,551,069	8,966,523	41,482,229	111,999,821
1917	69,955,275	27,061,875	59,711,869	156,729,019
1918	135,493,175	50,373,058	48,730,485	234,596,718

Source: TKA: A/1348 Tables supplied by Heinrich Kindt (GDK and CAO accountant), 17 May 1941.

the increase can be attributed to the rise in Konzern debt owed to the GDK, which rose from over 43 million to over 135 million marks and current accounts from 5.2 million to 50 million marks. These went mostly to the Stahlwerke Thyssen and Thyssen mining subsidiaries (Lohberg, Rhein, Jacobus). In a role formerly played by Thyssen & Co., the GDK increasingly acted as an internal credit bank for other Thyssen firms, who delayed their current account payments to the GDK.

Except for 1915–1916, the IG profit-pooling arrangement primarily supported the financial overextension of the GDK, its mining subsidiaries, and the Stahlwerke Thyssen.[10] The Machine Company retained a greater proportion of its profits because its employment skyrocketed. Table 11.2, based on internal CAO calculations, shows the considerable amount of cross-subsidies needed to cover wartime losses.

Especially after 1916, the Machine Company, the Rolling Mills, the AGHütt, and the *Press- und Walzwerke Reisholz* generated most of Thyssen's war profits. In 1915 and 1916, the GDK did transfer roughly 9 million and 4 million marks, respectively, through the IG. In 1916,

Table 11.2 IG financial redistribution among Thyssen firms, 1915–1918

Firm	1915		1916		1917		1918	
	Before IG	After IG	Before IG	After IG	Before IG	After IG	Before IG	After IG
Rolling Mills	1,028,681	1,560,583	7,240,875	2,672,361	13,172,787	3,142,862	6,848,839	0
Machine Co.	5,161,377	2,256,461	18,724,787	6,637,306	20,876,676	13,026,389	3,237,047	0
GDK	16,457,468	7,915,717	17,742,667	13,117,699	0	16,707,800[d]	−57,494,011	−24,311,182[e]
AGHütt	4,057,550	559,986	1,552,446	1,117,337	3,530,758[c]	2,221,174	2,482,590	0
Stahlwerke Thyssen	−4,748,568	0	−12,089,899	0	0	0	10,540,295	0
Gew. Jacobus	−1,104,467	0	−5,405,646	0	0	0	0	0
Gew. Lohberg	1,753,164	0	0	0	−988,038	0	−1,024,322	−2,008,888
Gew. Rhein	1,517,003	0	−51,988	0	−1,493,986	0	−2,386,785	−1,596,740
P & W, Reisholz							9,879,537	0
Konzern profits/ losses	17,581,873	12,292,746[a]	27,713,243	23,544,703[b]	35,098,197	35,098,225	−27,916,809	−27,916,809

Source: TKA: A/749/1–2, A/750/1, A/1348; MA: R 5 30 13.

a. An additional 5,289,127 Marks were transferred to the GDK and AGHütt for extraordinary losses.

b. An additional 4,168,540 Marks were transferred to the GDK and AGHütt for extraordinary losses.

c. The number includes both the profits of the GDK and AGHütt.

d. TKA: A/1348 Kindt reports a 12,707,800 Mark *loss* for the GDK in 1917. Treue, *Feuer Verlöschen Nie Verlöschen Nie*, p. 179 reports a profit of 15.7 million Marks.

e. TA: A/1348 Kindt reports a 26,353,275 Mark *loss* for the GDK in 1918.

the two Mülheim firms transferred 17 million marks to the Stahlwerke Thyssen and the Gewerkschaft Jacobus. In 1917, they transferred another 17 million marks to the GDK, which made no profit that year. In 1918, the GDK lost a remarkable 57.5 million marks before the IG transferred about 23 million marks to it, bringing its losses to 24 million marks. Increasingly, profits earned by the two Thyssen & Co. firms began subsidizing coal and crude-steel-making areas. Losses grew so great that Thyssen incorporated the *Press- und Walzwerke AG* in Reisholz into the 1918 IG financial statement to help compensate for losses at the GDK, Gew. Lohberg, and Gew. Rhein. The *Press- und Walzwerk Reisholz* thus became a new member of Thyssen's core group of firms. Moreover, the new IG contract, which added the Reisholz firm, contained a new clause explicitly dissolving the IG in the event that any participating firm was expropriated, "socialized," or any other change in ownership occurred.[11]

Before IG redistribution, the Thyssen & Co. Machine Company was especially profitable. It earned 10 million marks in 1915, about 12 million marks in 1916, peaking at a remarkable 26.4 million marks in 1917, before dropping back to 7.8 million marks in 1918. The Rolling Mills earned 1.8 million in 1915, about 11.5 million in 1916, 14.7 million in 1917, and 13.3 million marks in 1918.[12] Profits at the AGHütt tended to remain steady, but it still needed a number of financial transfers to compensate for extraordinary losses.

Thyssen made his profits at the high-value-added end of the steel goods spectrum. When the GDK began to lose money after 1917, the losses mounted dramatically—a particular problem of firms built on high-investment, high-fixed-asset, high-volume production. The relative profitability of finished goods producers foreshadowed a long-term structural shift in the German economy away from basic raw materials and semi-processed materials to finished goods. One can see the logic that drove heavy industrialists into a merger and acquisition mania for finished goods manufacturers after the war.

Thyssen resorted to high levels of depreciation on the balance sheets, which partially accounts for the high levels of loss. A good portion, however, was clearly justified because war production simply ground up plant and equipment. Throughout the Konzern, equipment fell into increasing disrepair because of the lack of proper maintenance. Equipment simply wore out from constant use. The book value of the fixed assets of the GDK actually declined from 173.8 million in 1914 to 147.2 million marks in 1918. The book value of the AGHütt's fixed assets declined from 19 million to 13.7 million marks during the war. Thyssen & Co. Rolling Mills' book value of its fixed assets rose slightly from 29.6 million in 1914 and 30.5 million marks by December 1917. The Machine Company's fixed assets, however, ballooned from 7.4 million to 21.1 million marks by the end of 1917. But jointly, the book value of Thyssen & Co. fixed assets declined from 37 million in 1914 to 29.5 million marks by the end of 1918. In the last year of the war, the book value of these fixed assets declined a remarkable 22.1 million, as Thyssen simply wrote down the costs of war-related equipment.[13] Every Thyssen enterprise established special reserve funds for future repairs or for dismantling wartime productive capacity, which also contributed to the loss figures. In short, Thyssen used his high war profits largely to compensate for extraordinary depreciation of his equipment and to prepare for future investment. War profits were tremendously high, but so were war expenses. (The exact proportion is subject to debate.) Thyssen's conservative accounting attempted to retain funds to prepare the Thyssen-Konzern for the competitive postwar world.

Here industrialists won advantages not available to ordinary people. Aside from outright cheating or blatant manipulation of accounting standards *à la* the Daimler Affair, big business had a range of options for minimizing the costs of the war, essentially by socializing expenses yet privately retaining profits.[14] For individuals, the loss of a wage-earning loved one, the psychological trauma of returning from the front, the depreciation of savings, the wearing out of clothes, the fatigue of the body from malnutrition, could not be written off as an accounting technique. But for Thyssen, one of the more visible "war profiteers," the war cannot be interpreted as an unqualified gain. The focus on the scale of war profits falls short. His enterprise lost far less than others did because he had more options to compensate for losses. But these losses nevertheless threatened the continuing financial viability of the Thyssen-Konzern.

The increasing financial interdependency among Thyssen firms through the IG and interlocking current accounts meant that the CAO accrued more power. By 1918, the CAO gained powers of executive command.[15] Despite the failure of the IG to create a central decision-making body, the CAO became a true central executive office. With Heinrich Kindt as his right-hand, Carl Rabes became executive director of the CAO, solidifying his key position in the center of the Konzern's financial control system.

Finally, the war permanently exposed the inevitable, irksome question of succession. On July 15, 1915, Joseph Thyssen tragically died. On his evening round across the factory grounds, a symbol of traditional, old-fashioned entrepreneurial authority, he inadvertently crossed between two passing railcars, which crushed him. In October 1915 Hans and Julius Thyssen joined Thyssen & Co.'s board of directors, but—even as the new proprietor/executives—they were explicitly excluded from direction of the firm.[16] The death of Joseph Thyssen also forced Thyssen to find a clear answer to another part of the succession problem, this one associated with August Thyssen, Jr. August, Jr.'s bankruptcy proceedings still threatened Thyssen & Co. On October 30, 1918, the Rolling Mills fused with the Machine Company into a new firm, the Thyssen & Co. AG.[17] The merger eliminated any potential legal claims by August, Jr.'s creditors on the private assets of the partnership, to which the 1885 divorce agreement applied. Explicit legal clauses in the firm's statutes voided any of August, Jr.'s financial or leadership claims on the new firm.[18] The incorporation effectively liquidated the original general partnership after nearly a half a century. Thyssen signed two other contracts in 1919 and 1921 with his sons, Fritz and Heinrich, which officially transferred ownership to them and ensured that they would take over the responsibility for Hedwig and August, Jr.'s settlements.[19]

The legal liquidation of the partnership ended Thyssen & Co.'s role as a financial holding company. Its financial condition just before its liquidation illustrates its altered role. The war had taken a great toll on the personal equity of the Thyssen brothers. At the end of 1913, their equity inside Thyssen & Co. had reached roughly 35 million marks. At the end of 1918, it amounted to just over 8 million marks. Much of the real estate assets had been transferred to the Machine Company or other firms. Thyssen also spread his stock securities around to other Thyssen firms, particularly the AGHütt and the Machine Company.[20] Before the war, liabilities or accounts payable to other Thyssen firms were quite small, and the partnership extended considerable amounts of credits to Thyssen firms, thus acting as a type of house bank for the

Konzern. By the end of the war, Thyssen & Co. became increasingly indebted to other firms in the Konzern, but passed on those financial
credits to the GDK. By 1918, Thyssen & Co. had credited the GDK with
54 million marks, making up half of its total accounts receivable. But
on the liabilities side, the AGHütt, the GDK Dinslaken, the Press- &
Walzwerk AG in Reisholz, and the Oberbilker Stahlwerk AG had credited Thyssen & Co. with 33 million marks. Bank credits made up an additional 7 million marks and equalled roughly the remaining equity inside Thyssen & Co. Much like a huge planet whose gravity attracts
matter, the GDK drew to it an increasing amount of the financial activity of the Konzern. Before the war, each firm had acted more autonomously because each firm could largely generate its own internal cash
flow after start-up investments.

Because both divisions now formed a single joint-stock company,
by law the company had to have a supervisory board and a managing board (Figure 11.1). Although the legal status of Thyssen & Co.
changed dramatically, the management of the new firm worked largely
as before. We will see this sort of organizational-legal maneuvering in
the future—changing as much as possible in order to change the management culture as little as possible, a type of creative conservatism.
The Rolling Mills and the Machine Company continued to act as independent, internal divisions, full profit centers. In the internal balances, management kept the two divisions' accounts distinct until consolidated into a published annual financial statement. They retained a
degree of formality in their business relations, although their central
offices were across the street from one another.[21] Each had separate
worker committees and factory councils. Not until December 1920
were some services (the wage, production cost, bookkeeping, and purchasing offices) subordinated to the Machine Company, that is, to Karl
Härle, with bad results. They shared the advertising office. The most
important centralization, however, was the auditing office, which was
now headed by Heinrich Dinkelbach. He became responsible for both
divisions' accounting procedures and managerial reporting.

The liquidation of the original Thyssen & Co. partnership marks a
major turning point in the history of the Thyssen-Konzern. Even before the war ended, even before the revolution broke out, and even before Thyssen lost the Stahlwerke Thyssen, the outlines of the postwar
world for the House of Thyssen became visible. A whole series of

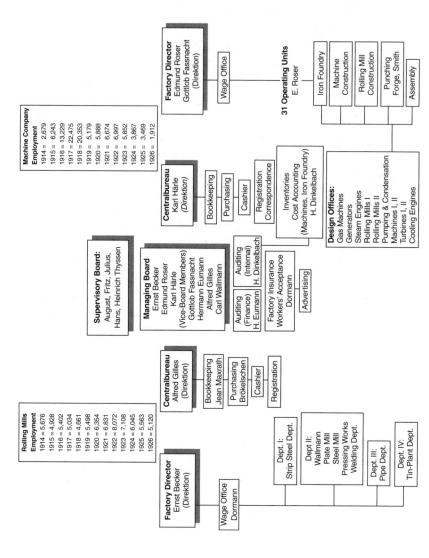

Figure 11.1 Thyssen & Co. AG, 1918—Steel and Rolling Mills Division; Machine Engineering Division

nearly intractable problems loomed on the horizon. The financial balance of the Konzern went awry, as not all the firms could financially sustain themselves alone—a fundamental Thyssen principle. The financial and strategic decision-making weight decisively shifted to the GDK, and especially, Wilhelm Späing, Carl Rabes, and Fritz Thyssen. The bipolar leadership role between Thyssen & Co. and the GDK ended. Finally, the problem of succession reared its ugly head. Thyssen sons appeared on all the Thyssen boards. An informal division of labor among the Thyssen sons began to evolve. Hans Thyssen supervised affairs in Mülheim, Julius the mines of Hamborn, Fritz the GDK steel works of Bruckhausen, and after returning to Germany from Hungary in early 1919, Heinrich the finishing, shipbuilding, and commercial export areas. In this respect, the death of Joseph Thyssen and the subsequent legal demise of the original partnership of the elder Thyssen brothers marked the end of an era. It also foreshadowed the demise of the Thyssen-Konzern, with its potent mix of finance and family.

Revolution and Reorganization

The November 9, 1918, democratic revolution sealed the fate of the Imperial era. It also brought fervent cries for the socialization of heavy industry, especially mining companies. Immediately, Thyssen took preventive measures to minimize the impact of the impending revolution on property rights. On the advice of Wilhelm Späing, Thyssen legally detached the GDK Hamborn mines from the GDK Bruckhausen steel works. On January 1, 1919, a few weeks after the revolution, he refounded his mining properties as the *Gewerkschaft Friedrich Thyssen*, naming it after his father. If mining companies were expropriated, the rest of the firm might escape socialization. An invaluable lawyer, Späing had found an old loophole in Prussian mining laws permitting two existing collieries to merge without incurring new land or company taxes, which were extremely high at the time. They renamed the former GDK steel works as the *August Thyssen-Hütte, Gewerkschaft* (ATH), a name it would carry for much of the 20th century. According to Späing, only after trying debates with Thyssen, who did not want to put his own name on a company, did executives convince him to rename the company after himself.[22] This name change signified the transfer of the center of the Thyssen-Konzern to the ATH (Figure 11.2).

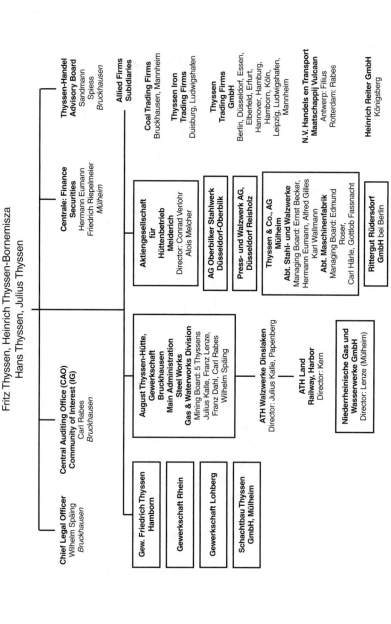

August Thyssen
Fritz Thyssen, Heinrich Thyssen-Bornemisza
Hans Thyssen, Julius Thyssen

Chief Legal Officer
Wilhelm Späing
Bruckhausen

Central Auditing Office (CAO)
Community of Interest (IG)
Carl Rabes
Bruckhausen

Centrale: Finance
Securities
Hermann Eumann
Friedrich Riepelmeier
Mülheim

Thyssen-Handel
Advisory Board
Sandmann
Spiess
Bruckhausen

Allied Firms
Subsidiaries

Coal Trading Firms
Bruckhausen, Mannheim

Thyssen Iron
Trading Firms
Duisburg, Ludwigshafen

Thyssen
Trading Firms
GmbH
Berlin, Düsseldorf, Essen,
Elberfeld, Erfurt,
Hannover, Hamburg,
Hamborn, Köln,
Leipzig, Ludwigshafen,
Mannheim

N.V. Handels en Transport
Maatschappij Vulcaan
Antwerp: Filius
Rotterdam: Rabes

Heinrich Reiter GmbH
Königsberg

Aktiengesellschaft
für
Hüttenbetrieb
Meiderich
Director: Conrad Verlohr
Alois Melcher

AG Oberbilker Stahlwerk
Düsseldorf-Oberbilk

Press- und Walzwerk AG,
Düsseldorf Reisholz

Thyssen & Co., AG
Mülheim
Abt. Stahl- und Walzwerke
Managing Board: Ernst Becker,
Hermann Eumann, Alfred Gilles
Karl Wallmann
Abt. Maschinenfabrik
Managing Board: Edmund
Roser,
Carl Härle, Gottlob Fassnacht

Rittergut Rüdersdorf
GmbH bei Berlin

August Thyssen-Hütte,
Gewerkschaft
Bruckhausen
Main Administration
Steel Works
Gas & Waterworks Division
Mining Board: 5 Thyssens
Julius Kalle, Franz Lenze,
Franz Dahl, Carl Rabes
Wilhelm Späing

ATH Walzwerke Dinslaken
Director: Julius Kalle, Papenberg

ATH Land
Railway, Harbor
Director: Kern

Niederrheinische Gas und
Wasserwerke GmbH
Director: Lenze (Mülheim)

Gew. Friedrich Thyssen
Hamborn

Gewerkschaft Rhein

Gewerkschaft Lohberg

Schachtbau Thyssen
GmbH, Mülheim

Figure 11.2 Thyssen-Konzern, 1919 (core firms only)

Simultaneously, they transformed the GDK mining construction department into a new firm called the *Schachtbau Thyssen GmbH,* with its seat in Mülheim. They also divided the GDK Gas- and Waterworks department into two separate firms. Those areas responsible for private households were turned into an independent firm, initially called the *Niederrheinische Gas- und Wasserwerke GmbH.* By 1921, the rest of the ATH gas and water works department, which serviced industry, became the *Gasgesellschaft mbH, Hamborn.* All of these new companies signed formal contracts with one another to ensure the continuity of long-term deliveries between one another. The war and Thyssen's advanced age forced a greater degree of formalization of long-standing practices. With the exception of the retirement of Franz Dahl in 1920, continuities dominated with respect to Thyssen's managerial organization in spite of this organizational maneuvering.

But the Treaty of Versailles restructured his Konzern against his will. Thyssen permanently lost his massive complex of steel works and iron-ore mines in Lorraine to the French. A consortium of French industrial consumers of iron and steel products, including Renault, Peugeot, and a number of heavy equipment and electrical machinery firms, took it over. For Thyssen, this meant an enormous loss, 246 million marks. Additionally, Thyssen lost all his foreign direct investments in Normandy, southern Russia, North Africa, and India, amounting to an estimated 88 million marks. In monetary terms, Thyssen lost the most compared to other heavy industrialists.[23] But unlike Gelsenkirchen (GBAG), which was a mining operation in Germany and a steel operation in (now) France, Thyssen could largely fall back to his 1910 condition. One executive remembered Thyssen being almost relieved to be rid of this "troubled child," which had never lived up to expectations.[24]

The Versailles Treaty delivered a sharp blow to the entire German economy, but especially to the steel industry. Germany lost half of Upper Silesia, most of Posen and East Prussia, the Saar, the left bank of the Rhineland, and Alsace-Lorraine (which the Germans had taken by force in 1871 from France). These border changes meant the loss of roughly 80% of German iron-ore supplies, 44% of pig-iron capacity, 36% of steel capacity, and 32% of rolled-steel-product capacity. In 1913, Lorraine iron and steel works alone had delivered 50% of total German pig-iron production. It contained 40% of German blast furnaces and steel works and 30% of German rolling mills, especially those for heavy plates. Although the figures are impressive, the French Lorraine plants were still more dependent in the long run on German coke than the other way around.[25]

In addition, the Versailles Treaty required Germany to deliver 25–40 million tons of coal yearly and 25% of its pharmaceutical and dye production until 1925 to France, Belgium, and Italy. All overseas assets of German companies in Allied countries were lost, without compensation. Moreover, Germany tariff sovereignty was denied until 1925. France, Belgium, and Luxembourg imposed a five-year tariff-free zone for all of their own iron and steel products, which became known as the so-called "hole in the West." The Versailles Treaty opened previously protected south German markets in particular to international competition. At the same time, a wave of international protectionism followed the war, and other countries raised tariffs against German exports.[26] International competition became fiercer, as other European countries built up their own steel production as a strategic industry. The German steel industry became heavily dependent on Swedish iron ore, which was imported and paid for with depreciating marks. In 1918, for instance, the GDK simply wrote off an extraordinary 50 million marks in losses due to the depreciation of the German mark (from $4.21 to $8.3 by December 1918), which made Swedish iron ore debts twice as expensive. (I state these figures not to evoke sympathy, but to present the real difficulties of restarting peacetime production under dramatically new competitive conditions. Recall Thyssen's own annexation claims in France and Russia.)

Finally, for Germans, the most hateful and humiliating aspect of the Versailles Treaty was the "war guilt" clause, which blamed Germany for starting the war and justified claiming reparations of GM 132 billion (Goldmarks). Reparations set the stage for the French occupation of the Ruhr and poisoned Weimar domestic politics. In protest, both August and Fritz Thyssen withdrew their support for the Center Party and Matthias Erzberger, who signed the hated treaty. Fritz Thyssen joined the DNVP and began his political drift to the far right.

On top of revolutionary strike activity and the loss of his Lorraine iron-ore fields, the rising inflation proved both a boon and a curse to Thyssen. While the decline in the value of the mark promoted German exports by making German goods cheaper on foreign markets, it also made German imports, especially the key input of quality iron ore, correspondingly more expensive. Thyssen depended heavily on Swedish iron-ore imports. Surprisingly, German steel industrialists could pay back most of their Swedish iron-ore debts incurred during the war by October 1920, mostly through increased exports, which provided hard currency. They made their credit rating with the Swedes a priority, as they wanted to present themselves as good customers. Additionally, German industrialists lobbied extensively for government compensation for these "indirect losses."[27]

For Thyssen, this dependence on Swedish iron ore and foreign currency led to a far-reaching rearrangement of his finances. He reopened many of his banking contacts overseas so that he could deal directly in foreign currencies. The *Bank voor Handel en Scheepvaart* in Rotterdam facilitated international trade relations and now took on an additional role as the main supplier of acceptance credits and foreign currency for the rest of the Konzern. The ATH also drew up a fifteen-year contract with the Thyssen trading firms in Antwerp and Rotterdam, as well as the *N. V. Handels- en Transport Maatschappij Vulcaan,* to secure their supply of iron ore. They set up a special account with the Dutch bank, the *N. V. H. Handelscompagnie Ruilverkeer,* whereby the Konzern debts from the iron ore were paid directly from the proceeds of export sales. The Dutch companies also provided a safe harbor from the battering of the mark. Thyssen's "intimate connections" with Dutch financial intermediaries, for example, helped attract the business of the International Acceptance Bank, a bank established by the important private bankers Max and Paul Warburg to bring large-scale investment capital to German industry.[28]

As German politics lost its balance, so did the Thyssen-Konzern. In April 1919, Thyssen sent a bleak letter to the Reich government. He emphasized how much production had dropped throughout the Konzern because of its "economic unity." His finished goods firms were dependent on a steady supply of intermediate-goods deliveries from the ATH and Friedrich Thyssen, which workers intermittently shut down. The necessity to pay off Swedish iron-ore debts to remain good customers with good credit standing, the incessant strikes, the interruptions in the coal supply, the low productivity, the loss of competitiveness, all led to this conclusion:

> We have also reached the end of our financial capacity. Our cash supply has long been exhausted. With all our strength, we will soon nei-

ther be able to meet the claims immediately due for wages and salaries, nor cover the debts that we were forced to take on during the war on the orders of the Reichsbank in the interest of the common good. . . . Without the financial support of the rest of the firms of the Thyssen-Group, the Gewerkschaft Deutscher Kaiser would have had to stop its payments long ago, but now their financial means are also exhausted. Because of this, this firm, built with over thirty years of laborious work and whose profits were always used for its further expansion, and whose owners never took out a single penny as a dividend, would be destroyed inside five months.[29]

Ending dramatically, Thyssen stated if the ATH shut down, it would take the entire Konzern down with its 40–50,000 jobs. Continuing production was thus in the public interest. He requested greater military protection against the Communists and wanted compensation for the strike losses.

The problems that Thyssen faced were severe. The ATH bled money, needing constant infusions of liquid capital. Thyssen even had to import high-priced American coal due to disruptions in 1921. Above all, between 1919 and 1923, the IG balanced out the losses racked up by the ATH and Thyssen mining companies.[30]

Defined by the IG, the core of the Thyssen-Konzern lost money in 1919–1920, earned money in 1921, before losing money again in 1922 (Table 11.3). According to profits before distribution, the ATH lost a huge amount of money in each of these years before the inflation made a mockery of such impressive-looking but increasingly meaningless figures. In 1921, the other firms in the IG transferred almost all their earnings to the ATH to balance out its losses. The mines took especially heavy losses in 1920 because of violence, but evened out thereafter. Profits derived largely from Thyssen & Co., the AGHütt, and the *Press- und Walzwerk AG*, but they could only partially compensate for these losses. The AGHütt proved to be a particularly steady performer. In 1919 and 1920, moreover, Thyssen & Co. profits came entirely from the Rolling Mills. The Machine Company incurred losses because of the expense of converting back to peacetime production. By 1921 the Machine Company turned a profit, but then the Rolling Mills slid into the red.[31] The addition of the *Press- und Walzwerk* in Reisholz proved particularly valuable for infusing new funds into the IG. High-end,

Table 11.3 IG financial redistribution among Thyssen firms, 1919–1922

Firm	1919		1920		1921		1922	
	Before IG	Transferred	Before IG	Transferred	Before IG	Transferred	Before IG	Transferred
Thyssen & Co. AG	4,639,350	−4,639,350	13,202,725	−13,202,725	11,050,102	0		0
AGHütt	3,400,753	−3,400,753	24,406,861	−24,406,861	28,176,220	−25,160,213		
ATH	−64,643,163	28,434,532	−3,545,451	2,433,950	−47,896,125	47,896,125	−13,787,110,670	1,639,850,010
Gew. Fried. Thyssen	−6,588,356	−6,782,564	−58,416,898	40,103,162	0	0	1,167,371,219	−1,167,371,219
Gew. Lohberg	−913,730	−3,233,546	−24,517,709	16,831,391	0	0	362,720,671	−362,720,671
Gew. Rhein I	−1,818,368	−1,364,859	−14,919,378	10,242,143	0	0	109,758,120	−109,758,120
Press- & Walzwerk	9,013,459	−9,013,459	32,001,060	−32,001,060	23,867,050	−22,739,633		
Schachtbau Thyssen					604,829	3,721		
Total Konzern	−56,910,054	0	−31,788,789	0	15,802,076	0	−12,147,260,660	0

Source: TKA: A/750/1–2. In 1922–23, Thyssen & Co. did not create financial statements.

quality-goods manufacturing essentially subsidized high-volume, commodity coal and steel production.

The ATH tapped into a broader array of financial sources, including foundations, mortgage banks, and real-estate credit banks. Between 1920 and 1922, these institutions (distinct from Thyssen's main banking partners) contributed an additional 39 million marks. In this respect, the inflation proved a boon for Thyssen, as these loans had relatively low interest rates and the sums quickly devalued. On the other hand, Thyssen also tried to float a 250-million mark bond in 1922, which never made it onto the market because inflation devalued the sum so quickly. Thyssen also tightened his banking relations with the Reichsbank, especially for current-account transactions. Once the Reichsbank instituted a tight monetary policy in 1924, these funds dried up.[32]

The intricate financial maneuverings had organizational implications. They strengthened the power of Rabes, who acted as the financial wizard of the Thyssen-Konzern, heading the CAO and controlling the crucial coal and iron ore trade. If the Thyssen-Konzern had had a single CEO in these years, the job would have fallen to Rabes.

Wilhelm Späing became the second crucial figure. Testifying to the way organizations "match" their environments with offices, in November 1921 Thyssen established the *Eigenschutz GmbH*. Its company name literally meant "for our own protection." Because of the mixture of legal and financial objectives, the managing directors were, not surprisingly, Rabes and Späing. Any compensation gained or expenses incurred were distributed according to the value of the individual firm's assets. Eigenschutz was a type of all-purpose insurance company with direct contact to official government agencies. It lobbied, negotiated, and coordinated all types of compensations, damages, reclamations, insurance, taxes, etc., for the Thyssen-Konzern with the German government and the French occupation forces (MICUM). During the period of passive resistance, Späing and Eigenschutz organized negotiations with MICUM. If Fritz Thyssen became a symbol of resistance, Späing and Rabes actually managed Thyssen's responses. Eigenschutz became a central information service for reporting the damage claims of each of the individual Thyssen firms. It also helped to formulate policy regarding specific reparation payments or deliveries in hard goods. Eigenschutz arranged the compensation for the loss of the

Stahlwerke Thyssen AG, estimated at 246 million marks. However, the government compensated Thyssen in 1922 marks, which by then were worth only GM 15 million (Goldmarks) or about 6% of the cost of building the Stahlwerke Thyssen. As compensation for the loss of his international assets, Thyssen received an impressive total of 334 million marks, but this sum too was worth GM 16.6, or just under 5% of its original value.[33] Thyssen did gain enormous advantages from the inflation, but it still cost him his financial solidity. The Great Inflation gave as it took away.

The inflation had one last implication for Thyssen's financial organization. As inflation rates accelerated, Thyssen's financial manipulations became increasingly opaque. One could say that in inverse proportion to the decline in value of the mark, the more the financial liquidity of the Thyssen-Konzern moved away from its domestic firms in the Ruhr to its international firms in Holland. Späing reported to a tax commission in 1928 that before the end of 1923, the Thyssen-Konzern had been "consciously drained of its financial blood" in favor of the Holland firms.[34] Other large industrial firms followed a similar strategy, but for Thyssen this had major implications for the history of the Thyssen-Konzern. Crucially, the Konzern's financial liquidity moved away from firms controlled by Fritz Thyssen to those run by Heinrich Thyssen-Bornemisza. Thyssen-Bornemisza had moved to The Hague in the Netherlands, basing his operations in Rotterdam. From there, he took over responsibility for Thyssen's foreign financial transactions. The hyperinflation and subsequent stabilization set up an increasing confrontation between the liquid-asset transactions and the fixed-asset needs of the coal and steel works, which became personified in the rivalry between Heinrich and Fritz. (This same inflation also endowed Thyssen-Bornemiscza with the strong financial base he needed to assemble one of the most distinguished art collections in the world). The inflationary years set the stage for confrontations between Fritz and Heinrich that would eventually bring Fritz's portion of his father's legacy into the VSt.

Inflationary Reconstruction and Rationalization

So far, I have stressed the challenges confronting the Thyssen-Konzern, yet it also drew tremendous advantages from the inflation.

First and foremost, the inflation cheapened debt and reduced the cost of investment, encouraging a flight into real goods.[35] Ruhr heavy industry went on a binge of mergers and acquisitions to reconstruct their vertically integrated structures. Unfortunately, the inflation allowed heavy industrialists to expand without regard to any accurate planning for present or future demand, but out of vaguely estimated financial and strategic considerations.

Above all, they vertically integrated into higher value-added manufacturing and diversified into machine engineering.[36] For instance, Phoenix took over a shipbuilding and machine engineering firm in Hamburg, a foundry for fittings in Düsseldorf, a railway equipment company, and began investing in Benz & Co. automobiles in Mannheim. The Haniel-controlled GHH went on a spectacular takeover spree of some of the most famous machine-engineering firms in Germany, including the *Machinenfabrik Esslingen AG, Fritz Neumeyer AG* in Nürnberg, the *Deutsche Werft AG* in Hamburg, and the *Zahnräderfabrik AG* in Augsburg. It also expanded its trading and shipping business. This acquisition wave culminated with the contentious takeover of MAN, one of Germany's largest and most renowned machine companies. Ruhr heavy industry thus spread its tentacles more strongly outside the region. Firms in finished steel goods and machine engineering viewed penetration of heavy industry into their sectors as a dangerous development. Many contemporary observers thought that the manufactured goods companies would go the way of pure rolling mills after the turn of the century and be absorbed into larger firms. Tensions between producers and consumers of steel rose considerably.

The single most dramatic example of inflation-driven empire-building, however, was carried out by the other "Merchant of Mülheim," Hugo Stinnes. Stinnes became known as the "Inflation King." He formed the *Siemens-Rheinelbe-Schuckert Union* (SRSU) as an *Interessengemeinschaft* (IG), uniting coal, steel, and electrical-engineering firms. Under Stinnes' initiative, three heavy industrial firms (Gelsenkirchen, Deutsch-Luxembourg, and the Bochumer Verein) formed the Rhein-Elbe-Union. Siemens-Schuckert then joined the Rhein-Elbe-Union as an "insurance contract" for reasons of "branch" and "territorial" security. "Branch" security meant insurance against material or capital shortages. "Territorial" security meant protection against political disruptions. Additionally, six other steel or metalworking firms joined the

SRSU, including an automobile company, a dental-equipment company, various machine-engineering firms, and a shipbuilding company. Altogether the SRSU became the largest conglomeration of enterprises in Germany during the early 1920s. Carl Friedrich von Siemens later admitted that he was embarrassed about the "obscure manipulations," unclear circumstances," and "carelessness" that had arisen from Siemens' attempt to deal with the inflation.[37] The overtly political considerations leading to the foundation of the SRSU, however, remained exceptional.

In organizational terms, the inflation period saw a boom in Konzern-building, true multisubsidiaries, because it was often difficult to incorporate these new acquisitions into a single corporation for personnel, tax, or legal reasons. Konzerne often became an *ad hoc* collection of varied interests and overlapping product lines that powerful individuals or companies brought under a very wobbly corporate roof (Haniel, Stinnes, Klöckner, Krupp, Henschel, Wolff, or Flick). At one point, Stinnes could honestly say that "yesterday the Rheinelbe-Union indirectly secured its control of the Bochumer Verein. You [Siemens] can consider Bochum as a Konzern work although its management still has no idea[!]"[38] Some Konzerne were manufacturing-oriented in that they tried to reduce the amount of product overlap by shutting down less efficient plants (so-called negative rationalization). Others opened more plants because of financial considerations (the conglomerates Stinnes or Flick). Publically, German entrepreneurs tended to justify these confusing structures on natural or technological grounds. Secondary factors included financial pooling, taxes, or the exchange of managerial experience or information (synergies in today's parlance). Others, more critically, argued that Konzerne primarily formed in the interest of monopoly profits, cartel quotas, financial pooling, financial hedging, profit manipulations, and finally "the striving for power and influence in order to participate in and shape economic conditions was a very important motivating force." After World War II, Heinrich Dinkelbach forcefully argued the latter case.[39]

The 1920s merger movement often brought numerous firms with different historical traditions, corporate cultures, and product markets under loose communities of interest (IGs).[40] German industrialists preferred IGs to American-style trusts because they allowed individual units a greater degree of independence, often important in overcoming organizational frictions with acquired firms. They were less functional, rigid, and centralized than American trusts. One business analyst, Ernst Schulze, argued that German firms were more supple organizations than American firms. Albert Vögler thought they respected the historical autonomy of their individual members and were more flexible.[41] Because Konzerne were messier, more historically haphazard, more vertically oriented, more diversified, less functional, and certainly less unified than American trusts, standardization, bureaucratization, centralization and rationalization moved more slowly in practice. Rationalization and Americanization became buzzwords in the 1920s precisely because German big business had less centralized, bureaucratic controls.[42] They needed to be created.

Thyssen chose a different route. The degree of organizational clarity inside the Thyssen-Konzern was exceptional, largely because Thyssen retained complete financial, strategic, and organizational control. The multisubsidiary structure grew out of conscious design and was reinforced by the desire for autonomy from individual senior managers, rather than strategic improvisation or shareholder resistance. In the postwar period, Thyssen did not participate in the acquisitions mania of the inflationary period, but instead concentrated on modernizing his core operations and improving his organizational capabilities. Contemporaries often contrasted Stinnes' strategy with that of Thyssen's. Business analysts today might say that Thyssen concentrated on his "core competencies."

Thyssen did not participate to a great extent in the vertical concentration of the immediate postwar period—partially because his Konzern already extended from coal to machine engineering. Thyssen rejected incorporation for incorporation's sake unless it directly fit in with his programs. The financial strain of the war precluded larger efforts. He did want to splinter his family holdings or offer equity, making greater expansion unlikely. Finally, Thyssen's strategy concentrated on renovating existing plant.[43] Thyssen did play a modest role in postwar vertical expansion. During the war, Thyssen had achieved majority holdings in some of the major shipbuilding firms such as the *Bremer Vulkan Schiffsbau- und Maschinenfabrik AG* and, just after the war, the *Flensburger Schiffbau AG*. He consolidated his hold on the *Press- und Walzwerk* in Reisholz, making it a core part of the Thyssen-Konzern. He also invested to a small degree in numerous other lignite and machine engineering companies to facilitate cooperation, but without attempting to integrate them.[44] Thyssen also concluded a number of joint ventures with the Klöckner-Konzern, including the *Krefelder Stahlwerk AG* and *Geisweider Eisenwerke AG.*

Above all, Thyssen management instrumentalized the inflation to reconstruct the Konzern on a new productive and organizational basis that preceded the more famous rationalization movement of mid-Weimar. Ironically, the constant production interruptions of the inflationary period provided management a chance to upgrade facilities and management, which might have been more difficult in times of continuous production. The VSt rationalization drive rested fundamentally on this inflationary reconstruction.

The impulsive, erratic Fritz Thyssen drove this wave of expensive—if not outsized and overextended—modernization. Thyssen, Sr., retired to his castle. He sometimes became disoriented during discussions of money in orders of magnitude that bore little relation to anything in his experience. (An apocryphal story once related that Thyssen was found standing confused outside a hotel because a woman in the wardrobe room demanded seven million marks from him to hang up his coat.)[45] According to one director, Thyssen, Sr., admitted "I am becoming old."[46] He was over eighty. While such stories exaggerate Thyssen, Sr.'s declining mental state, he was no longer as sharp as he had been. Fritz Thyssen took as much liquid capital as he could and transformed it into solid productive capacity. Fritz's never-ending requests for more capital to expand set up a simmering conflict between father and son, brother and brother.

Thyssen management launched a ten-year plan to expand and rationalize the Gewerkschaft Friedrich Thyssen and its affiliated mining fields. The plan foresaw a doubling of the 4.5 million tons mined in 1913. Like other mining firms, Thyssen placed a special emphasis on mechanizing the mines and drilling new shafts. By 1926, increasing mechanization and pneumatic jacks and hammers helped extract almost 66% of all coal in Ruhr mines in comparison with just 2% in 1913.[47] Thyssen helped lead the way. Thyssen also wanted to strengthen his hand in any future coal syndicate negotiations. Most coal producers (90%) agreed to join the 1924 extension, but Thyssen, backed by his modernized plant, refused to join, along with a number of other large mining companies. The government had to step in, but made concessions to the holdouts.[48]

In crude steel production, the modernization of the ATH was designed to offset the gaping hole in the supply of intermediate materials caused by the loss of Stahlwerke Thyssen. Lack of regular maintenance and repair during the war had left the ATH steelworks in disarray. In 1920, it began constructing a seventh blast furnace complex, finishing it by 1922, and completely renovated two other blast furnaces by 1925. Modeled on the state-of-the-art energy economies of the AGHütt, Thyssen's top technical director, Franz Bartscherer, added regenerative furnaces. By 1926, the ATH did not need a single ton of additional coal for crude steel or rolling mill production, because it used the ample gas energy coming from the coking and blast furnace processes. The combined improvements caused pig-iron production to double, while the use of coal sank by a dramatic *80%*.[49] The ATH added a long-planned sixth Thomas converter in 1923, which went into operation by 1925. Delayed since 1917, an entirely new Siemens-Martin plant was added, with two furnaces of 40 tons and four furnaces of 80 tons. In 1925, ATH shut down the first and original Siemens-Martin furnace built in 1891. Crude steel capacity almost doubled to 1.5 million tons. The weight of individual steel blocks rose dramatically.

Improvements in crude-steel manufacturing forced changes in steel-finishing stages. Thyssen managers modernized the entire rolling mills. They discontinued many of the old mill trains, in use since the 1890s. All of the new rolling-mill trains ran on electricity, and in 1923 and 1924, most of the new rolling mill trains went into operation. Rolling-mill capacity rose to just under one million tons per year. Mechanical conveyance systems across the whole works were introduced, such as slanted conveyer systems for raw materials, magnetic cranes, and scrap presses for crushing scrap into charges up to one ton.[50] At the AGHütt and the ATH Dinslaken, whose facilities had largely been completed just before the war, both firms had to content themselves with minor improvements in their facilities,

Thyssen's Mülheim Rolling Mills also underwent dramatic improvements. Led by Carl Wallmann, Rudolf Traut, and Martin Roeckner, the Thyssen & Co. Rolling Mills were entirely modernized. Thyssen & Co. managers had discussed some of these new projects for a decade before they could carry them out, beginning in 1921.

The Thyssen & Co. Machine Company returned to its old production program with all possible speed. Taking advantage of its engineering capabilities, the Machine Company bought out a troubled electrical machinery producer from Duisburg, the *Chr. Weuste & Overbeck GmbH,* and began manufacturing a new line of heavy electric dynamos. This firm's equipment moved into the halls of the old munitions factory and became an entirely new electro-technical department. The Machine Company purchased a special licensing agreement with a Swiss precision gear firm for electric dynamos. Thyssen then bought roughly 10 million marks of shares in the AEG with the intention of cooperating with it. By April 1921, the Machine Company exhibited huge steam turbines that could generate 12,000 kW of electricity. It could produce all ranges of gas and steam turbines for generating electricity. The Machine Company became the only firm in Germany which could supply the large flywheels for the electrical parts of the gas-powered electric dynamos. Inside the next few years, this department grew to be not only one of the most important departments inside the Machine Company, but in all of Germany. These new successes in generating electricity fed positively into the rationalization plans of the ATH. It was precisely in the realm of energy economies that the Thyssen-Konzern proved to be one of the leaders in the world. When a Siemens director toured Ruhr industry in April 1921, he found it "completely astonishing" that Thyssen was the only firm to use the gas-powered electric dynamo. These products successfully penetrated Siemens-Schuckert's traditional markets.[51] The Machine Company matched these technical achievements with the development of new quality controls and new advances in basic research and development.

Of equal importance with these clear technical achievements were Thyssen's organizational innovations, which placed the Konzern on the cutting edge of the German rationalization movement. Most of the voluminous literature about rationalization concentrates on shop-floor, labor, and production issues, especially the introduction of Taylorism.[52] There has been less coverage of managerial practice. Here I would like to highlight the work of just two people who represented a new guard of managers and of managerial technique: Franz Bartscherer and Heinrich Dinkelbach.

Franz Bartscherer stepped into the very large shoes of Franz Dahl, and in certain respects, Hans Richter.[53] In 1900, he graduated from the Technical University of Munich in machine engineering and immediately took a position at MAN, working there from 1901 to 1906 designing high-powered gas engines. (Bartscherer was at MAN at the same time as Richter when MAN delivered the first gas engine to the GDK.) Thyssen hired away Bartscherer to become the first director of manufacturing the GDK's massive, new array of gas engines in the central power plant. Thyssen promoted him quickly. By 1913, at thirty-five, he headed the machine facilities of the GDK blast furnaces in Hamborn and the coking operations in Bruckhausen, at the AGHütt in Meiderich, and the new Stahlwerke Thyssen in Lorraine. By 1917, Thyssen had named him a director, responsible for all of Thyssen's central power plants. By 1919, he was responsible for all of the machinery and equipment of the ATH. In 1924, Thyssen named Bartscherer works director of the ATH and chair of its technical board.

In the 1920s, his reputation as the "King of the Steelworks" grew. Bartscherer was tremendously competent and talented. He learned almost every detail of mechanical engineering, and iron and steel-making, and steel manufacturing. Branching out from his expertise in gas engines, he achieved patents across the full spectrum of blast-furnace operations, for rolling-mill trains, and for quality steel production. Even after his retirement, he remained active in experimental work in blast-furnace operations. Moreover, in 1921, the ATH completely renovated its chemical testing laboratory to incorporate higher levels of basic research on top of its older function of quality control, testing, and development. The ATH actively linked this laboratory with the education of university students. In 1937, Fritz Thyssen felt that Bartscherer was responsible for the ATH's reputation as the most technically advanced steelworks in Europe. Bartscherer would direct ATH until 1943. Many future ATH executives owed a good deal to Bartscherer, including Hans-Günther Sohl, the ATH director after World War II.

But it was how he ruled that made Bartscherer distinctive. He ruled through sober measurement and cold numbers. In 1920, Bartscherer founded the "Office for Power and Heat" at the ATH. Bartscherer hired numerous specialists to measure, test, experiment, and improve the efficiency of generators, machines, and the production process. At the ATH, the tremendous reduction of energy costs owed much to this commission. Other German steel firms also established similar offices, as did the Association of German Steelmakers, but none achieved quite Bartscherer's dramatic success, which he believed to be the most important change in steelmaking of the 1920s. These offices for energy efficiency acted as the seedbed of more comprehensive rationalization drives throughout the German steel industry. Bartscherer led the way in the ATH of broadening the scope of this investigative office to analyze systematically the entire production process. In 1925, he set up a central office of "Technical Factory Management," which attempted to capture the entire technical side of the production process from beginning to end in figures and ratios. According to Carl-Friedrich Baumann, "technical economy as a instrument of control for an entire steelworks is primarily an innovation of Bartscherer." One innovative aspect of the office was to put engineers and technical specialists in charge of cost control, instead of commercial accountants, who could measure input costs but did not have the technical know-how to measure, analyze, and improve the efficiency of conversion processes. The result of all of these measurements was a little black ring-binder that appeared on Bartscherer's desk every morning reporting on the firm's operations during the previous day and night shift. Bartscherer made decisions and scolded subordinates based on this evidence. He had the right numbers.

Beyond his technical competence, Bartscherer's reputation in German industry grew on the basis of his contributions to the practice of general management. From 1925 to 1946, he served on the executive board of the Association of German Steelmakers. He received an honorary doctorate in 1930 from the Mining Academy in Freiberg (Saxony). Again, the links among factory developments, industry associations, and universities characterized the German path of scientific management. While American and Taylorist principles certainly influenced German factory management, German scientific management had other roots, growing out of economies of energy rather than labor efficiency. It was also more system-oriented rather than workshop-oriented. But Bartscherer, and others of his generation, still found a way to distill the essence of a Taylorist spirit of technocratic control through machines and numbers.

In a different capacity but with similar tendencies, Heinrich Dinkelbach acted as a commercial counterpart to Bartscherer. Bartscherer was to technical rationalization at the ATH what Dinkelbach was to organizational rationalization at Thyssen & Co. In 1909, he entered the

Thyssen & Co. Machine Company. By 1912, Dinkelbach headed inventory accounting and even tried introducing the Hollerith punchcard machine. He would eventually perfect its use for the VSt after 1926. The war opened up a whole range of opportunities for Dinkelbach in the Machine Company when the army declared him unfit for service. When Härle went to the front, Dinkelbach took over its immense administrative responsibilities, which he handled superbly. During the war, Dinkelbach introduced American-style bookkeeping to Thyssen & Co., which again foreshadowed his work inside the VSt.[54]

After the war, he made himself invaluable. Dinkelbach implemented a whole set of new organizational innovations, which bound the two divisions more closely together as a single firm. He improved inventory tracking and valuations. Dinkelbach designed preformatted, standard forms for inventorying for each of the individual departments. Handwritten inventories of the Rolling Mill departments began to be typewritten. He introduced a card system. He completely reorganized the internal commercial process of both divisions for ordering, purchasing, shipping, and recording and controlling transactions. He also drew up standardized forms for internal control according to the rigid, functionalized principles that connected the work processes of all specialized offices across the firm into a single flow of information. For instance: "Principle: The supplier has the same organization as the receiver." This quote is also a good example of the modern, minimalist writing style that Dinkelbach cultivated. He reorganized Thyssen & Co.'s administration to standardize, monitor, and control the format of the orders among the purchasing department, bookkeeping, inventory bookkeeping, and current accounts. Changes in inventories could now be monitored on a monthly basis and incorporated into the monthly balances along with new investment costs. The innovations allowed monthly inventory evaluations to be cost-effective so that the monthly balances represented a more accurate assessment of the monthly net profits of the individual departments.[55] Handwritten trial balances were replaced by typewritten current accounts, classified into the most important categories of postings.[56] Analogous to the way engineers reorganized the shopfloor to improve the flow of materials and people, simplifying and standardizing activities, Dinkelbach reorganized and accelerated the flow of information. Such standardization provided the necessary basis for the eventual punchcard monitoring system introduced by the VSt after 1926.

The frequent shutdowns of the firm, especially in 1923, actually facilitated many of these organizational changes by providing a breathing space to introduce them. While the plant was still, many white-collar employees remained in their offices and had time to alter routines. Dinkelbach was the main liaison of Thyssen & Co. to the CAO in Bruckhausen, where he came into contact with Rabes and Fritz Thyssen. Rabes became a key sponsor of Dinkelbach's career within the Thyssen-Konzern and later the VSt. By the age of thirty, Dinkelbach headed the auditing department of one of the premier firms in Germany. In 1923, at thirty-two, he received power of attorney. In April 1925, Rabes transferred him to the CAO in Bruckhausen to help upgrade CAO auditing and information practices. There, Dinkelbach became privy to the negotiations to found the VSt, which began in the autumn of the same year.

Both Bartscherer and Dinkelbach are just exemplars of the collective work of many managers. They represented a new type of manager, enamored with science and system, objective information, and a faith in numbers so typical of the rationalizers of the 1920s.

Nowhere can this organizational rationalization be more dramatically conveyed than in the organization of the Machine Company (Figure 11.3). The Machine Company retained its central, functional organizational design, but added two main sets of offices to each product department designed to map out the production process more efficiently. The first set of offices signalled explicitly its chief aim and claim: the "Technical Central Office for Standardization and Progress." The office combined the setting of norms, orders, appointments, apprentice-training workshops, along with reserve parts, inventories, piece lists, work and material distribution. It provided a central information-clearing house for various production offices and production-planning offices. The production-planning offices concentrated largely on the specifics of their individual production workshops. What the design offices were to the construction of machines, the new planning offices were to the production process. Each operating unit had its own production-planning office except for the gas engine, steelworks machines and rolling-mill train, railway, rolling stock and pipeline workshops; these were centralized along with their respective production offices. Furthermore, all of the Machine Company's production departments were functional workshops, which generally had a production supervisor with his assistants, a production planning of-

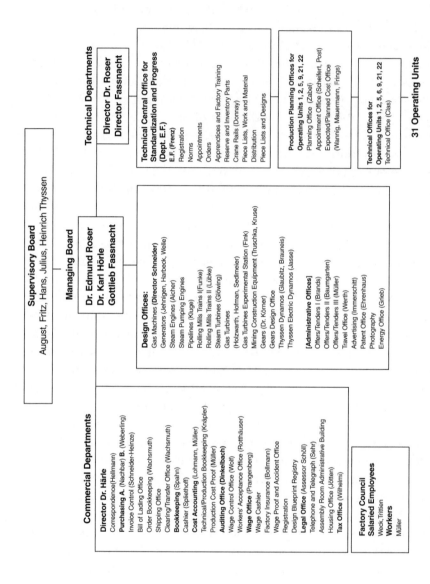

Supervisory Board
August, Fritz, Hans, Julius, Heinrich Thyssen

Managing Board
Dr. Edmund Roser
Dr. Karl Hörle
Gottlieb Fassnacht

Commercial Departments

Director Dr. Härle
Correspondence(Hellmann)
Purchasing A. (Nachbar) **B.** (Weberling)
Invoice Control (Schneider–Heinze)
Bill of Lading Office
Order Bookkeeping (Wachsmuth)
Shipping Office
Clearing/Transfer Office (Wachsmuth)
Bookkeeping (Spahn)
Cashier (Spliethoff)
Cost Accounting (Lohmann, Müller)
Technical/Production Bookkeeping (Knäpler)
Production Cost Proof (Müller)
Auditing Office (Dinkelbach)
Wage Control Office (Wolf)
Workers' Acceptance Office (Rotthäuser)
Wage Office (Prangenberg)
Wage Cashier
Factory Insurance (Bollmann)
Wage Proof and Accident Office
Registration
Design Blueprint Registry
Legal Office (Assessor Schöll)
Telephone and Telegraph (Sehr)
Assembly Room Administrative Building
Housing Office (Jötten)
Tax Office (Wilhelmi)

Factory Council
Salaried Employees
Weck, Trittien
Workers
Müller

Technical Departments

Director Dr. Roser
Director Fassnacht

Design Offices:
Gas Machines **(Director Schneider)**
Generators (Jehnigen, Harbeck, Welle)
Steam Engines (Aicher)
Steam Pumping Engines
Pipelines (Kluge)
Rolling Mills Trains I(Funke)
Rolling Mills Trains II (Lübke)
Steam Turbines (Glöwing)
Gas Turbines
(Holzwarth, Hofman, Sedlmeier)
Gas Turbines Experimental Station (Fink)
Mining Construction Equipment (Truschka, Kruse)
Gears (Dr. Körner)
Gears Design Office
Thyssen Dynamos (Glaubitz, Brauneis)
Thyssen Electric Dynamos (Jasse)

[Administrative Offices]
Offers/Tenders I (Brands)
Offers/Tenders II (Baumgarten)
Offers/Tenders III (Müller)
Travel Office (Werth)
Advertising (Immerschitt)
Patent Office (Ehrenhaus)
Photography
Energy Office (Grieb)

**Technical Central Office for
Standardization and Progress
(Dept. E.F.)**
E.F. (Frenz)
Registration
Norms
Appointments
Orders
Apprentices and Factory Training
Reserve and Inventory Parts
Crane Rails (Donnay)
Piece Lists, Work and Material
Distribution
Piece Lists and Designs

**Production Planning Offices for
Operating Units 1, 2, 5, 9, 21, 22**
Planning Office (Zabel)
Appointment Office (Scheifert, Post)
Expected/Planned Cost Office
(Wannig, Mauermann, Frings)

**Technical Offices for
Operating Units 1, 2, 5, 6, 9, 21, 22**
Technical Office (Clas)

31 Operating Units

Figure 11.3 Thyssen & Co. AG, Machine Engineering Division, 1922

Figure 11.4 Headquarters of the Thyssen & Co. rolling mills. Built by 1922, the Machine Company headquarters is located directly adjacent to it and connected by a bridge, symbolizing their divisional structure. Taken in 1983, this became the headquarters for the VSt Deutsche Röhrenwerke and eventually the Mannesmann-Röhrenwerke Mülheim headquarters (sign above). Note the Thyssen & Co. symbol above the main portal. (Reproduced with the permission of the Mannesmann-Archiv, Mülheim/Ruhr)

fice, a production office, a technical office, various workshops, and a shipping/loading office. Only the electrical machine department, like the rolling mills departments, included a commercial, wage calculation, and appointment office. The iron and metal foundries and gas central had their own laboratories for quality control.

Altogether, these organizational innovations after the fusion under Härle and Dinkelbach represented the most significant set of organizational reforms inside Thyssen & Co. since those of Ernst Nölle's in the early 1880s. Attesting to the close relationship between organizational innovation and its architectural housing, Thyssen & Co. built a new central office building for the Rolling Mills (Figure 11.4).

The building itself was designed along streamlined, functional lines, in the same way that Thyssen managerial systems were developing. The two Thyssen & Co. divisions each had their own office building, but the unity of the corporation was symbolized by the bridge between the two. In organizational terms, Dinkelbach bridged the two Thyssen & Co. divisions through the auditing and accounting offices; otherwise, the two divisions retained their organizational subcultures.

Dinkelbach's innovations in managerial control fused the auditing, bookkeeping, inventory, planning, and cost-accounting functions into a consistent, rational information system, epitomized by the name of the technical central office as "standardization and progress," along American lines. Bartscherer's and Dinkelbach's reforms are excellent examples of how rationalization, standardization, Americanization, and bureaucratization went hand-in-hand. Until the 1920s, German management used far fewer standardized forms and procedures than did American management.[57] Ironically, catching-up to these management techniques, made in America, meant generating more paperwork.

Thyssenhandel

At the end of the war, a far-reaching strategic discussion also began on how to reestablish the Thyssen-Konzern in peacetime world markets. A "new order" recast Thyssen marketing operations by expanding direct distribution channels and centralizing overall strategy in a corporate board known as *Thyssenhandel*. While that board formalized Thyssen marketing operations, they also reaffirmed the basic values and policies underlying Thyssen corporate culture.

In November 1916, a GDK board of directors reiterated Thyssen's basic policy of remaining as independent as possible from wholesalers. Large Berlin iron and steel wholesalers had just held a conference, in which they discussed binding together to counter the expected syndication of B-products by manufacturers in the Steel Works Association. As if they had never heard of such an idea, GDK directors agreed that they should "energetically" fight against such collusion, because producers would lose their autonomy and profits if wholesalers banded together.[58]

Thyssen's policy of principled independence became institutionalized in the expansion of the Thyssen trading firms during and after the war, to include Essen (1914), Mannheim and Hamborn-Duisburg

(1915),[59] Halle and Erfurt (1916), and Leipzig and Hamburg (1918). Unlike the prewar period, when Thyssen directed his expansion abroad and overseas, the postwar world was going to be considerably more domestically-oriented. Reflecting the leadership balance inside the Konzern, Thyssen & Co. had primary responsibility for the eastern areas of Germany, the GDK for trading firms in the west and south.[60]

Philip Neuhaus of Thyssen & Co. set the outlines for the debate about the nature and goals of Thyssen marketing operations in the postwar period.[61] The main point of contention was whether they should centralize postwar marketing operations. Neuhaus argued against a reorganization of Thyssen trading firms by appealing to historical continuity:

> Because, however, the trading firms, as they are operated, have proven themselves even from the standpoint of manufacturing, no compelling reason exists to change in one direction or the other. It must also be doubted, and rightly so, whether it is appropriate now during the war or after the peace treaty, to rearrange a decades-old foundation *(Grundlage)*, on which the Thyssen-Group's manufacturing and marketing have grown, in favor of another for which no experience exists.

Neuhaus contrasted Thyssen's arrangements favorably with the marketing operations of Rombach, Kneuttingen and Deutsch-Luxemburg, and the Königs- und Laurahütte. Neuhaus perfunctorily dismissed their arrangements and used them more as a rhetorical plea to stick to the tried and true.

Neuhaus argued against the creation of a central board for Thyssen marketing. He felt that a central office could not possibly coordinate regional trading firms; important cartel agreements (such as structural steel quotas) were negotiated regionally. Even the Steel Works Association did not impose unified guidelines on its regional offices, in the interest of holding the association together.[62] Neuhaus felt personnel problems would arise if a central representative not familiar with the details of the individual trading firms gave orders. Moreover, too many executives would feel passed over or injured. Neuhaus recommended that each manufacturing firm have a representative on the supervisory board of each marketing firm to enhance coordination and balance influence. This would promote "friendly, professional cooperation." If a new central board for Thyssen marketing were established,

Neuhaus felt that the executive in charge must be someone from the manufacturing works who would be "equally unbiased" and did not belong to any of the individual marketing offices. He must be based in an area:

> There, where the market is most comprehensive and mirrors most faithfully all types of incoming inquiries from domestic and foreign lands is the most fruitful basis [for a central director] to support Thyssen trading firms with informed advice, whose directors essentially know and see only their familiar area, that means, a more or less large cross-section of the market.

If a chief executive of Thyssen marketing stood too near any one of the branch offices, his appointment would only call forth accusations of favoritism. Neuhaus urged that these organizational "imponderables" be taken seriously. The final question addressed by Neuhaus concerned the proper delineation of boundaries between the various marketing firms. Apparently, considerable "unproductive frictions" among the trading firms existed regarding the size of their districts, especially between Cologne and Essen.

Neuhaus' memorandum turns a spotlight on the politicized nature of reordering Thyssenhandel. The proposed central board would shift the weight of marketing strategy to the GDK. A more decentralized structure would keep Mülheim—and Neuhaus—at a key organization point. The appointment and location of Thyssenhandel's director was an explicit organizational variable.

The May 1918 conference created a formal contract (like the IG) to reorder Thyssen marketing, but directors rejected or modified a number of Neuhaus' suggestions.[63] Neuhaus recommended fusing Hamborn with Cologne and making Cologne the center for the entire export trade. In the margins of Neuhaus' memo, August Thyssen personally and respectfully commented: "I would not recommend Cologne for the export trade. The export trade should have contact with both the firms and the shipping trade. Rotterdam or Antwerp would be particularly suitable as a seat for export." Thyssen's recommendation did not make it to the final agreement either. Duisburg became the site of the export trade, not Cologne, Rotterdam, or Antwerp. Among his top executives, Thyssen not only gave out advice but took it as well.[64]

The conference outlined spheres of activity precisely for each of Thyssen trading firms. As Neuhaus had suggested, the Hamborn trading firm fused with another trading firm, but with Duisburg, not Cologne. Duisburg gained responsibility for all of the export trade and for north, west, and middle Germany, where no other trading firm yet existed. Thyssen & Co., Berlin retained its pipe and tube customers in other domestic areas. Berlin, moreover, became responsible for the areas east of the Elbe, stretching up to the second main area, Heinrich Reiter in Königsberg and the trading firm in Halle. Königsberg retained its sales area, along with responsibility for the area brought under German control by the Brest-Litovsk treaty. Berlin's area would shrink once the new trading firms in Dresden or Leipzig and Magdeburg were established. Cologne, the third main area, became responsible for Rhineland-Westphalia; Mannheim for southern Germany; Halle and Erfurt split responsibility for middle Germany and Saxony.

Except for Halle and Erfurt, the contract called for each of these trading firms became the parent firm or head office for any other branch offices or new trading firms in their respective areas:

In those areas, the oldest and/or most proven subsidiary is the leader. It should be, so to speak, the parent company *(Mutterhaus)*, which brings together the general administrative and organizational questions of the trading houses which work in the same autonomous economic sphere. New firms should be founded and be administered by it without impinging on the [new trading house's] required freedom of action in business. The other trading houses, viewed as subsidiaries *(Tochtergesellschaften)*, should assume the responsibility themselves though for the line of business as such, that is, negotiations and transactions with Thyssen firms, other companies as well as with the customers.

The Thyssenhandel contract emphasized the need for freedom to maneuver and to operate the subsidiary of the parent firm "self-sufficiently." On the other hand, the parent firm decided important administrative and organizational questions. Again, we see that curious mixture of central supervision and decentralized decision-making, of authority and delegation inside the Thyssen-Konzern being reproduced among the regional trading firms.

With this reaffirmation of decentralized operations, the conference established a central board to administer the overall strategic direction of Thyssenhandel. It was responsible for all decisions concerning the establishment and expansion of new trading firms, as well as hiring new lead managers. It should act as a central informational and advisory committee for firms trading iron and steel products. Coal-trading firms (under Rabes) were excluded. The Thyssenhandel board of directors included Sandmann from the GDK Hamborn (who became chair), Kalle from Dinslaken, Gilles from Mülheim, and Spiess from Hagendingen. The AGHütt accepted the terms of the contract, but did not join the agreement. Verlohr thought it wise to wait until the end of the war when the move to Duisburg was complete, especially as the scrap trade needed special expertise.

All financial transactions for Thyssenhandel were routed through the Duisburg trading firm. As the conference agreement stressed, this arrangement should not jeopardize trading firms with late transfer payments or higher interest charges. Thyssen managers urged "pragmatism." They also recommended that Hamborn, Mülheim, and Hagendingen be included in the transfer of funds, with notification to the Reichsbank institute in Duisburg. Clearly, they were spreading income derived from current-account and revenue transactions to different cities.

Temporary exceptions to this "new order" were Thyssen & Co., Berlin, and Heinrich Reiter GmbH in Königsberg. Berlin was legally still a branch office of Thyssen & Co., not an independent firm, and Thyssen & Co. fully owned Heinrich Reiter. Berlin became an independent firm after the 1918 fusion of the Thyssen & Co. Rolling Mills and Machine Company. But after the Thyssenhandel conference, all its main contract negotiations went through Bruckhausen and Duisburg.[65] The Mülheim *Centralbureau* lost the control it had held since the 1880s. Probably feeling passed over, Neuhaus left Thyssen & Co. for Krupp that same year.[66]

As a result of the conference, a formal contract was made between the steel works and the Thyssen trading firms, spelling out the basic principles already governing Thyssen operations. Unlike the prewar arrangement, it provided a specific financial formula for regulating the relationship between manufacturing works and trading firms. These transfer prices are central to understanding the governance structure of the Konzern, and contained potent organizational-political implications.

Thyssen trading firms agreed to purchase from the manufacturing works at the most favorable market price for nonsyndicated goods and at cartel prices for syndicated goods; the contract termed this a "transfer sale price" *(Abschlagspreise)*. Trading firms could reduce this price by 1.5% to compensate for the salaries of their liaison officers present at the manufacturing works and any other costs arising from transactions, including revenue taxes. Thyssenhandel profits deriving from the sale of Thyssen products went to the manufacturing firms as a "transfer sum" *(Restkaufgeld)*, proportional to the quantities delivered to the trading firms. The transfer sum equalled the returns minus the transfer sale price, minus any payments to third parties, administrative and operational overhead, shortfalls, and depreciation.

The transfer sale price for nonsyndicated goods still rested on what the "most favorable market price" actually was. Judging from the correspondence, deciding this "most favorable market price" became subject to considerable and contentious debate. Setting the transfer price became a focal point of interorganizational negotiation, not a formal, rational procedure. Even the formal calculation of the transfer sum, which included various expenses incurred by the trading firm, was subject to interpretation, because included estimated costs, such as overhead and depreciation.

For the Thyssen-Konzern, the transfer-price formula forced the manufacturing units to make a profit on the most favorable market price and forced the trading firms to find customers willing to accept prices slightly higher than the most favorable price. Thyssenhandel firms had to concentrate on finding customers among small to middle size consumers, while the sales departments of the manufacturing firms dealt directly with the large commercial dealers and syndicates.[67]

Internal transfer prices were also based on syndicate prices. In effect, the cartel organization of German steel permeated the internal structure of the Konzern. This also meant that the Thyssen trading firms found no particular price advantage in the vertically integrated Konzern structure. This also kept profits from sales of syndicated goods, which were higher than market prices, largely inside the manufacturing units. The organizational bias of the Konzern remained with the manufacturing plants, forcing each trading firm to market even more effectively if it wanted to earn more profits. But this syndicate-set transfer price also held true for purchasing among Thyssen manufacturing works—as long as cartel agreements held. An American consulting firm found that various Thyssen steel works drew their coal at market rate (i.e., syndicate prices), not at an internal rate.[68] Coal was implicitly subsidized. This forced the steel works to remain efficient as possible and to minimize coal use. This incentive probably drove Bartscherer even harder to develop economies of energy at the ATH. In brief, the transfer pricing structure of the Konzern helped spread profits around the Konzern, and forced everyone to manufacture more efficiently and market more effectively, as if they were independent producers on the open market.

The advantages of this governance structure were clear. Thyssen retained a great degree of market pressure within a vertically integrated structure by assessing each module or subsidiary on market-based criteria and performance. The decentralization of decision-making ensured flexible responses to regional and local conditions, and gave a great deal of autonomy to the directors of the respective subsidiaries. The multisubsidiary form oriented to market prices built in a high degree of "pragmatism" and flexibility.

There were also disadvantages to such a governance structure. The incentive structure built on market transfer prices kept the Thyssen-Konzern immensely competitive, but depressed immediate profitability. (Thyssen's outstanding manufacturing efficiency would pay off during the negotiations to found the VSt.) Ironically, for a firm with a clear entrepreneurial point, central coordination and policy came together from a range of decentralized decisions. The new Thyssenhandel board helped solve some problems. In fact, at the end of the May 1918 conference, August Thyssen urged that more such meetings take place, "because they unmistakably could promote the effectiveness of the whole [Konzern]." Also a continuous, contentious stream of negotiation flowed among the sales departments, the manufacturing works, and trading firms: what was the most favorable market price for a given month? This heightened internal rivalries. Again the CAO played a key role in assessing whether each subsidiary bought and sold competitively.

Finally, and most importantly, the multisubsidiary form meant that each manufacturing and trading firm was a legal entity—but in postwar Germany, such interfirm trade was subject to taxation. This became a huge problem, as turnover and capital transfer taxes hit the Thyssen-Konzern hard. Eventually, they had to unify the Thyssen-Konzern legally into a single corporation.

Initially, Thyssen circumvented the effects of the revenue tax by passing it on to customers. As long as other firms did the same, the practice worked. Typically, German business created agreements to treat the tax consistently, but some firms, like Krupp and Gelsenkirchen, broke away. The turnover tax also opened up the question of how to handle the tax consistently *within* the Thyssen-Konzern. Each purchasing firm inside the Konzern assumed the costs of the tax, but passed it off to customers inconsistently, and individual purchasing offices or trading firms refused to accept the extra charge. In 1917, Späing took the point of view that the Thyssen-Konzern was a "unified whole," at least among those manufacturing and marketing firms owned completely by Thyssen, and thus should not be subject to the tax.[69] Although Späing's logic was impeccable, it contradicted existing German corporate law. Four years later, Späing reached an agreement with the Imperial Finance Court whereby sales arranged by Thyssenhandel, but not purchased or which did not pass through their warehouses, were exempt from the turnover tax.[70]

The turbulent postwar period gave new responsibilities to Thyssen trading firms. Some correspondence from 1910–1925 has survived from Thyssenhandel Duisburg, allowing us to see how these marketing arrangements worked in practice.[71] Duisburg was probably the most important Thyssenhandel firm because it handled all the export trade, the financial affairs of Thyssenhandel, and most of the materials delivery between the ATH and Thyssen & Co.[72] Thyssenhandel Duisburg became the new center of the Konzern scrap trade, which Thyssen & Co. had managed since the days of Franz Wilke. Becker left Mülheim in late 1920 to take over as director at Duisburg. He became known as the "scrap baron" of the Konzern.[73]

Thyssenhandel firms helped mediate financial and trading relationships among various manufacturing works, especially by helping set market transfer prices. Thyssenhandel Duisburg processed a constant stream of accusations, retorts, requests, reports, commissions, and contacts between Thyssen & Co. and the ATH. In December 1921, for instance, the ATH asked Thyssenhandel Duisburg to raise their transfer prices to Thyssen & Co. by 15%. Thyssenhandel checked with Thyssen & Co. to see if the new price was appropriate, but Thyssen & Co. replied that new, higher prices were only appropriate if deliveries were regular. Indeed, the strip-steel mill in Mülheim had to shut down two mill trains the next month because of irregular deliveries from the ATH. An aggravated Hermann Eumann suggested that Thyssenhandel Duisburg give in to the ATH in this particular case because "further negotiations with Bruckhausen are completely pointless."[74] In December, the Rolling Mills in Mülheim and Dinslaken negotiated with the ATH steel works to deliver particularly cheap intermediate materials for special export deliveries. Duisburg set the amount, the payment period, and price (in foreign currency). The ATH would supply additional amounts on the basis of the reigning domestic price.[75] Market transfer prices among Thyssen firms were constantly being negotiated. When the ATH again could not deliver, Duisburg arranged deliveries from the Bochumer Verein. But the steel quality was so poor that Thyssen & Co. had to scrap 76% of the manufactured product. Thyssen & Co. then initiated reclamation claims against the Bochumer Verein through Thyssenhandel Duisburg.[76]

Thyssenhandel scrounged for materials of all types in these difficult years. They arranged purchases from numerous other steel-producing firms if they could not get it internally. Duisburg also set up a considerable number of barter deals with other firms.[77] When in March 1922 Thyssen & Co.'s two new pilgrim's-step seamless pipe mills went into operation, Brökelschen and Härle asked Thyssenhandel Duisburg to scour the region for all possible supplies to build up reserves of material.[78] Deliveries from third-party firms, however, caused numerous problems, especially during the upheavals of the postwar period. In March 1922, for instance, Thyssen & Co.'s plate mill and strip-steel mill carried a backlog of non-deliveries from seven different firms. Arranged deliveries often never arrived because rival producers made internal deliveries to their own works a priority before they delivered to outside customers.[79] In April 1922 Krupp complained about slow deliveries from Thyssen & Co., but these deliveries awaited a shipment of intermediate material from Krupp![80]

In general, the ATH and Thyssen & Co. worked cooperatively through Thyssenhandel, but relations could become testy. Analogous to the CAO in the field of accounting and finance, Thyssenhandel played a similar role coordinating products and prices transferred among the subsidiaries. One example epitomizes the internal rivalry that the firms had with one another.[81] On April 18, 1923, the Thyssen & Co. Rolling Mills wrote to Thyssenhandel Duisburg that they had enough square stock in inventory for the strip steel department. They wanted to stop deliveries, although the supply of this intermediate good had consistently been in arrears over the last two years. The ATH wrote Duisburg that it was impossible to stop production at this point. Moreover:

> It is the same old experience that Mülheim completely stops purchases as soon as they have any sort of inventory, regardless of whether we suffer from it or not. Now they have the opportunity to create an inventory for which Mülheim has continually been deficient up to now and this opportunity should definitely be taken advantage of so as to avoid being placed immediately in an embarrassing situation again.[82]

The ATH requested that Thyssenhandel take this matter up with Thyssen & Co.

Thyssenhandel also mediated the manufacturing firms' relations with the syndicates. Thyssenhandel Hamburg convinced the Rhenisch-Westphalian Cement Association in January 1922 to allow cement from the Thyssen-owned firm, Rittergut Rüdersdorf, to be delivered to Thyssen & Co. The regional cement syndicates generally did not allow cross-regional deliveries. Thyssen received extraordinary treatment because of its influence in the syndicates, its property relations, and the postwar economy.[83]

Thyssenhandel illustrates in microcosm the corporate culture inside Thyssen and this study's theoretical concerns. Unlike Wilhelm Treue's exposition, Thyssen did not just delegate responsibilities to managers deriving from some Schumpeterian risk-venturing vision.[84] Thyssen's recommendations were not veiled orders, but true suggestions that could be overturned by reasoned objections. The whole negotiation process surrounding Thyssenhandel indicates a constantly evolving policy instead of a top-down strategy. Policy highlights the negotiated principles, the politicking among difficult tradeoffs. The specific marketing strategy of the Thyssen-Konzern emerged—more an end result of a decision-making evolution than a calculated set of objectives.[85] This negotiation process—including the setting of internal transfer prices—was a political process rather than a rationalization process. The transfer-price formula only helped to form the ground rules for internal debates over "most favorable price." These prices were not an indicator of bureaucratic, formal rationality, but instead reflected market conditions, cartel agreements, and internal political negotiations.

The constant tension among Thyssenhandel and the manufacturing works reproduce a tension between two different conceptions of organizing control inside business enterprises. Other firms' sales operations had a clear dominance in their internal organizations. Part of the genius of Thyssenhandel was that it allowed the trading firms to sell other firms' products to create revenue volume. After learning from years of bad experiences in Berlin, the Thyssen-Konzern realized that a trading firm could not be run as a company sales office. Conversely, the manufacturing firms could not simply act as suppliers for Thyssenhandel's sales strategies. The modular system allowed some degree of leeway to both strategies, although the core Thyssen manufacturing firms clearly had final say. Manufacturing and marketing had discrete logics and often contradicted one another. In short, there were tradeoffs to be managed.

Thus, there existed no single point toward which the Konzern could be rationalized. Instead, the choice lay between two different types of strategies, two types of organizing conceptions—two different rationales. (And here I have only discussed the tension between manufacturing and marketing, not finance and personnel issues.) Thyssen managers engaged in a highly political process to negotiate the inevitable tradeoffs.

Finally, one of the more striking aspects of these Thyssenhandel negotiations is the growing legal formality of interfirm agreements. These formal contracts placed in writing many of the Thyssen-Konzern's implicit policies. The agreements also ensured some degree of continuity across time; in particular, in the event of August Thyssen's death. But even more important, the formal contracts indicated the growing difficulty of squaring the legal autonomy of individual Thyssen firms with the Konzern's obvious "economic unity." The multisubsidiary form broke the legal bounds of what it meant to be one firm under German commercial law. These formal legal agreements (including the IG) helped ensure that the law recognized these arrangements. They would later have major legal, tax, and financial ramifications.

All of these organizational maneuverings and dilemmas brought to the fore the most important organizational question Thyssen faced in 1906, 1915, 1921, and again in 1924: should the Konzern be unified into a single large corporation?

One salient reason was the rising tax burden, especially capital transfer and unnerving turnover taxes. A turnover tax placed an extra charge on all sales between legally independent personages: for example, food sold by retail stores to their customers; machinery sold from one company to another; trade between a cartel and a member firm; but also sales from one Thyssen firm to another.

Another disadvantage of a decentralized structure was that certain things were duplicated, such as administrative headquarters buildings. Although little manufacturing overlap in pipe and tubes existed among Dinslaken, Reisholz, and Mülheim, each of these firms had its own sales force, which did duplicate efforts. This created confusion. Many customers could not figure out which Thyssen firm produced what sort of pipe or where to send their correspondence. Customers might order pipes from Thyssen & Co. and receive pipes from Dinslaken or Reisholz, which raised the suspicion that a mistake had occurred. To counter these problems, Thyssen management established a central office in July 1924 in Mülheim for all pipe and tube sales to facilitate communication and reduce staff costs. But they made this arrangement less effective by continuing to require customers to send separate letters for each type of pipes, because they kept the order registrations distinct among the three firms.[86] In 1923, they also finally established a consolidated product brochure, with hundreds of pages and photographs that displayed the entire range of Thyssen products in English and German.[87] But this was the extent of efforts at consolidation until the end of 1924.

An incident in 1921 explains why Thyssen did not unify and illuminates the underlying continuity of Thyssen-Konzern policy and culture which reinforced this strategic choice. Paul Silverberg of the *Rheinischen Braunkohlen-Aktiengesellschaft* (RBAG) offered to merge with the Thyssen-Konzern. Although Thyssen felt that the RBAG was an important firm, he felt that there were no long-term advantages for the Thyssen-Konzern. He thought that lignite (brown coal) would lose significance over time. A fusion would require founding of a joint-stock company whose shares would be publicly traded, which might splinter family ownership and lead to speculation. Silverberg had also confided that he wanted to be chair, but did not make it a condition of merger. But Thyssen's "greatest concern" was that Silverberg would build a top-heavy, rigid, general administration. This critique foreshadowed VSt's problems.

AGHütt directors agreed wholeheartedly with Thyssen. They established the principle that the Thyssen-Konzern would incorporate only with firms that could purchase or process Thyssen products. Such commitment to their core capabilities kept the Thyssen-Konzern largely out of the merger and acquisition movement of the early 1920s. Finally, provided the liquidity of the Konzern and the stock market value of the RBAG permitted it, they decided to purchase RBAG stock up to 25% to prevent rivals from any "uncomfortable" fusions. Thyssen then formally rejected the offer.[88]

The Silverberg offer discloses clearly the underlying principles of Thyssen's strategy. First, Thyssen considered the danger of losing family control. Second, he considered the long-term value of the product and its relation to his core industrial operations. Third, he stressed, possibly most of all, the importance of certain leadership qualities that could have been lifted straight from his reprimands of Emil Bousse in 1878. Fourth, both Thyssen and his managers stressed the danger of an overly rigid administration. Finally, he contemplated the risk of not controlling a market or company.

Early that same year, a special session of Konzern directors broached the question of unifying the Konzern. Two quandaries blocked it. *The* most controversial question was which directors would be appointed to the board of a unified firm, and which executive would be named *Generaldirektor.* None of the Thyssen directors was willing to subordinate himself to another. This was an even more heated question than the question of which firm should become the central holding company, or which Thyssen son would become chair of a unified board. Directorial independence and family tensions made a unified organization almost unthinkable.

Nevertheless, Späing had to think the unthinkable.[89] Turnover taxes threatened to make the decentralized organization an expensive conceit. Späing evaluated how to consolidate the Konzern without incurring more taxes. One early scheme foresaw leasing all of the core manufacturing firms to Thyssenhandel, creating a single company. But such a merger would end Thyssenhandel's tax privilege since they were legally considered mediating agents, not independent commercial houses. Other problems would arise with senior management, which Späing thought would not be "smooth." Finally, Späing warned that cities were beginning to tax these leasing arrangements to counter companies' clumsy attempts to circumvent new taxes. Taxes and tax law remained too much in flux, especially during the inflation. Späing concluded that such organizational maneuvering would be an "extremely dubious tax experiment."

In the end, the "great disorder" called the organization and finances of the Thyssen-Konzern into question. The inflation gave the Konzern much liquidity, but it also took away its financial solidity. Until the end of 1923, Germany played a losing game economically, socially, and politically. Great industrial firms such as Thyssen could more effectively play in this game and could play without losing proportionally as much, making them so-called winners in an overall losing game.[90] Trying to circumvent, minimize, manipulate, or take advantage of high inflation rates was ultimately not a good way to run a business— or a country. One of the biggest advantages gained by Thyssen from the inflation was the full-scale modernization of his manufacturing plant, built on relatively cheap debt. But the tremendous capacity created, especially at the ATH, quickly became overcapacity once inflation ended.

The incessant disputes between Thyssen, Sr., and his two sons revolved around such questions, especially as expansion, then overcapacity, strained the financial capabilities of the Konzern. Inflation economics irritated the already difficult tensions between father and son. Arguments among Thyssen, Sr., Fritz Thyssen, and Heinrich Thyssen-Bornemisza erupted with frequency and intense bitterness. According to Dinkelbach, Thyssen, Sr., hid certain large financial transactions from Fritz Thyssen.[91] Fritz Thyssen himself admitted to "conflicts."[92] Fritz Thyssen also allowed the ATH to draw money from wherever it could to finance the continuing expansion. Even Carl Rabes began to lose financial oversight.[93] As long as inflationary economics held sway, the Konzern retained financial room to maneuver. Once the mark was again worth a mark of gold instead of paper, the Thyssen-Konzern was plunged into a severe liquidity crisis.

CHAPTER 12

The Demise of the Thyssen-Konzern

I do not like this trust [the Vereinigte Stahlwerke]. This trust will
shatter a broadly conceived and extensive family enterprise.

Heinrich von Thyssen-Bornemisza to Fritz, Julius,
and Hans Thyssen, September 24, 1925

Since 1871, Thyssen had managed to successfully combine two cherished but sometimes contradictory strategic objectives: the desire to
lead the steel industry versus the desire for independent family control of his business. These goals defined the central tension of
Thyssen's long career, yet the decision to join the VSt forced Thyssen
to make a choice between them. Did the VSt represent the crowning
achievement of August Thyssen, the "American," who once said, "The
time of syndicates is past and we must move on to the time of trusts?"
Or did it represent the end of family enterprise in an age of anonymous corporations? How could this notoriously independent entrepreneur possibly join a firm that became known for its shady back-
room shareholding relations, its overbloated boards, and its heavy-
handed bureaucracy?

At the end of November 1923, a new currency, the Rentenmark, was
introduced, a step that ended the hyperinflation almost overnight.[1]
The Reichsbank president Hjalmar Schacht introduced a policy of
tight credit that caused the German economy to enter a major liquidity crunch, called the "stabilization crisis." The sudden tightening of
credit caught Thyssen in the middle of finalizing his expansion plans,
leading to a major liquidity crisis—the worst since the turn-of-the-
century recession. The 1925 crisis fused finance and family issues. The
sibling rivalry of Fritz Thyssen and Baron Heinrich von Thyssen-
Bornemisza also represented two potential but contradictory strategic
options.

478

Elsewhere, a wave of bankruptcies occurred throughout the period 1924–1925. German banks found it difficult to assemble enough capital to finance large-scale industrial projects. The Reichsbank no longer acted as a lender of last resort. At the same time, the Allies agreed to a program of reparations payments based on Germany's ability to pay. The Dawes Plan (named for its American architect) established a triangular system of debt payments among the U.S., the British and French, and Germany, stabilizing the international economy. Currency stability, tight credit, and international regulation paved the way for extensive American loans to German firms and cities, including the steel firms Krupp and Thyssen, who were the first private enterprises to take out loans directly from Wall Street. Financial issues forced the Thyssen-Konzern reluctantly to consolidate into a single, large corporation to eliminate turnover taxes on intra-Konzern deliveries and to become an attractive opportunity for American investment. Arcane but important legal questions and financing determined the strategy of the Thyssen-Konzern in the last two years of its existence.

The central figures managing this reordering were Wilhelm Späing, Carl Rabes, and Heinrich Dinkelbach—all of whom acted in the same capacity for the VSt in 1933–1934. Späing handled all tax and legal questions in cases involving the Reich Finance Court *(Reichsfinanzhof)*. Rabes negotiated directly with Dillon, Read & Co. in New York.[2] Moving over to the CAO, Dinkelbach worked closely with Price, Waterhouse & Co. to create a consolidated Konzern balance suited to American standards. It was a measure of the change in external environment that the German state (through its law, taxes, and courts) and American investors played a crucial role in the reorganization of the Thyssen-Konzern in 1924, the founding of the VSt in 1926, and the reorganization of the VSt in 1932–1934. As such, the issues discussed here act as a preview of the problems and solutions that the VSt would also confront (Part III).

Konzerne and German Corporate Law

What made the massive collection of individual Thyssen firms an "economic unity," or one corporation? In the eyes of the law, they were legally independent corporations (Figure 12.1).

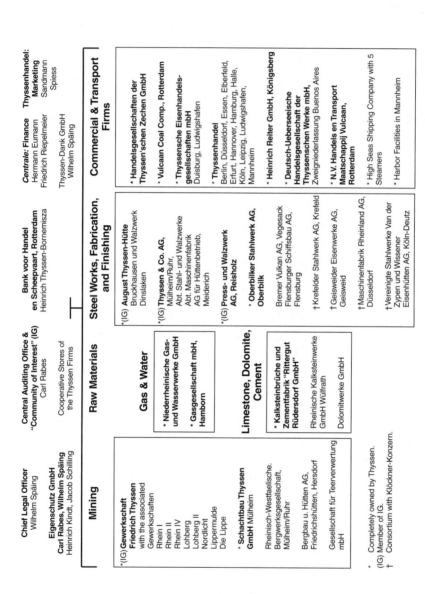

Figure 12.1 Extended Thyssen-Konzern, ca. 1924. *Sources:* W. Treue, *Die Feuer Verlöschen Nie*, p. 222; Paul Arnst, *August Thyssen und Sein Werk*, Anlage 1.

In the prewar period, such a question was merely academic. Thyssen once did run into trouble over the joint use of the GDK's harbor facilities, but serious troubles arose only with the advent of new taxes on corporations to cover the costs of the war. The Finance Ministry introduced an array of new taxes (war profit taxes, export taxes, revenue or turnover taxes, capital transfer taxes, and higher acquisition and incorporation taxes). The turnover tax and the capital transfer tax proved particularly irksome, as they were levied on transactions between legally independent corporations. All sales and capital transfers—including those firms within one Konzern, an IG, or between a cartel (also a legally independent company) and its member firms—were now taxable.[3] The Finance Ministry chose to tax turnover rather than profits because such taxes were easier to assess. A turnover tax avoided German industry's notorious ability to manipulate financial statements. As the Reich Finance Court itself admitted, the rapid expansion of corporate taxes had the unintended effect that firms simply chose their legal forms to create tax advantages, which did not necessarily improve their productivity and even hindered innovation.[4] Paradoxically, both turnover taxes and capital transfer taxes encouraged larger industrial concentrations, which was not necessarily popular.

The turnover tax hit the Thyssen-Konzern especially hard. The simplest solution would have been to unify the Konzern into one corporation, but the expensive costs of incorporation blocked this option. Other postwar Konzerne, which grew by merger and acquisition, also ran into the same problem on top of the usual transition costs associated with mergers. Then, because many industrialists preferred to maintain their managerial flexibility through an IG, turnover taxes affected their inter-Konzern transactions. German Konzerne were caught between two costly options.

The great German Konzerne undermined the basic tenets of a private-individual *(bürgerlich-rechtlich)* conception of the law, codified in the nineteenth century, and called into question what exactly constituted a single corporation. The 1920s wave of mergers, acquisitions, and alliances by German heavy industry created an impenetrable network of production, legal, financial, administrative, and property relations among German steel firms. Nineteenth-century corporate law simply was not designed to deal with such complicated business organizations. This yawning disjunction between the economic conception of the firm and the legal conception of the firm engendered a whole new area of corporate law known as the *Organschaftstheorie*, or the theory of corporate agency.

This body of law grew out of the discrepancy between formal legal independence and the economic unity of allied companies. It was the legal equivalent of trying to draw a circle around irregular shapes. The real winners were tax lawyers like Wilhelm Späing. Only with the background of the "theory of corporate agency" *(Organschaftstheorie)* does it become understandable why and how most of the Thyssen-Konzern was leased to the ATH on December 4, 1924, creating a single, legally unified corporation—which Thyssen management had resisted for twenty years.[5] A similar legal quandary confronted the VSt in 1932. As Späing said to the General Director of the VSt, Albert Vögler:

> Before we reached the Reich Finance Court decision mentioned above, we avoided revenue taxes in 1925 by having all of the Thyssen firms viewed as a unified set of operations *(Betriebsunternehmen)* due to the paramount personality of Mr. August Thyssen and unified through the August Thyssen-Hütte, Gewerkschaft. By leasing the Mülheim, Meiderich and other independently managed and legally independent firms to the August Thyssen-Hütte, Gewerkschaft, [we thereby] first created a corporate *(betriebliche)* unity.[6]

The 1924 arrangement was a measure designed to eliminate turnover taxes after 1925. In part, Späing chose a leasing arrangement to avoid high taxes on full mergers.

To understand the legal problems involved, it is necessary to briefly outline the German legal conception of the firm.[7] German commercial law turns archaically on the concept of "merchant" *(Kaufmann)*, rather than "enterprise" *(Unternehmen)* and, secondarily, on the concept of "commercial transaction" *(Handelsgeschäft)*, a distinction unreflexively adopted from the French *code de commerce* in the mid-nineteenth century.[8] Individuals, commercial partnerships, and companies become merchants when they practice a business activity or are entered into the commercial register. The merchant uses the name of the firm *(die Firma)* to conduct business or sign contracts. Moreover, it is *die Firma* as a legal concept, as a legal umbrella, that ensures the continuity of business relations, assets, and liabilities. Technically, *die Firma* cannot be sold since it is a legal entity only; it can only be transferred or liquidated. German private law does not recognize a business or its assets as a unit of property, and distinguishes sharply between the firm and its ownership even in a general or limited partnership. But unlike joint-stock (AG) or limited liability (GmbH) companies, a partnership has no legal personality apart from its owners. These principles were solidly in place by the time Thyssen began his first venture in 1871.[9]

German commercial law makes a clear distinction between the *internal* relationship between principal and agent, and the *external* relationship between the agent and a third party. The merchant (an individual or a company) is considered the principal and a salaried employee *(Angestellte)* an agent of the firm. A *Prokurist*, for instance, is an agent of the firm with power of attorney. A joint-stock company or a limited liability company, which have their own legal personality, operate through their organs or agents, that is, the general assembly, the supervisory board, and the managing board. Shareholders are thus owners of the firm in an *intermediate* way—mediated by these decision-making bodies or organs. In a partnership, the owners act as the agents of the firm *(Selbstorganschaft)*. Legally, the organs of the firm are also agents of the firm with powers of representation (an external relationship) and powers of management (an internal relationship). Hence, salaried employment, *Prokura,* and company institutional boards are conceptually all entwined on the basis of agency or organs in German law.[10] These esoteric legal distinctions have dramatic implications concerning the organizational form of the enterprise, the representation of the firm, and the relationship of one firm to another.

The key development in corporate law of the nineteenth century was to view joint-stock companies as supra-individual legal personages which could be freely incorporated without special concessions by the state and whose shareholders enjoyed limited liability for the actions of the company.[11] The key question answered in the 1920s was whether or not another firm (as a legal personage) could be considered the same as a salaried employee *(Angestellte)*, that is, an agent or organ of another firm. By 1934, the Reich Finance Court dropped the concept of *Angestellte* entirely in favor of the subsidiary/agency relationship *(Organverhältnis)*.[12] Unlike nineteenth-century corporate law, a subsidiary company did not have to be incorporated into the dominant company for the two to be considered one company. Even so, what criteria determined whether one firm was the organ or agent of another firm?

As it *emerged* throughout the 1920s and well into the 1930s, a company could be considered an agent of another company *only if* the subsidiary company was *financially, economically and organizationally dependent on the dominant company in a subordinate way.*[13] This phrasing is absolutely critical. A firm would have to act like a legally independent "department" *(Abteilung)* of a larger corporate complex.[14] Making matters more complicated, the *Organschaftstheorie* initially applied only to turnover taxes and corporate income taxes, but not capital transfer taxes.[15] Since the *Organschaftstheorie* began as an extension of the assumptions of natural persons, it began with a private individual's assumption of authority over another. Likewise, the dominant firm had to be able to make the subordinate company conform to its decisions or else no relationship of (organic) agency existed. A system of interlocking directories, financial participation or shareholding, close economic relations, legal fusion in the form of IG, joint ventures, long-term contracts, or even 100% ownership—*each one was not sufficient in itself to be considered one corporation.* (For instance, the ATH and Thyssen & Co., though 100% owned by August Thyssen, would not be considered a single enterprise.) The Reich Finance Court would decide if the *Organschaftstheorie* applied to firms only on a case-by-case basis.

Postwar Konzern-building put increasing pressure on the Finance Minister to expand this definition of the corporation. No steel Konzern had succeeded in having it applied to its business operations as a whole until Späing convinced the Finance Court of the appropriateness of the *Organschaftstheorie* for the Thyssen-Konzern on November 25, 1927. Previously, the Rheinische Stahlwerke and Gelsenkirchen had failed. This decision came only a few weeks after the crucial case in which the Reich Finance Court set final criteria for determining when a firm stood in a relationship of organic agency. Späing felt this ruling was one of the shining moments of his career.[16]

Späing reanimated the discussion of whether to consolidate the Konzern into one huge corporation in direct response to an October 1924 decision by the Reich Finance Court, which appeared to clarify the conditions in which the *Organschaftstheorie* applied to a leasing arrangement.[17] Späing designed a ten-year contract by which the ATH leased all other Thyssen companies' facilities, land, buildings, and employee housing, and contractually accepted the rights and responsibilities for their liabilities, employee contracts, inventories, and facilities. According to the Finance Court, in order to be considered an agent of the ATH, each firm had to become financially, economically, and organizationally dependent on the dominant company in a subordinate way.

For financial integration, Späing had little problem showing that Thyssen owned all of the shares of the company, but ownership alone was not sufficient.[18] The 1915 IG profit-pooling agreement also helped demonstrate that the Konzern acted as one financial unit, but the IG and ownership were still not sufficient.

For economic integration, Späing found little difficulty demonstrating the interrelatedness of Thyssen's manufacturing programs. Because of the court's existing criteria for interrelated production, he did not include the Machine Company, as it officially belonged to another industrial branch. At the time (1924), it was by no means clear that the Finance Court would agree that even core, consolidated Thyssen firms constituted a single firm. The Finance Court did not clarify this question until 1926.[19]

To establish organizational integration, the leasing arrangement granted *Prokura* (power of attorney) to all Thyssen executives in the leased firms. As required by law, Späing changed the official name *(die Firma)* of the Thyssen & Co. Rolling Mills, for instance, to the *August Thyssen-Hütte, Gewerkschaft, Abteilung Mülheimer Stahl- und Walzwerke.* Späing sent up a red flag to the Reich Finance Court that it should consider the Thyssen & Co. Rolling Mills dependent on the ATH by explicitly renaming Thyssen & Co. a "department" *(Abteilung)*. He then reworked the *Prokura* of Thyssen executives so that they worked *in the name of* the ATH. Späing designed the changes to signal clearly to authorities that all the organizational and personnel connections with the ATH were consistent with the theory of corporate agency.

The final criteria of the *Organschaftstheorie,* which required independent firms to be subordinate to the will of another, was assured through the formal structure of the new ATH board, which now included all Thyssen directors. The leasing contract made it clear that the ATH exercised "actual authority" over the formerly independent firms "in its own name." Späing highlighted that the leased firms produced, bought, and sold all of their goods in the name of the ATH to convince tax officials that they were dealing with a single enterprise *(Firma)*.

Externally, the ATH represented one corporation in the eyes of the law. The individual leased firms became internal divisions, subsidiary agents of the ATH. *Internally,* however, the previously independent Thyssen firms retained their full managerial autonomy. Späing's solution essentially transformed the Thyssen-Konzern from a multisubsidiary structure into a multidivisional structure. The Rolling Mills, the AGHütt, the mines, and the trading firms became internal divisions of the ATH, along the lines of the ATH Dinslaken (Figure 12.2).

Moreover, the Thyssen-Konzern merged legally without touching on many organizational "imponderables" a single, unified organization would entail. (The VSt would confront these difficulties in abundance.) Späing ingeniously sidestepped the perennial rivalries among Thyssen executives. In practice, decision-making within the Thyssen-Konzern remained *exactly the same,* each senior executive a "lord" over his respective area. Instead of being in charge of a legally independent subsidiary, each now ruled over an independent leased division of the ATH. The legal consolidation of the Thyssen-Konzern into the August Thyssen-Hütte then eased negotiations with American investment houses.

The care that Späing put into thinking through the logic of the Reich Finance Court's decisions and matching the new organization of the Thyssen-Konzern to its legal criteria was well taken. Thyssen needed it. The *Organschaftstheorie* was in such a state of flux that many actions by financial authorities, that is, the executive branches of the Finance Ministry, conflicted with the rulings of the Reich Finance Court. Various federal, regional, and local ministries did not yet follow a unified policy. Believing that they had done enough to convince the tax authorities, the Thyssen-Konzern did not pay taxes on intra-Konzern deliveries in 1925–1926 because they felt these were internal transfers of one corporation.

Importantly, the Reich Finance Court grounded its 1927 decision less on the complicated leasing consolidation of the ATH, but primarily on the fact that all firms were dependent on the property relations of the Thyssen family. That all financial, economic, and organizational threads of Thyssen's business passed through the ATH and the IG contract of 1915 was of great significance but of secondary import. According to the ruling, the *Organschaftstheorie* applied because the Thyssen-Konzern remained in the hands of one family. Still, the case

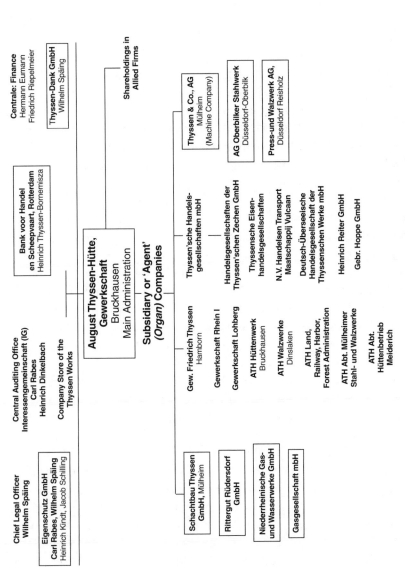

Figure 12.2 Consolidated Thyssen-Konzern, end of 1925 (boxed = not leased to the ATH and remained legally independent entities). *Sources:* TA: A/750/2, A/835/2; Treue, *Feuer Verloeschen Nie*, pp. 240–241.

set a precedent, subsequently built upon by the courts. The Thyssen-Konzern negotiations regarding the *Organschaftstheorie* provided a first template for the later VSt.[20]

Tax officials in Hamborn promptly launched a case against Thyssen. In 1928, they filed another. Preparing a report of over *two hundred pages* on the alleged accounting abuses and mismanagement of Thyssen finance between 1924 and 1926, they felt that the relations among the Thyssen family members had not been taken properly into account. They argued that Thyssen-Bornemisza—a naturalized Hungarian living in Holland—owned and controlled most of the foreign, finished goods manufacturers and utilities firms, while Fritz Thyssen owned and controlled the heavy industrial works on the Rhine and Ruhr. During the inflation years, most of the liquid capital of the Konzern had been converted to foreign currencies, without which the domestic heavy industry firms would not have survived. The tax officials interpreted this financial state of affairs (which was true enough) to mean that the foreign firms could not be dependent on the ATH, but rather the ATH was dependent on the foreign firms. Contrary to the decisions of Imperial Finance Court, they argued that the IG was not sufficient to uphold the *Organschaftstheorie*. On top of this, they accused Thyssen of not being an "orderly businessman," of committing accounting abuses, including not properly balancing his books. Ironically, Dinkelbach, who would become one of the key figures in establishing standards for the chartered accounting profession in Germany, and Price Waterhouse, had double-checked Thyssen's accounts to ensure their veracity for American bondholders!

The case brought by Hamborn tax officials was not upheld, because it contradicted the original decision of the Reich Finance Court, which based the application of the *Organschaftstheorie* on the property relations of the *family* and the *IG*, not the individual Thyssen brothers. August Thyssen retained full power *(Generalvollmacht)* over the property and direction of the Konzern—it was not shared with his two sons, Heinrich Thyssen-Bornemisza and Fritz Thyssen—based on the 1885 divorce agreement. (The divorce agreement continued to play strangely decisive roles at odd points in time.) Thus, while the first case wrestled with fundamental problems of economy and law, the second was a waste of everybody's time and money.

Throughout the 1920s, a civil, economic perspective on commercial law slowly replaced a private-individual perspective, just as an economic theory of the annual financial balance of an enterprise replaced a legal one. But the legal theory itself emerged slowly, stretching well into the 1950s. Individual firms continually had to prove before the courts that their subsidiaries were organic agents.[21] This theory of corporate agency had *direct* effects on the strategy, structure, and organization of German corporations. In this case, the law was not neutral, nor a foundation on which the economy operated more or less efficiently. It had its own logic that went beyond the economic logic of scale and scope, shaping entrepreneurial and organizational possibilities. Indeed, the interaction between law, cartel-distorted market competition, Konzerne, and corporate organizational change in the trajectory of the German steel industry is a story of unintentional consequences and paradoxes.

A Wall Street Encounter

Parallel to legal proceedings with the Reich Finance Court, the Thyssen-Konzern began negotiations with American investment bankers. Its legal consolidation occurred with one eye toward making the ATH the largest possible single legal-financial unit so as to attract as large a loan as possible. This section acts as a type of summary statement for the history of the Thyssen-Konzern at the time American consulting firms assessed the state of the enterprise before it joined the VSt and right before August Thyssen died. The negotiations with Dillon Read and Price Waterhouse exposed the financial weakness but manufacturing effectiveness of the ATH.

Financially, the Thyssen-Konzern never really recovered from the loss of the Stahlwerke Thyssen AG, but in terms of its manufacturing capabilities the ATH bounced back remarkably. By 1924, Thyssen suffered from a serious lack of working capital. Desperate, in early 1924 Thyssen sent a memorandum to other steel industrialists asking whether new German, European, or world-wide cartels were called for rather than the present "wild competition": "for me survival is at the moment the most necessary issue."[22] By mid-1925, steel industrialists managed to rebuild an extensive steel cartel as a stop-gap measure, but industry-wide overcapacity exacerbated Thyssen's shortage of cash. In January 1925, the Thyssens wrote a special management circular to each Thyssen firm:

> The momentary crisis is so serious, that the financial ramifications of every commercial transaction should be regarded first and foremost. You should abstain from business transactions that would cause losses or are connected with any sort of risk. . . . It is imperative that inventories should be reduced to minimum acceptable levels. You should refrain from new acquisitions, including those of raw materials.[23]

In the short term, they could expect little relief from domestic banks. Arguably, the great Berlin credit banks' alleged dominance of German industry, already greatly exaggerated in the contemporary press and historiographical literature, reached its nadir during Weimar.[24] Along with five other German heavy industrial firms, Thyssen looked toward the strongest financial market in the world: Wall Street.

We are well informed about the loan negotiations between Dillon Read and the Thyssen-Konzern because the leading German negotiators, Carl Rabes and Walter Barth, left a diary. They realized the historic importance of this transaction at the time. The historian William McNeil has used this diary extensively in his interpretation of German-American financial relations in the interwar period. McNeil highlights international policy aspects, especially the loan's relationship to the Dawes Plan.[25] Harold Wixforth used the diary to show that Thyssen had the financial clout to play banks off one another to his advantage (including American ones), thus reaffirming industry's independence from banking power.[26] While McNeil emphasizes the first phase of the negotiations and the difficulty of getting the loan (largely due to the instability of international monetary relations), Wixforth emphasizes the last phase, where Dillon Read fell all over itself trying to close the deal. Here I would like to analyze the negotiations as a cross-national business encounter.

At the beginning of April 1924, the ATH board of directors agreed to let Walter Barth, the director of the Cologne branch of the *Darmstädter- und Nationalbank,* send out feelers concerning a long-term loan or bond issue. In August, Barth made contact with the banking house W. A. Harriman & Co., which showed interest. But when

Harriman approached the Disconto-Gesellschaft to act as its agent and wanted to collect preliminary information, Thyssen abruptly rejected Harriman. Thyssen management felt the involvement of third-party domestic banks were "unnecessary" and "dispensable." He also probably worried that a domestic bank would divulge financial secrets. Thyssen wanted to negotiate directly with American investment firms.

In October 1924, Barth established contact with Dillon Read, which had one of the best reputations in the United States. The International Acceptance Bank established by the Warburg brothers owned one-third of Dillon Read, which eventually proved to be crucial. The stabilization of German currency, the success of the Dawes loan, and the "flight of the Zeppelin" all contributed to an improvement of German-American relations. One of Dillon Read's partners made the trip to Hamborn to meet Fritz Thyssen, and in November the Thyssens sent Rabes to New York with full negotiating powers.[27]

Greeted with "Yankee" customs, Rabes' and Barth's first impression was "not overwhelming." Both had their doubts about Clarence Dillon:

> Herr Dillon ruled in his firm as an autocrat. The deal appeared to interest [him] from the beginning. . . . The Americans got lost in endless details by German standards. . . . We had our doubts from the beginning if Dillon was the right man to carry out a project of this extent and of such eminent significance. Dillon came across to us as an excellent jobber (*Jobber*) in the good sense of the word, as a man who had an exceptional flair (*flair*). It was questionable to us, whether or not he would be capable of pioneering a truly great idea, whose fruit would perhaps ripen slowly.

It is surprising that Clarence Dillon struck Rabes as "autocratic," especially as Rabes worked with Thyssen. Their impressions convey an almost stereotypical conflict between industry and finance, long-term and short-term perspective, German solidity versus American financial "flair." And the Americans immediately dived into the "petty" details of the transaction, which surprised the Germans. As I will argue, this derived from the *more formally rational, bureaucratic* nature of American managerial controls, which emphasized calculable financial figures.[28]

For roughly a month, Dillon Read stalled, treating its negotiations "dilatorily." Dillon had his sights on a potential $100 million bond is-

sue (8% interest over twenty years) through the German-American Securities Company, formed by Dillon Read and a consortium of the
"Big Six" German heavy industrial Konzerne: Krupp, Deutsch-Luxembourg, Phoenix, Klöckner, Thyssen, and later, the GBAG. The sheer
size of the loan would make it more attractive to American investors
and would result in a large immediate profit for Dillon Read. Dillon
Read could not decide whether to issue bonds individually or collectively. Dillon Read even offered a ridiculously insufficient one-year,
short-term loan of $5 million that could be divided six ways. Rabes and
Barth grew frustrated. Moreover, Dillon Read appeared to offer only
new delaying tactics requiring new information or yet another expert.

On November 28, the bond sales department of Dillon Read gave
the go-ahead for the collective loan. Clarence Dillon, however, suddenly requested that Germany first had to pay off Dawes Plan debts (a
requirement of monumental political implications at the time) and
that his experts should inspect all the firms—once again. Unknow-
ingly, Dillon touched on one of the sorest points in German politics,
as heavy industrialists had reluctantly adhered to compulsory arbitration decrees in order to pay off their reparation duties.[29] Dillon Read
added another condition that all the firms needed to mortgage their
industrial property as collateral—a customary practice in the United
States. Rabes and Barth balked at this last requirement and the high
interest rate. They felt that the other firms in the consortium whose
names the Americans did not know, unlike Thyssen or Krupp, kept the
interest rate high. Then Clarence Dillon became sick "in reality or diplomatically." No else appeared empowered to continue negotiations.

As Dillon Read continually upped its loan conditions, Rabes wrote
to Fritz Thyssen on November 22 stating they would achieve better
terms and speed negotiations if they took out an individual loan. The
Americans considered Thyssen to be the number one steel company
in Germany. Späing agreed with Rabes. On December 6, the ATH
board of directors gave Rabes the go-ahead to negotiate individually.

The same day, Rabes gave one of Dillon Read's partners an ultima-
tum that they would look for a more eager investment bank. Clarence
Dillon still made himself scarce. Then it suddenly became public that
Krupp had finalized its bond issue through Goldman, Sachs & Co. The
notion of a consortium loan disappeared. Rabes and Barth established
contact with Goldman Sachs, who appeared enthusiastic about the

loan. Rabes then demanded from Dillon Read loan conditions similar to Krupp's. Rabes made clear to Dillon Read that:

> We are not accustomed to being at the mercy of the obvious reluctance of our client. . . . The Konzern has been courted by many quarters and what competitors are able to do, Dillon's firm—in accordance with their reputation—has to carry out in a contriving and gambling manner *(spielend)*. It has been made known to us that a loan secured by mortgages on goods has been offered to us on the part of the firm. We have been reminded that the formalities in this regard did not stand in any relationship to the extensive claims required for loans secured by mortgage. We had to insist, however, that we should be made at least the same offer at this point as Krupp. The differences in the documentation should now no longer play a role.

Dillon Read did everything possible to make up for lost time. Clarence Dillon personally reappeared, but the initiative had moved to Rabes. Dillon Read suddenly offered a $20 million bond issue over five years, 7% interest (instead of the original 8%), with raw materials and inventories as collateral.

Now Rabes' famous negotiating endurance returned great dividends. Two major points of dispute were decided completely in favor of Thyssen. Rabes refused to permit *any* public disclosure of income, capital, and profits. Rabes turned over the internal balances of the Thyssen-Konzern to Price Waterhouse, which created a consolidated balance along American accounting principles, only with the explicit confirmation that they would not pass them on to third parties.[30] Rabes also refused the usual American practice of securing a loan with a mortgage on raw materials or inventories, but instead offered only Thyssen's "Assets and Reputation." A respected Chicago-based industrial consulting firm, H. A. Brassert, Inc., added a glowing report to the bond prospect (immediately below).[31] Krupp settled for a Dresdner Bank trusteeship of all its unsold inventories. Krupp had to post signs on all of its warehouses declaring that the goods were "property of the trustee for the 1924 American bond." Krupp executives considered this an embarassment.[32] Rabes and Barth considered the Krupp bond a "mistake."

After many late nights of "extremely excited and bitter" negotiations, Rabes closed the deal on January 9, 1925, at three o'clock in the morning, six hours before the bond went on the market. He felt the bond issue was "pioneering work." One late-night debate concerned Dillon Read's attempt to secure exclusive rights on any future transactions by Thyssen in the United States. Rabes firmly rejected this. Rabes merely granted Dillon Read "first opportunity." Because of the lack of collateral on goods and inventories, Dillon Read reduced the amount of the bond issue from $20 to $12 million. Rabes and Thyssen had wanted $15 million. Both sides compromised. The final deal resulted in a bond issue of $12 million over five years at 7% with an underwriting rate of 93% and an emission rate of 98.5%. (Krupp's bond was $10 million over five years at 7% with an underwriting rate of 95 1/8% and an emission rate of 99¼%.)

The bonds sold out within hours. Rabes felt this was due to the "prestige of the Konzern." But the publically impressive-looking market demand actually resulted from participating banks buying up the entire stock of bonds for fear they would be left hanging in the wind. (Rabes neglected to mention this in his diary.) Rabes and Barth credited the support of the International Acceptance Bank (Paul and Max Warburg) and the Brassert report for overcoming Dillon Read's resistance. Thyssen immediately used the bulk of the new funds to consolidate short-term debt held by German and Dutch banks. Another $2.4 million went into completing the modernization of Thyssen's mining operations.

A New York legal firm, Appleton, Butler & Rice, who were involved with the drawing up of the final contract, complimented Rabes on his conduct of the loan negotiations:

> As I review the protracted negotiations, however, it seems to me that you and Mr. Barth by the use of great patience and tact under conditions which must at times have been exceedingly trying, and by standing firm at the right times and on the important point, succeeded in obtaining a very favorable contract and are to be congratulated upon a successful culmination of your efforts. I hope that the many tiresome delays and irritating incidents of the negotiations will not leave with you a permanently unpleasant impression of the methods here and that you will not find it too difficult to explain to your directors and to Mr. Thyssen the special customs and methods which prevail here. Whatever may be the practice in Germany it is certainly true that in ne-

gotiations and agreements of this kind here there is little disposition to consider the pride and feelings of those interested in the borrowing companies.[33]

Appleton, Butler & Rice hit upon on the enormous importance of pride and reputation to Thyssen and his corporate culture, which shines out of his correspondence as early as the 1870s. In spite of the statistical information required, intangible emotions still mattered and provided a powerful negotiating instrument.

The Thyssen–Dillon Read negotiations were not only a confrontation between American and German practices, but a confrontation between two styles of capitalism. Thyssen had traditionally worked on "assets and reputation" in the German banking environment, rather than disclosure. Some bankers like Carl Klönne gained some insight into the Thyssen-Konzern only by virtue of personal friendship, but even then Thyssen never told Klönne anything he did not want Klönne or the Deutsche Bank to know. In fact, the Deutsche Bank (Oskar Schlitter) felt betrayed by the Dillon Read loan, because Thyssen was locked in a dispute with the Deutsche Bank over a debt of £140,000 (pounds sterling), which he did not want to pay back. The Deutsche Bank appealed to Thyssen's "honor as a businessman," but to little avail.[34] Even so, Thyssen's bank-industry relations worked largely on the basis of his personal reputation.

To solve this problem of "assymetric information," Dillon Read had Price Waterhouse ensure that the Americans understood what Thyssen financial statements meant. Price Waterhouse created an "amalgamated consolidated balance sheet" in an American-style format, with American-style classifications. Price Waterhouse also required a "better commercial order" inside the ATH.[35] This meant reconstructing Thyssen's accounting system so as to generate financial figures along American lines. In April 1925, Rabes transferred Heinrich Dinkelbach from the Machine Company to join the CAO. From this point on, an informal division of labor between Rabes and Dinkelbach began, lasting well into the late 1930s. Rabes dealt with Dillon Read regarding external financial arrangements, while Dinkelbach coordinated relations with Price Waterhouse. Thus also began a long relationship between Dinkelbach and Price Waterhouse that would have tremendous implications for the future of German steel after World War II.

Above all, Dillon Read wanted full financial disclosure—hard figures and ratios. For the first time, Thyssen had to disclose his full financial condition even if Price Waterhouse kept those figures secret. From the beginning, Dillon Read had obsessed over the financial details, which so surprised Rabes and was contrary to his experience. (We should be skeptical about German relationship banking's informational advantage over arms-length stock markets.) Although Dillon Read used the differences in Krupp and Thyssen (and German) documentation as a negotiating ploy, the lack of reliable financial information signified a real problem of trust. Why should Dillon Read trust Rabes or Thyssen's figures? German financial accounting procedures were not as reliable or standardized across firms as American practices at the time. This Wall Street encounter forced Thyssen to alter underlying accounting categories so that both sides worked "on the same page." The formality of the categories, the "details," the "protracted negotiations," the additional talk, all ensured that Dillon Read and Rabes were clear about one another's intentions and financial conditions. The sociologist Anthony Giddens emphasizes how social systems "bracket time and space," particularly through "surveillance" as the "coding and retrieval of information" and as "direct supervision" of others. Development of trust in relationships depends on the ability of individuals to rely on "standardized procedural rules."[36] Rabes and Dillon essentially negotiated these new rules. Accounting conventions helped bridge German-American relations across the Atlantic.

Not only did the Americans demand common procedures and standards, they also valued different types of figures. In particular, the Americans wanted *profitability* figures. When the VSt discussed a possible loan from Dillon Read:

> Herr Rabes explained that it was absolutely imperative that the question of profitability had to be moved into the foreground and that overcapitalization would minimize disproportionately the available profits for [dividend] distribution. . . . An additional point: in the loan negotiations with the Americans, they placed great value on the relationship of crude steel production to share capital. A share capital of RM 500 million would result in a more favorable relationship to crude steel for us than the American steel trust [U.S. Steel] or the Bethlehem Steel Company. In America, they do not take exception to a secured debt at roughly the same level as the share capital.[37]

The information, "which, according to my [Rabes'] experience, is the *minimum* required," should be sent in triplicate and "the documentation has to be assembled into a unified whole and translated into English."[38]

The ratios deemed most significant and relevant betray assumptions on how to run a business. American investment banks considered the most important ratios to be dividends per share and crude steel production to share capital. The first needs little explanation, especially coming from an investment bank, but the second emphasized how scale related to owners' equity. The latter ratio implies that profitability derived from scale economies and how much or how little shareholders had to invest in the business to achieve such scale (implicitly, profits bore a direct relationship to scale). Both ratios imply a financial conception of control, that is, how money is earned from the point of view of capital markets and owners. Americans emphasized profitability. German steel's world of cartel-concern capitalism, however, stressed direct vertical control, diversification, capacity, cartel quotas, and manufacturing efficiency. As Brassert & Co. pointed out in a 1925 report on the Rhein-Elbe-Union for another Dillon Read loan, the cartel system emphasized that "the main factor in establishing low costs is therefore the efficiency of the plant and its management."[39] Manufacturing efficiency increased the difference between product costs and cartel prices, thereby increasing profits; of secondary import was the direct return on capital.

To be clear, I am not arguing that German industrialists were not interested in profitability or dividends. Instead, competition within the cartel system and conceptions of a firm (for instance the ideal of a self-sufficient, vertically oriented, balanced firm) altered priorities and the significance of some ratios versus other ratios. And those ratios imply strategies and means of organizing control. Just as importantly, none of these considerations (here ratios such as manufacturing efficiency versus investment profitability) are mutually exclusive. Achieving high manufacturing efficiency can lead to high financial profitability (defined as earnings per share), but one does not automatically lead to the other, especially in the short term. Ideally, German industrialists would have liked to integrate vertically and have high profitability, but in practice, the two strategies tended to diverge over time, especially if market demand weakened (not the least due to the high prices charged by cartels!) or the industry suffered from overcapacity. A ratio of crude steel production to equity glaringly exposed the inadequacies of this cartel-concern bargaining game. This was the gist of Albert Vögler's 1919 critique of the German steel industry, the intellectual foundation of the VSt. Finally, the quote about the importance of profitability alludes to how financial figures can be manipulated once certain ratios are deemed important targets. (By setting the VSt's equity fairly low, the dividend ratio could be improved and the company would appear to be more attractive on the stock market). In this case, stressing different ratios expose different institutional and cultural assumptions about how to run a business.

Financial Crisis

Price Waterhouse's financial statements offer a unique, comprehensive glimpse into the financial condition of the Thyssen-Konzern just before it ceased to exist. Price Waterhouse used the replacement value of current fixed assets, significantly inflating figures and bearing little relationship to internal Thyssen accounts that used historical book value. Thyssen figures provide a better sense of continuity with the prewar period, but the Price Waterhouse figures provide a better sense of the present value of the Thyssen-Konzern from the point of view of creditors. In both cases, absolute values are less important than relative values (ratios).

For the period after 1919, I have combined Thyssen's financial figures for the ATH and the Gewerkschaft Friedrich Thyssen to arrive at an approximation *as if* the original GDK had continued into the postwar period (Appendix A, Table A.6). Although the ATH is not equivalent to the Thyssen-Konzern, it was still the battleship in the Konzern convoy. Because it became a financial sore point, strain would be most evident here.

The period of inflation and stabilization created significant discontinuities in Thyssen financing practices. The inflation significantly distorted the first three columns (total assets, equity, and liabilities). Moreover, the Goldmark opening balance of January 1, 1924, obscures considerable arbitrariness so that generalizations are tenuous.[40] In the 1924 opening balance, total owners' equity easily covered total liabilities at a ratio of 2.79, which was unprecedented for the prewar period (and more a result of accounting manipulations). It quickly slipped below prewar relationships as Thyssen took on debt. In the prewar period, Thyssen's equity/debt ratio never dropped below one (one of the "golden rules of finance"), but after 1917 consistently fell below 0.5, indicating that creditors supplied a significantly higher proportion of funds. While inflationary excesses largely explain this poor ratio, the period after 1924 clearly shows that Thyssen was drawing down on the substance of the business (declining owner's equity) and drawing on outside debt. Thyssen had regularly broken another "golden rule," that owner's equity should always cover the value of total fixed assets, but the ratio slipped under 0.7 for the first time at the end of 1924, and below 0.5 in 1925. These low equity/fixed-asset ratios resulted despite permission from the Finance Ministry for Thyssen to take a significant devaluation of his 1924 total fixed assets. All these figures indicate that Thyssen was losing financial control.

In part, however, these worsening figures reflect heavy investment in plant modernization. His total assets exploded from just under RM 200 million to over RM 300 million in two years; total fixed assets rose by nearly RM 50 million in 1925. On the downside, growth of total assets also came as a result of accounts receivable (accounts owed to the ATH) expanding from RM 15.6 million to RM 61.5 million, and, more worryingly, the value of inventories expanding from RM 15 million to RM 55.2 million (see Appendix A, Table A.7).

A gloomier portrait emerges when one judges the results of these new investments in the last two years. The ATH–Friedrich Thyssen consistently ran losses between 1919 and 1924. Since Thyssen took no money out of the business, additions to reserves reflect net profits (after taxes and depreciation). This meant that these losses cut into the financial reserves and equity—the substance of the enterprise. In spite of higher levels of depreciation and accounting manipulations, if cash flow is placed in relation to total assets as a type of return-on-investment figure, Thyssen's cash flow was still negative in 1924, and a lowly 3.16% in 1925, nowhere near the prewar period, which averaged 8% after 1900. By 1925, internally generated cash flow covered little of Thyssen's expansion—one reason why Thyssen-Bornemisza and Thyssen, Sr., objected to this expansion.

Reflecting the most worrisome aspect of the stabilization crisis, the ATH auditing office prepared a long-term liquidity analysis of the GDK/ATH (Appendix A, Table A.7). Another dark present emerged.

Current assets and liabilities are figures measuring short-term accounts that can theoretically be liquidated within one year. Current assets include cash on hand, bank accounts, accounts receivable, and inventories—accounts that can be converted into cash. Current liabilities are outstanding short-term accounts owed to others (i.e., employees, banks, other firms, various other credits); they do not include long-term mortgages or loans. In theory, these creditors could demand immediate payment. The most important figures are the last three, which demonstrate the relationship between short-term assets or liabilities. (Not included in the above ratios is the column of credits from Thyssen & Co., which represented funds sent to the GDK.)

One of the most important measures of liquidity is the *current ratio,* which indicates whether a firm is capable of meeting its short-term obligations. As a rule of thumb, lenders generally apply a 2:1 proportion to view the firm as liquid. In other words, for every RM 1 payable in the near future, the firm has RM 2 of current assets that can be converted into payments. Throughout his history, Thyssen rarely came close to fulfilling this rule! Only in 1917 did Thyssen approach this ratio. Between 1897 and 1925, Thyssen averaged a ratio of just 1.06, indicating that he generally worked on the edge of liquidity. His best period was 1909–1916; after 1917 the ratio began to slide significantly. The current ratio, however, is merely a rule of thumb that can vary from industry to industry. Yet before 1913 the GDK/ATH current ratio fell significantly and consistently below the industry average.[41] The working capital column represents the absolute mathematical difference between current assets and current liabilities. If creditors were to demand immediately (as they nearly did in 1912) that Thyssen pay all debts, for a good portion of the GDK/ATH's history, Thyssen would have come up short.

The final liquidity figure is called the *quick ratio,* which is a more stringent test of liquidity. The reasoning behind this figure is that inventories cannot be easily transformed into immediate cash; the quick ratio represents almost instantly available cash. In addition, a high current ratio may just indicate a high level of inventories, which is not necessarily a sign of economic health. The general rule of thumb for the quick ratio is that a figure of 1 is satisfactory. Between 1897 and 1925, Thyssen averaged a fairly respectable 0.81. Again, the ATH was most liquid between 1910 and 1921. Before 1913 his average quick ratio was 0.76, whose story can clearly be divided into the start-up phase up to 1908 and then the period thereafter when the GDK matured. On average, the GDK actually had a higher ratio than the industry average in the prewar period, which hovered around 0.5. (Before the war, generally higher liquidity ratios could be found among the smaller firms such as Hoesch, the Rheinische Stahlwerke, or the Bochumer Verein, which did not have the same access to capital markets as larger firms.) In 1924, the ATH clearly faced the worst short-term liquidity crisis in its entire history. The quick ratio dropped below 0.4, not matched since the startup of the GDK. If creditors had demanded payment, Thyssen could not have paid them.

In brief, Thyssen always worked on the edge of normal liquidity guidelines, which confirms Dahl's impression of Thyssen as a man always short of cash, but by 1924–1925, at the end of a stunningly successful career, Thyssen faced the worst financial crisis of his long life. On the brighter side, the ATH figures do not include Thyssen's voluminous securities portfolio, which represented considerably undervalued assets which could be sold in a pinch, like the sale of Gladbeck in 1902. In addition, the ATH was arguably the most illiquid of Thyssen enterprises and depended considerably on cash funds from Thyssen-Bornemisza, so that the financial condition of the ATH overstates the difficult financial condition of the Konzern as a whole.

Price Waterhouse and Dillon Read required an "amalgamated consolidated" financial statement from Thyssen. Price Waterhouse drew up a complete balance sheet for the newly unified ATH, including all of its subsidiary or agent (*Organ*) companies (see Figure 12.2). This included all of Thyssen's mining operations, the Dinslaken rolling mills, the Rolling Mills in Mülheim, the AGHütt, and Thyssenhandel (which included most of the Thyssen coal and steel trading companies), and some miscellaneous small forest, quarry, and wood-haulage companies—in short, Thyssen's core manufacturing and trading firms. This consolidated financial statement did not correspond to the extended Thyssen-Konzern, and did not include firms eventually controlled by Thyssen-Bornemisza (Figure 12.1).

Price Waterhouse estimated the value of ATH plant and equipment at present or replacement value (see Appendix A, Table A.8). At the end of 1924, the total assets of the ATH amounted to RM 864,019,803; at the end of 1925, RM 901,957,557. If one compares the 1925 figure to American firms (at 4.2 RM/1$), the ATH was roughly one-third the value of Bethlehem Steel, roughly one and one-half times Republic Steel, and about the same as Jones & Laughlin Steel Corporation. In 1924, Price Waterhouse estimated the value of ATH fixed assets (properties and plant) at RM 678,567,202 and in 1925 at RM 711,702,485. Roughly the same proportions apply if one compares these values to the same American firms.[42] In short, one of the largest steel firms in Germany would be a large, independent firm in the United States, but did not approach the size of massive U.S. Steel. These figures are only a very rough guide because of considerable arbitrariness.

Above all, Price Waterhouse financial statements provide an excellent view into the state of Thyssen's finances. They highlighted the solvency (or liquidity) of the ATH, rather than its solidity. The financial portrait found by Price Waterhouse was not a pretty one, which is why Thyssen did not want them publicized, and why he needed a loan. In 1925, the ATH's finances noticeably slid. Although the value of ATH's fixed assets grew considerably by RM 33.1 million as a result of heavy investment in new plant, inventories also rose by RM 13 million, while accounts payable (owed) to the ATH declined by one-third. On the liabilities side, the growing indebtedness and poor financial performance of the ATH became evident. In the fiscal year 1924, the ATH posted a net profit of RM 18.6 million, but a net loss of RM 25.2 million in 1925, a huge negative difference of RM 43.8 million. It also showed that the ATH's total equity failed to accumulate. Simultaneously, long-term debt shot up astronomically from RM 5.2 million to RM 64.5 million, mostly as a result of the American loan. In addition, short-term debt through banks and acceptances grew by almost 10% from RM 94 million to RM 103 million.

From the Price Waterhouse's 1925 earnings statement, the ATH posted gross profits of almost RM 50 million on total sales worth RM 365 million, a gross profit margin of 13.6%. After administrative and sales expenses, the operating net profit margin on sales (without including interest income) amounted to 8.3%. Unfortunately for Thyssen, investment costs drove the ATH into the red (a loss of RM 25.2 million). Depreciation of plant amounted to RM 11.8 million, interest charges on debt amounted to RM 24.7 million, and extraordinary expenditures or charges amounted to RM 22.3 million. The ATH's largest interest charges included RM 10.6 million on bank overdrafts and suppliers' accounts, RM 8.4 million on bank acceptances and trade bills, and RM 3.4 million on a seller refunding mortgage loan. These charges indicate that the ATH was delaying payments to creditors. The largest extraordinary expenditures included RM 8.6 million for capital expenditure and heavy replacements, RM 4.3 million for a revalorization of mortgages, and RM 2.3 million for writing down investments and marketable securities. Other extraordinary charges, which hovered around the RM 2 million mark, included losses on cancelled contracts for iron ore, a payment to the coal syndicate for its sales operations during 1924, and other miscellaneous items. Softening these charges somewhat was RM 5.9 million in nonrecurring income, the bulk of which was RM 2.9 million from the German government to compensate the ATH for French confiscations.[43] One can see why Thyssen felt these compensations, while welcome, were a drop in the bucket.

A liquidity analysis similar to Table A.7 demonstrated similar cause for concern. The ATH had a current ratio of around 1 in 1924 and 1925, while its quick ratio dropped from 0.47 to 0.35. Satisfactory ratios are generally considered to be 2 and 1, respectively. The ATH's current ratio was actually worse in Thyssen's own figures, but the quick ratios roughly matched one another. In addition, the ATH's working capital appeared to be in good order, with a positive value of RM 8 million in 1924, but it slipped into the negative in 1925. Finally, if working capital is placed in relationship to total assets, which indicates a degree of financial room to maneuver, in 1924, working capital represented only about 1% of total assets, but essentially disappeared the next year. If one compares this ratio to the prewar period, in which the GDK's working capital ratio averaged 3.5%, the 1924 figure (let alone that of 1925), demonstrate how tight money had become for Thyssen. In the prewar period, Thyssen's GDK working capital ratio had consistently fallen below 1% before improving dramatically after 1909, lower than other Ruhr steel firms.[44] But this 1925 figure was still the worst ever. All these figures demonstrate that if creditors had demanded immediate payment, the ATH could not have paid them. Looking back long term, however, Thyssen regularly worked at the edge of his financial means, which implies that the 1924–1925 crisis, while severe, might have been overcome.

Finally, the last three figures in Table A.8 provide some measure of the ATH's total indebtedness. The debt to total assets ratio is an indicator of enterprise solvency, especially from the point of view of long-term creditors whose greatest concern would be whether Thyssen's enterprise could make its interest payments and repay the loan. In this case, indebtedness rose, but not significantly. Compared with an average of 0.4 between 1910 and 1913 (Table A.6), this had worsened, but not dramatically. In relationship to owner's equity, the level of debt rose by 11%, from 39% to 50%. Thyssen's personal equity and reserves, accumulated over the years, still contributed RM 2 for every RM 1 in outside debt. As a debt/equity (or equity/debt) ratio, this figure lay well within the bounds of the prewar period.[45]

Clearly, Thyssen suffered a short-term shortage of cash, not necessarily from long-term structural or managerial problems. Whatever risks he ran in the short term, Thyssen still gained the majority of his asset growth from personal funds. The equity and property of the plant were clear sources of collateral. Although the 1924–1925 liquidity crunch appeared to be the most severe of his career, from a long-term historical perspective, such ratios were not completely out of line with what Thyssen had faced before. The more the ratio oriented itself to short-term liquidity issues, the worse Thyssen looked.

Above all, the impressive report from Brassert & Co. proved decisive in closing the Dillon Read bond transaction. The report largely explains how Thyssen could rely on "assets and reputation." A German immigrant, H. A. Brassert had worked at Phoenix in 1895 when Thyssen first began building the GDK. He was one of the most important figures in German-American steel relations. To Brassert, the ATH was the most valuable steelworks in Germany. Excerpts from his report also provide a tribute and epitaph to "August Thyssen and his work." With great insight, Brassert highlighted some of the differences in constructing a competitive steel firm within the German institutional context:

> Giving due consideration to all important steel plants in the various countries, there are in my opinion none more favorably situated for the long pull, in regards to raw material supply, assembly manufacturing costs, than this August Thyssen plant. I make this statement because combined with its favorable geographical location, it is one of

the most modern and best equipped steel plants in the world. Competition from German or other plants can therefore be successfully and profitably met. . . .

Mr. August Thyssen who with members of his family owned and still owns the entire interests, has consistently followed the policy of reinvesting his large earnings in plant improvements, it being a matter of personal pride with him to have at all times the most advanced and best equipped plant. I personally know Mr. Thyssen and have been well acquainted with his son and his chief executives, who made frequent visits to the United States and kept themselves well informed as to our progress. They were at all times eager to exchange technical information and were the first in Europe to adopt our ideas of large production and labor saving. In respect to fuel economy, they were always in advance of the industry and today they lead the world in heat economy in the production of steel . . .

[On blast furnaces] These furnaces produce more iron than any foreign furnaces and are very well equipped with labor saving machinery, and particularly well equipped for fuel economy. . . . [On gas power station] This plant is only surpassed in magnitude by that of the United States Steel Corporation at Gary, Indiana. . . .

The Rolling Mill Plant of the August Thyssen Works has a capacity of 1,120,000 tons of finished product per year. It is more elaborate than plants of equal capacity in the United States, owing to the greater diversity of sizes and specifications required in the German trade and the world's market. . . .

[On housing] A considerable amount of the company's assets is represented by houses of which the company owns many thousands, having supplied a house for every four of its 10,000 employees at the steel plant and a house or living quarter for every one of its 20,000 miners. This is in accordance with the German law and the houses are very substantial and attractive, in marked contrast to our usual workmen's colonies. . . .

In conclusion I beg to state that the August Thyssen Steel Concern has as modern a type of plant as can be found anywhere and I consider them, all in all, the most efficient steel manufacturers of Europe. . . . In tonnage they are among the largest steel producers of Germany and have an enviable history of manufacturing and sales.[46]

Brassert highlights the labor-saving and scale achievements of the Thyssen-Konzern, which Americans found to be of special importance. Brassert's description generally reiterates most of the general strengths of the Thyssen-Konzern already discussed. While we might be skeptical about his comments about the quality of Thyssen company housing, which incidentally says more about American rather than German company quarters, there was little question that the Thyssen-Konzern remained one of the premier steel companies in the world.

The Brassert report has a number of important analytical dimensions for this study. First, the specific organizational structure and culture of the Thyssen-Konzern cannot be reduced to (although it was certainly influenced by) scale and scope economies, technology, markets, state or regulatory laws, or the overall complexity of business operations. All major German steel combines came to terms with these competitive conditions. At some point, the specific organizational form and capabilities of the Thyssen-Konzern must be traced to the collective *agency* of August Thyssen and his managers.

Second, a good portion of this collective agency derives from an intangible: pride. The Americans seemed genuinely surprised that pride was an issue. Thyssen's long-term success owed much to pride in his reputation, an important underlying if fuzzy corporate value. Often bordering on obsession, this psychological focus kept Thyssen at the forefront of technical, managerial, and commercial innovation in the steel industry. Thyssen's success thus derived from psychological and emotional wellsprings that went well beyond the desire to make money or maximize profit. As if it were ether, this pride suffused the corporate culture of the company. The fusion of pride in reputation *and* a sophisticated, systematic managerial hierarchy proved to be a source of Thyssen's strength over the "long pull."

Thyssen's Decision to Join the Vereinigte Stahlwerke

However, Brassert's report then leaves us with the central mystery. Why did Thyssen decide to merge this state-of-the-art, family-owned, managerial enterprise into the Vereinigte Stahlwerke? Like Andrew Carnegie and U.S. Steel before him, Thyssen had to decide to join this new "trust" which was, symmetrically, modeled on U.S. Steel. Thyssen and

Carnegie's lives paralleled one another in this respect. No direct documentation exists on this question. Apparently, Fritz and Heinrich discussed this merger quite literally at Thyssen, Sr.'s deathbed. Thyssen's work and Thyssen's personal life remained fused right up until the end. Why did August Thyssen sell out?

Many, if not most, contemporary analysts felt that the VSt finally realized Thyssen's vision of an American-style "trust."[47] In this interpretation, the VSt became his crowning achievement. Other contemporaries viewed the demise of the Thyssen-Konzern as the end of an era of heroic entrepreneurialism and the beginning of anonymous, joint-stock companies, if not monopoly capitalism. Yet considering his advocacy of "trusts," Thyssen never entertained the idea of forming larger mergers himself until the VSt. (He did help other firms form mergers, largely to simplify cartel negotiations and improve competitive conditions in the industry as a whole.) He consistently did *not* want to splinter the family property. He could have done more with the Schalker Verein, but instead started up the GDK. He adamantly refused to fuse with Silverberg. He despised joint-stock companies, which might limit his cherished "independence" and disclose his secrets. Up to the very end, Thyssen made few attempts to raise equity by offering shares, completely closing one path to alleviating the capital shortages he suffered in 1902 and 1925. Why not issue preferred shares or retain majority voting rights, which might keep him, or his family, as the ultimate decision-maker, à la Andrew Carnegie with his ironclad agreement? The one time he did issue a few shares in one of his core companies, it turned into an ugly battle with the GHH, filled with pigs and legal briefs.

We have some evidence that at the end of his career Thyssen toyed merging with Mannesmann, his archrival in the pipe and tube industry. In early 1925, Thyssen, Sr., tossed this idea out to Heinrich Thyssen-Bornemisza. In this plan, Thyssen would merge his high-end finishing firms with Mannesmann, including the *Press- und Walzwerke Reisholz,* the *Oberbilker Stahlwerke,* the Mülheim Rolling Mills (possibly also the Machine Company), the AGHütt, and the ATH Dinslaken. These finishing firms roughly equalled the size of Mannesmann. Thyssen and Mannesmann would each take a 50% share in the new firm. Together they would represent a dominant oligopoly in the pipe industry. Mannesmann or this new company would gain a secure source of intermediate supplies from the ATH through long-term contracts or cross-shareholding. The rest of the Konzern—mines, waterworks, crude and intermediate steel production, and Holland trading companies—would remain entirely in the hands of the Thyssen family. In its broad outlines, Thyssen's proposal remarkably resembled a division of labor between the ATH and Mannesmann forged in 1970.[48] Serious feelers, however, never went out to Mannesmann. The merger idea remained a throwaway.

Did the Thyssen-Konzern *have* to join the VSt? No. This was not the first time Thyssen suffered a liquidity crisis. According to the Brassert report, there was no better firm in Germany prepared for the long haul. Most importantly, Krupp, Hoesch, Klöckner, and Mannesmann, all of whom briefly entered and quit VSt negotiations, all managed to survive into the 1990s. Except perhaps Mannesmann, with its tight focus on a profitable seamless pipe business, all were financially weaker, or smaller, or less efficient firms at the time. Hoesch and Klöckner were smaller and less diversified, Klöckner less coherent and balanced. Krupp was the same size, but had lost its lucrative armament business; it remained in dire financial straits. It managed to survive with moderate amounts of state support, another American loan, and a ruthless abstention from any dividends until the mid-1930s—again not unheard of in Thyssen's career. Krupp took a hard road, but it survived without relying on its lucrative armament business until after the Depression.[49] Thyssen might have done the same. Thyssen also had an especially strong presence in finishing and machine engineering, which allowed other firms like the GHH to remain independent. Even Thyssen-Bornemisza's group of firms, which he pulled out of the VSt, and which corresponded to firms not included in the ATH Price Waterhouse balance sheet, continues to thrive independently—with revenues of a not insignificant $3 billion in the late-1990s and spread across four continents.[50]

Ultimately, and perhaps fittingly, Thyssen's decision to join the VSt came down to family quarreling and strategic differences. Family firms always have one crucial weakness: succession. In one respect, this is an ironic end because family played a distant role, with Thyssen, Sr., keeping his sons at arm's length until after the war. Thyssen, Sr., never really trusted his sons to run the family business. According to Albert Vögler, the general director of the new VSt: "August Thyssen had financial difficulties since the loss of Hagendingen. He had engaged himself strongly and the Deutsche Bank had become somewhat wary of him. This was only one reason. The other was that he had no trust in his sons, and his age."[51] August, Sr., Fritz, and Heinrich engaged in a triangular dispute about the future.[52]

The two brothers did not agree about the future strategic direction of the Thyssen-Konzern. The two brothers had dramatically different personalities as well as different visions about Thyssen, Sr.'s legacy. Fritz Thyssen was nationalistic, oriented to the Ruhr; Heinrich Thyssen-Bornemisza was internationally oriented, cosmopolitan. Fritz was bourgeois like his father; Heinrich was more aristocratic and elegant (somewhat of a perfumed dandy).[53] Fritz was blunt, impulsive, and moody in manner; Heinrich was diplomatic, smooth, and clever. However tempestuously, Fritz worked willingly with his father; Heinrich kept a cool distance. Fritz controlled the bulk of the fixed assets of the Konzern in its Ruhr stronghold; Heinrich controlled the liquid assets of the Konzern from Antwerp and Rotterdam. A large proportion of these liquid assets had been put into foreign currencies during the time of hyperinflation, and therefore into Heinrich's hands. Heinrich often threatened to block further credit to Fritz. This kind of activity dismayed Thyssen, Sr., who sometimes derided Heinrich as "only a banker," not a real industrialist.

On the other hand, Thyssen, Sr., could call Fritz a "spendthrift" as he laid out a considerable amount of capital for new plant and equipment with little regard for return, their costs, and the heavy debt incurred.[54] Up until the end of his life, Thyssen, Sr., like Fritz, continued to press for additional modernization and expansion, especially to compete with the Americans, but with a close regard to cost. He wrote Heinrich: "Either we find new, interest-free money to bring into the ATH in order to reduce the heavy expenses that it has and enable it to survive, or we have to join the trust which will produce more cheaply."[55] On his deathbed, he allegedly asked one executive to tell Härle not to allow the banks to charge high interest rates: "Money will become cheaper."[56] As money rarely came without interest, without the financial support of Heinrich's more liquid assets, and with heavily indebted fixed assets, Fritz had little choice but to join the VSt.

Heinrich adamantly refused to endorse the merger:

> I do not like this trust. This trust will shatter a broadly conceived and extensive family enterprise. The factories and companies I am respon-

sible for do not need this trust. Even in times of crisis these factories and companies have made it through without any significant outside help and hope to survive in the same manner in the future. In case the condition of the ATH is such that it must seek merger in this trust, then the board of directors and other authorized parties must assume exclusive responsibility for it. I will not accept such a responsibility. My warnings have not been heeded for years. My ideas were not taken into account.[57]

Heinrich thought like an international banker. Fritz thought like a German national industrialist, and was more than willing to work with other Ruhr industrialists. The ATH represented a first-class manufacturing operation, but financially, teetered on the edge. The two sons reflected the differing demands of two fingers on the hand of management (manufacturing vs. finance). They would have had to work together to keep the Thyssen-Konzern alive. If Fritz and Heinrich had had similar ideas about the strategic direction of the Thyssen-Konzern, it might have remained independent.

Still, it was a difficult decision. Up until the last minute, Thyssen, Sr., and Fritz Thyssen, as well as many managing directors, had reservations. Some Thyssen executives allegedly offered to reduce their salaries to help alleviate the financial strain if it could remain independent.

By May 1926, all resistance was finally overcome. Shareholders approved the VSt merger. But the withdrawal of Thyssen-Bornemisza's support meant that roughly half the assets of the Thyssen-Konzern never entered into the new VSt, weakening Fritz's negotiating position. The core steel facilities of the ATH (coal, pig iron, steel, rolled goods, trading companies) and the Machine Company controlled by Fritz joined. Heinrich kept the higher-value added and specialty firms independent. They included a number of untapped mining fields, an ongoing mining company (*Rheinisch-Westfälische Bergwerksgesellschaft*), the mineshaft construction company (*Schachtbau Thyssen*), specialty steel finishing firms (*Krefelder Stahlwerk, Press- und Walzwerk* in Reisholz, *Oberbilker Stahlwerk*), shipbuilding (*Flensburger Schiffsbau, Bremer Vulkan, Vegasack*), gas and waterworks (*Niederrheinische Gas- und Wasserwerke, Gasgesellschaft Hamborn*—both later the *Thyssensche Gas- und Wasserwerke*), and a number of Rotterdam-based trading and banking companies (*Bank voor Handel en Scheepvaart, Handels en Transport Mij. Vulcaan,* and the Vulcaan Coal Company). The type of companies they controlled fit their personalities: one large, imposing, concentrated in the Ruhr, based on fixed assets, scale, and commodity production; the other smaller, flexible, involved in high value-added manufacturing, and involved in fluid, foreign, financial transactions.

August Thyssen died on April 4, 1926, at the age of 84. His death and the inability of the two sons to work together effectively ended the Thyssen-Konzern. Thyssen, who had done so much to promote the VSt, especially as he saw that his sons did not see eye to eye, never witnessed the VSt's first general assembly, held in May 1926. In an unintentionally symbolic act, the first VSt shareholders meeting set its official founding date retroactively to April 1, 1926, three days before Thyssen's death.[58]

Ironically, the 1885 divorce agreement, which had caused a dark cloud of suffering between father and children for forty years, had a silver lining. Thyssen's children, who now could claim one of Germany's largest fortunes, paid a stamp tax of only RM 3. Because of the divorce agreement, tax lawyers agreed that August Thyssen's death had brought no actual transfer of ownership to his children because the 1885 divorce agreement had already transferred ownership (not control) to them. Legally, no inheritance took place, thus no inheritance taxes.[59]

Epitaph

Before moving on, it is useful to pause and reflect on Thyssen's long career. How did August Thyssen manage to compete as long as he did as a privately owned family enterprise in such a capital-intensive industry? Thyssen, Sr., had a combination of creative business qualities that appeared as if someone genetically separated them and placed them in two separate business heirs. (We will leave aside the ruthless, petty machinations of August, Jr., who inherited another less seemly character quality from his father.)

Thyssen, Sr., managed to combine apparent opposites throughout his business career. He attempted to build a family dynasty yet did not trust his sons. He had a sixth sense for hiring young managers and giving them extensive responsibilities, yet his own sons were quite old before they gained any decision-making powers. Like Heinrich, he wanted to maintain family independence, but like Fritz, spoke of the virtues of trusts and worked with other Ruhr industrialists. Thyssen, Sr., could criticize Heinrich as "only a banker," while criticizing Fritz for his "spendthrift" ways and outsized, overindebted investment strategy. Thyssen, Sr., always thought in terms of scale, but his financing practices always limited this scale in the interests of family control. Thyssen, Sr., combined a fierce patriotism, yet oriented himself internationally—a product of the gold standard internationalism of the pre-1914 world. Thyssen, Sr., exemplified the classic individualistic autocratic entrepreneur, yet built one of the more sophisticated managerial hierarchies in the world. While Fritz intervened impulsively and erratically in firm operations and Heinrich acted with the hands-off approach of a merchant-financier, Thyssen, Sr., delegated well yet paid close attention to matters of organizational control.

In the entire history of the Thyssen-Konzern, Thyssen, Sr., balanced continuous technical advancement with a strong commercial orientation. He retained a merchant mentality—or commercial mentality that overlaid his state-of-the-art industrial operations. This fundamental outlook was particularly important to retaining private financial control. It also moderated his expansion—above all, the renowned *balance* of the Thyssen-Konzern testified to this mentality. Scale or diversification without profits was unacceptable. Without commercial success, a product line, department, or firm "did not justify its existence." He always lavished considerable investment funds on justified technical improvements for his plants, yet maintained tight accounting controls over operating expenses, which gave him an unjust reputation for stinginess. He relied heavily on engineers for their technical expertise, but required cost and profit estimates from them. He hired the best engineers available, yet expected them to run their areas of responsibility with commercial acumen as "respectable businessmen." This attention to profitable performance also made Thyssen very skeptical of the German cartel system. He had a reputation for advocating "trusts" yet often helped build cartels. Thyssen, Sr., had a reputation for being an "American" yet was deeply "German." He was among the first to use American methods of production, yet pioneered typically German *Konzerne*. In short, Thyssen, Sr., managed to be nationalist and internationalist, an industrialist and a banker, a heavy industrialist and a finished-goods manufacturer, a trust-builder and a cartel-builder, an "Americanizer" yet "German," and ran a centralized but decentralized organization.

Thyssen's success cannot be attributed only to personal qualities. His managers made the Thyssen-Konzern successful. Full-time salaried managers primarily ran this family enterprise. As epitomized by Franz Wilke's, Albert Killing's, or Carl Wallmann's management in Mülheim, Otto Kalthoff's gruff leadership in Hamborn, Franz Dahl's activities in Bruckhausen and Hagendingen, Julius Kalle's in Dinslaken, and Conrad Verlohr's in Meiderich, Thyssen relied heavily on his managers to advise, formulate, and design whole companies. He encouraged active personal initiative from his managers. Thyssen retained his veto right, but could also allow executives to override him. Thyssen directed his companies with a fundamental respect for successful managers; he fired them quickly if they did not perform to his expectations. Dahl remembered Thyssen once saying: "I have large companies for which I am responsible, therefore I throw people out who don't perform."[60]

Thyssen demanded dynamic leadership personalities. Thyssen's letter enquiring about the qualities of a prospective hire illustrate just the type of qualities appropriate to his corporate culture:

> It is of particular interest to us to know, if Herr von Hagen possesses the capability, besides a sound [legal] scholarly education, to use his knowledge and ability with understanding and acumen *(Scharfblick)* while being able to differentiate accurately the essential from the inessential in concrete cases of practical life and thus to perform successful work. Also would you be so kind as to inform us, whether he is diligent, has the capacity of straightforward *(sachlicher)*, quick and insightful *(schlagfertiger)* discussion, and is skillful *(gewandt)* and correct in manner. Likewise we would be most grateful for your judgment about his character, in particular we would like to know if he would be an amicable and socially pleasant colleague. . . . [61]

The whole tone of Thyssen's correspondence left room for his advisors and department directors to act on their own judgment. He intervened only when the "results" contradicted his overall strategy. Thyssen also did not often order people to his office, but called upon them in their offices—with prior notification.[62] He visited his chief executives less to meddle in the business of his subordinates, but to inform himself. In its formal structure, all decisions radiated downwards; in practice, Thyssen firms generated decisions from the high middle of the hierarchy upwards. Moreover, he "wished that his managers would convince him and let himself be convinced."[63] All of his executives mentioned that he genuinely listened to them. If anything, he gave them too much responsibility.

Although Thyssen, Sr., ranked among the oldest of German entrepreneurs, his managerial organization remained young, on the cutting edge of organizational and technological developments. Although seniority was respected, the unbureaucratic nature of Thyssen's organization allowed talented young men (Hermann Eumann, Carl Rabes, Carl Wallmann, Julius Kalle, Franz Bartscherer, Rudolf Traut, Heinrich Dinkelbach, to name a few) to move quickly into positions of full responsibility. It indirectly testifies to the organizational culture in the Thyssen-Konzern that such strong-willed personalities could develop alongside August Thyssen.

Finally, just how "American" was August Thyssen? If by "American" one means an obsessive, often ruthless competitor, an individualist entrepreneur, and one who paid close attention to scale and the latest labor-saving methods through capital-intensive technological processes, then one could call August Thyssen an "Americanizer." But many German entrepreneurs would also fit this description. At least two major Thyssen executives (Dahl, Kalle) did not think he had American models in mind, although they agreed that Thyssen borrowed useful aspects from the United States, particularly technical innovations. Again, this was hardly unique among German industrialists.

Unlike Carnegie, who relentlessly focused on scale and prime costs (profits would naturally follow), Thyssen focused more intently on returns to investment, depreciation, and the build-up of reserves. One could say Victorian reputable solidity (more than financial liquidity or maximum profitability) was Thyssen's lodestar. Unlike Carnegie's attention to manufacturing scale, prime costs, and labor-saving devices, Thyssen paid utmost, precise attention to financial and organizational "imponderables," as epitomized by his personally composing the statutes of the CAO. Carnegie emphasized cost controls, Thyssen stressed financial and commercial control. Carnegie emphasized factory organization, Thyssen business organization. Unlike Carnegie's obsession with scale and mass production, Thyssen pushed for vertical integration and diversification. Aside from the fact that one needed a huge market for such Carnegie-like scale, such an American drive to scale and attention to prime costs would have forced Thyssen to issue shares. Carnegie was much more willing to work with shareholding partners, although he too worked with the so-called ironclad agreement granting him full control. Thyssen's attention to financial questions grew out of a self-imposed, personal choice to keep the firm in the family, under his complete control. Like Thyssen, Carnegie had little desire to sacrifice his company to so-called "speculators" and constantly reinvested his profits.

Most critically, if Thyssen was Germany's version of Andrew Carnegie, he operated in a significantly different economic and social environment. This made Thyssen behave much differently than his American counterpart. Thyssen worked in a fundamentally different institutional and competitive environment than did Carnegie. Joseph Schumpeter once wrote: "History is the record of 'effects' the vast majority of which nobody intended to produce."[64] Such was the case of the German steel industry. The cartel question pitted two central liberal values against one another: liberty of contract or freedom of competition. Cartels, which should have regulated competition in an orderly manner, led to perverse competitive practices that undercut their advocates' intentions. Steel industrialists willingly erected cartels—and then did everything possible to avoid their market distortions. Their attempts to circumvent the costs of their own cartels through vertical integration and product differentiation made their corporate organizations increasingly difficult to organize. Finally, multisubsidiary organizations or Konzerne, which became more prevalent in the German economy after World War I, inadvertently destroyed the legal conception of a firm. In real-world practice, affirming liberty of contract eventually subverted nineteenth-century notions of what if meant to be a single corporation. Although a good portion of public opinion after World War I protested big business, taxes levied on corporations inadvertently promoted larger mergers.

Cartels placed a premium on German-style vertical integration rather than Carnegie-style scale. In addition, a Carnegie-style drive to lower average unit costs through production scale was inappropriate to the much smaller German market and international European markets, which had a great diversity of product standards and protective systems. Carnegie or American-style drives for economies of scale were predicated on large, open domestic markets and relatively fluid capital markets. Cartels allowed the most efficient plants (Thyssen) to reap additional profits from the higher, stabilized prices. Thyssen then took advantage of these stabilized prices when he reached the margins of his financial liquidity.

Here then is the key to understanding Thyssen's cartel behavior. He did not think highly of cartels in principle, but instrumentalized them if they helped him earn money. Thyssen had little ideological stake in cartels—unlike other German industrialists and academic theorists. But unlike Andrew Carnegie, who made sure that both feet remained outside despised pools, Thyssen kept one "one foot in the syndicates, the other outside." Thyssen could live with them if he found them useful. Dahl actually thought that Thyssen was "cartel-friendly" because they stabilized prices; they provided Thyssen some relief from his persistent shortage of cash. Indeed, Thyssen did advocate larger trusts in the German steel industry because he thought them inevitable and they would simplify cartel negotiations by eliminating less efficient competitors. He advocated (and helped engineer) trusts for *others*.

The other major institutional difference was the existence of the great regional and Berlin universal banks. Using gymnastic financial methods, Thyssen remained independent of the banks. In the more traditional *Finanzkapital* view, one might interpret Thyssen as the "American," working valiantly without the stewardship of the big banks. But in recent historiography, Thyssen becomes an extreme version of the normal case. For *short-term* bursts of expansion, Thyssen relied heavily on the banks. They provided valuable services through their consulting, credit, and general information capacities—but not their ability to monitor borrowing or strategically direct investment. But because of their close institutional and personal relations with most large-scale industrial ventures ("development assistance to the strong"), banks made a Carnegie-style drive to scale or to monopoly more difficult in German steel. They had stakes in many firms and competed strongly with one another.

Thus, while Thyssen was Germany's *version* of Andrew Carnegie, the emphasis should be on the phrase "Germany's version." Thyssen had to follow the logic of German cartel-concern capitalism or else his firms would suffer a slow loss in their competitive position. Thyssen excelled less as a pioneer of vertical integration (he actually followed a half-step behind the others), than in his ability to *manage* extended vertical integration and product differentiation. Thyssen's achievement actually lay in the field of managerial organization and innovation. With these managerial and manufacturing capabilities, August Thyssen built one of the largest, most efficient enterprises in Europe. It is remarkable that the Thyssen-Konzern lasted as long as it did. Its long survival and success had less to do with family, than with the systematic development of its managerial capabilities, which lasted well beyond August Thyssen himself. The managerial legacy of the Thyssen-Konzern would decisively influence the organizational trajectory of the VSt.

PART III

The Vereinigte Stahlwerke, 1926–1936

With the Vereinigte Stahlwerke we enter into a very different sort of corporation. If Thyssen tried to keep his enterprise in the family, the VSt had shareholders to please. Thyssen delegated wide-ranging authority to powerful, vigorous managers and demanded leadership personalities; the VSt worked through management by committee. Rather than exercising veto power, the general director of the VSt, Albert Vögler, acted as a broker among powerful and divergent shareholder, stakeholder, and managerial interests. Unlike the Thyssen-Konzern, the VSt began as a single, unified corporation with high central overhead costs, unwieldy management boards, and unclear if not opaque lines of decision-making. While Thyssen kept his companies rich in substance but poor in appearance because he had no shareholders to please, the VSt desperately tried to show profitability and distribute dividends, often at the expense of substance. While Thyssen used negotiated market prices as transfer prices, the VSt created complicated bureaucratic procedures to determine internal prices; the VSt also stripped commercial costs out of its production cost calculations. Because of their different corporate strategies, organizational forms, internal corporate policies, decision-making processes, and accounting procedures, they were significantly different sorts of firm with different conceptions of control.

I will show how accounting and control imagine the corporation by informing, mediating, and guiding managerial decision-making inside the VSt. The VSt first constructed one type of control that looked more like other firms in German steel, then after 1933, reconstructed itself along multidivisional or multisubsidiary lines more like the Thyssen-Konzern. The 1933 reorganization also provides numerous parallels to reorganizations such as DuPont and General Motors.

The VSt represented a major attempt to rationalize the steel industry and create American-style mass-production economies. In a remarkable quote, Fritz Thyssen and Albert Vögler stated:

> Our model was the shining example of America. The riches of its natural world and its large market have promoted there the development of the most economically advantageous mass production. On this favorable basis, American scientists have made outstanding achievements. We first had to artificially create the foundation for such concentrated mass production by our own means.[1]

The founding of the VSt belongs to the wave of trust-building in the mid-1920s, which created such renowned firms as IG Farben, Daimler-Benz, and the fusion of the Deutsche Bank with the Disconto-Gesellschaft.[2] Indeed, like many contemporaries and historians before him, Alfred Reckendrees views the founding and development of the VSt as an important "component" or "contribution" to the Americanization of German industry.[3] The VSt was named the "United Steel Works" deliberately to invoke U.S. Steel, hoping it would become an oligopoly like U.S. Steel that could effectively manage competition in the entire steel industry. The venture would also be more likely to attract American capital. Like Thyssen, the VSt took out American loans through Dillon Read, and used an American accounting firm, Price Waterhouse. The VSt was one of the first major German firms to revamp its accounting system along American lines, and introduce mechanized punch-card methods of record-keeping using Hollerith (IBM) machines. The VSt also licensed American technologies. Finally, it moved to a version of the multidivisional structure during the depression, paralleling many U.S. firms of the 1920s and 1930s, including U.S. Steel. All in all, the VSt appears to represent one of the clearest cases of Americanization before the Americanization of German business before 1945.

But can one speak of the Americanization of German business and society in the 1920s, let alone after 1945, which was dominated by discussions of Americanization, Taylorism, Fordism, and rationalization?[4]

In spite of the obvious influence of America on Germany, the German economy still remains unfamiliar to most Americans, which makes sense, of course, because it is not really Americanized.

I want to undermine this notion of Americanization by analyzing the Vereinigte Stahlwerke (VSt), one of the salient examples of the Americanization of German business in the 1920s. As previously demonstrated, even August Thyssen, the most "American" of German steel industrialists, remained deeply "German." The VSt, too, remained a deeply German company, transforming American practices to fit its own specific organizational, economic, and political agenda. As shown earlier, the VSt remained embedded in a longer term trajectory of German managerial practice that had its own autonomous tradition, neither backward, as if waiting to be modernized and Americanized, nor unimportant for understanding its future organizational history.[5] I explore this process of organizational transfer, or rather, "Germanization" of American methods in six areas: the founding of the VSt, the rationalization of production, the transfer of an American licensed technology, the influence of American methods on VSt managerial and accounting practice, the move to a multidivisional form, and finally the figure of Heinrich Dinkelbach. This German-American encounter raises important methodological questions about how we can adequately describe cross-national, cross-cultural, and cross-organizational transfer in general.

I do not want to debate the success of the VSt in becoming Americanized—as if that were its goal—but to demonstrate how inadequate the concept of Americanization ultimately is, especially as a methodology of understanding institutional, organizational, or cultural learning. The concept of Americanization fails to show how selected ideas became embedded in long-standing—innovative, not backward—German institutional and business practices that carried into the Federal Republic of Germany after 1945. Americanization posits a one-way diffusion process from the most modern example and confuses innovative adaptation, selection, and transformation with mere imitation.[6] Unlike the concept of protoindustrialization, famously described as "industrialization before industrialization," Americanization offers little systematic set of concepts.

I first show how the Americanized productive rationalization of the VSt actually fits into the standard competitive dynamics of German steel. The VSt's best claim to being a successful "rationalization company" lay in its organization, auditing, and control system, which was organized along self-described "American" lines. Yet this new system of organizing control also grew out of Germany's distinct accounting and management tradition surrounding Eugen Schmalenbach, Germany's leading accounting and management theorist. The VSt's auditing and control system, built around Heinrich Dinkelbach, established a virtuous cycle of innovation between academic theory of the Schmalenbach school and applied business practice of the Dinkelbach school that recast American inspiration. Ironically, however, the VSt's new American practices exacerbated its internal rivalries and helped lame the company. In order to overcome its difficulties, the VSt evolved into a multisubsidiary structure that appeared to imitate the transition made at DuPont or U.S. Steel. But the remarkable similarities to the DuPont story were counterbalanced by VSt's different institutional and, especially, political context. Its reorganization created an unprecedented change in German corporate law, and was predicated on approval by the new Nazi state, which politicized it in a unique way. Finally, Heinrich Dinkelbach, whom historians have described as an "Americanizer" after 1945, actually drew on his earlier experiences in the VSt, dating from the 1920s, to break up German steel and to advocate codetermination based on Catholic social thought, ideas which were *not* inspired by America.

Until 1933, the VSt organized its control along the lines generally practiced in German steel before 1913. It resembled Phoenix or Krupp more than it did Thyssen. After 1933 the VSt *reinvents* (which is not to argue: imitates) the type of managerial control system (organizational form, accounting, and information issues) pioneered by the Thyssen-Konzern—the multisubsidiary form for its core steel operations combined with the tradition of the CAO in a conceptually more sophisticated and technologically savvy fashion.[7] By the 1920s, using a multisubsidiary form was hardly as uncommon as in the prewar period, but the VSt's methods of organizing control in its headquarters were cutting edge, the one area where the VSt gained a good reputation. Not surprisingly, the core team promoting this 1933 reorganization included Rabes, Späing, and Dinkelbach. Rabes and Dinkelbach, who had headed Thyssen's CAO, now headed the VSt's auditing and organizational offices.

CHAPTER 13

The "Rationalization Company"

[T]he possibility for creating manufacturing economies through specialization and concentration, the like of which did not exist in any other Konzern, resulted from this fusion whose founding was predominantly driven by financial considerations.

Heinrich Dinkelbach, Wilhelm Deist, et al.,
. . . *Report of the Steel Trustee,* 1954

The history of the Vereinigte Stahlwerke (VSt) is a story of unrealized potential found elsewhere in the "golden years" of the Weimar Republic. Just as so much modernist art or architecture appeared in the 1920s but did not become fully appreciated until the 1950s, the VSt foreshadowed many future industrial developments not fully realized until the 1950s. The VSt represented an attempt by German steel industrialists to create American-style mass production economies, rationalize the industry, and deliver productivity and profitability from their investments. The VSt attempted to break out of the logic of German cartel-concern capitalism, which rewarded capacity without production, vertical integration without profitability, and cartel formation without attention to market demand. With the merger of four major industrial *Konzerne* into the VSt, it became the largest industrial corporation in Germany (in terms of shareholder equity and total assets), slightly ahead of IG Farben, and the second largest steel corporation in the world behind U.S. Steel. As its name suggests, the VSt modeled itself explicitly on U.S. Steel with American-style objectives of horizontal integration. The whole project was designed to attract American investment capital.[1] Its strategic objectives went well beyond the rationalization of its own capabilities as it attempted to reorder the competitive dynamics of the whole steel industry.

Because of its symbolic character in the industrial history of Weimar, we are already well served by various booklets published by the VSt itself,[2] and through the accounts of contemporaries such as Paul

Ufermann[3] and Robert Brady[4], who immediately recognized the VSt's importance. These early accounts all emphasize its ability to rationalize it operations along American-style lines. In addition, other historians like Gert von Klass,[5] Wilhelm Treue and Helmut Uebbing,[6] Gerhard Mollin,[7] Wilfried Feldenkirchen,[8] and finally, Alfred D. Chandler, lent their insights to the history of the VSt.[9] Despite the glowing and rather heroic portrayals by Robert Brady, Wilfried Feldenkirchen, and Alfred Chandler, however, it is questionable just how successful a "rationalization company" *(Rationalisierungsgemeinschaft)* the VSt really became. Thomas Welskopp and Christian Kleinschmidt have called the rationalization of the VSt a "myth."[10] Reckendrees argues that it became less a successful "rationalization company" than a "rehabilitation company" for the four founding combines and their creditor banks. Diametrically divergent assessments of the VSt exist.[11]

Can we understand the VSt merger and subsequent rationalization as Americanization? While it had wide-ranging objectives to rationalize its own operations and tame the weird competitive dynamics of German steel industry and refashion them along American lines, the VSt did not achieve its professed objectives. The heavy "mortgage" (Reckendrees) of its founding, the role of its shareholders in the founding combines, internal managerial rivalries, and competition within German heavy industry undermined or reshaped basic ideas about American-style rationalization and horizontal integration. Rather than an example of ruthlessly streamlined Americanization, it remained a German company, indebted to its creditors and embedded in the cartel-concern order. For entirely different reasons, it actually acted too much like U.S. Steel, which followed almost a German style of vertical integration and cooperative capitalism.

On top of this, distinctively German shareholding, associational, and business–government relations played decisive roles in the birth of the VSt in 1926 and its "new order" in the unfortunate years 1933–1934. In order to found the VSt, the merging firms had to deal with a host of external stakeholders within the complicated associational life and political world of German capitalism. These included important individual firms, the finishing industry's association, cartels, American bondholders, local municipalities, and the central government. Ultimately, the founding of the VSt illustrates the vast discrepancy between German steel's business practices and its political rhetoric.

Founding the VSt

The roots of VSt failure lay in the manner in which the merger firms founded the VSt.[12] The founding Konzerne carried on their talks almost as glorified cartel negotiations, but they now debated about their proper shareholding quotas in the new company. They then institutionalized this rivalry into the organizational fiber of the new company. If one conceives so-called cooperative business relations as a spectrum, ranging from gentleman's agreements to IGs, then the VSt invented a new form. One might even view it almost as a cartel disguised in the garb of a joint-stock company.

The VSt founding negotiations also illustrate the lack of consistent bureaucratic control in German steel. The haggling derived in part from the inability of the founding combines to measure adequately the value of individual firms and plants in terms of financial, productivity, and cost accounting. Intensifying merger rivalries, the heterogeneity of accounting techniques made a mess of the negotiations. Formally rational techniques were not taken for granted but became the foundation on which executives fought politicized debates.

Inspired as much by IG Farben as by U.S. Steel, the intellectual foundation for the VSt derived from a 1919 memorandum written by Albert Vögler, the general director of Deutsch-Luxembourg.[13] Vögler's memorandum outlined a new strategy for the industry, which set off an important but inconclusive debate within the industry. Typically for heavy industrialists, Vögler translated the dysfunctional business *practice* of German steel into a *political* attack on the eight-hour day.

Echoing Thyssen's comments two decades before, Albert Vögler argued that "the time of the syndicates has passed." Vögler argued that the only sure way to raise productivity and reduce overcapacity was through an "alliance" of the steel industry in an IG. A unified organization should thoroughly rationalize the industry along horizontal lines: improve productivity coefficients, promote a better division of labor and standardized mass production, pool research and information capabilities, reduce administrative and marketing costs, and train a "first-class executive staff" in both technical and commercial fields. The traditional strategy of vertical integration had made German Konzerne mirror images of one another, with low productivity and low capacity use in all product lines. In 1925, Vögler had to repeat himself, as negotiations to found the VSt threatened to stall over petty haggling:

> A look in the list of the individual syndicates of the Pig Iron Association shows the disastrous diversity in the production program of each individual Konzern. One can maintain without great exaggeration that all great Konzerne of the west[ern Ruhr] manufacture the same steel products with few different points of concentration. Here definitely lies one of the reasons for the momentarily bad economies in the iron and steel factories. The [production] restrictions extend not only to single products but over the entire range of products, and thus all operating facilities are condemned to inefficiencies.[14]

Vögler's memorandum offered a vision of standardized mass production along horizontal rather than vertical lines geared to enhance international competitiveness and profitability. In 1919, Vögler condemned the jumble of inflationary plans to build new plants as well as the new wave of vertical integration, which threatened to extend the structural overcapacity of the basic steel industry into every branch of the finishing industry (shipbuilding, machine engineering, railway cars and locomotives, and automobiles).

One particularly dramatic but not uncommon case taken from the negotiations to found the VSt makes abundantly clear the effect of cartel distortions on the economics of German steel. Since it used seamless tubes, Thyssen-Dinslaken could potentially manufacture the cheapest steel tanks for compressed gas for a new "steel trust." Other companies merging into the VSt used a pressing technique that cost 5 RM more per tank than Thyssen; Thyssen-Dinslaken could also produce steel tanks in greater variety. Yet in the steel tank cartel, Phoenix had a 12.56% quota, Gelsenkirchen 13.08%, Thyssen-Dinslaken 12.56%, Mannesmann 27.26%, Rheinmetall 11.44%, Oberschlesische Eisenindustrie 9.15%, Borsig 6.98%, and Döhlen 6.97%. These steel tank quotas exemplified how the cartel system did not reward efficiency or low costs; they did not even reflect total production capacity. In a particularly good indicator of the enormous overcapacity extant in German steel, Thyssen's director, Julius Kalle, announced that Dinslaken could take over Phoenix's and Gelsenkirchen's share of the quota without any new investment in buildings or equipment, giving the new VSt a 38.2% quota. In steel tanks, the VSt could achieve a reduction of capital costs, reduce operating costs, gain higher quotas— and bolster profit margins—by simply letting Dinslaken run full.[15] And this was just in one product line. It is an especially trenchant example of how setting cartel quotas were an infinitely mysterious affair.

Vögler foresaw numerous problems with such a fusion. Merging rival companies was never easy. He already thought that the "most difficult" point would be assessing the value of each firm's fixed assets. He also thought that the appropriate organizational form of such an "alliance" would prove difficult. Reproducing the general German mistrust of American-style trusts, Vögler *rejected* an American-style fusion at the time because such a "rigid system of trusts" would inhibit innovation. Vögler envisioned a small IG central administration in the form of a limited liability company (GmbH), which would "eliminate external competition but continue and, if possible, promote it internally through the preservation of the individuality and the autonomy of the individual firms." The IG would primarily ensure that all divisions were "managed according to unified standpoints" and, most importantly, would retain the final right to approve any new investment. In this regard, Vögler's ideas foreshadowed the VSt reorganization of 1933–1934.

Circulated throughout the Ruhr, Vögler's memorandum found little favor. At an ATH board of directors meeting, however, August Thyssen and his executives unanimously supported such an "alliance"—without explicitly stating whether the Thyssen-Konzern would join it or not. Adding to his reputation as an "Americanizer," August Thyssen wholeheartedly endorsed Vögler at a Steel Works Association meeting a few days later—the only one to do so. At this time, Thyssen and his executives' support of the "alliance" owed more to his fear that the government would socialize all of heavy industry.[16]

But Vögler's ideas took on new meaning by the autumn of 1925, after the German economy entered a sharp recession.[17] German steelmaking capacity had climbed back to its prewar level, but without the corresponding level of demand. Like Thyssen, all of German steel suffered a capacity and liquidity crisis. Germany steel looked to the U.S. for liquidity, but additional American credit was still no solution to industry-wide overcapacity, poor productivity, and low profitability. Table 13.1, created by American consultants for the VSt, shows this crisis clearly.

Table 13.1 Capacity and production of the four VSt merger groups, 1925 (in millions of tons)

VSt group	Firms	Coal Capacity	Coal Prod.	Coke Capacity	Coke Prod.	Pig iron Capacity	Pig iron Prod.	Crude steel Capacity	Crude steel Prod.
Rhein-Elbe Union	Gelsenkirchen Bergwerks AG	11,688,000	58.1%	2,164,000	75%	1,015,000	39.1%	145,000	50.3%
	Deutsch-Lux	6,000,000	59.8%	2,400,000	60.5%	1,322,000	61%	1,199,500	68.0%
	Bochumer Verein	2,500,000	60.9%	850,000	51.1%	810,000	51.1%	880,000	48.1%
Thyssen-Konzern		8,000,000	66.9%	1,500,000	91.6%	2,200,000	63.5%	2,100,500	63.4%
Phoenix-Group	Phoenix	9,000,000	62.4%	1,950,000	84.3%	2,200,000	45.1%	2,191,000	60.0%
	van der Zypen	—	—	—	—	250,000	49.3%	303,000	53.3%
Rheinstahl		—	—	325,000	80.4%	1,241,000	52.2%	1,117,000	71.0%
Total capacity		37,188,000		9,189,000		9,038,000		7,936,000	

Source: MA: R 5 35 28 (1) "Handbuch für die Anleihen des Jahres 1926, Mit Anlage: Brassertsche Bewertungszahlen, Vereinigte Stahlwerke Aktiengesellschaft."

Each merging combine had slightly different points of concentration. The Rhein-Elbe Union, an IG of three firms, oriented itself more toward coal and coke, and Rheinstahl toward crude steel. Thyssen and Phoenix matched one another fairly evenly and were relatively balanced. In terms of crude steel production capacity, both Thyssen and Phoenix were comparable to the Republic Steel Company (1.45 million tons) or Jones & Laughlin (3.3 million tons) in the United States. The crude steel capacity of all four groups together roughly equaled Bethlehem Steel Corporation's production capacity (8.5 million tons).[18]

But capacity is not production. The discrepancy between capacity and production condemned German steel companies to poor profitability. Except for coking operations, most production hovered around 60% of capacity. In hot rolled mill products, use of capacity dropped below 60%, with Thyssen's capacity use reaching only 48.5%. In this respect, founding the VSt was a "negative" or defensive strategy (Reckendrees).[19] One must also interpret the inflationary modernization of the ATH in this light. Although the ATH developed state-of-the-art production facilities, it considerably overshot market demand. Although German heavy industrialists publically attributed their lack of profitability to rising wages and social benefits, as Vögler intimated, German heavy industry's injuries were largely self-inflicted.[20] This rhetorical disjunction between business practice and business politics became a political constant for the VSt.

As a result of this crisis in capacity, liquidity, profitability, and strategy, in July 1925 six major German steel combines began negotiations to form a "union of steel": Krupp, Thyssen, Phoenix, the Rheinische Stahlwerke (Rheinstahl), Hoesch, and the Rhein-Elbe-Union (an IG of Gelsenkirchen, Deutsch-Luxembourg, and the Bochumer Verein). In a series of backdoor maneuvers that would become all too commonplace for the VSt, Otto Wolff, an iron wholesaler and shareholder in the crisis-ridden Phoenix company, initiated discussions to form a "trust." Wolff was motivated by the desire for a cheaper supply of material and long-term delivery contracts for his wholesale trade. Hasslacher initially led direct discussions, a tactically effective maneuver for Wolff.[21] These nearly year-long negotiations were torturous, involving important but arcane points about the merger.

The main *internal*, interlocking set of questions discussed were the following:

- an appropriate organizational-legal form that would attract financing and allow the rationalization of production,
- the proper level of equity and capitalization for the new firm,
- the appropriate shareholding quotas for each of the founding combines in the new company,
- the proper valuation of the incoming properties,
- which properties would come into the new firm,
- the appropriate measures for determining the value and productivity of various plants, and
- where the company's headquarters should be located.

The decisive *external* variables were

- American financial support,
- the tax burden faced by the new company,
- its relationship to the government, and
- the new company's relations with manufacturing industries.

This internal-external distinction is important because it highlights the discrepancy between the VSt's actual business problems and its public representation of them. Moreover, a huge gulf existed between the most important dilemmas faced by the potential merger and the most vehemently discussed issues. It quickly became obvious that the VSt could only come into existence with American financial assistance and by means of a special arrangement regarding taxes, but there was little controversy since everyone agreed on these points. On the other hand, most of the initial debates turned on the proportion of shareholding quotas, the proper valuation of incoming properties, and the proper capitalization of the new company—areas in which the merging combines had some control and asserted themselves against one another.

Internal Debates

Although the firms agreed on the strategic goals of the new company, each Konzern brought its own interests to the negotiating table. Immediately dissatisfied and made skeptical by the new company's prospects, Hoesch dropped out.[22] As Vögler foresaw, the disputes about the value of incoming properties threatened to destroy the venture before they reached the more decisive stage of negotiations with the Americans or the German government. Each combine found ways to advantage itself, justified with accounting criteria. Which standard should provide the appropriate criterion for determining shareholding quotas? Hasslacher (Rheinstahl) wanted share capital, assets, and future profits allotted according to a quota system based on crude steel production. Naturally, this criterion advantaged Rheinstahl (see Table 13.1 above). Thyssen objected to a crude steel standard because it did not take into consideration favorable geographic and transport locations from which the new firm would ship to export markets—Thyssen's great advantage. Thyssen also emphasized its specialty goods production, especially the Machine Company. Like Thyssen, Krupp wanted its shareholding quota to take into consideration quality manufactured goods production—historically Krupp's great strength.

Allegedly simple statistics posed yet another problem. Clearly, Krupp had the highest crude steel production in the first half of 1925, followed by Phoenix, Thyssen, Rheinstahl, and the Dortmunder Union. But Thyssen had the lowest production costs and Phoenix the highest.[23] Phoenix had the second highest amount of production, but if the merger came about, the new company would shut down its facilities first because they were often the least productive. (Not surprisingly, it was also the company nearest bankruptcy.) Was not the purpose of the VSt to concentrate its production at the most efficient works? If so, the level of actual, present, or past production was not the proper criterion. The VSt's strategy of horizontal concentration dictated that productivity criteria (and its associated controls) be made paramount. In this respect, VSt strategy did usher in a new conception of control for German steel.

But once they agreed that productivity would act as the ultimate criteria, thus agreeing on a common standard, measuring productivity became an issue, as none of the firms calculated their production costs in the same way. Phoenix and Rheinstahl distributed their administrative and overhead costs according to wages across all manufacturing departments, including auxiliary departments. Krupp, however, used the same distribution formula, but allocated overhead only to direct manufacturing departments. The Dortmunder-Union allocated overhead only to manufacturing departments, but used a different formula that distributed 50% of the general overhead according to wages and 50% according to revenues. Finally, no one defined administration and overhead costs in the same way. Despite hours of discussion about the production cost of rails—the only product discussed—the five firms could not reach a consensus and gave up precision. Since Phoenix and Rheinstahl were the only firms to distribute their overhead costs to their auxiliary departments, those firms were asked to recalculate their figures. The lack of common financial and cost-accounting standards helped make negotiations more difficult. Even after share quotas had been allotted, such discussions continued with tedious regularity. Between January and April 1926, the cost-accounting committee of the study commission preparing the groundwork for the new company met *forty-one* times.[24] Deciding the most and least productive plants was absolutely crucial for the future of the VSt (more on this below).

A similar lack of standardization and debate affected financial statistics. Eventually, the five combines formed an independent central committee to establish common conventions for auditing the individual companies. These sorts of difficulties boosted the influence of accountants, including Dinkelbach (Thyssen) and Peter van Aubel (Phoenix), who moved into the center of such debates. Cost and financial accounting standards became a conceptual groundwork for the new corporation.

Much of the negotiation followed this same roundabout pattern. If they agreed on broad points, the question of standards set them back. If they agreed on the basic standards, then no one calculated the standards or defined their categories in the same manner, bringing them back to square one. Vögler urged everyone to keep negotiations simple, but to little avail. At issue was really power and control over the new corporation.

Initially, they conceived the new merger as a strengthened IG with control primarily over coal, coke, crude steel, and intermediate products (up to heavy steel plates), so-called A-products. In the interests of simplicity, initial discussion left out finished manufactured goods such as pipes and tubes, specialty steel products, or machine construction (B-products). In this way the VSt negotiations mirrored cartel discussions. In August 1925, they arrived at preliminary quotas based on coke, pig iron, and crude steel production: Rheinelbe would receive 28.03%, Thyssen 19.12%, Krupp 19.82%, Phoenix 18.71%, v.d.

Zypen 1.62%, and Rheinstahl 12.7%. Everyone agreed that these quotas were approximate. But Vögler, now representing Rheinelbe's interests, pointed out the impossibility of distinguishing Rheinelbe's crude steel production from the specialty cast iron goods of the Bochumer Verein. Fritz Thyssen indicated his unwillingness to exclude his profitable pipe and tube production. Krupp wanted to include its shipbuilding operations, the Bochumer Verein its specialty foundry production, and finally, Thyssen and Krupp wanted to include their machine engineering companies in any share quota valuation. With the inclusion of diverse product lines came a disproportionate increase in evaluation problems. August Thyssen recommended that Vögler become the primary intermediary for assessing the proper value of these properties.[25]

Until September, two months of negotiations had proceeded on the basis of rough production statistics, but suddenly Krupp demanded that the shareholding distribution formulas be shifted to revenues. Such a formula placed more value on their finished products, especially its specialty casting goods.[26] In rapid succession, Fritz Thyssen countered that they should value his mines based on their productive capacity. Thyssen had few collieries, but potentially higher productivity and production levels than other mining operations. He added that the whole point of the fusion was to center productive capacity on the most efficient plants.[27] Phoenix joined with Krupp to advocate a revenues formula, but demanded that absolute profits since the prewar period (i.e., a standard average) be used, just as IG Farben had done. Conveniently, this criteria would eliminate Phoenix's productivity disadvantage and emphasize the scale of its profits—not its profitability.[28] Again, each combine chose a criterion that advantaged itself.

Meanwhile, another line of debate pursued the absolute level of capitalization and how best to found the new company, which introduced difficult financing and tax issues. Early on, Hasslacher outlined three options: (1) a pure financial holding company that would take over the assets of the founding companies; (2) a new independent holding company, which would undertake a series of leasing arrangements with the older companies for use of their production facilities and profits distributed according to an arranged formula; (3) an entirely new company which would purchase outright the fixed assets of the older companies. The first two options would have created tax problems because of the existing German corporate law on capital transfer and turnover taxes. The third option would activate only a high but one-time fusion tax.[29] Another dilemma involved the particular modalities of founding the new firm. Hasslacher suggested fusing the other firms with Phoenix to save at least 20% of all the fusion costs, which would run RM 30–50 million. But this type of fusion would merely enrich Phoenix shareholders (Wolff, for instance) and would also enourage the perception that the new company was a "financial rehabilitation project." They eventually rejected an IG because it would not produce the "necessary simplification and cost reductions" needed. After some debate, the remaining five combines agreed that the Americans would lend money to the new company only if the company were a single corporate entity, not a financial holding or leasing operation.[30] The absolute level of shareholder equity then became an issue, which fluctuated between estimates of RM 500 million to RM 1 billion. In a portentous but typical move, while they could not agree on the appropriate level of equity for the new firm, they easily agreed to create preferred stock that would act as a guarantee of dividends.

By mid-September 1925, the negotiations threatened to stall on the details. Vögler brought the negotiations back on track. Vögler felt that debates about proper valuation were trivial, especially since most of them hovered around a mere 1% difference in share quotas. While he agreed that 1% represented a great sum if the new firm's share capital was high, it would make little difference if the firm proved unprofitable. (Vögler's comments intimated that shareholder and management interests might diverge.) Instead, Vögler urged:

> Decisive for handling the entire problem remains that:
> 1. the iron and steel production in Germany must be brought into accord with the demand,
> 2. the production of iron and steel products must be arranged more rationally,
> 3. the consolidation of similar lines of products will significantly reduce capital assets.
>
> The end result must then find expression in an increased efficiency and profitability *(Wirtschaftlichkeit)*. The last point of view is the only decisive factor. If all the participants are not convinced of this, then continuing the studies [for the merger] has no purpose.[31]

Vögler argued that the most efficient works had to be valued higher, but they would only become profitable if the merger succeeded. It was in everyone's interest to go ahead with it in spite of secondary differences of opinion. Impressed, August Thyssen apparently made the incorporation of his Konzern contingent on Vögler's being named general director for at least five years.[32]

Following his own advice, Vögler abandoned further discussions of quotas to "sketch" the organizational questions involved with the new company. Vögler envisioned six production groups *(Werksgruppen)* divided according to product lines. The first group encompassed the Dortmunder Union and the Hörder Verein which would concentrate on domestic intermediate materials, structural steel, heavy plates, merchant bars, construction materials, and other special steel of medium quality. The second group consisted of Krupp and the Bochumer Verein, which would produce all types of specialty castings and foundry products. The third group would concentrate on crude steel at the ATH, Krupp-Rheinhausen, Phoenix-Ruhrort, and Rheinstahl. The fourth production group would encompass finished goods such as wire, strip steel, medium and high grade sheets and plates. The fifth group would consolidate pipe and tube mills, and the sixth group would consolidate blast furnaces (ironmaking) with their affiliated foundries. Furthermore, "the machine engineering factories [of Thyssen and Krupp] cannot be separated from the other factories—the inspections showed that—because of technical, but above all, economic reasons. Therefore, they should be incorporated into the new company and accorded their full value." This vision roughly corresponded to the 1933 reorganization.[33]

Vögler did not envision the VSt as a monolithic block, but his ideas were impossible to realize. Bringing together long-standing rival companies so quickly and choosing executives to lead these groups from contending managers (who already headed their own plants) proved to be too difficult. Furthermore, the new company had to establish common financial, accounting, and administrative ground rules before it could regroup powerfully independent, centrifugal interests. Hours of controversial debates showed how few ground rules the VSt could assume. The future head of VSt general administration, Helmut Poensgen (Phoenix), later emphasized that the initial consolidation had to be rather simple and unified.[34]

In order to circumvent the valuation problem, Vögler made two other recommendations, both of which became institutionalized into VSt business practice. First, the new company would issue dividend certificates *(Genussscheine)* that linked rates of dividends paid to common stock, thereby compensating the founding combines for their "peak works" and other intangibles. They acted as a type of loan from the founding combines that had to be retired over time. Vögler invented a new financial mechanism for fine-tuning the direct method of valuation outside of shareholding quotas and helping "guarantee" a preferred return to shareholders.

Second, Vögler introduced the confusing but immensely important concept of "peak works" *(Spitzenwerke)*. (In German, *Spitzen* normally refers to the top or the best.) The unfortunately named concept did not refer to the most efficient works but to the second or third most efficient plants. With this suggestion the VSt established a basic policy of relying on one primary manufacturing site along with a "peak work" (to meet any excess demand during periods of peak demand). They would shut down remaining plants. In principle, this policy centered the VSt on its most efficient and profitable plants in terms of energy use, throughput, production costs, and geography. Vögler admitted that lower volume production schedules would impair the profitability of these "peak works," but other plants running at capacity would allegedly compensate for them.

In the short run, the concept of "peak works" helped break the deadlock, but in the medium term it diminished the impact of VSt's rationalization objectives. The plants saved as "peak works," moderately efficient plants held in reserve in case demand spiked, prevented a more ruthless American-style streamlining. These fixed costs remained on the VSt books, they had to spend additional money for maintenance, kept underused capacity, retained more staff, and left some overlap of product lines. The VSt then built an immensely complex internal quota scheme to compensate the founding combines for "peak works," which ran below capacity. This internal quota scheme further blurred clear calculations of performance and reduced overall profitability. "Peak works" thus ultimately contradicted VSt's primary strategic goal.

Conveniently, however, "peak works" helped retain the book value accorded the properties of the founding combines. As Reckendrees demonstrates, the VSt used most of the money from the American loan to purchase the properties, equipment, and inventories from the founding combines—at relatively high value, thus freeing the founding combines of their debt.[35] It cannot be stressed enough that this retention of plant capacity had little to do with VSt social policy or sympathy for laid-off workers, public relations, or even political considerations, but arose from internal rivalries among managers and financial considerations of shareholders. Vögler's recommendations did less to solve merger rivalries than to institutionalize them into the very fiber of VSt organizational and financial practices.

At the end of September, Krupp suddenly withdrew. Although its management remained sympathetic to the VSt, joining the VSt would have likely shut down a good part of its famous casting foundries, which its owner, Gustav Krupp von Bohlen und Halbach, could not bear to contemplate. In addition, Krupp received some state subsidies, which provided short-term relief. It remains a mystery if a timely visit by the new Reich President, Paul von Hindenburg, (and a promise of future army contracts) helped induce Krupp to remain independent. To survive, Krupp went on a disciplined rationalization drive. Like the VSt, it too took out another American loan, but—unlike the VSt—it plowed back all profits and abstained from dividends until the mid-1930s.[36]

Krupp's withdrawal temporarily unhinged the negotiations. After Krupp withdrew, the Thyssens turned difficult. They laid down a tough position, especially as the Rheinelbe Union now carried more negotiating weight. By the end of October, after many rounds of negotiations, the parties reached a temporary consensus on share quotas in the new firm. They agreed to issue roughly RM 600–800 million of common stock. They would value the Thyssen Machine Company at a straight 2% of the common stock. Although August and Fritz Thyssen wanted to use preferred stocks, the merging firms instead created a total RM 100 million of dividend certificates. The merging firms linked the dividend certificates to dividends on common stock, but these carried a limit of 7%; the new VSt could buy out these certificates as it saw fit at par value at a later date. Because of the ATH's special "geographical and economic position," they granted Thyssen RM 40 million (40%) of dividend certificates. The rest of the dividend certificates compensated the founding firms for their peak works, which would run at lower rates of capacity.

By the end of October, they settled on the name of the new company, the *Vereinigte Stahlwerke AG*. The anonymous, neutral name itself betrays its origin as the lowest common denominator; none of the founding combines found its traditional name favored. Its company logo became an abstract portrait of a union of chain links. They planned to locate the headquarters of the new company in the new Rheinstahl "thousand window" administrative building in Duisburg-Ruhrort. After composing a draft of the VSt's new statutes, Späing commented in October 1925 on how much more "cumbersome" the new VSt would become relative to the Thyssen-Konzern.[37]

External Relations

At the negotiating table, internal rivalries began to compromise the VSt's ability to rationalize itself. Now, after November, external shareholder and stakeholder interests intruded, threatening to destroy the consensus they had achieved on quotas. Since the VSt would control roughly 50% of Germany's steel production, its founding had economic and political consequences of the first magnitude, which extended well beyond the "three-pronged" investment and coordination of manufacturing, marketing, and management (Chandler). Industrial, associational, and political bargaining embedded VSt strategy in a web of compromises that circumscribed its strategy and further softened its rationalization drive.

In November 1925, IG Farben, which owned a good portion of Rheinstahl, entered VSt negotiations. IG Farben feared becoming dependent on the VSt for coal. Moreover, if Rheinstahl mines joined, IG Farben might lose its self-consumption rights in the coal syndicate. In spite of mediating efforts by banks, IG Farben refused to back down; Rheinstahl withdrew its mines. (The importance of IG Farben can be seen when the VSt created a special liaison office for it in 1927.)[38] With the loss of Rheinstahl's mines, Rheinelbe supplied approximately 50% of VSt coal. With greater leverage, Kirdorf and Vögler wanted a corresponding adjustment in the Rheinelbe quotas, which increased from 34% of VSt stock to 38%, largely at the cost of Rheinstahl, whose quota dropped from 14% to 9%.[39] The exemption of the Rheinstahl mines set off a new round of counterdemands, which nearly led to a "dead end" (Reckendrees). Moreover, because of adamant resistance to the VSt by Thyssen-Bornemisza, August and Fritz Thyssen could not bring in their unmined fields, the important gas and waterworks firms, and the Press- und Walzwerke in Reisholz.

Another company, Mannesmann, Germany's largest seamless pipe producer, briefly entered negotiations. Following the traditional logic of vertical integration, it planned to build its own integrated steel works at Huckingen. At the time Mannesmann still had no steel works and followed American-style development by concentrating on a few mass-production goods. Krupp and the Bochumer Verein supplied most of Mannesmann's intermediate goods so the VSt represented a potential hazard. The VSt made overtures for Mannesmann to join. Although the Deutsche Bank had great interest in the new steel trust, it had just as great an interest in Mannesmann's independence. (This is an especially good example of how banks' interests could conflict.) Mannesmann showed a willingness to join the VSt to secure its supply of inputs, but decided against the merger in order to maintain its independence, especially to maintain its reputable name overseas— an important reason for VSt's 1933 reorganization into subsidiaries. Mannesmann then began building the new Huckingen plant, which contradicted VSt's strategy of bringing industry capacity into line with demand. To stop it, the horrified VSt tried to take Mannesmann over in 1927, but to no avail. Not only did the VSt lose Mannesmann as a potential member and steady customer, but as demand dropped, its new steel plant dumped its excess production on the market. In this manner, the VSt unintentionally contributed to industry-wide overcapacity.[40]

Siemens-Schuckert then exerted pressure. Under the agreement, Siemens-Schuckert belonged to the Siemens-Rheinelbe-Schuckert-Union (SRSU) IG created by Hugo Stinnes, until the year 2000. Siemens-Schuckert supported the formation of the VSt in principle because it would cheapen input prices, but in practice Siemens could neither justify becoming an "appendage" of VSt, nor accede to the lowly quota of 38% being offered to the Rheinelbe-Union. It also predicated the dissolution of the SRSU on the VSt's good relationship with the finishing and electrical industry.[41] The backing of Siemens-Schuckert further strengthened Rheinelbe's hand. Rheinelbe then felt justified withdrawing Gelsenkirchen's Monopol mining company from the table. Van der Zypen, a small integrated combine, followed suit by withdrawing its lignite mines. In this manner, the VSt lost significant control over important mining fields, whose production would remain on the market. The resistance of individual big businesses reduced the VSt's ability to rationalize mining and pipe sectors.

In spite of its loss of leverage, Rheinstahl upped the ante. By December, the negotiations reached a complete standstill as Rheinstahl and Rheinelbe squared off. Kirdorf and Vögler refused to back down from their demand of at least 40% of VSt common stock, mostly at the expense of Rheinstahl. Despite the presence of the two grand old men, Emil Kirdorf and August Thyssen, who never got along, Rheinelbe could not justify its present quota to its stockholders, and discontinued negotiations. Even an offer of 39% with an extra RM 5 million of dividend certificates failed to move Rheinelbe. Negotiations again revolved around at most 1–2% of total VSt stock, as well as the amount and type of dividend certificates, reproducing the often petty disputes found in cartel negotiations.

The eventual compromise was to evenly distribute the contested 2% among the four combines.[42] This compromise produced final quotas of 39.5% for Rheinelbe, 26% for Phoenix and Thyssen, and 8.5% for Rheinstahl. In addition, the total value of dividend certificates (of two different sorts) was raised from RM 100 million to RM 125 million, to compensate for peak works, licenses, patents, and other important intangibles. Of these, Thyssen received RM 67 million (53%), Rheinelbe RM 36 million, Phoenix RM 15 million, and Rheinstahl RM 7 million. Considering that Thyssen-Bornemisza withdrew important ventures, Thyssen still got a highly favorable result—as the other firms duly noted. With this arrangement, the issue of appropriate shareholding quotas was settled.

On January 14, 1926, a VSt "study company" (*Vereinigte Stahlwerke Studiengesellschaft*) was founded to handle the practical questions of creating one organization out of the four rival Konzerne. (The first VSt financial report used January 14 as its official inception date.)[43] The study company made most of the early decisions about enterprise organization and manufacturing rationalization.

A new set of disputes immediately arose on the question of the VSt's relationship to coal, iron, and steel wholesalers. Vögler admitted that this was a highly "delicate point" and these negotiations stretched well into mid-1926. The negotiations were complicated by the fact that Otto Wolff was a powerful Phoenix shareholder, Thyssen and Rheinelbe had its own subsidiary trading companies, and Thyssen-Bornemisza controlled important Dutch trading companies with whom the VSt needed to cultivate good relations. All wished a secure and priority share of VSt turnover. Eventually, the VSt founded three independent joint-stock companies for the domestic market, which carried the old firms' names, Heinr. Aug. Schulte Eisen-AG, Thyssen Rheinstahl AG, Thyssen Eisen und Stahl AG. Then rivalries broke out over export trade exclusivity among Thyssen-Bornemisza's Vulcaan and N. V. Centrale Handelsvereniging firms in Holland, Raab-Karcher, and Otto Wolff's trading firms. The VSt bought off Wolff with extra financial compensations and a very lucrative set of long-term deals. Thyssen-Bornemisza reaped the rewards from being difficult and brought the N. V. Centrale Handelsvereniging (but not his logistics firm Vulcaan) into the new Stahlunion Export GmbH. Stahlunion Export handled all exports of VSt products.[44]

The VSt's relationship with Ruhr municipalities opened another question of where the VSt headquarters would locate, which tapped into the unresolved tax question. The four founding combines had temporarily agreed to locate the VSt's headquarters in the Rheinstahl administrative building in Duisburg-Ruhrort, which already existed. The size of the new building and the activist efforts of the mayor of Duisburg, Karl Jarres, who helped lobby the Reich Finance Ministry for a discount of taxes on the merger, played a decisive role. But other Ruhr municipalities competed to have the headquarters of the VSt in their city. It became a question of tax base, ability to influence VSt management, and sheer prestige. Additionally, the future site became an explicit organizational variable among the four rival combines. Hasslacher of Rheinstahl and Fritz Thyssen wanted the headquarters in Duisburg; Kirdorf and Vögler of Rheinelbe advocated Essen; Phoenix remained neutral.[45] Not surprisingly, Rheinelbe had its headquarters in Gelsenkirchen, Dortmund, and Bochum, all of which were closer to Essen, and both Rheinstahl and Thyssen had their main headquarters in Duisburg.

The VSt's financial power allowed it to play various Ruhr cities off of one another in an open competition for the lowest tax rates. Düsseldorf prided itself on having the lowest tax rates in the Ruhr and was already becoming the administrative seat of the Ruhr, as it remains today.[46] In March 1926, the VSt study commission officially announced that the new company would have its headquarters in Düsseldorf (Figure 13.1).

Düsseldorf already offered a home for a number of steel cartel

Figure 13.1 Corporate headquarters of the Vereinigte Stahlwerke, Düsseldorf. (Reproduced with the permission of the Mannesmann-Archiv, Mülheim/Ruhr)

adminstrations, including the important Steel Works Association and the pipe syndicate. The VSt's main administration was temporarily housed in the Steel Works Association's administrative building in Düsseldorf, called the "Steel Ministry" *(Stahlhof)*. Thereafter, as part of Düsseldorf's deal with the VSt, the city offered an adjacent building of the Stumm-Konzern to the VSt at cost and paid the expenses of furnishing it.[47] VSt main administration headquarters for its mining division, however, remained in Essen near the headquarters of the coal syndicate. Nothing symbolized the close relationship between *Konzerne* and *Kartelle* better than the location of VSt headquarters. Both still exist today as the old and new *Stahlhof* located on the Breite Strasse in the midst of regional banking headquarters.

VSt's relationship with the finishing industry exemplified these associational politics. Traditionally ensconced in their heavy industrial cartels like castle walls, this powerful new "alliance" of primary producers threatened to exacerbate already difficult relations between primary producers and finished goods manufacturers. The government predicated its tax break for the VSt on continuing good relations with finished goods manufacturers, who played a decisive role in shaping VSt strategy. Siemens played a particularly critical role in representing the manufacturing industry as it led the finishing industry's peak association and had leverage over the new VSt through its IG with Rheinelbe. The reader might note that in spite of the loud complaints about labor and the "political demands" of the state, the politics that affected the VSt the most came from business itself.

The AVI agreements concluded between 1924 and 1926 were an integral part of the compromise between crude steel producers (and the VSt) and other manufacturers.[48] AVI was the Working Community of the Iron Finishing Industry, led by the Association of German Machine Engineering Firms (VDMA). In expectation that Germany would regain tariff sovereignty, German heavy industrialists, led by Fritz Thyssen and Ernst Poensgen of Phoenix, had renewed negotiations to form the Crude Steel Association, established in November 1924. This new cartel not only syndicated A-products, but the more complicated B-products. This cartel encompassed 90% of all steel production. By contrast, prewar cartels syndicated approximately 50% of all steel products.

While the Crude Steel Association promised to stabilize prices in the interests of primary producers, these higher prices undercut the international competitiveness of manufacturers. Thus, parallel to steel cartel negotiations, in December 1924 German primary producers and manufacturers had finalized an agreement, the so-called "Paris agreement," whereby crude steel producers set up an open account to compensate the manufacturing industry's exports with the differential between the German domestic price and the world market price for basic steel. In July 1925, producers and manufacturers revised the agreement, especially determining the exact means of assessing this price differential, which took into account new tariffs. (Again they used calculation as control and compromise.) Fifteen different manufacturing associations signed the agreement, including the machine engineering, metalworking, electro-technical, automobile, railway, and bicycle industries.

When French–German diplomatic discussions threatened the AVI agreement by potentially providing French steel manufacturers easy access into the Saar, European steel producers began negotiations for the formation of an International Steel Cartel, established in September 1926, just after the VSt came into existence. This cartel set up international spheres of interest, which assured that each participating national steel industry controlled their respective home markets.[49] This European cartel would have serious ramifications for the VSt.

But the formation of the VSt threatened these agreements because of its potential influence on the price structure of the steel industry, the finishing industry, and the machine engineering industry through its direct control of the Thyssen Machine Company. Manufacturing associations felt that the VSt would manipulate internal transfer prices to favor its machine engineering works. (Internally, however, many VSt executives felt that they would have great difficulty marketing the Machine Company's products to rival companies.) To alleviate these fears, the VSt informally promised not to extend beyond its present market share into the finished goods industry.

After the formation of the International Steel Cartel, however, manufacturer and producer associations amended the AVI agreement to anchor this verbal promise in writing. In May 1926, the VSt signed a special agreement limiting itself to iron and steel production "in the interests of a healthy development of the national economy as well as a desirable cooperation and understanding." The VSt explicitly agreed no longer to follow the logic of "vertical trust building." If the VSt had any finished manufacturing plants, then it agreed to give them no special price advantages. Siemens-Schuckert pressured the VSt to sign this final AVI agreement by withholding agreement for the merger of the Rheinelbe Union into the VSt.[50] The manufacturing industry pressured the rest of German steel *Konzerne* to follow the lead of the VSt, but they did not. Hoesch, Krupp, and the GHH, for instance, retained their machine engineering companies. In this respect, only the VSt, which controlled roughly one-half of German crude steel production, broke with "vertical trust building." The VSt embedded itself in the existing industrial order, rather than fundamentally remaking it.

As a result, in a dramatic gesture of good will, the VSt sold the Thyssen Machine Company and the neighboring Friedrich-Wilhelms-Hütte to DEMAG, which the VSt then helped refound. The VSt listed DEMAG accounts in its balance sheets as a portfolio investment, not as a direct subsidiary, although through a secret pooling arrangement with the Deutsche Bank it controlled 51% of its shares. This surface independence aided DEMAG, since its customers were VSt rivals. It also assuaged the manufacturing industry, because cartels did not consider deliveries of steel to DEMAG as part of VSt self-consumption rights. (After 1929 the VSt purchased a majority of shares in DEMAG when it again wanted those self-consumption rights, thus tacitly abrogating parts of the AVI agreement.) DEMAG immediately shut down its former rival, the Thyssen Machine Company. In 1927, it sold its electric dynamo production to Siemens-Schuckert, costing Mülheim 1,500 jobs.[51]

The 1926 sale of the Thyssen Machine Company sent a clear signal to *die Wirtschaft* and the general public that the VSt would not leverage its way into the finishing industry or try to monopolize the steel industry. Much like U.S. Steel, which gave up market share in order to survive American antitrust legislation, the VSt rid itself of the Thyssen and Friedrich-Wilhelms-Hütte machine companies in order to win in the associational world of German capitalism.[52] This was an immensely important concession and strategic shift, as vertical growth had dominated German steel's strategy since the 1890s.

Complicated associational politics had contradictory effects on VSt strategy in the medium term. German steel had traditionally relied on exports, at minimum as a "safety valve," but the International Steel Cartel blocked imports from other nations' steel firms. International competition became fiercer as other nations (Netherland, Norway, Sweden) built or strengthened (France, Belgium) their steel industries. Increased competition combined with such a cartel agreement limited potential demand for a European industry already suffering from severe overcapacity. Henceforth, German steel had to rely on relatively weak domestic demand or export farther afield in poorer countries. Indeed, demand became so weak that the steel cartel could hardly sell its products at its official list prices at home.[53] The VSt's strategic goal of bringing industry capacity in line with demand thus grew further out of reach.

But in the short term, good relations with the manufacturing industry facilitated the special tax break from the German government. Jakob Hasslacher and Albert Vögler handled VSt's business–government negotiations. They lobbied through Hans von Raumer, a pro-business advocate in the German People's Party (DVP), former Reich Economic Minister, and a board member of the Central Association of the German Electrotechnical Industry. Von Raumer conducted talks with Hans Luther (Reich Economic Minister), Minister President Otto Braun, and Rudolf Hilferding (the SPD Finance Minister and author of *Das Finanzkapital*). Von Raumer found a sympathetic ear in all of them. Many leading government officials expected that the VSt would increase industry productivity, lower costs, and expand the trickle of American money into a flood. In October 1925, von Raumer advised Hasslacher that the VSt's argument for a tax break must emphasize the ability of the VSt to effect a cost reduction in primary steel products for the iron consuming industry, that is, finished goods manufacturers: "The iron producing industry should not conduct the battle, because it will appear in the struggle solely as a financially interested party. The battle can only be led by the iron consuming industry, which is pressing for measures reducing the cost of its primary products."[54] A few days later, Vögler wrote von Raumer thanking him for his "energetic" interventions on their behalf. At this juncture in the negotiations, Vögler thought that potential VSt firms were not carrying on the negotiations with the "necessary momentum" because everyone had visions of huge fusion costs. They originally expected a total tax burden of roughly RM 20 million. Vögler suggested to von Raumer a flat tax fee spread out over a number of years until the new VSt became more profitable.[55]

In order to justify a tax break on political grounds, the VSt appealed to manufacturer associations and sympathetic politicians to make its case. Throughout the course of VSt's negotiations with manufacturing associations and the central government, heavy industry's basic structural problems, largely deriving from its own cooperative-competitive practice, were being translated into a broader, more politicized field with a different rhetoric to accommodate other interests in the German economy and polity. Thus, while industry-wide structural problems and a financial liquidity crisis triggered VSt negotiations, and hardboiled financial/accounting dilemmas and power relations among the four rival Konzerne guided *internal* negotiations, in their *external* case to the Reich Finance Minister, the VSt blamed the French, the eight-hour day, the additional social costs of the Weimar state, and most cynically, the "inflation-dumping" [!] of the French and Belgians, for German steel's plight. Conveniently, in the final draft of the letter to the Reich Finance Minister, the VSt crossed out numerous references in the original draft to the rationalization envisioned by the new VSt— plant closings. Instead, Hasslacher stressed that the VSt would remain a rich tax base for the Reich (while arguing for a reduction in taxes) and would save roughly 200,000 jobs (while planning to cut them).[56] Gerald Feldman has correctly interpreted these arguments as a model of "heavy industry's capacity for disingenuousness."

The VSt's stance, epitomized by the letter to the Reich Finance Minister, illustrates the difficulty of using political-ideological arguments, meant to persuade outsiders—particularly politicians and the public— as to company motivations or interests. A process of translation from business *problems* to business *practice* to business *politics* occurred. The problems of the German steel industry arose from its own industrial order, best outlined in Vögler's 1919 memorandum. The 1925 merger negotiations stemmed from "financial and productivity standpoints" and not from alleged problems of the Weimar Republic. Heinrich Dinkelbach reflected on this after the war:

It becomes apparent how closely financial and productivity standpoints were bound up with the organizational development of the [VSt] Konzern. When in 1926 the Thyssen, Rheinstahl, Phoenix and Rhein-Elbe-Union groups merged, financial considerations in particular stood in the foreground. These perspectives remained dominant for the areas of activity of the holding company, which carried out an extensive centralization of finance and accounting. At the same time, the fusion of the different iron and steel concerns brought in numerous factories with the same or related lines of production, whereby a streamlining and rationalization of these production operations was assumed. The development of the Vereinigte Stahlwerke led to large-scale closings of inefficient lines of production in individual factories and to a tightened concentration on more appropriate operations. Moreover, an extensive coordination of product lines was initiated. Thus originated in this Konzern a vertically integrated entity, which extended from raw material production (coal, iron ore, limestone, etc.) and far into finishing, but allowed a far-reaching horizontal organization with the corresponding potential for rationalization in regards to the scope of the manufacturing workshops and product lines, in particular for mass production. Hence the possibility for creating manufacturing economies through specialization and concentration, the like of which did not exist in any other Konzern, resulted from this fusion whose founding was predominantly driven by financial considerations.[57]

Because of widespread support for its essential goals, the government proved largely willing to lower the tax burden on the new company.[58] Gustav Stresemann, for instance, viewed the new VSt favorably in diplomatic terms for strengthening Germany in international cartels and *vis-à-vis* France. The German parliament subsequently passed a "tax amelioration law" on March 22, 1926 to ease "necessary mergers." Eventually, the Finance Ministry agreed to a lump tax sum of RM 10.75 million payable over nine years, which carried an interest rate at 4 or 5% with a heavier burden at the end of the amortization period, which amounted to a generous tax break of roughly RM 40 million, or about 20% of the originally expected tax burden.

While generally sympathetic, various ministries found themselves in conflict with one another about the modalities of tax relief. To justify tax relief for the VSt, the Social Democrats demanded rent controls for a year. Above all, Ruhr cities that were about to lose major company headquarters with their associated financial transactions wanted higher real estate taxes, especially as Prussia passed on 96% of those taxes to the cities. Mayor Jarres, who had previously fought for tax reductions for the VSt in the expectation that the VSt would locate its headquarters in Duisburg, now advocated higher real estate taxes. (Such tense community relations would be another reason for the reorganization of the VSt.)

Paradoxically, the VSt attacked Weimar's politicians, who proved largely sympathetic to the VSt (though for varying reasons). For all its cynicism, the VSt merger *was* predicated on good relations with the finished goods and engineering industry, which decisively reoriented VSt strategy toward a strategy of horizontal rationalization. This American-style horizontal orientation, which led to the sale of the Thyssen Machine Company, resulted neither because its plant was obsolete, nor because the VSt followed an American-style strategy *per se,* but for complicated reasons of market order and the balance of power within the German economy. Instead of initiating a strong drive toward profitability and/or market share, the VSt remained caught in a web of countervailing interests—the least of which derived from labor opposition or wage issues. Instead of a ruthless drive for market share, lower production costs, and profitability, the VSt settled for internal compromises, further higgling and bargaining in associations and cartels, self-imposed market spheres, and dropping profitable lines of business (machine engineering). In this respect, the German "United Steel" acted too much like U.S. Steel, which also moderated its strategy by "losing to win."[59] Unlike the U.S., in Germany the rhetoric of rationalization was explicitly politicized. VSt's arguments may have been disingenuous or flat-out hypocritical, but industrialists expressed their interests as assaults on the Weimar system—a strange manner of rhetorical persuasion that attacked the government in order to convince it to grant a favor. This 1926 rhetoric contrasts dramatically with the effort to persuade Adolf Hitler's new government in 1933 for yet another tax break to save the VSt from economic depression, bankruptcy, and from itself.

The "Rationalization Company"

The VSt was designed to create American-style volume economies, to streamline its own operations, and to help the steel industry match production with demand. In terms of its strategy, manufacturing structure, and status in the industry, the VSt represented a convergence to the American model. Although it heralded a drive toward manufacturing rationalization, its achievements did not match its press.

After being assured a one-time tax break on the fusion costs to be paid in installments, the four combines finalized the merger. In May 1926, the VSt general assembly raised the share capital of the study commission company to RM 800 million. They chose the figure of RM 800 million to attract American capital and to (over)generously cover the incoming assets of the four founding combines. As Reckendrees demonstrates, the latter reason proved most important. Early in the negotiations, Vögler and Rabes had suggested a shareholding equity of RM 500 million, which would enhance VSt's profitability. With less equity one could pay out at a higher dividend rate and the VSt would cut a more impressive financial figure on the stock market. Moreover, in the Thyssen–Dillon Read negotiations, Rabes had stressed that the Americans placed particular weight on a crude-steel-production to share capital ratio and would not balk at a lower equity.[60] But a higher shareholding equity, let alone RM 125 million of dividend certificates, placed a higher value on the incoming assets of the founding combines (some of which would be shut down). Such a conflict of interest highlighted the potentially divergent goals between VSt shareholders and management, and that shareholders held the upper hand. So the new VSt—like U.S. Steel—began its existence financially overcapitalized. Its overcapitalization meant that return on equity ratios would suffer, yet VSt shareholders still expected an appropriate level of dividends. Thus, ironically, the VSt did take on what many German observers perceived as one of the great disadvantages of American-style trust-building: the "chronic birth mistake" of overcapitalization.[61]

Negotiations with Dillon Read made speedy progress after April 1926, with Carl Rabes (of Thyssen) and Oskar Sempell (of Deutsch-Lux) as experienced point men. At the end of June 1926, the VSt and Dillon Read closed their deal, worth nearly $71 million (RM 297 million). The VSt mortgaged its land and fixed assets as collateral, giving Dillon Read a veto right over their sale and use. The entire sum of the first loan covered the costs of the founding and the purchase of assets and inventories from the founding combines—assets that would have lost value if the founding firms had gone bankrupt.

In order actually to invest in modernization of plant and pay for strategic takeovers in the industry, Dillon Read issued another long-term loan worth an additional $30 million (RM 126 million). To Dillon Read, the VSt declared the sum would dissolve the dividend certificates. To the Reich Finance Ministry, the VSt declared that the money would go toward its rationalization program and *not* the dissolution of the dividend certificates, because the founding combines did not need funds for the time being. Instead, the founding combines' shareholders arranged for the VSt to delay regular amortization of their dividend certificates for four years and then repurchase them over the next five years. This loan further indebted the VSt, although it officially promised not to take on any more debt, and only postponed the amortization of the dividend certificates. Price Waterhouse's 1927 financial statement estimated that VSt's long-term debt against its founders was RM 200 million. The VSt entered the business world with commitments of RM 800 million in equity and RM 700 million in long-term debt.[62] This debt load contributed to the VSt's future fixed-cost crisis.

From its inception, the VSt was significantly overcapitalized and carried a heavy load of debt, while the founding combines regained financial maneuverability. For these reasons, Reckendrees argues that initially the VSt was less a successful "rationalization company" than a "rehabilitation company." The VSt managed to stop the "foreseeable bankruptcy of at least one of the four [founding] combines and initially secured their accumulated capital."[63] Hardly ringing praise. Moreover, in a typical move, shareholders demanded their cut of the dividends barely after the VSt began generating its own cash flow. For the first half-year balance, which showed a loss of RM 1 million (!), the VSt finance department (Rabes) recommended not showing a profit to forgo dividends and build reserves—an August Thyssen-like move. But shareholders demanded a 3% dividend for the sake of good publicity. In 1927, the VSt financial department (Rabes) again argued that the VSt should not show a profit and not pay out dividends to build reserves, but Rheinstahl shareholders refused; the VSt paid out dividends. In fact, until the Depression the founding combines decided that a 6% dividend was appropriate, then set a rough net profit figure to justify the dividends by manipulating depreciations and gross profit figures.[64] The VSt acted as a parody of shareholder value. As chair of the supervisory board, Fritz Thyssen did not act as though he had learned anything from his father.

As the flagship of German steel, the VSt claimed to bring industry capacity in line with demand and wanted to play a similar role in Germany that U.S. Steel did in the United States. The VSt represented a union of twelve major enterprises (four major Konzerne and five additional firms). The VSt and U.S. Steel held comparable market shares in their respective national markets. In this respect, we can speak of convergence.

In the crude steel cartel, the VSt represented almost one-half of German steel in cartel quotas and production. Krupp received the next highest quota with 10.5%, GHH 6.85%, Hoesch 5.27%, Klöckner 5.23%, and Mannesmann 2.56%. As did U.S. Steel at its inception, the VSt led with roughly 40–50% market share in almost every major category of steel products, except structural steel (Table 13.2). Additionally, before 1930 the VSt mined about 18% of all German coal (production, not cartel quotas). Thereafter, its market share dropped to 15%. Even before the Depression, the VSt did not maintain its quota share in the steel cartel. By 1929, its cartel quota shares for all

Table 13.2 VSt quotas in steel cartels, 1926 and 1929

Product	June 30, 1926	September 30, 1929
Pig iron	48.47%	38.45%
Crude steel	46.82%	38.30%
A. Products	48.96%	40.02%
1. Semi-processed materials	56.49%	45.91%
2. Structural shaped steel	28.04%	21.50%
3. Rails	55.77%	47.42%
Merchant iron	41.94%	30.72%
Strip steel/skelp	48.59%	38.96%
Rolled wire	38.75%	29.16%
Heavy plates	47.13%	39.74%
Pipes	50.20%	50.61%

Source: Die Vereinigte Stahlwerke A.-G.: Ihr Aufbau und ihre Bedeutung für Deutschland und die Weltwirtschaft, (Hg.) Schwarz, Goldschmidt & Co. (Berlin, 1926). Weisbrod, Schwerindustrie, pp. 98–100. Das Spezial-Archiv, Vereinigte Stahlwerke, 32. MA: R 1 40 35.1 "Bericht über das 4. Geschäftsjahr vom 1. Oktober 1928 bis 30. September 1929." Slight differences among the quota percentages exist.

goods except pipes dropped by 7–11%. A parallel story occurred with U.S. Steel.[65]

Why did the VSt not maintain market share? In this respect the VSt actually followed the American model too closely. To some extent this drop reflects a cartel effect, whereby the initial VSt quotas were a hold-over of quotas taken from the four founding combines. But there were two other crucial parts of this story. The first part of the story lies in the way it rationalized its own production operations. The second part is its failure to make its weight felt in the standard competitive dynamics of German steel.

Soon after it was founded, the VSt quickly acquired the AG Charlottenhütte, the AG Friedrichshütte, the Rombacher Hütten-werke, the Mitteldeutsche Stahlwerke, leased the properties of the Stumm-Konzern, and acquired stock in the Deutsche Edelstahlwerke AG.[66] Officially, the VSt took over these firms in the interests of eliminating less efficient plants and coordinating the more efficient plants to eliminate overlap. But behind the scenes, the first two Siegerland-based firms were part of Friedrich Flick's growing empire; he wanted to secure the value of his investments and increase his leverage over the VSt. Rombach was near bankruptcy and the government worried that a public bankruptcy would shake the confidence of foreign investors. Banks also turned to the "VSt-project" as a means of saving their invested capital. Located in the Saar, Stumm faced dire financial difficulties, but had received government help for diplomatic reasons *vis-à-vis* France, and the Deutsche Bank wanted to unload Stumm properties not located in the Saar. More positively, the VSt purchased control over the Mitteldeutsche Stahlwerke and consolidated its specialty steel plants into the Deutsche Edelstahlwerke AG to coordinate production. The VSt oriented the latter firm more toward series production and the burgeoning automobile industry.

In most of these cases, the VSt bore all the costs of incorporating these weaker firms at prices favorable to their previous owners, often to shut them down.[67] Such negative rationalization was not necessarily a flaw, but it cost the VSt more than necessary. Instead of letting firms go bankrupt for free and picking up valuable pieces at bargain-basement prices, the VSt saved the value of property for previous owners (some of whom were VSt shareholders). It did help streamline production in the industrial branch, but at the cost of carrying more corporate debt. American credit funded such actions. Because of this, the VSt's two strategic goals, to reduce industry capacity and to rationalize itself in the interest of profitability, wound up in conflict with one another, and, in any case, these maneuvers financially overtaxed the VSt.

Ironically designed to convince American investors of the value of the VSt, the following tables illustrate the many problems confronting the VSt as a "rationalization company."

In terms of the number of plants, U.S. Steel outweighed the VSt by two to three times in almost every major production area, particularly in iron, crude steel, and intermediate goods (Table 13.3). The VSt, however, had special strengths over U.S. Steel in its number of byproduct coking ovens, phosphate slag mills, seamless tube works, welded tubular goods departments, cold rolling mills, metal foundries, and forging departments. While major U.S. steel companies tended to have their weight in crude steel production combined with a concentration in particular specialty areas (Bethlehem in intermediate goods and heavy rolled products; Jones & Laughlin in structural and tin-plate steel; Youngstown Sheet & Tube in plates and welded pipes), the VSt (and other German companies) managed to cover almost the full

Table 13.3 Comparison of Vereinigte Stahlwerke with the four largest American steel companies (number of production plants)

Plants/mills/depts.	VST	U.S. Steel	Bethlehem	Jones & Laughlin	Youngstown Sheet & Tube
Coal mines	37	101	8	6	8
By product coke ovens	4,846	3,284	1,893	422	618
Bee hive coke ovens	—	13,305	—	1,208	—
Furnaces/blast furnaces	63	112	42	12	17
Steel plants, bessemer	33	34	17	7	4
S-M open hearth and electric furnaces	121	332	134	31	29
Puddling plants	2	—	21	—	25
Blooming, slabbing, large billet rolling mills	13	44	16	4	4
Small billet, sheet bar mills	14	15	8	3	4
Rail mills	8	8	5	—	—
Universal plate mills	8	7	2	1	—
Sheared plate mills	10	11	8	2	3
Structural shape mills	4	11	10	17	—
Wire rod mills	10	25	2	2	1
Skelp, hoop iron mills	18	20	2	1	6
Merchant mills	32	66	29	4	4
Hot mills, black plate for tinning	38	218	36	32	—
Sheet jobbing and plate mills	24	159	10	—	30
Wire mills, drawing depts.	9	23	2	1	1
Nail mills	5	15	2	1	1

Barbed and twisted fence depts.	3	13	1	2	2
Woven fence depts.	3	16	1	—	1
Spring works	4	3	—	—	—
Rope and electrical works	2	5	—	—	—
Pipe & tube works, welding pipe furnaces	9	55	—	5	22
Seamless tube mills	28	9	1	1	1
Welded tube and tubular goods depts.	4	—	—	—	—
Galvanizing depts.	7	35	2	2	8
Tinplate works	3	14	1	1	—
Bridge & structural plants	8	16	5	1	—
Splice bar, tie plate, or rail joint Finishing shops	2	7	2	—	—
Spike, nut, or bolt factories	5	7	4	1	—
Cold rolling mills	44	5	2	1	—
Iron, steel, or brass foundries	29	24	14	1	1
Sulphate of iron plants	2	12	—	—	—
Cement plants	3	5	5	—	—
Forging depts.	10	—	5	—	—
Phosphate slag mills	6	—	—	—	—
Miscellaneous works/depts.	48	49	20	2	10

Source: MA: R 5 35 28 (1) "Handbuch für die Anleihen des Jahres 1926."

Table 13.4 Approximate annual capacity of the VSt and four American companies, 1926

Product	VST	U.S. Steel	Bethlehem	Jones & Laughlin	Youngstown Sheet & Tube
Coal	37,188,000	31,475,568[a]	10,000,000	5,000,000	2,525,000
Coke	9,189,000	16,301,224[a]	7,369,900	2,800,000	2,600,000
Pig iron	9,038,000	18,940,000	6,850,000	2,400,000	3,053,000
Steel ingots and castings	7,936,000	22,750,000	7,600,000	3,000,000	3,240,000
Finished products	7,066,600	16,252,000	4,696,000	2,430,000	2,179,000

Source: MA: R 5 35 28 (1) "Handbuch für die Anleihen des Jahres 1926."

Notes: Figures used are 1925 production figures. VSt, metric tons. American companies, gross and net tons as per standard practice. 1 metric ton = .9842 ton.

a. No capacity figures published.

range of product lines from coal to foundries. In the extent of its vertical integration, U.S. Steel actually followed more of a German pattern.

As impressive as these figures appear at first glance, the number of plants was the major problem facing the VSt. With one-third the number of coal mines, the VSt had a stronger footprint in coal than U.S. Steel, but for most iron and steel production, the VSt was comparable to Bethlehem steel. If we compare pig-iron capacity (a constituent product for all downstream goods), the VSt could produce 9 million tons in 63 blast furnaces (Table 13.4). U.S. Steel could produce twice as much with twice as many blast furnaces, Bethlehem 1 million tons less than the VSt but with just two-thirds the number of blast furnaces. If we compare the largest and most efficient VSt steelworks, the ATH in Bruckhausen, with U.S. Steel's Gary works, in 1927 both works had comparable technologies and structures, but the ATH produced only 60% of its capacity. Unfortunately, the VSt operated significantly under capacity in coke, pig iron (ca. 53–69%), crude steel (ca. 60–74%), finished rolled products (44–55%) between 1926 and 1930—which only worsened during the Depression. At the time, both U.S. Steel and Bethlehem Steel operated at roughly 80% capacity. We should not idealize competitive conditions in American steel as the industry worked at roughly 60–75% capacity. U.S. Steel's strategy allowed "Little Steel" independents to grow swiftly around "Big Steel," ameliorating some of

Table 13.5 Comparison of 1925 production and revenues, VSt, U.S. Steel, Bethlehem Steel (in metric tons, RM)

	VST	U.S. Steel	Bethlehem
Coal production	22,885,888	31,979,177	6,432,546
Coke production	6,784,934	16,562,044	4,517,616
Pig iron production	4,776,994	15,035,783	4,091,619
Bessemer steel	4,920,016	19,201,076	5,430,139
Rolling and finished products (incl. self-consumption)	3,620,769	13,483,346	3,890,297
Revenues (incl. internal Konzern deliveries), RM	1,501,779,505	5,907,321,819	1,146,706,344
Salaries + wages, RM	467,392,170	1,918,309,491	452,642,186
Avg. salary/wage per year, RM	2,241	7,678	7,531
Total employment	208,546	249,833	60,098

Source: MA: R 1 35 28 (2)

American steel's overcapacity problems. Through its "losing to win" policy and infamous Gary dinners (an American example of German-style cooperative capitalism), U.S. Steel did not aggressively drive for more market share for fear of antitrust action, and due to the leadership of Elbert H. Gary. Indeed, Gary's biographer praised him for substituting "cooperation for defiance" and earning the "high title of Industrial Statesman," a rubric that would have made Emil Kirdorf or Gustav Schmoller proud.[68]

The next comparison illustrates VSt's potential for productivity gains. Although the VSt had more coal capacity with one-third the number of collieries as U.S. Steel, it produced just two-thirds of U.S. Steel's output—less than 60% of capacity (Table 13.5). Although the VSt had a capacity of 9 million tons of pig iron, it produced just over half that. Pig iron production did rise to 67% of capacity in the next year, but dropped to 60% by 1929. With just two-thirds of the VSt's pig-iron capacity, Bethlehem produced almost the same amount. Excepting its presence in coal, the VSt was roughly 60% the size of U.S. Steel and comparable to Bethlehem Steel. The bottom line was that the VSt began its existence with a a significantly lower level of production, had more overlap, less scale, and was less productive than American steel firms.[69] Such comparative figures clearly illustrated to German steel executives the value of mass-production techniques.

Table 13.6 Rationalization of production units of the VSt, 1926–1933

	Before VSt		In 1933	
Production facilities	Number of plants	In companies	Number of plants	In groups
Blast furnace plants	23	8	9	5
Siemens-Martin steel mills	20	8	8	6
Bar and profile iron mills	17	8	10	6
Strip iron mills	7	5	3	3
Wire mills	7	4	2	2
Plate and sheet mills	13	6	6	4
Pipe and tube mills	8	4	3	1
Pressing and hammer mills	8	6	4	3
Iron foundries	11	6	6	1
Steel foundries	10	6	4	4
Wire rod mills	9	5	4	1
Tin-plate mills	3	3	3	1
Wheel set mills	6	5	1	1
Fittings plants	3	3	3	1

Source: TKA: VSt/1588, 2966; MA: R 1 40 35.1 "Ausserordentliche Generalversammlung der Vereinigte Stahlwerke AG," 29 November 1933. Reprinted in Feldenkirchen, "Big Business," p. 425; Chandler, *Scale and Scope,* p. 555.

Although contemporaries and historians have harshly criticized the "negative rationalization" of the VSt,[70] the VSt's employment levels and labor intensity remained relatively high until the Depression. In principle, the corporate framework of the VSt permitted managers to undertake a far-ranging concentration of production in the most efficient factories. In practice, they did not go far enough.

The number of production plants rationalized out of existence was impressive (Table 13.6). Chandler relates how by 1930 the VSt closed 19 blast furnaces, 8 steel plants with 39 open-hearth furnaces, 16 mining pits, 11 rolling mills, and 1 coking furnace. Then Chandler adds: "After 1930 the depression brought further closings—closings that were carried out according to plans already instituted."[71]

But this impressive table conflates the period before the Depression with the reorganization of the VSt into a multisubsidiary structure after 1933. Using other sources, Reckendrees shows that the vast majority of VSt plant closings occurred by the end of 1926 (more than 206, which might include a small mill train or a whole plant). It shut down almost one-third of its blast furnaces in the first year—almost 10% of all those existing in Germany.[72] Most layoffs occurred with the VSt's founding, but by October 1927, the VSt still employed 198,409 people, its highest employment figure before World War II. It took the Depression to reduce most of the pre-VSt production sites by half. Of 39 original mining collieries, only 25 were still in operation after 1933.

The speed of plant closings slowed because of merger rivalries, the notion of peak works, and a favorable upturn in the business cycle. Early in 1926, the VSt established study committees with a representative from each of the founding combines to recommend which plants close. The committees operated on the principle of keeping one primary manufacturing site along with "peak works," and then shut down the rest of the plants. This policy should have centered the VSt on its most efficient plants in terms of energy use, throughput, production costs, and proximity. But plant closings affected the balance of power internal to the VSt and aggravated external relations with surrounding communities. By October 1926, VSt's total workforce had dropped to roughly 184,000 employees, a loss of 10%, a silent layoff. And decision-making to favor one plant or another often led to contentious exchanges within the study commissions, tapping into the now institutionalized merger rivalries within the VSt.

If we go inside the business firm to see how this decision-making process took place, a significantly qualified picture of VSt success and rationalization emerges. Making matters even more difficult for the study committees was that in 1926 the VSt lacked standard cost-accounting methods, which exacerbated tensions. Commonly, it was easy to decide which plants were most efficient, but troubles arose when deciding about "peak works," second or third-tier plants often comparable in statistical terms but not in qualitative terms. The following example from the plate-mill committee illustrates the type of reasoning operative in such committees; such discussions ranged from coal mines to specialty steel products. Decisions in some sectors proved easier than others; decisions regarding plate-mill locations proved to be more antagonistic, for instance, than those regarding pipes, strip steel, and cold rolling mills.[73]

Carl Wallmann (of Thyssen) recommended that Thyssen-Mülheim and one of the Phoenix plants in Hörde or Düsseldorf remain in operation for the production of heavy plates. (Note how VSt practice designated these plants.) Phoenix-Düsseldorf had a capacity of 11,400 tons/month, Phoenix-Hörde 10,650 tons/month, Rheinstahl-Duisburg 10,174 tons/month, and the Deutsch-Lux-Weber plant in Brandenburg 7000 tons/month. Without including the Brandenburg plant, located in a different regional market in eastern Prussia, the three combines had 50,000 tons of productive capacity in the heavy plate cartel—but with an estimated total market demand of only 60,000 tons and a quota of just 30% (or 20,000 tons) from the heavy plate cartel. Again production capacity, cartel quotas, and market demand proved to be dysfunctionally out of balance. Wallmann recommended that at least two plants be closed. The committee declared Phoenix-Hörde as the primary plant because it could use both scrap and pig iron. Because Thyssen-Mülheim produced special-quality heavy plates for boilers and welded tubes, it remained open as a peak works, with an expected capacity of 13,000–15,000 tons/month. The committee recommended closing the Rheinstahl-Duisburg and Phoenix-Düsseldorf plants.

For medium-grade plates, Wallmann also declared that Phoenix-Hörde would become the primary plant; Thyssen-Mülheim would become the peak work. For universal iron bars, Dortmunder Union and Thyssen-Mülheim would remain in operation. The Rheinstahl plant should be shut down. In water-gas welding, Thyssen-Mülheim would run full as the primary producer with Phoenix-Hörde as the peak work. They would also shut down Benrath and Eller but transfer their facilities to Mülheim. Wallmann presented a particularly strong case for the Mülheim welding department because it produced specialty, high-pressure drums, tanks and pipes. (However, location mattered in ambiguous cases. Thyssen-Mülheim took over the entire production of the VSt in pressing because it needed a pressing works on site for boiler plates and other such specialty production. This meant that the Phoenix-Hörde and Rheinstahl production lines would close.) In tin-plating, Wallmann's report favored Mülheim again because of its advanced technological capabilities; it could galvanize a variety of different goods and had extensive subcontracting capacity for outside firms. Except for some specialty tin-plating in fine grades of sheets, tin-plating centered on Mülheim, with Phoenix-Düsseldorf as the peak work. The committee generally agreed with most of Wallmann's recommendations, although executives in Benrath and Eller put up some resistance.

Wilhelm Esser of Rheinstahl seriously questioned Wallmann's assessment of universal bar iron production. He agreed that the Dortmunder Union should be the primary manufacturer, but felt that Rheinstahl's plant in Meiderich should be the peak work instead of Mülheim. Wallmann agreed that Rheinstahl's Meiderich mills were more efficient, but had recommended that the VSt close them because they were inflexible and entirely dependent on heavy structural steel contracts. They duplicated capacity already present at the Dortmunder Union and would only operate economically if demand existed for such a standardized, mass production product—ironically the main objective of the VSt. According to Wallmann, Rheinstahl-Meiderich was less appropriate as a peak work because it could not roll lighter, more varied types of goods. Thyssen-Mülheim had a broader range and could more easily complement Dortmund's main production line; it also had more modern technical facilities even if Mülheim had less horsepower than Rheinstahl's. Finally, Wallmann argued, the plate mills in Mülheim could produce specialty boiler plates in varied shapes, again supplementing heavy plate production of the Dortmunder Union. At the end of his rebuttal, Wallmann stressed that he tried to make his judgments on purely technical grounds.

The other technical directors agreed with Wallmann, but Esser managed to protect Rheinstahl-Meiderich's structural steel plant. By reassigning it as a peak work, and not closing it, the VSt hoped for an increase in market demand. Similarly, the VSt kept open a number of plants from firms it had taken over, Stumm, Rombach, Condordiahütte, and the Niederrheinische Hütte. After cost-accounting analyses and another dispute, the blast furnaces and heavy-plate plants of the Hörder Verein were also left open.[74] The VSt did manage to streamline some of its production capacity, but resistance from shareholders and management blunted an even more extensive streamlining.

The implications for VSt's rationalization drive were extensive. Production capacity and overlap waited for a market demand that never came. Extra plants required maintenance and the fixed capital remained on VSt's accounts. Additionally, the VSt built a complicated internal quota scheme for peak works because they ran at lower capacity levels. Thus, deep in the heart of the VSt rationalization process lay highly politicized reasoning.

Without question, the VSt made clear productivity gains. The VSt concentrated its coal-mining operations on its largest units: Thyssen-Hamborn and Gelsenkirchen-Essen. In pig iron and crude-steel production, there was no question as to which plant should be the primary manufacturer—the ATH. The ATH consistently had the lowest production costs for many of the key goods now in the VSt. For instance, the ATH could produce Thomas pig iron at 61.73 RM/ton, Phoenix-Ruhrort at 64.30 RM/ton, Krupp at 67.19 RM/ton, Deutsch-Lux at RM 67.60 RM/ton, Rheinstahl at 69.81 RM/ton, and Phoenix-Hörde at 74 RM/ton. Moreover, unlike the other firms, Thyssen included commercial costs such as overhead, debt, and depreciation expenses in its cost accounting.[75] Instead of nine different plants, the VSt concentrated the production of rails in only the ATH. The ATH also took over the VSt's export business, especially in the mass production of intermediate goods and shaped steel, because the ATH was the only plant to use English standards in its rolling mills and because of its favorable location. Thyssen-Meiderich (formerly AGHütt) also concentrated on exports of structural steel, rod iron, and specialty iron for intermediate materials, but the VSt now grouped it together with the rest of the ATH. While the VSt works in the western Ruhr concentrated on exports because of their low production costs and proximity to shipping routes, the major iron and crude steel works in Dortmund and Hörde in the eastern Ruhr specialized in intermediate goods for the domestic market, particularly since their primary customers were located directly in the area and domestic cartels would prop up prices. The western and eastern halves of the VSt each produced about 150,000 tons of crude steel per month.

Moving downstream, the VSt located its high-value-added finished products in the eastern area of the Ruhr where transportation costs were slightly higher. Intermediate products for the domestic market centered on Dortmund, while Bochum manufactured specialty casting and foundry goods, which gave the Bochumer Verein (along with its director) a unique position inside the VSt. It also supplied a good portion of the round blooms to outside pipe mills. The ATH, however, continued to act as the main internal supplier for VSt plate and pipe factories, especially for Thyssen-Mülheim.[76] The VSt concentrated heavy- and medium-grade plate production on Mülheim, Hörde, and Brandenburg. Sheets and fine-grade finished products concentrated in the Siegerland area.

The immediate effect of these rationalization measures was dramatic. The ATH became the "show horse" of the VSt. In the first year, crude steel production rose by 75% and coal production by 30% without any increase in employment. The next year saw a 35.6% increase in crude steel production. The newly consolidated works of Phoenix and Rheinstahl in Ruhrort-Meiderich produced 23% more pig iron and crude steel. The ATH also delivered a dramatic 41.2% increase in heavy rolling mill production for intermediate goods without a significant rise in employment. The ATH continued to increase its productivity until the Depression. As Wilhem Treue correctly points out, little wonder that VSt annual reports always stressed the economic performance of the ATH.[77] In the 1920s, even the otherwise unimpressed Robert Brady had to admit: "In but a very limited number of plants—the August Thyssenhütte alone of the Vereinigte Stahlwerke plants—has the technical reorganization been more or less completely rounded out."[78]

The ATH's success was not representative of the VSt as a whole. Across the VSt, productivity gains tended to be solid, but less than dramatic.[79] For instance, by 1929 productivity (production per labor hour) had risen, from a 1927 basepoint, 27% at the ATH, 12% at Hütte Ruhrort-Meiderich, and 7% at the Dortmunder Union/Hörder Verein. Rolling mills productivity followed a similar pattern at those same sites. Most of the VSt's productivity gains occurred as a result of plant closings, jumping 15–18%, depending on product. Thereafter, productivity rose yearly about 5% for steel works and 6% for rolling mills until the Depression. The number of workers employed by VSt steel mills actually dropped from 89,000 (its highest point) in 1927 to 86,000 by July 1929, although crude steel and rolling mill production rose by 6.8% and 12%, respectively. Productivity then obviously declined after the Depression.

Most importantly for this argument, the improvements in VSt productivity were often a result of previous capacity buildup and technological modernization undertaken *during the inflation years*—as a result a "flight into real values." Fritz Thyssen's outsized modernization plans before 1925, for instance, had favorable but unintended consequences for the VSt after 1926. The benefit from already existing modernizing efforts casts some doubt on the success achieved by the VSt itself. The golden years of the Weimar economy and VSt plant closings brought this previous expansion of capacity and technical advances to fruition —a product of the specifically German inflation years, not necessarily a result of Americanization or VSt-initiated rationalization plans. This was the gist of a comment by Ernst Poensgen, the second in command, when he maintained at the end of 1927 that the VSt "had not even rationalized, rather only consolidated."[80] In this sense, the VSt was continuous with specifically German inflationary reconstruction, rather than a break from it.

To be fair, as the counterpart to closing plants, the VSt continued to invest in new plant using an overly optimistic five year plan to further improve productivity. Until the business year 1930–1931, the VSt invested a total of RM 378 million—RM 193 million in mining (mechanization of collieries, infrastructural projects, coking operations, and regeneration economies), and RM 181 million in steel plants—on the assumption that demand would consistently rise. Demand, however, did not rise, further straining VSt's credit just when its interest and amortization payments jumped by 50% in 1929. The VSt had to resort to "financial chicanery" (Reckendrees) to raise new lines of credit. One of the founding combines, Phoenix, for instance, took out a loan from a Dutch bank and lent it to the VSt, which irritated Dillon Read.[81]

The new investment did not activate the same productivity increases the initial consolidation of manufacturing had caused. VSt pig-iron capacity shrank slightly between 1926 and 1930 from 10.3 to 10 million tons. Steel capacity also shrank slightly in the same period from 9.5 to 9.2 million tons.[82] Overall, "negative" rationalization offset "positive" rationalization in terms of capacity. In limiting capacity, improving unit costs, and increasing productivity, the VSt proved to be moderately successful.

This self-imposed constraint (also its lack of creditworthiness) explains in part why the VSt did not maintain its cartel quota share. As an individual firm strategy, its restraint, however, contradicted the VSt's other strategic goal—to act as a leader in the industry like U.S. Steel and bring industry capacity into line with demand. As Robert Brady, Gerald Feldman, and Harold James have argued, the rationalization of the VSt, however important, did not amount to a rationalization of the industry.[83] This second aspect of VSt strategy failed.

The second reason the VSt did not maintain its cartel quota share was the "second rationalization wave" in the German steel industry, which the VSt could not restrain. Most of the major firms independent of the VSt (ca. 50% of the industry) increased their productive capacity, in part because they felt compelled to compete with the cost advantages of the VSt and they continued to flesh out their vertically integrated structures. The pipe producer Mannesmann built an entirely new iron and steel works. Krupp, Hoesch, and the GHH built wholly modernized blast furnaces. The GHH restructured its high-value-added machine engineering to secure downstream demand more effectively. Klöckner doubled its steelmaking capacity. Instead of a better division of labor, overlap grew; industry capacity grew by roughly ten percent.

Like U.S. Steel, VSt's restraint only softened competition and allowed the independents to grow. In fact, VSt's capacity use shrank slowly before the onset of the Depression and remained below industry average. In October 1928, its best year, the VSt operated at 67% of capacity in pig iron, 74% in crude steel, and 72% in warm rolled products. In October 1929, the VSt operated at 60% of capacity in pig iron, just under 69% in crude steel, and 67% in warm rolled products.[84]

Capacity issues were only exacerbated by VSt's support for, and yes, leadership (Ernst Poensgen) in the (European) cartel system. The International Steel Cartel reserved domestic markets for their respective home industries, which circumscribed VSt's ability to export (its export revenues shrank between 1927 and 1929). Then domestic demand weakened so much that German producers could not sell at official cartel list prices.[85] By the Depression, the entire industry was suffering from overcapacity and the ensuing "fixed cost crisis" that went along with it.

Ultimately, the VSt was caught between an American-style horizontal drive to modernize plant, raise productivity, lay off workers, and lower prices, and a German-style cooperative strategy based on vertical integration and cartels. The VSt did not break out of the classic German cartel-concern setup, but instead fit into it and heightened tension within it.[86] Much like U.S. Steel, the VSt did not (or could not) use its weight to pressure the steel industry toward a better division of labor. Instead, it cleaned up the remnants at a cost to itself. The VSt was perhaps not American enough to leverage its weight in an old-fashioned price war against other German (European) steel companies by using its potential for mass production—but then again, neither was U.S. Steel, which followed part way a German-style amelioration of competition through cooperation.

The bottom line was that until 1936 the VSt suffered from a "profit squeeze" (Reckendrees): correct strategy and intentions, but wrong or incomplete execution. Clear improvements in productivity did not translate into effective financial performance. Below-average use of capacity combined with high levels of debt and high share equity kept VSt profitability below the industry average. Ironically, even those stable and "appropriate" dividends, were below average in the industry. Reflecting the dominance of shareholders, the VSt paid out more in dividends than it made in profits, and VSt creditors actually earned more than its shareholders did.[87]

As Reckendrees decisively demonstrates, the VSt founding carried a high "mortgage," from which it never really escaped. The high expectations placed on the VSt to save the invested capital of the founding combines, to bring industry capacity in line with demand, to streamline and modernize its own manufacturing capacity, to overcome organizational difficulties caused by the merger of four major rivals, and then to pay dividends, proved to be too much for it.

In order to found the VSt, the merging Konzerne fit themselves into the existing industry order rather than making a clean break with it. The VSt took its place firmly in this cartel order, epitomized by the parallel founding of the International Crude Steel Association in 1926 and symbolized by the location of VSt headquarters next to the *Stahlhof*. This failure to recast German steel's market order found its organizational counterpart inside the VSt, with the ongoing internal rivalry among the four founding combines, which limited a more fundamental rationalization of production. The founding combines swapped their debt and desperate financial straits for equity in a highly leveraged new company, thereby saving themselves at the cost of their new venture. Inter-firm rivalries and associational arrangements hobbled and circumscribed VSt performance.

The founding of the VSt did not act as an Americanization, as its executives claimed.[88] Its overcapitalization, however, did reproduce the perceived danger of American-style trusts. Indeed, the most dramatic example of the commitment to an American-style horizontal integration instead of German-style vertical integration came with the 1926 sale of the Thyssen Machine Company. But that important decision had more to do with complicated inter-associational bargaining with German finished goods manufacturers and getting a tax break from politicians than a fundamental commitment to American-style rationalization. And then the VSt cheated on the agreement by its secret control of DEMAG. The VSt controlled just under 50% of German steel production, but the rest of the industry chose not to follow its strategy. For the most part, steel Konzerne continued to justify their vertical integration primarily through the "natural and technical laws" of technology, often conflated with an "organic" notion of technology and economy. Secondary factors included financial pooling, tax questions, exchange of experiences, and so on. The decartelization trustees acting after the World War II, represented by Heinrich Dinkelbach, argued that vertically oriented Konzerne originated primarily in the interest of cartel quotas, financial pooling, cross-subsidies, financial hedging (as in the inflation years), tax advantages, profit manipulations, exchange of experiences, and finally, "the striving for power and influence in order to participate in the formation of economic conditions was a very important motivating force."[89]

Hence, only on the surface did the American-style productive rationalization of the VSt appear to be Americanization, when it was actually a new stage in the Germanization of (some) American business ideas. Intra- and inter-business politics transmuted American ideas. VSt productivity gains rested as much on the latent, inflationary achievements of the founding combines as much as on the accomplishments of the VSt. The VSt did, however, help actualize this inflationary reconstruction and ease some industry overcapacity, which would have been only more aggravating. It lost potential influence and cartel quota share because one part of VSt strategy, rationalizing the individual firm, unintentionally contradicted the other part of VSt strategy, bringing industry-wide capacity in line with market demand.

To be clear, there is nothing unique about high fixed costs and overcapacity generating low profits, but the VSt (and other German heavy industrialists) made numerous argumentative claims to the contrary. Contrary to German industrialists' laments about the rising costs of labor, social welfare expenses, and taxes, the fundamental problem of the German steel industry was a failure to set its own industrial house in order. Reckendrees definitively showed that VSt wage costs in relation to revenues remained stable or dropped. (If any cost rose, it was salaries.) Taxes and social policy costs also remained stable. The cost of debt servicing outweighed legal and voluntary social policy expenses.[90]

Still, the founding of the VSt introduced the intention (but not the reality) of a new strategy and conception of control, which sought to balance production directly with market demand and maximize profitability, but without breaking from the traditions of German steel. A German version of oligopoly capitalism began to form. Although it became renowned (or notorious) for its manufacturing rationalization, VSt actually excelled in the arena of commercial management. But, analogous to the way firm-level modernization paradoxically led to counterproductive industry-wide dynamics, VSt's organizational innovation perversely exacerbated internal tensions among the rival founding combines, which prevented the VSt from becoming a more successful company.

CHAPTER 14

Contested Terrain

1. to standardize, simplify, and reduce the costs of organizing the
Vereinigte Stahlwerke . . .
2. to avoid repeating mistakes by communicating the events along
with recommendations for improvements to all relevant positions.

VSt organizational goals, from "Guidelines for the Auditing Department,
March 13, 1926, composed by Carl Rabes and Heinrich Dinkelbach

The VSt could best lay claim as a "rationalization company" in the
realm of accounting, information, and control—that is, corporate
management rather than factory management. This was done in a
suite of offices (auditing, bookkeeping, Hollerith information, and organization) that collectively came to be known as *Büro Dinkelbach*.[1]
Heinrich Dinkelbach, Peter van Aubel, and Leo Kluitmann, the cream
of the German accounting profession, designed VSt's information and
control systems. These executives made organization itself a subject of
self-reflection and a source of corporate improvement alongside production, finance, personnel, and marketing functions.

The VSt called these new control routines "American." VSt finance
and auditing executives (Carl Rabes, Erich Deleurant, and Heinrich
Dinkelbach) emphasized the need to unite auditing, bookkeeping, inventory, and cost accounting "according to the American model."[2]
The VSt fused operational bookkeeping and cost accounting functions, placing both functions under the purview of one person, "according to American practice."[3] The new VSt provided an opportunity to reinvent accounting and managerial practices from scratch,
creating best-practice guidelines that then contributed to industry-
wide standards. The VSt represents a case of Americanization that
came before the Americanization beginning in 1945.

American ideas contributed to the VSt guidelines, but the innovations were also based on the people, journals, and ideas surrounding
the leading light of the German accounting and a business economics

profession, Eugen Schmalenbach, at the University of Cologne.[4] Germans had a distinct, autonomous accounting and management tradition, and the Schmalenbach Society remains one of the most important forums for German management theory and practice. Thus, a feedback loop between the German accounting profession and VSt organizational practice recast any American-influenced practices.

The first three sections of this chapter describe VSt's manner of organizing control, while the last section focuses on the adoption of the Fretz-Moon process, a technical innovation for welding "made in America." The Fretz-Moon process acts as a trenchant metaphor for the transmutation of American ideas and shows how deep merger rivalries permeated VSt decision-making. Rather than acting as a rational or taken-for-granted guide for decision-making, the innovative VSt cost-accounting measures provided an informational foundation for highly politicized debates. These standardized—"Americanized"—organizational practices paradoxically exacerbated VSt's reputation for clay-footedness. Just as rationalization measures in manufacturing intensified merger rivalries and community relations, these state-of-the-art organizational and technical innovations did the same.

Creating a Managerial Organization

Wilfried Feldenkirchen identified two phases in the history of the VSt.[5] Between 1926 and 1931, the VSt concentrated on productive rationalization, but after 1931 on "administrative decentralization." Reckendrees has called for more nuance in this portrayal. He stresses the continuing administrative autonomy of local plant executives and that the VSt retained a good deal of administrative decentralization. He views the 1933 reorganization as further consolidating the number of manufacturing plants into fewer profit centers. While Feldenkirchen focuses on the shift from a single unified corporation to a multisubsidiary form, Reckendrees stresses the continuing degree of decentralization within this unified structure. Rather than viewing the two periods as centralized decentralization and then "decentral centralization" (Reckendrees) or productive rationalization then "administrative decentralization" (Feldenkirchen), it can be helpful to view the first five years as setting standardized ground rules or routines—controls—on which the later reorganization, however conceived, rested. The VSt had to construct a new head office, which centralized and homogenized routines along common standards to create a new system of organizing control.[6] A considerable amount of administrative centralization occurred before 1933. Such centralization supervised and partially checked the autonomy of formerly independent plant directors. The reader should recognize numerous parallels with Thyssen & Co.'s early reforms of the 1880s. These "guidelines" helped make the VSt, still a half-merged messy amalgamation of founding combines and plants, a semi-coherent corporation.

On the surface, the VSt introduced an impressively streamlined, unitary, functionally organized administration—matching closely Chandler's multiunit ideal-type, cut from the cloth of the American business experience (Figure 14.1). This chart acts as an important self-representation of the firm and its organizational goals, yet this formal outline did not reveal the immense difficulties of forging a single corporation from four former rivals.

The problems of the VSt began at the top. Fritz Thyssen chaired the supervisory board. (The reader might remember my discussion of Fritz Thyssen.) The general director of Phoenix, Walther Fahrenhorst, became vice-chair. In 1926, the supervisory board had 23 board members and by 1931, 31 board members, representing many major figures in German industry and banking. Two members of the factory council also had seats but exercised little to no influence.

The VSt acted as a "conglomerate" of former rivals, more along the line of an IG in joint-stock company clothing. The VSt's nickname, *der Stahlverein,* "steel association," was more appropriate than contemporaries realized. Behind the supervisory board floated the original founding combines as ghost holding companies, which constantly haunted the results of any VSt decision for its impact on shareholders. Until the 1933 reorganization—and a major reason for it—VSt strategic decision-making had to take into consideration the interests of these ghost combines, particularly those of Friedrich Flick. These ghost companies controlled roughly 90% of VSt shares; various banks held the rest. Few VSt shares traded publicly and the VSt shareholders agreed through a pooling arrangement not to sell them on the open market.

To make matters more complicated, each of the founding combines held stock in the others (excepting Thyssen). A network of back-

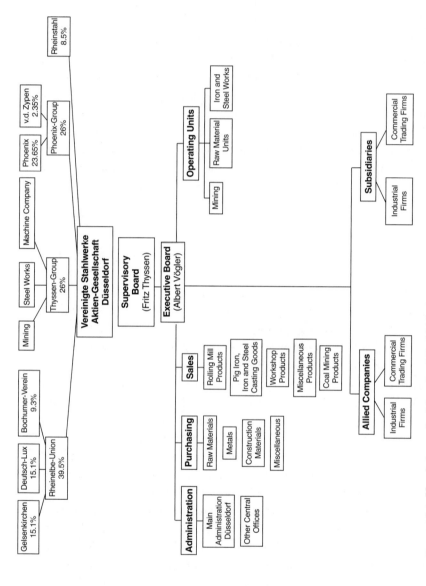

Figure 14.1 Vereinigten Stahlwerke AG, 1930. *Source: Zeitschrift für Organisation* Jg. 4, Heft 4, 24.2.1930, S.91–92.

room negotiations existed behind the VSt. For instance, Thyssen's direct VSt shareholding actually declined, but he asserted himself indirectly on the VSt by purchasing Phoenix shares. In 1926, the notorious Friedrich Flick suddenly appeared on VSt's supervisory board. And then, by purchasing cross-shareholdings from his AG Charlottenhütte through Gelsenkirchen (GBAG) and later Phoenix, Flick became the VSt's largest controlling shareholder, although he held few VSt shares directly. Flick controlled 42% of VSt shares in 1930 through the GBAG alone, and attained the crucial privilege of receiving dividends tax free with shareholding above 25%. It was one measure of the tension between the goals of shareholders and the VSt that one Phoenix shareholder threatened to build a rival pipe plant and break the pooling arrangement, a demand designed to "blackmail" the VSt. Flick and Thyssen purchased Phoenix shares to block this blackmail attempt and thus increased their control over the VSt. Until 1932, Fritz Thyssen, Flick, and Vögler, the "triumvirate" (Reckendrees), had strategic control over the VSt. Many important decisions were a result of informal, personal, mysterious arrangements among them.[7] But these back-room, cross-shareholding pyramidal relations became a public relations disaster. One of the few things that the Communists, Socialists, and the Nazis could agree upon was that such dark, labyrinthian, interlocking financial directorates *(Verschachtelung)* were a nefarious influence on the Germany economy.

Reflecting the continuing power of the ghost combines, the supervisory board retained a great deal of formal power over the executive board. According to Späing, the company statutes were "gratifyingly short and limited to the most necessary conditions" and supposedly strictly delineated the relationship between the supervisory board and executive board. But they did not. The supervisory board reserved the right to intervene in any matter of "fundamental significance."[8] The last clause gave a good deal of leeway for myriad micro-interventions. In a move all too typical for the VSt, shareholders formed a subcommittee of supervisory board members, known as the "industrial commission," which hammered out proposals for the rest of the board to approve. With people like Flick and Fritz Thyssen on it, it proved a powerful forum. It met monthly to discuss major strategic issues with Vögler [or primary representatives like Ernst Poensgen (Phoenix), Rabes (Thyssen), or Gustav Knepper (Deutsch-Lux)]. This board determined how the VSt behaved strategically as a unitary actor on the market and in the industry.[9]

The size of the VSt executive board best expressed the slapped-to-gether nature of the VSt and its simmering internal conflicts. In 1926, the managing board consisted of 40 regular board members and an additional 12 vice-board members. Carl Rabes' son remembered that someone told his father that the VSt was richly endowed with directors, whereupon his father replied: "Rest easy, they will all die out."[10] By the end of 1931, the VSt did reduce the executive board to 34 directors and 6 vice-directors. Although in principle the VSt distinguished central strategy and administration from day-to-day operations, each plant director sat on the central managing board, effectively eliminating this distinction in organizational terms.

Because of his notable powers of persuasion and personality, Vögler acted as the decision-making hub of the VSt, not as an anchor, as had August Thyssen. He especially had to take into consideration the myriad demands of Flick and Fritz Thyssen as well as willful directors below him. Vögler chaired the managing board, along with representatives Poensgen, Rabes, and Knepper. These four executives worked collegially with a loose but overlapping division of labor. Vögler became responsible for the overall strategy of the VSt, Poensgen for VSt's external relations with cartels and sociopolitical associations, Rabes for internal financial, accounting, and organizational questions, and Knepper for VSt mining operations.[11]

Realizing the unwieldy nature of the managing board, Vögler set up smaller technical committees as decision-making boards to streamline the negotiation process. The VSt initially intended to establish five committees: mining, steel works, administration, blast furnace/foundry, and sales committees. The VSt reduced these to three: mining, iron and steel works, and administration committees.[12] These committees conformed to VSt's three main centers (Exhibit 14.1). Headquarters sat in Düsseldorf, Vögler's office in Dortmund, and the mining administration in Essen. Also making decisions for the raw material units, the steel works committee became the most important decision-making body inside the VSt. The administration committee quickly faded away. The mining committee (*Bergausschuss*) maintained its independence as much as possible.

Such organizational devolution did little to alleviate the existing problems. Chaired by Vögler, the steel works committee regularly had 26 works directors present at meetings, a reduction of about half. In general, the steel works committee discussed market and production trends, dealt with subsidiaries, compared statistical information, set investment budgets, and set internal transfer prices—the latter always a difficult issue. The committee provided Vögler with forum for disseminating decisions, keeping plant directors informed (a fundamental VSt corporate principle), and discussing important issues.

A perusal of the committee's protocols over time shows a motley agenda, indicating that the VSt did not have a well-defined structure of decision-making or a clear sense of priorities or clean lines of responsibility.[13] This added to the information overload in central forums. In one meeting, the steel works committee might debate major investment decisions, plant closings, and rationalization measures alongside minor business: for instance, whether or not Mülheim could receive RM 2,000 of VSt donations, or discuss whether the VSt should support the incorporation of new towns into the district of Düsseldorf. Works directors often had to wait until the central committees decided minor matters such as community donations or major matters such as new investment decisions or transfer pricing. The lack of priorities in the central committees antagonized VSt's relationship with Ruhr municipalities—strained by the impact of plant closings and when the Depression struck. Decision-making inside the VSt organization was ponderous and increasingly distant.[14] The meeting protocols also indicate a constant jockeying among factory directors for position, new investment, and operating funds. Because of the nature of decision-making within the central committees, favoring one community or works director automatically appeared to disadvantage another, who desired equitable treatment. Such forums managed to politicize the decision-making process inside the VSt (shareholder decision-making had different dynamics). The VSt in effect created an internal culture of begging, endless negotiation, and *quid pro quos* that had more to do with organizational politics than performance. It provided a voice to powerful plant directors, but such committees also opened a space for dissent.

In order to construct the new corporation, the VSt had to design procedures for channeling information, clarifying lines of authority, creating and refining standard operating procedures, and establishing clear standards of evaluation and performance. In principle, these paralleled the problems Thyssen faced in constructing his own nascent industrial bureaucracy in the early 1880s. But its sheer scale, its merger rivalries, its importance in the general economy, the number of administrative layers between ownership, management, and workers, its geographical dispersion of manufacturing sites, administration, and sales, the complexity of information technologies, and the growing distance between company and community made the VSt a qualitatively different type of corporate organization from that of Thyssen & Co. or even from that of the founding combines, which had grown organically and historically. In fact, the attention the VSt brought to administration, information, accounting and control matters indicated the difficulties of coordination in such a large corporation. In direct proportion to the level of organizational complexity, the degree of central codification and standardization—of system—also grew.

In its formal structure, the VSt operated by a staff-line organization and created an American-style general staff in Düsseldorf. The central office had formal control over most financial, cost-accounting, general informational/statistical, sales, legal, tax, land sales, patents, and purchasing questions. The VSt worked with four functional operating groups: mining, raw materials, steel manufacturing, and sales (Figure 14.1).

The staff-line organization gained a *geographic* dimension as key management functions resided in Düsseldorf or Dortmund, and day-to-day plant management were located in cities across the Ruhr, creating a physical distance—and a tension—between central control at headquarters and on-site responsibilities in the factories. Except for critical control functions (finance, auditing, and cost accounting), the exact degree of task responsibilities and competencies between central office and plant management remained contested.[15]

The VSt headquarters had three main areas: purchasing, sales, and general administration (Figure 14.2). The VSt organized both purchasing and sales according to product line. Most of the sales offices, especially for steel products, were relocated to Düsseldorf because most of the major iron and steel cartels had their headquarters there. But the mining group in Essen handled its coal and coke sales autonomously, or rather through the syndicate, also located in Essen. Still, the VSt spread responsibility for specialized and non-cartelized prod-

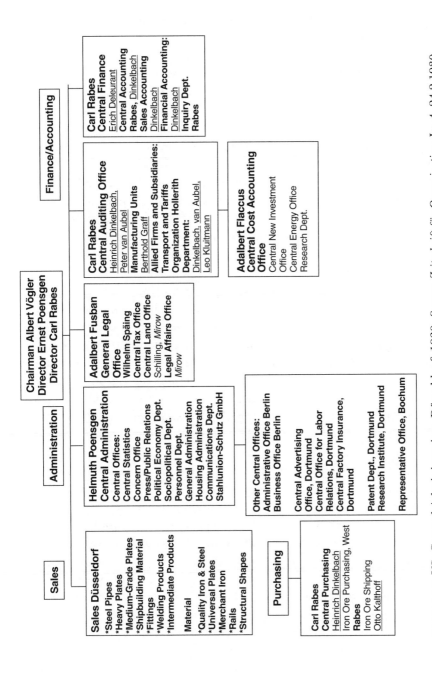

Figure 14.2 VSt Central Administration, Düsseldorf, 1930. *Source: Zeitschrift für Organisation,* Jg. 4, 24.2.1930, 91–81; MA: R 2 50 02 VSt.

ucts throughout the Ruhr (such as tempered foundry goods of the Bochumer Verein), which helped limit the degree of centralization and kept sales directly in the hands of experienced line-managers. Under Carl Rabes, the central purchasing department concentrated on special purchases of key goods or bulk goods, the most important being the purchase of iron ore and scrap. The iron ore purchasing offices, moreover, were subdivided into two centers in Dortmund and Düsseldorf which corresponded to the two main areas of steel production in Hamborn and Dortmund.[16] Moreover, Rabes officially headed finance and auditing offices. Under Rabes, Erich Deleurant was the most important person in finance, while Heinrich Dinkelbach, Peter van Aubel from Phoenix, and Leo Kluitmann designed the VSt's financial accounting, information, and reporting systems. Adalbert Flaccus directed the critical cost-accounting office with its important control function over new investment.

The central VSt legal offices were jointly led by Adalbert Fusban, who handled general legal questions, and Wilhelm Späing, who dealt with problems of taxes, land, corporate, and international law. The legal department had eight local legal offices tied to works groups. Helmuth Poensgen (Phoenix), brother of Ernst Poensgen, headed the general administrative offices *(Generalsekretariat):* statistical, Konzern relations, public relations, political economy, sociopolitical, general administration, personnel, housing, and communications offices. This main administrative center acted as a central assembly point for general information.

The offices themselves need little explanation, but a few represent some of the more innovative aspects of the VSt. The statistical office, in conjunction with cost-accounting and auditing departments, prepared daily, monthly, and yearly statistical reports on just about every aspect of the VSt. Alongside normal monthly balances and cost accounting statistics, each of the individual manufacturing units, for instance, submitted descriptive year-end reports on the course of the business year to this office. The statistical office created encyclopedia-scale confidential production statistics on the monthly production of each department in each individual manufacturing unit. These alone showed the amount of information processed inside the VSt.[17] The statistical office also increased the mechanization of administration with adding machines, letter opening and stamping machines, copying machines, booking machines, and coding devices for confidential materials. Moreover, the increasing use of punchcards, filing cards, and machines depended entirely on newly standardized classification codes for everything ranging from a code for the individual factory to office supplies.

Such mechanization produced another one of VSt's dubious achievements—its immense capacity to generate paper. This grew out of the combination of internal managerial rivalries and its innovative yet bureaucratic methods. VSt central administration produced forms, questionnaires, circulars, and statistics as never before, just in order to keep everyone informed. *Nineteen* copies of all circulars, "except to the interested parties [*sic*]" had to be sent to each of the administrative centers of the VSt: eight to the central office in Düsseldorf, four to the Berlin office, five to the mining offices in Essen and its subgroups, and two to Vögler in Dortmund. Additionally, each of these main offices created its own numerically ordered circulars. (Indeed, Vögler simply gave up reading them all after a year and a half.)[18] One of the implicit organizing principles of VSt corporate culture was that everyone should be kept as informed as possible so as not to slight someone. Explicitly stated by the VSt social policy office, the idea was to "unify and centralize."

The public relations, political economy, and social policy offices together provided an internalized news and information service for the VSt. These illustrate an increased awareness, if not always sensitivity, of executives to the VSt's important place in the rest of the economy. The public relations office also scoured the newspapers and journals for press coverage. This office then clipped, pasted, numbered, dated, and sent to the individual factory directors its findings, so that all VSt executives would be aware of the impression their actions made on the local, regional, and national press. One example of such circulated information described a poor worker who fell into the blast furnace of the Friedrich-Wilhelm-Hütte and was instantly incinerated. They tapped the converter and cast a small iron block with the name of the worker and the day of his death. The block was buried in his place, as usual. The public relations department also published a company magazine called *Das Werk*, which ran a full complement of articles ranging from the economic state of the VSt to cultural affairs.[19]

The political economy *(Volkswirtschaftliche Abteilung)* and social policy offices were closely related, but had slightly different points of emphasis. Initially, the VSt united both offices, but quickly decided that the intricacies of social policy questions needed a separate office. While the political economy office dealt with business cycles, transportation, tariffs, taxes, or changes in corporate law, the social policy office provided a central clearing house for information to "unify and centralize" the VSt's corporate responses to industrial relations. (It laid out its objectives explicitly when it had to justify its existence during the Depression.) It kept executives updated on legal and working relations, participated in regional meetings, ascertained the effect of social policies on the VSt, negotiated with government authorities, and created circulars and reports for the rest of the VSt. In 1929, it even produced a relatively insightful special report on the rise of the Nazi party.[20] These reports and offices were designed not only to inform, centralize, and unify, but also helped to mold opinion within the VSt.

The VSt also had a political office in Berlin (as did IG Farben), as a type of economic embassy, headed by Oskar Sempell. Any large German enterprise had to cultivate personal contacts in parliament, ministries, the bureaucracy, the Imperial Railways, and with various industrial peak associations. This office, too, received at least four copies of every circular and had a telegraph address named "Ruhrunion"—another apt description of the VSt.[21]

The VSt also maintained a good number of important offices outside Düsseldorf. Vögler kept the VSt advertising office, a center for labor relations, the factory insurance policy office (which largely advised the plant directors who remained in charge), the patent office, and an innovative central research institute close to him in Dortmund. Vögler's commitment to open, basic research remained a constant throughout his life. He generously supported the Kaiser-Wilhelm-Gesellschaft. (The secretive August Thyssen thought Vögler would ruin the iron and steel industry with his commitment to technical information exchange.)[22] The research department encouraged the important "plant technical committees" among the individual works managers and engineers, which created a cross-lateral informative, educational, and decision-making forum. These proved immensely popular, but "cost-intensive."[23]

Vögler also vigorously promoted close contact with Karl Arnhold, the infamous director of the "German Institute for Technical Industrial Training" (DINTA) and later one of the leading figures in the Nazi-run German Workers' Front (DAF). Research and DINTA worker-training centers were Vögler's pet projects. DINTA professed a strongly Taylorist, but skill-oriented training program with a focus on "human economies," "factory communities," and the "industrial leadership of men" *(industrielle Menschenführung)*. Characteristically, Vögler thought that literature on efficiency and economy neglected the psychological, human factor of work. Unlike Taylor, Arnhold built in a psychological, social, and human relations aspect that stressed the harmony of workers and management, but with extremely nationalist overtones. Although not necessarily Nazi, it was a short step from a "bonding to a firm" *(Werksverbundenheit)* under a military, male model of camaraderie, to a Nazi "people's community" *(Volksgemeinschaft)*.[24]

In spite of the centralization of key administrative functions, powerful plant directors *(Werksleiter)* in so-called "work groups" provided the basis for internal decision-making. Many of them retained a high degree of autonomy within the VSt's organization as the "central administration's possibility of influence often ended at the plant gates" (Reckendrees).[25] In Essen, the mining group remained relatively autonomous and was run almost as an independent division, but it did not control investment and financial accounting questions; sales went through the syndicate. It too made a typically German distinction between commercial and technical directors (along such lines as Thyssen & Co. or Phoenix departments). It was further subdivided into four operating subgroups: Dortmund, Bochum, Gelsenkirchen, and Hamborn. In Dortmund, the raw materials group also had its own centralized administration and sales functions. The factory directors retained autonomy over local management, sales of non-cartelized goods, some legal offices, and personnel decisions.

These plant directors greatly resisted Düsseldorf's encroachment, especially the mining division under Gustav Knepper, the Bochum plant under Walter Borbet, and Thyssen-Bruckhausen under Franz Bartscherer. Central staff functions had little authority over powerful plant directors, who often saw themselves as advocates of their plants first, rather than members of the VSt. The Düsseldorf public relations office once tried to take over the mining group's public relations affairs, but to no avail. Indicatively, the plant directors retained their old affiliation with the founding combines and city, such as Phoenix-Lierenfeld or Thyssen-Mülheim. Factory executives sometimes ignored directives from the steel works committee. One of the most assertive was Bartscherer of the former ATH. Bartscherer once admitted to Vögler that he had carried out new construction above and beyond the approved investment credits, but he was not the only one who carried out "black" construction projects. Many of the plant directors attempted to circumvent VSt's strict financial policy of covering all new investment with depreciation, or to book new investment as operating expenses. (The same problem that Thyssen & Co. faced in the 1880s.) Vögler's exhortations proved to be limited. Echoing Thyssen's complaints of an earlier era, Price Waterhouse and the VSt central finance offices were upset at the distortions and obfuscations in the accounts. On a secondary matter, Bartscherer objected to the centralization of VSt phone service, but gave his complaint to Späing, instead of going through official, formal channels. This example shows that the VSt remained laced with personal networks from the merged firms (see the Fretz-Moon process example below).[26]

Why did VSt management choose this type of organization, especially as Vögler had recommended an alternative? VSt executives chose it by default. The VSt's first business report openly stated that they sought to minimize administrative centralization:

> The organization or our company has been carried out by avoiding any centralization not entirely necessary. The manufacturing sites have been consolidated according to geographical and technical viewpoints and stand under the responsible direction of individual managing board members. In a similar manner, sales, purchasing, and administration have been organized. We believe by means of this division of labor to have given the leading persons more possibilities of acting independently *(selbständig)* and responsibly than had been the case in the individual concerns.[27]

Reckendrees nicely summarized the idea that the more decisive the senior corporate function, the more central it became, yet the VSt retained a good deal of decentral decision-making in less important functions. Above all, financial and accounting controls were centralized, especially as the diversity of administrative and accounting methods of the former combines needed harmonizing. According to

Helmut Poensgen, they had little choice, given the confusing variety of corporate procedures, standards, people, and cultures of the founding combines: "We did not have the opportunity to have the best and the finest [organizational form]. Fifty-seven executive board members was an impossibility. The unified state was necessary. We did not know the people yet, did not know who would rise to the top, or if this or that factory would be closed. Also the cost comparisons were all still very rough."[28] Indeed, the merger put a premium on central and standard organizational controls to set new organizational ground rules for co-operation—or contestation—within the VSt.

Inside the VSt, ongoing organizational tension resulted from rivalries among shareholders in the ghost companies, from a tension between shareholder and management interests, from an unwieldy superstructure that special committees bypassed (in both the supervisory and executive boards), from a tension between the Düsseldorf and Dortmund central offices and on-site local management, and from an extensive management by committee. The new organization failed to eliminate the clash of corporate cultures inherent in fusing four major Konzerne, each steeped in its own corporate culture. As Dinkelbach cryptically noted: "The head of the VSt [was] too large. No real responsibilities. Always had to ask a lot of questions. Divided minds."[29] While the Thyssen-Konzern's decision-making process was characterized as well by competitive negotiation among strong personalities, those "lords" ruled over clearly defined areas of responsibility and autonomy. The VSt had a contentious management by committee. Unlike at Thyssen, where the buck stopped at the strategic level, Vögler had to take into account the machinations of various shareholders, especially the erratic Fritz Thyssen and the ever mobile and opportunistic Friedrich Flick. Below him, plant executives resisted encroachments on their autonomy. Diverging interests and the lack of trust within the VSt found expression in the immense amount of talk, paperwork, questioning, haggling, and bargaining needed to move the VSt forward. Everybody felt they needed to be in the loop so as not to be disadvantaged. Ironically, instead of an efficient, swift American-style steel trust, the new VSt quickly gained a reputation as a top-heavy, lumbering dinosaur in just a few years. This had little to do with problems of labor and state intervention, as VSt (and German steel) industrialists commonly argued, but with internal problems of shareholding and management as well as universal dilemmas associated with any merger of major rivals.

On paper, VSt management created a unitary, functional administration complete with an American-style general management. Befitting the attention drawn to advances in managerial technique during the rationalization craze of the 1920s, VSt managers eagerly propagated their accomplishment in the *Zeitschrift für Organisation,* a new journal oriented to organizational issues. Anonymous VSt managers sent in the 1930 organizational chart (Figure 14.1), outlining the lines of authority and structure of competencies within the VSt. It was the first organizational map to appear in the journal's survey. The VSt charts are the first ones available drawn up by the firm itself, so it acts as a form of self-representation; the Thyssen-Konzern never used such organizational charts. The VSt introduced such charts in the interest of transparency, clarifying areas of responsibility and accountability—"unify and centralize," but also in the broader interest of rationalization, that is, as a way to advance the science of management as practiced in Germany. Such rationalization did mean greater bureaucracy, but this bureaucracy grew not out of an underlying preindustrial German tradition or a vague psychological tendency for order, but out of short-term organizational necessity, new means of information technology and organization often borrowed from America, and the need to bind former rivals together.

Accounting for Control: Büro Dinkelbach

The cutting edge information, accounting, and reporting system of the VSt was at the center of its organizational efforts to "unify and centralize." In principle, VSt management faced similar issues of accounting for control as did Thyssen, Killing, and Nölle in their 1882–1884 reforms. The VSt had to collect basic information about expenses and production across the firm and its many plants and offices, and then deliver it to the appropriate people in a timely fashion. It had to set appropriate standards and measures for assessing profitability, efficiency, and performance. Then, it had to place the relevant pieces of data in relation to one another and interpret the information in order to make decisions. As described earlier, a conception of control was a loosely coupled relationship linking the overall strategic objectives of the firm, its organizational structure, and accounting and information principles that provided key signals to chief executives about its performance. The sheer size of the VSt and the volume of information processed generated a qualitative change of the first order. These problems pushed a new breed of systems managers to the forefront. These same managers conceived of the firm less as a set of productive/engineering relations than as an abstract financial and organizational entity, expressed by the charts and data they created. They then propagated those innovative procedures through business associations and academic contacts to the rest of the industry.

The accounting and control measures they developed provided an informational service and an implicit conceptual pattern for the VSt—the corporation as construction. If VSt factories and machines represent the girders and beams of a building, accounting and information provided its plumbing and electrical wires. Managers made important decisions (like plant closings) based on cost accounting and profitability estimates. Accounting measures arbitrated intrafirm disputes (such as the debate over the Fretz-Moon process below) without overdetermining the outcome. A discussion of VSt accounting and control thus provides an insightful glimpse into the best practice construction of a firm in the 1920s.

The VSt assembled a first-class collection of talent inside its auditing and organization offices. The five people most responsible for designing the organizational, financial, and accounting procedures were Carl Rabes, Heinrich Dinkelbach, Peter van Aubel, Erich Deleurant, and Leo Kluitmann. As the third highest ranking executive board member behind Vögler and Poensgen, Rabes provided the organizational clout to implement these managerial innovations. Rabes tended to concentrate on external financial affairs, while Dinkelbach and van Aubel concentrated on internal matters. Rabes officially headed both the VSt auditing and finance offices. In practice, Dinkelbach and van Aubel headed the auditing department, while Deleurant directed the finance department. All of them worked closely with Dillon Read and Price Waterhouse, sending regular reports on the performance of individual works to them.[30] After leaving the VSt in 1931, van Aubel founded his own management consultancy that specialized in auditing public administration. On Dinkelbach's suggestion, van Aubel and Herbert Rätsch founded a new auditing firm, the Kontinentale Treuhandgesellschaft, which replaced Price Waterhouse as the chartered accountant for the VSt and hired many former Price Waterhouse employees.[31]

Although the Americans influenced VSt's accounting methods, auditing and financial departments also stood in direct administrative and personnel continuity with Thyssen's CAO, and had close ties to Eugen Schmalenbach. Almost the entire central, sales, and bookkeeping, purchasing, finance, auditing, and organization departments were in the hands of Rabes and Dinkelbach, and they spread their influence throughout the VSt main administration just as they did at Thyssen. Rabes' renowned ability to occupy key organizational places inside the Thyssen-Konzern extended to the VSt. Dinkelbach's ambition allied him to Rabes. But unlike the Thyssen-Konzern, where strong individuals guided the firm, the VSt was more of a collective or team effort. Other key figures inside the VSt organization and accounting offices included Leo Kluitmann, Berthold Graff, and Heinrich Kindt. Graff and Kindt had worked side-by-side with Rabes and Dinkelbach in Thyssen's CAO. Graff, the main auditor for the manufacturing works, became head of the VSt auditing department after 1933. Like van Aubel, Graff had taken his doctorate under Schmalenbach. Kindt had long worked with Rabes in the CAO when it moved to Bruckhausen in 1906; he remained chief of the ATH accounting departments well into the 1930s. Kluitmann transferred from the banking house Simon Hirschland and had also studied with Schmalenbach. This talent, for which these names stand only as a few signposts, worked together as teams to organize (and then reorganize) the VSt. My focus here on Büro Dinkelbach should be thought of as a shorthand for the collective work of this team.

When the VSt was founded, none of the major steel companies operated with the same financial standards. To overcome this mess, VSt "guidelines" gave priority to the assembly of "experiences" with the "final objective:"

1. to standardize, simplify, and reduce the costs of organizing the Vereinigte Stahlwerke as well as in its subsidiaries and affiliated firms.

2. to avoid repeating mistakes by communicating the events along
   with recommendations for improvements to all relevant positions.[32]

Rabes and Dinkelbach composed these VSt guidelines while still
at Thyssen's CAO in Hamborn. Preparing the groundwork for the
VSt, the study commission (Rabes, van Aubel, Dinkelbach) established
most of the basic cost guidelines and definitions for the accounting system with the goals, neatly summarized by Kluitmann in a 1928
report:

> to create a standardized and homogenous form, whereby we strived to
> minimize the increased costs, which a large-scale internal accounting
> apparatus necessarily generated up to now for smaller economic enti-
> ties, but could be reduced on the other hand through appropriate
> technical aids and procedures available to a large enterprise.[33]

The administrative objectives of the VSt mirrored those in manufacturing, which sought to minimize production costs through greater
economies of scale. The new scale of the VSt, its new organizational
procedures, and its introduction of office machinery would create new
breakthroughs in the quantity and quality of information available to
VSt executives. The statement also nicely highlights the tradeoff between the costs of collecting information and the advantages of having
that information. Information costs money.

The most innovative aspect of the VSt auditing department was its
establishment of a distinct office for *Organisation* and its associated
Hollerith (IBM) office designed to mechanize the paperwork of the
VSt down to the workshop level. Establishing a distinct office for such
matters testifies to a self-reflective consciousness about the significance
of organizational design itself. As a specialist in office machines, Leo
Kluitmann developed standardized reports which mechanized the
collection of information across the entire firm using the Hollerith system. He created the key assessment device, voluminous, but standardized monthly balance reports *(Bilanzmappe)* for each of the manufacturing units and sales offices. Kluitmann related how Dinkelbach
called Kluitmann and van Aubel in the day before a holiday in 1926
to complain about the inadequacy of VSt's financial reporting.
Dinkelbach wanted suggestions for a new accounting system by the

next day. Van Aubel brought in a version of the standard handwritten account journal broken down by factory and cost categories. Kluitmann brought in a pre-formatted balance form in DIN A4 size (the new paper size recently set by the German Association for Norms), whose postings could be typed in and whose columns could be torn out along perforated lines, then glued into a central account journal for each manufacturing works, and sales and administration offices. While "pleasantly smiling to van Aubel," Dinkelbach accepted Kluitmann's version.

In principle, these reports were equivalent to the monthly balance reports introduced by Nölle in the 1880s, but they bore little relationship in their organization, detail, mechanization, or sophistication. The Hollerith computing machinery could calculate the monthly and cumulative postings of almost every revenue or expense of the VSt with unprecedented levels of precision and reproduce these figures almost at will. For the manufacturing units, the monthly balances accounted for its operating assets, liabilities, and a profit-loss statement for each month. These monthly reports also included, on separate worksheets, income from the factories' housing, changes in inventories, an overview of sales costs, and an overview of general expenses. These account formats with their expense classifications provided a model for numerous German firms even fifty years later; the printer of these forms still did a brisk business with them in 1967.[34]

The Hollerith accounting system produced balance sheets that represented a surveillance or control system *par excellence.* Top executives could easily compare expenses according to area and type across the entire VSt. For example, in November 1929 administration costs for the VSt's Thyssen-Mülheim rolling mills came to exactly RM 33,920.71 and they spent RM 2,052.12 in telephone fees. In February 1930, the Mülheim sales office spent RM 537.58 for "representation" purposes, up over RM 200 RM from the previous month. In May 1930, it used RM 92.65 for advertising. By 1930, these expense categories had expanded to over 24 pages of expense category areas, and were subdivided into as many as fifty expense types on each page—one for each of the manufacturing and sales sites—each month. The mechanized balance sheet reports might be said to express a collision of obsessive American cost controls and German thoroughness.

Although Kluitmann designed the basic format, the VSt's account structure was actually a collective effort extended and refined over many years. In order for the Hollerith process to work, the Hollerith office had to encode the whole organization of the VSt into standard categories. The VSt organization and auditing office stressed that all initial entries should be posted on loose-leaf, standardized forms, or punch cards. It took many years to design all the appropriate forms. For instance, in 1930 the format for administration costs was revised because it mixed together expense areas and expense types too indiscriminately, making comparison difficult. Instead of one worksheet, three worksheets separated expense areas and expense types, then later recombined them.[35] The task of codifying all expenses in a homogenous way was so great that the VSt initially had to compromise. At first, the VSt allowed manufacturing units to work as usual without harming the "transparency of the production costs," but wanted to unify standards as quickly as possible. In the first two years, VSt concentrated on subsuming the older combines' accounting techniques into the new ones, but the next three years the VSt auditing department concentrated on improving its own system, largely by mechanizing, norming, and encoding its account statements. At Thyssen-Mülheim, for instance, the transition from the old Thyssen system to the new VSt system occurred between 1926 and 1928; the former Thyssen system remained in use until September 1927. Other areas of the VSt were even slower to make this shift, but they made steady progress. After 1928–1929, Büro Dinkelbach introduced separate, six-page account books for sales offices.[36] VSt mining executives, for instance, did not want to introduce the process until the steel works proved its effectiveness. As late as July 1932, Price Waterhouse could still complain that not all plants had unified financial accounts, and the ATH only moved to the VSt cost-accounting scheme with the 1933 reorganization.[37]

The VSt managed to mechanize the creation of monthly balance statements from the beginning, although the initial reports sent from the manufacturing units were handwritten, then typed to punch cards in the central administration (by young female secretaries). By 1930, the VSt headquarters in Düsseldorf included 850 male managers and 170 female support staff. About one half worked in export and sales offices, and about one-quarter in financial, statistical, and purchasing functions (Figure 14.3).[38]

Figure 14.3 The "Modern Office:" VSt's Hollerith department, 1933. Note the increasing utilization of women inside company offices. (Reproduced with the permission of the Mannesmann-Archiv, Mülheim/Ruhr)

VSt managers realized that the punchcard process became economical only for sectors where a great deal of statistics arose from the volume of activity. With the VSt experience behind him, van Aubel became one of the leading figures in industry-wide discussions about the mechanization and standardization *(Normung)* of accounts, which included such luminaries as Walter Gropius, the famous Bauhaus architect, who also weighed in on the advantages of standardization.[39]

While the mechanization and standardization of statistics might have had American or Fordist inspirations, the categorization of the account scheme ultimately rested on a combination of van Aubel's classification scheme inspired by Schmalenbach. The VSt released its classification of expenses *(Kontenrahmen)* in 1927, the same year that Schmalenbach published his first draft of an accounting scheme. Reproducing an industry-wide debate, VSt executives also discussed how best to classify expenses. After years of discussion, both practical and academic discussions influenced one another until the first industry-wide accounting and expense classification scheme for the iron and steel branch appeared in 1940. Working closely with Schmalenbach, Kluitmann was a central figure in this endeavor.[40]

With these advances, VSt could now minutely track expenses, revenues, and production. The volume of information grew so great that senior management could no longer grasp it all. The auditing, finance, bookkeeping, organization, information, and Hollerith threads came together in a set of offices that collectively became known as *Büro Dinkelbach*. Büro Dinkelbach became the key link in this information processing circuit. He acted as the crucial organizational and interpretive filter that sifted out the most relevant information for senior executives, management committees, and shareholders. The 1926 guidelines also explicitly made the auditing office the central information and mediating service between the VSt executives and shareholders. Büro Dinkelbach became the center of control, the surveillance eye of the VSt.

As such it acted as an office of knowledge creation for Vögler and Poensgen, who knew about the operations of the VSt through its information service. The auditing office called attention to problem areas by sending monthly reports to Vögler. It also sent innumerable copies (naturally according to VSt corporate culture) to plant directors. Price Waterhouse received similar reports, emphasizing the burden on individual product costs from the interest on the American loan. Rabes, van Aubel, Knies, and Dinkelbach signed these reports in some combination, but Dinkelbach's signature always appeared. The reports to Vögler presented overall performance figures on the gross and net profits of each individual manufacturing plant, along with sales figures, stoppage costs, and other such information. Because of the volume of information, the auditing department sampled product lines by summarizing data regarding production, revenues, production costs, sales (domestic and foreign), and profit margins by comparing them to the previous month. If product lines showed little or no fluctuation compared to the previous month, then they were not included. Büro Dinkelbach highlighted potential problem areas, calling them to the attention of senior executives, and implicitly introduced the principle of management by exception. Additionally, the auditing department designed graphics for all facets of an individual plant or its product lines over time.[41] Without overdetermining the outcome, the organization of information inside the VSt shaped decision-making at the top.

Büro Dinkelbach essentially became a source of knowledge creation inside the VSt. The auditing office conceptually reattached the functional pieces (manufacturing, sales, financial, personnel expenses) together into a coherent evaluation of company, managerial, and product-line performance and profitability. Büro Dinkelbach played a critical role in arbitrating disputes. Dinkelbach's swift rise within the VSt attests to this link between information, knowledge, and power.

Büro Dinkelbach not only acted as an internal knowledge circuit, but also as a conduit for the latest organizational, management, and economic theories being disseminated in a growing body of academic literature. It thus helped establish a virtuous circle among company practice, business associations, and academia that had long existed for engineers. For instance, the 1930 VSt organizational chart (Figure 14.1) appeared in the most important journal for organization, the *Zeitschrift für Organisation* (ZfO), one week after they began publishing the results of their survey of organizational charts. The magazine represented a cutting edge combination of management theory and practice; it provided an open forum for academics and active managers alike. It remained open to international international developments before the Nazi seizure of power. The ZfO wanted to standardize technical symbols for organizational charts and place them on a par with technical drawings of machinery so that organizational studies could become a "science." Van Aubel of the VSt auditing office wrote in the VSt company magazine, *Das Werk,* that "one should name the *ZfO* the German journal of organization."[42] Such charts then influenced the VSt. In lectures, Dinkelbach placed particular emphasis on the use of organizational charts, flow charts, graphics, preformatted and standardized forms, office machines, and most importantly, the accounting system itself. VSt's system was considered state of the art.[43] VSt auditing and financial offices also maintained contact with the nascent accounting profession. Through their continuing connections with Price Waterhouse and Schmalenbach, Dinkelbach and van Aubel took a particular interest in the creation of an Institute for Public Chartered Accountants *(Institut der Wirtschaftsprüfer).* In this respect, Büro Dinkelbach acted as a source of organizational learning that foreshadowed the *1950s.*

Such organizational, financial, and accounting innovations placed VSt management in the firmament of the rationalization movement. Although even the VSt termed such innovations "American," they had just as much to do with an autonomous German tradition. While the mechanization of information was clearly inspired by America, the classification of accounts rested on Schmalenbach's ideas. The VSt influenced industry-wide financial and cost accounting influence, which slowly formed industry-wide conventions, that is, common norms that made cost accounting and financial reporting comparable and meaningful across diverse firms. In this respect, VSt management innovations had more influence on the industry than its manufacturing rationalization.

Institutionalizing Standard Costs, Standard Values

How exactly did the VSt classify its expenses? These accounts institutionalized a code or language, a conception of control, defining costs, efficiency, and profits. They created and measured value. As we saw in the negotiations to found the VSt, the founding combines could not agree on a common set of standards to assess the proper value of their firms. For the VSt (and any business firm), the cost accounting, financial reports, balance sheets, the company statutes, the organizational charts, employment contracts, and office procedures encoded its organizational principles and the values governing it, its manner of organizing control.

The VSt created new guidelines *(Richtlinien)* to administer it. These guidelines codified the principles underlying standard operating procedures or routines. As used here, codification pertains to the increasingly explicit and broadening application of agreed-upon principles or policies. Standardization refers to the set of norms designed to ensure the application of uniform and accurate classification, permitting the reproduction of the same tasks, materials, or technologies. The concepts of standardization and codification shade into one another, but codification focuses on the principles or values underlying norms, operating routines, or standardized classifications. Eventually the specific norms become conventions, a conventional way of thinking about and organizing information.

These conventions eventually become a set of "unobtrusive controls" (Charles Perrow), designed to ensure some degree of regularity and provide measurable standards of performance. These conventions, codes, and standards both delimit and empower. To use a familiar analogy, the American use of a 110-volt, flat-pronged electrical socket establishes a fixed set of codes and standards that allow a great deal of flexibility of use in everyday life. One can only imagine the disorganization if one had to adjust constantly to different sockets, prong sizes, or electrical currents. When one travels overseas, these ordinary, hidden conventions suddenly stand out by their absence. At present, the current diversity in computer hardware and software is a good example of an industry without clearly set standards. (It is entirely another question whether setting fixed standards at this stage of product development would help or harm innovation.) Once standards become set, however, they become a taken-for-granted part of the technical, organizational, or social operating system. They subtly construct the world by limiting options and empowering those who control and have access to them. At one time, for instance, the choice of a 110-volt, flat-pronged electrical socket standard blocked alternatives and eliminated other designs and competitors. Establishing standards or controls creates winners and losers. But these unobtrusive controls provide a basis for establishing trust and comparison, ultimately permitting a greater delegation of decision-making and expanding flexibility.[44]

Thus, the construction of the VSt accounting system provides a unique glance into this institutionalization of organizational controls, precisely because setting these conventions, codes, and standards was an obtrusive process. The VSt faced an enormously difficult task of homogenizing and standardizing (classic 1920s corporate goals) these accounting standards.

None of the merging firms operated with the same accounting norms. The Thyssen-Konzern, for instance, was the only combine that mixed commercial, financial, and technical costs in its cost accounting. As shown, this arrangement resulted from Thyssen's market-oriented conception of the firm and the modular/subsidiary management structure underpinning Thyssen operations, but it was a decidedly less effective way of classifying costs in a firm organized in a unitary fashion and oriented to improving manufacturing efficiency. For instance, VSt overhead expenses and services of the central administration in Düsseldorf were less directly tied to individual manufacturing facilities as they would in a subsidiary; in effect, the costs of central administration were 'socialized' across the whole firm. The Thyssen system of cost accounting also had real disadvantages. Thyssen calculated auxiliary department expenses into the workshop results. They mixed in estimates of general overhead or interest charges in with direct manufacturing costs. While such a scheme offered a more comprehensive, conservative measurement of production costs (minimizing profit margins), it mixed up indirect, less precisely assessed variables with direct manufacturing costs. Thyssen's system was more comprehensive, but less precise.

Consistent with van Aubel's theoretical recommendations, Phoenix had a classification scheme based on expense types *(Kostenarten)* combined with a series of adjunct auxiliary department calculations. Rheinstahl, however, used expense areas *(Kostenstellen)* subdivided by expense types. The internal VSt debate reproduced a contemporary debate between academic theorists favoring expense types or expense areas.[45] Furthermore, none of the founding combines categorized their expense areas in precisely the same manner. For instance, a complete difference of opinion existed where blooming mills ended, that is, the extent of the cost area. Some firms included the shears and assembly room, others did not. The differences in expense areas were so great that the VSt study commission gave up trying to figure out which of the founding combines produced most cheaply because it entailed too much additional work to recalculate. For the VSt, they agreed that a rolling mill train expense area included the cutting shears, but not beyond. In essence, they reconceived the firm into distinct imaginative areas for the purposes of recording costs. Once standardized, they could create comparable cost figures and encode expenses using new mechanical methods.

Each of the above methods, cost types, or expense areas were valid methods of cost classification with advantages and disadvantages. Tradeoffs were inevitable. For instance, classifying expenses into broad cost areas meant considerably less effort and cost in recording expenses, collecting information, and fewer staff positions, but a concomitant loss of precision. Accounting for expense types resulted in greater degree of detail, a greater isolation of potential costs, and a perhaps a reduction in the level of recording mistakes, but it also meant longer lists, more time involved, and more staff employees to record the expenses, making it considerably more expensive. Rabes objected to the classification scheme proposed by van Aubel for the Thomas and Siemens-Martin works because of the level of detail it entailed, but van Aubel wanted this classification in the interests of clear cost comparisons. Everyone objected to Thyssen's classification scheme because it was too static and broad. Thyssen did not calculate and apportion costs according to each individual product piece, but to the workshop area or product line as a whole. But this method kept Thyssen's staff costs leaner (deriving in part from his corporate culture), although it was much less accurate. More cost-accounting precision also meant more calculations and machinery and more staff, which, of course, cost more money and raised overhead—one of the most difficult expense types to estimate and allocate properly. Everyone in the VSt auditing commission agreed that the new scheme would enlarge personnel costs, especially in Thyssen firms, but would enable a better comparison and control of expenses.

It was often no less easy to make a decision about expense types. For instance, the study commission debated at great length whether waste steam energy should be included as an expense. Thyssen & Phoenix managers agreed; Rheinstahl & Deutsch-Lux did not agree. Overhead costs proved to be the most ambiguous category, and such costs provide the clearest example of the problems in categorizing expenses. Eventually, the VSt central auditing office drew up *ten pages* classifying overhead and sales costs; five pages alone defined the monthly statistical material required by the central administration.[46]

Perhaps more important than the type of cost recording was whether everyone agreed to a set of cost conventions in which subsequently recorded postings remained consistent in a "homogeneous" scheme. It also created a great number of standard expense classification forms to regulate proper coding and posting. The type of classification scheme altered the findings of any evaluation and the ability of managers to isolate problem areas—making costs visible. If, for instance, they included the assembly area beyond the plate or pipe shears in the expense area (and it was not clearly subdivided), a manager would find it that much more difficult to *see* where costs for plates or pipes arose. Including the more labor-intensive assembly area meant that the complete product carried more weight than the raw pipe or plate manufacturing process. Classification thus affected how managers saw their areas, made judgments, and performed. As at Thyssen, adding interest, sales, or overhead expenses into the cost accounting of manufactured goods meant that the profit margins were squeezed. Managers became sensitive to the effect of overhead or sales expenses. If, however, cost accounting stripped out such expenses, the department chief's attention and orientation shifted to pure manufacturing efficiencies.

Ultimately, the VSt settled on a combination of van Aubel's and VDE's recommendations. It distinguished three primary levels of accounting: the operating unit or product-line workshop; the factory or manufacturing unit; and central administration (including sales). The operating unit's accounting concentrated on monitoring and assessing conversion costs, factory accounting on a complete rendering of the total on-site production and administrative costs (say Mülheim or Dortmund), and the central administration's expense in Düsseldorf. The bookkeeping, accounting, and auditing system itself corresponded closely to the staff-line functional model of administration, although the management of the VSt was messier than its accounting scheme. The VSt also fused operational bookkeeping and cost accounting functions, placing both functions under the purview of one person, Adalbert Flaccus, "according to American practice."[47] Rabes and Dinkelbach stressed the need to unite auditing, bookkeeping, inventory, and cost accounting "according to the American model."[48] In classic, modernist fashion, VSt organizers claimed to be presenting a "true mirror" of the VSt's operations rather than representing it.

The central accounting and auditing offices conceptually amalgamated the various units, functions, and levels of the VSt into monthly and yearly balances which reflected the profits and losses of its individual units. Most of the correspondence went through Dinkelbach and van Aubel in central administration.[49] VSt management prepared extensive monthly lists of accounts receivable and payable, new investment expenses, and inventories. Ten copies of the monthly unit balances were sent in, first by handwritten methods, then later by typewriter or machine punch cards. The number of copies and regular monthly due dates for general statistics, inventories, bookkeeping, and factory balances defined work rhythms. As in the 1882 Thyssen & Co. reforms, timing and circulation of pertinent information was just as important as ever. For the accounting departments in the manufacturing units and the central accounting offices, it was imperative to have all of them "absolutely finished" (*fix und fertig*) by the fifteenth of the next month. The central accounting office had to make it possible that the entire profit/loss statement of each manufacturing unit was finished seven days later of the same month, and a complete cumulative yearly balance within two months of closing.

The monthly financial reports provided a balance statement of the assets and liabilities of each individual manufacturing works including inventories (current accounts) to cash accounts and detailed expense accounts. It also provided an operating profit-loss statement (with a breakdown) for the month in question, the year to date, and the total from the previous year. The profit-loss statement for each manufacturing unit also included revenues. The next broad category was an account of general manufacturing unit's overhead, which they distributed to the operating departments, to the factory as a whole, or to general administrative costs (the three basic levels of VSt organization). Inventory breakdowns for each individual product followed. The monthly balance sheets ended with an overview of other miscellaneous expenses. Additional accounts tallied up an income/expense statement for housing administration and sales expenses. *In accounting terms,* the manufacturing works were conceived largely as operating units with sales expenses attached to them, not semi-autonomous technical-commercial modules as at Thyssen & Co. or Phoenix, or complete divisions such as at the ATH Dinslaken. As mentioned before, in reality many manufacturing works retained some sales responsibilities.

The conceptual issues involved in placing sales, administrative, manufacturing, and financial expenses into meaningful accounting statements were immense. For instance, the mechanization of bookkeeping could easily track overhead costs (a classic 19th century problem), but how overhead expenses should be apportioned to product lines or manufacturing units remained a thorny accounting question. Suddenly, the central accounting office might arbitrarily distribute a certain level of overhead costs to the manufacturing units, which lay outside their control yet affected their overall profitability. Ironically, the VSt magnified the problem of overhead because of the costs of its huge executive board and its information-collection system which required the development of middle-management staff, let alone additional machines.

The relationship between accounting, organization, and organizational micropolitics became particularly clear in the question of overhead (general administrative expenses). The proper distribution formula conceptually attached central overhead and factory overhead expenses to manufacturing units as well as to individual product lines.

Setting this formula highlights the potential arbitrariness involved in evaluating manufacturing efficiency, internal transfer prices, and product profitability.

VSt accountants identified four types of expenses for cost accounting:

- workshop manufacturing costs *(Betriebs-Selbstkosten);*
- operating production costs *(Herstellselbstkosten)* of the manufacturing plant, which included factory overhead *(Werksverwaltungskosten or Werksumlage)*, that is, the common expenses of a collection of workshops at one local site such as technical and commercial salaries, receiving, shipping, the fire department, factory police, factory administration, and any taxes assessed directly to the factory;
- total production costs *(Gesamtselbstkosten)* of the manufacturing unit, which included central overhead expenses such as taxes and administration; and
- central costs *(Zentralkosten)* of the firm-level central administration.

Sales accounts remained functionally separate for cost-accounting purposes and were viewed as a reduction in profit margins.

VSt accountants wrestled with the question of how to allocate factory overhead properly. Then, the question of overhead distribution tapped into the "peak works" dilemma. Initially, the study commission allocated factory overhead according to the proportion of total wages used by an individual manufacturing site, but van Aubel objected that the most efficient works employing a full contingent of workers would carry more of the general costs, making their products disproportionately more costly, although they were most efficient. Less efficient factories with lower wage bills would not bear their full share of common factory costs, which might remain stable regardless of capacity use. In effect, an allocation formula based on total wages would act as a silent method of cross-subsidization.

Van Aubel instead recommended a "normal or standard wage sum" *(normalisierte Lohnsumme)* based on the normal full employment of each manufacturing unit. But others quickly raised objections. First, they would have to book factory overhead costs to closed workshops or factories, which the VSt held in reserve as "peak works" or had not yet written off. Counterintuitively, they would be charged on a full-employment basis although the VSt might have shut them down. Previously at Phoenix, van Aubel had simply posted the overhead costs of closed plants to the profit/loss statement as the costs of closings (*Stillstandkosten*). But not everyone in the merged combines operated with such accounts; and their representatives refused to accept such methods. Van Aubel insisted that the VSt introduce this type of distribution formula at a later date, and he did manage to introduce such a factory overhead allocation formula based on wage levels at normal employment levels.[50] We can quickly see how such abstract and arcane matters as distribution formulas slipped into the riptide of VSt organizational politics.

Allocation of general administrative and sales expenses was another complicated problem area. The VSt moved most its major sales offices for the steelworks to its central headquarters in Düsseldorf, but a number of specialized product sales offices remained dispersed at the various manufacturing sites around the Ruhr. Rabes wanted the VSt to subsume all sales expenses under the costs of general administration because it was "impossible" to assess and reallocate the appropriate relative weight of the central headquarters according to each manufacturing unit; it was also not easy to distinguish a sales expense from a general administrative expense because most sales operations went through Düsseldorf. Rabes recommended a rule of thumb: that 50% of central administrative costs be considered sales expenses; the VSt would distribute the other 50%, for such activities as purchasing and general operating expenses, to factory overhead. Others objected that this was too imprecise.

The VSt eventually gave up trying to redistribute central administrative costs as a basis for cost accounting because that could only be achieved by distributing the expenses according to a rough formula, which the commission felt too arbitrary.[51] Instead, they distinguished as clearly as possible cost accounting (for assessing manufacturing or operating efficiency) from financial accounting (for measuring plant profitability). The VSt's accounting guidelines distributed factory overhead expenses to the individual operating units according to a plant's normalized wage levels. The VSt did not use other alternative distribution formulas such as salaries, revenues, or fixed costs.

As a result (see Table 14.1), operating costs of a given workshop equaled its manufacturing costs plus allocated factory expenses. Total factory costs (which included central administrative costs, but not

Table 14.1 Basic expense categories of the VSt

Allocated general factory expenses

Operating production costs =
Workshop manufacturing costs + allocated general factory expenses =
Internal transfer price (factory to factory)

Central administrative costs
(Central administration and taxes)

Total factory production costs =
Operating production costs + central administrative costs allocated as a
proportional surcharge
(Not used as a cost accounting measure)

Sales accounts
(Not used in cost accounting, but considered a "reduction of profit
margins")

Source: MA: R 1 35 32 (3) Rundschreiben 1, Hauptkostenabteilung, gez. Schirner,
Osterloh.

sales) were also not used to determine the transfer price or manufacturing efficiency of a plant.

Central (general administration, interest charges, taxes, depreciation, representation, etc.) and sales expenses did not appear in cost accounting calculations at all, but only in financial reports for internal use only. The central office calculated total factory production costs, that is, operating costs plus central costs, as a percentage of normed wage levels. The central accounting office regularly informed factory accounting offices of the central costs they needed to add to total factory production costs. VSt auditors emphasized over and over again to plant directors that operating or factory production costs did not represent goods' full production cost.[52]

Finally, the VSt gave up attaching sales expenses to any operating, factory, or central costs. Instead, they divorced central sales expense accounts completely and considered them a "reduction of profit margins or proceeds." Insofar as the central sales offices directly sold the factory's goods, their costs would be transferred to the factories' sales accounts according to a monthly revenue formula for financial, but not cost accounting, purposes.[53]

What did such an accounting system say about the VSt? First the

VSt's formal organizational design, not its actual or informal decision-making paths, inscribed itself on its information system. In effect, VSt executives imagined the corporation through its organizational charts and accounts. This act of imagining was based on certain—contested—assumptions about the relationship of the parts to the whole. Product sales expenses and manufacturing costs became distant from one another in accounting terms as well as in geographical location.

Second, as expressly stated in its accounting guidelines, the VSt "Americanized" its account structure with a strong cost-accounting emphasis on manufacturing or workshop efficiency (by contrast, compare Thyssen's modular conception). The VSt simply divorced difficult problems of allocating central or sales costs in the interests of correctly assessing manufacturing efficiency. True to the VSt's prime strategic objective of improving manufacturing productivity, the accounting system shifted attention to manufacturing efficiencies at the plant level, which provided the main basis for determining internal transfer prices. Executives' focus shifted to manufacturing criteria and they had to be reminded that the full cost of the product was not properly taken into account. Implicitly, profits would naturally follow if manufacturing costs were kept low. Thus, a particular conception and construction of the firm linked strategy, structure, organization, and system of accounts—its conception of control.

Moreover, VSt's cost accounting guidelines and standards do represent a clear case of a convergence to an American model. In the 1920s, Americans tended to have an advantage in developing methods of factory cost accounting (particularly standard rates, efficiency cost accounting, and budgetary analysis), while the Germans tended to have an advantage in the area of general costs, depreciation, and internal transfer prices, that is, areas of managerial administration. Not surprisingly, when the VSt turned to a centralized, horizontally oriented, functional form, it too began to reproduce the cost accounting techniques and manufacturing biases associated with U.S. firms. While one could make this argument in terms of cost accounting, in financial accounting, Germans have retained a good deal of distinct methodology to the present day. Conservative accounting, high levels of depreciation, generous reserve policies, the cultivation of hidden reserves, all are hallmarks of German financial reporting history. If we speak of

Americanization of the VSt, then this Americanization applied to cost accounting, not financial reporting.[54]

Third, the "story" the accounting and information system told about the VSt and the relationship of individual VSt manufacturing units to one another had implications for its financial and organizational dynamics. The accounting system helped laid down the fault lines around which conflicts arose. One of these issues played itself out inside the VSt with the issue of new investment versus operating costs and internal transfer prices, just as it did inside Thyssen & Co. in the 1880s. Vögler and the auditing office had immense difficulties ensuring that those powerful plant executives properly distinguished between new investment and operating costs.[55]

Internal transfer prices were another issue. By clearly distinguishing cost accounting from sales and central financial expenses, the VSt greatly simplified the calculation of internal transfer prices. The VSt used the average operating production cost of the previous month (see Table 14.1) to set prices for most inputs except coal, crude steel, scrap, and high-end products such as wire, pipes, and forged goods. Unlike transfers from divisions of subsidiaries of the Thyssen-Konzern, bureaucratic cost accounting procedures determined transfer prices for the VSt, instead of market price levels mediated by interpersonal negotiations. For the above exceptions, the VSt had slightly different procedures. The VSt set coal and coke prices at the syndicate price minus any revenue taxes; this also corresponded to the mining group's special status within the VSt, and effectively amounted to a subsidy. The cost-accounting department added a special surcharge for special quality crude steel to compensate for the differences in quality. The VSt also credited a manufacturing unit producing scrap at market prices by setting up a special account. Finally, high-value-added steel goods such as wire and pipes were sold to internal customers at their full domestic price minus any revenue taxes. Any other pricing method caused difficulties with cartels and led to difficulties with setting prices for widely differentiating quality and types of pipes. (Again, cartel considerations nestled themselves into the deepest parts of organizational life in German steel.) Factories producing high-value-added goods also sold their goods with a percentage of central administration costs included in their prices, even to other VSt units.

This extensive, highly bureaucratic system of internal transfer prices, however, caused fundamental problems of evaluating the performance of various manufacturing plants. These internal (plant-to-plant) transfer prices did not really correspond to total factory production costs. Reducing production costs became the manufacturing units' executives' chief aim. But since factory transfer prices for intermediate goods did not include central administrative expenses, those works delivering goods to downstream factories were at a disadvantage because central accounting still charged them with a portion of central administrative expenses. If these central overhead charges were equally distributed across each manufacturing unit, upstream units would undercharge downstream VSt factories for their goods. Since the VSt distributed these charges proportionately based on their total average wage bill (and lower end goods such as coal or crude steel operations tended to have larger working staffs because of their necessary scale), internal suppliers bore a disproportionate share of central overhead charges. For this reason, the central finance office charged manufacturing units producing intermediate goods with a smaller percentage of the total central administration costs. In effect, the Düsseldorf central headquarters had to create yet another internal accounting loop to compensate for one of the disadvantages of internal transfer prices in an integrated firm.

This calculation of internal transfer prices was not necessarily to the advantage of intermediate goods suppliers, who delivered a great proportion of their orders to other VSt factories, as they earned no profit. Yet each manufacturing unit generated revenues as an indicator of performance. In the worst-case scenario, if all supplier firms oriented themselves to the delivery of internal intermediate materials, profits would essentially come out at the top of the manufacturing process— i.e., pipes, wire, or other such high-value-added goods. Another administrative financial loop could possibly send profits back down to the other stages of production in some manner. If suppliers of intermediate goods sold to other VSt firms at cost, one direct incentive to produce more efficiently was lost. Manufacturers such as the ATH works, which consistently produced more cheaply than other VSt suppliers, derived no advantages unless they sold goods directly on the market. Bartscherer of the ATH continuously complained to Vögler that the ATH had too many orders for input materials for other VSt factories.[56]

In effect, the VSt decoupled its internal intermediate goods producers from the pressures of market competition. (Cartels accomplished this for coal and coke, but they received syndicate prices.) Unlike the Thyssen-Konzern, which kept market or cartel prices mediating the economic relationship among its firms (at the cost of much negotiation), the VSt completely internalized the market for intermediate goods by supplying at cost most of the goods it produced to other parts of the VSt (and really less than total factory production costs). A massive volume of statistical material substituted for whole markets. This internalized market eliminated the advantage of allowing certain divisions to buy from cheaper competitors (as did the Thyssen-Konzern, which kept pressure on internal suppliers to remain cost competitive). Internalizing the market through internal transfer prices also increased the number of central staff personnel and technologies needed to calculate costs and internal transfer prices. This central staff not only had to process an ever-increasing load of information, but also had to build a series of corrective loops into such procedures. On the other hand, internal transfer prices provided a higher degree of regularity and speed with little or no haggling, and they were not subject to rapid, possibly disruptive, fluctuations in market prices. Since manufacturing costs were largely stripped of other variables, the pricing system focused the attention of manufacturing units' managers on producing efficiently. Although profits did not accrue directly to the individual manufacturing unit or its management, they eventually accrued to the VSt as a whole. But the final goal of the VSt venture, to improve overall profitability, receded into the distance for its plant managers. The VSt heightened control by making most plant executives accountable for improving manufacturing ratios, not profitability ratios. In this respect (only), the two strategic objectives of the VSt—to improve profitability by improving manufacturing productivity—actually became detached from one another in organizational practice.

Finally, power shifted to the central finance and accounting offices (that is, to those office run by Rabes, Dinkelbach, and Flaccus), which substituted for the open market. These central offices inserted themselves into the relationship of one factory executive to another by bureaucratic procedures and calculations based on certain assumptions and not others. Sometimes additional expenses affecting factory performance appeared as if from high, as the VSt administratively and geographically disconnected senior management of the manufacturing units from a significant part of their costs and performance (sales and overhead). Central headquarters, which reallocated costs and determined internal transfer prices, gained a clear informational advantage over the manufacturing units and their executives. This became one of the most significant criticisms of the VSt before it reorganized.

The way VSt organized control—its form, its accounting codes, its codified and standard norms, and its routines, which bound together its manufacturing units, sales offices, and central administration in an information network—expressed an implicit organizational "rules of the game." These codes, measures, and procedures provided the ground rules for contestation within the VSt. Managers resorted to the accounting figures as a source of legitimacy for decision-making. The dry language of accounting helped to shape internal collective action. Yet, as we have seen, constructing this system of accounts depended on a whole mixture of debatable assumptions, latest theoretical advances, particular corporate strategies, general policy objectives such as creating an "American" system, practical cost constraints, the practicality and cost of new technologies, internal organizational politics, and corrective administrative and accounting loops. Far from being rational in the Weberian sense, these internal transfer prices disguised their assumptions, their costs, and their politics.

These American methods of cost accounting and organization had unintended results, by helping spawn a whole new set of middle managers, who contributed to its overhead and start-up costs. The VSt's huge supervisory and executive board did not help reduce central overhead costs either. Ironically, these new, state-of-the-art Americanized procedures contributed to gridlock inside the VSt. The amount, precision, and quality of information available to the VSt did not always lead to clear-cut, objective decision-making. Sometimes, this information merely fueled rivalries inside the VSt.

Made in America? The Fretz-Moon Process

The introduction of the Fretz-Moon pipe-welding process provides an inside look at one of the most important investment decisions of the VSt during Weimar.[57] The Fretz-Moon process represents only a fraction of VSt new investment outlays, but is a trenchant metaphor for the process of technological transfer and transmutation of American ideas. Calling into question a simple process of Americanization, the Fretz-Moon adoption was a creative *fusion* of German and American technical practices. Furthermore, the decision to purchase the license became entwined with the internal rivalries of the VSt and the vagaries of the German cartel system, and illustrates the highly politicized use of rational cost accounting measures in practice.

On a technical tour of the United States in 1929, a VSt engineer, formerly of Phoenix, Paul Inden, visited the Fretz-Moon Tube Company in Butler, Pennsylvania.[58] Inden wrote directly to Ernst Poensgen, the VSt vice-chairman, his uncle, and a former senior director of Phoenix, about a continuous, electric-arc welding process. The process enabled the Fretz-Moon company to produce a continuous pipe from tubing strips for over 38 straight hours with only five men. Moreover, the weld appeared to be even stronger than the strip steel tubing itself. In quality tests the metal tube split before the seam; the Fretz-Moon company had not had one return in over a year. If Inden's reports were true, and they sounded too good to be true, then the invention was the most significant advance in pipe manufacture since the Mannesmann seamless process.

Poensgen sent Inden's reports to the head of the cost accounting department, Adalbert Flaccus. Flaccus was also a former Phoenix managing director, who then sent them to the VSt pipe committee, made up of Walter Borbet (Bochumer Verein), Heinrich Esser (Phoenix), and Julius Kalle and Carl Wallmann (Thyssen). He also sent copies of the reports to Julius Lamarche (Phoenix), Hermann Possehl, and Albert Vögler. It was a typical process of VSt management by committee so as not to exclude any relevant parties from the original founding combines. The key figures became, however, Heinrich Esser, Carl Wallmann, and Rudolf Traut (of Thyssen-Mülheim). Phoenix and Thyssen had been major rivals in pipes for the last fifty years. Esser was then director of Phoenix-Lierenfeld (near Düsseldorf), which had an even longer tradition in pipes than Thyssen-Mülheim. Moreover, Julius Lamarche, along with a relative of Paul Inden, Alfred Inden, headed the steel pipe and fittings sales groups. They, too, came from Phoenix. As such, the discovery of the Fretz-Moon process was almost entirely a Phoenix affair.

A month after they circulated Inden's reports, Wallmann wrote

Flaccus that the VSt should purchase the Fretz-Moon license immediately. Wallmann began to make arrangements with Traut, his most experienced rolling mill designer, to provide hall space for the equipment so that if the VSt purchased the license, they could quickly bring it into operation in Mülheim.[59] Esser assessed the process more skeptically and thought it might be profitable only for conduit pipes of small diameters. He questioned Inden's figures and did not think that German Thomas steel would work as well as American Bessemer steel. Finally, Esser asked the important question. If the process was so good, why did other big American producers not use it?

Traut immediately replied, stressing the advantages of the process, which required only a few unskilled people. Only the welder, who regulated the speed and the temperature of the oven, had to be a skilled worker. The weld was free of slag, and the completely automated process required no physical strength. In present processes, a highly coordinated rolling mill team of over twenty people was necessary.[60] Moreover, Traut was convinced that the technology would also be effective with larger diameter pipes of greater thickness. Both Wallmann and Traut wanted the basic technology, not the finished production process.

Both Traut (Thyssen-Mülheim) and Esser (Phoenix-Lierenfeld) agreed, however, that German Thomas strip steel, which was more difficult to weld properly than American Bessemer material, first needed testing with the Fretz-Moon process. Inden sent another glowing report in June 1929, which Esser viewed skeptically because Inden did not differentiate the thickness of the pipe metal. Traut attacked Esser's logic and Phoenix-Lierenfeld's cost-accounting estimates. Traut argued that since Thyssen-Mülheim made pipes with American thicknesses and diameters, they had made a more accurate and comparable cost-accounting assessment.[61] After numerous minor delays, Ernst Poensgen personally ordered two members of the central cost-accounting department to test Thyssen-Mülheim-produced Thomas steel tubing strips at the Fretz-Moon Company in Pennsylvania. At the same time, Vögler wrote the Brassert consulting company for their view of electric-arc welding. Brassert thought this process would be the future of pipe welding.[62] By February 1930, the first experimental pipes had returned to Mülheim for quality control.

Traut immediately wrote a full report on the virtues of the Fretz-

Moon process and recommended purchasing it, provided the licensing fees were not too steep. Traut evaluated the process positively, arguing that it would:

- reduce personnel from 22 to 5
- require only one observer/regulator instead of two welders who performed extremely hard work
- mechanize the entire process
- reduce the price of pipes up to three-quarters of an inch in diameter, and keep the production cost for pipes up to one inch as roughly equivalent.[63]

A cost accounting specialist (Wiegand) at headquarters also concluded that the Fretz-Moon process was cheaper for pipes up to three-quarters of an inch. But Esser felt that the results did not "provide enough basis for a safe judgment about the efficiency of this process." Esser felt that the waste was too high (and it was higher at the time), the product was not useful for gas or water pipes used in Germany, and potentially only of use for conduits because of the threat of leaks. He also questioned Wiegand's figures and assumptions. Esser recommended waiting ten years until the patent rights terminated. Traut and Wiegand prepared another detailed rebuttal, which argued that there would be significant cost savings and the process was also good for gas and water pipes.[64]

After a flurry of memoranda, Poensgen (Phoenix) gave the green light to begin negotiations over the licensing fees, which dragged on for a full year. In March 1930, they also intended to erect the new plant *in Mülheim*. At issue were the amount of the fee, set at $500,000 (ca. RM 2.1 million), the sudden takeover of the Fretz-Moon company by Republic Steel and Spang Chalfant, conflicting patent-right negotiations in France and Belgium, continuing doubts by Phoenix representatives, the weak financial state of the VSt, and the depressingly poor demand for pipes because of the international economy. Cost-accounting calculations assumed a demand of 120,000 tons, but Lamarche argued that they could expect only 80,000 tons of sales.[65]

In December 1930, Traut traveled to Pennsylvania to cast aside the last objections to the Fretz-Moon process made by Phoenix executives. In order to eliminate their objections, Traut planned further cost reductions. Traut felt only three workers were needed instead of five. He also planned to improve the oven and burners to reduce the level of scrap. Finally, Traut answered the vexing question as to why American companies did not use the process. Before its takeover, the Fretz-Moon Company had demanded a domestic market licensing fee of nine million dollars. Even interested parties, like the pipe producer Jones & Laughlin, had dropped negotiations. After the takeover, Republic Steel and Spang Chalfant planned to introduce the process to their Youngstown and Pittsburgh plants.[66] Traut, moreover, struck up a good personal working relationship with the Americans.

Back in the Ruhr, the Thyssen-Mülheim cost-accounting office (Maxrath) backed Traut up. Esser continued to object, and even proposed a completely unproven, uneconomical process as a serious alternative. Traut quickly shot down his ideas based on cost considerations, but his objections set off yet another round of cost calculations.[67] The central cost accounting office confirmed Mülheim's calculations over Lierenfeld's, though its estimates were not quite as favorable as Mülheim's.[68] Carl Wallmann then wrote Vögler that they had carried on the debate "exhaustively" enough and that the license would "mean a progress that cannot be underestimated and recommend once again the purchase of the patent."[69] The last round of cost calculations and Wallmann's intervention clinched the decision. In April 1931, the VSt bought the exclusive rights for Germany for $200,000. The agreement set no limits on the number of facilities the VSt could build in Germany or where it could sell its pipes.[70]

The final decision to purchase the license, however, touched off a major row between Phoenix-Lierenfeld and Thyssen-Mülheim. Both sides felt that the VSt should place the Fretz-Moon process at their respective sites. The new Fretz-Moon plant would make the other plant's welded pipe production superfluous and the stakes were high, given the Depression. Recently, the VSt had closed a gas pipe mill in Mülheim in favor of the Lierenfeld factory.[71] Moreover, Vögler reminded directors that they still needed to adhere to the five-year plan's new investment budget limits—any new investment funds in one area meant a corresponding loss in another.[72]

As usual, the debate first went to a committee, consisting of Lamarche and Esser of Phoenix, and Kalle and Wallmann of Thyssen. The committee agreed to submit to the judgment of the VSt central cost-accounting office, as a type of neutral, objective observer, based on four explicit criteria:

1. Which factory had the most favorable production costs for the Fretz-Moon tubing strips?
2. At which factory could the necessary renovation of the strip steel mill trains and the new construction of the Fretz-Moon facility be carried out with the least expense?
3. Which factory has the most favorable situation of the existing and future facilities for the material flows from input materials to the finished pipe?
4. Which factory has the most favorable transport situation for delivery of materials and shipping?[73]

But the cost-accounting results remained inconclusive. Above all, they could not answer the first question with any determinacy, *because the new plant would offer a disruptive technology did not yet exist.* This was a bet on the future. Lierenfeld objected because its existing tubing strip mill was more efficient than Mülheim's. Indeed, the Lierenfeld gas pipe operations stayed in operation throughout the Depression and Mülheim's did not. The answers to the third and fourth questions cancelled each other out. Mülheim was slightly more favorable for input supply due to its long-term relationship with the ATH, while Lierenfeld could ship the final product more favorably.

Both sides made disingenuous and inconsistent arguments against the other.[74] Traut, for instance, argued that wages in Düsseldorf were higher, yet stressed that the new process would largely eliminate workers, making this question less compelling. Although the VSt had shut down the Mülheim gas pipe operation in favor of Lierenfeld because of a better transportation situation, Traut still argued that Lierenfeld's advantage was not actually true. Both sides did not seem to know the location of each other's tin-plate mills or if the other had enough hall space.

The complicated cartel order of German steel nearly decided where the Fretz-Moon plant would locate. When the VSt was founded, the VSt signed cartel agreements retaining the quotas and self-consumption rights of its member factories. The head of the VSt legal office, Adalbert Fusban (of Phoenix), reminded everyone all the way up to Fritz Thyssen that self-consumption rights for strip steel were limited to tubing strips processed in Düsseldorf (Oberbilk, Lierenfeld). The VSt also agreed not to take advantage of the cartel agreement by shifting quotas around internally, thus making it impossible to locate the

Fretz-Moon process in Mülheim without the loss of VSt self-consumption rights or breach of contract. (In fact, the VSt was cheating on the cartel already by shutting down the Thyssen-Mülheim gas pipe mill in favor of Lierenfeld. The VSt should have reported an increase in its self-consumption production. It was risking a fine of RM 20,000). Moreover, the VSt had to consider the trade-off between its quotas in the strip steel cartel and those in the gas pipe cartel. If the VSt lost more money by giving up its strip steel quota than it gained from altering its gas pipe quota, then the strip steel quota for Düsseldorf should be retained. Eventually, the head of the VSt strip steel sales office, Franz Heumüller (of Thyssen) negotiated a transfer of self-consumption privileges to Thyssen-Mülheim.[75]

The decisive factor appeared to be hall space. Traut's plans used Mülheim's space more effectively than Lierenfeld, which would have placed the new Fretz-Moon furnace and rolling mills within existing facilities and material flows, which Esser argued was an advantage. The decision to place the Fretz-Moon process in Mülheim came down to Traut's innovative plant design (not his arguments) as well as Traut's and Wallmann's advocacy and entrepreneurial initiative. It is remarkable that there was any debate at all given Esser's consistent denigrations.

Traut designed an entirely new Fretz-Moon plant in which not a single crane or a single human hand touched the tubing trips and pipes until the finished product. Traut took out ten patents on the improvements made on the original American facilities. The Americans delivered only the designs for the furnace and the immediately adjacent milling machine. The whole process, from the coils to cooling beds, the saw, water tester, threading machine, bundle table, to the weighing scale in the end assembly room *(Adjustage)*, was completely automated. Everything was timed to the speed of the weld, which could produce pipes at roughly five km/hr, a good walking pace. Traut's new mill needed five workers in the welding hall (not three), and only one of them skilled. The skilled worker merely acted as an observer who adjusted the speed of the welding.

In May 1932, the Fretz-Moon plant began operations. Within a month, Traut had worked out most of the bugs in the process—an unusually short time for any new technical innovation.[76] Traut's good working relationship with the Americans sped up the introduction. After June, the VSt cost accounting office checked the plant's efficiency and profitability. Instead of finding the expected RM 5–8/ton of savings, the cost reduction amounted to RM 20–30/ton. The Fretz-Moon facility proved to be 50% cheaper to operate than the Lierenfeld gas pipe works in both variable and fixed costs, and at different levels of capacity. Within one year—during the Depression—the profits generated by the new plant paid off the entire building costs as well as the remaining licensing fees owed to the Americans.[77] The VSt permanently shut down the Lierenfeld gas pipe works after the Fretz-Moon facility started operation.

Within a few months, the director of Republic Steel could write: "I hope to have the pleasure of seeing the rolling mill in operation, for it is the most perfect and best laid out gas pipe mill which has ever been built." Traut's designs eventually influenced American developments, just as Willy Trapp's had done before. That same year, Republic Steel also sold to the British pipe firm, Stewarts & Lloyds, the patent rights to the Fretz-Moon process. When the director of Stewarts & Lloyds, Graham Satow, toured Mülheim in September 1932, he could write: "The Fretz-Moon plant, in the way in which you have arranged it, is a revolution in one's ideas of tube manufacture. I was exceedingly impressed with the attention which had been paid to detail, particularly the furnace and welding controls. It is a fine layout in every way."[78] Satow purchased the design of the entire mill from the VSt.

In 1934 and 1935, Traut constructed two more Fretz-Moon plants, which could produce all pipe sizes up to two inches in diameter, of varying thicknesses. The advantage of the process was not just mass production of a few sizes, but flexible mass production of a whole range of diameters and wall thicknesses by a completely automated process. Mülheim became the VSt center for mass-production welded pipes and was very profitable; Lierenfeld subsequently concentrated on specialty, seamless pipes. Because of this decision, Mülheim remains one of the leading centers of welded pipe production on the European continent today.

What exactly does this licensing of an American invention illustrate? First, the convoluted and contentious decision-making process exemplifies how much the VSt did *not* supersede the interests or corporate cultures of the ghost companies controlling it. Tellingly, Phoenix-Lierenfeld's letter rebutting the VSt cost-accounting department's evaluation constantly referred to the Mülheim works as "at Thyssen" (*bei Thyssen*). Not surprisingly, an informal network among former company managers continued to exist. Interventions from superiors, right up to Fritz Thyssen, broke down along former Phoenix or former Thyssen lines. The VSt committees appeared to be less designed to provide a panel of experts than to ensure that all sides were included. The VSt resorted to objective offices at headquarters, which could not offer clear-cut, cost-rational alternatives. They did, however, help construct the terms of the debate. Cost-accounting results were ambiguous precisely because the new processes were innovative. Moreover, the German cartel system played a strange role right in the heart of the enterprise: The distribution of self-consumption rights affected investment strategy and location of manufacturing plants.

Second, although the invention of the Fretz-Moon process was "made in America," a good portion of the process innovation was "made in Germany." Traut's innovations reverberated back to England and America itself. The transfer of an American invention had to pass a number of tests and barriers. Was it cost effective? Could it use German steel? (A resource barrier.) Should one adopt it during a depression with limited demand? (A timing issue, even if the technology was good.) Was it appropriate to the VSt? (An organizational issue of the first magnitude for VSt, Phoenix or Thyssen advocates.) Additionally, the institutional, contractual world in which the VSt was embedded affected how, when, and where the process was transplanted. Finally, the transplant, let alone improvements, owed much to the initiative of an individual, Rudolf Traut. (Historians speak of agency.) Even at the organizational leve, this filter and transfer process was complex, and not a straightforward process of Americanization.

If we think of this technical transfer (as well as Büro Dinkelbach's organizational innovations) as a metaphor for the transfer of American ideas, models, or innovations, we certainly can speak of a convergence, *but not necessarily to an American model.* Germans improved the Fretz-Moon process, which moved back to America and England as an "international style" of pipe plant. If we took this reverse process as seriously as we take the Americanization of German practices, we would have to speak of the Germanization of British and American pipe plants. That would be silly. Classic American *film noir* owes much to the great German directors of the 1920s. Might this be construed as the

Germanization of Hollywood? Did Otto Preminger, Fritz Lang, Friedrich Murnau, or Billy Wilder help redefine American cinema? Postwar American intellectual life owes much to European émigrés. Is this the Europeanization of American intellectuals? Should we talk about the Germanization of American architecture by Bauhaus architects, when Walter Gropius and Mies van der Rohe emigrated from Germany in the 1930s?

Walter Gropius, who participated in the rationalization debates of the 1920s, brings us back to the issue of the VSt as a rationalization company. The VSt achieved less in its manufacturing rationalization than contemporaries and historians have attributed to it, and more in terms of managerial innovation than contemporary public opinion gave it credit for. In this respect, the VSt acted as an industry model—in spite of itself. As long as the VSt could not overcome its merger rivalries, the innovative aspects of the VSt simply raised the sophistication of debates. Instead of arguing with no comparable cost data, now they could argue among themselves with comparable cost data.

In short, an incomplete organizational founding also marred the financially "mortgaged" VSt. It would have to be refounded; many VSt executives actually used the term "refounding" *(Umgründung)*. Its supervisory, executive, and main committee boards had too many people. And the network of backroom negotiations made decision-making byzantine and opaque. According to Dinkelbach, even Fritz Thyssen became so frustrated with the VSt that he considered pulling his Thyssen plants back out of it.[79] The VSt operated by management by committee. With no clear lines of responsibility, the commissions, boards, and committees kept inter-firm merger conflicts, literally, at the negotiating tables. The VSt created a corporate culture of informing and including all senior executives *not* as a commitment to collegial decision-making, but instead as a way to keep the four original combines in the decision-making loop. Nearly every top executive was involved before the investment for Fretz-Moon pipes could be approved; then, recommendations broke along lines of the former combines. The VSt retained a strong informal network that channeled information along those lines as well. No wonder the contemporary business press (only somewhat unfairly) called the VSt a heavy-handed, overly bureaucratic "colossus." Ironically, the innovative reporting methods produced bureaucracy and paperwork, and contributed to decision-making delays. The VSt fully caught up to American business with this level of paperwork—to its own detriment. Instead of coming from an allegedly German state-bureaucratic tradition, bureaucratization and Americanization went hand in hand.

But we should not blame Americanization either. Particularly through the financial, auditing, and organizational offices run by Büro Dinkelbach, the VSt introduced "American-style" accounting methods built around the Hollerith calculating machine and implemented a higher degree of homogenization of accounting standards. The VSt introduced best-practice statistical, accounting, and reporting routines, experimented with and implemented new managerial methods, and led the industry in terms of information processing. Its close connection to Schmalenbach, moreover, created a virtuous loop between academic theory and industry practice. This virtuous loop, however, also kept the VSt (and future German managerial practices) from becoming a mirror-like imitation of American practices. If there existed a convergence to an American model, then it applied to cost accounting, not financial accounting. But, more importantly, just as the introduction of the American Fretz-Moon process transmuted a technological transfer, although the inspiration may have come from America, the actual organizational and technological innovations were made in Germany. Indeed, the particular organizational dynamics and corporate culture of the VSt, as well as the professional trajectory of the German accounting system, actively filtered and institutionalized American ideas in ways that transformed the basic ideas and their effect into something else—sometimes in unintended ways.

Ultimately, the 1926 founding of the VSt created a financial and administrative overhead that contributed to its fixed cost crisis, and a corporate culture that could neither react effectively nor deal with the depths of the world economic crisis of the 1930s. The real losers were Ruhr communities. Instead of having a major firm in their midst, more or less responsive to their local needs, they lost direct contact, worked through a perceived distant central headquarters, and lost a portion of their tax base. Depression-era plant closings damaged the VSt's relations with surrounding communities as well as exacerbated internal rivalries. In one instance in 1930–1931, despite the entreaties of the mayor of Duisburg, Karl Jarres, the VSt shut down Phoenix-Ruhrort and Rheinstahl-Meiderich in favor of Thyssen-Hamborn (for-

merly the ATH) and Thyssen-Meiderich (formerly the AGHütt) because they had duplicate production lines. Ruhrort lost 2,600 jobs;
Meiderich lost 8,000 jobs. (Even Thyssen-Meiderich's factory council
reminded Vögler that there was "no doubt" that Thyssen-Meiderich
was more profitable than Rheinstahl-Meiderich). The closing sparked
debates inside the VSt as to whether they could have avoided the
duplication of effort in intermediate materials in both plants—tacitly
admitting that rationalization measures did not go far enough. Both
Thyssen-Hamborn and Thyssen-Meiderich continued operation throughout the Depression at a considerably reduced rate and with loss of
employment. But when Bartscherer announced the plan to close
Rheinstahl-Meiderich, the public thought that Thyssen firms were favored because Fritz Thyssen was chair of the VSt supervisory board.
Then, Rheinstahl-Meiderich's director, Wilhelm Esser, who had suffered injuries in a 1929 car accident, committed suicide in January
1932. Gloom and bitterness descended on the city of Meiderich. Considering the virulently nasty press the VSt received, let alone the cost
of RM 17 million to shut down and then reopen Ruhrort-Meiderich
three years later, the Depression did no one any good except the Nazis, who pressured the VSt to reopen the factory. When the VSt began
hiring workers again, the Nazis got the credit.[80] Such merger rivalries
not only injured VSt economic performance, hobbled the effectiveness of innovative organizational routines, and slowed the adoption
of new technologies, but they also made for extremely poor public
relations.

CHAPTER 15

Business Practice and Politics

> The subsidiaries should form genuine, autonomous, and fully re-
> sponsible units within the framework of the VSt. This holds true for
> the management of (a) manufacturing, (b) sales, (c) personnel. As
> much as possible these units should be genuinely market-oriented,
> which means that they ought to be placed on the same basis as
> independent firms of the same type in their essential economic
> conditions.
>
> Heinrich Dinkelbach, "Fundamental Guidelines," November 7, 1933

The Great Depression plunged the VSt into desperate straits, nearly
bankrupting it. By September 1930, revenues of its steel business had
sunk almost 50%, compared to May 1929, but then appeared to stabilize. Yet once again, and against the adamant arguments of Vögler,
in January 1931 owners demanded dividends from the sinking ship
that was losing money in the fiscal year 1930–1931. A major banking
crisis in July 1931, which led to a state takeover of major banks, made
clear that this was no ordinary downturn. Vögler met with creditors
to assure them that the VSt would remain solvent. By January 1932, VSt
revenues from its steel business sank to just one-fifth its 1929 level; revenues from coal to one-half. The VSt did not even bother to disclose its
financial statements for the next two fiscal years. (In fact, the VSt lost a
huge RM 38 million in the next fiscal year, yet managed to earn a small
profit in the next on because of tax relief, accounting manipulations,
and lower interest payments due to the fall of the U.S. dollar.) It still
suffered from a "catastrophal lack of liquidity" by September 1932.[1]

The Great Depression triggered a major financial, organizational,
and public relations crisis in the VSt, forcing it to undertake a fundamental reflection, an organizational learning process, to resolve the
underlying problems incurred by its 1926 founding. Vögler, who had
recommended a consolidated group organization for the VSt back
in 1925, provided the necessary initiative, enthusiasm, and authority.
Heinrich Dinkelbach, sitting in the surveillance eye of the VSt, subse-

quently designed, planned, and executed the devolution of the VSt into a multisubsidiary form. It was largely his "brainchild" (Felden-kirchen). Dinkelbach acted as a sort of corporate architect.[2] The combination of Vögler's authority and Dinkelbach's planning pushed through the reorganization against great obstacles.

The 1933–1934 reorganization was one of the most complex undertakings in German business history. Its two major elements consisted of refounding the VSt parent company to eliminate overcapitalization, indirect shareholding, and ghost holding companies. The second element was creating legally independent subsidiaries that united the management of manufacturing, marketing, sales, and financing under one product-oriented roof. Feldenkirchen described this process as administrative decentralization, while Reckendrees views it entirely in the opposite manner as "decentral consolidation" *(dezentrale Zentralisierung)* because the VSt planned to consolidate the number of manufacturing units into fewer groups. Reckendrees argues that "'decentralization' was not an essential component of the restructuring" because he stresses the continuing high level of staff, staff functions, and autonomy in local plants. Only (cartelized) sales, R&D, cost and financial accounting, and portions of purchasing had been previously centralized. Otherwise consolidation was the "fundamental principle of this reorganization."[3] Still, the legal decentralization and creation of Konzern subsidiaries away from a unified corporation required major changes in German law and posed enormous organizational challenges. Even VSt executives had trouble finding the proper term to describe the undertaking: dissolution *(Auflösung)*, devolution *(Aufteilung)*, detaching *(Loslösung)*, decentralization *(Dezentralisierung)*, centralization *(Zentralisierung)*, refounding *(Umgründung)*, restructuring *(Umbildung)*, and reorganization *(Umorganiserung)*—precisely because of the complicated interlocking quality of the centralizing and decentralizing elements of this move.

The contradictory combination of centralization and decentralization was a standard characteristic (sometimes confusion) of a multidivisional/subsidiary form. The VSt reorganization appears to be a remarkable imitation of American models, similar in principle and in practice to the multidivisional story of DuPont or General Motors. VSt executives were also aware at least of U.S. Steel's simultaneous move to a multidivisional form.

But the formal similarities were counterbalanced by some peculiar differences. The reorganization stretched the corporate theory of agency *(Organschaftstheorie)*, that is, what it meant to be a single corporation, because the VSt opted for subsidiaries rather than internal divisions. The VSt had to consider its relationships with myriad cartels. It also had to consider the interests of American firms (Dillon Read and Price Waterhouse) and bondholders represented by various American and German banking trustees, who held veto rights. After bailing out Friedrich Flick in May 1932, the German Reich became a direct VSt shareholder (not just a stakeholder), controlling roughly 25% of its stock. Because of its shareholding privilege, it too had veto rights over any VSt strategic decision. Negotiations between VSt executives and ministers of the central government were unusually direct, including such Finance Ministry officials and the new Reichsbank director, Hjalmar Schacht. Just as in 1926, VSt's reorganization depended on another tax break from the government, which became known as *Lex Stahlverein*.[4] Last but not least, the 1933–1934 negotiations with the German government replicated the constellation of interests, people, and issues seen in the 1924 Thyssen-Konzern reorganization and the 1926 VSt merger—except now the new Nazi regime (after January 31, 1933) were involved. Unlike the DuPont or General Motors story as told by Chandler, the VSt was embedded in a web of external stakeholding arrangements.

Furthermore, the remarkable synchronicity of the VSt's "new order" with the ugly new order of German politics fundamentally altered the *meaning* of the corporate reorganization. The new tax law can be interpreted as a negotiated settlement between big business and the Nazi regime. And unlike the VSt's attack on the state of Weimar in 1926 to convince its officials to grant a tax break, the VSt flattered the new government. Finally, the language used by Dinkelbach and Vögler to sell their plan could all too easily be linked to Nazi economic ideology. In this respect, the Nazi regime did not "synchronize" *(gleichgeschalten)* the VSt; the VSt actively accommodated itself to the new regime. Thus, VSt's institutional and political context gives this near classic story of corporate reorganization a unique political spin.

Recommendations and Resistance

Financial and organizational issues provided the motivation for the complete overhaul. The first initiatives to reorganize the VSt appeared in *June 1931* (the date will become important), and came from two independent directions. In June 1931 Erwin Daub, an aide to Oskar Sempell in VSt's Berlin office, recommended fusing the VSt, GBAG, and Phoenix. The plan would have created paper profits to save the poor financial condition of Flick, who controlled the VSt through the GBAG ghost company. Vögler rejected it, especially as Flick would have transferred GBAG debts to the VSt—just as the founding firms had done in the merger.[5] This suggestion, however, foreshadowed the 1933 refounding of the VSt holding.

Simultaneously, Heinrich Dinkelbach proposed a reorganization of VSt internal management. Excessive *administrative* costs triggered, but did not cause, this rethinking. With its precise Hollerith accounting, Büro Dinkelbach quickly became aware that administrative expenses were not keeping pace with reductions in production, revenues, or wages. The VSt did not lay off white-collared employees at the same rate as it did blue-collar workers. In March 1931, Vögler sent a form letter prepared by Büro Dinkelbach to each manufacturing works outlining their administrative costs in relation to their revenues for the last quarters of 1929 and 1930. Thyssen-Mülheim's administrative costs, for instance, rose by 8.4% while its revenues dropped by 47%, doubling from 2.8% to 5.8% of revenues. Other internal figures showed that salary costs (as a proportion of total revenues) rose from about 4% between 1927 and 1929 to 6.8% in 1931–1932, while wages dropped slightly from 24% to 22%. In the steelmaking sector as a whole, the proportion of salary costs rose from about 3.6% to 7.5% in the same period, while wage costs remained relatively stable, rising slightly from 17.8% to 18.6%. By contrast, interest payments on the American loan rose from 1.9% to 5%, depreciation from 3.6–4.9% to 15.6%.[6] Publicly, steel industrialists complained loudest about taxes, the costs of social policy benefits, and wages, all of which rose the least. In effect, the corporate apparatus of the VSt produced the same amount of paperwork and had to make large interest payments on debt (let alone pay out dividends to shareholders), whether it sold any goods or none at all.

Taking the initiative, in June 1931 Dinkelbach wrote his first memorandum to "simplify the commercial organization" of the VSt.[7] Dinkelbach felt that the VSt's commercial organization of the VSt had not kept pace with its technical rationalization. The original units retained a good deal of commercial or administrative staff, as it was "understandable that it was not possible to organize in the most simplified and most economical arrangement after the founding." Only a few consolidations had taken place, such as Phoenix-Ruhrort with Rheinstahl-Meiderich or the Dortmunder Union with the Hörder Verein, or in few cases in the administration, such the finance department. The VSt could not reduce its central administration because of the amount of statistical work required. Before the consolidation of VSt finishing firms in 1930 into Group Siegerland, the VSt processed over 50 works balances from 30 administrative units. Group Siegerland consolidated a great number of VSt's geographically peripheral and miscellaneous finishing firms. Vögler and Rabes drove its amalgamation.[8] Still, in 1931, not including the mining and raw materials departments, the VSt steel works produced 23 works balances and 16 sales balances. Dinkelbach wanted to reduce the 23 main manufacturing works to 6 groups, oriented primarily around product lines and secondarily around geographic relations, as pioneered by Group Siegerland or Ruhrstahl AG. (In March 1930 Vögler and Rabes pushed the founding of Ruhrstahl AG in Witten to consolidate various smaller foundries and finishing subsidiaries.) The VSt would then spread the administration of these six groups throughout the Ruhr, largely on the basis of available administration buildings. For mining and raw material operations, a certain degree of "group" organization already existed. Dinkelbach argued that the VSt could thus reduce the circulation of paper by a ratio of even more than 23:6 because personal and oral communication within each group or manufacturing unit could replace written correspondence, which now had to be sent to the Düsseldorf headquarters. Such reforms would also improve correspondence with customers and suppliers, provide a better overview, and simplify business administration.

In an important respect this first memorandum differed greatly from the final reorganization plan. Dinkelbach recommended folding the *entire* commercial organization into the Düsseldorf central administration, largely stripping the manufacturing works of commercial/ administrative duties, but consolidating their number, such as with Group Siegerland. He felt that this would lead to an improved central supervision of accounts payable and receivable, eliminate the mass of information processed by the headquarters, and ease VSt's financial management (*finanzielle Dispositionen*). In short, Dinkelbach initially proposed a more streamlined, *functional* organization that would consolidate existing manufacturing plants into a smaller number of pure *manufacturing* groups like Siegerland. The VSt would have organized itself more along the lines of Krupp or Hoesch. But the final devolution of the VSt was based on legally independent subsidiaries with full control over manufacturing, commercial, personnel, and financial functions.

Dinkelbach's memorandum got the management side of the reorganization rolling and placed him in the center of planning. An internal commission was formed to examine the question in more detail. The steel works committee discussed the proposal in August 1931, which recommended further consolidation of office staff, but did not decide for or against the idea of building groups. In fact, someone reading the meeting notes wrote "Groups" in red and placed a large red exclamation point after the phrase "building of groups" as if it were a surprise or questionable. Three days later, Gustav Knepper of the mining department formulated the first objections to the plan. He felt strongly that it would endanger the autonomous status of the mining department by pulling its commercial staff away from it, subordinate it to Düsseldorf, and allow the steel works to extend its influence over it, which might endanger its finances.[9]

By the end of 1931, Büro Dinkelbach prepared a series of reports on the newly consolidated Siegerland Group. Vögler then asked Dinkelbach to prepare a two-hour presentation for a February 15, 1932, meeting of the steel works committee. Vögler presented the basic outlines of the proposed groups. He highlighted two main points. First, they should plan the reorganization of the VSt so that "autonomous *(selbständige)* groups result inside the VSt, which might become legally independent firms. Whether or not legal corporations develop should not yet be touched upon." Tremendous corporate legal and tax issues blocked the possibility of considering legally independent subsidiaries for the time being (see below), but the government had passed some key tax provisions that might allow larger firms to create subsidiaries operating at lower tax rates. In between June 1931 and February 1932, Vögler appears to have reconceived the idea of turning consolidated manufacturing groups into (at least) internal product groups, uniting manufacturing, sales, and administration functions.

Second, probably under Dinkelbach's influence, Vögler stressed that they would have to execute the reorganization in a completely uniform *(einheitlich)* manner. Indeed, in each one of his recommendations over the next two years, Dinkelbach stressed that the new VSt organization rested entirely on the uniform centralization of organization, accounting, control measures, procedures, guidelines, and policies developed since the 1926 fusion. After finishing preliminary statistical work by the end of 1932, Dinkelbach prepared a detailed financial and organizational statement for each of the new groups, which now had actually grown to fifteen. At the end of these group portraits, Dinkelbach emphasized: "It should be noted for all organizational questions regarding the consolidation of the individual works into production groups or into independent companies that the fundamental VSt concept *(der Gesamt V.St. Gedanke)* with its advantages resulting from cooperation must remain anchored in place."[10]

The new VSt groups would be "independent" *(selbständig)* within certain bounds. Just what those bounds were became subject to a complex negotiating process over the next two years. Dinkelbach made clear that the decentralization of key powers to the groups did not mean the dissolution of the VSt, but its transformation into a different type of business organization. A classic tension between centralized and decentralized decision-making made itself manifest here. Clearly, the Düsseldorf central headquarters would retain responsibility for overall strategy, policies, and control over the new groups.

Vögler empowered Dinkelbach with planning. He would work closely with the directors, and a liaison for each of the proposed groups was chosen who would make recommendations, stay informed, and report their opinions back to Dinkelbach, who then made further adjustments. Dinkelbach worked particularly closely with Bartscherer, but Rabes and Vögler felt compelled to remind Bartscherer at one point that Dinkelbach would have authority over the administrative work. Dinkelbach's right-hand aide, Leo Kluitmann, later related: "The cooperation between Vögler and Dinkelbach, which I experienced, was outstanding. With the overwhelmingly simple portrayals, which Dinkelbach designed to depict this enormously complicated economic process and which Vögler convincingly presented, the transaction was carried off smoothly."[11] But Kluitmann's retrospective assessment leaves out a considerable number of obstacles facing the reorganization.

The Vögler-Dinkelbach plan met some resistance from other VSt executives. As Reckendrees relates, precisely those executives who most "stubbornly" held onto their autonomy were chosen as directors of the new groups to help bring them on board; their powers would expand.[12] But this also implies that other executive board members would lose some of their decision-making capacity. (A reduction from twenty-two plants to six groups meant that sixteen directors lost out.) From February to December 1932, Dinkelbach and Vögler spent their time working out the plan's viability and dealing with the fallout from Flick's Gelsenberg deal.

It is important to sketch these objections in more detail because they point out the real complexities of reorganization. As simple as the restructuring sounded on paper (consolidate according to product and geography), it was complicated to execute in real life. The objections also highlight the advantages and disadvantages of a single unified corporation versus a multisubsidiary one. Finally, the debate pitted a manufacturing conception of control against an emerging financial conception of control.

Carl Wallmann of Thyssen-Mülheim wrote a thoughtful counter-argument.[13] Wallmann felt the plan was "without precedence and its final effects could not be foreseen." If they intended the plan as a quick solution to the Depression, then such a "thorough reorganization" would only cost a great deal of money in the short term. Even from a long-term perspective, Wallmann felt it was either too complicated or entirely superfluous. On one hand, consolidation would eliminate healthy competition among the manufacturing works. On the other hand, if they wanted to reduce an "uneconomical duplication of production," then the recent closing of two Mülheim plants already eliminated overlap; moreover, the Fretz-Moon process would eliminate two more in Lierenfeld. What further gains could be expected by combining various pipe factories into a single group? For the potential pipe group at least (but not others), Düsseldorf had already centralized sales and purchasing. Regardless of their group affiliation, VSt pipe plants would still have to duplicate personnel positions because they were geographically distant from one another.

Wallmann recognized one of the plan's premier difficulties: "It is illuminating that the more radical a detachment *(Loslösung)* and the more diversified a corresponding plant unity, the more difficulties it will cause." How would various departments, mills, or plants, separated from one another in geographic terms yet united in an organizational group on paper, act as an autonomous unit?

For instance, the three main product departments of the Thyssen-Mülheim and Thyssen-Dinslaken factories could belong to three different groups: a strip steel group, a plate and sheet group, and a pipe group. (Indeed, the pipe group incorporated the strip steel and plate mills of Thyssen-Mülheim because they largely produced either tubing strips or plates for welded pipes, but the Thyssen-Dinslaken factory ended up belonging to three different companies.) Since the strip steel mill had supplied tubing strips to the Mülheim pipe mill for over fifty years, how and why should it belong to another group, possibly another firm? To which group should various auxiliary departments belong? If they combined the Mülheim pipe mill with another (rival) pipe mill, the new pipe group would have to set up its own quality control and testing laboratory, now presently shared with the plate mill, which would increase personnel costs.

Wallmann concluded that *if* the reorganization went forward, the VSt should incorporate the other pipe mills like Düsseldorf-Lierenfeld (Phoenix) and Höntrop (Bochumer Verein) into Mülheim (Thyssen), since those plants were less dependent on their local, affiliated works. Wallmann quickly asserted his own interests. Not surprisingly, Walter Borbet of the Bochumer Verein objected vehemently to this consolidation for its pipe works. Furthermore, in a new pipe group Mülheim and Lierenfeld managers would have to learn to work together. The plan touched upon sensitive rivalries within the VSt.

A similar problem arose in March and April 1932 with placing blast furnaces and casting foundries into the appropriate group. This discussion pitted two different conceptions of management, and two managers (Dinkelbach and Adolf Wirtz) against one another. Dinkelbach's original plan assigned the Meiderich blast furnaces to Bartscherer's steel works group west, but its foundries to the foundry group. Bartscherer, Wirtz (the technical director of the Friedrich-Wilhelms-Hütte), Schuh (the technical director of Meiderich), and Vögler disagreed because about three-quarters of both Meiderich's pig iron *and* foundry production went to the new steel works group. The head VSt cost accountant backed Dinkelbach by arguing that this violated the principle of organizing groups according to end products and would make cost accounting more difficult. Admitting it as a conceptual "blemish," Vögler suggested that the Meiderich foundry work only for the new steel works group. Now Dinkelbach, Flaccus, and Schuh objected. They thought this would limit Meiderich's range of production, raise its production costs, make financial and cost controls more difficult, and make its management more complicated. They thought they might move Meiderich's blast furnace operations to the new foundry group, but found it impossible for cost reasons to distinguish the Thyssen-Meiderich and ATH blast furnaces because of shared gas economies. In April 1932, Vögler unilaterally assigned the Meiderich blast furnaces operations to the steel works group west and the foundries to the new foundry group.

Wirtz objected to this sort of Dinkelbachian reshuffling. He felt it only made sense for the commercial side of the business, not for manufacturing operations: "where not expense accounting areas, but thinking human beings matter." He objected to the Schmalenbach-based "schematism," which oriented itself to cost and profitability criteria rather than technical efficiency. In Schmalenbach's management thinking, every department of a firm should operate as profitably as an outside supplier, or else it should not exist, which was essentially August Thyssen's notion. Wirtz thought this less important than interlocking vertical integration of the manufacturing operations. As an engineer, he did not want responsibility for financial functions in his group, and pleaded with Vögler to change as little as possible. He pointed out the financial costs of the Düsseldorf headquarters and the psychological costs of too much paperwork. Such objections illustrated a fundamental conflict between commercial/financial and manufacturing conceptions of control, a tension that Thyssen engineers always had to face. Wirtz's complaints foreshadow the same type of objections that *Heinrich Dinkelbach* would face post-1945 when he restructured the West German steel industry.[14]

The objections of Wallmann and Wirtz highlight the abstract, schematic quality of Dinkelbach's planning. The groups existed only as dots and arrows on organizational charts, rows of vital statistics and financial figures, and a fictional balance sheet and profit-loss statement for the new groups as if they were building blocks. He paid special attention to derived financial ratios such as fixed assets, inventories, working capital, profit/losses, and proportion of VSt equity and debt in relation to net revenues and to VSt equity. If the groups should be near equivalents of independent companies, Dinkelbach needed to project their individual financial figures, profitability rates, and their effects on the overall profitability of the VSt. Such ratios also provided the preliminary basis for setting the correct level of capitalization should the groups become legally independent firms.[15] As Wirtz clearly noted (and objected to), Dinkelbach primarily considered financial profitability the organizing principles of the new groups. Dinkelbach used *a financial and organizational conception of the firm* to reorganize the VSt, instead of a manufacturing conception of control, dominant since the turn of the century. Thus, if manufacturing efficiency and productivity ratios centered the VSt on its most productive plants after 1926, profitability, return on investment/equity, and liquidity ratios guided its reorganization after 1932.

In November 1932, Dinkelbach concluded in a second major memorandum that the task ahead was to shift from a "manufacturing rationalization" to an "administrative rationalization:"

> [T]he investigation proved that it was as inevitable as it was also effective to combine works with similar products administratively and to form a resulting organization *(Organisation)*, consisting of production, sales and administration, which acts as much as possible as an autonomous economic unit *(eine möglichst selbständige wirtschaftliche Einheit)*. The construction of groups should be equivalent in their economic effect to independent legal persons. The combination of the production, sales, and administrative functions into an economic unity and as an area of responsibility guarantees maneuverability *(Beweglichkeit)* and the maximum success *(bestmöglichen Erfolg)* for the whole enterprise.[16]

In no uncertain terms, Dinkelbach proposed that the new groups unite the "three-pronged" investment in manufacturing, marketing, and management. Dinkelbach "preferred" the founding of legally independent subsidiaries in the interest of sales, financing, and good business management *(Geschäftsführung)*, but realized that significant obstacles remained. But by creating legally independent firms, the VSt could increase its financial maneuverability.

Dinkelbach's November memorandum opened up another whole set of issues that the VSt would debate throughout 1933. Rather self-consciously, he stated that a number of severe *external* challenges still faced the VSt: cartels, German corporate law, trustees of the American loan, and tax questions, especially the level of taxes for the refounded holding. On top of these questions, further *internal* questions remained, including the relationship of one group to another, deliveries, transfer prices, sales, housing, and the appropriate financial relationship and control between central administration and the groups. This memorandum sparked the most difficult opposition yet.

The Limits of the Law

Throughout 1933, the subsequent debate turned on the question whether to turn the consolidated groups into legally independent subsidiaries.[17] Devolving an entire, unified corporation into independent subsidiaries was an unprecedented step in German business history and corporate law. Indeed, the *Konzern* form advocated by Vögler and Dinkelbach was not economically viable for the above reasons. Moreover, they also planned to reform the corporate holding company financially to reduce its overcapitalization and eliminate the ghost holding companies.[18] At its core, a team of Vögler, Fusban (reluctantly), Späing, Rabes, Dinkelbach, and Sempell handled the intricacies of the reorganization. The discussion here illuminates the dense institutional web of German capitalism, which delimited just how independent the new subsidiaries could be. Since many decisions occurred through a *process* of negotiation, a narrative is most appropriate here.

It is one measure of resistance that the highest-ranking executive in the legal department, Adalbert Fusban, fired the opening salvo.[19] Fusban did not approve of the consolidated groups in general and the attempt to make them into legally independent subsidiaries in particular. Fusban offered *fifty* pages of counterarguments. Fusban's specific counterarguments made two broad points. What did "independence" or "self-sufficiency" *(Selbständigkeit)* mean? (Conceptually, this is similar to defining the "self-sufficiency" of department heads in Thyssen & Co., and inside the Thyssen-Konzern). The second line of argument defended the alleged advantages of the German way of doing business, which emphasized profit-sharing, quota distribution, and amelioration of market pressure through formal, bureaucratic arrangements. A single unified corporation enhanced these methods, and Fusban's objections accurately outline the considerable challenges involved with the reorganization.

Fusban thought Dinkelbach did not clearly perceive the purpose of the groups. Did he want a consolidation for technical reasons to improve "flexibility" or to create additional financing opportunities? For instance, the VSt might make profits by selling parts of itself to new companies it established. If Dinkelbach wanted restructuring for technical reasons, he did not need legally independent companies. Fusban saw only one advantage of the groups—they eliminated inter-factory rivalries. Fusban argued, however, the groups would only increase sectoral particularism within the VSt by shifting conflicts to financial arenas instead of manufacturing areas. Each of the groups would compete with one another for investment funds and for their share of depreciation.

Fusban thought a decentralized VSt would lose financial and managerial control. If Dinkelbach wanted to open greater financing options, then he had not yet arrived at the proper opening value of the new groups or their relationship to one another, which would decisively affect their profitability as well as any short-term gains accruing from the sale of such groups. If Dinkelbach wanted greater financial maneuverability, the mutual financial arrangements binding the groups together and to the parent company would contradict the notion of their being independent companies. Fusban felt it impossible to treat legally independent companies as "departments" *(Abteilungen);* they would act in their own particular interests, not in the interests of the whole. If the VSt bound the new companies through long-term contracts, these contracts would abolish or limit the firms' flexibility. If the VSt bound the firms together in an IG arrangement, then the IG would only increase tensions among profitable and unprofitable units. Legally independent companies would remain in the IG only insofar as they gained advantages from it. Finally, as more executives gained power of attorney in the decentralized units, the VSt would lose control over its subsidiaries. In short, Fusban stressed the danger of delegation without proper supervision, but if the VSt supervised too closely, then the subsidiaries were not independent. Fusban touched upon classic issues of locating decision-making and control in any complex organization.

Above all, Fusban thought that the reorganization would eliminate "all of the advantages of integrated combines" in a unified corporation. The VSt and its new subsidiaries would lose their ability to balance fluctuations in the business cycle and to compensate internally for unprofitable sectors. If the VSt founded new subsidiaries as joint-stock companies, disclosure laws would come into effect and expose the weak sectors (coal) and the strong product lines (pipes). Disclosure laws could only harm profitable subsidiaries in their wage negotiations. An IG might possibly level off some of the differences through its profit-loss statements, but introducing competitive market transfer prices *(Konkurrenzpreise)* to inter-subsidiary deliveries instead of internal transfer prices *(Werksverrechnungspreise)* would block any significant effort to compensate for less profitable sectors. Fusban's logic was the exact opposite of that governing the Thyssen-Konzern.

Fusban then continued with *external* challenges, which were even more daunting. The VSt would have to renegotiate all of its cartel quotas; Fusban gave *37 pages* of examples. It might lose its self-consumption rights for its coal because they would become "pure coal companies" instead of being inside an integrated combine. Hidden among the forest of its subsidiaries, the VSt would lose its "prestige value" of being the most powerful firm in the cartels. Fusban showed just how much German cartel-concern capitalism replaced American-style drives for profitability and market share with extensively structured lobbying efforts for quota shares.

Even *if* the VSt could circumvent these problems, the proposed multisubsidiary form was not financially viable. Under the existing state of German corporate law, all inter-subsidiary deliveries, all capital transfers among the subsidiaries and between the subsidiaries and the parent holding company would be taxed. The costs of founding the new subsidiaries and refounding the VSt corporate holding were still separate but still just as costly issues. The reorganized VSt would collapse under the weight of new taxes. Fusban was entirely correct.

Although the mining group was already one of the autonomous areas, its directors weighed in with an eighteen-page report. Twelve pages dealt with the problems of cartel contracts and self-consumption rights. How to regulate production quotas with other VSt subsidiaries was another issue. They stressed that they needed to have new financial offices in Essen if they were independent and warned against more consolidations, which "should not be exceeded, otherwise a greater bureaucratization with all its incalculable shadow sides would be unavoidable." But their most decisive objection to the plan attacked the intention of establishing independent housing management companies, which would separate 54,000 company houses. They argued that the VSt had a "considerable interest in being able to influence the accommodations of their employees, both salaried employees as well as workers, even when there was no housing shortage." After Vögler and Rabes threatened to lower depreciation rates and internal transfer prices for coke by 11%, decoupling it from the syndicate prices that subsidized its profit rates, they backed down.[20]

Unlike Fusban, who wanted to halt the reorganization in its tracks, Wilhelm Späing weighed in with more constructive criticism. Späing had consistently extolled the virtues of smaller executive boards and approved of the plan in principle. But he too reminded Vögler that the plan was not feasible. The "theory of corporate agency" *(Organschaftstheorie)* only extended to certain types of taxes (revenue but not capital transfers), which would complicate the legal relationship between the central parent company and its subsidiaries. If Dinkelbach and Vögler preferred to make the groups legally independent firms, then the Reich Finance Ministry would have to rule more extensively on the theory of corporate agency for the VSt. Späing hinted that if the VSt could find a legal solution acceptable to the courts and the government, the arrangement might disentangle VSt subsidiaries' relations with the cartels. In another letter, Späing assured Vögler that the trustees for the American loan would have little trouble with independent firms because VSt's plans were similar to U.S. Steel's and "are just now belatedly doing what has already been done there for years."[21] Clearly, the VSt was aware of American organizational developments.

Späing highlighted the "dilemma or double game" *(Doppelspiel)* that the plan entailed because he had acted in the same capacity for the Thyssen-Konzern in 1924–1925. In January 1933, he notified Vögler how to promote the reorganization in the eyes of the law. Späing agreed that increasing the autonomy *(Selbständigkeit)* of the groups as joint-stock companies would increase the clarity of financial relations, raise the degree of personal initiative, and limit the level of outside intervention from other directors in the firm—implying that this had been a problem. But while certain officials in government ministries might sympathize with the VSt's need for added flexibility, the Reich Finance Ministry's tax lawyers would not. They would "stick to the letter of the law and their prejudices" as they had with Thyssen. Any further discussions should emphasize the remaining "dependency" of the

subsidiaries as "organs," rather than the advantages of greater autonomy. Government tax lawyers had to agree that VSt subsidiaries were
legally *internal* to the VSt. In short, the *boundary* of the VSt would be
under scrutiny, and based on legal assumptions, not economic ones.[22]

To make matters more complicated, on March 18, 1932, the German government purchased RM 110 million of Gelsenkirchen
(GBAG) stock, one of the VSt's ghost holding companies (with 36% of
VSt shares), to bail out Friedrich Flick. Flick controlled the GBAG
through his nearly wholly owned but nearly bankrupt Charlottenhütte. This sum was three times existing share value. The "Gelsenberg-
Deal" outraged the public when it became known in June. An additional RM 15 million in GBAG shares were held by the Dresdner bank,
which the government also took charge of when it took over the failing
Dresdner. The government appeared to have socialized and bailed out
the VSt. Behind the scenes, the government bailed out Flick because
he controlled some of the most important heavy industrial firms in
Upper Silesia and Poland. For geopolitical reasons, the government
wanted to maintain German control of this lost steel industry—even
using Swiss and American holding companies as cover. Flick received
secret state financial support (specifically from the Foreign Ministry),
as any government attempt to control Polish industry would prove offensive. Knowing this, Flick leveraged his geopolitical position into a
bailout for his "precarious" empire, built on opaque cross-shareholdings and debt. Indeed, Flick had even threatened to sell his stakes to
various unnamed French, American, or Swedish interests if he did not
receive German help. The government justified the bailout on politically correct, nationalist grounds.

At one surprising stroke the German government became the VSt's
largest indirect shareholder through Flick's interlocking directories
that controlled the GBAG and Phoenix ghost companies. Flick had
left Vögler (and Fritz Thyssen) completely in the dark. The Finance
Ministry told Vögler to treat the matter as a "state secret." Government
ownership of the VSt caused great dissension among Ruhr industrialists themselves. The conservative, pro-business government of Chancellor von Papen was also left in an awkward position. Vögler was so
embarrassed that he tried to resign from all his outside honorary offices and industry positions, but Ernst Poensgen refused to send the
letter.[23]

If anything, the VSt became free of Flick's constant demand for dividends. The government was a more benevolent stockholder than Flick or Thyssen had been, so Vögler actually gained more autonomy. With Flick out, reform of the corporate holding was eased. Although the government had control, the state actually influenced VSt corporate strategy more *after* it sold its shareholding. Government had more influence on the VSt through its laws and taxes, and later through its moratorium and rearmament policies. Hjalmar Schacht, the new Reichsbank and Economics Minister, made this clear at an October 24, 1933 meeting. When the VSt broached the subject of the state's shareholding, Schacht warned that the state did not need a single share of stock to make the VSt carry out its wishes.[24]

The government placed Privy Counselor Hans von Flotow (of the banking firm Hardy & Co.) on VSt's supervisory board. He acted largely on the VSt's behalf, smoothing the path with government ministries. In February 1933, Dinkelbach and von Flotow discussed the potential impact of taxes on the fusion of the holding and on inter-subsidiary sales under the planned reorganization. Von Flotow estimated an expected tax burden of approximately RM 3.8 million per year on RM 190 million of turnover, that is, four times the tax level in 1931. Without a tax solution, the reorganization was dead on arrival, but von Flotow still felt confident that a compromise could be found. As Späing pointed out, the state earned less as a shareholder than as a tax collector because it received few dividends, but received a guaranteed 100% of the taxes levied on the VSt.[25] Executives might desire to reduce the level of state-owned shares in principle, but they did not want to press the issue, which might jeopardize a favorable ruling on tax issues. In any case, the VSt had little free cash to repurchase state-owned shares.

The VSt could also count on the support of key government officials such as Alfred Hugenberg, Economics Minister in Hitler's new cabinet. The Finance Ministry showed a good deal of empathy, but felt it could hardly reduce taxes in the midst of a depression, most of which went to Ruhr cities. Vögler and von Flotow contended that many Ruhr cities expressed a desire to have a major steel company headquarters in their midst once again, which would also shore up their tax bases. But the Finance Ministry argued that another tax break was out of the question, especially because the VSt still owed three tax installments from the 1926 merger. Special consideration would set a dangerous political precedent.

The VSt negotiated on the principle that they would not request extraordinary tax breaks, but that the VSt should not incur additional tax burdens resulting from organizational changes. (They were still asking for a tax break.) Initially, the Finance Ministry would not offer the VSt a one-time tax break on the establishment of subsidiaries and the reorganization of the new VSt holding. But they did agree that the theory of corporate agency could apply to subsidiaries if the VSt properly formulated the contractual relationship between the parent company and its subsidiaries.[26] This was an immensely difficult task because of the state of flux in the theory of corporate agency. Although it appeared likely that the VSt would receive some sort of tax break, the final amount remained up in the air. Späing took the lead in this matter and arrived at the final version of the subsidiary contracts just one month before Vögler announced in November 1933 to the VSt general assembly that they would carry out the reorganization.

Späing considered three options for the subsidiaries: leasing firms, so-called "management companies," and "product corporations." A discussion of these options is important because the final organizational form of the VSt depended on the limits of the German legal system, the sympathy of key figures in the Finance Ministry, trustees for the American loan, and the calculating creativity of VSt directors—a confluence of politics, law, banking influence, managerial innovation, and personalities.[27]

Until May 1933, the legal department worked with the idea of leasing VSt facilities to newly established companies. The VSt would form an IG to ensure that the new subsidiaries were financially, economically, and organizationally dependent on the dominant company (a reformed holding company) in a subordinate way. The 1924 Thyssen leasing contracts provided a model.[28]

But this solution had a number of problems. Under the theory of corporate agency, leasing arrangements still did not cover *capital transfers* between the parent and subsidiary companies. A recent decision by the Reich Finance Court reaffirmed that capital transfers were taxable (October 26, 1932). Second, the theory of corporate agency assumed that one company was subordinated to another company, yet a leasing arrangement assumed that both parties were equal and independent legal personages who could sign contracts. Unlike the Thyssen-Konzern, which was already a collection of legally independent firms, the VSt had to establish legally independent companies *prior* to leasing VSt facilities back to the VSt. Logically, these firms were either equal, independent legal entities or they were subordinate and not independent. If the company had no independent will, then one could not lease facilities to it. In effect, the VSt would be leasing facilities to itself. Such transparent machinations would hardly convince the state's tax lawyers. Vögler also remained dissatisfied. If the holding company retained ownership of property, a leasing arrangement simply inserted another tier of hierarchy. Finally, transferring VSt property to new companies, subordinate or independent, was a breach of contract with trustees of the American loan.[29]

The legal department subsequently dropped the idea of leasing contracts in favor of "management companies" *(Gestionsgesellschaften)*. Späing named the companies after the Latin word *gestio,* to manage.[30] Under this second option, the new subsidiaries would not directly own VSt property, but manage VSt property and assets. The theory of corporate agency assumed that a legal personage (i.e., a company) could act as a salaried employee of another company, as an agent of the merchant principal. This was the legal principle behind *Prokura* (or power of attorney) but only a living person could hold *Prokura.* Hence Späing proposed to equip the new subsidiaries with a circumscribed version of *Prokura,* the power to act in the VSt's name with full powers *(Handlungsvollmacht).* By transforming the groups into a specific type of salaried employee, Späing sought to outflank the law by specifying agency more precisely.

According to Späing, these "management companies" had a number of advantages. They could appear on the stock market (with a recommended share capital of RM 500,000) to avoid negative publicity arising from VSt financial and legal contortions. The property would remain property of the VSt, thus avoiding problems with trustees of the American loan and German tax officials. The management companies could easily be transformed later into full-fledged companies that owned property. This would solve the issue of reducing the number of people on executive boards in the groups—one of the main goals of the reorganization. Finally, all uniform accounting procedures and financial balances practices could be maintained; the new companies would balance internally in their own names.[31]

But the solution failed to address the primary issues of financing and organization. The concept did not sufficiently clarify the lines of authority between the corporate holding company and the operating groups. Superficially, the management companies' boards were smaller, but they remained completely dependent on the approval of central VSt boards—already the problem. They would not be fully responsible for the financial disposition of their assets, thus less accountable. Finally, in the eyes of the law, a "management company" could not hire or fire its own employees because it was considered a salaried employee itself, not a real company. Clauses in the proposed subsidiaries' contracts, which stated that each new company received no salary for its services, showed how much Späing stretched the law.[32]

Vögler and Dinkelbach preferred a third solution: full-fledged "product subsidiaries" (*Werksgesellschaften* or *Betriebsgesellschaften*) that independently managed their own finances, production, sales, and employees—the four main functional areas that every independent business firm must coordinate. According to this plan, the obligation to pay off American loans to the VSt and GBAG would be divided among the new subsidiaries. But the trustees for the American loan strongly objected to any contractual changes involving their securities.

Led by Rabes, Sempell, and Dinkelbach, the VSt began negotiating with Dillon Read, Price Waterhouse, and trustees of the loan in late February 1933. (They included Chase National Bank, American Exchange Irving Trust Company, National City Bank, the Dresdner Bank, and the Deutsche Kreditsicherungs AG.) The VSt informed Dillon Read and Price Waterhouse of their plans to reorganize, after the question of the legal independence of the new subsidiaries became pressing. Dillon Read appeared carefully conciliatory, while Price Waterhouse representatives showed great enthusiasm for the project as long as it did not affect repayments to bondholders. Both, however, thought that the trustees would be less than enthusiastic. Price Waterhouse even volunteered to attend negotiations between the VSt (Oskar Sempell) and the trustees in New York in support. German trustees were sympathetic as long as the reorganization did not affect repayments. Between May and July, Sempell negotiated in New York and corresponded almost daily with Vögler, Rabes, and Dinkelbach. But to little avail. The American trustees rejected the plan outright. They stressed that each of the new subsidiaries had to be held liable for the entire loan *(Solidarhaftung)*. Although they felt the Vögler-Dinkelbach plan in principle was "excellent," they could not justify risking the real possibility of VSt default. They were afraid that the VSt could shuffle debts or profits off to legally independent firms, potentially leaving American bondholders with a bankrupt firm. VSt managers felt that this requirement would limit, if not close off, financing opportunities on the part of the subsidiaries—one of the main purposes of the reorganization. One director of Price Waterhouse independently recommended that the VSt establish "management companies" similar to those advocated by Späing. Vögler, Rabes, and Dinkelbach felt dissatisfied with "management companies" because they could only *represent* the VSt and would not be fully accountable for their financial performance. In spite of this, they agreed to finalize planning on this basis. They considered it a temporary solution until the Americans could approve the transfer of property.[33] (After 1937, the VSt began transferring property to the subsidiaries, but the war interrupted the process.)

A second sticking point with the trustees concerned the disposition of another loan to the GBAG, which in the reform of the VSt corporate holding would be exchanged for new securities. The GBAG still owned some mining properties, used as loan collateral in 1928. On top of this, after June 9, 1933, the Nazi regime introduced a moratorium on all currency transactions and interest payments; they subsequently set up a currency board. In effect, this made the German mark inconvertible and stopped loan payments. Now the VSt needed the personal intervention of Economics Minister Schacht to approve the transfer of hard currency; through personal contacts, Vögler got approval. (The VSt got the approval of the currency board for its loan repayments.) The VSt also made payments through Dutch and Swiss subsidiaries to maintain its contractual obligations. This commitment eased the minds of most of the trustees except for the American Exchange Irving Trust Company, which only compromised after Dillon Read and Price Waterhouse intervened in favor of the VSt.[34]

On the home front, in August 1933, the Finance Ministry and VSt lawyers *jointly* drafted six versions of the legal relationship of the new VSt parent holding company with the subsidiaries. The ministers accepted only the last two versions, which cleared inter-subsidiary deliveries from turnover taxes. However, the government ministers and lawyers disagreed among themselves on whether or not the theory of corporate agency extended to capital transfers. Capital transfer taxes would particularly affect the transfer of inventories, share equity, and loans to the subsidiaries from the parent holding company.[35]

At this point, some disagreement arose among those most enamored of the idea of fully independent subsidiaries. Vögler, Rabes, and Dinkelbach wanted the subsidiaries to act in their own name with responsibility for their own *financial* accounts—at minimum, inventories, current accounts, and some level of equity. As legally independent subsidiaries, they could expand their financing capacity and arrange their own operational financing, while the VSt parent would hold them accountable for their financial performance. Under Späing's "management company" plan, the new groups could only *represent* the VSt, but were not fully responsible for their own financial operations. The relationship between parent and subsidiary was symbolized by the contractual formulation for the management companies, which could sign "as a representative of the Vereinigte Stahlwerke AG [printed small], the DEUTSCHE RÖHRENWERKE AG [capitalized]." Despite the attempt to express the independence of the new companies through capital letters and font sizes, they remained tied to the consent of the VSt central headquarters for their financial arrangements. Vögler, Dinkelbach, and Rabes wanted a clearly delineated financial relationship between the VSt parent company and subsidiaries.

Späing agreed in principle with the advantages of full legal independence for a "product subsidiary," but could not justify the tax risk involved, particularly regarding capital transfer taxes. Over the full month of September 1933, Dinkelbach and Späing argued back and forth. Dinkelbach wanted the subsidiaries to have a high equity account to improve their financial maneuverability and credit rating; this would make subsidiary directors directly responsible for their profitability. Späing kept reminding Dinkelbach that all capital transfers, be they equity or long-term operating loans *(Betriebsdarlehen)*, would suffer from costly taxes. Even if the VSt granted its subsidiaries taxable one-time loans, which Dinkelbach was willing to tolerate, they would complicate negotiations with the Finance Ministry about the lump-sum tax payment for the refounding of the VSt parent company. Without a clear statement about a tax break regarding capital transfers between the VSt holding and its subsidiaries, or a fundamental change in corporate law, Späing could not justify the danger. Moreover, at a

September 15th meeting with state finance ministers and tax lawyers, the idea of merging the one-time flat rate fusion taxes and any future capital transfers for the subsidiaries did not register appeal.[36]

Von Flotow, the government's representative, found the eventual solution regarding the new subsidiaries.[37] Von Flotow finessed the quandary with this formulation: the *"results of the accounts* go to the VSt,*"* while the *"means for the operations management* belong to the subsidiary.*"* The subsidiary could own and control all of its own *operating* assets as property *except* its fixed assets (land, buildings, equipment), which the VSt holding company legally owned. The VSt would set up a separate credit line *(Tredefina)* to ensure that the VSt parent company transferred inventories to the management companies. Since the transfer of VSt funds to the subsidiaries would be considered as share capital, such funds would not be taxed in the same way as long-term loans, thus eliminating a good portion of the initial tax burden. The VSt would also be taxed only once.

But the Finance Ministry still had to approve the plan. The clearest justification for the VSt's "intended new order" appeared in August 1933.[38] In October, von Flotow and Späing set up a series of meetings to tackle both taxes on the reform of the parent company and capital transfers to the subsidiaries. A great number of questions, including the level of equity for the new subsidiaries, remained in the air. The VSt suggested distributing the taxes in installments as they had done in the 1926 merger, but von Flotow stressed that the government would approve the reorganization as long as the state did not lose its veto rights over the VSt. This affected the future level of capitalization of the new VSt. Rabes and Dinkelbach estimated that the VSt needed a minimum shareholder equity of RM 536 million (down from RM 774 million) for financing purposes. Since one of the main objectives of the refounding was to lower its capitalization, the Reich would only gain more control. Until June 1933, in fact, the government insisted that it would have to retain an absolute majority in conjunction with Thyssen's shareholdings to allow the fusion. Otherwise, any reorganization would appear as a cagey attempt to reduce the power of the state. Indeed, many VSt shareholders saw the fusion of the parent company as an opportunity to reduce government control. In March 1933, Ernst Poensgen marketed the "freeing" *(Loslösung)* of the VSt to his industrial colleagues as a means of reducing state influence over the VSt.

For reasons unknown, but associated with the June resignation of Economics Minister Hugenberg and with Hitler's personal permission, the government switched its adamant demand for a majority to a controlling minority position of at least 25%, which still guaranteed it veto rights.[39]

Taxes on future capital transactions proved once again to be the main source of controversy because, by law, they were still taxable. The debate turned on the legal question of whether fully owned but legally independent VSt subsidiaries were external or internal to the VSt—in short, the economic and legal concept of the firm diverged from one another. One Finance Minister refused to discuss the issue of capital transfer taxes in the context of the one-time flat tax break for the VSt holding company because they could not predict the future level of capital transfer taxes. Späing retorted that the VSt planned to raise the level of equity in the subsidiaries in the interests of financial flexibility and better credit, which von Flotow and the ministers themselves recommended. The VSt needed to be sure that taxes on unforeseen capital transfers would not unduly burden it. The Finance Ministry refused to compromise.[40]

The VSt–Finance Ministry negotiations were furthered muddied by competing interests within the state. The Reich made it clear that it wanted to retain its veto rights in the VSt. Justice Ministry officials did not agree with Finance Ministry officials on how far they could stretch corporate tax law. The Prussian Finance Ministry did not immediately agree with the position of the Reich Finance Ministry to allow the VSt to pay its taxes in stock because it was responsible for the tax revenues of Ruhr municipalities. Finally, the Reich and the Prussian state competed with one another for quotas of VSt stock. The documentation makes abundantly clear that the state was less a unified actor than an arena of competing interests.

The Finance Ministry, however, compromised within the next month on the one-time flat fee to cover taxes arising on capital transfers, although the exact amount was not decided until May 1934. By November 1933, Reich Economic Ministry (RWM) began drawing up a draft of the law called the "Law regarding the New Order of the Steel Union-Concern." One VSt lawyer tried to convince von Flotow to intervene with the Economic Ministry to name the law more broadly, "similar to the tax relief law" of 1926. After discussions, the Economic

Ministry rejected this request on the grounds that German banks were already the object of a specific law and a more vaguely worded law was inappropriate.

As part of the refounding the VSt holding company, the Reich accepted stock in the VSt in lieu of direct financial payments, which allowed it to retain its veto rights, although its shareholding share dropped to 26.5%. The next largest shareholder, Fritz Thyssen, owned 17.9% of of the new VSt equity of RM 560 million. For the transfer of land to the four newly founded housing and land management companies, the state accepted another one-time tax fee of RM 7.7 million.[41] In their final legal form, the new VSt production groups became nineteen legally independent subsidiaries with seven sales clearing houses (Kontoren). Thus, the projected consolidation and reduction in paperwork from twenty-three manufacturing units to six groups appeared much less than originally intended. The management companies owned and controlled the working capital for general operations, inventories, and current accounts, but only controlled the use of land, buildings, equipment, and inventories in the name of the VSt. The subsidiaries operated in their own name, but were accountable to the VSt (im eigenen Namen aber für Rechnung der VSt). The trustees of the American loan effectively blocked a complete transfer of capital assets to the subsidiaries. Instead, the VSt parent company retained legal ownership of all capital assets—land, building, equipment, and inventories. All the subsidiaries listed RM 1 in their financial balances as the value of their fixed assets. The VSt subsidiaries, therefore, were something more than management companies, but less than a full product subsidiaries.

The government's viewing the multisubsidiary VSt as "one corporation" greatly facilitated the subsidiaries' acceptance by the cartels. The VSt remained a cartel member in each one of them as an "organic whole" (Ernst Poensgen). The VSt negotiated with each one of the cartels to clarify its subsidiaries' legal relationship to them, but remained present in the cartels through special sales companies with limited-liability status. The statutes of each of the new management companies carried five pages or more of dense clauses concerning its legal relationship to the cartels.

Thus, reorganizing the VSt depended entirely on a carefully crafted, complex process of negotiation that had to master the intricate relations between politics, law, competition, internal organizational change, and shareholder interests. Instead of a straightforward economizing impulse based on industry "structures" or company interests, a team of executives actively formulated corporate strategies in a complex process of policy formation, arising out of competing claims by external stakeholders and internal strategic goals. Neither VSt executives nor state ministers necessarily agreed with one another. The negotiations illustrate, moreover, the intimate institutional connections among the state, industry, and cartels in Germany. Surprisingly, in spite of the dramatic political events in Germany (the Nazis became the only legal political party, labor unions were dissolved, and Germany withdrew from the League of Nations), VSt negotiations with the Reich Finance or Economics Ministry remained on an intimate but formally legalistic, not strictly political, basis. They followed well trodden, if arcane and complicated, paths of business-government-legal relations developed throughout the 1920s.

Reorganizing the VSt

Two years of detailed planning and exasperating discussion allowed the VSt to execute its decentralization rapidly. Unlike U.S. Steel, which restructured haltingly, VSt's reorganization took place within a few months. The complete restructuring consisted of seven main parts:

1. establishing four housing and land management companies;
2. transforming company cooperative stores into independent companies;
3. establishing *Essener Steinkohlenbergwerke AG* in Essen to consolidate all subsidiary mining properties;
4. fusing eight companies into a tightened VSt holding company, thereby eliminating the ghost holding companies;
5. creating nineteen new subsidiaries and seven sales companies;
6. legally and financially transferring ownership and control of VSt properties to the new subsidiaries along with a corresponding rise in share equity to be arranged at a later date after trustees of the American loan permitted it;
7. creating a securities management company, called the *Stahlverein GmbH für Bergbau- und Industriewerte* in Berlin.

On Dinkelbach's suggestion and over the objections of the mining executives, the VSt consolidated its land and housing assets into four separate management companies. Housing assets represented a considerable capital asset and collateral for loans, but they also depressed the *profitability* of the subsidiaries. Making them independent helped reduce fusion taxes, increased the possibility of selling them, and opened new lines of credit—and conveniently the VSt made a paper profit on their founding. This move also loosened one of the traditional forms of social discipline prevalent in German heavy industry, thus transforming VSt housing administration into a modern, functional administration oriented to market conditions rather than a patriarchal form of labor discipline. Walter Cordes, an executive director of the ATH between 1951 and 1969, testified to the long-term effectiveness of this move. He felt the legal decoupling of the housing management companies eliminated many of the problems faced by German heavy industrial firms in the 1960s caused by the separation of mining from steel.[42]

By the same logic, the VSt established in October 1933 a company cooperative store, the *Westdeutsche Haushalt-Versorgung AG, Bochum* (Wehag), which consolidated VSt company stores in the Ruhr. Another one, *Siegerländer Haushaltversorgung GmbH*, consolidated individual stores in that region. The VSt also established a securities management company, the *Stahlverein GmbH für Bergbau- und Industriewerte* in Berlin in February 1934. This firm administered all VSt securities not directly *(organisch)* related to the VSt's core operations. Such organizational and legal maneuvers allowed for a cleaner and more rational administration.

By far the most complicated and financially important aspect of the reorganization involved the fusion of the GBAG, Phoenix, van der Zypen, and the old VSt holding company. It eliminated cross-shareholding of the ghost holding companies, clarifying shareholder decision-making, reduced the capitalization of the VSt, created new financial opportunities, especially for depreciation (about RM 221 million), improved profitability ratios, enabled a better assessment of the financial condition of the VSt, and altered the shareholding weight of the Reich, which had indirectly controlled a majority of VSt shares through the GBAG and Phoenix. Vögler neatly described the fusion or refounding process as a "crisis press" whereby the fusion squeezed out of the VSt the inflated, unsavory aspects of the 1926 merger. For instance, it squeezed out *112* supervisory directors from Phoenix, the GBAG, and the VSt combined.[43] After the fusion, for instance, the VSt had just 27 supervisory board members. Fusion negotiations began in earnest in early 1933, and remained secret from most VSt shareholders until October.

In order to reduce the taxes associated with refounding the VSt, the GBAG and the VSt founded the *Essener Steinkohlen-Bergwerke AG* in November 1933 to transfer all GBAG mining assets to it through a complex series of loan and stock exchanges. The VSt then merged with the GBAG (now a pure holding company) by transferring all of its assets to it. The old VSt in Düsseldorf then liquidated itself, whereupon the GBAG, Essen changed its name into the (new) Vereinigte Stahlwerke AG and moved its headquarters back to Düsseldorf (Figure 15.1).[44]

By the end of the year, the first new product subsidiaries entered the commercial register as legally independent companies.[45] Once founded, the subsidiaries acted in all but a narrow legal sense as independent companies responsible for their own financing, sales, production, and employment policies within the overarching strategy and policy of the VSt.

For the VSt, the subsidiaries once again carried their traditional firm names, reestablishing a degree of continuity with customers and reasserting their reputable brand presence. For instance, the August Thyssen-Hütte AG (ATH) reappeared as a consolidation of all of the Rhine-based iron and steel works, including those factories shut down during the Depression. New companies subsumed old rivalries. The Deutsche Röhrenwerke AG (DRW) combined the Lierenfeld and Mülheim pipe works, now called Werk Thyssen and Werk Poensgen. Others like the Bochumer Verein AG reconfirmed previous production entities. The reorganization divided other companies dramatically. The three manufacturing departments in the former ATH Dinslaken now belonged to three different companies: the Deutsche Röhrenwerke (pipes), *Bandeisenwalzwerk AG* in Dinslaken (strip steel), and the *Westfälische Union AG für Eisen- und Drahtindustrie* in Hamm (wire).

The reorganization also set up a number of sales clearing houses *(Verkaufskontoren)* for maintaining direct contact with the cartels and associations, keeping accounts with the product subsidiaries, and dis-

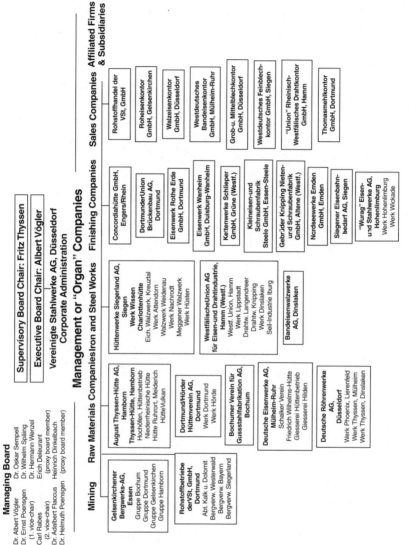

Managing Board

Dr. Albert Vögler Dr. Oskar Sempell
Dr. Ernst Poensgen Dr. Wilhelm Späing
(1. vice-chair) Dr. Hermann Wenzel
Carl Rabes Erich Deleurant
(2. vice-chair)
Dr. Adalbert Flaccus (proxy board member) Heinrich Dinkelbach
Dr. Helmuth Poensgen (proxy board member)

Supervisory Board Chair: Fritz Thyssen

Executive Board Chair: Albert Vögler
Vereinigte Stahlwerke AG, Düsseldorf
Corporate Administration

Management or "Organ" Companies

Mining

Gelsenkirchener Bergwerks-AG, Essen
Gruppe Bochum
Gruppe Dortmund
Gruppe Gelsenkirchen
Gruppe Hamborn

Rohstoffbetriebe der VSt, GmbH, Dortmund
Abt. Kalk u. Dolomit
Bergverw. Westerwald
Bergverw. Bayern
Bergverw. Siegerland

Raw Materials Companies

August Thyssen-Hütte AG, Hamborn
Thyssen-Hütte, Hamborn
Hochöfen, Hüttenbetrieb
Niederrheinische Hütte
Hütte Ruhrort, Meiderich
Hütte Vulkan

Dortmund/Hörder Hüttenverein AG, Dortmund
Werk Dortmund
Werk Hörde

Bochumer Verein für Gussstahlfabrikation AG, Bochum

Deutsche Eisenwerke AG, Mülheim-Ruhr
Schalker Verein
Friedrich Wilhelms-Hütte
Giesserei Hüttenbetrieb
Giesserei Hilden

Deutsche Röhrenwerke AG, Düsseldorf
Werk Phoenix, Lierenfeld
Werk Thyssen, Mülheim
Werk Thyssen, Dinslaken

Iron and Steel Works

Hüttenwerke Siegerland AG, Siegen
Werk Wissen
Charlottenhütte
Eich. Walzwerk, Kreuztal
Werk Attendorn
Walzwerk Weidenau
Werk Nachrodt
Meggener Walzwerk
Werk Hüsten

WestfälischeUnion AG für Eisen-und Drahtindustrie, Hamm (Westf.)
Westf. Union, Hamm
Werk Lippstadt
Drahtw. Langendreer
Drahtw. Knipping
Werk Dinslaken
Seil-Industrie Iburg

Bandeisenwalzwerke AG, Dinslaken

Finishing Companies

Concordiahütte GmbH, Engers/Rhein

DortmunderUnion Brückenbau AG, Dortmund

Eisenwerk Rothe Erde GmbH, Dortmund

Eisenwerk Wanheim GmbH, Duisburg-Wanheim

Kettenwerke Schlieper GmbH, Grüne (Westf.)

Kleineisen-und Schraubenfabrik Steele GmbH, Essen-Steele

Gebrüder Knipping Nieten- und Schraubenfabrik GmbH, Altena (Westf.)

Nordseewerke Emden GmbH, Emden

Siegener Eisenbahnbedarf AG, Siegen

"Wurag" Eisen- und Stahlwerke AG, Hohenlimburg
Werk Hohenlimburg
Werk Wickade

Sales Companies

Rohstoffhandel der VSt, GmbH

Roheisenkontor GmbH, Gelsenkirchen

Walzeisenkontor GmbH, Düsseldorf

Westdeutsches Bandeisenkontor GmbH, Mülheim-Ruhr

Grob-u. Mittelblechkontor GmbH, Düsseldorf

Westdeutsches Feinblechkontor GmbH, Siegen

"Union" Rheinisch-Westfälisches Drahtkontor GmbH, Hamm

Affiliated Firms & Subsidiaries

Thomasmehlkontor GmbH, Dortmund

Figure 15.1 Vereinigte Stahlwerke AG, 1934. *Source: MA: R 2 50 02 "Unterschriften-Verzeichnis" 1 Juli 1934; TA: VSt/2996.*

tributing contracts to them.[46] The VSt established these trading firms as small limited-liability companies (GmbHs) which closed their books without profit or loss. The sales companies solved many of the difficult problems pointed out by Wallmann. For example, the VSt could not concentrate certain products in one specific location. The DRW Werk Thyssen, for instance, continued to produce heavy plate and strip steel for sale. It sold these goods through the *Grob-u. Mittelblechkontor* in Düsseldorf. Such trading companies or clearing houses included the raw materials firm in Dortmund, pig iron in Düsseldorf, strip steel in Mülheim, rolled goods in Düsseldorf, fine sheets in Siegen, and wire products in Hamm. To preserve their interests, each of the individual subsidiaries' directors formed an advisory panel in each of the trading firms. All of these trading firms sold their exported goods through the Stahlunion-Export GmbH.

Since the VSt parent company still retained legal ownership of all fixed assets, the subsidiaries did not have any fixed assets on their balance sheets. The VSt finance and auditing office set up a so-called "clearing office" *(Abwicklungsstelle)* to manage the joint accounts for the subsidiaries' fixed assets and bond interest payments, "as if they already belonged to the subsidiaries."[47] For internal use, Büro Dinkelbach allocated the American bond debt interest expenses to the subsidiaries, as if they were directly responsible for its amortization. The VSt holding company remained legally responsible for interest payments. On the basis of these joint accounts, Büro Dinkelbach calculated the profitability and liquidity of VSt subsidiaries according to "legal unity" and "economic unity." Again, the system of accounting corresponded closely to the property relations within the VSt and its manner of organizing control.

Only after mid-1937 did the trustees permit the VSt to legally transfer property to the subsidiaries. Thereafter Dinkelbach began transferring VSt fixed assets to its subsidiaries, along with a proportion of the American debt load, using a complicated accounting procedure and loan exchange. When the war broke out, however, Dinkelbach had completed fusing the "economic unity" with the "legal unity" of the subsidiaries for only four of the subsidiaries.[48] VSt property and financial relations were so complicated that only a handful of people really understood them—*one of the reasons why Price Waterhouse recommended that Heinrich Dinkelbach act as trustee of the Ruhr steel industry after the war.*

By 1939, the VSt had paid off $26.1 million (40%) of the original $65.8 million owed to the Americans through a complicated buyback scheme regulated by the government.[49]

The founding of the subsidiaries moved along relatively smoothly, but the VSt suffered from centrifugal tendencies. Walter Borbet of the Bochumer Verein, for example, objected to the transfer of its Höntrop pipe works to the DRW. He refused to sign the management contract with the VSt because the contract forbade the Bochumer Verein from producing any types of pipes "now or in the future." At minimum, the Bochumer Verein wanted the DRW to purchase the facilities from them so as to compensate the Bochumer Verein for its "loss." Dinkelbach reminded Borbet, however, that neither the DRW or the Bochumer Verein owned the facilities, but rather the VSt activated its ownership of the Höntrop works at the DRW through its accounts. (The complex property relations of the VSt apparently confused many executives.) Borbet had quickly come to view his subsidiary as an independent company, which Fusban had warned about. Because of Borbet's resistance, within two months after the founding of the DRW, the Bochumer Verein managed to pull its Höntrop pipe works from DRW control.

The German cartel system complicated matters with Höntrop, and again influenced corporate policy. The VSt could not permit the Höntrop pipe works under the auspices of the Bochumer Verein to sell any products included in the pipe association agreements. The DRW had exclusive rights of sale. VSt central management only permitted the transfer of the Höntrop pipe works back to the Bochumer Verein under the condition Höntrop manufacture no pipes of any sort. The Bochumer Verein could use the facilities for other products. Moreover, the DRW could commandeer any type of equipment needed for pipes. These transfers threw a monkey wrench into Dinkelbach's original planning and he had recalculate DRW's pipe quotas. Borbet of the Bochumer Verein promptly objected that they were not sufficient. In addition, since the value of Höntrop's fixed assets went back to Bochumer Verein's (internal) accounts, Dinkelbach also had to recalculate the value of the fixed capital assets for both the DRW and the Bochumer Verein as well their percentage share interest on the American loan. They debated these calculations fervently for over two months. Borbet ultimately managed to pressure Vögler, Dinkelbach, and Lamarche to guarantee the Bochumer Verein a fixed 20% quota of the DRW supply of round cast iron bars for pipes. Having "won," Borbet was left with a state-of-the-art pipe plant that was not permitted to produce pipes. Borbet then aggressively transformed the Höntrop works into a major center for munitions production for Hitler's expansionary schemes.[50]

On top of this, cartel quotas affected the financing and profitability of the new subsidiaries. Undertaking an immensely complicated accounting task, Dinkelbach had to redistribute loan interest payments to each subsidiary, which carried them in their financial statements. Typically, they could not agree on the proper distribution formula and debated this internally for nearly a year. VSt managers could not decide which set of quotas should provide the basis for the new calculations: the quotas of the founding combines in the cartels before the founding of the VSt, or those based on the peak performance years 1927–1928. Dinkelbach's original plan used the peak performance quotas of 1927–1928, but the final allocation formula used cartel quotas of the founding combines *before* 1926—expressing the power of ghost holding companies and continuing merger rivalries. Plant closings and shifts in production among VSt works between 1926 and 1933 further complicated this difficult accounting task. For instance, since the VSt closed the Ruhrort/Meiderich plants during the Depression, Büro Dinkelbach had to distribute these plants' original quotas and maintenance costs to each of the new subsidiaries. In the functional structure of the VSt, such financial quotas did not affect the operations of individual plants, but under the new multisubsidiary form, the VSt parent company compensated the subsidiaries for manufacturing works closed or working at less than capacity through subsidiary financial accounts. Using the original quotas allowed the stronger sectors to compensate for manufacturing works closed or working at less than capacity through subsidiary accounts (i.e., weaker sectors), thus confronting some of the original objections presented by Fusban. In any case, the complexity of accounting and financial calculations again placed the responsibility for planning squarely on the shoulders of Büro Dinkelbach.[51] And once again the VSt never quite overcame its original merger rivalries.

Despite these complicated last minute delays, the founding of the management subsidiaries moved relatively quickly forward on the basis of the detailed, uniform organizational planning. The major differences in the subsidiaries' respective founding contracts pertained to their respective cartel and association agreements. After consulting with all the subsidiaries, the DRW received organizational "recommendations" from Büro Dinkelbach, which mapped out the firm in detailed organization charts.[52]

To take one example, the recommendations of the VSt organization office focused primarily on the proper functioning of the DRW and its commercial-administrative offices. The VSt organization office emphasized the need for a "standardization of the accounting system as well as a congruent functional *(organische)* division of responsibilities and connections among tasks." Even within the DRW, the DRW administration in Düsseldorf centralized purchasing, commercial bookkeeping, and accounting *(zentrale Bearbeitung)*, while the geographically decentralized manufacturing plants retained the operating bookkeeping, cost accounting, and miscellaneous commercial offices to handle wages, salaries, inventories, and shipping *(dezentrale Bearbeitung)* according to "uniform standards." The VSt office for organization abstractly mapped out the DRW according to lines of authority and function. The VSt office for organization also supplied a detailed expense classification chart with Hollerith codes, and created two further graphics, which charted the functional position of each of the major office supervisors and the exact proper division of labor within the general accounting office.

These organizational maps depicted "a systematic local and functional *(örtliche und sachliche)* division of responsibilities" . . . in order to bring about and ensure a faultless cooperation among all offices of the central administration with one another and with the subsidiaries *(Werken)*." Indeed the column headings divided the firm by function, the row headings along "local" areas of authority. The circles represented where specific functions took place, the dots where some secondary work took place, and the crosses where monitoring and supervision took place. These graphical charts, moreover, resembled those propagated by surveys in Germany's premier journal for organization *(Zeitschrift für Organisation)*. The planning was so meticulous that the VSt organization department recommended using specific machines for bookkeeping and statistical compilation.[53] Business management strove to become an engineering science.

Finally, the recommendations of the VSt organization office paid particular attention to the relationship between the decentralized accounts of the individual divisional groups and the centralized accounts of the VSt corporate holding company. The purchasing, accounting, and sales offices of the DRW received special instructions. For instance, all inter-subsidiary deliveries were still booked to a transitory corporate account of the VSt, not directly across the subsidiary groups themselves, although prices for such transfers were now market transfer prices. This bookkeeping arrangement allowed the auditing departments to track more readily subsidiary transactions, and kept the central office as a mediator in case of dispute.

The meticulously uniform and standardized planning eased decentralization of the VSt, and testified to the importance that Dinkelbach, Kluitmann and others placed on organizational matters, on systematic control. Delegate as much as possible but supervise. Büro Dinkelbach controlled especially through financial ratios, cost accounting, sales and production statistics, and the mapping of the entire VSt, expressed in graphics, charts, tables, figures, and statistics. These charts expressed a new, modern business sensibility at the advent of the Third Reich. The micro-planning hints at an obsession with managerial routines rather than shopfloor manufacturing considerations—one could say the difference between a Henry Ford and an Alfred Sloan (of GM). The executives working in Büro Dinkelbach represented a new type of systems manager, more at home with financial and organizational criteria in the central office, rather than on the productive criteria of the factory floor. This sensibility affected how they accounted for control, how they supervised the decentralized subsidiaries.

Accounting for Control

The essence of a multidivisional/subsidiary form was not just the decentralization of decision-making to product divisions organized under self-sufficient chief executive responsible for the bottom line, but its central surveillance system of controls. The strict distinction between overall corporate planning and central supervision in the VSt parent company from the operational management of its subsidiaries, which was unclear in the previous incarnation of the VSt, introduced a *financial conception of the control* as the dominant organizing principle. If the 1926 founding was designed to generate *productivity* gains (and thereby improve profits), the 1933 refounding of the VSt (triggered by financial and management issues: the cost of capital, overcapitalization, a fixed cost crisis, high debt levels, and rising salary and administrative costs), turned attention to the productivity of capital investment, or *profitability*. The VSt holding company judged the bottom-line performance of its subsidiaries primarily by financial criteria. A financial conception of control superseded (but did not eliminate) a manufacturing conception of control, the dominant managing rationale since the turn of the century.

One of the final steps in the reorganization of the VSt involved the codification of a series of new "fundamental guidelines." Prepared by Dinkelbach, Kluitmann, and the relevant directors of the main departments, they clarified the lines of authority between the parent company and subsidiaries. They essentially reminded the subsidiaries' managers that common VSt interests had priority over the interests of individual firms. This general principle echoed similar exhortations by August Thyssen. In internal correspondence, they phrased this principle in various ways: "the communal idea means that the common interests of the Konzern must be preserved," or "the whole," or the "common interests" of the VSt, and even the more notorious slogan: "common interest before private interest" *(Gemeinnutz geht vor Eigennutz)* popularized by the Nazis. The latter is a good example of how general principles of a multidivisional form could be expressed in Nazified ways.

The parent company maintained control over the number and type of product lines and the use of fixed assets "in accordance with the interests of the whole." The corporate holding arbitrated any disputes among the subsidiaries regarding production, sales, financing, or transfer pricing questions. For all cartel questions, the VSt negotiated as a whole. The sales clearing houses represented the VSt in individual cartel negotiations, but remained subordinated to Ernst Poensgen, who continued to act as the VSt's main liaison figure with the major cartels. The corporate holding company continued to distribute contracts to individual subsidiaries, especially for syndicated goods, so that "maximum returns for the whole could be achieved." This allowed the VSt parent company to allocate contracts to the most efficient works.

(Still, the VSt central cost-accounting office compensated underused manufacturing sites for their lack of orders based on internal quotas). With the introduction of competitive pricing (often cartel prices in the German system), VSt subsidiaries did not have to purchase products from one another, but the guidelines reminded subsidiary executives they should "unconditionally strive" to give priority to other VSt subsidiaries—a policy similar to that of the Thyssen-Konzern. Most of the other organizational instances such as the sociopolitical office, statistics, financing, purchasing (where less expensive), auditing, general legal questions, patents and licenses, press, insurance, land, and so on, remained the same as before 1933. As usual, the general guidelines stressed the creation of a unified, homogenous system of financing and accounting controls in the interests of comparison of a "full overview of the profitability *(Wirtschaftlichkeit)* of the new subsidiaries."[54]

Other general administration executives composed detailed guidelines for their areas. Continuities with Thyssen-Konzern practices cropped up in the VSt legal department. Späing, for instance, chose not to write formal guidelines describing the division of responsibilities between the central legal department and the subsidiaries' legal offices because he felt that the "agency relationship" *(Organschaftsverhältnis)* made such questions sufficiently clear. Späing also rejected an explicit subordination of the subsidiaries' legal officers to himself, "for he [the undersigned] placed considerably more value on a friendly, collegial cooperation than a personal subordination of colleagues in the legal departments of the divisions." Späing, however, had ultimate responsibility for all major legal questions, especially those concerning land, fixed assets, and patent and tax questions. Any transfer of fixed assets endangered VSt's relationship with the Americans. Vögler's assent was needed for patent questions. Finally, Späing attempted to counteract an apparent mood *(Zeiterscheinung)* within the VSt expressed by the "curious phrase" "break away from Düsseldorf" *(los von Düsseldorf)*. Späing stressed that this phrase contradicted the authority of the corporate holding company over VSt subsidiaries, which the legal theory of corporate agency or "organic" relationship required.[55] Some executives misunderstood the combination of central control and delegation of decision-making.

Rabes and Deleurant called the VSt corporate holding the "house bank of the concern" *(Hausbank des Konzerns)*, which best expressed its new role. This was a key quality of "M-form" firms in general. In legal terms, VSt subsidiaries had no credit distinct from the VSt holding company and carried no bank accounts except for a checking account and a line of credit. The VSt holding also controlled all foreign currency exchanges. Rabes and Deleurant explained that for the time being the illiquidity of the VSt and the insolvency of regional banks made strict control by the VSt corporate holding company more necessary than ever, especially since banks were eager to open accounts with the new VSt subsidiaries—one of the reasons why subsidiaries had more financial maneuverability, in theory. Rabes and Deleurant warned that this zeal on the part of banks would not necessarily mean cheaper credit for the VSt. The close financial monitoring by the VSt parent company reflected its serious financial condition as well as its fundamental role in the Konzern. Rabes and Deleurant stressed that the VSt holding company already had numerous accounts, so the subsidiaries could attain "quickest and cheapest" credit through the parent company. Moreover, Rabes felt the VSt information service *(Auskunftei)* could provide a better consulting service than banks. Similarly, the VSt purchasing department could also provide better service for critical inputs. Rabes headed the VSt central purchasing department. (At the time, the VSt considered spinning off the purchasing department as an independent company as well.) The VSt holding company, not third-party banks, would provide loan guarantees and other such liabilities. Except for *Tredefina* credits, which transferred inventory accounts to the subsidiaries, the VSt holding company had to approve of all special credits, loans, or acceptances, including those credited to third-party customers and other subsidiaries.[56]

In addition, the reorganization consolidated the VSt accounting, Hollerith balance bookkeeping, auditing, and organization offices (or *Büro Dinkelbach*) into two main offices: a *Konzern* bookkeeping and a *Konzern* auditing office. The Konzern auditing office subsumed the organization and Hollerith offices. The auditing and organization offices remained independent of the VSt bookkeeping office. Organizationally, this made the auditing and organization office a more self-reflexive forum:

> The auditing office is the internal evaluatory instance for all departments and intervenes in particular to check the diverse work of the

accounting system. The organization office evaluates the knowledge gained on the basis of a thorough examination with simultaneous consideration of the latest ideas from academia and practice for the firm's organization. It strives to increase a rational arrangement of the offices with most effective work procedures, [to provide] a fast and frictionless work sequence by formatting *(Schematisierung)* the paperwork and by simplifying operating procedures.[57]

Dinkelbach explicitly conceived of the auditing office as a fusion of applied business experience and academic advances; in a sense it played an analogous role to that of an in-house R & D office. With office mechanization and information services used to advise and transform subsidiaries' routines, the auditing and organization offices provided a clear overview and were "organically built into the gearworks *(Räderworks)* of a modern industrial firm."[58] The auditing office provided the informational lubricant for a "frictionless" organization. This image of interlocking gears or clockworks tapped into a long metaphor about bureaucracies going back to Frederick the Great's famous comment about armies. But the image of gears conceals the *manner* in which the auditing office evaluated the VSt. This manner differed greatly from the Prussian State bureaucracy and even from prior means of organizing control prevalent in German business firms before the 1920s.[59]

The homogenization and standardization of VSt accounts and organizational routines—its bureaucratization—was designed to ensure *comparable* measures of *financial* data. The VSt auditing office evaluated VSt's market performance as a whole, and of its individual subsidiaries, primarily on uniform profitability and liquidity ratios. It was less interested in the product subsidiaries' efficiency or productivity (that was left to the subsidiaries' managers). The accounting and information reports to the VSt holding stressed more heavily profitability, liquidity, sales, and the level of future orders in year-end reports of its subsidiaries. By 1935, the Konzern auditing department formatted these reports so subsidiary executives could enter pertinent financial data in a consistent manner. Supervised by Price Waterhouse, these reports and balances often provided over twenty pages of detailed financial analysis.

The auditing office constructed *two* balances or financial statements for each subsidiary: one according to its *legal* unity for official publication, and one (for internal use) according to its "economic" unity *as if* the subsidiary directly owned its fixed assets. After each of the subsidiaries submitted its individual balances and business reports, the Konzern auditing office and Price Waterhouse consolidated them into a single, public balance statement for the VSt. But the internal report provided a more accurate assessment of individual subsidiaries' economic performance. These reports paid particular attention to changes in the financial relationship between the parent and the subsidiary, especially changes in the profitability of different product lines, net revenues, total profits, and current accounts. The latter two figures formed the basis for calculating profitability and liquidity ratios. Manufacturing issues and figures played a secondary role. Then the reports used visual graphics to chart yearly and monthly changes in the most important financial posts. Before 1933, the monthly reports stressed changes in production and revenues.[60]

A dynamic balance analysis as advocated by Eugen Schmalenbach underlaid this reporting scheme. Unlike nineteenth-century accounting practice or "organic" balance analyses popular even in the 1920s, the VSt's financial analysis centered on a profit-loss statement— the firm's success. Dinkelbach called them "performance figures" *(Leistungszahlen)*. Such an analysis paid less attention to the value of the corporation as represented by the size of its assets or its manufacturing efficiency, than to the financial return it achieved from its assets or investment, or the firm's financing ability measured in terms of liquidity ratios. Moreover, the essence of Schmalenbach's balance analysis was to compare performances of various firms over time, which would control for the effects of business cycles and industry. A 1939 report prepared by Dinkelbach used the same principles to compare the performance of the VSt with other coal and steel concerns such as Klöckner, GHH, Hoesch, and Krupp. Moreover, by comparing *profitability* rates, the parent company could evaluate whether one firm or subsidiary performed more effectively than another. Manufacturing was abstracted away. The reports prepared by Büro Dinkelbach compared profit rates, the level of internal and external financing, liquidity rates, reserves, social spending, wages, employment, and so on, in absolute terms and in relation to total investment, equity, units of production, revenues, and social benefit expenditures.[61]

The decisive evaluative role the auditing and organization department played within the VSt, the separation of corporate supervision and control from divisional operations, and these types of financial analyses, clearly show that the VSt operated with a financial conception of control as its underlying organizing principle. In contrast to 1926, which emphasized manufacturing efficiency and productivity, a financial/organizational conception of control (and of the firm) replaced a manufacturing/engineering conception of control. In corporate practice, management conceived the firm less as a collection of factories, or as an organization of *production,* than as an organization of *financial arrangements.* Dinkelbach highlighted this shift in his trustee report on the VSt after the World War II, when he said that the reorganization of the VSt was intended to achieve "greater economies in management, not greater efficiencies in manufacturing."[62]

Under Schmalenbach's accounting advances and Dinkelbach's technocratic vision, the business firm became a complex "system" that internalized a number of abstracted activities, units, and offices, which could be properly arranged (and rearranged), coordinated, and supervised to assure financial control (and hopefully success). His initial 1931–1932 preparatory planning for the VSt product groups simply deconstructed, reshuffled, and reconstructed the entire VSt—people, products, equipment, plants, assets, inventories, cash, debt, mortgages, profits, and losses—on paper, in abstract statistical and financial form.[63] Manufacturing was just one business activity under others, subsumed into financial and accounting statistics. The business firm had moved away from being an entrepreneurial expression of personal property (*à la* Thyssen) to a managerially organized expression of institutionalized property *relations*—financial, organizational, shareholding, social, or otherwise.[64]

Dinkelbach was not an organizational engineer, but an organizational architect. As shown especially in Dinkelbach, authority in the corporation did not necessarily derive from ownership (Thyssen) or even formal hierarchical authority (Vögler, Poensgen), but *from the ability to persuade, control, and organize information and create knowledge.* Only by making the link between information, knowledge, and power can we explain how a mid-tier, young accountant—an accountant, this bears repeating, an *accountant*—became such a central figure. The fact that Dinkelbach was a relatively young staff *Prokurist* often caused problems of rank and seniority. Obviously having Vögler and Rabes as key supporters backed up Dinkelbach's formal authority. But the rise of Dinkelbach within the VSt, who eventually succeeded Carl Rabes on the executive board, illustrates how the multidivisional corporation "increases the volume of financial information and control . . . [and] places it more firmly in the province of the accounting profession."[65]

Reinventing the (American or German?) M-Form

The VSt reorganization paralleled the most advanced American organizational developments. Simultaneously, however, the VSt reinvented a particular German corporate form, the Konzern.

On the surface, the development of this classic centralized-decentralized form appears to be a clear case of imitating "best practice" American models. Plausibly, through Dillon Read and Price Waterhouse, VSt managers might have been made aware of similar reorganizations at DuPont, GM, Sears, or U.S. Steel. VSt executives were well aware of U.S. Steel's plans to decentralize into a multidivisional form.[66] This restructuring perfectly confirms the theoretical advantages of the M-form. The redefinition of the VSt parent as "house bank of the concern" *(Hausbank des Konzerns)* utilized a phrasing that would make Oliver Williamson proud. Williamson saw this "house bank" quality as *the* central virtue of multidivisionals because it is an "internal quasi-capital market to monitor and discipline top managers of vertically integrated organizations."[67]

Moreover, the VSt reorganization stunningly confirms Chandler's three-stage explanation for the transition to the multidivisional corporation in the United States.[68] Chandler's *Strategy and Structure* analysis can explain *why* and *how* the reorganization took place, and *who* arrived at the plan. First, the structural "conditions for innovation" had to exist, resulting primarily from the inadequacies of the traditional central office (functional) structure that could no longer cope with the intricacies of diversified product lines, the complexity of transactions, and the volume of information. There is little question that this description fit the VSt, although the VSt's organization was messier than a strictly functional form. DuPont, too, found creating autonomous divisions the most difficult part of the process, though for very different reasons.

Second, managers had to initiate a "process of innovation" that went beyond a mere "adaptive response" offered by Tayloristic scientific management. Taylorism refined existing practices on the operational level of the manufacturing "field units" and at most improved central office monitoring procedures. Instead, according to Chandler, executives had to introduce a fundamentally "creative innovation," while the "process of innovation" depended on the specific circumstances of the individual companies. GM and U.S. Steel, for example, had to create a stronger general office; DuPont and the VSt needed to establish divisions or subsidiaries. All original proposals for reorganization met varying degrees of resistance. Vögler embraced Dinkelbach's streamlining proposal, but transformed it into full product-oriented subsidiaries. Moreover, Chandler found a direct relation between the degree of internal organizational planning and the speed with which the multidivisional structure was carried out. The VSt implemented its reorganization with exceeding rapidity on the basis of extensive microplanning by Büro Dinkelbach. Chandler claims in *Strategy and Structure* that the multidivisional form also implied that the central office had a more objective or rational perspective on the business as a whole than others. So did Dinkelbach's rational systems mentality.

In the third stage of his analysis, Chandler offers a clear sense as to who became "aware" and who initiated the "process of innovation." All the *Organisatoren* (the contemporary German phrase) or "organization builders" (Chandler's phrase) were young junior staff executives, who possessed a high degree of professional managerial skill, and took a rational, systematic approach to industrial administration. Both DuPont (Donaldson Brown) and General Motors (Donaldson Brown, Alfred Sloan) had junior level-staff officers like Dinkelbach who treated organization self-reflexively as an independent variable. The VSt institutionalized organizational questions into a distinct office. Chandler's analysis fits so closely that it practically predicts the age of the organizers. Alfred Sloan was forty-four at the time of the GM reorganization; Heinrich Dinkelbach was forty-two. Like Sloan, Dinkelbach hired assistants such as Leo Kluitmann or Walter Cordes who were even younger than himself. Thus, in contrast to most assessments of the backwardness of German business, particularly those *bêtes noires* of German capitalism, German heavy industry, VSt innovations were entirely comparable to those in the most advanced American firms.

But the theoretical similarities with the DuPont story especially are counterbalanced by some crucial differences. First, the VSt operated in a very different legal and institutional environment. VSt executives had to take into consideration a number of other actors, including a state with its shareholding, Finance Ministries, Ruhr communities, and cartels. Cartel contracts affected VSt's overall strategy and limited its organizational options. Then, the central government became a Nazi government (discussed immediately below). Second, the restructuring was one of the most complex undertakings in German business history, because it pushed the bounds of what it meant to be a corporation under German corporate law. While it was common enough to consolidate peripheral firms or take over other firms into a Konzern, no other major German corporation had so self-consciously devolved its core operations in this manner. Third, the motivations for the reorganization went well beyond Chandler's functional-structural perspective (see below). It addressed overcapitalization, financing issues, and merger rivalries. It even attempted to improve company–community relations. The VSt viewed itself as part of a larger social system (community, region, nation), which one should not conflate with an older paternalism. The reorganization superseded old-style social paternalism by turning housing management and cooperative stores into separate companies that operated on market-based criteria rather than on social discipline.

Fourth, the VSt *reinvented* a familiar form of *German*, not American, corporate organization—the *Konzern* (multisubsidiary organization) or an IG (with some degree of central control over independent firms). In certain respects, VSt's *initial* organization between 1926 and 1933 was the exception to the rule in German steel, as it consciously drew on American business models. As previously argued, this unification, bureaucratization, and Americanization exacerbated merger rivalries inside the VSt. Vögler and Dinkelbach also "preferred" German-style legally independent subsidiaries rather than American-style internal divisions to open up new lines of credit, to give them more flexibility on financial markets, to tie executive responsibility more closely to true market performance, and to create self-sufficient areas of decision-making with clear accountability. What differentiated the VSt from earlier Konzerne after its reorganization was the quality of its central administration and its tight, standardized financial and accounting controls over its subsidiaries.

By the 1920s, Konzern-building *per se* was not novel, but it applied mostly to heavy industrial companies, such as Krupp, Klöckner, or Hoesch, which incorporated machine engineering or peripheral finishing firms as satellites around a core firm. The Haniel-Konzern had also formed a wide-ranging Konzern with a central office. But even within the Haniel-Konzern, the core firm, the GHH, remained a legally unified corporation; an equivalent move would have divided the GHH into subsidiaries. IG Farben and the Siemens-Konzern followed paths similar to the VSt's, but they were always collections of independent firms, and did not devolve their managements. Like GM, they created overarching central offices and routines, which developed more or less standardized sets of controls. In this regard, VSt's manner of organizing control conformed most to the Thyssen-Konzern, which had always kept all of its core firms legally distinct from one another until forced to legally, but not administratively combine. All of Vögler and Dinkelbach's reasons for reorganizing the VSt had precedents inside the Thyssen-Konzern, especially in its finance (acceptances, current-account flexibility, market transfer prices) and organization (responsiveness to product markets, clear decision-making areas, and financial accountability), and its corporate culture's stress on individual initiative and leadership.

Especially in the key offices that organized control (finance, auditing, and accounting) were continuities with Thyssen particularly strong. Späing was the chief legal officer for tax issues inside both the Thyssen-Konzern and the VSt; he played a crucial role in extending the "theory of corporate agency" to the VSt. Rabes acted as the one of the negotiators for American loans for the Thyssen-Konzern and the VSt. Dinkelbach acted as chief liaison with Price Waterhouse for Thyssen and the VSt. Along with Dinkelbach, Rabes occupied the same key internal organizational position he had in the Thyssen CAO.

Thyssen's CAO should also be viewed as the direct precursor of the auditing, financial accounting, and organizational offices of the VSt. Dinkelbach clearly admired Heinrich Hofs, the first head of the CAO, and made himself indispensable to Rabes, eventually replacing him on the VSt executive board. He was replaced as head of the VSt central auditing office by Berthold Graff. Graff, too, had begun his career in the Thyssen CAO. Symbolically, as they planned the new guidelines for the reorganized VSt, Graff requested the 1906 Thyssen CAO statutes composed by August Thyssen. Graff wanted it as a guide for the *new, post-*

1933 VSt central auditing office.[69] Later, Dinkelbach argued that he
had arrived at the fundamental idea to reorganize the VSt from his experience inside Thyssen & Co., which had been organized as two entirely independent internal companies or divisions, where he was chief
auditor: "Dinkelbach wanted decentralization, but supervision of the
execution [of the reorganization] and to ensure that everything was
handled the same in a decentralized manner so that it would be comparable. It was his Mülheim experience where Dinkelbach had already
given tasks to the operating units. (Delegate as much as possible, but
supervise)."[70]

But drawing a direct line from Thyssen & Co. to the VSt is misleading. Reckendrees shows that the 1930–1931 Group Siegerland consolidation provided the immediate prototype for a more extensive consolidation of the VSt, but Siegerland remained an internal division of the
VSt, not a fully independent subsidiary. Vögler's role in creating legally independent subsidiaries was decisive. But in conceptual terms,
the devolution of the VSt into a multisubsidiary arrangement reinvented the basic organizational *principles* consistently governing the
Thyssen-Konzern.

The major difference with Thyssen lay in the sophistication of VSt's
corporate administration. The few overarching corporate offices of
the Thyssen-Konzern hardly compared with the extent or the level
of mechanized techniques of the new VSt holding company. August
Thyssen acted as the "house bank" of the Konzern, while the CAO only
financially controlled it. They hardly compared to the control measures and routines of the VSt. The Thyssen CAO also used return on
investment (ROI) figures to evaluate company performance, implying
a nascent financial conception of control, but the VSt finance and auditing office used such financial techniques *as the primary structuring element* for organizing and evaluating its subsidiaries. And unlike the
Thyssen-Konzern, which was run by strong individual personalities,
the VSt was more of a collective managerial effort, if not "management
by committee" (sometimes to its disadvantage).

Ultimately, the VSt reorganization derived from the specific financial deficiencies and organizational dynamics originating with the incomplete 1926 merger. German institutional conditions constrained
the reorganization, and German models of corporate life inspired it.
The VSt reorganization acts as a parallel to, not a slavish imitation of,

American models. Moreover, the vaunted multidivisional form, one of the indicators of twentieth-century best-practice management is again not necessarily "made in America." Similar organizational forms, more or less coherent, could be found at Thyssen, Siemens, IG Farben, or Haniel *before* antitrust eliminated cartels, *before* the intervention of Americans, and *before* American-style oligopoly competition became firmly institutionalized in post-1945 West Germany. VSt organizational innovations tapped into German trends reaching back to the turn of the century. Nowhere can this be seen more clearly than in the figure of Dinkelbach, who played a critical role after World War II. Dinkelbach proved to be one of the main "Americanizers" of German industry and epitomized the new type of "systems manager"—more prevalent in the 1950s and 1960s—*before* Americans taught Germans allegedly American models of business.

Business Rhetoric and Business Politics

Finally, although the VSt reorganization offered amazing American parallels, the timing of the Nazi "new order" and the VSt's "new order" significantly altered the *meaning* of it. Why did Vögler and Dinkelbach undertake immense organizational, legal, financial, and political changes in the midst of a major depression and political upheaval? Because the state indirectly held a majority of VSt stock, they had to sell their plan to the government and its ministries. Their persuasive rhetoric illuminates their motives in the dramatic year of 1933.

Dinkelbach's "intended new order" memorandum and Vögler's speeches were semi-public statements about VSt's new objectives that rhetorically tied VSt's new order to that of Germany's "new order." Moreover, in February 1933, Späing wrote that "the advantages of a devolution *(Aufteilung)* from an individual economic standpoint *(privatwirtschaftlicher)* could also be achieved by the building of [internal] groups and that their legal independence should only be carried out in the national economic interest and in accord with the economic tendencies of the [Nazi] government."[71]

Indeed, the language of the Vögler-Dinkelbach plan did conform to tendencies in the new government and did react to public criticism. Some wings of the Nazi movement launched vicious assaults on the VSt for being indebted to international capital, for its opaque interlocking directories, for its anonymity and bureaucracy, and for its lack of direct personal ownership control. The Nazi movement harbored significant resentment of big business for its allegedly Jewish internationalism and the insidious influence of big Berlin banks. In general, Nazi economic ideology directed itself against liberal, "egoistic" profit-seeking that placed private interest before the common national interest; the Nazi slogan "common interest before private interest" concisely captured this attitude. In general, the inchoate Nazi corporate reform movement tended to advocate the devolution of large joint-stock companies back into smaller, personal or partnership forms with direct owner control. In the early 1930s, the Finance and Economic Ministries also heatedly debated a new comprehensive joint-stock company law that would clarify lines of control in businesses under a clear "leader" *(Betriebsführer)*.[72]

Finally, a number of senior VSt figures (Fritz Thyssen, Ernst Brandi, Erich Winnaker) were active supporters of the Nazis. Most, however, were conservatives of varying shades of black, like Vögler or Poensgen. In general, the VSt's top echelons acted ambivalently toward the Nazis. They generally thought the new conservative-dominated cabinet would constrain and tame Hitler.[73] This wariness on the part of the VSt could express itself in small ways. For instance, in mid-1933 Vögler and Poensgen purchased numerous copies of *Mein Kampf* so the Nazis would stop harassing the VSt about its loyalty. They *confidentially* directed other VSt executives to refrain from purchasing more copies of this book "as well as other books from this publishing house."[74] But because they crossed paths with the Nazis at the highest levels of government—at minimum to enable VSt's own plans—rumors arose about strong VSt support for Hitler. Yet, at one point Vögler had the audacity personally to criticize Hitler and Göring for their attitude toward and verbal assaults on Jews. Poensgen was unimpressed by the Nazis, especially by their claptrap about a national corporatist society, advocated by Fritz Thyssen.[75]

Because they were wary does not imply that they would not work with the new regime. As long as the Nazis respected the principles of private property, contained the threat of Communism, constrained union demands, and permitted the reorganization, the VSt found enough common ground to work with them.

Dinkelbach composed his August 1933 memorandum to persuade

government tax officials to back VSt's reorganization. In October 1933, the VSt sent *one hundred copies* of Dinkelbach's plan to the Reich Finance Ministry. The Prussian Ministry of Justice requested an additional *one hundred* and the Prussian Finance Ministry an additional *twenty* copies! This was a well-read document.[76] At the end of November 1933, Vögler described the full outline of the reorganization at an extraordinary session of the VSt general assembly. Prepared by Dinkelbach and Kluitmann, Vögler's speech contained nine graphics designed to present as simply as possible the entire reorganization to shareholders—a hallmark of Büro Dinkelbach.[77] In his speech, Vögler attributed the VSt's reorganization to the "firm leadership" and "calm and order" provided by the new government. In his memorandum, Dinkelbach's first point linked the two phases of the VSt's organizational history:

> After the reorganization of production has been carried out, the legal independence of the firms makes a simple and clear administration possible. Competition among individual factories *(Werken)* will not exist. Where certain products are still produced in different places, the sales activity will be uniformly regulated in a corresponding way.[78]

The Depression helped resolve the controversy over remaining overlap in the production facilities of the VSt. By transforming newly consolidated production groups into legal entities, each subsidiary could concentrate on specific lines of product and have clear zones of responsibility and administration. The subsidiaries could manage operations in their own house without having to navigate the politics of central headquarters. New sales companies would act as clearing houses for similar (cartelized) products manufactured in different subsidiaries such as heavy and medium-grade plates or strip steel, thus confronting such objections as those posed by Wallmann.

Vögler's pet interest in training the next generation made itself felt:

> With the departure of the present people, the replacement of senior directors in the company as a whole will be very difficult. After the formation of separate legal entities *(Rückbildung in juristische Personen)*, it will be relatively simple to find correspondingly competent people in both technical and commercial areas. Indeed, a solution to the personnel question propels the reorganization immensely just as it is of ut-

most importance to build a good and competent new generation of executives.

Vögler felt the younger generation of managers did not have the same all-around training in technical, financial, and commercial sides of the business as had the previous generation. The VSt reorganization worked against greater specialization in big business. Vögler thought the younger generation was more expert than his, but they did not have a chance in large firms to gain an overview of the business or assume positions of responsibility until late in their careers. In smaller firms, young managers would "automatically" gain experience more quickly.

Specialization was just one aspect of the problem. A good many senior executives in the VSt (such as Vögler, Poensgen, Rabes, Bartscherer, Kalle, and Wallmann, to name just a few) had had their formative experiences during the Imperial period. Ernst Brökelschen, for instance, who headed the VSt purchasing office in Mülheim in 1934, provided this study with some of the earliest accounts of factory life in Thyssen & Co. A similar aging elite dominated Weimar society and political culture, allowing the Nazi party to forge its image as a party of youth and dynamism. The VSt even conducted internal studies on the generational makeup of the company to analyze this problem. In effect, a generational "glass ceiling" existed in the VSt, similar to the Weimar Republic as a whole. A new wave of senior executives would come of age in the Third Reich.[79]

The reorganization expanded financing possibilities and addressed the inadequate definition of areas of responsibility within the VSt:

> Financing will be extremely simplified. In certain circumstances, mutual deliveries could be financed through current account acceptances *(Warenakzepte)*. Each firm director would again feel directly the financial burden and will thereby be forced to economize further. The product groups will remain free of all unnecessary shareholdings *(Beteiligungen)* stemming from the past and will represent pure manufacturing operations. Their leading directors will have a clear-cut activity and will no longer feel burdened with other tangential work.

Since they were legally independent firms, the subsidiaries (under control of headquarters) could extend current account credits and acceptances to other VSt subsidiaries as well as to third-party companies. This arrangement clearly echoed the notorious financing policy of the Thyssen-Konzern, which was built on acceptances and current-account credits. Within the limits of central headquarters control, the subsidiary directors would manage their own financing. The legal decentralization of the VSt also expanded the financing possibilities of the subsidiaries—one of the main objectives for the cash-strapped VSt. By clearly delineating product lines based largely, but not exclusively, on financial accountability, managerial responsibility would conform more closely to market or financial criteria. Subsidiary directors would gain a clear overview of the success or failure of their manufacturing, commercial, and financial strategies as if they were independent firms. In another memorandum from November 1933, Dinkelbach argued:

> The subsidiaries should form genuine, autonomous, and fully responsible units within the framework of the VSt. This holds true for the management of (a) manufacturing *(Betriebsführung)*, (b) sales, (c) personnel *(Menschenführung)*. As much as possible these units should be genuinely market-oriented. That means that they ought to be placed on the same basis as independent firms of the same type in their essential economic conditions.[80]

Although financing remained tightly supervised by the corporate holding company, Dinkelbach and Vögler required that the new subsidiaries combine the four main functional areas of any business firm: financing, manufacturing, sales, and personnel management. The double use of the term "genuine" by Dinkelbach stressed that these subsidiaries should pose as fully autonomous firms underneath the holding company. In his planning, Dinkelbach compared and highlighted the financial condition of the subsidiaries' main rivals, so that the subsidiaries could compete with them, in particular regarding the financing and profitability of their operations.[81] This methodology was similar to the CAO's planning before spinning off the Thyssen Machine Company as an independent firm. Finally, the reorganization eliminated the annoying habit of VSt executives in the manufacturing units of continuing to work on the securities management of their former ghost holding combines, which distracted them and complicated VSt's financial relationships. Separating out real estate and housing did the same, as well as generating profits from their establishment.[82]

In principle, Vögler and Dinkelbach introduced negotiated market transfer prices for VSt products, similar in concept to Thyssen practices. Market prices were often cartel-set prices, which differed significantly from internally set prices *(Werksverrechnungspreise)* built on cost-accounting procedures for assessing production costs in a unitary corporation. In a triangular negotiation, the VSt headquarters set prices in consultation with the subsidiaries, prices which roughly conformed to market rates, then adjusted them from time to time. In practice, after the Nazis imposed wage and price controls, the Reich Commissioner set prices.[83] But in principle, each VSt subsidiary was to become responsive to changes in product markets. Market (or cartel) transfer prices also meant that subsidiaries producing intermediate goods could turn more of a profit on internal deliveries—eliminating one of Bartscherer's most significant complaints.

The reorganization would address the psychology and organization of human relations:

> The direct connection among the factory director *(Werksleiter)* with his workers and salaried employees will be substantially strengthened in contrast to present circumstances. The regulation of working conditions in smaller units with more unified production bases is easier and healthier than in large mixed combines.

Clarifying lines of authority in the corporate holding company caused the backroom network of the ghost holding companies to disappear. Decisions became more transparent, as executives (in theory) had direct responsibility for policies governing their subsidiaries. Employees would know who made decisions for them and who was responsible for their needs. Employment policies would more easily conform to the particularities of the product and the location of the firm. In large, vertically integrated firms inequities resulted from standard guidelines. Employment policies appropriate for steelworkers in Bruckhausen was not necessarily good for tin-plate workers in Hamm or coal miners in Gelsenkirchen. Furthermore, the reorganization would put the face of authority closer to the factory floor, making it personal.

These straightforward ideas gain insidious overtones in the context of 1933. National Socialism translated common fears about big business in particular ways. Nazi economic ideologists had vague but firm ideas about how National Socialist firms would be organized. One central concept was that of the *Betriebsführer,* or factory leader. Linguistically, the term *Betriebsführer* harkened back to the workshop, department, or factory directors before the 1880s. (Thyssen & Co. used this idea, but more commonly used the term *Betriebschef).* The term implied a personal authority over workers allegedly based on the comradely bonds of a unified and harmonious work group with its firm, gruff, but ultimately sympathetic boss. (Americans might imagine this person as a type of grizzled, veteran football coach or boot camp drill sergeant.) But the Nazi version militarized the notion of the *Betriebsführer* into a platoon commander. By making the "factory leader" analogous to the role of the *Führer* in the nation; all powers and goals radiated downward. Employees became known as the *Gefolgschaft,* or followers. In Nazi rhetoric, the factory became known as a "working community" *(Arbeitsgemeinschaft),* a productive cell or unit, of the larger "national people's community" *(Volksgemeinschaft),* a racist conception of the nation that excluded outsiders *(Asozialen)* such as Jews or Communists or homosexuals. The *Betriebsführer* acted for the good of the factory community and ran the factory personally—suffering no anonymous rules, no interlocking directors, no class divisions—and in the national interest (as defined by the goals of Adolf Hitler and the Nazi party)—national (common) interest, not (individual) private interest. Nazi economic ideology offered a vision of a militarized, hierarchical, racially pure society whereby individual interest became subordinated to the national interest.[84]

Although the systems functionalism and general tone of Dinkelbach's memo is analytically distinguishable from the Nazi platoon-like comradeship between the factory director and his followers, at this historical conjuncture the two notions easily slid into one another. As found in VSt corporate statutes of 1934, required by law, Dinkelbach's phrase "works director" easily shifted to *Betriebsführer.* By 1934, Dinkelbach couched his ideas in this rhetoric by using the loaded term *Betriebsführer* instead of the neutral *Werksleiter.* In one speech, the "spiritual revolution" of 1933 "woke living spirits affecting the organization of the economy" and expressed itself in the "idea of leadership" *(Führeridee),* which gave the responsible leadership personality greater personal initiative within the ordered framework of the people and state.[85] After rhetorically embedding the reorganization of the VSt into such Nazi terminology in this speech, however, Dinkelbach slipped back into his standard technocratic language about the appropriate size of economic units, the development of information technology, the proper delineation of responsibility areas, the need for trained chartered accountants, and then essentially backed industry's position against the government's tax officials.

Dinkelbach also tied the reorganization of the VSt in this memorandum and later speeches to the notion of "corporate estate," the "concept of estates," and "estate honor" *(Stand, Ständeidee, Standesehre).*[86] The VSt reorganization would help solve frustrating problems of the VSt with Ruhr communities:

> Smaller firms are better integrated into local and regional economic life than one large company; this holds particularly true for its integration in the structure of estates *(in den ständischen Aufbau)*. The location of the administrations of the individual works will be distributed over the entire Ruhr. This decentralization should certainly be in the interests of communal associations. The seat of the individual firms will be: Düsseldorf, Duisburg-Hamborn, Mülheim, Essen, Bochum, Witten, Dortmund, Hamm, Siegen. If possible, the companies should again take up their old company names and thereby continue the good traditions of the previous firms, which is, above all, of particular significance for transacting business with customers.

Instead of suppressing the traditions of the founding combines inside its corporate structure, the reorganization tried to build on them. By accentuating reputable names for the new subsidiaries, the VSt allowed itself to be perceived as continuing in the "tradition" of these firms, effectively reversing previous policy. For this reason, Mannesmann had not joined the VSt. Commercially, it allowed the brand names of the companies to reappear for customers. For instance, Thyssen-Hamborn and Thyssen-Meiderich again became the ATH, and the Bochumer Verein reappeared. No wonder some plant executives interpreted the reorganization as a move "away from Düsseldorf." The Bochumer Verein celebrated by raising flags and ringing bells![87] But other firms became even more anonymous and were geographically subsumed inside new firms: the unexcitingly named Deutsche Eisenwerke, Deutsche Röhrenwerke, or the Bandeisenwalzwerke. Thyssen-Mülheim and Phoenix-Lierenfeld became known as Werk Thyssen and Werk Poensgen inside the DRW. In general, the more the new subsidiaries submerged former rivals, the duller became the subsidiary name.

The devolution of the VSt also had public relations and tax advantages for cities that once again had a major company in their fold. Reorganizing the VSt restructured the financial relations between the VSt and Ruhr communities. Under the previous governance structure, Düsseldorf or the Prussian State collected VSt tax revenues. With a major volume of business transactions passing through individual subsidiaries, Ruhr cities regained part of their tax base (similar to the GDK's relationship with Hamborn). When the centralized VSt did agree on donations or financial sponsorship of municipal events or communal associations, it decided in a distant, slow, and seemingly arbitrary process. The reorganization made the subsidiaries theoretically more responsive to the local needs of communities.

Such company–community problems are by no means unique to Germany, but Dinkelbach's phrasing resonated with Nazi social corporatism in the same way as the term *Betriebsführer.* The term "estates" *(Stände)* evoked a healthy middle class world of guilds and small proprietors, based on an idealized notion of an organic but hierarchical social community existing prior to the divisive social leveling and alienating effects of liberal capitalism, let alone Marxism. This corporatist idiom was one of the most powerful appeals in middle class political discourse at the time.[88] Paradoxically, Vögler and Dinkelbach situated the distinctly modern organizational innovation of the VSt in a language of pre-industrial rhetoric and imagery, or, turning it around, the pre-industrial political rhetoric concealed a fundamentally modern industrial content. This conjunction was epitomized by Vögler's speech to shareholders in October 1933, which announced the details of the fusion and subsidiary foundings for the first time. All of Dinkelbach's modernist graphs, tables, and slides—the foundation of today's business presentation style—ended with Vögler giving credit to the tremendous work it took to create them and to the new "resolute" *(entschlussfreudige)* regime, which enabled the reorganization of the German economy and the VSt. By viewing it as "thoroughly organic," the regime undertook the "serious attempt" to bring people and work together again in the "rebuilding of Germany."[89]

Finally, as Dinkelbach emphasized over and over again in almost all other memoranda, the process of decentralization remained "anchored" in the "VSt-idea" of centralizing, rationalizing, and standardizing evaluative controls, which made the statistical and financial results of all the decentralized subsidiaries comparable. The reorganization built upon these achievements: "Along with these advantages, the good results, accrued from experiences inside the Konzern up to now, will be retained in an undiminished manner."

This last point, above all, reproduced the paradox found in this study of centralization and standardization of important financial controls and information reporting, and decentralized decision-making and responsibility.

Was the VSt reorganization driven by Nazi ideological tenets? Although there are similarities, the answer would be "no." The best evidence comes from across the Atlantic, as American firms wrestled with similar problems of organizational complexity and arrived at a similar multidivisional answer (though the process was by no means the same). The parallels drawn should be viewed as a sales pitch. Internal documentation clearly shows that the reorganization was a response to VSt financial and organizational problems. Rough ideas and sketches of the reorganization had appeared in 1931. In *1931* Dinkelbach had suggested relocating group headquarters back to Ruhr cities to better use available administrative buildings. In *1933,* he rhetorically positioned this aspect of the plan as a manner of upholding corporate, organic, middle-class society itself. VSt executives had debated the plan throughout 1932 in financial and administrative terms, but in 1933 VSt managers willingly linked its economic new order with the political new order. This verbal flattering of the Third Reich contrasts dramatically with the verbal assault on the Weimar Republic.

To conclude, there are two intriguing stories here: one involving the VSt's business practice, the other involving its business politics. In spite of VSt's ambivalent relationship to the Nazis, it actively and rhetorically aligned its reorganization with the Nazi "new order." The new political order, however, did not propel VSt's reorganization. The restructuring was primarily a response to the Depression and an organizational solution to its own considerable financial and managerial difficulties.

In spite of the dramatic takeover of Germany by the Nazis, VSt's negotiations with the government in 1933–1934 follow well trodden, if complicated, paths of business–government relations developed throughout the 1920s. This continuity with Weimar tends to confirm Harold James' interpretation of the early years of the Nazi regime as having more in common with previous Weimar governments than commonly assumed.[90] Even during the Third Reich, historians should not reduce business–government relations to big business's relationship to the Nazi party. Especially under the Nazis, government was a complex, polycratic arena of contradictory interests, impulses, and personalities.

Understanding the *formation* of VSt interests is of crucial importance to assessing its stance toward the Nazis. No one VSt executive had a fixed idea of VSt's true interests. Instead, VSt interests, as usual, were forged through incessant negotiation. The VSt formed its strategy and policy in a complex *process* of negotiation using different *rationales* to legitimize any major decision. Business interests were not self-evident and did not derive in a linear fashion from a firm's structural position in the market, profit-maximizing impulse, or from its leading personalities. We need to deconstruct analytically these "interests," especially in relation to a firm's business practices. Just as the VSt had to fuse its business objectives with its political context, historians need to show how business practices informed business politics and how business politics affected business practice. It is quite surprising to note that given the noisy public debate about the destructive effects of high wages, the entire debate *internal* to the VSt turned on the costs of its own heavy debt load, overcapitalization, administration, and its own managerial deficiencies at the executive level. These factors explain its less than stellar business performance. For the same reason, it is difficult to posit a clearly delineated rationalization process because there existed no single point of view toward which the VSt could rationalize all of its operations. The term "rationalization" disguises myriad points of view, range of reasons, inherent trade-offs, and negotiated solutions. Instead, VSt interests were formed over time through a complex process of negotiation that eventually forged its corporate policy and strategy—and took into consideration "the economic tendencies of the [Nazi] government."

The other story is a less dramatic story of continuity. The reorganization of the VSt reinvented (which is not to argue imitated) the basic principles of modular management found in the Thyssen-Konzern

and the general advantages of the Konzern design found in other German firms in the 1920s. The VSt introduced a nearly classic version of
the multidivisional firm implemented by America's most modern business firms. Even if the VSt had American inspirations, from which
Traut introduced the Fretz-Moon process, the VSt transformed them
to fit their own organizational practice and institutional context. Instead, the remarkable parallels show that big business around the
world confronted similar problems of *organizational complexity* caused
by their vertical integration, sheer size, geographic spread, product
and market diversification, financial difficulties, economic and political weight in the economy, and even the high level of information being processed by new data technologies.

The ascension of the Nazis to power altered the *meaning* of these
general corporate changes in Germany. Herein lies the peculiarity of
the VSt. In the United States the terminology of managerial change remained oriented to economic efficiency. In Germany, although the
language was relatively neutral in internal discussions, the rhetoric was
explicitly politicized (much like talk of the eight-hour day). Ultimately,
the VSt's arguments for a tax break may have been cynical, self-serving,
or disingenuous in *both* 1926 and 1933, but the VSt embedded its interests in a rhetoric that attacked the Weimar Republic in 1926—in itself
a strange way of persuading those who held the legislative strings—but
praised the 1933 regime. Even Dinkelbach, who typically had a modern, functional, business-bullet-style of writing, used the rhetoric of the
Arbeitsgemeinschaft if it suited.

The VSt paid dearly for this accommodation. VSt's business practices and its business politics were not entirely congruent. This conflict came to a dramatic head in the 1936–1937 Reichswerke crisis.
Ironically, the Reichswerke crisis occurred just after the VSt liberated
itself from the state. By May 1936, the government had sold its shares
back to the VSt, making Fritz Thyssen the largest single shareholder of
the VSt (26%).[91] In October 1936, Hermann Göring launched a Four
Year Plan to lessen Germany's dependence on foreign imports and to
prepare for war. Göring wanted the VSt to mine domestic iron ore in
Salzgitter, but the VSt refused to consider mining "uneconomic" iron
ore and smelting such "technically questionable" low-quality iron ore.
The Reichswerke contradicted VSt's central strategy of bringing industry capacity in line with demand. The VSt also wanted to reassert it-

self in international export markets. In the Four Year Plan memorandum Hitler wrote: "But if the private economy believes that it is not competent to do this [mine domestic ore] then the National Socialist state will know how to solve it on its own." In December 1936, Göring condemned capitalist employers for not plunging into this venture: "if anyone cannot decide himself on the exploitation of the mines, he must sell his property, so that other people can do so." The VSt greeted Göring's speech with "hilarity."

Göring had the last laugh. Like a "bolt from the blue" (Poensgen), in July 1937 Göring announced the founding of the state-owned Reichswerke AG Hermann Göring. The Reichswerke would not only mine and smelt this iron ore, but also manufacture finished steel goods. Göring condemned "capitalistic methods" and "the crassest economic egoism" demonstrated by employers.[92]

In typical associative fashion, Vögler and Poensgen went about finding friends to support their memorandum condemning the Reichswerke plan. Allying themselves with Reichsbank President Schacht and a number of other Ruhr steel industrialists, they quietly planned an August 1937 conference to sign a joint declaration of protest. Göring got wind of their plans through wiretaps, hidden microphones, and spies. He nearly arrested Vögler and Poensgen for conspiracy. Instead—without notifying the VSt—he sent telegrams to nine other industrialists on the morning of the meeting warning them that their plans bordered on "sabotage." He also offered Krupp special financial advantages if it cooperated. At the meeting, Vögler and Poensgen lost out. The industrial front split apart. Göring had crushed Germany's single most powerful economic lobby. Göring later reminded Vögler and Poensgen of their near-treasonous acts by playing back secret tapes of their "intrigues."

The VSt lost its massive Salzgitter iron ore fields to the Reichswerke; thereafter, the Reichswerke forced the sale of VSt's majority shareholding in the Austrian iron and steel firm, Alpine Montangesellschaft. It thereby set a "precedent" for the Reichswerke to take over other firms in annexed territories. Finally, once Fritz Thyssen had "deserted" the Third Reich after September 1939—largely as a result of these economic defeats and disappointments as well as opposition to the war—the state confiscated all of Thyssen's shareholdings (managed through two financial management companies: Thyssen & Co.

AG and the August Thyssen-Hütte, Gewerkschaft, both hollow remnants of the original firms). In August 1940, the Reichswerke got its hands on the Thyssen Schachtbau company, the mining construction firm. Once again, the state became one of VSt's leading shareholders. The Reichswerke had badly defeated the leaders of German heavy industry. The VSt lost market share, production, influence in cartels, and its political clout.[93]

At the heart of the intersection of these two stories about business practice and business politics is the underlying and difficult question of how to relate changes in social (or corporate) organization to particular regime policies. For instance, IG Farben and Daimler-Benz maintained a close relationship to the German government throughout the Third Reich, as did the Imperial Chemical Industries to Britain's government and DuPont and General Motors to the U.S. government. Not surprisingly, industrial societies go to war with their industrial firms. The difference is, of course, that IG Farben, Daimler-Benz, and the VSt worked with a fundamentally murderous regime—and this transforms the context and meaning of structural relationships. In the Third Reich, meaning becomes more important than structure. Similarly, Hitler helped establish the Volkswagen plant in Wolfsburg, the most modern, most Fordist, most Americanized plant in Germany. The so-called "Americanization" or "modernization" of the German automobile industry apparently went along with Hitler's murderous plans of conquest.[94] A number of broad social, economic, and technological trends that could also be found elsewhere occurred during Hitler's Third Reich, more or less quickly, more or less intentionally than under peacetime conditions. But only by stripping structural changes, technical procedures, industrial relations, or social policy measures undertaken during the Third Reich from their specific political and cultural meanings at the time can one speak of a long-term modernization process.

Here, the modernity of VSt management practices—as technocratic and state-of-the-art as Alfred Sloan's organizational innovations at General Motors—must be integrated into VSt's business politics during the Third Reich. In fact, the most unnerving aspect of this story is that the systems rationality of Heinrich Dinkelbach, one of the best informed people in the VSt between 1926 and 1945, provided the designs for the VSt during the Third Reich as well as for the German steel industry during the Bonn Republic.

CHAPTER 16

Heinrich Dinkelbach, Organization Man

> If we want to economize correctly, we must create arrangements
> that communicate knowledge to us whether we have correctly
> economized so far. . . . But not only directors, owners, or board
> members have the need to be informed about the economic state
> of their enterprise. Everyone somehow associated with the enter-
> prise rather has an equal and justified interest [in it], its employ-
> ees, its creditors, and finally, the entire national economy.
>
> Heinrich Dinkelbach, "Nature and Construction of
> Konzern Balances," 1941

The juxtaposition of August Thyssen and Heinrich Dinkelbach illustrates the transition from Victorian entrepreneur to organization man,
reflecting the changing nature of business. What Thyssen represented
to late-nineteenth century entrepreneurial business, Dinkelbach represented for mid-twentieth century managerialism. Both were hardly
typical, as if being representative were the most important factor. They
epitomized business excellence at different points in time. Moreover,
the continuity in their ideas about corporate organization provided an
influential model for German management.

In 1952, *Fortune* magazine named Dinkelbach one of the eighteen
most important personalities in German industry.[1] Dinkelbach acted
as Ludwig Erhard's counterpart in Ruhr steel. They worked together
to transform the West German economy.[2] Marie-Laure Djelic argues
that the Americans "co-opted" people or "marginal" groups like Ludwig Erhard and the Freiburg School in order to impose their ideas
about competition policy.[3] John Gillingham and Volker Berghahn view
Dinkelbach as the "one potential Americanizer." Thomas Lux calls
Dinkelbach's ascent to the heights of the German steel industry an
"American career."[4] One of the ironies of German business history
is that Dinkelbach helped reconstruct the VSt in 1933 and deconstructed it in 1953. Dinkelbach proved willing to break with classic patterns of German industrial practice. He questioned the extent of verti-

cal integration, especially the alleged necessity to link coal and steel. He helped to realize August Thyssen's long-standing critiques of Germany's expensive cartel system. Regarding cartels, he stood in the Americanizing tradition that August Thyssen came closest to symbolizing in German steel.

For purposes of argument, let us assume that Djelic's view of Erhard as a marginal co-opted pawn for the American project is correct. The same cannot be said of Dinkelbach, who ranked third in the hierarchy of the VSt, one of Germany's flagship firms. As his postwar correspondence indicates, many regarded him as the *de facto Generaldirektor* of the VSt in 1945. His advocacy of decartelization, deconcentration, and codetermination marginalized him after the 1950s. If one follows the career of Heinrich Dinkelbach as a practitioner and signifier for innovations inside German business, an alternative continuity is disclosed within the heart of German industry that looks more American than the standard portrayal of German business permits. Leo Kluitmann felt that a full biography of Dinkelbach's life was needed to do justice to his considerable influence on German industry, especially one that would focus on his organizational innovations. Only by understanding how an accountant managed to command organization, information, and knowledge to accrue power can one explain how Dinkelbach rose to the heights of German industry. Moreover, Dinkelbach's legacy stands as one of the clearest examples of continuity in German business history. Ideas about allegedly American forms of corporate organization simmered inside German business long before the Americanization of German industry after 1945. And Dinkelbach (Figure 16.1) became one of the few German employers to promote that very un-American institution of codetermination, which placed him in a crossfire of controversy.

As typical as Thyssen's career was before his thirtieth birthday, Dinkelbach's was not. Can one consider Dinkelbach representative of Germany's twentieth-century managerial class? Even if we could answer that question in a more satisfying empirical way, the answer would still be "no." His career was exceptional.

Heinrich Dinkelbach was born a Catholic in Mülheim/Ruhr in January 1891 into the lower middle class, almost working class. His father worked as a leather tanner; his mother as a seamstress. From 1897 to 1905, Dinkelbach studied at the local Catholic public school in

Figure 16.1 Heinrich Dinkelbach. (Reproduced with the permission of the ThyssenKrupp Corporate Archives, Duisburg)

Mülheim. He excelled so well that he skipped two grade levels. Later in life, he credited these elementary schoolteachers for providing the motivation and educational basis for his high-flying career. (Characteristically, he later noted that those six years constituted exactly 10% of his life, yet only 3% in the life of the school—a statistical point only Dinkelbach might choose to highlight. He had a self-professed weakness for such calculations, which regularly occur in his letters.)[5]

His family could not afford higher education or university, which foreclosed the possibility of his becoming a teacher, his first career choice. Instead he apprenticed as a commercial clerk in 1905 at a local construction company and received a commercial education certificate in a school for continuing studies. At eighteen, in 1909, he joined the Thyssen & Co. Machine Company. He worked directly under Karl Härle and Gottlob Fassnacht. He had initial difficulties with Fassnacht, who nearly fired him, but Härle entrusted him with more and more responsibilities. In 1912, Härle charged him with developing a Hollerith department for inventory accounting, one of the first of its kind in

Germany. In 1913, at a mere twenty-two years of age, he was named by
Härle chief of the bookkeeping and internal auditing offices. There
his work brought him into direct contact with Heinrich Hofs, Heinrich
Kindt, Berthold Graff, Carl Rabes, and Hermann Eumann, all of
whom were key figures in the Thyssen accounting system. Dinkelbach
credited Hofs for educating him about accounting and organization,
and Härle and Rabes for furthering his career.

During World War I, Dinkelbach became a crucial figure at Thyssen
& Co. Declared unfit for service, he remained with the Machine Company. With Härle at the front until 1917, Dinkelbach managed the Machine Company's accounting system. He introduced American-style
bookkeeping procedures. After both Thyssen & Co. companies fused
in 1918, he revamped the entire accounting system for both Thyssen &
Co. divisions. In contrast to his industrial relations policy after World
War II, Dinkelbach organized the lockout of Thyssen & Co. workers in
1923. In doing so, he actually overstepped his authority. His bosses formally reprimanded him, but not for his effective organization of the
lockout. By thirty, Dinkelbach headed the auditing department of one
of the premier engineering firms in Germany. At thirty-two he received power of attorney *(Prokura)*. Impressed, Rabes transferred him
to the main CAO headquarters in April 1925, just before negotiations
to form the VSt, which made him privy to insider information. There
he came to the attention of Fritz Thyssen.

Theodor Gessel, who worked with Dinkelbach in the ATH and the
VSt, argued: "Looking back it seems to me that the former supremacy
of Mülheim in the Thyssen complex disappeared with the transfer of
Herr Dinkelbach to Hamborn, and the preeminence of the August
Thyssen-Hütte, Hamborn, should be dated from this point on."[6]
Gessel's interpretation goes too far (ATH's precedence inside the
Thyssen-Konzern dates to World War I), but his comment indicates
the important role that Dinkelbach began to play. He became acting
head of the Thyssen CAO, concentrating primarily on the internal accounting affairs of the Konzern, while Rabes focused on external financial relations. Rabes dealt directly with Dillon Read, while Dinkelbach worked closely with Price Waterhouse. His contacts with various
Price Waterhouse managers would play a key role in Dinkelbach's
overall career and in the history of the German steel industry. Because
accounting and financial criteria played such an important role in

founding the VSt, his star rose even further, as Dinkelbach assembled the statistical data used by Thyssen to debate VSt share quotas.[7] In those debates, he came into contact with a whole series of executives from the other merged companies, who became lifelong colleagues and friends—for instance, Peter van Aubel.

Dinkelbach sat in the surveillance eye of the VSt, the self-described *Büro Dinkelbach*, which gave him an authority well beyond his formal place in the hierarchy. Along with his colleagues, Dinkelbach introduced a distinct systems sensibility into VSt's organization. His memoranda for the 1933 reorganization best expressed his method of thought. Dinkelbach used greatly simplified terminology, almost bullet-pointing, and functionally organized his thoughts into clean paragraph blocks, which then built logically on one another. All his organizational recommendations for the new product subsidiaries used the same format to provide standardized portraits of each. In themselves, these planning memorandums acted as models of modular thinking, reminiscent of functionalist Bauhaus architecture. Such pared-down modernist memos would fit into any business today. The memoranda testify to Dinkelbach's technocratic systems orientation, which consistently broke down larger issues into cleanly delineated smaller concepts, which he would then build up to form an (allegedly) harmonized, perfectly consistent, rationalized whole.

After VSt's reorganization, Dinkelbach became a proxy member of the executive board at forty-two. In 1936, he succeeded Rabes, becoming a full-fledged member of the board and senior commercial director of the VSt. His formal authority now corresponded to his informational authority. Walter Cordes, one of Dinkelbach's closest friends and colleagues—and later the commercial director of the ATH between 1951 and 1969—felt that Dinkelbach always maintained a close contact with former Thyssen enterprises inside the VSt.[8]

One example brilliantly illustrates the new role Dinkelbach played in the reorganized VSt and highlights a continuity with the Thyssen-Konzern. Franz Bartscherer, director of the VSt subsidiary, August Thyssen-Hütte AG, once complained to Dinkelbach that the transfer prices set for intermediate materials delivered to the Deutsche Röhrenwerke AG (DRW) disadvantaged his subsidiary. According to Bartscherer, the DRW had taken advantage of the newly released prices set by the Reich Commissioner to lower their purchase prices for ATH goods. (At the time, the Nazis controlled important materials and foodstuff prices.) Bartscherer wanted to alter retroactively the transfer prices to the previous level. Dinkelbach tried to resolve the dispute by means of a personal letter:

> We have known each other so long, that you should have the conviction about me that I have an objective and proper attitude about all [such] questions. Concerning the question of prices . . . I must safeguard the interests of the Aug. Thyssen-Hütte as well as the interests of the Deutsche Röhrenwerke. . . . After the Deutsche Röhrenwerke asserted their claims for price reductions in time . . . I cannot presume upon the Deutsche Röhrenwerke to recognize the position taken by you, even less so, because the Aug. Thyssen-Hütte justifies its stance with an earlier price regulation, which has nothing to do with the present price question. . . . I ask of you to review the context once again and to agree kindly with my recommendation, whereby I ask you to regard as well that the Deutsche Röhrenwerke has always taken a generous viewpoint in the setting of prices for the intermediate goods deliveries of the Aug. Thyssen-Hütte for the production of steel pipes. I would naturally have nothing against it, if you arranged yourself to sway the Deutsche Röhrenwerke to accept your point of view for the materials deliveries for the production of cartridges, only I cannot presume upon the Deutsche Röhrenwerke from here due to reasons of principle.
>
>   When I spoke recently with Herr Director Scheifhacken about the present matter, I had the impression as if you held the view that Herr Director Kreis, who is my advisor in these questions, did not always take a consistent and friendly point of view for you. Insofar as I can see the matter from here, I can only say the opposite about the attitude of Herr Director Kreis. The treatment of such questions in the Konzern is not always easy, because completely contradictory positions have to be reconciled *(überbrückt)*. We try to take into consideration sympathetically the interests of the [individual] works in question with respect to the preservation of the entire interests of the Konzern. It is extraordinarily important to me that you also are convinced that we have preserved the above principles. If you have reason to think differently, then I would be extraordinarily grateful to you, if you, Herr Kreis and I could have the opportunity to clear up all the misunderstandings—and

they could only be misunderstandings—in this regard as soon as possible in a personal meeting.

Bartscherer wrote back a week later agreeing rather heavily to Dinkelbach's "recommendations." According to Bartscherer, the particular amount of loss was of no consequence, but "we only see once again that we should be disadvantaged with this decision as well, just as we almost always have been in the course of the years." Bartscherer left the matter with a "feeling of unfairness." The ATH lost.[9]

In effect, Heinrich Dinkelbach was the evolutionary heir to August Thyssen, playing the same mediating role between the ATH and DRW that Thyssen, and later the CAO, played between the GDK and Thyssen & Co. (Indeed, both these subsidiaries were successor firms to the GDK and Thyssen & Co.) Dinkelbach's attempt to stress the interests of the whole firm versus the interests of individual firms, harks back to Thyssen's reprimand in the dispute between Thyssen & Co., Berlin and the GDK in 1898. The dispute also echoes similar long-standing conflicts about transfer prices between the GDK/ATH and Thyssen & Co., which Bartscherer knew all too well. It also highlights the critical organizational-political problem of transfer prices within any enterprise. Finally, the tone of the letter reproduced Thyssen's tone of polite but professional correspondence. Dinkelbach's tone sounded more ingratiating, more interested in papering over irreconcilable differences, rather than the civil but authoritative correspondence of Thyssen. But Dinkelbach's rational, conciliatory tone also left little room for other opinions. Misunderstandings could arise, but they could be only irrational misunderstandings. Once all factors had been considered, as Dinkelbach implied he did, "objectively" there could be little other choice but see it his way.

Dinkelbach did not gain authority in Thyssen & Co., the ATH, and the VSt because of his background, education, or ownership, but because of his expertise with information. He had a remarkable memory. Cordes remembered: "I have known very few people who commanded the great art of portraying the economic possibilities so sensibly through a combination of figures that everyone, who had to make decisions afterwards, were convinced by the correctness of the ideas presented. Dinkelbach could juggle numbers until the sweat dripped from the brows of his subordinates."[10] This did not always work to his advantage. Walter (Panzer) Rohland related one anecdote with glee. Rohland succeeded Ernst Poensgen as chair of the VSt executive board, headed Albert Speer's organizational "ring" for tank production, and was one of Speer's closest colleagues. Rohland remembered how Dinkelbach gave one lecture so studded with impenetrable statistics, so boring his audience, that Poensgen simply cut off his presentation. Relations between Dinkelbach and Rohland were tense, especially after 1945. Rohland remained unrepentant, insisting in his autobiography that forced laborers lived a tolerable life in the armament factories of the Third Reich and that the victimization of Germans "settled the score" for the genocide of Jews.[11] Dinkelbach fundamentally changed his life and world-view after the war. Not surprisingly, Rohland was one of the very few German executives who did not reenter industry after war's end.

If Dinkelbach's influence had extended only to the Thyssen-Konzern and the VSt, no mean accomplishment for an individual career, he would remain a lesser-known figure. But in his associational role in the zone between public and private spheres, Dinkelbach's activities greatly influenced broader patterns of German business.[12] Dinkelbach's ambition to combine the latest techniques of *praxis* with the newest ideas of the academy gave him an extremely high but quiet profile in the national economy before 1945.

Perhaps his lack of formal education made him particularly eager to anchor his ideas in academia, but he also remained a teacher at heart. Büro Dinkelbach maintained close contact with academic and professional societies, an explicit strategic objective of VSt guidelines. VSt's pioneering accounting and organizational innovations influenced academic theory and set new standards for the entire industry.[13]

The University of Cologne was the leading center for theoretical research on auditing, accounting, and economics. With the avid support of Konrad Adenauer, Cologne became in 1919 the first university in Germany endowed with a chair for economics. In 1941, the University of Cologne named Dinkelbach an "honorary senator" in economics because he "designed the entire organization and accounting system in model fashion in one of the largest German enterprises and thereby also helped to bring the theoretical research of the Cologne economics research into practice."[14] The VSt experience, in turn, influenced the theoretical work of the Schmalenbach Society. In this respect, Büro Dinkelbach achieved its mission.

His formative Thyssen and VSt experiences influenced his management ideas, which he disseminated into academia through formal and informal means. In his speeches from the *1930s,* Dinkelbach emphasized the proper "delineation of spheres of responsibility" to avoid "organizational frictions" and to enhance personal initiative. Good organizational form should link responsibility centers directly to performance and profit—a classic Thyssen virtue. Dinkelbach constantly stressed that organization, especially of large enterprises, had to be clearly and self-reflexively designed. Above all, the accounting and information system—through strategic, task, and process plans and aided by technical means—represented a critical "instrument of knowledge" and learning.[15] He sought to enable large enterprises to react to the market as swiftly as did smaller enterprises by organizing according to "building blocks" *(Bausteine)*—one of his favorite phrases—and by delegating direct responsibility to talented people lower in the hierarchy.

Dinkelbach (and other important VSt figures such as van Aubel, Kluitmann, Graff) also contributed by setting new standards for the nascent German chartered accounting profession. Dinkelbach was a talented autodidact. Van Aubel, Kluitmann, Graff, and Cordes, who were all Dinkelbach's subordinates, had all studied under Schmalenbach.[16] Reinforced by their connections with Price Waterhouse, Dinkelbach and van Aubel took a particularly strong interest in the creation of an Institute for Public Chartered Accounts, which has ensured professional standards to this day. Both Dinkelbach and van Aubel participated in the advisory committee for the milestone accounting act of 1931, which more or less institutionalized Schmalenbach's recommendations for joint-stock company financial disclosure. The act was one of the most significant regulatory acts for joint-stock companies since 1884, codifying standards so that corporate financial statements would become comparable and meaningful.[17] This activity kept them in continuing contact with Schmalenbach throughout the Third Reich and into the postwar period.[18]

In the early 1930s, Dinkelbach became a member of the commission for testing new chartered accountants at the University of Cologne and Münster. Between 1935 and 1945, Dinkelbach sat on advisory boards regarding balance, accounting, and testing standards for the Academy of German Law as well as in the central committees in the Reich Justice, Finance, and Economic Ministries. In 1934, Dinkelbach became a member of the Schmalenbach Society. *Before* the American-ization of German business after 1945, Dinkelbach lectured at the yearly conference of steel industrialists and engineers and at the Düsseldorf Academy of Administration to explain the organizational implications of the multidivisional/multisubsidiary firm, with its strange mixture of centralizing and decentralizing tendencies. In his lectures, Dinkelbach emphasized the need for clearly organized com-petencies to avoid redundancy and to reduce bureaucracy, rigidity, and stasis. Dinkelbach placed particular emphasis on the use of orga-nizational charts, flow charts, graphics, preformatted and standard-ized forms, office machines, and most importantly, the accounting sys-tem itself. All of these were particularly important for running a large-scale operation. Dinkelbach stressed the systematization and study of corporate management itself.[19]

He also stressed new ideas regarding the proper disclosure of Konzern balances, which he felt were less well developed in contrast to the United States, the "motherland of trusts." He criticized German law's tendency to treat corporations as separate legal entities rather than economic unities, except under the complicated theory of corpo-rate agency. (Not until 1996 did German regulatory reforms address this issue.) Dinkelbach complained that half of chartered accountants' work consisted of revising "heterogenous" postings. Without unifor-mity, financial statements were just masses of meaningless numbers. He particularly objected to the disarray of accounting standards within any one Konzern. It should be treated as an "economic unity" with a consolidated balance sheet. Dinkelbach credited the need to turn to American capital markets with improvement in Konzerne financial statements—a neat parallel with the 1990s. He was speaking of the Thyssen-Konzern and VSt in the 1920s. Moreover, appearing in 1941, his statement was somewhat remarkable because it credited interna-tional capital, rather than disparaged it. Dinkelbach's thinking about Konzern financial statements appeared in Schmalenbach's *Journal of Commercial Research,* which Schmalenbach personally edited until 1933.

> If we want to economize correctly, we must create arrangements that communicate knowledge to us whether we have correctly economized so far. These arrangements depend on the size and type of economic entities to be assessed. At first the director and the owner of the enter-

prise have an interest to have clear knowledge about the economic processes [of the firm]. In most enterprises, because of their legal form board members or shareholders substitute for the role of the single proprietor. But not only directors, owners, or board members have the need to be informed about the economic state of their enterprise. Everyone somehow associated with the enterprise rather has an equal and justified interest [in it], its employees *(Gefolgschaft)*, its creditors, and finally, the entire national economy.[20]

Today, we would say that corporate governance issues interested Dinkelbach, who always viewed accounting, knowledge, and financial reporting as being at its heart.

At present, the available evidence is too sketchy to form a solid judgment of Dinkelbach's ideological position during the Third Reich. Throughout the Third Reich, Dinkelbach tended to concentrate on arcane (for political historians), but important matters (for business historians). His public statements during the Third Reich concentrated on technical issues regarding the proper management of large enterprises. Professionally, Dinkelbach managed to concentrate on VSt finances right up until the end of the war, even though bombs had razed his own home. In 1944, he became the VSt chief financial officer, taking over for Deleurant. He appears to have largely ducked the burning political issues of his day, remaining an organizational insider. In a *private* letter from 1947, a friend wrote Dinkelbach about an informal talk they had had in 1943 on the street where they felt they simply "had the wrong colors and that our time has not yet come."[21]

There are some traces of weak support for the Nazi party, but as with most Catholics, Dinkelbach appears to have been immune to the dubious appeals of Nazism. In 1933 he gave a voluntary contribution to the SS, and continued doing so irregularly until 1935. He gave donations amounting to RM 20/month to the Nazi party, which he later explained was a result of constant Nazi "begging." Like many other leading Germans, he became a member of mass Nazi organizations such as the German Workers' Front or the National Socialist Association of German Technicians. After consulting a priest (a sign in itself), he belatedly joined the Nazi party in December 1938 at the urging of a fellow colleague in the VSt. Joining may have had something to do with the Reichswerke-VSt crisis of 1937, where VSt executives' loyalty came into question. Dinkelbach received a temporary card. According to Dinkelbach, he transferred his membership to another Nazi district because he knew the leader there would not drag him further into "party-political" affairs. What all this actually meant to him is still a matter of speculation. Unlike the leading, symbolic figures of the VSt such as Albert Vögler, Ernst Poensgen, or Walter Rohland, Dinkelbach remained one of the key behind-the-scenes figures without great public profile. During the 1930s and 1940s he remained active in various committees and ministries regarding chartered accounting and public financial statements. In 1941, he joined a special commission of the Reich Finance Court to discuss consolidated balances.

Dinkelbach wore a cloak of grey-suited ambivalence towards the regime. On one hand, he objected to one Nazi attempt to pass a new joint-stock company law that would make the chair of the executive board a political decision. On the other hand, one can clearly find some affinities to Nazi ideology in his speeches. Dinkelbach's ideas, such as promoting young talent, the decentralization of large firms into smaller, advocating less bureaucratic units which better fit the "estate" (Stände) order of communities, delineating clearer lines of authority under the "leader of the firm" (Betriebsführer), and viewing the firm as the "cell of the economy," all found resonances with Nazi economic ideology. However, these ideas also prefigure his behavior in the new West Germany.

From personal letters explaining himself after Germany's defeat (and thus needing a degree of skepticism), Dinkelbach appeared as a rather passive participant in the Third Reich, who went along without overt resistance or dissent. He neither aggressively took advantage of the opportunities the new regime offered, nor did he retreat into an inner exile. Instead, Dinkelbach was among those who kept the VSt and the Third Reich working to the very end by going about their business. One must also remember that he was one of the best-informed members of the VSt throughout the war. He knew about the Jews forced out of the VSt; he knew about the conflict with the Reichswerke; he knew about the VSt's interests in occupied territories; and he knew about the use of slave laborers.

Dinkelbach would have especially known about the persecution of Schmalenbach for having a Jewish wife. In 1933, the Nazis forced Schmalenbach to retire. In 1941, helped by friends, Schmalenbach went into hiding to save his wife.[22] In a private letter to Berthold Graff's wife, Dinkelbach admitted that Graff (VSt chief of auditing after 1933) was always a sympathetic listener when they needed to find a place for persecuted Jews—possibly a reference to Schmalenbach's case. On the other hand, Dinkelbach did not disavow himself from dealing with Schmalenbach's successor, who was an overt Nazi. Dinkelbach joined the Schmalenbach Society just after Schmalenbach was forced out. Cordes' edited volume on Schmalenbach's life and influence inexplicably does not mention Dinkelbach at all, let alone refer to any direct support for Schmalenbach during the Third Reich (van Aubel, Kluitmann, and Potthoff all play important roles). Yet Cordes remained close with Dinkelbach into the late 1950s and considered Dinkelbach his honorable mentor.[23] Because Dinkelbach's motives and actions were so unclear, Dinkelbach gave the impression that he was simply an ambitious opportunist—an accusation that would continue to haunt him.

Immediately following the war, Dinkelbach maintained good relations with a diverse array of people. He was on speaking terms with some figures thoroughly tainted by Nazism (Walter Rohland, Karl Arnhold of DINTA, or Friedrich Flick), but also with a number of Jews.[24] Returning from exile, one former VSt Jewish director felt comfortable enough with him to complain about continuing anti-Semitic rhetoric and asked Dinkelbach to intervene on his behalf.[25] In 1947, Dinkelbach asked a half-Jewish executive, Landau Remy, to take a director's seat in a new company, but Remy turned the position down because of persistent anti-Semitism lurking just below the surface. Dinkelbach agreed.[26] Dinkelbach's personal openness and political tractability allowed him to gain new friends easily, but this same flexibility also acted as a lightning rod for suspicion.

Most important to understanding his behavior and political direction, Dinkelbach remained devoutly Catholic. He attended a Catholic church regularly during the Third Reich and engaged in charitable causes as the war progressed. During the war, Dinkelbach (among others) underwent a reaffirmation of his Catholic ideals or, more strongly, a conversion to Catholic social thought. By the end of the war, he viewed himself as a Catholic entrepreneur, joining the Association of Catholic Entrepreneurs in 1949.[27]

Whatever Dinkelbach's involvement in one of Germany's most

prominent firms, it did not cast a long shadow over his postwar career. Dinkelbach moved squarely into the public spotlight for the first time. The Ruhr fell first under the control of the Americans, then under British occupation authorities. The British quickly rehabilitated him, considering him clean of Nazism. Dinkelbach was the *only* VSt board member not arrested in December 1945.[28] By default, he became General Director until October 1946 when the British appointed him trustee of the steel industry. It is still not entirely clear how Dinkelbach gained the confidence of the British so rapidly, but Price Waterhouse executives, with whom Dinkelbach had had contact since 1924, were critical for the British action.[29] His wide-ranging knowledge of the steel industry, especially his knowledge of the complicated and unclarified financial state of the VSt, made him absolutely invaluable. Moreover, in 1945 Schmalenbach came out of hiding and immediately appointed him to a special commission of public accountants for the politically and racially persecuted. They both discussed the future intensely in the immediate aftermath of the war.[30] For Dinkelbach, Zero Hour ushered in a new era of opportunity. In a letter to van Aubel, Dinkelbach associated the "reconstruction of the economy" with the "reconstruction of souls." He once thought: "Much energy, trust, and love is necessary. Above all, we need love. Only it provides us the necessary protection."[31] His economic expertise fused with a revitalized religious conscience to give him strength to carry on. He would need it.

Before the war ended (May 1945), Dinkelbach and others began ruminating about the future of the VSt and the German steel industry. In June 1945, he and Hans-Günther Sohl helped Rohland prepare a deeply apologetic memorandum about the role of Ruhr industry in the Third Reich to convince authorities to rebuild it, but the memo failed to persuade even many Ruhr industrialists.[32] Three months later, while most Ruhr industrialists began coalescing around a self-described "Sohl-Kreis" that advocated restarting coal and steel production on the same "unbroken dynamic" basis, in October 1945 Dinkelbach presented an alternative "new order" for the German steel industry.[33] This so-called Dinkelbach plan would break up the great steel *Konzerne* and *Kartelle* into small, market-oriented, flexible units that could begin manufacturing as quickly as possible. Dinkelbach called them "building blocks."

From this point on, Dinkelbach worked at odds with most of his fellow colleagues. Dinkelbach often had to remind his critics that on the basis of the July 1945 Potsdam agreement, the Allies mandated the dissolution of large firms. Germany had no choice. Dinkelbach viewed the defeat as an opportunity to reshape the German steel industry, or at least guide the inevitable deconcentration into productive and socially acceptable channels.[34]

The plan also expressed Dinkelbach's notion that the VSt (and other German Konzerne) were too vertically integrated, too complicated, and too large for their own good. The "building block" model appealed to his technocratic tendency to delineate responsibility into small, efficient, market-oriented—and now socially responsible—economic units. At minimum, he felt smaller firms would be able to start up operations more quickly, thereby providing employment and contributing to their communities. This appealed to his resurgent religiosity and new-found empathy for workers. Dinkelbach leaned on ideas taken from social Catholicism, which stressed the building of a new theologically based community among men, and a vague third way between capitalism and socialism. In his vision, private property would remain largely untouched, but become capitalism with a human face. Such religious underpinnings would also help rehabilitate German industry.[35]

Only loosely can Dinkelbach be called an "Americanizer." At minimum, these ideas meshed well with Allied plans to decartelize and deconcentrate German heavy industry, which they blamed for the success of Nazism.[36] One must remember that standard Allied explanations at the time for the rise of Nazism rested on the assumed insidious political results of economic cooperation among cartels, concerns, and banks, which we would now associate with a Marxist interpretation of German acceptance of the Nazis.

As a result of this memorandum and because of recommendations from Price Waterhouse figures, William Harris-Burland, the British military head (a chartered accountant in private life), appointed Dinkelbach in October 1946 to the position of trustee of the British North German Iron and Steel Control Board (*Treuhandverwaltung* or Treuhand). Throughout the coming ordeal, Dinkelbach became close, lifelong friends with British authorities such as Harris-Burland, Brian Robertson, Sir Reginald Wilson, J. B. Clark, and George Cusworth (the latter became a particularly good friend). The board became a model of British-German cooperation—or "collaboration" as some of his colleagues felt.[37]

In December 1946, Dinkelbach presented another deconcentration plan. His fellow industrialists were mortified, for it would liquidate the historic Konzerne, eliminate their vertical integration, and dismantle a great number of key plants. Moreover, with the support of the British Labour government, this plan appeared to be the first step toward socializing Ruhr heavy industry. The financing and operations of these new, smaller companies, called "management companies" (Betriebsführungsgesellschaften)—shades of the VSt—would enable them to begin operations. Dinkelbach reiterated over and over that these smaller companies were mere "building blocks," which could begin constructing a new economic house, whose ultimate form could be decided later by the German people. Beginning production swiftly, more or less efficiently, was in the interest of industrialists, workers, and the public at large. Furthermore, he argued that breaking up old structures would provide a "foundation" for a "new order." Dinkelbach tried to explain that his plan merely executed decisions decreed by British occupation authorities and made no final decisions regarding decartelization, the constitution of the new Germany, or the role of private property.[38] At a supervisory board meeting of the Hüttenwerk Oberhausen AG in 1947, Dinkelbach also expressed misgivings about the lack of political clarity, but stressed adamantly that they must make the best of things and not wait until all the largest questions were decided.[39] In a 1954 radio interview, Dinkelbach continued to defend himself:

> One had to have the courage to work where it was possible in order to employ people, find sales, to take care of things in order to have the means to carry out the whole thing. These considerations had nothing whatever to do with the attempt to reconstruct the German economy, in particular the German steel industry, and steer it onto particular rails. I have always said that one should collect building blocks.[40]

In private, Dinkelbach debated the pros and cons of private property with the Catholic intellectual, Peter Wilhelm Haurand, in which he defended it, but thought it should be tempered by social considerations. His extensive correspondence with Haurand demonstrates the extent to which Catholic social thought informed Dinkelbach's advocacy of codetermination.[41]

Judging from his past and later behavior, he did favor smaller, economically efficient production units that oriented themselves to market signals, rather than traditional cartel pricing or bureaucratic planning that he learned to distrust within the VSt. At a lecture to the Schmalenbach Society in March 1948, Dinkelbach argued that many small companies would be more difficult to socialize than larger ones, although this did not appear to be a driving consideration in 1946. He stressed that the new management companies would be of optimal size and felt it important to reestablish freedom of contract among firms. But he rejected the alleged necessity for complete vertical integration, distancing himself from most of his fellow steel industrialists, who argued that technical and energy economies required it and "forbid the schematic application of business economics principles."[42]

At the end of 1946, Dinkelbach's subtler points were by no means obvious. Backed by the British, Dinkelbach's plan became official policy. He became one of the most controversial figures in the German economy. Industrialists assaulted it as the first step to socialization, a violation of their property rights, or at least a step toward the elimination of the German steel industry as a competitive force in world markets.

The attacks became personal. One friend spoke of near "incessant irritations and harassment," which Dinkelbach had to weather over the next seven years.[43] Haurand's daughter, who worked as Dinkelbach's personal translator, experienced the incredible "bitterness" surrounding his office.[44] Hermann Reusch (son of Paul Reusch, director of the GHH, and now leader of the main Iron and Steel Trade Association) egregiously accused Dinkelbach and his Treuhand employees of engaging in orgies at work. He, and others, fallaciously equated Allied deconcentration measures with the Aryanization of Jewish property.[45] Others attacked Dinkelbach as a traitor or collaborator. More mildly, others accused him of promoting VSt interests against other German firms. At minimum, almost all fought against the dissolution of the old Konzerne as economically unsound.[46]

The slings and arrows of former colleagues only added to his physical and mental agony, further harming his health. In 1947, Dinkelbach complained to British authorities about his deteriorating health and relations with fellow colleagues. His position as trustee put him in the awful position of listening to public attacks on his person or his policies by former colleagues, yet receiving innumerable letters from the same people wanting to return as executives in the new companies—Rohland being especially persistent.[47] To one former VSt executive, he described the job as "extraordinarily difficult, requiring much work, patience, and nerves."[48] On top of this, his wife, too, fell ill frequently. The Allies did not release his son from a POW camp until October 1946. Finally, obituaries of former colleagues filled his correspondence, which probably added to a sense of his own mortality. Over the next fifteen years, Dinkelbach was constantly readmitted to hospitals or convalescent spas for intestinal problems and exhaustion.

Heightening tensions of the Cold War shifted British occupation policy, particularly regarding the socialization of the Ruhr. In January 1947, the British and American zones merged into the Bizone. American policies took the upper hand, which advocated deconcentration but with a firm commitment to private enterprise. The Marshall Plan of June 1947 to reconstruct German industry placed Dinkelbach's plans on a whole new basis. The Americans began to take a greater interest in Dinkelbach, whose intentions initially baffled them:

> According to reports, which I have been receiving for some time now, Dinkelbach is described as an opportunist who has known how to adapt himself to changing conditions and ingratiate himself with the-power-that-be, regardless of principles. It has been evident for some time now that Dinkelbach has been changing his course since it became obvious to him that the United States Government was about to gain more influence on economic affairs in the Ruhr. This has caused him to depart rather ostentatiously from a policy [socialization] which he evidently hoped would please the British and he is now pursuing a more "capitalistic" policy which he evidently believes will gain the favor of the Americans. This seems to be borne out by the fact that he now nominates former German industrialists as managing directors of works to be separated. He is reported to pay no attention to the denazification of these industrialists who were even attacked by him during the stages of his earlier career.[49]

Among others whom Dinkelbach wanted to rehabilitate, the U.S. Consul General specifically named Walter Rohland and Hans-Günter

Sohl. Sohl would eventually become the first general director of the new ATH. For his role as head of the tank ring, the Russians ensured that Rohland would never return to West German business life. Rohland remained embittered, especially toward Dinkelbach, although Dinkelbach did not have authority over such matters (the Allies did) and was personally not averse to allowing Rohland back in.[50] Over time, Dinkelbach gained the trust of the Americans. Again Price Waterhouse contacts such as with Jack W. F. Neill helped overcome this initial suspicion.

While Dinkelbach introduced his Catholic social ideas to no great enthusiasm and his deconcentration plans to great consternation, his near single-handed promotion of codetermination for Ruhr heavy industry earned him lasting enmity. Initially, his advocacy of labor representation appeared to indicate that he supported socialism. At the time, Ruhr industrialists managed to conflate codetermination with both the Nazi "seizure of power" and a Communist "dictatorship of the proletariat." His outspoken stance on codetermination surprised even union leaders, but it cost him some of his closest friends.[51] Because his colleagues largely dissociated themselves from him, Dinkelbach has had a low profile in the history of German steel.

Codetermination for the coal and steel industry began with the Treuhand itself. Dinkelbach employed a great number of former VSt personnel from its auditing and organization offices into the Treuhand, contributing to the common complaint that his plans advantaged the VSt. The Treuhand also included a good number of union leaders and Social Democratic party members (committed to socialization at the time). The Treuhand included Social Democrats such as Heinrich Deist, an expert in economic affairs, Heinrich Meier, and Erich Potthoff. Potthoff was not only chief of the economic institute for the German Association of Unions (DGB), but also one of Schmalenbach's closest friends; their relationship went back two decades.[52] Also an expert on auditing and financial statement, Potthoff was one of the most consistently strong defenders of codetermination throughout the Federal Republic and eventually found a professorship at the University of Cologne. Potthoff and Dinkelbach too remained close friends till the end of Dinkelbach's life.

By March 1947, the first four of Dinkelbach's "building blocks" of his "new order" in Ruhr steel went back into operation as best they could. Each of them had five members of management and five members from labor represented on their boards. The Treuhand itself acted as the eleventh board member and potential tie-breaker. By 1948, Dinkelbach planned to divide eight major Ruhr Konzerne, including the VSt, into 24 operating units (80% of West Germany's total steel capacity), whose funds came from public and private sources and whose boards would also include union representatives.[53]

In November 1948, the Allies formed a new Steel Treuhand (*Stahltreuhändervereinigung*) for all of West Germany. The Steel Treuhand had three chief directors, of which Dinkelbach acted as leading figure. Although the Allies had decreed decartelization and deconcentration, the actual form it took was Dinkelbach's work. This process, too, was not simply an Americanization of German industry, as he bent it to German advantage. They kept largely the same personnel and plans of the British Treuhand, but phased out plans to dismantle German steel.

The dismantling of the ATH, in particular, engendered a huge political controversy at the highest levels of state and diplomacy. The ATH became one of the most potent symbols of the contradictions inherent to the occupation period. Counterproductively, the Marshall Plan proposed to rebuild the German economy, but the Allies still planned to dismantle its industrial capacity.[54] Leading Ruhr industrialists stressed the importance of the ATH to the Marshall Plan. They argued that the productive superiority of the ATH would save American taxpayers more in the long run. They listed all of the classic virtues of Thyssen operations, especially its huge export volume which would help Germany balance its inevitable trade deficit and currency weakness. They quoted the 1925 Brassert report to Dillon Read. Finally, they reminded American occupation authorities that the VSt-ATH subsidiary still acted as collateral for the American trustees of VSt bondholders, as it had a lien on its assets. Not only did the war obviously "impair" its worth, but the "impending dismantling of the Thyssen-Hütte, undoubtedly, also constitutes an encroachment on the rights of the American creditors." American trustees would have to approve of dismantling. The VSt still had over $39.7 million of outstanding debts to American creditors (the original amount was $65.8 million), most of which was in the hands of the Russians since the Dresdner Bank held these bonds in Berlin.[55] This VSt debt also helps explain why Dinkelbach, who had worked with Price Waterhouse, became such a crucial figure.

The ATH controversy stretched up to Konrad Adenauer, the new (Catholic) West German Chancellor, who in November 1949 managed to reach an agreement with the Americans that set a definitive end to dismantling. By 1950, dismantling ended, but not before the ATH lost most of its steelmaking capacity and rolling mill capacity (more than strategic bombing had caused); it retained only its blast furnace or ironmaking capacity.[56]

Once dismantling ceased, the Steel Treuhand restructured the entire German coal and steel industry, dissolving the old Konzerne.[57] Industrialists' arguments against Dinkelbach largely mirrored the arguments made by Fusban against the VSt reorganization. Over great objections, Dinkelbach created twenty-four new companies, often reuniting different pieces of different firms together inside new enterprises. Dinkelbach dissolved the VSt into thirteen different companies.

Successor Firms to the VSt
Rheinische Röhrenwerke AG, Mülheim (Ruhr)
Gussstahlwerke Oberkassel AG, Düsseldorf
Hüttenwerke Ruhrort-Meiderich (later Phoenix) AG, Duisburg-
    Ruhrort
Gussstahlwerk Witten AG, Witten
Niederrheinische Hütte AG, Duisburg
Dortmund-Hörder Hüttenunion AG, Dortmund
Stahlwerke Südwestfalen AG, Geisweid
Deutsche Edelstahlwerke AG, Krefeld
Gusstahlwerke Bochumer Verein AG, Bochum
Ruhrstahl AG, Hattingen
Hüttenwerke Siegerland AG, Siegen
Rheinisch-Westfälische Eisen- und Stahlwerke AG, Mülheim
August Thyssen-Hütte AG, Duisburg-Hamborn

These new companies did not initially own their own assets; the Steel Treuhand did. As management companies, they leased their fixed assets from the Steel Treuhand and operated with a minimum equity capital of just DM 100,000—similar to the VSt's 1933 reorganization. Critics noted that experts, economists, technicians, and representatives of unions sat on the steel Treuhand, but no representatives of owners. They accused Dinkelbach of paving the way for "exaggerated theories" of American decartelization specialists, who could not even apply their pet theories in their own country.[58]

But Dinkelbach's ideas grew out of his experiences inside the VSt, and codetermination bore little relationship to American ideas. As one American colleague warned Dinkelbach: codetermination was "a serious mistake and will be a serious deterrent to American capital ever investing in German industry. It might be good politics in Germany, but it is unsound business and bad internationally."[59] His actions, however, stirred up bad politics in the Ruhr, so controversial that owners and directors of the former Konzerne refused to sign the new contracts. Dinkelbach signed these contracts himself in the name of the Treuhand *and* the new companies.

But Dinkelbach's actions allowed these firms to begin manufacturing and rebuilding. The Steel Treuhand acted on the supervisory and managing boards for the new management companies and chose the new directors in conjunction with Allied authorities. Dinkelbach proved critical for reinstating numerous executives, many of whom intensely disagreed with him. Bearing all the signature marks of Dinkelbach's business philosophy, the Steel Treuhand implemented a higher degree of standardization in their management principles, their cost-accounting policy, and in organization for the whole steel industry that had not existed before.[60]

After regulating all of the immensely complicated ownership and property questions, between June 1951 and May 1953, the Steel Treuhand officially founded twenty-three new firms which now fully owned and controlled their assets. This action ended the deconcentration process and inaugurated a process of reconcentration for the West German steel industry.

The last firm to be established was the successor company of the GDK/ATH, now renamed the August Thyssen-Hütte AG, Duisburg-Hamborn. The new ATH, however, contained only some of its original plants of the VSt-ATH, although its core manufacturing plants could be traced back to the GDK. Three of its five main plants were now dismantled or belonged to different firms. For instance, the Hüttenwerke Ruhrort-Meiderich (later Hüttenwerk Phoenix) contained the manufacturing capacity of the former AGHütt, which had been included in the VSt-ATH subsidiary. The Rheinische Röhrenwerke AG, Mülheim/Ruhr contained the production capacity of the Thyssen & Co. Rolling Mills and the pipe capacity of the former GDK Dinslaken. The Allies dismantled the VSt strip steel subsidiary into oblivion (the strip steel operations of the former GDK Dinslaken). Moreover, in the course of reconcentration in the 1950s and 1960s, a number of former VSt subsidiaries or plants drifted into other firms. For instance, the Hüttenwerke Siegerland drifted into Hoesch; Krupp incorporated the Gussstahlwerke Bochumer Verein.

The new rump ATH would become the focal point for the postwar rise of Thyssen back to the height of the German steel industry.[61] The first directors of the refounded ATH were Hans-Günther Sohl as general director, Walter Cordes as commercial director, and Alfred Michel as technical director. Fritz Thyssen's heirs proved decisive for the pattern of its reconcentration. With Fritz Thyssen's death in 1951, the Allies ordered that the Thyssen family's 21% of the former VSt share capital be divided equally between Fritz's heirs: his wife, Amélie Thyssen, and her daughter, Countess Anita Zichy-Thyssen. Through private investment trusts, their share portfolios came to be concentrated in firms that had contained pieces of the old Thyssen-Konzern. The Thyssen family portfolio not only provided a secure capital base for the new companies, but also facilitated the consolidation of these former Thyssen-Konzern companies (among others) into a new firm. A close advisor of Chancellor Konrad Adenauer and now chairman of the ATH supervisory board, Robert Pferdmenges of the private investment bank, Sal. Oppenheim Jr., also played a crucial role in reestablishing the ATH.

Sohl put the ATH onto a crash expansion course by focusing on flat rolled steel (of immense importance for its future linkage to the automobile industry) and fleshing out a diversified line of products. With the help of "counterpart" (Marshall aid) funds and generous state (Länder) investment programs for coal and steel, the new ATH invested heavily in new plant. Sohl once half-joked in the 1980s that the "only unmodern aspect" of the ATH was its blast furnaces, the only plants not dismantled.[62] Within a few years, the ATH began to pay dividends and it expanded through retained earnings. When the ATH's new hot warm sheet rolling mills went into production in 1955, replacing the capacity dismantled at Dinslaken, it was considered such an event that Adenauer and Erhard participated in the ceremony. At the ceremony, Adenauer reminisced about how he had toured the original ATH plant years before with August Thyssen. By 1965, a mere dozen years after its reestablishment, it produced 8.6 million metric tons of steel, the largest single-company total in Europe and the fourth-largest in the world. By 1967, the ATH's revenues made it the third-largest company in Germany, behind Volkswagen and Siemens.[63]

Unlike Thyssen's old policy of internal expansion through private means, the new ATH rebuilt its position in the German steel industry through a policy of merger and acquisition. Facilitated by the Thyssen family investment trusts, by 1965 the ATH had managed to reunite many of the former parts of the old Thyssen-Konzern in its operations. In 1955, it incorporated the Niederrheinishe Hütte, an important rolled wire producer that had belonged to the VSt. In 1957–1958, it annexed the Deutsche Edelstahlwerke, a quality steel goods producer that substituted for the ATH's dismantled electric-arc steel capacity; it belonged formerly to the Thyssen-Konzern (Krefelder Stahlwerke) and the VSt. In 1960–1961, the ATH annexed the Handelsunion AG, a consolidation of trading firms, including such former Thyssen and VSt firms as the important VSt subsidiary, the Stahlunion-Export. After overcoming difficulties with the High Authority of the European Coal and Steel Community, in 1964 the ATH managed to incorporate the Phoenix-Rheinrohr AG (a 1955 merger of the Hüttenwerk Phoenix AG and the Rheinische Röhrenwerke). With this acquisition, parts of the former AGHütt, Thyssen & Co. and the pipe production of GDK Dinslaken again came under the ATH umbrella. Unlike old August Thyssen's adamant personal control, by 1964 the ATH had over 90,000 shareholders, almost as many shareholders as employees. Moreover, unlike August Thyssen's strategy, Sohl did not build on coal.

One of the most visible signs of German steel's recovery was the erection of two major skyscrapers in Germany, which towered over Düsseldorf (Figure 16.2). The first was Mannesmann's, finished in 1955 (and now of Vodafone), followed in 1960 by a gleaming building for the Phoenix-Rheinrohr AG. Known as the "three-pane house" (*Dreischeibenhaus*) for its appearance of three imposingly vertical rectangles pressed up against one another, its façade consisted of plate glass and chromium steel. Inside it incorporated columns of steel pipe produced by the owning company, which owned the original Thyssen & Co. plant in Mülheim. With the takeover of the Phoenix-Rheinrohr AG, the ATH moved its main headquarters there. This central headquarters was now clearly distinct and geographically separate from the soot-darkened smokestacks of the Duisburg-Hamborn area. The

Figure 16.2 Thyssen headquarters, Düsseldorf, 1950s. (Reproduced with the permission of the ThyssenKrupp Corporate Archives, Duisburg)

streamlined modernism of its International Style architecture expressed the new world of corporate system for the ATH.

Although greatly criticized by his colleagues, by placing the German steel industry firmly on the ground of the new geopolitical situation, Dinkelbach allowed it to rehabilitate itself quickly after Germany's devastating defeat. It remains an open question how much Dinkelbach's "building block" scheme helped or harmed the German steel industry over the medium and long term. Similar to the great German universal banks, by the 1960s the German steel industry quickly consolidated into a constellation of oligopolies with prewar roots led by ATH, Krupp, Hoesch, Klöckner, Rheinstahl, and Mannesmann. At the turn of the century, August Thyssen had once stated the "time of cartels had passed" and advocated an American, oligopoly-based economic order. In this sense, Dinkelbach helped carry it out.

In another respect, Dinkelbach also stepped into the shoes left by Hugo Stinnes and the formation of the *Zentralarbeitsgemeinschaft* (ZAG) in 1918, which created a *modus vivendi* between employers and labor. After much maneuvering, debate, and counterpositioning by both labor and management, the coal and steel codetermination law of May 1951 was promulgated, one of the most significant signs that a basis for social partnership existed in the new Federal Republic. The administrative constellation of the Treuhand also echoed that of the ZAG. Unlike Stinnes, however, Dinkelbach's inclusion of union representation on the boards of German coal and steel companies was not cynically motivated. It rested on his belief "that the many complicated problems in the modern economy can no longer be solved by a single person, but only through teamwork *(Teamarbeit)*."[64] It was precisely in his initiation of codetermination that he broke most dramatically with Thyssen's and older German management principles. Dinkelbach was a crucial figure on the employer side for shifting German economic life from a stockholding concept of the firm to that of a stakeholding one. As early as 1941, Dinkelbach's work in making corporate financial statements meaningful expressed the thought that "everyone somehow associated with the enterprise" has "an equal and justified interest" in knowing the economic and financial state of the corporate enterprise.

These controversial positions and health condition caused him to withdraw. After 1954, he largely retired from active life in business except as chairman of the supervisory board for a few firms, mostly associated with Rheinstahl. However, on the occasion of Dinkelbach's death in 1967, Cordes commented on Dinkelbach's lasting influence on West German industry. He remained deeply skeptical of Dinkelbach's policies, especially codetermination. Their friendship had grown distant, though still polite, by the late 1950s. Yet Cordes could still argue: "I personally think his greatest achievement is probably that his numerous colleagues spontaneously formed a circle to preserve his body of thought which he has conveyed to us." Indeed, after 1948 members of the VSt auditing and organization offices voluntarily organized a yearly reunion of about fifty people in the Düsseldorf Industry Club to celebrate their time together.[65] Cordes felt the "school" that had evolved around Dinkelbach over the last thirty years developed into a "genuine training center for future managing directors" for the

West German economy. Cordes called Dinkelbach a "true role model," who always wanted "capable young people to move into positions of authority more quickly than has so far been the case"—much like August Thyssen or Albert Vögler. These words were not mere niceties at Dinkelbach's funeral, for Cordes had often privately conveyed his "pride in coming from the Dinkelbach School" and being "his thankful student." He sometimes turned to Dinkelbach for advice and solace.[66] Carl Buz, who had worked with Dinkelbach since the days of the Thyssen Machine Company, also privately thanked him for "having the luck to have grown up in the Dinkelbach School" where he gained his career skills.[67] Indeed, the list of Dinkelbach students reads like a who's who of postwar leading executive directors in the Ruhr. They knew that they had stood at the cutting edge of German management practice.

The phrase, "Dinkelbach School," was well-chosen. Dinkelbach was once asked if he felt a loss when good colleagues left for other jobs elsewhere. Dinkelbach corrected the interviewer arguing "the more young people I give up, the more come to me. That is not idealism, but rather practical realism."[68] Spoken like the teacher he had first wanted to be. Dinkelbach himself thought that the influence of the "school of the VSt had at least in regards its accounting system and organization" had a "good name."[69]

Through former "students" such as Krähe, Kluitmann, van Aubel, Cordes, Potthoff—all of whom joined the Schmalenbach Society—the practical experience of *Büro Dinkelbach* diffused into German corporate management practices after 1945. These ideas found theoretical expression in the Krähe Circle of the Schmalenbach Society for corporate management, which published significant works on management theory and organization design in the 1950s. Named for Dr. Walter Krähe, one of Schmalenbach's students *and* a former subordinate of Dinkelbach's, this group was formed in 1942.[70] The Krähe circle became the most influential think-tank for postwar German management. Kluitmann, who headed the VSt organization and Hollerith departments, later became one of the executive directors of the Schmalenbach society. In addition, van Aubel played a critical role in restarting the chartered accounting profession in West Germany. Van Aubel became president of the Schmalenbach Society between 1960 and 1962. Erich Potthoff, who worked closely with Dinkelbach in the

Steel Treuhand, became president of it between 1968 and 1971. Walter Cordes, a friend, a former direct subordinate, and after 1953 the commercial director of the ATH, also became president between 1971 and 1978.[71] Büro Dinkelbach had a quiet but powerful bearing on the construction of the institutional framework for German business in the Weimar Republic, in the Third Reich, and in the Bonn Republic.

After the war, Dinkelbach maintained close contact with the various members of this group as well as professors at the University of Cologne when he had time.[72] They attempted to maintain contact with one another, exchanging pleasantries, life experiences, memories, books, articles, and ideas—insofar as Dinkelbach's health permitted.[73] For instance, before Potthoff gave the closing speech to the Schmalenbach Society in 1956 concerning corporate governance issues in German big business—a surprisingly relevant speech today—he first ran the speech by Dinkelbach.[74] Dinkelbach's 1920s–1930s organizational accomplishments would have fit in perfectly with the American movement of systems men who sought to revamp managerial decision-making by improving information flows popular in the 1950s and 1960s.[75]

Because Dinkelbach's health suffered (he often went to work in pain), he did not actively play a large role in the economic miracle. But he never regretted what he accomplished as Steel Treuhand. The vehement hatred engendered by his actions have made his subsequent presence as a historical figure quite slight. Dinkelbach's importance to the West German economy, however, lies in the way he subtly influenced German managerial practices—especially those organizational methods found in the corporate headquarters of the German economic miracle, softwired into the architectural monuments of our industrial time.

Intriguingly, Eugen Schmalenbach delivered the most succinct description of Thyssen's and Dinkelbach's modular management principles built on the principle of delegate but supervise. The thrust of Schmalenbach's whole exposition on good organizational design argued vigorously against bureaucratic methods of business organization or continual micro-interventions by top management, which he found all too prevalent in German industry. In 1941, before going into hiding and before Americans arrived with their Marshall Plan commissions, Schmalenbach outlined the theoretical fundamentals of the *Divisionalization of Concerns* based on *prewar* German business practice; this work was later published in 1948.

Schmalenbach was well aware of VSt organizational practices and its problems through Dinkelbach, van Aubel, Graff, Cordes, and Kluitmann. After Schmalenbach's death, Dinkelbach acknowledged that he had "learned to know and appreciate the old master of economic theory through long professional and personal collabora-tion."[76] In 1945–1946, Schmalenbach, van Aubel, and Dinkelbach spent hours discussing issues with one another. In 1948, they planned a birthday celebration for Schmalenbach.[77] In mid-1950, Kluitmann and Krähe (among the authors) sent Dinkelbach a copy of their new book regarding Konzern organization—explicitly understood as a multisubsidiary association. Dinkelbach then passed this book on to members of the Steel Treuhand to study. The book concerned itself with the "delineation and division of functions between the headquarters and units, in particular the question of centralization and decentralization." It divided Konzerne into two types: owner or "personally led Konzerne" (such as Krupp, Thyssen, Stinnes, Siemens) and "real [anonymous] Konzerne" (such as the VSt or IG Farben), which tended to form through mergers because of economic considerations. The authors thought that personally led combines tended to centralize few functions, relying on subsidiary directors, while "anonymous" combines tended to be divided functionally, with a tendency toward centralization. While personally led firms might lead to bad decision-making, particularly in personnel questions, anonymous firms faced the "danger of bureaucratization and overorganization."[78] The authors might as well have been speaking of Thyssen and the VSt. Finally, the book focuses on whether functions should be integrated or outsourced from the Konzern, and how much should firms follow a path of vertical or horizontal integration—classic transaction cost questions popular today. In general, they tried to clarify the advantages and disadvantages of different organizational arrangements in large enterprises.

In a later book, *Leitungsorganization,* which Kluitmann immediately sent to Dinkelbach, the Schmalenbach Society shifted its focus focused to strategic management. Potthoff's 1956 speech to this society, on which Dinkelbach commented beforehand, provided some background to this study, published two years later. Potthoff argued that

Germans needed to place more emphasis on strategy so as to improve the long-term management of the firm. The larger the organization, the more problematic the question becomes whether to direct the enterprise more centrally or more decentrally. Potthoff offered no "general recipe," especially as examples of both tendencies could be found in other countries, including the United States. However, the tasks of top management should primarily focus on setting "guidelines" necessary for establishing this strategy, including the "planning, organization, coordination, management *(Disposition)*, and finally control." He stressed most strongly that a clearer distinction between "long-term strategic decisions" and "routine events" *(laufende Geschehen)* needed to take place:

> *We need to have the courage to make it a priority* for top executives *(Spitzenkräfte)* of large enterprises *to have the time to reflect* as it says in a text by the large American chemical company, Du Pont de Neumours. [underlining by Dinkelbach] "The top executives have 'time to think,' without the burden of management detail." [original in English]. This is only possible when the executive board *is freed from all routine administrative duties* [underlined by Potthoff] so that they can devote themselves to strategy *(Geschäftspolitik)*. Naturally, one should not understand this as a multiplication of meetings in a multiplication of committees of national or supranational conferences. Even here one must have more courage to delegate responsibility.

Potthoff thought that the "strongest impulse" for reform of the German executive board came from America, but that the Krähe Circle had been dealing with these issues for years.[79]

Schmalenbach's own organizational studies advocated a multidivisional or multisubsidiary form built around guided, "pretial management," that is, the use of market transfer prices or internal transfer prices that reflected true marginal costs so that profit centers would form. The key organizational figure in his argument was the divisional or subsidiary director:

> The essence of pretial direction of firms *(Betriebslenkung)* is that the highest instance allows subordinate positions to have far-reaching autonomy and retains only the especially important decisions; but in return evaluates the success *(Leistung)* of the positions in general on the

basis of departmental performance calculations *(Erfolgsrechnungen)*. By using pretial management the operations directors are able to do what they want except for a few restrictions, but they should present at the end of the accounting period a good result. To accomplish this, the type of accounting, in particular the choice of transfer prices, has to see to it that that no departmental profits arise, which are not profits in the sense for the whole firm.[80]

Standard, uniform accounting classifications underlay those departmental performance evaluations. The headquarters of the firm should manage its departments by strategically using transfer prices among the units.

Schmalenbach disagreed with Dinkelbach's claim that the firm had to be a "harmonic organism."[81] Schmalenbach realized that tensions within the firm could never be completely smoothed over, while Dinkelbach's rational systems thinking and conciliatory tone implied that they could through objective accounting statistics (see his answer to Bartscherer above). Dinkelbach had more faith in technocratic planning using objective information. While Thyssen typified the image of the individual owner-entrepreneur *par excellence,* Dinkelbach ushered in the age of the technocratic systems manager. Dinkelbach typifies a type of executive most comparable to an Alfred Sloan (CEO of GM) or Robert MacNamara (CEO of the Ford Motor Company).

Clearly, the practical experiences—both good and bad—of the VSt strongly informed these works by the Schmalenbach Society, whose presidents tended to be former VSt executives, students of theory through Schmalenbach's teaching, and self-proclaimed students of practice who passed through the "Dinkelbach School." Indirectly then, Thyssen corporate principles flowed into Dinkelbach's organizational teachings and over to his students. After 1918, Thyssen & Co. had two internal divisions united by the legal structure of the corporation and its accounting system, which Dinkelbach ran. In turn, through his students, Schmalenbach's theories shaped VSt organizational practice. (Incidentally, one of Schmalenbach's students, Paul Arnst, wrote his dissertation on August Thyssen.)

Thus, this virtuous, circular network of people and ideas, the interaction between theory and practice—between the Schmalenbach Society and the Dinkelbach School—created one of the most influential impulses for German business management in the early postwar period. In short, they formalized the lessons learned through concrete organizational practice. If one follows the trajectory of Dinkelbach's career from the beginning of the century, his methods were derived less from an impulse from America, although he was certainly aware of American practices, than from a autonomous tradition of German management practice and thinking—and as a solution to their dysfunctions. (Following a telephone interview in 1947, Dinkelbach made a number of points about the importance of creating a "clear order" by dissolving the old Konzern, which clearly drew on his own VSt experience, to reorganize German steel.)[82] This body of management theory created by this network of individuals resonated in the long term as one of the most important lines of *continuity* in German business history.

To be absolutely clear, I am not arguing that such ideas came solely from them, nor that there was some sort of unmediated straight line leading from the Thyssen CAO (let alone Thyssen & Co.), nor that other company practices had no lasting impact (IG Farben's clearly did), nor that American influences were unimportant. Instead, these management practitioners and theorists helped to clarify crucial dilemmas of modern corporate life that many other large-scale business organizations confronted, but drew on their own experiences, especially those made by Thyssen and the VSt, and then formalized their own theories rather than just imitating or co-opting America ones.

The postwar encounter with America did give Dinkelbach the leverage to implement his ideas more swiftly and thoroughly than they otherwise would have, but a straightforward Americanization thesis obscures this important intellectual and organizational legacy. Everything that appears as American was not necessarily so—even the introduction of the vaunted multidivisional form and its principles. It was also a German invention. An Americanization thesis obscures the way in which obvious American impulses became refracted and institutionalized in the German context. Once German firms and banks reconsolidated themselves, they could draw upon this prewar legacy of institutional knowledge, organizational practice as well as personnel continuities. The ascension of Walter Cordes to commercial director of the new ATH, a self-described Dinkelbach "student," placed him in a clear line of succession beginning with Nölle/Killing, Hofs/Rabes, and Dinkelbach.

Finally, Dinkelbach's advocacy of German codetermination has little place in any story of Americanization. Codetermination grew out of German political compromises stemming from World War I. For Dinkelbach personally, Catholic social thought contributed to this rethinking. (And one of the coincidences of the story line of this book is that the most important people in this story were Catholic: August Thyssen and Heinrich Dinkelbach, hardly confirming Max Weber's *Protestant Ethic*.) In one of the many ironies of history, in 1923 it was Dinkelbach who organized Thyssen & Co.'s lockout and return to the ten-hour day, but by 1953 he helped to promote codetermination because he felt modern companies and modern societies were too complex to be managed by a single person. August Thyssen must have rolled over in his grave one more time.

Conclusion

We have come a long way from puddling, Albert Killing's warm handshake and disdain for typewriters, the letterpress journal, and Thyssen's bakehouse headquarters. The physical construction and geographical location of central headquarters built this narrative; they expressed the relationships among owners, company, managers, factory, and community. August Thyssen's father's banking business was located directly inside his home. The first and second administrative buildings of Thyssen & Co. were cramped structures located directly adjacent to the manufacturing facilities. With the diversification of production in the 1880s, Thyssen & Co. dispersed the commercial and technical offices of its five main product departments throughout the factory grounds next to the manufacturing areas, reproducing its departmental management organization. Thyssen had his home adjacent to the factory grounds in a comfortable villa, but had to breathe his own smoke and sleep through the rumblings of nearby freight traffic. His directors, Franz and August Wilke, had the privilege of cleaner living in a nearby manor on the river Ruhr.

The turn of the century marked a profound shift in business management for the Thyssen-Konzern. His management shifted from a merchant-entrepreneurial conception of control to a manufacturing conception of control built around productive efficiency. Architecture and buildings expressed this shift in management style. "Scientific management"—which one cannot subsume under Taylorist, Fordist, or so-called American ideas—found expression in the new halls of structural steel and corrugated sheet metal that replaced nineteenth-century brick mills. Buildings internalized girders, replacing the bricks and external support structures, just as industrial bureaucracies internalized transactions that markets once carried out. These new factory buildings permitted a reflexively designed manufacturing space to appear that permitted a greater scale and rationalization of production. Plant directors such as Franz Dahl or Franz Bartscherer designed best practice manufacturing operations around flows of material, energy, and people. Managers (largely engineers) turned their attention to the proper arrangement of a vast array of interlocking machinery and equipment; they increasingly controlled this energy and machinery through electrical systems, dials, monitors, and gauges, which created new measures of flows and output expressed in productive statistics and cost accounting efficiency ratios. This *Metropolis*-like vision of factory life owes much to a manufacturing conception of control that became the dominant means of managing—and of imagining—corporations for much of the twentieth century.

Even though Thyssen retained full possession of his firms, an "immense" management apparatus had grown between Thyssen and his firms, as Franz Dahl lamented. Marking the greater separation of ownership from control, even in a family firm, Thyssen moved to nearby Schloss Landsberg as if to underscore this transition. Joseph Thyssen moved to a stately villa in Mülheim overlooking the Ruhr river. Fritz Thyssen built a sumptuous Tudor-style home in a Mülheim garden suburb, distant from his main office at the GDK in Hamborn-Bruckhausen.[1] Schloss Landsberg, Thyssen & Co., and the GDK central offices, however, remained key sites for strategic decisions.

Senior management and a proliferation of new central staff functions became housed in sparkling, sometimes imposing, administrative headquarters. Finished by 1907, a new central office building for the GDK allowed it to move out of a makeshift old schoolhouse; the GDK also moved out from under its subsidiary status to Thyssen & Co. The GDK's organizational structure, with its three "fortresses" of mining, steelmaking operations, and commercial administration found expression in the location of its head offices. Still, the GDK administrative building remained on site, adjacent to the main steelmaking plant, even somewhat endangered by its own coal-mining operations.

The GDK Dinslaken, the Thyssen & Co. Machine Company, Rolling Mills, and AGHütt had its own headquarters. All remained close to factory grounds.

Given the new needs and wealth created by big business, it is not surprising that this brave new industrial world inspired architects such as Peter Behrens (AEG Turbine Hall) or Walter Gropius (Fagus Schoe Factory) to create new forms of architectural design.[2] Specializing in department stores, the architect for the 1911 Machine Company headquarters stripped away the heavy ornamentalism of Wilhelmine Germany in favor of thick functional lines made possible by vertical, reinforced steel concrete pillars, which permitted large windows and sunlit interior spaces. Only the block tower evoked an older era of town-hall architecture. This new building also reinforced the staff-line functionalism of the Machine Company. The architect of the Thyssen & Co. Rolling Mills headquarters built it along relentlessly rectangular, cubist lines, juxtaposing horizontal and vertical lines, and eschewing the prewar neo-Gothicism of the GDK's headquarters or the turret of the Machine Company. The front of the building suggested a classical façade of pillars, as if superimposed on a massive rectangle. All of these buildings represented a growing distinction between administration and manufacturing, white-collar and blue-collar work. They expressed an architectural and managerial trend to functionalist modernism.

In terms of the Thyssen-Konzern, all the buildings symbolized the multisubsidiary autonomy of individual Thyssen firms. They articulated the idea that each firm could manage its own affairs "self-sufficiently" within Thyssen's overall strategy. The architecturally most elaborate headquarters, located in Mülheim and Bruckhausen, represented the dual centers of the Thyssen-Konzern before World War I. The GDK's central office, housing the new CAO, swiftly became the information and coordination center for the entire Konzern.

Thyssen's decentralized management structure remained largely intact until it merged into the VSt. The 1926 fusion of four major steel Konzerne moved the VSt's corporate administration to the "house of steel" (Stahlhaus) in downtown Düsseldorf, adjacent to the Steel Works Association headquarters, the so-called "court of steel" (Stahlhof). The VSt corporate headquarters was now divorced from any VSt manufacturing sites. The VSt formed a capitalist organization that reorganized how economic and political decisions were made across the entire

Ruhr. The VSt further increased the social and geographic distance between ownership and management, business administration and factory management, and marketing and manufacturing. To bridge this geographical distance, to overcome merger rivalries, and to create corporate time, the VSt built an increasingly elaborate management system filled with new accounting procedures, timetables, deadlines, statutes, guidelines, regulations, and organizational maps to coordinate and control a vast array of manufacturing sites spread throughout the Ruhr. The VSt broke with the Thyssen-Konzern multisubsidiary principle of "delegate but supervise." Its ownership was more diluted as well, being spread among four interlocking ghost holding companies and then among numerous shareholders, including the Reich government. Unlike Thyssen's home adjacent to his firm, the homes of VSt shareholders did not necessarily bear any relation to the four original combines, the VSt, or its factories. Indeed, few shareholders owned VSt shares directly. The VSt nearly detached ownership from control, being led by Albert Vögler, a salaried manager. The VSt Düsseldorf headquarters fully expressed this managerial revolution.

However, the VSt proved incapable of coping with the 1930s world depression or its own shareholders effectively. Merger rivalries, back-room cross-shareholding, high fixed costs, heavy debt load, the costs of administration, and dysfunctional decision-making—its incomplete and "mortgaged" founding (Reckendrees)—exacerbated this crisis. The VSt proved incapable of adeptly managing its corporate relations with the myriad communities of the Ruhr, partially because of its distant headquarters. Its unitary legal form also meant that most taxes levied on VSt transactions went to one city, Düsseldorf, rather than many. In addition, Vögler worried that the next generation of managers were too specialized, and not given enough all-around responsibility. As a result, Vögler and Dinkelbach planned to refound the VSt holding company and decentralize the VSt into a number of product-oriented subsidiaries under the financial control of corporate headquarters.

The reorganization spread subsidiary headquarters throughout the Ruhr. In this manner, it reunited the manufacturing plants with their former corporate headquarters, with their communities, and with their historic, reputable names, which had been lost with the merger. These local firms were pillars of employment and symbols of these municipalities' economic health. The Bochumer Verein was most enthusiastic about this change.

At the same time, however, other new subsidiary headquarters, such as the Deutsche Röhrenwerke AG with its headquarters in Düsseldorf, combined geographically separate and traditionally rival manufacturing operations in Lierenfeld, Dinslaken, and Mülheim. More dramatically, the Westfälische Union AG combined numerous different wire-producing plants even outside the Ruhr. Thus, the reorganization simultaneously affirmed the traditions of pre-VSt business firms while reinventing the nature of the firm as an abstract entity primarily bound together by sophisticated financial, accounting, and organizational methods. These techniques made the corporation cohere.

The move to a multisubsidiary design helped improve VSt's organization by localizing subsidiary decision-making under the overarching financial control of the corporate holding—"coordinated decentralization" in the classic words of Alfred Sloan. The reorganization simultaneously tightened the relationship between management and municipality, but made corporate controls more abstract. Dinkelbach's fundamental organizational innovation was to manage VSt operations through complex, financial accounts that highlighted rates of profitability and liquidity, rather than manufacturing data. The VSt cohered primarily through statistical, accounting, organizational, and financial information—its surveillance system—which made the collection of geographically spread manufacturing sites, commercial offices, trading companies, and administrative headquarters viable, "self-sufficient" modular units, that is, subsidiaries. On paper, Dinkelbach deconstructed, reconstructed, and then after 1945 deconstructed the VSt once again, based on abstract organizational, financial, and accounting criteria—by the numbers. The information required by this managerial and financial conception of control came together in the ten-story corporate headquarters in Düsseldorf. Unlike the management of manufacturing efficiency, Dinkelbach sought to control corporate management itself. In his words, the VSt reorganization should activate "greater economies in management, not greater efficiencies in manufacturing." Organizational design became a distinct, self-reflexive economic variable. He helped inaugurate a new managerially oriented, financial conception of control—a new form of rationalization that became more influential in German business after the World

War II. We have moved a long way from Thyssen's personal letters and face-to-face communication.

Rethinking German Management

Throughout this story, I have deconstructed four interlocking themes: our dominant understanding about German managerial styles; the concept of the Americanization of German business; Alfred Chandler's influential classification schemes for big business; and Weberian notions of bureaucratization and rationalization. More constructively, I have developed a rough typology of organization change built around three conceptions of control.

I have tried to reconceptualize German business management. Because his firms remained privately held and because of August Thyssen's great entrepreneur reputation, it came as a surprise that he developed one of the more sophisticated managerial systems in Germany—and in the world. Thyssen's great achievement was in the management of a well-balanced Konzern complete with relatively sophisticated control measures epitomized by the CAO. He was one of Germany's premier *Organisatoren*. Since the Thyssen-Konzern is comparable to other German steel firms in terms of size, technology, product diversification, markets, state and regulatory laws, complexity of its operations, and so on, its particular organizational design and capabilities must, in part, be explained by the collective agency of August Thyssen and his managers.

We should call into question the classic, preindustrial, peculiarly German, authoritarian model of entrepreneurship. We still need considerably more research into German management, but Thyssen's decentralized *Rechtstaat* model of management does not fit the Kruppian absolutist ruler paradigm or the Siemens-based, Prussian state-bureaucratic model (according to Kocka's portrayal, not Feldenkirchen's), or IG Farben's Hapsburg Monarchy model. I do not argue that Thyssen should be placed in their stead. We need more systematic internal studies to argue this point on grounds of representativeness. It appears that a variety of German models of management could exist alongside one another, influenced by personality, region, product type, size of enterprise, and eventually a growing management profession that disseminated corporate experiences. Arguably, Thyssen's Catholic,

Rhineland background with its strong Belgian influence made a difference. Possibly this made him more freewheeling, more internationally oriented, more willing to accept markets, more meritocratic, and more objective; the latter two qualities because of his experience of Catholic persecution. But this hypothesis needs more grounding in biography.

My argument moves well beyond questions of representativeness. Tellingly, those large-scale companies personally led by owner-entrepreneurs with a *Herr in Haus* mentality did not make it far into the 1880s and 1890s without crises of leadership—as at Krupp and Siemens. Such captains of industry ran aground. As shown by his close attention to the reorganization of the early 1880s, his personal composition of the CAO statutes, and the on-again-off-again debates about decentralization or centralization, Thyssen reflected on organizational design and attempted to manage change proactively.

Ultimately, Thyssen's success rested less on his entrepreneurial vision than on his ability to choose good people and to create a coherent managerial system that allowed these talented people wide-ranging autonomy: "delegate as much as possible, but supervise." Unlike Werner von Siemens, who had considerable difficulty delegating responsibility to non-family members, Thyssen delegated easily to non-family members—sometimes too easily, as his Berlin experience showed—and not well at all to his family. Most Thyssen innovations did not derive from August Thyssen. The accounting and organizational sophistication of the Thyssen-Konzern owes much to Ernst Nölle, Albert Killing, Heinrich Hofs, and Carl Rabes. The GDK/ATH and Stahlwerke Thyssen depended largely on Franz Dahl's design genius and Franz Bartscherer's scientific management of energy. Julius Kalle commanded the highly profitable GDK Dinslaken. The development of high-powered gas engines owed much to Hans Richter and Edmund Roser. Conrad Verlohr succeeded in achieving long-term profitability at the AGHütt. The importance of the Mülheim pipe factory today originated with Carl Wallmann and Rudolf Traut. Wilhelm Späing smartly managed legal affairs.

Thyssen demanded leadership personalities. Thyssen consistently worked with strong-willed personalities, who could contradict Thyssen in reasoned ways. Thyssen once privately criticized Emil Kirdorf's "irresponsible" and "all-powerful" behavior toward his executives and supervisory board, who could not have an independent opinion that would require them to say "no" instead of only "yes."[3] All of his executives pointed out Thyssen's ability to lead people, listen to them, and manage very contradictory characters. The success of the Thyssen Machine Company, in spite of the fact that none of its leading directors were friendly with one another, testifies to this quality. None of his managers ever complained that they felt cramped by his presence. If anything, they probably felt they had too much responsibility and knew the consequences if they failed. Such ambitious leadership traits actually prevented a fusion of the Thyssen-Konzern.

Thyssen's corporate culture also allowed for young managers to move quickly into positions of responsibility and leadership. Thyssen managers moved upward in his organization not because of their subaltern mentality or seniority, but rather because of their personal initiative, willingness to work hard, to take on responsibility for their tasks, and for their civil collegiality. The lack of upward mobility became a problem inside the VSt, which the reorganization tried to address. Thyssen's incentive policy oriented itself to performance measures: production, profit margins, net profits, or cash flow. A decidedly anti-bureaucratic mentality permeated Thyssen corporate culture.

Thyssen's managerial system grew out of the attempts of a Bismarckian merchant to master the new challenges of scale and scope—of growth itself. Historians have underestimated this strong merchant–commercial tradition in German business. Ironically, Kocka presented an alternative model of merchant *(Kaufmann)* instead of civil servant. Thyssen maintained a commercial–financial orientation in his strategic thinking, and then institutionalized this orientation into his Konzern. By contrast, Siemens retained a strong technical or engineering bias. Siemens & Halske acknowledged itself as a "technical holding," a place where ideas, inventions, knowledge, and innovations flowed into the parent company, just as a financial holding company pools profits.[4] Siemens focused on creating new inventions and spoke contemptuously about the "massification of technology" *(Verpöbelung der Technik)*. The Siemens brothers had disdain for merchants and organizational matters. Werner Siemens once called Georg Siemens, who later became director of the Deutsche Bank: "My son, the clerk."[5] Thyssen was just the opposite, placing technology in the service of commerce and firing technically competent people regardless of their inventions. Thyssen kept trying to transform engineers into "respectable businessmen."

Thyssen's organization was also not influenced by state bureaucratic models. One limit on the bureaucratization of German big business was their product diversity and vertical integration within their individual organizations (for numerous reasons). The diversity of product lines, small batch production, economies of scope, vertical integration, the emphasis on self-sufficiency, and acquisitions of very different types of related companies, all frustrated general bureaucratic controls, cost accounting, or organizational procedures. Kocka, who argues so strongly for the influence of bureaucratic models, provides a legion of evidence to the contrary, in describing Siemens wrestling with difficulties of decentralization and diversity.[6] If anything, German firms tied decision-making more tightly to product departments and engineers, who "make things." The engineering and craft-skill bias of many German firms pushed authority downwards to powerful department heads and shopfloor foremen; product diversification only reinforced their authority, built around technical *Kompetenz*. Because of syndicates, German heavy industry did not internalize marketing functions as quickly as did American firms, possibly hindering sales executives from achieving greater power.

This internal diversity slowed the development of an American-style middle management (not necessarily bad). The American focus on scale and standardization of products for a large market eased organizational centralization and uniformity. Not surprisingly, as American firms diversified after World War I, they confronted managerial dilemmas that had been already faced by German firms. The U.S. multidivisional form was one response to managing *diverse* product lines. Meanwhile, German firms wrestled with problems of *centralizing* control within their organizations. Konzerne tended to have less central control, less general management, and less formalized bureaucracy than American-style firms. Mergers and acquisitions, especially under IG arrangements, left considerable room for autonomy within vertically integrated steel firms. Such administrative controls had to be asserted over very independent departments, subsidiaries, or acquired firms—a difficult agenda, as the experience of the VSt demonstrated. Ironically, it was the VSt, which developed a classic American-style middle management, which contemporary Germans derided. Perhaps the

German stress on bureaucracy in management literature indicated the problem, not the reality?

A tendency to bureaucracy did not necessarily stem from preindustrial, state-bureaucratic traditions, but from modern American managerial methods, such as Taylorism or the Hollerith (IBM) machine. Bureaucratization and Americanization went hand in hand in the history of German business. For instance, the organizationally innovative DuPont had extensive written codes and regulations. In DuPont's "Standard Practice Book," a manager was required to submit eight copies of the application form, No. 16822 *(sic)*, to apply for small experiments costing under $500.[7] How might this be interpreted in Germany?

It is useful to contrast Thyssen's management of men with Frederick Taylor's. Taylorism is also predicated on highly bureaucratic controls of supervision.[8] While Thyssen delegated tasks and expected managers to achieve certain objectives or "results," Taylor's management principles had managers and workers run through a checklist of motions or functions to be fulfilled in order to achieve a certain objective. By analogy, the American army tends to follow a chain of command based on following orders *(Befehlstaktik),* while the German army classically used orders to achieve objectives *(Aufgabetaktik).* In this respect, American methods are more authoritarian and controlling. As one GDK document stated:

> In general: individual departments are headed by supervisors and managers have to unconditionally follow the orders of their supervisor or in his absence the orders of their representative. The supervisor gives the orders in general form, while the managers have to carry it out in an otherwise self-sufficient manner with the greatest possible precision and punctuality as well as accepting the responsibility for it. The supervisor has naturally the right to allocate to his managers other corresponding work in circumstances.[9]

Clearly, a top-down command hierarchy did form (I am not arguing that Thyssen ran some sort of democracy), but one that accorded responsibility and decision-making flexibility to subordinate managers.

These differences are another reason why the classic *Herr im Hause* concept is misleading as a means of analysis because it neglects the actual practice of German entrepreneurialism and management by focusing exclusively on entrepreneurs' political stances or attitudes, especially toward democracy or the labor movement. Entrepreneurs' acceptance of cartels was a solution to a very modern problem of high fixed costs and ultimately rested on *liberal* legal principles about freedom of association or contract—not preindustrial hankerings for guilds. German companies' paternalist social welfare policies might well be labeled a modern rather than a preindustrial, authoritarian response.[10] Calling an entrepreneur authoritarian is an effective debating technique to advocate a greater voice for labor or to critique industrialists' pitiful support of democracy, but it is not an effective means of analyzing corporations from an historical perspective. Otherwise, Carl Rabes, of all people, could not have called Clarence Dillon an autocrat. The tendency of many business histories to use the great entrepreneur (nowadays the cult of the CEO) to personify their firms has blocked a better understanding of German management. This has very little to do with the way entrepreneurs have managed large-scale German firms since the 1880s and 1890s, but a good deal more to do with public debate, entrepreneurial hagiography, and the discourse of the history profession. At minimum, historians need to deconstruct this concept of *Herr im Hause* more precisely in comparative, cultural terms. Here is where cultural history and business history could fruitfully intersect. Leadership *(Führung),* for instance, has a long and honorable tradition in American management literature and was a mainstay in pre-1945 German management literature until Hitler tainted the term. The concept of entrepreneur *(Unternehmer)* had particular cultural valencies in Germany that did not exist elsewhere.[11]

As I have argued throughout this study, August Thyssen maintained "ultimate authority" not because of some *Herr im Hause* attitude, but because of highly modern modes of organizing control. Paradoxically, because of the weird property relations of the Thyssen family, August Thyssen might be construed as one of Germany's premier salaried managers because he did not actually own the Thyssen-Konzern, but acted as his childrens' trustee of the family property. But such a reformulation still cannot effectively analyze the company's managerial hierarchy.

The Thyssen-Konzern was a modern managerial enterprise, which happened to have an entrepreneur at its head just as many *Mittelstand* firms today have succeeded in global markets in spite of (because of?) family ownership. They still have mysteriously developed organizational capabilities, which permitted them to finance, market, manufacture, employ, and manage their expansion abroad. Thyssen developed a cohesive, coherent Konzern because of a unified central direction, a more or less uniform set of financial standards (cost accounting apparently moved less quickly forward), formal institutional arrangements such as the IG and inter-firm contracts for deliveries, a coherent overall manufacturing and marketing strategy best expressed by balanced and controlled vertical integration (unlike other Konzerne), and a pervasive corporate culture characterized by flexibility, improvisation, speed, delegation of responsibility, lateral communication (in spite of a formal hierarchy), politeness and collegiality (in spite of cross-cutting interests), and clear performance standards based on the profitability of departments and firms. This extension of systematic organization allowed Thyssen to expand successfully into sectors such as machine engineering or gas and water supply (but not banking). Thyssen's CAO, as modern as anything in the United States, became the key supervisory instance for the whole Konzern. The CAO assembled statistical and financial information, recommended organizational changes as an in-house consulting forum, and monitored the complicated financial relations among the Thyssen firms. The Thyssen-Konzern (and Mitsui) outlined the basic principles of the multidivisional form slightly before U.S. firms did. From this perspective, it is less than surprising that key Thyssen executives (Rabes, Späing, Dinkelbach) were among the core team to reorganize the VSt into a multidivisional firm; former Thyssen CAO executives played a leading role in VSt's finance, auditing, accounting, and organizational offices—areas of organizing control where August Thyssen excelled.

I have focused more intently on the development of this management organization to reconceptualize our understanding of German business. The dominance of American historiography and making U.S. developments the ultimate yardstick by which to judge other national business trajectories has contributed to misleading conclusions. (This is a running critique by British business historians, who argue that British business was not in decline, family enterprises are not inherently dysfunctional, and that it neglects the dynamics of financial and service industries, one of Britain's perennial strengths.) A confluence of writing business history as entrepreneurial history, American business classifications, modernization theory, and Weberian methodology has channeled researchers into thinking that Germany did not have a modern managerial revolution and was somehow backward. To catch up or become modern (and normal), German business must converge to a best-practice American model.

First, this perspective ignores the ongoing dialogue and exchange that constituted German-American business relations. Carnegie's early success depended on German engineers and chemists. In technical matters, Americans made pilgrimages to German steel companies regarding German-style "economies of energy." German firms often had more advanced forms of managerial and financial accounting methods than American firms, such as depreciation, overhead cost-allocation methods, and internal transfer pricing. They also had more experience managing scope, technologically diverse products, and vertical integration.

As demonstrated most closely by the purchase of the Fretz-Moon license (or for the VSt more generally), one could just as well call borrowing from the United States the Germanization of (some) American techniques, rather than Americanization. After Fretz-Moon was moved to Germany as an American invention, Traut significantly improved upon it as a German innovation, and then this hybrid moved back to England and to the United States. We see the creation of a nascent "international style" of pipe-making or business practice, not necessarily a convergence to an American model. Well-known examples such as Walter Gropius (architecture) or Billy Wilder (Hollywood) show how much the so-called American model was transformed by this exchange.

Second, a straightforward Americanization thesis simply obscures autonomous trajectories within German business itself and recognizes them as backward. All that appears as Americanization was not necessarily American—not August Thyssen the Americanizer, not the vaunted M-form, not the Fretz-Moon process, not the horizontal rationalization of the VSt, not the VSt accounting methods, and not Heinrich Dinkelbach, the "one potential Americanizer." All had roots in an autonomous, evolving German management tradition, which filtered American impulses through a semiotic process of perception, reception, interpretation, selection, channels of organizational transfer, and

creative adaptation based on an organization's own historical trajectory. The VSt remained a fully German company for all its attempts to
model itself after U.S. Steel. Without question, many of the inspirations for the new corporation did stem from a vision of America, yet
the selection of what constituted the American model and its implementation in practice made the VSt deviate substantially from anything found in America. On the other hand, many institutional, professional, and organizational developments were true parallels, rather
than slavish imitations of an American example.

In short, if it is a mixture, then it is not a linear Americanization,
and we need to understand the other side of this process, which remains largely unexplored. One important aspect of this Germanization process depends on the virtuous circle of formal and informal
linkages and cooperation among industrial firms, business associations, and academia (in management, accounting, and engineering)
that characterized a German way of doing business, a national innovation system. This web of intellectual and personnel linkages and business traditions kept German accounting norms from becoming a mere
copy of American methods. In the realm of financial accounting, the
Germans have maintained a distinctly modern but alternative institutional tradition that has recently found its limits when some German
firms sought to place their securities on Wall Street in the 1990s, just as
in the 1920s.

Third, the notion of Americanization runs into interpretive difficulties for understanding German history. If we take the Americanization and modernization of German business to mean one built on
Fordist mass-production assembly-line models, and use it as an "indicator of modernity," then, the most Americanized corporation in Germany was probably Volkswagen, a Nazi project with Hitler's personal
stamp of approval. For just this reason, debates surrounding the modernity of the Third Reich have caused a good deal of consternation
among German historians.[12] The systems modernity of VSt business
practices, as advanced as U.S. practices, must be squared with the VSt's
business politics with the Third Reich. But trends in German managerial practices cannot be tied directly to the politics of a particular regime or the export of the American model. They had their own trajectory that converged with political regimes but also diverged from them
in particular ways. As shown by the career of Heinrich Dinkelbach, this

modernity of German managerial practices operated through the Third Reich as well as into the Federal Republic. Büro Dinkelbach kept the VSt producing for the Third Reich until the very end of the war but it also acted as a "genuine training center" for West German industry. The managers of Dinkelbach's generation and organizational capabilities provide one source of continuity in German business history across the great divide of 1945. If one follows this trajectory, then German management during the Third Reich appears more modern than a preindustrial tradition would imply, and German management appears more American than the standard portrayal of German industrial practice allows.

Without denying the great asymmetry and dominance of America in the world economy, if we want to understand exchange, transfers, or encounters prior to the age of globalization, we need to rethink the unilinear model of Americanization, which is too broad to be of good analytical use except as loose shorthand. The best case for Americanization can be made for the decartelization measures of the 1950s, but that is just one aspect of a complex economy. Other important differences such as works councils, codetermination, or the German house bank system were strengthened after 1945, that is, *diverged* even more from American practices. Likewise, Japanese *keiretsu*, enterprise unions, industrial relations, and manufacturing processes diverged from American ones after the occupation rather than becoming similar. In short, these methodologies are not an appropriate way for analyzing cross-cultural interactions. Understanding the creative process of encounter is even more important as we (maybe) move to a globalized (rather than international) world and away from simplistic development models of Americanization, Westernization, and modernization, which the postwar period conflated.

Americanization is one "concept too many" to paraphrase D.C. Coleman's comment on the theory of protoindustrialization. Unlike protoindustrialization, which has an enormous heuristic value for organizing research because of its intellectual hypotheses, the concept of Americanization offers little except a loose sense of convergence. The theory of protoindustrialization systematically links commercialization of the countryside, cottage industry, demographic change, and industrialization. Recent work on protoindustrialization has undermined the clear links presented by earlier proponents of the theory, but the theory still links disparate elements together into a coherent research program.[13] Americanization, however, is not a theory, but a grab-bag of signifiers. It offers little except a quick reference to the adoption of this or that institution, practice, idea, consumer good, or sign (be they rock and roll, McDonald's arches, a baseball cap, Fordist mass production, oligopolies, or the M-form). None of these artifacts Americanize a country or a company. The VSt clearly adopted aspects of the American model, but selected only certain aspects, implemented them in particular ways, and finally had to deal with the unintended consequences. The concept of Americanization ultimately obscures the process of cultural exchange and institutional translation.

Weber's theories of rationalization and bureaucratization have underpinned much business history, but there was no single point toward which the Thyssen-Konzern or the VSt could be rationalized. One cannot conceive the Thyssen-Konzern as an internally consistent bureaucracy or "production function" built around a single will. Lujo Brentano once criticized Max Weber by saying that a rationalization toward an irrational mode of life is hardly rational.[14] But even this critique falls short, as the Thyssen-Konzern or the VSt was a collection of many points of view. How did a business arrive at a strategy towards which the firm could be rationalized? For whom was that strategy rational? How did a firm manage the inevitable trade-offs in the type of rationalization that proceeded? What were the implicit assumptions on which that strategy rested? The term "rationalization" disguises myriad points of view, varied reasons, inherent trade-offs, and negotiated solutions. Thyssen and VSt executives formed strategy and policy in a complex process of negotiation with people of different points of view and used different *rationales* to legitimize strategies, decisions, and policies.

Corporate goals, interests, strategies, policies, and their execution were continually negotiated, contested, and eventually defined through a complex communicative process, patterned after the formal structure of the organization, informed by reporting techniques, and constructed by measures of performance and informal personal interaction in both Thyssen and the VSt. Both firms were contested terrains, but the process of negotiation was structured in very different ways over time. Thyssen & Co. of the 1880s was a very different creature than the Thyssen-Konzern of the 1920s or the VSt of the early 1930s. Even in a firm led by August Thyssen, who represented a clear

anchor of authority, strategy and policy emerged from competitive negotiation and an organizational learning process that was not free
from mistakes. Organizational and technological change often bub-
bled from the middle of the hierarchy on up, not only from the top
down.

Not surprisingly, conflicts over strategies and objectives grew with
large supervisory boards, majority and minority shareholders, bank
representation, and large managing boards. The organizational structure of the VSt formed out of contesting claims from outside stakeholding agencies as well as internal objectives formulated by VSt management. The VSt's decision-making process was characterized by a
highly fluid political process revolving around Albert Vögler, who had
to take into consideration the aggressive desires of major shareholders, strong-willed subordinate directors, and a number of external
stakeholders, ranging from other important business firms, cartels,
business associations, the central government, American bondholders,
Price Waterhouse and Dillon Read, and finally the communities of the
Ruhr. Those top managers of the VSt who could negotiate and fuse
these various claims on the firm into an acceptable corporate policy
and strategy became leading managers.

A concept of rationalization simply obscures how business firms formulate and execute strategy. As we saw with the VSt, contradictions
could lie within its basic strategy as it attempted to bring capacity in
line with demand. It proved moderately successful in rationalizing and
limiting its own growth in capacity, but its formation terrified other
firms into expanding their capacity to compete with the new giant,
thus negating its other strategic goal of bringing industry capacity in
line with demand. It also took over other firms' manufacturing capacity to streamline them, but this strained its financing capacity. Here
two of its basic business functions, producing and financing, ended up
in conflict with one another. It sought to stabilize profits (through cartels) and dividends (because of shareholder interests), but cartels reduced demand and those dividends harmed its financial substance.
Contradictions and conflicts could arise in the execution of a rational
strategy as well. Not only did workers object to the VSt's "negative rationalization," but so did some managers, who felt that the productivity figures did not take into account key qualitative aspects of the
factory (or because they might lose their positions). Was it rational

to purchase the license for the Fretz-Moon process and locate it in Mülheim in the middle of a depression with a poor outlook for future demand? Despite the use of rational, objective cost-accounting techniques, it was an immensely contentious decision.

Weber also viewed modern capital accounting as the epitome of formal rationality, yet as I have stressed throughout, the formally rational, technical procedures are chock-full of conceptual content ("substantive rationality" in his terms) that construct organizational reality and guide action. These formally rational techniques varied from firm to firm because it was not clear how best to construct them. There was no "one best way" to "mirror" operations or find value in spite of the claims of accountants. This caused conflicts among the merged firms of the Vst as well as difficulties among VSt accountants trying to establish appropriate standards. Even with proper standards, both Thyssen and VSt managers mobilized these formally rational techniques in very different ways as well as questioned the way they were calculated. Internal transfer prices in real-world business practice became political points of contention, not signifiers of formal, instrumental rationality or a formal, value-neutral technique without content. At Thyssen & Co., internal transfer prices for key goods remained the domain of the owners and senior executives, precisely because of their potential politicization, and they reinforced the owner's ultimate authority over his managers.[15]

Rationalization from the highest level of strategy to the lowest level of cost calculation obscures the point of view, the standards, and reasoning used by participants to justify a particular action. The concept also stakes a larger claim to being the optimal solution and relegates other positions to being irrational or inconsistent deviations from rational operations. It is, in fact, inherently authoritarian because it makes a claim that a single, correct perspective guides the whole, while other viewpoints are condemned to irrationality or irrelevance. Dinkelbach's systems rationality took this position as well.

If rationalization is virtually a meaningless concept, then bureaucratization is merely vague. If we apply Weber's notion of bureaucracy strictly, we note a strong anti-bureaucratic element in business organization. This was one of Kocka's great insights. The entrepreneur or senior management usually resisted submitting to bureaucratic formality, preferring to retain their individual autonomy. In addition, a market orientation differentiates business management from Weberian bureaucratic administration; performance counts more than adherence to rigid rules. Firms develop a flexible hierarchical structure rather than the strict, homogenous hierarchy oriented to internally consistent rules. Indeed, the tension between fluid market performance and rules (designed to make an organization consistent and reliable) is constituent of the business enterprise.[16]

However, if we apply the concept of bureaucratization too loosely, thereby reducing it to the growth of a set of offices, written rules, files, hierarchical status relations, career paths, and so on, then we cannot differentiate organizations as diverse as universities, business enterprises, public bureaucracies, non-profit organizations, the Catholic Church, or the local gun club. In fact, most of contemporary society is bureaucratized in some manner. If bureaucratization and the alleged rationalization of modern society were major social concerns at the turn of the twentieth century, then, for the twenty-first century we need to differentiate these concepts to describe twentieth-century organizational life. We need new historical categories of thought to distinguish social change after society has been completely bureaucratized, commodified, rationalized, or urbanized. The rich field of organizational theory has gone a long way to differentiate Weber's theory of bureaucracy and theorize these organizational dynamics.

In order to distinguish the evolution of corporate management more effectively than an ideal-typical approach focusing on the person at the head of the corporation, or a vague rationalization or bureaucratization process, I have focused on how the system of organizing control inside the Thyssen-Konzern and the VSt evolved between 1871 and 1934. Throughout, I have focused on the *construction* of corporate organization (in its physical and discursive sense), its internal decision-making process, the development of managerial methods, and the assumptions by which various routines governed the business enterprise.

A business enterprise is distinguished by its accounting and reporting system, which defines how management knows about processes and performance inside the firm. Accounting helps constitute organizational reality by imaginatively reconstructing the corporation itself in facts and figures. It betrays a particular perspective on the business because it selects the pertinent information most relevant to management. A loosely coupled relationship of the organization of the firm, the structure of responsibility, and its accounting system can be delineated that links information, knowledge, and power. I term this relationship of strategy, organization, and accountability the firm's *conception of control*. The conception of control underpinning a business firm is central to understanding corporate governance and how it attempts to realize the universal priority of business enterprise: to earn profits. A firm's accounting system is not just a rational technique for generating information, but a system of maintaining control—of creating accountability. This conception of control generates a system of surveillance that binds the firm together as a coherent organizational entity.

This study has found three analytically distinct conceptions of control—ways of managing a business. The advantage of these conceptions of control is that they historicize dominant notions of how managers think they can generate profits (strategy), for whom does the firm work, and how they conceive of their firm or what a business enterprise is. This system of accountability implies a specific concept of the corporation itself.

A mercantile/commercial model dominated Thyssen & Co. from the 1870s to the turn of the century. As a partnership, the business firm was conceived as an expression of entrepreneurial will and property assets. German commercial law and financial disclosure laws conceived of the firm as a legal umbrella covering the property assets of the merchant. Indicating the tight links between the entrepreneur and his company, when marketing his firm's products, Thyssen stressed the reputation of his name, which fused Victorian-era family reputation with modern brand marketing.

Initially, problems associated with the transformation of a small-to-middling-sized merchant-run business into a large-scale business operation dominated Thyssen & Co.'s agenda. If Thyssen & Co. wanted to make the transition to a larger scale of business, it needed to manufacture new products of varied specifications using experimental, difficult, and untested technologies, find new markets for its goods, develop ways of coordinating manufacturing and marketing so that these goods made it to the customer on time, ship these products around the globe in the cheapest manner, finance the growing levels of capital equipment, labor costs, and debt, and hire people who would probably be unwilling to work long hours in dirty conditions and under a strong disciplinary regime. The inherent conflicts and trade-offs among manufacturing, marketing, personnel, and financial matters led to unprecedented problems of complexity, coordination, timing and control. Overcoming these challenges was not easy; both Krupp and Siemens went through major organizational crises. Managers had to learn to manage diverse processes and people across time and space; they had to learn to manage time itself. Not surprisingly, much of the tension between department chiefs and the central office revolved around the timing of accounting and statistical reports. Much of the dialogue inside the firm in the 1880s consisted of how best to accomplish and enforce these new rules. Many of Thyssen & Co.'s organizational innovations sprang from improvisations, mistakes, and conflicts. This transition to an industrial bureaucracy should not be interpreted only as a means of maintaining Thyssen's personal authority.

As a result of the early 1880s reforms, *new*—not preindustrial or premodern—methods of organizing control arose. (Symbolically, in 1884 Thyssen ended the preindustrial custom of managers congratulating the owners at the end of a year.) This type of accounting was qualitatively different than a bureaucratic recording of transactions, since it places figures in relation to other figures and tracks new types of expenses. Ernst Nölle "took into account" new concepts such as fixed costs, depreciation, interest on debt, and overhead. Backed by Thyssen, these accounts ruthlessly distinguished between new investment and operating expenses. Nölle's monthly departmental profit reports represented the crucial reporting innovation (but not the only one), which determined the ultimate results. Implicitly, these procedures evaluated departmental managers by subtracting many types of expenses (including commercial expenses) from sales revenues to obtain a measure of profits. These reports emphasized growth in sales and cumulative profits generated by the departments to date. Although engineers usually had formal authority over the departments, these reports checked their power and defined their performance in terms of commercial success. Thyssen institutionalized a commercial orientation into the organization and tried to turn his engineers into respectable businessmen. This merchant rationale controlled for absolute profits and savings—reproducing a type of Victorian frugality; by reducing expenditures one theoretically made more profits. Unlike an Andrew Carnegie who viewed his firm as a manufacturing operation that would make profits if he could drive down prime costs or average unit costs to their lowest possible level, August Thyssen stressed running full but within the framework of his personal finances and sales orientation. Thyssen's cost accounting incorporated commercial costs into production cost and conversion cost figures.

A manufacturing conception of control emerged more fully after Thyssen moved the bulk of his operations to the GDK. Symbolically, Thyssen had to break away from the Mülheim model of operations and bring in new executives such as Franz Dahl to make the GDK profitable. This manufacturing conception of control became entirely dominant in the German coal and steel industry after the turn of the century. As Christian Kleinschmidt has argued, the German rationalization movement correctly begins with the recession at the turn of the century. The productive rationalization of the VSt also fit into this manufacturing conception of control, until the Depression hit.

Above all, this productivist conception of control as the dominant rationale or strategy stressed technical efficiency. By manufacturing as efficiently ("rationally") as possible, one reduced operating and fixed costs per unit produced and theoretically generated additional profits. Rationalized efficiency was also a relative value (profit margins per unit cost or output per labor hour), rather than a broader, absolute value such as "savings" implicit in the merchant rationale. One could spend more on the latest technical equipment, yet profits might increase because of the greater productivity of a new (manufacturing) process. The central strategy consisted mainly of expanding economies of scale and scope by spending money on ever-larger capacities and technically efficient (usually labor saving) equipment. In the historiographical literature, this type of strategy fits most closely to the common notion of a business firm as *factory,* as a "production function" or as an "organization of production," rather than as a commercial house. This conception of control (and of the firm) conflated the business firm with factory operations, the firm as rationalized factory. Not surprisingly, this conception of the firm gave rise to Taylorism and Fordism, and films such as *Metropolis* or *Modern Times* or *Á Nous la Liberté.*

The achievements of this manufacturing conception of control were demonstrated by the sheer scale of new operations and reflected in astonishing rises in manufacturing productivity. For many products,

German productivity levels reached their highest point before 1913 and were not surpassed until the 1930s. Electricity and the high-powered gas engine transformed manufacturing operations. New management of factory operations created new types of techniques to measure manufacturing efficiency—and measurement meant more control. Around the turn of the century, both Thyssen & Co. and the GDK placed great stress on new cost-accounting methods. Eventually, these methods became more elaborate and expressed themselves in Bartscherer's small notebook summing up the previous day's operations that appeared on his desk the next morning. Within commercial administration, Dinkelbach's internal accounting innovations at Thyssen & Co. and the VSt highlighted the increasing use of technical equipment (Hollerith), standardization of preformatted information sheets, and comprehensive coding of internal processes. New technical equipment drove down information costs and increased the volume of data processed. New central administrative offices proliferated. New financial reporting methods were formulated.

Business firms (at least industrial ones) became progressively biased toward manufacturing. The age of engineers with their claims and catchwords of efficiency, productivity, and rationalization had arrived. These new business methods fed into academic theories, which fed back into companies' practices, so that a new science of "factory economy" *(Betriebswirtschaftslehre)* was born. Universities all across Germany founded new chairs for economics and management. Management became increasingly professionalized. Professionals discussed accounting practices and slowly standardized them inside the firm and across the industry.

Indeed, at this time we might speak about the Americanization of German business. Many Germans viewed American labor saving equipment and technical cost-accounting methods (not other aspects of business management) as state of the art. American firms tended to pay more attention to labor costs because of higher wages. Because of the size of the American market, American firms could usually focus on the manufacture of a single, relatively homogenous product, which eased the standardization of managerial methods and cost accounting. Scale practically became a virtue unto itself, and America led the way. Fritz Thyssen, Julius Kalle, or Franz Dahl among hundreds of other Germans made business trips to the United States to examine American management practices. Obligatory business trips to America multiplied in the 1920s, especially to Ford's River Rouge plant, one of the eight wonders of the business world. They came back with ideas about factory management, especially regarding technical aspects of American manufacturing, which they then integrated into an already sophisticated managerial system with its own historical trajectory. Only in this respect can we speak of the Americanization of German business.

Even within this dominant manufacturing conception of control, significant differences between German and American management practices still existed. Germans developed a type of "scientific management" that differed from Taylor's obsessive shopfloor and labor cost focus or Fordist serial production. German management focused more on the systematic integration of factories' operations through technical measures and controls, especially to develop "economies of energy." The relative cost of coal probably played a role here. The science and research-based engineering advances in German steel rested on the systematic exchange of people and ideas among firms, engineering societies, and academia that created a virtuous cycle of constant innovation and kept it distinct from U.S. practices. While Americans concentrated on economies of scale and speed, the Germans pioneered in economies of scope and vertical integration. One could speak of a certain convergence by the 1920s, as American steel firms moved into multiactivity operations (economies of scope), while German steel firms placed more emphasis on economies of scale.

The complicated, competitive dynamics of cartel-concern capitalism and diversity of export markets placed a premium on vertical integration and product differentiation, forcing Germans to come to terms with the problems of managing multiactivity operations long before the Americans. The Thyssen-Konzern followed this logic in an ideal-typical manner. Cartels slowed greater American-style merger movements, but did not prevent them. By the mid-1920s, the German steel industry reached a limit in its vertical integration and it no longer had the scale to compete effectively. As a result, four major steel combines merged into the VSt. But the VSt fit right into the German (really European) cartel world. American-style drives to greater oligopolies, standardization, and scale as represented by the VSt did not contradict a desire to form cartels.

Overall, cartels significantly altered the strategy and the type of competition in German steel, but not its manufacturing conception of control, even enhancing it in particular ways since it rewarded manufacturing efficiency and scope. Engineers tended to remain in leading positions, while finance and marketing people tended to move into leadership in American firms.[17] In part, cartels reinforced engineers' positions within firms as they syndicated a good portion of their steel products. In the United States profitability and market share (limited by antitrust laws) became key measures of competitive success, while in Germany, quota share and vertical self-sufficiency became primary virtues. These differences between the United States and Germany are critical in developing a theory of German entrepreneurship. Both countries developed different sorts of managerial capitalism; for America this meant general manager capitalism, while for Germany it meant technical or operations manager capitalism.

What did alter the manufacturing conception of control inside the VSt was the Great Depression, when the VSt's fixed costs (debt, interest, administration, and overhead) failed to respond as quickly as other costs. The VSt reorganization ushered in a technocratic systems conception of control oriented to financial and organizational information to control for profitability and management itself, not manufacturing. It was entirely equivalent to the rise of "systematic management" in U.S. firms in the 1940s and 1950s, which slowly distinguished itself from engineering rationales and metaphors.[18]

Instead of engineering or manufacturing rationales, financial and organizational rationales underlay the VSt reorganization. The type of figures considered most important by senior management implies the type of reasoning used to control the firm, and these new methods highlighted the costs of business management and capital itself. To measure and hold accountable is to control. This (managerial) financial conception of control oriented itself to measuring the profitability of investment and the financial liquidity of the VSt as a whole and its individual subsidiaries. Like efficiency or productivity, profitability is a relative value, but it emphasizes the efficient use of investment capital itself. By orienting more towards investment profitability, one asks if the costs of improving the technical efficiency of equipment brings an adequate return relative to other investment options. Liquidity ratios especially addressed the VSt's chronic levels of debt. The new multisubsidiary design clearly distinguished central corporate staff positions responsible for overall policy and strategy from the individual product subsidiaries responsible for individual product markets. Dinkelbach paid particular attention to financial ratios (particularly ROI and liquidity ratios) when planning the product subsidiaries. The VSt parent company became the "house bank" for its subsidiaries. Subsidiary directors became responsible for returning adequate profits on VSt investment and were held accountable. Productive efficiency probably remained a key virtue in the product subsidiaries, but not for overall subsidiary or company performance.

Moreover, to survey is to map so as to manage. At first, Büro Dinkelbach designed the new VSt entirely on paper, as functional and localized lines of authority and statistics on a chart, rearranging the firm as a set of financial, statistical, and organizational assets. Büro Dinkelbach evaluated, deconstructed, and reconstructed the VSt largely "by the numbers" and with organizational charts. This planning abstracted people, activities, products, work processes, factories, headquarters, individual offices, and tasks into account statistics that could be arranged, rearranged, then coordinated and controlled by headquarters' standard managerial methods. Geography or manufacturing capacity became less important than the appropriate arrangement of financial figures and assets to generate appropriate levels of profitability and liquidity.

Statistical and financial information about management itself becomes a key variable in running a modern enterprise, not just engineering expertise on the shopfloor. Grey-suited accountants—organization men—vie with engineers for leadership inside the business firm. Dinkelbach's rise in the VSt hierarchy indicates the relationship between information and power. Objections to Dinkelbach's central planning for the Vst and later the attack on his postwar reorganization of the German steel industry reflected the tension created by Schmalenbach-based "schematism," which oriented itself to cost and profitability criteria, rather than to technical efficiency of manufacturing.

This typology offers a positive alternative to the standard *Herr im Hause* characterization, rationalization, or bureaucratization models, as well as Chandler's typology of personal, entrepreneurial, or managerial enterprises. It places the evolution of managerial practices squarely on center stage and links them to general strategy, the structure of accountability, and a definition of performance. There is no clean transition from one to the other, even within one business firm, which must manage all four functional areas adequately to succeed. This concept of control focuses on the dominant ordering principles, but competing rationales continued to exist inside firms. Obviously, the transitions among these conceptions of control varied from firm to firm, and the typology here is cut to the firms studied here. More research is needed. The available literature leads me to suspect that the VSt transition to a (managerial) financial conception of control remained largely exceptional until the late 1950s, delayed by the war, deconcentration, and reconstruction. VSt practices foreshadow postwar West German management.[19] The VSt at least had a good reputation for innovation in accounting, financial, and organizational matters, and Büro Dinkelbach acted as a "training ground" for future West German managers.

But why did the Thyssen-Konzern develop an early version of the multidivisional or a financial conception of control? Why did it develop a relatively sophisticated set of financial controls through the CAO? Because August Thyssen relied almost exclusively on his own financial means and largely refused to offer equity, his financing capacity remained more constrained. Always apparently short of cash, Thyssen's money was at stake. Thyssen had to use his investment capital in the most productive manner possible. Engineers always had to turn in cost-benefit analyses of their projects that took into account projected costs and interest charges; manufacturing efficiency was never a sufficient criterion. His multisubsidiary system with negotiated market transfer prices built in a high degree of financial clarity (to insiders), kept the subsidiaries competitive, and made sure that each individual firm or department justified its financial existence. Funds moved from one Thyssen firm to another carried interest charges just like any other debt. And finally Thyssen paid attention to such organizational matters, even the intangibles. Such complicated financial relations led to the founding of the CAO. What began as an act of improvisation and community relations turned into a sophisticated central control office that acted as an in-house organizational and financial consulting operation.

The ability of the Thyssen-Konzern to maintain a relatively decentralized structure and decision-making process rested on the CAO's ability to control, to check, to supervise, to survey, and to watch over (*überwachen*) the independent judgments of its subsidiary managers. Precisely because Thyssen established impersonal means of control, he did not have to resort to frequent calls for loyalty to his person, or intervene directly in relatively self-sufficient operations as a meddling, authoritarian *Herr im Hause*. He intervened when his control system informed him that the resulting performance suffered. By creating an organizational base of control, Thyssen could delegate.

Conrad Verlohr put his finger on the essential problem of all organizations when had to apologize for a bribery scandal at the AGHütt during World War I: "I regret deeply, as well as on the behalf of Herr Schuh, Scheifhacken, and Schroeder, to have to report to you about the above case. One is simply powerless against such a breach of confidence by a trusted high executive."[20] This failure of control triggered the strengthening of the CAO's powers over individual Thyssen firms. Why should any of the firms' directors act in the interest of the whole and not in their own interests? The CAO helped align individuals' (or individual firms') interests to Thyssen's overall goals.

The CAO and Büro Dinkelbach exemplify a larger issue about how control is established in organizations more generally. While specific modes and measures of control changed over time, this system of organizational controls, or accountability, helped create organizational coherency. They addressed the perennial tension between centralization and decentralization. This tension played itself out inside Thyssen & Co. in the early 1880s, in the debates about unifying the Thyssen-Konzern in 1906, 1921, and 1924, and in the decision to devolve the VSt in 1934. Throughout this study, managers have had to find ways of developing overall strategy (no easy feat in itself), yet ensure control over the various "self-sufficient" parts of the organization in the interests of the whole. Senior management had to maintain an overall sense of direction, while simultaneously allowing other managers in different product markets, departments, firms, or (eventually) in different areas of the globe, decision-making autonomy. Too much centralization curtailed the flexibility of the organization. Too much decentralization and the organization ceased to exist—as with Nölle in Berlin or the AGHütt scandal, or when some VSt managers interpreted its reorganization as "away from Düsseldorf." Fritz Thyssen and top VSt executives swiftly reminded subordinates that they remained responsible to the "whole" enterprise. The CAO and the VSt corporate offices checked and controlled these centrifugal tendencies in the double sense of the verbs.

Paradoxically, uniform central controls enabled greater decentralization just as a centralized electrical power plant allowed greater flexibility on the shopfloor. Behind the push-pull of centralization or decentralization was the dilemma of ensuring coherent policies over broader areas of organizational life in order to manage complexity. Although cheating is a running threat to any organization, ensuring a degree of reliability in the reputation of the company's products, assuring that those products are desirable, arrive on time (sometimes around the world), and are made with the proper specifications is critical for the long-term success of any company. New types of information collection, computerization, and reporting allowed a greater expansion of organizational scale. The basic problem was less one of ensuring personal power or generating efficiency gains than one of creating generalized, reliable, and impersonal trust across space and time. The firm's conception of control embodied in its surveillance system maintains control—in the double meaning of the word. Surveillance and trust are two sides of the same coin.

The Institutionalization of the Business Corporation

In this crucial period for modern capitalism, from August Thyssen to Heinrich Dinkelbach, the nature of the business corporation changed dramatically. Classically, one can interpret this transition as a managerial revolution whereby salaried managers replaced owners-entrepreneurs, thereby separating control from ownership. This description falls short of grasping numerous changes in the nature of the corporation itself. In this period, the business enterprise transmuted from being conceived as a collection of personal assets under a single proprietor to an institutionalized one with numerous shareholders and stakeholders.

In 1925, a bitter editorial asked why "poverty-stricken" Ruhr industrialists received over 715 million Goldmarks as compensation for losses incurred during the French occupation. According to the author, August Thyssen had earned a mere 300 million Goldmarks in the previous ten years. He had a total wealth of an estimated one billion

Goldmarks. The Americans had just appraised the Thyssen-Konzern as valued at over $166 million. Thyssen owned the largest privately-held expanse of coalfields in Germany. On top of this, he took out inflation-aided cheap loans, taken the last extra "pennies" from workers' wages, gained extra coal profits from cartels, and then received huge loans from the Americans. Now, astonishingly, the government arranged a bailout. The author indignantly asked why taxpayers should pay for these "indigent" and suffering" industrialists.[21]

I do not want to debate the fairness of this compensation (and given the sacrifices most Germans made over that decade, it was not), but question why the German government felt obliged to bail out Thyssen and Ruhr industry. First, Ruhr heavy industry did gain special favors from the government because of its political connections and national-strategic importance. Second, the Thyssen-Konzern suffered from a major liquidity crisis. The Thyssen-Konzern had high value, but teetered on the edge of bankruptcy. Third, these business enterprises had become major sources of employment. Indirectly, the compensation represented a type of (inefficient) social subsidy. Business enterprises such as Thyssen's had transformed the Ruhr from one of peaceful agricultural fields and small villages where rabbits could peaceably live out their lives to a raging industrial inferno that lit up the night sky with gas fires surrounded by sooty, overcrowded cities where people could not live out their lives very peaceably. No matter how much individual industrialists conceived of their enterprises as their own, big business found itself in the strange position of being the property of single owners or a few shareholders and also being a major economic institution of modern society.

Over time, the Thyssen-Konzern had to formulate its strategy and coordinate its company policies with a variety of external, organized groups, including other firms, business associations, professions (accounting, engineering, commercial), labor unions, local communities, regional governments, and the central government—whether August Thyssen liked it or not. The rise of Wilhelm Späing, a lawyer, tax expert, social policy coordinator, and all-around political negotiator might be the best illustration of how private enterprise had to take seriously and match its environment. For the VSt, the process of forming corporate strategy and policies included an even broader array of shareholders and stakeholders. Its top executives attempted to fuse these internal and external claims, which often conflicted with one another, into a relatively coherent corporate strategy that would allow the VSt to earn profits. Gradually, large-scale German business shifted further away from an owner-shareholder to a stakeholder conception of the firm. Dinkelbach again continually urged the greater regulation of corporate financial statements so the public or other stakeholders could meaningfully inform themselves about the state of the enterprise. This advocacy of corporate transparency was light years away from the Sphinx-like August Thyssen.

As the business enterprise mutated from a merchant-entrepreneurial collection of assets to an institutionalized economic organization, newly woven webs of social, political, professional, and legal relations entangled the business enterprise. Government regulations regarding everything from labor laws to corporate governance shaped what business could and could not do. Even through its commercial laws, such as the "theory of corporate agency," it helped determine the legal limits of the firm and reconceived the corporation as an abstract set of economic and financial relations, not just as property of a merchant.

However, it would be wrong to view these new institutions connecting firms to society as purely statist in origin. For instance, the chartered accounting profession grew out of the dearth of transparency in company financial statements, harming industrialists and investors themselves. New professional practices, eventually backed by state authority, institutionalized financial accounting procedures across firms, regulating and standardizing their behavior. Academia, accounting professionals, and individual managers introduced best-practice cost-accounting procedures across industries, enclosing individual business firms in a new web of norms. In conjunction with industry, the German Institute for Norms (DIN) standardized everything down to paper sizes. German engineering societies disseminated knowledge about technologies, research, and operations across individual firms. The Kaiser-Wilhelm Institute (now Max-Planck-Institute) pooled industry resources in the interest of primary research. Academia contributed to individual firms' organizational capabilities through their tight links to corporate practices in both engineering and commercial capacities (such as with Lenze and water management, Bartscherer and energy economies, Vögler and DINTA, Dinkelbach or van Aubel and accounting). Journals, such as the *Zeitschrift für Organisation* or

Stahl und Eisen, disseminated models, experiences, and ideas to a range of academic and company managers. Business associations helped coordinate the steel industry's relations with the finishing industry and its politics with the central government. Often these new institutions grew out of the attempt by industrialists to regulate themselves so the state would not intervene in their affairs.

These institutions, associations, and professions external to the individual firm altered its internal organizational decision-making process, thus helping to shape corporate strategy and policies. In this respect, the business firm proved to be a porous entity. Drawing a sharp distinction between markets or hierarchies does not do justice to the ways such non-statist institutions or associations mediate markets and permeate company hierarchies. In addition, VSt management clearly saw itself as part of a larger social system, not just as the personal property of owners. In part, this new perception resulted from its sheer size, its strategic prominence in the German steel industry, its economic and political power in the Ruhr, and its diluted shareholding (in contrast to Thyssen). Community relations, which are usually not factored into business histories, provided a major impulse for restructuring Thyssen's finances in 1906 and the decentralization of the VSt in 1934. This reorganization moved well beyond a straightforward paternalism, foreshadowing the notion of corporate rational beneficence of the 1950s and 1960s. Corporate responsibility became a key element in legitimizing VSt's reorganization. Managerial decision-making could no longer legitimately focus only on narrowly defined economic concerns in forming its strategy and policies (which is not to argue that management did not often view its relations with external agencies in economic, instrumental terms).

For better or for worse, these outside institutions helped create the internal organizational capabilities of individual firms. A wide variety of social relations and institutions embedded business, enabling, influencing, and constraining their internal decision-making. In line with new institutional theory: "Organizational forms, structural components, and rules, not specific organizations, are institutionalized. Thus whereas the old institutionalism viewed organizations as organic wholes, the new institutionalism treats them as loosely coupled arrays of standardized elements."[22] Because management had to answer to diverse and sometimes contradictory pressures, one cannot construe the

internal world of management, its organizational dynamics, as fulfilling a single will or having a single direction. Organizational dynamics
and processes that formulated the interests of an individual firm were
as much an end result as a beginning. Furthermore, the lack of internal consistency among a managers' objectives or desires, a firm's policies, the debates about central strategy, the ongoing internal organizational tradeoffs, the running politicking (an apparent constant inside
any organization), the uneven distribution of power and information
internal to any firm, the rivalries among primary actors, or the sophistication of one sector of the firm versus an alarming lack of sophistication in another area, make a mockery of Weber's bureaucratization
concept. Bureaucracies are not an instrument, or a technology of efficiency and domination characterized by rationalized procedures, but
rather an field of intense, interpersonal interaction. A diverse array of
codes, regulations, routines, institutionalized practices, social interests, specific tasks, and individuals' self-interest permeate any business
organization. In this view, the individual enterprise becomes a site or
locus of decision-making and the specific selection of institutionalized
components helps shape the specific decision-making process within
it. This meant that business organizations were *bric-a-brac* constructions
of old and new elements that often derived from external influences
or sources filtered through the expectations, interests, and objectives
of the participants within the firm.

There is little question that the formal lines of authority inside a
company act as a script structuring the decision-making process. This
script empowers certain people (managers) and disempowers others
(workers). August Thyssen's rights as owner empowered him to intervene where he wanted, but the formal hierarchy or script did not determine where initiatives or decisions originated. Informal jockeying
for position around August Thyssen ensued. Above all, Carl Rabes
made himself indispensable. He capitalized on his close relationship
with the Thyssens, allowing him to occupy key organizational positions
in the Thyssen-Konzern and later the VSt. Rabes' position had the un-
foreseeable effect of catapulting Heinrich Dinkelbach into key positions. The VSt had a less clear decision-making point revolving around
the "triumvirate" of Fritz Thyssen, Flick, and Vögler with Vögler acting
as a hub for divergent shareholder and management interests. Yet only
by understanding the nature of VSt's accounting and information sys-

tem can one explain how a junior staff executive with little formal authority could become one of the major players in VSt's reorganization,
let alone the effective *Generaldirektor* of the VSt at the end of the war.

In brief, the screenplay does not make the movie. Formal lines
of authority or rules do not entirely determine organizational dynamics: they cannot explain the continuing importance of puddlers in the
initial success of Thyssen & Co.; the influence of a young engineer,
Rudolf Traut, on its post–World War I expansion; whether the VSt
would purchase the Fretz-Moon process; the backroom negotiating
process among shareholders and rival managers in the VSt; or the influential interaction between the Dinkelbach practical school of management and theories of the Schmalenbach. Formal lines of authority
cannot explain the informal network of personal relations that spins itself around the formal process based on the formal script.

Bureaucracy (business or otherwise) should not be conceived as an
iron cage or systematic panopticon or harmonic entity, in spite of the
many claims of organization-builders themselves. And it is certainly
not an internally consistent, organic whole directed by some charismatic personality. Business organizations are more like elastic nets
with many rips, holes, conflicts of interest, and contradictions. They
are messy precisely because the people in the nets have knives and can
cut, retie, and alter (partially) the nets in which they are caught. People outside the nets also cut, tie and retie them. In spite of his self-per-
ception as an independent entrepreneur, August Thyssen too became
caught in these complicated webs.

But unlike new institutionalist theory, the creative agency of individual managers or the collective agency of an individual organization
should also be taken into account. Precisely because such "standardized elements," components, or rules were constantly evolving and
"loosely coupled," individual agency still played a huge role in how
they fit together. Management discussed and debated each organizational change. They did not merely accept one best-practice model or
another. They selected and transformed certain aspects of American
practice. They did not passively accept or conform to contemporary legal limits of the firm; instead they actively sought to change the law.
Accounting methodologies and the resulting figures did not overdetermine organizational action; executives always questioned their results. They found some pieces of information more relevant or sig-

nificant than others, often based on their own organizational interests or place inside the firm. Even in the Thyssen-Konzern, with a clear entrepreneurial point of authority, the business firm was a contested terrain.

One of the keys to the success of German business over time was the growth of a professional managerial class. Although historians have researched the German bourgeoisie, their studies still focus on leading directors or entrepreneurs. We still know little about the immensely important class of people who ran the companies on a day-to-day basis and constituted an ever greater proportion of the middle class. Instead of static social stratification studies, we need to know a great deal more about such individuals: the Nölles, Dahls, Rabes, Wallmanns, Späings, Kluitmanns, or Dinkelbachs of this world. We need to know more about what they did as businessmen, let alone as fathers or community members, which gave them great influence inside and outside their business. These people made the modern German business corporation.

Their professional work lay at the core of their personal identity. One of the unintentional effects of the three conceptual models introduced here has been to reproduce some of the primary gender models for men in the twentieth century: the dynamic merchant or entrepreneur, the technically rational engineer, and the technocratic, white-collar organization man. This typology might describe their personal identity better than their (often) dubious forays into politics. The tens of thousands of personal meetings, millions of tiny decisions, decisions to locate in a particular place, the type of professional practices and decision-making inside business firms have collectively altered our world as much as their overt interventions into state politics. German industry's success also rests on firms' organizational competencies and the capabilities of workers and managers that stretched across two world wars. Arguably, many German businesses survived over a century in spite of their political actions.

Finally, because these economic institutions and professional managers depend upon broad arrangements in political economy as well as specific institutions of modern capitalism, they cannot be isolated from the rest of society. If a society could invent and support such modern forms of economic and social life, then it is a modern society. They could not exist as islands of modernity in a sea of backwardness.

Private corporations are unique governance systems of this modern world because civil and commercial laws of capitalist societies guarantee in principle rights of property, allowing them to have an internal logic all of their own. Modern capitalist enterprises are unthinkable without a public social order that protects a space governed by relatively secure private property and respect for contracts. The real intellectual and social innovation about property rights is not their security, or their ability to allow individuals to capture the fruits of their labor, or to reduce transaction costs (as important as these are), but the crucial shift in understanding them as private. This, in turn, implies a notion of the public, a new type of political culture, and a new type of subjectivity.[23] Unlike small businesses, big business is rarely possible without limited liability or joint-stock company laws, which allow firms to assemble large amounts of capital, commercial laws, and courts to enforce contracts. Only credible institutions can establish such rules of the game, so business corporations, markets, and the modern state are inextricably and bound together. Clearly, even within capitalist societies, this general social contract is, of course, by no means a natural political arrangement.

Big business became a problem precisely because private organizations have transformed public space in dramatic ways, ranging from sooty pollution to shining new skyscrapers. As Ronald Coase has argued, business grew large because it internalized a great number of (previously) market-determined transactions, superseding, but not eliminating market mechanisms. By 1926, VSt managers created routines that spanned the entire Ruhr, marking a qualitative change for the region. The VSt could transfer employment possibilities, investment funds, or new equipment from department to department, subsidiary to subsidiary, community to community according to its managerial will. Although the VSt still had to react to the market, management mediated this relationship. Simultaneously, VSt managers created a worldwide export network known as the Stahlunion-Export, with 175 firms "situated in practically every country of the world."[24]

VSt's managerial organization linked consumption in the world market to the individual manufacturing plants of the Ruhr, mediating the relationship between the global and the local. A drop in the demand of rail goods in Argentina or Brazil could affect the number of orders the ATH had, which might possibly lead to layoffs. A large-scale business enterprise (and others like it) asymmetrically embedded itself between international markets and regional economies.

When the VSt shut down factories during the Depression, the layoffs were based not only on structural conditions of the international economy, but also on managerial decisions. Managerial choice (and sometimes organizational infighting) coordinated the relationship between international and regional markets. Shifts in employment or where to place a new plant were not directly the result of market changes, but of managerial decision-making on grounds of greater rationalization, greater efficiency, lower costs, and market relations—as managers defined it, largely but not exclusively through financial and cost accounting criteria.

Through the organizational decision-making process and the coded transmission belts of the accounting, information, and reporting methods of the business corporation, that is, through its managerial control system, sales orders overseas were translated into manufactured goods and jobs back in the Ruhr. VSt managers, moreover, could check to see if the customer received the same manufactured goods at the specified price, and evaluate whether they had profited from the transaction. The corporation did become more responsive to material and capital flows overseas in product or financial markets (the U.S. loan) than the needs of the regional or national economy—just one reason why the Nazis did not like the internationalism implicit in big business. As the reorganization showed, the VSt reshuffled factories among different companies throughout the Ruhr. It transferred workers and salaried employees from factory to factory, from city to city, yet they remained in the same company. The company became responsive to its own internal control system than perhaps the region around it. Based on internal efficiency and profitability calculations, the VSt could shut down or build new plants, transfer orders to other firms, expand or reduce product lines, and start new ventures.

We need to understand better the internal organizational dynamics that have such powerful impacts on the external world. Business enterprises are still black boxes conceived as maximizers of profits, reducers of transaction costs, and/or exploiters of workers. These views still beg the question of how they go about accomplishing these objectives. Above all, the increasingly "visible hand" of management has steered the course of the firm on the basis of that encoded information. In a world of multinational or transnational corporations, this internal decision-making—and not just the overt political manipulations or business-government relations of huge corporations—can lead to the creation and destruction of whole cities or regions. Ready or not, like it or not, they have become an intimate part of our lives, as ubiquitous as the products or their advertising, and as imposing as their skyscrapers on our major city skylines.

APPENDIXES

NOTES

INDEX

Appendix A: Tables

Table A.1 Selected financial statistics of the GDK, 1892–1913

Year	Gross assets	Total equity	Total liabilities	Equity/ liabilities	Fixed assets (mining)	Fixed assets (coking)	Fixed assets (steel)
1892	15.87	11.16	4.72	2.36	5.07	—	7.23
1893	17.72	12.54	5.18	2.42	6.79	—	8.04
1894	19.53	13.94	5.59	2.49	7.93	—	8.36
1895	23.01	14.51	8.50	1.71	9.01	—	9.24
1896	29.83	20.28	9.55	2.12	10.61	—	13.27
1897	43.52	27.59	15.94	1.73	13.74	0.87	19.77
1898	50.63	30.15	20.47	1.47	14.97	2.22	20.97
1899	56.35	35.87	20.48	1.75	18.34	2.95	21.77
1900	59.82	39.76	20.06	1.98	20.43	3.45	22.66
1901	63.42	43.96	19.46	2.26	21.65	3.19	22.40
1902	69.72	51.72	18.00	2.87	27.20	2.95	21.61
1903	78.17	54.32	23.86	2.28	32.68	2.58	21.55
1904	102.87	58.12	44.75	1.30	39.71	4.63	23.10
1905	115.62	69.56	46.06	1.51	47.02	6.83	23.89
1906	144.70	80.36	64.33	1.25	55.46	8.58	25.30
1907	154.23	91.59	62.64	1.46	61.65	9.03	25.64
1908	161.90	100.68	61.22	1.64	66.35	10.85	25.03
1909	183.73	112.09	71.64	1.56	73.60	9.84	26.33
1910	199.47	123.78	75.70	1.64	75.27	10.40	28.92
1911	243.97	144.44	99.53	1.45	77.00	9.36	34.45
1912	275.56	169.06	106.50	1.59	75.22	8.42	38.40
1913	249.93	126.89	123.03	1.03	74.38	7.58	44.28

Source: TKA/A1754; Feldenkirchen, Eisen- und Stahlindustrie, Tab. 83. Total fixed Assets from Feldenkirchen, Eisen- und Stahlindustrie, Tab. 83 (includes railway, harbor and subsidiary shareholding).

Total equity capital = share capital (after 1899 constant at RM 30 million) + owner deposits + various reserve funds

Total liabilities = creditors + acceptances + mortgages

Depreciation includes depreciation on subsidiaries.

Fixed assets (Dinslaken)	Total fixed assets	Equity/ total fixed assets	Depre-ciation	Additions to reserves	Cash flow or gross profits	Net profits/ equity	Cash flow to total assets	Cash flow to increase in fixed assets
—	13.38	0.83	0.34	—	0.34	—	2.14	
—	12.98	0.97	0.20	—	0.20	—	1.10	(0.48)
—	15.80	0.88	0.33	—	0.33	—	1.71	0.12
—	17.32	0.84	0.56	—	0.56	—	2.45	0.37
—	22.38	0.91	0.86	—	0.86	—	2.88	0.17
—	32.15	0.86	1.10	—	1.10	—	2.53	0.11
—	39.77	0.76	1.74	1.87	3.61	6.20	7.13	0.47
—	44.62	0.80	1.97	2.91	4.88	8.11	8.67	1.01
—	48.05	0.83	2.03	4.41	6.44	11.08	10.76	1.88
—	48.78	0.90	1.99	4.86	6.85	11.05	10.80	9.41
—	56.69	0.91	2.41	4.26	6.67	8.23	9.56	0.84
—	65.16	0.83	3.85	2.98	6.83	5.48	8.73	0.81
—	85.06	0.68	4.12	2.51	6.63	4.32	6.44	0.33
—	96.62	0.72	4.64	3.40	8.04	4.88	6.96	0.70
4.77	110.52	0.73	5.55	6.55	12.10	8.15	8.36	0.87
4.75	119.95	0.76	6.12	7.22	13.34	7.89	8.65	1.41
4.84	132.85	0.76	6.77	6.27	13.04	6.23	8.05	1.01
5.21	141.50	0.79	7.52	8.07	15.59	7.20	8.48	1.80
6.28	147.52	0.84	8.60	8.43	17.03	6.81	8.54	2.83
6.63	170.09	0.85	9.48	9.93	19.41	6.88	7.96	0.86
7.31	174.71	0.97	9.75	11.11	20.87	6.57	7.57	4.52
9.38	180.91	0.70	10.13	10.80	20.93	8.51	8.37	3.38

Table A.2 Thyssen & Co. credits and debits to the Thyssen-Konzern, 1909–1914

	1909	1910	1911	1912	1913	1914
Assets						
August Thyssen Acct. II, Schloss Landsberg						7,775,602
Machine Company	9,459,694	9,459,694	1,769,207	8,550,524	11,067,926	3,420,905
Thyssen & Co., total						
Steam turbine facility		450,000	693,795	693,795	693,795	693,795
Central generator						651,873
GDK, Bruckhausen, Total	26,326,507	31,908,928	44,480,206	59,267,474	66,596,450	66,146,667
Wasserwerk Thyssen & Co., total	3,049,238	2,409,341	3,593,363	5,320,504		
Gas & Wasserwerk, Hamborn					101,798	227,470
Kalkwerk T&C, Wüelfrath, total	1,332,699	1,145,645	966,421	759,120	916,969	1,004,524
Thyssen-Konzern Central Co-op Store	482,894	470,463	20,958	22	40	412
Berlin subsidiary	313,791	391,531	1,394,397	1,912,972	987,728	1,087,224
Berlin supplementary acct.		40,000				
Berlin subsidiary, capital acct.	1,000,000	1,000,000	1,200,000	1,235,238	1,235,238	1,300,000
Heinrich Reiter, total						1,050,514
Mengelbier & Co.	100,000	100,000	120,000	120,000	120,000	120,000
Stahlwerk Thyssen AG, total			2,251,765	1,118,408		
Bad Töennistein, total			116,352	137,581	162,580	162,558
Gewerkschaft Lohberg			42,218	21,477	12,444	18,311
AG fr. Hüettenbetrieb, total	7,906,136	4,716,361	3,923,953			
Gewerkschaft Rhein				2,472	26,707	11,836
GDK, Dinslaken						89,137
Gewerkschaft Jacobus						37,113
Thyssen Trading Co., Cologne						377,522
Thyssen Trading Co., Essen						5,631
Thyssen'sche Trading companies, total				28,243	269,208	
Total Thyssen-Konzern credits	49,970,959	52,091,964	60,572,636	79,167,829	82,190,884	76,405,491

Liabilities

August Thyssen	12,411,365	12,640,433	15,614,255	19,959,977	26,504,440	5,533,513
Joseph Thyssen	4,626,412	4,689,849	6,093,217	7,756,036	9,605,116	1,113,606
GDK, Dinslaken	1,515,534	663,806	2,277,499	2,121,574	1,785,434	7,840,299
AG fr. Hüettenbetrieb, total	0	0	0	447,688	2,876,287	
Gewerkschaft Jacobus				74,268		
Machine Company Thyssen & Co.	1,786,674	693,834				
Spülversatz Hamborn		7,346	21,292	47,546	111,134	64,773
Stahlwerk Thyssen AG, accept.-acct.						2,301,868
Total Thyssen-Konzern debits	3,302,208	1,364,985	2,298,790	2,691,077	4,772,855	10,206,940

Source: MA: R 5 30 12–13; R 5 35 15–18.

Notes: Figures for December 31 of each year. Postings for 1909–1911 not final; those for 1912–1914 final.

Table A.3 CAO-prepared Thyssen-Konzern financial statement, 1912 (December 31)

	Mining			Steel works, Stahlwerk Thyssen	Mining, steel works, GDK	Blast furnaces, AGHütt	Steel & rolling mills, Thyssen & Co.	Machine engineering comp., MF Thyssen & Co.	Trading firm, Vulcaan AG	Total
	Gew. Lohberg	Gew. Rhein	Gew. Jacobus							
Assets										
Fixed assets	16,305,516	7,474,355	18,616,104	29,972,613	140,286,688	20,048,229	29,247,601	6,124,349	1,638,778	269,714,234
Mortgages	0	0	0	0	0	0	0	0	44,982	44,982
Running accounts	12,000	4,800	187,520	778,920	0	192,500	0	0	0	1,175,740
Subsidiaries	100,000	100,000	366,300	0	25,471,042	1,483,728	0	0	0	27,521,070
Banks	0	0	0	0	0	0	1,415,942	0	82,861	1,498,803
Thyssen-Concern	152,142	51,711	2,216,519	2,639,353	79,283,381	0	70,722,184	0	1,385,879	156,451,169
Other acct. receivable	880,919	947,300	2,612,241	23,977,163	23,546,920	3,017,307	17,703,806	4,182,446	857,590	77,725,692
Total acct. receivable	1,033,061	999,011	4,828,760	26,616,516	102,830,301	3,017,307	89,841,933	4,182,446	2,326,330	235,675,664
Inventory	1	0	2,797,354	2,898,281	6,391,060	4,071,050	2,085,508	5,137,185	0	23,380,438
Securities	0	0	0	8,545	0	0	2,558,390	0	8,500	2,575,434
Cash, bills	0	0	20,924	74,161	585,087	11,186	241,712	2,293	4,901	940,266
Profit/loss account	223,978	96,255	40,120	0	0	0	0	0	0	360,353
Outstanding stock	0	0	0	0	0	0	0	0	765,000	765,000
Total assets	17,674,556	8,674,421	26,857,082	60,349,036	275,564,180	28,824,000	123,975,143	15,446,273	4,788,491	562,153,182

Liabilities

										Total
Equity accounts	0	0	0	1,000,000	30,000,000	4,500,000	28,614,890	1,000,000	1,700,000	66,814,890
Bonds—loans	0	0	0	0	0	0	2,792,000	4,000,000	0	6,792,000
Mortgages	0	0	0	0	44,551,573	7,557,789	2,009,473	84,500	0	54,203,335
Guaranteed/ Del Credere	0	0	0	0	0	0	1,731,263		0	1,731,263
Acceptances	0	0	0	0	13,211,903	7,857,003	11,326,516	0	0	32,395,423
Banks	516,465	0	526,789	2,500,000	20,134,422	3,743,304	36,794,184	0	0	64,215,163
Thyssen-Concern	17,015,089	8,627,434	21,008,232	49,476,851	52,824,499	2,097,190	569,503	4,832,372	0	156,451,169
Other acct. payable	131,052	42,187	2,295,440	5,263,466	14,356,534	844,402	10,338,310	3,145,442	1,304,566	37,721,398
Total acct. payable	17,662,606	8,669,621	23,830,461	57,240,317	87,315,454	6,684,895	47,701,996	7,977,814	1,304,566	258,387,730
Outstanding wages	0	0	0	110,189	3,743,424	203,622	328,020	170,245	0	4,555,499
Depreciation account	0	0	2,839,051	1,210,464	0	0	20,102,000	782,448	181,277	25,115,239
Employee support funds	0	0	0	9,147	4,098,855	0	2,408,109	100,435	0	6,616,545
Joint public accounts	0	0	0	0	0	0	329,850	0	0	329,850
Reserves	0	0	0	0	74,028,470	150,980	300,021	352,158	6,766	74,838,394
Reserve funds	0	0	0	0	7,500,000	0	1,608,481	245,769	663,341	10,017,591
Running accounts	12,000	4,800	187,520	778,920	0	192,500	0	0	0	1,175,740
Net profits	0	0	0	0	11,114,500	2,627,119	3,772,616	732,904	932,542	19,179,682
Total liabilities	17,674,606	8,674,421	26,857,031	60,349,036	275,564,180	29,773,908	123,025,235	15,446,273	4,788,491	562,153,181
Check	17,674,556	8,674,421	26,857,082	60,349,036	275,564,180	28,824,000	123,975,143	15,446,273	4,788,491	562,153,182
Discrepancy	50	0	-51	0	0	949,908	-949,908	0	0	-1

Source: TKA: A/814/3.

Table A.4 Thyssen & Co. banking relations, 1908–1914 (unless otherwise noted, as of December 31 of each year)

Account	1908 Current acct. (Jan. 1)	1908 Sub-acct. (Dec. 31)	1909 Sub-Acct.
Bank füer Handel und Industrie, Berlin	1,010,423	1,029,117	873,696
Barmer Bankverein, Hinsberg, Fischer & Co., Barmen	998,211	997,250	994,706
Bergisch Märkische Bank, Duesseldorf	1,002,761	979,998	1,367,138
S. Bleichroeder, Berlin	1,003,517	1,005,162	1,004,298
Credit Lyonnais, Bruessel	113,438		
Commerz- und Disconto Bank, Berlin			993,524
Deutsche Bank, Berlin	141,575	−494,157	524,813
Deutsche Bank, Tratten-Kto (Draft-Acct.)	4,367,267	4,551,350	3,744,338
Deutsche Bank, Succursal du Bruxelles, Bruessel			
Disconto-Gesellschaft, Berlin	650,287	−27,537	137,733
Disconto-Gesellschaft, Berlin, Tratten-Kto (Draft Acct).	2,230,000	2,800,000	1,650,000
Disconto-Gesellschaft, Essen			
Disconto-Gesellschaft, Frankfurt a/M.	501,492	486,330	502,827
Dresdner Bank, Dresden/Berlin	640,358	−125,580	−630,045
Dresdner Bank, Tratten-Kto (Draft Acct.)	3,600,000	4,515,000	4,825,000
Dresdner Bank, Pfund-Konto			
Dresdner Bank, Separat-Konto, Berlin (Saar u. Mosel)	3,735,740	3,810,455	3,810,403**
Essener Credit Anstalt, Essen	−1,304	−125,377	−48,482
Essener Credit Anstalt, Separat-Konto			
Essener Credit Anstalt, Tratten-Kto.	990,000	1,125,000	1,050,000
Alfred Gans & Cie., Paris	155,231	290,243	87,701
von der Heydt-Kersten & Söhne, Elberfeld		797,357	802,450
Nationalbank füer Deutschland, Berlin	757,286	744,607	731,951
Niederrheinische Bank, Düsseldorf	750,164		
Rheinische Bank, Müelheim-Ruhr	681,459	516,246	539,265
Rheinische Bank, Essen	244,789		
Rheinische Bank, Separat-Konto, Essen			
A. Schaaffhausen Bankverein, Cöln/Berlin	−37,886	−39,307	117,778
A. Schaaffhausen Bankverein, Tratten-Kto (Draft Acct.)	4,300,000	4,440,000	4,200,000
Comptoir National d' Ecompte du Paris, Paris			
E. von der Heydt & Cie., London			
Schweizerische Bankverein, Zürich			
Deutsche Bank, Suca du Br. Vorschuss-Kto, Bruessel (Advance Acct.)			
Kleinwort Sons & Co., London			
Simon Hirschland, Essen			
Lazard Brothers & Cie, London			
A. J. Stern & Co., Paris			
Centralbanken for Norge, Christiania			
Deutsche Effecten & Wechsel Bank, Frankfurt a/M		708	−1,000
C. G. Trinkhaus, Düsseldorf	1,055,682	953,262	
Banque du Bruxelles, Bruessel	666,311		
Norddeutsche Creditbank			
Deutsche Bank, Lombard-Konto, Berlin			
Total banks	29,556,802†	28,230,127†	27,278,093†
Reichsdarlehnskasse, Mülheim-Ruhr			
Great Investment Banks, Berlin	21,896,543	21,690,278	21,482,018
% of total funds from investment banks	74.08	76.83	78.75
Delcredere-Konto			2,071,360
Sconto-Konto (Discount)			175,000
Accepte-Konto	1,696,186	3,702,442	3,031,047
GDK. Accepte-Kto	6,260,000	5,000,000	3,900,000
Total Accepte	7,956,186	8,702,442	6,931,047

*Source 3: MA: R 5 30 12–13; R 5 35 15–18.   **Fol. 41—was not included in the original bank list. Placed in after along with Bank fuer Handel & Industrie, Conto septimo.   †Foreign banks possibly under a different account system; matches the figures used on Fol. 39–40.   ‡This account represents the only significant difference between the preliminary balance and the final balance except for the accounts with Stahlwerke Thyssen.

1910 Sub-Acct.	1911 Sub-Acct.	1912 Sub-Acct.	1913 Sub-Acct.	1914 Sub-Acct.	Final post
983,343	993,675	975,603	982,253	994,735	
1,014,977	1,036,687	1,001,409	940,709	1,006,267	
1,330,096	1,388,168	1,372,421	1,331,778		
1,002,380	1,998,174	2,009,093	2,008,662	1,996,096	
995,675	994,264	980,461	984,021	1,005,882	
91,076	−180,084	−105,426	−11,894	−651,889	
4,431,050	5,187,938	5,238,063	4,962,375	6,794,200	
		11,446	−26,666	282,784	
−399,011	−72,385	−153,370	−53,962	−94,147	
2,800,000	2,920,000	2,300,000	2,150,000	1,850,000	
		487,239	474,702	499,470	
499,774	501,133	489,176	477,867	486,881	
−164,577	−358,398	−1,535,812	−328,764	−226,465	
4,565,000	5,305,000	8,555,000	8,340,000	8,420,000	
				−8,607	
	2,813,536				
−143,148	−78,219	−3,102	−56,084	−22,122	
		1,018,767		1,036,700	
1,130,000	1,125,000	1,020,000	970,000	1,000,000	
−225	266,667	392,291	398,162	401,798	
776,846	805,112	802,633	794,404	799,153	
754,187	995,214	1,005,051	988,848	1,013,097	
620,734	1,096,046	754,264	595,466	739,964	
967,880	989,441	3,217	330,919	219,538	
			21,224		
−330,015	−84,628	−181,902	−488,030	−257,083	
4,740,000	4,985,000	4,750,000	4,730,000	4,750,000	
		398,784	392,864	395,803	
		260,425	179,448	46,481	
		394,237	393,059	397,812	
		800,000			
		1,655,746	1,026,129	1,031,551	
			1,197,578	1,210,352	
			1,337,108	313,625	
			800,000	800,000	
			−6,294		
			852		
				118,974	
		2,098,470	1,051,484		
25,666,042†	32,627,340†	36,794,184	36,888,220	36,350,849	36,350,849
					3,750,000
18,966,502	24,000,265	25,713,999	24,232,234	24,858,858	
73.90	73.56	69.89	65.69	68.39	
2,147,713	1,649,751				1,696,689
175,000	175,000		175,000‡		175,000
4,539,571	6,233,912	8,726,516	11,203,716	28,911,146	
3,600,000	3,300,000	2,600,000	2,250,000	2,100,000	
8,139,571	9,533,912	11,326,516	13,453,716	31,011,146	31,011,146

Table A.5 Thyssen-Konzern balance analysis, 1909–1913 (as of December 31 of each year)

	1909 (%)	1910 (%)	1911 (%)	1912 (%)	1913 (%)
Gross profits					
Stahlwerk Thyssen			0	1,210,464	8,500,000
				(3.98)	*(21.44)*
GDK	15,587,599	17,028,945	19,413,372	20,068,969	20,129,135
	(76.70)	*(79.97)*	*(74.86)*	*(66.03)*	*(50.78)*
AGHütt	1,632,341	1,773,994	2,390,393	3,571,871	4,429,446
	(8.03)	*(8.33)*	*(9.22)*	*(11.75)*	*(11.17)*
Thyssen & Co.	3,101,592	2,492,380	3,186,863	4,150,049	4,881,151
	(15.26)	*(11.70)*	*(12.29)*	*(13.65)*	*(12.31)*
MF Thyssen			942,737	1,391,766	1,698,392
			(3.64)	*(4.58)*	*(4.28)*
Thyssen-Konzern	20,321,533	21,295,319	25,933,365	30,393,118	39,638,124
	(100.00)	*(100.00)*	*(100.00)*	*(100.00)*	*(100.00)*
Net profits					
Stahlwerk Thyssen	0	0	0	0	0
GDK	8,070,857	8,425,996	9,934,300	11,114,500	10,797,985
	(79.24)	*(79.16)*	*(76.95)*	*(64.08)*	*(64.50)*
AGHütt	313,059	281,719	509,646	1,724,788	2,399,765
	(3.07)	*(2.65)*	*(3.95)*	*(9.94)*	*(14.34)*
Thyssen & Co.	1,802,015	1,936,178	2,008,148	3,772,616	2,448,513
	(17.69)	*(18.19)*	*(15.56)*	*(21.75)*	*(14.63)*
MF Thyssen	0	0	457,687	732,904	1,094,322
			(3.55)	*(4.23)*	*(6.54)*
Thyssen-Konzern	10,185,931	10,643,894	12,909,781	17,344,809	16,740,584
	(100.00)	*(100.00)*	*(100.00)*	*(100.00)*	*(100.00)*
Fixed assets					
Stahlwerk Thyssen			7,047,700	29,972,613	58,162,000
GDK	141,495,193	147,522,870	170,090,930	174,712,201	180,912,224
AGHütt	13,961,417	16,382,448	20,134,868	20,048,229	19,355,103
Thyssen & Co.	27,271,397	28,445,954	29,367,168	29,110,020	27,594,895
MF Thyssen		3,500,000	5,100,610	6,124,349	7,254,918
Thyssen-Konzern	182,728,007	195,851,272	231,741,276	259,967,412	293,279,141

Table A.5 (continued)

	1909 (%)	1910 (%)	1911 (%)	1912 (%)	1913 (%)
Net profits: fixed assets					
Stahlwerk Thyssen			0.00	0.00	0.00
GDK	5.70	5.71	5.84	6.36	5.97
AGHütt	2.24	1.72	2.53	8.60	12.40
Thyssen & Co.	6.61	6.81	6.84	12.96	8.87
MF Thyssen		0.00	8.97	11.97	15.08
Thyssen-Konzern	5.57	5.43	5.57	6.67	5.71
Cash flow (net profits + depreciation + increase in reserves)					
Stahlwerk Thyssen			0	2,108,719	8,500,000
				(5.89)	*(19.58)*
GDK	15,587,599	17,028,945	19,413,373	20,868,970	21,633,113
		(82.48)	*(73.06)*	*(58.29)*	*(49.83)*
AGHütt		1,422,067	2,228,753	4,884,245	6,132,187
		(6.89)	*(8.39)*	*(13.64)*	*(14.12)*
Thyssen & Co.		2,080,452	3,132,246	5,305,233	3,593,587
		(10.08)	*(11.79)*	*(14.82)*	*(8.28)*
MF Thyssen		115,034	1,798,957	2,634,224	3,558,379
		(0.56)	*(6.77)*	*(7.36)*	*(8.20)*
Thyssen-Konzern		20,646,498	26,573,329	35,801,391	43,417,266
		(100.00)	*(100.00)*	*(100.00)*	*(100.00)*
Net increase in fixed assets					
Stahlwerk Thyssen			7,047,700	24,135,377	36,689,387
GDK	16,043,139	14,630,627	23,368,056	14,100,342	16,640,856
AGHütt		3,496,002	5,074,759	1,244,985	803,587
Thyssen & Co.		2,669,557	1,029,214	1,117,852	-841,830
MF Thyssen		3,500,000	1,260,561	1,466,138	1,654,046
Thyssen-Konzern		24,296,186	37,780,290	42,064,694	54,946,046
Cash flow: net increase in fixed assets					
Stahlwerk Thyssen				0.09	0.23
GDK	0.97	1.16	0.83	1.48	1.30
AGHütt		0.41	0.44	3.92	7.63
Thyssen & Co.		0.78	3.04	4.75	-4.27
MF Thyssen		0.03	1.43	1.80	2.15
Thyssen-Konzern		0.85	0.70	0.85	0.79

Table A.5   (continued)

	1909 (%)	1910 (%)	1911 (%)	1912 (%)	1913 (%)
Company fixed assets as a percentage of total Konzern fixed capital					
Stahlwerk Thyssen	0.00	0.00	3.04	11.53	19.83
GDK	77.43	75.32	73.40	67.21	61.69
AGHütt	7.64	8.36	8.69	7.71	6.60
Thyssen & Co.	14.92	14.52	12.67	11.20	9.41
MF Thyssen	0.00	1.79	2.20	2.36	2.47
Thyssen-Konzern	100.00	100.00	100.00	100.00	100.00
Redistributed share or equity capital					
Stahlwerk Thyssen			1,912,271	7,942,298	15,063,683
GDK	43,484,542	43,312,595	46,151,216	46,296,140	46,855,411
AGHütt	4,290,646	4,809,873	5,463,246	5,312,483	5,012,880
Thyssen & Co.	8,381,092	8,351,709	7,968,270	7,713,723	7,146,948
MF Thyssen		1,027,597	1,383,962	1,622,861	1,878,990
Thyssen-Konzern	56,156,280	57,501,774	62,878,965	68,887,506	75,957,912
Return to (redistributed) owners equity (ROE)					
Stahlwerk Thyssen			0.00	0.00	0.00
GDK	18.56	19.45	21.53	24.01	23.05
AGHütt	7.30	5.86	9.33	32.47	47.87
Thyssen & Co.	21.50	23.18	25.20	48.91	34.26
MF Thyssen			33.07	45.16	58.24
Thyssen-Konzern	18.14	18.51	20.53	25.18	22.04
Total assets or investment					
Stahlwerk Thyssen			20,844,900	60,349,036	79,417,500
GDK	183,729,189	199,473,616	243,969,012	275,564,180	249,925,226
AGHütt	24,395,304	24,815,959	31,522,615	31,382,389	30,655,473
Thyssen & Co.	89,040,013	91,519,258	103,792,383	123,538,327	130,559,293
MF Thyssen		11,233,921	12,115,323	15,446,273	19,382,065
Thyssen-Konzern	297,164,506	327,042,754	412,244,233	506,280,205	509,939,557
Return on investment (ROI)					
Stahlwerk Thyssen			0.00	0.00	0.00
GDK	4.39	4.22	4.07	4.03	4.32
AGHutt	1.28	1.14	1.62	5.50	7.83
Thyssen & Co.	2.02	2.12	1.93	3.05	1.88
MF Thyssen		0.00	3.78	4.74	5.65
Thyssen-Konzern	3.43	3.25	3.13	3.43	3.28

Table A.5 (continued)

	1909 (%)	1910 (%)	1911 (%)	1912 (%)	1913 (%)
Growth or financing potential (cash flow: total investment × 100)					
Stahlwerk Thyssen			0.00	3.49	10.70
GDK	8.48	8.54	7.96	7.57	8.66
AGHütt		5.73	7.07	15.56	20.00
Thyssen & Co.		2.27	3.02	4.29	2.75
MF Thyssen		1.02	14.85	17.05	18.36
Thyssen-Konzern		6.31	6.45	7.07	8.51
Cash flow to fixed assets					
Stahlwerk Thyssen			0.00	7.04	14.61
GDK	11.02	11.54	11.41	11.94	11.96
AGHütt		8.68	11.07	24.36	31.68
Thyssen & Co.		7.31	10.67	18.22	13.02
MF Thyssen		3.29	35.27	43.01	49.05
Thyssen-Konzern		10.54	11.47	13.77	14.80

Source: MA: R 5 30 12–13; R 5 35 15–18; P 7 77 00–08. Feldenhirchen, *Eisen -und Stahlindustrie. Handbuch der deutschen Aktiengesellschaften.*

Table A.6 Selected financial statistics of the GDK, 1910–1918, and ATH/Friedrich Thyssen, 1919–1925 (in Marks, after 1924 in RM millions)

Year	Total assets	Total equity	Total liabilities	Equity/ liabilities	Fixed assets Mining	Coking	Steel	Dinslaken
1910	199.47	123.78	75.70	1.64	75.27	10.40	28.92	6.28
1911	243.97	144.44	99.53	1.45	77.00	9.36	34.45	6.63
1912	275.56	169.06	106.50	1.59	75.22	8.42	38.40	7.31
1913	249.93	126.89	123.03	1.03	74.38	7.58	44.28	9.38
1914	253.43	131.80	121.63	1.08	73.39	6.92	46.21	9.40
1915	266.20	140.91	125.30	1.12	75.41	6.44	44.76	8.18
1916	279.42	152.44	126.98	1.20	74.29	5.98	40.54	6.50
1917	315.36	167.97	147.39	1.14	72.26	5.39	35.07	6.19
1918	422.23	176.28	245.95	0.72	73.80	5.06	33.81	5.84
ATH+Gew. Friedrich Thyssen								
1919	427.25	143.04	284.21	0.50	93.81	4.50	31.73	5.21
1920	1,122.04	203.58	918.46	0.22	146.02	4.53	74.74	6.49
1921	1,768.28	200.63	1,567.65	0.13	100.09	4.69	65.27	7.55
1922	47,906.47	12,006.86	59,866.90	0.20	533.08	4.23	1,078.32	17.71
1923								
1.1.1924	197.60	145.43	52.18	2.79	78.99	4.69	41.65	4.61
1924	240.71	99.37	140.17	0.71	74.44	5.32	24.48	4.37
1925	311.47	92.69	216.83	0.43	93.16	7.95	57.25	4.15

Source: TKA/A1754; Feldenkirchen, Eisen- und Stahlindustrie, Tab. 83. Total fixed assets from Feldenkirchen, Eisen- und Stahlindustrie, Tab. 83 (includes railway, harbor and subsidiary shareholdings). After 1914 from TKA/A1754.

Total equity capital = share capital (after 1899 constant at RM 30 million) + owner deposits + various reserve funds

Total liabilities = creditors + acceptances + mortgages

Depreciation includes depreciation on subsidiaries.

Total fixed assets	Equity/ total fixed assets	Depre- ciation	Additions to reserves	Net profits (loss)	Cash flow or gross profits	Net profits/ equity	Cash flow to total assets	Cash flow to increase in fixed assets
147.52	0.84	8.60	8.43		17.03	6.81	8.54	(0.39)
170.09	0.85	9.48	9.93		19.41	6.88	7.96	0.86
174.71	0.97	9.75	11.11		20.87	6.57	7.57	4.52
180.91	0.70	10.13	10.80		20.93	6.57	7.57	4.52
173.81	0.76	9.47	5.24		14.71	3.97	5.80	(2.07)
166.96	0.84	13.84	7.92		21.76	5.62	8.17	(3.17)
154.94	0.98	16.04	13.12		29.16	8.61	10.44	(2.43)
146.12	1.15	12.54	15.71		28.25	9.35	8.96	(3.20)
147.15	1.20	8.24	8.51	(9.61)	(26.35)	4.83	(6.24)	(25.60)
171.96	0.83	7.42	9.86	(3.52)	(9.13)	(2.46)	(2.14)	(0.37)
248.09	0.82	17.34	70.76	(1.73)	69.78	(0.85)	6.22	0.92
228.52	0.88	16.01	91.13	3.35	102.44	1.67	5.79	(5.23)
6,536.15	1.84	130.43	15,373.63	12,160.50	15,279.01	101.28	31.89	2.42
		—	—	—	—			
163.67	0.89	—	—	—	—	—	—	—
143.70	0.69	10.93	(4.86)	(5.74)	(15.08)	(5.77)	(6.27)	0.76
191.11	0.49	3.76	13.62	15.57	6.68	16.80	2.15	0.14

Table A.7 Liquidity analysis of the GDK/ATH, 1897–1925

Year	Accounts receivable	Inventories	Current assets	Accounts payable
1897	2,862,201	4,706,093	7,654,672	8,669,911
1898	5,540,755	5,195,394	10,856,764	11,779,421
1899	6,403,087	5,201,213	11,726,157	10,813,428
1900	5,693,653	5,871,320	11,774,107	10,028,040
1901	6,031,489[a]	3,832,471	10,007,544	9,161,695
1902	7,016,857	5,376,402	12,605,898	5,279,705
1903				
1904	8,541,582	8,846,468	17,809,812	17,260,975
1905	12,740,681	6,124,090	19,008,484	18,263,058[b]
1906	20,741,065	6,032,840	27,073,843	34,870,019
1907	21,335,747	6,042,609	27,722,694	31,479,223
1908	22,645,245	6,135,379	29,056,813	28,456,652
1909	31,351,528	10,334,351	42,233,996	31,697,197
1910	37,952,295	13,336,031	51,950,743	29,738,305
1911	74,085,254	7,636,211	82,557,155	44,191,058
1912	102,830,301	6,391,060	109,806,449	44,995,421
1913	64,387,417	10,232,044	75,863,655	53,864,016
1914	58,793,799[c]	9,961,272	70,761,815	39,195,230[d]
1915	87,027,148	11,306,645	99,239,753	62,501,081
1916	110,999,821	11,239,110	124,474,230	59,871,022
1917[e]	156,729,019[f]	11,923,294	169,142,572	
1918	234,596,718[g]	12,510,345	248,729,807	
August Thyssen-Hütte (ATH)				
1919	217,246,015[h]	10,613,878	237,085,954	200,564,488
1920	718,265,071[i]	92,461,524	815,894,823	702,383,754
1921	1,159,250,793[j]	298,315,992	1,476,873,097	1,379,588,126
1922	33,417,912,280	5,911,592,281	41,243,975,294	52,181,314,072
1923				
1 Jan. 1924	15,639,372	15,029,947	32,460,738	43,065,286[m]
1924	50,053,877[k]	42,831,270	93,769,327	132,593,570
1925	61,501,386[l]	55,191,123	118,067,872	158,769,089
1 Mar. 1926		70,710,432	71,713,067	74,045,325[n]

Source: TKA: A/1754.

a. Of which RM 4,638,014 owed by Thyssen & Co.
b. Of which RM 7,936,239 owed to banks.
c. Thyssen-Konzern = RM 42,238,875
d. Of which RM 23,826,628 owed to banks.
e. After IG redistribution. Accounts payable not given.
f. Thyssen-Konzern = RM 69,955,275.
g. Thyssen-Konzern = RM 135,493,175
h. Thyssen-Konzern = RM 71,745,513.
i. Thyssen-Konzern = RM 566,265,097.
j. Thyssen-Konzern = RM 14,763,477,704.
k. Thyssen-Konzern = RM 15,390,435.
l. Thyssen-Konzern = RM 28,722,547.
m. Thyssen-Konzern = RM 3,871,711.
n. Represents a balance in this amount.

Current liabilities	Thyssen & Co.	Current ratio	Quick ratio	Working capital
10,126,201	11,598,838	0.76	0.29	−2,471,529
14,476,984	3,191,848	0.75	0.39	−3,620,220
14,584,804	996,992	0.80	0.45	−2,858,647
13,764,918	659,330	0.86	0.43	−1,990,811
12,486,206	0	0.80	0.49	−2,478,662
7,827,853	1,380,038	1.61	0.92	4,778,045
20,760,796	3,481,609	0.86	0.43	−2,950,984
21,838,162	11,913,649	0.87	0.59	−2,829,678
39,403,373	10,645,242	0.69	0.53	−12,329,530
36,787,794	16,760,828	0.75	0.59	−9,065,100
33,825,302	21,050,276	0.86	0.68	−4,768,489
38,456,696	24,794,428	1.10	0.83	3,777,300
37,294,243	28,159,171	1.39	1.04	14,656,500
55,295,767	39,096,358	1.49	1.35	27,261,388
61,950,748	52,824,499	1.77	1.67	47,855,701
68,020,053		1.12	0.96	7,843,602
51,173,834		1.38	1.19	19,587,981
69,793,791		1.42	1.26	29,445,962
64,372,511		1.93	1.76	60,101,719
147,588,027		1.15	1.07	21,554,545
245,950,740		1.01	0.96	2,779,067
207,208,979		1.14	1.09	29,876,975
714,967,650		1.14	1.01	100,927,173
1,413,310,377		1.04	0.83	63,562,720
59,196,031,416		0.70	0.60	−17,952,056,122
44,323,140		0.73	0.39	−11,862,402
133,990,358		0.70	0.38	−40,221,031
161,602,153		0.73	0.39	−43,534,281
80,415,607		0.89	0.01	−8,702,540

Table A.8 Financial analysis of the ATH, 1924–1925 (Price Waterhouse figures)

ATH Consolidated (including trading firms)	Dec. 31, 1924	Dec. 31, 1925	Change
Assets			
Fixed assets (properties/plant)	678,567,202	711,702,485	33,135,283
Investments in affiliated companies	19,453,715	27,384,894	7,931,179
Inventories	90,734,923	103,702,104	12,967,181
Affiliated companies in debit	23,016,571	12,565,921	−10,450,650
Trade debtors	28,182,407	26,537,738	−1,644,669
Accounts receivable	65,195,321	43,693,388	−21,501,933
Current assets	165,134,401	158,837,680	−6,296,721
Total assets/liabilities	864,019,803	901,957,557	37,937,754
Liabilities			
Share capital	30,300,000	30,300,000	0
Accumulated surplus (at beg. of year)	631,583,765	643,795,841	12,212,076
Profit/loss for year	18,595,800	−25,183,863	−43,779,663
Owner's capital and surplus	680,479,565	648,911,979	−31,567,586
Minority interest in Gebr. Hoppe	206,402	212,345	5,943
Total proprietary capital or equity	680,685,967	649,124,324	−31,561,643
Lease obligation to affiliated companies	2,805,522	10,051,424	7,245,902
Funded long-Term debt	5,231,653	64,463,858	59,232,205
of which five year 7% sinking fund gold bond		45,360,000	45,360,000
Floating debt	104,013,077	103,677,018	−336,059
of which bank loans and acceptances	94,056,086	103,473,018	9,416,932
Affiliated companies in credit	12,363,272	6,947,580	−5,415,692
Trade creditors	14,622,415	14,462,126	−160,289
Trade acceptances	7,316,218	13,833,221	6,517,003

Total accounts payable	51,018,918	53,842,139	2,893,221
Current liabilities	157,122,614	159,549,609	2,426,995
Total sales revenues		364,999,510	
Profit/loss statement			
Gross profit		49,680,006	
Administrative/selling expenses		28,374,369	
Interest income		6,735,090	
Net profit (before interest and depreciation)		28,040,727	
Depreciation and rent of plant (including leased)		11,756,331	
Interest charges (all types)		24,746,227	
Preliminary balance		-8,461,832	
Profits tax		268,231	
Nonrecurring income		5,983,543	
Nonrecurring expenditure and special charges		22,343,725	
Interest proportion of profits in Gebr. Hoppe		-93,618	
Net profits/losses	18,595,800	-25,183,863	-43,779,663
Ratio analysis			
Gross profit margin on sales		13.61	
(Operating) net profit margin on sales		8.33	
Net profits: fixed assets	2.74	-3.54	-0.06
Current ratio (current assets/current liabilities)	1.05	1.00	
Quick ratio (current assets − inventories)/current liabilities	0.47	0.35	-0.13
Working capital (current assets − current liabilities)	8,011,787	-711,929	-8,723,716
Working capital (*100): total assets	0.93	-0.08	-1.01
Debt: total assets	0.31	0.36	0.06
Debt: owner's equity	0.39	0.50	0.11
Owner's equity: debt	2.56	1.98	-0.57

Source: TKA: A/833/2; A/835/1.

Appendix B:
Accounting as Symbolic Practice

For readers unfamiliar with accounting, let alone "new accounting theory," this appendix outlines some of the new approaches. Furthermore, it makes explicit some of the ideas underlying the methodology of this book, whose premises were deeply informed by newer approaches to accounting and organization theory, but whose interpretation remains framed by debates of German history and business history.

By treating accounting as a procedural artifact, a remnant of a lost organizational order, I tracked the evolving conception of control operating inside the management systems of Thyssen & Co., the Thyssen-Konzern, and the VSt. Unlike earlier views about accounting that stressed its documentary, neutral character, as if it held a mirror up to the enterprise, new postmodern theories of accounting treat it as a social, institutional, and organizational practice. This postmodern approach also calls into question Max Weber's modernist conception of accounting as a formally rational procedure. In this approach, accounting helps constitute organizational reality, creating "specific patterns of organizational visibility" and imaginatively reconstructs the corporation itself.[1] Accounting does not just provide an information-processing service, but rather creates and organizes knowledge about the firm, thus mediating managerial decision-making. In short, the information and accounting system of a business is a key part of a complex communicational process, allowing the firm to coordinate and control, thereby creating organizational coherency and constructing the corporation.

The accounting and information system acts as at least one critical component of the organizational capabilities of the business firm. If the competence of the firm is "a measure of a firm's ability to solve both technical and organizational problems," then this information system provides the crucial set of signals to management about those problems.[2] While these procedures are certainly bureaucratic techniques binding the firm together in a series of organizational routines, they construct knowledge about the firm. If the successful firm is a learning organization, as modern organizational theory emphasizes, then this reporting system provides an "account"—it tells a story—about the firm's activities so that managers can learn. The communication procedures and types of information collected affect recognition, transmission of knowledge, and decision-making throughout the organization.[3] August Thyssen knew about his firm through this information system; he traveled frequently and so judged his managers from accounting reports. He paid an amazing amount of attention to financial and organizational matters, best represented by his personal composition of the statutes for the CAO. Analogous to the way accounts track and record the activity of a firm over time, I took the alterations in this information and reporting system as the best signifiers for the evolution of management and managerial knowledge that made firms' operations intelligible.

Financial and managerial accounting help create organizational coherence inside the business enterprise by connecting the actions of its employees across time and space. The critical question is how the enterprise (or enterprise system) is conceived as a coherent unified whole that makes sense of the business firm's activities and performance. What concept of control governs the firm and how is the firm implicitly conceived?[4] This concept of the firm refers to a sometimes unreflexive, seemingly natural preunderstanding of what a business should do, whom it should work for, and what a business is. One should view the concept of a corporation not as a free-floating cultural metaphor, but rather as an assumption embedded in a firm's practices, shaped by the firm's individual strategies. Like archaeological artifacts, one can interpret such business practices not only as instrumental techniques, but also as signifiers of the social, organizational, and conceptual world they express. Historians might find this approach similar to Richard Biernacki's, who showed how broader cultural meanings in Britain and Germany fabricated the practice of labor commodification inside firms. Because of different understandings about labor, British and German textile firms measured and accounted for labor in different ways. Although similar in sensibility, I did not embed the accounting analysis in a discussion of culture as did Biernacki, but instead understood it as a social, institutional, and communicational process within organizations. More work linking German business culture to its business practices still needs to be accomplished.[5]

Accounting as Symbolic Practice

How does a firm account for itself? A system of accounts discursively re-presents the firm as classification schemes, financial statements, and reports, whose numerical figures illuminate the processes and relationships of the firm, and provides a basis for evaluating the firm's performance. It makes the enterprise transparent, generating visibility in order to manage and to regulate, thereby disciplining managers and workers into a system of accountability.[6] It affects the very mentality and discourse of entrepreneurs and management.[7] Accounting is much more than a system of formal rules or a signifier of calculative rationality as Max Weber interpreted it, but rather an analytical, interpretive, communicational, and symbolic practice. As the familiar adage goes, the "language of business is accounting."

Once treated like language, accounts become more or less standardized codes built around conventions and institutionalized practices, which help transform perception and create organizational reality.[8] Accounts are a major part of management's conceptual lenses, forming premises for decision-making. As a form of communication, moreover, accounts always have an audience, which often reshapes the presentation of information. (One can call them genres.) For instance, it is common to distinguish between financial accounting and managerial accounting.[9] Financial accounting reports primarily to audiences external to the firm, and thus come under the purview of owners, bankers, bondholders, professional accounting societies, disclosure laws, national public opinion, municipalities, and state regulation. But internal managerial accounting, because its audience varies so greatly depending on industry, firm, product, or managers, has a significant diversity of practice. Financial accounting is much more institutional-

ized (i.e., embedded in social and professional circles rather than organizational contexts), but still varies considerably from country to
country today. Present controversies about international accounting
standards or the reform of German accounting norms testify to how
financial reporting is such a crucial part of corporate governance, especially if firms want to attract outside investors.

Max Weber described "capital accounting" as "formally the most rational means of orienting economic activity" because it provides a
quantitative calculation for transacting, recording, and assessing economic activity. In his theory, it is *the* central indicator of the formally
rational nature of economic action, distinctive to (Western) capitalist
enterprise and modernity. By contrast, "substantive rationality" is the
degree to which actions are consistent with the ends or "ultimate values," be they authoritarian, feudal, political, ethical, hedonistic, etc.,
or associated with a specific social group or interest. (The historiography of German entrepreneurs clearly has its roots in Weber's
thought.) Precisely because capitalist firms orient themselves to markets to earn profits—and money and markets are already rationalized
abstractions—he felt that these characteristics made capital accounting the most formally rational form of human interaction, so much so
that "through a system of individual accounts the fiction is here created that different departments within an enterprise, or individual accounts, conduct exchange operations with each other, thus permitting
a check in the technically most perfect manner on the profitability of
each individual step or measure."[10] For Weber, formal capital accounting is instrumental, objective, a value-neutral tool oriented to earning
profits. Significantly, Weber chose internal transfer pricing among organizational departments within the enterprise to show the highest
form of rationality, yet as we saw, setting internal transfer prices can
be one of the most problematic and politicized aspects of corporate
organization. Moreover, the conscious or unconscious manipulation
of internal transfer prices inside multinational corporations to avoid
taxes or national regulations is one of the most controversial topics
today.

To be fair, Weber was well aware of the enormous social tension between the formal rationality of economic actors and the substantive rationality oriented to the needs, ends, and values of society. Indeed, the
growth of big business or state bureaucracies (instrumental rational-

ity) threatening traditional values of communities (the "lifeworld" in Habermas) or social needs of workers (class) has been the primary source of discontent or open conflict in modern society. Weber also noted the tension between the economic rationality of the enterprise (management) and the substantive rationality of ownership (family). A Weberian approach would interpret the sour relations inside the Thyssen family as a symptom of such a tension. This tension between the two rationalities constitutes the essence of Weber's thought.

Yet, in his underlying theory—not as a scholar or human being—Weber analytically detached means from ends, technique from decisions, technical or formal rationality from substantive rationality, form from content, value neutrality from ultimate values. For most of the twentieth century (and still in many textbooks), accounting is portrayed as a neutral, value-free reporting technique. It provides feedback that informs individuals of an optimal strategy or decision so that they can make an informed, rational choice.[11] Not surprisingly, the practice of accounting immediately loses its credibility, its "aura," precisely when accounts seem "cooked" or manipulated.[12] The power of accounting as a decision-making instrument is destroyed when it fails to seem neutral and objective. Thus, the more naturally categorized or consistently rational or objective accounts appear, the more they silently guide organizational action.

This modernist view of economic and accounting rationality has come under attack. In an influential article, John Meyer and Brian Rowan argued against conceiving rationalized "formal structures" of organizations as a means of efficient control or coordination. Instead, "institutionalized products, services, techniques [accounting], policies, and programs function as powerful myths, and many organizations adopt them ceremonially." Organizational structures, best-practice manufacturing processes, or technical procedures become "taken-for-granted means to accomplish organizational ends. Quite apart from their efficiency, such institutionalized techniques establish an organization as appropriate, rational, and modern."[13] (One could interpret the VSt's explicit introduction of an American Hollerith-based accounting system as a ceremonial emblem of rationalization and modernity). Meyer and Rowan view accounting as a means of creating organizational legitimacy, tapping into broadly accepted social virtues and myths about rationality, efficiency, and objectivity. Bruce Carruthers called accounting the "quintessential rationalized myth."[14]

Guided by this approach, for instance, Wendy Espeland and Paul Hirsch have argued that the symbolic power of accounting rhetorically legitimized the U.S. conglomerate movement of the late 1960s and 1970s and reinterpreted the corporation as a financial unit. With a financial conception of the firm, power moved to financial officers and creative accountants.[15]

Meyer and Rowan accentuate the dark side of Weber's often forgotten fears—that bureaucratic rationality forms a particular type of legitimate domination, the "iron cage," rather than a benign technocratic efficiency.[16] Unlike Weber, however, Meyer and Rowan view organizations not as regular, rationalized, and internally consistent wholes, but rather as artifacts embedded in a set of social institutions such as professions, policies, or programs. They do not view techniques as rational instruments, but as historically institutionalized procedures, borrowed from the outside. Best-practice accounting procedures, for instance, grew out of the hands of individual organizations and into sophisticated, professional societies. According to Meyer and Rowan, business managers use these typified professional routines ceremonially inside an individual organization to create legitimacy, rather than as rational instruments. Sometimes new state-of-the-art procedures begin as rational solutions to specific problems, but over time become more ritualistic than rational.

For other such "neo-institutional" analysts, the incorporation of professionalized routines explains to a large extent why industrial practices and forms converge over time ("institutional isomorphism"). Pushed to an extreme, this approach actually calls into question an individual decision-making point and regards decisions as embedded in ritualized social, institutional, and organizational practices, which decide *for* managers.[17] The accounting system tells managers when and where they have turned a profit or loss. This knowledge embeds individual managers inside the firm into a broader institutional context that they themselves do not make, trains them to think in particular ways, and constructs the options available to them. Those professional norms and practices influence—if they do not determine—decision-making and express socially institutionalized conventions and values. Unlike economic, rational choice, transaction cost, or modernization theories, organizations converge through institutional, imitative, ritualistic, or cultural processes.

Significant theoretical problems, however, arise in viewing accounting practices as myth and ceremony. This idea assumes that participants blindly or tacitly accept the accounting rules as legitimate. The social construction of reality approach tends to break down when participants go "behind the numbers" to question how the accounting system generates results. Accounting research offers numerous cases where participants either instrumentalize certain account information (and not others) for their own ends, or deconstruct the methodology of the techniques, or question the validity of the figures generated. In addition, financial reports or the bottom line, as one "text" among many, can also be read "openly" and interpreted by management in different ways as a center of an intertextual, often politicized, organizational project.[18] Accounting information provides just one set of signals, rules, or resources for managerial decision-making. Managers can often play one set of signals or rules off of another, contesting their validity in specific contexts at specific times. Often there are alternative, legitimate institutionalized formal techniques, accounting methods, organizational forms, or production processes available that managers can wield inside their organization. Outside the firm, academics or accountants can debate the efficacy of particular methods, such as the common use of return on investment (ROI) ratios.[19] Even judged by purely technical criteria, considerable ambiguity can exist about the relative efficiency of various, competing institutionalized procedures, "scripts," or "templates." Accounting reports can generate contradictory results and signals. Managers can then deem certain signals or criteria more significant or relevant than other signals. In short, there is a reflexive "interpretive act" in reading accounts.[20] Making accounting (or other institutionalized practices) a myth overstates how much is taken for granted, and overdetermines decision-making. Finally, pushed down its logical path, viewing accounting as myth and ceremony eventually cannot explain change in organizations or institutions.

Recent postmodern accounting theorists, drawing on the usual suspects—Jacques Derrida,[21] Roland Barthes,[22] Michel Foucault,[23] Anthony Giddens,[24] Walter Benjamin,[25] Jürgen Habermas,[26] H. Richard Niebuhr and Paul Ricoeur,[27] and Clifford Geertz[28]—or analyzing it as rhetoric,[29] information, or culture, have brought a whole battery of intellectual approaches to reinterpret accounting. The free-floating set of theoretical approaches testifies to the new accounting theory's intellectual vibrancy, but also to the difficulty in finding an appropriate analytical approach.[30] All these broadly postmodern, culturalist approaches have a common deficiency in that they have difficulty explaining historical change in accounting practice over time (even at the level of meaning) or the diversity of accounting approaches across individual organizations or societies. For my purposes, we need not decide conclusively that accounting is either a formal, instrumentally rational technique of efficient coordination or a celebratory myth of legitimizing ritual. Instead, I instrumentalized a few core ideas to analyze the conception of control governing Thyssen & Co., the Thyssen-Konzern, and the VSt.

Information, Organization, and Conception of Control

Belying its reputation as bean-counting, accounting is fundamentally an act of imagination. The accounting system provides "cognitive maps" of an enterprise's relationships (other firms, labor, the state), processes (such as manufacturing activity or financial flows), cost or profit centers (particular internal areas), its performance over time, and the overall state of the enterprise.[31]

Alfred Chandler argued that accounting remained fairly much the same as it was in fourteenth-century Italy, until the advent of railroads. Others have placed the transition to modern accountancy in the 1880s or with the American textile mills in the 1850s, or at Springfield Armory of the 1830s, or at Wedgwood and Boulton & Watt, pushing its advent back into the British industrial revolution.[32] In any event, in the 1880s, let alone the 1920s, accounting conventions were hardly standardized procedures in Germany or anywhere else in the industrializing world. Accounting practices varied greatly from firm to firm. A nascent public profession of accountants in the 1880s concerned themselves with how to set up a new system of accounts with the proper categories. These accounting firms propagated and standardized procedures across firms. According to the available literature, corporate industrial practice appears to have been more sophisticated than the published literature of the profession at least until the mid-twentieth century, perhaps earlier (by the 1920s) in Britain and the United States.

Until the advent of large-scale organizations with high fixed costs, capital accounting was essentially mercantile bookkeeping *(Buch-führung)*, a recording and monitoring device to control people (for fraud) and track transactions. German commercial law viewed book-keeping as a set of archival records, which required appropriate care in account journals as a legal basis for claims and counterclaims. At root, it is a bureaucratic procedure, which is why Weber could make it central to his theory of rational bureaucracy. But accounting is not bookkeeping. What bookkeeping is to bureaucracy, accounting is to capitalist enterprises. Accounting is a management device, not just a bureaucratic technique.

German organizational practice, for instance, distinguished be-tween bookkeeping *(Buchführung)*, accounting *(Buchhaltung)*, and au-diting *(Revision)*.[33] Thyssen & Co. clearly distinguished between an ac-counting and an auditing office. Thyssen later added the CAO for his whole complex of firms, which acted more as an outside consulting and auditing firm. Bookkeeping allows firms to record, register, and reckon expenses and transactions, but accounting implies a system-atic order to create transparency. The appropriate connections among various bookkeeping journals of the firm allow a series of meaning-ful statements to emerge, most importantly year-end balance sheets, profit-loss statements, income statements, cost-accounting schedules, and sales summaries. Some of the earliest German organizational manuals concentrated on the proper and orderly linking of the vari-ous bookkeeping journals to create an early version of industrial *System* or *Organisation*.[34] In brief, accounting implies a more comprehensive system—how all the books combined create meaningful statements.

Finally, auditing moves one step further in abstraction by not only cross-checking and controlling for the basic accounting figures, but by also interpreting the methodologies and accounting measures them-selves—not only for their veracity but for their implications for the business firm. The auditing office acts as a second tier of control, inter-pretation, and reflexive self-analysis. By its nature, auditing questions the accounting procedures themselves. Not surprisingly, professional, independent auditing firms developed quickly into powerful, external consulting firms, which gained greater power as legislation required certain standards of financial disclosure.[35]

Thus, the analysis and judgment associated with accounting differ-entiate it from mere bookkeeping in theory as well as in organizational practice because it is a fundamentally interpretive act, not just one of recording. Indeed, the more accounting conventions become institutionalized, the more they appear routine, formal, calculative, and technical, and thereby disguise their conceptual foundation in interpretation and imagination. Yet one can construct accounts in very different ways, with different categorizations, different principles, different conventions, and different theoretical premises underlying the calculable figures and ratios. Evolving and changing modes of accounting can lead to different results and different profit levels—the ultimate arbiter of business performance. Peter Miller nicely called this emergence the "genealogies of calculation."[36]

How is accounting an act of interpretation and imagination? The second sentence of a German textbook on business states: "The picture of numbers *(Zahlenbild)* of the accounting system mirrors the firm's activity."[37] These numbers purport to offer a faithful portrait of the firm over a given period of time. Accounting systems manufacture knowledge about the organization's past as if it were a mirror, a slew of figures truthfully lined up in columns or a summary of salient ratios. These accounts represent a complex four-dimensional firm in a two-dimensional paper representation of reality, using black and white numbers: in reports, statistics, graphics, figures, and ratios—what Edward Tufte called "flatland."[38] Historians confront a similar problem. Roland Barthes once scathingly described written histories as "an inscription of the past pretending to be a likeness of it, a parade of signifiers masquerading as a collection of facts."[39] Correctly, historians cannot squeeze a four-dimensional (space-time) past with a cast of hundreds of millions onto black-and-white pages, no matter how thick the tome and sophisticated the historian. Likewise, Tufte's "flatland" highlights the unbridgeable difference between the three-dimensional world and its two-dimensional representation, reality and the numbers, the world and the word, and the signified and the signifier. This act of representation and system of signification is fundamentally creative. Obviously, escaping "flatland" can be more or less accomplished, more or less persuasive.

As a representation of the activity of a four-dimensional enterprise across time, certain orientations and principles guide the construction of this image (and not others.) For instance, all accounting information begins with the act of classifying costs so they can be recorded consistently. Yet the act of classifying already presumes judgments and preconceptions, a way of thinking, because classifying accounts constructs a figurative taxonomy of the enterprise and its transactions.[40] Certain principles (and not others) "order things" and costs according to their similarities and differences so that they appear in the same class or genus or species or account book. Varying degrees of ambiguity enter with the first stroke of the recording act.

For instance, all accounting conventions need to define an expense area (i.e., a secretarial office pool or a functional workshop) or an expense type (specific sorts of office supplies, mailings, services, energy, or other inputs). In the 1920s, German accountants and engineers heatedly debated whether they should define expenses by areas or types.[41] There are advantages and disadvantages to both. Broad expense areas are easier to account for, but less precise. Expense types are more precise, but involve more expense in tracking them. Overhead and administrative costs are also notoriously difficult to calculate as well as to allocate across specific activities or expense areas. Even delineating where an expense area begins or ends is not necessarily easy. For instance, in a plate mill, where does the production process end? Does it include the plate shears that cut the rolled metal or not? Or does it extend to the point where the finished product is prepared for shipping in the final assembly room? Ultimately, the exact extent of the cost area or category is probably less important than emerging, more or less agreed-upon conventions that are consistent and comparable over time—one reason why all accounting textbooks stress the importance of balance continuity in financial statements. Classifying costs in a particular way not only can bring the expense of an activity out of invisibility, but it can also make some of them disappear once again. In this respect, accounting does not just make costs transparent but fundamentally creates them. Classifying expenses in certain ways makes costs. Constructing cost schemes thus appear as cognitive maps of company expenses.

Such ruminations might appear banal or unnecessarily abstract, but they have major implications for business enterprises. No German steel firm answered these questions in precisely the same way until the 1930s, and such questions played a major role in forming the VSt. Even year-end financial statements that helped guide major investments and stock speculation had few ground rules for their formatting, so that a tremendous amount of variety and leeway for manipulation existed. Not until the 1930s did legislation in Germany begin to standardize financial statements more closely. Contemporaries could not take their numbers at face value. Neither can historians. Because of this, certain financial statements cannot necessarily be trusted.[42] Accounting standards are crucial for establishing trust—one reason why the Enron-Arthur Anderson scandal struck at the heart of capitalism itself.

Even if one solves the issue of standardization and conventions, what information as a representation of company performance is of utmost importance to entrepreneurs, managers, investors, or stakeholders? The selection of critical information implies a core strategy, a manner of organizing control, as well as a particular conception of the firm. Does the firm emphasize profit margins, production costs, labor productivity, output, return on sales, earnings per share, return on assets, return on investment, cash flow ratios, and so on?

Key pieces of information or figures deemed important by the actors themselves divulge a particular strategy, a concept of control, and a conception of the firm. Andrew Carnegie, for instance, felt profits would follow naturally if he ruthlessly drove down prime costs (direct labor and materials costs). Thyssen focused on monthly reports and production costs that incorporated various commercial and financial costs (esp. amortization, depreciation, and overhead). DuPont and General Motors later focused on return on investment ratios, which indicated that profits would follow if they used their investment capital most efficiently. Both primary indicators of strategy controlled for and turned attention to very different activities of the business firm. Carnegie essentially conceived of the firm as a manufacturing operation that makes profits, while DuPont or General Motors conceived of the firm as a financial organization that makes profits. This is why it is somewhat shocking to read Alfred Sloan describing General Motors as not in the business of making cars, but of making money. Obviously, both companies manufactured products and used capital (as well as hired people and sold their products to customers)—the four functional "fingers" of the firm, but their strategies and conceptions of control, their "thumbs," differed dramatically.

Companies can also change what they stress over time as their strategies change. When Dow Chemical launched a new strategy oriented

toward product and process innovation to increase market share
rather than collude with the bromine pool, they reinvented their organization and flows of information. They created new reports focusing especially on quality of product, manufacturing efficiency (i.e.,
pounds of bleach per ampere day), average cost of product, and after
1903 unit earnings for each product (measured two different ways).
Reflected and reinforced by accounting information, the company
reconceived itself as an adaptive, proprietary firm oriented toward
making satisfactory profits by "keeping expenses as low as possible that
is if we can do it without having to add to the plant" to one based on
constant innovation and new investment, especially to expand plant to
gain new manufacturing efficiencies and market share. They also began offering new products. Dow reconceived itself as a chlorine producer (of many products), rather than as just a bleach producer. They
designed informative reports to promote "innovative investing."[43] Information followed strategy.

In the 1990s, it became commonplace to criticize the conglomerate
movement for reconceiving a firm merely as a stream of assets, financial flows, or as a portfolio rather than as an enterprise for making
things. Financial ratios increasingly guided strategic decisions. In this
case, market price of a share, dividends per share, earnings per share
(EPS), or price/equity (P/E) ratios might be deemed most appropriate.

For our purposes, what do these figures of performance communi-
cate? They indicate fundamentally what performance is and how it is
calculated; they imply a strategy and specific organizational behaviors;
they also imply an audience to which company reporting is directed.
For instance, the financial reporting to improve earnings per share or
price/equity ratios is an expression of maximizing "shareholder value"
for investors, which pressures the firm into improving these measures
of performance (first) and not others. Importantly, one can evaluate a
complex organization by a number of criteria, but some are more
compelling than others inside a given business enterprise or in various
business cultures. These criteria and performance measures disclose
different means of organizing control.

A contrast of two Italian Renaissance firms, using even simplified
double-entry bookkeeping, offers a perspective on this issue. Frederic
Lane noted how Venetian venture accounting differed from Tuscan

business accounting. Venetian venture accounting oriented itself toward tracking obligations and claims, a single venture's profit-and-loss, the firm's choice of commission agents, and the price of sales overseas. By contrast, Tuscan business accounting attended more to the short-term needs of partnerships, specifically in order to calculate short-term profits and distribute them regularly to shareholders. Unlike most Venetian firms, Tuscan accounting also distinguished between the firm as a temporary, contractual entity and its partners. Venetian accounting had difficulty preparing periodic financial statements at any point in time for a business, but instead focused on the beginning and ending of a voyage, the individual venture. Venetian accounting proved very suitable for testing whether its sales agents traded with the largest potential profit margins, and was adept at tracking agent's sales commissions. Maximizing profits and minimizing sales commissions meant profits would follow. Both types of accounting kept their agents honest, but the concept of control differed significantly. Tuscan accounts, however, were primed to assess surpluses at regular intervals and redistribute them to the partners. One operated as a sales-oriented organization, the other as a financial organization. They also differed in their conception of a firm as a series of discrete ventures organized by a family, versus a temporary partnership with an implicit separation of shareholders from the firm's management. Context and audience shaped the *construction* of these accounts and divulged these two firms' concept of control.

How has a firm's accounting system constructed performance and profitability? Different calculative measurements of profits yield different results, different levels of profit. Measuring returns, making costs transparent, assessing the capital, discovering the value of an enterprise are surprisingly tricky calculations. Accounts take some things, processes, costs, or flows into account better than other things, processes, costs, flows, or intangible intellectual property. The difficulty of valuing knowledge-based firms such as computer software companies is a recent case in point. Share price or balance sheets may not properly value a company or its intangibles, indicating a potential disjunction between price and value.[44]

All these questions highlight a theoretical problem with Weber's conception of capital accounting. Weber posits a rather unproblematic notion of profit, which is disembodied from social, institutional, and organizational contexts and which allows him to conceive of the profit-orientation of capitalist enterprises as formal, contentless market rationality. Even if we grant the calculative, instrumental act of accounting as a formally rational system and even if we assume the enterprise is a profit-maximizing venture, the question of which information or figures are most meaningful to management is still an important question that lies outside the boundaries of the formally rational. The very measure of profit provides content, or, in Weber's terms, contains substantive rationality. It conceals a conceptual understanding of the corporation, its performance, how it should work, and toward what it works. Instead of taking the maximization of profits or profit-orientation at face value, we need to deconstruct it. Allegedly, formally rational accounting techniques and figures remain entwined with the strategy and conception of the enterprise. The fact that Weber uses internal transfer prices as the premier expression of formal rationality indicates this blind spot because they are one of the most problematic aspects of managerial accounting practices. Deep in the heart of capitalist enterprise lies a conceptual and substantive structuring element that creates order. It is precisely here that postmodern approaches to accounting and organization are most valuable because they highlight or deconstruct the assumptions of the dominant way of ordering knowledge, and thereby show alternatives and give "voice and legitimacy to those tacit and oftentimes unpresentable forms of knowledge that modern epistemologies inevitably depend upon yet conveniently overlook or gloss over in the process of knowledge creation."[45]

Traditionally, academics have conceived the field of management control as a tool to assess whether the organization achieves its strategic objectives, as if it were a "thermostat" that management regulates. This (implicitly Weberian) distinction between strategy and control, formulation and implementation, ends and means analytically distinguishes the two concepts as if managers formulated strategy somehow separately from their information system.[46] Yet this control system helps reinforce strategy because crucial information (allegedly) is taken into account.[47] A strict delineation between ends and means makes managerial choice a sequence of independent, more or less informed, decision-making acts instead of a complex, ongoing feedback process. The "thermostat," the accounting control, tell management if their strategy is succeeding or failing. The control system actively shapes strategy formulation as well as internal organizational behavior precisely because it provides incentives and data about the direction of the company. This approach does not analyze the particular construction of accounts, for what the information system was explicitly or implicitly accounting or controlling.

Moreover, once institutionalized into organizational practice, measurement alters organizational action as managers orient themselves toward these controls and indicators—and not necessarily for the better. Educators have experienced a similar problem with standardized testing scores: education means teaching to the test. One frustrated financial controller argued: "The minute you say that 'that' is what you are measuring, if you haven't a balance and a check within the system [i.e., other measurements], 'it' will get better!"[48] Named after the London School of Economics professor, Charles Goodheart, Goodheart's law maintained that any observed statistical regularity will tend to collapse once pressure is placed upon it for control purposes; once a variable is incorporated into policy-making, it tends to lose its explanatory power, although the variable itself gains power as people orient themselves to it. The common objection that orientation to short-term share price regardless of other variables actually undermines the health of an enterprise has its roots in this idea. Ironically, often the more complex the formal controls inside an organization for checks and balances, the more difficulty the organization has with maintaining control; moreover, the expense and time involved in collecting such information rises. Many office workers have had the experience of spending more time reporting on their work than doing the work itself.

From the point of view of a historian, if the remnants of this management control system are analyzed as conceptual and procedural remnants of a previous organizational order, they can provide an insight into key measures of performance, linking the information system to firm strategy and core organizational values.[49] Accounting information provides a feedback loop for contemporaries within the managerial organization and betrays a particular perspective on the business. A business firm may aim the antennae of its accounting and information system to signal some changes in performance more sensitively than other issues. These performance indicators are then intimately linked to firm strategy, its system of control, its organizational form, its internal governance system, who the firms works for, and an implicit conception of the firm itself.[50] This approach is particularly useful in earlier periods, precisely because of the lack of professionalized and institutionalized procedures, because it discloses an inside perspective on the individual business firm.

I termed this relationship of strategy, organization, information, and accountability the firm's conception of control, which provides a means of ensuring accountability and trust—organizing control. This conception of control underpinning the business firm is central to understanding corporate governance and how it attempts to realize the universal priority of business enterprise: to make profits. Thus, unlike Weber, this perspective makes profit-making the beginning, not the end, of inquiry. Ultimately, the conception of control provides a system of surveillance, whose task, however, is not only to monitor or discipline, but is also part and parcel of the organizational capabilities of the firm. This surveillance system is not total or uniform, but has biases, blindspots, and points of priority. It is also loosely coupled to corporate strategy and the highlighted statistics act as signals, which help construct organizational reality. I stress the term "loosely coupled" because senior management may decide upon a new strategy, and the alignment of the organization along with its routines and accounting measures (Chandler's structure) may not follow immediately.

To be clear, by no means does an accounting system overdetermine managers' thinking or action. To paraphrase Karl Marx, managers might not make their own accounts, but their accounts do not quite make them. Framed, constrained, and guided by (more or less) institutionalized accounting procedures, managers retain an active, interpretive, reflexive agency. The accounting and information system provides a set of meaningful signals to contemporaries. If contemporaries treat these signals as good, relevant, or rational, the accounts structure the field of debate within the organization even if participants disagree with the results. Accounting provides information on which to base reasonable assertions, a way of constituting knowledge without overdetermining action and eliminating agency. In this case, managers may even use these figures as "ammunition machines" in their own politicized battles, as VSt managers did with the Fretz-Moon process. As we saw with this debate or in the negotiated debates about internal transfer prices, the accounting system acts as a symbolic or rhetorical ground for making decisions, helping constitute and frame the internal dialogue of a firm.[51] At minimum, the accounting reports help frame the terms of reasoned debate. Exactly how an organization uses such information is a matter for empirical analysis.

Thus, "reading" the accounting and control system inside a business firm provides the historian with an insightful method for entering into the life of an organization. Contemporaries took these accounts seriously. People's ideas and (pre)conceptions became embedded in the standard operating procedures of firms. This operating conception of control essentially describes how a firm's organization thinks, decides, and learns. This methodology provides a way of grasping changes in the managerial system itself, rather than relying on the figure in charge of the business firm as a signifier of an ideal-type. From this system of controls, with its implicit values and concerns and with its explicit routines and procedures, one can read the evolving, historical nature of the business enterprise. We need a good deal more work on the history of European management inside the business firm, not just more business histories that assume the firm is a unitary actor on the market.

Finally, throughout this book I tried to show how financial and accounting criteria, accounting conventions, and financial ratios inform organizational decision-making and confer power. They help guide the formulation of business strategy as they provide a set of information for competing strategies and rationales. Traut's presentation to Thyssen, which stressed the needed cost and future profitability of his plan, is one example. In the VSt study commission, the numbers helped decide which plants should stay in operation and which ones should be shut down. As in Dinkelbach's career, accounting information confers organizational legitimacy on those managers who can present signals that participants find most persuasive and compelling. Those who gather, frame, and report this information gain special power within the business organization. With this in mind, there is little wonder that discussion about the proper organization of the firm in Thyssen & Co., the Thyssen-Konzern, and the VSt were closely associated with central auditing offices. This link between organizational knowledge and power held particularly true for Albert Killing (inside Thyssen & Co.), Carl Rabes (inside the Thyssen-Konzern and VSt), and finally, Heinrich Dinkelbach (inside the VSt).

Notes

Introduction

1. R. H. Coase, "The Nature of the Firm (1937)," in *The Nature of the Firm: Origins, Evolution, and Development,* ed. Oliver E. Williamson and Sidney G. Winter (Oxford: Oxford University Press, 1991), pp. 18–33.

2. Alfred D. Chandler, Jr., *The Visible Hand: The Managerial Revolution in American Business* (Cambridge, Mass.: Belknap Press of Harvard University Press, 1977); and *Scale and Scope: The Dynamics of Industrial Capitalism* (Cambridge, Mass.: Belknap Press of Harvard University Press, 1990).

3. William Lazonick, *Business Organization and the Myth of the Market Economy* (Cambridge: Cambridge University Press, 1991).

4. Harold James, *A German Identity* (New York: Routledge, 1989).

5. Hermann Simon, *Hidden Champions: Lessons from 500 of the World's Best Unknown Companies* (Boston: Harvard Business School Press, 1996), p. 18. W. R. Smyser, *The German Economy: Colossus at the Crossroads* (New York: St. Martin's Press, 1993), pp. 67–101.

6. Olivier Zunz, *Making America Corporate, 1870–1920* (Chicago: University of Chicago Press, 1990). There is no equivalent in German historiography.

7. To name a few of the most outstanding, Jürgen Kocka, *Unternehmensverwaltung und Angestelltenschaft am Beispiel Siemens 1847–1914: Zum Verhältnis von Kapitalismus und Bürokratie in der deutschen Industrialisierung* (Stuttgart: Klett-Cotta, 1969); Peter Hayes, *Industry and Ideology: IG Farben in the Nazi Era* (Cambridge: Cambridge University Press, 1987); Gottfried Plumpe, *Die I. G. Farbenindustrie AG: Wirtschaft, Technik und Politik 1904–1945* (Berlin: Duncker and Humblot, 1990); Lothar Gall et al., *The Deutsche Bank, 1870–1995* (London: Weidenfeld and Nicolson, 1995); Hartmut Berghoff, *Zwischen Kleinstadt und*

Weltmarkt: Hohner und die Harmonika, 1857–1961 (Paderborn: Ferdinand Schöningh, 1997); Wilfried Feldenkirchen, *Siemens, 1918–1945* (Columbus: The Ohio State University Press, 1999); Neil Gregor, *Daimler-Benz in the Third Reich* (New Haven: Yale University Press, 1998); Alfred Reckendrees, *Das "Stahltrust" Projekt: Die Gründung der Vereinigte Stahlwerke AG und ihre Unternehmensentwicklung, 1926–1933/34* (München: C. H. Beck, 2000); Lothar Gall, *Krupp: Der Aufstieg eines Industrieimperiums* (Berlin: Siedler, 2000); Christopher Kobrak, *National Cultures and International Competition: The Experience of Schering AG, 1851–1950* (Cambridge: Cambridge University Press, 2002).

8. See the excellent comparative work by Thomas Welskopp, *Arbeit und Macht im Hüttenwerk: Arbeits- und industrielle Beziehungen in der deutschen und amerikanischen Eisen- und Stahlindustrie von den 1860er bis zu den 1930er Jahren* (Bonn: Verlag J. H. W. Dietz, 1994).

9. See Victoria de Grazia, "Introduction," in *The Sex of Things: Gender and Consumption in Historical Perspective,* ed. Victoria de Grazia with Ellen Furlough (Berkeley: University of California Press, 1996), pp. 1–10.

10. Richard R. Nelson and Sidney G. Winter, *An Evolutionary Theory of Economic Change* (Cambridge, Mass.: Harvard University Press, 1982). See also M. Dierkes, A. Berthoin Antal, J. Child, and I. Nonaka, eds., *Handbook of Organizational Learning* (Oxford: Oxford University Press, 2001). My contribution to the *Handbook* offers a theoretical exposition of my approach (see "Thinking Historically about Organizational Learning," pp. 162–191), and the volume as a whole offers a rich palette of approaches toward organizational theory. See also Haridimos Tsoukas and Christian Knudsen, eds., *The Oxford Handbook of Organization Theory: Meta-Theoretical Perspectives* (Oxford: Oxford University Press, 2003).

11. The following literature represents the best overviews of the story of the Thyssen-Konzern: Conrad Matschoss, "August Thyssen und Sein Werk: Zur Erinnerung an die Begründung des ersten Werkes am 1. April 1871," *Zeitschrift des Vereines deutscher Ingenieure,* Nr. 14 (Berlin, 2. April 1921); Paul Arnst, *August Thyssen und Sein Werk* ed. Dr. E. Schmalenbach (Leipzig: G. A. Gloeckner, 1925); Walter Däbritz, *Geschichte der Deutschen Röhrenwerke Aktiengesellschaft Werk Thyssen in Mülheim-Ruhr* (Unpublished manuscript) ([1930s]), Mannesmann-Archiv (MA); Walter Däbritz, *August Thyssen* (unpublished manuscript): Mannesmann & Thyssen-Archiv ([1944]); Walter Däbritz, "August Thyssen: Zum Gedächtnis an seinen Geburtstag, den 17. Mai 1842," *Werkszeitung Deutsche Röhrenwerke A. G. Werk Thyssen,* Mülheim-Ruhr, 17. Jg., special issue (May), ed. in cooperation with the Society for Arbeitspädagogik in agreement with the German work front

(1942); Wilhelm Treue, *Die Feuer Verlöschen Nie: August Thyssen-Hütte, 1890–1926*, 1 (Düsseldorf/Wien: Econ, 1966); Wilhelm Treue and Helmut Uebbing, *Die Feuer Verlöschen Nie: August Thyssen-Hütte, 1926–1966*, 2 (Düsseldorf/Wien: Econ, 1969); Helmut Uebbing, *Wege und Wegmarken: 100 Jahre Thyssen, 1891–1991*(Berlin: Siedler, 1991); Manfred Rasch, "August Thyssen: Der Katholische Grossindustrielle der Wilhelminischen Epoche," *August Thyssen und Hugo Stinnes: Ein Briefwechsel, 1898–1922* ed. Manfred Rasch and Gerald D. Feldman (München: C. H. Beck, 2003), pp. 14–107.

12. Alfred D. Chandler, Jr., "The United States: Seedbed of Managerial Capitalism," in *Managerial Hierarchies: Comparative Perspectives on the Rise of the Modern Industrial Enterprise*, ed. Alfred D. Chandler, Jr., and Herman Daems (Cambridge, Mass.: Harvard University Press, 1980), pp. 9–40.

13. Hidemasa Morikawa, *Zaibatsu: The Rise and Fall of Family Enterprise Groups in Japan* (Tokyo: Tokyo University Press, 1992), pp. 105–114.

14. Oliver E. Williamson, *Markets and Hierarchies: Analysis and Antitrust Implications: A Study in the Economics of Internal Organization* (New York/London: Free Press, 1975); Oliver E. Williamson, "The Modern Corporation: Origins, Evolution, Attributes," *Journal of Economic Literature*, XIX (December 1981), pp. 1537–1568; and Oliver E. Williamson, *The Economic Institutions of Capitalism: Firms, Markets, Relational Contracting* (New York: Free Press, 1985), pp. 279–297. See also H. Thomas Johnson and Robert S. Kaplan, *Relevance Lost: The Rise and Fall of Management Accounting* (Boston, Mass.: Harvard Business School Press, 1991), p. 99. On the development of the multidivisional enterprise, see Alfred D. Chandler, Jr., *Strategy and Structure: Chapters in the History of the Industrial Enterprise* (Cambridge, Mass.: MIT Press, 1962). In brief, see *Scale and Scope: The Dynamics of Industrial Capitalism* (Cambridge, Mass.: Belknap Press of Harvard University Press, 1990), pp. 36–45.

15. Ulrich Wengenroth, "Germany: Competition Abroad—Cooperation at Home 1870–1990," in *Big Business and the Wealth of Nations,* ed. Alfred D. Chandler, Jr., Franco Amatori, and Takashi Hikino (New York: Cambridge University Press, 1997), pp. 139–175.

16. Michel Albert, *Capitalism vs. Capitalism* (New York: Four Walls Eight Windows, 1993).

17. On the concept of the firm and its relationship to organizational capabilities, see Jeffrey R. Fear, "Constructing Big Business: The Cultural Concept of the Firm," *Big Business and the Wealth of Nations,* ed. Alfred D. Chandler, Jr., Franco Amatori, and Takashi Hikino (Cambridge: Cambridge University Press, 1997), pp. 561–569.

18. William H. Sewell, Jr., "Toward a Post-Materialist Rhetoric for Labor

History," in *Rethinking Labor History*, ed. Lenard R. Berlanstein (Urbana: University of Illinois Press, 1993), pp. 15–38.

19. Gerhard Mollin, *Montankonzerne und 'Drittes Reich': Der Gegensatz zwischen Monopolindustrie und Befehlswirtschaft in der deutschen Rüstung und Expansion, 1936–1944* (Göttingen: Vandenhoeck & Ruprecht, 1988).

20. Classic texts are Ralf Dahrendorf, *Society and Democracy in Germany* (New York: Norton, 1967); Hans-Ulrich Wehler, *The German Empire 1871–1918* (Lexington Spa: Berg, 1985); and David Blackbourn and Geoff Eley, *The Peculiarities of German History: Bourgeois Society and Politics in Nineteenth-Century Germany* (Oxford: Routledge, 1984).

21. Volker R. Berghahn, *The Americanisation of West German Industry, 1945–1973* (New York: Cambridge University Press, 1986).

22. Alexander Gerschenkron, *Economic Backwardness in Historical Perspective* (Cambridge, Mass.: Belknap Press of Harvard University Press, 1966); Henry Rosovsky, ed., *Industrialization in Two Systems: Essays in Honor of Alexander Gerschenkron* (New York: Wiley, 1966); Clive Trebilcock, *The Industrialization of the Continental Powers, 1780–1914* (London/New York: Longman, 1981); and Richard Sylla and Gianni Toniolo, eds., *Patterns of European Industrialization: The Nineteenth Century* (New York: Routledge, 1991). See also Douglass Bennett and Kenneth Sharpe, "The State as Banker and Entrepreneur: The Last Resort Character of the Mexican State's Economic Intervention, 1917–1970," in *Brazil and Mexico: Patterns in Late Development*, ed. Silvia Ann Hewlett & Richard S. Weinert (Philadelphia: Institute for the Study of Human Issues, 1982), pp. 169–211.

23. Gerschenkron, *Economic Backwardness,* p. 14.

24. See Gerschenkron's classic, *Bread and Democracy in Germany* (Berkeley: University of California, 1943). See also William N. Parker, "Europe in an American Mirror: Reflections on Industrialization and Ideology," *Patterns of European Industrialization: The Nineteenth Century,* ed. Richard Sylla and Gianni Toniolo (London: Routledge, 1991), pp. 80–91.

25. The more general literature on German history is too vast to be given note here. Some examples of this view that give special attention to German business can be found in Dahrendorf, *Society and Democracy in Germany,* pp. 49–54, 162–171; Heinz Hartmann, *Authority and Organization in German Management* (Princeton: Princeton University Press, 1959). Hans-Ulrich Wehler, *Das Deutsche Kaiserreich, 1871–1918* (Göttingen: Vandenhoeck & Ruprecht, 1973); Toni Pierenkemper, *Die Westfälischen Schwerindustrielle, 1852–1913: Soziale Struktur und unternehmerischer Erfolg* (Göttingen: Vandenhoeck & Ruprecht, 1979), pp. 72–81; Eckehard J. Häberle, *Strukturwandel der Unternehmung: Unter-*

suchungen zur Produktionsform der bürgerliche Gesellschaft in Deutschland von 1870–1914 (Frankfurt/Main: Haag & Herchen, 1979); Gerhard A. Ritter und Klaus Tenfelde, *Arbeiter im deutschen Kaiserreich 1871–1914* (Bonn: J. H. W. Dietz, 1992); Susanne Hilger, *Sozialpolitik und Organisation: Formen Betrieblicher Sozialpolitik in der Rheinisch-Westfälischen Eisen- und Stahlindustrie set der Mitte des 19. Jahrhunderts bis 1933* (Stuttgart: F. Steiner Verlag, 1996); and Barbara Wolbring, *Krupp und die Öffentlichkeit im 19. Jahrhundert* (München: C. H. Beck, 2000). For a lucid exception to the rule, see Dick Geary, "The Industrial Bourgeoisie and Labour Relations in Germany," *The German Bourgeoisie: Essays on the Social History of the German Middle Class from the Late Eighteenth to the Early Twentieth Century,* ed. David Blackbourn and Richard J. Evans (London: Routledge, 1991), pp. 147–152.

26. For skeptical discussions, see Hartmut Kaelble, "Wie feudal waren die deutschen Unternehmer im Kaiserreich? Ein Zwischenbericht," *Beiträge zur quantitativen vergleichenden Unternehmensgeschichte,* ed. Richard Tilly (Stuttgart: Klett-Cotta, 1985), pp. 148–171. Also Dolores Augustine, *Patricians and Parvenus: Wealth and High Society in Wilhelmine Germany* (Oxford: Berg, 1994). The most recent research has tended to reverse this position entirely. In English, see especially the collection of articles in *Bourgeois Society in Nineteenth-Century Europe,* ed. Jürgen Kocka and Allan Mitchell (Oxford/Providence: Berg, 1993). As Kocka summarizes, the "aristocratic-*haut bourgeois* symbiosis" was more or less common to all European countries but was decidedly "less advanced" in Germany than in France or England (but not Austria and Italy), and certainly not as much as the feudalization thesis would suggest. In spite of the exact opposite reasoning, the German *bourgeoisie* remained more backward, weaker, decidedly less liberal, more dependent and allied to state-bureaucratic traditions, more isolated, and less alluring to other classes in Germany relative to other West European countries. Kocka no longer speaks of a lack of *embourgeoisement* characterizing German society, but of the *bourgeoisie*'s limits or weaknesses or *"unbourgeois"* features. In spite of these massive revisions, the "core of the *Sonderweg* thesis" still applies (see esp. pp. 21–32).

27. Hartmann, *Authority and Management,* pp. 5–11. For a more differentiated assessment of authority relations inside German firms, see Patrick Fridenson, "Authority Relations in German and French Enterprises, 1880–1914," *Bourgeois Society in Nineteenth-Century Europe,* ed. Jürgen Kocka and Allan Mitchell (Oxford/Providence: Berg, 1993), pp. 323–345.

28. Hartmann, *Authority and Management,* pp. 22–78, quote from p. 190.

See also Peter A. Schlenzka, *Unternehmer, Direktoren, Manager: Krise der Betriebsführung?* (Düsseldorf: Econ Verlag, 1954). Schlenzka attempts to upgrade the term *management*. Ironically, this distinction between leadership and management, entrepreneurialism and administration, creative change and mundane routine has come roaring back in American management literature. For examples, see John P. Kotter, *A Force for Change: How Leadership differs from Management* (New York: Free Press, 1990), and Abraham Zaleznik, "Managers and Leaders: Are They Different?" *Harvard Business Review* (March-April 1992), pp. 126–135.

29. Hans Jaeger, "Unternehmensgeschichte in Deutschland seit 1945: Schwerpunkte—Tendenzen—Ergebnisse," *Geschichte und Gesellschaft,* 18 (1992), pp. 107–132. Jaeger provides a detailed, though somewhat more positive portrayal of the literature. In general, he calls for a more reflective, theoretical, and synthetic approach to business history. Kocka's articles have recently been collected in an edited volume available in English: Jürgen Kocka, *Industrial Culture and Bourgeois Society: Business, Labor, and Bureaucracy in Modern Germany, 1800–1918* (New York: Berghahn Books, 1999).

30. Jürgen Kocka, *Unternehmensverwaltung und Angestelltenschaft am Beispiel Siemens, 1847–1914: Zum Verhältnis von Kapitalismus und Bürokratie in der deutschen Industrialisierung* (Stuttgart: Klett-Cotta, 1969).

31. Kocka: *Unternehmensverwaltung,* pp. 463–544.

32. This thesis has been more fully developed in Jürgen Kocka, "Bürgertum und Bürgerlichkeit als Probleme der deutschen Geschichte vom späten 18. zum frühen 20. Jahrhundert," in *Bürger und Bürgerlichkeit im 19. Jahrhundert* ed. Jürgen Kocka (Göttingen: Vandenhoeck & Ruprecht, 1987); and Jürgen Kocka, "Bürgertum und bürgerliche Gesellschaft im 19. Jahrhundert: Europäische Entwicklungen und deutsche Eigenarten," in *Bürgertum im 19. Jahrhundert: Deutschland im europäischen Vergleich,* 1, ed. Jürgen Kocka (München: DTV, 1988).

33. Others have approached industrial organization in a case-study format using a social-structural framework: Günther Schulz, *Die Arbeiter und Angestellten bei Felten & Guilleaume: Sozialgeschichtliche Untersuchung eines Kölner Industrieunternehmens im 19. und beginnenden 20. Jahrhundert* (Wiesbaden: F. Steiner Verlag, 1979); Hermann-Joseph Rupieper, *Arbeiter und Angestellte im Zeitalter der Industrialisierung: eine sozialgeschichtliche Studie am Beispiel der Maschinenfabriken Augsburg und Nürnberg* (M. A. N.), *1837–1914* (Frankfurt/New York: Campus, 1982); Hannes Siegrist, *Vom Familienbetrieb zum Managerunternehmen: Angestellte und industrielle Organisation am Beispiel der Georg Fischer AG in Schaff-*

hausen, 1797–1930 ed. Helmut Berding, Jürgen Kocka, and Hans-Ulrich Wehler (Göttingen: Vandenhoeck & Ruprecht, 1981); and Heidrun Homburg, *Rationalisierung und Industriearbeit: Arbeitsmarket—Management—Arbeiterschaft im Siemens-Konzern Berlin 1900–1939* (Berlin: Haude & Spener, 1991). These studies provide a bridge to the study of the professionalization of white-collar workers, or the effect of corporate industrial policies on labor relations and employee social policies.

34. Jürgen Kocka, "Family and Bureaucracy in German Industrial Management, 1850–1914: Siemens in Comparative Perspective," *Business History Review*, 45, 2 (Summer 1971), pp. 133–56.

35. Jürgen Kocka, *Unternehmer in der deutschen Industrialisierung* (Göttingen: Vandenhoeck & Ruprecht, 1975). An English summary of his arguments can be found in "Entrepreneurs and Managers in German Industrialization," in *Cambridge Economic History of Europe, Volume VII: The Industrial Economies: Capital, Labour, and Enterprise*, ed. Peter Mathias and M. M. Postan (Cambridge: Cambridge University Press, 1978), pp. 492–589.

36. Jürgen Kocka, "Grossunternehmen und der Aufstieg des Manager-Kapitalismus im späten 19. und frühen 20. Jahrhundert: Deutschland im internationalen Vergleich," *Historische Zeitschrift*, 232 (1981), 39–60; Jürgen Kocka, "The Rise of the Modern Industrial Enterprise in Germany" in *Managerial Hierarchies: Comparative Perspectives on the Rise of the Modern Industrial Enterprise*, ed. Alfred D. Chandler, Jr., and Herman Daems (Cambridge, Mass.: Harvard University Press, 1980), pp. 77–116, esp. 107–110.

37. Kocka, "Rise," pp. 88–92, 107–109.

38. Jürgen Kocka, "Industrielles Management: Konzeptionen und Modelle in Deutschland vor 1914," *Vierteljahrschrift für Sozial- und Wirtschaftsgeschichte*, 56, 3 (Oktober 1969), pp. 332–372.

39. Kocka, "Rise" and "Industrielles Management."

40. Alfred D. Chandler, Jr., "The United States: Seedbed of Managerial Capitalism," *Managerial Hierarchies: Comparative Perspectives on the Rise of the Modern Industrial Enterprise*, ed. Alfred D. Chandler, Jr., and Herman Daems (Cambridge, Mass.: Harvard University Press, 1980), pp. xx–xx; Alfred D. Chandler, Jr., and Herman Daems, "Administrative Coordination, Allocation and Monitoring: Concepts and Comparisons," *Recht und Entwicklung der Grossunternehmen im 19. und frühen 20. Jahrhundert: Wirtschafts-, sozial- und rechtshistorische Untersuchungen zur Industrialisierung in Deutschland, Frankreich, England und den USA* ed. Norbert Horn and Jürgen Kocka (Göttingen: Vandenhoeck &

Ruprecht, 1979), pp. 28–54. Also reprinted in *The Essential Alfred Chandler,* ed. Thomas K. McCraw (Boston: Harvard Business School Press, 1988), pp. 398–424.

41. Jürgen Kocka and Hannes Siegrist, "Die hundert grössten deutschen Industrieunternehmen im späten 19. und frühen 20. Jahrhundert: Expansion, Diversifikation und Integration im internationalen Vergleich," in *Recht und Entwicklung der Grossunternehmen im 19. und frühen 20. Jahrhundert: Wirtschafts-, Sozial- und Rechtshistorische Untersuchungen zur Industrialisierung in Deutschland, Frankreich, England und den USA* ed. Norbert Horn, Jürgen Kocka (Göttingen: Vandenhoeck & Ruprecht, 1979), pp. 55–122.

42. The section on Germany in *Scale and Scope* rests on the extensive but uneven narratives in German anniversary issues and on the exemplary work of Wilfried Feldenkirchen, Ulrich Wengenroth, Robert Brady, Gerald Feldman, and especially, Jürgen Kocka. See also the review essay by Christopher Schmitz, "Cooperative Managerial Capitalism: Recent Research in German Business History," *German History,* 10, 1 (1992), pp. 91–103. Schmitz argues that "there has been no satisfactory work of synthesis which goes any way towards offering a balanced appraisal of the nature of German capitalism." It is illuminating that the underlying *theoretical* foundation for German business organization has been implicitly grounded on Chandler's works: *Strategy and Structure* (1962), the *Visible Hand* (1977), and *Scale and Scope* (1990).

43. See Chandler, *Scale and Scope,* pp. 393–395, 587–592, for a summary of the differences in German capitalism.

44. See the collection of articles including Kocka's in *Organisierter Kapitalismus* ed. H. A. Winkler (Göttingen: Vandenhoeck & Ruprecht, 1974). For a skeptical assessment of this concept, see Gerald Feldman, "Der deutsche Organisierte Kapitalismus whrend der Kriegs- und Intlationsjahre, 1914–1923" in *Deutsche Wirtschaftsgeschichte im Industriezeitalter: Konjunktur, Krise, Wachstum* ed. Werner Abelshauser und Dietmar Petzina (Düsseldorf: Athenäum-Verlag, 1981), pp. 299–323. The concept is still controversial. For more debate, see Hans-Jürgen Puhle, "Historische Konzepte des entwickelten Industriekapitalismus: 'Organisierter Kapitalismus' und 'Korporatismus,'" *Geschichte und Gesellschaft,* 10 (1984), pp. 165–184; Volker Hentschel, "German Economic and Social Policy, 1815–1939," *Cambridge Economic History of Europe, Volume VIII,* ed. Peter Mathias and Sidney Pollard (Cambridge: Cambridge University Press, 1989), pp. 752–813; Jeffrey Fear, "German Capitalism," *Creating Modern Capitalism: How Entrepreneurs, Com-*

panies, and Countries Triumphed in Three Industrial Revolutions ed. Thomas K. McCraw (Cambridge, Mass.: Harvard University Press, 1997), pp. 135–182.

45. Chandler, *Scale and Scope,* p. 295.

46. Jürgen Kocka, "Scale and Scope: A Review Colloquium," *Business History Review* 64 (Winter 1990), pp. 690–735, quotes from p. 714.

47. Bernd Dornseifer and Jürgen Kocka, "The Impact of the Preindustrial Heritage: Reconsiderations on the German Pattern of Corporate Development in the Late 19th and Early 20th Centuries," in *Industrial and Corporate Change,* 2, 2 (1993), pp. 233–248.

48. Michael E. Porter, "Capital Disadvantage: America's Failing Capital Investment System," *Harvard Business Review* (Sept.-Oct. 1992), Reprint No. 92508.

49. Hans H. Hinterhuber and Wolfgang Popp, "Are You a Strategist or Just a Manager?" *Harvard Business Review* (Jan.-Feb. 1992), pp. 105–113.

50. Gary Herrigel, *Industrial Constructions: The Sources of German Industrial Power* (Cambridge: Cambridge University Press, 1996); Simon, *Hidden Champions;* Günter Rommel, Jürgen Kluge, Rolf-Dieter Kempis, Raimund Diederichs, and Felix Brück, *Simplicity Wins: How Germany's Mid-Sized Industrial Companies Succeed* (Boston, Mass.: Harvard Business School Press, 1995). Big business is just *one* aspect of Germany's long-term economic competitiveness: Jeffrey R. Fear, "German Capitalism," *Creating Modern Capitalism: How Entrepreneurs, Companies, and Countries Triumphed in Three Industrial Revolutions,* ed. Thomas K. McCraw (Cambridge, MA: Harvard University Press, 1997), pp. 135–182.

51. For an American critique, see Walter Licht, *Industrializing America: The Nineteenth Century* (Baltimore: John Hopkins University Press, 1995); Philip Scranton, *Endless Novelty: Specialty Production and American Industrialization, 1865–1925* (Princeton: Princeton University Press, 1997).

52. This statement might even hold true for allegedly free-market Britain: see John Brewer, *The Sinews of Power: War, Money and the English State 1688–1783* (New York: Knopf, 1989); Nancy Koehn, *The Power of Commerce: Economy and Governance in the first British Empire* (Ithaca: Cornell, 1994); Chalmers Johnson, *MITI and the Japanese Miracle: The Growth of Industrial Policy, 1925–1975* (Stanford: Stanford University Press, 1982); and Alice Amsden, *Asia's Next Giant: South Korea and Late industrialization* (Oxford: Oxford University Press, 1989).

53. This is one of the clear results of the contributions found in Chandler, Amatori, and Hikino, eds. *Big Business and the Wealth of Nations.*

54. Kocka and Dornseifer cite Michael E. Porter, *The Competitive Advantage of Nations* (New York: Free Press, 1990).

55. Peter Hayes, "Industrial Factionalism in Modern German History," *Central European History*, 24, 2 (1991), pp. 122–131.

56. John Gillingham, *Coal, Steel, and the Rebirth of Europe 1945–1955: The Germans and French from Ruhr Conflict to Economic Community* (Cambridge: Cambridge University Press, 1991).

57. Mollin, *Montankonzerne und 'Drittes Reich'*. Mollin depicts Ernst Poensgen and Albert Vögler as ideal-type representatives of economically rational behavior rather than as flesh-and-blood human beings. See also David Abraham, *The Collapse of the Weimar Republic: Political Economy and Crisis* (New York: Holmes & Meier, 1986).

58. Fritz Thyssen, *I Paid Hitler* (New York: Farrar & Rinehart, 1941).

59. Hayes, in "Industrial Factionalism," suggests: "In consequence, understanding the interests and behavior of large firms must start from a close analysis of each corporation's business, not from aggregate national or branch-specific data that blur critical issues. Moreover, in conducting such analyses, researchers need to remember that interests are definitions, not concrete objects, and that they exist in the minds of managers, minds which weigh data differently and vary in their perspicacity. All this means that patient examinations of individuals who run corporations is as vital as scrutiny of their commercial calculations."

60. Berghahn, *Americanisation of West German Industry*. A brief exposition is in Volker R. Berghahn, "West German Reconstruction and American Industrial Culture, 1945–1960," in *The American Impact on Postwar Germany*, ed. Reiner Pommerin (Providence: Berghahn Books, 1997), pp. 65–81. See also Volker R. Berghahn, ed. *Quest for Economic Empire: European Strategies of German Big Business in the Twentieth Century* (Providence: Berghahn Books, 1996).

61. Berghahn, "West German Reconstruction," p. 78.

62. Thomas K. McCraw, *The Essential Alfred Chandler: Essays Toward a Historical Theory of Big Business* (Boston, MA: Harvard Business School Press, 1988), pp. 18–21, 301–306.

63. D. C. Coleman, "The Uses and Abuses of Business History," *Myth, History and the Industrial Revolution*, ed. D. C. Coleman (London: The Hambledon Press, 1992), pp. 203–219; and Jaeger, "Unternehmensgeschichte in Deutschland seit 1945"; Morikawa, *Zaibatsu*. Less so for Latin America; see Carlos Dávila and Rory Miller, eds. *Business History in Latin America: The Experience of Seven Countries* (Liverpool: Liverpool University Press, 1999).

64. Feldenkirchen, *Eisen- und Stahlindustrie*, pp. 304–324; Kocka/Siegrist, "Hundert"; and Kocka, "Unternehmer," pp. 14, 115–122. In "Un-

ternehmer," p. 171, Kocka terms the joint-stock companies Krupp and Siemens, "veiled family enterprises" *(verkappten Familienunternehmen)*, as they were joint-stock companies with most of the shares owned by family members. See also Hilger, *Sozialpolitik und Organisation.*

65. Chandler, *Visible Hand,* pp. 381–382, and especially pp. 411–414. All quotes are from these pages.

66. For a critique in international perspective, see Fear, "Constructing Big Business," pp. 555–561.

67. Uwe Kessler, *Zur Geschichte des Managements bei Krupp: Von den Unternehmensanfängen bis zur Auflösung der Fried. Krupp AG (1811–1945),* pp. 306–7.

68. Harold James, "The German Experience and the Myth of British Cultural Exceptionalism," *British Culture and Economic Decline,* ed. Bruce Collins and Keith Robbins (New York: St. Martin's Press, 1990), pp. 115–122; quote from p. 120.

69. John F. Wilson, *British Business History, 1720–1994* (Manchester: Manchester University Press, 1995), p. 75.

70. A similar argument can be found for Japan; see Hidemasa Morikawa, "Japan: Increasing Organizational Capabilities of Large Industrial Enterprises, 1880s–1980s," *Big Business and the Wealth of Nations,* pp. 316–321.

71. Chandler, *Scale and Scope,* pp. 235–237, 389–392; for the Pilkington example, see pp. 591–592, which significantly ends the section on Germany. British business historians have not taken this critique lying down. Ironically for Chandler, the Pilkington example, which acted as such a devastating critique of British personal capitalism in *Scale and Scope,* turned out quite well for the company. Despite its rather quaint decision-making process, the new "family" hire did create the float glass technique that kept Pilkington on the postwar industrial map. Geoffrey Jones even argued that Pilkington's great advantage was *being* a family firm because it did not have to answer to shareholders. See also the critiques in Roy Church, "The Family Firm in Industrial Capitalism: International Perspectives on Hypotheses and History," *Business History,* 35, 4 (1993), pp. 17–43. Geoffrey Jones, "Great Britain: Big Business, Management, and Competitiveness in Twentieth-Century Britain," *Big Business and the Wealth of Nations,* pp. 102–138; Maurice W. Kirby and Mary B. Rose, eds. *Business Enterprise in Modern Britain from the Eighteenth to the Twentieth Century* (London: Routledge, 1994); and Wilson, *British Business History, 1720–1994,* esp. pp. 62–132.

72. The development of the term "organizational capabilities" is a major and still underappreciated intellectual shift for Chandler, see *Scale and*

Scope, esp. pp. 594–605. See the collection of individual country articles in Alfred D. Chandler, Jr., Franco Amatori, and Takashi Hikino eds. *Big Business and the Wealth of Nations* (Cambridge: Cambridge University Press, 1997), esp. the excellent comments by Giovanni Dosi, pp. 465–479. The country articles in this volume generally confuse the *Visible Hand* and *Scale and Scope* classifications.

73. Susanne Hilger, *Sozialpolitik und Organisation: Formen betrieblicher Sozialpolitik in der rheinisch-westfälischen Eisen- und Stahlindustrie seit der Mitte des 19. Jahrhunderts bis 1933* (Stuttgart: Franz Steiner Verlag, 1996), pp. 102–107.

74. Jürgen Kocka, "Industrielles Management: Konzeptionen und Modelle in Deutschland vor 1914," *Vierteljahrschrift für Sozial- und Wirtschaftsgeschichte,* 56, 3 (Oktober 1969), pp. 332–372.

75. Youssef Cassis, *Big Business: The European Experience in the Twentieth Century* (Oxford: Oxford University Press, 1997), pp. 157–167.

76. Morikawa, *Zaibatsu;* Hilger, *Sozialpolitik und Organisation;* and Uwe Kessler, *Zur Geschichte des Managements bei Krupp: Von den Unternehmensanfängen bis zur Auflösung der Fried. Krupp AG (1811–1943)* (Stuttgart: Franz Steiner Verlag, 1995).

77. Jürgen Kocka, "Scale and Scope: A Review Colloquium," *Business History Review* 64 (Winter 1990), p. 714.

78. Alfred D. Chandler, Jr., "Organizational Capabilities and the Economic History of the Industrial Enterprise," *Journal of Economic Perspectives,* 6, 3 (1992), pp. 79–100. Alfred D. Chandler, Jr. and Takashi Hikino, "The Large Industrial Enterprise and the Dynamics of Modern Economic Growth," *Big Business and the Wealth of Nations,* ed. Alfred D. Chandler, Jr., Franco Amatori, and Takashi Hikino (Cambridge: Cambridge University Press, 1997), pp. 34–37.

79. Nick Tiratsoo, "British Management 1945–64: Reformers and the Struggle to Improve Standards," *Japanese Success? British Failure? Comparisons in Business Performance since 1945,* ed. Etsuo Abé and Terry Gourvish (Oxford: Oxford University Press, 1997), p. 78. For similar points, see Mark W. Fruin, *The Japanese Enterprise System: Competitive Strategies and Cooperative Structures* (Oxford: Clarendon Press, 1994), pp. 130–131. Michael Best, *The New Competition: The Institutions of Industrial Restructuring* (Cambridge, Mass.: Harvard University Press, 1990), p. 144.

80. Naomi R. Lamoreaux and Daniel M. G. Raff, "Introduction," *Coordination and Information: Historical Perspectives on the Organization of Enterprise,* ed. Naomi R. Lamoreaux and Daniel M. G. Raff (Chicago: University of Chicago Press, 1995), pp. 3–4. I have been strongly influ-

enced by the general approach of this book, which seeks a dialogue among economics, management theory, and history. See also Peter Temin, ed. *Inside the Business Enterprise: Historical Perspectives on the Use of Information* (Chicago: University of Chicago Press, 1991).

81. Even Hayes' excellent work on IG Farben explicitly excluded discussions of labor relations, managerial styles, and the internal operations of its factories. Hayes, *Industry and Ideology,* p. xix. See also Plumpe, *Die I. G. Farbenindustrie AG,* pp. 509–510.

82. See especially Chandler, "Business History as Institutional History" in *The Essential Alfred Chandler: Essays toward a Historical Theory of Big Business,* ed. Thomas K. McCraw (Boston: Harvard Business School Press, 1988), pp. 301–306. It should be emphasized, however, that Chandler's new formulation "organizational capabilities" implicitly calls into question this older view of organizations and their leadership.

83. Max Weber, *Economy and Society: An Outline of Interpretive Sociology,* ed. Guenther Roth and Claus Wittich (Berkeley: University of California Press, 1979), pp. 212–241, 941–1005. For a critique of Weber's basic notions, see Jürgen Habermas, *Theory of Communicative Action, Vol. 1: The Reason and the Rationalization of Society,* trans. Thomas McCarthy (Boston: Beacon Press, 1984), pp. 143–286.

84. Charles Perrow, *Complex Organizations: A Critical Essay* (New York: McGraw-Hill, 1983); see also Charles Perrow, "Economic Theories of Organization," *Structures of Capital: The Social Organization of the Economy* (Cambridge: Cambridge University Press, 1990), pp. 121–152. Perrow takes up the idea that organization is an "instrument" as well, but for its powerholders, and attacks particularly the agency and transaction-costs theorists, who use efficiency-based explanations.

85. Joseph A. Schumpeter, *Capitalism, Socialism and Democracy* (New York: Harper & Bros., 1942). Not surprisingly, Chandler counts Schumpeter as one of his intellectual influences.

86. See especially Kocka, *Siemens,* pp. 547–559.

87. See the debate between Stephen Marglin, "What do Bosses Do? The Origins and Functions of Hierarchy in Capitalist Production," *The Review of Radical Political Economy,* 6 (Summer 1974), pp. 60–112, and David Landes "What Do Bosses Really Do?", *Journal of Economic History* 46, 3 (September 1986), pp. 585–623.

88. In terms of German industrial relations and social policy, German labor historians make the distinction between "primary" (personal) and "secondary" (constitutional, functional, and modernized) patriarchalism. See the discussion in Gerhard A. Ritter and Klaus Tenfelde,

Arbeiter im Deutschen Kaiserreich 1871 bis 1914 (Bonn: Verlag J. H. W. Dietz, 1992), pp. 409–422.

89. Thyssen Krupp Archiv (TKA): A/1774 Franz Dahl to Walter Däbritz.

90. See Neil Fligstein, *The Transformation of Corporate Control* (Cambridge, Mass.: Harvard University Press, 1990).

91. Werner Kirsch, *Unternehmenspolitik und Strategische Unternehmensführung* (München, 1990), esp. pp. 55–130.

92. See Fear, "Thinking Historically about Organizational Learning"; and Karl Lauschke and Thomas Welskopp, "Einführung: Mikropolitik im Unternehmen: Chancen und Voraussetzungen bezihungsanalytischer Ansätze in der Industrie- und Arbeitergeschichte," *Mikropolitik im Unternehmen: Arbeitsbeziehungen und Machtstrukturen in industriellen Grossbetrieben des 20. Jahrhunderts,* ed. Karl Lauschke and Thomas Welskopp (Essen: Klartext, 1994), pp. 10–13.

93. Weber, *Economy and Society,* pp. 86–100.

94. Peter Miller, "Accounting as Social and Institutional Practice: An Introduction," *Accounting as Social and Institutional Practice,* ed. Anthony G. Hopwood and Peter Miller (Cambridge: Cambridge University Press, 1994), pp. 1–39. John Roberts, "The Possibilities of Accountability," *Accounting, Organizations and Society* 16, 4 (1991), pp. 355–368.

95. Richard Biernacki, *The Fabrication of Labor: Germany and Britain, 1640–1914* (Berkeley: University of California Press, 1995). Biernacki shows how cultural meanings affected the practice and understanding of labor in British and German textile firms. The approach used here is similar, but I do not embed it into a discussion of culture as does Biernacki, but instead as a social, institutional, and communicative process within organizations.

96. For an exploratory survey, see Mark Covaleski and Michael Aiken, "Accounting and Theories of Organizations: Some Preliminary Considerations," *Accounting, Organizations and Society,* 11, 4/5 (1986), pp. 297–309; and Levenstein, *Accounting for Growth.*

97. Dermer, "Control and Organizational Order." For an empirical example, see Gordon Boyce, "Corporate Strategy and Accounting Systems: A Comparison of Developments at Two British Steel Firms, 1898–1914," *Business History,* 34, 1 (Jan. 1992), pp. 42–65.

98. Werner Plumpe, "Statt einer Einleitung: Stichworte zur Unternehmens-Geschichtsschreibung," *Unternehmen zwischen Markt und Macht: Aspekte deutscher Unternehmens- und Industriegeschichte im 20. Jahrhundert,* ed. Werner Plumpe and Christian Kleinschmidt (Essen: Klartext Verlag, 1992), pp. 9–13.

99. Jerry Dermer, "Control and Organizational Order," *Accounting, Orga-*

nizations and Society, 13, 1 (1988), pp. 25–36. See also Neil Fligstein, *Transformation of Corporate Control.*

100. Gareth Morgan, *Images of Organization* (London: Sage, 1986); Peter M. Senge, *The Fifth Discipline: The Art and Practice of the Learning Organization* (New York: Doubleday, 1990), pp. 292–300; John W. Thompson, "The Renaissance of Learning in Business," *Learning Organizations: Developing Cultures for Tomorrow's Workplace,* ed. Sarita Chawla and John Renesch (Portland, Oregon: Productivity Press, 1995), pp. 85–99; Michael J. Marquardt, *Building the Learning Organization: A Systems Approach to Quantum Improvement and Global Success* (New York: McGraw-Hill, 1996); M. Dierkes, A. Berthoin Antal, J. Child, and I. Nonaka, eds. *Handbook of Organizational Learning;* Tsoukas and Knudsen, eds. *The Oxford Handbook of Organization Theory: Meta-Theoretical Perspectives.*

1. August Thyssen, Victorian Entrepreneur

1. ThyssenKrupp Archive (TKA): A/1771 Däbritz Interview with (Thyssen & Co. Director) Carl Wallmann, 4 Nov. 1940.

2. Dolores L. Augustine, *Patricians and Parvenus: Wealth and High Society in Wilhelmine Germany* (Oxford: Berg, 1994).

3. These newspaper articles can be found in the Mannesmann Archive (MA): R 2 30 00.

4. See Hartmut Kaelble, *Berliner Unternehmer während der frühen Industrialisierung* (Berlin: de Gruyter, 1967); Dolores L. Augustine, "Arriving in the upper class: the wealthy business elite of Wilhelmine Germany," in *The German Bourgeoisie: Essays on the social history of the German middle class from the late eighteenth to the early twentieth century,* ed. David Blackbourn and Richard J. Evans (London: Routledge, 1991), pp. 46–86. Augustine relies on Carl-Friedrich Baumann, "August Thyssen: Ein Bürger Mülheims," in *Thyssen & Co. Mülheim a. d. Ruhr: Die Geschichte einer Familie und ihrer Unternehmung,* ed. Horst A. Wessel (Stuttgart: F. Steiner, 1991), pp. 179–198.

5. Brief biographies can also be found in the following: Manfred Rasch, "August Thyssen: Der Katholische Grossindustrielle der Wilhelminischen Epoche," in *August Thyssen und Hugo Stinnes: Ein Briefwechsel 1898–1922,* ed. Manfred Rasch and Gerald D. Feldman (München: Verlag C. H. Beck, 2003), pp. 17–107; Carl-Friedrich Baumann, *Schloss Landsberg und Thyssen,* ed. Thyssen Aktiengesellschaft and August Thyssen-Stiftung Schloss Landsberg [Duisburg/Mülheim (Ruhr), 1993]; Carl-Friedrich Baumann, "August Thyssen—Ein Bürger Mülheims," pp. 179–198, and Stephan Wegener, "Die Familie Thyssen

Aachen-Eschweiler-Mülheim a. d. Ruhr," both in *Thyssen & Co.*
Mülheim a. d. Ruhr: Die Geschichte einer Familie und ihrer Unternehmung,
ed. Horst A. Wessel (Stuttgart: F. Steiner, 1991), pp. 13–52; Walter
Däbritz, *August Thyssen* (unpublished manuscript): Mannesmann &
ThyssenKrupp Archive (ca. 1944); Lutz Hatzfeld, "Schwester Balbina
und August Thyssen," *Thyssenrohr* (Werkzeitschrift), p. 97, 25 found
in MA: R 2 30 00.4. See also Lutz Hatzfeld, *Die Begründung der Deutschen
Röhrenindustrie durch die FA. Poensgen & Schöller, Mauel 1844–1850*
(Wiesbaden: F. Steiner, 1962).

6. TKA: A/1771: Däbritz Interview with Kern, 5. Nov. 1940. Rasch, "August Thyssen," pp. 17–23.

7. For his version of the causes for the Anglo-German trade rivalry, which
conforms to his life experience, see August Thyssen, "Offener Brief
an den Herausgeber, 19 June 1912," *Nord und Süd*, 36, 142 (1912),
pp. 75–79. For a good discussion on continental emulation, see David
S. Landes, *The Unbound Prometheus: Technological Change and Industrial
Development in Western Europe from 1750 to the Present* (Cambridge: Cambridge University Press, 1969). See also Clive Trebilcock, *The Industrialization of the Continental Powers 1780–1914* (London/New York:
Longman, 1981), pp. 29–34. On the Rhineland, see Jonathan Sperber,
*Rhineland Radicals: The Democratic Movement and the Revolution of 1848–
1849* (Princeton: Princeton University Press, 1991) and Richard Tilly,
Financial Institutions and Industrialization in the Rhineland, 1815–1870
(Madison: University of Wisconsin Press, 1966).

8. Wilhelm Helmrich, "August Thyssen: Ein Unternehmer des
Ruhrreviers" [Druck] "Ehrenbürger Dr. ing. August Thyssen an die
Mülheimer Zeitung, Mülheim a. d. Ruhr, den 3. März 1922," reprinted
in *Tradition: Zeitschrift für Firmengeschichte und Unternehmerbiographie*
(ZfUG), 3. Jahrgang Heft 3 (August 1958), pp. 140–150. Henceforth
August Thyssen (1922).

9. August Thyssen (1922). Rasch, "August Thyssen," pp. 26–27.

10. The letter is reprinted in Walter Däbritz, "August Thyssen: Zum
Gedächtnis an seinen Geburtstag, den 17. Mai 1842," *Werkszeitung
Deutsche Röhrenwerke A. G. Werk Thyssen*, Mülheim-Ruhr, Jg. 17 (May),
ed. in cooperation with the Society for Arbeitspädagogik in agreement with the German work front (1942), p. 2. Conrad Matschoss,
"August Thyssen und Sein Werk: Zur Erinnerung an die Begründung
des ersten Werkes am 1. April 1871," *Zeitschrift des Vereines deutscher
Ingenieure*, 14 (Berlin, 2. April 1921), p. 10; Hatzfeld, "Werks- und
Firmengeschichte," pp. 54–60.

11. Toni Pierenkemper, *Die westfälischen Schwerindustrielle 1852–1913:*

Soziale Struktur und unternehmerischer Erfolg (Göttingen: Vandenhoeck & Ruprecht, 1979). A summary of his results along with additional information concerning textile industrialists can be found in Hans-Jürgen Teuteberg, "Industriestaat," *Rheinland-Westfalen im Industriezeitalter,* ed. Kurt Düwell and Wolfgang Köllmann, 2 (Wuppertal: Hammer, 1984), pp. 266–273. See also Wilfried Feldenkirchen, *Die Eisen- und Stahlindustrie des Ruhrgebiets 1879–1914: Wachstum, Finanzierung und Struktur ihrer Grossunternehmen* (Wiesbaden: F. Steiner, 1982), p. 17; Friedrich Zunkel, *Der Rheinisch-Westfälische Unternehmer 1834–1879* (Köln: Westdeutscher, 1962). Augustine, *Patricians and Parvenus,* pp. 26–60, has a good summary of the social-history literature on business elites.

12. Pierenkemper, *Schwerindustrielle,* pp. 39–42; and Teuteberg, "Industriestaat," pp. 266.

13. For a discussion, see Augustine, *Patricians and Parvenus,* pp. 32–35. Max Weber's famous *Protestant Ethic and the Spirit of Capitalism* (New York: Charles Scribner's Sons, 1958; first published in 1904–1905) took as its starting point this discrepancy.

14. TKA: A/1771 Anton Mittler, butler, *Erinnerungen,* 1944.

15. Wegener, "Familie Thyssen," pp. 29–31, and Barbara Maas, *Im Hause des Kommerzienrats* [Mülheim (Ruhr): Edition Werry, 1990]. Maas offers an excellent, richly documented architectural history.

16. Baumann, "Ein Bürger Mülheims," p. 186.

17. TKA: A/1771: Däbritz Interview with Dahl, 28 Jan. 1939.

18. TKA: A/1771: Däbritz Interview with Wallmann, 4 Nov. 1940.

19. Konrad Adenauer, future Chancellor of West Germany, had to have them typed before he could read them; see Hans-Peter Schwarz, *Adenauer, Der Aufstieg: 1876–1952* (Stuttgart: Deutsche Verlags-Anstalt, 19863), p. 180. The collection of letters published in Rasch und Feldman, *August Thyssen und Hugo Stinnes,* was partially inspired by the difficulty of deciphering his letters.

20. TKA: A/1727: Däbritz Interview with Härle and Küpper, 11 July 1938.

21. TKA: A/1727: Däbritz Interview with Bankdirektor Hilger, 28 June 1938.

22. See, for instance, regarding the expansion of the RWE, Thyssen to Stinnes, 1 Jan. 1902, in Rasch/Feldman, *August Thyssen und Hugo Stinnes,* pp. 214–215. Regarding negotiations surrounding the merger of the GBAG and the Schalker Verein, see Feldman, *Hugo Stinnes,* pp. 82–92.

23. Quoted in Feldman, *Hugo Stinnes,* p. 851.

24. As in the case of Ernst Nölle in Berlin in Chapter 3.

25. August Thyssen (1922).

26. TKA: A/1727: Däbritz Interview with Rabes, *et al.*, 5 Dec. 1938.

27. TKA: A/1773 Letter from Wilhelm Späing to Walther Däbritz, 3 Feb. 1941.

28. Fritz Thyssen, *I Paid Hitler,* pp. 120–127.

29. TKA: A/1771: Däbritz Interview with Wallmann, 4 Nov. 1940.

30. TKA: A/3614: Landrat des Kreises Ruhrort, Wülfing on Thyssen in 1907; Baumann, "Ein Bürger Mülheims," p. 194.

31. See George Grosz's sketch, "Stinnes and Co., or the Hagglers Over Men," reproduced in Beth Irwin Lewis, *George Grosz: Art and Politics in the Weimar Republic* (Princeton: Princeton University Press, 1991), Fig. 43, 139.

32. Treue, *Feuer Verlöschen Nie,* tends to perpetuate this image. For a whole collection of anecdotes, see Lutz Hatzfeld, "Anekdoten um August Thyssen," *Thyssen & Co. Mülheim a. d. Ruhr: Die Geschichte einer Familie und ihrer Unternehmung,* ed. Horst A. Wessel (Stuttgart: F. Steiner, 1991), pp. 199–211.

33. Baumann, "Ein Bürger Mülheims," p. 186.

34. MA: R 2 30 09 "Geehrter Herr Bellmann," 15 Feb. 1894, Fol. 307–308, Aug. Thyssen. For the "injured" reaction of Bellmann, see "Geehrter Herr Bellmann," 15 Feb. 1894, Fol. 309–310, Aug. Thyssen; "Sehr geehrter Herr Bellmann," 18 Dec. 1894, Fol. 349–350, Aug. Thyssen.

35. MA: R 2 30 10 "Herrn A. Gilles," 3 May 1903, Fol. 409, Thyssen & Co.

36. No less a personage than Konrad Adenauer related such stories; see Schwarz, *Adenauer,* p. 71.

37. Schacht, *Confessions,* pp. 133–35. Schacht relates how Thyssen carried his own bags, traveled in third-class coaches, "second-rate" hotels, and would bargain about the price of the hotel room.

38. Quote from Clara Stinnes' diary, 1 May 1904, in Feldman, *Hugo Stinnes,* p. 69.

39. Kurt Wiedenfeld, *Zwischen Wirtschaft und Staat aus den Lebenserinnerungen* (Berlin: de Gruyter, 1960), pp. 21–22. Wiedenfeld was one of the best respected and informed scholars on the German economy. See also his *Kapitalismus und Beamtentum* (Berlin: de Gruyter, 1932).

40. Arnst, *August Thyssen.* See TKA: A/1770. Letter to Dr. Paul Arnst from Thyssen, forwarded to W. Däbritz, 24 Nov. 1942.

41. *Konzerne der Metallindustrie: Eine Darstellung der Entwicklung und des gegenwärtigen Standes der grossen Konzerne der deutschen Metallindustrie,* ed. vom Vorstand des Deutschen Metallarbeiter-Verbandes (Stuttgart, 1924), pp. 250–254.

42. TKA: A/1771: Däbritz Interview with Wallmann, 4 Nov. 1940.

43. Quoted in Baumann, "Ein Bürger Mülheims," p. 183, from TKA: A/9578 "Conrad Verlohr," 10 Dec. 1905.

44. TKA: A/1727: Däbritz Interview with Fritz Thyssen, 22 Aug. 1938.

45. Harold C. Livesay, *Andrew Carnegie and the Rise of Big Business* (New York: Harper & Row, 1975), p. 2.

46. TKA: A/1771: Däbritz Interview with Carl Wallmann, 4 Nov. 1940.

47. Gisbert Knopp, *Schloss Landsberg* [Duisburg/Mülheim (Ruhr): Thyssen AG, 1993].

48. Quote from Clara Stinnes' diary, 2 July 1905, in Feldman, *Hugo Stinnes*, p. 68.

49. Gertrud Milkereit, "August Thyssen und Auguste Rodin," *Unsere ATH*, Heft 12 (1966), pp. 20–1.

50. Baumann, *Schloss Landsberg und Thyssen*, pp. 43–49.

51. Table conversation from 1912, in Wegener, "Familie Thyssen," p. 42; TKA: A/1771: Däbritz Interview with Wallmann, 4 Nov. 1940. See also the incident related in Nievelstein, *Zug nach der Minette*, pp. 355–6.

52. MA: R 1 30 25 (1): Bericht der Handelskammer Mülheim-Ruhr, 1890.

53. MA: R 2 30 00.3: Thyssen to Geheimrat von Schönebeck, 22 Aug. 1919.

54. MA: R 1 35 06: Thyssen to Reichskanzler Joseph Wirth, reprinted in *Mülheimer Zeitung*, 14 Oct. 1922.

55. Hugo Stehkämper, *Konrad Adenauer: Oberbürgermeister von Köln* (Köln: Rheinland Verlag, 1976), p. 784, fn. 165; Henning Köhler, *Adenauer, Eine politische Biographie* (Berlin: Propyläen, 1994), p. 202.

56. MA: R 2 30 09 Circulair, 31 Oct. 1883, Fol. 138–139, Killing.

57. He suggested that Hugo Stinnes build a Catholic church in a predominantly Catholic area—Feldman, *Hugo Stinnes*, p. 311; TKA: A/9578, Letter to Conrad Verlohr, 6 Feb. 1898; TKA: A/1771, Däbritz Interview with Franz Dahl, 28 Jan. 1939.

58. Fritz Thyssen, *I Paid Hitler* (New York: Farrar & Rinehart, 1941), p. 215.

59. MA: R 2 30 10, "An den Königlichen Landrath. Herrn Dr. Lembke, 11. Oct. 1900," Fol. 247–253, Aug. Thyssen. At Thyssen & Co., thirteen senior executives were Catholic and nineteen Protestant. At the GDK, ten of forty-eight senior executives were Catholic. They also conducted a survey of Thyssen & Co. The religious breakdown of the plate mill can be found in R 2 30 22 (2): forty-two were Catholic; forty-nine were Protestant (thirteen were unaccounted for). For a summary of Catholic representation in Germany, see Thomas Nipperdey, *Deutsche Geschichte 1866–1918, Band I: Arbeitswelt und Bürgergeist* (München: C. H. Beck, 1990), pp. 449–451.

60. Quote from a letter from Hugo Stinnes to the RWE, in Feldman, *Hugo Stinnes*, p. 282.

61. August Thyssen, "Offener Brief an den Herausgeber, 19 June 1912," *Nord und Süd*, 36, 142 (1912), pp. 75–79. Compare the more bellicose justification for a German Navy from Hugo Stinnes in the same volume, pp. 50–52. Treue, *Feuer Verlöschen Nie*, pp. 79–91. See the debate over the meaning of this type of international investment activity by Carl Strikwerda and Paul Schroeder in the AHR Forum, *American Historical Review*, 98, 4 (October 1993), pp. 1106–1142.

62. Rasch, "August Thyssen," pp. 96–98; Treue, *Feuer Verlöschen Nie*, pp. 182–190 ; Fritz Fischer, *Germany's Aims in the First World War* (New York: Norton, 1967), pp. 108–10, 257–9, 479–487, 563–6. Treue tends to pull the fangs from Thyssen's proposals, interpreting them merely as a response to losses caused by national confiscations, while Fischer places Thyssen wrongly in the pan-German, imperialist camp. Fischer also overemphasizes Thyssen's ability to influence policies by the central government. See the recent discussion in Feldman, *Hugo Stinnes*, pp. 384–396.

63. MA: T 2 30 00.3 Thyssen to Geheimrat Franz von Schönebeck, 30 July 1918.

64. See the letter to Alfred von Tirpitz, 8 Nov. 1917, reproduced in Rasch und Feldman, *August Thyssen und Hugo Stinnes*, p. 576, fn. 2041.

65. Fritz Fischer, *Krieg der Illusionen: Die deutsche Politik von 1911 bis 1914* (Düsseldorf: Droste, 1969), pp. 742–44. At dinner in 1912, Thyssen argued that "We must ally ourselves with France against England," in Wegener, "Die Familie Thyssen," p. 42.

66. Treue, *Feuer Verlöschen Nie*, pp. 188–90.

67. Many of these issues regarding Thyssen and Erzberger were aired publicly in 1920 when Erzberger sued the former Director of the Deutsche Bank (1908–15) and Treasury and Interior Minister (1915–18), Karl Helfferich, for defamation of character. For details see Klaus Epstein, *Matthias Erzberger and the Dilemma of German Democracy* (Princeton: Princeton University Press, 1959), esp. Appendix V; Theodor Eschenburg, *Matthias Erzberger: Der grosse Mann des Parlamentarismus und der Finanzreform* (München: R. Piper, 1973), pp. 154–165; and John G. Williamson, *Karl Helfferich 1872–1924: Economist, Financier, Politician* (Princeton: Princeton University Press, 1971), pp. 312–329. In the trial against Helferrich, Thyssen defended Erzberger with a favorable affidavit.

68. MA: T 2 30 00.3: Thyssen an Geheimrat Franz von Schönebeck, 24 May 1917. See also the letter to Alfred von Tirpitz, 8 Nov. 1917, repro-

duced in Rasch und Feldman, *August Thyssen und Hugo Stinnes,* p. 576, fn. 2041.

69. Feldman, *Hugo Stinnes,* p. 468. Nievelstein, *Zug nach der Minette,* pp. 345–354. An ex-Thyssen director, Alfons Horten, managed the captured de Wendel firm during the war. Incidentally, the de Wendel family faced similar problems as the Thyssen family. Henri de Wendel, the owner-director, accused his nephews of not being capable of running the firm, excessively spending his money, and suffering from mental incapacity.

70. Däbritz, *August Thyssen,* p. 18; Hatzfeld, "Balbina."

71. TKA: A/1727 Däbritz Interview with Frau Scholten-Bagel (Klara Bagel), 2 Nov. 1938.

72. TKA: A/1771 Däbritz Interview with Wallmann, 4 Nov. 1940.

73. TKA: A/1727 Däbritz Interview with Eumann, 26 April 1939.

74. TKA: A/1727 Däbritz Interview with Frau Scholten-Bagel (Klara Bagel), 2 Nov. 1938.

75. TKA: A/1727 Däbritz Interview with Hasslacher, 7 Nov.1939.

76. Rasch, "August Thyssen," p. 99, fn. 301.

77. Fritz Thyssen, *I Paid Hitler,* pp. 123, 138.

78. TKA: A/1727 Däbritz Interview with Frau Scholten-Bagel (Klara Bagel), 2 Nov. 1938.

79. TKA: A/1771 Däbritz Interview with Anton Mittler (fragment), 1944.

80. Quote from Rasch, "August Thyssen," p. 103. John R. Harvey, *Men in Black* (Chicago: University of Chicago Press, 1995); Philippe Perrot, *Fashioning the Bourgeoisie: A History of Clothing in the Nineteenth Century* (Princeton: Princeton University Press, 1994).

81. TKA: A/889 Gutachten des Geh. Justizrates Ernst, Berlin, 26 Jan. 1907.

82. Quoted in Baumann, *Schloss Landsberg und Thyssen,* p. 54.

83. TKA: A/1727 Däbritz Interview with Jakob Hasslacher, 7 Nov. 1939.

84. Wegener, "Die Familie Thyssen," p. 33.

85. Quoted in Wegener, "Die Familie Thyssen," p. 50 fn. 20 from TKA: A/195 70 Schriftwechsel Carl Klönne/Thyssen.

86. TkA: A/1801: Däbritz Interview with Albert Vögler, 11 Jan. 1943 and with Dinkelbach, Dec. 1942 and 2 March 1943.

87. Feldman, *Hugo Stinnes,* p. 205.

88. Günter Buchstab, "Fritz Thyssen (1873–1951), *Zeitgeschichte in Lebensbildern* (Band 9: Aus dem deutschen Katholizismus des 19. und 20. Jahrunderts), ed. Jürgen Aretz, Rudolf Morsey, and Anton Rauscher (Münster: Aschendorff, 2003), pp. 115–133.

89. Wegener, "Die Familie Thyssen," pp. 39–44.

90. Quoted in Treue, *Feuer Verlöschen Nie,* p. 164 from mid-July 1902.

91. Thyssen to Klönne, 11 July 1902, quoted in Wegener, "Die Familie Thyssen," p. 37.

92. TKA: A/195 70 Schriftwechsel Carl Klönne/Thyssen, 9 July 1900.

93. MA: R 2 30 00.4 (1): "Der Roland von Berlin," 24 Nov. 1904–2 Feb. 1905 and *Berliner Tageblatt,* 16 Nov. 1904. Dolores Augustine cites a letter from August, Sr., to August, Jr., from 1910: "I have never thought of putting you into an insane asylum, and besides I would have had no legal basis for doing so," from TKA: A/886, Anlage 12: August, Sr., to August, Jr., 22 May 1910 and 30 May 1910. But Wegener, "Familie Thyssen," for instance, reports that it took place; Rasch, "August Thyssen," thinks some version of this story took place; Baumann argues that there is no evidence for it; Augustine is skeptical about the first alleged attempt, but cites Arnst, *August Thyssen,* which might not be the best source, as evidence of the second attempt.

94. These included the Rheinische Bank, the Mülheimer Bergwerksverein (mining), the Saar- und Mosel-Bergwerksgesellschaft (mining), and the Rheinisch-Westfälische Elektrizitswerke (RWE). For their correspondence, see Rasch und Feldman, *August Thyssen und Hugo Stinnes.* On the ins and outs of these joint ventures from the point of view of Hugo Stinnes, see Gerald D. Feldman, *Hugo Stinnes: Biographie eines Industriellen 1870–1924* (München: C. H. Beck, 1998), pp. 41–55, 118–141. For an example of their rivalry over the Grey license for girders, see pp. 181–184; in the cartels, pp. 224–225, 326–332; and with ore fields, pp. 352–356.

95. Wegener, "Familie Thyssen," p. 37 who cites the Archiv der Konrad Adenauer Stiftung, Nachlass Hugo Stinnes, I 220–294/3, 20 March 1906, 24 Nov. 1910.

96. Quote from Clara Stinnes' diary, 1–3 April 1906 in Feldman, *Hugo Stinnes,* p. 69. See also Rasch and Feldman, *August Thyssen und Hugo Stinnes,* pp. 117–119, 347–348.

97. Rasch and Feldman, *August Thyssen und Hugo Stinnes,* p. 504, fn. 1788.

98. Quoted in Augustine, *Patricians and Parvenus,* p. 133, from TKA: A/886.

99. MA: R 2 30 00.4 (1) *Berliner Tageblatt,* 28 Oct. 1910, among others; Rasch and Feldman, *August Thyssen und Hugo Stinnes,* pp. 563–564, from May 1914.

100. See the numerous articles in MA: R 2 30 00.4 (1).

101. TKA: A/1806.

102. Arnst, *August Thyssen und Sein Werk,* p. 66.

103. Rasch and Feldman, *August Thyssen und Hugo Stinnes,* pp. 502–504, from Feb. 1911.

104. MA: R 2 30 00.4 (1) Rheinisch Westfälische Zeitung, 11 July 1913. Rasch and Feldman, *August Thyssen und Hugo Stinnes*, pp. 563–564, from May 1914.

105. MA: R 2 30 00.4 for articles about his death; MA: R 1 30 10 Handelsregister; and Wegener, "Familie Thyssen," pp. 45–46.

106. Wegener, "Familie Thyssen," p. 39; MA: R 5 35 10 (1) Letters: "Herren Thyssen & Co." 6 June 1918, 1 Oct. 1918, 10 Oct. 1918; see also R 1 30 10, R 1 35 01, R 1 35 05, R 5 35 15.

107. Thyssen to Stinnes, 25 Sept. 1905, in Rasch and Feldman, *August Thyssen und Hugo Stinnes*, pp. 331–332.

108. Augustine, *Patricians and Parvenus*, pp. 125–156; Carl Schorske, *Fin-de-siècle Vienna: Politics and Culture* (Cambridge: Cambridge University Press, 1981).

109. Augustine, *Patricians and Parvenus*, Chapters 2–3.

110. Augustine, *Patricians and Parvenus*, p. 147.

111. For an evocative portrait of France, see Eugen Weber, *France Fin de Siècle* (Cambridge, Mass.: Belknap Press of Harvard University Press, 1986). See also the collections of essays by August Nitschke, Gerhard A. Ritter, Detlev J. K. Peukert, and Rüdiger vom Bruch, eds. *Jahrhundertwende: Der Aufbruch in die Moderne 1880–1930* (Hamburg: Rowohlt, 1990); and Lutz Niethammer, u.a., ed. *Bürgerliche Gesellschaft in Deutschland* (Frankfurt/Main: Fischer Taschenbuch, 1990). Miller, *Bon Marché*. For discussions on the nature of the German *bourgeoisie*, see the diametrically opposed interpretations about the notion of a German *Sonderweg* using the same social-historical evidence in Augustine, *Patricians and Parvenus*, 1–17, 243–254; and Kocka, "The European Pattern and the German Case," 21–32. See also Youssef Cassis, *Big Business: The European Experience in the Twentieth Century* (Oxford: Oxford University Press, 1997), pp. 187–230; and David Blackbourn and Geoff Eley, *The Peculiarities of German History: Bourgeois Society and Politics in Nineteenth-Century Germany* (New York: Routledge, 1984), pp. 181–2, 232–7. On consumption, see Warren Breckman, "Disciplining Consumption: The Debate about Luxury in Wilhelmine Germany 1890–1914," *Journal of Social History*, 24 (1991), pp. 485–505.

112. TKA: A/1727: Däbritz Interview with Rabes, *et al.*, 5 Dec. 1938.

2. If I Rest, I Rust

1. Thomas J. Misa, *A Nation of Steel: The Making of Modern America 1865–1925* (Baltimore: The Johns Hopkins University Press, 1995).

2. See Reinhard Spree, *Wachstumstrends und Konjunkturzyklen in der deutschen Wirtschaft von 1820 bis 1913: Quantitativer Rahmen für eine*

Konjunkturgeschichte des 19. Jahrhunderts (Göttingen: Vandenhoeck & Ruprecht, 1978).

3. Except for larger coal mining, steel, and railroad companies, most businesses remained dependent on family financing. See Toni Pierenkemper, "Zur Finanzierung von Industriellen Unternehmensgründungen im 19. Jahrhundert—mit einigen Bermerkungen über die Bedeutung der Familie," *Zur Geschichte der Unternehmensfinanzierung,* ed. Dietmar Petzina (Berlin: Duncker & Humblot, 1990), pp. 37–55.

4. Mannesmann-Archiv (MA): R 1 30 10. Also ThyssenKrupp Archive (TKA): A/1086: [Hauptbuch], pp. 2–4. Däbritz, *August Thyssen,* p. 14. August Thyssen (1922), pp. 143–150. TKA: F/Alb28; Hatzfeld, "Werks- und Firmengeschichte," p. 59. *Mülheim: Denkschrift,* pp. 246, 255–258. Rasch, "August Thyssen," pp. 27–32.

5. On the growth of the Ruhr railway net, see Wiel, *Ruhrgebiet,* pp. 359–363; Horst A. Wessel, *Das Werk Mülheim: Eine Chronik in Stichworten* (Düsseldorf, [no date]); Teuteberg, "Industriestaat," pp. 222–234; Hermann Korte, "Die Entfaltung der Infrastruktur," *Das Ruhrgebiet im Industriezeitalter* (Düsseldorf: Schwann, 1990), pp. 576–581; Wolfram Fischer, "Der Ausbau des Verkehrsnetzes im Spiegel der Handelskammerberichte," *Wirtschaftliche Nachrichten,* (1965), pp. 696–708; Wolfram Fischer, *Herz des Reviers: 125 Jahre Wirtschaftsgeschichte des Industrie- und Handelskammerbezirks Essen-Mülheim-Oberhausen* (Essen: R. Bacht, 1965), pp. 147–157. See *Mülheim a. d. Ruhr 1808–1908: Denkschrift zur Hundertjahrfeier der Stadt Mülheim an der Ruhr 1908,* ed. vom Geschichtsverein Mülheim a. d. Ruhr e.V. [Mülheim a. d. Ruhr, 1983 (1908)], pp. 238, 269–271.

6. See Fischer, *Herz,* pp. 27–60. *Mülheim: Denkschrift,* pp. 113–114, 234–246. Styrum was mostly working-class. In 1878, Styrum numbered 14,503 people; in 1890, 21,679; in 1897, 30,153; and in 1902, roughly 40,000. For the effect of incorporation, see *Mülheim: Denkschrift,* pp. 115–124. Wiel, *Ruhrgebiet,* pp. 22–65, 115, 179. Weber, "Entfaltung der Industriewirtschaft," pp. 220–228. Hatzfeld, "Werks- und Firmengeschichte," p. 55. Also Dietmar Bleidick, "Steinkohlenbergbau in Mülheim 1800–1870: Die Anfänge des Tiefbaus und das Aufkommen der Mergelzechen" in *900 Jahre Mülheim an der Ruhr 1093–1993* (Zeitschrift des Geschichtsvereins Mülheim a. d. Ruhr, Nr. 66) (Mülheim/Ruhr, 1993), pp. 363–385.

7. Lutz Hatzfeld, "Anekdoten um August Thyssen," pp. 199–200.

8. Figures and discussion are based on Feldenkirchen, *Eisen- und Stahlindustrie,* pp. 34–51, Tab. 11, 33, and Spree, *Wachstumstrends und Konjunkturzyklen,* pp. 352–363, 372, 464, 470. Also Wilfried Felden-

kirchen, "Banking and Economic Growth: Banks and Industry in Germany in the Nineteenth Century and their Changing Relationship during Industrialisation" in *German Industry and German Industrialisation: Essays in German Economic and Business History in the Nineteenth and Twentieth Centuries* (London: Routledge, 1991), pp. 116–147; also Richard Tilly, "Banking Institutions in Historical and Comparative Perspective: Germany, Great Britain and the United States in the Nineteenth and Early Twentieth Century," *Journal of Institutional and Theoretical Economics* (JITE), 145, (1989), pp. 189–209.

9. TKA: A/1086 Letter to the Chamber of Commerce, Mülheim a. d. Ruhr, Herr Heinrichs, 29. Sept. 1876; MA: 1 30 25 Letter Book, p. 108, Thyssen & Co. [Aug.]

10. Hatzfeld, "Thyssen & Co.," p. 61.

11. TKA: A/1086.

12. Hatzfeld, "Werks- und Firmengeschichte," p. 65. Also Hatzfeld, *Die Begründung der deutschen Röhrenindustrie.* Düsseldorf became the main center for pipe and tube production, especially when Albert Poensgen, the "father" of German pipe production, moved there.

13. MA: R 1 30 25: Bürgermeister Rheinen, 24. Juli 1876, gez. Thyssen & Co. [Aug.] The request was granted to Thyssen & Co. on August 31, 1876. See TKA: F/Alb 28. Photographs of the early mill appear in Hatzfeld, "Werks- und Firmengeschichte," p. 66.

14. For the work dynamics engendered by the skills required by puddlers, see Thomas Welskopp, *Arbeit und Macht im Hüttenwerk: Arbeits- und industrielle Beziehungen in der deutschen und amerikanischen Eisen- und Stahlindustrie von den 1860er bis zu den 1930er Jahren* (Bonn: J. H. W. Dietz, 1994), pp. 61–141. For a vivid description of puddling in English, see David Montgomery, *The Fall of the House of Labor: The Workplace, the State, and American Labor Activism, 1865–1925* (New York: Cambridge University Press, 1987).

15. One of the best overviews of steelmaking processes available to Germans at the time is Oskar Simmersbach, *Die Eisenindustrie* ed. Van der Borght, Schumacher, and Stegemann (Leipzig/Berlin: B. G. Teubner, 1906). See also various issues of the *Gemeinfassliche Darstellung des Eisenhüttenwesens,* ed. Verein Deutscher Eisenhüttenleute in Düsseldorf (Düsseldorf: Bagel, 1901). Note the importance of the Bagel publishing house for the steel industry.

16. Hatzfeld, "Werks- und Firmengeschichte," pp. 68–69. For a brief history of the pipe syndicate and its history see Robert Nyssen, *Das Röhrensyndikat und seine Entwicklung* (Düsseldorf: Droste Verlag, 1949), pp. 5–11.

17. MA: R 1 30 25: An Herrn Landrat von Rosenberg-Gruszezinski, ppa Thyssen & Co., gez. F. Wilke, Killing. An den Königlichen Regierungs- und Baurat, Herrn Danninghoff, 16 Aug. 1878, ppa Thyssen & Co., gez. F. Wilke, Killing.

18. For instance, over a 32-year period 233 ship boilers exploded in the United States, killing 2,563 people. In the ten years before the invention of the seamless pipe process (1886), 155 steam boilers blew up in Germany; numerous splits and breaks were unrecorded. Figures are drawn from Wessel, *Kontinuität und Wandel*, pp. 20–23. For a description of the production process, see Hatzfeld, "Werks- und Firmengeschichte," pp. 71–74.

19. MA: R 1 30 25; Concessionsgesuche, "An Herrn Bürgermeister Tschoepke, 23 March 1882. MA: M 30 109 VDI-Verlag, "Die Entwicklung der Einrichtungen für die Herstellung von Kesselbaumaterial bei der Firma Thyssen & Co. in Mülheim a. d. Ruhr" (Berlin, ca. 1922), provides the best technical history of the plate mill, steel mill, pressing works, and welding workshop, which became known as "Department II," and details the interrelationship between the plate and welding department.

20. See Ulrich Wengenroth, *Unternehmensstrategien und technischer Fortschritt: Die deutsche und die britische Stahlindustrie 1865–1895* (Göttingen: Vandenhoeck & Ruprecht, 1986), pp. 23–43 for a succinct discussion on the various types of steel processes available during this period. In English, Ulrich Wengenroth, *Enterprise and Technology: The German and British Steel Industries 1865–1895* (Cambridge: Cambridge University Press, 1994). See also *Gemeinfassliche Darstellung des Eisenhüttenwesens*.

21. MA: R 5 30 95: Herrn Rechtsanwalt Westermann, 11 March 1882, pr.pa. Thyssen & Co., [illegible]. Hatzfeld, "Werks- und Firmengeschichte," pp. 79–80. Hatzfeld suggests that Poensgen's Lierenfeld factory was the model for this expansion.

22. TKA: F/Alb28. See Fear, *Thyssen & Co.*, pp. 36–49, Appendix C for more discussion and sources.

23. Quoted in Däbritz, *August Thyssen*, pp. 22–23 and Hatzfeld, "Werks- und Firmengeschichte," p. 65.

24. Rasch, "August Thyssen," pp. 29–30. Hatzfeld, "Werks- und Firmengeschichte," pp. 60–64. Wiel, *Ruhrgebiet*, p. 263. Arnst, *August Thyssen*, pp. 6–7. Wilhelm Treue, *Die Geschichte der Ilseder Hütte* (Peine, 1960), pp. 149–153. Emil Müssig, *Eisen- und Kohlen-Konjunkturen seit 1870: Preisentwicklung in der Montanindustrie unter Einwirkung von Technik, Wirtschaft und Politik* (Augsburg: T. Lampart, 1925), pp. 34–35. According to Müssig, coal prices followed a similar price development as pig iron.

25. MA: R 5 30 18 Effekten-Kontobücher 1882–1921.

26. Däbritz, *August Thyssen,* pp. 27–31. TKA: A/1727 Däbritz Interview with Rabes, et al., 5. Dec. 1938. Rasch, "August Thyssen," pp. 36–39.

27. Rasch, "August Thyssen," pp. 36–39. Däbritz, *August Thyssen,* pp. 31–33; Walther Däbritz, *Denkschrift zum 50jährigen Bestehen der Essener Credit-Anstalt in Essen* (Essen: ECA, 1922).

28. TKA: A/1727 Däbritz Interview with Hermann Eumann, 26 April 1939.

29. Carnegie had similar problems with his outside investors, including his brother. Wall, *Andrew Carnegie,* pp. 322, 506, 635–637. Harold C. Livesay, *Andrew Carnegie and the Rise of Big Business* (New York: Harper-Collins Publishers, 1975), pp. 170–173. Rasch, "August Thyssen," pp. 38.

30. Matschoss, *Thyssen,* p. 11; Däbritz, *August Thyssen,* p. 23.

31. Däbritz, *August Thyssen,* p. 18; Hatzfeld, *Balbina;* Hatzfeld, "Werks- und Firmengeschichte," pp. 65 ff. For a comparative discussion about the role of family, see Jeffrey R. Fear, "Constructing Corporations: The Cultural Conception of the Firm," *Big Business and the Wealth of Nations,* ed. Alfred D. Chandler, Jr. and Takashi Hikino (Cambridge, Mass.: Harvard University Press, 1997), pp. 546–574.

32. August Thyssen (1922), p. 146.

33. MA: R 5 30 09: Herr Lesenberg, Fol. 149–150, 27 Dec. 1883, Thyssen & Co. [Aug.] and Fol. 191, 23 May 1884, Thyssen & Co. [Aug.].

34. Hatzfeld, "Werks- und Firmengeschichte," p. 81.

35. MA: R 2 30 09 Letter to Hermann Löhrer, department chief (and all other departmental heads), 19 Jan. 1884," Fol. 157–159, Thyssen & Co. [Aug.].

36. TKA: A/1727 Däbritz Interview with Directors Rabes, et al., 5. Dec. 1938. See the anniversary collections in the Thyssen Archive. TKA: F/Alb28 covers Thyssen & Co.

37. Chandler's most important insight is that big business tends to rise in certain industries and not others because of underlying technology and market conditions, almost irregardless of national cultures. See Chandler, *Scale and Scope,* p. 19, Table 5.

38. Quoted in Livesay, *Andrew Carnegie and the Rise of Big Business,* p. 116.

39. The discussion generally follows Chandler, *Scale and Scope,* pp. 14–31; and Lazonick, "Business Organization and Competitive Advantage," *Business Organization and the Myth of the Market Economy,* pp. 92–111. The discussion is designed to highlight Thyssen's early behavior, not to offer a complete theoretical exposition of economies of scale. See also James P. Hull, "From Rostow To Chandler to You: How Revolutionary was the Second Industrial Revolution?," *The Journal of European Economic History,* 25, 1 (Spring 1996), pp. 191–208.

40. Wengenroth, *Enterprise and Technology*, pp. 11–30, 157–166, 176–204, 243–246 offers an excellent discussion of the technological options.
41. Hatzfeld, "Werks- und Firmengeschichte," pp. 79–84. August Thyssen (1922), p. 146. For the reprimands, see MA: R 2 30 09 To Ober-Ingenieur Deussen, 30 April 1884," Fol. 179–182; 3 May 1884, 182a; 7 May 1884, 184; 26 May 1884, 192; 6 June 1884, 194–195; 7 June 1884, 196; 23 June 1884, 197.
42. MA: R 1 30 25 (1) Report to the Mülheim Chamber of Commerce, 1890.
43. MA: R 2 30 11 (1) Letter to the Styrum Mayor Tschoepke, 11 May 1889, Fol. 165–167 and 26 April 1890, Fol. 179–180, pr. pa. Thyssen & Cie., F. Wilke.
44. For complete runs of statistics, see Fear, *Thyssen & Co.*, Appendices.
45. Jersch-Wenzel, Krengel und Martin, *Die Produktion der deutschen Hüttenindustrie 1850–1914*, p. 128 and Hoffmann, Grumbach und Hesse, *Das Wachstum der deutschen Wirtschaft*, pp. 172–174; Felden-kirchen, *Eisen- und Stahlindustrie*, App. Tab. 20. See also the internal report prepared by Department II on the "Entwicklung des Grobblechpreises in der Zeit 1902–1914 in MA: R 5 30 95. Until today, crude steel production parallels world economic growth quite closely, although world steel production has been decoupled from *individual* nations' economic growth.
46. MA: R 1 30 25 (1).
47. MA: R 1 30 70 (8) Wallmann's Ringtaschenbuch and R 5 30 02 Bilanzkopierbuch.
48. MA: R 2 30 10 Letters to various *Meister*, 11 Dec. 1901, Fol. 275–281, Thyssen & Co. [Aug.] and "Herrn Betriebs-Direktor Matzek, Hier, den 31 March 1904," Fol. 482–484, [none, probably Thyssen]. In 1904, Thyssen notified *Betriebs-Direktor* Matzek that he was satisfied with the results in the steel mill, but worried that the plate mill was not being directed with the necessary "thoroughness and safety, which we feel desirable for the further development of this department."
49. MA: R 2 30 00.3: Thyssen an Geheimrat von Schönebeck, 22 Aug. 1919.
50. TKA: A/1086 Thyssen & Co. Maschinenfabrik to the GDK, and AGHütt. The letter provides a brief description of the "Thyssen-Conzern," author not given.
51. Advertising brochures from 1887–1923 can be found in MA: R 5 30 60–65.
52. MA: R 1 30 70 (8); R 1 35 28 (1).
53. MA: M 30.109 "Entwicklung der Einrichtungen für die Herstellung

von Kesselbaumaterial bei der Firma Thyssen & Co. in Mülheim a. d. Ruhr," ed. VDI-Verlag (Berlin, 1922). Hatzfeld, "Thyssen & Co. Mülheim—Werks- und Firmengeschichte," pp. 81–82, 152–153.

54. TKA: F/Alb28.

55. See the list of international projects in MA: R 5 35 87.

56. MA: R 5 30 83; R 5 30 90 (3). Brown was the District Sales Manager for the William B. Pollock Company of Youngstown, Ohio, but worked in New York. MA: R 5 30 84, 85 1910/11 contains correspondence between Thyssen & Co. and Drummond, McCall & Co., who helped Thyssen & Co. break into the Mexican market with its lapwelded steel pipes and Thyssen's iron making company penetrate into the Canadian market. At one time Drummond, McCall & Co. helped Thyssen & Co. maneuver around the German corrugated furnace cartel. By requesting specific firm's products, rather than generic syndicated products, the product was exempted, 1 March 1911 (Confidential).

57. MA: R 1 30 70 (8) Wallmann's Ringtaschenbuch. See MA: R 5 30 66 for an advertising brochure with photographs.

58. TKA: F/Alb 28. Also Fear, *Thyssen & Co.*, pp. 121–128, 180–184, Graph 19, Appendix C.

59. MA: R 5 30 64 Rolling Mills, Department III: Tube Works Prospect ca. 1912–1914, p. 33.

60. Fear, *Thyssen & Co.*, pp. 180–184, Graph 20, Appendix C.

61. See Horst A. Wessel, *Kontinuität im Wandel,* p. 135 for quotes and a fuller discussion of the development of the seamless pipe process.

62. Hatzfeld, "Werks- und Firmengeschichte," pp. 136–7, 154–6.

63. Joachim Radkau, *Technik in Deutschland,* p. 174.

64. Wilfried Feldenkirchen, *Werner von Siemens: Inventor and International Entrepreneur* (Columbus: Ohio State University Press, 1994), pp. 8, 31, quote from 186, fn. 23.

65. MA: M 30.111 Walter Däbritz, *Geschichte der Deutschen Röhrenwerke Akriengesellschaft, Werk Thyssen in Mülheim-Ruhr* (unpublished manuscript), p. 69, and Hatzfeld, "Werks- und Firmengeschichte," p. 148. Feldenkirchen, *Eisen und Stahl,* Tab.: 60a, b. See Table 16 of Horst A. Wessel, "Finanzierungsprobleme in der Gründungs- und Ausbauphase der Deutsch-Österreichischen Mannesmannröhren-Werke AG 1890–1907," *Zur Geschichte der Unternehmensfinanzierung,* ed. Dietmar Petzina (Berlin: Duncker & Humblot, 1990), pp. 119–171.

66. See Feldenkirchen, *Eisen- und Stahlindustrie,* Tab. 60b.

67. Martin Fiedler, "Die 100 grössten Unternehmen in Deutschland— nach der Zahl ihrer Beschäftigten—1907, 1938, 1973 und 1995," *Zeitschrift für Unternehmensgeschichte (ZUG),* 44, 1 (1999), pp. 32–66.

Fiedler uses Hatzfeld's figure of 6,489. See also the figures provided by Cassis, *Big Business*, Appendix, pp. 238–266, and Hannah, "Marshall's 'Trees' and the Global 'Forest;" pp. 36–39.

3. Creating Management

1. Kessler, *Zur Geschichte des Managements bei Krupp*, pp. 55–88. Hilger, *Sozialpolitik und Organisation*, pp. 83–85. Kocka, *Unternehmensverwaltung*, pp. 233–254.
2. ThyssenKrupp Archive (TKA): FA/Alb 28. See Baumann, "Ein Bürger Mülheims," p. 188.
3. See Jürgen Kocka, "The Rise of the Modern Industrial Enterprise in Germany," *Managerial Hierarchies: Comparative Perspectives on the Rise of the Modern Industrial Enterprise*, ed. Alfred D. Chandler, Jr., and Herman Daems (Cambridge, Mass.: Harvard University Press, 1980), pp. 77–116, and Kocka, "Industrielles Management," pp. 332–372.
4. Mannesmann Archive (MA): R 2 30 60 (2). The first direct sign of his role appears in the protocol of the sickness insurance meetings after August 1875, identified by his distinctive handwriting. MA: R 2 30 07 Salair-Buch 1881–1882, also with his handwriting.
5. MA: 30.174 Ernst Brökelschen: *50 Jahre Werkserinnerungen* (unpublished manuscript, 1940), p. 10. Brökelschen was the head of the purchasing office. He entered the firm in April 1890 and left in 1939.
6. Hatzfeld, "Werks- und Firmengeschichte," pp. 109–111.
7. MA: R 2 30 09 "Frau Director F.Wilke, Schloss Styrum," 20 April 1891, Fol. 100–101, Thyssen [Aug.].
8. MA: R 2 30 11, Wilke's letter journal. MA: R 2 30 26 (1) Entlassungsregister 1881–1883. Of the 155 people with written reasons, Wilke fired almost 100; another 120 were left blank.
9. MA: R 1 30 25 "Herrn Landrat von Rosenberg-Gruszezinski," 27 May 1878, ppa. Thyssen & Co., gez. F. Wilke, Killing. "Königlichen Regierungs- und Baurat, Herrn Dannighoff," 16 Aug. 1878, ppa. Thyssen & Co., gez. F. Wilke, Killing. MA: R 2 30 11 "Herrn Director Sach," 10 Dec. 1884, Fol. 25, F. Wilke; On the selling of allegedly tainted beer, see "Herrn Bürgermeister Tschoepke," 19 Dec. 1885, Fol. 39–41, 20 June 1880, Fol. 123–4, 20 June 1888, Fol. 125–9, 8 Aug. 1888, Fol. 136–7, 15 Aug. 1888, Fol. 138–143, 22 July 1890, Fol. 181–3, F. Wilke; "Königliche Regierung in Düsseldorf" [and to Tschoepke regarding pollution and complaints of a local baker 1885–1887], 14 May 1885, 18 Aug. 1885, 22 Nov. 1886, 14 March 1887, 23 May 1887, 19 April 1887, F. Wilke. On complaints of bad cooking by a local boarder, see "Frau Meissner," 10 Jan. 1888, Fol. 114–5, F. Wilke.

10. Kocka, "Management in der Industrialisierung," pp. 143–145.

11. MA: 2 30 07 Salair-Buch 1881–1882.

12. MA: R 1 30 10, Handelsregister. The merchant is considered the "principal" and the *Prokurist* as the "agent" of the firm *(die Firma)*.

13. Kessler, *Zur Geschichte des Managements bei Krupp*, pp. 44–60.

14. MA: 30.174 Ernst Bröckelschen, *Werkserinnerungen*, p. 10. MA: R 2 30 00: *Hütte Werkszeitung der Stahl- und Walzwerke Thyssen und der Friedrich Wilhelmshütte, Mülheim-Ruhr*, 4 Dec. 1926.

15. See MA: R 30 09 "Zeugnis!" [Fritz Olpe], Fol. 69, Killing. Olpe worked in the central office Jan. 1877 to May 1879.

16. MA: 30.174 Brökelschen, *Werkserinnerungen*, p. 3.

17. JoAnne Yates, *Control through Communication: The Rise of System in American Management* (Baltimore: The Johns Hopkins University Press, 1989), pp. 26–28. Until 1897, the German commercial code, § 28, required business enterprises to keep letter press books. For Thyssen & Co., much of the early materials have been lost or destroyed except for the worker rolls, the *Copierbücher,* and a lone monthly balance book.

18. Scholl, *Ingenieure*, pp. 397–406, 424–430.

19. Thomas Welskopp, *Arbeit und Macht*, pp. 123–128, 149–153, 201–204, 233–236, 324–334, 535–541.

20. MA: R 1 30 10 *Reglement für die Meister und Arbeiter des Walzwerkes von Thyssen & Co. in Styrum*, 6 Oct. 1871. Although not required by law until 1891, the creation of work statutes was by no means unusual for industry. They went by a whole host of names: *Arbeitsordnung, Betriebsordnung, Fabrik-Ordnung, Statuten, Reglement*, etc. After 1891, the official legal term became "Order of Work" *(Arbeitsordnung)*. See Gerhard A. Ritter and Klaus Tenfelde, *Arbeiter im Deutschen Kaiserreich 1871 bis 1914* (Bonn: J. H. W. Dietz, 1992), pp. 397–425 for a discussion of the statutes with a useful bibliography.

21. See MA: R 2 30 09 "Herrn Aug. Schmitz," 11 Nov. 1882, Fol. 86–89, [none]. See also MA: R 2 30 07 "Salair-Buch" 1881–1882.

22. Dornseifer, "Zur Bürokratisierung deutscher Unternehmen," pp. 76–77. MA: R 5 30 09 "Herrn Herm. Löhrer," 18 Dec. 1882, Fol. 103, Thyssen.

23. See Hatzfeld: "Werks- und Firmengeschichte," pp. 89–91 for more information concerning Bad Tönnistein. See MA: R 5 30 08 "Herrn Thyssen & Co., Mülheim a. d. Ruhr II," 24 Aug. 1886, Strassburger.

24. MA: R 2 30 11 (2). There are numerous letters to the GDK and the Schalker Gruben- und Hüttenverein between 1895–1903. All are labelled as "secret," which leads one to believe that Thyssen firms were avoiding cartel stipulations.

25. MA: R 2 30 11 (1), 15 July 1891; R 2 30 11 (2) "Herrn Jul. Pintsch," 18

July 1905, Vertraulich!, Fol. 138, A. Wilke. MA: R 2 30 11 (1) "Herrn Carl Bader," 11 Dec. 1905," Fol. 330, Thyssen & Co.: In Vollmacht, A. Wilke.

26. The letter is reprinted in Hatzfeld, "Firmen- und Werksgeschichte," p. 98. Three more (Heinrich Martini, Alfred Gilles, and Otto Garrey) received collective procura in the 1890s. Philip Neuhaus, Killing's successor in 1904, and Hans Richter in 1905.

27. MA: R 5 30 60 Thyssen & Co. 1906, 1908.

28. MA: R 5 30 60, R 5 30 64, R 5 30 65, R 5 30 66.

29. MA: M 30.174 Brökelschen, *50 Jahre Werkserinnerungen*, pp. 2–7.

30. MA: R 2 30 09 "Circulair: Zur Circulation . . . Killing," 12 Dec. 1883, Fol. 146–148, Thyssen & Co. [Aug.]

31. MA: R 2 30 09 "Circular: Zur Circulation . . . Killing," 4 March 1884, Fol. 165–166, Thyssen & Co. [Aug.] "Circular! . . . zum Central-Büreau," [no date], Fol. 222, Killing. "Circular! . . . u. Central-Bureau," 30 Dec. 1887, Fol. 422, Killing. "Circular! . . . Killing," 28. Febr. 1885, Fol. 259–260, [none].

32. MA: R 5 30 09 "Circulair II . . . Wilke," 26 May 1882, Fol. 28–31, Thyssen [Aug.].

33. MA: R 2 30 09 "Circular! . . .Killing," 4 Dec. 1884, Fol. 227–228, [none]. MA: R 2 30 10 To all the departments, 13 June 1903, Fol. 422–431, [none]. MA: R 2 30 10 "Herrn Direktor Wilke, 3 Jan. 1903," Fol. 327, Thyssen & Co. [Aug.]. Complete inventory lists between 1908–1925 can be found in MA: R 5 30 12–13 and R 5 35 15–18.

34. On trends in social policy in Ruhr heavy industry, see especially Hilger, *Sozialpolitik und Organisation.*

35. MA: R 2 30 09 "Rundschreiben!," 2 July 1891, Fol. 120, Thyssen & Co. [Aug.].

36. MA: R 1 30 76 Belegschaftsstatistik Wellrohrbau March 1906–Feb. 1908, Presswerk March 1907–March 1908, "Aufstellung der Wellrohrbau in Stunden und Löhnen und Tonnen"; MA: R 2 30 27 "Übersicht über den Arbeiterbestand Zu- und Abgang," 1 Jan. 1906–31 Dec. 1926 & 1 Jan. 1927–31 Dec. 1935. MA: R 2 30 15. The folder contains confidential correspondence, statutes, and negotiation protocols. Most of the correspondence was directed to Phoenix and the GHH. Another Thyssen firm, the Aktiengesellschaft für Hüttenbetrieb, Meiderich (AGHütt) refused to join because they would have had to reorganize their employment office.

37. MA: R 2 30 10 "H. An die Herren Oberingenieure und Ingenieure der Abteilungen Blechwalzwerk einschliesslich Stahlwerk, Röhrenwerk, Verzinkerei und Eisenwalzwerk," 22 May 1907, Fol. 339, Thyssen & Co. [Jos.]

38. MA: R 2 30 10 Circular to the departments, 1 April 1908, Fol. 406, Thyssen & Co. [Aug.].

39. For organizational charts of these departments, see Fear, *Thyssen & Co.*, Appendix B.

40. The autonomy of the department and the necessity for close coordination between the commercial and technical side of the plate department can be seen in the correspondence between Martini and the municipality of Steglitz in Berlin. MA: R 5 30 75 (1, 2, 3) Vertrag: Thyssen & Co. and Gemeinde Steglitz, Berlin with all correspondence between 1913–1920 [mainly] Martini, Schwenke. This is a very important collection of letters, which show the day-to-day level of business required to complete a project at this very difficult time. Also see the problems dealt with by Wallmann directly in MA: R 5 30 78 Korrespondenzen.

41. MA: R 5 30 12–13 and R 5 35 15–18. See the "Bewertung des Röhrenwerks" in 1910 in R 4 30 95 (1) and R 4 30 95: "Bewertung der Gemeinschaftlichen-Betriebs-Einrichtungen RW 1912."

42. MA: R 4 30 95 "RW Betriebsunkosten 1910–1914."

43. Chandler, *Scale and Scope*, p. 16.

44. Dornseifer, "Zur Bürokratisierung deutscher Unternehmen," p. 78, 80–81, quote from p. 81.

45. Hilger, *Sozialpolitik und Organisation*, pp. 79–102. See also Fear, *Thyssen & Co.*, Appendix B.5-B.11, pp. 520–526

46. Paul J. DiMaggio and Walter W. Powell, "Introduction," *The New Institutionalism in Organizational Analysis* ed. Walter W. Powell and Paul J. DiMaggio (Chicago: Chicago University Press, 1991), pp. 11–15.

47. Killing wrote all of the correspondence analyzed here, presumably with Wilke's input since the letters dealt mostly with the department chiefs under his command, which Thyssen then signed. If Thyssen wanted to make a matter especially urgent, he wrote the letter himself or signed it with his personal signature, not the official Thyssen & Co.

48. MA: R 5 30 09 "Herrn Ingenieur Bousse, 31 Dec. 1881," Fol. 6, Thyssen & Co. [Aug.].

49. MA: R 5 30 09 "An die Abteilung Röhrenwalzwerk zu Händen des Herrn E. Bousse," 13 May 1882, Thyssen & Co. [Aug.].

50. MA: R 5 30 09 "Herrn Ingeniur E. Bousse," 27 May 1882, Fol. 32–35, Thyssen & Co. [Aug.].

51. MA: R 5 30 09 "Herr Georges Chandoir," Fol. 65–68, 12 Sept. 1882, Privation!/Secret, [none]. "Herrn Ingeniur E. Bousse," 17 and 19 June 1882, Thyssen & Co. [Aug.] MA: R 2 30 07 Salair-Buch 1881–1882. Bousse's salary ranged between 4,500–5,000 marks per year with free housing, making him the third highest-paid person in the firm behind Wilke and August Schmitz, and putting him ahead of Killing.

"Herrn Emil Bousse zu Styrum," 30 Jan. 1883, Fol. 108. Thyssen & Co. [possibly Joseph]. Bousse's final recommendation *(Zeugnis)* can be found on Fol. 116.

52. MA: R 2 30 10 "Sehr geehrter Herr Trapp!" 27 April 1904, Fol. 500, Aug. Thyssen.

53. MA: R 5 30 09 Correspondence with "Herrn Aug. Schmitz," 29 April 1882, Fol. 12–13, [none, probably Wilke]; 7 May 1882, Fol. 15–17, [none]; 23 Sept. 1882, Fol. 69, 17 Oct. 1882, Fol. 76–77, 30 Oct. 1882, Fol. 78–85, 11 Nov. 1882, Fol. 86–89, 15 Nov. 1882, Fol 90–91, 20 Nov. 1882, Fol. 91, 22 Nov. 1882, Fol. 92–96, Thyssen & Co. [Aug.]; last quotes from a letter from 3 Aug. 1882, Fol. 49–50, [none].

54. MA: R 2 30 09 "Herrn Ober-Ingenieur Deussen," 30 April 1884, Fol. 179–182; 3 May 1884, Fol. 182a; 7 May 1884, Fol. 184; 26 May 1884, Fol. 192; 6 June 1884, Fol. 194–195; 7 June 1884, Fol. 196; 23 June 1884, Fol. 197.

55. On Löhrer, see MA: R 2 30 09 "Herrn H. Löhrer," 12 July 1884, Fol. 202; 18 Dec. 1885, Fol. 299–300, 306–307, 312. See also "Zeugnis! [Herm. Löhrer BW]," 12 April 1887, Fol. 371, [no signature]. Löhrer's recommendation is brief and terse. On Schmidt, see MA: R 2 30 09 "Thyssen & Co.," 13 March 1886, Paul Schmidt. A complete resumé and a very good recommendation are included here. "Herrn Paul Schmidt," 30 Dec. 1887, Fol. 424–425, 3 Jan. 1888, Fol. 430, Thyssen & Co. [Aug.] Schmidt's contract can be found on Fol. 360–362. Also MA: R 5 30 08 "Herrn Paul Schmidt," 30 April 1890. Eumann wrote Schmidt to make sure that the sketches and designs stemming from a trip England be handed over to Thyssen & Co., because they paid for the trip. For some time, the plate mill was without a department head after Schmidt left.

56. TKA: A/1771 Däbritz Interview with Wallmann, 4 Nov. 1940.

57. See Hatzfeld, "Werks- und Firmengeschichte," pp. 77–78 for a brief discussion about tin-plating. MA: R 2 30 08 "Vertrag!" [Bruno Heil], 21 March 1883, Thyssen & Co. [Aug.], Bruno Heil.

58. MA: R 2 30 09 "Herrn Bruno Heil," 5 Jan. 1884, Fol. 154–156.

59. MA: R 2 30 09 "Circulair" to Schmidt, Bene, Rauxlot and back to Wilke, 26 Jan. 1884, Fol. 160–161.

60. MA: R 2 30 09 "Zeugnis!" [Adolf Reussner], Fol. 231. Hatzfeld, "Werks- und Firmengeschichte," p. 78 reprints part of the recommendation. Reussner left the galvanizing plant at the end of 1884. Thyssen regretted that Reussner had decided to move back to Saxony but recommended him highly and "warmly."

61. MA: R 2 30 09 Herrn B. Heil, 23 Oct. 1884, Fol. 893–894 [between Fol. 222–223], Thyssen & Co.[Aug.]

62. MA: R 2 30 09 "Herrn Ingenieur Surmann, M. F.," 12 Sept. 1890, Fol. 69, Thyssen & Co. [Aug.]

63. MA: R 2 30 09 "Herrn Friedr. Overdieck, Betriebs-Chef," 27 March 1887, Fol. 357–359. Fritz Wilke proved to be a critical figure in the history of the GDK, a position which he held until 1931. Hatzfeld, "Werks- und Firmengeschichte," pp. 83–85.

64. MA: R 2 30 09 "Herrn E. Schwarz," 27 March 1893, Fol. 274–276, Thyssen & Co. [Aug.]. Reflecting the special status of the machine engineering department, Schwarz was not subordinated to August Wilke.

65. TKA: A/1767 Däbritz Interview with Späing, 28 Oct. 1940.

66. MA: R 2 30 09 "Herrn Thyssen & Co.," 25 Jan. 1891, Fol. 90–92, E. Münsterberg.

67. MA: R 2 30 09 "Herrn J. Wallmann," 5 Jan. 1884, Fol. 153, Thyssen [Aug.] See as well the case of F. Pahl MA: R 2 30 09 "Herrn F. Pahl, 12 Juli 1884," 16 July 1884, Fol. 204, 206, Thyssen & Co.

68. MA: R 2 30 10, Letters to Richter, 3 March 1908, [no date, early 1908], Fol. 401–403, Aug. Thyssen.

69. MA: R 2 30 09 "Sehr geehrte Herr Nölle, Berlin," 23 Dec. 1886, Fol. 337–338, Thyssen & Co. [Aug.]. Killing wrote most of the letters, then Thyssen signed them. In this letter, August Thyssen corrected an omission from the original, implying that the Berlin correspondence belongs as much to Killing as Thyssen.

70. TKA: A/643 [Denkschrift]: "Die Thyssen'schen Handelsniederlassungen, ihr entstehen, ihr Wesen und ihre Aufgabe," 26 Jan. 1918 [prepared by P. Neuhaus].

71. MA: R 1 30 10 Handelsregister.

72. MA: R 2 30 09 "Sehr geehrte Herr Nölle," 19 Feb. 1891, Fol. 95–97 [none].

73. MA: R 2 30 09 "Sehr geehrte Herr Nölle," 17 June 1891, Fol. 114, [none, Killing].

74. MA: R 2 30 09 "Sehr geehrte Herr Nölle," 28 Oct. 1891, Fol. 139–143, Aug. Thyssen; "Sehr geehrte Herr Nölle," 17 Nov. 1891, Fol. 148–150, Aug. Thyssen.

75. MA: R 2 30 09 "Sehr geehrte Herr Nölle," 5 Nov. 1891, Fol. 144–148, [none].

76. MA: R 2 30 09 "Sehr geehrte Herr Nölle," 30 Nov. 1891, Fol. 153–154, Aug. Thyssen. Yet much later, R 2 30 10 "Herrn Thyssen & Cie, Berlin, *Privat!*," 9 Feb. 1897, Fol. 33, Thyssen & Co. Georg Richtsteig, *Geschichte des Deutschen Eisen- und Stahlhandels* (Bochum: Verlag der Verbriebsgesellschaft des Bundesverband Deutscher Stahlhandel, 1975), p. 175. In 1921, Steffens & Nölle formed a joint venture with the GHH to form an iron and steel wholesaler in the Ruhr. See Harald

Wixforth, *Banken und Schwerindustrie in der Weimarer Republik* (Köln: Böhlau Verlag, 1995), p. 128

77. MA: R 2 30 09 "Geehrter Herr Oparka, *Streng vertraulich!*," 22 Dec. 1891, Fol. 159, Thyssen & Co. [Aug.]; "Geehrter Herr Bellmann, *Streng vertraulich!*,," 22 Dec. 1891, Fol. 160, Thyssen & Co. [Aug.]; "Herrn Nölle," 29 Dec. 1891, Fol. 166, Thyssen & Co. [Aug.]; "Sehr geehrte Herr Nölle," 3 May 1892, Fol. 182, pr. pa. Thyssen & Co., Killing; "Sehr geehrter Herr Nölle," 10 May 1892, Fol. 186–7, Thyssen & Co. [Aug.]; "Sehr geehrte Herr Buff," 2 Feb. 1893, Fol. 255–256, [none, Killing].

78. MA: R 2 30 09 "Geehrter Herr Bellmann," 15 Feb. 1894, Fol. 307–308, Aug. Thyssen. For the "injured" reaction of Bellmann, see "Geehrter Herr Bellmann," 15 Feb. 1894, Fol. 309–310, Aug. Thyssen; "Sehr geehrter Herr Bellmann," 18 Dec. 1894, Fol. 349–350, Aug. Thyssen. "Sehr geehrter Herr Buff," 18 Dec. 1894, Fol. 349–350, Thyssen & Co. [Aug.]. "Herr W. Bellmann," 16 Jan. 1895, Fol. 359–360, Thyssen & Co. [possibly Joseph]. Thyssen, however, was careful to keep Buff informed of the correspondence so there would be no question of going over his head. At first, Bellmann objected because Buff was told of these reprimands, but Thyssen & Co. reminded him that Buff was his superior and needed to know.

79. MA: R 2 30 09 "Sehr geehrter Herr Buff!," 22 April 1896, Fol. 446–447, Aug. Thyssen; 24 April 1896, Fol. 448–449, Aug. Thyssen; "Herrn P. Oparka," 24 April 1896, Fol. 450–451, Aug. Thyssen; "An die Herrn H. Eumann u. O. Garrey," 2 May 1896, Fol. 452–455, [none].

80. MA: R 2 30 10 "Herren Thyssen & Cie, Berlin," 14 Dec 1896, Fol. 39, Thyssen & Co. [Aug.]. MA: R 2 30 09 "An die Herrn H. Eumann u. O. Garrey," 4 May 1896, Fol. 456–457, Thyssen & Co., [Joseph?]; "Herrn Thyssen & Cie, Berlin zu Händen des Vorstehers Herrn Aug. Buff," 4 May 1896, Fol. 458–459, [Aug.]; "Herrn P. Oparka," 9 May 1896, Fol. 460–461, [?]; "Sehr geehrter Herr Garrey," 12 June 1896, Fol. 474–475, Thyssen & Co. [Aug.]. Thyssen asked Garrey to find a new position for Oparka before the end of his contract. MA: R 2 30 10 "Herrn P. Oparka," 19 Dec. 1896, Fol. 18–19, [none]. In December, Oparka was 'retired' once again, after which they went to court (Fol. 22). MA: R 2 30 09 "Einschreiben: Herrn Aug. Buff," 9 May 1896, Fol. 462–463, Thyssen & Co. [Aug.]; "Herrn Aug. Buff [and] Herrn Thyssen & Cie in Berlin," 11 May 1896, Fol. 464, [none]; "Herrn P. Oparka," 11 May 1896, Fol. 465, [none]; "Herrn Aug. Buff," 13 May 1896, Fol. 466, Thyssen & Co. [Aug.]; "Herrn Aug. Buff," 20 May 1896, Fol. 470–471, [none]; "P. P." [Garrey named Prokurist], 12 June 1896, [none]. MA: R 2 30 09 "Herrn Thyssen & Cie, Berlin," 6 Oct. 1896, Fol. 499, [none, written by H. Eumann].

81. MA: R 2 30 09 "Sehr geehrter Herr Garrey," 12 June 1896, Fol. 474–475, Thyssen & Co. [Aug.]; "Herrn Thyssen & Cie, Berlin," 26 June 1896, Fol. 476–477, Thyssen & Co. [Aug.]; "Herr O. Garrey," 3 Oct. 1896, Thyssen & Co. [Jos.]

82. MA: R 2 30 10 "Herr Aug. Thyssen, jr., Berlin," 29 March 1897, Fol. 46–47 [none, probably Killing due to "Geehrte" and "Sie" form of address].

83. MA: R 2 30 10 "Herrn Th. Neuhaus," 24 April 1904, Fol. 496–97 [none, Thyssen].

84. TKA: F/Alb28. Statistics for the Berlin commercial office only begin to be available after 1897.

85. MA: R 2 30 10 "Herrn Johannes Biesold," 14 Aug. 1902, Fol. 302; "Sehr geehrter Herr Garrey!," 28 Aug. 1902, 2 Sept. 1902, Fol. 309–310, 311–312, Aug. Thyssen.

86. MA: R 2 30 10 "Herr Prokurist Otto Garrey," 13 March 1906, Fol. 254–257, Thyssen & Co. [Aug.]; "Herrn Prokurist Otto Garrey," 21 Dec. 1905, Fol. 217–223, Thyssen & Co. [Aug.].

87. MA: R 2 30 10 "Herrn Prokurist Otto Garrey," 5 May 1907, Fol. 336; "Herrn Julius Lampmann," 19 June 1907, Fol. 348–349; "Herrn Otto Garrey," 19 June 1907, Fol. 350–351, Thyssen & Co. [Aug.].

88. MA: R 5 30 13 Abteilung II, WK [an] Buchhaltung Th. & Co., 8 May 1918, Gilles, Wallmann. Also MA: M 30.109 [Author unknown] "Entwicklung der Einrichtungen für die Herstellung von Kessel-baumaterial bei der Firma Thyssen & Co. in Mülheim a. d. Ruhr," VDI-Verlag, Berlin (ca. 1922). MA: R 1 35 25 (3) "Zusammenstellung der für den Neubau der Abteilung Wellrohrbau seit 1911 gemachten Entwürfe." MA: R 4 35 35 "Entwurf für einen Umbau der Abteilung W. B. Juli 1921," 8 Aug. 1921; "Verkleinerter Entwurf Juli 1921," 11 July 1921. "Besprechung über Erweiterungsbauten der Abteilung Blech-werk und Neubau der Abteilung Wellbau," 10 Aug. 1921. "Betrifft: Besprechung über Erweiterungs-Bauten der Abteilung B. W. und Neubau der Abteilung Gas-Schweisserei, 12 Aug. 1921." MA: R 4 35 05 [Layout] Regierungsbezirk Düsseldorf, Plan No. H VII 13, 1922.

89. MA: R 4 35 35 (1), R 1 35 70 (1) [Besprechung] "Aktennotiz: Betr: Vergrösserung und Modernisierung des Blechwalzwerkes," 9 Sept. 1918, Wallmann. "Prüfung der Möglichkeit der Abgabe eines Teiles der Gebäude von P. B. an M. F. und an R. W.," 12 Sept. 1918, MR [Martin Roeckner]. "Abteilung Blechwalzwerk, z.H. des Herrn Direktor Wallmann," 24 Sept. 1918, pr. pa. Thyssen & Co.: Becker; "Betr. Bohrrohrfabrikation," 30 Sept. 1918, MR [Martin Roeckner].

90. See the profitability calculations of the plate department in 1920 for heavy plates in MA: R 5 30 95 (3).

91. MA: R 4 35 35 (1) "Betr.: Herstellung von Bohrrohre." 17 July 1918, [none, Wallmann or Roeckner]. "Betr.: Bohrrohrfabrikation," 4 Sept. 1918, MR [Martin Roeckner]. "Erläuterung zum Entwurf einer Wassergasschweisserei mit Bearbeitungswerkstätte" 21 Jan. 1918," MR [Martin Roeckner]. "Kostenanschlag nach Entwurf VI," 5 Sept. 1918, MR [Martin Roeckner].

92. MA: R 4 35 35 "Entwurf für einen Umbau der Abteilung W. B. Juli 1921," 8 Aug. 1921; "Verkleinerter Entwurf Juli 1921," 11 July 1921. "Besprechung über Erweiterungsbauten der Abteilung Blechwerk und Neubau der Abteilung Wellbau," 10 Aug. 1921. "Betrifft: Besprechung über Erweiterungs-Bauten der Abteilung B. W. und Neubau der Abteilung Gas-Schweisserei," 12 Aug. 1921, Roeckner. Present: August Thyssen, Hans Thyssen, Alfred Gilles, Grossweischede, Roeckner, and Wallmann.

93. MA: M 30.109 "Entwicklung der Einrichtungen"; Hatzfeld, *Werks- und Firmengeschichte,* 168–169.

94. MA: R 4 35 05 Regierungsbezirk Düsseldorf, Plan No. H VII 13, 1922. Before World War II, the city government gave permission to build beyond the Hüttenstrasse only in the interests of war production.

95. MA: R 1 35 70 (1) "Niederschrift der Besprechung über die Errichtung von neuen Pilgerstrassen," 11 Oct. 1920 [none, probably Wallmann]. Present: August Thyssen, Hans Thyssen, Dir. Dr. Roser, Betr.-Dir. Traut, Schaaphaus, Stiepel.

96. MA: R 1 25 70 (1) "Bericht über die Besprechung bei der Demag betr. Neubau Pilgerwalzwerke," 30 Oct. 1920 and "Niederschrift der Besprechung über den Neubau der Pilgerstrassen," 28 Oct. 1920, Traut.

97. MA: R 5 35 31 Röhren-Verband 1921–1926 [Rundschreiben, Korrespondenzen].

98. TKA: A/1727: Däbritz Interview with Rabes, *et al.,* 5 Dec. 1938. These *documented* negotiations confirm the memories of his managers that he genuinely listened to them.

99. Kocka, "Industrielles Management," p. 346.

100. Scholl, *Ingenieure,* 336–367. The quote can be found on p. 356. Kessler, *Zur Geschichte des Managements bei Krupp.* Wolfram Bongartz, "Unternehmensleitung und Kostenkontrolle in der Rheinischen Montanindustrie vor 1914: Dargestellt am Beispiel der Firmen Krupp und Gutehoffnungshütte (Teil II)," *Zeitschrift für Unternehmensgeschichte* (ZUG), 29, 2 (1984), pp. 86–97. Wolbring, *Krupp und die Öffentlichkeit.* Lothar Gall, *Krupp: Der Aufstieg eines Industrieimperiums* (Berlin: Siedler Verlag, 2000).

101. Scholl, too, compares Krupp's organization directly to Siemens, as described by Kocka, *Unternehmensverwaltung und Angestelltenschaft*. Both had the final goal of making their chief director/owners "dispensable." Quote from Jürgen Kocka, "Entrepreneurs and Managers in German Industrialization," *The Cambridge Economic History of Europe, Volume VII: The Industrial Economies: Capital, Labour, and Enterprise; Part I: Britain, France, Germany, and Scandinavia*, ed. Peter Mathias and M. M. Postan (Cambridge/New York, 1978), p. 575. The article is essentially a summary of Jürgen Kocka, *Unternehmer in der deutschen Industrialisierung* (Göttingen, 1975). The German quote can be found on p. 112.

102. Kocka, *Unternehmensverwaltung*, pp. 292–297, quote from p. 292.

103. Kocka, *Unternehmensverwaltung und Angestelltenschaft*, esp. pp. 233–254, quote from pp. 251–252.

104. Kocka, *Unternehmensverwaltung*, p. 486, fn. 90.

4. Accounting for Control

1. Theodor M. Porter, "Information Cultures: A Review Essay," *Accounting, Organizations and Society*, 20, 1 (1994), pp. 83–92, quote from p. 88. Porter reviews Temin's *Inside the Business Enterprise*, whose general approach informs this book considerably. Also influential for my general interpretation is the collection of articles in Lamoreaux and Raff's *Coordination and Information*. Yates, *Control through Communication*. Levenstein, *Accounting for Growth*. Jones, *Accounting and the Enterprise*, pp. 124–128, on accounting, control, and agency theory. Anthony Giddens, "Time and Social Organization," *Social Theory and Modern Sociology* (Stanford: Stanford University Press, 1987), pp. 140–165, esp. 153–160.

2. Dornseifer, "Zur Bürokratisierung deutscher Unternehmen," p. 91.

3. Yates, *Control through Communication*, pp. 65–100. Also JoAnne Yates, "Investing in Information: Supply and Demand Forces in the Use of Information in American Firms, 1850–1920," *Inside the Business Enterprise: Historical Perspectives on the Use of Information*, ed. Peter Temin (Chicago: Chicago University Press, 1991), pp. 117–152.

4. Hayden White, "The Historical Text as Literary Artifact," *History and Theory: Contemporary Readings*, ed. Brian Fay, Philip Pomper, and Richard T. Vann (Oxford: Blackwell Publishers Ltd., 1998), p. 17.

5. C. Edward Arrington and Jere R. Francis, "Giving Economic Accounts: Accounting as Cultural Practice," *Accounting, Organizations and Society*, 18, 2/3 (1993), pp. 107–124.

6. Mannesmann Archive (MA): R 5 30 09 "P. P.," 26 May 1882, Fol. 27, Thyssen [Aug.]. Lutz Hatzfeld, "Geschichte der Unternehmensverwaltung und -Organisation als Voraussetzung für Wertung, Ordnung und Verzeichnung in Werksarchiven," Ordnung und Information: Vorträge vor dem 7. Lehrgang des VDWW and der Archivschule Marburg-Institut für Archivwissenschaft vom 5.-16 Feb. 1973, *Archiv und Wirtschaft: Mitteilungsblätter für das Archivwesen der Wirtschaft,* 1 (Dortmund, 1974), pp. 153–171.

7. Kocka, *Unternehmensverwaltung,* p. 298, 340.

8. Yates, *Control through Communication,* pp. 66–71, 107–8, 119–122, 168–176, 202–227. Another American firm, Scovill, introduced similar methods of systematic reporting in the 1890s.

9. MA: R 5 30 09 "Circulair II: . . . zurück zu Händen des Herrn Director Wilke," 26 May 1882, Fol. 28–31, Thyssen [Aug.].

10. Yates, *Control through Communication,* pp. 172–176.

11. MA: R 5 30 09 "Circulair IV . . . zurück zu Händen des Herrn Director Wilke," 6 June 1882, Fol. 38–40, Killing.

12. MA: R 2 30 09 "Circulair VII . . . zurück zu Händen des Herrn Director Wilke," 5 Jan. 1883, Fol. 107, [none]. "Circulair IX . . .: zurück an die Firma zu Händen des Herrn Director Wilke!," 10 May 1883, Fol. 117, Thyssen & Co. [Aug.].

13. MA: R 5 30 09 "Circulair!," 12 Sept. 1882, [An alle Beamte], Fol. 62, Thyssen & Co. [Aug.].

14. MA: R 5 30 09 "Circulair VI: . . . zurück an die Firma zu Händen des Herrn Director Wilke," 12 Sept. 1882, Fol. 63–64, Thyssen & Co. [Aug.].

15. MA: R 2 30 07 Salair-Buch 1881–2.

16. MA: R 2 30 09 "Circular!: . . . zurück zum Central-Büreau zu Händen Herrn Killing!," Fol. 216–217, Thyssen & Co. [Aug.].

17. MA: R 5 30 09 "Circulair III: . . . zurück zu Händen des Herrn Director Wilke," 30 May 1882, Fol. 36—37, [none, probably Thyssen]. No examples of the old *Schema* from before 1885 exist.

18. MA: R 2 30 09 "An die Maschinenfabrik (Abt. V)," 9 May 1885, Fol. 271, Thyssen & Co. [Aug.].

19. MA: R 2 30 09 "Circular! . . . zurück nach dem Central-Büreau zu Händen des Herrn Eumann," 5 June 1885, Fol. 275–276, Thyssen & Co.[Aug.].

20. MA: R 2 30 09 "Circular! . . . . zurück zu Händen des Herrn A. Killing!," Fol. 185–186, [none]. The old, and now new, working hours were 7:30–12:30 and 2:30 to 6:30. Mannesmann introduced these "English" hours for its office employees in 1912. See Wessel, *Kontinuität,* p. 170.

21. Phrase used by Max Haushofer, *Der Industriebetrieb: Ein Handbuch der Geschäftslehre für technische Beamte, Industrielle, Kaufleute, etc. sowie zum Gebrauche an technischen Schulen* (München: Eduard Koch, 1904), p. 365. Only after its financial crisis of 1874 and mistake-laden financial statements did Krupp establish a similar office as well. On Krupp, see Wolfram Bongartz, "Unternehmensleitung und Kostenkontrolle in der Rheinischen Montanindustrie vor 1914: Dargestellt am Beispiel der Firmen Krupp und Gutehoffnungshütte (Teil II)," *Zeitschrift für Unternehmensgeschichte* (ZUG), 29, 2 (1984), pp. 86–97.

22. MA: R 2 30 09 "Circular!: . . . zurück zu Händen des Herrn Killings," 30 Jan. 1885, Fol. 255, Killing.

23. MA: R 5 30 09 "Circulair V: . . . zurück zu Händen des Herrn Director Wilke," 28 June 1882, Fol. 45–46, [none, probably Thyssen].

24. ThyssenKrupp Archive (TKA): A/1783 Carl Härle to the Königliche Stempel- & Erbschaftssteueramt, Düsseldorf, 22 March 1913, No. 4577 [none, Härle].

25. MA: R 2 30 07 Salair-Buch 1881–2. More managers drew a salary, but, according to this salary list, were obviously not considered senior management.

26. MA: R 2 30 09 "Circular!: . . .," Fol. 382, [none]; and "Rundschreiben! . . . zurück zum CB [Centralbureau]," 3 June 1891, Fol. 111–112, pa. pa. Thyssen & Cie., Killing.

27. MA: R 2 30 10 "An den Staatssecretär des Reichspostes," 24 May 1898, Fol. 124–127, Thyssen & Co. & Gewerkschaft Deutcher Kaiser, Jos. Thyssen. MA: R 2 30 12. The recommendations for Albert Meyer, 7 April 1915 (Fol. 255), and Hermann Unger, 30 June 1915 (Fol. 270), indicate that until the war most of the telephone operators were male. See MA: R 1 31 05 for the telephone directory. These telephone books are central sources for the organization of the firm.

28. MA: R 2 30 12 Letter, 31 March 1901, Fol. 139, Eumann. MA: R 2 30 11 (2) Letter 3 Jan. 1903, Fol. 52, A. Wilke. Hatzfeld, "Werks- und Firmengeschichte," pp. 100, 159.

29. Yates, *Control through Communication*, pp. 39–45, 131, 167–168, 209–211.

30. Kocka, *Unternehmensverwaltung*, p. 341.

31. On the high degree of similarity of workshop practices in the American and German steel industries, see Welskopp, *Arbeit und Macht*.

32. Kocka, *Unternehmensverwaltung*, pp. 237–254. Wilfried Feldenkirchen, *Werner von Siemens: inventor and International Entrepreneur* (Columbus: Ohio State University Press, 1994), pp. 89, 135–140. Bongartz, "Unternehmensleitung und Kostenkontrolle," pp. 73–83.

33. A discussion of financial accounting follows in Chapter 9. Thyssen &

Co. financial statements are not available for the years prior to 1909 and make more sense in the context of the Thyssen-Konzern. For an overview of the typical set of journals used in German firms, see Max Haushofer, *Der Industriebetrieb,* pp. 328–367.

34. For a historical example, see Gordon Boyce, "Corporate Strategy and Accounting Systems: A Comparison of Developments at Two British Steel Firms, 1898–1914," *Business History,* 34, 1 (Jan. 1992), pp. 42–65.

35. MA: R 5 30 09 "Circulair III: . . . zurück zu Händen des Herrn Director Wilke," 30 May 1882, Fol. 36–37, [none, probably Thyssen]. I found no examples of the pre-1885 classifications. "Circular!: . . . zurück zum Central-Büreau zu Händen des Herrn Killing!," 4 Dec. 1884, Fol. 227–228, [none].

36. MA: R 2 30 09 "Circular!: . . . zurück nach dem Central-Büreau zu Händen des Herrn Killing," 5 March 1885, Fol. 263, [none].

37. See Albin Kerth and Jakob Wolf, *Bilanzanalyse und Bilanzpolitik* (München/Wien: C. Hanser, 1986).

38. Hatzfeld, "Werks- und Firmengeschichte," p. 96. Hatzfeld emphasizes this same point.

39. Such regular reporting and the strict distinction between current expenses and "betterments and additions" did not exist until after 1898 at the Midland (Dow) Chemical Company, see Levenstein, *Accounting for Growth,* pp. 100–107.

40. MA: R 5 30 02 Bilanzkopierbuch. Only the monthly balances for the steel mill between January 1887–March 1890, the plate and sheet department between December 1886–March 1890, and the machine department between November 1886–November 1905 still exist. The nail department also briefly appears.

41. MA: R 2 30 08 "Vertrag! Bruno Heil," 24 May 1884, Thyssen & Co. [Aug.], B. Heil. This is the only contract available in which the method of calculating 'net profits' was precisely outlined. Article §2 stipulated.

42. Newer, more efficient technology might actually reduce the number of workers yet increase the general overhead costs incurred by the firm (if it went heavily in debt to purchase the equipment). The more fixed capital (machinery and equipment) drove overall costs—which did become a crucial problem by the 1920s—the less accurate the number of employees might be as an allocation key.

43. Richard Colignon and Mark Covaleski, "A Weberian Framework in the Study of Accounting," *Accounting, Organizations and Society,* 16, 2 (1991), pp. 141–157. For a discussion of the problem of allocating joint costs such as overhead at Dow Chemical, which caused difficulties, see Levenstein, *Accounting for Growth,* pp. 150–157.

44. Other methods of computing depreciation include a units-of-output, declining balance, and the sum-of-the-years'-digits method. I found no evidence that Thyssen used any other method than straight-line depreciation. See Levenstein, *Accounting for Growth*, pp. 142–150 for a discussion of depreciation.

45. MA: R 2 30 08 "Vertrag! Bruno Heil," 24 May 1884, Thyssen & Co. [Aug.], B. Heil. For instance, the tin-plate department depreciated 18,000 marks per year in monthly installments.

46. MA: R 4 30 95 (1) Bewertung des Röhrenwerks 1910 and R 5 30 12–13; R 5 35 15–18 [Inventur 1908–1925]. The pipe and tube department's capital account was divided into buildings, machines, and general operating areas (such as technical office and storage areas, and general social welfare areas like shower rooms). Each of the above was subdivided into the various workshops of the pipe department. The pipe department inventories broke down into individual products whose values were calculated at near constant values between 1908–1923.

47. MA: R 5 35 17–18. See the "Monatliche Abschlüsse," 1924–1925. Unfortunately, it is impossible to tell if the overall balance statements for these years included overhead or depreciation estimates. Central firm-level accounts for general overhead, depreciation, and interest exist.

48. B. Penndorf, *Geschichte der Buchhaltung in Deutschland* (Leipzig: G. A. Gloeckner, 1913). Albert Ballewski and C. M. Lewin, *Der Fabrikbetrieb* (Berlin: Julius Springer, 1912), esp. pp. 37–69, 207–210. Richard Woldt, *Der industrielle Grossbetrieb: Eine Einführung in die Organisation moderner Fabrikbetriebe* (Stuttgart: F. Steiner, 1911), pp. 66–79.

49. Richard P. Brief, "Nineteenth Century Accounting Error," *Journal of Accounting Research* (Spring 1965), pp. 12–31, quote from p. 18. On American Tobacco Company, see Chandler, *Visible Hand*, p. 257, 274, 279, 386.

50. Chandler, *Visible Hand*, pp. 267–9. Bongartz, "Unternehmensleitung und Kostenkontrolle," pp. 86–89.

51. Levenstein, *Accounting for Growth*, pp. 140–163. Also Margaret Levenstein, "The Use of Cost Measures: The Dow Chemical Company, 1890–1914" in *Inside the Business Enterprise: Historical Perspectives on the Use of Information*, ed. Peter Temin (Chicago: Chicago University Press, 1991), pp. 71–116.

52. Johnson and Kaplan, *Relevance Lost*, pp. 66–75.

53. Baker Library, Harvard Business School, MSS: 5, Fall River Iron Works, Fall River Mass. 1821–1909, Case 3. Henceforth: Fall River, (Mill) and (Box number). Fall River, Iron Works, DA-2. I discuss only the period after 1870.

54. In this style, the left page of the open account journal entered transactions in chronological fashion, but the opposite right page was entered in double-entry form. The Metacomet Mill followed this form of bookkeeping. See Fall River, Metacomet Mill, Journals, BA-8. More sophisticated versions subdivide the right hand page into types of accounts. Penndorf, *Geschichte der Buchhaltung,* pp. 197–201; Ballewski/Lewin, *Fabrikbetrieb,* pp. 23–25. Early German critics of this method thought it was too detailed, too time-consuming, and had too many columns. However, the method began its "triumphant march" (Penndorf) in the last decade of the nineteenth century. On Dinkelbach, see TKA: PA (Presse) "Der Dinkelbachkreis," Dr. Theodor Gessel, 27 Oct. 1967.

55. Fall River, Case 4.

56. MSS: 526 Lowell Machine Shop 1845–1912, MSS 52: Stanley Manufacturing Company 1888–1919, Portland Company 1846–1902.

57. Fall River, Machine Shop, AK-2.

58. Fall River, Annawan Manufactory, L-1, M-1, N-1; the Metacomet Mill had a similar account structure, EA (1–3), GB-7, HB-1, KB-8, KC-(1–3), Case 4, "Metacomet Run of Mill 1848–63." Weekly statements are in GC-(1–3).

59. Johnson, "Managing by Remote Control," p. 49–50. Krass, *Carnegie,* pp. 137–139.

60. Chandler, *Visible Hand,* p. 279.

61. Quotes from Johnson and Kaplan, *Relevance Lost,* pp. 63–65, 89 fn. 6. Levenstein, *Accounting for Growth,* pp. 20–39. Also Kocka, "Industrielles Management," p. 340.

62. Kocka and Siegrist, "Hundert Grössten Deutschen Industrieunternehmen," esp. pp. 69–72, Tables 1, 2, 4.

63. "Industrielles Rechnungswesen in den Vereinigten Staaten von Amerika und Deutschland," *Technik und Wirtschaft* ed. Verein deutscher Ingenieure, 20, 10 (October 1927), pp. 289–290. Kurt Schmaltz, *Bilanz- und Betriebsanalyse in Amerika* (Stuttgart: C. E. Poeschel, 1927).

64. Penndorf, *Geschichte der Buchhaltung,* p. 227 relates that more than 800 works and 500 articles appeared about bookkeeping in Germany alone in the first decade of the 20th century. See Ballewski-Levin, *Fabrikbetrieb* for a good survey of these new techniques. For a bibliography, see Kocka, "Industrielles Management," pp. 347–353.

65. MA: R 4 35 37 (2) Selbstkosten 1904–1920. It is also most likely that the departments kept some sort of record of the conversion costs of individual products, but none are available before 1904.

66. Richard Woldt, *Der Industrielle Grossbetrieb: Eine Einführung in die Organisation moderner Fabrikbetriebe* (Stuttgart: J. H. W. Dietz, 1911), pp. 67–78. Woldt also indicated the difficulty, but paramount importance, of accurately assessing indirect costs and depreciation, especially for multi-activity firms.

67. See the discussion in Johnson and Kaplan, *Relevance Lost,* esp. pp. 48–58. Bongartz, "Unternehmensleitung und Kostenkontrolle," pp. 86–89. Dow began including such costs after 1900, but never included depreciation in product costs. See Levenstein, *Accounting for Growth,* pp. 160–161.

68. On the link between strategy and accounting see the nice discussion comparing two British steel firms by Boyce, "Corporate Strategy and Accounting Systems," pp. 55–61.

69. MA: R 2 30 10 "Herrn E. Becker," 5 June 1902, Fol. 296–297, [none].

70. This conforms to Christian Kleinschmidt's interpretation, *Rationalisierung als Unternehmensstrategie,* pp. 36–41. Also Bhimani, "Accounting and the Emergence of 'Economic Man'," pp. 655–658. Bhimani finds a similar transition in three French companies at the turn of the century, but focuses on workers' subjectivity and shifts in methods of organizational control.

71. Chandler, *Visible Hand,* pp. 272–279.

72. MA: R 2 30 09 "Circular!: . . . zurück zu Händen des Herrn Killing!," 30 Dec. 1884, Fol. 233–234, Thyssen & Co. [Aug.].

73. Kocka, *Unternehmensverwaltung,* p. 297.

74. Kocka, *Unternehmensverwaltung,* p. 392.

75. Kocka, "Industrielles Management," pp. 356–360.

76. Dent, "Accounting and Organizational Cultures," pp. 726–729.

77. Kocka, "Industrielles Management," pp. 368–369.

78. TKA: A/1771 Däbritz Interview with Dr. Schoell, 6 Sept. 1954.

5. Sustaining Innovation

1. ThyssenKrupp Archive (TKA): A/1783 Königliche Stempel- & Erbschaftssteueramt, 22 March 1913, No. 4577 [none, Härle].

2. See especially Christian Kleinschmidt, *Rationalisierung als Unternehmensstrategie: Die Eisen- und Stahlindustrie des Ruhrgebiets zwischen Jahrhundertwende und Weltwirtschaftskrise* (Essen: Klartext, 1993), pp. 41–59, 142–158. A short summary can be found in Christian Kleinschmidt, "'Amerikanischer Plan' und Deutscher Weg: Technische Rationalisierung in der Rekonstruktionsphase nach dem Ersten Weltkrieg, dargestellt an Beispielen aus der Dortmunder *Eisen- und*

Stahlindustrie" in *Die Eisen- und Stahlindustrie im Dortmunder Raum: Wirtschaftliche Entwicklung, soziale Strukturen und technologischer Wandel im 19. und 20. Jahrhundert* (Dortmund: Gesellschaft für Westfälische Wirtschaftsgeschichte, 1992), pp. 355–374. The general discussion on the gas-powered engine is largely based on his exposition. On U.S. steel companies, see Chandler, *Scale and Scope*, p. 139.

3. For an excellent analysis using an evolutionary model inspired from biology, see Johan Peter Murmann, *Knowledge and Competitive Advantage: The Coevolution of Firms, Technology, and National Institutions* (Cambridge: Cambridge University Press, 2003). Also Otto Keck, "The National System for Technical Innovation in Germany," *National Innovation Systems: A Comparative Analysis,* ed. Richard R. Nelson (Oxford: Oxford University Press, 1993), pp. 115–157. Robert R. Locke, *The End of the Practical Man: Entrepreneurship and Higher Education in Germany, France, and Great Britain, 1880–1940* (Greenwich, Conn.: JAI Press, 1984). David S. Landes, *The Unbound Prometheus: Technological Change and Industrial Development in Western Europe from 1750 to the Present* (Cambridge: Cambridge University Press, 1969).

4. The figures are from Keck, "The National System of Technical Innovation in Germany," p. 123. See also Clive Trebilcock, *Industrialization of the Continental Powers 1780–1914* (London: Longman, 1981), p. 63. Scholl, *Ingenieure in der Frühindustrialisierung,* pp. 406–430, the figures are from p. 422. Radkau, *Technik in Deutschland,* pp. 40–45 and 155–171, is more skeptical about the success of the polytechnical schools.

5. Wessel, *Kontinuität und Wandel,* p. 27. Radkau, *Technik in Deutschland,* pp. 165–167.

6. Richard Nelson, ed., *National Innovation Systems: A Comparative Analysis* (Oxford: Oxford University Press, 1993).

7. Giovanni Dosi, David J. Teece, and Sidney Winter, "Toward a Theory of Corporate Coherence: Preliminary Remarks," *Technology and Enterprise in a Historical Perspective,* ed. Giovanni Dosi, Renato Giannetti, Pier Angelo Toninelli (Oxford: Oxford University Press, 1992), pp. 185–211. For a contrary response, see Bruce Kogut, Gordon Walker, and Jaideep Anand, "Agency and Institutions: National Divergences in Diversification Behavior," *Organization Science,* 13, 2 (2002), pp. 162–178.

8. A number of articles have been written on the Thyssen & Co. Machine Company. See especially Hatzfeld, "Werks- und Firmengeschichte," pp. 128–149 for internal development of this department. Mannesmann Archive (MA): M30.112 A. Wallichs, "Die Entwicklung der Maschinenfabrik Thyssen & Co. A. G. in Mülheim-Ruhr," *Stahl und*

Eisen, 32, 21 (23 May 1912), pp. 851–856. MA: M30.140: K. Schneider, "Die Entwicklung der Grossgasmaschine der Maschinenfabrik Thyssen," in *50 Jahre Ingenieurarbeit zwischen Rhein und Ruhr 1872–1922,* ed. *Ruhr-Bezirksverein des Vereins deutscher Ingenieure* (Essen: VdI, 1922), pp. 41–65. Schneider focuses on the technical aspects of the machines themselves. MA: M30.141 *Das Mülheimer Werk der Siemens-Schuckertwerke A. G.: Dampfturbinen, Tubosätze,* ed. von der Siemens-Schuckertwerke A. G. (Berlin: V. D. I.-Verlag, 1937).

9. MA: R 2 30 09 "Duisburger Maschinenbau Actien-Gesellschaft, Theod. Keetmann," 22 May 1882, Fol. 22–25, [none].

10. MA: R 5 30 18 "Effekten-Konto Bücher."

11. MA: R 2 30 09 "Herrn R. Meyer," 28 July 1883, Fol. 120–122; 24 Aug. 1883, Fol. 134; 12 Oct. 1883, Fol. 136; 16 Oct. 1883, Fol. 137, "Der Aufsichtsrat, Aug. Thyssen."

12. MA: R 2 30 09 "An die Abteilung V," 11 Aug. 1884, Fol. 211–212, [none].

13. MA: R 2 30 09 "An die Maschinenfabrik (Abt. V)," 9 May 1885, Fol. 271, Thyssen & Co. [Aug.]; "Herrn A. Baertl," 23 Feb. 1886, Fol. 314, Thyssen & Co. [Aug.].

14. MA: R 2 30 08 "Herren Thyssen & Co.," 29 Jan. 1886, A. Baertl; R 2 30 09 "Herrn Aug. Baertl," 1 June 1887, Fol. 372–373, Thyssen & Co. [Aug.] and "Zeugnis!," 1 Sept. 1887, Fol. 390–91, [none].

15. Däbritz, *Thyssen,* pp. 62–68.

16. MA: R 2 30 12 "Sehr geehrter Herr Kommerzienrath! [no name]," 18 Sept. 1891, Fol. 52–53.

17. MA: R 2 30 09 Letter to Widekind, 12 Nov. 1888, Fol. 462–463, Aug. Thyssen; R 2 30 08 E. Widekind, 15 June 1889, Thyssen & Co. [Aug.]; R 2 30 09 W. Surmann, 1 Jan. 1890, Fol. 37–37, Thyssen & Co. [Aug.] and 12 Sept. 1890, Fol. 69, Thyssen & Co. [Aug.]; R 2 30 09 M. Thesing, Fol. 233, [none].

18. MA: R 2 30 10 "Vertrag [R. Hoffmann]," 15 May 1899, Fol. 176–179; 30 Jan. 1903, Fol. 348–349, [none].

19. MA: R 2 30 10 "Direktor Hoffmann," 20 Aug. 1904, Thyssen & Co. [Aug.]; 24 Sept. 1904 and 5 Oct. 1904, Aug. Thyssen (both written by Thyssen himself); 25 Feb. 1905, Fol. 136; 27 Feb. 1905, Fol. 138–139, Aug. Thyssen. Hoffmann still received a good recommendation from Thyssen, Fol. 140.

20. "Hans Richter," *Stahl und Eisen,* 27 April 1910, p. 727.

21. Thyssen-Stinnes correspondence, 21–22, 24 April 1905; 15, 18 June 1905; 23, 26 July 1905; 15 Jan. 1906 in Rasch/Feldman, *August Thyssen und Hugo Stinnes,* pp. 282–283, 286–290, 298–300, 306–314, 345–346.

22. Schneider, "Die Entwicklung der Grossgasmaschine," p. 44.

23. Thyssen to Stinnes, 26 Nov. 1907 and 31 Dec. 1907 in Rasch/Feldman, *August Thyssen und Hugo Stinnes,* pp. 392–393, 398. At this juncture, Thyssen sold over 1.75 million marks of RWE stock (par value) to the city of Essen in order to make key payments.

24. MA: P 7 77 02 "General-Versammlung," 29 June 1906.; "Bericht des Vorstandes," 23 May 1905; "Bericht des Aufsichtsrats," 24 May 1905. Hatzfeld, "Werks- und Firmengeschichte," pp. 139–141.

25. Stinnes to Thyssen, 25 Dec. 1907 in Rasch/Feldman, *August Thyssen und Hugo Stinnes,* pp. 396–397, fn. 1246.

26. "Hans Richter," *Stahl und Eisen,* 27 April 1910, p. 727.

27. MA: R 4 30 52 Report to August Thyssen, Gasversorgung Mülheim, 20 March 1911, Maschinenfabrik Thyssen & Co., Dr. Roser.

28. TKA: A/1774 Letter from Franz Dahl. On this trend to "full mechanization," see Kleinschmidt, *Rationalisierung als Unternehmensstrategie,* pp. 59–66. Welskopp, *Arbeit und Macht,* pp. 437–466.

29. See Kleinschmidt, *Rationalisierung als Unternehmensstrategie,* esp. pp. 41–65, 142–158.

30. See especially MA: R 5 30 65 (1912). Unfortunately, much of the statistical material for the development of the machine engineering company was destroyed. In 1926, the company was sold to DEMAG and most of the records went to that company. They were then lost in a bombing raid during World War II.

31. MA: R 2 30 10 Letters to Richter, [undated mid-1908], Fol. 401; 3 March 1908, Fol. 402–3; 30 May 1908, Fol. 420–1; 8 June 1908, Fol. 423—all signed Aug. Thyssen. Hatzfeld, "Werks- und Firmengeschichte," p. 142.

32. TKA: A/1783 Königliche Stempel- & Erbschaftssteueramt, 22 March 1913, No. 4577 [none, Härle]. Hatzfeld, "Werks- und Firmensgeschichte," pp. 141–143. The quoted phrase is from Härle himself.

33. TKA: A/635/19 "Entwürfe zum Gesellschaftsvertrag und Statuten der Ehrhardt-Sehmersche Maschinenfabriken GmbH 1908." In A/681/1 is a partial copy of the draft of the contract; A/635/19 "Rabes u. Hopmann [an] Herrn August Thyssen, Schloss Landsberg," 3 Oct. 1908; TKA: A/1783 Königliche Stempel- & Erbschaftssteueramt, March 1913, No. 4577 [none, Härle].

34. TKA: A/635/19 (§1).

35. "Fusionsbewegung in der Verfeinerungsindustrie" in *Kartellrundschau: Zeitschrift für Kartellwesen und verwandte Gebiete,* 6, 8 (August 1908), 640.

36. TKA: A/681/1. Articles 7 and 8 detailed the exact accounting measures through which the net profits would be assessed, and, probably more than any other clause, showed just who was driving the venture on.

37. TKA: A/681/1 (§ 12). A/635/19 Letter to August Thyssen, Rabes u. Hopmann, 3 Oct. 1908.

38. TKA: A/1083 "Herrn Direktor Dr. Drawe," 30 June 1908, gez. Erhardt & Sehmer GmbH: Ed Sehmer, Th. Ehrhardt, Thyssen & Co. [Aug.]. MA: R 2 30 1 "Herrn Friedr. Falck," 18 May 1908, Fol. 415–417 [none].

39. TKA: A/1783 Königliche Stempel- & Erbschaftssteueramt, 22 March 1913, No. 4577 [none, Härle].

40. TKA: A/1783 Königliche Stempel- & Erbschaftssteueramt, 22 March 1913, No. 4577 [none, Härle].

41. MA: R 2 30 10 "Herrn Thyssen & Co., Abt. Maschinenfabrik," 15 March 1909, Fol. 467, Thyssen & Co. [Aug.].

42. "Aus den Erinnerungen von Dr. Ing. Roser" in *Unsere ATH*, 3, (March 1960), p. 26. "Edmund Roser," *Lebensbilder aus dem Rheinisch-Westfälischen Industriegebiet*, 1962–1967, ed. Dr. Fritz Pudor (Baden-Baden: Nomos Verlagsgesellschaft, 1977), pp. 83–85. On his activities at Thyssen & Co., see MA: R 4 30 52 "Herrn August Thyssen," 20 March 1911 [Betr.:] Gasversorgung Mülheim, Dr. Roser. MA: R 4 35 36 for a history of the 'energy economies' in Mülheim prepared by Roser; MA: R 4 35 37 (1) on the central boiler facility 1911–1923.

43. TKA: A/1806 Däbritz Interview with Heinrich Dinkelbach, 11 Aug. 1954. A/1806–1807 Letter from Karl Fuss, 23 Oct. 1957 and the unpublished manuscript from Walter Däbritz. Fritz Pudor, ed., *Nekrologe aus dem Rheinisch-Westfälischen Industriegebiet, Jahrgang 1939–1951* (Düsseldorf: August Bagel Verlag, 1955), pp. 189–190. Härle was active in the Chambers of Commerce in Essen for thirty years, and especially active in the creation of the nascent chartered accountant's profession. He was also an internationally renowned collector of medieval Christian art; he had so many sculptures that they would not all fit into his house.

44. MA: R 1 35 06 Letter to Heinrich Thyssen-Bornemisza, 18 Jan. 1925, Aug. Thyssen. TA: A/1806 Däbritz Interview with Heinrich Dinkelbach, 11 Aug. 1954.

45. TKA: A/1783.

46. MA: R 1 35 05 "Maschinenfabrik Thyssen & Co. Aktiengesellschaft Mülheim-Ruhr: Statuten" [1911]. In comparison with the 1918 statutes, the managing board had to get the approval of the supervisory board in only seven decision areas. The 1911 statutes implied that the managing board acted essentially as executors of the supervisory board, but the 1918 statutes implied that the managing board did most of the strategy formulation.

47. TKA: A/681/1 "An den Vorsitzenden des Aufsichtsrates . . . Herrn August Thyssen, Bad Gastein," 8 Aug. 1912, Maschinenfabrik Thyssen & Co. Aktien-Gesellschaft, Direktion, Str., [none, Str.].

48. The Hollerith machine was the "real business basis" of the growth of International Business Machines (IBM). See David Mercer, *IBM: How the World's Most Successful Corporation is Managed* (London: K. Page, 1987), pp. 25–26; Saul Engelbourg, *International Business Machines: A Business History* (New York: Arno Press, 1976). On Hollerith himself, see Geoffrey D. Austrian, *Herman Hollerith: Forgotten Giant of Information Processing* (New York: Columbia, 1982), esp. pp. 197–211, 238–257. American business firms began introducing the Hollerith machine after 1903. A German company, the Deutsche Hollerith Maschinen Gesellschaft in Berlin (DEHOMAG) was established around 1910 (pp. 327–328).

49. TKA: PA (Presse) "Der Dinkelbachkreis," 27 Oct. 1967 by Leo Kluitmann.

50. TKA: A/681/1 Herrn Direktor Rabes, Gewerkschaft Deutscher Kaiser, 11 April 1913, R[oser]. The quotas were based on the firm's three best years of their choice. Their main competitors were the Elsässische Maschinenbau-Gesellschaft, which received 6.117 %; Maschinenbau-A. G. vorm. Gebr. Klein, Dahlbruch 6.005%; Pokorny & Wittekind, Maschinenbau A. G. 0.462%; Donnersmarckhütte 0.820%; Aschersslebener Maschinenbau AG 1.349%; Gutehoffnungshütte 1.338%; Deutsche Maschinen-Fabrik AG 1.198%; Friedrich-Wilhelms-Hütte 4.415%; Haniel & Lueg 5.814%; Société Anonyme John Cockerill 9.931%; Maschinenfabrik Augsburg-Nürnberg AG 22.798%; Maschinenfabrik Thyssen & Co. AG 20.075%; Gasmotorenfabrik Deutz 3.374%; Dingler'sche Maschinenfabrik AG 0.323%; Ehrhardt & Sehmer GmbH 7.493%; Siegener Maschinenbau-AG & Gebr. Körting AG 8.488%; and the Maschinenbau-Anstalt Humboldt. As befits the complicated nature of German cartel negotiations, the Thyssen Machine Company received a lower quota because inner-Konzern deliveries were only valued at 60% of their original value. The machine department directors, who negotiated with the syndicate, felt this quota was still a good result because Konzern orders were so high that they could still produce at the same capacity as M. A. N.

51. TKA: A/1783 "Mitteilung von Dr. Roser" [no date]. See also the discussion in Brigitte Ingeborg Schluter, *Verwaltungsbauten der Rheinisch-Westfalischen Stahlindustrie 1900–1930* (Bonn: Rheinischen Friedrich-Wilhelms Universitat, 1991).

52. See Hatzfeld, "Werks- und Firmengeschichte," pp. 89–91 for a discussion of Bad Tönnistein and pp. 92–93 for Thyssen & Co. Abt. Wülfrath.

53. TKA: F/Alb 27 "Wasserwerk Thyssen & Cie., GmbH, Mülheim-Ruhr-

Styrum" for a chronology as well as maps and statistics on its development. Rasch, "August Thyssen," pp. 63–66. Hatzfeld, "Werks- und Firmengeschichte," pp. 91–2. Däbritz, *August Thyssen,* pp. 201–02.

54. MA: R 2 30 10 Herrn W. Pouch, 24 Feb. 1899, Fol. 160–162. This complicated contract lays out precisely how Pouch's year-end bonuses would be calculated as a percentage of profits. Gas and waterworks expenses were distinguished strictly from one another. Pouch received 4000 marks per year and a 1% share of profits.

55. TKA: Personnel Files. "Franz Lenze," *Stahl und Eisen,* 57, 48, p. 1372. Gertrud Milkereit, "Franz Lenze: Der Fachmann für Gas und Wasser," *Niederrheinkammer* (Jan. 1987), p. 40. "Kleine Chronik Thyssengas 1921–1981," *Thyssengas Intern* (Duisburg: Thyssen Gas GmbH PR, 1981), p. 3.

56. Rasch and Feldman, *August Thyssen und Hugo Stinnes.* See Feldman, *Hugo Stinnes,* esp. pp. 118–141, 242–260, 276–289. The discussion generally follows Feldman's portrayal as well as that of Hans Pohl, *Vom Stadtwerk zum Elektrizitätsgrossunternehmen: Gründung, Aufbau und Ausbau der 'Rheinisch-Westfälischen Elektrizitätswerk AG' (RWE) 1898–1918* (Stuttgart: Franz Steiner Verlag, 1992), esp. pp. 9–36.

57. Stinnes to Thyssen, 24 April 1905 in Rasch and Feldman, *August Thyssen und Hugo Stinnes,* p. 290.

58. Thyssen to Stinnes, 21 July 1905 in Rasch and Feldman, *August Thyssen und Hugo Stinnes,* p. 303.

59. Thyssen to Stinnes, 21 Dec. 1902 in Rasch and Feldman, *August Thyssen und Hugo Stinnes,* p. 226.

60. Thyssen to Stinnes, 1 Nov. 1902 in Rasch and Feldman, *August Thyssen und Hugo Stinnes,* p. 214. MA: P7 77 15 (1) "Landrat Graf von Meerveld, Recklinghausen, und die angeblich Stinnes-Thyssenschen Monopol-Bestrebungen," 24 April 1906. Von Meerveld attacked Thyssen's and Stinnes' attempt to supply water to Mülheim, causing a "lively echo" in public opinion.

61. Thyssen to Stinnes, 21 Nov. 1902 and 27 Dec. 1905 in Rasch and Feldman, *August Thyssen und Hugo Stinnes,* pp. 220–221 and 342, respectively.

62. See especially Feldman, "Zwischen Zusammenarbeit und Konflikt," pp. 111–126.

63. Quoted in Feldman, *Hugo Stinnes,* pp. 136–7.

64. MA: R 4 30 51 (1), Vertrag 27 Feb. 1905. The file is filled with draft contracts. TKA: F/Alb27.

65. MA: R 4 30 51 (1), Letter to the machine department from the Wasserwerk, 7 July 1906.

66. Feldman, "Zwischen Zusammenarbeit und Konflikt," pp. 126–131,
67. Feldman, *Hugo Stinnes,* pp. 279–282, quote from p. 280. Peter Wulf, *Hugo Stinnes,* pp. 26–27.
68. See the map reproduced in Rasch and Feldman, *August Thyssen und Hugo Stinnes,* p. 518. Rasch, "August Thyssen," pp. 64–65
69. Wall, *Andrew Carnegie,* pp. 267–268, 338–340. Wall, *The Andrew Carnegie Reader,* pp. 52–53, 58–61
70. For a theoretically-informed perspective on this same virtuous loop, see Murmann, *Knowledge and Competitive Advantage,* esp. pp. 69–79.
71. Dosi, Teece, and Winter, "Toward a Theory of Corporate Coherence: Preliminary Remarks," pp. 185–211.
72. David Landes in *Unbound Prometheus* provides a similar vision of technological change.
73. Dosi, Teece, and Winter, "Toward a Theory of Corporate Coherence," pp. 198–207.
74. Kogut, Walker, and Anand, "Agency and Institutions."
75. Louis Galambos, "The Innovative Organization: Viewed from the Shoulders of Schumpeter, Chandler, Lazonick, et al.," *Business and Economic History,* 22, 1 (Fall 1993), pp. 86–89.

6. Cartels and Competition

1. Richard H. K. Vietor, *Contrived Competition: Regulation and Deregulation in America* (Cambridge, Mass.: Belknap Press of Harvard University Press, 1994). The impact of state-sponsored industrial regulation on many American firms acts as a counterpart to German industrial self-governance by private associations. Vietor's case study on American Airlines offers surprising parallels to the German steel industry.
2. Harm Schröter, "Small European States and Cooperative Capitalism, 1920–1960," *Big Business and the Wealth of Nations,* ed. Alfred D. Chandler, Jr., and Takashi Hikino (Cambridge, Mass.: Belknap Press of Harvard University Press, 1997), pp. 176–204; *idem,* "Cartelization and Decartelization in Europe, 1870–1995: Rise and Decline of an Economic Institution," *The Journal of European Economic History,* 25, 1 (Spring 1996), pp. 129–153. Also see the contributions in Alfred D. Chandler, Jr., and Takashi Hikino ed., *Big Business and the Wealth of Nations* (Cambridge: Cambridge University Press, 1997). Alfred D. Chandler, Jr., *Scale and Scope: The Dynamics of Industrial Capitalism* (Cambridge, Mass.: Belknap, 1990), pp. 72–73. Tony Freyer, *Regulating Big Business: Antitrust in Great Britain and America 1880–1990* (Cambridge: Cambridge University Press, 1992). Also Tony Freyer, "Legal Restraints

on Economic Coordination: Antitrust in Great Britain and America, 1880–1920," *Coordination and Information: Historical Perspectives on the Organization of Enterprise,* ed. Naomi R. Lamoreaux and Daniel M. G. Raff (Chicago: University of Chicago Press, 1995), pp. 183–202.

3. Friedrich Kleinwächter, *Die Kartelle: Ein Beitrag zur Frage der Organisation der Volkswirtschaft* (Innsbruck: Wagner, 1883).

4. Lujo Brentano, *Über die Ursachen der heutigen sozialen Not: Ein Beitrag zur Morphologie der Volkswirtschaft* (Leipzig: Duncker & Humblot, 1889).

5. Karl Bücher, "Die wirtschaftlichen Kartelle," *Verhandlungen der am 28. und 29. September 1894 in Wien abgehaltenen Generalversammlung des Vereins für Socialpolitik über die Kartelle und über das ländliche Erbrecht* (Schriften des Vereins für Socialpolitik, 61) (Leipzig: Duncker & Humblot, 1895), pp. 138–157; quote from p. 154.

6. Friedrich List, *Das Nationale System der Politischen Ökonomie* (Tübingen: Kykles, 1959 [1841]).

7. Quoted in Karl-Heinz Fezer, "Die Haltung der Rechtswissenschaften zu den Kartellen bis 1914," *Kartelle und Kartellgesetzgebung,* ed. Hans Pohl (Stuttgart: F. Steiner, 1985), pp. 50–68.

8. Freyer, *Regulating Big Business,* pp. 121–149. Rudolph J. R. Peritz, *Competition Policy in America, 1888–1992: History, Rhetoric, Law* (New York: Oxford University Press, 1996), pp. 13–18.

9. Hovenkamp, *Enterprise and American Law 1836–1937* (Cambridge, Mass.: Harvard University Press, 1991), pp. 293–295.

10. Fritz Blaich, *Kartell- und Monopolpolitik im Kaiserlichen Deutschland: Das Problem der Marktmacht im deutschen Reichstag zwischen 1879 und 1914* (Düsseldorf: Droste, 1973), pp. 43–47, views the 25 June 1890 decision by the Imperial court as the decisive case permitting cartels. The case concerned the German booksellers' association.

11. *Entscheidung des Reichsgerichts in Civilsachen,* 38, 4 Feb. 1897 (Leipzig: Veit & Co., 1897), pp. 155–162. See also Blaich, *Kartell- und Monopolpolitik* and the contributions in *Kartelle und Kartellgesetzgebung in Praxis und Rechtsprechung vom 19. Jahrhundert bis zur Gegenwart,* ed. Hans Pohl (Stuttgart: F. Steiner, 1985). There is unfortunately no good comparative intellectual-legal study of these fundamental decisions in the 1890s.

12. The term "self-government" *(Selbstverwaltung)* has a long history and a particularly German resonance. It refers mostly to the wide-ranging autonomy of free towns and cities in Germany. Martin Parnell, *The German Tradition of Organized Capitalism: Self-Government in the Coal Industry* (Oxford: Clarendon Press, 1994). Parnell makes self-government "THE fundamental organizing principle of German-style capitalism."

But Parnell tends to see self-government as a statist philosophy of the "substantial, intimate, and possibly necessary role of the state in industrial affairs" (p. 237). He also tends to generalize the relationship business-government relationship of the coal industry in the second half of the twentieth century to other industries and to other periods of German history.

13. Blaich, *Kartell- und Monopolpolitik,* pp. 97, 132–33. See the debate in 1906 between Gustav Schmoller and Emil Kirdorf, the director of the Rheinisch-Westfalian Coal Syndicate, which is reproduced in Ludwig Kastl, ed., *Kartelle in der Wirklichkeit* (Köln: Heymann, 1963), pp. 89–110. It can also be found in the *Verhandlungen der Generalversammlung in Mannheim 1905* (Schriften des Vereins für Socialpolitik, 116) (Leipzig: Duncker & Humblot, 1906). Klaus J. Bremer, "Die Kartellverordnung von 1923: Entstehung, Inhalt und praktische Anwendung," *Kartelle und Kartellgesetzgebung in Praxis und Rechtsprechung vom 19. Jahrhundert bis zur Gegenwart,* ed. Hans Pohl (Stuttgart: F. Steiner, 1985), pp. 111–128. On Britain, see Tony Freyer, "Legal Restraints on Economic Coordination: Antitrust in Great Britain and America, 1880–1920," *Coordination and Information: Historical Perspectives on the Organization of Enterprise,* ed. Naomi R. Lamoreaux and Daniel M. G. Raff (Chicago: Chicago, 1995), pp. 183–202, quote from p. 201. In the United States the Sherman Act even allowed for imprisonment and the expropriation of property. Peritz, *Competition Policy in America,* pp. 20–26. These intellectual divisions took on very real contours during the so-called Hibernia affair. Blaich, *Kartell- und Monopolpolitik,* pp. 97, 132–33. Dietmar Bleidick, *Die Hibernia-Affäre: Der Streit um den Preussischen Staatsbergbau im Ruhrgebiet zu Beginn des 20. Jahrhunderts* (Bochum: Deutsches Bergbau-Museum, 1999). Charles Medalen, "State Monopoly Capitalism in Germany: the Hibernia Affair," *Past and Present,* 78 (February 1978), pp. 82–112.

14. Blaich, *Kartell- und Monopolpolitik* offers the best overview of the political spectrum and the various debates and commissions on cartel behavior. Fritz Blaich, "Die Rolle der amerikanischen Antitrustgesetzgebung in der Wirtschaftspolitischen Diskussion Deutschlands zwischen 1890 und 1914," *ORDO,* 22 (1971), pp. 229–254. Peritz, *Competition Policy in America,* pp. 29–37.

15. Robert Liefmann, *Die Unternehmerverbände (Konventionen, Kartelle): Ihr Wesen und Ihre Bedeutung,* ed. Carl Johannes Fuchs, Heinrich Herkner, Gerhard von Schulze-Gävernitz, and Max Weber (Freiburg i.B.: J. C. B. Mohr, 1897). For a bibliography of contemporary German theory about the logic of fixed costs, see Theodor Becker, *Die Bedeutung der Rationalisierung für die Kartellbildung* (Emsdetten, Westfalen: Lechte,

1932), pp. 8–15. Literature on cartel theory can be found in Hans Merten, *Perioden der Kartellforschung in Deutschland* (Kiel: Dissertation Christian-Albrechts Universität, 1933). Walter Braeuer, *Kartell und Konjunktur, der Meinungsstreit in fünf Jahrzehnten* (Berlin: Carl Heymanns Verlag, 1934). Harry Lieser, *Kartelle und Konjunktur in ihrer wechselseitigen Beeinflussung* (Wien/Leipzig: M. Perles, 1934). A whole series of critical assessments came out after 1929 that began to undercut standard assumptions, especially by future, 'neo-liberal' theorists of the social market economy. Franz Böhm, *Wettbewerb und Monopolkampf: Eine Untersuchung zur Frage des wirtschaftlichen Kampfrechts und zur Frage der rechtlichen Struktur der geltenden Wirtschaftsordung* (Berlin: Carl Heymanns Verlag, 1933, repr. in 1964); *idem Kartelle und Koalitionsfreiheit* (Berlin: Carl Heymanns Verlag, 1933). Walter Eucken wrote his dissertation about cartels in the shipping industry, *Verbandsbildung in der Schiffahrt* (München: Duncker & Humblot, 1914). Eucken and Böhm founded the neo-liberal journal *ORDO* at the end of 1945. See also A. J. Nicholls, *Freedom with Responsibility: The Social Market Economy in Germany 1918–1963* (Oxford: Clarendon Press, 1994), esp. Chapter 2 on the origins of neo-liberalism.

16. Robert Liefmann, *Kartelle und Trusts und die Weiterbildung der volkswirtschaftlichen Organisation* (Stuttgart: Moritz, 1910), esp. pp. 109–142. Various editions available. Indeed, German steel firms' overall employment levels achieved steadier figures than did American steel firms, who frequently laid off more than 20% of their work forces, something unheard of in German firms. Compare the average employment levels between 1907–1914 in Wilfried Feldenkirchen, *Die Eisen- und Stahlindustrie des Ruhrgebiets 1879–1914: Wachstum, Finanzierung und Struktur ihrer Grossunternehmen* (Wiesbaden: F. Steiner, 1982), Table 104 a/b, with Gertrude G. Schroeder, *The Growth of Major Steel Companies, 1900–1950* (Baltimore: John Hopkins, 1953), pp. 216–218. Average yearly employment levels do not take into consideration the considerable turnover rates of German workers. Contemporaries (and some historians) claimed that cartels made German industrial growth less volatile than the that of the United States or Britain. See Alexander J. Field, "The Relative Stability of German and American Industrial Growth, 1880–1913: A Comparative Analysis," *Historische Konjunkturforschung*, ed. Wilhelm Heinz Schröder and Reinhard Spree (Stuttgart: Klett-Cotta, 1980), pp. 208–233.

17. The discussion is based on Liefmann, *Kartelle und Trusts,* esp. pp. 109–142. Also Lon LeRoy Peters, *Cooperative Competition in German Coal and Steel 1893–1914* (Dissertation: Yale University, 1981), pp. 44–78.

18. For a discussion about Standard Oil that raged through Parliament be-

tween 1895–1897 and after 1911, see Blaich, *Kartell- und Monopolpolitik,* pp. 74–92, 185–206.

19. *Stenographische Berichte über die Verhandlungen des Deutschen Reichstags,* 159, p. 107 ff. quoted in Fritz Blaich, "Die Rolle der amerikanischen Antitrustgesetzgebung," p. 231.

20. Gustav Schmoller, *Grundriss der Allgemeinen Volkswirtschaftslehre,* Erster Teil (Leipzig: Duncker & Humblot, 1900), pp. 450–454.

21. One contemporary American critic of U.S. antitrust legislation put his finger on this point. It took "no account of intent, methods, and results of combination . . . In prohibiting combination agreements it has gone far to drive corporations directly to the most extreme and complete form of consolidation." Herbert Knox Smith quoted in Herbert Hovenkamp, *Enterprise and American Law,* p. 243.

22. Quoted in Blaich, *Kartell- und Monopolpolitik,* p. 31. Blaich, "Die Rolle der amerikanischen Antitrustgesetzgebung." A similar reasoning could also be found in the United States as Louis Brandeis argued for the efficacy of cartels for preserving the independence of small business and thus political and "industrial liberty." See Freyer, *Regulating Big Business,* pp. 66–67. See also Neil Fligstein, *The Transformation of Corporate Control* (Cambridge, Mass.: Harvard University Press, 1990), pp. 75–115. Fligstein argues that the Sherman Act created a new dominant "manufacturing conception of control" that subverted anti-trust.

23. Wilfried Feldenkirchen, "Concentration in German Industry 1870–1939," *The Concentration Process in the Entrepreneurial Economy since the late 19th Century,* (*Zeitschrift für Unternehmensgeschichte,* 55), ed. Hans Pohl and Wilhelm Treue (Stuttgart: Franz Steiner, 1988), p. 126.

24. Peter Hüttenberger, "Wirtschaftsordnung und Interessenpolitik in der Kartellgesetzgebung der Bundesrepublik 1949–1957," *Vierteljahrshefte für Zeitgeschichte,* 24, 3 (1976), pp. 287–307.

25. For a list of cartel types, see Wolfgang Korndörfer, *Allgemeine Betriebswirtschaftslehre* (Wiesbaden: Gabler, 1988), pp. 128–132 and Feldenkirchen, "Concentration Process," pp. 113–115. See *The Economist*'s review of Andrew Dick, "If Cartels Were Legal, Would Firms Fix Prices?," (Antitrust Division, U.S. Department of Justice, 1997), in *The Economist* (August 9, 1997), p. 68.

26. Feldenkirchen, "Concentration in German Industry," p. 120.

27. Feldenkirchen, *Eisen- und Stahlindustrie,* pp. 112–117, 154–161; Feldenkirchen, "Concentration in German Industry," pp. 119–124. Archibald Stockder, *Regulating an Industry: The Rheinisch-Westphalian Coal Syndicate 1893–1929* (New York: Columbia, 1932). Kurt Wiedenfeld, *Das Rheinisch-Westfälische Kohlensyndikat* (Bonn: Marcus &

Weber, 1912). Peters, *Cooperative Competition in German Coal and Steel*, pp. 127–136.

28. Feldenkirchen, *Eisen- und Stahlindustrie*, pp. 118–120, 169–186. Arthur Klotzbach, *Der Roheisen-Verband: Ein geschichtlicher Rückblick auf die Zusammenschlussbestrebungen in der deutschen Hochofen-Industrie* (Düsseldorf: Stahleisen, 1926).

29. See Chandler, *Scale and Scope*, 138, Table 11, which lists the market share of U.S. Steel for various product lines between 1901–27.

30. The steel cartel's legacy, in fact, extends through the International Steel Cartel of 1926 until the European Coal and Steel Community. John Gillingham, *Coal, Steel, and the Rebirth of Europe 1945–1955: The Germans and French from Ruhr Conflict to Economic Community* (Cambridge: Cambridge University Press, 1991).

31. Feldenkirchen, *Eisen- und Stahlindustrie*, pp. 120–124, 144–147, 186–212. Peters, *Cooperative Competition in German Coal and Steel* and L. L. Peters, "Are Cartels Unstable?: The German Steel Works Association before World War I," *Technique, Spirit and Form in the Making of the Modern Economies*, ed. Gary Saxonhouse and Gavin Wright (Greenwich, Conn.: JAI Press, 1984), pp. 61–85.

32. Frank B. Tipton, Jr., *Regional Variation in the Economic Development of Germany during the Nineteenth Century* (Middletown, Conn.: Wesleyan University Press, 1976). Hubert Kiesewetter, *Industrielle Revolution in Deutschland 1815–1914* (Frankfurt/Main: Suhrkamp, 1989). Regional cartels could affect internal entrepreneurial strategy as well. One of Thyssen's trading firms in Hamburg had to get special permission to clear the delivery of cement from the Thyssen-owned firm in the eastern part of Germany, the Rittergut Rüdersdorf, because the Rhineland-Westphalian Cement Association normally did not allow cross-regional deliveries. See Mannesmann Archive: R 5 35 63 Thyssen Handelsgesellschaft, Hamburg to Thyssen & Co., Jan. 1922.

33. Steven B. Webb, "Tariffs, Cartels, Technology, and Growth in the German Steel Industry, 1879 to 1914," *Journal of Economic History*, 40, 2 (June 1980), pp. 309–329.

34. Only Britain maintained open borders for steel products. Even the United States had higher tariff barriers until World War II, as well as an uncontested domestic market additionally protected by high transportation costs. Paul Bairoch, *Economics and World History: Myths and Paradoxes* (Chicago: Chicago University Press, 1993), pp. 30–55, esp. Table 3.3.

35. Gerschenkron, *Economic Backwardness in Historical Perspective* (Cambridge, Mass.: Belknap Press of Harvard University Press, 1966), p. 15.

Gerschenkron largely followed the interpretations of Otto Jeidels, Jakob Riesser, and Rudolf Hilferding.

36. Lothar Gall, Gerald D. Feldman, Harold James, Carl-Ludwig Holtfrerich, Hans E. Büschgen, *Die Deutsche Bank 1870–1995* (München: C. H. Beck, 1995), pp. 44–48.

37. Quoted in Volker Wellhöner, *Grossbanken und Grossindustrie im Kaiserreich* (Göttingen: Vandenhoeck & Ruprecht, 1989), p. 125. Horst A. Wessel, *Kontinuität und Wandel: 100 Jahre Mannesmann 1890–1990* (Düsseldorf: Droste, 1990), pp. 100–103. Peters, *Cooperative Competition in German Coal and Steel*, pp. 288–294.

38. Even Gerschenkron noted the declining importance of banks for industry financing after 1895. Jeremy Edwards and Sheilagh Ogilvie, "Universal Banks and German Industrialization: A Reappraisal," *Economic History Review*, 59, 3 (1996), pp. 427–446. Gall et al., *Deutsche Bank*, pp. 48–52.

39. The following discussion is based on Wellhöner, *Grossbanken*, pp. 80–87.

40. Kamp to Lantz (Director of Phoenix), 23 March 1904 and to Gaedicke (Verwaltungsrat) from 2 March 1904, quoted in Wellhöner, *Grossbanken*, p. 86.

41. In October 1903, Carl Klönne wrote nearly identical lines to Baare (Bochumer Verein), F. Goecke (Rheinische Stahlwerke), Lueg (GHH), Meyer (Peiner Stahlwerk), Schmidt (Krupp), Später (Rombacher Hütte), and August Thyssen, (ZStA Potsdam, 80 BA 2, Nr. 21026). Quoted in Wellhöner, *Grossbanken*, p. 264, fn. 31.

42. Kamp to Lantz (exact date unknown), quoted in Wellhöner, *Grossbanken*, p. 87.

43. ThyssenKrupp Archive (TKA): A/1727: Däbritz Interview with Jakob Hasslacher, 7 Nov. 1939.

44. Hugo Hartung, the representative of the Schaffhausen'sche Bankverein in Phoenix, to Heinrich Kamp, the General Director of Phoenix, 14 June 1906. Quoted in Wellhöner, *Grossbanken*, pp. 80–84.

45. Gerald D. Feldman, *Hugo Stinnes: Biographie eines Industriellen 1870–1924* (München: C. H. Beck, 1998), pp. 82–91. Manfred Rasch and Gerald D. Feldman, eds., *August Thyssen und Hugo Stinnes: Ein Briefwechsel 1898–1922* (München: C. H. Beck, 2003), pp. 117–122. 240–250. Wilhelm Treue, Treue, Wilhelm, *Die Feuer Verlöschen Nie: August Thyssen-Hütte 1890–1926*, 1 (Düsseldorf/Wien: Econ, 1966), pp. 69–74. Walter Däbritz, *August Thyssen* (unpublished manuscript), available in the ThyssenKrupp Archive and Mannesmann Archive (ca. 1944), pp. 153–161.

46. Kirdorf, "Verhältnis der Kartelle zum Staate," pp. 109–110.

47. See the chronologies in Feldenkirchen, *Eisen und Stahlindustrie* and in Arnold Tross, *Der Aufbau der Eisen- und eisenverarbeitenden Industrie-Konzerne Deutschlands: Ursachen, Formen und Wirkungen des Zusammen-schlusses unter besonderer Berücksichtigung der Maschinen- Industrie* (Berlin: J. Springer, 1928).

48. Christian Kleinschmidt and Thomas Welskopp, "Zu viel 'Scale' zu wenig 'Scope:' Eine Auseinandersetzung mit Alfred D. Chandlers ana-lyse der deutschen Eisen- und Stahlindustrie in der Zwischen-kriegszeit," *Jahrbuch für Wirtschaftsgeschichte*, 2 (1993), pp. 251–297, here p. 261.

49. George Ebner, *Die Kartellgeschichte der deutschen Röhrenindustrie* (Berlin: Deutscher Montan-Bund GmbH, 1913), pp. 18–22. Peters, *Cooperative Competition in German Coal and Steel*, pp. 288–294.

50. Steven B. Webb, "Tariffs, Cartels, Technology, and Growth in the Ger-man Steel Industry, 1879 to 1914," *Journal of Economic History*, 40, 2 (June 1980), pp. 309–329. Webb also argues that cartels contributed to German steelmakers' productivity.

51. See Ulrich Wengenroth, "Germany: Competition Abroad—Coopera-tion at Home," *Big Business and the Wealth of Nations*, ed. Alfred D. Chandler, Jr., and Takashi Hikino (Cambridge, Mass.: Harvard Univer-sity Press, 1997), pp. 141–143.

52. Feldman, *Hugo Stinnes*, pp. 327–329.

53. Harvard Business School, Baker Library: GO: 301 B82. H. A. Brassert & Company (Consulting Engineers): *Report on Gelsenkirchener Bergwerks Aktiengesellschaft, Deutsch-Luxemburgische Bergwerks und Hütten Aktien-gesellschaft and Bochumer Verein für Bergbau and Gussstahlfabrikation* (Dillon, Read & Co., December 1925). A similar point in Siegfried Tschierschky, *Kartell und Trust: Vergleichende Untersuchungen über deren Wesen und Bedeutung* (Göttingen: Vandenhoeck & Ruprecht, 1903), p. 61.

54. Patrick Fridenson, "France: The Relatively Slow Development of Big Business in the Twentieth Century," *Big Business and the Wealth of Na-tions*, ed. Alfred D. Chandler, Jr., and Takashi Hikino (Cambridge, Mass.: Harvard University Press, 1997), pp. 225–226.

55. Feldenkirchen, *Eisen- und Stahlindustrie*, pp. 93, 232, Table 20. Before 1900, the ratio was roughly 80 percent; between 1900–1908 it was roughly 65 percent. German export potential also should not be re-duced to its cartel system because it increased its world market share in various uncartelized industries. Germany also manufactured 90 per-cent of all dyestuffs sold on world export markets, 30 percent of all

pharmaceuticals, 35 percent of electrical goods, 27 percent of chemicals, 29 percent of machine-tools, and 17 percent of internal combustion engines. See Otto Keck, "The National System for Technical Innovation in Germany," pp. 115–157.

56. See Gerald Feldman, "The Collapse of the Steel Works Association, 1912–1919," *Sozialgeschichte Heute. Festschrift für Hans Rosenberg zum 70. Geburtstag*, ed. Hans-Ulrich Wehler (Göttingen: Vandenhoeck & Ruprecht, 1974), pp. 575–593.

57. MA: R 5 30 64 Thyssen & Co. Department III: Tube Works English Brochure 1912–1914, p. 4.

58. Blaich, Kartell- und Monopolpolitik, pp. 152–159.

59. Gerald D. Feldman, "The Collapse of the Steel Works Association." Hermann Schäfer, "Kartelle in der Zeit des ersten Weltkrieges: Funktionen im Rahmen von Kriegswirtschaft und Sozialisierung," Kartelle und Kartellgesetzgebung, ed. Hans Pohl (Stuttgart: F. Steiner, 1985), pp. 81–99.

60. Gerald Feldman, *Iron and Steel in the German Inflation 1916–1923* (Princeton, N.J.: Princeton University Press, 1977), p. 215.

61. Fligstein, *Transformation of Corporate Control*, p. 23. Also Neil Fligstein, "The Structural Transformation of American Industry: An Institutional Account of the Causes of Diversification in the Largest Firms, 1919–1979," *The New Institutionalism in Organizational Analysis* ed. Walter W. Powell and Paul J. DiMaggio (Chicago: University of Chicago Press, 1991), pp. 311–336. Fligstein argues that U.S. antitrust legislation drove American firms into a "manufacturing conception of control" because cartels were outlawed. Yet German steel firms developed a similar "manufacturing conception of control" with different points of emphasis, despite being able to resort to cartels.

62. Feldenkirchen, "Concentration," pp. 119–129.

63. Fear, "August Thyssen and German Steel," *Creating Modern Capitalism: How Entrepreneurs, Companies, and Countries Triumphed in Three Industrial Revolutions*, ed. Thomas K. McCraw (Cambridge, Mass.: Harvard University Press, 1997), Figures 6.4–6.5, pp. 223–224.

64. Youssef Cassis, *Big Business: The European Experience in the Twentieth Century* (Oxford: Oxford University Press), pp. 11, 33, 232.

65. There is still considerable debate on the productivity levels between German and British firms. The 'environmental' advantages for German firms are impossible to factor out. See the contributions by Steven Tolliday and Rainer Fremdling in *Changing Patterns of International Rivalry: Some Lessons from the Steel Industry* (Tokyo: Tokyo University Press, 1991).

66. Quoted from Thyssen/Klönne correspondence, 18 Dec. 1902 in Treue, *Die Feuer Verlöschen Nie*, p. 140.

67. Treue, *Feuer Verlöschen Nie*, pp. 140–141; Gall *et al.*, *Deutsche Bank*, pp. 44–48.

68. This was the main thesis of Paul Arnst, *August Thyssen und Sein Werk* (Leipzig: G. A. Gloeckner, 1925).

7. Rushing Forward and Backward

1. Christian Kleinschmidt, *Rationalisierung als Unternehmensstrategie: Die Eisen- und Stahlindustrie des Ruhrgebiets zwischen Jahrhundertwende und Weltwirtschaftskrise*, (Essen: Klartext, 1993), p. 68.

2. Leslie Hannah, "Marshall's 'Trees' and the Global 'Forest:' Were 'Giant Redwoods' Different?," Centre for Economic Performance, Discussion Paper No. 318 (January 1997), pp. 36–39, Appendix A.

3. Martin Fiedler, "Die 100 grössten Unternehmen in Deutschland—nach der Zahl ihrer Beschäftigten—1907, 1938, 1973 und 1995," *Zeitschrift für Unternehmensgeschichte (ZUG)*, 44, 1 (1999), pp. 32–66, 44

4. Quoted in Däbritz, *August Thyssen*, p. 24.

5. Wilhelm Helmrich, "August Thyssen: Ein Unternehmer des Ruhrreviers: Ehrenbürger Dr. ing. August Thyssen an die Mülheimer Zeitung, Mülheim a. d. Ruhr, den 3. März 1922" [Nachdruck], *Tradition: Zeitschrift für Firmengeschichte und Unternehmerbiographie* (ZUG), 3, 3 (August 1958), pp. 140–150. Henceforth August Thyssen (1922).

6. Däbritz, *August Thyssen*, pp. 54, 98. Erhard Lucas, *Zwei Formen von Radikalismus in der deutschen Arbeiterbewegung* (Frankfurt/Main: Roter Stern, 1976). Detlev Vonde, *Revier der grossen Dörfer: Industrialisierung und Stadtentwicklung im Ruhrgebiet* (Essen: Klartext, 1989), esp. pp. 76–98. James H. Jackson, Jr., *Migration and Urbanization in the Ruhr Valley, 1821–1914* (New Jersey: Humanities Press, 1997). David Crew, *Town in the Ruhr: A Social History of Bochum 1860–1914* (New York: Columbia University Press, 1979). Geoff Eley neatly summarizes Crew's basic argument concerning the relationship of industrialists to the communities in David Blackbourn and Geoff Eley, *The Peculiarities of German History: Bourgeois Society and Politics in Nineteenth-Century Germany* (New York: Routledge, 1984), pp. 105–113. Jürgen Reulecke, *Geschichte der Urbanisierung in Deutschland* (Frankfurt a/Main: Suhrkamp, 1985) provides a useful overview of the urbanization process in Germany.

7. Mannesmann Archive (MA): R 5 30 18 Thyssen Securities Portfolio. Däbritz, *August Thyssen*, pp. 43. Gertrud Milkereit, "Einige Überlegungen zum Verhältnis zwischen Industrie und Banken" in *Wirt-*

schaftskräfte und Wirtschaftswege, III. Auf dem Weg zur Industrialisierung ed. von Jürgen Schneider, *et al.* (Stuttgart: Klett-Cotta, 1978), pp. 521–528. See Helmut Uebbing, *Wege und Wegmarken: 100 Jahre Thyssen 1891–1991,* ed. Thyssen AG (Berlin: Siedler, 1991), p. 8.

8. Däbritz, *August Thyssen,* p. 63.

9. *Thyssen-Bergbau am Niederrhein 1871 bis 1921* (Hamborn, 1922). This pamphlet provides a detailed technical history of the difficulties confronted by the GDK in this area. Däbritz, *August Thyssen,* pp. 36–56. Arnst, *August Thyssen,* pp. 17–22.

10. Däbritz, *August Thyssen,* p. 51–2 from the Gelsenkirchener Bergwerks-AG, *Zechen-Zeitung,* 16 Nov. 1937.

11. The following discussion is based on Däbritz, *August Thyssen,* pp. 167–174; Rasch, "August Thyssen: Der Katholische Grossindustrielle der Wilhelminischen Epoche," *August Thyssen und Hugo Stinnes: Ein Briefwechsel 1898–1922,* ed. Manfred Rasch and Gerald D. Feldman (München: C. H. Beck, 2003), pp. 48–49; August Thyssen (1922).

12. A more detailed technical and financial history can be found in Däbritz, *August Thyssen,* pp. 64–74 or Treue, *Feuer Verlöschen Nie,* pp. 39–44. Lutz Hatzfeld, "Thyssen & Co., Mülheim—Werks- und Firmengeschichte," *Thyssen & Co. Mülheim a. d. Ruhr: Die Geschichte einer Familie und ihrer Unternehmung,* ed. Horst A. Wessel (Stuttgart: F. Steiner, 1991). p. 84.

13. See Gertrud Milkereit, "Innovation, Know-How, Rationalization and Investments in the German Mining and Metal-Producing Industries, including the Iron and Steelmaking Industry (1868/71–1930)," *Innovation, Know How, Rationalization and Investment in the German and Japanese Economies 1868/1871–1930/1980,* ed. Hans Pohl and Wilhelm Treue (Wiesbaden: Franz Steiner, 1982), pp. 151–179 provides a brief overview of metallurgical innovation. See also Wengenroth, *Unternehmenstrategien,* p. 184, and Oskar Simmersbach, *Die Eisenindustrie* (Leipzig/Berlin: B. G. Tuebner, 1906).

14. Feldenkirchen, *Eisen- und Stahlindustrie,* p. 187. Rainer Fremdling, "The German Iron and Steel Industry in the 19th Century," *Changing Patterns of International Rivalry: Some Lessons from the Steel Industry,* ed. Etsuo Abe and Yoshitaka Suzuki (Tokyo: University of Tokyo Press, 1991), pp. 118–130.

15. ThyssenKrupp Archive (TKA): A/1774 Reply of Franz Dahl to Walter Däbritz.

16. TKA: A/1727 Däbritz Interview with Kalle, 25 July 1939.

17. TKA: A/1771 Däbritz Interview with Franz Dahl, 28 Jan. 1939.

18. Technical details can be found in Däbritz, *August Thyssen,* pp. 78–81.

19. TKA: PA Press Biographies. Carl-Friedrich Baumann, "Franz Dahl: Reorganisator und Planer der Hüttenwerke von August Thyssen," *Niederrheinische Unternehmer* (February 1987), p. 104. "Bericht über die Hauptversammlung vom 6–7. Nov. 1920," *Stahl und Eisen* (25 Nov.–2 Dec. 1920), p. 1585. Carl-Friedrich Baumann, "Franz Dahl" *Stahl und Eisen* (1950), p. 632.

20. Däbritz, *August Thyssen,* p. 26 and Treue, *Feuer Verlöschen Nie,* p. 48 reproduces the full text. See as well, Markus Nievelstein, "Lothringen im Kalkül der rheinisch-westfälischen Schwerindustrie vor dem Ersten Weltkrieg" in *Unternehmen zwischen Markt und Macht: Aspekte deutscher Unternehmens- und Industriegeschichte im 20. Jahrhundert,* ed. Werner Plumpe und Christian Kleinschmidt (Essen: Klartext, 1992), pp. 14–28. The report also mentions that Thyssen was contemplating locating the new pig iron production in Lorraine; he did not venture there until 1912.

21. Däbritz, *August Thyssen,* pp. 86–87; Treue, *Feuer Verlöschen Nie,* p. 50.

22. MA: R 2 30 09 "Herrn Ingenieur Kalle," 17 Dec 1895, Fol. 410–412, 418–420, [none]. Däbritz, *August Thyssen,* pp. 101–104; Treue, *Feuer Verlöschen Nie,* pp. 55–56. On Julius Kalle see Gertrud Milkereit, "Julius Kalle," *Neue Deutsche Biographie,* 11, (1977) and Carl-Friedrich Baumann, "Julius Kalle: Ein Leben für Bandeisen," *Niederrheinische Unternehmer* (February 1991), p. 112.

23. MA: R 2 30 11 (1) "Herrn Bürgermeister Berg, Dinslaken, *Streng vertraulich!,*" 12 Sept. 1895, Fol. 323–324, A. Wilke; R 2 30 09 "Herrn Ingenieur Kalle," 17 Dec. 1895, Fol. 410–412, 418–420 [none].

24. Baumann, "Kalle," p. 112.

25. Feldenkirchen, *Eisen- und Stahlindustrie,* Table 60.

26. Feldenkirchen, *Eisen- und Stahlindustrie,* pp. 98–109, quoted from p. 100, fn. 54. TKA: Thyssen to Klönne, 2 Dec. 1901. TKA: A/1727 Däbritz Interview with Klara Scholten-Bagel, 2 Nov. 1938.

27. Bleidick, *Die Hibernia-Affäre.* Medalen, "State Monopoly Capitalism in Germany: The Hibernia Affair."

28. Stinnes/Thyssen correspondence, 22–23 Nov. 1902 in Rasch and Feldman, *August Thyssen und Hugo Stinnes,* pp. 220–221.

29. Feldenkirchen, *Eisen und Stahlindustrie,* p. 101, fn. 55. TKA: Thyssen to Klönne, 14 Feb. 1902.

30. Däbritz, *August Thyssen,* pp. 120–122, 129–131; Treue, *Feuer Verlöschen Nie,* pp. 56–58; TKA: F/Alb 30; Uebbing, *Wege und Wegmarken,* pp. 14–19.

31. MA: P 7 77 00–07 for year-end balances. MA: P 7 77 00 Generalversammlung, 29 June 1903, Aug. Thyssen/C. Verlohr.

32. MA: R 1 35 06 Letter to Heinrich [Thyssen-Bornemisza], 18 Jan. 1925, Aug. Thyssen.

33. Letter from Thyssen to Verlohr, 15 February 1904, quoted in Treue, *Feuer Verlöschen Nie,* p. 125

34. TKA: A/84815.

35. For the time being, this firm remained separate from Thyssen & Co., Wülfrath. See MA: P 7 77 01 "Bilanz," 31 Dec. 1903; "Bericht des Vorstandes," 29 March 1904; "Bericht des Aufsichtsrats," 30 March 1904, Sültemeyer, Verlohr; Aug. Thyssen.

36. Uebbing, *Wege und Wegmarken,* pp. 22, 188.

37. A more detailed discussion can be found in Treue, *Feuer Verlöschen Nie,* pp. 94–105, 146–160.

38. Däbritz, *August Thyssen,* pp. 222–223; Kleinschmidt, *Rationalisierung als Unternehmensstragie.* Christian Kleinschmidt, "'Amerikanischer Plan' und Deutscher Weg': Technische Rationalisierung in der Rekon-struktionsphase nach dem Ersten Weltkrieg, dargestellt an Beispielen aus der Dortmunder Eisen- und Stahlindustrie," *Die Eisen- und Stahl-industrie im Dortmunder Raum: Wirtschaftliche Entwicklung, soziale Strukturen und technologischer Wandel im 19. und 20. Jahrhundert* (Untersuchungen zur Wirtschafts-, Sozial- und Technikgeschichte, 9) ed. Ottfried Dascher and Christian Kleinschmidt (Dortmund: Gesell-schaft für Westfälische Wirtschaftsgeschichte, 1992), pp. 355–374. Thyssen & Co. also arranged with the FWH to build a tunnel under-neath the street (the Friedrich-Ebert-Strasse) between the FWH and Thyssen & Co., which enabled a direct supply of pig iron from the FWH blast furnaces to Thyssen & Co. See Carl-Friedrich Baumann, "August Thyssen: Ein Bürger Mülheims," *Thyssen & Co. Mülheim a. d. Ruhr: Die Geschichte einer Familie und ihrer Unternehmung,* ed. Horst A. Wessel (Stuttgart: F. Steiner, 1991), pp. 179–198, here p. 183.

39. TKA: F/Alb 29 for a chronology and statistics.

40. TKA: A/1727 Däbritz Interview with Kalle. Treue, *Feuer Verlöschen Nie,* p. 56.

41. Kleinschmidt, *Rationalisierung als Unternehmensstrategie,* pp. 54–55.

42. TKA: A/6377, Nachlass F. Bartscherer. Lecture to the VDESI, 18 March 1927. Reproduced in Kleinschmidt, *Rationalisierung als Unter-nehmensstrategie,* pp. 191–193.

43. Chandler, *Scale and Scope,* pp. 139.

44. Däbritz, *August Thyssen,* pp. 150–152; Treue, *Feuer Verlöschen Nie,* pp. 141.

45. Arnst, *August Thyssen,* p. 40, fn. 2.

46. MA: P 7 77 00 Generalversammlung, 29 June 1903, Aug. Thyssen/C.

Verlohr. Treue, *Feuer Verlöschen Nie,* pp. 141, states that the AGHütt received only 88,980 tons or 6.6 percent. The report from Verlohr, however, states that the AGHütt received 90,000 tons or 7.59 percent.

47. Treue, *Feuer Verlöschen Nie,* p. 144; more detailed is Feldenkirchen, *Eisen- und Stahlindustrie,* Tables 28–29, 52.

48. TKA: A/1727 Däbritz Interview with Jakob Hasslacher, 7 Nov. 1939.

49. Quoted in Wellhöner, *Grossbanken und Grossindustrie,* p. 83.

50. TKA: A/1771 Däbritz Interview with Franz Dahl, 28 Jan. 1939.

51. TKA: A/1767 Däbritz Interview with Julius Lamarche, 19 Oct. 1940. TKA: A/1727 Däbritz Interview with Jakob Hasslacher, 7 Nov. 1939. The best inside look on Thyssen's long-term relationship to the cartels is Wolfgang Pieper, *Theodor Wuppermann und die Vereinigung Rheinisch-Westfälischer Bandeisenwalzwerke,* ed. Rheinisch-Westfälischen Wirtschaftsarchiv zu Köln (Köln: R-W Wirtsschaftsarchiv, 1963). Wolfgang Pieper, "Thyssen als Aussenseiter in der deutschen Kartellentwicklung: Ein Rückblick in die Unternehmensgeschichte," *Bänder Bleche Rohre,* 8 (August 1964), pp. 453–456.

52. Peters, *Cooperative Competition in German Coal and Steel* and *idem,* "Are Cartels Unstable?"

53. Klönne to Thyssen, 16 Oct. 1913, quoted in Wellhöner, *Grossbanken und Grossindustrie,* p. 210.

54. TKA: A/1771 Däbritz Interview with Dr. Kern, 5 Nov. 1940.

55. Harald C. Livesay, *Andrew Carnegie and the Rise of Big Business* (New York: Harper Collins, 1975), p. 171.

56. TKA: A/1771 Däbritz Interview with Dr. Kern, 5 Nov. 1940.

57. Quoted in Markus Nievelstein, *Der Zug nach der Minette. Deutsche Unternehmen in Lothringen 1871–1918. Handlungsspielräume und Strategien im Spannungsfeld des deutsch-französischen Grenzgebietes* (Bochum: N. Brockmeyer, 1993), p. 150. Also Nievelstein, "Lothringen im Kalkül," p. 23. From TKA: A/9569 Thyssen to Klönne, 16 July 1902.

58. Nievelstein, *Zug nach der Minette,* pp. 162–166. For a detailed elucidation of the Pröhm-Thyssen affair, see Jacques Maas, "August Thyssen und die luxemburgische Minenkonzessionsaffäre von 1912," *900 Jahre Mülheim an der Ruhr 1093–1993,* ed. Zeitschrift des Geschichtsvereins Mülheim a. d. Ruhr, 66 (Mülheim (Ruhr), 1993), pp. 433–466.

59. Rasch, "August Thyssen," pp. 52–53, 56–59. Treue, *Feuer Verlöschen Nie,* pp. 79–91. See the debate over the meaning of this type of international collaboration by Carl Strikwerda and Paul Schroeder in the *American Historical Review,* 98, 4 (October 1993), pp. 1106–1142.

60. TKA: A/751/6. See Nievelstein, "Lothringen im Kalkül," p. 24, fn. 39.

61. The following discussion is based on Rasch, "August Thyssen," pp. 53–

56; Däbritz, *August Thyssen,* pp. 246–253; Treue, *Feuer Verlöschen Nie,* pp. 114–119; and Nievelstein, *Zug nach der Minette.* Franz Dahl gave a detailed technical description of the steel works in "Die Anlagen des Stahlwerks Thyssen A. G. in Hagendingen (Lothr.)" in Stahl und Eisen, 21, 13 (1921), pp. 430–443.

62. Nievelstein, *Zug nach der Minette,* pp. 355–356.

63. Nievelstein, *Zug nach der Minette,* pp. 366–372. For Thomas pig iron at 44.5 m/ton, roughly 10 m/ton cheaper than the GDK; Thomas steel at 53.40 m/ton, about 14 m/ton cheaper than at the GDK; and Thomas steel blocks/ingots at 57.40 m/ton, roughly 15 m/ton cheaper than the GDK.

64. Nievelstein, *Zug nach der Minette,* pp. 215–221.

65. Nievelstein, *Zug nach der Minette,* pp. 274–279.

66. Nievelstein, *Zug nach der Minette,* pp. 239–250.

67. TKA: A/1771 Däbritz Interview with Directors Rabes, *et al.,* 5 Dec. 1938.

68. Statistics from Feldenkirchen, *Eisen- und Stahlindustrie,* Table 52a–b, 56 a–b; TKA: A/613/1,2, A614/1,2; A/1790.

8. Managing a Konzern

1. On the problems and virtues of families and managerial capitalism, see Mary Rose, "The Family Firm in British Business, 1780–1914," *Business Enterprise in Modern Britain: From the Eighteenth to the Twentieth Century,* ed. Maurice W. Kirby and Mary B. Rose (New York: Routledge, 1994), pp. 61–87, and Jeffrey R. Fear., "Constructing Corporations: The Cultural Conception of the Firm," *Big Business and the Wealth of Nations,* ed. Alfred D. Chandler, Jr., and Takashi Hikino (Cambridge, Mass.: Harvard University Press, 1997), pp. 555–561.

2. Hidemasa Morikawa, *Zaibatsu: The Rise and Fall of Family Enterprise Groups in Japan* (Tokyo: Tokyo University Press, 1992), esp. pp. 17–18.

3. Wilfried Feldenkirchen, *Siemens 1918–1945* (Columbus: Ohio State University Press, 1995), p. 49.

4. ThyseenKrupp Archive (TKA): A/1773 Letter from Wilhelm Späing, 3 Jan. 1941.

5. TKA: A/1801 Däbritz Interview with Dinkelbach, Dec. 1942.

6. Its entire organization is laid out in the telephone books, see Mannesmann Archive (MA): R 1 31 05 *Privat-Fernsprech-Verzeichnung . . . der Thyssen'schen Werke* (August 1914). TKA: A/1773 Letter from Wilhelm Späing to Däbritz, 13 Feb. 1941.

7. TKA: A/1784.

8. TKA: A/1801 Däbritz Interview with Dinkelbach, Dec. 1942.

9. Maximilian Müller-Jabusch, *Oscar Schlitter* (Berlin: R. Scherpe [1938], 1955), pp. 52–54.

10. Arnst, *August Thyssen*, p. 66.

11. Däbritz, *August Thyssen*, pp. 169–171, 174–179.

12. The following discussion is based on this important memorandum. TKA: A/643, [Denkschrift], "Die Thyssen'schen Handelsniederlassungen, ihr Entstehen, ihr Wesen und ihre Aufgabe," 26 Jan. 1918 [prepared by Neuhaus].

13. TKA: A/760/5 "Vereinbarung zwischen den Werken des Thyssen-Concern . . . bezüglich Ausführung von Lieferungen" [ca. 1911].

14. See esp. TKA: A/760/5.

15. TKA: A/848/4, [Brief 96] "An die Gewerkschaft Deutscher Kaiser, Bruckhausen, Privat!," 12 Feb. 1898, Thyssen. Also MA: R 2 30 10 "Herren Thyssen & Co., Berlin," 12 Feb. 1898, Fol. 98–101, [none]. Also TKA: A/828/2 [Brief 42:] Letter to the GDK, 1 Feb. 1895 [handwritten by Killing], Thyssen & Co. [Aug.]

16. TKA: A/828/1 [Brief 27:] Letter to the GDK, 12 Nov. 1893 and [Brief 28:] Letter to the GDK, 14 Nov. 1893 [both handwritten by Killing], Aug. Thyssen.

17. TKA: A/828/2 [Brief 44:] Letter to the GDK, 30 March 1895, Aug. Thyssen.

18. MA: R 2 30 12 "Central Bureau," 28 Sept. 1896, Fol. 117, Thyssen & Co. [Aug.] TKA: A/828/2 [Brief 58:] "An die 'Gewerkschaft Deutscher Kaiser'," 1 Dec. 1896 [handwritten by Killing], Aug. Thyssen.

19. TKA: A/828/3 [Brief 82:] "An die Gewerkschaft Deutscher Kaiser . . .," 30 Nov. 1897 [handwritten by Killing], Aug. Thyssen.

20. TKA: A/828/4 "Vertraulich nur für Herrn Director Raabes & Herrn Director Dahl bestimmt, Gewerkschaft Deutscher Kaiser," 5 Jan. 1898, Aug. Thyssen.

21. TKA: A/848/4 [Brief 90:] "An die Gewerkschaft Deutscher Kaiser," 3 Feb. 1898 [handwritten by Killing], Aug. Thyssen.

22. See Edmond Landauer, "Fernlenkung von Betrieben," *Zeitschrift für Organisation* (ZfO), 3, 14, 25 July 1929, pp. 383–387. Landauer wrote this article particularly as a response to the problem of how to direct a firm with numerous facilities spread over a great distance.

23. MA: R 2 30 10 Fol. 342. The term *"Centrale"* first appears in the archives after 6 June 1907. MA: M 30.174 Ernst Brökelschen, *50 Jahre Werkserinnerungen* (unpublished manuscript), p. 10.

24. Däbritz, *August Thyssen*, p. 200. MA: P 7 77 00–07.

25. MA: R 2 30 17 (1) "An das Militärbüro der Firma Thyssen & Co . . .,"
30 June 1917, Thyssen & Co. [Aug.]. R 2 30 12 "An die Handelskammer . . .," 4 June 1918, H. Eumann, W. Kocks.

26. MA: R 2 30 11 (2) "Gewerkschaft Deutscher Kaiser, Vertraulich, 3 Jan.
1903, Fol. 7, and "Herrn Noether & Cie, Mannheim," Fol. 24–25, 31,
A. Wilke.

27. MA: R 2 30 11 (1) See especially Fol. 351 and 457 for examples.

28. MA: R 2 30 11 (2) "W. Abteilung Baubureau, Vertraulich!," 25 Sept.
1906, Wilke; "Abschrift! Herren Thyssen & Co., Mülheim-Ruhr," 19
May 1906, Fol. 180–181, Actiengesellschaft für Hüttenbetrieb.

29. TKA: A/1773 Letter to Däbritz, 3 Jan. 1941, Späing. "Wilhelm Späing,"
*Nekrologe aus dem Rheinisch-Westfälischen Industriegebiet Jahrgang 1939–
1951,* ed. Dr. Fritz Pudor (Düsseldorf: August Bagel, 1955), pp. 116–
117.

30. See the letterhead TKA: A/7772 "Herrn Generaldirektor Dahl,
Betr.: Pensionsversicherung!, Vertraulich," 16 Aug. 1910 [mit An-
lage:] "Grundzüge einer Beamten=Versicherung der sämtlichen
Thyssen'schen Werke," 29 June 1910, Thyssen & Co., Der Justitiar
[Härle]

31. TKA: A/1773 Letter to Däbritz, 13 June, 1940, 3 Jan. 1941, Späing. For
an example of Späing's wide-ranging activities, see the correspondence in TKA: A/813/1 esp. 4 Apr. 1914.

32. TKA: A/828/6 [Brief 159:] "An Herrn Dr. Lembke, Oberbürgermeister," 8 Aug. 1910, GDK. Thyssen was prepared to offer Professor
Harnack of the University of Berlin a donation of 100,000 marks,
spread over yearly installments of 4000 marks, to induce a more favorable ruling.

33. MA: P 7 77 03 [Briefwechsel der Aktionären], 31 Dec. 1909. Erich
Maschke, *Es entsteht ein Konzern* (Tübingen: Wunderlich, 1969),
pp. 55–56.

34. MA: P 7 77 04. The case can be followed quite precisely from these
documents. Also see TKA: A/1773 Letter to Däbritz, 3 Jan. 41, Späing.
Justizrat Dr. Hermann Veith-Simon helped prepare and notarized for
the Thyssen. Simon wrote the standard work on the use of financial
balance statements in late nineteenth-century Germany. See Herman
Veit Simon, *Die Bilanzen der Aktiengesellschaften und der Kommanditgesellschaften auf Aktien* (Berlin: J. Guttentag, 18993). The specific case is
from the *Reichsgericht,* 12 Nov. 1913. For its present use, see Norbert
Horn, Hein Kötz, and Hans G. Leser, *German Private and Commercial
Law: An Introduction* (Oxford: Clarendon Press, 1982), pp. 256–257.

35. MA: R 5 30 75 (1,2,3) Correspondence with Steglitz, Berlin, 1913–
1920 [mainly] Martini, Schwenke.

36. Quoted in Treue, *Feuer Verlöschen Nie*, p. 125 from 1905.

37. TKA: PA Carl Rabes. TKA: A/1773 Letter to Däbritz, 3 Feb. 1941, Späing. "Carl Rabes," *Nekrologe aus dem Rheinisch-Westfälischen Industriegebiet Jahrgang 1939–1951*, ed. Dr. Fritz Pudor (Düsseldorf: August Bagel, 1955), pp. 69–70.

38. Rasch, "August Thyssen," pp. 59–63; Treue, *Feuer Verlöschen Nie*, pp. 133–136; Däbritz, *August Thyssen*, pp. 257–259.

39. TKA: A/1773 Letter to Däbritz, 3 Feb. 1941, Späing.

40. TKA: A/1801 Däbritz Interview with Dinkelbach, Dec. 1942, regarding the founding of the VSt.

41. TKA: A/639/2 Letters to August Thyssen, 21 Feb. 1906, 17 March 1906, and 19 March 1906, Heinrich Hofs. Letter to the Einkommensteuer-Berufungskommission zu Düsseldorf, 6 Aug. 1906, Heinrich Hofs. TKA: A/1801 Däbritz Interview with Dinkelbach, Dec. 1942. TKA: A/501/4 for Hofs 1909 salary contract.

42. MA: R 1 31 05 "Geschäftsordnung für das Revisions-Büro der Thyssen'schen Werke," 1 Dec. 1906.

43. TKA: A/701/1 "Bericht über die Prüfung der Wagenstands-geldrechnung . . . für Monat November 1917," 17 Jan. 1918, Revisionsbüro der Thyssen'schen Werke: i.a. H. Kindt.

44. TKA: Personal-Akten, "Zeugnis" Rudolf Krautheim, 15 Nov. 1911, Revisionsbüro der Thyssen'schen Werke, Der Vorstand: Hofs. Krautheim concerned himself mainly with the annual balances of the Konzern firms, profitability rates, and production cost calculations. I would like to thank Arno Mietschke for pointing out this document to me.

45. See MA: R 1 35 83 "Bericht über die Revision der Bilanz der Firma: Thyssen & Comp., Berlin für das Jahr 1913," 1 July 1914 Revisionsbüro, Der Thyssen'schen Werke. Annual reports carry through to 1916 here.

46. For a good example, see TKA: A/681/1 Firma Maschinenfabrik Thyssen & Co. . . . zu Händen des Herrn Direktor Dr. Härle," 14 Nov. 1913, H. Kindt, and A/681/2 "Bericht über die Revision der Bilanz der Maschinenfabrik Thyssen & Co., A. G., Mülheim-Ruhr für das Jahr 1913," Revisions-Büro der Thyssen'schen Werken, Hofs.

47. TKA: A/701/2 "Jahres-Bericht über die Tätigkeit des Revisionsbüros" [1910–1912], 14 Dec 1910, 15 Dec. 1911, 31 Dec 1912, Revisions-Büro der Thyssen'schen Werke, Hofs.

48. TKA: A/681/1 "An das Revisionsbureau der Thyssen'schen Werke," 11 Nov. 1912, Maschinenfabrik Thyssen & Co. Aktiengesellschaft: H[ärle], R[oser].

49. For examples see TKA: A/698/2 "Revision des Wasserwerk Thyssen &

Co., GmbH, 1910," 26 July 1911, Hofs. TKA: A/681/2 "Revision der 'Maschinenfabrik' Thyssen & Co., 1910," Revisions-Büro der Thyssen'schen Werke [none]; "Revision der Bilanz der Maschinen-fabrik Thyssen & Co., 1913," Revisions-Büro der Thyssen'schen Werken: Hofs. MA: R 1 35 83 "Revision der Bilanz der Firma: Thyssen & Comp., Berlin für das Jahr 1913," 1 July 1914 Revisionsbüro, Der Thyssen'schen Werke, [none]. This document collection includes other auditing reports.

50. H. Thomas Johnson and Robert S. Kaplan, *Relevance Lost: The Rise and Fall of Management Accounting* (Boston: Harvard Business School, 1991), pp. 52–80.

51. TKA: A/760/5 Correspondence regarding the royalties of Härle, Roser, Fassnacht, 1911–1916; C. Rabes, Dr. Roser, Dr. Härle, H. Hofs.

52. MA: R 5 30 12–13, R 5 35 15–18 for Thyssen & Co. inventories. In Mülheim, inventories were valued at constant prices between 1908–1923.

53. Hatzfeld, "Werks- und Firmengeschichte," p. 161.

54. Vonde, *Revier,* pp. 84–85, 89.

55. Lucas, *Radikalismus,* pp. 132–136.

56. See Vonde, *Revier,* pp. 76–98.

57. Thyssen also favored a greater Duisburger region that would encompass most of his firms, but this too never happened. Such districting also caused difficulties with the telephone. Telephone calls became long-distance calls between Mülheim and Hamborn-Bruckhausen. Thyssen requested that the post office make an exception for Thyssen & Co. and the GDK, which "belong together as part of a single property holding." Eventually, Thyssen set up a private company network. See MA: R 2 30 10 "An den Staatssecretair des Reichspostamts, Herrn von Podbielski, Excellenz zu Berlin," 24 May 1898, Fol. 124–127, Thyssen & Co.[Aug.] and from the GDK, Jos. Thyssen.

58. MA: R 2 30 10 "Herrn Reichsbankdirektor Schmid," 30 July 1909, Aug. Thyssen. Also "An das Reichsbank-Direktorium," 30 July 1909, Thyssen & Co. [Aug]. Stephan Wegener, "Die Familie Thyssen Aachen-Eschweiler-Mülheim a. d. Ruhr" in *Thyssen & Co. Mülheim a. d. Ruhr: Die Geschichte einer Familie und ihrer Unternehmung,* ed. Horst A. Wessel (Stuttgart: F. Steiner, 1991), p. 44.

59. TKA: A/813/2 GDK, "An die Herren Mitglieder des Gruben-vorstandes der Gewerkschaft Deutscher Kaiser," 12 Jan. 1917, Der Justitiar: Späing; "An die Herren Mitglieder des Grubenvorstandes der Gewerkschaft Deutscher Kaiser," 28 Nov. 1918, gez. Rabes. Including "Abschrift! "Entwurf einer Geschäftsordnung für das Revisions-Bu-

reau der Thyssen'schen Werke, Hamborn," Späing. Also the repentant letter "Sehr geehrter Herr Thyssen," 29 Sept. 1918, Verlohr.

60. Däbritz, *August Thyssen*, p. 69. MA: R 5 30 18 Thyssen Securities Portfolio. Thyssen & Co. owned 910 shares of the GDK, August Thyssen 70 shares, and Joseph Thyssen 20 shares. TKA: A/782/1 "An die Gewerkschaft Deutscher Kaiser," 28 April 1904, pr. pa. Thyssen & Co., Killing [handwritten by Eumann]. After April 1904, Thyssen & Co. owned only ten GDK shares.

61. On its design, see Brigitte Ingeborg Schluter, *Verwaltungsbauten der Rheinisch-Westfälischen Stahlindustrie 1900–1930* (Bonn: Dissertation Rheinischen Friedrich-Wilhelms Universitat, 1991).

9. Organizing Financial Control

1. Wellhöner, *Grossbanken und Grossindustrie im Kaiserreich*, p. 197.

2. Classic works include Rudolf Hilferding, *Finance Capital: A Study of the Latest Phase of Capitalist Development* (London: Routledge, 1981 [1910]). Gerschenkron, *Economic Backwardness in Historical Perspective*. Still useful classic works on German banking are Jacob Riesser, *Die Deutschen Grossbanken und ihre Konzentration* (Jena: G. Fischer, 1910), in English: *The German Great Banks and their Concentration* (Washington, D.C.: Government Printing Office, 1911); and Otto Jeidels, *Das Verhältnis der deutschen Grossbanken zur Industrie* (Leipzig: Duncker und Humblot, 1905). For an early critical view contradicting the power of the banks on supervisory boards, see the neglected Richard Passow, *Die Aktiengesellschaft: Eine Wirtschaftswissenschaftliche Studie* (Jena: Gustav Fischer, 1922²), esp. pp. 387–461. Recent works stressing the important interdependency of universal banks and heavy industry, see Richard Tilly, "On the Development of German Big Banks as Universal Banks in the 19th and 20th Centuries: Engine of Growth or Power Block?" *German Yearbook on Business History 1993*, ed. German Society for Business History (München: K. G. Saur, 1994), pp. 110–130. *Idem*, "Banking Institutions in Historical and Comparative Perspective: Germany, Great Britain and the United States in the Nineteenth and Early Twentieth Century," *Journal of Institutional and Theoretical Economics*, 145 (1989), pp. 189–209; *idem*, "German Banking, 1850–1914: Development Assistance to the Strong," *Journal of European Economic History*, 15 (1986), pp. 113–152. *Idem*, "An Overview on the Role of the Large German Banks up to 1914," *Finance and Financiers in European History, 1880–1960*, ed. Youssef Cassis (Cambridge: Cambridge University Press, 1992), pp. 92–112. Wilfried Feldenkirchen, "Banking and Eco-

nomic Growth: Banks and Industry in Germany in the Nineteenth Century and Their Changing Relationship during Industrialisation," *German Industry and German Industrialisation,* ed. W. R. Lee (London: Routledge, 1991), pp. 116–147. For a political, rather than an economic, explanation for the origins of universal banks, see Daniel Verdier, "The Political Origins of Banking Structures," *The Policy History Newsletter,* 2, 3 (1997), pp. 1–10.

3. Wellhöner, *Grossbanken und Grossindustrie.* For the 1920s, see Harald Wixforth, *Banken und Schwerindustrie in der Weimarer Republik* (Köln: Böhlau Verlag, 1995). Harald Wixforth and D. Ziegler, "Bankenmacht: Universal Banking and German Industry in Historical Perspective," *The Evolution of Financial Institutions and Markets in Twentieth-Century Europe,* ed. Youssef Cassis, Gerald Feldmann, and U. Olsson (Aldershot: Scholar Press, 1995), pp. 249–272. Harald Wixforth and D. Ziegler, "The Niche in the Universal Banking System: The Role and Significance of Private Bankers within German Industry 1900–1933," *Financial History Review,* 1 (1994), pp. 99–119. Charles W. Calomiris, "The Costs of Rejecting Universal Banking: American Finance in the German Mirror 1870–1914," *Coordination and Information,* ed. Naomi Lamoreaux and Daniel Raff (Chicago: University of Chicago, 1995) pp. 257–321. Jeremy Edwards and Sheilagh Ogilvie, "Universal Banks and German Industrialization: A Reappraisal," *Economic History Review,* 49, 3 (1996), pp. 427–446. Caroline Fohlin, "The Rise of Interlocking Directorates in Imperial Germany," *Economic History Review,* 52, 2 (1999), pp. 307–333. Caroline Fohlin, "Relationship Banking, Liquidity, and Investment in the German Industrialization," *Journal of Finance,* 53 (October 1998), pp. 1737–1758, see p. 1738.

4. ThyssenKrupp Archive (TKA): A/760/5 "Rentabilitätsziffern der deutschen Maschinenbau-Actiengesellschaften im Jahre 1910."

5. Gallhofer and Haslam, "The Aura of Accounting," pp. 495–499. See Herman Veit Simon, *Die Bilanzen der Aktiengesellschaften und der Kommanditgesellschaften auf Aktien* (Berlin: J. Guttentag, 18993).

6. See R. Fischer, *Die Bilanzwerte: Was Sie Sind und Was Sie nicht Sind* (Leipzig: Dielerich'sche Verlagsbuchhandlung, 1905).

7. At the same time, Schmalenbach also worked on improving cost accounting methods in the name of manufacturing efficiency. See the literature cited in Eugen Schmalenbach, *Dynamische Bilanz* (Köln/ Opladen: Westdeutscher [1919] 196213), Vorwort. The original edition first appeared in 1919. The best introduction to Schmalenbach's thinking and career is Max Kruk, Erich Potthoff, and Günter Sieben, *Eugen Schmalenbach: Der Mann—Sein Werk—Die Wirkung* ed. Walter

Cordes im Auftrag der Schmalenbach Stiftung (Stuttgart: Fachverlag für Wirtschafts- und Steuerrecht Schäffer GmbH & Co., 1984). Regarding the "dynamic balance," see esp. pp. 303–317. In English, David A. R. Forrester, *Schmalenbach and After: A Study of the Evolution of German Business Economics* (Glasgow: Strathclyde Convergencies, 1977). A brief overview can be found by Erich Potthoff and Günter Sieben, "Eugen Schmalenbach (1873–1955)," *Twentieth-Century Accounting Thinkers,* ed. John Richard Edwards (London: Routledge, 1994), pp. 79–94.

8. TKA: A/1801 Däbritz Interview with Dinkelbach, Dec. 1942.

9. Alfred D. Chandler, Jr., *The Visible Hand: The Managerial Revolution in American Business* (Cambridge, Mass.: Belknap Press of Harvard University Press, 1977), pp. 444–450. The first quote is from p. 445. The second quote is from Johnson and Kaplan, *Relevance Lost,* p. 65.

10. See Johnson and Kaplan, *Relevance Lost,* pp. 195–206. Both Du Pont and General Motors used the ROI in the Twenties as only *one* means of evaluating divisional performance. Their overarching thesis argues that the heavy reliance on ROI figures for both short-term and long-term performance evaluation, particularly in manufacturing, has depressed long-term investment activity in favor of short-term returns. Contemporary (American) cost accounting, which centers on this ratio, can no longer properly evaluate the internal efficiency or effectiveness of manufacturing operations.

11. Feldenkirchen, *Eisen- und Stahlindustrie,* Table 113a,b for net profits of major steel firms. Däbritz, *August Thyssen,* pp. 55, 69–71, 90–91.

12. TKA: A/828/3 [Briefe 63–64] Formular, GDK, 12 April 1897, Vertraulich [handwritten by H. Eumann]. For more details, see Wellhöner, *Grossbanken und Grossindustrie,* pp. 197–211.

13. Milkereit, "Überlegungen," p. 527. Feldenkirchen, *Eisen- und Stahlindustrie,* pp. 276–277, ftnt. 37.

14. The summary of the sale is based on Däbritz, *August Thyssen,* pp. 126–129; Milkereit, "Überlegungen," pp. 526–527; Feldenkirchen, *Eisen- und Stahlindustrie,* pp. 98–102, 276–277, fn. 37; Treue, *Feuer Verlöschen Nie,* pp. 59–63. The key parts of the correspondence are also quoted directly in each of these sources. See also Mannesmann Archive (MA): R 5 30 18 Securities Portfolio 1882–1918.

15. Feldenkirchen, "Concentration Process."

16. Wellhöner, *Grossbanken und Grossindustrie,* p. 201.

17. TKA: A/786 Gewerkensammlung, 30. Dez. 1905.

18. TKA: A/1773 Letter to Däbritz from Späing, 13 June 1940.

19. On the 'merger wave' in German banking, see Manfred Pohl, *Deutsche*

Bankengeschichte, Band 2: Festigung und Ausdehnung des deutschen Bankwesens zwischen 1870 und 1914 (Frankfurt/Main: Fritz Knapp Verlag, 1982), pp. 271–287. On American practices, see Naomi Lamoreaux, *Insider Lending: Banks, Personal Connections, and Economic Development in Industrial New England* (Cambridge: Cambridge University Press, 1994), esp. 52–62.

20. Wellhöner, *Grossbanken und Grossindustrie*, p. 203–204, quote from p. 204.

21. Treue, *Feuer Verlöschen Nie*, pp. 156–157.

22. For figures, see Feldenkirchen, "Concentration Process," and Christopher Schmitz, "The World's Largest Industrial Companies of 1912," *Business History*, 37, 4 (1995), pp. 85–96. Present values are calculated by dividing the 1913 sum by 4.2 and using the CPI historical calculator found at http://www.eh.net. One dollar in 1913 equaled $18.40 in 2003.

23. Strangely, the exact figure in the securities column (2,558,390 marks) of Thyssen & Co. can be found in the official published financial statements of the AGHütt between 1907–1912. In 1913, however, it disappeared from the AGHütt balances. The transfer, moreover, epitomizes the fluid financial structure of the Konzern.

24. Hatzfeld, "Werks- und Firmengeschichte," p. 147.

25. Müller-Jabusch, *Oscar Schlitter*, pp. 52–54. See Chapter 9 for the quote.

26. For the GDK, see Feldenkirchen, *Eisen- und Stahlindustrie*, Tables 97b and 98b; for the AGHütt see MA: P 7 77 00–11, esp. P 7 77 05, 11; for the Machine Company, see TKA: A/681/1, A/814/3.

27. The depreciation account refers to depreciation account A for the four main rolling mill departments. Account B was added when the Waterworks fixed assets accounts were added to Thyssen & Co. accounts.

28. The figure of 5 percent can be found in TKA: A/1783 Königliche Stempel- & Erbschaftssteueramt," 22 March 1913, [none, Härle].

29. TKA: A/9569 Thyssen to Klönne, 6 Dec. 1903. Quoted in Feldenkirchen, *Eisen- und Stahlindustrie*, p. 286, fn. 69.

30. Albin Kerth and Jakob Wolf, *Bilanzanalyse und Bilanzpolitik* (München/Wien: C. Hanser, 1986), pp. 191–200.

31. TKA: A/760/5 [Korrespondenzen betreffs Tantieme Machine Company: Härle, Roser, Fassnacht], 1911–1916, C. Rabes, Dr. Roser, Dr. Härle, H. Hofs. The CAO used a basic equation to estimate cash flow: net profits equal the year-end balance plus depreciation, plus the value of half-finished goods, minus miscellaneous reserves held over from previous years. Bonuses for Härle amounted to 1 percent, for

Roser 2 percent of cash flow. In addition, Härle and Roser received an additional 1 mark (later 2 marks) per 1000 marks of sales that went to the Thyssen-Konzern because the Machine Company turned no profit on Thyssen-Konzern sales. Similar problems arose with other directors, including Heinrich Reiter, GmbH. See MA: R 1 35 86 (2) [Briefwechsel vom 10. Dez. 1913—30. Juli 1918 with] Fritz Nagel. Nagel addressed his correspondence to "Herren Thyssen & Co., Centrale." For the Thyssen trading firms in the east, Phillip Neuhaus dealt with the discontented director as head of the Mülheimer *Centrale.*

32. Feldenkirchen, *Eisen- und Stahlindustrie,* Table 101b.

33. Alfred D. Chandler, Jr., *Strategy and Structure: Chapters in the History of the Industrial Enterprise* (Cambridge, Mass.: MIT, 1962). Oliver Williamson, *The Economic Institutions of Capitalism: Firms, Markets, Relational Contracting* (New York: Free Press, 1985), pp. 279–284. The quote is from Williamson, p. 279. For more skeptical views on the organizational efficiency of the multidivisional form, especially its use as an indicator of being the most modern organization, see J. Cable and M. J. Dirrheimer, "Hierarchies and Markets: An Empirical Test of the Multidivisional Hypothesis in West Germany," *International Journal of Industrial Organization,* 1 (1983), pp. 43–62. Bruce Kogut and David Parkinson, "The Diffusion of American Organizing Principles to Europe," *Country Competitiveness: Technology and the Organizing of Work* (New York: Oxford University Press, 1993), pp. 179–202.

34. John F. Wilson, *British Business History, 1720–1994* (Manchester: Manchester University Press, 1995), p. 137.

35. An organizational chart of the ideal-typical form can be found in Chandler, *Scale and Scope,* p. 44.

36. Donaldson Brown, "Centralized Control with Decentralized Responsibilities," *Annual Convention Series No. 57* (New York: American Management Association, 1927), pp. 3–24.

37. Walther Kunze, *Der Aufbau des Phoenix-Konzerns* (Dissertation: Universität Frankfurt a. Main, 1926).

38. MA: R 1 10 22 Ernst Poensgen to Phoenix Zentraldirektion," 21 March 1911, 27 March 1911.

39. *Handbuch der Deutschen Aktien-Gesellschaften: Jahrbuch der deutschen Börsen* (Berlin: Verlag für Börsen und Finanzliteratur AG, 1914), pp. 385–391.

40. MA: P 1 25 35 1908–1916. Geschäftsanweisungen für den Vorstand und für die Abteilungsleitung.

41. MA: R 5 10 00, R 5 10 09 Richtlinien für Organisation und Verwaltung for examples from Abt. DREW.

42. MA: R 1 10 20 Anlagen zum Geschäftsberichte und Geschäftsbericht 1910–1916. See as well the outside auditing report in MA: P 5 25 28.1– 6 Prüfungs-Bericht der Treuhand-Vereinigung Aktiengesellschaft, Berlin, 30 June 1911 der Zentral-Buchhaltung der 'Phoenix'. See as well the criticisms of Phoenix bookkeeping from Price Waterhouse in MA: P 5 25 29 "Memorandum der Notwendigen Vorbereitungen für die Revision per 31. Dezember 1924" from Price, Waterhouse & Co.: Chartered Accountants. In a second audit investigation of Phoenix, completed on 13 February 1926 in preparation for the loan to the VSt, Price Waterhouse concluded: "The Company's Accounting System as at present operated, is however, not suited to the production of Earnings Statements on the lines of those presented herewith, and consequently, a very considerable amount of time was required both for their production and for their verification . . . [PW wants Phoenix to amend this]." "Special difficulty was experienced during the investigation in segregating the purely operating figures from transfers to and from Reserves, and other items of a Non-Operating nature, and generally the book results have been obscured by reasons of unscientific Works Accounting. While we believe that the attached Earnings Statements give an accurate view of the operations during the periods covered thereby, yet it has not been possible to offer as full information as would have been possible if the records had been properly suited to these requirements." Obviously some criticism is due to an alternative set of accounting conventions required by Price Waterhouse, but their criticisms testify to the difficulty of distinguishing both accounting practices and delegated responsibilities of the departments from the central administration, and new investment accounts from operating expenses.

43. MA: P 5 25 20 Hörder Verein, see especially the correspondence from August 1907. MA: P 5 25 21 "Monatliche Zusammenstellungen des Gewinn- und Verlust-Kontos 1907–1923."

44. MA: R 5 10 20 Finanzübersichten der Phoenix AG "Protokolle über Kassen-Revision bei der Abt. Düsseldorfer Röhren- und Eisenwalzwerke 1910–1914."

45. MA: R 5 10 09 Richtlinien für Organisation und Verwaltung.

46. For other Ruhr steel firms, Susanne Hilger, *Sozialpolitik und Organisation: Formen betrieblicher Sozialpolitik in der rheinisch-westfälischen Eisen- und Stahlindustrie seit der Mitte des 19. Jahrhunderts bis 1933* (Stuttgart: F. Steiner, 1996), pp. 79–107. The Krupp discussion is based on Uwe Kessler, *Zur Geschichte des Managements bei Krupp: Von den Unternehmensanfängen bis zur Auflösung der Fried. Krupp AG (1811–1943)* (Stuttgart: Franz Steiner Verlag, 1995), esp. pp. 88–151. Bongartz and

Wolfram, "Unternehmensleitung und Kostenkontrolle in der Rhein-
ischen Montanindustrie vor 1914: Dargestellt am Beispiel der Firmen
Krupp und Gutehoffnungshütte (Teil II)," *Zeitschrift für Unternehmens-
geschichte* (ZUG), 29, 2 (1984), pp. 86–97. *Handbuch der Deutschen
Aktien-Gesellschaften: Jahrbuch der deutschen Börsen* (Berlin: Verlag für
Börsen und Finanzliteratur AG, 1914), pp. 349–354.

47. Barbara Wolbring, *Krupp und die Öffentlichkeit im 19. Jahrhundert*
(München: C. H. Beck. 2000).

48. Erich Maschke, *Es Ensteht ein Konzern: Paul Reusch und die GHH*
(Tübingen: Wunderlich, 1969). Tross, *Der Aufbau der Eisen- und eisenverarbeitenden Industrie-Konzerne Deutschlands.* Bongartz, "Unternehmensleitung und Kostenkontrolle," pp. 107–110.

49. See the organizational charts in Feldenkirchen, *Siemens,* pp. 61, 65.
The discussion is based on Jürgen Kocka, *Unternehmensverwaltung und
Angestelltenschaft am Beispiel Siemens 1847–1914: Zum Verhältnis von
Kapitalismus und Bürokratie in der deutschen Industrialisierung* (Stuttgart:
Klett-Cotta, 1969), pp. 408–459. Jürgen Kocka, "Family and Bureaucracy in German Industrial Management 1850–1914: Siemens in Comparative Perspective," *Business History Review,* 45, 2 (Summer, 1971),
pp. 133–156. Wilfried Feldenkirchen, "Big Business in Interwar Germany: Organizational Innovation at Vereinigte Stahlwerke, IG Farben,
and Siemens," *Business History Review,* 61 (Autumn 1987), pp. 417–451,
esp. 440–443. Feldenkirchen, *Werner von Siemens: Inventor and International Entrepreneur* (Columbus: Ohio State University Press, 1994),
pp. 132–160.

50. Feldenkirchen, *Siemens,* p. 49–50.

51. Feldenkrichen, *Siemens,* p. 283.

52. For more on Siemens & Halske's internal organization, esp. into the
1920s, see Feldenkirchen, *Siemens,* pp. 205–218.

53. Feldenkirchen, *Siemens,* pp. 58–60, 240–245. Kocka, *Unternehmensverwaltung,* p. 451–452, 457–8.

54. Kocka, *Unternehmensverwaltung,* pp. 388–389.

55. Feldenkirchen, *Siemens,* p. 596, ftn. 24.

56. Kocka, *Unternehmensverwaltung,* p. 441.

57. See John G. Roberts, *Mitsui: Three Centuries of Japanese Business* (New
York: Weatherhill, 1973).

58. The discussion is based on W. Mark Fruin, *The Japanese Enterprise System: Competitive Strategies and Cooperative Structures* (Oxford: Clarendon
Press, 1994), pp. 89–125. Morikawa, *Zaibatsu,* esp. pp. 106–114. The
quotes are based on Mitsui internal memorandum quoted in Morikawa. See especially the organizational chart on p. 107.

59. Morikawa, *Zaibatsu,* pp. 12–15, 22–24, 28–35, 52–54, 111–114. See the

Mitsubishi organizational charts in Fruin, *Japanese Enterprise System*, p. 100.

60. Fruin, *Japanese Enterprise System*, pp. 113–121. Bernd Dornseifer, "Zur Bürokratisierung deutscher Unternehmen im späten 19. und frühen 20. Jahrhundert," in *Jahrbuch für Wirtschaftsgeschichte* (1993), pp. 72–73.

10. Revolutionizing Industrial Relations

1. Irmgard Steinisch, *Arbeitszeitverkürzung und Sozialer Wandel: Der Kampf um die Achtstundenschicht in der deutschen und amerikanischen Eisen- und Stahlindustrie 1880–1929* (Berlin: de Gruyter, 1986), p. 451.

2. See especially Gerald D. Feldman, *The Great Disorder: Politics, Economics, and Society in the German Inflation, 1914–1924* (Oxford: Oxford University Press, 1993) and Gerald D. Feldman, *Army, Industry and Labor in Germany 1914–1918* (Princeton: Princeton University Press, 1966). See also Richard Bessel, *Germany after the First World War* (Oxford: Clarendon Press, 1993), pp. 1–48, with its literature citations; Werner Milert and Rudolf Tschirbs, *Von den Arbeiterausschüssen zum Betriebsverfassungsgesetz: Geschichte der betrieblichen Interessenvertretung* (Cologne: Bund-Verlag, 1991); Eberhard Kolb, *The Weimar Republic* (London: Unwin Hyman, 1988); Detlev Peukert, *The Weimar Republic: The Crisis of Classical Modernity* (New York: Hill & Wang, 1992); and Jürgen Kocka, *Facing Total War: German Society 1914–1918* (Cambridge, Mass.: Harvard University Press, 1984). For the regional level, see Jürgen Reulecke, "Der Erste Weltkrieg und die Arbeiterbewegung im rheinisch-westfälischen Industriegebiet," in *Arbeiterbewegung an Rhein und Ruhr: Beiträge zur Geschichte der Arbeiterbewegung in Rheinland-Westfalen*, ed. Jürgen Reulecke (Wuppertal: Hammer, 1974); Reinhard Rürup, "Einleitung," in *Arbeiter- und Soldatenräte im rheinisch-westfälischen Industriegebiet: Studien zur Geschichte der Revolution 1918/19*, ed. Reinhard Rürup (Wuppertal: Hammer, 1975), pp. 7–38; Werner Abelshauser and Ralf Himmelmann, eds., *Revolution in Rheinland und Westfalen: Quellen zu Wirtschaft, Gesellschaft und Politik 1918–1923*, (Essen: Klartext, 1988); and Stefan Goch, *Sozialdemokratische Arbeiterbewegung und Arbeiterkultur im Ruhrgebiet: Eine Untersuchung am Beispiel Gelsenkirchen 1848–1975* (Düsseldorf: Droste, 1990). Goch has a rich bibliography.

3. Werner Plumpe, *Betriebliche Mitbestimmung in der Weimarer Republik: Fallstudien zum Ruhrbergbau und zur Chemischen Industrie* (München: R. Oldenbourg Verlag, 1999). Bernard P. Bellon, *Mercedes in Peace and War: German Automobile Workers, 1903–1945* (New York: Columbia,

1990), p. 3: "I know of no other work which illuminates wartime and revolutionary events from the perspectives of conditions and conflicts within a factory." Werner Plumpe, "Die Betriebsräte in der Weimarer Republik: Eine Skizze zu ihrer Verbreitung, Zusammensetzung und Akzeptanz," *Unternehmen zwischen Markt und Macht: Aspekte deutscher Unternehmens- und Industriegeschichte im 20. Jahrhundert,* ed. Werner Plumpe and Christian Kleinschmidt (Essen: Klartext, 1992), p. 42: "The history of the factory councils in the Weimar Republic has not been researched." Also Werner Plumpe, "Mikropolitik im Unternehmen: Die Reaktion der Farbenfabriken vorm. Bayer & Co. in Leverkusen auf die Novemberrevolution 1918/19," *Mikropolitik im Unternehmen: Arbeitsbeziehungen und Machtstrukturen in industriellen Grossbetrieben des 20. Jahrhunderts,* ed. Karl Lauschke and Thomas Welskopp (Essen: Klartext, 1994), pp. 123–160. Also see Matthias Freese, "Betriebsrat und Betriebsrätetätigkeit zwischen 1920 und 1960: Handlungsspielräume und –muster betrieblicher Interessenvertretung am Beispiel der Carl-Freudenberg-Werke in Weinheim a. d. Bergstrasse," in same, pp. 161–185.

4. See the critique by Jonathan Zeitlin, "From Labour History to the History of Industrial Relations," *Economic History Review,* II: 40, 2 (1987), pp. 159–184. For a highly sophisticated systems approach, which seeks to bridge the shopfloor and class formation models, see Thomas Welskopp, *Arbeit und Macht im Hüttenwerk: Arbeits- und industrielle Beziehungen in der deutschen und amerikanischen Eisen- und Stahlindustrie von den 1860er bis zu den 1930er Jahren* (Bonn: J. H. W. Dietz, 1994). Two books on other countries manage to analyze both sides. See Elizabeth Perry, *Shanghai on Strike: The Politics of Chinese Labor* (Stanford: Stanford University Press, 1996), and Ann Farnsworth-Alvear, *Dulcinea in the Factory: Myths, Morals, Men, and Women in Colombia's Industrial Experiment 1905–1960* (Durham: Duke University Press, 2000).

5. Plumpe, *Betriebliche Mitbestimmung,* pp. 1–32.

6. Milert/Tschirbs, *Von den Arbeiterausschüssen,* pp. 45–51.

7. Kocka, *Facing Total War,* pp. 16–75, esp. the related charts on pp. 16–26. Jürgen Reulecke, "Der Erste Weltkrieg und die Arbeiterbewegung im rheinisch-westfälischen Industriegebiet," in *Arbeiterbewegung an Rhein und Ruhr: Beiträge zur Geschichte der Arbeiterbewegung in Rheinland-Westfalen,* ed. Jürgen Reulecke (Wuppertal: Hammer, 1974), 205–239, esp. the chart on wages and prices on p. 219. *Revolution in Rheinland und Westfalen,* p. 188ff.

8. The Christian Metalworker Unions were nationalist, Catholic, and associated with the Center Party (Thyssen's party), and rejected the idea

of class struggle. In 1912, for instance, the Catholic union rejected the attempt by other unions to start a general strike and publicly called for military intervention against the strikers. See Erhard Lucas, *Märzrevolution im Ruhrgebiet: Vom Generalstreik gegen den Militärputsch zum bewaffneten Arbeiteraufstand. März-April 1920, Band I* (Frankfurt/Main: März Verlag, 1970), p. 23. John J. Kulczycki, *The Polish Coal Miners' Union and the German Labor Movement in the Ruhr, 1902–1934: National and Social Solidarity* (Oxford: Berg, 1997).

9. Mannesmann Archive (MA): R 2 30 15 "An die verehrl. Direktion der Firma Thyssen & Co.," 28 Aug. 1915.

10. See Werner Plumpe, "Unternehmerverbände und industrielle Interessenpolitik seit 1870," in *Das Ruhrgebiet im Industriezeitalter: Geschichte und Entwicklung, Band I,* ed. Wolfgang Köllmann, Hermann Korte, Dietmar Petzina, and Wolfhard Weber (Düsseldorf: Schwann im Patmos, 1990). Feldman, *Iron and Steel,* pp. 43–49. Elaine Glovka Spencer, *Management and Labor in Imperial Germany: Ruhr Industrialists as Employers 1896–1914* (New Brunswick, N.J.: Rutgers, 1984), pp. 102–109.

11. MA: R 2 30 15 "An den Arbeitgeber-Verband . . .," 1 March 1915, 9 March 1915. MA: R 2 30 18 (1) "An die Herren des Vorstandes und Ausschusses!," Vertraulich!, 13 Oct. 1915, Dr. E. Hoff; "Herrn Dr. E. Hoff," 17 Oct. 1915; Herren Thyssen & Co., 17 Oct. 1915, Surmann. Also Feldman, *Army, Industry and Labor,* p. 92.

12. MA: R 2 30 15 "Abschrift!," 31 Jan. 1916, gez. Harr, Pilz, Esser, Goedecke.

13. See the dispute between Thyssen & Co. and the GDK, Bergbau in MA: R 2 30 18 (1), 24 July 1915, 26 July 1915, 7 Aug. 1915. They vehemently discussed the proper interpretation of the orders concerning re-employment of workers discharged from active service. Also see correspondence, 4 July 1917, Roser, Fassnacht//Becker, Wallmann.

14. A good example of its activity can be found in MA: R 2 30 17 (1) Letters and documents from 28 May 1915, 8 Jan. 1916, 23 March 1916, 7 June 1915, 16 Nov. 1915, and 9 Jan. 1917, Pardon.

15. ThyssenKrupp Archive (TKA): A/1806 Däbritz Interview with Heinrich Dinkelbach, 11 Aug. 1954.

16. For similar problems and developments at Bayer, see Plumpe, *Betriebliche Mitbestimmung,* pp. 78–95.

17. MA: R 2 30 18 (1) Correspondence between Thyssen & Co. and Krupp, 8–23 July 1915; "An das Königliche Generalkommando Münster," 23 July 1915, pr. pa. Thyssen & Co., Becker.

18. MA: R 2 30 17 (2) Letter to the GDK board of directors, 25 May 1916, Der Justitiar: Späing.

19. MA: R 2 30 18 (2) "Abschrift," 5 July 1918, von Gayl. The General-kommando found the secret agreements controlling labor turnover a direct violation of the Auxiliary Service Law. MA: R 2 35 12 "An die Firma August Thyssen," 22 Aug. 1917, von Gayl; [Reply] Gilles to GDK (Dahl), 14 Sept. 1917, G[illes].

20. Feldman, *Army, Industry and Labor,* pp. 507–508. MA: R 2 30 15 "An unsere Mitglieder! Die auf Verkürzung der Arbeitszeit gerichteten Bestrebungen der Gewerkschaften," 25 March 1918, Dr. E. Hoff.

21. See MA: R 2 35 12 Quote from "An die Firma Thyssen & Co.," 21 Oct. 1916, Giffenig. For Thyssen & Co.'s response, see MA: R 2 30 17 (2) "An die Firma Thyssen + Comp.," 6 May 1916, Giffening with reply "An das stellvertr. Generalkommando des VII Armeekorps," 20 May 1916, [none]; "Abschrift," 10 Feb. 1916 with appendix describing the war committees.

22. Steinisch, *Arbeitszeitverkürzung,* pp. 332–358. She attributes this moderation to the ability of large firms to provide better food supplies, their harsh disciplinary regimes, the industry's good relations with the Military Command, the lack of a "broad unionized organization" in the steel industry (unlike mining), and the relative support of unions for the wartime "social truce."

23. MA: R 2 35 12 "Gewerkschaft Deutscher Kaiser," Vertraulich, 26 Oct. 1916, pr. pa. Thyssen & Co.: gez. Becker; "Firma Thyssen & Co.," *Vertraulich!,* 27 Oct. 1916, Rabes; "An das stellvertretende Generalkommando," 3 Nov. 1916, gez. Becker. MA: R 2 30 15 "An unsere Mitglieder! Die auf Verkürzung der Arbeitszeit gerichteten Bestrebungen der Gewerkschaften," 25 March 1918, Dr. E. Hoff.

24. For a good example see the discussion between the GDK, Thyssen & Co., and the Generalkommando concerning financial support for workers discharged from the army in MA: R 2 30 17 (2) 16 May 1916; "An die Firma Thyssen & Co.," 19 May 1916, Dahl; "Stellungnahme," 22 May 1918, Becker.

25. For the political and interest group negotiations leading up to the bill see Feldman, *Army, Industry and Labor,* pp. 149–249. For its general effect on industry with a focus on Rhineland-Westphalen, see Steinisch, *Arbeitszeitverkürzung,* pp. 302–358.

26. See MA: R 2 30 17 (2) "Verfahren vor dem Schlichtungsausschuss," [Jan 1917]; "An Herrn Direktor Becker," 9 Jan. 1917, [Mayor] Lembke.

27. MA: R 2 30 15 "Firma Thyssen & Co.," 6 Feb. 1917, Nordwestliche Gruppe, Dr. E. Hoff.

28. For the lists of elected workers, see MA: R 1 35 40; MA: R 2 30 17–18 (2) Arbeiterausschuss; MA: R 1 35 41 Angestelltenausschuss 1917–

1919. The latter file contains a well-ordered and chronological set of reports, letters, and protocols.

29. Unfortunately, most of the Machine Company's records have been lost or destroyed. For a comprehensive view of women at war, see Ute Daniel, *The War from Within: German Working-Class Women in the First World War* (Oxford: Berg, 1997). For the implications of gender on shop-floor practices, see Laura Lee Downs, *Manufacturing Inequality: Gender Division in the French and British Metalworking Industries 1914–1939* (Ithaca: Cornell University Press, 1995). For white-collar women, see Ellen Lorentz, *Aufbruch oder Rückschritt? Arbeit, Alltag und Organisation weiblicher Angestellter in der Kaiserzeit und Weimarer Republik* (Bielefeld: Kleine Verlag, 1988).

30. MA: R 2 30 27 provides detailed monthly employment figures with turnover rates.

31. Irmgard Steinisch, "Linksradikalismus und Rätebewegung im westlichen Ruhrgebiet: Die revolutionären Auseinandersetzungen in Mülheim an der Ruhr" in *Arbeiter- und Soldatenräte im rheinisch-westfälischen Industriegebiet,* ed. Reinhard Rürup (Wuppertal: Hammer, 1975), pp. 155–237, p. 161. Jürgen Mengler, *Werkskolonien in Mülheim an der Ruhr: Entstehung und Wandel—dargestellt an vier Beispielen* (Mülheim/Ruhr: Zeitschrift des Geschichtsvereins Mülheim a. d. Ruhr, 1982). Gerold Olsen, "Von einer unauffälligen Ruhrgebietsstadt zu einem syndikalistischen Zentrum: Sozialgeschichtliche Voraussetzungen für den Syndikalismus in Mülheim an der Ruhr" *Arbeit und Alltag im Revier: Arbeiterbewegung und Arbeiterkultur im westlichen Ruhrgebiet im Kaiserreich und in der Weimarer Republik,* ed. Ludger Heid and Julius H. Schoeps (Duisburg: W. Braun, 1985), 241–248, p. 247. Also Lucas, *Arbeiterradikalismus,* pp. 137–149, 155–192.

32. Feldman, *Great Disorder,* p. 124. Jürgen Tampke, *The Ruhr and Revolution: The Revolutionary Movement in the Rhenish-Westphalian Industrial Region 1912–1919* (London: Croom Helm, 1979), pp. 33–43.

33. Treue, *Feuer Verlöschen Nie,* p. 172.

34. MA: R 2 30 18 (2) "An den Obmann Lohschelder," 9 Aug. 1918.

35. MA: R 2 30 18 (2) "Lohnbüro," 20 Feb. 1917, Becker, Wallmann. "An die Firma Thyssen & Co.," 9 March 1917, Lembke. "An die wohll. Direktion der Firma Thyssen u. Co.," 26 Aug. 1918 [10 signatures]; Protokoll: Sitzung, 3 Sept. 1918, Vertreter der Firma: Klink, Arbeiterausschuss: Friedr. Monning; "Herrn Oberingenieur Klinck," 17 July 1918, [15 signatures]. MA: R 1 35 42 (1) "Ab 12. November 1918 wird unter Aufhebung früherer Vereinbarungen bis auf Weiteres folgende Regelung getroffen.: (Für die 8stündige Schicht.)," D[ormann].

36. MA: R 2 30 18 (2) "An die löbliche Direktion der Firma Thyssen & Cie.," 8 April 1918, [8 signatures].

37. MA 2 30 18 (2) "Herrn Oberingenieur Klinck," 17 July 1918, [15 signatures].

38. MA: R 2 30 18 (2) "An Herrn Direktor Becker," 22 May 1918, Abt. II, Wallmann. Likewise at Bayer, see Plumpe, *Betriebliche Mitbestimmung*, pp. 82–86.

39. Steinisch, "Linksradikalismus und Rätebewegung," p. 162. MA: R 2 30 18 (2) "An die Direktionen der Firma Thyssen & Co.," 2 July 1918, der Arbeiterausschuss [8 signatures]. Plumpe, *Betriebliche Mitbestimmungen*, pp. 98–100.

40. Quoted in Plumpe, "Mikropolitik im Unternehmen," p. 134.

41. Dokument 11: "Streikversammlung bei Thyssen/Mülheim," 18 July 1918 in *Revolution in Rheinland und Westfalen*, pp. 20–24.

42. TKA: A/1806 Däbritz Interview with Heinrich Dinkelbach, 11 Aug. 1954; A/1806–1807 Letter from Karl Fuss, 23 Oct. 1957; NDI/4 Dinkelbach's Note for Härle's Denazification, 9 Sept. 1947. TKA: PA Walter Däbritz, unpublished manuscript on Härle, ca. 1957. Fritz Pudor, ed., *Nekrologe aus dem Rheinisch-Westfälischen Industriegebiet, Jahrgang 1939–1951* (Düsseldorf: August Bagel Verlag, 1955), pp. 189–190.

43. Plumpe, *Betriebliche Mitbestimmung*, pp. 265–284 discusses the escalation of strikes in mining.

44. Steinisch, "Linksradikalismus und Rätebewegung" is the best account of the postwar radicalization of the Mülheim working class. J. Reulecke, "Der erste Weltkrieg und Arbeiterbewegung," pp. 228–234. Olsen, "Von einer unauffälligen Ruhrgebietsstadt," pp. 241–248.

45. Plumpe, *Betriebliche Mitbestimmung*, pp. 102–107.

46. Erhard Lucas, *Arbeiterradikalismus*, pp. 155–192. Peter von Oertzen, *Die Probleme der wirtschaftlichen Neuordnung und der Mitbestimmung in der Revolution von 1918, unter besonderer Berücksichtigung der Metallindustrie* (Frankfurt/Main: Europäische Verlag, 1965), pp. 42–45. Peter von Oertzen, *Betriebsräte in der Novemberrevolution: Eine politikwissenschaftliche Untersuchung über Ideengehalt und Struktur der betrieblichen und wirtschaftlichen Arbeiterräte in der deutschen Revolution 1918/19* (Düsseldorf: Droste, 1963). Reinhard Rürup, "Einleitung" in *Arbeiter- und Soldatenräte im rheinisch-westfälischen Industriegebiet: Studien zur Geschichte der Revolution 1918/19*, ed. Reinhard Rürup (Wuppertal: Hammer, 1975), pp. 7–38.

47. Gerald D. Feldman, "German Business between War and Revolution: The Origins of the Stinnes-Legien Agreement," in *Entstehung und Wandel der Modernen Gesellschaft*, ed. Gerard A. Ritter (Berlin: De

Gruyter, 1970), pp. 312–341. Gerald D. Feldman and Irmgard Steinisch, *Industrie und Gewerkschaften 1918–1924: Die überforderte Zentralarbeitsgemeinschaft* (Stuttgart: Deutsche Verlags-Anstalt, 1985). Feldman, *Army, Industry and Labor*, pp. 522–533. Steinisch, *Arbeitszeitverkürzung*, pp. 358–376.

48. MA: R 2 30 15 "Erläuterungen," 23 Nov. 1918, gez. Dr. E. Hoff, gez. Karl Spiegel.

49. MA: R 1 35 42 (1) Bekanntmachung: "An unsere Arbeiter!," 16 Nov. 1918; "An die Firma Thyssen & Co.," 20 Nov. 1918, Arbeiter- & Soldatenrat Mülheim-Ruhr, gez. Herm. Lauterfeld, Gerhard Serfort; [reply from Machine Company], 22 Nov. 1918, [none, Roser, Härle].

50. Steinisch, "Linksradikalismus," pp. 182–183.

51. Lucas, *Märzrevolution im Ruhrgebiet*, pp. 25–30. Tampke, *Ruhr and Revolution*, pp. 102–113. Plumpe, *Betriebliche Mitbestimmung*, pp. 286–296.

52. Steinisch, "Linksradikalismus," p. 195. Lucas, *Märzrevolution*, p. 29.

53. On the violent social psychology of the *Freikorps*, see the fascinating work by Klaus Theweleit, *Male Fantasies* (Minneapolis: University of Minnesota Press, 1987).

54. Tampke, *Ruhr and Revolution*, p. 112.

55. TKA: A/1774 Correspondence concerning the Jacob affair, 10 Jan. 1919, 27 Jan. 1919, and 12 Feb. 1919. TKA: A/1771 Däbritz Interview with Dr. Kern (GDK), 5 Nov. 1940. Quote from Feldman, *Hugo Stinnes*, p. 205. Cläre referred to a 1909 incident in the Saar-Mosel mining company, a Thyssen and Stinnes' joint-venture, regarding its director Johann Flake. See the correspondence in Rasch and Feldman, *August Thyssen und Hugo Stinnes*, pp. 426–457, 571

56. Lucas, *Märzrevolution*, pp. 39–44; Tampke, *Ruhr and Revolution*, pp. 117–129. Steinisch, "Linksradikalismus," p. 205–208. Plumpe, *Betriebliche Mitbestimmung*, pp. 296–303.

57. Quoted in Tampke, *Ruhr and Revolution*, p. 130.

58. Steinisch, "Linksradikalismus," pp. 210–216.

59. MA: R 1 35 41 (2) "Kürass.-Zug im Frei-Korps Schulz," *Mülheim General-Anzeiger*, 14 March 1919.

60. Tampke, *Ruhr and Revolution*, pp. 138–140.

61. Tampke, *Revolution in the Ruhr*, pp. 151–158.

62. Tampke, *Revolution in the Ruhr*, p. 140.

63. MA: R 2 35 12 "Protokoll: *1. Sitzung Arbeitsgemeinschaft*," 17 June 1919, signed by labor unions; "An die Direktionen der Mülheimer Metallwerke," Betr. Arbeitsgemeinschaft, 27 June 1919, signed by labor unions.

64. MA: R 1 35 42 (1) "Betrifft: Löhne Maschinenfabrik und Hüttenwerk," 15 Oct. 1919; "Lohnabkommen," 16 Oct. 1919.

65. MA: R 1 35 42 (3) "Abschrift: An unsere Mitlgieder! Rundschreiben

Nr. 3/20," 22 Jan. 1920, Dr. E. Hoff; "Richtlinien für die Auslegung und Durchführung des Betriebsrätegesetzes," 19 May 1920, Dr. E. Hoff; "An unsere Mitglieder!, "Bezirkliche Regelung der Löhne," Rundschreiben Nr. 41/20, 11 May 1920, Dr. E. Hoff.

66. MA: R 2 35 10 "Herrn Direktor Wallmann," 2 March 1920," Der Justitiar: gez. Dr. Späing.

67. MA: R 2 35 42 (3) "An unsere Mitglieder!, Rundschreiben Nr. 15/20, *Aussschussbeschluss,* Betr. Rahmentarifvertrag," 16 Feb.1920, Dr. Hoff. R 2 35 11 "An die Direktion der Fa. Thyssen & Co. z.H. Herrn Direktor Becker," 23 July 1920, signatures of union and factory council representatives. MA: R 1 35 42 (3) "Vertraulich! Bericht. Betr.: Zweite Besprechung über Lohnfragen mit den Vertretern der Gewerkschaften, der freien Arbeiterunion und den vereinigten Arbeiterräten," 13 Aug. 1920.

68. See especially MA: R 1 35 41 (2) with its wealth of correspondence on the escalation of events and the demands of white-collar employees.

69. A similar incident occurred at Bayer after Jan. 1921, but ended in the lockout of Bayer workers. See Plumpe, *Betriebliche Mitbestimmung,* pp. 150–165.

70. MA: R R 1 35 41 (2). See the various newspaper articles from 6 March 1919.

71. MA: R 2 35 10 "Herrn Dir. Wallmann, Dir. Gilles," 20 Nov. 1919, B[ecker].

72. MA: R 2 30 12, 16 Nov. 1918, various signatures for unions. See especially the recommendation for Wilhelmine Kemper, 2 Jan. 1919, Fol. 333–341, 344, ppa. Horst, W. Stiepel. MA: R 2 30 06 (1) contains recommendations from 1914–1926. MA: R 1 35 41 (3) "Angestellten-Forderungen," 3 April 1919, Roser, Härle, and Wallmann, with signatures of the various committee members. MA: R 1 35 41 (3) "Sitzung des Angestellten-Ausschusses mit der Direktion," 28 April 1919; "An die Direktion der Firma Thyssen & Co A. G.," 15 May 1919, Gröschner, G. Barth; "Bericht der Sitzung mit der Direktion," 26 May 1919, Gröschner, Barth. The employee committee explicitly named those women who should leave. A similar process took place at Bayer. See Plumpe, *Betriebliche Mitbestimmung,* pp. 110–112.

73. MA: R 2 35 10 "Neuregelung der Einkommensverhältnisse der Angestellten der Firma Thyssen & Co.," 11 Oct. 1919, gez. Dr. Härle, gez. Gröschner-Schmitz. MA: R 2 35 19 (2) Rahmentarifverträge für die Angestellten, 1921, 1924, 1927, 1928, 1930. Plumpe, *Betriebliche Mitbestimmung,* p. 421.

74. MA: R 2 35 10 "Sitzungsprotokoll," 15 Sept. 1919, die Geschäftsstelle. A good early example of this process can be found in MA: R 2 35 10

"Herrn Direktor Becker, Betr.: Gehaltsregelung f. Angestellte," 25 Nov. 1919, [?]; "Protokoll über die Sitzung mit dem Angestellten-Ausschuss," 13 Feb. 1920; "An die Direktion der Thyssen & Co. Abt. Stahlwalzwerk," 19 Feb. 1920, ATH; "Schiedsspruch!," 22 Jan. 1920, gez. Severing. The best extended discussion on state arbitration is Johannes Bähr, *Staatliche Schlichtung in der Weimarer Republik: Tarifpolitik, Korporatismus, und industrieller Konflikt zwischen Inflation und Deflation 1919–1932* (Berlin: Colloquium Verlag, 1989). Specifically on miners, see Rudolf Tschirbs, *Tarifpolitik im Ruhrbergbau 1918–1933* (Berlin: de Gruyter, 1986).

75. See the descriptions of the American Quaker missions to the Ruhr in Feldman, *Great Disorder,* pp. 220–222. Richard Bessel, *Germany after the First World War* (Oxford: Clarendon Press, 1993), pp. 111–116.

76. The Severing discussion is based on Lucas, *Märzrevolution,* pp. 51–57. Quote from Feldman, *Great Disorder,* p. 197–198.

77. MA: R 2 35 10 "Bekanntmachung," 16 March 1920, Becker, Eumann; "Mitteilung an alle Angestellten!," 18 March 1920, Angestellten-Ausschuss MF & S-W, Direktion. Lucas, *Märzrevolution* provides the most detailed account of the Kapp-Putsch and the general strike from a decided leftist bent. For industrialists' responses to the putsch, see Feldman, *Great Disorder,* pp. 207, 212–214.

78. Lucas, *Märzrevolution,* pp. 280–310. Treue, *Feuer Verlöschen Nie,* pp. 198–200. TKA: PA Carl Rabes for a short unpublished biography of Rabes, 10 March 1941.

79. Karl Rohe, Wolfgang Jäger, and Uwe Dorow, "Politische Gesellschaft und politische Kultur," in *Das Ruhrgebiet im Industriezeitalter,* pp. 476–486. In the Ruhr, the SPD, which had received 37.2 percent of all votes in 1919, dropped spectacularly in June 1920 to 14.7 percent of the vote, losing most of their votes to the Independent Socialist Party (17.7 percent). Communists received just 3.7 percent of the vote. After the hyperinflation ended, the Communist Party received 21 percent of the vote, while the Social Democrats received just 11.3 percent of the votes on the left. Thereafter, the Communist Party in the Ruhr received a roughly consistent 8–10 percent more voters than in Germany as a whole.

80. For the legal history of the Factory Council Law and its stipulations, see Plumpe, *Betriebliche Mitbestimmung,* pp. 37–65. Also see von Oertzen, *Die Probleme der wirtschaftlichen Neuordnung,* pp. 51–70. Plumpe, "Die Betriebsräte," pp. 42–60. *Die Betriebsräte in der Weimarer Republik: Von der Selbstverwaltung zur Mitbestimmung,* 1, 2, ed. R. Crusius, G. Schiefelbein, and M. Wilke (Berlin: Olle & Wolter, 1978), esp. 2, pp. 75–152.

81. Quoted in Plumpe, *Betriebliche Mitbestimmung*, p. 44.

82. Plumpe, *Betriebliche Mitbestimmung*, pp. 73–74.

83. MA: P 7 77 07 "Direktion der Aktiengesellschaft für Hüttenbetrieb," 30 Oct. 1919, Härle; Maschinenfabrik Thyssen & Co. Aktiengesellschaft Mülheim-Ruhr, 'Statuten' [revised and also used for the AGHütte, 19 Dec. 1919.

84. MA: R 1 35 42 (5) "An den Vorsitzenden des Aufsichtsrats der Firma Thyssen & Co., A. G., Herrn August Thyssen, Betr. Entsendung von Betriebsratsmitgliedern in den Aufsichtsrat," 5 July 1922, Betriebsrat, gez. Wilh. Rautenberg; "An den Vorsitzenden des Aufsichtsrats der Firma Thyssen & Co., A. G. Herrn August Thyssen," 23 Dec. 1922, Der Betriebsrat: gez. Sensenbusch, Dietrich. The first two worker members of the supervisory board were Wilhelm Rautenberg from the Rolling Mills and Weck from the Machine Company. Weck left in December 1922 and was replaced by Heinrich Bleichardt.

85. MA: R 2 35 10 "Herrn Direktor Wallmann," 2 March 1920, Der Justitiar: gez. Dr. Späing. All salaried employees could vote as long as they did not hold *Prokura*.

86. MA: R 2 35 10 "An die Direktion der Firma Thyssen & Co., AG, Abtlg. Stahl- u. Walzwerk," 14 May 1920, Angestelltenrat, I. Vorsitzender: gez. Gröschner, Schriftführer: gez. H. Schmitz.

87. MA: R 1 35 42 (3) "Betr. Sitzung v. 26.März 1920," Grossweischede; "Entwurf zu Lohnvereinbarungen," 26 March 1920, [various factory council and union representatives].

88. MA: R 1 35 41 (3) "An die Direktion der Firma Thyssen & Co A. G.," 15 May 1919, Angestellten-Ausschuss, Gröschner, G. Barth. R 2 35 10 "Herrn Direktor Becker," 10 Oct 1919, Angestelltenausschuss: Gröschner, Schmitz; "An die Firma Thyssen & Co. Herrn Direktor Becker," 12 Jan. 1920, Angestellten-Ausschuss: Gröschner, Schmitz; "An den Angestellten-Ausschuss der Fa. Thyssen & Co. AG, Abtlg. Stahl- & Walzwerke, z.Hd. des Obmanns Herrn Gröschner," 13 Jan. 1920, Becker.

89. TKA: PA Carl Wallmann. "Carl Wallmann," *Stahl und Eisen,* 72, 26 (1952), p. 1696. See the newspaper clippings in MA: R 2 41 81 (1–2). Wallman once had to mediate soup line disputes that broke down largely along religious lines. One of his solutions was to standardize the soup and its ingredients. One member of the Protestant Church actually pulled his soup out of the Emergency Aid commission for "reasons of conscience," objecting to such a "schematization" of the soup.

90. See the Duisberg quote from 8 Nov. 1919 in Plumpe, *Betriebliche Mitbestimmung*, p. 130.

91. MA: R 1 35 42 (2) "Niederschrift: Betriebsrats-Sitzung," 15 May 1920, Der Vorsitzende: Abrath; Der Schriftführer: Gröschner.

92. MA: R 1 35 42 (2) "Niederschrift über die Arbeiterrats-Sitzung am 19.Mai 1920," Der Schriftsführer: Schmitz. The owner-director of the Carl Freudenberg-Werke in Baden also chaired the factory council, but only after difficult negotiations. See Matthias Freese, "Betriebsrat und Betriebsrätetätigkeit," p. 170.

93. MA: R 1 35 42 (2) "Niederschrift über die Arbeiterrats-Sitzung am 19. Mai 1920," Der Schriftsführer: Schmitz. MA: R 2 35 10 "Sitzung des Angestelltenrats v. 18 May 1920," 19 May 1920, gez. Wallmann. The factory council also reminded management that the gold watches for twenty-five years of service were overdue to many employees, which indicates a level of self-identification with the firm.

94. MA: R 2 35 14 (1) "An die Direktion der Firma Thyssen & Co. A.-G., Abt. Stahl- & Walzwerke," 8 Feb. 1923, der Angestelltenrat: Gröschner, Dornhaus. Härle remained in charge of these offices.

95. MA: R 1 35 42 (4) "Bekanntmachung!," 30 Sept. 1921, Betriebsrat: Rautenberg.

96. MA: R 1 35 42 (2) "Sitzung mit der Direktion am 16. November 1920," die Direktion. MA: R 1 35 42 (5) "An den Betriebsrat der Firma Thyssen & Co. A. G., Abteilung Stahl- und Walzwerke," 16 Oct. 1922; "Bekanntmachung," 16 Oct. 1922, Die Direktion: gez. Wallmann. In this instance, Wallmann sent out an announcement in response to Saturday wildcat strikes; the firm would no longer tolerate such actions. He wanted the factory council to use its influence to stop them.

97. MA: R 2 35 19 (1) "Arbeits-Ordnung der Firma Thyssen & Co. Aktien-Gesellschaft, Abteilung Stahl- und Walzwerke," in effect after 1 March 1921, Die Werksleitung: gez. Wallmann, Der Vorsitzende des Arbeiter-rates: gez. Siepmann. Geprüft, 22 Feb. 1921, Gewerbeaufsichtsamt Mülheim-Ruhr: gez. Strauven.

98. MA: R 1 35 42 (2) "Engere Ausschuss-Sitzung 26. May 1921, Rühl."

99. MA: R 2 35 11 "Kurze Besprechung" 28 Sept. 1920, Für die Firma: Becker, Wallmann, Der Schriftführer: Abrath. H. Schmitz.

100. MA: R 1 35 42 (5) "Niederschrift über die Sitzung mit dem engeren Ausschuss des Betriebsrates," 4 Nov. 1922, Lenz.

101. MA: R 1 35 42 (5) Letters and reports, 29 Aug. 1923, 30 Aug. 1923, and 3 Sept. 1923 [none]; An den Betriebsrat Abteilung Stahl- und Walzwerke, Betr. Kartoffel-beschaffung," 5 Sept. 1923, Die Direktion [none]. A great deal of dispute surrounded the fact that Thyssen & Co. did not disclose its 1922 and 1923 annual financial statements, because none were ever created. The factory council, however, did not believe this.

102. MA: R 1 35 42 (5) Correspondence 12 April 1923, 15 May 1923, gez.

Wallmann, gez. ppa. Grossweischede, Schuldensky; "Niederschrift über die Besprechung mit den Betriebsräten der Maschinenfabrik und der Abteilung Stahl- und Walzwerke betreffend die Besetzung des Werkes am 18. Juli 23 durch die Besatzungsmächte," [none]. Treue, *Feuer Verlöschen Nie,* pp. 202–204.

103. Plumpe, *Betriebliche Mitbestimmung,* p. 2.

104. For a political overview, see Feldman, *Great Disorder,* pp. 631–697, 746–751, 770–72, 798–800, 828. For the steel industry's involvement, see Gerald D. Feldman, *Iron and Steel in the German Inflation 1916–1923* (Princeton: Princeton, 1977), pp. 346–444, and Charles S. Maier, *Recasting Bourgeois Europe: Stabilization in France, Germany, and Italy in the Decade after World War I* (Princeton: Princeton University Press, 1988 [1975]), pp. 356–420. For Fritz Thyssen's views and the effect of the invasion on Hamborn-Bruckhausen, see Treue, *Feuer Verlöschen Nie,* pp. 204–207. On Stinnes' maneuverings and bad press, see Feldman, *Hugo Stinnes,* pp. 894–922. From the point of view of labor and Thyssen & Co. on MICUM and the occupation ordinances, see MA: R 1 35 42 (5) "Bericht über die Verhandlungen beim General Degoutte am 24 Oct. [1923] Deutscher Metallarbeiter-Verband." See also MA: R 1 35 24 (1); R 1 35 23 (2); R 2 35 14 (1); and TKA: A/726/1–3.

105. MA: R 1 35 06. Thyssen to Chancellor Joseph Wirth, confidential letter reprinted in *Mülheimer Zeitung,* 14 Oct., 1922.

106. Feldman, *Iron and Steel,* pp. 427–444. Steinisch, *Arbeitszeitverkürzung,* pp. 464–489, 530–576.

107. Feldman, *Great Disorder,* pp. 799, 807–808.

108. MA: R 2 35 14 (1) "Angestelltenrat 10/11/1923," [none, Roser].

109. Dinkelbach first received *Prokura* in August 1924. MA: R 2 35 15 "Lohnbüro," 28 Nov. 1923, Rev. Büro: Dinkelbach; "Betr. Vergütung für Kurzarbeit," 30 Nov. 1923, Rev. Büro: Dinkelbach; "Der Regierungs-Präsident. Demobilmachungskommissar, Wiederaufnahme der Arbeit . . .," 5 Dec 1923, gez. von Stein; "Herrn Direktor Wallmann," 7 Dec. 1923. Also R 2 35 14 (2) 8 May 1924.

110. MA: R 1 35 42 (5) "An den Vorsitzenden des Gewerbegerichts Herrn Dr. Loos, Betrifft: Lohnfrage," 26 Oct/ 1923, [none]. See MA: R 2 35 15 for the dispute's legal resolution on 17 Sept. 1924 and the court decision from 23 July 1924. This settlement totalled 1,750 marks.

111. MA: R 2 35 19 (1) Bekanntmachung, Arbeitsordnung, 30 Nov. 1923, Thyssen & Co. AG, Abteilung Maschinenfabrik, Dr. Roser, Dr. Härle.

112. MA: R 2 35 16, Rundschreiben, 28 Dec. 1923.

113. Plumpe, *Betriebliche Mitbestimmung,* p. 404.

114. Thyssen/Stinnes correspondence, 12–13 April 1908, quoted in Rasch/Feldman, *August Thyssen und Hugo Stinnes,* pp. 417–418.

115. Plumpe, "Betriebsräte der Weimarer Republik," pp. 51–60.

116. Plumpe, *Betriebliche Mitbestimmung,* pp. 69–78, quote from p. 248. Plumpe, "Mikropolitik im Unternehmen," pp. 156–160.

117. Bellon, *Mercedes in Peace and War,* pp. 128–9, 152–160, 164–166, 173–184, 191–203.

118. This is perhaps the only difference of interpretation within Plumpe's analysis. Plumpe, *Betriebliche Mitbestimmung,* pp. 434–440, places more weight on the "technically determined organizational structures," which probably arises from the stark contrast between chemical and coal industrial branches.

119. Richard Locke, Thomas Kochan, and Michael Piore, "Reconceptualizing Comparative Industrial Relations: Lessons from International Research," *International Labour Review,* 134, 2 (1995), pp. 139–161. They, too, point to an increasing need for focus on the enterprise.

120. Plumpe, *Betriebliche Mitbestimmung,* pp. 217–223, 247–248.

121. These are good examples of how organizations "match" their environments with corresponding internal offices; offices are touchpoints for dealing with the external world. See the classic Paul R. Lawrence and Jay Lorsch, *Organization and Environment* (Cambridge, Mass.: Harvard University Press, 1967).

11. Centralization or Decentralization?

1. August Thyssen, quoted in Carl-Friedrich Bauman, *Schloss Landsberg und Thyssen,* ed. Thyssen Aktiengesellschaft und August Thyssen-Stiftung Schloss Landsberg (Duisburg/Mülheim (Ruhr), 1993), p. 15.

2. ThyssenKrupp Archive (TKA): A/9568 Denkschrift des Reichsmarineamtes: Abschrift zu K IV a 7905/19: "Verhandlungen mit Thyssen über Aufnahme der Panzerplatten-Herstellung" 1906–1910, May 1913.

3. TKA: A/1771 Däbritz Interview with Carl Wallmann, 4 Nov. 1940.

4. Treue, *Feuer Verlöschen Nie,* 172–176.

5. TKA: A/1783 Geschäftsberichte der Maschinenfabrik Thyssen u. Co., AG, Mülheim-Ruhr. TKA: A/681/1 Bilanz, 31 Dec 1916; TKA: A/1086 "Inspektion," 28 Feb. 1918. TKA: A/1727 Däbritz Interview with Rabes et al., 5 Dec. 1938.

6. TKA: A/681/1 "Erhöhung des Aktienkapitals und Bildung einer Jnteressen-Gemeinschaft mit der Firma Thyssen & Co.," 24 Nov. 1915, Maschinenfabrik Thyssen & Co., [none].

7. TKA: A/635/12 "Entwurf" [Interessengemeinschaftsvertrag], 15 Dec. 1915, Späing.

8. TKA: A/747/1 "Jnteressengemeinschaftsvertrag," 20 Dec 1915, Thyssen & Co. [Aug.], Roser, Fassnacht, Kalle, Filius, Verlohr, Melcher, Theis, Späing, Dahl, F. Thyssen, Jacob, Julius Thyssen.

9. Feldman, *Iron and Steel*, pp. 55, 92–94, 140–146. Also Maier, *Recasting Bourgeois Europe*, p. 518 for a useful overview about the international flows of coal, iron, and steel between 1910–1930. Treue, *Feuer Verlöschen Nie*, p. 180.

10. Mannesmann Archive (MA): P 7 77 06 [Briefwechsel der Aktionären], 31 Dec. 1916. If the company distributed dividends as it did in 1916, the GDK also received the bulk of the dividends from the AGHütt.

11. TKA: A/747/1 "Interessengemeinschaftsvertrag," 30 April 1919, [signatures from all firms].

12. TKA: A/815/2; MA: R 5 30 16 for 1915; TKA: A/681/1; MA: R 5 30 16 for 1916; TKA: A/749/2; MA: R 5 35 10 for 1917; TKA/750/1; MA: R 5 30 13, R 5 35 10 (3), R 5 35 15,16 for 1918. The pipe department provided the bulk of the profits.

13. Figures from MA: P7 77 06 for the AGHütt, R 5 35 10; TKA: A/749/2 for the Thyssen & Co. Rolling Mills; TKA: A 814/3, A/749/2 for the Machine Company; and MA: R 1 35 04 for the fused Thyssen & Co. AG.

14. Bellon, *Mercedes in Peace and War,* pp. 102–114. Gallhofer and Haslam, "The Aura of Accounting in the Context of a Crisis: Germany and the First World War," pp. 487–520.

15. TKA: A/813/2 Letter from Späing to the GDK Board of Directors, 28 Nov. 1918 with "Entwurf einer Geschäftsordnung für das Revisions-Bureau der Thyssen'schen Werke, Hamborn."

16. MA: R 2 30 00.4 for articles about his death. MA: R 1 30 10 Handelsregister. Wegener, "Familie Thyssen," pp. 45–46.

17. MA: R 1 30 10, R 1 35 01, R 1 35 05.

18. Wegener, "Familie Thyssen," p. 39. MA: R 5 35 10 (1) Letters "Herren Thyssen & Co." 6 June 1918, 1 Oct. 1918, 10 Oct. 1918. Also MA: R 5 35 15. The first consolidated balance is in MA: R 1 35 04.

19. Rasch, "August Thyssen," pp. 103–106.

20. MA: R 1 35 00 "An die Abteilung Buchhaltung, Mülheim," 15 July 1918, pr. pa. Thyssen & Co.: Thyssen. MA: R 5 30 18 Securities Portfolio.

21. MA: R 5 35 63 Letter from Rolling Mills to the Machine Company, 12 Jan. 1920.

22. Treue, *Feuer Verlöschen Nie,* pp. 212–214. TKA: A/1773 Letter from Späing to Däbritz, 3 Jan. 1941.

23. Treue, *Feuer Verlöschen Nie,* pp. 196–197. Arnst, *August Thyssen,* p. 54,

fn. 1. The government commission valued the losses of Rombacher Hütte at 235 million, Lothringen Hüttenverein 196 million, Deutsch-Luxembourg at 192 million, and Gelsenkirchen (GBAG) at 111 million marks.

24. TKA: A/1727 Däbritz Interview with Rabes, et al., 5 Dec. 1938.

25. Feldman, *Iron and Steel*, p. 84. Maier, *Recasting*, pp. 517–520.

26. Bernd Weisbrod, *Schwerindustrie in der Weimarer Republik: Interessenpolitik zwischen Stabilisierung und Krise* (Wuppertal: Peter Hammer Verlag, 1978), pp. 36–51; Feldman, *Iron and Steel*, pp. 11–15; Gustav Stolper, Karl Häuser [and] Knut Borchardt, *The German Economy 1870 to the Present* (New York: Harcourt, Brace & World, 1967), pp. 74–78.

27. Feldman, *Iron and Steel*, pp. 55–56, 94, 140–43, 146.

28. Wixforth, *Banken und Schwerindustrie*, pp. 215–221. The quote is from p. 218, fn. 24. On the Warburg family, see Ron Chernow, *The Warburgs: The Twentieth-Century Odyssey of a Remarkable Jewish Family* (New York: Vintage Books, 1993), p. 224.

29. TIA: A/564/7 "Betrifft: *Wirtschaftliche Lage der Werke der Thyssen-Gruppe*," 29 April 1919, GKD: Aug. Thyssen, Hans Thyssen.

30. MA: R 5 35 16 "Abt. Buchhaltung," 24 Feb. 1921, Eumann. Wixforth, *Banken und Schwerindustrie*, Table 5 uses the final balances of the ATH *after* the IG profit redistribution. Wixforth's table shows that the ATH earned profits in each year between 1919–1923. See MA: R 5 25 15,16.

31. MA: R 5 35 10 (2), R 5 35 16.

32. TKA: A/540/6 [Bekanntmachung]: "M. 250.000.000 4 1/2% Teilschuldverschreibung der Thyssen & Co. A. G.," 7 Jan. 1922, Direction der Disconto-Gesellschaft. "August Thyssen-Hütte, Gew. "Vertraulich," 23 Feb. 1922, Thyssen & Co. Abt. Buchhaltung: Härle, Eumann. Wixforth, *Banken und Schwerindustrie*, pp. 218–220.

33. TKA: A/557/7 [Gründungsakten] Eigenschutz GmbH, 28 Nov. 1921. For the role of Eigenschutz and the course of the Ruhr occupation on Thyssen & Co., see MA: R 2 35 14, R 2 35 16, R 1 35 22–24, R 1 35 23. The documentation is extremely rich. Wixforth, *Banken und Schwerindustrie*, p. 206. Treue, *Feuer Verlöschen Nie*, p. 232.

34. TKA: A/599/6 Reports by the Finanzamt, from 27 March 1928 to 13 June 1928 and from 6 Aug. 1928 to 29 Sept. 1928, Reichslisten-Nr. 10589; with corresponding letters from Späing to Härle, Rabes, and Dinkelbach, 3 June 1929.

35. The banking sector also underwent a major wave of consolidation under the largest Berlin universal banks. Manfred Pohl, *Entstehung und Entwicklung des Universalbankensystems: Konzentration und Krise als wichtige Faktoren* (Frankfurt/Main: Knapp, 1986), pp. 67–69. Manfred

Pohl, *Konzentration im deutschen Bankwesen 1848–1980* (Frankfurt/ Main: Knapp, 1982), pp. 285–330. Gerald Feldman, "Banks and banking in Germany after the First World War: strategies of defence," in *Finance and Financiers in European History, 1880–1960* ed. Youssef Cassis (Cambridge: Cambridge University Press, 1992), pp. 243–262.

36. The classic, most useful account is still Tross, *Der Aufbau der Eisen- und Eisenverarbeitenden Industrie-Konzerne Deutschlands.* The best account in English is Feldman, *Iron and Steel,* pp. 210–279. He concentrates on two case studies, the GHH/MAN merger and the building of the Stinnes-Konzern, the Siemens-Rheinelbe-Schuckert-Union (SRSU).

37. Feldman, *Iron and Steel,* pp. 210–279. Feldman, *Great Disorder,* p. 841. Feldman, *Hugo Stinnes,* pp. 662–667. Feldenkirchen, *Siemens,* pp. 153– 157, pp. 559–563, esp. p. 562, fn. 61.

38. Quoted in Feldman, *Hugo Stinnes,* p. 660.

39. For the post-World War II debates on the virtues of the self-sufficient, vertically-integrated steel: "Konzerne in Stellungnahme der Treuhandverwaltung im Auftrag der North German Iron and Steel Control: Die Entflechtung und Neuordnung der Eisenschaffenden Industrie," in *Die Neuordnung der Eisen- und Stahlindustrie im Gebiet der Bundesrepublik Deutschland: Ein Bericht der Stahltreuhändervereinigung* (München: C. H. Beck, 1954), pp. 15–26, 528–539, 567–570.

40. See Tross, *Der Aufbau der Eisen- und eisenverarbeitenden Industrie-Konzerne Deutschlands.*

41. Ernst Schulze, *Organisatoren und Wirtschaftsführer* (Leipzig: F. A. Brockhaus, 1923), pp. 22–23. See also Albert Vögler's comments: MA: R 1 35 32 (6) "Dortmunder Denkschrift über einen Zusammenschluss in der Stahlindustrie," Albert Vögler, reprinted in Gerald Feldman and Heidrun Homburg, *Industrie und Inflation: Studien und Dokumente zur Politik der deutschen Unternehmer 1916–1923* (Hamburg: Hoffmann und Campe, 1977), pp. 219–225. Richard Rosendorff, *Die rechtliche Organisation der Konzerne* (Berlin: Spaeth und Linde, 1927), esp. pp. 11– 33, 113–119.

42. Mauro F. Guillén, *Models of Management: Work, Authority, and Organization in a Comparative Perspective* (Chicago: University of Chicago, 1994). Mary Nolan, *Visions of Modernity: American Business and the Modernization of Germany* (New York: Oxford University Press, 1994).

43. Treue, *Feuer Verlöschen Nie,* 212–228. Wixforth, *Banken und Schwerindustrie,* p. 200. Feldman, *Iron and Steel in the German Inflation,* pp. 244–250, 262.

44. MA: R 5 30 18 Thyssen Securities Portfolio.

45. Baumann, *Thyssen und Schloss Landsberg,* pp. 51–52. Lutz Hatzfeld,

"Anekdoten um August Thyssen," *Thyssen & Co. Mülheim a. d. Ruhr: Die Geschichte einer Familie und ihrer Unternehmung*, ed. Horst A. Wessel (Stuttgart: F. Steiner, 1991), p. 208, Anekdote 24.

46. TKA: A/1771 Däbritz Interview with Dr. Kern, 5 Nov. 1940.

47. Werner Abelshauser, "Wirtschaft, Staat und Arbeitsmarkt 1914–1945," *Das Ruhrgebiet im Industriezeitalter: Geschichte und Entwicklung*, 1, ed. Werner Abelshauser and Wolfgang Köllmann (Düsseldorf: Schwann im Patmos, 1990), p. 460. John Ronald Shearer, *The Politics of Industrial Efficiency in the Weimar Republic: Technological Innovation, Economic Efficiency, and their Social Consequences in the Ruhr Coal Mining Industry 1918–1929* (PhD Dissertation: University of Pennsylvania, 1989), pp. 239–246, 345–372, esp. p. 358, Table 6.1.

48. Shearer, *The Politics of Industrial Efficiency*, pp. 325–327. Archibald Stockder, *Regulating an Industry: The Rheinisch-Westphalian Coal Syndicate 1893–1929* (New York: Columbia, 1932), pp. 91–110

49. TKA: PA Franz Bartscherer. Carl-Friedrich Baumann, "Franz Bartscherer: Vom Maschinenbauer zum 'Hüttenkönig,'" *Niederrheinkammer* (January 1985), p. 30. TKA: A/9417, A/6377, A/3214. Kleinschmidt, *Rationalisierung als Unternehmensstrategie*, pp. 142–158, esp. Table 28.

50. Treue, *Feuer Verlöschen Nie*, pp. 214–225. Gertrud Milkereit, "Die ATH und der Thyssen-Konzern nach dem ersten Weltkrieg" in *Unsere ATH: Werkszeitschrift* (April 1965), pp. 22–24.

51. Quoted from Feldman, *Iron and Steel*, pp. 260–261. MA: M 30.141 *Das Mülheimer Werk der Siemens-Schuckertwerke AG*. Hatzfeld, "Werks- und Firmengeschichte," pp. 166–167. Kleinschmidt, *Rationalisierung als Unternehmensstrategie*, pp. 142–158. For a history of the energy economy in the rolling mills in Mülheim, see MA: R 4 35 36 Roser an Direktor Wallmann, 14 June 1921, 17 June 1921. A complete report on the energy economy of Thyssen & Co. AG can be found in MA: R 4 35 36 "Bericht: Besprechung der Kohlenwirtschaft bei Thyssen & Co, A. G.," 15 April 1919, gez. Roser.

52. See especially Mary Nolan, *Visions of Modernity*. See also Guillén, *Models of Management*, pp. 91–121; Heidrun Homburg, *Rationalisierung und Industriearbeit: Arbeitsmarkt—Management—Arbeiterschaft im Siemens-Konzern Berlin 1900–1939* (Berlin: Haude & Spener, 1991); Thomas V. Freyberg, *Industrielle Rationalisierung in der Weimarer Republik: Untersucht an Beispielen aus dem Maschinenbau und der Elektroindustrie* (Frankfurt: Campus Verlag, 1989); and the classic by Robert Brady, *The Rationalization Movement in German Industry* (Berkeley: University of California, 1933).

53. The discussion is based on TKA: PA Franz Bartscherer. Carl-Friedrich Baumann, "Franz Bartscherer: Vom Maschinenbauer zum 'Hüttenkönig,'" *Niederrheinkammer* (Januar 1985), p. 30. TKA: A/9417, A/6377, A/3214. Kleinschmidt, *Rationalisierung als Unternehmensstrategie,* pp. 142–158.

54. TKA: PA (Presse) "Der Dinkelbachkreis," Dr. Theodor Gessel.

55. TKA: A/8970 Nachlass Dinkelbach: "Kurze Erläuterung betreffend ausgehende und eingehende Rechnungen!" Revisions-Büro, 13 Sept. 1919, D[inkelba]ch.

56. MA: R 5 30 13, 15–17.

57. Bernd Dornseifer, "Zur Bürokratisierung deutscher Unternehmen im späten 19. und frühen 20. Jahrhundert," in *Jahrbuch für Wirtschaftsgeschichte,* (1993), pp. 69–91. Bryn Jones, *Forcing the Factory of the Future: Cybernation and Societal Institutions* (Cambridge: Cambridge University Press, 1997), pp. 23–50.

58. TKA: A/813/1 Letter to the GDK board, 15 Nov. 1916, Späing. For the conflict between the iron and steel producers and their industrial customers during the war, see Feldman, *Iron and Steel,* pp. 71–81.

59. MA: R 1 35 86,2 (1) "Herrn Eduard Stier, Halle," 3 Dec 1915, Aug. Thyssen.

60. TKA: A/749/2. See the financial statements of Thyssen & Co. for the capital accounts of the trading firms. TKA: A/756/4 "Herrn Direktor Hofs, Revisionsbüro der Thyssen'schen Werke," 12 Oct. 1916, ppa. Thyssen & Co.: H. Eumann. Heinrich Reiter GmbH, Königsberg sent their correspondence to Eumann; Eumann then informed Hofs.

61. TKA: A/643, [Denkschrift], "Die Thyssen'schen Handelsniederlassungen, ihr Entstehen, ihr Wesen und ihre Aufgabe," 26 Jan. 1918 [prepared by Neuhaus].

62. Feldman, "Collapse of the Steel Works Association."

63. MA: R 1 35 86 (6): "Gemeinschafts-Sitzung der Thyssen'schen Werke und Thyssen'schen Handels-Niederlassungen," 14 May 1918; "Thyssen'sche Handelsniederlassungen. Neuordnung ab 1. Juli 1918," 14 May 1918; "Vertrag" among Thyssen manufacturing firms and Thyssenhandel. The agreement took effect retroactively on 1 Jan. 1918.

64. In a separate case, Thyssen wanted to exchange some of his stock shares for new ones in a new company, but his executives disagreed with him. He abstained and let himself be overridden. TKA: A/847/7 "Niederschrift über die Aufsichtsratssitzung der Aktiengesellschaft für Hüttenbetrieb," 3 Feb. 1921, Verlohr, Scheifhacken. TKA: A/ A/1727 Däbritz Interview with Rabes, et al., 5 Dec. 1938.

65. MA: R 1 35 86 (2) Correspondence from 10 Dec. 1913–30 July 1918 with Fritz Nagel. Until this point, Nagel addressed his correspondence to "Herren Thyssen & Co., Centrale."

66. TKA: A/1805 Nachlass Däbritz Personal-Angaben.

67. See TKA: A/643 "Protokoll über die Sitzung der Thyssen'schen Handelsgesellschaften," 23 Jan. 1919, Sandmann (with all present). This division of labor was explicitly discussed at this meeting.

68. MA: R 1 35 32 (5) H. A. Brassert, Inc. Reporting-Consulting-Operating Iron and Steel Industries Report (Brassert-Report).

69. TKA: A/813/2 Letter to the GDK board, 12 Jan. 1917, Späing.

70. TKA: A/639/2 Gutachten, Vertraulich, 20 May 1921, Späing, Gilling.

71. MA: R 5 35 63 Contains reports and correspondence from the purchasing department (Ernst Brökelschen), Direktor Wallmann, the ATH and the Thyssenhandel Duisburg. See also MA: R 5 35 85 for accounts of Thyssen sales operation in Argentina and Brazil, R 5 35 87 for the Soviet Union, and R 5 35 88 for the USA, especially for drilling pipes in Texas.

72. See TKA: A/643 "Protokoll über die Sitzung der Thyssen'schen Handelsgesellschaften," 23 Jan. 1919, Sandmann.

73. TKA: A/1805 Däbritz interview with Riepelmeier and Wilhelmi, 5 Jan. 1945.

74. MA: R 5 35 63 Thyssenhandel Duisburg, 10 Jan. 1922, Eumann.

75. One of the better examples of the complex negotiations that went on among Thyssen firms can be found in MA: R 5 35 63 "An den Thyssen-Eisenhandel, *Lieferung von billigerem Halbzeug für Mülheimer- und Dinslakener Exportaufträge,*" 27 Dec. 1922, ATH, Sandmann, Wibbeke; also Letter from 6 Jan. 1923.

76. MA: R 5 35 63 Letter to Thyssen & Co. Rolling Mills, 20 Feb. 1922, Thyssen-Eisenhandel. The ATH received 6,660 m/ton for crude steel used for pipes; Krupp delivered them for 6250 m/ton. It is impossible to say if prices were consistently higher. Quality was also a major issue, especially for specialty steel for tubing strips and pipes. Letter to Thyssen-Eisenhandel Duisburg, 28 Dec. 1921, Thyssen & Co. Einkauf, [Brökelschen].

77. MA: R 5 35 63 Direktor Wallmann, 10 Nov. 1921, Thyssen & Co., Einkauf. Thyssen & Co. (Eumann, Brökelschen), 13 Jan. 1922, Thyssen-Eisenhandel, Duisburg.

78. MA: R 5 35 63 Thyssen-Eisenhandel Duisburg, 15 March 1922, Thyssen & Co., Brökelschen, Härle.

79. MA: R 5 35 63 Thyssen & Co., 9–10 Jan. 1922, Thyssenhandel Duisburg.

80. MA: R 5 35 63 Thyssen-Eisenhandel, Duisburg, 5 April 1922, Thyssen & Co., Eumann, Brökelschen.

81. For an example of the intricate financial maneuverings of the ATH and the level of cooperation among Thyssen firms, see MA: R 5 35 63 Thyssen & Co. AG, 1 May 1922, ATH, gez. Rabes, gez. Späing.

82. MA: R 5 35 63 Thyssen'sche Eisenhandelsgesellschaft, Duisburg, *Halbzeuglieferung für Mülheim,* 18 April 1923, ATH, gez. Sandmann, Wibbeke. The Machine Company, moreover, cancelled all deliveries to the Rolling Mills in July 1923 because of "higher powers." See Thyssen & Co., Abt. Stahl- und Walzwerke, 26 July 1923, [signatures].

83. MA: R 5 35 63 Thyssen & Co., Jan. 1922, Thyssen Handelsgesellschaft, Hamburg.

84. Treue, *Feuer Verlöschen Nie,* pp. 120–129.

85. Similarly, the strategy of annual model changes at General Motors evolved slowly throughout the 1920s and was not recognized as an explicit concept until the 1930s. See Alfred P. Sloan, Jr., *My Years with General Motors* (Garden City, NY: Doubleday, 1972), pp. 188–193.

86. MA: R 1 30 10 "Bekanntmachung" Thyssen & Co. AG, Abt. Verkaufsstelle der Thyssen'schen Röhrenwerke, June 1924; "An die Handelsregister," 1 June 1924, Thyssen & Co. AG, Abt. S-W.

87. MA: R 5 30 66 The entire 1923 catalogue of Thyssen products is also presented in English.

88. TKA: A/847/7 "Niederschrift. Gelegentlich der Gründung der Gasgesellschaft mbH, Hamborn," 25 Jan. 1921, Verlohr, Schuh, Scheifhacken. I would like to thank Dr. Arno Mietschke for directing me to this document.

89. TKA: A/639/2 Vertraulich [Gutachten zur Frage, ob es sich empfiehlt, die Betriebe der Konzernwerke in einer Gesellschaft mit eigener Rechtspersönlichkeit zusammenzufassen 1. nach zivilrechtlichen und handelsrechtlichen 2. nach steuerrechtlichen Gesichtspunkten], 20 May 1921, Späing, Gilling.

90. Dieter Lindenlaub, *Maschinenbauunternehmen in der deutschen Inflation 1919–1923: Unternehmenshistorische Untersuchungen zu einigen Inflationstheorien* (Berlin/New York: de Gruyter, 1985). Feldman, *Great Disorder,* pp. 281–305.

91. TKA: A/3271 Däbritz Interview with Dinkelbach, 1 April 1960.

92. TKA: A/1771 Däbritz Interview with Dahl, 28 Jan. 1939; Däbritz Interview with Dr. Schöll, 6 Sept. 1954. TKA: A/3271 Edgar Kuepper to Scheifhacken, 20 April 1960. TKA: A/1727 Däbritz interview with Fritz Thyssen, 22 Aug. 1938.

93. TKA: A/1801 Däbritz Interview with Dinkelbach, 2 March 1943.

12. The Demise of the Thyssen-Konzern

1. Feldman, *Great Disorder,* pp. 708–725 for various preliminary plans; pp. 832–835 on the credit stop. For the economic and social impact of the stabilization, see Steven B. Webb, *Hyperinflation and Stabilization in Weimar Germany* (New York: Oxford University Press, 1989). Michael L. Hughes, *Paying for German Inflation* (Chapel Hill: University of North Carolina Press, 1988).

2. ThyssenKrupp Archive (TKA): A/831/2 [Amerika-Anleihe] "Tagebuch," 9 Jan. 1925, C. Rabes, W. Barth.

3. Ums[atz]St[euer]G[esetz] 1919 §1 Nr. 1. V. Senat, 9 Dec. 1924, VA 47/24, *Reichsfinanzhof: Sammlung der Entscheidungen und Gutachten des Reichsfinanzhofs,* ed. Reichsfinanzhof (München, 1919ff.), pp. 136–143.

4. VI. Senat. Urteil, 3 Dec. 1924, VIeA 188/24, *Reichsfinanzhof,* pp. 15–20.

5. TKA: A847/7, 4. Dec. 1924; Mannesmann Archive (MA): P 7 77 08 "Pachtvertrag," 28 Nov. 1924; MA: R 1 35 09, R 1 30 10 "August Thyssen-Hütte, Gewerkschaft, Abteilung Mülheimer Stahl- und Walzwerke," 15 Dec. 1924.

6. TKA: VSt/957 Späing to Linz and Vögler, 31 July 1933.

7. Useful surveys of this literature are Thomas Raiser, "The Theory of Enterprise Law in the Federal Republic of Germany," *The American Journal of Comparative Law,* 3 (1988), pp. 111–129. Richard Rosendorff, *Die rechtliche Organisation der Konzerne* (Berlin: Spaeth & Linde, 1927), pp. 34–112. Franz Bauer, *Das Organschaftsverhältnis im Steuerrecht als Problem der betriebswirtschaftlichen Steuerlehre,* 2, 46, ed. F. Schmidt, (Berlin, 1930). Heinrich Friedländer, *Konzernrecht: Das Recht der Betriebs- und Unternehmens-Zusammenfassungen* (Mannheim/Berlin/Leipzig: J. Bensheimer, 1927). Dr. Gablers, *Wirtschafts-Lexikon,* 2, 8, ed. R. Sellien and H. Sellien (Wiesbaden: Gabler, 1971), pp. 579–587. *Handwörterbuch der Betriebswirtschaft,* 3, ed. Hans Seischab and Karl Schwantag (Stuttgart: C. E. Poeschel, 1960). Norbert Horn, Hein Kötz, and Hans G. Leser, *German Private and Commercial Law: An Introduction* (Oxford: Clarendon University Press, 1982), esp. pp. 239–281. The decisions of the RFH can be found in *Reichsfinanzhof: Sammlung der Entscheidungen und Gutachten des Reichsfinanzhofs,* ed. Reichsfinanzhof (München, 1919ff.). The latter were the tax bibles of German business in the 1920s.

8. Rolf Hagenguth, *Die Anknüpfung der Kaufmannseigenschaft im internationalen Privatrecht* (München: Dissertation Universität München, 1981). For early cases in *Zeitschrifte für das gesammte Handelsrecht*

(Erlangen, 1858ff). This definition led to enormous legal difficulties in the 1860s. For instance, if a person sold wood to a neighbor could that person potentially be sued on the basis of German commercial code?

9. Horn/Kötz/Leser, *German Private and Commercial Law*, pp. 211–225 for basic commercial legal concepts, and pp. 243–251.

10. Horn/Kötz/Leser, *German Private and Commercial Law*, pp. 225–242.

11. For a comparative overview of the joint-stock companies legal development, see Norbert Horn, "Aktienrechtliche Unternehmensorganisation in der Hochindustrialisierung (1860–1920): Deutschland, England, Frankreich und die USA im Vergleich" in *Recht und Entwicklung der Grossunternehmen im 19. und frühen 20. Jahrhundert: Wirtschafts- sozial- und rechtshistorische Untersuchungen zur Industrialisierung in Deutschland, Frankreich, England und den USA*, ed. Norbert Horn and Jürgen Kocka (Göttingen: Vandenhoeck & Ruprecht, 1979), pp. 123–189.

12. *Dr. Gablers Wirtschafts-Lexikon*, p. 579. The collection of judgments by the Reich Finance Court regarding the *Organschaftstheorie* are listed under salaried employees *(Angestellte)* in the appendix.

13. I. Senat. Urteil, 11. November 1927, I A 75/27, *Reichsfinanzhof*, "Zur Frage, wann eine gewerblich tätige juristische Person, z.B. eine Gesellschaft m.b.H., steuerrechtlich der Selbständigkeit entbehrt, d.i. als blosses Glied (Organ) oder Angestellter eines anderen geschäftlichen Unternehmens gelten kann." This crucial phrasing can hardly be found in Friedländer's 1925 book on Konzern law. Bauer, *Das Organschaftsverhältnis*, p. 43, thought this November 1927 judgment to be the key decision of the 1920s because it clearly outlined the criteria needed to consider an independent firm an agent of another.

14. 1. Senat. Beschluss, 23. November 1925, I B 101/26, *Reichsfinanzhof*, pp. 46–50. The RFH referred to Rosendorff's interpretation, *Die rechtliche Organisation der Konzerne*, p. 109 in their decision.

15. Horn, *German Private and Commercial Law*, p. 280. Bauer, *Das Organschaftsverhältnis*, pp. 11, 54, 70, 74–78, 113–115. Rosendorff, *Organisation der Konzerne*, pp. 108–112.

16. TKA: A/1773 Späing to Däbritz, 3 Jan 1941, Späing. Theodore Wuppermann and Rheinstahl AG set up an IG, but failed to convince the RFH that the *Organschaftstheorie* applied. Gelsenkirchen (GBAG) also tried and failed see *Reichsfinanzhof*, 15, p. 136, and 18, pp. 75ff., respectively. Also Friedländer, *Konzernrecht*, pp. 371–373.

17. 1. Senat, Urteil 10 Oct. 1924, IA 71/24, *Reichsfinanzhof*, 14, pp. 303–310

18. 1. Senat, Beschluss, 4. März 1927 I B 3 /27, *Reichsfinanzhof*. The deci-

sion confirmed that two firms owned by a single individual did not make them a single, 'organic' company.

19. I. Senat. Beschluss, 23 Nov. 1926, I B 101/26, *Reichsfinanzhof,* 20: "Zur Frage, unter welchen Voraussetzungen eine juristische Person, z.B. die Gesellschaft m.b.H., als Angestellte—als blosses Organ—eines anderen geschäftlichen Unternehmens, z.B. einer Aktiengesellschaft, angesehen werden kann." Another federal state finance office *(Landesfinanzamt)* brought a similar case before the Senate two years only after the Thyssen fusion. The Senate affirmed that related firms did not have to be in the same trade, but had to be dependent and subordinate on the dominant firm.

20. TKA: A/599/6 Reports/Letters from 27 March 1928 to 13 Juni 1928 [and] 6 Aug. 1928 to 29 Sept. 1928; 3 June 1929; Härle, Späing, Dinkelbach, Rabes.

21. Raiser, "The Theory of Enterprise Law in the Federal Republic of Germany," pp. 111–119. Gareth P. Dyas and Heinz T. Thanheiser, *The Emerging European Enterprise: Strategy and Structure in French and German Industry* (Boulder: Westview Press, 1976), pp. 55, 100. The German state replaced the turnover tax in 1968 by a value-added tax, which decreased the need for complicated legal decisions about the *Organschaftstheorie.*

22. TKA: A/1802, 12 Jan. 1924, quoted in Alfred Reckendrees, *Das «Stahltrust»-Projekt: Die Gründung der Vereinigte Stahlwerke AG und ihre Unternehmensentwicklung 1926–1933/34* (München: C. H. Beck, 2000), p. 131.

23. Quoted from Wixforth, *Banken und Schwerindustrie,* p. 212. Cite from TKA: A/847/4 Brief von Fritz, "Hans und Julius Thyssen an alle Direktoren und Leiter der Thyssen-Unternehmen vom 15.1.1925."

24. Feldman, "Banks and Banking;" Harold James, "Banks and Bankers in the German Interwar Depression" in *Finance and Financiers in European History 1880–1960,* ed. Youssef Cassis (Cambridge: Cambridge University Press, 1992), pp. 263–281. Also the collection of essays in *Zur Geschichte der Unternehmensfinanzierung,* ed. Dietmar Petzina (Berlin: Duncker & Humblot, 1990).

25. William C. McNeil, *American Money and the Weimar Republic: Economics and Politics on the Eve of the Great Depression* (New York: Columbia University Press, 1986), pp. 70–77. The diary can be found in TKA: A/831/2 [Amerika-Anleihe] "Tagebuch," New York, 9 Jan. 1925, C. Rabes, W. Barth. McNeil attributes the negotiations largely to Barth, but there is no way that Thyssen would allow an out-of-work banker not associated with his firm to negotiate with full powers for a loan. Späing attributes the course of negotiations entirely to Carl Rabes.

26. Wixforth, *Banken und Schwerindustrie*, pp. 224–232. The following discussion rests on Wixforth's discussion and my own research.

27. TKA: A/1773 Späing to Däbritz, 3 Feb. 1941. Späing confirmed that the "interesting financial negotiations in New York were his own work."

28. The American emphasis on specific, formal financial figures and ratios can also be seen in one Japanese-American business culture encounter, see Tomoko Hamada, *American Enterprise in Japan* (Albany: State University of New York Press, 1991), esp. pp. 99–100, 129–130, 147–149, and 164–169. On Japanese use of accounting and financial figures and by contrast the American use, see Toshiro Hiromoto, "Another Hidden Edge—Japanese Management Accounting," *Japanese Business: Cultural Perspectives*, ed. Subhash Durlabhji and Norton E. Marks (Albany: State University of New York Press, 1993), pp. 345–352. My argument is not that one is better or worse in this context, but that the use of such statistics is embedded in specific organizational, institutional, and cultural contexts.

29. See Fritz Thyssen's letter to Reich Chancellor Wilhelm Marx, 24 May 1924, cited in Bähr, *Staatliche Schlichtung*, p. 113.

30. TKA: A/833/2 August Thyssen-Hütte 29 Dec. 1924, Price, Waterhouse Co.

31. TKA: A/833/2 [Prospect:] "$12,000,000 August Thyssen Iron and Steel Works, Five-Year 7% Sinking Fund Mortgage Gold Bonds of January 1, 1925, due January 1, 1930, Dillon, Read & Co.," Carl Rabes. MA: R 1 35 32 (5) "H. A. Brassert, Inc. Reporting-Consulting Report, Jan. 1, 1925," H. A. Brassert. Other reports used are in MA: R 1 35 32 (5) "Engineer-Report by Dr. Ing. Petersen" and "Engineer-Report by Geheimrat Professor A. Schwemann and Oberbergrat Dr. jur. Schlueter: Valuation of Thyssen Mining Property," 10 Oct., 1924, A. Schwemann, Dr. Schlueter.

32. Wixforth, *Banken und Schwerindustrie*, pp. 118–121.

33. TKA: A/831/1 "Appleton, Butler & Rice Cousellors at Law [to] Carl Rabes, Esq. Hamborn, Rhineland [concerning] Thyssen Bonds, January 13, 1925," Appleton, Butler & Rice: Lee J. Ferrin.

34. Related in Gerald D. Feldman, "Die Deutsche Bank vom Ersten Weltkrieg bis zur Weltwirtschaftskrise 1914–1933," *Die Deutsche Bank* ed. Lothar Gall, et al., pp. 231–232.

35. TKA: A/835/1. Price Waterhouse prepared a balance sheet for 1925 as well by August 1926 in preparation for a 1926 loan. For details on the 1926 loan negotiations, see Wixforth, *Banken und Schwerindustrie*, pp. 230–232. A more detailed description of differences between American and German accounting methods will be discussed in the

next chapter when Rabes and Dinkelbach set up the American-style accounting system of the VSt. TKA: A/1801 Däbritz Interview with Dinkelbach, Dec. 1942.

36. See Anthony Giddens, "Time and Social Organization" in *Social Theory and Modern Sociology* (Stanford: Stanford University Press, 1987), 140–165.

37. TKA: RSW 1 70 00/1/a/2 [Werksbesprechung], Essen, den 17 September 1925.

38. TKA: RSW 1 70 00/1/a/1 Rheinische Stahlwerke, Vereinigte Stahlwerke Aktiengesellschaft, Düsseldorf 1926–1944; 1. Vorverhandlungen, Gründung, Verträge und Satzungen ATH Direktion Rabes [an] Herrn Generaldirektor Dr. Hasslacher m/Br. Rheinische Stahlwerke, Dsbg.-Meiderich, Hamborn, d. 17 August 1925, Rabes.

39. Harvard Business School, Baker Library: GO: 301 B82 H. A. Brassert & Company (Consulting Engineers): *Report on Gelsenkirchener Bergwerks Aktiengesellschaft, Deutsch-Luxemburgische Bergwerks und Hütten Aktiengesellschaft and Bochumer Verein für Bergbau and Gussstahlfabrikation* (Dillon, Read & Co., December 15, 1925). Incidentally, Thyssen & Co. Machine Company supplied all of the Schalker Verein's gas compressors and turbines.

40. More detailed discussions on the Gold Mark Opening Balance Law can be found in Lindenlaub, *Maschinenbauunternehmen,* pp. 35–45; also Feldenkirchen, *Siemens,* pp. 324–327.

41. See Feldenkirchen, *Eisen- und Stahlindustrie,* pp. 299–301, Table 132a/b.

42. See Schroeder, *Growth of Major Steel Companies,* pp. 216–217, Appendix Tables 1–4.

43. TKA: A/835/1 Price Waterhouse, 31 Dec., 1925, Exhibit III, IV, V.

44. See Feldenkirchen, *Eisen- und Stahlindustrie,* pp. 301–2, Table 134a/b.

45. See Feldenkirchen, *Eisen- und Stahlindustrie,* Table 119a/b.

46. MA: R 1 35 32 (5) "H. A. Brassert, Inc. Reporting-Consulting-Operating Iron and Steel Industries 310 South Michigan Ave. Chicago (H. A. Brassert, President, E. L. Ives, Vice President, A. J. Boynton, Vice President) to Messrs. Dillon, Read & Co., Nassau and Cedar Streets, New York, New York," 1 January 1925, H. A. Brassert.

47. Paul Arnst, *August Thyssen und Sein Werk.* Most analysts followed Arnst's interpretation, which appeared one year before Thyssen died.

48. MA: R 1 35 06 Letter from Thyssen to Heinrich Thyssen-Bornemisza, 18 Jan. 1925. Uebbing, *Wege und Wegmarken,* pp. 82–84.

49. Reckendrees, *Das «Stahltrust»-Project,* pp. 171–180, 572.

50. Baumann, *August Thyssen und Schloss Landsberg,* p. 31.

51. TKA: A/1801 "Mitteilungen von Generaldirektor Dr. Ing. Albert Vögler, Dortmund betr. der Gründung der Vereinigten Stahlwerke vom 11.1.1943."

52. TKA: A/1727 Däbritz Interview with Dr. Härle and Dr. Küpper, 11 July 1938. TKA: A/3271 Däbritz Interview with Scheifhacken and Dinkelbach, 19 Feb. 1960.

53. TKA: A/1771 Däbritz Interview with Dr. Schöll, 6 Sept. 1954.

54. Quoted in Baumann, *Schloss Landsberg und Thyssen,* pp. 70–1.

55. Quoted in Baumann, *Schloss Landsberg und Thyssen,* p. 17.

56. MA: R 1 35 06 Letter from Thyssen to Heinrich Thyssen-Bornemisza, 18 Jan. 1925. TKA: A/1727: Däbritz Interview with Director Rabes, Schleifhaken, Murrmann, Dr. Späing, Dr. Rekate, Dr. Küpper, 5 Dec. 1938.

57. Quoted in Wegener, "Die Familie Thyssen," p. 46.

58. MA: R 1 35 29 (2) "Mitteilung der Direktion! An die Vereinigte Stahlwerke Akt.-Ges. gehen *nicht* über:," M.-R., den 24 March 1926, gez. Dr. Härle. At Thyssen's side since the early 1880s, Hermann Eumann too retired from service. The VSt turned Thyssen's office in Mülheim over for the exclusive use of his family or VSt board members. Härle withdrew from the VSt board with the sale of the Machine Company and became the trustee for Thyssen's estate.

59. TKA: A/1807 unpublished manuscript on Karl Härle by Walter Däbritz.

60. TKA: A/1771 Däbritz Interview with Dahl, 28 Jan. 1939.

61. MA: R 2 30 10 "Aktien-Gesellschaft Schalker Gruben- & Hütten-Verein, Gelsenkirchen, 30. Januar 1906, Vertraulich," Fol. 169–170, Thyssen & Co. [Aug.]

62. TKA: A/1801 Däbritz Interview with Dinkelbach, Dec. 1942. TKA: A/1774: Jacob an Thyssen, 12 Feb. 1919.

63. Conrad Matschoss, "August Thyssen und Sein Werk: Zur Erinnerung an die Begründung des ersten Werkes am 1. April 1871," *Zeitschrift des Vereines deutscher Ingenieure,* 14, (2 April 1921), p. 38.

64. Joseph Schumpeter, *Business Cycles: A Theoretical, Statistical, and Historical Analysis of the Capitalist Process* (New York, 1939), p. 1045, fn. 1.

III. The Vereinigte Stahlwerke, 1926–1936

1. Quoted in Alfred Reckendrees, "Die Vereinigte Stahlwerke A. G. 1926–1933 und 'das glänzende Beispiel Amerika,'" *Zeitschrift für Unternehmensgeschichte (ZUG),* 41, 2 (1996), pp. 159–186; quote from p. 159 from ThyssenKrupp Archive (TKA): VST/3049.

2. Alfred D. Chandler, Jr., *Scale and Scope: The Dynamics of Industrial Capitalism* (Cambridge, Mass,: Belknap Press of Harvard University Press, 1990), pp. 506–592. Wilfried Feldenkirchen, "Concentration in German Industry 1870–1939," *The Concentration Process in the Entrepreneurial Economy since the Late 19th Century* (ZUG, Beheift 55) ed. Hans Pohl (Stuttgart, 1988), 113–146. For a list of the mergers since the end of 1925 to July 1926, see Richard Rosendorff, *Die rechtliche Organisation der Konzerne* (Berlin: Spaeth & Linde, 1927), pp. 184–197.

3. Alfred Reckendrees, *Das «Stahltrust»-Projekt: Die Gründung der Vereinigte Stahlwerke AG und ihre Unternehmensentwicklung 1926–1933/34* (München: C. H. Beck, 2000), p. 584.

4. Mary Nolan, *Visions of Modernity: American Business and the Modernization of Germany* (New York: Oxford University Press, 1994); Volker R. Berghahn, *The Americanisation of West German Industry 1945–1973* (New York: Berg, 1986); Reiner Pommerin, ed., *The American Impact on Postwar Germany* (Providence, RI: Berghahn Books, 1997); Michael Ermarth, *America and the Shaping of German Society 1945–1955* (Providence, RI: Berg, 1993); Marie-Laure Djelic, *Exporting the American Model: The Postwar Transformation of European Business* (Oxford: Oxford University Press, 1998).

5. Reckendrees, *Das «Stahltrust»-Projekt,* p. 584, hints at an "autonomous development of production and organizational forms" that was similar to "American models."

6. My approach parallels that advocated in Jonathan Zeitlin and Gary Herrigel, eds., *Americanization and Its Limits: Reworking US Technology and Management in Post-War Europe and Japan* (Oxford: Oxford University Press, 2000); see especially the theoretical exposition in the introduction.

7. This final section by no means offers a comprehensive history of the VSt. Alfred Reckendrees has published an excellent reconstruction of the VSt. He focuses more on VSt's shareholder relations and strategic-financial decisions, while I focus more on the manner of organizing below Albert Vögler, not above him. I am more interested in organizational dynamics inside the VSt, to contrast VSt's organization with that of Thyssen's, and to question the idea of Americanization. Because of these different agendas, we stress different issues at different points in time. I do not claim that organizational or accounting issues were the main problem facing the VSt (financial issues were), but only that they caused significant difficulties that had financial consequences. I am uncovering and exploring this "autonomous development," or a line of continuity in German management practice, and outlining the ten-

sions involved in building a coherent corporate organization. My portrayal is more interpretive, more thematic, and more stylized than his.

13. The "Rationalization Company"

1. Reckendrees, *Das «Stahltrust»-Projekt,* pp. 250–259, 574.
2. Mannesmann Archive (MA): V1S. Das Spezial-Archiv der deutschen Wirtschaft, Vereinigte Stahlwerke Aktiengesellschaft, Düsseldorf 1927: Aufbau Werke, Zechen u. Rohstoffbetriebe Konzern- u. Gründer-Gesellschaften, Statistik & Finanzen (Berlin, 1927). Allgemeiner Führer, ed. Vereinigte Stahlwerke AG (Ausgabe 1930). *Coal, Iron and Steel: A Review of the Vereinigte Stahlwerke Aktiengesellschaft,* ed. Vereinigte Stahlwerke AG, Presseabteilung (Düsseldorf, 1937).
3. Paul Ufermann, *Der Deutsche Stahltrust* (Berlin: Verlagsgesellschaft des Allgemeinen Deutschen Gewerkschaftbundes, 1927). Ufermann emphasizes its alleged monopolistic tendencies. Also H. Apfelstedt, *Konzerne der deutschen Eisen- und Stahl-Industrie, Interessengebiete und Verflechtungen* (Berlin: R. & H. Hoppenstedt, 1933). *Die Vereinigte Stahlwerke AG: Ihr Aufbau und Ihre Bedeutung für Deutschland und die Weltwirtschaft,* ed. Schwarz, Goldschmidt & Co. (Berlin: R. & H. Hoppenstedt, August 19264).
4. Robert Brady, *The Rationalization Movement in German Industry: A Study in the Evolution of Economic Planning* (Berkeley: University of California, 1933). Brady argues that the VSt exemplified the German rationalization movement in the 1920s.
5. Gert von Klass, *Albert Vögler: Einer der Grossen des Ruhrreviers* (Tübingen: Rainer Wunderlich, 1957).
6. Wilhelm Treue und Helmut Uebbing, *Die Feuer Verlöschen Nie: August Thyssen-Hütte 1926–1966* (Düsseldorf/Wien: Econ-Verlag, 1969).
7. Gerhard Mollin, *Montankonzerne und 'Drittes Reich': Der Gegensatz zwischen Monopolindustrie und Befehlswirtschaft in der deutschen Rüstung und Expansion 1936–1944* (Göttingen: Vandenhoeck & Ruprecht, 1988). Mollin concentrates on the complicated and antagonistic relations between the VSt and the Reichswerke Hermann Göring, particularly after 1936. Gustav-Hermann Seebold, *Ein Stahlkonzern im Dritten Reich: Der Bochumer Verein 1927–1945* (Wuppertal: Hammer Verlag, 1981). Seebold provides a history of the VSt's Bochumer Verein subsidiary and concentrates on how 'nazified' it became.
8. Wilfried Feldenkirchen, "Big Business in Interwar Germany: Organizational Innovation at Vereinigte Stahlwerke, IG Farben, and Siemens," *Business History Review,* 61 (Autumn 1987), pp. 417–451.

9. Chandler, *Scale and Scope,* pp. 550–561.

10. Christian Kleinschmidt and Thomas Welskopp, "Zu viel 'Scale' zu wenig 'Scope': Eine Auseinandersetzung mit Alfred D. Chandlers Analyse der deutschen Eisen- und Stahlindustrie in der Zwischenkriegszeit," in *Jahrbuch für Wirtschaftsgeschichte,* 2 (1993), pp. 251–81.

11. Reckendrees, *Das «Stahltrust»-Project,* pp. 275, 589; for these assessments, see pp. 44–52.

12. This is Reckendrees' central argument, *Das «Stahltrust»-Project,* pp. 144–275, esp. 268–275.

13. MA: R 1 35 32 (6) Vögler Denkschrift. Reprinted in Gerald Feldman and Heidrun Homburg, *Industrie und Inflation: Studien und Dokumente zur Politik der deutschen Unternehmer 1916–1923* (Hamburg: Hoffmann & Campe, 1977), document 10, pp. 219–225. On the Rhein-Elbe-Schuckert-Union, see especially Gerald D. Feldman, *Iron and Steel in the German Inflation 1916–1923* (Princeton: Princeton, 1977), pp. 213–279, and esp. pp. 244–279 for a "balance sheet of vertical concentration." Gerald D. Feldman, *Hugo Stinnes: Biographie eines Industriellen 1870–1924* (München: C. H. Beck, 1998), pp. 634–687. Reckendrees, *Das >Stahltrust<-Project,* pp. 95–108. On Vögler, see Manfred Rasch, "Über Albert Vögler und sein Verhältnis zur Politik," in *Mitteilungsblatt des Instituts für Soziale Bewegungen: Forschungen und Forschungsberichte,* 28 (Essen: Klartext-Verlag, 2003), pp. 127–156.

14. ThyssenKrupp Archive (TKA): RSW 1 70 00/1/a/2 Vögler Denkschrift, 18 Sept. 1925.

15. TKA: RSW 1 70 00/1/b/1 Studiengesellschaft, 19 Feb. 1926. TKA: RSW 1 70 1, A/1801 Werksbesprechung, 23 July 1925.

16. TKA: A/1801 "Konzentrationspläne," 14 July 1919. Gerald D. Feldman and Heidrun Homburg, *Industrie und Inflation: Studien und Dokumente zur Politik der deutschen Unternehmer 1916–1923* (Hamburg: Hoffmann & Campe, 1977), document 10, 16 July 1919, pp. 225–230. Reckendrees, *Das «Stahltrust»-Project,* p. 121.

17. For an overview of the crisis, see William C. McNeil, *American Money and the Weimar Republic: Economics and Politics on the Eve of the Great Depression* (New York: Columbia, 1986), pp. 97–133. Also Reckendrees, *Das «Stahltrust»-Project,* pp. 135–144.

18. Gertrud G. Schroeder, *The Growth of Major Steel Companies, 1900–1950* (Baltimore: Johns Hopkins, 1953), pp. 216–219.

19. Reckendrees, *Das «Stahltrust»-Project,* p. 148, p. 392, Table 6.9, pp. 566–569.

20. See the excellent discussion in Bernd Weisbrod, *Schwerindustrie in der Weimarer Republik: Interessenpolitik zwischen Stabilisierung und Krise*

(Wuppertal: Hammer, 1978), pp. 31–51, 63–92. Also Eugen Schmalenbach, "Die Betriebswirtschaftslehre an der Schwelle der neuen Wirtschaftsverfassung," *Zeitschrift für Handelswissenschaftliche Forschung,* 5 (1928), pp. 241–251, which has been reprinted in *Deutsche Sozialgeschichte 1914–1945: Ein historisches Lesebuch,* ed. Werner Abelshauser, Anselm Faust and Dietmar Petzina (München: C. H. Beck, 1985), pp. 38–42. For an overview on the Borchardt debate on whether or not wages were too high during Weimar, see Ian Kershaw, ed., *Weimar: Why did German Democracy Fail?* (New York: St. Martin's Press, 1990). Borchardt's original contributions can be found in English in Knut Borchardt, *Perspectives on Modern German Economic History and Policy* (Cambridge: Cambridge University Press, 1991).

21. TKA: RSW 1 70 00/1/a/1, A/1801 Werksbesprechung, 11 July 1925; A/1801 Däbritz interview with Albert Vögler, 11 Jan. 1943; Däbritz Interview with Dinkelbach, 2 March 1943; Däbritz interview with Helmuth Poensgen, 8 April 1943. Reckendrees, *Das «Stahltrust»-Project,* pp. 149–156, 570.

22. TKA: RSW 1 70 1, A/1801 Werksbesprechung, 17 July 1925. See Reckendrees, *Das «Stahltrust»-Project,* pp. 161–199 for a richer discussion.

23. TKA: RSW 1 70 1, A/1801 Werksbesprechung, 23 July 1925.

24. TKA: RSW 1 70 00/1/a/1 Selbstkostenvergleichs von Schienen, 27 July 1925, Esser (Phoenix). See also "Grundsätze und Termine der Zahlenrevision," 26 Aug. 1925, Ernst Poensgen (Phoenix) chaired. Heinrich Dinkelbach represented Thyssen, Peter van Aubel for Phoenix. Reckendrees, *Das «Stahltrust»-Project,* p. 208, fn. 205 from TKA: A/608–4.

25. TKA: RSW 1 70 1, A/1801 Werksbesprechung, 14 Aug. 1925, 22 Aug. 1925; TKA: RSW 1 70 00/1/a/1ATH Letter to Hasslacher (Rheinstahl) 17 Aug. 1925, Rabes.

26. TKA: RSW 1 70 00/1/a/1 "(Vertraulich!), Berücksichtigung des Umsatzes in den Eisenfabrikaten bei der Schlüsselfestsetzung," 12 Sept. 1925, Fried. Krupp, Das Direktorium Kl./D.

27. TKA: RSW 1 70 00/1/a/2 Sitzung 16 Sept. 1925.

28. TKA: RSW 1 70 00/1/a/1,2 Letter to Hasslacher, Thyssen, Vögler, Funcke, Borbet, Klotzbach, 15 Sept. 1925, Fahrenhorst, pa. Poensgen (Phoenix) and 16 Sept. 1925, Fahrenhorst.

29. TKA: RSW 1 70 00/1/a/1 "Rechtsform des Zusammenschlusses," 11 Sept. 1925, Keil.

30. TKA: RSW 1 70 00/1/a/2 Werksbesprechung, 17 Sept. 1925.

31. TKA: RSW 1 70 00/1/a/2 [Vögler Denkschrift] 18 Sept. 1925, Vögler.

Reckendrees, *Das «Stahltrust»-Project,* p. 168–170 views the negotiations more positively at this juncture. He describes them as "clearly approaching their goal through mutual readiness to compromise," although numerous questions remained open. Still, he argues that Vögler's initiative was a "breakthrough" (p. 170).

32. Thyssen wrote Vögler personally. The letter, which has been lost, had been in the possession of Dinkelbach and Späing. Vögler, Dinkelbach, and Späing all independently confirm its existence. TKA: A/3271 Däbritz interview with Schiefhacken and Dinkelbach, 19 Feb. 1960; TKA: A/1801 Däbritz interview with Dinkelbach, Dec. 1942. Also von Klass, *Albert Vögler,* p. 143.

33. TKA: A/1801 Däbritz interview with Vögler, 11 Jan. 1943 and with Dinkelbach, 2 March 1943. Vögler argued to Däbritz that the term "refounding" *(Umgründung)* was wrong because the firm first had to go into operation before it could be reorganized. Dinkelbach argued that the idea for a decentralized reorganization did not yet exist—which is also not correct.

34. TKA: A/1801 Däbritz Interview with Helmuth Poensgen, 8 April 1943.

35. Reckendrees, *Das «Stahltrust»-Project,* pp. 251–274–275

36. TKA: RSW 1 70 00/1/a/3 19.12.1925. Reckendrees, *Das «Stahltrust»-Project,* pp. 171–180, 572. Feldman, *Iron and Steel,* pp. 460–461. Harald Wixforth, *Banken und Schwerindustrie in der Weimarer Republik* (Köln: Böhlau, 1990), pp. 101–114. Krupp possibly wanted to pursue its armament production in spite of its present "meagre" orders; based on a letter from Krupp to Vögler, 20 Sept. 1925, quoted in Weisbrod, *Schwerindustrie,* p. 97.

37. TKA: RSW 1 70 00/1/a/2 A. Vögler [und Dr. Fahrenhorst, Dr. Hasslacher], 10 Oct. 1925, Rabes; Herrn Dr. Fritz Thyssen, 11 Oct. 1925, Hasslacher; Dr. Hasslacher, 12 Oct. 1925, ATH Direktion: Fritz Thyssen; Werksbesprechung, 16 Oct. 1925, 21 Oct. 1925, 23 Oct. 1925. On the draft statutes, see TKA: A/596/2 (Gutachten) 2 Nov. 1925, Späing. Reckendrees, *Das «Stahltrust»-Project,* pp. 180–185.

38. Reckendrees, *Das «Stahltrust»-Project,* p. 284, fn. 30.

39. TKA: RSW 1 70 00/1/a/3 See the notes from the meetings of 10, 11, and 26 Nov.; 5 Dec. (both August Thyssen and Emil Kirdorf were present on this day); and 15 Dec. 1925, Baum, Hasslacher, Fahrenhorst.

40. Reckendrees, *Das «Stahltrust»-Project,* p. 187, 346–350. Horst A. Wessel, *Kontinuität und Wandel: 100 Jahre Mannesmann 1890–1990* (Düsseldorf: Droste, 1990), pp. 189–195. TKA: RSW 1 70 00/1/a/3 Werksbesprechung, 4 Nov. 1925.

41. Quote from Feldman, *Iron and Steel,* p. 456, fn. 18. On its complicated

position, see Reckendrees, *Das «Stahltrust»-Project,* pp. 189, 197, 239–244.

42. On the last minute maneuvering, see Reckendrees, *Das «Stahltrust»-Project,* pp. 194–199.

43. MA: R 1 40 35.1 1. Geschäftsjahr, 14 Jan.—30 Sept. 1926, 30 March 1927.

44. For more details, see Reckendrees, *Das «Stahltrust»-Project,* pp. 213–222.

45. TKA: RSW 1 70 00/1/a/3 Werksbesprechung 11 Nov. 1925, also Fahrenhorst to Hasslacher, 11 Dec. 1925.

46. TKA: RSW 1 70/00/1/b/2 "Besprechung" with Mayor Dr. Lehr and Dr. Odenkirchen with Fusban and Niemeyer, 13 March 1926, gez. Fusban.

47. Reckendrees, *Das «Stahltrust»-Project,* pp. 204, fn. 194.

48. TKA: VSt/1388 Materialian zu AVI-Abkommen und VSt. Ulrich Nocken, "Inter-Industrial Conflicts and Alliances as Exemplified by the AVI-Agreement," *Industrielles System und politische Entwicklung in der Weimarer Republik,* ed. Hans Mommsen, Dietmar Petzina, and Bernd Weisbrod (Düsseldorf: Droste, 1974), pp. 693–704. Weisbrod, *Schwerindustrie,* pp. 114–119. Reckendrees, *Das «Stahltrust»-Project,* pp. 259–262.

49. John Gillingham, *Coal, Steel, and the Rebirth of Europe, 1945–1955: The Germans and French from Ruhr Conflict to Economic Community* (Cambridge: Cambridge University Press, 1991), pp. 17–28. Ervin Hexner, *The International Steel Cartel* (Chapel Hill: University of North Carolina Press, 1943). George W. Stocking and Myron W. Watkins, *Cartels in Action: Case Studies in International Business Diplomacy* (New York: Twentieth Century Fund, 1947).

50. TKA: A/1801 Däbritz Interview with Vögler, 11 Jan. 1943, Däbritz Interview with Dinkelbach, 2 March 1943.

51. TKA: VSt/4148 Letter to Vögler, 1 June 1926, E. Poensgen. According to DEMAG's longtime director, Wolfgang Reuter, the perception was widespread that the VSt unduly favored DEMAG and that DEMAG did not guarantee its service to the same degree as it did for the VSt. DEMAG sales also tended to suffer from the perception that it would divulge company secrets or new plans to the VSt. In 1936, Reuter arranged a leveraged buyout of VSt shareholders in the interests of "liberating" DEMAG from the VSt and especially from the influence of Fritz Thyssen. In retrospect, Reuter felt that this "liberation" was his "greatest achievement." See TKA: VSt/2697, "Haupt-Buchhaltung, Betrifft: Demag A. G.," 29 Jan. 1927, Haupt-Revisions: L . . .; TKA: A/

1801 "Aus Geschäfts- und Betriebsberichten;" VSt/4148 Letter to Dinkelbach, "Beteiligung bei der Demag bezw. Ausnutzung des Selbstverbrauchrechts," 23 Dec 1927, Sekr. Dir. Sch. For public perceptions of the VSt/DEMAG relationship, see Ufermann, *Stahltrust,* who argues that the VSt tried to turn the DEMAG into an in-house machine supplier. For a synopsis of the history of DEMAG, see Wessel, *Kontinuität und Wandel,* pp. 440–456. TKA: A/1801 Aus den persönlichen Erinnerungen Wolfgang Reuter's. TKA: VSt/4148 Mietvertrag between the VSt Thyssen-Mülheim and Demag, 8 May 1928, Demag AG: gez. Stutz, Meyer; VSt AG: gez. Wallmann, ppa Brökelschen. Reckendrees, *Das «Stahltrust»-Project,* pp. 336–339. The agreement stipulated that the DEMAG would supply the bulk of the machinery for the VSt and the VSt would supply all foundry supplies to DEMAG.

52. Thomas K. McCraw and Forest Reinhardt, "Losing to Win: U.S. Steel's Pricing, Investment Decisions, and Market Share, 1901–1938, *Journal of Economic History* (Sept. 1989), pp. 593–619.

53. Reckendrees, *Das «Stahltrust»-Project,* pp. 123–129, 271, 416–422.

54. TKA: RSW 1 70 00/1/a/2 Letter to Hasslacher, 2 Oct. 1925, Reichsminister: H.v. Raumer; Letters to v. Raumer, and Reichsfinanzminister Dr. v. Schlieben, 24 Oct. 1925, Hasslacher. Quoted in Feldman, *Iron and Steel,* pp. 457–459.

55. TKA: RSW 1 70 00/1/a/1 Letter to von Raumer, 14 Sept. 1925, Vögler.

56. TKA: RSW 1 70 00/1/a/1 [Draft] Letter to Reichsfinanzminister, 12 Nov. 1925. The letter was actually sent on 27 Nov. 1925.

57. *Die Neuordnung der Eisen- und Stahlindustrie im Gebiet der Bundesrepublik Deutschland: Ein Bericht der Stahltreuhändervereinigung* (München: C. H. Beck, 1954), pp. 20–21.

58. Reckendrees, *Das «Stahltrust»-Project,* pp. 222–238, 272, 573–574. For the VSt's relationship to the SPD and unions, pp. 262–267. Reckendrees underestimates the importance of taxes for the founding of the VSt, calling them "insignificant" *(belanglos)* (p. 574) or of "no influence on the form of merger" (p. 272), while simultaneously maintaining that these laws represented a significant change in the "institutional framework." Rewriting these tax laws, however, involved important issues of corporate strategy. The VSt engaged in a sort of legal entrepreneurialism to change them. The tax issue also broached VSt industry-political relations to individual companies, industry associations, municipalities, and the state. The financial sum was less important than these other interrelated dimensions.

59. McCraw and Reinhardt, "Losing to Win." Chandler, *Scale and Scope,*

pp. 131–140. For Chandler, U.S. Steel provides the best example of a company that *failed* to realize its potential economies of scale and scope. Christian Kleinschmidt and Thomas Welskopp, "Zu viel 'Scale' zu wenig 'Scope:' Eine Auseinandersetzung mit Alfred D. Chandlers analyse der deutschen Eisen- und Stahlindustrie in der Zwischenkriegszeit," *Jahrbuch für Wirtschaftsgeschichte*, 2 (1993), p. 290, mistakenly argue that Chandler views U.S. Steel as the prototype of the successful large enterprise.

60. RSW 1 70 00/1/a/2 [Werksbesprechung], 17 Sept. 1925.

61. See for example Siegried Tschierschky, *Kartell und Trust: Vergleichende Untersuchungen über deren Wesen und Bedeutung* (Göttingen: Vandenhoeck & Ruprecht, 1903), pp. 92–93.

62. Wixforth, *Banken und Schwerindustrie*, pp. 453–461, 493–497 for an overview of the course of the negotiations with an eye toward its banking relations. Also Reckendrees, *Das «Stahltrust»-Project*, pp. 250–259, 364–373, 430–432 for more financial details. Wilfried Feldenkirchen, "Concentration in German Industry 1870–1939," *The Concentration Process in the Entrepreneurial Economy since the Late 19th Century* (ZUG, Beheift 55) ed. Hans Pohl (Stuttgart, 1988), 113–146 and "Big Business" implies that bankers drove on the formation of the VSt with the phrase "the bankers' view prevailed." German banks tended to remain interested spectators with some influence on the course of the negotiations. For bond details, see especially MA: R 5 35 28 (1) Handbuch, Brassertsche Bewertungszahlen) and R 5 51 01 (1) "Prospekt. . ." This "reference work" is a 250-page overview of the loan conditions and provides one of the best descriptions of the VSt in 1926, in both English and German. The VSt issued three series of bonds.

63. Reckendrees, *Das «Stahltrust»-Project*, pp. 275, 413, 573, 589.

64. Reckendrees, *Das «Stahltrust»-Project*, p. 367; on profitability issues, pp. 422–433.

65. Feldenkirchen, "Concentration," pp. 128–129, Graph 4. Chandler, *Scale and Scope*, p. 138, Table 11. On U.S. Steel's problems, see Kenneth Warren, *Big Steel: The First Century of the United States Steel Corporation 1901–2001* (Pittsburgh: University of Pittsburgh Press, 2001), pp. 86–97, 123–131.

66. MA: R 1 40 35.1 First and second VSt Geschäftsberichte 30 Sept. 1926, 30 Sept. 1927.

67. Reckendrees offers a richer discussion, *Das «Stahltrust»-Project*, pp. 244–250, 330–336, 364–373.

68. Thomas Welskopp, *Arbeit und Macht im Hüttenwerk: Arbeits- und industrielle Beziehungen in der deutschen und amerikanischen Eisen- und*

Stahlindustrie von den 1860er bis zu den 1930er Jahren (Bonn: J. H. W. Dietz, 1994), pp. 468, Table 19. Kleinschmidt/Welskopp, "Zu viel 'Scale' zu wenig 'Scope,'" Table 4. Reckendrees, *Das «Stahltrust»-Project*, p. 392, Table 6.9. Bela Gold, William S. Peirce, Gerhard Rosegger, and Mark Perlman, *Technological Progress and Industrial Leadership* (Lexington, Mass.: LexingtonBooks, 1984), pp. 579–592, esp. Tables 21–1, Figures 21–1, 21–2. McCraw and Reinhardt, "Losing to Win." Chandler, *Scale and Scope*, pp. 131–140. Warren, *Big Steel*, pp. 125–128.

69. MA: R 1 40 35.1 VSt 2. Geschäftsbericht. 30 Sept. 1927. Kleinschmidt/ Welskopp, "Zu viel "Scale" zu wenig "Scope," pp. 259–267. Reckendrees, *Das «Stahltrust»-Project*, pp. 206–207, 377–378, Tables 4.6, 6.6.

70. Weisbrod, *Schwerindustrie*, pp. 52–62. Nolan, *Visions of Modernity*, pp. 73, 139–140, 145–146. Harold James, *The German Slump: Politics and Economics 1924–1936* (Oxford: Clarendon, 1986), pp. 146–161.

71. Chandler, *Scale and Scope*, p. 138, also Table 11.

72. Reckendrees, *Das «Stahltrust»-Project*, pp. 374–378, Table 6.5, p. 388.

73. TKA: RSW 1 70/00/1/b/2 See Kalle's "Bericht über Röhrenwerke, Bandeisen- und Kaltwalzwerke," 6 March 1926; "Besprechung des Technischen Ausschusses . . .," 11 March 1926. MA: R 1 35 26 (2) "An die Hauptverwaltung des 'Phönix', Wallmann. TKA: RSW 1 70/00/1/ b/2 Besprechung des Technischen Ausschusses . . .," 11 March 1926. MA: R 1 41 10 "Zum Bericht über die Auswirkung des Zusammenschlusses auf die Betriebe des Dezernates Wallmann" [no date, about July 1926]. MA: R 1 35 32 (6) Letter to Direktor Esser and Klinkenberg 15 May 1926, Wallmann.

74. Reckendrees, *Das «Stahltrust»-Project*, pp. 376.

75. TKA: RSW 1 70 1 Werksbesprechung, 23 July 1925

76. TKA: RSW 1 70/00/1/b/2 Studiengesellschaft, Rundschreiben, 1 March 1926. MA: R 1 40 35.1 First VSt Geschäftsbericht bis 30 Sept. 1926.

77. Treue/Uebbing, *Feuer Verlöschen Nie*, pp. 26–36. MA: R 1 40 35. First VSt Geschäftsbericht bis 30 Sept. 1926. MA: R 5 35 28 (1) Handbuch, Brassertsche Bewertungszahlen, p. 203.

78. Brady, *Rationalization*, p. 115

79. Reckendrees, *Das «Stahltrust»-Project*, pp. 397–403.

80. Reckendrees, *Das «Stahltrust»-Project*, p. 378.

81. Reckendrees, *Das «Stahltrust»-Project*, pp. 379–388, esp. Table 6.7.

82. Reckendrees, *Das «Stahltrust»-Project*, pp. 388–396, esp. Table 6.7. Kleinschmidt/Welskopp, "Zu viel 'Scale' zu wenig 'Scope,'" Tables 3–4 wrongly claim that capacity expanded.

83. Feldman, *Iron and Steel*, p. 460. Brady, *Rationalization Movement in German Industry*, pp. 103–138. James, *The German Slump*, pp. 146–152. James relies on Seebold, *Ein Stahlkonzern im Dritten Reich*. The Bochum plant concentrated on specialty steels and castings so that it is probably not the best indicator.

84. Reckendrees, *Das «Stahltrust»-Project*, p. 392, Table 6.9.

85. Reckendrees, *Das «Stahltrust»-Project*, pp. 413–422.

86. Kleinschmidt/Welskopp, "Zu viel 'Scale' zu wenig 'Scope'," pp. 280–283.

87. Weisbrod, *Schwerindustrie*, pp. 114–119. Reckendrees, *Das «Stahltrust»-Project*, pp. 422–435, quote from p. 586.

88. Feldenkirchen, "Big Business in Interwar Germany," p. 426. *Die Neuordnung der Eisen- und Stahlindustrie*, pp. 20–21. Kleinschmidt/Welskopp, "Zu viel "Scale" zu wenig "Scope," pp. 273–275.

89. *Die Neuordnung der Eisen- und Stahlindustrie*, pp. 15–26, 528–539, 567–570; quote from p. 568.

90. Reckendrees, *Das «Stahltrust»-Project*, pp. 403–413.

14. Contested Terrain

1. Reckendrees, *Das «Stahltrust»-Projekt*, pp. 578–584. We both agree that the VSt introduced an "innovative corporate organization," but Reckendrees refers mainly to the multidivisional structure after 1933.

2. Mannesmann Archive (MA): R 1 35 32 (4) "Richtlinien für die Revisions-Abteilung," 13 March 1926, Rabes, Dinkelbach.

3. MA: R 1 35 32 (2) "Richtlinien für die Buchhaltung," 18 March 1926, Rabes, Schirner, Osterloh, Bruss.

4. Peter van Aubel, *Selbstkostenrechnung in Walzwerken und Hütten* ed. Eugen Schmalenbach (Leipzig: G. A. Gloeckner, 1926). Eugen Schmalenbach, *Dynamische Bilanz* (Köln und Opladen: Westdeutscher, (1919) 1962). The best introduction to Schmalenbach's thinking and career is Max Kruk, Erich Potthoff, and Günter Sieben, *Eugen Schmalenbach: Der Mann—Sein Werk—Die Wirkung*, ed. Walter Cordes im Auftrag der Schmalenbach Stiftung (Stuttgart: Fachverlag für Wirtschafts- und Steuerrecht Schäffer GmbH & Co., 1984). In English, David A. R. Forrester, *Schmalenbach and After: A Study of the Evolution of German Business Economics* (Glasgow: Strathclyde Convergencies, 1977). A brief overview can be found by Erich Potthoff and Günter Sieben, "Eugen Schmalenbach (1873–1955)," *Twentieth-Century Accounting Thinkers*, ed. John Richard Edwards (London: Routledge, 1994), pp. 79–94.

5. Feldenkirchen, "Big Business," p. 426.

6. Reckendrees, *Das «Stahltrust»-Projekt,* p. 578.

7. Reckendrees, *Das «Stahltrust»-Projekt,* pp. 278–291, quote from p. 293. Reckendrees' major achievement is to clearly divulge these relations.

8. ThyssenKrupp Archive (TKA): A/596/2 Gutachten, 2 Nov. 1925, Der Justitiar, [Späing]; MA: R 1 35 32, R 1 50 00.2 "Gesellschaftsvertrag"; TKA: A/5506 Personal-Angelegenheiten, 28 May 1926, Vögler, Poensgen.

9. Reckendrees, *Das «Stahltrust»-Projekt,* pp. 291–297 has examples how this commission worked.

10. TKA: NDI/1 Letter from Rudolf Rabes to Heinrich Dinkelbach, 29 Aug. 1945.

11. For Poensgen's activities, see Weisbrod, *Schwerindustrie,* pp. 173–179.

12. TKA: A/5526 VSt Protokoll, 12 May 1926.

13. TKA: A/5740-A/5744. Good examples of the wide-ranging assortment of points discussed can be found in the Steel Works Committee meetings from 3 Feb. 1928, 18 Sept. 1928, and 19 Nov. 1929. After November 1929, the VSt classified the protocols as confidential. See also Reckendrees, *Das «Stahltrust»-Projekt,* pp. 298–302. Reckendrees and I differ in our assessment on the role of these central committees. In the dissertation, I went so far as to suggest that every type of decision had to have the approval of everyone on the committee (implying a consensus), but Reckendrees views these forums as a place where Vögler announced his "presidial" decisions. Why are all those committees needed inside the VSt if decision-making was so top-down? How does this assessment square with Reckendrees' portrayal of powerfully independent plant directors? Surely they were not silent on important issues affecting their operations, such as new investments and transfer pricing, which Reckendrees notes. Also, one of the main objectives of the 1933 reorganization was to reduce the size of the central executive boards, so those boards must have caused problems. In part, this difference in interpretation derives from the style of the protocols. The protocols merely relate the issues discussed, not the debates. For instance, see the frustrating documentation about an important "long discussion" on 10 October 1933 about the "Aryanization question" in TKA: VSt/1573. That is the extent of the protocol. My point is that issues and decisions were *discussed,* not just announced. If decision-making was so top-down, the steel works and mining committees would not have been so important. They would have been made irrelevant like the administrative committee. There exists a clear tension be-

tween Reckendrees' description of the VSt as "top-down" (p. 302) from the "triumvirate" (p. 293) of Flick, Thyssen, and Vögler, and as having an organization based on "management by committee" and the fiercely independent, "decentralized" decision-making of plant directors. The "triumvirate" clearly carried more weight at the strategic-financial level where the VSt acted as a unitary actor on the market, but less so inside the organization and underneath Vögler. Reckendrees argues that "enterprise management acted as loyal agent of the private owners" and views Vögler as the decisive "center of power" (p. 575) in the VSt executive board. True enough. Yet the conclusion reduces Vögler to a loyal "asset trustee" of Fritz Thyssen and Friedrich Flick, although Vögler would often rather not pay out dividends and build reserves. As trustees, "conflicts were therefore the exception" (p. 575). This is surprising given the welter of claims and objectives of the VSt, which he overtaxed it, *even if* Vögler viewed himself as a loyal trustee. Reckendrees' own evidence hints at a misalignment of agent-owner interests and internal managerial tensions.

14. For examples, see VSt relations with Mülheim MA: R 2 41 81 (1–2) and R 2 41 00 (2) "Beitragszahlung an Vereine" 4 Jan. 1926, VSt Hauptstelle Generalsekretariat. Also MA: R 1 40 07 [Rundschreiben] Vorschüsse und Darlehn an Angestellte, 21 Dec. 1926, gez. Poensgen, gez. Possehl.

15. For more detail, see Reckendrees, *Das «Stahltrust»-Projekt,* pp. 303–328. In the dissertation, I overemphasized the purity of this staff-line distinction. Reckendrees stresses the continuing level of decentralization of staff functions in the original plants, but I still think this staff-line distinction as a general principle holds true. Finance, accounting, purchasing, and most importantly, sales of cartelized steel goods were centralized at Düsseldorf. The sale of cartelized goods for steel made up a good portion of VSt sales; the administrative staff for coal remained in Essen. For this reason, Reckendrees views the 1933 reorganization primarily as a centralization or consolidation into groups.

16. "Konzern-Aufbau der Vereinigten Stahlwerke," *Zeitschrift für Organisation,* 4, 4 (24 Feb. 1930), pp. 91–92. Feldenkirchen, "Big Business," p. 424. TKA: A/608/7 "Vorschläge für die Einrichtung des Einkaufs der Vereinigte Stahlwerke," 20 March 1926; also "Niederschrift," 20 March 1926, Rabes.

17. MA: R 1 40 06 VSt. For examples, see the descriptive annual reports from Thyssen-Mülheim. MA: R 1 40 40–46 VSt "Tagesberichte," 31 May 1926—31 June 1933, Vertraulich. TKA: A/9415 Herrn Direktor Schuh, 30 Jan. 1928, Steuerstatistik VSt. Hauptstelle.

18. TKA: A/5529–30 Betrifft: Rundschreiben, 9 June 1926, Poensgen, Dr. Poensgen. MA: R 5 40 08 about the monthly balance reports for plants. Also Reckendrees, *Das «Stahltrust»-Projekt,* p. 301, fn. 89.

19. MA: R 2 41 83, R 1 40 56 VSt Presseabteilung [Zeitungsausschnitte] 1927–1942. This sad example can be found in the *Metallarbeiter-Zeitung,* 50, 10 Dec. 1932 (MA: R 1 40 56). Susanne Hilger, *Sozialpolitik und Organisation: Formen betrieblicher Sozialpolitik in der rheinisch-westf-älischen Eisen- und Stahlindustrie seit der Mitte des 19. Jahrhunderts bis 1933* (Stuttgart: F. Steiner, 1996), pp. 345–351.

20. TKA: VSt/4 Sozialpolitische Abteilung 1926–1945, esp. 6 Dec. 1926, 19 Aug. 1927, 11 July 1928, 9 Feb. 1929, 28 March 1929, 25 April 1929, and 11 Nov. 1929, 30 Sept. 1930. MA: R 1 40 47.2–3 Sozialpolitischer Bericht, 9–37, Dr. Bretschneider.

21. MA: R 1 40 07 VSt. "Anschriftenverzeichnis," 1 Dec. 1926, gez. Poensgen, gez. i.V. Weidemann. Peter Hayes, *Industry and Ideology: IG Farben in the Nazi Era* (Cambridge: Cambridge 1987), pp. 29–31.

22. Manfred Rasch, "Industrieforschung im Dritten Reich: Die Kohle- und Eisenforschung GmbH der Vereinigte Stahlwerke AG 1934–1947: Enstehung—Entwicklung—Ende," *Die Eisen- und Stahlindustrie im Dortmunder Raum,* ed. Ottfried Dascher and Christian Kleinschmidt (Dortmund: Gesellschaft für Westfälische Wirtschaftsgeschichte, 1992), pp. 375–400.

23. Reckendrees, *Das «Stahltrust»-Projekt,* pp. 311–312.

24. See von Klass, *Albert Vögler,* pp. 290–305, and Nolan, *Visions of Modernity,* pp. 30–82, 179–205; also see the literature citations of same, pp. 312–313. John Gillingham, "The Deproletarianization of German Society: Vocational Training in the Third Reich," *Journal of Social History,* 9, 3 (1986), pp. 423–432.

25. Reckendrees, *Das «Stahltrust»-Projekt,* p. 315.

26. Reckendrees, *Das «Stahltrust»-Projekt,* pp. 309–310, 315–16, 380–381, quote from p. 381. Given such evidence for powerful plant directors, it is surprising that Reckendrees concludes that conflicts were "exceptional" (p. 575).

27. MA: R 1 40 35.1 VSt annual report 14 Jan.–30 Sept. 1926.

28. TKA: A.1801 Däbritz Interview with Helmuth Poensgen, 8 April 1943.

29. TKA: A/1801 Däbritz Interview with Heinrich Dinkelbach, Dec. 1942.

30. MA: R 5 40 08 (16), R 5 40 14 (14), and R 5 40 23 (4) for examples.

31. Konrad Mellerowicz and Jörg Bankmann, eds., *Wirtschaft und Wirt-schaftsprüfung* (Stuttgart: C.E. Poeschel Verlag, 1966), p. 5.

32. MA: R 1 35 32 (4) "Richtlinien für die Revisions-Abteilung," 13 March 1926, Rabes, Dinkelbach.

33. TKA: PA (Presse) Kluitmann: Errinerung an Heinrich Dinkelbach. Kluitmann quoted a report from the department "H. R., Organisation', 1.10.1928."

34. TKA: PA (Presse) Kluitmann: Erinnerung an Heinrich Dinkelbach

35. MA: R 1 40 33 "An alle Geschäftsbuchhaltungen, An alle Kostenabteilungen," 20 Oct. 1930, ppa Dinkelbach, ppa. [?]. MA: R 1 35 32 (3) Betr. Buchhaltung der Vereinigten Stahlwerk, 24 April 1926, ppa. Dinkelbach, p. 18.

36. MA: R 5 40 01–03, 08 (14), 10, 16 (1), 18–19, 22–23, 25 (13), 31–32, 37–38, 43 (15), 44, 50, 53. MA: R 1 40 32 VSt Hollerithabteilung, H. R. Organisation, Betreff: Lochkartenorganisation, Sitzung, 19 April 1928, ppa Dinkelbach, van Aubel. This document provides a state of the punchcard process in the VSt to date. Herrn Maxrath, Sitzung, Betrifft: Kunden-Schlüsselung am 23 June 1927, 25 June 1927, ppa Dinkelbach, i.V. Backhaus. "Firmenschlüssel," May 1928, Hollerithabteilung. MA: R 1 40 07 "Herrn Krum, Betreff Umdruckverfahren und lochkartenmässige Bearbeitung der Düsseldorfer Abrechnungsstellen," 24 Sept. 1929, Hauptrevision, Organisation: Kluitmann. MA: R 1 40 33 "Rundschreiben Nr. 100," Betreff: Werkskontenplan 1930, 14 Nov. 1930, Organisation: ppa Dinkelbach, ppa [?].

37. Reckendrees, *Das «Stahltrust»-Projekt,* p. 456, fn. 61.

38. J. Hausen, "Das moderne Büro. Technische Neuerungen von der 6. Internationalen Büroausstellung zu Berlin," *Das Werk: Monatschrift der 'Vereinigte Stahlwerke Aktiengesellschaft,* 8, 10 (1934), 440–443. For a cultural history, see Ludwig Gorm, "Das Büro: Einkulturhistorische Studie," pp. 435–439 in the same volume. MA: R 2 40 00 (1) for the problems of transferring white-collar employees to Düsseldorf.

39. Introducing punchcard operations occupied a great deal of space in industry journals, see Dr. Ing. Schäfer, "Normung in der Bürotechnik," *Technik und Wirtschaft,* 20, 1 (January 1927), pp. 4–7 (and an accompanying article by Walter Gropius); Georg Brandl, "Grundsätze für Einführung des Lochkartenverfahrens im industriellen Rechnungswesen," *Technik und Wirtschaft,* 20, 10 (October 1927), pp. 283–287.

40. TKA: PA (Presse) Kluitmann: Errinerung an Heinrich Dinkelbach. TKA VSt/5989 Leo Kluitmann, "Das Rechnungswesen," *Eisenhüttenwesen (betriebswirtschaftlich)* (unpublished manuscript), ca. 1931–32.

41. MA: R 5 40 53 (1) Berichte 1927–1933.

42. "Ein Jahr ZfürO," ZfO, 2, 1 (15 Jan. 1928), pp. 1–2. The ZfO reprinted van Aubel's comments from *Das Werk,* 9, 1927. The survey of organiza-

tions began in 1929. The VSt remained close to *ZfO* until the Nazis "synchronized" it and took an expressly anti-VSt stance. See Bernard Köhler, "Nationalsozialistische Rationalisierung," *ZfO*, 10, 5 (25 May 1936), pp. 173–177. Köhler argued that the founding of the VSt and IG Farben were mistakes because technical improvements were financed with foreign money. In his view, the rationalization wave financed with loans simply earned profits for foreign financial houses at the cost of German workers.

43. TKA: FWH-200–30-A/2 Die Volksparole, 48, 17 February 1934: "Organisationsfragen der Wirtschaft: Ein beachtenswerter Vortrag von Direktor Dinkelbach;" "Grundsätze und Gedanken der Wirtschafts-organisation: Organisationsfragen—Zwei Vorträge," in *Düsseldorfer Tageblatt*, 52, 22 Feb. 1934; "Betriebliche Organisation" in *Berliner Börsen-Zeitung*, 556, 26 Nov. 1936.

44. Charles Perrow, *Complex Organizations: A Critical Essay* (New York: McGraw-Hill, 1986), pp. 128–131.

45. van Aubel, *Selbstkostenrechnung in Walzwerken und Hütten*. See A. Ackermann, "Betriebsvergleich nach Kostenarten oder nach Kosten-stellen?" *Betriebswirtschaftliche Rundschau*, 5 (1928), pp. 191–192 and the debates therein.

46. See MA: R 1 35 32 (2) Eisenwerk & Verzinkerei, Blechwalzwerk, Einkauf, 1 April 1926, [none].

47. MA: R 1 35 32 (2) "Richtlinien für die Buchhaltung," 18 March 1926, Rabes, Schirner, Osterloh, Bruss.

48. MA: R 1 35 32 (4) "Richtlinien für die Revisions-Abteilung," 13 March 1926, Rabes, Dinkelbach.

49. See MA: R 5 40 08–09 for the amount of work needed to prepare monthly balance sheets.

50. TKA: RSW 1 70/00/1/b/1 Studiengesellschaft Kostenausschuss, 28 u. 29 Sitzung, 23 Feb. 1926; MA: R 1 35 32 (3) "Richtlinien für die Buchhaltung," 31 March 1926, p. 13, §1o-q.

51. TKA: RSW 1 70/00/1/b/1 Studiengesellschaft Kostenausschuss, 28 u. 29 Sitzung, 23 Feb. 1926; MA: R 1 35 32 (3) Richtlinien für die Buchhaltung: Entwurf der Einzelvorschriften für die Betriebsbuchhal-tung, 31 March 1926, p. 13, §1o-q.

52. MA: R 1 35 32 (3) Buchhaltung der Vereinigten Stahlwerke, 24 April 1926, ppa. Dinkelbach.

53. MA: R 1 35 32 (3) Rundschreiben 1 der Hauptkostenabteilung, Bilanzpreise, Werksumlage, Herstellselbstkosten, gez. Schirner, ppa. Osterloh. MA: R 1 35 32 (3) Buchhaltung der Vereinigten Stahlwerke, 24 April 1926, ppa. Dinkelbach.

54. "Industrielles Rechnungswesen in den Vereinigten Staaten von Amerika und Deutschland," *Technik und Wirtschaft* ed. Verein deutscher Ingenieure, 20, 10 (October 1927), pp. 289–290. Kurt Schmaltz, *Bilanz- und Betriebsanalyse in Amerika* (Stuttgart: C. E. Poeschel, 1927).

55. Reckendrees, *Das «Stahltrust»-Project*, pp. 380–381.

56. MA: R 1 35 32 (3) "Rundschreiben 1: Abänderung der Betriebs-buchhaltungsvorschrift, Bilanzpreise, Werksumlage, Herstellselbst-kosten," gez. Schirner, ppa. Osterloh. MA: R 1 35 32 (3) Buchhaltung, 24 April 1926, ppa. Dinkelbach. Treue/Uebbing, *Feuer Verlöschen Nie*, pp. 26–28.

57. Lutz Hatzfeld, "50 Jahre Fretz-Moon-Anlage in Mülheim (Ruhr), Jubiläum bei den Mannesmannröhren-Werken AG," *Stahl und Eisen*, 8 (5 April 1982), p. 134. Rudolf Traut provides a concise overview of the process in MA: R 4 53 42 (4) "Das Fretz-Moon-Verfahren," 28 June 1933.

58. MA: R 4 20 30 Korrespondenz Dr. Inden und E. Poensgen betreffs Fretz-Moon-Verfahren der Fretz Moon Tube Co., Jan. 1929—May 1930, Inden, Poensgen.

59. MA: R 6 40 51 (4) "Chronologische Entwicklung der Fretz-Moon Angelegenheit," 17 May 1930, Tr[aut]. The chronology, however, should be used with care. Traut states that Wallmann received the report from Flaccus on 19 February 1929. Wallmann replied positively two days later. Yet from the original correspondence between Inden and Poensgen, Poensgen sent the reports directly to the pipe committee. MA: R 6 40 51 (2) "Herrn Dir. Dr. Flaccus," 21 Feb. 1929, Wallmann.

60. MA: R 6 40 51 (2) "Aktennotiz zu dem Bericht des Herrn Dr. Inden über das kontinuierliche Stumpfschweissverfahren Fretz-Moon, Tr/Ba," 1 March 1929, [Traut]; Herrn Dir. Dr. Flaccus, 21 Feb. 1929, Wallmann; "Aktennotiz: Betr. Stumpfgeschweisste Gasrohre Moon'sches Verfahren," 28 Feb. 1930, Nachtrag zur . . . , 14 March 1930, 2. Nachtrag zur 21 March 30 [Traut].

61. MA: R 6 40 51 (2) Bericht, 6 July 1929, Esser and "Aktennotiz: Betr. Stumpfgeschweisste Gasrohre Moon'sches Verfahren," 25 July 1929, Traut.

62. MA: R 4 20 30 A. Brassert & Co. to Vögler, 14 Dec. 1929.

63. MA: R 6 40 5 (2) "Denkschrift zur Würdigung des Fretz-Moon-Verfahrens für die Herstellung stumpfgeschweisster Gasrohre," 28 Feb. 1930, Tr[aut].

64. MA: R 6 40 51 (3) Herrn Ernst Poensgen, 17 March 1930, Sekretariat:

Esser; Ernst Poensgen, 24 March 1930, Direktion: [Wallmann, Traut]; Dr. E. Poensgen Betr. *Fretz-Moon-Verfahren,* 25 March 1930, gez. Wiegand [Hauptkostenstelle VSt]. Herrn Ernst Poensgen, 24 March 1930, Flaccus; Herrn Ernst Poensgen, Fretz-Moon-Verfahren, 24 March 1930, Direktion: [Wallmann, Traut]; "Herrn Direktor Dr. E. Poensgen, Betr. Fretz-Moon-Verfahren," 25 March 1930, gez. Wiegand.

65. MA: R 4 53 51, R 6 40 51 (4). TKA/5740–5744 35 Sitzung des Hüttenausschusses, 18 March 1930, Vertraulich!. TKA/5740–5744 37 Sitzung des Hüttenausschusses, 19 May 1930; MA: R 6 40 51 (4) 1 May 1930 Niederschrift. Present were H. Esser (Esser II), Flaccus, Kalle, Lamarche, Wallmann—copies to Vögler, E. Poensgen, Rabes, Koppenberg, Wiegand.

66. MA: R 4 53 50 "Bericht über die Amerikareise Dezember 1930," Traut. R 6 40 51 (5) "2. Denkschrift . . . Fretz-Moon-Verfahren," 29 Dec. 1930, Tr[aut].

67. MA: R 6 40 51 (5) "Aktennotiz: Betr. Herstellung nahtloser Gasrohre," 3 Jan. 31, Tr[aut]; "Nachtrag," 19 Jan. 1931, Traut. See Wessel, *Kontinuität und Wandel,* pp. 90–99. Esser used the same arguments for the seamless pipe process that Max Mannesmann had used in 1898 to attempt to block the production of welded pipes in his company for fear of losing their influence in the company as the Deutsche Bank began taking it over. I am grateful to Dr. Wessel for this tip.

68. MA: R 6 40 51 (5) "Hauptkostenabteilung: Ihr Schreiben vom 19 Jan. 1931," K/Schm., Betr.: Fretz-Moon-Verfahren, gez. Wiegand.

69. MA: R 6 40 51 (2) Wallmann an Vögler, 14 Feb. 1931.

70. MA: R 6 40 51 (1) Kaufvertrag, 9 April 1931, ppa. Brökelschen, Riepelmeier.

71. Hatzfeld, "50 Jahre Fretz-Moon-Anlage in Mülheim (Ruhr)," *Stahl und Eisen,* p. 134.

72. TKA: A/5740–5744 37. Sitzung des Hüttenausschusses, 19 May 1930, Poensgen.

73. MA: R 4 20 42 "Betr. Aufstellung des Fretz-Moon-Verfahren," [March 1931] (pro-Lierenfeld, with draft of letter); R 6 40 51 (2) "Aktennotiz: Betr. Fretz-Moon-Verfahren," 20 Feb. 1931, [Traut or Wallmann] (pro-Mülheim); R 6 40 51 (4) "Je besonders: Lamarche, Heumüller, Unsere Bandeisen-Eigenbedarfs-Privilegien. Ihre gestrige Rücksprache mit dem Rechtsunterzeichneten," 28 Feb 1931, Dr. L./Be.

74. MA: R 6 40 51 (2) "Aktennotiz," 20 Feb. 1931; R 6 40 51 (4) Unsere Bandeisen-Eigenbedarfs-Privilegien . . . ," 28 Feb. 1931; R 4 20 42 "Betr. Aufstellung des Fretz-Moon-Verfahren, and the rebuttal from central cost accounting office's position from 5 March 1931. For a

side-by-side comparison, see Jeffrey R. Fear, *Thyssen & Co., Mülheim (Ruhr) 1871–1934: The Institutionalization of the Corporation, Vol. II* (Dissertation: Stanford University 1993), p. 416, Table 34.

75. MA: R 6 40 51 (4) "Herrn Dr. Fritz Thyssen, Dr. Ernst Poensgen, Dr. Borbet, Bochum, Dr. Flaccus, (Heinrich) Esser II, Kalle, Wallmann, "Betr. Bandeisenprivileg der Vereinigten Stahlwerke," 5 March 1931, Lamarche (mit Anlage) Dr. L/?, "Lamarche, Heumüller, "Unsere Bandeisen-Eigenbedarfs-Privilegien. Ihre gestrige Rücksprache mit dem Rechtsunterzeichneten," 28 Feb. 1931, Fusban, ppa. Linz.

76. For the startup problems see MA: R 4 53 50 (1) 30 Dec. 1931, 27 May 1932.

77. MA: R 4 53 42 (4) "Das Fretz-Moon-Verfahren," 28 June 1933, Traut. Hatzfeld, "50 Jahre Fretz-Moon-Anlage." MA: R 4 41 22 (2) Abschrift! Herrn Lamarche im Hause, Betreff: Selbstkostenvergleich Fretz-Moon-Anlage-Lierenfeld für geschweisste Gasrohre," 6 June 1932, gez. Flaccus (copies to Vögler, E. Poensgen, Esser, Wallmann). MA: R 4 41 22 (1) Gasrohrschweisswerke, Geschäftsjahr 1931/32. TKA: A/5554 "Röhrenausschusses" (esp. 4 July 1933).

78. MA: R 4 53 53 "Herr Traut," 30 Sept. 1932, Graham Satow.

79. TKA: A/3271 Däbritz Interview with Scheifhacken and Dinkelbach, 19 May 1960.

80. Treue/Uebbing, *Feuer Verlöschen Nie,* pp. 44–50.

15. Business Practice and Politics

1. Reckendrees, *Das «Stahltrust»-Projekt,* pp. 436–453, 460–461, quote from p. 448.

2. The quote is from Feldenkirchen, "Big Business," p. 426. Reckendrees, *Das «Stahltrust»-Projekt,* p. 467 disagrees with this choice of words, but instead calls Dinkelbach the "leading *Organisator.*" The entire reorganization might not be his "child," but he was certainly the processing "brain" behind it. By using the term "brainchild," one need not believe that every idea derived from Dinkelbach. As this study analyzes organization, I highlight the "leading *Organisator's*" role more than Reckendrees does, since Dinkelbach's use of organization and management design was especially innovative. This is an example where our respective agendas diverge and influence our analysis. Almost the entire planning process went through Büro Dinkelbach, and this planning influenced Vögler and the final results. Dinkelbach was much more than a personal planning secretary for Vögler; other managers did not just execute Vögler's ideas.

3. Reckendrees, *Das «Stahltrust»-Projekt,* p. 466–467.

4. Passed in March 1934, *Reichsanzeiger,* 63, 15 March 1934. ThyssenKrupp Archive (TKA): VSt/1616: To Vögler, Sempell, Späing (copies to H. Poensgen, Dinkelbach, Linz), 7 Nov. 1933, Daub

5. Reckendrees, *Das «Stahltrust»-Projekt,* pp. 455.

6. Mannesmann Archive (MA): R 1 40 33 "Herrn Wallmann . . . Betreff: Senkung der Verwaltungsausgaben," 24 March 1931, Vögler. Wallmann complained, see "Dr. Vögler . . . Senkung der Verwaltung-sausgaben," 31 March 1931, [Wallmann]. Also "Rundschreiben Nr. 119, Betreff Repräsentationskosten," 26 May 1931, Rabes, ppa. Dinkelbach. MA: R 5 40 53 Erfolgsrechnung 1927–1931. Reckendrees, *Das «Stahltrust»-Projekt,* p. 406, Table 6.15.

7. TKA: VSt/1567–1595 contains almost the whole process of reorganiz-ing the VSt between 1931–1933. Here VSt/1575–1587 [Vorarbeiten, Statistiken 1931–1933 zur Gruppenbildung], esp. VSt 1575 "Vorschlag für eine Vereinfachung der kaufmännischen Organisation," 23 June 1931, Dinkelbach.

8. For details, see Reckendrees, *Das «Stahltrust»-Projekt,* pp. 456–463.

9. VSt/1575–1587 Vorarbeiten, Statistiken 1931–1933. TKA: A/5741 VSt Hüttenausschuss Protokoll, 17 Aug. 1931. Reckendrees, *Das «Stahltrust»-Projekt,* p. 458–459 argues that the decision was "in princi-ple" made at this point, yet the quote he cites states "perhaps in the form of groups."

10. MA: R 1 50 02 (1) "Einzel-Vorschläge betr. Gruppenbildung," Betr. Röhrengruppe, [Dinkelbach].

11. TKA: VSt/1576 Dinkelbach's draft for Vögler's presentation, 15 Feb. 1932. PA (Presse) Leo Kluitmann on Heinrich Dinkelbach.

12. Reckendrees, *Das «Stahltrust»-Projekt,* pp. 463–469, 516–522. Reckendrees argues that there were "few fundamental problems" (p. 463) and little internal resistance to the plan: "During the entire time [pre-Nov. 1932], VSt executive directors hardly had possibility (and apparently little interest), in articulating their position to the plans (p. 516)." But he provides at least four examples of senior execu-tives dissatisfied with it for various reasons. He views these objections to the plan as minor, exceptional, or merely "tactical" (p. 517). In my dissertation, I may have overstated the degree of internal resistance to the plan, but my goal is not to generalize from a few dissatisfied execu-tives about the rest, rather it is to show the real difficulties confronting the reorganization. Our different agendas cause us to weight these dis-cussions differently.

13. MA: R 1 40 19 (1) "Gedanken über die beabsichtigte Zusammen-fassung der Röhrenwerke," 8 April 1932, [Carl Wallmann].

14. Reckendrees, *Das «Stahltrust»-Projekt,* pp. 464–466 who discovered this exchange.

15. See especially MA: R 1 40 19 (2) group 4. Also MA: R 1 50 02 (1) "Einzel-Vorschläge betr. Gruppenbildung," Betr. Röhrengruppe, [Dinkelbach]. MA: R 1 50 03 (4). TKA: VSt/1575–1587. The DRW "template" is in VSt/1584.

16. TKA: VSt/1576–1577 Vorarbeiten zur Gruppenbildung, 14 Nov. 1932, (Büro Dinkelbach).

17. Reckendrees, *Das «Stahltrust»-Projekt,* pp. 508–519. Reckendrees and I tend to differ in our view of Albert Vögler. Vögler is clearly the great "presidential" authority in the VSt, but according to Reckendrees, Vögler essentially gives "marching orders" (p. 519) or "decides," and then actions result that conform to his orders. I view Vögler more as a hub or arbiter of competing strategies, views, and interests. In Reckendrees' view, Vögler's subordinates become mere executors of Vögler's will, rather than active formulators of VSt policy. For instance, Reckendrees argues that Vögler had already decided in favor of legally independent subsidiaries, while Dinkelbach treated the legal independence of the subsidiaries as secondary. However, Dinkelbach clearly "preferred" legally independent subsidiaries, especially for financial and accounting purposes; these reasons differ from Vögler's reasons. Reckendrees finds the decision in favor of legally independent subsidiaries as falling in January 1933, when von Flotow assured Vögler that he could view the tax question as "settled" (p. 513). But no final decision was possible at this time because of the enormous legal-political difficulties regarding taxes. The subsequent negotiating *process,* not Vögler, made the 'decision.'

18. TKA: A/3482, A/9415 "Abschliessende Darstellung der Umorganisation der Vereinigte Stahlwerke A.G," 25 April 1934, Späing, i.V. Schilling. MA: R 1 40 35.1 Ausführungen des Herrn Dr. Vögler, 29 Nov. 1933. MA: R 1 50 03 (1) "Die Gliederung der Vereinigte Stahlwerke A. G. nach dem jetzigen Stande und nach der beabsichtigten Neuordnung," 4 Aug. 1933. And TKA: VSt/950 "Die Gliederung der Vereinigte Stahlwerke A. G. nach dem jetzigen Stande und nach der beabsichtigten Neuordnung" [Letzte Fassung], 7 Oct. 1933, Dinkelbach. These provide the best overviews of the reorganization.

19. TKA: VSt/963 "Gruppenbildung. Zur Denkschrift Dinkelbach vom 14 Nov. 1932," 4 Jan. 1933, Dr. L/Se; "Gruppenbildung und Verbände. 1. Ergänzung zur ersten summarischen Äusserung der Hauptrechtsabteilung vom 4.1.33," 11 January 1933, VSt Hauptrechts-

abteilung: Fusban, ppa. Linz. Reckendrees, *Das «Stahltrust»-Projekt,* pp. 516–518 argues that Fusban's critiques were merely a reflection of "personal motives" and oriented "exclusively [to] technical details."

20. TKA: VSt/963 "Stellungnahme der Abteilung Bergbau," 17 Feb. 1933, Knepper, Kauert, quotes from this source. Reckendrees, *Das «Stahltrust»-Projekt,* pp. 520–523. For these plans, see TKA: VSt/963 "Gründung der Pachtgesellschaften . . . ," 13 April 1933, Dr. Linz, Sempell. VSt/1612 "Herrn Direktor Rabes, Herrn Direktor Dinkelbach (Organisation)," 24 June 1933: "*Organisationsplan* für die Hauptsteuerabteilung und Hauptgrundstücksabteilung des Konzerns," Späing, Schilling.

21. TKA: VSt/963 To Dr. Linz, 30 Dec. 1932, Späing. Reckendrees, *Das «Stahltrust»-Projekt,* p. 514, quoted from TKA: VSt/1616 To Vögler, 16 Dec. 1932, Späing.

22. TKA: VSt/963 To Vögler," 17 Jan. 1933, Späing. VSt/957 [Henceforth "Gestionsgesellschaften?"] To Linz and Vögler, 31 July 1933, Späing [mit] Anlagen: I. Wie kamen wir zu den Gestionsgesellschaften?, Sind Pachtbetriebsgesellschaften nicht vorzuziehen? II: "An die Deutsche Röhrenwerke Aktiengesellschaft, Düsseldorf" (Entwurf), III: "Zusammenfassung und Ergebnis" eines Rechtsgutachtens Dr. Mirow vom 31.7.1933 über Steuerfragen der Pachtbetriebsgesellschaften." The legal extent of the firm, or its boundaries, has major implications for transaction-cost theory. In Oliver Williamson's theory, transaction-costs arise in the process of exchange. Yet what constitutes an exchange, a transaction crossing some theoretical boundary, depends critically on the legal code. See Scott E. Masten, "A Legal Basis for the Firm," *The Nature of the Firm: Origins, Evolution, and Development,* ed. Oliver E. Williamson and Sidney G. Winter (New York: Oxford University Press, 1991), pp. 186–212.

23. For an fascinating discussion of this "deal," see Reckendrees, *Das «Stahltrust»-Projekt,* pp. 471–507; for VSt shareholding figures, see pp. 539–540, Table 7.5. On Flick, see Henry Ashby Turner, *German Big Business and the Rise of Hitler* (New York/Oxford: Oxford, 1985), pp. 231, 254–258. Mollin, *Montankonzern,* pp. 48, 52–54.

24. Mollin, *Montankonzern,* pp. 48–51, 276–279. Bundesarchiv Potsdam, *Reichsfinanzministerium* (RFM), B7279, S. 4105–4032: "Umorganisation der Vereinigten Stahlwerke." The records here are less comprehensive than those in the ThyssenKrupp archives. TKA: VST/958 "Besprechung im Reichsfinanzministerium," 24 Oct. 1933.

25. TKA: VSt/963 Vögler, 17 Jan. 1933, Späing. VSt/957 Gestionsgesellschaften?, 31 July 1933, Späing.

26. TKA: VSt/956 Besprechung von Flotow, Sempell, Dinkelbach, 3 March 1933, Dinkelbach. "Aussprache im Reichsfinanzministerium, 10 March 1933, Späing. "Entwurf an den Herrn Reichsminister der Finanzen," 13 March 1933, Späing.

27. The legal department used the future pipe group company, the Deutsche Röhrenwerke (DRW: Thyssen-Mülheim/Phoenix-Lierenfeld/Bochum-Höntrop), as a template for the rest of the subsidiaries because the pipe group had the least number of cartel clauses.

28. TKA: VST/963 "Gründung von Pachtgesellschaften zur Vorbereitung der Gruppenbildung. 1. Entwürfe der Hauptrechtsabt," 8 April 1933; To Vögler, Rabes, Knepper, Lamarche, Späing, Dinkelbach, Vertraulich!, 13 April 1933, Lenz, Sempell. This package includes a legal commentary on the drafts.

29. On these issues, see TKA: VSt/963 "To Dr. Vögler," 13 April 1933, Späing with "Abschrift. Der Reichsminister der Finanzen S 4105–4032 III," 7 April 1933. VSt/964 "Herrn Rabes," 2 May 1933, Späing; "Direktor Rabes" 20 July 1933, gez. Sempell. VSt/963 "To Vögler," 17 Jan. 1933, Späing. VSt/957 Gestionsgesellschaften?, 31 July 1933, Späing.

30. TKA: VSt/964 To Späing, Dinkelbach, "Gründung von Studiengesellschaft zur Vorbereitung der Gruppenbildung," 8 May 1933, Fusban, Linz.

31. TKA: VSt/957 Gestionsgesellschaften?, 31 July 1933, Späing.

32. MA: R 1 50 00.1 To Lamarche, Deutsche Röhrenwerke A. G., 14 June 1933, Fusban, ppa. Linz. MA: R 1 50 01–02 (2) To Vögler, E. Poensgen, Rabes, Fusban, Flaccus, Späing, Lamarche, H. Poensgen, Esser, *Wallmann*, Deleurant, Dinkelbach, Betreff: Werksgesellschaften, 28 June 1933, Rabes, ppa. Dinkelbach. These documents have complete drafts, recommendations for balances, sales companies *(Kontoren)*, profit/loss statements, and quotas for the future Deutsche Röhrenwerke AG. The same contracts for each of the groups can be found in TKA: A/5510.

33. TKA: VSt/964 To Rabes, 20 July 1933, gez. Sempel; to Rabes," 21 July 1933, Späing.

34. The discussion is based on Reckendrees, *Das «Stahltrust»-Projekt*, pp. 527–539.

35. TKA: VSt/964 To Rabes, 21 July 1933, Späing.

36. TKA: VSt/964 To Dinkelbach, Linz, Daub "Rechtsgutachten des Herrn Dr. Mirow über die Frage der Kapitalverkehrsteuer der Betriebsgesellschaften," 13 Sept. 1933, Späing. To Linz, 21 Sept. 1933, Späing. TKA: VSt/957 "Besprechung im Reichsfinanzministerium," 15 Sept. 1933, Daub, Späing. TKA VSt/1617 Besprechungen Späing, Dinkelbach, 22 Sept. 1933, 27 Sept. 1933.

37. MA: R 1 50 02 (2) "Besprechung [Vögler, Dinkelbach] mit Herrn von Flotow, Betr. Kapital für die Betriebsgesellschaften," 28 Sept. 1932, gez. Dinkelbach. To Späing, "Betr.: Betriebsgesellschaften," 29 Sept. 1933, [Dinkelbach]. A special line of credit from the "Treuhandverwaltung für das deutsch-neiderländische Finanzabkommen, GmbH, Berlin," *Tredefina*, was set up, which charged to the accounts of the subsidiaries the value of the inventories used by the subsidiaries. See especially, MA: R 1 50 00.1 (1) "Gründungs-Akten der Deutsche Röhrenwerke AG," "Gründungsurkunde und Satzung nebst Anlagen," Anlage II, III.

38. MA: R 1 50 03 (1) "Die Gliederung der Vereinigte Stahlwerke," 4 Aug. 1933, Dinkelbach. TKA: VSt/1616 Besprechungen mit dem Preussisches Finanzministerium, Betr. Fusion/Gruppenbildung/ Steuern/Gerichtskosten, 1 Nov. 1933, Späing, Daub.

39. For more detail, see Reckendrees, *Das «Stahltrust»-Projekt*, pp. 526–527, 539–552. Seebold, *Ein Stahlkonzern*, pp. 61–63. Seebold argues that the reorganization was designed to reduce the influence of the state. This assertion cannot be upheld.

40. TKA: VSt/958 "Besprechung mit Herrn von Flotow," Betr. Fusion Gruppenbildung Steuern und Gerichtskosten," 23 Oct. 1933, Linz. "Besprechung" in RFM, Btr. Fusion Gruppenbildung Steuern, 24 Oct. 1933, gez. Daub.

41. *Reichsanzeiger*, 63, 15 March 1934. TKA: VSt/1616: To Vögler, Sempell, Späing, 7 Nov. 1933, Daub. TKA: A/3482 Rechtsabteilungen der VSt, 25 May 1934. "Der Reichsminister der Finanzen S 5114-V. 39 III, Auf die Eingaben vom 31 Aug. 1933, 10 Nov. 1933, 15 March 1934, 3 April 34 und 18 April 34 wegen Pauschalierung der Reichssteuern anlässlich der Neuordnung des Stahlverein-Konzerns," 18 May 1934, VSt Hauptsteuerabteilung [Späing, Schilling], gez. Schlüter.

42. Hilger, *Sozialpolitik und Organisation*, pp. 314–330. Reckendrees, *Das «Stahltrust»-Projekt*, p. 522. TKA: PA (Presse) Ausführungen by Dr. Cordes, 27 Oct 1967.

43. TKA: VSt/952 "Vorschlag betr. eine Fusion der Gesellschaften," 15 March 1933, Dinkelbach. See the richer discussion in Reckendrees, *Das «Stahltrust»-Projekt*, pp. 497–498, 539–552. By not discussing the fusion more in depth, I do not mean to imply that this was less important than the creation of subsidiaries.

44. TKA: A/3482, A/9415 Abschliessende Darstellung der Umorganisation der Vereinigte Stahlwerke AG, 25 April 1934, Späing, i.V. Schilling. Also Vögler's speech to shareholders, 29 November 1933. Some minor changes occurred between November 1933 and April 1934.

45. MA: R 1 50 03, R 1 50 04, R 2 50 02.

46. MA: R 1 50 03 (7) "Verkaufsplan nach Verkaufsstellen" (pre-1933), "Verkaufsplan nach Werksgruppen und Erzeugnissen" (post-1933).

47. TKA: VSt/1612 "Vorschlag für die Bearbeitung der Beteiligungen," 10 Jan. 1934, Dch/He. A/3482 VSt. Bilanzbuchhaltung Rundschreiben Nr. 146, "Betreff: Organisation des Rechnungswesens ab 1 Jan. 1934, 22 Dec. 1933," Rabes, Dinkelbach, Buz.

48. MA: R 5 51 01 (3) To Flaccus, Lamarche, H. Poensgen, Scheifhacken, Sempel, Späing, Betreff: Konversion der Umtausch-Anleihen," Dinkelbach.

49. National Archives (NA): RG 59 862.6511/6–1648 Letter to the Secretary of State, regarding the proposed dismantling of the ATH in Hamborn, 16 June 1948, Maurice W. Altaffer. Adam Klug, *The German Buybacks, 1932–1939: A Cure for Overhang?* (Princeton: Princeton University International Finance Section, November 1993), pp. 5–21, figure from p. 21. The amount paid off by the VSt was in line with other industrial bonds.

50. TKA: VSt/953 Korrespondenz Dec. 1933–Feb. 1934, Rabes, Späing, Linz, Dinkelbach, Lamarche, Borbet. MA: R 1 50 03 (7) "An die Geschäftsführung der Walzeisenkontor GbmH, Direktor Scheifhacken," 12 Dec. 1934, Rabes, Dinkelbach. Seebold, *Ein Stahlkonzern,* pp. 142–145.

51. MA: R 1 50 03 (4) "Interne Quoten und Vergütungen," 14 Feb. 1933, [Dinkelbach]. MA: R 1 50 03 (5) "Betr.: Ergebnisrechnung für die Werksgruppen," 1 July 1933, Dinkelbach. To Vögler, E. Poensgen, Rabes, Fusban, Flaccus, Späing, Lamarche, H. Poensgen, Deleurant, Dinkelbach, "Besprechung über den Ausgleich der Gruppenrentabilität durch Quotenvergütungen," 17 July 1933, VSt Hauptkostenabteilung, [no signature].

52. MA: R 1 50 00.1 (1) "Gründungs-Akten der Deutsche Röhrenwerke Aktiengesellschaft 1933–34." MA: R 1 50 04 "Handelsregister" DRW 1933–1951. MA: R 1 50 03 (5) "Besetzung der Vorstände," 19.6.1933. MA: R 1 50 03 (2) "Vorschläge für die sich bei der Bildung der Deutsche Röhrenwerke AG ergebenden organisatorischen Änderungen," Ausfertigung 5, Bericht 3401, 2 Feb. 1934, mit Organisationsgraphik, gez. Ciliax, Mesmann, Petzold. Reproduced in Fear, *Thyssen & Co.,* p. 453 with a discussion on pp. 452–456 and Reckendrees, *Das «Stahltrust»-Projekt,* p. 557. I am indebted to Lutz Budrass for turning my attention to the similarities between these VSt organizational charts and those propagated by the *Zeitschrift für Organisation.*

53. See as well MA: R 5 50 08 "Bericht vom 15. August 1935 über den

Büromaschinenbestand der Deutsche Röhrenwerke AG," VSt Abt. Organisation.

54. TKA: VSt/1611 [Grundsätzliche Richtlinien, Dch/W., 7 Nov. 1933, 4 Nov. 1933, [Dinkelbach]. "Richtlinen für die Zusammenarbeit der in der Vereinigte Stahlwerke AG zusammengeschlossenen Unternehmungen," 24 Feb. 1934, Kl[uitmann]/Nt.

55. TKA: VSt/1612 To Fahrenhorst, Rabes, Helmut Poensgen, Dinkelbach, 30 Jan. 1934, Späing.

56. TKA: VSt/1612 To Vögler, "Richtlinien der Hauptfinanzverwaltung: Grundsätze für den Verkehr zwischen den Gesellschaften des V.St.-Konzerns und der Hauptfinanzverwaltung" [prepared by Deleurant and includes earlier drafts from July], 6 Nov. 1933, Rabes, gez. Deleurant.

57. TKA: A/5373 "Organisation des Rechnungswesens, ca 1934, [none].

58. TKA: VSt/1612 "Vorschlag für die Bearbeitung der Beteiligungen," 10 Jan. 1934, Dinkelbach. "Richtlinien für Revision: Prüfungen im Auftrag des Vorstands oder des Aufsichtrates," 16 June 1933, Dinkelbach; To Dinkelbach, "Umstellung der Konzern-Organisation," 19 June 1933, Backhaus. Also A/3482 VSt Bilanzbuchhaltung Rundschreiben Nr. 146, "Organisation des Rechnungswesens ab 1 Jan. 1934," 22 Dec. 1933, Rabes, Dinkelbach, Buz.

59. Gareth Morgan, *Images of Organization* (Newbury Park/London: Sage, 1986) provides a useful survey on the various metaphors employed to describe organizations and their implications.

60. MA: R 1 5 20–22, 25 Geschäftsberichte, Bilanzen der DRW 1934–1939. See R 5 50 05 for complete handwritten balances in the old boundbook format. MA: R 1 40 35.1–2 VSt AG: Berichte über das Geschäftsjahr 1934–1939.

61. MA: R 5 50 31 (1) To Lamarche, "Vergleich Montan-Abschlüsse 30.6.1939," 29 Nov. 1939, Dinkelbach (prepared by Bilanzbuchhaltung: Buz, Dinkelbach). "Vergleich der Jahresabschlüsse," 16 Feb. 1940, Buz, Dinkelbach. To Lamarche, "Betriebsvergleich," 24 March 1939, Dinkelbach (prepared by Haupt-Revision: Cordes, Brune).

62. TKA: VSt/2996 "Konzernübersicht der Vereinigte Stahlwerke AG (Bericht Nr. 61), ed. Stahltreuhändervereinigung, 2 March 1950.

63. MA: R 1 40 19 (2) group 4: Bilanzen zum 30 Sept. 1931. Also MA: R 1 50 01, R 1 50 02 (2) Bilanz zum 31 March 1933.

64. My argument loosely confirms Charles Maier's "Between Taylorism and Technocracy: European Ideologies and the Vision of Industrial Productivity in the 1920s," *In Search of Stability: Explorations in Historical Political Economy* (Cambridge: Cambridge University Press, 1987), pp. 19–69.

65. Peter Armstrong, "The Rise of Accounting Controls in British Capitalist Enterprises," *Accounting, Organizations and Society,* 12, 5 (1987), pp. 415–436, quote from p. 430.

66. Reckendrees, *Das «Stahltrust»-Projekt,* p. 559. MA: R 4 50 00 "Bericht über den Besuch amerikanischer Röhrenwerke, Block-und Breitbandstrassen in der Zeit vom 20. März bis 13. Mai 1939," Paul Inden, Wilhelm Schmidt. Inden and Schmidt supplied an organizational description of U.S. Steel on pp. 167–169 of this report. U.S. Steel finished its reorganization in 1937.

67. TKA: VSt/1612 "Richtlinien der Zusammenarbeit," 6 Nov. 1933, Rabes, gez. Deleurant. Oliver Williamson, *The Economic Institutions of Capitalism* (New York: Free Press, 1985), pp. 279–297. Quote from H. Thomas Johnson and and Robert S. Kaplan, *Relevance Lost: The Rise and Fall of Management Accounting* (Boston: Harvard Business School, 1991), p. 99.

68. Alfred D. Chandler, Jr., *Strategy and Structure: Chapters in the History of the Industrial Enterprise* (Cambridge, Mass.: MIT, 1962), pp. 283–323.

69. TKA: A/1345 To Kindt at ATH, 1 Dec. 1932. VSt Hauptrevision Dr.Gr/ He [Dr. Graff].

70. TKA: A/1801 Däbritz Interview with Dinkelbach, Dec. 1942. In the dissertation, I made a stronger argument for continuity with Thyssen & Co. implied by the term "blueprint" of the VSt.

71. Reckendrees, *Das «Stahltrust»-Projekt,* pp. 514–515, quoted from TKA: VSt/1592 6 Feb. 1933.

72. Avraham Barkai, *Nazi Economics: Ideology, Theory, and Policy* (New Haven: Yale University Press, 1990). Bundesarchiv Potsdam: RWM: Reform des Aktienrechts, B17568, 31.01 9974, 1006, 17569–70 and RFM, 21.01 B6008, B7648–9. Although the Nazis spearheaded such reforms, we should be careful to attribute this to uniquely German conditions. Adoph Berle and Gardiner Means' classic work on the disparaging consequences of the separation of ownership from control, *The Modern Corporation and Private Property* (New York: MacMillan, 1932), appeared at the same time. See as well Richard Rosendorff, "The New German Company Law and the English Companies Act, 1929," *Journal of Comparative Legislation and International Law,* 14 (1932), 94–100; 15 (1933), 112–116, 242–254. Rosendorff makes the important point that this was an international movement. Dinkelbach played a critical role in representing industry interests and the relatively new field of the chartered accounting profession in these discussions. See Bundesarchiv Potsdam: RWM 31.01 9974, Bl. 159–175 "Referat: Zur Reform des Bilanzsteuerrechts—Berichterstatter: Direktor Dinkelbach." Also TKA: FWH-200–30-A/2 *Die Volksparole,* 48, 17 Feb. 1934;

Düsseldorfer Tageblatt, 52, 22 Feb. 1934; and *Berliner Börsenzeitung,* 556, 26 Nov. 1936.

73. On big business reactions to the new cabinet, see Turner, *German Big Business and the Rise of Hitler,* pp. 326–339. Also Rasch, "Über Albert Vögler und sein Verhältnis zur Politik," pp. 131–143. We need more research on lower levels of VSt and other enterprises' management. For a beginning, see Harold James, "Die Deutsche Bank und die Diktatur 1933–1945," *Die Deutsche Bank 1870–1995* ed. Lothar Gall, et al. (London: Weidenfeld & Nicolson, 1995), pp. 340–344.

74. MA: R 1 40 06 VSt. Generalsekretariat: Rundschreiben 170, 18 May 1933; Rundschreiben 173, 17 June 1933; Rundschreiben 177, Vertraulich!, 31 July 1933, H. Poensgen.

75. Turner, *German Big Business and the Rise of Hitler,* pp. 204–219. See his discussions about other VSt executives such as Thyssen, Brandi, Winnacker, Vögler, and Poensgen.

76. MA: R 1 50 03 (1) "Die Gliederung der Vereinigte Stahlwerke," 4 Aug. 1933, Dinkelbach.

77. MA: R 1 40 35.1 "Ausführungen des Herrn Dr. Vögler . . ." 29 Nov. 1933. Albert Vögler, "Die betriebsorganisatorische Umbau der Vereinigte Stahlwerk A.-G . . . am 29 Nov 1933," *Das Werk: Monatsschrift der Vereinigte Stahlwerk Aktiengesellschaft,* 13 (1933), pp. 483–492. TKA: PA (Presse) Leo Kluitmann on Dinkelbach, 27 Oct. 1967.

78. MA: R 1 50 03 (1) "Die Gliederung der Vereinigte Stahlwerke," 4 Aug. 1933, Dinkelbach. The numerically ordered reasons in the text are indented in the following discussion and stem from this document.

79. TKA: A/1801 Däbritz Interview with Albert Vögler, 11 Nov. 1943. VSt/ 3053 "Rede Dr. Vögler auf der gemeinsamen Sitzung der Aufsichtsräte von: VSt. AG, Phoenix, van der Zypen," 27 Oct. 1933. TKA: VSt/728 "Fragebogen über die Altersgliederung und Betrtiebszugehörigkeit der Angestellten einschl. der leitenden Angestellten," 10 Jan. 1929. Detlev Peukert, *The Weimar Republic: The Crisis of Classical Modernity* (New York: Hill & Wang, 1991), pp. 7–12, 89–95.

80. TKA: VSt/1611 [Grundsätzliche Richtlinien], 7 Nov. 1933, 4 Nov. 1933, [Dinkelbach].

81. MA: R 1 50 02 (2) "Vergleichsbilanzen Röhrengruppe . . . [usw.]," 28 Sept. 1933. Here Dinkelbach compared the capital requirements of the new pipe subsidiary, the DRW, to those of Mannesmann and its quota in the pipe syndicate.

82. Reckendrees, *Das «Stahltrust»-Projekt,* p. 522 stresses the financial opportunities of the reorganization.

83. Reckendrees, *Das «Stahltrust»-Projekt,* pp. 556, fn. 409. After 1926, in-

ternal transfer prices were not based on market or cartel prices except for a few exceptional goods. Cartels did set prices for third parties.

84. Alfred Hueck, Hans-Carl Nipperdey, and Rolf Dietz, *Gesetz zur Ordnung der nationalen Arbeit und Gesetz zur Ordnung der Arbeit in Öffentlichen Verwaltungen und Betrieben. . . . :Kommentar,* (München: C. H. Beck, 1939). Also Helmut Trischler, "Führerideal und die Formen faschistischer Bewegungen: Industrielle Vorgesetztenschulung in den USA, Grossbritannien, der Schweiz, Deutschland und Österreich im Vergleich," *Historische Zeitschrift,* 251 (1990), pp. 45–88.

85. TKA: FWH-200–30-A/2 *Die Volksparole,* 48, 17 Feb. 1934; *Düsseldorfer Tageblatt,* 52, 22 Feb, 1934; and *Berliner Börsenzeitung,* 556, 26 Nov. 1936. MA: R 4 53 35 "Betriebsordnung der Deutsche Röhrenwerke Aktiengesellschaft: Werk Thyssen Mülheim (Ruhr)," 29 Sept. 1934. See also Bundesarchiv Potsdam: RWM 31.01 9974, Bl. 159–175 "Referat: Zur Reform des Bilanzsteuerrechts—Berichterstatter: Direktor Dinkelbach."

86. TKA: FWH-200–30-A/2 *Die Volksparole,* 48, 17 Feb. 1934.

87. Seebold, *Ein Stahlkonzern,* p. 72.

88. Thomas Childers, "The Social Language of Politics in Germany: The Sociology of Political Discourse in the Weimar Republic," *American Historical Review,* 95, 2 (April 1990), pp. 331–358.

89. TKA: VSt/3053 Rede Dr. Vögler, 27 Oct. 1933.

90. Harold James, "Innovation and Conservatism in Economic Recovery: The alleged 'Nazi recovery' of the 1930s," *Capitalism in Crisis: International Responses to the Great Depression,* ed. W. R. Garside (New York: St. Martin's Press, 1993), pp. 70–95, quote from p. 90.

91. Mollin, *Montankonzern,* pp. 53–54.

92. All quotes are based on Richard Overy, "Heavy Industry in the Third Reich: The Reichswerke Crisis," *War and Economy in the Third Reich* (Oxford: Clarendon Press, 1994), pp. 93–118. The discussion is based on Overy, "Heavy Industry in the Third Reich," and Mollin, *Montankonzern,* pp. 102–109.

93. Mollin, *Montankonzern,* pp. 115–133.

94. See the controversy over Plumpe's history of IG Farben during the Third Reich: Peter Hayes, "Zur umstrittenen Geschichte der I. G. Farbenindustrie AG," *Geschichte und Gesellschaft,* 18, 3 (1992), pp. 405–417. And Thomas Sandkühler and Hans-Walter Schmuhl, "Noch Einmal: die I. G. Farben und Auschwitz," *Geschichte und Gesellschaft,* 19, 2 (1993), pp. 259–267. On the controversial topic of the modernity of the Third Reich, see Jeffrey Herf, *Reactionary Modernism: Technology, Culture, and Politics in Weimar and the Third Reich* (Cambridge: Cam-

bridge University Press, 1984). Michael Prinz and Rainer Zitelmann, eds., *Nationalsozialismus und Modernisierung* (Darmstadt: Wissenschaftliche Buchgesellschaft, 1994). For a critical take on Prinz and Zitelmann's interpretation, see Norbert Frei, "Wie modern war der Nationalsozialismus?" *Geschichte und Gesellschaft*, 19, 3 (1993), pp. 367–387. Also Neil Gregor, *Daimler-Benz in the Third Reich* (New Haven: Yale University Press, 1998), pp. 2–5, 247–252.

16. Heinrich Dinkelbach, Organization Man

1. "Eighteen German Businessmen . . . and how they made their astonishing comeback," *Fortune* (March 1952), pp. 112–165. ThyssenKrupp Archive (TKA): NDI/33 *Tagesspiegel* to Dinkelbach, 3 March 1952.
2. See TKA: NDI/8 Meeting with Erhard, 6 and 9 Dec. 1948. NDI/12 Dinkelbach to Erhard, 7 Oct. 1949.
3. Gillingham, *Coal, Steel, and the Rebirth of Europe 1945–1955,* pp. 197–205, quote from p. 197. Djelic, *Exporting the American Model,* pp. 103–111, 162–3. Berghahn, *Americanisation of German Industry.*
4. Thomas Lux, "Heinrich Dinkelbach—Vom Lehrling zum Generaldirektor: Eine amerikanische Karriere," in *900 Jahre Mülheim an der Ruhr 1093–1993* (Zeitschrift des Geschichtsvereins Mülheim a. d. Ruhr, 66, 1993), pp. 569–587.
5. TKA: NDI/60 Dinkelbach to Leo Kluitmann, 1 Aug. 1956; NDI/76 Dinkelbach to Peter van Aubel, 5 June 1959.
6. TKA: PA (Presse) "Der Dinkelbachkreis," 27 Oct. 1967 by Theodor Gessel.
7. TKA: A/606 also used by Reckendrees, *Das «Stahltrust»-Project,* pp. 163–166, fn. 52–62.
8. TKA: PA (Presse) "Der Dinkelbachkreis," 27 Oct. 1967 by Walter Cordes.
9. TKA: A/5055–56 Bartscherer-Dinkelbach correspondence, Betr.: Preise für Halbzeug zur Herstellung von Ronden für Kartuschen und Patronen," 11 Sept. 1942 [also 18 Sept. 1942 and 29 Oct. 1942], Dinkelbach, Bartscherer.
10. TKA: PA (Presse) "Der Dinkelbachkreis," 27 Oct. 1967 by Walter Cordes. NDI/71 Dr. Jr. G. Freiherr von Falkenhausen to Dinkelbach, 21 Jan. 1958.
11. Manfred Rasch, "Walter Rohland zwischen Kaiserreich und Bundesrepublik. Eine biografische Skizze," in *Findbuch zum Nachlass Walter Rohland* (1898–1981), ed. Manfred Rasch (Duisberg: Veroffentlichungen zus dem Archiv der ThyssenKrupp AG, 5: 2001), pp. 3–61. Walter Rohland, *Bewegte Zeiten: Erinnerungen eines Eisenhüttenmannes* (Stutt-

gart: Seewald, 1978), pp. 63–64. S. Jonathan Wiesen, *West German Industry and the Challenge of the Nazi Past, 1945–1955* (Chapel Hill: University of North Carolina Press, 2001), pp. 224–225.

12. Mannesmann Archive (MA): R 2 25 07 "Bedeutung der Persönlichkeit des Herrn Direktor Heinrich Dinkelbach für den wirtschaftliche Prüfungswesen," 5 Jan. 1951. Henceforth "Bedeutung Dinkelbach,"

13. TKA: PA (Presse) "Der Dinkelbachkreis," 27 Oct. 1967 by Leo Kluitmann.

14. TKA: FWH/458, clipping from the *Kölnische Zeitung*, 20 April 1941.

15. TKA: FWH/458 "Betriebliche Organisation," clipping from the *Berliner Börsen-Zeitung*, 26 Nov. 1936. "Organisationsfragen der Wirtschaft: Ein beachtenswerter Vortrag von Direktor Dinkelbach"; "Grundsätze und Gedanken der Wirtschaftsorganisation: Organisationsfragen— Zwei Vorträge gehalten von Direktor H. Dinkelbach (Vereinigte Stahlwerke) am 15. und 19. Februar," *Die Volksparole*, 48, 17 Feb. 1934, also clippings from the *Düsseldorfer Tageblatt*, 52, 22 Feb. 1934.

16. MA: R 2 25 07 "Bedeutung Dinkelbach," 5 Jan. 1951.

17. Friedrich-Wilhelm Henning, "Die externe Unternehmensprüfung in Deutschland vom 16. Jahrhundert bis zum Jahre 1931," *Vierteljahrschrift für Sozial- und Wirtschaftsgeschichte*, 77, 1 (1990), pp. 1– 28. Also Hugh B. Markus, "Der Wirtschaftsprüferberuf: Eine geschichtliche Kurzfassung," *Wirtschaftsprüferkammer Mitteilungen*, 31 (February 1992), pp. 1–44.

18. TKA: NDI/30 Institut der Wirtschaftsprüfer to Dinkelbach, 7 March 1952. Dinkelbach and van Aubel served in the top advisory board along with people such as Hermann J. Abs. Also NDI/32 Herbert Rätsch to Dinkelbach, 3 July 1952.

19. TKA: FWH/458 "Organisationsfragen der Wirtschaft," *Die Volksparole*, 48, 17 Feb. 1934; in *Düsseldorfer Tageblatt*, 52, 22 Feb. 1934. Also "Betriebliche Organisation" in *Berliner Börsen-Zeitung*, 556, 26 Nov. 1936. MA: R 2 25 07 "Bedeutung Dinkelbach," 5 Jan. 1951.

20. Heinrich Dinkelbach, "Das Wesen und der Aufbau der industriellen Konzernbilanz," *Zeitschrift für Handelswissenschaftliche Forschung*, 35, 1/2 (1941), pp. 55–66.

21. TKA: NDI/11 Dinkelbach to Hans Boeckler, 1 April 1949. Lux, "Heinrich Dinkelbach," pp. 577, 587, fn. 72.

22. Kruk, Potthoff, and Sieben, *Eugen Schmalenbach*, pp. 150–188.

23. TKA: NDI/23 Walter Cordes to Dinkelbach 21 July 1951 and 18 Nov. 1951. Lux, "Heinrich Dinkelbach," p. 576, fn. 35. Kruk, Potthoff, and Sieben, *Eugen Schmalenbach*.

24. TKA: NDI/28 Dr. Karl Arnhold to Dinkelbach, 30 Dec. 1952; NDI/35 Arnhold to Dinkelbach, 7 Aug. 1953; NDI/36 Dinkelbach to Friedrich Flick, 9 July 1953; NDI/43 Friedrich Flick to Dinkelbach, 15 July 1954.

25. TKA: NDI/26 Siegried Seelig to "Generaldirektor" Dinkelbach, streng persönlich und privat, 10 Jan. 1951. See also NDI/74 Seelig to Dinkelbach 21 April 1958. Lux, "Heinrich Dinkelbach," p. 575–576.

26. TKA: NDI/5 Letters Remy/Dinkelbach, 20 Jan. 1947, 25 March 1947.

27. Lux, "Heinrich Dinkelbach," p. 578.

28. See Klaus-Dietmar Henke, *Die Amerikanische Besetzung Deutschlands* (München: R. Oldenbourg Verlag, 1995), pp. 449–571, esp. pp. 560–571 on the dramatic effect of these arrests.

29. TKA: NDI/5 John W. F. Neill to Dinkelbach, 27 Oct. 1947. Dinkelbach attributed his appointment to a Mr. Caspers, one of the Allied controllers and a member of Price Waterhouse, see TKA: PA (Presse) Bayerische Rundfunk interview, 20 Sept. 1954.

30. TKA: NDI/6 Dinkelbach to Schmalenbach, 20 Dec. 1946. Frank Golczewski, *Kölner Universitätslehrer und der Nationalsozialismus: Personengeschichtliche Ansätze* (Köln: Böhlau, 1988), pp. 205–207.

31. TKA: NDI/1 Dinkelbach to van Aubel, 31 Dec. 1946.

32. Henke, *Die Amerikanische Besetzung*, pp. 521–527.

33. Toni Pierenkemper, "Hans-Günther Sohl: Funktionale Effizienz und autoritäre Harmonie in der Eisen- und Stahlindustrie," in *Deutsche Unternehmer zwischen Kriegswirtschaft und Wiederaufbau: Studien zur Erfahrungsbildung von Industrie-Eliten,* ed. Paul Erker and Toni Pierenkemper (München: R. Oldenbourg Verlag, 1999), pp. 53–107, esp. 72–75.

34. Letter to the GHH, Klöckner-Werke, Otto Wolff, 29 Jan. 1947, Dinkelbach; reproduced in *Die Neuordnung der Eisen- und Stahlindustrie,* 5, pp. 611–612.

35. TKA: NDI/4 Press Interviews Jan. 1947. Also Lux, "Heinrich Dinkelbach," p. 579. On this new religious economic culture, see the excellent discussion in Wiesen, *West German Industry and the Challenge of the Nazi Past,* pp. 123–127, esp. 149–155 for the attempted rehabilitation of Albert Vögler by Thyssen executives including Dinkelbach. On Gert von Klass's work, see Manfred Rasch, "Von Festschrift und Hagiographie zur theorie—und methodengeleiteten Darstellung? Unternehmens- und Unternehmergeschichtsschreibung zur Stahlindustrie im Ruhrgebiet in den letzten hundert Jahren," in *Ferrum,* 74 (May 2002), pp. 26–27.

36. See Isabel Warner, "Allied-German Negotiations on the Deconcentration of the West German Steel Industry," *Reconstruction in Post-War Germany: British Occupation Policy and the Western Zones 1945–55,* ed. Ian D. Turner (Oxford: Berg, 1989), pp. 155–185.

37. Berghahn, *Americanisation of West German Industry,* pp. 96–97. Lux, "Heinrich Dinkelbach," p. 586, fn. 65. On British occupation policy in

general, see Ian D. Turner, ed., *Reconstruction in Post-War Germany: British Occupation Policy and the Western Zones 1945–55* (Oxford: Berg, 1989). Dietmar Petzina, "Wirtschaft und Arbeit im Ruhrgebiet 1945 bis 1985" in *Das Ruhrgebiet im Industriezeitalter: Geschichte und Entwicklung,* ed. Wolfgang Köllmann (Düsseldorf: Schwann, 1990), pp. 500–505. On Dinkelbach's postwar activities, Gabriele Müller-List, *Neubeginn bei Eisen und Stahl im Ruhrgebiet: Die Beziehungen zwischen Arbeitgebern und Arbeitnehmern in der nordrhein-westfälischen Eisen- und Stahlindustrie 1945–1948* (Düsseldorf: Droste Verlag, 1990), esp. pp. 93–119.

38. TKA: NDI/4 Press Interview with Mr. Haeth (U.S. journalist) and Mr. Gilmon (British), 31 Jan. 1947; meeting with Harris-Burland and Cusworth 30 Jan. 1947; and telephone interview with M. C. Müller, 31 Jan. 1947. Also see Warner, "Allied-German Negotiations," p. 158. Müller-List, *Neubeginn,* document 73a,b. TKA: PA (Presse) "Der Dinkelbachkreis," 27 Oct. 1967 by Walter Cordes. Bayerischen Rundfunk interview, 20 Sept. 1954. Letter to the GHH, Klöckner-Werke, Otto Wolff, 29 Jan. 1947, Dinkelbach. Reproduced in *Die Neuordnung der Eisen- und Stahlindustrie,* p. 612.

39. TKA: TNO/302 Aufsichtsratsitzung, 29 April 1947.

40. TKA: PA (Presse) Bayerischen Rundfunk interview, 20 Sept. 1954.

41. TKA: NDI/19 for extensive correspondence in 1950.

42. Peter Hubsch, "DGB Economic Policy with Particular Reference to the British Zone 1945–9," *Reconstruction in Post-War Germany,* pp. 271–300. Letter from the GHH to the DGB, 18 Jan. 1947 in Erich Potthoff, *Der Kampf um die Montan-Mitbestimmung* (Köln: Bund-Verlag, 1957), p. 42.

43. TKA: NDI/10 Adolf Wirtz to Dinkelbach, 2 Dec. 1948.

44. TKA: NDI/19 Haurand to Dinkelbach, 17 April 1950; letter of reference for Elisabeth Haurand, 26 July 1950.

45. Wiesen, *West German Industry and the Challenge of the Nazi Past,* pp. 56–59.

46. Pierenkemper, "Hans-Günther Sohl," pp. 84–90.

47. See the numerous job requests in TKA: NDI/22, NDI/14 Gustav Knepper to Dinkelbach, 5 April 1949, 9 Oct. 1949; Heinrich Kindt to Dinkelbach, 7 March 1949; Max Nantulle to Dinkelbach, 1, 4, and 10 Oct. 1949.

48. TKA: NDI/3 Dinkelbach to van Aubel, 15 April 1947; meeting with Herr Bungeroth and Dr. Gnoth, 14 Feb. 1947; and Dinkelbach to Erwin Daub, 14 June 1947 for quote.

49. National Archives (NA): RG 59 800.515/1–3048 Letter to the Secretary of State, Feb. 10, 1948, Maurice W. Altaffer, American Consul General.

50. TKA: NDI/21 Notiz Betr. Dr. Rohland, 28 March 1950. Other corre-

spondence between Dinkelbach and Rohland in NDI/9 Dinkelbach to Herr Meier, regarding Rohland 23 Aug. 1948; Rohland to Dinkelbach 27 June 1949, 31 Jan. 1950

51. Berghahn, *Americanisation,* p. 97, 203–230. Hubsch, "DGB Economic Policy with Particular Reference to the British Zone 1945–9," pp. 285–288. TKA: PA (Presse) "Der Dinkelbachkreis," 27 Oct. 1967 by Walter Cordes. On this heated controversy and its relation to the Nazi past, see Wiesen, *West German Industry and the Challenge of the Nazi Past,* pp. 179

52. Müller-List, *Neubeginn,* pp. 109, 311. Also Kruk, Potthoff, and Sieben, *Eugen Schmalenbach,* pp. 80–1, 162–3, 171–184.

53. Warner, "Allied-German Negotiations," p. 158.

54. On the German reaction toward dismantling, see Wiesen, *West German Industry and the Challenge of the Nazi Past,* pp. 60–67.

55. NA: RG 59 862.6511/6–1648 Letter to the Secretary of State, June 16, 1948, Altaffer.

56. Uebbing, *Wege und Wegmarken,* pp. 50–53. Treue/Uebbing, *Die Feuer Verlöschen Nie,* pp. 131–156.

57. *Neuordnung der Eisen- und Stahlindustrie,* esp. pp. 523–620. See the position paper by members of the old Konzerne, defending their way of doing business, and the one by the Steel Treuhand, which critiqued the old manner of doing business.

58. K. H. Herchenröder, Joh. Schäfer, und Manfred Zapp, *Die Nachfolger der Ruhrkonzerne* (Düsseldorf: Econ-Verlag, 1953), pp. 13–15.

59. TKA: NDI/23 Raoul E. Desvernine (Washington representative for major U.S. steel companies) to Dinkelbach, 6 Feb. 1951.

60. Petzina, "Wirtschaft und Arbeit," p. 501. *Neuordnung der Eisen- und Stahlindustrie,* pp. 71–75.

61. This brief discussion is based on Uebbing, *Wege und Wegmarken,* pp. 55–67. Treue/Uebbing, *Die Feuer Verlöschen Nie,* pp. 168–234. Pierenkemper, "Hans-Günther Sohl," pp. 93–98.

62. Pierenkemper, "Hans-Günther Sohl," p. 84.

63. Uebbing, *Wege und Wegmarken,* p. 70.

64. TKA: PA (Presse) "Der Dinkelbachkreis," 27 Oct. 1967 by Walter Cordes.

65. Cordes' quotes all from from TKA: PA (Presse) "Der Dinkelbachkreis," 27 Oct. 1967 by Walter Cordes. TKA: NDI/26 VSt Hauptrevision 1926–1933 to Dinkelbach, 16 Nov. 1951; NDI/32 Dr. Hans-Wilhelm Rudhart to Dinkelbach 25 Nov. 1952; NDI/37 Rudhart to Dinkelbach 26 Oct. 1953, VSt Hauptrevision to Dinkelbach, 23 Oct. 1953; NDI/68 Rudhart to Dinkelbach 6 Sept. 1957; NDI/74 14 Nov. 1958. The 1953 letter contains a list of these members.

66. Quote from TKA: NDI/23 Cordes to Dinkelbach, 21 June 1951; but also NDI/64 Cordes to Dinkelbach, 7 April 1957; NDI/71 Cordes to Dinkelbach 17 June 1958.

67. TKA: NDI/76 Buz to Dinkelbach 29 Sept. 1959. Buz succeeded Dinkelbach in the Thyssen Machine Company and was later director of the accounting office in the VSt, see Dinkelbach to Buz, 21 Sept. 1959.

68. TKA: PA (Presse), Bayerische Rundfunk interview, 20 Sept. 1954.

69. Letter from Dinkelbach to Oskar Gierke quoted in Lux, "Heinrich Dinkelbach," p. 584, fn. 23.

70. TKA: NDI/45 Dinkelbach to Krähe, 31 July 1954.

71. Arbeitskreis Dr. Krähe der Schmalenbach-Gesellschaft, *Konzern-Organisation: Aufgaben- und Abetilungsgliederung im industriellen Unternehmungsverbund* (Köln/Opladen: Westdeutscher Verlag, 1952). *Ibid.,* *Unternehmungsorganisation: Aufgaben- und Abteilungsgliederung in der industriellen Unternehmung* (Köln/Opladen: Westdeutscher Verlag, 1954). *Ibid., Leitungsorganisation. Die Organisation der Unternehmungsleitung* (Köln/Opladen: Westdeutscher Verlag, 1958). Eugen Schmalenbach, *Dienststellengliederung im Grossbetriebe* (Köln/Opladen: Westdeutscher Verlag 1959 [1941]). On the origins this group and works, see Kruk, Potthoff, and Sieben, *Eugen Schmalenbach,* pp. 171–174.

72. TKA: NDI/10 Schmalenbach Society 5 April 1948. NDI/30 Dr. Heyde to Dinkelbach, 23 Jan. 1952. NDI/27 Dr. G. Schmölders (Finanzwissenschaftliches Forschungsinstitut) to Dinkelbach 28 April 1951. Schmölders wanted to continue their "long-time cooperation" regarding the effect of turnover taxes. NDI/30 Dr. Heyde (Sozialpolitisches Seminar) to Dinkelbach, 23 Jan. 1952. Dinkelbach donated to Cologne as well, see NDI/45 Rektor der Universität Köln to Dinkelbach, 23 Nov. 1954.

73. See TKA: NDI/45 Dinkelbach to Kluitmann, 19 July 1954, 9 Dec. 1954; Walter Krähe to Dinkelbach 6 Aug. 1954. NDI/48 Dinkelbach to Schmalenbach-Gesellschaft, 3 Nov. 1954. NDI/53 Kluitmann to Dinkelbach, 2 Aug. 1955. NDI/56 Schmalenbach-Gesellschaft (Krähe) to Dinkelbach, 10 March 1955. NDI/60 Dinkelbach to Kluitmann, 16 April 1956. NDI/60 Dinkelbach to Kluitmann, 16 April 1956. NDI/73 Kluitmann (privately and in the service of the Schmalenbach-Gesellschaft) to Dinkelbach, 7 Nov. 1958, 4 Aug. 1958; Dinkelbach to Kluitmann 12 May 1958; Krähe to Dinkelbach 2 Sept. 1958. NDI/74 Dinkelbach to Potthoff, 11 Feb. 1958. NDI/77 Kluitmann to Dinkelbach, 29 July 1959. NDI/84 Krähe to Dinkelbach, 25 Aug. 1960. NDI/85 Potthoff to Dinkelbach, 3 June 1960.

74. TKA: NDI/62 Potthoff to Dinkelbach, 12 April 1956. Potthoff's speech is also included.

75. Thomas Haigh, "Inventing Information Systems: The Systems Men and the Computer, 1950–1968," *Business History Review,* 75, 2 (Spring 2001), pp. 15–61.

76. TKA: NDI/56 Dinkelbach to Herrn Inhaber der Treuhand-Kommandit-Gesellschaft Hartkopf & Rentrop, 26 Feb. 1955.

77. TKA: NDI/6 Dinkelbach to Schmalenbach, 20 Dec. 1946, 16 Jan. 1947. Also see the correspondence with van Aubel in 1945 in NDI/1 and NDI/8 Dinkelbach to van Aubel, 12 Aug. 1948. Dinkelbach attempted to place Schmalenbach's son, Fritz, as a director of an art museum in Düsseldorf, which did not succeed, see TKA: NDI/48 Correspondence Dinkelbach, Fritz Schmalenbach, Eugen Schmalenbach, Präsident des Landtags Nordrhein-Westfalen and Oberbürgermeister J. Gockeln, Oct. 1954.

78. Arbeitskreis Dr. Krähe, *Konzern-Organisation;* quote from preface, see esp. pp. 16–17. This edition was a supplement and continuation of the 1950 edition given to Dinkelbach.

79. Quotes from TKA: NDI/62 Potthoff to Dinkelbach, 12 April 1956. Also NDI/73 Dinkelbach to Kluitmann, 12 May 1958. Arbeitskreis Dr. Krähe der Schmalenbach-Gesellschaft, *Leitungsorganisation: die Organisation der Unternehmungsleitung* (Köln: Westdeutscher Verlag, 1958).

80. Schmalenbach, *Dienststellengliederung im Grossbetriebe* ([1941], 1959) and *Pretiale Wirtschaftslenkung, Band 1: Die optimale Geltungszahl* and *Band 2: Pretiale Lenkung des Betriebes* (Bremen: W. Dorn, 1948). See the discussion and quote from 1, pp. 8–17. Also Hannelore Ludwig, *Die Wirtschafts- und Sozialwissenschaftliche Lehre in Köln von 1901 bis 1989/1990* (Köln: Böhlau, 1991), pp. 63–67. Erich Potthoff und Günter Sieben, "Eugen Schmalenbach (1873–1955)," in *Betriebswirte in Köln,* ed. Friedrich-Wilhelm Henning (Köln: Böhlau Verlag, 1988), pp. 1–33, esp. 24–25.

81. Schmalenbach, *Pretiale Lenkung des Betriebes: Band 2* (Bremen: W. Dorn, 1948), Einleitung.

82. TKA: NDI/4 Anrof M. C. Mueller, 31 Jan. 1947.

Conclusion

1. Barbara Maas, *Im Hause des Kommerzienrats* (Mülheim/Ruhr: Werry, 1990), pp. 49–53.

2. Brigitte Ingeborg Schluter, *Verwaltungsbauten der Rheinisch-Westfälischen Stahlindustrie 1900–1930* (Bonn: Dissertation Rheinischen Friedrich-Wilhelms Universitat, 1991).

3. Thyssen to Stinnes, 21 Aug. 1904 in *August Thyssen und Hugo Stinnes: Ein Briefwechsel 1898–1922,* ed. Manfred Rasch and Gerald D. Feldman (München: C. H. Beck, 2003), pp. 258–259.

4. Wilfried Feldenkirchen, *Siemens: 1918–1945* (Columbus: Ohio State University Press, 1995), p. 283.

5. Jürgen Kocka, *Unternehmensverwaltung und Angestelltenschaft am Beispiel Siemens 1847–1914: Zum Verhältnis von Kapitalismus und Bürokratie in der deutschen Industrialisierung* (Stuttgart: Klett-Cotta, 1969), pp. 88–89, 157–166, 171–190, quote from p. 172.

6. Jürgen Kocka, "Industrielles Management: Konzeptionen und Modelle in Deutschland vor 1914," *Vierteljahrschrift für Sozial- und Wirtschaftsgeschichte,* 56, 3 (Oktober 1969), 332–372. Kocka, *Unternehmensverwaltung,* p. 297.

7. Bernd Dornseifer, "Zur Bürokratisierung deutscher Unternehmen im späten 19. und frühen 20. Jahrhundert," in *Jahrbuch für Wirtschaftsgeschichte* (1993), pp. 72–77, example from p. 89. Dornseifer makes the same argument using different examples, especially from Siemens and IG Farben,

8. Bryn Jones, *Forcing the Factory of the Future: Cybernation and Societal Institutions* (Cambridge: Cambridge University Press, 1997), pp. 23–50.

9. TKA: A/643 "Geschäfts-Ordnung für Gewerkschaft Deutscher Kaiser, Abteilung Eisen, [probably ca. 1914]. I am grateful to Don Abenheim for pointing out this distinction between American and German military models. Manfred Rasch, "August Thyssen: Der Katholische Grossindustrielle der Wilhelminischen Epoche," *August Thyssen und Hugo Stinnes: Ein Briefwechsel 1898–1922,* ed. Manfred Rasch and Gerald D. Feldman (München: C. H. Beck, 2003), p. 23 also views Thyssen practice as conforming to the organization of the Prussian military.

10. Dick Geary, "The Industrial Bourgeoisie and Labour Relations in Germany 1871–1933," *The German Bourgeouisie: Essays in the Social History of the German Middle Class from the Late Eighteenth to the Early Twentieth Century,* ed. David Blackbourn and R. J. Evans (London: Routledge, 1991), pp. 147–152. Patrick Fridenson, "Authority Relations in German and French Enterprises, 1880–1914," in *Bourgeois Society in Nineteeth-Century Europe,* ed. Jürgen Kocka and Allan Mitchell (Oxford: Berg, 1993), pp. 323–345.

11. Wiesen, *West German Industry and the Challenge of the Nazi Past.*

12. Prinz/Zitelmann, *Nationalsozialismus und Modernisierung.*

13. Sheila Olgilvie and Markus Cerman, *European Proto-Industrialization* (Cambridge: Cambridge University Press, 1996).

14. Max Weber, *The Protestant Ethic and the Spirit of Capitalism* (New York: Scribner's Sons, 1958), pp. 193–194.

15. For a similar view, see John W. Meyer, "Sources and Effects of Decisions: A Comment on Brunsson," *Accounting, Organizations and Society,* 15, 1 (1990), pp. 61–65.

16. Kocka, *Unternehmensverwaltung,* pp. 552–555.

17. Peter Lawrence, *Managers and Management in West Germany* (New York: Croom Helm, 1980). Neil Fligstein, *Transformation of Corporate Control* (Cambridge, Mass.: Harvard University Press, 1990).

18. Yehouda A. Shenhav, *Manufacturing Rationality: The Engineering Foundations of the Managerial Revolution* (Oxford: Oxford University Press, 1999).

19. Erwin Grochla, *Unternehmungsorganisation: Neue Ansätze und Konzeptionen* (Hamburg: Rowohlt, 1972), p. 204. Gareth P. Dyas and Heinz T. Thanheiser, *The Emerging European Enterprise: Strategy and Structure in French and German Industry* (Boulder: Westview Press, 1976).

20. TKA: A/813/2 To the GDK, 28 Nov. 1918, Rabes: "Entwurf einer Geschäftsordnung für das Revisions-Bureau der Thyssen'schen Werke," Späing; Letter to Thyssen, 29 Sept. 1918, C. Verlohr.

21. MA: R 2 35 13.1 (3). The Wellrohrkesselmaterial-Verband, GmbH, 20 February 1925: "Ein notleidender Ruhrindustrieller: Thyssen verdient in 10 Jahren über 300 Millionen Goldmark."

22. Sharon Zukin and Paul DiMaggio, "Introduction," *Structures of Capital: The Social Organization of the Economy,* ed. Sharon Zukin and Paul DiMaggio (Cambridge: Harvard University Press, 1990), p. 14.

23. The evolution of this distinction is most famously outlined in Jürgen Habermas, *Structural Transformation of the Public Sphere: An Inquiry into a Category of Bourgeois Society* (Cambridge, Mass.: MIT Press, 1989).

24. MA: R 1 40 35.2 VSt Annual Report, 1936.

Appendix B

1. Peter Miller, "Accounting as Social and Institutional Practice: An Introduction," *Accounting as Social and Institutional Practices,* ed. Anthony G. Hopwood and Peter Miller (Cambridge: Cambridge University Press, 1994), pp. 1–39, quote from p. 6. Also T. Colwyn Jones, *Accounting and the Enterprise: A Social Analysis* (London: Routledge, 1995), pp. 25–33, 118–143. See also the journal *Accounting, Organizations and Society* with its eclectic set of approaches.

2. I am following the definition of an enterprise as a learning organization implied by Chandler's latest work and explicitly defined by Giovanni Dosi, David J. Teece, and Sidney Winter, "Toward a Theory of Corporate Coherence: Preliminary Remarks," *Technology and Enter-*

prise in a Historical Perspective, ed. Giovanni Dosi, Renato Giannetti, and Pier Angelo Toninelli (Oxford: Oxford University Press, 1992), pp. 185–211; the quote is from p. 198.

3. A visual counterpart to this approach might be Edward R. Tufte, *The Visual Display of Quantitative Information* (Cheshire, Conn.: Graphics Press, 1983) and *idem, Envisioning Information* (Cheshire, Conn.: Graphics Press, 1990). The literary counterpart to this approach would be Hayden White, *Tropics of Discourse: Essays in Cultural Criticism* (Baltimore: Johns Hopkins University Press, 1978). Hayden White, "The Historical Text as Literary Artifact," *History and Theory: Contemporary Readings,* ed. Brian Fay, Philip Pomper, and Richard T. Vann (Oxford: Blackwell Publishers Ltd., 1978), pp. 15–33, quote from p. 17. For a critique see Noël Carroll, "Interpretation, History, and Narrative," in the same volume, pp. 34–56.

4. This approach finds its predecessor in Peter Drucker's *Concept of the Corporation* (New York: John Day, 1972 [1946]). See as well the criticism of Chandler's *Scale and Scope* by Hidemasa Morikawa, "The View from Japan," *BHR,* 64 (Winter 1990), pp. 716–725. For a hint how this approach may work in an international perspective, see Jeffrey R. Fear, "Constructing Big Business: The Cultural Concept of the Firm," *Big Business and the Wealth of Nations,* ed. Alfred D. Chandler, Jr., Franco Amatori, and Takashi Hikino (Cambridge: Cambridge University Press, 1997), pp. 561–569.

5. Richard Biernacki, *The Fabrication of Labor: Germany and Britain 1640–1914* (Berkeley: University of California Press, 1995).

6. Peter Miller and Ted O'Leary, "Accounting and the Construction of the Governable Person," *Accounting, Organizations and Society,* 12, 3 (1987), pp. 235–265.

7. Alnoor Bhimani, "Accounting and the Emergence of 'Economic Man'," *Accounting, Organizations and Society,* 19, 8 (1994), pp. 637–674.

8. John Roberts, "The Possibilities of Accountability," *Accounting, Organizations and Society,* 16, 4 (1991), pp. 355–368.

9. H. Thomas Johnson and Robert S. Kaplan, *Relevance Lost: The Rise and Fall of Management Accounting* (Boston: Harvard Business School, 1991), pp. 32–43. H. Thomas Johnson, "Managing by Remote Control: Recent Management Accounting Practice in Historical Perspective," *Inside the Business Enterprise: Historical Perspectives on the Use of Information,* ed. Peter Temin (Chicago: Chicago, 1991), pp. 48–52. In the late nineteenth and early to mid-twentieth century, this distinction governed most German and American firms. Johnson uses Andrew Carnegie and argues against the post–World War II practice of American

firms of increasingly using financial information to guide manufacturing operations, thus eliding the difference between managerial and financial accounting.

10. Max Weber, *Economy and Society: An Outline of Interpretive Sociology*, ed. Guenther Roth and Claus Wittich (Berkeley: University of California,1979), pp. 85–100, quotes from pp. 85, 93. Richard Colignon and Mark Covaleski, "A Weberian Framework in the Study of Accounting," *Accounting, Organizations and Society*, 16, 2 (1991), pp. 141–157. I am concentrating on accounting's rationality at an institutional and organizational level, not at a social or political level.

11. For an insightful critique, see James G. March, "Ambiguity and Accounting: The Elusive Link between Information and Decision-Making," *Decisions and Organizations* (Oxford: Basil Blackwell, 1988), pp. 384–408.

12. Sonja Gallhofer and James Haslam, "The Aura of Accounting in the Context of a Crisis: Germany and the First World War," *Accounting, Organizations and Society*, 16, 5/6 (1991), pp. 487–520.

13. John W. Meyer and Brian Rowan, "Institutionalized Organizations: Formal Structure as Myth and Ceremony," *The New Institutionalism in Organizational Analysis*, ed. Walter W. Powell and Paul J. DiMaggio (Chicago: Chicago University Press 1991), pp. 41–62. Originally published in the *American Journal of Sociology*, 83, 2 (1977), pp. 340–363. Miller, "Introduction," pp. 9–13. Jan Mouritsen, "Rationality, Institutions and Decision Making: Reflections on March and Olsen's Rediscovering Institutions," *Accounting, Organizations and Society*, 19, 2 (1994), pp. 193–211.

14. Bruce G. Carruthers, "Accounting, Ambiguity, and the New Institutionalism," *Accounting, Organizations and Society*, 20, 4 (1995), pp. 313–328, quote from p. 326.

15. Wendy Nelson Espeland and Paul M. Hirsch, "Ownership Changes, Accounting Practice, and the Redefinition of the Corporation," *Accounting, Organizations and Society*, 15, 1/2 (1990), p. 80.

16. Paul J. DiMaggio and Walter W. Powell, "The Iron Cage Revisited: Institutional Isomorphism and Collective Rationality in Organizational Fields," *The New Institutionalism in Organizational Analysis*, ed. Walter W. Powell and Paul J. DiMaggio (Chicago: University of Chicago Press, 1991), pp. 63–82.

17. Edward C. Arrington and William Schweiker, "The Rhetoric and Rationality of Accounting Research," *Accounting, Organizations and Society*, 17, 6 (1992), pp. 511–533, esp. p. 518, Table 1. Dean Neu, "The Social Construction of Positive Choices," *Accounting, Organizations and Society*,

17, 3–4 (1992), pp. 223–237. Mouritsen, "Rationality, Decision-Making and Decision Making," pp. 201–202. Nils Brunsson, "Deciding for Responsibility and Legitimation: Alternative Interpretations of Organizational Decision-Making," *Accounting, Organizations and Society,* 15, 1 (1990), pp. 47–59. See also the intelligent critique by John W. Meyer, "Sources and Effects of Decisions: A Comment on Brunsson," in same, pp. 61–65.

18. Christine Cooper and Anthony Puxty, "Reading Accounting Writing," *Accounting, Organizations and Society,* 19, 2 (1994), pp. 129–131.

19. Johnson and Kaplan, *Relevance Lost,* have questioned the efficacy ROI ratios as a good indicator of internal managerial performance.

20. Richard J. Boland, Jr., "Accounting and the Interpretive Act," *Accounting, Organizations and Society,* 18, 2/3 (1993), pp. 125–146.

21. C. Edward Arrington and Jere R. Francis, "Letting the Chat out of the Bag: Deconstruction and Accounting Research," *Accounting, Organizations and Society,* 14, 1 (1989), pp. 1–28.

22. Cooper and Puxty, "Reading Accounting Writing." Miller and O'Leary, "Accounting and the Construction of the Governable Person."

23. Bhimani, "Accounting and the Emergence of 'Economic Man'," pp. 651–654.

24. N. B. Macintosh and R. Scapens, "Structuration Theory in Management Accounting," *Accounting, Organizations and Society,* 15, 5 (1990), pp. 455–477, but also see the critique by Boland, "Accounting and the Interpretive Act," in same.

25. Gallhofer and Haslam, "The Aura of Accounting in the Context of a Crisis," pp. 487–520.

26. Richard C. Laughlin, "Accounting Systems in Organisational Contexts: A Case for Critical Theory," *Accounting, Organizations and Society,* 12, 5 (1987), pp. 479–502.

27. Arrington and Francis, "Giving Economic Accounts."

28. Jeremy F. Dent, "Accounting and Organizational Cultures: A Field Study of the Emergence of a New Organizational Reality," *Accounting, Organizations and Society,* 16, 8 (1991), pp. 705–732.

29. Arrington and Schweiker, "The Rhetoric and Rationality of Accounting Research," and Graham Thompson, "Is Accounting Rhetorical? Methodology, Luca Pacioli and Printing," *Accounting, Organizations and Society,* 16, 5/6 (1991), pp. 572–599. Mary Poovey, *A History of the Modern Fact: Problems of Knowledge in the Sciences of Wealth and Society* (Chicago: University of Chicago Press, 1998), Chapter 2, pp. 29–91.

30. Gareth Morgan, "Accounting as Reality Construction: Towards a New

Epistemology for Accounting Practice," *Accounting, Organizations and Society*, 13, 5 (1988), pp. 477–485.

31. Espeland and Hirsch, "Ownership Changes, Accounting Practice, and the Redefinition of the Corporation." See the critique of their thesis by Robert P. Crum, "Accounting Magic and Corporate Control: A Discussion of Espeland and Hirsch," in same, pp. 97–105.

32. Alfred D. Chandler, Jr., *The Visible Hand: The Managerial Revolution in American Business* (Cambridge, Mass./London: Belknap, 1977), pp. 36–42, 109–120. For a different periodization for the United States, see Margaret Levenstein, *Accounting for Growth: Information Systems and the Creation of the Large Corporation* (Stanford: Stanford University Press, 1998), pp. 20–39. Richard K. Fleischman and Thomas N. Tyson, "Cost Accounting during the Industrial Revolution: The Present State of Historical Knowledge," *Economic History Review*, 46, 3 (1993), pp. 503–517. Keith Hoskin and Richard Macve, "Writing, Examining, Disciplining: The Genesis of Accounting's Modern Power," *Accounting as Social and Institutional Practice*, ed. Anthony G. Hopwood and Peter Miller (Cambridge: Cambridge University Press, 1994), pp. 67–97.

33. Kurt Schmaltz, *Bilanz- und Betriebsanalyse in Amerika* (Stuttgart: C. E. Poeschel Verlag, 1927), pp. 4–9.

34. For examples, C. G. Otto, *Die Buchführung für Fabrik-Geschäfte: Ein Neues System* (Berlin: Julius Springer, 1850). Adolph Busch, *Die Organisation und Buchführung des Eisengiesserei- und Maschinenbau-Betriebes* (Nordhausen: Adolph Büchling, 1854).

35. Albert Ballewski and C. M. Lewin, *Der Fabrikbetrieb: Praktische Anleitungen zur Anlage und Verwaltung von Maschinenfabriken und ähnlichen Betrieben sowie zur Kalkulation und Lohnverrechnung* (Berlin: Julius Springer, 1912), pp. 252–259 on auditing. Paul Montagna, "Accounting Rationality and Financial Legitimation," *Structures of Capital: The Social Organization of the Economy*, ed. Sharon Zukin and Paul DiMaggio (Cambridge: Cambridge University Press, 1990), pp. 227–260. See also, Michael Power, "The Audit Society," *Accounting as Social and Institutional Practices*, ed. Anthony G. Hopwood and Peter Miller (Cambridge: Cambridge University Press, 1994), pp. 299–316.

36. Miller, "Introduction," p. 20.

37. Rudolf Seÿffert, *Wirtschaftslehre des Handels* (Köln: Westdeutscher Verlag, 1951), p. 441.

38. Edward R. Tufte, *Envisioning Information* (Cheshire, Conn.: Graphics Press, 1990), pp. 12–35. Also Morgan, "Accounting as Reality Construction."

39. Quoted in Richard Evans, *In Defence of History* (London: Granta Books, 1997), p. 94.

40. Alan Roberts, "The Very Idea of Classification in International Accounting," *Accounting, Organizations and Society*, 20, 7/8 (1995), pp. 639–664.

41. A. Ackermann, "Betriebsvergleich nach Kostenarten oder nach Kostenstellen?," *Betriebswirtschaftliche Rundschau*, 5 (1928), pp. 191–192 and the debate therein.

42. Reinhardt Hanf, "Veröffentlichte Jahresabschlüsse von Unternehmen im deutschen Kaiserreich; Bedeutung und Aussagewert für Wirtschaftshistorische Analysen" in *Zeitschrift für Unternehmensgeschichte*, 23, 3 (Herbst, 1978), pp. 145–172. This held true well into the 1920's in both Germany and the U.S. In Germany, the standardization of account formats of all types played a central role in the rationalization debates of the Twenties. See H. Thomas Johnson, "Managing by Remote Control" in *Inside the Business Enterprise: Historical Perspectives on the Use of Information*, ed. Peter Temin (Chicago: Chicago University Press, 1991), pp. 41–69, esp. 48–52.

43. Levenstein, *Accounting for Growth*, pp. 164–195; quotes from p. 172 and p. 195.

44. James K. Glassman, "Michael Milken, Looking Beyond the Bottom Line," *Washington Post*, (28 Sept. 1997), H1, H14. "A Star to Sail By?" *The Economist* (2 Aug. 1997), pp. 53–55.

45. Robert Chia, "Organization Theory as a Postmodern Science," *Oxford Handbook of Organization Theory: Meta-Theoretical Perspectives*, ed. Haridimos Tsoukas and Christian Knudsen (Oxford: Oxford University Press, 2003), pp. 113–140, quote from p. 127.

46. Jerry Dermer, "Control and Organizational Order," *Accounting, Organizations and Society*, 13, 1 (1988), pp. 25–36.

47. Robert Simons, "The Role of Management Control Systems in Creating Competitive Advantage: New Perspectives," *Accounting, Organizations and Society*, 15, 2 (1990), pp. 127–143, esp. Table 1 on "strategic archetypes." See also the critique of his approach by Barbara Gray, "The Enactment of Management Control Systems," in same, pp. 145–148. Jeremy Dent, "Strategy, Organization, and Control: Some Possibilities for Accounting Research," *Accounting, Organizations and Society*, 15, 1 (1990), pp. 3–25.

48. Jones, *Accounting and Management*, pp. 123–4.

49. For an exploratory survey, see Mark Covaleski and Michael Aiken, "Accounting and Theories of Organizations: Some Preliminary Considerations," *Accounting, Organizations and Society*, 11, 4/5 (1986), pp. 297–

309. Levenstein, *Accounting for Growth*. I am grateful to Jonathan Steinberg for pointing out Goodheart's law to me.

50. Dermer, "Control and Organizational Order." For an empirical example, see Gordon Boyce, "Corporate Strategy and Accounting Systems: A Comparison of Developments at Two British Steel Firms, 1898–1914," *Business History*, 34, 1 (Jan. 1992), pp. 42–65.

51. Jones, *Accounting and the Enterprise*, pp. 121–123. Martha S. Feldman and James G. March, "Information in Organizations as Signal and Symbol," *Decisions and Organizations* (Oxford: Basil Blackwell, 1988), pp. 409–428.

Index

Abrath, Hermann, 413, 415; factory councils and, 425

Academia, 17, 225, 741–742; industry practice and, 616; Dinkelbach and, 684

Acceptances, 349, 356, 360–361

Accountability, 173–174

Accounting, 9; as communication, 35, 772–773; structure via, 35–36; as control, 36–37, 150–189, 338–343, 651–658; Thyssen & Co., 41; letter-press journals and, 110; product departments and, 117, 120–121; commercial offices and, 120–121; monthly department reports in, 155–157, 163–170; development of, 161–189; investments in, 162; operating expenses in, 162; guidelines for, 162–163, 586–587, 652–653; overhead in, 166–168; depreciation in, 166–170; American practices in, 170–175, 187; biases from, 173–174; cost vs. financial, 174–175; Americanization of, 174–176, 602–603; central production-cost office, 175–185; corporate culture and, 184; employment contracts and, 184–185; decision-making and, 185–187, 774–776, 787; enterprise reconceptualized by, 187–189; machine department, 194; Hollerith system, 213, 215, 587–590; quota negotiations and, 256; *Centralbureau*, 315–316; Central Auditing Office, 324–336, 338–343; standardization of, 328–329, 496–498, 593–606; organization of, 337–343; spreadsheet for, 339–342; profitability ratios in, 340–343; in Phoenix, 367–368; in Krupp, 369; in Siemens, 373; rationalization and, 459–461, 464, 773–776; Dillon

Read and, 489–498; VSt, 519–520, 569–617; in the VSt, 559; mechanization and, 578–579; Büro Dinkelbach, 584–593; goals in, 587; classification in, 589, 590, 593–606, 779–781; advantages and disadvantages of different systems in, 594–597; levels of VSt, 597; monthly financial reports in, 597–598; organizational structure and, 598–600, 602; expense types in, 599; administrative expenses in, 600–601; sales expenses in, 600–601; transfer prices and, 603–605; power and, 605–606; middle management and, 606; for subsidiaries, 647–648; subsidiaries and, 650–651; auditing and, 654–657; bookkeeping vs., 654–657, 778; chartered, 685–686; conceptions of control and, 729–739, 777–787; as symbolic practice, 770–787; financial vs. managerial, 772–773; as myth/ceremony, 774–776; neutrality in, 774–776; postmodern theory on, 776–777; as interpretation, 778–780; performance construction through, 782–783; Venetian vs. Tuscan, 782–783

Adenauer, Konrad, 55, 697, 699

Administrative expenses, 600–601, 621

AG Charlottenhütte, 552–553

Agency, 150; multisubsidiary form and, 297, 299; corporate, 482–488, 632–633, 635–636; collective, 506, 716–717, 744–745; VSt reorganization and, 632–633

AG Friedrichshütte, 552–553

AGHütt. *See* Aktiengesellschaft für Hüttenbetrieb in Ruhrort-Meiderich (AGHütt)

935

AG Oberbilker Stahlwerke, 279
Aktiengesellschaft für Hüttenbetrieb in
　Ruhrort-Meiderich (AGHütt), 276–279;
　director of, 277; in anti-cartel plans,
　277–278; gas engines and, 198, 199;
　growth of, 278–279
Alpine Montangesellschaft, 675
America: as yardstick for modernity, 21,
　722–726; antitrust legislation, 239–241;
　Great Merger Movement, 242; horizon-
　tal integration in, 258, 378; special path
　in, 378
American Exchange Irving Trust Com-
　pany, 638
Americanization, 6–7, 22–24; Sonderweg
　and, 12; Dinkelbach in, 23, 521, 522,
　663; of accounting, 174–176; Thyssen in,
　260, 286–287, 512–513, 514–517; at
　GDK, 282; CAO and, 335–336; mass pro-
　duction and, 520; VSt and, 520–522,
　566–568; routines in, 569; accounting
　and, 602–603; technology transfer and,
　606–617; mutual influence in, 614–617,
　723–724; Hitler and, 676; bureaucratiza-
　tion and, 720; reevaluation of, 722–726,
　733–734
Annexationism, 56–57
Appleton, Butler & Rice, 494–495
Arbitration, 424; councils, 388; wage/sal-
　ary negotiations and, 408; eight-hour
　day and, 421–422
Architecture/buildings: pipe mill, 98–99;
　Machine Company, 216; GDK, 273;
　CAO, 335; innovation and, 463–464;
　Mannesmann, 700–701; postwar, 700–
　701; narrative and, 711–714
Armaments, 432–433
Arnhold, Karl, 580–581
Arnst, Paul, 43–44
Assets: financial statement on, 339–343;
　owner's equity and, 344–345; Thyssen-
　Konzern, 358–359; debt and, 503–504;
　personal, 504–505; VSt, 644; of subsidiar-
　ies, 647–648
Association of German Machine Engi-
　neering Firms (VDMA), 543
Association of German Steelmakers, 459
ATH. See August Thyssen-Hütte,
　Gewerkschaft (ATH)
Audits: Eumann and, 157; year-end, 326,
　327–330

Audits, 597, 778; VSt, 654–657. See also Ac-
　counting
August Thyssen-Hütte, Gewerkschaft
　(ATH), 443, 455–456; Bartscherer and,
　458; Thyssenhandel and, 472–473;
　Thyssen-Konzern leased to, 482; recov-
　ery of, 489–490; long-term liquidity anal-
　ysis of, 499–501; in VSt, 562, 563; dis-
　mantling and reorganization of, 696–
　700; headquarters, 700–701; financial
　statements, 764–769
Authoritarian entrepreneurs, 5–6, 716–
　717, 720–721; late industrialization and,
　13–14
Authority: cultural values and, 14–15; orga-
　nizational structure and, 121–122; for-
　mal line vs. pragmatic operations, 130–
　131; ultimate, 150, 721; managerial au-
　tonomy and, 301–302; CAO, 333–334;
　VSt, 575–579, 668; decision-making and,
　743
Auxiliary Service Law, 387–388
AVI agreements, 543–544, 545

Backwardness, 12–14; Kocka on, 16–17
Bad Tönnistein, 112, 217
Baertl, August, 193–194
Bagel, Klara, 59, 275
Bank für Handel und Industrie, 351
Bank–industry relations, 15; cartels and,
　248–253; Phoenix and, 249–252
Bank voor Handel en Scheepvaart, 447
Barth, Walter: Dillon Read and, 490–498;
　Goldman Sachs and, 492–493
Barthes, Roland, 779
Bartscherer, Franz, 210, 456, 457–459, 581;
　Dinkelbach and, 681–683
Baumann, Carl-Friedrich, 459
Bayer, 426–427
Becker, Ernst, 118–119, 413; contract for,
　184–185; Richter and, 207; scrap trade
　and, 316, 471–472; Northwest Group
　and, 385; arrest of, 399; factory councils
　and, 413; on IG board, 434
Behrens, Peter, 713
Bellmann, W., 135–136
Berghahn, Volker, 12, 23–24, 677
Berlin branch, 112, 133–139; Nölle and,
　134–136; Eumann and, 136–138; Garrey
　and, 136–138; marketing, 305–306; audit
　of, 329; Thyssenhandel and, 468

Bethlehem, Fritz, 99–100
Betriebsführer, 669
Bicheroux, Désiré, 45–46, 58, 82
Biernacki, Richard, 771–772
Bismarck, Otto von, 3, 53
Blasberg, Robert, 126
Bochumer Verein, 648–649; origins of, 254
Bohr- und Schachtbau-Gesellschaft, 206, 266
Bookkeeping, 597, 778; double-entry, 171; VSt, 654–657. *See also* Accounting
Borbet, Walter, 581, 607–608; reorganization and, 626; property transfers and, 648–649
Borden, Richard, 171
Bornemisza, Margareta, 69–70
Bosch, Robert, 381
Bousse, Emil, 78–79; failure of, 122–126
Brady, Robert, 523–524, 563, 564
Brandi, Ernst, 664
Brassert, H. A., 504–506
Braun, Otto, 546
Brauns, Heinrich, 421–422, 423
Bread and Democracy in Germany (Gerschenkron), 13–14
Bremer Vulkan Schiffsbau- und Maschinenfabrik AG, 454
Brentano, Lujo, 236, 239
Britain: as yardstick for modernity, 21; German firms compared with, 258–259
Brökelschen, Ernst, 116, 666
Bruckhausen. *See Gewerkschaft Deutscher Kaiser* (GDK)
Bücher, Karl, 236
Buddenbrooks (Mann), 66, 71
Buff, August, 136, 137
Burbacher Hütte, 268, 269
Bureaucracy, 9, 744; Weber on, 29–31, 728–729; Thyssen & Co., 84–85; communication in, 152–161; at Siemens, 186–187, 371–372; boards and, 300; in German steel, 525; VSt, 615–616; accounting and, 655–656; limits on German, 719–720; Americanization and, 720
Burger, Franz, 211, 279
Büro Dinkelbach, 569, 584–593; information processing in, 590–591; knowledge creation in, 591–592; reorganization and, 621–624; systems management in, 650–651; conceptions of control and, 736; control through, 738–739

Business–government relations, 22; VSt negotiations and, 545–549
Business historiography: *Sonderweg* in, 11–24; backwardness theory in, 12–14, 16–17; Chandler on, 17–19

Capacity, 85, 100–101; economies of scale and, 86–88; excess, 256–257; exports and excess, 256–257; in *Konzerne,* 525–528; in VSt, 527–529; VSt, 556–557
Capitalism: Rhine model of, 6–7; competitive managerial, 18–19; cooperative managerial, 18–19; organized, 18–19; cartels and, 235–236, 240–241; American vs. German, 495–498; VSt and, 524–530; oligopoly, 568
Capitalization: VSt negotiations and, 533–534, 549–550; VSt, 549–551, 566–567, 567, 629, 640–641
Capital markets, 362
Capital transfers, 480–481, 635–636, 638–639
Carnegie, Andrew: Thyssen compared with, 7, 43–44, 506–507, 514–517; labor and, 27; accounting and, 36; economies of scale and, 86; prime costs and, 182; Kloman and, 224; cartels and, 288
Cartels: August Thyssen on, 78; capacity and, 87; GDK and, 135, 261, 262–263, 273–274; M.A.N. and, 199
Cartels, 231–232, 235–260; capitalism and, 235–236, 240–241; competition in, 235–236, 247, 259, 287–288; goals of, 236, 242; German view of, 236–241; freedom of association vs. competition and, 237–239; self-regulation and, 237–239; monopolies and, 238, 240–241; public perception of, 239; trusts vs., 239–241; size of, 241; in practice, 241–253; communities of interest as, 242; Düsseldorf Pig Iron Syndicate, 242, 244–245; Steel Works Association, 242, 245–247; types of, 242; Rhenish-Westphalian Coal Syndicate, 242–244; self-consumption rights in, 244, 253; stability of, 247–248; tariffs and, 248; universal banks and, 248–249, 248–253; Phoenix and, 249–252; diversification and, 253; vertical integration and, 253, 515–517; steel-firm strategy and, 253–260; niche strategy and, 254; quotas, 254–255, 284–285, 526–527;

Cartels *(continued)*
    competition mechanisms in, 254–257;
    syndicated vs. non-syndicated goods in,
    255; strategic incentives and, 255–256;
    exports and, 256–257; combines and,
    257; entrepreneurship and, 257; consoli-
    dation and, 257–258; pricing in, 258;
    economic performance and, 258–259;
    value questions and, 259; mergers vs.,
    259–260; strategy and, 261; Thyssen's ef-
    forts against, 261–295, 284–288, 512–
    513; Carnegie and, 288; Stahlwerke
    Thyssen and, 288–295; overproduction
    and, 292; decentralization and, 304–305;
    Rabes and, 323; profitability and, 343,
    497–498; *Thyssenhandel* and, 473; distor-
    tions from, 525–527; VSt and, 565–568,
    648–649; Fretz-Moon and, 611–612; VSt
    reorganization and, 631; VSt subsidiaries
    and, 642; Dinkelbach and, 678, 690–694;
    conceptions of control and, 734–735
Cash flow, 354, 357–359
Cassis, Youssef, 28
Castle Landsberg, 52–53
Catholic Center Party, 54–55, 58, 446
Cement syndicates, 473
Central Auditing Office (CAO), 231, 722;
    transparency and, 304; intersubsidiary
    conflicts and, 310–311; Hofs and, 324–
    336; organization of, 325; procedures of,
    325–326; as mediator, 326, 327, 335; sub-
    sidiaries' interaction with, 326; year-end
    audits of, 326, 327–330; pricing and,
    327; organizational studies by, 328–329;
    annual financial reports, 329–330; com-
    munity relations and, 331–333; standard-
    ization by, 333, 335–336; authority of,
    333–334; power of, 333–334; supervisory
    board, 334; building for, 335; control
    through, 338–343, 738–739; in IG, 433–
    434; the IG and, 439–440; Rabes in, 440;
    VSt and, 661–662
Centralbureau: Killing and, 106–107; func-
    tions of, 109–110, 155, 159; ordering
    and, 116–117; modernization of, 117–
    118; Berlin branch and, 136; managerial
    oversight by, 145; control through, 148–
    149, 314–316; reporting and, 155–157;
    decentralization and, 185–187; Thyssen-
    Konzern and, 311–316; transfer pricing
    and, 315–316

Central production-cost office, 175–185
Chandler, Alfred D., Jr., 1, 17–19; classifica-
    tion system of, 7–8, 24–31; on through-
    put, 87; on functional division, 121; on
    M-form, 232, 361–362, 658–659; on the
    VSt, 524; on accounting, 777
Chartered accounting, 685–686, 741
Chr. Weuste & Overbeck GmbH, 457
Christ and Madelaine (Rodin), 53
Church, Alexander Hamilton, 183
Circulairs, 153–155, 186
Clark, J. B., 691
Classification: Chandler's enterprise sys-
    tem of, 7–8; interpretation in, 779–781
Coal Syndicate. *See* Rhenisch-Westphalian
    Coal Syndicate
Coase, Ronald, 1, 746
Codetermination, 692–693, 695–696, 698,
    702, 709
Coking process: gas engines in, 202; gas
    from, 219; GDK and, 270; energy econo-
    mies and, 282–283
Collective bargaining, 388, 397–398, 405–
    407, 424; regional, 407–408
Commercial law, 482–483
Commerz- und Disconto-Gesellschaft
    Bank, 351
Communication: accounting as, 35, 772–
    773; routines for, 151; business genres,
    151–152; centralization of, 152–161;
    standardization of, 152–161; manage-
    ment circulars for, 153–155; monthly de-
    partment reports in, 155–157; factory
    councils in, 415–416
Communism, 403–405
Communities of interest. *See*
    Interessengemeinschaft (IG)
Community relations, 331–333, 336, 742;
    VSt, 541–542, 670–671; taxes and, 548
Competency, 228–229
Competition: intra-organizational, 145;
    cartels and, 235–260, 243–244, 247, 254–
    257, 259, 287–288; freedom of associa-
    tion vs., 237–239; coal syndicate, 243–
    244; Versailles Treaty and, 446; transfer
    prices and, 604–605
Conceptions of control, 8, 729–739; manu-
    facturing/productivist, 8, 41, 731–735;
    mercantile/commercial, 8, 41, 730–731;
    technocratic systems, 8, 735–736; ac-
    counting and, 35–36, 771–772; Thyssen

& Co., 41; VSt reorganization and, 627–628, 656–657; manufacturing, 731–735; definition of, 786

Continuity, 2; crises and, 4–5; management, 112, 114

Continuous pipe production, 281–282

Control: accounting as, 36–37, 150–189; as performance management, 37–38; Berlin branch and, 136–139; decentralization and, 148–149, 185–187, 737–739; delegation and, 150–151; efficiency and, 188–189; innovation and, 191–192; coherence and, 228–229; Thyssen-Konzern, 311; Central Auditing Office, 324–336; financial, 337–379; in Phoenix, 365–367; *Thyssenhandel* and, 474; VSt, 519–520, 522, 569–617; Büro Dinkelbach and, 584–593; Hollerith system in, 588; institutionalization of, 593–594; standardization and, 593–594; accounting standardization and, 593–606; strategy and, 784–787. *See also* Conceptions of control

Conventions, 593–594

Conversion costs, 176–182

Cooperative entrepreneurial capitalism, 25

Cooperative managerial capitalism, 18–19

Cordes, Walter, 699, 702–703, 704, 708

Core capabilities, 475–476

Corporate culture, 40, 41; intra-organizational competition in, 145; managerial qualities and, 146–147, 718; merchant-entrepreneurial, 146–148; accounting and, 184; coherence and, 228–229; multisubsidiary form and, 297, 299; expanding, 313–314; labor relations and, 385–386; *Thyssenhandel* and, 473–474; VSt, 583

Corporate estate, 670–671

Corporate law, 318–320, 479–489

Corporations, 1–2, 28–29; five fingers of, 32–35; Dinkelbach on, 686–687

Cost centers, 170

Craft/guild traditions, 19–20

Credit, 303–304, 338; among Thyssen firms, 350–351; GDK in, 436; liquidity crises and, 478–479; VSt manipulations in, 564, 653–654

Crude Steel Association, 543

Cusworth, George, 691

Dahl, Franz, 32–33, 55; Thyssen's relationship with, 73; GDK and, 268–270, 269–270; American trip of, 279; GDK and, 279–281; on cartels, 286; Stahlwerke Thyssen and, 290; autonomy of, 301–302; Späing and, 301–302; CAO and, 334; on IG board, 434; retirement of, 445

Daimler, Gottlieb, 196

Daimler-Benz, 427, 676

Darmstädter- und Nationalbank, 490

Das Werk, 579, 592

Dawes Plan, 479, 490, 492

Debt, 85; liquidity crisis and, 344–345; expansion and, 355–356; inflation and, 452; ATH, 503–504; allocation of VSt, 647–648

Decartelization, 23

Decentralization: management and, 111–114, 299–311; overall strategy and, 133–139; *Centralbureau* control and, 148–149; control and, 189; Thyssen-Konzern, 233, 299–311; financial advantages of, 303–304; cartels and, 304–305; market sensitivity and, 305–311; in M-forms, 362; labor and, 428–430; the IG and, 433–443; duplication and, 475; disadvantages of, 475–477; of decision-making, 582–584; coordinated, 715

Decision-making, 30; tradeoffs in, 33–34; investment strategy and, 139–149; accounting and, 185–187, 774–776, 787; market sensitivity and, 309–311; factory councils and, 412–413; in the IG, 435; in the VSt, 559–561, 574–575, 581–582, 582–584; decentralized, 582–584; Fretz-Moon process and, 613–614; authority and, 743

Deconcentration, 690–694

Deist, Heinrich, 695

Deleurant, Erich, 578, 584–585

DEMAG, 144, 193; VSt and, 544–545, 567

Department heads, 110–111, 229. *See also* Managers

Depreciation, 166–170; American practices on, 170–175; corporate culture and, 184; Thyssen-Konzern, 349–350; profit levels and, 352, 353–354; GDK, 438–439; postwar, 438–439

Deussen, Wilhelm, 127–128

Deutsche Bank: cartels and, 248; Phoenix and, 250

Deutsche Bank, 260, 351; Dillon Read and, 495

Deutsche Edelstahlwerke AG, 552–553, 700

Deutsche Grammophon-Gesellschaft, 370

Deutsche Röhrenwerke AG, 715

Deutsche Werft AG, 370, 452

Deutsch-Luxembourg: production in, 293

Deutsch-Überseeische Handelsgesellschaft der Thyssenschen Werke mbH, 323

Dillon, Clarence, 491, 492, 493

Dillon Read, 489–498; VSt and, 549–550; VSt accounting and, 584–585; VSt negotiations with, 637–638

Dinkelbach, Heinrich, 3, 677–709; Americanization and, 23, 521, 522, 663, 691, 708–709; on control, 37; Thyssen compared with, 44; on Fritz Thyssen, 63; double-entry bookkeeping and, 171; Härle and, 213, 215, 679–680; on Härle, 394–395; lockout and, 422–423; auditing office and, 441; on Konzerne, 452–453; rationalization and, 459–461; in reorganization, 479; Read Dillon and, 495; influence of, 521, 677, 684–687, 702–703; on tax negotiations, 547–548; Büro Dinkelbach and, 569, 584–593, 681; VSt accounting and, 584–585; in VSt reorganization, 618–619, 621–624; Vögler and, 624; conception of the firm and, 627–629; on product subsidiaries, 639–642; conceptions of control and, 657; as organizational architect, 657–658; business rhetoric of, 663–676; on leadership, 669–670; on corporate estate, 670–671; cartels and, 678; career of, 678–679; education of, 678–679; Fassnacht and, 679–680; WWI and, 680; Price Waterhouse and, 680–681; systems management and, 681, 707; VSt reorganization and, 681–683; authority of, 683–684; memory of, 683–684; Rohland and, 684; Schmalenbach and, 684, 690, 703–708; academia and, 684–685; chartered accounting and, 685–686; Nazi Germany and, 687–690; as Catholic, 689, 691, 692–693, 709; postwar career of, 689–690; deconcentration and, 690–694; British cooperation with, 691–695;

codetermination and, 692–693, 695–696, 698, 709; on private property, 692–693; attacks against, 693–694; health of, 693–694, 704; Cold War and, 694–695; Steel Treuhand and, 696–699; VSt dismantling by, 697–700; retirement of, 702–703

Dinkelbach School, 703, 707

Dinslaken, 272–274, 281–282, 302, 526

Disconto-Gesellschaft, 249–250, 251–252, 260, 343, 351, 491

Diversification: Thyssen & Co., 79, 80, 91–103; related, 80; cartels and, 253; at GDK, 280–281; managing, 378; bureaucratization and, 719–720

Dividends: Thyssen's forgoing of, 82; spreadsheet analysis for, 339–341; GDK, 345; per share, 497; ratios, 498; certificates, 535–536, 550; VSt, 535–536, 551, 566

Divisionalization of Concerns (Schmalenbach), 704–705

Djelic, Marie-Laure, 677

Dornseifer, Bernd, 19–22, 121–122, 150

Dow Chemical Company, 170–171, 781–782

Drieschner, Alfred, 97, 98, 100

Drummon, McCall & Co., 94

Duisberg, Carl, 397; factory councils and, 426–427

Duisburger Maschinenfabrik AG, 193

DuPont, 160, 171; branch offices, 330; return on investment at, 342, 343; innovation in, 658–659; VSt compared with, 660–661; Standard Practice Book, 720

Du Pont, Lammot, 153

Düsseldorfer Eisen- und Röhrenindustrie, 193, 364–365

Düsseldorf Pig Iron Syndicate, 242, 244–245, 278

Ebeling, C., 195–196

Ebert, Friedrich, 399

Economic Backwardness in Historical Perspective (Gerschenkron), 12–14

Economic conditions: 1873 stock-market crash, 76–77; 1889 slowdown, 89–90; WWI and, 232–233; Thyssen's financial crises and, 274–276; Versailles Treaty and, 445–446; Great Depression, 563, 616–617

Economics: cartels and, 236–237
Economies of energy, 190, 204–206; at GDK, 282–283
Economies of scale, 41, 732; expansion and, 76–81; Thyssen & Co., 85–91; GDK, 271; Stahlwerke Thyssen and, 290–291
Economies of scope, 254
Economies of speed, 87
Edison, Thomas, 100
Efficiency, 188–189; eight-hour day and, 421
Ehrhardt & Sehmer, 207–209, 322
Eigenschutz GmbH, 450–451
Eight-hour day, 156, 380–381, 399; demise of, 419–430; Vögler on, 525, 526
Electric-arc furnaces, 204
Electricity: machine department and, 202–203; factory operations and, 202–204; sales of surplus, 205–206; RWE and, 219–223; coherence and, 226; gas-powered dynamos and, 457
Elektrizitätswerke AG vorm W. Lahmeyer & Co., 220–223
Employer Association, 382, 384–385, 406
Employment contracts, 131–133, 184–185; grace periods in, 124–125, 132
Engineers: in management hierarchy, 110–111; entrepreneurship by, 143–145; Traut, 143–145; power of, 188; Thyssen's reliance on, 224–225
Entrepreneurial/personal enterprises, 24, 25–26
Entrepreneurs: German style of, 5–6; Weber on, 29–31; August Thyssen's views on, 54; managers as, 105; strategic control and, 139; engineers as, 143–145
Entrepreneurship, 25; cartels as, 257; authoritarian model of, 716–717
Environmental considerations, 740–748
Equity: debt levels and, 344–345, 499
Equity, 360; WWI impact on, 440–441; owner's, 499
Erhard, Ludwig, 677
Erzberger, Matthias, 55, 57, 58, 446; on IG board, 434
Essener Credit Anstalt, 343
Essener Steinkohlen-Bergwerke AG, 645
Esser, Heinrich, 607, 608, 609–610
Esser, Wilhelm, 561
Eumann, Hermann, 59, 114, 155, 156–157, 343; Berlin branch and, 136–138; RWE

and, 222; Thyssenhandel and, 472; Dinkelbach and, 680
Expansion: scale economies and, 76–81; tradeoffs in, 140–149; electricity delivery and, 220–221; GDK, 269–271, 279–284; financial crises and, 274–276; financing, 351–352, 354–356, 378–379
Exports, 82, 92–93; steel industry, 254, 256–257; VSt negotiations on, 541; reliance on, 545

Factory cost accounting, 174–175
Factory Council Law, 411–419
Factory councils, 381–382, 411–419; trade unions vs., 383; pragmatism of, 425–428
Factory-management systems, 4, 17
Fahrenhorst, Walther, 571
Fall River Iron Works, 171–173
Family-led enterprises, 6, 24–29, 28; zaibatsu, 296–297, 373–377; Konzerne, 377–378
Fassl, Aloys, 97, 100
Fassnacht, Gottlieb, 210, 212; Machine Company and, 213
Fasssnacht, Gottlob, 679–680
Feldenkirchen, Wilfried, 337, 344, 355, 524, 570–571, 619
Feldman, Gerald, 547, 564
Finance Ministry, 640, 641–643
Financial statements, 339–343; GDK, 346–348, 433–438, 752–753, 764–767; Price Waterhouse, 495–498, 501–504; balance sheet, 501–504; VSt negotiations and, 532; VSt standardized, 587–589; classification in, 589, 590–591; auditing and, 655–656; Dinkelbach and, 686–687, 702; Thyssen-Konzern, 754–757, 760–763
Financing: decentralization and, 303–304; Thyssen-Konzern, 343–361; debt levels and, 344–345; self-, 344–345, 504–505; banks in, 345–346, 351, 379, 447; Reichsbank in, 346; acceptances in, 349; expansion, 352–355, 378–379; outside funding in, 355; WWI and, 360–361; capital allocation and, 378–379; war production and, 433–440; postwar, 447–451; the IG in, 448–449; Wall Street in, 489–498; inflation and, 498–500; VSt manipulations in, 564
Finanzkapital (Hilferding), 338
Finishing industry, 542–546

Fixed costs: definition of, 86–87; capacity and, 86–88

Flaccus, Adalbert, 578, 607–608

Flensburger Schiffbau AG, 454

Flick Friedrich, 552–553, 571, 573, 583

Ford, Henry, 33

Forward integration, 320–324

Fossoul, Noel, 45–46

Franz Haniel & Cie, 25, 370

Freiburg School, 677

Freikorps, 400–401, 403–405, 409–411

Fretz-Moon process, 570, 606–617, 723

Friedrich Wilhelms-Hütte (FWH), 76, 199, 202; sale of, 544–545

Fulfillment policy, 419–420

Functional lines of organization, 32–35

Fusban, Adalbert: VSt legal offices and, 578; Fretz-Moon and, 611; reorganization and, 629–632

FWH. *See* Friedrich Wilhelms-Hütte (FWH)

Garrey, Otto, 136–138

Gas delivery, 218–220, 222–223

Gas engines, high-horsepower, 190, 196–206, 215; standardization of, 200; applications of, 201–202; electrification and, 202–203; success of, 202–204; coherence and, 226; at GDK, 283

Gasgesellschaft mgH, Hamborn, 445

Gas-powered electric dynamos, 457

Gas-turbines, 210

Gas- und Wasserwerke Gewerkschaft Deutscher Kaiser, 224

GDK. *See* Gewerkschaft Deutscher Kaiser (GDK)

Geisweider Eisenwerke, 455

Gelsenberg Deal, 633–634

Gelsenkirchener Bergwerks AG, 252

Gelsenkirchen (GBAG), 445, 633–634

Gender, 745

German Association of Unions (DGB), 695

German Fatherland Party, 409

German Imperial Court: on cartels, 237–239, 241

German Institute for Norms (DIN), 741

German Institute for Technical Industrial Training (DINTA), 580–581

Germanization, 521–522, 614–617, 723–724

German Metalworkers Association, 51

German National People's Party, 382–383

German People's Party (DVP), 317, 382–383

German Workers' Front (DAF), 580–581

Gerschenkron, Alexander, 21, 338; on *Sonderweg*, 12–14; on cartels, 248

Gessel, Theodor, 680

Gewerkschaft Deutscher Kaiser (GDK), 39, 82, 231, 261–276; founding of, 92; Nölle and, 135; machine department and, 194–195; high-horsepower gas engines and, 196–206, 283; origins of, 235–236; exports by, 256–257; in anti-cartel strategy, 261, 262; size of, 261, 272–273; in Thyssen's strategy, 261; founding of, 263; mining, 263–265; Kalthoff and, 264–265; mineshaft construction, 265–266; Schachtbau, 265–266; slag recycling, 265–266; internal demand and, 266; production at, 267–268; Bruckhausen, 267–271, 279–284; iron and steel, 267–271; Dahl and, 268–270, 269–270; pig-iron production, 269–270; expansion of, 269–271, 279–284; railway network, 270; rolling mills, 271–274, 280–281; strip steel, 271–274; seamless pipes, 272; Dinslaken, 272–274, 281–282, 302, 526; administration building, 273, 712–713; vertical integration of, 273; Thyssen's financial crisis and, 274–276; diversification at, 280–281; railway workshop, 281; continuous pipe production process, 281–282; managerial autonomy in, 301–302; *Centralbureau* control of, 311–316; Central Auditing Office and, 324–336; community relations and, 331–333; financing, 343–348; growth of, 344; dividends, 345; financial statements of, 346–348; Thyssen-Konzern finances and, 359–360; wartime labor in, 390–391; working conditions in, 390–391; strikes at, 398–399; in the IG, 435–438; postwar finances of, 435–438; depreciation in, 438–439; as financial center, 441; long-term liquidity analysis of, 499–501; financial statements, 752–753, 764–767

Gewerkschaft Friedrich Thyssen, 443, 455

Gewerkschaft Graf Moltke, 277

Gewerkschaft Lohberg, 206

Giddens, Anthony, 496

Gilles, Alfred, 120

Gilles, Heinrich, 416–417

Gillingham, John, 23, 677
Goldman, Sachs & Co., 492–493
Goodheart's law, 785
Göring, Hermann, 674–676
Graff, Berthold, 586, 661–662, 680
Graf Moltke, 217
Great Depression, 563, 616–617, 665, 735–736
Great Merger Movement, 242, 284–285
Grillo, Friedrich, 81, 82
Gropius, Walter, 615, 713
Gröschner, Heinrich, 406–407, 413, 416
Grosz, George, 50
Group Siegerland, 622, 623, 662
Gutehoffnungshütte (GHH), 76, 196, 269, 369–370; origins of, 254; Walsum harbor and, 319–320

H. A. Brassert, Inc., 492–493, 497
Hamborn, 91–92; GDK and, 263, 331–333; community relations with, 331–333; wartime migration to, 390; Workers' and Soldiers' Council, 399–400; tax case of, 488
Haniel, August, 319
Haniel, Franz, 76
Haniel-Konzern, 369–370
Hannah, Leslie, 102
Härle, Carl: August, Jr. and, 68–69; on transfer prices, 158–159; on delegation, 189; Maschinenfabrik and, 209, 210–212; profit calculations and, 330; strikes and, 394–395; worker committees and, 395; arrest of, 399; salary negotiations and, 406–408; factory councils and, 412–413; Dinkelbach and, 679–680
Harris-Burland, William, 691
Hartmann, Heinz, 14–15
Hasslacher, Jakob, 59–60, 62; tax break and, 545–549
Hatzfeld, Lutz, 77, 107
Haurand, Peter Wilhelm, 692–693
Heil, Bruno, 129–130
Heinrich Reiter GmbH, 323; *Thyssenhandel* and, 468
Helle, Amelie Zur, 64
Herr im Hause image, 5–6, 27, 717; backwardness and, 14; August Thyssen and, 73; rethinking, 720–721; conceptions of control and, 736–737
Heumüller, Franz, 612

Hibernia Affair (1904), 275
Hilferding, Rudolf, 18, 338, 546
Hilger, Suzanne, 27, 121–122
Hindenburg, Paul von, 51, 537
Hindenburg Program, 387–389
Hoesch, 293. *See also* Vereinigte Stahlwerke AG (VSt)
Hoffman, R., 197–198
Hofs, Heinrich, 324–336, 339, 342; Dinkelbach and, 661, 680
Hollerith system, 213, 215, 460, 520; VSt, 587–590, 650, 654–657
Holley, Alexander, 268
Hoover, Herbert, 421
Hörder Verein, 196, 251, 364
Horizontal integration, 258, 378; VSt, 523
Horten, Alfons, 291
Hours-of-work decrees, 421–422, 423
Hugenberg, Alfred, 634
Hyperinflation, 232–233

Ideal-types, 9, 21, 24
IG Farben, 426, 538, 676
IGs. *See Interessengemeinschaft* (IG)
Incentives, 122–126; grace periods, 124–125, 132; bonuses, 138; Jacob and, 401–402
Inden, Paul, 607
Independent Social Democrats, 382–383
Industrial relations, 380–430; factory councils, 381–382, 411–419; actors in, 382–384; forced corporatism in, 384–396; Military Command and, 386–388, 395; collective bargaining, 388, 397–398; government and, 388–389; transition to peacetime and, 395–396; revolution and, 396–405; Stinnes-Legien agreement, 397–398; military intervention in, 400–401, 403–405; institutionalization of, 405–411; eight-hour day and, 419–430; layoffs and, 422–423
Inflation: advantages and disadvantages of, 446–447, 451–464, 477; postwar, 446–447; stabilization crisis, 478–479; financing and, 498–500; VSt and, 563–564
Information: technology and, 151, 159–161; flow, 460, 495–496; VSt flow of, 575–579, 654; Büro Dinkelbach and, 590–591

Innovation, 190–229; commercial goals and, 200; engineers in, 224–225; coherence and, 226–228; feedback loops and, 228; steel industry, 254; architecture and, 463–464; in the VSt, 578–581; Fretz-Moon process and, 614–615; conditions for, 658–659; process of, 659; managers in, 717–720

Institute for Public Chartered Accountants, 592

Institutional isomorphism, 775

Institut Supérieur du Commerce de l'Etat, 45

Interessengemeinschaft (IG): with Ehrhardt-Sehmer, 207–209; as cartels, 242; *Konzerne* and, 296; war production and, 433–440; Stinnes', 452–453; trusts vs., 453–454; VSt as, 532–533; profits and, 630–631

International Acceptance Bank, 447, 491, 494

International Steel Cartel, 22, 544; exports and, 545; VSt and, 565

Intra-organizational competition, 145, 309–311

Inventory control, 117; reserve materials and, 154; office for, 157–158; CAO and, 328; valuation in, 330; Dinkelbach and, 460; VSt, 598

Investments: strategy formulation for, 139–149; accounting for, 162; GDK and, 263; ROE/ROI and, 342–343; inflation and, 452; liquidity and, 501

Iron ore supplies: Stahlwerke Thyssen and, 290–292; Rabes and, 322–323; Swedish, 447

Jacob, Arthur, 301–302, 400; CAO and, 334; fired, 401–402; on IG board, 434

Jacobus fields, 289–290, 291–292

James, Harold, 564

Jarres, Karl, 541, 616–617

Johnson, H. Thomas, 183

Joint-stock companies, 212–213, 483–484; AGHütt, 276; Stahlwerke Thyssen, 290; Thyssen on, 507

Joint ventures: with Stinnes, 199; with Ehrhardt-Sehmer, 207–209; Klöckner-Konzern, 455

Jones & Laughlin, 553–557, 610

Jordan & Meyer, 192–193

Journal of Commercial Research (Schmalenbach), 686–687

Kaiser-Wilhelm Institute, 741

Kalle, Julius: Thyssen's relationship with, 73; GDK and, 268; strip-steel mine and, 271–274; managerial autonomy of, 302; on IG board, 434; on Dinslaken, 526; Fretz-Moon and, 607

Kalthoff, Otto, 264–265

Kaplan, Robert S., 183

Kapp, Wolfgang, 409

Kapp Putsch, 409–411

Killing, Albert: Thyssen's relationship with, 73

Killing, Albert, 106–107, 108–109; Nölle and, 134; Berlin branch and, 137–138; *Circulairs* by, 153; telephones/typewriters and, 159–161; GDK and, 311–315

Kindt, Heinrich, 325, 326, 435, 586; CAO and, 334, 440; Dinkelbach and, 680

Kirdorf, Emil, 252, 255, 717–718

Klass, Gert von, 524

Kleinschmidt, Christian, 524

Kleinwächter, Friedrich, 236, 239

Klöckner, Peter, 211, 279

Klöckner-Konzern, 455

Kloman, Andrew, 224

Klönne, Carl, 63; August, Jr. and, 65; divorce contract and, 66; Deutsche Bank and, 248; Phoenix and, 250; on cartels, 287–288; Dillon Read and, 495

Kluitmann, Leo, 569, 624; VSt accounting and, 584–585, 587–589; on Dinkelbach, 678

Knepper, Gustav, 403, 574, 581, 623

Kocka, Jürgen, 15–17; on preindustrial influences, 19–22; on Chandler, 28–29; on bureaucratization, 30–31, 728–729; on Siemens, 147, 187; Dornseifer on, 150; on accounting, 174

Kontinentale Treuhandgesellschaft, 586

Konzerne: as multisubsidiaries, 6

Konzerne, 232; definition of, 296–297; pre- and postwar, 369–370; *zaibatsu* compared with, 373–377; capital allocation in, 378–379; inflation and, 452–453; German corporate law and, 479–489; vertical integration in, 525–528; reinvention of, 658–663; Dinkelbach plan for, 690–694, 705

Krähe Circle, 703–704
Krefelder Stahlwerke, 211, 279, 432, 455
Krupp: employment by, 74; managerial
  trust at, 108–109; corporate culture at,
  146–147; *General Regulations*, 147; reorganization at, 161; origins of, 254; size
  of, 258–259; production in, 293; organization of, 368–369; accounting in, 369;
  bond issue, 492–493. *See also* Vereinigte
  Stahlwerke AG (VSt)
Krupp, Alfred, 5; Villa Hügel, 52; patriarchal style of, 146–147
Krupp von Bohlen und Halbach, Gustav,
  537

Labor, 27, 233, 380–430; eight-hour day
  and, 156, 380–381, 399, 419–430, 525,
  526; specialization of, 362; factory councils, 381–382, 411–419; corporatism and,
  384–396; employment policies, 385–386;
  shortages of, 385–386; arbitration and,
  388; collective bargaining, 388, 397–398;
  turnover rates of, 389–390; housing and,
  390; overtime and, 392; strikes, 392–396;
  military intervention and, 400–401, 403–
  405; layoffs, 422–423; management redefined by, 428–430; commodification of,
  771–772
Labor Ministry, 421–422
Labor unions, 239; political parties and,
  382–384; military and, 386–388; transition to peacetime and, 395–396; wage
  rates and, 405–407; Weimar and, 408–
  410
Lane, Frederic, 782–783
Langnamverein, 317
Lapwelded pipes, 79
Law regarding the New Order of the Steel
  Union-Concern, 641–642
Lazonick, William, 1–2
Leadership: managers in, 127–128, 146–
  147, 301–302, 476, 513–514; machine
  department, 209–210; *Betriebsführer,* 669–
  670
Legal issues: Späing and, 316–320; corpo-
  rate law, 318–320, 479–489;
  Thyssenhandel and, 474; VSt, 578; VSt re-
  organization and, 629–643
Legien, Carl, 397–398, 411
Leitungsorganization (Schmalenbach), 705–
  706

Lenze, Franz, 219, 225
Letter-press journals, 110
Lex Stahlverein, 620
Licensing, 607–617
Liefmann, Robert, 239–240
Liquidity: crises in, 344–345, 478–479
Liquidity, 451; long-term analysis of, 499–
  501; quick ratio in, 500–501; VSt and,
  507–508; ATH, 766–767; GDK, 766–767
List, Friedrich, 236–237
Lockouts, 422–423, 424
Lux, Thomas, 677

M.A.N., 198, 199, 215; takeover of, 452
Management: tradeoffs and, 32–35;
  around product departments, 40–41; development of, 104–149; Thyssen & Co.,
  104–149; modular, 105, 119–121, 673–
  674; hierarchy in, 110–111; *Meister* in,
  110–111; authority and, 111; reforms of,
  111–114; *Centralbureau* and, 118–119;
  monitoring of, 145; growth of, 159; redefined by labor, 428–430; rationalization
  and, 457–464; VSt, 570–584; accounting
  and, 606; architecture and, 711–714;
  owner distance from, 713–714; reevaluation of German, 716–739; middle, 719–
  720; strategy vs. control in, 784–787
Management circulars, 153–155, 186
Management companies, 635–637, 638
Managerial enterprises, 24, 26
Managers: modern corporations and, 1–2;
  systems, 3; Thyssen's relationships with,
  72–73, 105, 145; entrepreneurship of,
  105, 122–126, 133; strategy formulation
  by, 108–109, 133–139, 295; incentives
  for, 122–126; performance and, 122–
  126; Thyssen's evaluation of, 123–128;
  grace periods for, 124–125; productivity
  demands on, 125–127; leadership qualities in, 127–128, 146–147, 301–302, 513–
  514; as role models, 128; collegiality
  among, 128–131; formal authority vs.
  pragmatic operations and, 130–131; professional behavior of, 131–133; self-sufficiency of, 131–133, 146; salaries of,
  132; investment strategy and, 139–149;
  rivalries among, 301–302; as policy makers, 428–430; middle, 606; innovation
  and, 659; professionalization of, 745
Mann, Thomas, 66, 71

Mannesmann, 99–100, 507–508; origins of, 254; cartels and, 287; VSt and, 539; skyscraper of, 700–701

Manufacturing/productivist conception of control, 8, 41, 731–735

Marketing: Thyssen & Co., 82; capacity and, 87–88; exports, 100–101; Berlin branch and, 139; coherent strategy in, 295; *Thyssenhandel*, 305, 464–477; war production and, 433; Neuhaus in, 465–467

Markets: sensitivity to, 305–311; transfer prices and, 604–605

Marshall Plan, 23, 694, 696

Maschinenfabrik Thyssen & Co., AG, 40, 209–216, 441; high-horsepower gas engines, 190, 196–206; regeneration economies of, 190, 196–206; R&D at, 191; origins of, 192–209; accounting in, 194; GDK and, 194–195; quality issues in, 197–198; expansion of, 200; employees in, 201; ownership of, 212; strike against, 212; as Swabian, 212; as joint-stock company, 212–213; Hollerith system, 213, 215; organization of, 213–215; sales of, 215; buildings of, 216; education system and, 216; coherence and, 227–228; marketing by, 228; contract negotiations for, 309–311; spreadsheet analysis for, 339–342; wartime labor and, 391–392; strikes at, 393–395; postwar finances of, 437, 438; modernization of, 456–457; rationalization in, 461–464; sale of, 544–545

McNeil, William, 490

Measurement, impact of, 785

Mechanization, 589–590

Meister, 110–111, 154

Melcher, Aloys, 277; on IG board, 434

Mercantile conception of control, 8, 41, 730–731

Merchant-business enterprise model, 189, 512, 717–719

Mergers and acquisitions: Great Merger Movement, 242, 284–285; cartels vs., 258–260; Phoenix, 363–368; postwar, 438; IGs and, 452–454; inflation and, 452–455; Thyssen-Konzern, 475–476; VSt, 524–530; ATH, 700; autonomy and, 719–720

Metzmacher, Franz: plate mill and, 93–94

Meyer, Rudolf, 193

MICUM *(Mission Interalliée des Mines et des Usines)*, 419–420, 450–451

Military Command, 386–388, 395, 400

Military influences, 5–6, 74; line of command, 111; in labor relations, 386–388, 409–411

Mineshaft construction, 265–266

Mitsubishi, 373, 375–377

Mitsui, 6, 373–375

Mitteldeutsche Stahlwerke, 552–553

Modernization, 455–457; welding shop, 142–143; inflation and, 477; financial conditions and, 499; VSt and, 550, 563–564

Modular management, 105, 119–121, 673–674, 704–705

Mollin, Gerhard, 524

Moltke, Helmuth von, 20

Monopolies, 88; electricity, 220–221; cartels and, 238, 240–241. *See also* Cartels; Trusts

Monthly departmental reports, 155–157, 163–170; machine department, 193; at GDK, 314–315

Morgan Construction Company, 195, 281–282

Mülheim, 75–76, 91–92; Workers' and Soldiers' Council, 398–404; strikes in, 403–405

Multidivisional structure (M-form), 6, 8; accounting and, 174–175; Thyssen-Konzern as, 231, 232, 361–379; *Konzerne* as, 232; Konzerne, 296–297; Thyssen's preference for, 297, 299; Späing and, 318–320; importance of, 361–362; advantages of, 362; unified corporations vs., 365, 625–629; Japanese, 373–377; international perspective on, 373–378; family-led, 377–378; VSt as, 618–619; reinvention of, 658–663; Dinkelbach and, 686–687; Schmalenbach on, 705–707

Murmann, Johann Peter, 225

N. V. Handels en Transport Maatschappij Vulcaan, 322, 447

Nationalbank für Deutschland, 351

National identity, 2

Nazi Germany, 11; big business and, 620; as VSt shareholder, 620, 633–634, 640–641; moratorium of, 638; VSt business rhetoric and, 663–676; supporters of, 664; economic theory in, 668–669; VSt accommodation to, 674–676; Dinkelbach and, 687–690; Schmalenbach and, 688–689

Neill, Jack W. F., 695

Nelson, Richard, 4, 40

Neo-institutional analysis, 774–776

Neuhaus, Philip, 134, 305, 307; RWE and, 222; marketing and, 465–467, 468

Niederrheinische Gas- und Wasserwerke GmbH, 445

Nölle, Ernst, 155; Berlin branch and, 112, 134–136; accounting guidelines of, 162–163, 169; monthly report structure and, 163–170; conceptions of control and, 731–732

Norms, 593–594

North German Iron and Steel Control Board, 691–692

Northwest Group, 382, 384–385, 406; Military Command and, 387; wage standardization and, 406

Noske, Gustav, 401, 404, 405

November revolution (1918), 380–381, 393, 443, 445

Oberbilker Stahlwerk, 206, 432

Oparka, P., 135–136, 137

Open-hearth process. See Siemens-Martin process

Oppenheim, Sal. Jr., 699

Ordering process: Thyssen & Co., 114–117; delivery dates and, 123–126

Organiserter Kapitalismus, 18–19

Organizational culture, 122–133; personality and, 514

Organizational learning, 4, 28–29, 217, 334; tradeoffs and, 33–34; postmodern theory on, 37–38; organizational culture and, 122–133; Thyssen & Co., 122–133; Büro Dinkelbach and, 591–592; accounting and, 771

Organizational structure: commercial vs. technical offices in, 105–106, 145; product departments in, 112–113; function in, 121–122; Machine Company, 213–215; multidivisional, 231, 232; comparisons of, 361–379; heterogeneity of German, 373; war production and, 433–440; clarity of, 454; transfer prices and, 468–

471; VSt, 535, 576–579, 715–716; accounting and, 598–600, 602; economic vs. legal concepts in, 641–643; VSt reorganization and, 650–651

Organschaftstheorie (theory of corporate agency) 482–488, 744–745; leasing arrangements and, 484–488, 635–636; taxes and, 484–488; VSt reorganization and, 620, 632–633; capital transfers and, 635–636, 638–639; Späing and, 661, 741

Overdieck, Diedrich, 131, 132

Overhead, 166–168; allocating, 167–168; American practices on, 174; CAO distribution of, 329–330; VSt, 598–600

Patriarchy, 54, 71–72, 186; at Krupp, 146–147

Peak works, 536–537, 559, 561–562; overhead and, 599

Performance: accounting for, 35–37, 168–169; control and, 37–38; incentives for, 122–126; Thyssen's definition of, 122–126; employment contracts and, 184–185; enterprise reconceptualization and, 188–189; market, 305–311; evaluation of, 575–579; in the VST, 575–579; transfer prices and, 604; accounting as construction of, 782–783; measuring, 785

Perrow, Charles, 593–594

Personnel issues: product departments and, 117; Deussen and, 127–128

Personnel issues, 154; women employees, 160, 389, 390, 391, 407; machine department, 197–198; worker committees and, 407–408. See also Industrial relations; Labor

Pferdmenges, Robert, 699

Phoenix, 249–252, 363–368; origins of, 254; production in, 293; control in, 365–368. See also Vereinigte Stahlwerke AG (VSt)

Phoenix-Rheinrohr AG, 700

Pickhardt, Moritz, 155, 157–158, 218

Pig Iron Syndicate, 284–285

Plumpe, Werner, 381–382, 408, 429

Poensgen, Albert, 193

Poensgen, Ernst, 364–365, 564; in VSt decision-making, 574; Fretz-Moon and, 607, 609; reorganization and, 640–641; sales clearing houses and, 652; Göring and, 675–676

Poensgen, Helmuth, 578, 583
Political economy office, 579–580
Politics, 22; August Thyssen's, 53–58; profitability and, 90; accounting and, 162–163; decision-making and, 309–311; industrial relations and, 382–384; Kapp Putsch and, 409–411; tax negotiations and, 546–548; VSt and, 663–676
Porter, Michael, 20
Portland Company, 172
Potthoff, Erich, 695, 703–704, 705–706
Pouch, Walter, 218, 221, 222
Power of attorney (*Prokura*), 108–109, 114, 120
Preindustrial traditions, 14, 19–22
Press- und Walzwerke Reisholz, 143, 432, 448, 450, 454
Price Waterhouse, 489–498; balance sheet by, 501–504; VSt accounting and, 584–585; VSt negotiations with, 637–638; Dinkelbach and, 680–681, 695
Pride, 51–52, 123, 128, 506
Prime costs, 174, 182–183
Process improvements, 97–99
Production, 4; scientific professionalization of, 191; small-batch, 232; exports and, 256–257; research and, 282–283; Stahlwerke Thyssen, 291; Bartscherer and, 459; Dillon Read and, 497; Thyssen on, 512–513; in VSt, 527–529
Production costs: sales price vs., 80–81; accounting and, 173–174, 176–183; standardization of, 328
Production engineering perspective, 256
Productivity: expansion and, 80; manufacturing improvements and, 96–97; under Bousse, 124–125; in *Konzerne*, 525–528; measuring, 531–532; VSt, 557–565; VSt reorganization and, 651–652; accounting as construction of, 782–783
Product subsidiaries, 635, 637–643
Profitability: business politics and, 90; managers' responsibility for, 123–126; factors in assessment of, 145; transfer prices and, 157–159, 470, 605; savings as, 188–189; Machine Company, 215; spreadsheet analysis of, 339–343; cartels and, 343; Thyssen-Konzern, 352–355; profits vs., 353–354; return on equity and, 356–

361; return on investment and, 357; WWI and, 360–361; postwar, 435–438; Dillon Read and, 496–498; VSt reorganization and, 644, 651–652, 656
Profit centers, 170
Profit-pooling, 433–440
Profits: reports on, 155–157; overhead and, 166–168, 184; depreciation and, 166–170, 184; cartels and, 256; CAO calculation of, 330; return on investment and, 340–341; Thyssen-Konzern, 352–355; Weber on, 782–783
Protoindustrialization, 725–726
Prussian Mining Authority, 265, 275
Purchasing office, 157–158

Quality issues: machine department, 197–198, 207; gas engines and, 200
Quick ratio, 500–501
Quotas, 254–255; buying/selling, 255–256; accounting and, 256; VSt, 532–533; VSt reorganization and, 631; peak works and, 649; subsidiaries and, 649

Rabes, Carl: Thyssen's relationship with, 73; Verlohr and, 278; *Thyssenhandel* and, 320–324; CAO and, 325, 334, 440; employment policies and, 386; on IG board, 434; financial manipulations by, 450; Dinkelbach and, 461, 680; inflation and, 477; in reorganization, 479; Dillon Read and, 490–498; Goldman Sachs and, 492–493; in VSt decision-making, 574; VSt central purchasing and, 578; VSt accounting and, 584–585; decision-making and, 743
Radkau, Joachim, 191
Rathenau, Emil, 101
Rationality, 9; formal vs. substantive, 36; ROE/ROI and, 342–343; substantive vs. formal, 773–774
Rationalization: manufacturing/productivist conception of control and, 8, 41, 731–735; German path of, 40–41; of space, 99; accounting and, 184–185; economies of energy and, 190, 204–206; quotas and, 255–256; GDK, 279–281, 282–283; CAO in, 335–336; WWI and, 432; technical, 457–459; Thyssen-Konzern, 457–459, 464; Dinkelbach and, 459–461; Machine Company, 461–464;

architecture and, 463–464; transfer prices and, 473–474; VSt, 520, 523–568; Americanization and, 521–522; peak works and, 536–537; horizontal, 548–549; negative, 553, 558; problems in, 553–559; production unit, 557–558; second wave of, 565; Büro Dinkelbach and, 592–593; manufacturing vs. administrative, 628–629; organizational design as, 715–716

Rätsch, Herbert, 586

Raumer, Hans von, 545–546

Reckendrees, Alfred, 524, 558–559, 567–568, 570–571, 619, 662

Regeneration economies, 190, 196–206, 204–206

Reichsbank, 346

Reichsgruppe Industrie, 317

Reichswerke AG Hermann Göring, 675–676

Rentenmark, 478–479

Rents, 165–166

Reorganization: Thyssen-Konzern, 443–451; VSt, 618–676

Reports: monthly departmental, 155–157, 163–170; VSt financial, 587–589, 597–598

Republic Steel, 609, 610

Research and development, 191, 283; VSt, 580–581

Return on equity (ROE), 340–341, 356–361

Return on investment (ROI) ratios, 171, 340–341; DuPont, 342, 343

Reusch, Hermann, 693

Reusch, Paul, 320, 369–370

Reussner, Adolf, 129–130

Rhein-Elbe-Union, 539–540. *See also* Vereinigte Stahlwerke AG (VSt)

Rheinische Bank, 345–346

Rheinische Kalksteinwerke, GmbH, Wülfrath, 279

Rheinischen Braunkohlen-Aktiengesellschaft (RBAG), 475–476

Rheinische Stahlwerke, 293. *See also* Vereinigte Stahlwerke AG (VSt)

Rheinisch-Westfälische Elektrizitätswerke (RWE), 205–206, 219–223

Rheinstahl, 539–540

Rhenisch-Westphalian Cement Syndicate, 473

Rhenisch-Westphalian Coal Syndicate, 240, 242–244, 284–285; pricing in, 243; competition in, 243–244; self-consumption rights in, 244; GDK and, 263–265

Richter, Hans, 190, 198–201, 457–458; gas engines and, 200–206; Becker and, 207; Stinnes and, 221–222

Rittergut Rüdersdorf, 67, 68, 278

Rodin, Auguste, 53

Roeckner, Martin, 139–140, 142–143

Rohland, Walter, 684, 694–695

Rolling Mills: Machine Company and, 216; GDK, 271–274; wartime labor and, 389–390, 391–392; in Thyssen & Co. AG, 441; modernization of, 456; architecture of, 463–464; headquarters, 713. *See also* Gewerkschaft Deutscher Kaiser (GDK)

Rombacher Hüttenwerke, 552–553

Roser, Edmund, 144, 202, 210, 212; profit calculations and, 330; worker committees and, 395; arrest of, 399; salary negotiations and, 406–408; war production and, 432; on IG board, 434

Routines, 4; failure and, 122–126; communication and, 151; management circulars on, 154; machine department and, 229; VSt, 569, 575–579; accounting and, 775–776

Rubber shaft loophole, 243, 244

Ruhr Iron Lockout (1928), 424

Ruhr Struggle (1923), 212, 418–420; eight-hour day and, 420–421

RWE. *See* Rheinisch-Westfälische Elektrizitätswerke (RWE)

Sales: reports on, 155–157; machine department, 207; Erhardt & Sehmer and, 208; Machine Company, 215; *Thyssenhandel* and, 320–324; expense allocation for, 600–601; clearing houses, 645, 647, 652

Scale and Scope (Chandler), 18, 19, 25–29

Schaaffhausen'sche Bankverein, 249–250, 251–252, 343, 351

Schacht, Hjalmar, 47, 634

Schachtbau Thyssen GmbH, 445

Schalker Gruben- und Hüttenverein, 81–82, 252

Schlitter, Oscar, 303–304, 495

Schloss Landsberg, 52–53, 712

Schmalenbach, Eugen, 339–343, 342, 570; VSt accounting and, 586, 590–591, 616; balance analysis by, 656; Nazi Germany and, 688–689; Dinkelbach and, 690, 703–708; schematism and, 736

Schmalenbach Society, 570, 684, 703–708

Schmid, Eduard, 332, 333, 346

Schmidt, Paul, 128

Schmitz, August, 126–127

Schmoller, Gustav, 239–241, 241

Schneider, Karl, 200

Schulze, Ernst, 454

Schumpeter, Josef, 30, 515

Scientific management: energy economies and, 204–206; Carnegie and, 224; innovation and, 659; architecture and, 711–712; German vs. American, 734

Scientific professionalization, 191

Scrap trade, 316, 471–472

Seamless pipes, 99–100

Sebold, Heinrich, 410–411

Self-consumption rights, 244; steel industry, 253; excess capacity and, 257; Fretz-Moon and, 611–612

Self-regulation, 237–239

Sempell, Oskar, 580, 637–638

Severing, Carl, 404, 408–409

Shareholders: German law and, 483; VSt, 519, 533, 538–549, 566, 571, 573; combines and, 551

Sherman Antitrust Act, 239, 241

Siegrist, Hannes, 17

Siemens: Kocka on, 15; corporate culture at, 146–147; management circulars at, 153; reorganization at, 161; organization of, 370–373; Managerial Secretariat, 372; accounting in, 373; factory councils, 426; technical bias in, 718

Siemens, Carl Friedrich von, 371, 453

Siemens, George von, 248, 718

Siemens, Werner von, 101, 147–148, 718

Siemens, Wilhelm von, 187

Siemens & Halske, 147–148, 186–187, 370–373

Siemens-Martin process, 79; start-up problems with, 88–89; quality improvements in, 96; electrification and, 206; at GDK, 267–271, 279–281

Siemens-Rheinelbe-Schuckert Union (SRSU), 452–453

Siemens-Schuckertwerke (SSW), 370–373, 539

Silverberg, Paul, 475–476

Simon, Herman Veit, 341

Sloan, Alfred, 659, 715

Smith, Adam, 236–237, 253

Social Democratic Party (SPD), 382–383, 397–398

Social Democrats, 239, 380–381

Socialism: August Thyssen's views on, 53–54; mines socialized and, 402–404; Ruhr industry and, 693–695

Social policy, 233, 318, 406; VSt, 579–580. See also Industrial relations

Sohl, Hans-Günther, 458, 690, 694–695, 699

Sohl-Kreis, 690

Sonderweg (special path), 11–24, 378

Späing, Wilhelm, 301–302, 316–320; Rabes and, 324; on CAO objectives, 333–334; employment policies and, 386; IG formation and, 433–435; on IG board, 434; reorganization and, 443, 445; financial manipulations by, 450; unification and, 476–477; in reorganization, 479; corporate agency and, 482; in Organschaftstheorie and taxes, 484–488; VSt legal offices and, 578; VSt reorganization and, 632–633, 635–641; on product subsidiaries, 639–642; environmental issues and, 740–748

Spang Chalfant, 609, 610

Spartacist movement, 401

Special path. See Sonderweg (special path)

Spiegel, Karl, 398

Stabilization crisis, 233, 478–479, 498–500

Stahl und Eisen, 215, 741–742

Stahlunion-Export, 700

Stahlverein GmbH für Bergbau- und Industriewerte, 644

Stahlwerke Thyssen AG: August, Jr. and, 67–68

Stahlwerke Thyssen AG, 246, 288–295; loss of, 361, 489–490

Standardization: of communication, 152–161; of gas engines, 200; CAO in, 328–329, 335–336

Standardization, 333; in Phoenix, 368; wages/salaries, 385–388, 391–392, 405–407; wage, 406; of financial statements,

495–498; VSt negotiations and, 532; in reporting, 587–589; VSt financial reports, 587–589
Standard Oil, 171, 240
Standard operating procedures, 575–579
State-bureaucratic model, 5, 14, 719–720; Kocka on, 15–17
State Mining Authority, 292
Steel industry, 74; coal syndicate and, 253; vertical integration in, 253–254; cartels and, 253–260, 525–527; production in, 293; Versailles Treaty and, 445–446; bureaucratic control in, 525; finishing industry, 542–546; German vs. U.S., 553–557; Fretz-Moon and, 611–613; codetermination in, 695–696; Dinkelbach's restructuring of, 695–702
Steel Treuhand, 696–699
Steel Works Association: Phoenix and, 249–252
Steel Works Association, 284–285; Thyssen in, 287–288; regional offices, 308
Steffens & Nölle, 135, 370
Steinisch, Irmgard, 420
Stewarts & Lloyds, 613
Stinnes, Clara, 51, 52, 56, 223, 402
Stinnes, Hugo, 5; home of, 47; on Thyssen's personality, 49; caricature of, 50; on Fritz Thyssen, 63; divorce contract and, 67; August, Jr. and, 68–69; Friedrich Wilhelms-Hütte, 199, 202; joint ventures with, 199; Richter and, 206; Rheinisch-Westfälische Elektrizitätswerke and, 219–223; RWE and, 227; Phoenix and, 251–252; on cartels, 257; Deutsch-Luxembourg, 359; postwar labor and, 397–398; MICUM and, 419–420; mergers by, 452–453; ZAG and, 702
Stinnes-Legien agreement, 397–398, 399
Strategy and Structure (Chandler), 658–659
Strategy formulation: tradeoffs in, 33–34; Killing in, 108–109; managers in, 108–109, 133–139, 295; Wilke in, 108–109; for investment, 139–149; coherent, 295; in M-forms, 362; VSt and, 508–511; rationalization and, 726–728; Thyssen-Konzern, 740–748; accounting and, 781–782; control and, 784–787

Stresemann, Gustav, 548
Strikes: Machine Company, 212; Workers' and Soldiers' Councils and, 396–397; postwar, 398–404, 403–405; military intervention in, 400–401, 403–405; general, 411; Ruhr Struggle and, 418–420
Strip steel, 271–274, 281–282
Stumm Konzern, 552–553
Succession issues, 433–434, 440
Sültemeyer, Fritz, 269, 276
Surmann, W., 130–131, 385
Syndicalist movement, 397
Syndicated/non-syndicated goods, 255, 287
Syndicates. See Cartels
Systems managers, 3, 584–585, 650–651; Dinkelbach and, 681, 707

Tariffs, 248, 446
Taxes: Späing and, 316–320; Hamborn and, 332–333; transfer prices and, 470–471
Taxes, 475; unification and, 476–477; corporate law and, 479–489; capital transfer, 480–481, 635–636, 638–639; turnover, 480–481; Organschaftstheorie and, 484–488; VSt negotiations and, 533–534, 541, 545–549; community relations and, 548; Lex Stahlverein, 620; VSt reorganization and, 631, 634–635
Taylor, Frederick, 183, 720
Taylorism, 17
Technical education system, 191, 210, 216; innovation and, 224–225
Technocratic systems conception of control, 8, 735–736
Technology, 79; strategy and, 101; Thyssen's attitude toward, 128; information, 151, 159–161; practical experience and, 191–192; commercial goals and, 200; coherence and, 226–228; mechanization and, 578–579; Fretz-Moon process, 606–617; transfers of, 606–617; disruptive, 611
Telephones, 159–161
Thomas steel, 267, 269–271, 280; Fretz-Moon process and, 608
Thyssen, August: Carnegie compared with, 7, 43–44, 506–507, 514–517; Chandler on, 26–27; relationship of his children with, 39, 43, 61–72, 477

Thyssen, August, 43–73; background of, 44; education of, 44–45; foreign influences on, 45–46; Bicheroux and, 45–46; early businesses of, 45–46; marriage of, 46, 60–61; career path of, 46–47, 511–517; home of, 47, 52–53; personality of, 47–53; workers' relationships with, 49; frugality of, 50–51; secrecy of, 51; pride of, 51–52, 123, 128, 506; Schloss Landsberg, 52–53, 712; politics of, 53–58; Catholicism and, 54–55; annexationism of, 56–58, 292; Joseph Thyssen and, 58–60; divorce contract of, 61–62, 70–72, 71–72, 488, 511; managerial relationships with, 72–73, 145, 513–514, 717–720; drive of, 74–103; cartels and, 78, 284–288; investments of, 81–82; financial control vs. expansion and, 83; financing techniques of, 83–84, 85; strategies of, 85; leadership style of, 148–149; Krefelder Stahlwerke and, 211; death of, 233, 440, 511; Steel Works Association and, 246; Phoenix and, 249–252; as Americanizer, 260, 286–287, 512–513, 514–517, 527; as enemy of cartels, 260; financial crises of, 274–276, 344, 478–479; on consolidation, 285–286; arrest of, 399; Jacob and, 401–402; labor relations and, 401–402; as war profiteer, 431; succession and, 433–434, 440; in IG, 434; retirement of, 455; reputation and, 494–495; decision to join VSt, 506–511; evaluation of, 511–517; authority of, 721; postwar compensation to, 739–740

Thyssen, August, Jr., 61, 64–69, 275; Rittergut Rüdersdorf and, 67, 68; bankruptcy of, 68–69, 440, 442; Berlin branch and, 137

Thyssen, Balbina, 45, 58, 82

Thyssen, Foussoul & Co., 45–46

Thyssen, Friedrich, 44, 82

Thyssen, Fritz: Third Reich and, 22, 64; home of, 47, 712; Hedwig and, 62; relationship of with his father, 62–64; divorce contract and, 65–67; Heinrich and, 233; American trip of, 279; Dahl and, 301–302; CAO and, 334; arrest of, 399; on IG board, 434; succession and, 440; postwar resistance by, 450; conflicts with Heinrich, 451; modernization under, 455–457; inflation and, 477; disputes about VSt and, 508–511; on America, 520; in VSt, 571; machinations of, 583; VSt equity of, 642; Nazis and, 664, 674–676

Thyssen, Hans, 69, 440

Thyssen, Hedwig Pelzer, 46, 59, 60–61; divorce contract and, 61–62, 66, 67

Thyssen, Joseph, 58–60, 193; divorce contract and, 66; death of, 69; ownership by, 212; home of, 712

Thyssen, Julius, 69, 434, 440

Thyssen, Katharina, 44

Thyssen-Bornemisza, Heinrich: divorce contract and, 65–67

Thyssen-Bornemisza, Heinrich, 69–70, 233; on IG board, 434; succession and, 440; conflicts with Fritz and, 451; liquidity and, 451; disputes about VSt and, 508–511

Thyssen & Co.: departments of, 39–40; corporate culture of, 40, 41; Thyssen and, 43–73; as private partnership, 58; divorce contract and, 61–62; as joint-stock company, 69; capitalization of, 75, 82–84; family financing in, 75, 82–83; founded, 75; location of, 75–76; expansion of, 76–81, 140–149; hoop iron/strip steel at, 77–78, 90; puddling furnaces, 77–78; pipes and tubes, 78–79, 90, 97–99, 140–149; Siemens-Martin mills, 79, 88–89; vertical integration in, 79, 81, 82; galvanizing plant, 79–80, 90, 143; employment by, 84, 102–103; scale strategies and, 85–91; raw materials at, 88, 89–90; profitability of, 90–91; diversification in, 91–103; GDK and, 91–103; product range of, 91–103; scope strategies and, 91–103; advertising, 92; welding tube workshop, 93–94; plate-mill department, 93–96; size of, 101–103; management of, 104–149; modular management in, 105, 119–120, 120–121; headquarters of, 105–106, 109; as entrepreneurial, 111; *Reglement,* 111; management reforms, 111–114; Berlin branch, 112, 133–139; product departments, 112–113, 114–117; ordering in, 114–117; organizational culture at, 122–133; WWI effects on, 140; water-gas pipe-welding, 141–149; accounting in, 150–189; control in, 150–189, 185–187; management circulars, 153–155, 186; central production-cost office, 175–185; as managerial enterprise, 186–187; machine department, 190–209, 309–311; innovation at, 190–229; coherence in, 226–228; origins of, 254; in Thyssen-Konzern, 337, 343–344, 348, 350–351; worker committee, 393; factory council, 411–419; as holding company, 440–441; liquidation of, 440–443; *Thyssenhandel* and, 472–473; banking relations of, 758–759

Thyssen & Co. Abteilung Wülfrath, 217

Thyssen & Co. AG, 440, 441, 442

Thyssen & Compagnie, Commanditgesellschaft, Styrum bei Mülheim a/d/ Ruhr, 46

Thyssenhandel, 305, 320–324, 464–477; Neuhaus in, 465–467; contract for, 466–467; structure of, 467–468; boards, 468; transfer prices and, 468–472; taxes and, 476–477

Thyssen-Konzern: founded, 3; energy economies in, 204–206; Central Auditing Office (CAO), 231, 324–336

Thyssen-Konzern, 231–517; cartels and, 235–260; GDK, 261–276; AGHütt, 276–279; Stahlwerke Thyssen, 288–295; coherence in, 295; parent company in, 296–297; managing, 296–336; decentralization in, 299–311; advantages of various legal forms in, 299–311; boards in, 300; oversight of, 302; market sensitivity in, 306–311; control in, 311; *Centralbureau* and, 311–316; Centrale, 315; Späing and, 316–320; *Thyssenhandel*, 320–324, 464–477; Thyssen & Co. in, 337, 343–344, 348, 350–351; financial control in, 337–379; financing, 343–361; liquidity crisis in, 344–345; accounts receivable/payable, 347–348; depreciation in, 349–350; financial advantages of, 349–350; financial state of, 350–351; expansion of, 351–352, 378–379; profitability in, 352–355; international historical perspective on, 361–379; as multidivisional form, 361–379; vertical integration in, 361–379; Phoenix compared with, 363–368; industrial relations in, 380–430; labor competition in, 385–386; WWI labor and, 389–391; postwar finances of, 431–443, 447–451; central-ization vs. decentralization in, 431–477; war production by, 432–433; as IG, 433–440; reorganization of, 443–451, 451–464, 475–477; Versailles Treaty and, 445–446; financial manipulations in, 447–451; liquidity of, 451; inflation and, 451–464, 477; rationalization and, 451–464, 726–727; mergers by, 452–455; organizational clarity in, 454; vertical concentration in, 454–455; modernization in, 455–457; Rheinischen Braunkohlen-Aktiengesellschaft and, 475–476; demise of, 478–517; corporate law and, 479–489; Wall Street and, 489–498; financial crisis of, 498–506; decision to join VSt, 506–511; architecture and, 713; conceptions of control in, 737–739; strategy formulation in, 740–748; financial statements, 754–757, 760–763

Thyssen Patent Pipes, 79

Tiefbohr-AG vorm. Hugo Lubisch, 266

Tilly, Richard, 27

Trade unions, 383–384

Trading firms, 305, 307–308

Transaction costs: Coase on, 1

Transfer prices: definition of, 157–158; internal, 157–159, 469–470; accounting and, 166, 603–605; trading firms and, 308–309; *Centralbureau* and, 315–316; CAO in, 327; *Thyssenhandel* and, 468–472; rationalization and, 473–474; VSt and, 544, 575, 603–605, 668; competition and, 604–605

Trapp, Willy, 97, 126

Traut, Rudolf, 139–140, 143–145, 607; Fretz-Moon and, 607, 608–610, 611, 612, 613; Fretz-Moon process and, 614–615

Treaty of Versailles, 54, 419; Thyssen-Konzern and, 445–446

Treue, Wilhelm, 473, 524

Treuhandverwaltung, 691–692, 695–696

Trusts: cartels vs., 239–241; Thyssen on, 288, 506–507, 512–513; IGs vs., 453–454; VSt and, 520; vertical, 544

Tufte, Edward, 779

Typewriters, 160–161

Uebbing, Helmut, 524

Ufermann, Paul, 523–524

Universal banks, 13, 516; cartels and, 248–249; Thyssen-Konzern and, 338

U.S. Steel, 241, 506–507, 520, 523, 553–557; restraint by, 565

Vacation shifts, 398
Values: *bourgeois,* 71–72; family life changes and, 71–72; cartels and, 259
Van Aubel, Peter, 532, 569; VSt accounting and, 584–585, 590; on overhead, 599–600
Vereinigte Stahlwerke AG (VSt): founding of, 3, 525–530; August Thyssen and, 43–44; as crowning achievement vs. failure, 506–511; decision to join, 506–511; Thyssen-Bornemisza and, 508–511; shareholders, 519, 533, 538–549, 566; control in, 519–520, 522, 569–617, 651–658
Vereinigte Stahlwerke AG (VSt), 519–709; rationalization and, 520, 523–568, 592–593, 726–727; U.S. Steel and, 520, 523; Americanization and, 520–522, 524, 566–568; cartels and, 523, 565, 648–649; stakeholders in, 524–530, 538–549; failure of, 525, 714; capacity in, 527–529, 556–557, 563–564; production in, 527–529, 551–553; negotiations for, 527–549; external relations of, 530, 538–549, 628–629; private vs. public representation in, 530; valuing properties for, 530–532, 534–536; internal issues facing, 530–538, 629; productivity in, 531–532, 557–565; quotas in, 532–533, 551–553, 564–565; organization of, 535, 571–573, 576–584; peak works in, 536–537, 559, 561–562, 599; name selection for, 537–538; headquarters of, 538, 541–542, 576–580; stock distribution, 539–540; study company, 540; wholesalers and, 540–541; community relations and, 541–542, 670–671; finishing industry and, 542–546; tax break for, 545–549; horizontal rationalization in, 548–549, 565–568; capitalization of, 549–550, 549–551; overcapitalization of, 549–551, 566–567, 629, 640–641; market share of, 551–553; negative rationalization in, 553, 558; U.S. Steel compared with, 553–557; rationalization problems in, 553–559; employment by, 558, 559; plant closings in, 558–565; decision-making in, 559–561,

581–582, 582, 743–744; study committees in, 559–561; rationalization drive in, 561–565; ATH in, 562, 563; finished products in, 562–563; expansion, 563–564; restraint by, 564–565; second rationalization wave and, 565; vertical integration in, 565–568; profit squeeze in, 566; Büro Dinkelbach, 569, 584–593; accounting in, 569–617; managerial organization of, 570–584, 713–716; shareholder conflict in, 571, 573; supervisory board of, 571, 573–574; ghost combines in, 571–574, 582, 583–584, 629, 644–645; organizational chart of, 572, 584, 592; executive board of, 573–574; managing board in, 574; technical committees in, 574–575; transfer prices, 575, 603–605, 668; information flow in, 575–579, 654; general administrative offices, 578; statistical office, 578–579; innovation in, 578–581; paper generated by, 579; public relations and, 579–580; research institute, 580–581; work groups, 581–582; centralization in, 582–584; conflicts in, 582–584, 603–605; Hollerith system in, 587–589, 650, 654–657; expense classification in, 589–590, 593–606; monthly financial reports, 597–598; Fretz-Moon process, 606–617; bureaucracy in, 615–616; refounding of, 615–616; internal rivalries in, 616–617; Great Depression and, 618–619; reorganization of, 618–676; government shares in, 620, 633–634, 640–641; recommendations for change to, 620–629; groups in, 623–624, 626–629, 629–632; resistance to reorganization of, 623–633; legal issues facing, 629–643; taxes and reorganization of, 634–635; capital transfers and, 635–636, 638–639; reorganization options for, 635–641; Dillon Read and, 637–638; subsidiary setup in, 643–651; property transfers, 647–649; common interests in, 652–653; continuities in, 653, 661–662; internal purchases by, 653; house bank for, 653–654, 658; reinvention of M-form in, 658–663; DuPont compared with, 660–661; corporate administration in, 662–663; business rhetoric and, 663–676; Nazis and, 663–676; politics and, 663–676;

areas of responsibility in, 666–668; Nazi accommodation to, 674–676; dismantling of, 697–700; decentralization and, 713–716; strategy formulation in, 727–728; conception of control in, 735–736

Verlohr, Conrad: Thyssen's relationship with, 73

Verlohr, Conrad, 199, 738; AGHütt and, 276, 277–278; Rabes and, 321; on IG board, 434

Vertical integration: Thyssen & Co., 79, 81, 82; diversification and, 80; cartels and, 231–232, 253, 515–517; of GDK, 273; AGHütt and, 279; Stahlwerke Thyssen and, 290–291; Thyssen-Konzern, 292, 293–295, 361–379; inflation and, 452–455; in *Konzerne*, 525–528; Dinkelbach on, 691, 692; bureaucratization and, 719–720

Verwissenschaftlichung, 191

Visible Hand (Chandler), 17–19, 24–31

Vögler, Albert: on Fritz Thyssen, 63; Rabes and, 321; on trusts, 454; corporate agency and, 482; critique of steel industry by, 498; on VSt, 508–509; on America, 520; eight-hour day and, 525, 526; VSt founding and, 525–526; on Dinslaken, 527; VSt property valuation and, 534–536; tax break and, 545–549; in VSt decision-making, 574–575; Arnhold and, 580–581; Fretz-Moon and, 607; on reorganization, 623–624, 626–627; Dinkelbach and, 624; business rhetoric of, 663–676; on training, 665–666, 714; Göring and, 675–676

Von Watter, Oskar, 403–405, 409–411

VSt. *See* Vereinigte Stahlwerke AG (VSt)

Vulcaan Coal Company, 322

W. A. Harriman & Co., 490–491

Wages/salaries: Thyssen & Co., 84; office for, 118; managerial, 132; deductions from, 154–155; accounting for, 166; standardization and, 385–388, 391–392, 405–407; cost-of-living raises, 386; Stinnes-Legien agreement and, 398; white-collar, 406–408; collective bargaining and, 407–409; hyperinflation and, 424

Wallmann, Carl: on Joseph Thyssen, 59

Wallmann, Carl, 119–120, 140; on setbacks, 128; drilling pipes and, 141–142; Traut and, 144; in cartels, 287; factory councils and, 413, 414–415, 416, 425; war production and, 432; on plant closings, 559–561; Fretz-Moon and, 607–608, 610; on reorganization, 625–626

Wallmann, Julius, 132

Warburg, Max, 447

Warburg, Paul, 447

War committees, 387–388

Wasserwerke Thyssen & Co., GmbH, 40, 217–229; gas delivery by, 218–220, 222–224; Rheinisch-Westfälische Elektrizitätswerke and, 219–223; pipelines, 223–224; coherence and, 226

Webb, Steven, 248

Weber, Max, 9, 29–31; ideal-types, 9, 21, 24; *Sonderweg* and, 12; on accounting, 35, 770–787; on rationality, 726–728; on bureaucracy, 728–729

Weimar Republic: industrial relations and, 380; central working association, 397–398; as union state, 408–411; factory councils and, 411–419; labor in, 424–425

Wellhöner, Volker, 337

Welskopp, Thomas, 524

Wengenroth, Ulrich, 6

Westfälische Union AG, 363–364, 715

White, Hayden, 152

White-collar class, 15; salaries and, 406–408; working council for, 408

Widekind, Edgar, 194

Wilhelm II (Kaiser), 53, 58, 292, 396

Wilke, August, 107, 108, 112, 114, 160, 316

Wilke, Franz, 73, 90, 93, 106, 107–109

Wilke, Fritz, 154

Wilke, Robert, 126

Williamson, Oliver, 232, 361–362

Wilson, John, 25

Winter, Sidney, 4

Wirtz, Adolf, 626, 627

Wixforth, Harold, 490

Wolff, Otto, 527, 540

Women employees, 160, 389, 390, 391, 407, 589

Worker committees, 393, 395

Workers' and Soldiers' Councils, 396–397, 398–400, 402–404

Working-class formation, 428–429

Working Community of the Iron Finishing
  Industry (AVI), 543
World War I: annexationism and, 56–58
World War I, 140–141, 232–233;
  Stahlwerke Thyssen and, 292; financial
  impact of, 360–361, 431–443; labor relations and, 380, 385–396; black markets
  in, 390; strikes and, 392–396, 398–404;
  transition to peacetime and, 395–396;
  Ruhr Struggle and, 418–420; reparations, 446; Dinkelbach and, 680; compensation after, 739–740

Yates, JoAnne, 151
Yatoro, Iwasaki, 376
Youngstown Sheet & Tube, 553–557

Zahnräderfabrik Augsburg, 370, 452
Zaibatsu, 6, 296–297, 373–377
Zeitschrift für Organisation, 584, 592, 741–
  742
Zentralarbeitsgemeinschaft (ZAG), 421, 424,
  702
Zichy-Thyssen, Anita, 699
Zunz, Olivier, 2

Harvard Studies in Business History

1. John Jacob Astor, Business Man, *by Kenneth Wiggins Porter*
2. Jay Cooke, Private Banker, *by Henrietta M. Larson*
3. The Jacksons and the Lees: Two Generations of Massachusetts Merchants, 1765–1844, *by Kenneth Wiggins Porter*
4. The Massachusetts–First National Bank of Boston, 1784–1934, *by N. S. B. Gras*
5. The History of an Advertising Agency: N. W. Ayer & Son at Work, 1869–1949, *revised edition, by Ralph M. Hower*
6. Marketing Life Insurance: Its History in America, *by J. Owen Stalson*
7. History of Macy's of New York, 1858–1919: Chapters in the Evolution of the Department Store, *by Ralph M. Hower*
8. The Whitesmiths of Taunton: A History of Reed & Barton, 1824–1943, *by George Sweet Gibb*
9. Development of Two Bank Groups in the Central Northwest: A Study in Bank Policy and Organization, *by Charles Sterling Popple*
10. The House of Hancock: Business in Boston, 1724–1775, *by W. T. Baxter*
11. Timing a Century: History of the Waltham Watch Company, *by C. W. Moore*
12. Guide to Business History: Materials for the Study of American Business and Suggestions for Their Use, *by Henrietta M. Larson*
13. Pepperell's Progress: History of a Cotton Textile Company, 1844–1945, *by Evelyn H. Knowlton*
14. The House of Baring in American Trade and Finance: English Merchant Bankers at Work, 1763–1861, *by Ralph W. Hidy*
15. The Whitin Machine Works since 1831: A Textile Machinery Company in an Industrial Village, by *Thomas R. Navin*
16. The Saco-Lowell Shops: Textile Machinery Building in New England, 1813–1949, *by George Sweet Gibb*
17. Broadlooms and Businessmen: A History of the Bigelow-Sanford Carpet Company, 1825–1953, *by John S. Ewing and Nancy P. Norton*
18. Nathan Trotter: Philadelphia Merchant, 1787–1853, *by Elva Tooker*
19. A History of the Massachusetts Hospital Life Insurance Company, *by Gerald T. White*
20. The Charles Ilfeld Company: A Study of the Rise and Decline of Mercantile Capitalism in New Mexico, *by William J. Parish*

21. The Rise and Decline of the Medici Bank, 1397–1494, *by Raymond de Roover*
22. Isaac Hicks: New York Merchant and Quaker, 1767–1820, *by Robert A. Davison*
23. Boston Capitalists and Western Railroads: A Study in the Nineteenth-Century Railroad Investment Process, *by Arthur M. Johnson and Barry E. Supple*
24. Petroleum Pipelines and Public Policy, 1906–1959, *by Arthur M. Johnson*
25. Investment Banking in America: A History, *by Vincent P. Carosso*
26. Merchant Prince of Boston: Colonel T. H. Perkins, 1764–1854, *by Carl Seaburg and Stanley Paterson*
27. The Maturing of Multinational Enterprise: American Business Abroad from 1914 to 1970, *by Mira Wilkins*
28. Financing Anglo-American Trade: The House of Brown, *by Edwin J. Perkins*
29. British Mercantile Houses in Buenos Aires, 1810–1880, *by Vera Blinn Reber*
30. The British Shipbuilding Industry, 1870–1914, *by Sidney Pollard and Paul Robertson*
31. Moving the Masses: The Evolution of Urban Public Transit in New York, Boston, and Philadelphia, 1880–1912, *by Charles W. Cheape*
32. Managerial Hierarchies: Comparative Perspectives on the Rise of Modern Industrial Enterprise, *edited by Alfred D. Chandler, Jr., and Herman Daems*
33. Big Business in China: Sino-Foreign Rivalry in the Cigarette Industry, 1890–1930, *by Sherman Cochran*
34. The Emergence of Multinational Enterprise: American Business Abroad from the Colonial Era to 1914, *by Mira Wilkins*
35. Kikkoman: Company, Clan, and Community, *by W. Mark Fruin*
36. Family Firm to Modern Multinational: Norton Company, a New England Enterprise, *by Charles W. Cheape*
37. Citibank, 1812–1970, *by Harold van B. Cleveland and Thomas F. Huertas*
38. The Morgans: Private International Bankers, 1854–1913, *by Vincent P. Carosso*
39. Business, Banking, and Politics: The Case of British Steel, 1918–1939, *by Steven Tolliday*
40. Enterprising Elite: The Boston Associates and the World They Made, *by Robert F. Dalzell, Jr.*
41. The History of Foreign Investment in the United States to 1914, *by Mira Wilkins*
42. News over the Wires: The Telegraph and the Flow of Public Information in America, 1844–1897, by *Menahem Blondheim*
43. The History of Foreign Investment in the United States, 1914–1945, *by Mira Wilkins*
44. Dilemmas of Russian Capitalism: Fedor Chizhov and Corporate Enterprise in the Railroad Age, *by Thomas C. Owen*
45. Organizing Control: August Thyssen and the Construction of German Corporate Management, *by Jeffrey R. Fear*